ROBOT VISION

Edited by

ALEŠ UDE

Robot Vision

Edited by Aleš Ude

Republished by InTech

Janeza Trdine 9, 51000 Rijeka, Croatia

Additional hard copies can be obtained from orders@intechopen.com

Robot Vision, Edited by Aleš Ude
p. cm.
ISBN 978-953-307-077-3

For EU product safety concerns:
IN TECH d.o.o., Prolaz Marije Krucifikse Kozulić 3, 51000 Rijeka, Croatia,
info@intechopen.com or visit our website at intechopen.com.

Meet the editor

I am the head of Department of Automatics, Biocybernetics and Robotics, Jožef Stefan Institute, Ljubljana, Slovenia, and the founder of the Humanoid and Cognitive Robotics Lab, which operates within the department. I am also associated with ATR Computational Neuroscience Laboratories in Kyoto, Japan. My main research interests are in applying the results of the research on human motor control and perception to the creation of cognitive agents, such as for example humanoid robots. My research focuses on various issues in robot learning, especially imitation learning and learning by exploration, where I combine statistical learning techniques and reinforcement learning to increase the efficiency and autonomy of the acquisition of new sensorimotor behaviors. I am also interested in humanoid robot vision with the focus on learning object representations, object recognition, and foveated vision. Finally, I study mechanisms to integrate active perception and manipulation in robots that operate in natural environments. I have been a principal investigator at Jožef Stefan Institute for several European projects (STREPs and IPs), bilateral projects with ATR, and national projects. My publication record consists of over 100 papers in referred journals and conferences. I have been involved with the preparation of major robotics conferences such as ICRA, IROS, Robotics: Systems and Science, and Humanoids for many years. In 2011 I was a general chair of IEEE-RAS International Conference on Humanoid Robots (Humanoids). I co-organized more than 10 workshops at Humanoids and ICRA.

Preface

The purpose of robot vision is to enable robots to perceive the external world in order to perform a large range of tasks such as navigation, visual servoing for object tracking and manipulation, object recognition and categorization, surveillance, and higher-level decision-making. Among different perceptual modalities, vision is arguably the most important one. It is therefore an essential building block of a cognitive robot. Most of the initial research in robot vision has been industrially oriented and while this research is still ongoing, current works are more focused on enabling the robots to autonomously operate in natural environments that cannot be fully modeled and controlled. A long-term goal is to open new applications to robotics such as robotic home assistants, which can only come into existence if the robots are equipped with significant cognitive capabilities. In pursuit of this goal, current research in robot vision benefits from studies in human vision, which is still by far the most powerful existing vision system. It also emphasizes the role of active vision, which in case of humanoid robots does not limit itself to active eyes only any more, but rather employs the whole body of the humanoid robot to support visual perception. By combining these paradigms with modern advances in computer vision, especially with many of the recently developed statistical approaches, powerful new robot vision systems can be built.

This book presents a snapshot of the wide variety of work in robot vision that is currently going on in different parts of the world.

March 2010

Aleš Ude

Contents

1

Design and fabrication of soft zoom lens applied in robot vision

Wei-Cheng Lin[a], Chao-Chang A. Chen[b], Kuo-Cheng Huang[a] and Yi-Shin Wang[b]

[a] *Instrument Technology Research Center, National Applied Research Laboratories Taiwan*

[b] *National Taiwan University of Science and Technology Taiwan*

1. Introduction

The design theorem of traditional zoom lens uses mechanical motion to precisely adjust the separations between individual or groups of lenses; therefore, it is more complicated and requires multiple optical elements. Conventionally, the types of zoom lens can be divided into optical zoom and digital zoom. With the demands of the opto-mechanical elements, the zoom ability of lens system was dominated by the optical and mechanical design technique. In recent years, zoom lens is applied in compact imaging devices, which are popularly used in Notebook, PDA, mobile phone, and etc. The minimization of the zoom lens with excellent zoom ability and high imaging quality at the same time becomes a key subject of related efficient zoom lens design. In this decade, some novel technologies for zoom lens have been presented and they can simply be classified into the following three types:

(1)Electro-wetting liquid lens:

Electro-wetting liquid lens is the earliest liquid lens which contains two immiscible liquids having equal density but different refractive index, one is an electrically conductive liquid (water) and the other is a drop of oil (silicon oil), contained in a short tube with transparent end caps. When a voltage is applied, because of electrostatic property, the shape of interface between oil and water will be changed and then the focal length will be altered. Among the electro-wetting liquid lenses, the most famous one is Varioptic liquid lens.

(2) MEMS process liquid lens:

This type of liquid lens usually contains micro channel, liquid chamber and PDMS membrane which can be made in MEMS process, and then micro-pump or actuator is applied to pump liquid in/out the liquid chamber. In this way, the shape of liquid lens will change as plano-concave or plano-convex lens, even in bi-concave, bi-convex, meniscus convex and meniscus concave. It can also combine one above liquid lens to enlarge the field of view (FOV) and the zoom ratio of the system.

(3)Liquid crystals lens:

Liquid crystals are excellent electro-optic materials with electrical and optical anisotropies. Its optical properties can easily be varied by external electric field. When the voltage is applied, the liquid crystals molecules will reorient by the inhomogeneous electric field which generates a centro-symmetric refractive index distribution. Then, the focal length will be altered with varying voltage.

(4)Solid tunable lens:

One non-liquid tunable lens with PDMS was increasing temperature by heating the silicon conducting ring. PDMS lens is deformed by mismatching of bi-thermal expansion coefficients and stiffness between PDMS and silicon. Alternatively the zoom lens can be fabricated by soft or flexible materials, such as PDMS. The shape of soft lens can be changed by external force, this force may be mechanical force like contact force or magnetic force; therefore the focal length will be altered without any fluid pump.

All presented above have a common character that they process optical zoom by changing lens shape and without any transmission mechanism. The earliest deformed lens can be traced to the theory of "Adaptive optics" that is a technology used to improve the performance of optical systems and is most used in astronomy to reduce the effects of atmospheric distortion. The adaptive optics usually used MEMS process to fabricate the flexible membranes and combine the actuator to make the lens with the motion of tilt and shift. However, there has not yet a zoom lens with PDMS that can be controlled by the fluid pressure for curvature change. In this chapter, PDMS is used for fabricating the lens of SZL and EFL of this lens system will be changed using pneumatic pressure.

2. PDMS properties

PDMS, Dow Corning SYLGARD 184, is used because of its good light transmittance, a two-part elastomer (base and curing agent), is liquid in room temperature and it is cured by mixing base and curing agent at 25°C for 24 hour. Heating will shorten the curing time of PDMS, 100 °C for 1hour, 150°C for only 15 minutes. PDMS also has low glass transition temperature (-123 °C), good chemical and thermal stability, and contain flexibility and elasticity from -50 to 200°C. Since different curing parameter cause different Young's Modulus and refractive index, this section introduces the material properties of PDMS, including Young's Modulus, reflection index (n) and Abbe number (v) in different curing parameter.

2.1 PDMS mechanical property (Young's Modulus)

Young's Modulus is the important mechanic property in the analysis of the maximum displacement and deformed shape of PDMS lens. In order to find the relationship of curing parameter and Young's Modulus, tensile test is used, master curing parameters is curing time, curing temperature and mixing ratio.

The geometric specification of test sample is define as standard ASTM D412 98a , the process parameter separate as 10:1 and 15:1, cured at 100 °C for 30, 45, 60 minutes and 150 °C for 15, 20, 25 minutes. As the result, in the same mixed ratio, higher curing temperature and long curing time cause larger Young's Modulus; in the same curing parameter, in mixed ratio 10:1 has larger Young's Modulus than 15:1. The mixed ratio 15:1 is soft then 10:1 but is weaker, so the fabrication of PDMS lens will use the ratio 10:1.

2.2 PDMS optical property (Refractive index and Abbe number)

Refractive index (n) and Abbe number (v) is the essential optic parameter of material optical properties in optical design. Spectroscopic Ellipsometer is used to inspect the n in wavelength 587nm, then discuss the nPDMS of mixed ratio 10:1 and 15:1 cured at 100°C for 30, 40, and 60min. The v is defined as follows:

$$V_d = \frac{n_d - 1}{n_F - n_C} \quad (1)$$

nF, nC, and nd is the refractive index at 486.1、656.3 and 587.6nm. The nd and ν d of PDMS is calculated according to the data by using least square method. As the result, curing parameter is not the key point that influences the optical properties of PDMS material; mixed ratio has more influence on optical properties. 10:1 has larger n and ν than 15:1. In this research, the n 1.395 and v 50 is used. Table.1 shows the comparison with PDMS and the other most used optical materials.

Materials	BK7	PMMA	COC	PC	PS	PDMS
Refractive index (n)	1.517	1.492	1.533	1.585	1.590	1.395
Abbe number (v_d)	64.17	57.442	56.23	29.91	30.87	50

Table. 1. Optical property of PDMS and common optical material

3. Methodology

This section introduces the design process of pneumatic SZL system; this system is divided into SZL unit and pneumatic control unit. As the PDMS material properties is obtained, then the optical design, optical mechanism, PDMS lens mold and mold inserts is consequently designed and experimentally fabricated. After assembly of the PDMS lens and optic mechanism, the SZL system is presented and investigated for its optical performance of desired EFL.

3.1 Design of pneumatic soft zoom lens unit

Components of the SZL unit are shown in Fig.1. The SZL unit includes BK7 lens and PDMS lens, the PDMS lens were designed with flat and spherical lens. The EFL is 33.56mm when using PDMS spherical lens and the EFL is 32.55mm when using PDMS flat lens. In order to simply verify this idea, optical performance of the SZL system is not the main purpose, thus diffractive optical elements and correct lens is a good choice to modify the aberration for better optical performance in this system. Mechanisms of SZL unit will be devised as barrel, O-ring, cell, retainer and spacer.

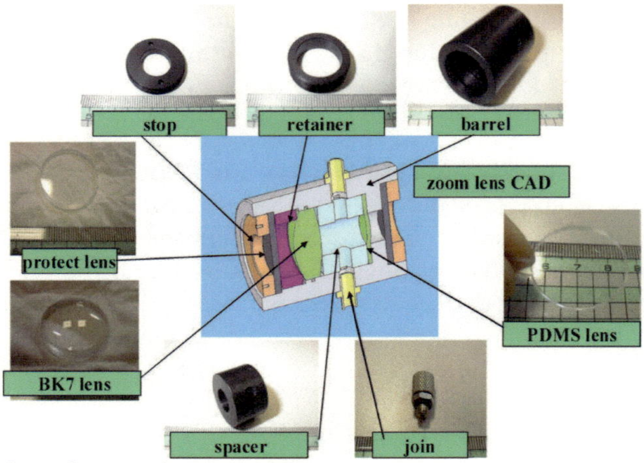

Fig. 1. Components of the soft zoom lens system.

3.2 SZL system

The SZL system assembly procedure is following these steps as show in Fig.2.: (1) PDMS lens is put into the barrel, (2) the spacer which constrain the distance between PDMS lens and BK7 lens is packed, (3) O-ring is fixed which can avoid air to escape, (4) BK7 lens is loaded and mounted by retainer, (5) BK7 protect lens is equipped with at both end of the SZL, and finally, the SZL system is combined with the SZL unit and pneumatic control unit with a pump (NITTO Inc.), a regulator, a pressure gauge and also a switch.

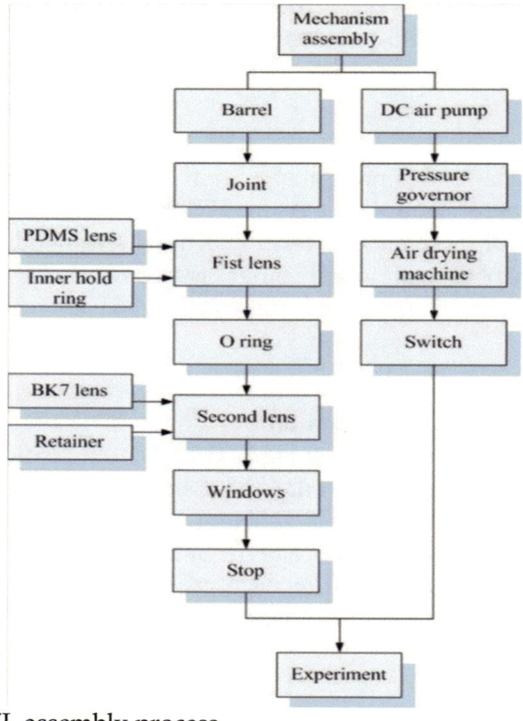

Fig. 2. Flow chart of SZL assembly process.

Fig. 3. Soft zoom lens system contain pneumatic supply device for control unit.

Fig.4. shows the zoom process of SZL system for variant applied pressures. The principle of SZL system is by the way of pneumatic pressure to adapt its shape and curvature, the gas input is supplied with NITTO pump and max pressure is up to 0.03 MPa. The regulator and pressure gauge control the magnitude of applied pressure, and there are two switches at both end of the SZL, one is input valve and the other is output valve.

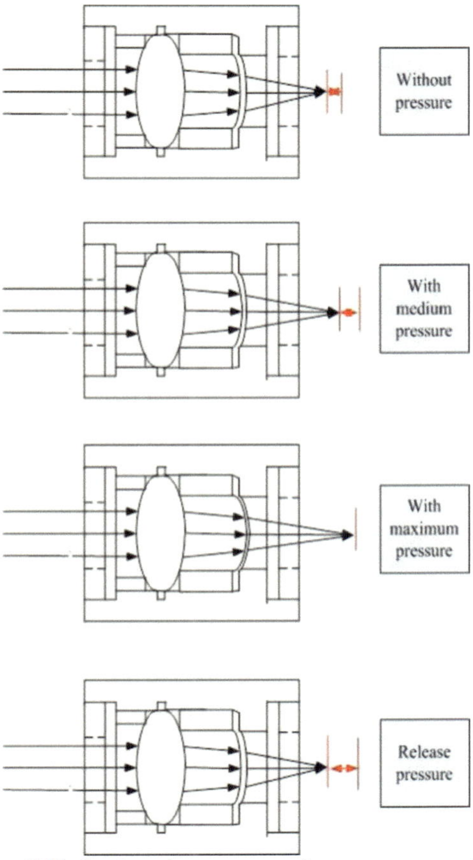

Fig. 4. Zoom process of the SZL during the pneumatic pressure applied.

3.3 PDMS lens mold and PDMS soft lens processing

The lens mold contains two pair of mold inserts, one pair is for PDMS spherical lens and another is for PDMS flat lens. Each pair has the upper and the lower mold inserts. The material of mold insert is copper (Moldmax XL) and is fabricated by ultra-precision diamond turning machine. Fig.4. shows the fabrication process. Since the PDMS lens is fabricated by casting, the parting line between the upper and the lower mold inserts need have an air trap for over welling the extra amount PDMS. At the corner of the mold are four guiding pins to orientate the mold plates.

The fabrication processes is shown at Fig.5. The fabrication process of PDMS lens is mixing, stirring, degassing and heating for curing. At first, base A and curing agent B is mixed and stirred with 10:1 by weight, then degas with a vacuum pump. After preparing the PDMS, cast PDMS into the mold cavity slowly and carefully, then close the mold and put into oven for curing. As the result, at curing temperature 100°C, PDMS lens can be formed after 60 min. Fig.6. is the PDMS lens of SZL unit. There are spherical lens and flat lens for experimental tests and they are fabricated at the same molding procedure.

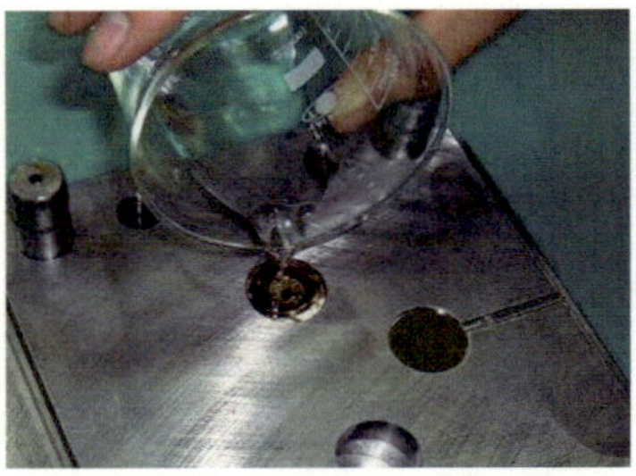
(a) PDMS cast into mold cavity

(b) Mold cavity full of PDMS

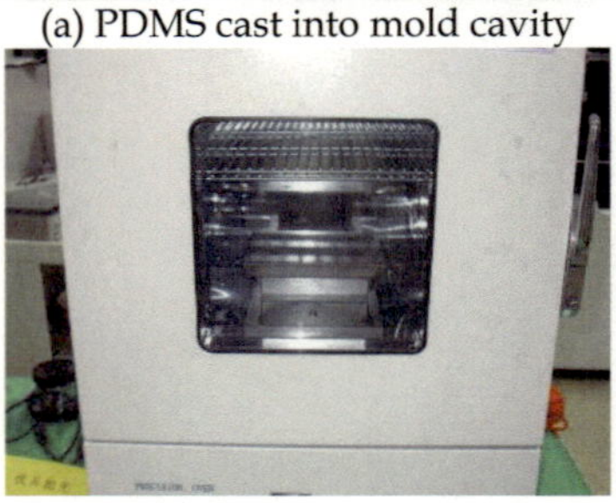
(c) Curing in oven

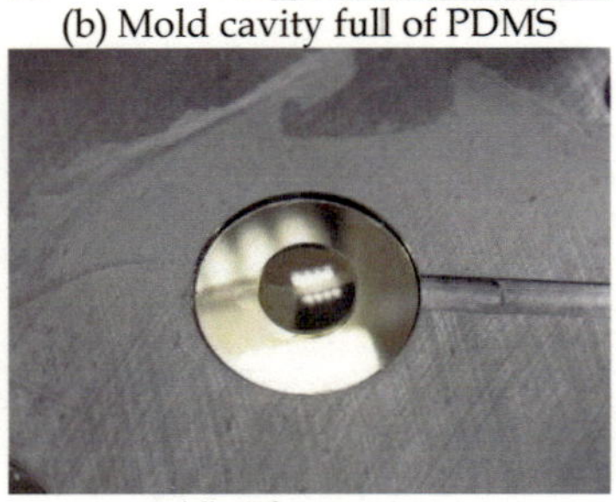
(d) After curing

Fig. 5. Fabrication processes of PDMS lens.

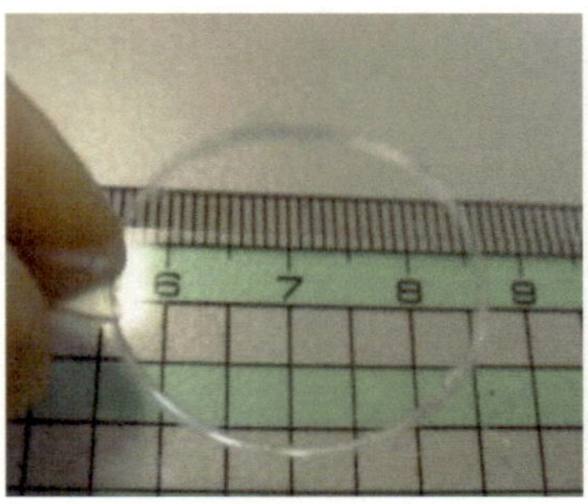
(a) PDMS flat lens

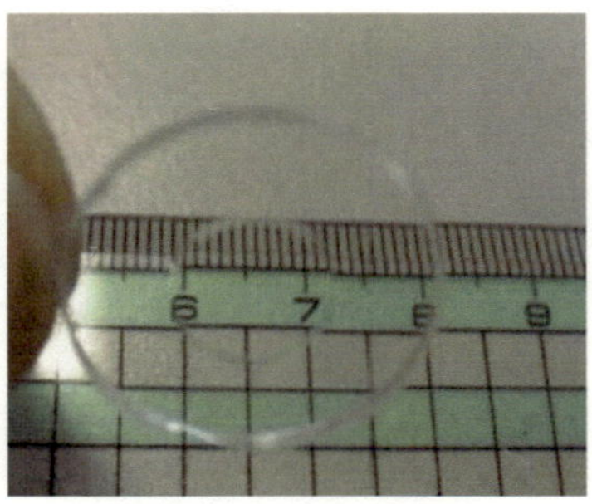
(b) PDMS sphere lens

Fig. 6. PDMS lens of soft zoom lens system.

3.4 Deformation analysis of PDMS lens

In the deformation analysis of PDMS lens, the measured Young's Modulus and Poisson's Ratio of PDMS are inputted to the software and then set the meshed type, boundary condition and loading. The boundary condition is to constrain the contact surface between the PDMS lens and mechanism like barrel and spacer, and the load is the applied pressure of pneumatic supply device. Fig.7. shows the analysis procedure. As the result of the deformation analysis, comparing to the SZL with PDMS flat and spherical lens, the flat lens has larger deformation with the same curing parameter of both PDMS lens. Fig.8. shows the relationship of the maximum displacement versus the Young's Modulus of PDMS flat lens and spherical lens.

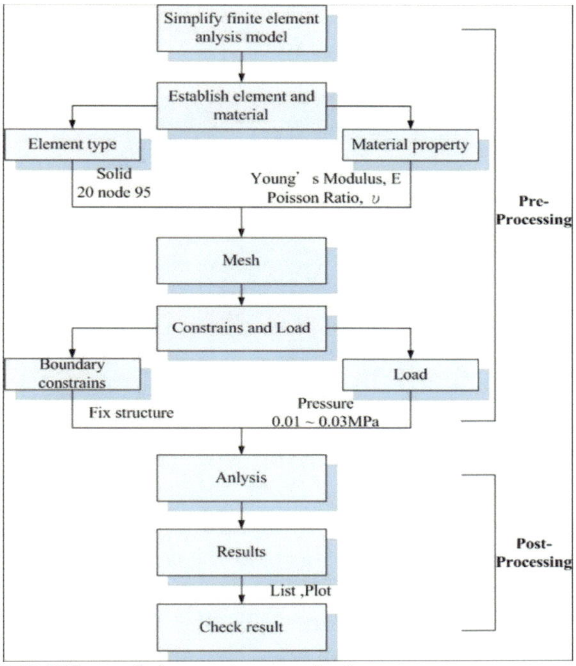

Fig. 7. Flow chart of PDMS lens deformation analysis.

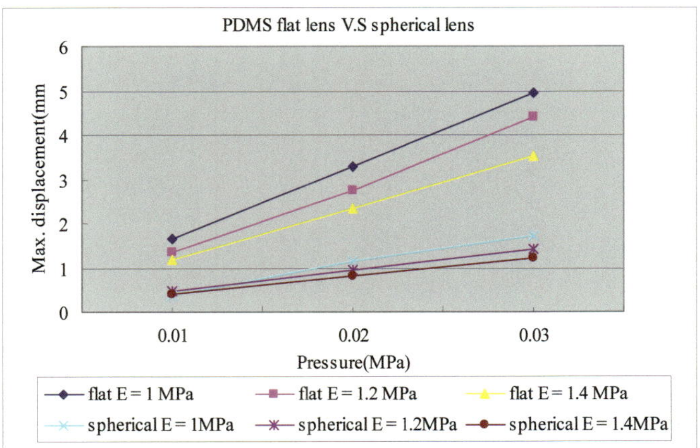

Fig. 8. Relationship of PDMS lens Young's Modulus and maximum displacement.

4. Results and Discussion

The EFL of soft zoom lens system is inspected by an opto-centric instrument (Trioptics OptiCentric) in a transmission mode show as Fig.9. The lens system with PDMS spherical lens are cured at 100°C for 60, 70 min and separately inspected at five conditions as 0, 0.005, 0.01, 0.015 and 0.02 MPa. The EFL of soft zoom lens with PDMS lens cured at 100°C for 60 min changes from 33.440 to 39.717 mm or increasing 18.77% during the applied pressure from 0 to 0.02 MPa. The EFL of soft zoom lens with PDMS lens cured at 100°C for 70 min changes from 33.877 to 39.189 mm or increasing 15.68%. PDMS lens cured at 150°C for 45 min changes from 33.254 to 37.533 mm or increasing 12.87%. The longer curing time or larger curing temperature affects the stiffness of elastomer and the Young's modulus increases for less deformable by the external force.

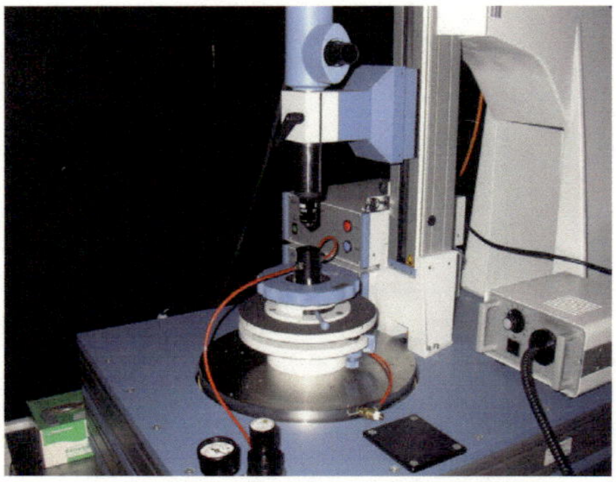

Fig. 9. The effective focal length measurement by using Trioptics.

For the PDMS flat lens cured at 100°C for 60 min, the EFL of this SZL system changes from 32.554 to 34.177mm or increasing 4.99%. Fig.10. is the relationship of applied pressure and EFL of soft zoom lens system. Fig.11. shows the relationship of applied pressure and system zoom ratio. The EFL of the SZL system with flat PDMS lens seems not changing conspicuously as that with PDMS spherical lens. The variation of thickness of the flat lens is not so obvious than that of the spherical lens due to the deformation induced by the pneumatic pressure. The repeatability of the soft zoom lens is also inspected for the SZL with PDMS spherical lens and is measured for 100 times. Result is shown in Fig.12.

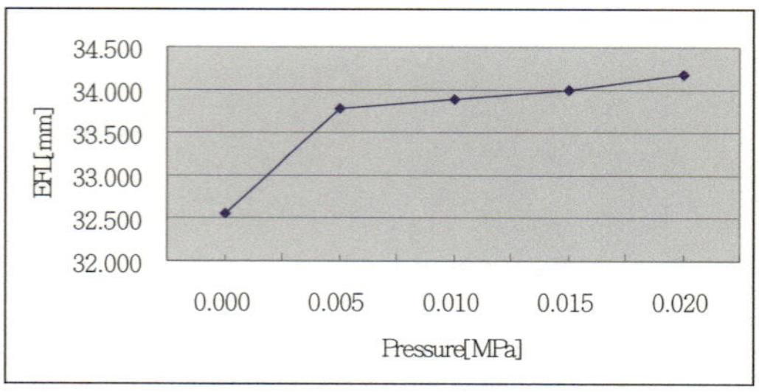

(a) 100 °CPDMS flat lens

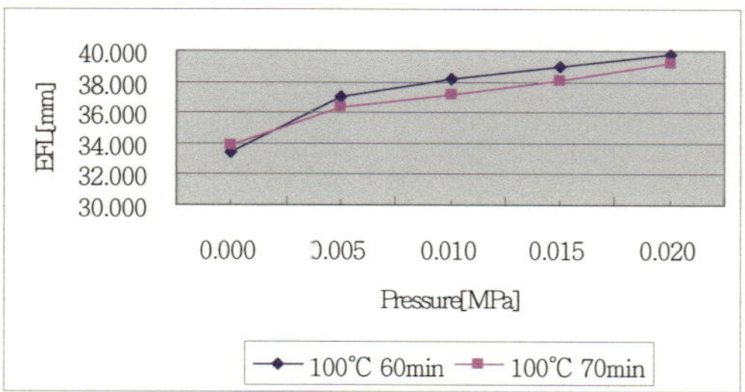

(b) 100 °CPDMS spherical lens

Fig. 10. The relationship of applied pneumatic pressure and effective focal length with PDMS lens cured at 100°C.

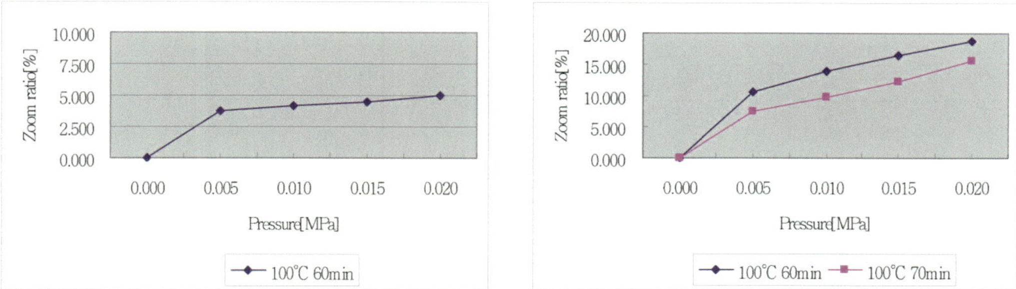

(a) PDMS flat lens (b) PDMS spherical lens

Fig. 11. The relationship of applied pneumatic pressure and zoom ratio with different shape of PDMS lens.

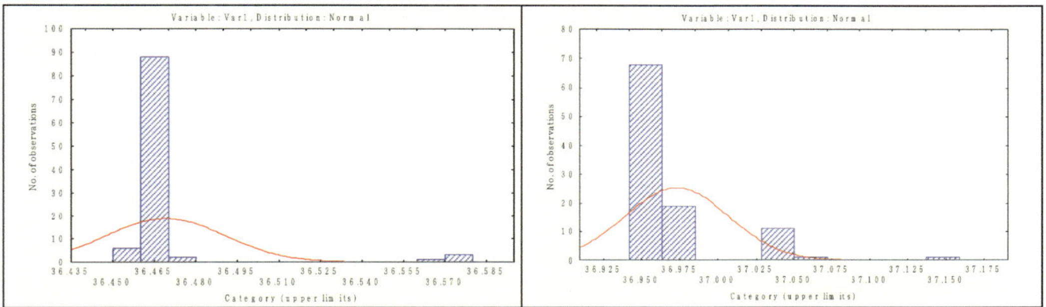

(a) EFL repeatability at 0.16 kg/cm²	(b) EFL repeatability at 0. 2 kg/cm²

Fig. 12. The repeatability of the SZL system.

In order to comprehend the variation of EFL with zoom effect of the developed SZL system, a CCD imaging experiment was performed for verification. A mechanical adapter was design to assemble the SZL unit onto the CCD camera. Fig.13. shows the experimental setup of this imaging experiment. In this experiment, the ISO 12233 pattern was used and the object length from the pattern to the SZL unit was fixed to observe the acquired image from the CCD camera for the pneumatic pressure applied from 0 to 0.02 MPa. The captured image during the pressure applied for each applied pressure is from clear to indistinct as show in Fig.14. It is obviously verified the zoom effect of this developed SZL system with the fabricated PDMS lens.

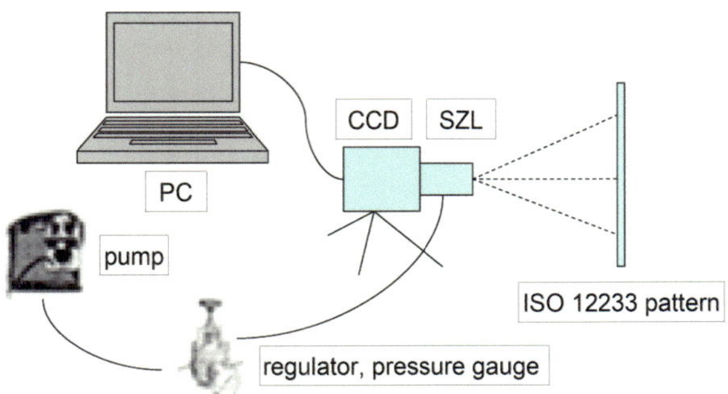

Fig. 13. The experimental setup of the soft zoom lens system imaging.

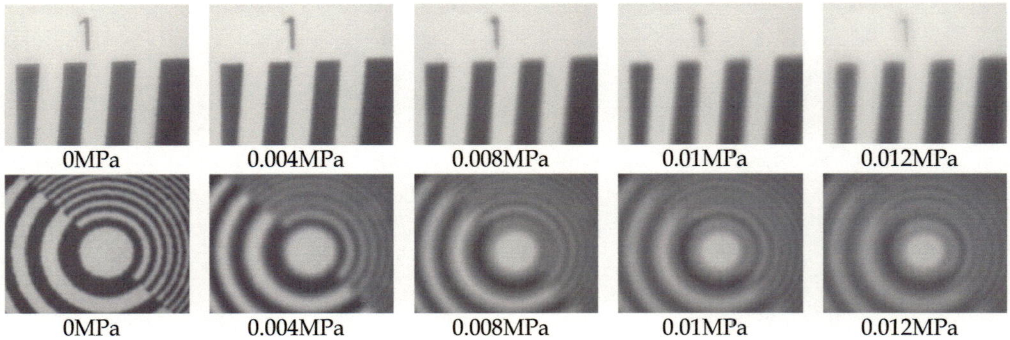

Fig. 14. The image of soft zoom lens system from the image test.

As a summary of experimental results and discussion, EFL is direct proportion to the magnitude of the applied pressure during the EFL inspection. When the pressure is applied, the EFL of the system and shape of PDMS lens change. The major EFL variation occurs in the beginning of applied pressure. For example, when the pressure is applied from 0 to 0.005MPa the EFL variation of PDMS lens cured at 100°C for 60min is 3.577mm, then when the applied pressure is up to 0.02MPa the variation of EFL is 6.277mm, the variation between 0.015 to 0.02MPa is only 0.749mm. Fig.15. shows the relationship of EFL variation and pressure. Comparing to the SZL with PDMS flat and spherical lens, the flat lens has larger deformation with the same curing parameter, but the zoom ratio does not as good as spherical lens. According to the experimental result, the thickness, curing parameter and the geometry shape of the PDMS lens can influence zoom ability. Therefore, the imaging experiment was performed by the SZL system with spherical PDMS lens and the obtained image has been verified for its feasibility of zoom effect.

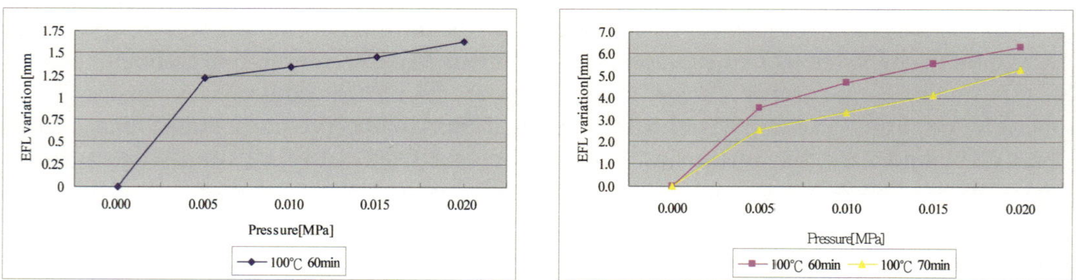

(a) 100°C PDMS flat lens (b) 100°C PDMS spherical lens

Fig. 15. The relationship of applied pneumatic pressure and variation of effective focal length.

5. Conclusion

Based on the experimental results, the novel design of this SZL system has been proved effectively for its zoom effects for image. The EFL of SZL system with PDMS lens cured at 100°C for 60 min changes from 33.440 to 39.717 mm or increasing 18.77% for the applied pressure from 0 to 0.02 MPa. The curing temperature and time significantly affects the stiffness of the PDMS lens and causes different results of EFL. Experimental results also show that zoom effects of the developed SZL system are significantly affected by the shape, thickness of PDMS soft lens. The SZL system has been verified with the function of zoom ability.

In future, the deformed shape of PDMS lens after applied pressure needs to be analyzed and then the altered lens's shape can be obtained to be fit and calculated. It can be imported to the optical software to check the EFL variation after applying the pressure and also compare with the inspection data. Furthermore, it can find the optimized design by the shape analysis of PDMS lens when the pneumatic pressure is applied, then the correct lens is obtained to modify the optical image property. On the operation principle, we should find other actuator instead of fluid pump to change the shape of PDMS lens and EFL of SZL with external pressure for zoom lens devices. Further research will work on the integration of the SZL system with imaging system for mobile devices or robot vision applications.

6. Future work

As the result, the pneumatic control soft zoom lens can simply proof our idea that the effective focal length of zoom lens will be altered through the deformation varied by changing the pneumatic pressure. As we know, the deformed lens whether in pneumatic system or MEMS micro-pump system is not convenient to apply in compact imaging devices. In order to improve this defect, we provide another type of soft zoom lens whose effective focal length can be tuned without external force. Fig.16. shows one of the new idea, flexible material are used to fabricate the hollow ball lens then filled with the transparent liquid or gel. The structure like human eyes and its shape can be altered by an adjustable ring, thus the focal length will be changed.

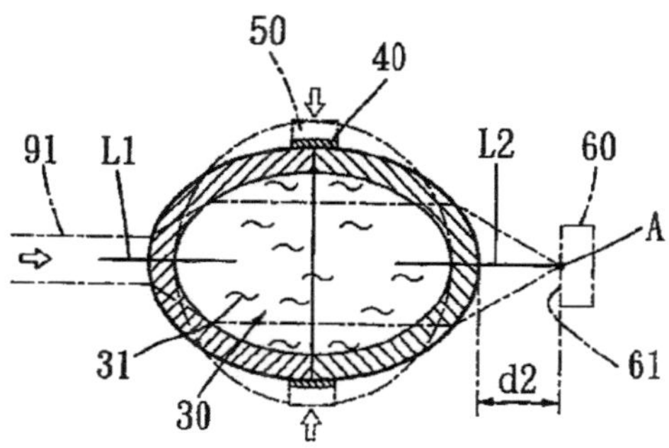

Fig. 16. The structure of artificial eyes.

Another one of the improvement of pneumatic control soft zoom lens is showed in Fig.17. This zoom lens can combine one and above soft lens unit, each unit has at least one soft lens at both end and filled with transparent liquid or gel then seal up. The zoom lens with two and above soft lens unit can be a successive soft zoom lens and the motion is like a piston when the adjustable mechanism is moved, the fluid that filled in the lens will be towed then the lens unit will be present as a concave or convex lens. Due to different combination, the focal length is changed from the original type. Those two type soft zoom lens will be integrated in imaging system which can applied in robot vision.

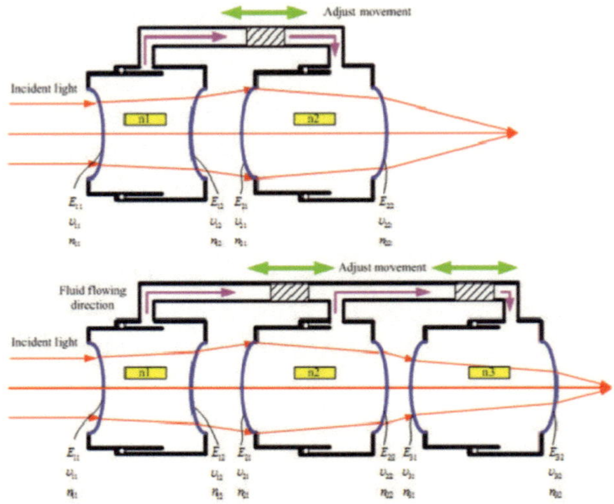

Fig. 17. The structure of successive soft zoom lens.

7. References

Berge, Bruno, Peseux, Jerome, (1999). WO 99/18456, USPTO Patent Full-Text and Image Database , 1999

Berge B. ,Varioptic, Lyon, (2005). Liquid lens technology : Principle of electrowetting based lenses and applications to image, 2005

Chao Chang-Chen, Kuo-Cheng, Huang, Wei-Cheng Lin, (2007) US 7209297, USPTO Patent Full-Text and Image Database, 2007

Dow Corning, (1998). Production information-Sylgard® 184 Silicone Elastomer, 1998

David A. Chang-Yen, Richard K. Eich, and Bruce K. Gale, (2005). A monolithic PDMS waveguide system fabricated using soft-lithography techniques," Journal of lightwave technology, Vol. 23, NO. 6, June (2005)

Feenstra, Bokke J., (2003). WO 03/069380, USPTO Patent Full-Text and Image Database, 2003

Huang, R. C. and Anand L., (2005). Non-linear mechanical behavior of the elastomer polydimethylsiloxane (PDMS) used in the manufacture of microfluidic devices, 2005

Jeong, Ki-Hun, Liu Gang L., (2004). Nikolas Chronis and Luke P. Lee, Turnable microdoublet lens array, Optics Express 2494, Vol. 12, No. 11, 2004

Peter M. Moran, Saman Dharmatilleke, Aik Hau Khaw, Kok Wei Tan, Mei Lin Chan, and Isabel Rodriguez, (2006). Fluidic lenses with variable focal length, Appl. Phys. Lett. 88, 2006

Rajan G. S., G. S. Sur, J. E. Mark, D. W. Schaefer, G. Beaucage, A. (2003). Preparation and application of some unusually transparent poly (dimethylsiloxane) nanocomposites, J. Polym. Sci., B, vol.41, 1897–1901

R.A. Gunasekaran, M. Agarwal, A. Singh, P. Dubasi,P. Coane, K. Varahramyan, (2005). Design and fabrication of fluid controlled dynamic optical lens system, Optics and Lasers in Engineering 43, 2005

2

Methods for Reliable Robot Vision with a Dioptric System

E. Martínez and A.P. del Pobil
Robotic Intelligence Lab., Jaume-I University, Castellón, Spain
Interaction Science Dept., Sungkyunkwan University, Seoul, S. Korea

1. Introduction

There is a growing interest in Robotics research on building robots which behave and even look like human beings. Thus, from industrial robots, which act in a restricted, controlled, well-known environment, today's robot development is conducted as to emulate alive beings in their natural environment, that is, a real environment which might be dynamic and unknown. In the case of mimicking human being behaviors, a key issue is how to perform manipulation tasks, such as picking up or carrying objects. However, as this kind of actions implies an interaction with the environment, they should be performed in such a way that the safety of all elements present in the robot workspace at each time is guaranteed, especially when they are human beings.

Although some devices have been developed to avoid collisions, such as, for instance, cages, laser fencing or visual acoustic signals, they considerably restrict the system autonomy and flexibility. Thus, with the aim of avoiding those constrains, a robot-embedded sensor might be suitable for our goal. Among the available ones, cameras are a good alternative since they are an important source of information. On the one hand, they allow a robot system to identify interest objects, that is, objects it must interact with. On the other hand, in a human-populated, everyday environment, from visual input, it is possible to build an environment representation from which a collision-free path might be generated. Nevertheless, it is not straightforward to successfully deal with this safety issue by using traditional cameras due to its limited field of view. That constrain could not be removed by combining several images captured by rotating a camera or strategically positioning a set of them, since it is necessary to establish any feature correspondence between many images at any time. This processing entails a high computational cost which makes them fail for real-time tasks.

Despite combining mirrors with conventional imaging systems, known as catadioptric sensors (Svoboda et al., 1998; Wei et al., 1998; Baker & Nayar, 1999) might be an effective solution, these devices unfortunately exhibit a dead area in the centre of the image that can be an important drawback in some applications. For that reason, a dioptric system is proposed. Dioptric systems, also called fisheye cameras, are systems which combine a fisheye lens with a conventional camera (Baker & Nayar, 1998; Wood, 2006). Thus, a conventional lens is changed by one of these lenses that has a short focal length that allows cameras to see objects in an hemisphere. Although fisheye devices present several advantages over catadioptric sensors

such as no presence of dead areas in the captured images, a unique model for this kind of cameras does not exist unlike central catadioptric ones (Geyer & Daniilidis, 2000).
So, with the aim of designing a dependable, autonomous, manipulation robot system, a fast, robust vision system is presented that covers the full robot workspace. Two different stages have been considered:

- moving object detection
- target tracking

First of all, a new robust adaptive background model has been designed. It allows the system to adapt to different unexpected changes in the scene such as sudden illumination changes, blinking of computer screens, shadows or changes induced by camera motion or sensor noise. Then, a tracking process takes place. Finally, the estimation of the distance between the system and the detected objects is computed by using an additional method. In this case, information about the 3D localization of the detected objects with respect to the system was obtained from a dioptric stereo system.
Thus, the structure of this paper is as follows: the new robust adaptive background model is described in Section 2, while in Section 3 the tracking process is introduced. An epipolar geometry study of a dioptric stereo system is presented in Section 4. Some experimental results are presented in Section 5, and discussed in Section 6.

2. Moving Object Detection: A New Background Maintance Approach

As it was presented in (Cervera et al., 2008), an adaptive background modelling combined with a global illumination change detection method is used to proper detect any moving object in a robot workspace and its surrounding area. That approach can be summarized as follows:

- In a first phase, a background model is built. This model associates a statistical distribution, defined by its mean color value and its variance, to each pixel of the image. It is important to note that the implemented method allows to obtain the initial background model without any restrictions of bootstrapping
- In a second phase, two different processing stages take place:
    - First, each image is processed at pixel level, in which the background model is used to classify pixels as foreground or background depending on whether they fit in with the built model or not
    - Second, the raw classification based on the background model is improved at frame level

Moreover, when a global change in illumination occurs, it is detected at frame level and the background model is properly adapted.
Thus, when a human or another moving object enters in a room where the robot is, it is detected by means of the background model at pixel level. It is possible because each pixel belonging to the moving object has an intensity value which does not fit into the background model. Then, the obtained binary image is refined by using a combination of subtraction techniques at frame level. Moreover, two consecutive morphological operations are applied to erase isolated points or lines caused by the dynamic factors mentioned above. The next step is to update the statistical model with the values of the pixels classified as background in order to adapt it to some small changes that do not represent targets.

At the same time, a process for sudden illumination change detection is performed at frame level. This step is necessary because the model is based on intensity values and a change in illumination produces a variation of them. A new adaptive background model is built when an event of this type occurs, because if it was not done, the application would detect background pixels as if they were moving objects.

3. Tracking Process

Once targets are detected by using a background maintenance model, the next step is to track each target. A widely used approach in Computer Vision to deal with this problem is the Kalman Filter (Kalman & Bucy, 1961; Bar-Shalom & Li, 1998; Haykin, 2001; Zarchan & Mussof, 2005; Grewal et al., 2008). It is an efficient recursive filter that has two distinct phases: **Predict** and **Update**. The predict phase uses the state estimate from the previous timestep to produce an estimate of the state at the current timestep. This predicted state estimate is also known as the *a priori* state estimate because, although it is an estimate of the state at the current timestep, it does not include observation information from the current timestep. In the update phase, the current *a priori* prediction is combined with current observation information to refine the state estimate. This improved estimate is termed the *a posteriori* state estimate. With regard to the current observation information, it is obtained by means of an image correspondence approach. In that sense, one of most well-known methods is the Scale Invariant Feature Transform (SIFT) approach (Lowe, 1999; Lowe, 2004) which shares many features with neuron responses in primate vision. Basically, it is a 4-stage filtering approach that provides a *feature* description of an object. That feature array allows a system to locate a target in an image containing many other objects. Thus, after calculating feature vectors, known as SIFT keys, a nearest-neighbor approach is used to identify possible objects in an image. Moreover, that array of features is not affected by many of the complications experienced in other methods such as object scaling and/or rotation. However, some disadvantages made us discard SIFT for our purpose:

- It uses a varying number of features to describe an image and sometimes it might be not enough
- Detecting substantial levels of occlusion requires a large number of SIFT keys what can result in a high computational cost
- Large collections of keys can be space-consuming when many targets have to be tracked
- It was designed for perspective cameras, not for fisheye ones

All these approaches have been developed for perspective cameras. Although some research has been carried out to adapt them to omnidirectional devices (Fiala, 2005; Tamimi et al., 2006), a common solution is to apply a transformation to the omnidirectional image in order to obtain a panoramic one and to be able to use a traditional approach (Cielniak et al., 2003; Liu et al., 2003; Potúcek, 2003; Zhu et. al (2004); Mauthner et al. (2006); Puig et al., 2008). However, this might give rise to a high computational cost and/or mismatching errors. For all those reasons, we propose a new method which is composed of three different steps (see Fig. 1):

1. The minimum bounding rectangle that encloses each detected target is computed
2. Each area described by a minimum rectangle identifying a target, is transformed into a perspective image. For that, the following transformation is used:

$$\phi = c/R_{med} \tag{1}$$

$$R_{med} = (R_{min} + R_{max})/2 \tag{2}$$

$$c_1 = c_0 + (R_{min} + r) \sin \phi \tag{3}$$

$$r_1 = r_0 + (R_{min} + r) \cos \phi \tag{4}$$

where (c_0, r_0) represent the image center coordinates in terms of column and row respectively, while (c_1, r_1) are the coordinates in the new perspective image; ϕ is the angle between Y-axis and the ray from the image center to the considered pixel; and, R_{min} and R_{max} are, respectively, the minimum and maximum radius of a torus which encloses the area to be transformed. These radii are obtained from the four corners of the minimum rectangle that encloses the target to be transformed. However, there is a special situation to be taken into account. It is produced when the center of the image is in the minimum rectangle. This situation, once it is detected, is solved by setting R_{min} to 0.

On the other hand, note that only the detected targets are transformed into its cylindrical panoramic image, not the whole image. It allows the system to reduce the computational cost and time consumption. Moreover, the orientation problem is also solved, since all the resulting cylindrical panoramic images have the same orientation. In this way, it is easier to compare two different images of the same interest object

3. The cylindrical panoramic images obtained for the detected targets are compared with the ones obtained in the previous frame. A similarity likelihood criterion is used for matching different images of the same interest object. Moreover, in order to reduce computational cost, images to be compared must have a centroid distance lower than a threshold. This distance is measured in the fisheye image and is described by means of a circle of possible situations of the target having as center its current position and as radius the maximum distance allowed. In that way, the occlusion problem is solved, since all parts of the cylindrical panoramic images are being analyzed.

(a) Original Image | (b) Image from Segmentation Process | (c) Minimum rectangle that encloses the target | (d) Corresponding cylindrical panoramic image | (e) Matching process

Fig. 1. Tracking Process

This method is valid for matching targets in a monocular video sequence. Thus, when a dioptric stereo system is provided, the processing is changed. When an interest object firstly appears in an image, it is necessary to establish its corresponding image in the other camera of the stereo pair. For that, a disparity estimation approach is used. That estimation is carried out until the interest object is in the field of view of both stereo cameras. In that moment, the same identifier is assigned to both images of the interest object. Then, matching is done as a monocular system in a parallel way, but as both images have the same identifier it is possible to estimate its distance from the system whenever it is necessary. As it is performed in a parallel way and processing is not time-consuming, a real-time performance is obtained.

4. Experimental Results

For the experiments carried out, a mobile manipulator was used which incorporates a visual system composed of 2 fisheye cameras mounted on the robot base, pointing upwards to the ceiling, to guarantee the safety in its whole workspace. Fig. 2 depicts our experimental setup, which consists of a mobile Nomadic XR4000 base, a Mitsubishi PA10 arm, and two fisheye cameras (Sony *SSC-DC330P 1/3-inch color cameras* with *fish-eye vari-focal lenses Fujinon YV2.2x1.4A-2*, which provide 185-degree field of view). Images to be processed were acquired in 24-bit RGB color space with a 640x480 resolution.

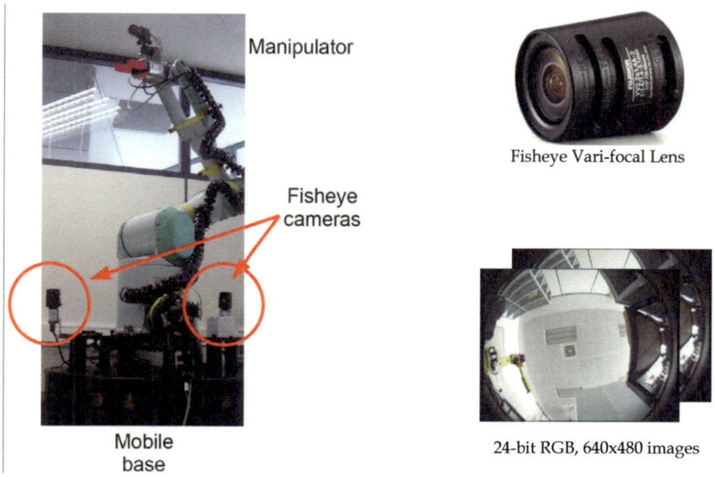

Fig. 2. Experimental Set-up

Different experiments were carried out obtaining a good performance in all of them. Some of the experimental results are depicted in Fig. 3. where different parts of the whole process are shown. The first column represents the image captured by a fisheye camera, then the binary image generated by the proposed approach appears in the next column. The three remaining columns represent several phases of the tracking process, that is, the generation of the minimum bounding rectangle and the cylindrical panoramic images. Note that in all cases, both the detection approach and the proposed tracking process were successful in their purpose, although some occlusions, rotation and/or scaling had occurred.

5. Conclusions & Future Work

We have presented a dioptric system for reliable robot vision by focusing on the tracking process. Dioptric cameras have the clear advantage of covering the whole workspace without resulting in a time consuming application, but there is little previous work about this kind of devices. Consequently, we had to implement novel techniques to achieve our goal. Thus, on the one hand, a process to detect moving objects within the observed scene was designed. The proposed adaptive background modeling approach combines moving object detection with global illumination change identification. It is composed of two different phases, which consider several factors which may affect the detection process, so that constraints in illumination conditions do not exist, and neither is it necessary to wait for some time for collecting enough data before starting to process.

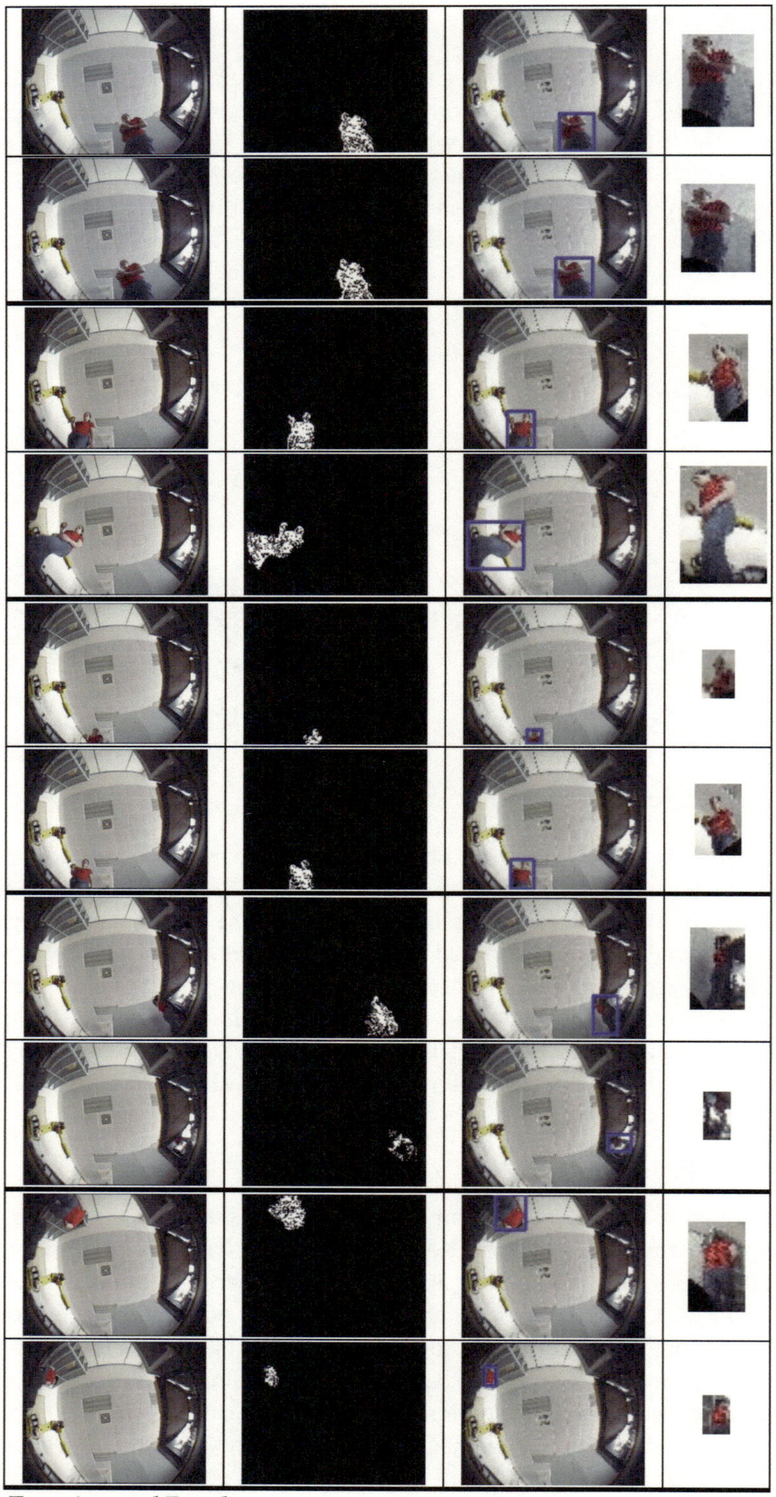

Fig. 3. Some Experimental Results

On the other hand, a new matching process has been proposed. Basically, it obtains a panoramic cylindrical image for each detected target from an image in which identified targets where enclosed in the minimum bounding rectangle. In this way, the rotation problem has disappeared. Next, each panoramic cylindrical image is compared with all the ones obtained in the previous frame whenever they are in its proximity. As all previous panoramic cylindrical images are used, the translation problem is eliminated. Finally, a similarity likelihood criterion is used for matching target images at two different times. With this method the occlusion problem is also solved. As time consumption is a critical issue in robotics, when a dioptric system is used, this processing is performed in a parallel way such that correspondence between two different panoramic cylindrical images of the same target taken at the same time for both cameras is established by means of a disparity map. Therefore, a complete real-time surveillance system has been presented.

6. Acknowledges

This research was partly supported by WCU (World Class University) program through the National Research Foundation of Korea funded by the Ministry of Education, Science and Technology (Grant No. R31-2008-000-10062-0), by the European Commission's Seventh Framework Programme FP7/2007-2013 under grant agreement 217077 (EYESHOTS project), by Ministerio de Ciencia e Innovación (DPI-2008-06636), by Generalitat Valenciana (PROMETEO/2009/052) and by Fundació Caixa Castelló-Bancaixa (P1-1B2008-51).

7. References

Baker, S. & Nayar, S.K. (1998). A Theory of Catadioptric Image Formation. *Proceedings of International Conference on Computer Vision (ICCV)*, pp. 35–42, 1998, Bombay, India

Baker, S. & Nayar, S.K. (1999). A Theory of Single-Viewpoint Catadioptric Image Formation. *International Journal on Computer Vision*, Vol. 2, No. 2, (1999), page numbers (175-196)

Bar-Shalom, Y. and Li X-R (1998). *Estimation and Tracking: Principles, Techniques and Software*, YBS Publishing, ISBN: 096483121X

Cervera, E.; Garcia-Aracil, N.; Martínez, E.; Nomdedeu, L. & del Pobil, A. Safety for a Robot Arm Moving Amidst Humans by Using Panoramic Vision. *Proceedings of IEEE International Conference on Robotics & Automation (ICRA)*, pp. 2183–2188, ISBN: 978-4244-1646-2, May 2008, Pasadena, California

Cielniak, G.; Miladinovic, M.; Hammarin, D. & Göranson, L. (2003). Appearance-based Tracking of Persons with an Omnidirectional Vision Sensor. *Proceedings of the 4th IEEE Workshop on Omnidirectional Vision (OmniVis)*, 2003, Madison, Wisconsin, USA

Fiala, M. (2005). Structure from Motion using SIFT Features and the PH Transform with Panoramic Imagery. *Proceedings of the 2nd Canadian Conference on Computer and Robot Vision (CRV)*, pp. 506–513, 2005

Geyer, C. & Daniilidis, K. (2000). A Unifying Theory for Central Panoramic Systems and Practical Applications. *Proceedings of 6th European Conference on Computer Vision (ECCV)*, pp. 445–461, ISBN: 3-540-67686-4, June 2000, Dublin, Ireland

Grewal, M., Andrews, S. and Angus, P. (2008) *Kalman Filtering Theory and Practice Using MATLAB*, Wiley-IEEE Press, ISBN: 978-0-470-17366-4

Haykin, S. (2001). *Kalman Filtering and Neural Networks*. John Wiley & Sons, Inc. ISBN: 978-0-471-36998-1

Kalman, R.E. and Bucy, R.S. (1961). New Results in Linear Filtering and Prediction Theory. *Journal of Basic Engineering* (1961)

Liu, H.; Wenkai, P.I. & Zha, H. (2003) Motion Detection for Multiple Moving Targets by Using an Omnidirectional Camera. *Proceedings of IEEE International Conference on Robotics, Intelligent Systems and Signal Processing*, pp. 422–426, October 2003, Chansgsha, China

Lowe, D.G. (1999). Object recognition from local scale-invariant features, *Proceedings of International Conference on Computer Vision*, pp. 1150–1157, September 1999, Corfu, Greece

Lowe, D.G. (2004). Distinctive image features from Scale-Invariant Keypoints. *International Journal of Computer Vision*, Vol. 60, No. 2, (2004), page numbers (91-110)

Mauthner, T.; Fraundorfer, F. & Bischof, H. (2006). Region Matching for Omnidirectional Images Using Virtual Camera Planes. *Proceedings of Computer Vision Winter Workshop*, February 2006, Czech Republic

Murillo, A.C.; Sagüés, C.; Guerrero, J.J.; Goedemé, T.; Tuytelaars, T. and Van Gool, L. (2006). From Omnidirectional Images to Hierarchical Localization. *Robotics and Autonomous Systems*, Vol. 55, No. 5, (December 2006), page numbers (372 – 382)

Potúcek, I. (2003). Person Tracking using Omnidirectional View. *Proceedings of the 9th International Student EEICT Conference and Competition*, pp. 603–607, ISBN: 80-214-2370, 2003, Brno, Czech Republic

Puig, L.; Guerrero, J. & Sturm, P. (2008). Matching of Omnidirectional and Perspectiva Images using the Hybrid Fundamental Matrix. *Proceedings of the Workshop on Omnidirectional Vision, Camera Networks and Non-Classical Cameras*, October 2008, Marseille, France

Svoboda, T.; Pajdla, T. & Hlavác, V. (1998). Epipolar Geometry for Panoramic Cameras. *Proceedings of the 5th European Conference on Computer Vision (ECCV)*, pp. 218–231, ISBN: 3-540-64569-1, June 1998, Freiburg, Germany

Tamimi, H.; Andreasson, H.; Treptow, A.; Duckett, T. & Zell, A. (2006). Localization of Mobile Robots with Omnidirectional Vision using Particle Filter and Iterative SIFT. *Robotics and Autonomous Systems*, Vol. 54 (2006), page numbers (758-765)

Wei, S.C.; Yagi, Y. & Yachida, M. (1998). Building Local Floor Map by Use of Ultrasonic and Omni-directional Vision Sensor. *Proceedings of IEEE International Conference on Robotics & Automation (ICRA)*, pp. 2548–2553, ISBN: 0-7803-4300-X, May 1998, Leuven, Belgium

Wood, R.W. (1906). Fish-eye Views. *Philosophical Magazine*, Vol. 12, No. 6, (1906), page numbers (159–162)

Zarchan, P. and Mussof, H. (2005) *Fundamentals of Kalman Filtering: A Practical Approach*, American Institute of Aeronautics & Ast (AIAA), ISBN: 978-1563474552

Zhu, Z.; Karuppiah, D.R.; Riseman, E.M. & Hanson, A.R. (2004). Keeping Smart, Omnidirectional Eyes on You [Adaptive Panoramic StereoVision]. *IEEE Robotics and Automation Magazine – Special Issue on Panoramic Robotics*, Vol. 11, No. 4, (December 2004), page numbers (69–78), ISSN: 1070-9932

3

An Approach for Optimal Design of Robot Vision Systems

Kanglin Xu
New Mexico Tech
USA

1. Introduction

The accuracy of a robot manipulator's position in an application environment is dependent on the manufacturing accuracy and the control accuracy. Unfortunately, there always exist both manufacturing error and control error. Calibration is an approach to identifying the accurate geometry of the robot. In general, robots must be calibrated to improve their accuracy. A calibrated robot has a higher absolute positioning accuracy. However, calibration involves robot kinematic modeling, pose measurement, parameter identification and accuracy compensation. These calibrations are hard work and time consuming. For an active vision system, a robot device for controlling the motion of cameras based on visual information, the kinematic calibrations are even more difficult. As a result, even though calibration is fundamental, most existing active vision systems are not accurately calibrated (Shih et al., 1998). To address this problem, many researchers select self-calibration techniques. In this article, we apply a more active approach, that is, we reduce the kinematic errors at the design stage instead of at the calibration stage. Furthermore, we combine the model described in this article with a cost-tolerance model to implement an optimal design for active vision systems so that they can be used more widely in enterprise. We begin to build the model using the relation between two connecting joint coordinates defined by a DH homogeneous transformation.We then use the differential relationship between these two connecting joint coordinates to extend the model so that it relates the kinematic parameter errors of each link to the pose error of the last link. Given this model, we can implement an algorithm for estimating depth using stereo cameras, extending the model to handle an active stereo vision system. Based on these two models, we have developed a set of C++ class libraries. Using this set of libraries, we can estimate robot pose errors or depth estimation errors based on kinematic errors. Furthermore, we can apply these libraries to find the key factors that affect accuracy. As a result, more reasonable minimum tolerances or manufacturing requirements can be defined so that the manufacturing cost is reduced while retaining relatively high accuracy. Besides providing an approach to find the key factors and best settings of key parameters, we demonstrate how to use a cost-tolerance model to evaluate the settings. In this way, we can implement optimal *design for manufacturing*(DFM) in enterprises. Because our models are derived from the Denavit-Hartenberg transformation matrix, differential changes for the transformation matrix and link parameters, and the fundamental algorithm for estimating depth using stereo cameras, they are suitable for any manipulator or stereo active vision system. The remainder of this article is organized as follows. Section 2 derives the model for analyzing the effect of parameter errors on robot poses. Section 3 introduces the extended kinematic error model for an active vision system. It should be noted that this extended model is the main contribution of our article and that we integrate the robot differential kinematics into an active vision system. Section 4 provides more detailed steps describing how to use our approach. Section 5 discusses some issues related to the design of active vision systems and DFM. Section 6 presents a case study for a real active vision system and cost evaluation using a cost-tolerance model. Finally, Section 7 offers concluding remarks.

2. Kinematic Differential Model Derived from DH Transformation Matrix

A serial link manipulator consists of a sequence of links connected together by actuated joints (Paul, 1981). The kinematical relationship between any two successive actuated joints is defined by the DH (Denavit-Hartenberg) homogeneous transformation matrix. The DH homogeneous transformation matrix is dependent on the four link parameters, that is, θ_i, α_i, r_i, and d_i. For the generic robot forward kinematics, only one of these four parameters is variable. If joint i is rotational, the θ_i is the joint variable and d_i, α_i, and r_i are constants. If joint i is translational, the d_i is the joint variable and θ, α_i, and r_i are constants. Since there always exist errors for these four parameters, we also need a differential relationship between any two successive actuated joints. This relationship is defined by matrix $d\mathbf{A}_i$ which is dependent on $d\theta_i$, $d\alpha_i$, dr_i, and dd_i as well as θ_i, α_i, r_i, and d_i. Given the relationship between two successive joints $\mathbf{A}_i$ and differential relationship between two successive joints $d\mathbf{A}_i$, we can derive an equation to calculate the accurate position and orientation of the end-effector with respect to the world coordinate system for a manipulator with N degrees of freedom(N-DOF).
In this section, we will first derive the differential changes between two successive frames in subsection *2.1*. We then give the error model for a manipulator of N degrees of freedom with respect to the world coordinate system in subsection *2.2*.

2.1 The Error Relation between Two Frames

For an N-DOF manipulator described by the Denavit-Hartenberg definition, the homogeneous transformation matrix $\mathbf{A}_i$ which relates the *(i-1)*th joint to ith joint is (Paul, 1981)

$$\mathbf{A}_i = \begin{bmatrix} c\theta_i & -s\theta_i\, c\alpha_i & s\theta_i\, s\alpha_i & r_i c\theta_i \\ s\theta_i & c\theta_i\, c\alpha_i & -c\theta_i\, s\alpha_i & r_i s\theta_i \\ 0 & s\alpha_i & c\alpha_i & d_i \\ 0 & 0 & 0 & 1 \end{bmatrix} \tag{1}$$

where s and c refer to sine and cosine functions, and θ_i, α_i, r_i, and d_i are link parameters.
Given the individual transformation matrix $\mathbf{A}_i$, the end of an N-DOF manipulator can be represented as

$$\mathbf{T}_N = \mathbf{A}_1 \mathbf{A}_2 \cdots \mathbf{A}_{N-1} \mathbf{A}_N \tag{2}$$

We will also use the following definitions. We define $\mathbf{U}_i = \mathbf{A}_i \mathbf{A}_{i+1} \cdots \mathbf{A}_N$ with $U_{N+1} = I$, and a homogeneous matrix

$$\mathbf{A}_i = \begin{bmatrix} \mathbf{n}_i & \mathbf{o}_i & \mathbf{a}_i & \mathbf{p}_i \\ 0 & 0 & 0 & 1 \end{bmatrix} \tag{3}$$

where $\mathbf{n}_i$, $\mathbf{o}_i$, $\mathbf{a}_i$ and $\mathbf{p}_i$ are 3×1 vectors.
Given the ith actual coordinate frame $\mathbf{A}_i$ and the ith nominal frame $\mathbf{A}_i^0$, we can obtain an additive differential transformation $d\mathbf{A}_i$

$$d\mathbf{A}_i = \mathbf{A}_i - \mathbf{A}_i^0. \tag{4}$$

If we represent the ith additive differential transformation $d\mathbf{A}_i$ as the ith differential transformation $\delta\mathbf{A}_i$ right multiplying the transformation $\mathbf{A}_i$, we can write

$$d\mathbf{A}_i = \mathbf{A}_i\,\delta\mathbf{A}_i. \tag{5}$$

In this case, the changes are with respect to coordinate frame $\mathbf{A}_i$.
Assuming the link parameters are continuous and differentiable we can represent $d\mathbf{A}_i$ in another way, that is

$$d\mathbf{A}_i = \frac{\partial\mathbf{A}_i}{\partial\theta_i}d\theta_i + \frac{\partial\mathbf{A}_i}{\partial\alpha_i}d\alpha_i + \frac{\partial\mathbf{A}_i}{\partial r_i}dr_i + \frac{\partial\mathbf{A}_i}{\partial d_i}dd_i. \tag{6}$$

Comparing (5) with (6), we obtain

$$\begin{aligned}\delta\mathbf{A}_i &= \mathbf{A}^{-1}\Big(\frac{\partial\mathbf{A}_i}{\partial\theta_i}d\theta_i + \frac{\partial\mathbf{A}_i}{\partial\alpha_i}d\alpha_i \\ &+ \frac{\partial\mathbf{A}_i}{\partial r_i}dr_i + \frac{\partial\mathbf{A}_i}{\partial d_i}dd_i\Big).\end{aligned} \tag{7}$$

For the homogeneous matrix, the inverse matrix of $\mathbf{A}_i$ is

$$\mathbf{A}_i^{-1} = \begin{bmatrix} \mathbf{n}_i^t & -\mathbf{p}_i\cdot\mathbf{n}_i \\ \mathbf{o}_i^t & -\mathbf{p}_i\cdot\mathbf{o}_i \\ \mathbf{a}_i^t & -\mathbf{p}_i\cdot\mathbf{a}_i \\ \mathbf{0}_{1\times 3} & 1 \end{bmatrix} \tag{8}$$

By differentiating all the elements of equation (1) with respect to θ_i, α_i, r_i and d_i respectively, we obtain

$$\frac{\partial\mathbf{A}_i}{\partial\theta_i} = \begin{bmatrix} -s\theta_i & -c\theta_i\,c\alpha_i & c\theta_i\,s\alpha_i & -r_i\,s\theta_i \\ c\theta_i & -s\theta_i\,c\alpha_i & s\theta_i\,c\alpha_i & r_i\,c\theta_i \\ 0 & 0 & 0 & 0 \\ 0 & 0 & 0 & 0 \end{bmatrix} \tag{9}$$

$$\frac{\partial\mathbf{A}_i}{\partial\alpha_i} = \begin{bmatrix} 0 & s\theta_i\,s\alpha_i & s\theta_i\,c\alpha_i & 0 \\ 0 & -c\theta_i\,s\alpha_i & -c\theta_i\,c\alpha_i & 0 \\ 0 & c\alpha_i & -s\alpha_i & 0 \\ 0 & 0 & 0 & 0 \end{bmatrix} \tag{10}$$

$$\frac{\partial\mathbf{A}_i}{\partial r_i} = \begin{bmatrix} 0 & 0 & 0 & c\theta_i \\ 0 & 0 & 0 & s\theta_i \\ 0 & 0 & 0 & 0 \\ 0 & 0 & 0 & 0 \end{bmatrix} \tag{11}$$

$$\frac{\partial\mathbf{A}_i}{\partial d_i} = \begin{bmatrix} 0 & 0 & 0 & 0 \\ 0 & 0 & 0 & 0 \\ 0 & 0 & 0 & 1 \\ 0 & 0 & 0 & 0 \end{bmatrix} \tag{12}$$

Substituting equations (8), (9), (10), (11) and (12) into (7), we obtain

$$\delta\mathbf{A}_i = \begin{bmatrix} 0 & -c\alpha_i\,d\theta_i & s\alpha_i\,d\theta_i & dr_i \\ c\alpha_i\,d\theta_i & 0 & -d\alpha_i & u \\ -s\alpha_i\,d\theta_i & d\alpha_i & 0 & v \\ 0 & 0 & 0 & 0 \end{bmatrix} \tag{13}$$

where $u = r_i\ c\alpha_i\ d\theta_i + s\alpha_i\ dd_i$ and $v = r_i\ s\alpha_i\ d\theta_i + c\alpha_i\ dd_i$. Since $d\mathbf{A}_i = \mathbf{A}_i\ \delta\mathbf{A}_i$, therefore (Paul, 1981)

$$\begin{pmatrix} dx_i \\ dy_i \\ dz_i \end{pmatrix} = \begin{pmatrix} dd_i \\ d_i\ c\alpha\ d\theta_i + s\alpha_i\ dr_i \\ -d_i\ s\alpha\ d\theta_i + c\alpha_i\ dr_i \end{pmatrix} \tag{14}$$

$$\begin{pmatrix} \delta_{x_i} \\ \delta_{y_i} \\ \delta_{z_i} \end{pmatrix} = \begin{pmatrix} d\alpha_i \\ s\alpha\ d\theta_i \\ c\alpha\ d\theta_i \end{pmatrix} \tag{15}$$

where $(dx_i \quad dy_i \quad dz_i)^t$ is the differential translation vector and $\left(\delta_{x_i} \quad \delta_{y_i} \quad \delta_{z_i}\right)^t$ is the differential rotation vector with respect to frame $\mathbf{A}_i$.
Let $\mathbf{d}_i = (dx_i\ dy_i\ dz_i)^t$ and $\boldsymbol{\delta}_i = (\delta_{x_i}\ \delta_{y_i}\ \delta_{z_i})^t$. The differential vectors $\mathbf{d}_i$ and $\boldsymbol{\delta}_i$ can be represented as a linear combination of the parameter changes, which are

$$\mathbf{d}_i = \mathbf{k}_i^1\ d\theta_i + \mathbf{k}_i^2\ dd_i + \mathbf{k}_i^3\ dr_i \tag{16}$$

and

$$\boldsymbol{\delta}_i = \mathbf{k}_i^2\ d\theta_i + \mathbf{k}_i^3\ d\alpha_i \tag{17}$$

where $\mathbf{k}_i^1 = (0 \ \ r_i c\alpha_i \ \ -r_i s\alpha_i)^t$, $\mathbf{k}_i^2 = (0 \ \ s\alpha_i \ \ c\alpha_i)^t$ and $\mathbf{k}_i^3 = (1\ 0\ 0)^t$.

2.2 Kinematic Differential Model of a Manipulator

Wu (Wu, 1984) has developed a kinematic error model of an N-DOF robot manipulator based on the differential changes $d\mathbf{A}_i$ and the error matrix $\delta\mathbf{A}_i$ due to four small kinematic errors at an individual joint coordinate frame.
Let $\mathbf{d}^N$ and $\boldsymbol{\delta}^N$ denote the three translation errors and rotation errors of the end of a manipulator respectively where $\mathbf{d}^N = (d\mathbf{x}^N\ d\mathbf{y}^N\ d\mathbf{z}^N)$ and $\boldsymbol{\delta}^N = (\boldsymbol{\delta}_x^N\ \boldsymbol{\delta}_y^N\ \boldsymbol{\delta}_z^N)$. From (Wu, 1984), we obtain

$$\begin{aligned} \begin{pmatrix} \mathbf{d}^N \\ \boldsymbol{\delta}^N \end{pmatrix} &= \begin{pmatrix} \mathbf{M}_1 \\ \mathbf{M}_2 \end{pmatrix} d\boldsymbol{\theta} + \begin{pmatrix} \mathbf{M}_2 \\ \mathbf{0} \end{pmatrix} d\mathbf{r} \\ &+ \begin{pmatrix} \mathbf{M}_3 \\ \mathbf{0} \end{pmatrix} d\mathbf{d} + \begin{pmatrix} \mathbf{M}_4 \\ \mathbf{M}_3 \end{pmatrix} d\boldsymbol{\alpha} \end{aligned} \tag{18}$$

where

$$\begin{aligned} d\boldsymbol{\theta} &= (d\theta_1 \quad d\theta_2 \quad \ldots \quad d\theta_N)^t \\ d\mathbf{r} &= (dr_1 \quad dr_2 \quad \ldots \quad dr_N)^t \\ d\mathbf{d} &= (dd_1 \quad dd_2 \quad \ldots \quad dd_N)^t \\ d\boldsymbol{\alpha} &= (d\alpha_1 \quad d\alpha_2 \quad \ldots \quad d\alpha_N)^t \end{aligned}$$

and $\mathbf{M}_1$, $\mathbf{M}_2$, $\mathbf{M}_3$ and $\mathbf{M}_4$ are all $3 \times N$ matrices whose components are the function of N joint variables. The ith column of $\mathbf{M}_1$, $\mathbf{M}_2$, $\mathbf{M}_3$ and $\mathbf{M}_4$ can be expressed as follows:

$$\mathbf{M}_1^i = \begin{bmatrix} \mathbf{n}_{n+1}^u \cdot \mathbf{k}_i^1 + (\mathbf{p}_{i+1}^u \times \mathbf{n}_{i+1}^u) \cdot \mathbf{k}_i^2 \\ \mathbf{o}_{i+1}^u \cdot \mathbf{k}_i^1 + (\mathbf{p}_{i+1}^u \times \mathbf{o}_{i+1}^u) \cdot \mathbf{k}_i^2 \\ \mathbf{a}_{i+1}^u \cdot \mathbf{k}_i^1 + (\mathbf{p}_{i+1}^u \times \mathbf{a}_{i+1}^u) \cdot \mathbf{k}_i^2 \end{bmatrix}$$

$$\mathbf{M}_2^i = \begin{bmatrix} \mathbf{n}_{n+1}^u \cdot \mathbf{k}_i^2 \\ \mathbf{o}_{i+1}^u \cdot \mathbf{k}_i^2 \\ \mathbf{a}_{i+1}^u \cdot \mathbf{k}_i^2 \end{bmatrix}$$

$$\mathbf{M}_3^i = \begin{bmatrix} \mathbf{n}_{n+1}^u \cdot \mathbf{k}_i^3 \\ \mathbf{o}_{i+1}^u \cdot \mathbf{k}_i^3 \\ \mathbf{a}_{i+1}^u \cdot \mathbf{k}_i^3 \end{bmatrix}$$

$$\mathbf{M}_4^i = \begin{bmatrix} (\mathbf{p}_{i+1}^u \times \mathbf{n}_{i+1}^u) \cdot \mathbf{k}_i^3 \\ (\mathbf{p}_{i+1}^u \times \mathbf{o}_{i+1}^u) \cdot \mathbf{k}_i^3 \\ (\mathbf{p}_{i+1}^u \times \mathbf{a}_{i+1}^u) \cdot \mathbf{k}_i^3 \end{bmatrix}$$

where $\mathbf{n}_{i+1}^u$, $\mathbf{o}_{i+1}^u$, $\mathbf{a}_{i+1}^u$ and $\mathbf{p}_{i+1}^u$ are four 3×1 vectors of matrix $\mathbf{U}_{i+1}$ which is defined as $\mathbf{U}_i = \mathbf{A}_i \mathbf{A}_{i+1} \cdots \mathbf{A}_N$ with $\mathbf{U}_{N+1} = I$.

Using the above equations, the manipulator's differential changes with respect to the base can be represented as

$$d\mathbf{T}_N = \begin{bmatrix} d\mathbf{n} & d\mathbf{o} & d\mathbf{a} & d\mathbf{p} \\ 0 & 0 & 0 & 1 \end{bmatrix} \tag{19}$$

where

$$\begin{aligned} d\mathbf{n} &= \mathbf{o}_1^u \, \delta_z^N - \mathbf{a}_1^u \, \delta_y^N \\ d\mathbf{o} &= -\mathbf{n}_1^u \, \delta_z^N + \mathbf{a}_1^u \, \delta_x^N \\ d\mathbf{a} &= \mathbf{n}_1^u \, \delta_y^N - \mathbf{o}_1^u \, \delta_x^N \\ d\mathbf{p} &= \mathbf{n}_1^u \, d\mathbf{x}^N + \mathbf{o}_1^u \, d\mathbf{y}^N + \mathbf{a}_1^u \, d\mathbf{z}^N \end{aligned}$$

and $\mathbf{n}_1^u$, $\mathbf{o}_1^u$, $\mathbf{a}_1^u$ are four 3×1 vectors of matrix $\mathbf{U}_1$.

Finally, the real position and orientation at the end of the manipulator can be calculated by

$$\mathbf{T}_N^R = \mathbf{T}_N + d\mathbf{T}_N \tag{20}$$

where $\mathbf{T}_N = \mathbf{A}_1 \mathbf{A}_2 \cdots \mathbf{A}_N$.

3. Extended Model for an Active Visual System

An active vision system, which has become an increasingly important research topic, is a robot device for controlling the motion of cameras based on visual information. The primary advantage of directed vision is its ability to use camera redirection to look at widely separated areas of interest at fairly high resolution instead of using a single sensor or array of cameras to cover the entire visual field with uniform resolution. It is able to interact with the environment actively by altering its viewpoint rather than observing it passively. Like an end effector, a camera can also be connected by a fixed homogeneous transformation to the last link. In addition, the structure and mechanism are similar to those of robots. Since an active visual system can kinematically be handled like a manipulator of N degrees of freedom, we can use the derived solutions in the last section directly.

In this section, we will first introduce the camera coordinate system corresponding to the standard coordinate system definition for the approaches used in the computer vision literature and describe a generic algorithm for location estimation with stereo cameras. We will then integrate them with the kinematic error model of a manipulator.

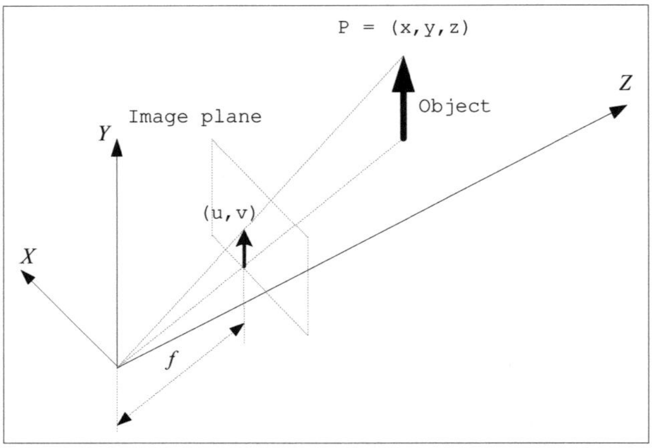

Fig. 1. The camera coordinate system whose x- and y-axes form a basis for the image plane, whose z-axis is perpendicular to the image plane (along the optical axis), and whose origin is located at distance f behind the image plane, where f is the focal length of the camera lens.

3.1 Pose Estimation with Stereo Cameras

We assign the camera coordinate system with x- and y-axes forming a basis for the image plane, the z-axis perpendicular to the image plane (along the optical axis), and with its origin located at distance f behind the image plane, where f is the focal length of the camera lens. This is illustrated in Fig. 1. A point, ${}^{c}\mathbf{p} = (x, y, z)^t$ whose coordinates are expressed with respect to the camera coordinate frame C, will project onto the image plane with coordinates $\mathbf{p}_i = (u, v)^t$ given by

$$\pi(x, y, z) = \begin{pmatrix} u \\ v \end{pmatrix} = \frac{f}{z}\begin{pmatrix} x \\ y \end{pmatrix} \tag{21}$$

If the coordinates of ${}^{x}\mathbf{p}$ are expressed relative to coordinate frame X, we must first perform the coordinate transformation

$${}^{c}\mathbf{p} = {}^{c}\mathbf{T}_x {}^{x}\mathbf{p}. \tag{22}$$

Let ${}^{a}\mathbf{T}_{c1}$ represent the pose of the first camera relative to the arbitrary reference coordinate frame **A**. By inverting this transformation, we can obtain ${}^{c1}\mathbf{T}_a$, where

$${}^{c1}\mathbf{T}_a = \begin{bmatrix} {}^{c1}r_{11} & {}^{c1}r_{12} & {}^{c1}r_{13} & {}^{c1}t_x \\ {}^{c1}r_{21} & {}^{c1}r_{22} & {}^{c1}r_{23} & {}^{c1}t_y \\ {}^{c1}r_{31} & {}^{c1}r_{32} & {}^{c1}r_{33} & {}^{c1}t_z \\ 0 & 0 & 0 & 1 \end{bmatrix} \tag{23}$$

For convenience, let

$${}^{c1}\mathbf{R}_1 = ({}^{c1}r_{11}\ {}^{c1}r_{12}\ {}^{c1}r_{13}) \tag{24}$$
$${}^{c1}\mathbf{R}_2 = ({}^{c1}r_{21}\ {}^{c1}r_{22}\ {}^{c1}r_{23}) \tag{25}$$
$${}^{c1}\mathbf{R}_1 = ({}^{c1}r_{31}\ {}^{c1}r_{32}\ {}^{c1}r_{33}) \tag{26}$$

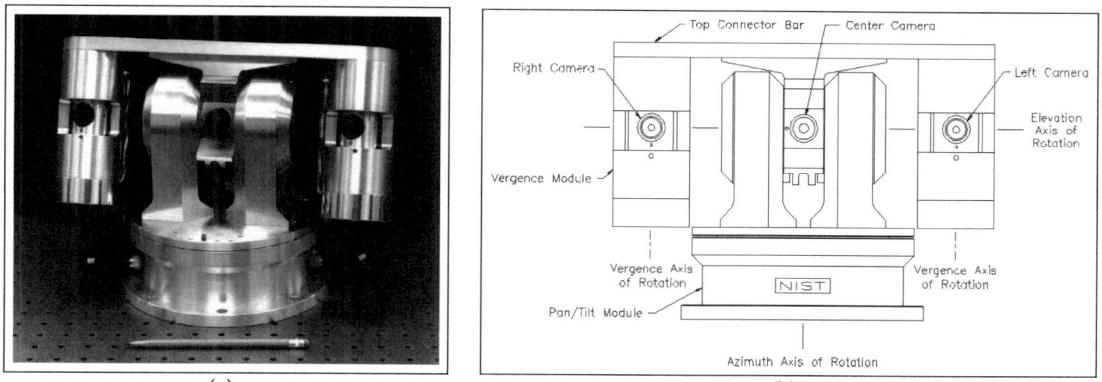

(a) (b)

Fig. 2. *The TRICLOPS Active Vision System has four axes. They are pan axis, tilt axis, left vergence axis and right vergence axis. The pan axis can rotate around a vertical axis through the center of the base. The tilt axis can rotate around a horizontal line that intersects the base rotation axis. The left and right vergence axes intersect and are perpendicular to the tilt axis. These two pictures come from Wavering, Schneiderman, and Fiala (Wavering et al.). We would like to thank to the paper's authors.*

Given the image coordinates, Hutchinson, Hager and Corke (Hutchinson et al., 1996) have presented an approach to find the object location with respect to the frame **A** using the following equations:

$$\mathbf{A}_1 \cdot {}^a\mathbf{p} = \mathbf{b}_1 \tag{27}$$

where

$$\mathbf{A}_1 = \begin{pmatrix} f_1\,{}^{c1}\mathbf{R}_1 - u_1\,{}^{c1}\mathbf{R}_3 \\ f_1\,{}^{c1}\mathbf{R}_2 - v_1\,{}^{c1}\mathbf{R}_3 \end{pmatrix} \tag{28}$$

$$\mathbf{b}_1 = \begin{pmatrix} u_1\,{}^{c1}t_z - f_1\,{}^{c1}t_x \\ v_1\,{}^{c1}t_z - f_1\,{}^{c1}t_y \end{pmatrix} \tag{29}$$

Given a second camera at location ${}^a\mathbf{X}_{c2}$, we can compute ${}^{c2}\mathbf{X}_a$, $\mathbf{A}_2$ and ${}^a\mathbf{p}$ similarly. Finally we have an over-determined system for finding ${}^a\mathbf{p}$

$$\begin{pmatrix} \mathbf{A}_1 \\ \mathbf{A}_2 \end{pmatrix} {}^a\mathbf{p} = \begin{pmatrix} \mathbf{b}_1 \\ \mathbf{b}_2 \end{pmatrix} \tag{30}$$

where $\mathbf{A}_1$ and $\mathbf{b}_1$ are defined by (28) and (29) while $\mathbf{A}_2$ and $\mathbf{b}_2$ are defined as follows:

$$\mathbf{A}_2 = \begin{pmatrix} f_2\,{}^{c2}\mathbf{R}_1 - u_2\,{}^{c2}\mathbf{R}_3 \\ f_2\,{}^{c2}\mathbf{R}_2 - v_2\,{}^{c2}\mathbf{R}_3 \end{pmatrix} \tag{31}$$

$$\mathbf{b}_2 = \begin{pmatrix} u_2\,{}^{c2}t_z - f_2\,{}^{c2}t_x \\ v_2\,{}^{c2}t_z - f_2\,{}^{c2}t_y \end{pmatrix}. \tag{32}$$

3.2 Pose Estimation Based on an Active Vision System

As mentioned before, assuming that the camera frames are assigned as shown in Fig. 1 and that the projective geometry of the camera is modeled by perspective projection, a point ${}^c\mathbf{p} = ({}^cx\ {}^cy\ {}^cz)^t$, whose coordinates are expressed with respect to the camera coordinate frame will project onto the image plane with coordinates $(u\ v)^t$ given by

$$\begin{pmatrix} u \\ v \end{pmatrix} = \frac{f}{{}^cz} \begin{pmatrix} {}^cx \\ {}^cy \end{pmatrix} \tag{33}$$

For convenience, we suppose that f - the focal length of lens, does not have an error. This assumption is only for simplicity purposes and we will discuss this issue again in Section 5. Another problem is that the difference between the real pose of the camera and its nominal pose will affect the image coordinates. This problem is difficult to solve because the image coordinates are dependent on the depth of the object which is unknown. If we assume $f/{}^cz \ll 1$, we can regard them as high order error terms and ignore them. From these assumptions, we can obtain the real position and orientation of the left camera coordinate frame which is

$${}^a\mathbf{T}_{c1} = \mathbf{T}_1^R \mathbf{A}_{c1} \tag{34}$$

and those of the right camera coordinate frame which is

$${}^a\mathbf{T}_{c2} = \mathbf{T}_2^R \mathbf{A}_{c2} \tag{35}$$

In the above two equations, $\mathbf{T}_1^R$, $\mathbf{T}_2^R$ are the real poses of the end links and $\mathbf{A}_{c1}$, $\mathbf{A}_{c2}$ are two operators which relate the camera frames to their end links.
Given Equation (34) and (35), we can invert them to get ${}^{c1}\mathbf{T}_a$ and ${}^{c2}\mathbf{T}_a$. Then we can obtain an over-determined system using the method mentioned before. This system can be solved by the least squares approach as follows (Lawson & Hanson, 1995):

$${}^a\mathbf{p} = \left[(\mathbf{A}^T\mathbf{A})^{-1}\mathbf{A}^T \right] \mathbf{b} \tag{36}$$

where

$$\mathbf{A} = \begin{pmatrix} f_1\ {}^{c1}\mathbf{R}_1 - u_1\ {}^{c1}\mathbf{R}_3 \\ f_1\ {}^{c1}\mathbf{R}_2 - v_1\ {}^{c1}\mathbf{R}_3 \\ f_2\ {}^{c2}\mathbf{R}_1 - u_2\ {}^{c2}\mathbf{R}_3 \\ f_2\ {}^{c2}\mathbf{R}_2 - v_2\ {}^{c2}\mathbf{R}_3 \end{pmatrix} \tag{37}$$

$$\mathbf{b} = \begin{pmatrix} u_1\ {}^{c1}t_z - f_1\ {}^{c1}t_x \\ v_1\ {}^{c1}t_z - f_1\ {}^{c1}t_y \\ u_2\ {}^{c2}t_z - f_2\ {}^{c2}t_x \\ v_2\ {}^{c2}t_z - f_2\ {}^{c2}t_y \end{pmatrix} \tag{38}$$

If the superscript a in equations (34) and (35) indicates the world frame, we can calculate the position of $\mathbf{P}$ in world space.

4. Optimal Structure Design for Active Vision Systems

In the previous section, we derived an equation to calculate the real position when using a active vision with kinematic errors to estimate the location of a point P in the world space. Given this equation, it is straightforward to design the structure of an active vision system optimally. First, we can use $\mathbf{T}_1$ and $\mathbf{T}_2$ to replace $\mathbf{T}_1^R$ and $\mathbf{T}_2^R$ in equations (34) and (35). We then invert the resulting ${}^a\mathbf{T}_{c1}$ and ${}^a\mathbf{T}_{c2}$ to get ${}^{c1}\mathbf{T}_a$ and ${}^{c2}\mathbf{T}_a$. Finally we solve the over-determined system by the least squares approach to obtain the nominal pose of the cameras $\mathbf{P}^N$. The difference between these two results, *i.e.*

$$\mathbf{E} = \mathbf{P} - \mathbf{P}^N, \tag{39}$$

is the estimation error.

Note that the estimation errors are dependent on the joint variables and are a function of these joint variables. Consequently, a series of estimation errors can be obtained based on different poses of the stereo vision system. A curve describing the relationship between estimation errors and joint variables can be drawn. This curve can help us to analyze the estimation error or to design an active vision system. Inspired by the eyes of human beings and animals, we usually select a mechanical architecture with bilateral symmetry when we design a binocular or stereo active vision system. In this way, we can also simplify our design and manufacture procedures, and thus reduce the our design work and cost. We summarize our method described in the previous sections as follows:

1. Calculate transformation matrix $\mathbf{A}_i$ for each link based on the nominal size of the system and use them to calculate $\mathbf{U}_1, \mathbf{U}_2, \cdots, \mathbf{U}_{N+1}$, where $\mathbf{U}_i = \mathbf{A}_i\mathbf{A}_{i+1}\cdots\mathbf{A}_N$, $\mathbf{U}_{N+1} = I$ and $\mathbf{T}_1 = \mathbf{U}_1$.
2. Calculate the operator $\mathbf{A}_{c1}$ which relates the camera frame to its end link and multiply it with $\mathbf{T}_1$ to obtain the nominal position and orientation of the camera coordinate frame $\mathbf{T}_{c1}$.
3. Repeat the above two steps to obtain the nominal position and orientation of the other camera coordinate frame $\mathbf{T}_{c2}$.
4. Invert frames $\mathbf{T}_{c1}$ and $\mathbf{T}_{c2}$ to obtain ${}^{c1}\mathbf{T}$ and ${}^{c2}\mathbf{T}$. Here we assume that $\mathbf{T}_{c1}$ represents the pose of the first camera relative to the world frame. Since they are homogeneous matrices, we can guarantee that their inverse matrices exist.
5. Derive Equation (36), an over-determined system using ${}^{c1}\mathbf{T}$ and ${}^{c2}\mathbf{T}$ and solve it by the least squares approach to find nominal location estimation $\mathbf{P}^N$.
6. Calculate four $3 \times N$ matrices $\mathbf{M}_1$, $\mathbf{M}_2$, $\mathbf{M}_3$ and $\mathbf{M}_4$ in Equation (18), which are determined by the elements of matrices in $\mathbf{U}_i$ obtained in the first step. Since $\mathbf{U}_i$ is dependent on i^{th} link parameters θ_i, α_i, r_i and d_i, these four matrices are functions of the system link geometrical parameters as well as of the joint variable $\boldsymbol{\theta}$.
7. Based on performance requirements, machining capability and manufacturing costs, distribute tolerances to the four parameters of each link. Basically, the three geometrical tolerances $d\boldsymbol{\alpha}$, $d\mathbf{d}$, and $d\mathbf{r}$ affect manufacturing and assembling costs while the joint variable tolerance $d\boldsymbol{\theta}$ affects control cost.
8. Given four matrices $\mathbf{M}_1$, $\mathbf{M}_2$, $\mathbf{M}_3$, $\mathbf{M}_4$ and tolerances for each link, we can use Equation (19) to compute the total error with respect to the base frame. By adding it to the $\mathbf{T}_1$ obtained in the first step, we can have $\mathbf{T}_1^R$, the real position and orientation of the end link for the first camera. Similar to *Step 2*, we need to use the operator $\mathbf{A}_{c1}$ to do one more transformation to find the real position and orientation of camera coordinate frame $\mathbf{T}_{c1}^R$.

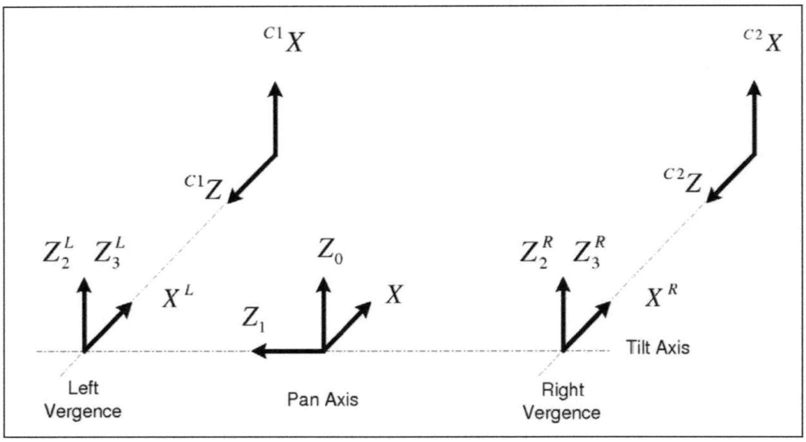

Fig. 3. Coordinate Frames for TRICLOPS - *Frame 0* for world frame; *Frame 1* for Pan; *Frame 2(left)* for left tilt; *Frame 2(right)* for right tilt; *Frame 3(left)* for left vergence; *Frame 3(right)* for right vergence. There are also two camera frames C_1 and C_2 whose original are located at distance f behind the image planes.

9. Repeating *Step 6*, *Step 7* and *Step 8* for the second camera, we can obtain $\mathbf{T}_{c2}^{R}$. As mentioned above, we usually have a symmetry structure for a stereo vision system. We assign the same tolerances $d\boldsymbol{\alpha}$, $d\boldsymbol{\theta}$, $d\mathbf{d}$ and $d\mathbf{r}$ for the two subsystems. Otherwise, the subsystem with low precision will dominate the whole performance of the system, and therefore we will waste the manufacturing cost for the subsystem with highest precision.
10. Similar to *Step 4* and *Step 5*, we can obtain the inverse matrices of $\mathbf{T}_{c1}^{R}$ and $\mathbf{T}_{c2}^{R}$, and use them to build another over-determined system. Solving it, we can have real pose $\mathbf{P}$ with respect to the world frame. The difference between $\mathbf{P}$ and $\mathbf{P}^{N}$ is the estimation error.
11. Repeat the above ten steps using another group of joint variables $\boldsymbol{\theta}_1, \boldsymbol{\theta}_2, \cdots, \boldsymbol{\theta}_N$ until we exhaust all the joint variables in the $\boldsymbol{\Theta}$ domain.
12. After exhausting all the joint variables in the $\boldsymbol{\Theta}$ domain, we have a maximum estimation error for assigning tolerances. Obviously, if this maximum does not satisfy the performance requirement, we need to adjust tolerances to improve the system precision and then go to *Step 1* to simulate the result again. On the other hand, if the estimation errors are much smaller than that required, we have some space to relax tolerance requirements. In this case, we also need to adjust tolerance in order to reduce the manufacturing cost and go to *Step 1* to start simulation. After some iterations, we can find an *optimal* solution.

Like many engineering designs, while it is true that we can learn from trial and error, those trials should be informed by something more than random chance, and should begin from a well thought out design. For example, we can initialize the tolerances based on the previous design experience or our knowledge in the manufacturing industry. The theory and model described in this article provide a tool for the design of such an active vision system.

Plan #	$d\theta$	$d\alpha$	$d\mathbf{d}$	$d\mathbf{r}$
1	$(.8^\circ\ .8^\circ\ .8^\circ)^T$	$(.8^\circ\ .8^\circ\ .8^\circ)^T$	$(.005\ .005\ .005)^T$	$(.005\ .005\ .005)^T$
2	$(.8^\circ\ .8^\circ\ .5^\circ)^T$	$(.8^\circ\ .8^\circ\ .5^\circ)^T$	$(.005\ .005\ .005)^T$	$(.005\ .005\ .005)^T$
3	$(.8^\circ\ .5^\circ\ .8^\circ)^T$	$(.8^\circ\ .5^\circ\ .8^\circ)^T$	$(.005\ .005\ .005)^T$	$(.005\ .005\ .005)^T$
4	$(1.1^\circ\ 1.1^\circ\ .5^\circ)^T$	$(1.1^\circ\ 1.1^\circ\ .5^\circ)^T$	$(.005\ .005\ .005)^T$	$(.005\ .005\ .005)^T$
5	$(.8^\circ\ .8^\circ\ .8^\circ)^T$	$(.8^\circ\ .8^\circ\ .8^\circ)^T$	$(.05\ .05\ .05)^T$	$(.05\ .05\ .05)^T$
6	$(.8^\circ\ .8^\circ\ .8^\circ)^T$	$(.8^\circ\ .8^\circ\ .8^\circ)^T$	$(.5\ .5\ .5)^T$	$(.5\ .5\ .5)^T$

Table 1. The Tolerances for Link Parameters (length unit: *in* and angle unit: *deg*)

Feature Category	A	k	δ_0	g_0	δ_a	δ_b
Ext. Rotational Sur	3.96	-22.05	0.0	0.79	0.0038	0.203
Hole	1.8	-20.08	-0.025	1.55	0.0038	0.203
Plane	1.73	-12.99	-0.025	0.79	0.0038	0.203
Location	0.68	-12.20	0.0	1.25	0.0038	0.203

Table 2. The parameters of Exponential Function A, k, δ_0, g_0, δ_a, δ_b (δ unit: mm) for four common manufacturing process (Dong & Soom, 1990)

5. Some Issues about Design of Active Vision Systems

As mentioned, the estimation errors are dependent on four link parameters $\boldsymbol{\theta}$, $\boldsymbol{\alpha}$, $\mathbf{r}$, $\mathbf{d}$ and their errors $d\boldsymbol{\theta}$, $d\boldsymbol{\alpha}$, $d\mathbf{r}$, $d\mathbf{d}$. Besides, they are also dependent on the focal length of the camera lens and its error. Note that although, for simplicity purposes, we do not include the errors of focal length in our model, adding them is straightforward. Since the cameras are located in the most end frames, we can obtain the effect of error of focal length directly by substituting the nominal focal length for the real one.

The four link parameters affect the structure and performance of active vision system. For example, the parameter $\boldsymbol{\theta}$ can determine the motion range of each link, and therefore affect the view space and domain of the vision system. These parameters should be given based on specification and performance requirements. The errors of link parameters affect not only pose estimation precision and performance but the manufacturing process, and therefore the manufacturing cost as well.

Basically, $d\boldsymbol{\alpha}$ is orientation tolerance while $d\mathbf{r}$ and $d\mathbf{d}$ are location tolerances. They affect manufacturing cost and assembly cost. The joint variable $d\boldsymbol{\theta}$ affects control cost. When we assign errors of link parameters, the bottom line is to satisfy the function requirement of the active system. In other words, "*...tolerances must be assigned to the component parts of the mechanism in such a manner that the probability that a mechanism will not function is zero...*"[1].

On the other hand, we must consider manufacturing cost when we design active vision systems since even for the same tolerances, different tolerance types can also affect manufacturing cost. For example, form tolerances are more difficult to machine and measure than size tolerances, and so are holes tolerances more difficult than shaft tolerances.

The final factor discussed in this article, which affects the systems precision and cost, is the focal length of camera. Since the differences between prices and performances for different cameras in the current market are big, selecting and purchasing a suitable camera is also a primary task for the system design. To do trade-off studies before the active system is built,

[1] Evans(1974)

we need a simulation tool for evaluating and optimizing our design. We need to use it to increase the understanding of how each error affects system performance and design the active vision system in terms of various parameters. Fortunately, the model in this article makes this simulation possible. Actually, we have developed a C++ class library to implement a simple tool. With it we can do experiments with various alternatives and obtain data indicating the best settings of key parameters.

6. TRICLOPS - A Case Study

In this section, we apply the model described above to a real active vision system - *TRICLOPS* as shown in Fig. 2[2]. First, we provide six design plans with tolerances assigned for all link parameters and analyze how the tolerances affect the pose estimation precision using our approach. We then compare the cost of each design plan based on an exponential cost-tolerance function. Please note that we do not give a complete design which is much more complicated than described here, and therefore beyond this article's range. We just want to demonstrate how to use our model to help to design active vision systems or analyze and estimate kinematic error.

TRICLOPS has four mechanical degrees of freedom. The four axes are: pan about a vertical axis through the center of the base, tilt about a horizontal line that intersects the base rotation axis and left and right vergence axes which intersect and are perpendicular to the tilt axis (Fiala et al., 1994). The system is configured with two $0.59(in)$ vergence lenses and the distance between the two vergence axes is $11(in)$. The ranges of motion are $\pm 96.3(deg)$ for the pan axis, from $+27.5(deg) to - 65.3(deg)$ for the tilt axis, and $\pm 44(deg)$ for the vergence axes. The image coordinates in this demonstration are arbitrarily selected as $u = -0.2$ and $v = 0.2$. The assigned link frames are shown in Fig. 3.

6.1 Tolerances vs. Pose Estimation Precise

As mentioned, the errors are dependent on the variable parameters. We let the three variables change simultaneously within their motion ranges, as shown in Fig 4. In this experiment, we have six design plans as shown in Table 1. The results corresponding to these six plans are shown in Fig. 5 in alphabetical order of sub-figures. If all the translational parameter errors are $0.005(in)$ and all angular parameter errors are $0.8(deg)$, from Fig. 5(a), we know that the maximum relative error is about 6.5%. Referring to Fig. 5(b), we can observe that by adjusting $d\theta_3$ and $d\alpha_3$ from 0.8(deg) to 0.5(deg), the maximum relative error is reduced from 6.5% to 5.3%. But adjusting the same amount for α_2 and θ_2, the maximum percentage can only reach 5.8%, as shown in Fig. 5(c). So the overall accuracy is more sensitive to α_3 and θ_3. As shown in Fig. 5(d), if we improve the manufacturing or control requirements for α_3 and θ_3 from $0.8(deg)$ to $0.5(deg)$ and at the same time reduce the requirements for α_1, α_2, θ_1 and θ_2 from 0.8(deg) to 1.1(deg), the overall manufacturing requirement is reduced by 0.6 (deg) while the maximum error is almost the same. From an optimal design view, these tolerances are more reasonable. From Fig. 5(e), we know that the overall accuracy is insensitive to translational error. From the design point of view, we can assign more translational tolerances to reduce the manufacturing cost while retaining relatively high accuracy.

[2] Thanks to Wavering, Schneiderman, and Fiala (Wavering et al.), we can present the TRICLOPS pictures in this article.

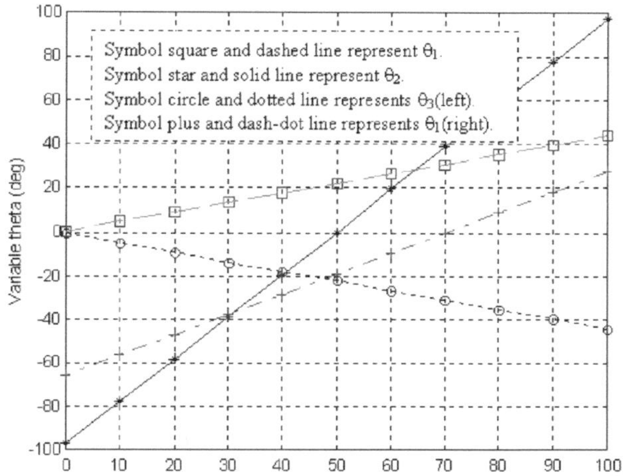

Fig. 4. Simulation Points - The pan axis whose range is from $-96.3°$ to $+96.3°$, tilt axis whose range is from $-65.3°$ to $+27.5°$, and two vergence axes whose ranges are from $-44°$ to $+44°$ rotate simultaneously.

6.2 Tolerances vs. Manufacturing Cost

For a specific manufacturing process, there is a monotonic decreasing relationship between manufacturing cost and precision, called the *cost tolerance relation,* in a certain range. There are many cost tolerance relations, such as *Reciprocal Function, Sutherland Function, Exponential/Reciprocal Power Function, Reciprocal Square Function, Piecewise Linear Function,* and *Exponential Function.* Among them, the *Exponential Function* has proved to be relatively simple and accurate (Dong & Soom, 1990). In this section, we will use the *exponential function* to evaluate the manufacturing cost. The following is the mathematical representation of the exponential cost-tolerance function (Dong & Soom, 1990).

$$g(\delta) = Ae^{-k(\delta-\delta_0)} + g_0 \quad (\delta_0 \leq \delta_a < \delta < \delta_b) \tag{40}$$

In the above equation, A, δ_0, and g_0 determine the position of the cost-tolerance curve, while k controls the curvature of it. These parameters can be derived using a curve-fitting approach based on experimental data. δ_a and δ_b define the lower and upper bounds of the region, respectively, in which the tolerance is economically achievable. For different manufacturing process, these parameters are usually different. The parameters are based on empirical datum for four common feature categories *external rotational surface, hole, plane,* and *location,* shown in Table 2 are from (Dong & Soom, 1990) . For convenience, we use the average values of these parameters in our experiment. For angular tolerances, we first multiply them by unit length to transfer them to the length error, and then multiply the obtained cost by a factor 1.5 [3]. With these assumptions, we can obtain the relative total manufacturing costs, which are

[3] Angular tolerances are harder to machine, control and measure than length tolerances.

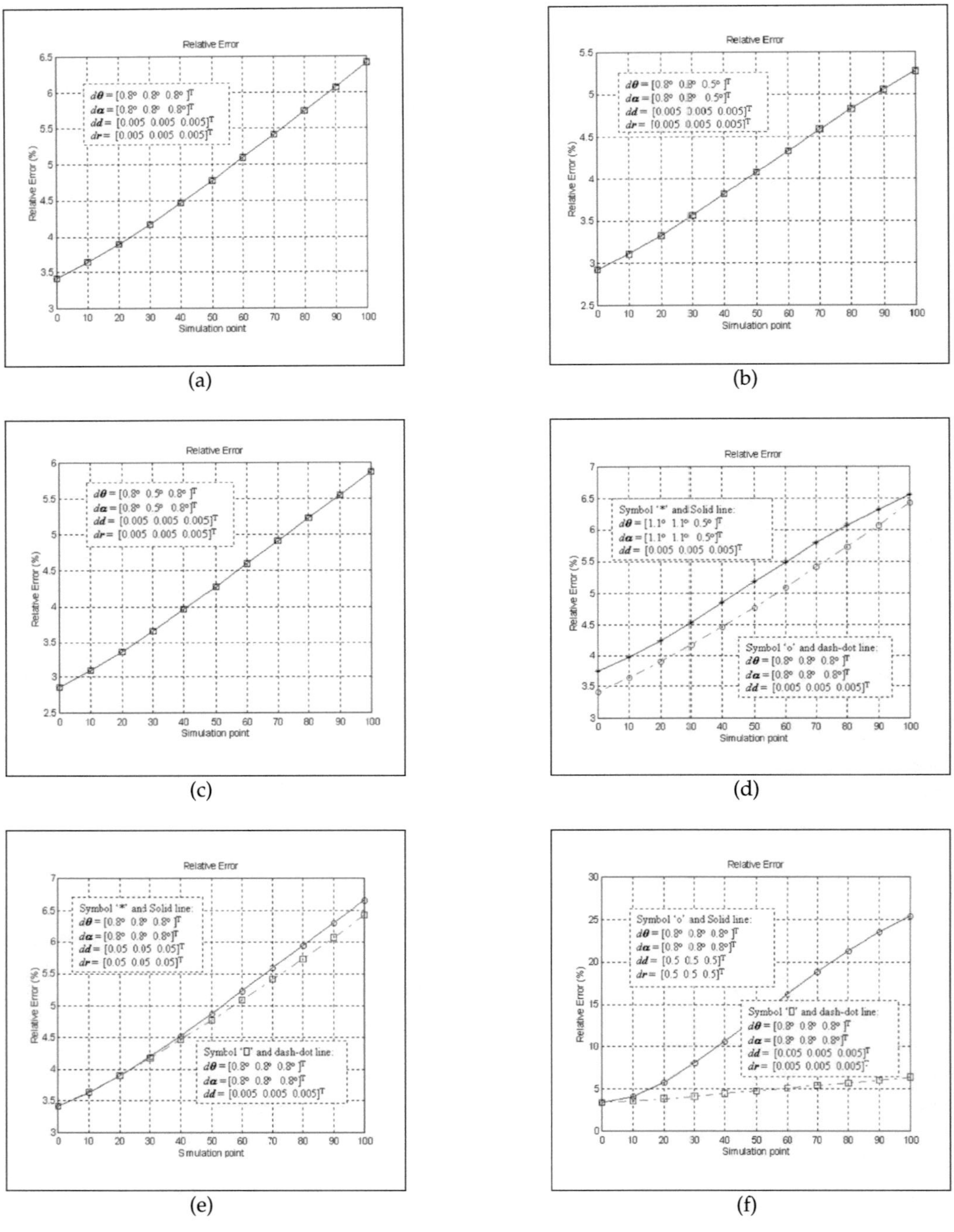

Fig. 5. *Experimental Results*

14.7, 14.9, 14.9, 14.5, 10.8 and 10.8 for the plans one through six mentioned above, respectively. Note that for *Plan 5* and *Plan 6* the length tolerances, after unit conversion, are greater than parameter δ_b, and therefore are beyond the range of *Exponential Function*. So we can ignore the *fine* machining cost since their tolerance may be achieved by rough machining such as forging. Compared with *Plan 1*, *Plan 2*, *Plan 3* and *Plan 4* do not change cost too much while *Plan 5* and *Plan 6* can decrease machining cost by 26%. From the analysis of the previous section and Fig. 5(e), we know that *Plan 5* increases system error a little while *Plan 6* is obviously beyond the performance requirement. Thus, *Plan 5* is a relatively optimal solution.

7. Conclusions

An active vision system is a robot device for controlling the optics and mechanical structure of cameras based on visual information to simplify the processing for computer vision. In this article, we present an approach for the optimal design of such active vision systems. We first build a model which relates the four kinematic errors of a manipulator to the final pose of this manipulator. We then extend this model so that it can be used to estimate visual feature errors. This model is generic, and therefore suitable for analysis of most active vision systems since it is directly derived from the DH transformation matrix and the fundamental algorithm for estimating depth using stereo cameras. Based on this model, we developed a standard C++ class library which can be used as a tool to analyze the effect of kinematic errors on the pose of a manipulator or on visual feature estimation. The idea we present here can also be applied to the optimized design of a manipulator or an active vision system. For example, we can use this method to find the key factors which have the most effect on accuracy at the design stage, and then give more suitable settings of key parameters. We should consider assigning high manufacturing tolerances to them because the accuracy is more sensitive to these factors. On the other hand, we can assign low manufacturing tolerances to the insensitive factors to reduce manufacturing cost. In addition, with the help of a cost-tolerance model, we can implement our *Design for Manufacturing* for active vision systems. We also demonstrate how to use this software model to analyze a real system *TRICLOPS*, which is a significant proof of concept. Future work includes a further analysis of the cost model so that it can account for control errors.

8. Acknowledgments

Support for this project was provided by DOE Grant *#DE-FG04-95EW55151*, issued to the UNM Manufacturing Engineering Program. Figure 2 comes from (Wavering et al., 1995). Finally, we thank Professor Ron Lumia of the Mechanical Engineering Department of the University of New Mexico for his support.

9. References

Dong, Z. & Soom, A. (1990). Automatic Optimal Tolerance Design for Related Dimension Chains. *Manufacturing Review*, Vol. 3, No.4, December 1990, 262-271.

Fiala, J.; Lumia, R.; Roberts, K.; Wavering, A. (1994). TRICLOPS: A Tool for Studying Active Vision. *International Journal of Computer Vision*, Vol 12, #2/3, 1994.

Hutchinson, S.; Hager, G.; Corke, P. (1996). A Tutorial on Visual Servo Control. *IEEE Trans. On Robotics and Automation*, Vol. 12, No.5, Oct. 1996, 651-670.

Lawson, C. & Hanson, R. (1995). *Solving Least Squares Problems*, SIAM, 1995.

Mahamud, S.; Williams, L.; Thornber, K.; Xu, K. (2003). Segmentation of Multiple Salient Closed Contours from Real Images. *IEEE Transactions on Pattern Analysis and Machine Intelligence*, Vol. 25, No. 4, April 2003.

Nelson, B. & Khosla, P. (1996). Force and Vision Resolvability for Assimilating Disparate Sensory Feedback. *IEEE Trans. on Robotics and Automation*, Vol 12, No. 5, October 1996, 714-731.

Paul, R. (1981) *Robot Manipulators: Mathematics, Programming, and Control*, Cambridge, Mass. MIT Press, 1981.

Shih, S.; Hung, Y.; Lin, W. (1998). Calibration of an Active Binocular Head. *IEEE Trans. On Systems, Man , and Cybernetics - part A: Systems and Humans*, Vol 28, No.4, July 1998, 426-442.

Wavering, A.; Schneiderman, H.; Fiala, J. (1995). High-Performance Tracking with TRICLOPS. *Proc. Second Asian Conference on Computer Vision, ACCV'95*, Singapore, December 5-8, 1995.

Wu, C. (1984). A Kinematic CAD Tool for the Design and Control of a Robot Manipulator, *Int. J. Robotics Research*, Vol. 3, No.1, 1984, 58-67.

Zhuang, H. & Roth, Z. (1996). *Camera-Aided Robot Calibration*, CRC Press, Inc. 1996.

Visual Motion Analysis for 3D Robot Navigation in Dynamic Environments

Chunrong Yuan and Hanspeter A. Mallot
Chair for Cognitive Neuroscience
Eberhard Karls University Tübingen
Auf der Morgenstelle 28, 72076 Tübingen, Germany

1. Introduction

The ability to detect movement is an important aspect of visual perception. According to Gibson (Gibson, 1974), the perception of movement is vital to the whole system of perception. Biological systems take active advantage of this ability and move their eyes and bodies constantly to infer spatial and temporal relationships of the objects viewed, which at the same time leads to the awareness of their own motion and reveals their motion characteristics. As a consequence, position, orientation, distance and speed can be perceived and estimated. Such capabilities of perception and estimation are critical to the existence of biological systems, be it on behalf of navigation or interaction.

During the process of navigation, the relative motion between the observer and the environment gives rise to the perception of optical flow. Optical flow is the distribution of apparent motion of brightness patterns in the visual field. In other words, the spatial relationships of the viewed scene hold despite temporal changes. Through sensing the temporal variation of some spatial persistent elements of the scene, the relative location and movements of both the observer and objects in the scene can be extracted. This is the mechanism through which biological systems are capable of navigating and interacting with objects in the external world.

Though it is well known that optical flow is the key to the recovery of spatial and temporal information, the exact process of the recovery is hardly known, albeit the study of the underlying process never stops. In vision community, there are steady interests in solving the basic problem of structure and motion (Aggarwal & Nandhakumar, 1988; Calway, 2005). In the robotics community, different navigation models have been proposed, which are more or less inspired by insights gained from the study of biological behaviours (Srinivasan et al., 1996; Egelhaaf & Kern, 2002). Particularly, vision based navigation strategies have been adopted in different kinds of autonomous systems ranging from UGV (Unmanned Ground Vehicles) to UUV (Unmanned Underwater Vehicles) and UAV (Unmanned Aerial Vehicles). In fact, optical flow based visual motion analysis has become the key to the successful navigation of mobile robots (Ruffier & Franceschini, 2005).

This chapter focuses on visual motion analysis for the safe navigation of mobile robots in dynamic environments. A general framework has been designed for the visual steering of UAV in unknown environments with both static and dynamic objects. A series of robot vision algorithms are designed, implemented and analyzed, particularly for solving the following problems: (1) Flow measurement. (2) Robust separation of camera egomotion and independent object motions. (3) 3D motion and structure recovery (4) Real-time decision making for obstacle avoidance. Experimental evaluation based on both computer simulation and a real UAV system has shown that it is possible to use the image sequence captured by a single perspective camera for real-time 3D navigation of UAV in dynamic environments with arbitrary configuration of obstacles. The proposed framework with integrated visual perception and active decision making can be used not only as a stand-alone system for autonomous robot navigation but also as a pilot assistance system for remote operation.

2. Related Work

A lot of research on optical flow concentrates on developing models and methodologies for the recovery of a 2D motion field. While most of the approaches apply the general spatial-temporal constraint, they differ in the way how the two components of the 2D motion vector are solved using additional constraints. One classical solution provided by Horn & Schunck (Horn & Schunck, 1981) takes a global approach which uses a smoothness constraint based on second-order derivatives. The flow vectors are then solved using nonlinear optimization methods. The solution proposed by Lucas & Kanade (Lucas & Kanade, 1981) takes a local approach, which assumes equal flow velocity within a small neighbourhood. A closed-form solution to the flow vectors is then achieved which involves only first-order derivatives. Some variations as well as combination of the two approaches can be found in (Bruhn et al., 2005). Generally speaking, the global approach is more sensitive to noise and brightness changes due to the use of second-order derivatives. Due to this consideration, a local approach has been taken. We will present an algorithm for optical flow measurement, which is evolved from the well-known Lucas-Kanade algorithm.

In the past, substantial research has been carried out on motion/structure analysis and recovery from optical flow. Most of the work supposes that the 2D flow field has been determined already and assumes that the environment is static. Since it is the observer that is moving, the problem becomes the recovery of camera egomotion using known optical flow measurement. Some algorithms use image velocity as input and can be classified as instantaneous-time methods. A comparative study of six instantaneous algorithms can be found in (Tian et. al., 1996), where the motion parameters are calculated using known flow velocity derived from simulated camera motion. Some other algorithms use image displacements for egomotion calculation and belong to the category of discrete-time methods (Longuet-Higgins, 1981; Weng et al., 1989). The so-called n-point algorithms, e.g. the 8-point algorithm (Hartley, 1997), the 7-point algorithm (Hartley & Zisserman, 2000), or the 5-point algorithm (Nister, 2004; Li & Hartley, 2006), belong also to this category. However, if there are less than 8 point correspondences, the solution will not be unique.

Like many problems in computer vision, recovering egomotion parameters from 2D image flow fields is an ill-posed problem. To achieve a solution, extra constraints have to be sought after. In fact, both the instantaneous and the discrete-time method are built upon the principle of epipolar geometry and differ only in the representation of the epipolar constraint. For this reason, we use in the following the term image flow instead of optical flow to refer to both image velocity and image displacement.

While an imaging sensor is moving in the environment, the observed image flows are the results of two different kinds of motion: one is the egomotion of the camera and the other is the independent motion of individually moving objects. In such cases it is essential to know whether there exists any independent motion and eventually to separate the two kinds of motion. In the literature, different approaches have been proposed toward solving the independent motion problem. Some approaches make explicit assumptions about or even restrictions on the motion of the camera or object in the environment. In the work of Clarke and Zisserman (Clarke & Zisserman, 1996), it is assumed that both the camera and the object are just translating. Sawhney and Ayer (Sawhney & Ayer, 1996) proposed a method which can apply to small camera rotation and scenes with small depth changes. In the work proposed in (Patwardhan et al., 2008), only moderate camera motion is allowed.

A major difference among the existing approaches for independent motion detection lies in the parametric modelling of the underlying motion constraint. One possibility is to use 2D homography to establish a constraint between a pair of viewed images (Irani & Anadan, 1998; Lourakis et al., 1998). Points, whose 2D displacements are inconsistent with the homography, are classified as belonging to independent motion. The success of such an approach depends on the existence of a dominant plane (e.g. the ground plane) in the viewed scene. Another possibility is to use geometric constraints between multiple views. The approach proposed by (Torr et al., 1995) uses the trilinear constraint over three views. Scene points are clustered into different groups, where each group agrees with a different trilinear constraint. A multibody trifocal tensor based on three views is applied in (Hartley & Vidal, 2004), where the EM (Expectation and Maximization) algorithm is used to refine the constraints as well as their support iteratively. Correspondences among the three views, however, are selected manually, with equal distribution between the static and dynamic scene points. An inherent problem shared by such approaches is their inability to deal with dynamic objects that are either small or moving at a distance. Under such circumstances it would be difficult to estimate the parametric model of independent motion, since not enough scene points may be detected from dynamic objects. A further possibility is to build a motion constraint directly based on the recovered 3D motion parameters (Lobo & Tsotsos, 1996; Zhang et al., 1993). However such a method is more sensitive to the density of the flow field as well as to noise and outliers.

In this work, we use a simple 2D constraint for the detection of both independent motion and outliers. After the identification of dynamic scene points as well as the removal of outliers, the remaining static scene points are used for the recovery of camera motion. We will present an algorithm for motion and structure analysis using a spherical representation of the epipolar constraint, as suggested by (Kanatani, 1993). In addition to the recovery of the 3D motion parameters undergone by the camera, the relative depth of the perceived scene points can be estimated simultaneously. Once the position of the viewed scene points are localized in 3D, the configuration of obstacles in the environment can be easily retrieved.

Regarding the literature on obstacle avoidance for robot navigation, the frequently used sensors include laser range finder, inertial measurement unit, GPS, and various vision systems. However, for small-size UAVs, it is generally not possible to use many sensors due to weight limits of the vehicles. A generally applied visual steering approach is based on the mechanism of 2D balancing of optical flow (Santos-Victor, 1995). As lateral optical flow indicates the proximity of the left and right objects, robots can be kept to maintain equal distance to both sides of a corridor. The commonly used vision sensors for flow balancing are either stereo or omni-directional cameras (Hrabar & Sukhatme, 2004; Zufferey & Floreano, 2006). However in more complex environments other than corridors, the approach may fail to work properly. It has been found that it may drive the robot straight toward walls and into corners, if no extra strategies have been considered for frontal obstacle detection and avoidance. Also it does not account height control to avoid possible collision with ground or ceiling. Another issue is that the centring behaviour requires symmetric division of the visual field about the heading direction. Hence it is important to recover the heading direction to cancel the distortion of the image flow caused by rotary motion.

For a flying robot to be able to navigate in complex 3D environment, it is necessary that obstacles are sensed in all directions surrounding the robot. Based on this concept we have developed a visual steering algorithm for the determination of the most favourable flying direction. One of our contributions to the state-of-the-art is that we use only a single perspective camera for UAV navigation. In addition, we recover the full set of egomotion parameters including both heading and rotation information. Furthermore, we localize both static and dynamic obstacles and analyse their spatial configuration. Based on our earlier work (Yuan et al., 2009), a novel visual steering approach has been developed for guiding the robot away from possible obstacles.

The remaining part is organized as follows. In Section 3, we present a robust algorithm for detecting an optimal set of 2D flow vectors. In Section 4, we outline the steps taken for motion separation and outlier removal. Motion and structure parameter estimation is discussed in Section 5, followed by the visual steering algorithm in Section 6. Performance analysis using video frames captured in both simulated and real world is elaborated in Section 7. Finally, Section 8 summarizes with a conclusion and some future work.

3. Measuring Image Flow

Suppose the pixel value of an image point $p(x, y)$ is $f^t(x, y)$ and let its 2D velocity be $\mathbf{v} = [u, v]^T$. Assuming that image brightness doesn't change between frames, the image velocity of the point $\mathbf{p}$ can be solved as

$$\mathbf{v} = \begin{bmatrix} u \\ v \end{bmatrix} = \mathbf{G}^{-1}\mathbf{b}, \tag{1}$$

with

$$\mathbf{G} = \sum_{(x,y)\in W} \begin{bmatrix} f_x^2 & f_x f_y \\ f_x f_y & f_y^2 \end{bmatrix} \tag{2}$$

and

$$\mathbf{b} = -\sum_{(x,y)\in W} \begin{bmatrix} f_t f_x \\ f_t f_y \end{bmatrix}. \tag{3}$$

Here f_x and f_y are the spatial image gradients, f_t the temporal image derivative, and W a local neighbourhood around point $\mathbf{p}$.

The above solution, originally proposed in (Lucas & Kanade, 1981), requires that $\mathbf{G}$ is invertible, which means that the image should have gradient information in both x and y direction within the neighbourhood W. For the reason of better performance, a point selection process has been carried out before $\mathbf{v}$ is calculated. By diagonalizing $\mathbf{G}$ using orthonormal transform as

$$\mathbf{G} = \mathbf{U}^{-1} \begin{bmatrix} \lambda_1 & 0 \\ 0 & \lambda_2 \end{bmatrix} \mathbf{U}, \tag{4}$$

the following criterion can be used to select point $\mathbf{p}$:

1. λ_1 and λ_2 should be big.
2. The ratio of λ_1 / λ_2 should not be too big.

For the purpose of subpixel estimation of $\mathbf{v}$, we use an iterative algorithm, updating f_t sequentially as follows:

$$f_t = f^{t+1}(x+u, y+v) - f^t(x, y). \tag{5}$$

The initial value of $\mathbf{v}$ is set as $\mathbf{v} = [u, v]^T = [\mathbf{0,0}]^T$. To handle large motion, a further strategy is to carry out the above iterative steps in a pyramidal fashion, beginning with the smallest scale image and refining the estimates in consecutive higher scales.

Once a set of points $\{\mathbf{p}_i\}$ has been selected from image $\mathbf{f}^t$ and a corresponding set of $\{\mathbf{v}_i\}$ is calculated, we obtain automatically a set of points $\{\mathbf{q}_i\}$ in image $\mathbf{f}^{t+1}$, with $\mathbf{q}_i = \mathbf{p}_i + \mathbf{v}_i$. In order to achieve higher accuracy in the estimated 2D displacement $\mathbf{v}_i$, we calculate a new set of backward displacement $\{\hat{\mathbf{v}}_i\}$ for $\{\mathbf{q}_i\}$ from image $\mathbf{f}^{t+1}$ to $\mathbf{f}^t$. As a result we get a set of backward projected point $\{\hat{\mathbf{p}}_i\}$ with $\hat{\mathbf{p}}_i = \mathbf{q}_i + \hat{\mathbf{v}}_i$.

For an accurately calculated displacement, the following equation should hold:

$$e_i = \left\| \hat{\mathbf{p}}_i - \mathbf{p}_i \right\| = 0 . \quad (6)$$

For this reason, only those points whose $e_i < 0.1$ pixel will be kept. By this means, we have achieved an optimal data set $\{(\mathbf{p}_i, \mathbf{q}_i)\}$ with high accuracy of point correspondences established via $\{\mathbf{v}_i\}$ between the pair of image $\mathbf{f}^t$ and $\mathbf{f}^{t+1}$.

4. Motion Separation

While the observing camera of a robot is moving in the world, the perceived 2D flow vectors can be caused either entirely by the camera motion, or by the joined effect of both camera and object motion. This means, the vector $\mathbf{v}_i$ detected at point $\mathbf{p}_i$ can come either from static or dynamic objects in the environment. While static objects keep their locations and configurations in the environment, dynamic objects change their locations with time.

Without loss of generality, we can assume that camera motion is the dominant motion. This assumption is reasonable since individually moving objects generally come from a distance and can come near to the moving camera only gradually. Compared to the area occupied by the whole static environment, the subpart occupied by the dynamic objects is less significant. Hence it is generally true that camera motion is the dominant motion.

As a consequence, it is also true that most vectors $\mathbf{v}_i$ come from static scene points. Under such circumstance, it is possible to find a dominant motion. The motion of static scene points will agree with the dominant motion. Those scene points whose motion doesn't agree with the dominant motion constraint can hence be either dynamic points or outliers. Outliers are caused usually by environmental factors (e.g. changes of illumination conditions or movement of leaves on swinging trees due to wind) that so far haven't been considered during the 2D motion detection process. The goal of motion separation is to find how well each vector $\mathbf{v}_i$ agrees with the dominant motion constraint.

4.1 Motion constraint

Using the method proposed in Section 3, we have gained a corresponding set of points $\{(\mathbf{p}_i, \mathbf{q}_i)\}$ with i=1 to N. In order to explain the 2D motion of n static points between $\mathbf{f}^t$ and $\mathbf{f}^{t+1}$, we use a similarity transform $\mathbf{T} = (R, t, s)$ as the motion constraint, where R is a 2D rotation matrix, t a 2D vector and s a scalar. Since $\mathbf{p}_i$ and $\mathbf{q}_i$ are the 2D perspective projections of a set of n static points in two images, the applied constraint is an approximation of the projected camera motion. The transform parameters can be found by minimizing the following distance measure:

$$\varepsilon(R,t,s) = \sum_{i=1}^{n} \| \mathbf{q}_i - (s\mathbf{R}\mathbf{p}_i + \mathbf{t}) \|^2 . \qquad (7)$$

We may solve the transform parameters using a linear yet robust minimization method designed by (Umeyama, 1991). Once the parameters of the transform $\mathbf{T}$ are calculated, it can be used to determine whether the scene points agree with the approximated camera motion.

4.2 Motion classification

Since a vector $\mathbf{v}_i$ corresponding to a static scene point is caused by the camera motion, while the $\mathbf{v}_i$ corresponding to a moving scene point is the result of independent motion, the separation of the two kinds of motion is equivalent to classify the set of mixed $\{\mathbf{v}_i\}$ into different classes. Altogether there are three classes: static scene points, dynamic scene points and outliers.

Based on the motion constraint $\mathbf{T} = (R,t,s)$, a residual error can be calculated for each of the points as:

$$d_i = \| (\mathbf{p}_i + \mathbf{v}_i) - (s\mathbf{R}\mathbf{p}_i + \mathbf{t}) \|^2 . \qquad (8)$$

We can expect that:

1. $d_i = 0 \Rightarrow \mathbf{v}_i$ is correct (inlier), $\mathbf{p}_i$ is a static point
2. d_i is small $\Rightarrow \mathbf{v}_i$ is correct (inlier), $\mathbf{p}_i$ is a dynamic point
3. d_i is very big $\Rightarrow \mathbf{v}_i$ is incorrect, $\mathbf{p}_i$ is an outlier

The remaining problem consists of finding two thresholds k_1 and k_2, so that:

1. if $d_i \le k_1$, $\mathbf{p}_i$ is a static point
2. $k_1 \prec d_i \le k_2$, $\mathbf{p}_i$ is a dynamic point
3. $d_i \succ k_2$, $\mathbf{p}_i$ is an outlier

This belongs to a typical pattern classification problem, which can be solved by analyzing the probabilistic distribution of the set of distance errors $\{d_i\}$. The most direct way is to quantize the distance measures $\{d_i\}$ into L+1 levels, ranging from 0 to L pixels. Following that, a residual distance histogram h(j), j=0 to L, can be calculated. If h(j) is a multimodal histogram, two thresholds k_1 and k_2 can be found automatically for motion separation.

An automatic threshold algorithm has been implemented earlier for the two-class problem (Yuan, 2004). Using this algorithm, we can find a threshold k_1 for separating the points into two classes: one class contains static points; the other is a mixed class of dynamic points and outliers. In case that k_1 doesn't exist, this means there is only a single motion which is the camera motion. If k_1 does exist, then we will further cluster the remaining mixed set of both dynamic points and outliers by calculating another threshold k_2.

5. Motion & Structure Estimation

Now that we have a set of n points whose image flow vectors are caused solely by the 3D rigid motion of the camera, we can use them to recover the 3D motion parameters. Denoting the motion parameters by a rotation vector $\omega = (r_x, r_y, r_z)^T$ and a translation vector $\mathbf{t} = (t_x, t_y, t_z)^T$, the following two equations hold for a perspective camera with a unit focal length (Horn, 1986):

$$u = \frac{t_x - xt_z}{Z} + [-r_x xy + r_y(x^2+1) - r_z y], \tag{9}$$

$$v = \frac{t_y - yt_z}{Z} + [r_y xy - r_x(y^2+1) + r_z x], \tag{10}$$

where Z is the depth of the image point $\mathbf{p}$. As can be seen, the translation part of the motion parameter depends on the point depth, while the rotation part doesn't. Without the knowledge of the exact scene depth, it is only possible to recover the direction of $\mathbf{t}$. For this reason, the recovered motion parameters have a total of five degrees of freedom.

As mentioned already in Section 2, we use a spherical representation of the epipolar geometry. Let $\mathbf{u}$ be a unit vector whose ray passes through the image point and $\mathbf{v}$ a unit flow vector whose direction is perpendicular to $\mathbf{u}$, the motion of the camera with parameter $(\omega, \mathbf{t})$ leads to the observation of $\mathbf{v}$ which is equal to

$$\mathbf{v} = -\omega \times \mathbf{u} - (\mathbf{I} - \mathbf{u}\mathbf{u}^T)\mathbf{t}/Z. \tag{11}$$

The goal of motion recovery is to find the motion parameter $(\omega, \mathbf{t})$ that minimizes the following term: $\left\| \mathbf{v} + \omega \times \mathbf{u} + (\mathbf{I} - \mathbf{u}\mathbf{u}^T)\mathbf{t}/Z \right\|$. Using a linear optimization method (Kanatani, 1993), it has been found that the solution for $\mathbf{t}$ is equal to the least eigenvector of a matrix $\mathbf{A} = (\mathbf{A}_{\mathbf{ij}})$, i, j=1 to 3 and that

$$\mathbf{A}_{ij} = \mathbf{L}_{ij} - \sum_{k,l,m,n=1}^{3} \mathbf{M}_{ikl} \mathbf{N}_{\mathbf{klmn}}^{-1} \mathbf{M}_{jmn}, \tag{12}$$

with

$$\mathbf{L}_{ij} = \int_{\Omega} \mathbf{v}_i^* \mathbf{v}_j^* d\Omega, \tag{13}$$

$$\mathbf{M}_{ijk} = \int_{\Omega} \mathbf{v}_i^* \mathbf{v}_j \mathbf{v}_k d\Omega, \tag{14}$$

$$\mathbf{N}_{ijkl} = \int_{\Omega} \mathbf{v}_i \mathbf{v}_j \mathbf{v}_k \mathbf{v}_l d\Omega, \tag{15}$$

where

$$\mathbf{v}^* = \mathbf{u} \times \mathbf{v}. \tag{16}$$

Once $\mathbf{t}$ is recovered, the solution for ω can be computed as:

$$\omega = \frac{1}{2}\left[tr(\mathbf{K}) + 3\mathbf{t}^T\mathbf{K}\mathbf{t}\right]\mathbf{t} - 2\mathbf{K}\mathbf{t}, \tag{17}$$

where $tr(\,)$ is the trace of a matrix and

$$\mathbf{K} = (\mathbf{K}_{ij}), \tag{18}$$

$$\mathbf{K}_{ij} = -\sum_{k,l,m,n=1}^{3} \mathbf{N}_{ijkl}^{-1} \mathbf{M}_{mkl} \mathbf{t}_m. \tag{19}$$

Subsequently, the depth Z of a scene point $\mathbf{p}$ can be estimated as

$$Z = \frac{1 - (\mathbf{u}^T\mathbf{t})^2}{\mathbf{u}^T(\omega \times \mathbf{t}) - \mathbf{v}^T\mathbf{t}}. \tag{20}$$

If $(\omega, \mathbf{t})$ is a solution, then $(\omega, -\mathbf{t})$ can also be a solution. The correct one can be chosen based on the cheirality constraint, by assuring positive scene depth (Z>0).

6. Visual Steering

6.1 Obstacle detection

After the motion parameters as well as the relative scene depths of the static points are calculated, we now obtain the viewing direction of the camera together with the location of a set of 3D scene points relative to the camera.

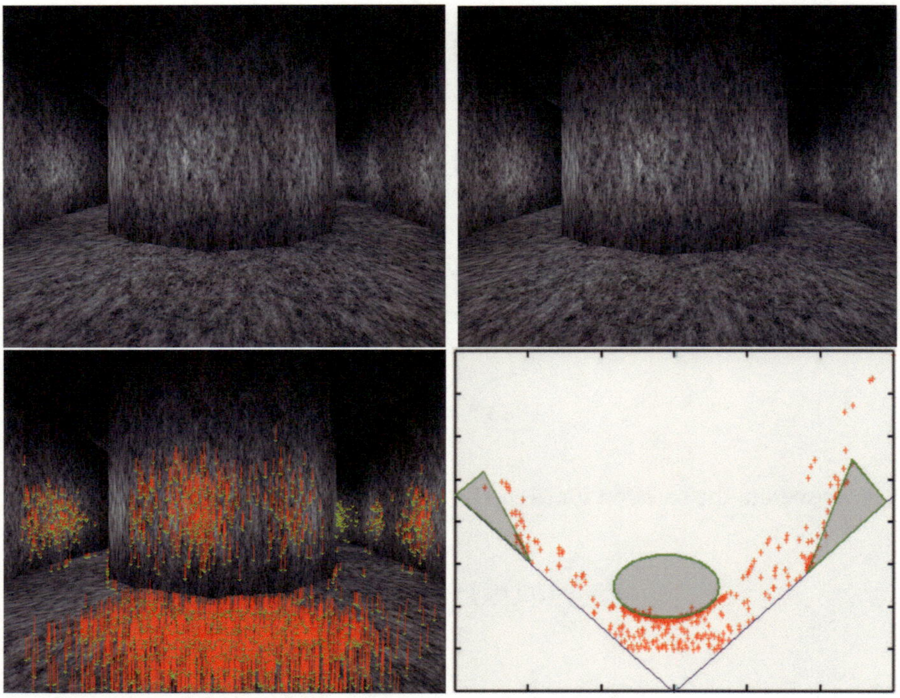

Fig. 1. Configuration of detected 3D scene points relative to the camera.

Shown in Fig. 1 is an illustration of the visual processing results so far achieved. In the top row are two images taken by a camera mounted on a flying platform. The result of image flow detection is shown on the left side of the bottom row. Obviously the camera looking in the direction of the scene is flying upward, since the movement of the scene points are downward, as is shown by the red arrows with green tips. The image on the bottom right of Fig. 1 shows the configuration of detected 3D scene points (coloured in red) relative to the camera. Both the location and orientation of those 3D scene points and the orientation of the camera have been recovered by our motion analysis algorithm. The blue \/ shape in the image represents the field-of-view of the camera. The obstacles are shown in solid shape filled with colour gray. They are the left and right walls as well as the frontal pillar. The goal of visual steering is to determine in the next step a safe flying direction for the platform.

As shown by Fig. 1, each image point $\mathbf{p_i}$ in $\mathbf{f^t}$ corresponds to a 3D point $\mathbf{P_i}$ with a depth Z_i. This distance value indicates the time-to-contact of a possible obstacle in the environment. Our visual steering approach exploits the fact that the set of depth values reveals the distribution of obstacles in different directions. Specifically, we use a concept built upon directional distance sensors to find the most favourable moving direction based on the distance of nearest obstacles in several viewing directions. This is done through a novel idea of cooperative decision making from visual directional sensors.

6.2 Directional distance sensor

A single directional sensor is specified by a direction $\mathbf{d}$ and an opening angle α that defines a viewing cone from the camera center. All the scene points lying within the cone defines one set of depth measurements. Based on the values of these depth measurements, the set can be further divided into a few depth clusters. The clustering criterion is that each cluster K is a subset with at least s scene points whose distances to the cluster center are below δ. The parameter s and δ are chosen depending on the size of the viewing cone and the density of depth measurements.

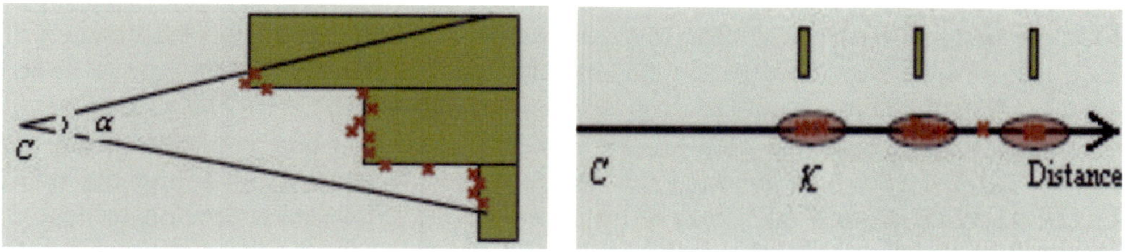

Fig. 2. A directional distance sensor and scene points with corresponding depth clusters.

Shown in Fig. 2 on the left is a directional distance sensor (located at camera center *c*) with the set of detected scene points lying within the viewing cone. The set is divided into three depth clusters, as is shown on the right of Fig. 2. Note that it is possible that some points may not belong to any clusters, as is the case of the points lying left to the rightmost cluster.

Once the clusters are found, it is possible to find the subset K whose distance to the viewing camera is shortest. In the above example, the nearest cluster is the leftmost one. With the nearest cluster K identified, its distance to the camera, represented as D_K, can be determined as the average distance of all scene points belonging to K. In order to determine whether it is safe for the UAV to fly in this direction, we encode D_K in a fuzzy way as near, medium and far. Depending on the fuzzy encoding of D_K, preferences for possible motion behaviours can be defined as follows:

1. Encoded value of D_K is far, flying in this direction is favourable
2. Encoded value of D_K is medium, flying in this direction is still acceptable
3. Encoded value of D_K is near, flying in this direction should be forbidden.

If we scan the viewing zone of the camera using several directional distance sensors, we may obtain a set of nearest depth clusters K_i together with a corresponding set of fuzzy-encoded distance values. By assigning motion preferences in each direction according to these distance values, the direction with the highest preferences can be determined. Built exactly upon this concept, novel visual steering strategies have been designed.

6.3 Visual steering strategies

Three control strategies are considered for the visual steering of the UAV: horizontal motion control, view control and height control.

The purpose of view control is to ensure that the camera is always looking in the direction of flight. By doing so, the principle axis of the camera is aligned with the forward flight direction of the UAV so that a substantial part of the scene lying ahead of the UAV can always be observed. Because the camera is firmly mounted on the UAV, changing the viewing direction of the camera is done by changing the orientation of the UAV. Here we would like to point out the relationship between the different coordinate systems. A global coordinate system is defined whose origin is located at the optical center of the camera. The optical axis of the camera is aligned with the z axis pointing forward in the frontal direction of the UAV. The image plane is perpendicular to the z axis, with the x axis pointing horizontally to the right side of the UAV and the y axis pointing vertically down. View control is achieved by rotating the UAV properly, which is done by setting the rotation speed of the UAV around the y axis of the global coordinate system. Obviously this is the yaw speed control for the UAV.

The main part of visual steering is the horizontal motion control. We have defined five motion behaviours: left (←), forward and left (↖), forward (↑), forward and right (↗) and right (→). Once the flying direction is determined, motion of the UAV is achieved by setting the forward motion speed, left or right motion speed and turning speed (yaw speed). The yaw control is necessary because we want to ensure that the camera is aligned with the direction of flight for maximal performance of obstacle avoidance. Hence a left motion will also result in modifying the yaw angle by rotating the UAV to the left via the view control.

In order to realize the horizontal motion control as well as the view control, it is necessary to select one safe flying direction from the five possibilities defined above. We define five virtual directional distance sensors which are located symmetrically around the estimated heading direction. This corresponds to a symmetric division of the visual field into far left, left, front, right and far right, as is shown in Fig. 3.

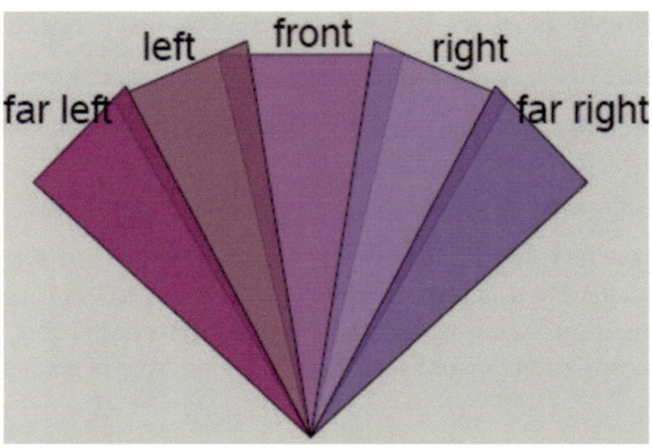

Fig. 3. A symmetric arrangement of five directional distance sensors for visual steering.

As mentioned in Section 6.1, each of these five directional sensors perceives the nearest obstacles in a particular direction. Depending on the nearness of the obstacles detected, every directional sensor will output one preference value for each of the five possible motion behaviours. Three preference values have been defined. They are favourable (FA), acceptable (AC) and not acceptable (NA).

Each directional sensor has its own rules regarding the setting of the preference values. An example of rule setting for the front sensor is given in Table 1. Table 2 shows another example for the far left sensor. As can been seen, once a fuzzy encoded distance measure is determined, a directional sensor outputs a total of five preference values, with one for each possible moving direction.

Distance	Behavioural preferences for each of the five motion directions				
	←	↖	↑	↗	→
far	AC	AC	FA	AC	AC
medium	AC	FA	AC	FA	AC
near	FA	AC	NA	AC	FA

Table 1. Preference setting rules for the front distance sensor.

Distance	Behavioural preferences for each of the five motion directions				
	←	↖	↑	↗	→
far	FA	AC	AC	AC	AC
medium	AC	FA	AC	AC	AC
near	NA	AC	FA	AC	AC

Table 2. Preference setting rules for the far left distance sensor.

From all the five directional sensors shown in Fig. 3, we have got altogether a set of 25 preferences values, five for each moving direction. By adding the preference values together, the motion behaviour with the highest preference can be selected as the next flying direction.

Suppose the fuzzy distance values of the five directional sensors (from left to right) are near, far, far, medium and near, the preference values for each motion behaviour can be determined individually, as shown in Table 3. If we take all the sensors into account by adding all the preference values appearing in each column, the final preference value for each motion direction can be obtained, as is shown in the second last line of Table 3. Apparently, the highest preference value is achieved for the forward direction. Hence the safest flying direction is moving forward.

Sensor	Distance	Behavioural preferences for each of the five motion directions				
		←	↖	↑	↗	→
far left	near	NA	AC	FA	AC	AC
left	far	AC	FA	AC	AC	AC
front	far	AC	AC	FA	AC	AC
right	medium	AC	AC	FA	AC	AC
far right	near	AC	AC	FA	AC	NA
All sensors		1 NA 4 ACs	1 FA 4 ACs	4 FAs 1 AC	5 ACs	1 NA 4 ACs
Decision				O		

Table 3. Decision making based on the fuzzy encoded distance values of all five sensors.

As for the height control of the UAV, a single directional distance sensor looking downwards is used. It estimates the nearness of obstacles on the ground and regulates the height of the UAV accordingly. In addition, we take into account the vertical component of the estimated motion parameter of the camera, which is t_y. The direction of t_y can be up, zero or down. The goal is to let the UAV maintain approximately constant distance to the ground and avoid collision with both ground and ceiling. This is performed by increasing/decreasing/keeping the rising/sinking speed of the UAV so as to change the height of the UAV. Decision rules for the height control of the UAV can be found in Table 4.

ty	Estimated distance to ground		
	near	medium	far
up	no speed change	decrease rising speed	decrease rising speed
zero	increase rising speed	no speed change	increase sinking speed
down	increase rising speed	increase rising speed	no speed change

Table 4. Using a vertical directional sensor and t_y for height control.

7. Experimental Evaluation

The proposed approach has been implemented using C++ running on a Samsung M60 laptop. For each pair of frames ($\mathbf{f}^t, \mathbf{f}^{t+1}$), we first detect 3000 features in frame $\mathbf{f}^t$ and try to find their correspondences in $\mathbf{f}^{t+1}$. Depending on the nature of the input frames, the found number of point correspondences N ranges from a few hundreds to a few thousands. Thanks to the linear methods used, a frame rate of 15 frames/s can be achieved for images with a resolution 640x480, including both motion analysis and visual steering steps.

Both indoor and outdoor experiments have been carried out for evaluation purpose. We have captured videos using both hand-held camera and the camera mounted on a flying robot. Shown in Fig. 4 is the AR-100 UAV we have used, which is a kind of small-size (diameter < 1m) drone whose weight is below 1kg. The onboard camera inclusive the protecting case is ca. 200g. The images captured by the camera are transmitted via radio link to the laptop on which our motion algorithm is running. The UAV has a remote control panel. In manual flight mode, controlling commands are triggered by human operation. In auto-flight mode, the controlling commands for avoiding detected obstacles are calculated by our visual steering algorithm and sent via radio transmission to the drone. Through a switch on the control panel, the mode can be changed by the human operator.

Fig. 4. The AR-100 UAV with the camera mounted beneath the flight board.

In the following we analyze the results achieved, concentrating on one particular aspect in a single subsection.

7.1 Performance on motion separation

For the evaluation of our motion separation algorithm, we have used several video sequences captured by mobile cameras navigating in the natural environment. The images in the first video sequence are taken on a sunny day in an outdoor environment, using the camera on the drone. The dynamic objects to be detected are people moving around the drone. Some example images with people moving are shown in Fig. 5. As can be seen clearly from the second image, the quality of the transmitted image is not perfect. Altogether there are 3082 frames in the video sequence. Among them, there are 1907 frames which consist only of static scenes. In each of the remaining 1175 frames, there are either one or two objects moving.

Fig. 5. Some images in video sequence 1.

Shown in Fig. 6 on the left is one example image together with the detected 2D displacement vectors and the result of motion separation. There are a few outliers in the static background as well as on the moving person. This is due largely to illumination variations. Those long vectors (with colour yellow) are the outliers. The vectors shown in colour black come from the static background. The two moving persons have been identified correctly, as can be seen clearly from the vectors shown as red lines with green tips. Another example is shown in Fig. 6 on the right, where neither independent motion nor outliers occur. In both cases, it is obvious from the visualized flow vectors that the camera motion consists of both rotation and translation component.

Fig. 6. Examples of detection result in sequence 1.

Sequence 2 is captured with a hand-held camera. The moving object to be detected is the AR-100 flying drone. There are also some people moving in the background. In Fig. 7 on the left we can see one input frame, where the moving drone is even difficult to perceive with human eyes. Shown on the right is the result of detection. Three moving objects have been identified. They are the flying drone as well as two persons moving behind the tree. The purpose of performance evaluation with sequence 2 is to find how our algorithm will behave in case the size of the object is very small compared to the visual field of the camera. All together there are 80 frames, with the drone moving all the time in the scene.

Fig. 7. Examples of detection result in sequence 2.

Shown in Fig. 8 are two examples of detection results achieved on the third video sequence (video available at http://robots.stanford.edu/). The moving object is a robot car running on the road. Altogether there are 303 frames. Each frame has a single moving object in it.

Fig. 8. Examples of detection result in sequence 3.

On all three sequences, we have achieved an average separation accuracy of 83.3%. This means, among all those flow vectors detected, 83.3% of them have been correctly classified. Particularly, the flow vectors coming from static scene points have been identified with a precision of 90%, while those form dynamic scene points with an accuracy of slightly over 70%. The false alarm rate of moving object detection is below 5%. Considering that the dynamic objects are either small or moving at far distances and that we use only the last and current frame for motion separation, the results are quite encouraging.

7.2 Performance on motion estimation

Once the flow vectors coming from static scene points have been identified, we use RANSAC together with the approach presented in Section 5 to refine the inliers for correct estimation of motion parameters.

In order to estimate the accuracy of the estimated motion parameters, we need to have the ground truth values of them. This is nearly impossible when a camera is moving freely in space. For this reason we use a simulated environment where the ground truth is available. During the flight of an agent in a virtual world, real images are rendered continuously, with the motion between consecutive frames known. Using these images, we extract flow vectors and compute the motion parameters of the flying agent. They are then compared with the known ground truth to compute the precision of our algorithm. The images rendered from the virtual world have a horizontal field of view of 110 degrees, which is slightly larger than that of the camera on the real robot. To be compatible with real-world situations, we vary the illumination of the virtual world to simulate the lighting changes appeared usually in the real world.

A corridor environment has been constructed and two tests have been performed. The first test consists of a simple rotation around the vertical axis. The agent rotates first 360 degrees clockwise and then 360 degrees anticlockwise. It has been found that the deviation of the estimated final heading direction lies within 1 degree. In Fig. 9 a, the white line shows the heading direction of the agent relative to the corridor.

Fig. 9. Results of motion estimation.

The second test consists of a flight through the corridor, where the agent computes its translation and rotation parameters from image flow measurements. The average accuracy of the estimated heading direction is 2 degrees. In Fig. 9 b and c, one can observe the difference between the estimated and the ground truth motion of the agent. We project the estimated heading direction into the image and mark it with a red 'x'. The projected point of the ground truth direction of the heading is shown as a red '+'.

Further performance analysis on motion estimation has been carried out through the reconstruction of real-world camera motion. We first calculate the real camera motion from images captured by the flying robot in the outdoor environment. The calculated motion parameters have been used to generate images simulating a virtual camera moving in a textured environment. By observing synchronously the real and virtual videos, the quality of the motion estimation can be visually observed. The fact that no difference has been perceived between the two videos indicates that our algorithm on motion estimation has achieved similar results using real-world images.

7.3 Performance analysis on visual steering

The first visual steering experiment is carried out in the above corridor. A top view of the whole corridor is shown with red colour in Fig. 10 on the left. After the motion and scene depth have been calculated from two initial images, the UAV is set to move in the direction determined by our visual steering algorithm. Then the UAV captures the next frame, determine its next moving direction and moves accordingly. During the experiment, we have recorded the trajectory of the UAV. Shown in Fig 10 on the left in colour green is the recorded trajectory of the UAV. As demonstrated by this green curve, the vehicle is able to navigate through the corridor without any collision.

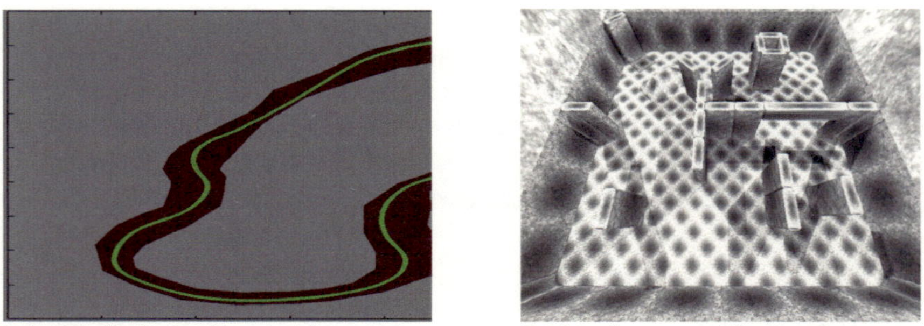

Fig. 10. Left: 3D flight in the corridor environment. Right: the maze-like environment.

Further experiments are carried out in a maze-like environment with irregular configurations of obstacles, as is shown in Fig. 10 on the right. In the beginning, the vehicle is placed randomly within the maze. The flying direction is set to the viewing direction of the camera, i.e., the forward direction. Several experiments with different starting positions show that the vehicle is capable of navigating safely within the maze by finding its way automatically. Particularly, it is able to regulate both flying direction and height to avoid collision with walls, corners, buildings, the ground, the arch etc. Some images showing the path of the drone during its navigation are shown in Figure 11.

As shown in Fig. 11 a to b, one can observe that the vehicle has found free space for navigation and change its flying direction toward the arch to avoid collision with walls and corners. From there, the agent is flying through the arch, as can be read out from Fig 11 image b, c and d. Following that, the vehicle is able to prepare the turning around the corner shown in image e. Having turned around the corner, the vehicle is guided by our visual steering algorithm to fly along the wall and adjust height due to the level of terrain and the obstacle floating in the air, as is shown by image f.

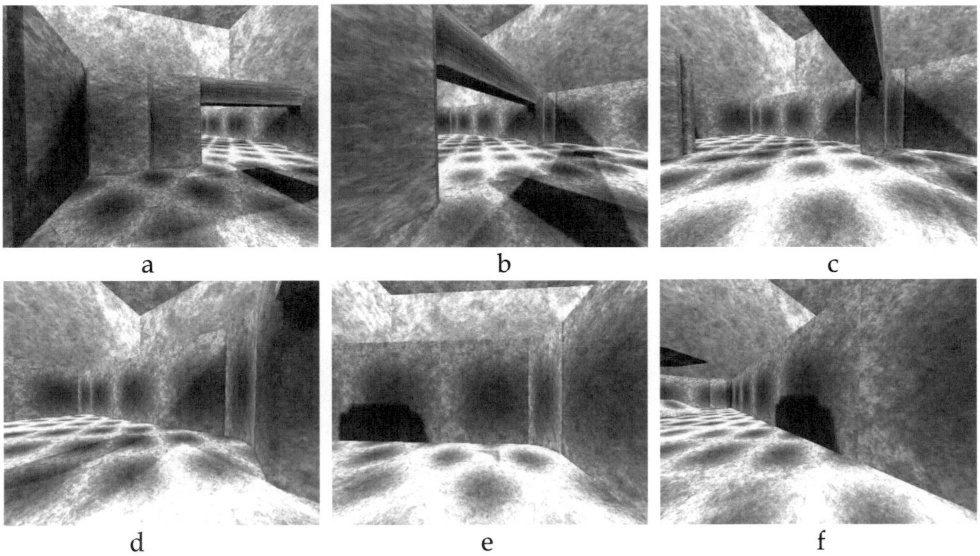

Fig. 11. 3D Flight within the maze.

Further experiments are carried out in an office experiment, which is a T-shaped corridor with isolated obstacles. As can be seen from Fig. 12, the environment is not entirely static, as the doors may be closed and opened. This is indeed an unknown dynamic environment with general configuration of obstacles. In this sense, performance in this environment indicates the effectiveness of our whole visual steering approach, including robust image flow calculation, motion separation, motion and depth estimation, and the determination of flying direction.

In Fig.12 we show one example of the experiments made in this environment. Both the visual path of the flying platform and the decisions made by our algorithm can be viewed.

Based on the output of our visual steering algorithm, the vehicle is able to maintain constant distance to the ground. The decision for horizontal motion control has been shown with red arrows, indicating the next flying direction. The length of the arrows is set in inverse proportion to the distance of obstacles. A longer arrow indicates a shorter distance to the detected obstacle and hence a faster speed needed by the UAV for flying away from it. As can be seen, the platform has been kept safely in the middle of the free space.

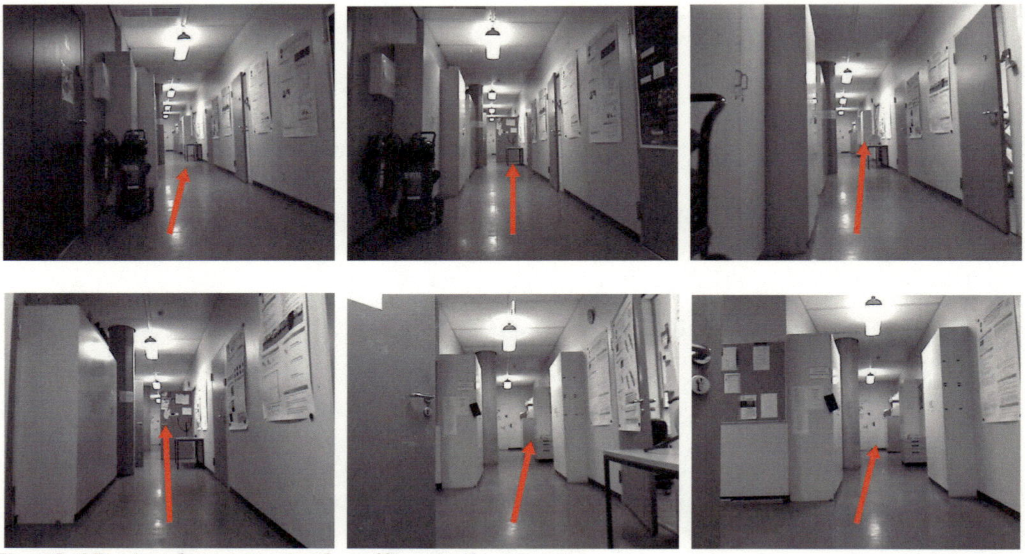

Fig. 12. 3D visual steering in the office environment.

8. Conclusion

This chapter concentrates on visual motion analysis for the safe navigation of mobile robots in dynamic environment. The aim is to build one of the important navigation abilities for robot systems: the detection of obstacles for collision avoidance during the 3D autonomous flight of UAVs. In dynamic environment, not only the robot itself but also some other objects are moving. With the proposed approach, we have shown a robot vision system capable of understanding the natural environment, analyzing the different motions and making appropriate decisions.

Most motion estimation algorithms work well with perfect image flow measurement but are very sensitive to noise and outliers. To overcome this problem, we have designed a complete computational procedure for robust 3D motion/structure recovery. A well-known image flow algorithm has been extended and improved for the robust detection of image flow vectors. In order to estimate the camera motion, we proposed a novel approach for the separation of independent motion and removal of outliers. The motion parameters of the camera and the 3D position and orientation of scene points are then recovered using a linear estimation approach. With the output of our visual motion analysis, we are able to facilitate a flying platform with obstacle detection and avoidance ability. As a result, safe and autonomous navigation of UAV systems can be achieved.

As mentioned already, the UAV has both manual and auto flight mode. However, our visual steering algorithm runs independent of the mode chosen. Even in manual mode, the human pilot can observe the visual processing results. Alerted by the decision made by our algorithm, the pilot can hence avoid possible errors and trigger correct operation. In this sense, the robot vision system developed can be used as a pilot assistance system as well. Currently we provide only a primitive visualization of the dynamic/static objects in the environment together with the decision made by our algorithm for the horizontal motion control. Visualization of the decision made for height control is omitted for the purpose of simplicity. We plan to improve the way of information presentation for better human robot interaction.

In the vision system presented, we use always two frames, the current and the last one, for making a decision. While quite efficient, its drawback is that the valuable visual processing results achieved in the past are not considered in the current analysis step. Such results can be used for example for the detection of independent motion. If a moving object is detected in several past frames, it may be more advantageous to switch from detection to tracking method for localizing the object in the current frame. This will probably improve largely the performance regarding the detection of dynamic objects. By tracking dynamic objects continuously, it is also possible to estimate their 3D motion parameters constantly. With the heading direction of the dynamic objects known, a more advance and effective visual steering strategy can be designed.

Another future research direction is to combine the visual steering approach with that of camera-based SLAM (simultaneous localization and mapping). We are updating our UAV system to have two cameras mounted on it. While the available camera looks ahead in the flying direction, another camera will point downwards to the ground. Through the second camera, more features on the ground can be observed. Together with the forward-looking camera, motion as well as location of the UAV can be estimated more accurately. A more elaborate 3D motion constraint can be derived for better motion separation and analysis. At the same time, both safer and efficient navigation of UAV can be achieved by combining the current way of reactive steering with that of goal-directed motion planning.

9. Acknowledgement

This work originates from research activities carried out on the project μDrones (Micro drone autonomous navigation for environment sensing). Funding from the European Union is gratefully acknowledged.

10. References

Aggarwal, J. K. & Nandhakumar, N. (1988). On the computation of motion from sequences of images --- A review, *Proceedings of the IEEE,* Vol. 76, No. 8 (August 1988) pp (917-935), ISSN 0018-9219

Bruhn, A.; Weickert, J. and Schnörr, C. (2005). Lucas/Kanade meets Horn/Schunck: Combining local and global optical flow methods, *Int. Journal of Computer Vision,* Vol. 61, No. 3 (March 2005) pp (211-231), ISSN 0920-5691

Calway, A. (2005). Recursive estimation of 3D motion and structure from local affine flow parameters, *IEEE Trans. Pattern Analysis and Machine Intelligence,* Vol. 27, No. 4 (April 2005) pp (562-574), ISSN 0162-8828

Clarke, J. C. & Zisserman, A. (1996). Detecting and tracking of independent motion, *Image and Vision Computing,* Vol. 14, No. 8 (August 1996) pp (565-572), ISSN 0262-885

Egelhaaf, M. & Kern, R. (2002). Vision in flying insects. *Current Opinion in Neurobiology,* Vol. 12, No. 6 (December 2002) pp (699-706), ISSN 0059-4388

Gibson, J. J. (1974). *The perception of the visual world,* Greenwood Press, ISBN 0-8371-7836-3, Westport, Connecticut, USA.

Hartley, R. I. (1997). In defense of the eight-point algorithm, *IEEE Trans. Pattern Analysis and Machine Intelligence,* Vol. 19, No. 6 (June 1997) pp (580-593), ISSN 0162-8828

Hartley R. I. and Zisserman, A. (2000). *Multiple View Geometry in Computer Vision,* Cambridge University Press, ISBN 0-5216-2304-9, Cambridge, UK.

Hartley, R. I. & Vidal, R. (2004). The multibody trifocal tensor: motion segmentation from 3 perspective views, *Proceedings of Int. Conf. on Computer Vision and Pattern Recognition (CVPR 2004),* pp. 769-775, ISBN 0-7695-2158-4, Washington DC, USA, July 2004, IEEE Computer Society, Washington, DC.

Horn, B. K. P. & Schunck, B. G. (1981). Determing optical flow. *Artificial Intelligence,* Vol. 17, No. 1-3 (August 1981) pp (185-203), ISSN 0004-3702

Horn, B. K. P. (1986). *Robot Vision,* Mit Press, ISBN 0-2620-8159-8, Cambridge, MA, USA.

Hrabar, S. & Sukhatme, G. S. (2004). A comparison of two camera configurations for optic-flow based navigation of a UAV through urban canyon, *Proceedings of 2004 IEEE/RSJ Int. Conf. on Intelligent Robots and systems (IROS 2004),* 2673-2680, ISBN 0-7803-8463-6, Sendai, Japan, September 2004, IEEE press.

Irani, M. & Anadan, P. (1998). A unified approach to moving object detection in 2D and 3D scenes, *IEEE Trans. Pattern Analysis and Machine Intelligence,* Vol. 20, No. 6 (June 1998) pp (577-589), ISSN 0162-8828

Kanatani, K. (1993). 3-D interpretation of optical flow by renormalization, *Int. Journal of Computer Vision,* Vol. 11, No. 3 (December 1993) pp (267-282), ISSN 0920-5691

Li, H. & Hartley, R. (2006). Five point motion estimation made easy, *Proceedings of Int. Conf. on Pattern Recognition (ICPR 2006),* pp. 630-633, ISBN 0-7695-2521-0, Hongkong, China, August 2006, IEEE Computer Society, Washington, DC.

Lobo, N. & Tsotsos, J. (1996). Computing egomotion and detecting independent motion from image motion using collinear points. *Computer Vision and Image Understanding,* Vol. 64, No. 1 (July 1996) pp (21-52), ISSN 1077-3142

Longuet-Higgins, H. C. (1981). A computer algorithm for reconstructing a scene from two projections, *Nature,* Vol. 293, No. 5828 (September 1981) pp (133-135), ISSN 0028-0836

Lourakis, M.; Argyros, A. & Orphanoudakis, S. (1998). Independent 3D motion detection using residual parallax normal flow field, *Proceedings of the sixth Int. Conf. on Computer Vision (ICCV 1998)*, pp. 1012-1017, ISBN 8-1731-9221-9, Bombay, India, January 1998, Narosa Publishing House, New Delhi, India.

Lucas, B.D. & Kanade, T. (1981). An iterative image registration technique with an application to stereo vision, *Proceedings of the 7th Int. Joint Conf. on Artificial Intelligence (IJCAI'81)*, pp. 674-679, ISBN 1-5586-0044-2, Vancouver, British Columbia, Canada, August 1981, William Kaufmann, Los Altos, CA.

Nister, D. (2004). An efficient solution to the five-point relative pose problem, *IEEE Trans. Pattern Analysis and Machine Intelligence*, Vol. 26, No. 6 (June 2004) pp (756-770), ISSN 0162-8828

Patwardhan, K.; Sapiro, G. & Morellas, V. (2008). Robust foreground detection in video using pixel layers, *IEEE Trans. Pattern Analysis and Machine Intelligence*, Vol. 30, No. 4 (April 2008) pp (746-751), ISSN 0162-8828

Ruffier, F. & Franceschini, N. (2005). Optic flow regulation: the key to aircraft automatic guidance. *Robotics and Autonomous Systems*, Vol. 50, No. 4 (March 2005) pp (177-194), ISSN 0921-8890

Santos-Victor, J. ; Sandini, G.; Curotto, F. & Garibaldi, S. (1995). Divergent stereo for robot navigation: A step forward to robotic bee, *Int. Journal of Computer Vision*, Vol. 14, No. 2 (March 1995) pp (159-177), ISSN 0920-5691

Sawhney, H.S. & Ayer, S. (1996). Compact representations of videos through dominant and multiple motion estimation, *IEEE Trans. Pattern Analysis and Machine Intelligence*, Vol. 18, No. 8 (August 1996) pp (814-830), ISSN 0162-8828

Srinivasan, M. V.; Zhang, S.W.; Lehrer, M. & Collett, T.S. (1996). Honeybee navigation en route to the goal: visual flight control and odometry. *The Journal of Experimental Biology*, Vol. 199, No. 1 (January 1996) pp (237-244), ISSN 0022-0949

Tian, T.Y.; Tomasi, C. & Heeger, D.J. (1996). Comparison of approaches to egomotion computation, *Proceedings of Int. Conf. on Computer Vision and Pattern Recognition (CVPR 1996)*, pp. 315-320, ISBN 0-8186-7258-7, Washington, DC, USA, June 1996, IEEE Computer Society, Washington, DC.

Torr, P.; Zisserman, A. & Murray, D. (1995). Motion clustering using the trilinear constraint over three views, *Proceedings of the Europe China Workshop on Geometric Modelling and Invariants for Computer Vision (GMICV'95)*, 118-125, ISBN 7-5656-0383-1, Xian, China, April 1995, Xidian University Press, Xian.

Umeyama, S. (1991). Least-squares estimation of transformation parameters between two point patterns, *IEEE Trans. Pattern Analysis and Machine Intelligence*, Vol. 13, No. 4, (April 1991) pp (376-380), ISSN 0162-8828

Weng, J.; Huang, T. S. & Ahuja, N. (1989). Motion and structure from two perspective views: algorithms, error analysis and error estimation, *IEEE Trans. Pattern Analysis and Machine Intelligence*, Vol. 11, No. 5 (May 1980) pp (451-476), ISSN 0162-8828

Yuan, C (2004). Simultaneous tracking of multiple objects for augmented reality applications, *Proceedings of the seventh Eurographics Workshop on Multimedia (EGMM 2004)*, 41-47, ISBN 3-9056-7317-7, Nanjing, China, October 2004, Eurographics Association.

Yuan, C.; Recktenwald, F. & Mallot, H. A. (2009). Visual steering of UAV in unknown environment, *Proceedings of 2009 IEEE/RSJ Int. Conf. on Intelligent Robots and Systems (IROS 2009)*, pp. 3906-3911, ISBN 978-1-4244-3803-7, St. Louis, Missouri, USA, October 2009, IEEE press.

Zhang, Z.; Faugeras, O. and Ayache, N. (1993). Analysis of a sequence of stereo scenes containing multiple moving objects using rigidity constraints, *Proceedings of Int. Conf. on Computer Vision (ICCV 1993)*, pp. 177-186, ISBN 0-8186-3870-2, Berlin, Germany, May 1993, IEEE Computer Society, Washington DC.

Zufferey, J. C. & Floreano, D. (2006). Fly-inspired visual steering of an ultralight indoor aircraft, *IEEE Trans. Robotics*, Vol. 22, No. 1, (January 2006) pp (137-146), ISSN 1552-3098

5

A Visual Navigation Strategy Based on Inverse Perspective Transformation

Francisco Bonin-Font, Alberto Ortiz and Gabriel Oliver
University of the Balearic Islands
Spain

1. Introduction

Vision-Based Navigation Techniques can be roughly divided in map-based and mapless systems. Map-based systems plan routes and their performance and are labeled as deliverative, while mapless systems analyze on-line the environment to determine the route to follow (Bonin et al., 2008). Some reactive vision-based systems include the implementation of local occupancy maps that show the presence of obstacles in the vicinity of the robot and try to perform a symbolic view of the surrounding world. The construction of such maps entails the computation of range and angle of obstacles in a particularly accurate manner. These maps are updated on-line and used to navigate safely (Badal et al., 1994) (Goldberg et al., 2002).
Many of the local map-based and visual sonar reactive navigation solutions are vulnerable to the presence of shadows or inter-reflections and they are also vulnerable to textured floors, since they are mostly based on edge computation or on texture segmentation. Solutions based on homography computation fail in scenarios that generate scenes with multiple planes. Some road line trackers based on Inverse Perspective Transformation (*IPT*) need to previously find lines in the image that converge to the vanishing point. Some other *IPT*-based solutions project the whole image onto the ground, increasing the computational cost.
This chapter presents a new navigation strategy comprising obstacle detection and avoidance. Unlike previous approaches, the one presented in this chapter avoids back-projecting the whole image, presents a certain robustness to scenarios with textured floors or inter-reflections, overcomes scenes with multiple different planes and combines a quantitative process with a set of qualitative rules to converge in a robust technique to safely explore unknown environments. The method has been inspired on the visual sonar-based reactive navigation algorithms and implements a new version of the Vector Field Histogram method (Borenstein & Koren, 1991) but here adapted for vision-based systems.
The complete algorithm runs in five steps: 1) first, image main features are detected, tracked across consecutive frames, and classified as obstacle or ground using a new algorithm based on *IPT*; 2) the edge map of the processed frames is computed, and edges comprising obstacle points are discriminated from the rest, emphasizing the obstacle boundaries; 3) range and angle of obstacles located inside a Region of Interest (*ROI*), centered on the robot and with a fixed radius, are estimated computing the orientation and distance of those obstacle points that are in contact with the floor; 4) a qualitative occupancy map is performed with the data computed in the previous step; and 5) finally, the algorithm computes a vector which steers the robot towards world areas free of obstacles.

This chapter is structured as follows: related work is presented in section 2, the method is outlined in Sections 3, 4 and 5, experimental results are exposed and discussed in Section 6, and finally, conclusions and forthcoming work are given in Sections 7 and 8, respectively.

2. Related Work

2.1 Feature Detection and Tracking

Visual techniques for detecting and tracking significant elements of the scene, so called features, have been extensively improved over the last years and used for localization and/or navigation purposes. Significant scene features are categorized using the concept of distinctiveness. The distinctiveness notion is related with the size of the window used to define the neighborhood captured by the feature descriptor and with the amount and type of information processed and extracted from the feature neighborhood. Distinctive features can be characterized by a vector of values including location, scale, orientation, intensities and gradients in several directions. Distinctive features can be tracked without using a motion model and more accurately than the nondistinctive features.

Harris (Harris & Stephens, 1988) and Shi and Tomasi (Shi & Tomasi, 1994) are early and fast techniques to find and/or track little discriminative features. Zhou and Li (Zhou & Li, 2006) detected features located on the ground plane grouping all coplanar points that have been found applying the Harris corner detector. Nister *et al.* estimated the motion of mobile robots tracking nondistinctive Harris corners. Saeedi *et al* (Saeedi et al., 2006) presented a stereo vision-based 3-D trajectory tracker for localization of mobile robots in unexplored environments. This work proposed a new corner detector to extract image features. Features were matched in consecutive frames minimizing the mean-squared error and searching for the highest cross correlation as a similarity measure. Rabie *et al* (Rabie et al., 2001) used a feature-based tracking approach to match in consecutive images nondistinctive points detected using the Shi and Tomasi algorithm. The algortihm was applied for traffic flow speed estimation in a system addressed to automatically monitor traffic conditions.

Lowe (Lowe, 2004) developed the Scale Invariant Feature Transform (SIFT) method to extract high discriminative image features. SIFT is robust to image scaling, rotation, illumination changes or camera view-point changes. Stephen *et al.* performed global simultaneous localization and mapping in mobile robots tracking distinctive visual SIFT landmarks in static environments (Stephen et al., 2005). Rodrigo *et al.* (Rodrigo et al., 2009) combined a set of selected relevant distinctive SIFT features with a collection of nondistinctive features to perform a robust navigation algorithm based on feature or landmark tracking. SIFT features were used to compute the homographies of the different planar structures in the scene. Nondistinctive features were used to refine the motion model. Once the homographies of the different planes were computed it was possible to determine the motion of nondistinctive features across consecutive images.

Mikolajczyk and Schmid (Mikolajczyk & Schmid, 2005) compared the performance of different descriptors for image local regions. Experimental results of different matching approaches used to recognize the same region in different viewing conditions showed that SIFT yields the best performance in all tests.

2.2 Inverse Perspective Transformation-based Obstacle Detection

To detect obstacles, Mallot *et al* (Mallot et al., 1991) analyzed variations on the optical flow computed over the Inverse Perspective Mapping (*IPM*) of consecutive images. Bertozzi and Broggi (Bertozzi & Broggi, 1998) projected two stereo images onto the ground applying the

IPM concept. Then, they subtracted both projections to generate a non-zero pixel zone that evidenced the presence of obstacles. Batavia *et al* (Batavia et al., 1997) used the *IPT* and the camera ego-motion to predict future frames and compare them with the corresponding new real frames. Differences between the predicted and real images showed the presence of obstacles. The system was designed to detect vehicles in the blind spot of the cars rear-view mirror. Shu and Tan (Shu & Tan, 2004) also employed the *IPM* to detect road lanes for self-guided vehicles. Ma *et al* (Ma et al., 2007) presented an automatic pedestrian detection algorithm based on *IPM* for self-guided vehicles. The system predicted new frames assuming that all image points laid on the floor. The distorted zones of the predicted image corresponded to objects. Simond combined the *IPM* with the computation of the ground plane super-homography from road lines to discriminate obstacles from road in an autonomous guided vehicle application (Simond & Parent, 2007).

2.3 Visual Sonar

Some other researchers explored the idea of Visual Sonar. Visual Sonar techniques provide depth and orientation of elements in the scene, using visual sensors in an analogous way to ultrasonic sensors (Horswill, 1994) (Choi & Oh, 2005) (Martin, 2006). In some cases, the application of the visual sonar concept results in the computation of local occupancy maps (Lenser & Veloso, 2003) (Fasola et al., 2005).

3. Obstacle Detection: Overall Description

3.1 The Inverse Perspective Transformation

The Perspective Transformation is the method for mapping three-dimensional points onto a two-dimensional plane called the plane of projection. This Perspective Transformation models the process of taking a picture, being the image plane the plane where the spatial scene is projected. The line that connects a world point with the camera lens intersects the image plane defining the corresponding and unique image point of that world point. The inverse process, that is, the projection of every image point back to the world is modeled by the Inverse Perspective Transformation. The back projected point will be somewhere in the line that connects the image point with the center of projection (camera lens).
The direct and the inverse perspective projections are usually modelled assuming a pinhole camera and a flat ground (Duda & Hart, 1973) (Hartley & Zisserman, 2003). Three coordinate systems are involved: the world, the camera and the image coordinate systems. The linear mapping between world to image points, both expressed in homogeneous coordinates, can be written as (Hartley & Zisserman, 2003):

$$\begin{bmatrix} x_p \\ y_p \\ f \end{bmatrix} = \begin{bmatrix} 1 & 0 & 0 & 0 \\ 0 & 1 & 0 & 0 \\ 0 & 0 & 1 & 0 \end{bmatrix} T_w^c \begin{bmatrix} x \\ y \\ z \\ 1 \end{bmatrix}, \tag{1}$$

where (x_p, y_p) are the image point coordinates, f is the focal length, (x, y, z) are the corresponding scene point world coordinates and T_w^c is the 4×4 transformation matrix from world to the camera coordinates.
It is possible to compute the scene point world coordinates corresponding to an image point knowing either the distance between the camera and the point in the space or any of the (x, y, z) world coordinates, as for example, for points lying on the floor (z=0). The expressions

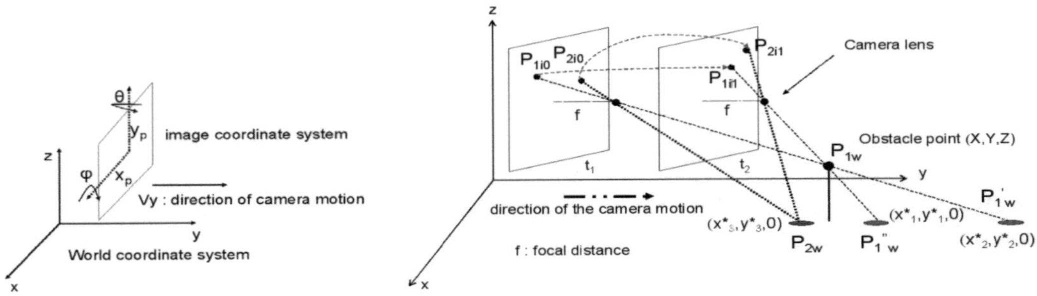

(a) (b)

Fig. 1. (a) Coordinate frame conventions. (b) The IPT-based obstacle detection.

in closed form to calculate the world coordinates for points lying on the floor are (Duda & Hart, 1973):

$$x^* = X_0 - \frac{Z_0 x_p cos\theta + (y_p sin\varphi - f cos\varphi)(Z_0 sin\theta)}{y_p cos\varphi + f sin\varphi} \tag{2}$$

$$y^* = Y_0 - \frac{Z_0 x_p sin\theta - (y_p sin\varphi - f cos\varphi)(Z_0 cos\theta)}{y_p cos\varphi + f sin\varphi} \tag{3}$$

where (x^*,y^*) are the ground point world coordinates, (X_0, Y_0, Z_0) are the camera world coordintes at the moment in which the frame has been taken, and θ and φ are the camera yaw and pitch angles, respectively. Coordinate system conventions and notation are illustrated in figure 1-(a).

3.2 Discrimination Between Obstacle and Ground Points

The (x^*,y^*) values computed by means of equations (2) and (3) for an image point that corresponds to a point lying on the floor are equal when they are computed from two consecutive images, and exactly correspond to the point (x, y) world coordinates. However, for an image point that belongs to an object protruding vertically from the floor, the assumption $z = 0$ is incorrect and the (x^*,y^*) values turn out to be different when they are calculated from two consecutive images, and different to the object point real (x, y) world coordinates. Hence, one can distinguish if the point belongs to an obstacle or to the floor assuming $z = 0$ and comparing the distance between the resulting (x^*,y^*) values calculated for two consecutive images:

$$(discrepancy) \quad D = \sqrt{(x_2^* - x_1^*)^2 + (y_2^* - y_1^*)^2} \Rightarrow \begin{cases} if D > \beta \Rightarrow \text{obstacle}, \\ if D \le \beta \Rightarrow \text{ground}. \end{cases} \tag{4}$$

where (x_1^*,y_1^*) and (x_2^*,y_2^*) correspond to instants t_1 and t_2, respectively, and β is the threshold for the maximum difference admissible between (x_1^*,y_1^*) and (x_2^*,y_2^*) to classify the feature as ground point. Ideally β should be 0.

The idea is illustrated in figure 1-(b). Two frames of a scene are taken at instants t_1 and t_2. Point P_{2w} is on the floor. Its projection into the image plane at instants t_1 and t_2 generates, respectively, the image points P_{2i0} and P_{2i1}. The Inverse Transformation of P_{2i0} and P_{2i1} generates a unique point P_{2w}. P_{1w} is an obstacle point. Its projection into the image plane at t_1 and t_2 generates, respectively, the points P_{1i0} and P_{1i1}. However, the Inverse Transformation of P_{1i0} and P_{1i1} back to the world assuming $z = 0$ (e.g. projection onto the ground plane), generates two different points on the ground, namely, P'_{1w} and P''_{1w}.

3.3 Feature Detection and Tracking

The first key step of the algorithm is to detect a sufficiently large and relevant set of image features and match them across consecutive images. SIFT features (Lowe, 2004) have been chosen as the features to track because of their robustness to scale changes, rotation and/or translation as well as changes in illumination and view point. Wrong correspondences between points in consecutive frames are filtered out in four steps, using RANSAC and imposing the epipolar constraint: $x'_p F x_p = 0$, where x'_p and x_p are the point image coordinates in two consecutive frames, and F is the fundamental matrix (Hartley & Zisserman, 2003):

1. Compute SIFT features and match them in the two consecutive images,
2. starting with 7 correspondences randomly generated, compute the Fundamental Matrix taking the one with the lowest standard deviation of inliers (RANSAC robust estimation),
3. re-compute F from the correspondences classified as inliers,
4. update the correspondences using the updated F.

Steps 3 and 4 can be iterated until the number of correspondences is stable.

4. Obstacle Detection: Enhanced Feature Classification

4.1 Direct Identification of Some Obstacle Points

The set of scene points that map to a given image point can be written as (Duda & Hart, 1973):

$$p = p_l + \lambda(p_p - p_l) \tag{5}$$

where p is the scene object point (x, y, z), p_l is the camera center (X_0, Y_0, Z_0), p_p is the image point corresponding to the scene point p, expressed in the world coordinate system,

$$p_p = \begin{bmatrix} X_0 \\ Y_0 \\ Z_0 \end{bmatrix} + \begin{bmatrix} x_p cos\theta - f cos\varphi sin\theta + y_p sin\varphi sin\theta \\ x_p sin\theta + f cos\varphi cos\theta - y_p sin\varphi cos\theta \\ f sin\varphi + y_p cos\varphi \end{bmatrix}, \tag{6}$$

and λ is a free parameter leading to a certain world point somewhere on the image point-lens line. The idea is illustrated in figure 2-(a).

The back-projection onto the ground of all these image features (p_p) which correspond to scene points (p) located below the plane parallel to the flat ground and that contains the lens center (p_l) requires a positive λ, while λ has to be negative for all image features corresponding to scene points located above the mentioned plane. The idea is illustrated in figure 2-(b). p_1 is a point lying on the floor, and its corresponding image point is p_{p1}. In equation (5) p_1 is obtained from p_{p1} with $\lambda > 0$. Likewise, p_2 and p'_{2w} result from p_{p2} for $\lambda > 0$. However, p_{p3} leads to a point on the ground p'_{3w} for which λ is < 0

Clearly, image points with λ negative necessarily correspond to scene points above the ground, while image points with λ positive can correspond either to elevated points or to points lying on the floor. Consequently, the process of inverse projection and discrepancy computation can be omitted for all these image features that need a $\lambda < 0$ to be projected onto the ground, as they can be directly classified as obstacle points.

The goal then is to find which is the location in the image of all these features that can be directly classified as obstacle points. Doing some manipulations on equation (5), the z world coordinate of a scene point can be calculated as (Duda & Hart, 1973):

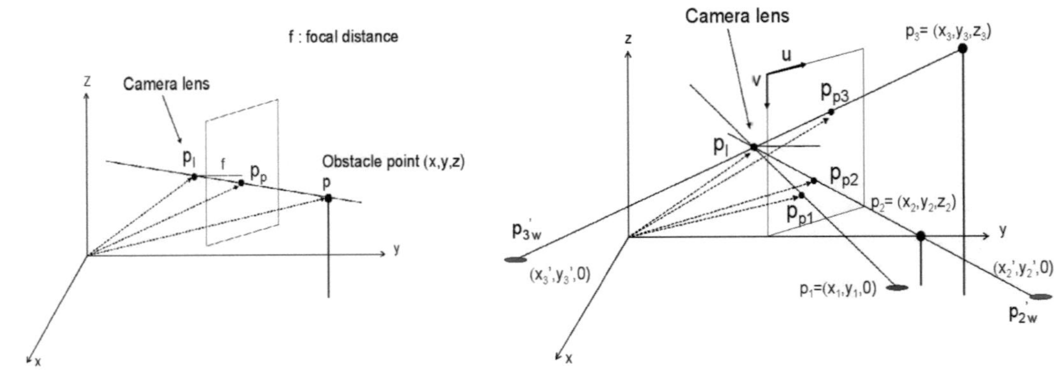

(a) (b)

Fig. 2. (a) The *IPT*: $p = p_l + \lambda(p_p - p_l)$ (b) $\lambda's$ positives and negatives

$$z = Z_0 + \lambda(fsin\varphi + y_p cos\varphi) \tag{7}$$

where λ determines the exact position of the scene point in the inverse perspective projecting ray.
If $z = 0$, we can solve for λ:

$$\lambda = \frac{-Z_0}{fsin\varphi + y_p cos\varphi}. \tag{8}$$

Making $\lambda < 0$ means that $(fsin\varphi + y_p cos\varphi) > 0$, then solving for y_p:

$$y_p > -f \tan \varphi. \tag{9}$$

Expressing the y_p image coordinate in pixels and translating the origin of the image coordinate system from the image center to the upper left corner (see figure 3), we obtain that:

$$v < v_0 + k_v f \tan \varphi \tag{10}$$

where k_v factor is the relation $[pixels/length]$ of the used images.
Therefore, all image points with a vertical coordinate v lower that $v_0 + k_v f \tan \varphi$ pixels correspond to obstacle points of the scene.

4.2 Selection of Threshold β

Those image features that do not admit a direct identification as obstacles must be classified using equation (4). In order to select an appropriate value for β in this equation, we have studied the behavior of discrepancy D for all the pixels of one image under reasonable conditions of application in the navigation strategy. More precisely: a) the distance between the camera and a scene point (DST) was fixed to a constant value for all pixels of one image, and tested with 1000mm, 1500mm and 2000mm, b) according to the experimental setup, the camera separation between two consecutive images was 31mm along the direction of motion, the image resolution was set to 256×192 pixels, the focal length was set to 3.720mm, and the camera angles φ and θ were set to -9° and 0°, respectively, c) the rotation matrix R representing the orientation of the camera in the world coordinate system was defined for rotation only around the x_p axis.

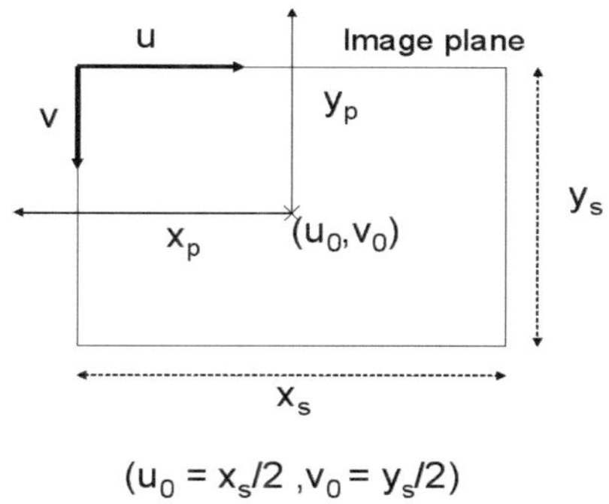

Fig. 3. Image plane coordinate system, where x_s and y_s are respectively, the horizontal and vertical image resolution

This section describes next the algorithm to compute the discrepancy D for each pixel of one image, under the aforementioned conditions.

I) We start from two consecutive images. First, given a point in the first image with coordinates (x_{p1}, y_{p1}), the world coordinates of its corresponding scene point are calculated assuming that the distance between the camera and the point of the scene (DST) is known. The relation between the coordinates (X_{c1}, Y_{c1}, Z_{c1}) of a scene point expressed in the coordinate system attached to the camera and its corresponding image point (x_{p1}, y_{p1}) is (Hartley & Zisserman, 2003):

$$X_{c1} = \frac{x_{p1} Z_{c1}}{f} \qquad Y_{c1} = \frac{y_{p1} Z_{c1}}{f}. \tag{11}$$

The distance between the camera and the point of the scene (DST) can be calculated as:

$$DST = \sqrt{Z_{c1}^2 + Y_{c1}^2 + X_{c1}^2}, \tag{12}$$

combining (12) with (11), we obtain:

$$Z_{c1}^2 = \frac{DST^2}{1 + (\frac{y_{p1}^2}{f^2}) + (\frac{x_{p1}^2}{f^2})}. \tag{13}$$

The euclidean transformation between the world and camera homogeneous coordinates can be expressed as:

$$\begin{bmatrix} x \\ y \\ z \\ 1 \end{bmatrix} = T_c^w \begin{bmatrix} X_{c1} \\ Y_{c1} \\ Z_{c1} \\ 1 \end{bmatrix}, \tag{14}$$

where

$$T_c^w = \begin{bmatrix} R & T_1 \\ 0^T & 1 \end{bmatrix}, \tag{15}$$

being R the 3×3 rotation matrix, and $T_1 = (X_{01}, Y_{01}, Z_0)$ (the camera position at the first image). Knowing R and T_1, we can obtain the world coordinates (x, y, z) of the scene point corresponding to the chosen image point.

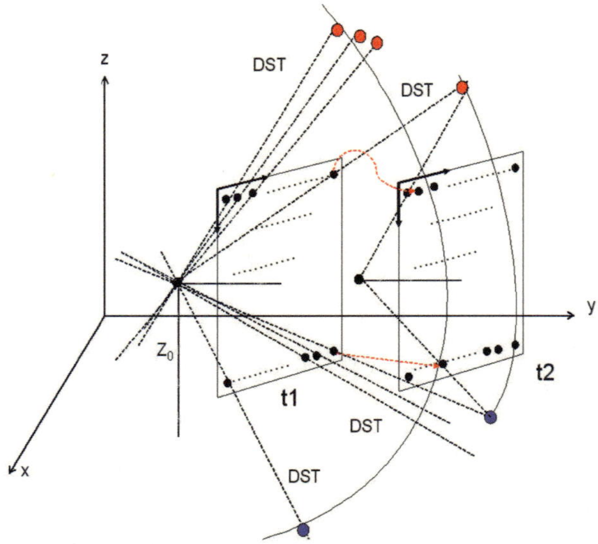

Fig. 4. All image points over a sphere of a defined radius DST are projected in the image plane, and then tracked in two consecutive images, at instants t_1 and t_2.

II) Next, this scene point (x, y, z) is projected onto the second image, obtaining the point coordinates (x_{p2}, y_{p2}) in the second frame. The camera position at the instant of taking the second image is $T_2 = (X_{02}, Y_{02}, Z_0)$. Assuming that R does not change, with the new camera position and the calculated world point coordinates (x, y, z), the scene point expressed in the new camera coordinates (X_{c2}, Y_{c2}, Z_{c2}) can be calculated using the equation (14). With (X_{c2}, Y_{c2}, Z_{c2}), the image coordinates (x_{p2}, y_{p2}) can be calculated using equations (11).
III) Finally, (x_{p1}, y_{p1}) and (x_{p2}, y_{p2}) are back-projected onto the floor using equations (2) and (3) to obtain (x_1^*, y_1^*) and (x_2^*, y_2^*), which are used to calculate the discrepancy D defined in equation (4).
The so far described process is illustrated in figure 4. Assuming a constant DST for all image points means that all points located in the surface of a sphere surrounding the camera, with a radius of DSTm are projected onto the image. If the radius is sufficiently long, the sphere will intersect the plane $z = 0$. All points of the sphere that intersect this plane are on the floor, and are projected at the bottom of the image.
Figure 5 plots three cases of function $D(x_p, y_p)$ for all pixels of one image of 256×192 pixels, using DST=1000mm, DST=1500mm and DST=2000mm, and setting the rest of parameters (f, φ and θ) as stated at the beginning of this section. Note in plots (d) and (f) how pixels at the bottom of the image present discrepancies equal to 0. These pixels correspond to those scene points located on the floor or below the $z = 0$ world plane.
Figure 6 plots $D(x_p, y_p)$ for images with a resolution of 1024×768 pixels and the same parameters as stated previously in this section. D values reach their maximum around v=50 pixels for images with a resolution of 256 × 192 pixels and v=200 for images with a resolution of 1024 × 768 pixels.
As can be observed in figures 5 and 6, discrepancy D exhibits different behavior depending on the image pixel location. The dependance of D with the position of the feature in the image suggests that the β threshold defined in equation (4) can be also dependent on the image feature position. Adjusting β to a low value for image features near the bottom or to a

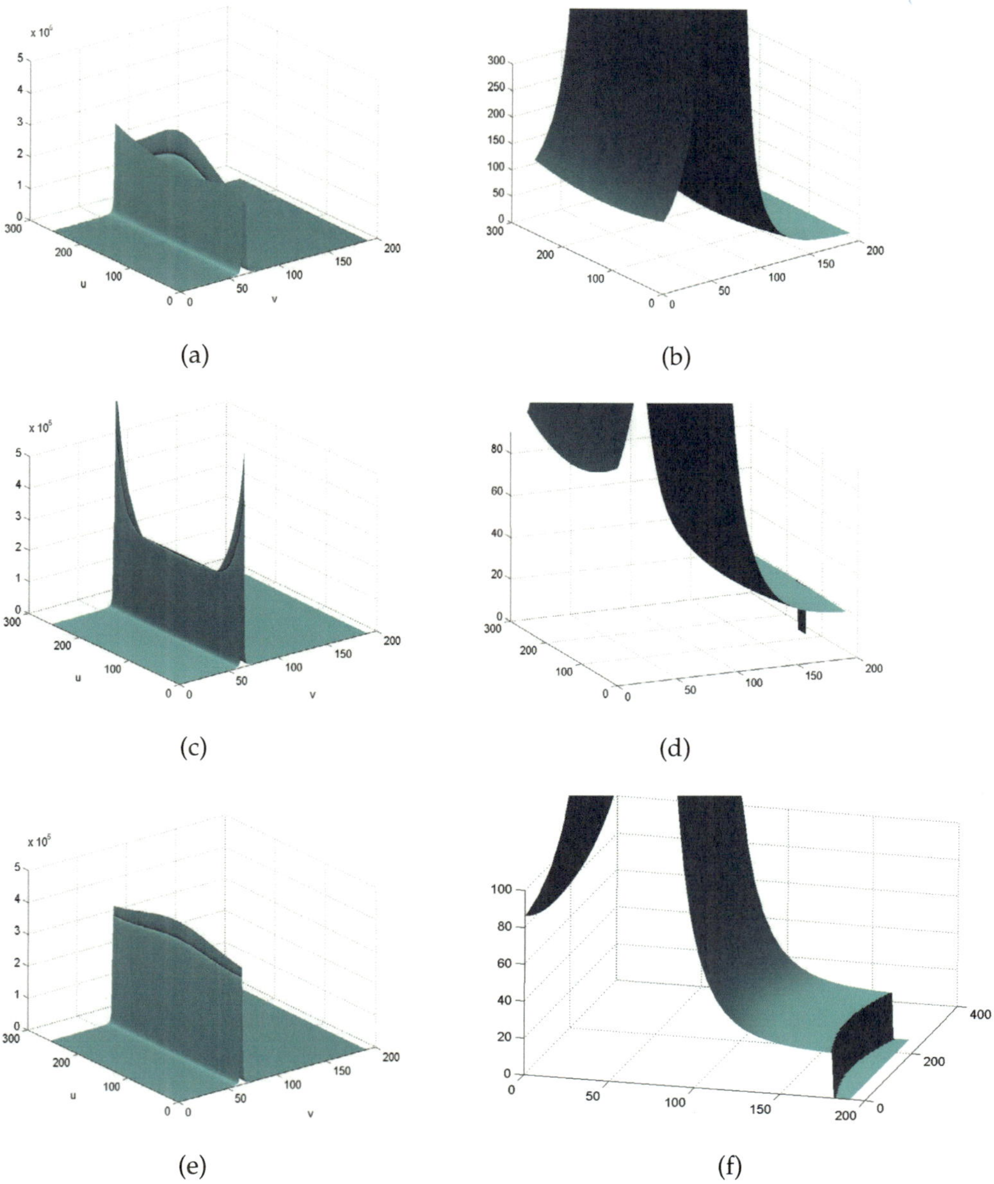

Fig. 5. (a), (c) and (e), plot of $D(x_p, y_p)$ function for DST=1m, DST=1.5m and DST=2.0m, respectively, for a resolution of 256×192 pixels. (b), (d) and (f): respectively, detail of (a), (c) and (e). In plots (c), (d), (e) and (f), $D = 0$ for world points lying on the sphere surface with radius DST and such that $z \leq 0$

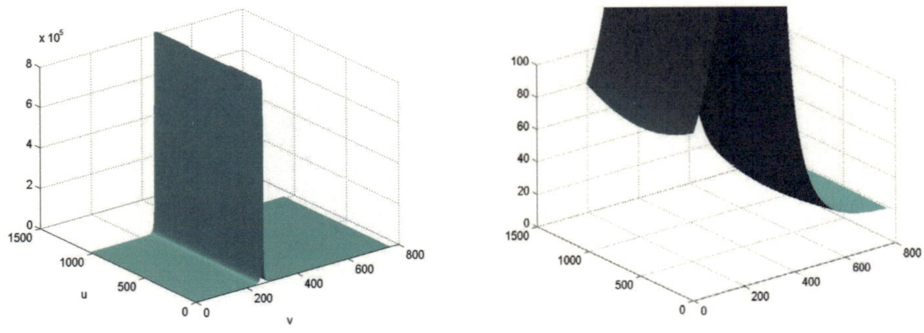

(a) (b)

Fig. 6. (a) D graphic for DST=1.5m and image resolution of 1024×768. (b) detail of (a) for D (discrepancy) low levels

higher value for image features near the zone with maximum D should decrease the number of missclassified SIFT features.

5. The Navigation Strategy

5.1 Obstacle Profiles

SIFT features are usually detected at regions of high gradient (Lowe, 2004), thus they are likely to be near or belong to an edge. Besides, features classified as obstacles are most likely to be contained or near a vertical edge belonging to an obstacle. Hence, the next step of the algorithm is the computation of edge maps and the association of such edges with real obstacle points. This process permits isolating the obstacle boundaries from the rest of edges and getting a qualitative perception of the environment.
In order to combine a high degree of performance in the edge map computation with a relatively low processing time, the edge detection procedure runs in two steps (Canny, 1986):

1. First, the original image is convolved with a 1D gaussian derivative horizontal kernel. This permits detecting zones with high vertical gradient from smoothed intensity values with a single convolution.
2. Next, a process of hysteresis thresholding is applied. Two thresholds are defined. A pixel with a gradient above the highest threshold is classified as edge pixel. A pixel with a gradient above the lowest threshold is classified as edge if it has in its vicinity a pixel with a gray value higher than the highest threshold. In this way, edge pixels with low gradient are not filtered if the threshold is defined too high, and noise is not considered as an edge if the threshold is defined too low.

The algorithm locates every image feature classified as obstacle and then searches for all edge pixels which are inside a window centered at the feature image coordinates. Then, every edge is tracked down starting from the object point position until the last edge pixel or a ground point is found. This will be considered as to be the point(/s) where the object rests on the floor. This process permits isolating the obstacle boundaries from the rest of edges and to get a qualitative perception of the environment.

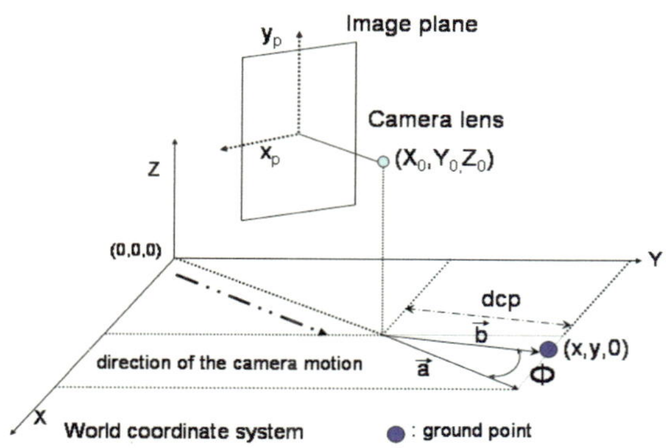

Fig. 7. Distance and orientation of an obstacle point with respect to the camera

5.2 Building the Local Occupancy Map

Knowing the camera position and the world coordinates of a point on the floor, the distance *dcp* between the vehicle and the floor point and the angle ϕ defined by the direction of motion and the relative orientation of this point with respect to the camera can be calculated as:

$$dcp = \sqrt{(x - X_0)^2 + (y - Y_0)^2}$$
$$\phi = \arccos\left(\frac{\vec{a} \cdot \vec{b}}{|\vec{a}||\vec{b}|}\right) \quad (16)$$

where $(x, y, 0)$ are the world point coordinates, $\vec{a}$ is a vector with the same direction as the vector from the world coordinate system origin to point $(X_0, Y_0, 0)$, $\vec{b}$ is the vector from point $(X_0, Y_0, 0)$ to point $(x, y, 0)$, and $\vec{a} \cdot \vec{b}$ is the dot product between both vectors. The idea is illustrated in figure 7.

The orientation and distance of obstacles with respect to the robot can then be qualitatively estimated computing the distance and orientation between the camera and those obstacle points in contact with the floor, using equations (16).

5.3 The Navigation Strategy

A semicircular area on the ground plane, of a fixed radius and centered at the robot position, is defined as the Region of Interest (*ROI*). Only obstacles detected inside this *ROI* are considered to be avoided. The *ROI* is in turn divided in angular regions. Histograms of obstacle-to-ground contact points at each polar direction of the *ROI* are computed. Those polar directions corresponding to angular regions occupied by a set of obstacle-to-ground contact points are labeled as forbidden and those free of obstacle-to-ground contact points are included in the set of possible next movement directions. This process results in a qualitative polar occupancy map of free and occupied zones in the vicinity of the robot. Obstacle-free polar regions which are narrower than a certain threshold (determined empirically and depending on the robot size) are excluded from the possible motion directions. If all angular regions are narrower than the defined threshold, the algorithm concludes that all space in front is occupied by obstacles and returns a stop order.

The next movement direction is given as a vector pointing to the center of the widest polar obstacle-free zone. Positive angles result for turns to the right and negative angles for turns to the left.

6. Implementation and Experimental Results

6.1 Overall Performance of the Classifier

To test the proposed strategy, a Pioneer 3DX robot with a calibrated wide angle camera was programmed to navigate in different scenarios, such as environments with obstacles of regular and irregular shape, with textured and untextured floor, and environments with specularities or under low illumination conditions. The operative parameter settings were: robot speed=40mm/s; the radius of the *ROI*=1'5m; for the hysteresis thresholding, low level= 40 and high level= 50; camera height= 430mm; $\varphi = -9°$; initial $\theta = 0°$, and finally, $f = 3.720mm$. For each scene, the complete navigation algorithm was run over successive pairs of 0.77-second-separation consecutive frames so that the effect of *IPT* was noticeable. Increasing the frame rate decreases the *IPT* effect over the obstacle points, and decreasing the frame rate delays the execution of the algorithm. Frames were originally recorded with a resolution of 1024×768 pixels but then they were down-sampled to a resolution of 256×192 pixels, in order to reduce the computation time. All frames were also undistorted to correct the error in the image feature position due to the distortion introduced by the lens, and thus, to increase the accuracy in the calculation of the point world coordinates. The implementation of the SIFT features detection and matching process was performed following the methods and approaches described in (Lowe, 2004). The camera world coordinates were calculated for each frame by dead reckoning, taking into account the relative camera position with respect to the robot center.

First of all, the classifier performance was formally determined using *ROC* curves (Bowyer et al., 2001). These curves were computed for every pair of consecutive images and plot the *recall* of classified points vs the *fall-out*, varying the threshold β:

$$recall(\beta) = \frac{TP(\beta)}{TP(\beta) + FN(\beta)} \qquad fallout(\beta) = \frac{FP(\beta)}{FP(\beta) + TN(\beta)}, \tag{17}$$

where TP is the number of true positives (obstacle points classified correctly), FN is the number of false negatives (obstacle points classified as ground), FP is the number of false positives (ground points classified as obstacle) and TN is the number of true negatives (ground points classified correctly). For every *ROC* curve, its Area Under the Curve (AUC) (Hanley & McNeil, 1982) was calculated as a measure of the success rate. The optimum β value was obtained for every pair of images minimizing the cost function:

$$f(\beta) = FP(\beta) + \delta FN(\beta). \tag{18}$$

During the experiments, δ was set to 0.5 to prioritize the minimization of false positives over false negatives. For a total of 36 different pairs of images, corresponding to a varied set of scenes differing in light conditions, in the number and position of obstacles and in floor texture, a common optimum β value of 21mm resulted.

Figure 8 shows some examples of the classifier output. Pictures [(1)-(2)], [(4)-(5)], [(7)-(8)], [(10)-(11)] show several pairs of consecutive frames corresponding to examples 1, 2, 3 and 4, respectively, recorded by the moving robot and used as input to the algorithm. Pictures (2), (5), (8) and (11) show obstacle points (in red) and ground points (in blue). Although some ground points were wrongly classified as obstacles, the AUC of the ROC curves for examples 1 to 4 (plots (3), (6), (9) and (12) of figure 8) suggest success rates of 97%, 94%, 92% and 95%, respectively. Notice that all scenes present inter-reflections, shadows and specularities, although they do not affect the classifier performance.

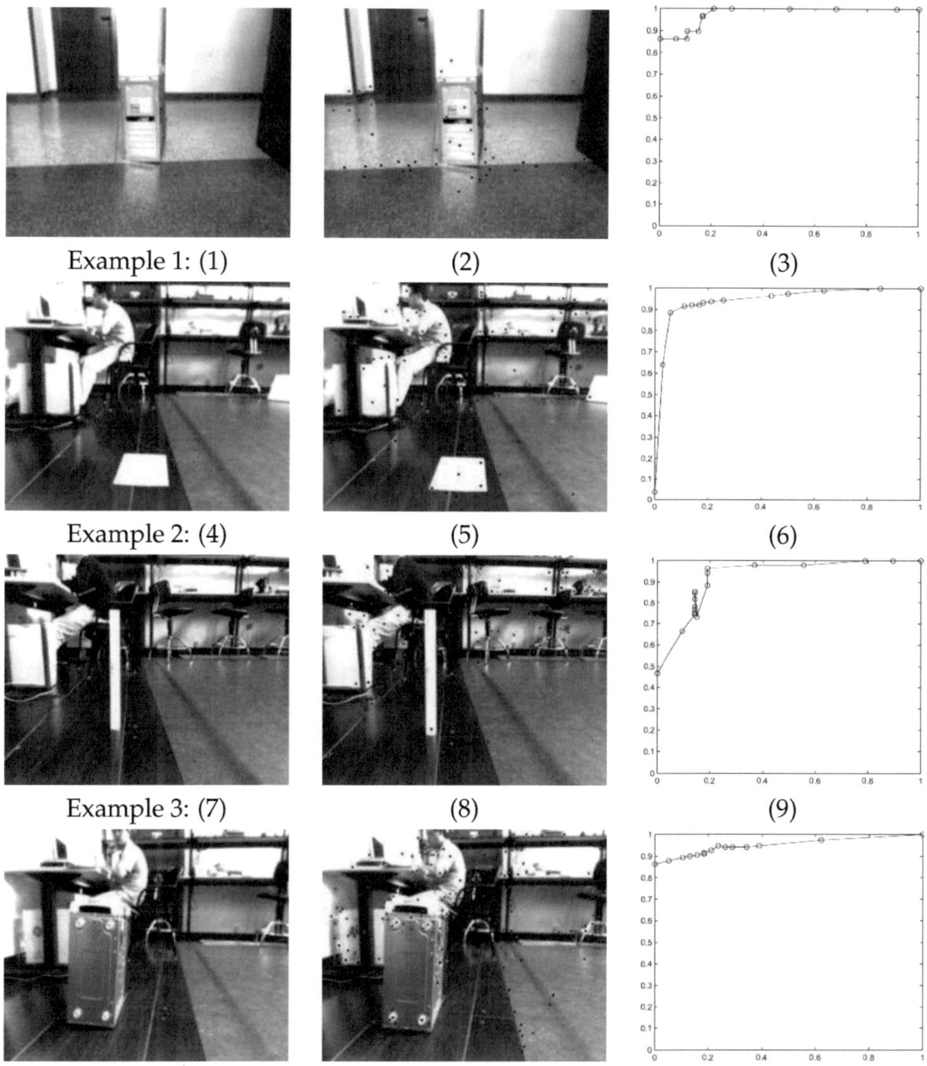

Example 4: (10) (11) (12)

Fig. 8. (1),(4), (7) and (10): undistorted first frame of examples 1, 2, 3 and 4, respectively. (2), (5), (8) and (11): undistorted second frame. (3), (6), (9) and (12): ROC curves for examples 1, 2, 3 and 4, respectively (AUC_1=0'9791, AUC_2=0'9438, AUC_3=0'9236, AUC_4=0'9524).

6.2 The Classifier Refinement Routine

Features corresponding to points lying on the floor but classified as obstacle points can induce the detection of false obstacles. In order to filter out as much *FPs* as possible, the threshold β

was varied with the feature image location and according to the concepts and results outlined in section 4.2.

Taking the same values of f, φ, camera height, image resolution, robot speed, ROI and frame rate as stated in section 6.1, and with a k_v=1000/(4 ∗ 4,65) (taking into account that 1 pixel=4.65μm for the original image resolution of 1024 × 768 pixels, then, for the down-sampled images with a resolution of 256 × 192 pixels, 1 pixel=4*4.65μm), from equation (10) resulted v <65 pixels. All features located between the top of the image and v=65 pixels were directly classified as obstacle points.

Since the yaw angle of the camera with respect to the direction of motion was 0 and the camera pitch angle was $-9°$, it was defined a rotation matrix corresponding to a unique rotation around the x_p camera axis. The transformation from camera to world coordinates T_c^w was set to:

$$T_c^w = \begin{bmatrix} 1 & 0 & 0 & X_0 \\ 0 & \sin\varphi & \cos\varphi & Y_0 \\ 0 & \cos\varphi & -\sin\varphi & Z_0 \\ 0 & 0 & 0 & 1 \end{bmatrix} \qquad (19)$$

The radius of the ROI was set to 1.5m, so the DST (see equation (12)) reference value was also set to 1.5m.

In a previous training phase, a number of image sequences were recorded in different scenarios with the moving robot remotely controlled. 36 image pairs were used to train the β adjustment. Every image was then virtually divided in four sectors, 1) zone 3, from v=0 to v=65, where all points were automatically classified as obstacle points; 2) zone 2, from v=65 to v=90, which is the zone where D reaches abruptly its maxima values; 3) zone 1, from v=90 to v=169, where D changes gradually with the image v coordinate and 4) zone 0, from v=169 to v=192, where D has a nearly constant value of 21mm, for a DST=1.5m. The threshold β used to determine the maximum discrepancy admissible for a feature to be classified as ground point was set differently for the different image zones: a) 21mm in zone 0, b) in zones 1 and 2, the β value was chosen to minimize the number of $FP(\beta) + 0.5FN(\beta)$ in each image zone, and for each different scenario. For example, scenario 2 required a higher β in zone 2 than scenario 1. In zone 1, βs resulted in a 20mm to 30mm range, and in zone 2, βs resulted in a 30mm to 150mm range.

Also during the training phase, histograms accounting for the number of FP and TP for each D value where computed over a number of pre-recorded images of different scenarios. Figure 9 shows some examples of these histograms. TP located in zone 2 are shown in green, TP in zone 1 are shown in blue, FP in zone 1 are shown in red and FP in zone 2 are shown in magenta. The majority of TP are located in zone 2 and have high D values. Only a few obstacle points are located in zone 1. FP in the zone 2 do not affect our navigation algorithm since they are out of the ROI. FP in the zone 1 can be inside the ROI and have to be filtered out. For all the analyzed scenarios, all FP of zone 1 presented discrepancies (D) in a 20mm and 85mm range.

Once β had been configured for every image zone and scenario, and the filtering criteria had been defined, the algorithm could be run during the autonomous navigation phase. During this autonomous process and for all tested scenes, all features of zone 1 that presented a discrepancy between 20mm and 85mm were not classified. Combining the aforementioned filter with a β changing at each different image zone, nearly all ground points classified as obstacles were filtered out and some other points were well re-classified. This reduced the risk

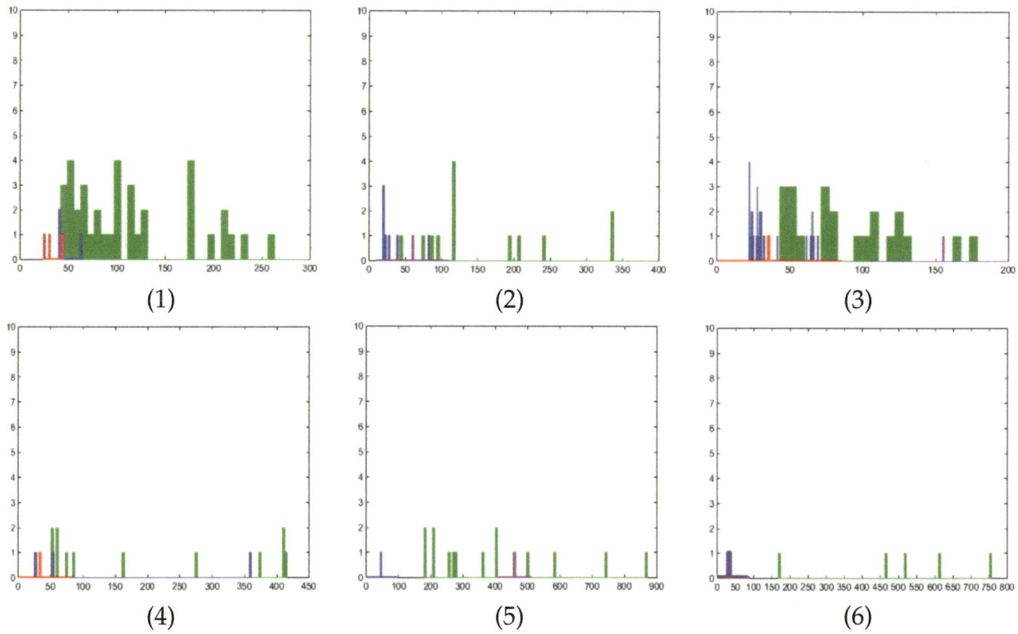

Fig. 9. (1), (2) and (3): Examples of histograms corresponding to scenario 1. (4) and (5): Example of histograms corresponding to scenario 2. (6): Example of histogram corresponding to scenario 3.

of detecting false obstacles, and although some true obstacle points were also removed, the remaining ones were sufficient to permit the detection of those obstacles.

Figure 10 shows several results of the refinement routine. Pictures (1), (3), (5), (7), (9) and (11) show images recorded during some navigation tests in different scenarios. Obstacle points are shown in red and ground points in blue. Pictures (2), (4), (6), (8), (10) and (12) show the corresponding images after the refinement routine was applied. See as in all these images false obstacles in zone 1 were filtered out.

Table 1 shows some numerical results to compare the classifier assessment using a single β and no filtering process vs the results obtained using a changing β and the filtering routine. Columns $FPAF/Nbr$ and FP/Nbr show the percentage of FP with respect to the total number of features at each scene, with and without the refinement process, respectively. In all cases this percentage either maintains the value or decreases. The column AUC shows the area under the ROC curve without the refinement process. All values suggest a classifier success rate greater than 90%. The *Fall Out* for the optimum β in each image zone, calculated when the refinement process was applied, decreases or maintains the value with respect to the *Fall Out* computed with the single optimum β (21mm) without the refinement process.

6.3 The Complete Navigation Strategy

After image features have been classified, the algorithm successfully identifies the relevant part of the obstacle contour. A 9×15 pixel window is used to find edge pixels near an obstacle point and to track down the obstacle contours. The window is longer in the vertical direction to overcome possible discontinuities in the obstacle vertical borders.

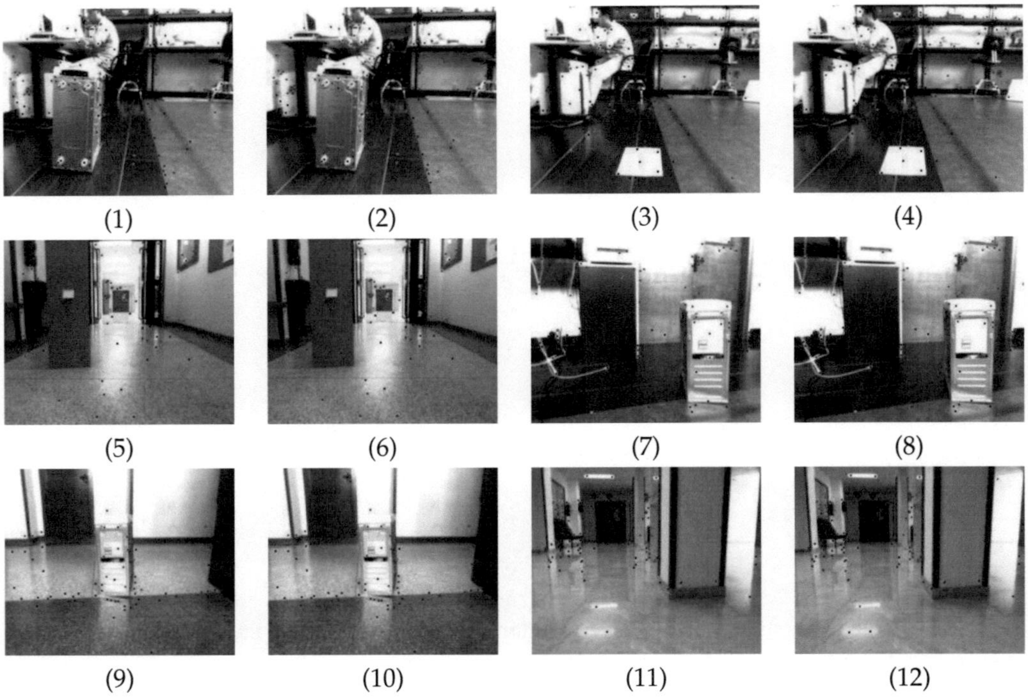

Fig. 10. (1), (3), (5), (7), (9) and (11): Image with SIFT features classified. (2), (4), (6), (8), (10) and (12): Image with SIFT features filtered and reclassified.

Scene	FP/N_{br}	AUC	*Fall-Out* for a unique β	*Recall* for a unique β	FPAF /N_{br}	*Fall Out* with refine-ment	*Recall* with refine-ment
scene 1	0.0078	0.9482	0.0600	0.9467	0.0042	0.0286	0.9415
scene 2	0.0275	0.9412	0.1500	0.8998	0.0096	0.0625	0.9034
scene 3	0.0313	0.9434	0.1156	0.9857	0.0108	0.0400	0.9850
scene 4	0.0081	0.9554	0.0416	0.7653	0.000	0.0000	0.7700
scene 5	0.0088	0.9834	0.0830	0.9010	0.0089	0.0833	0.9000
scene 6	0.0115	0.9376	0.0331	0.9818	0.0120	0.0357	0.9818
scene 7	0.0091	0.9827	0.0272	0.9315	0.0000	0.0000	0.9090
scene 8	0.0066	0.9350	0.0621	0.9700	0.0068	0.0625	0.9700
scene 9	0.0231	0.9100	0.1421	0.9459	0.0047	0.0294	0.9325
scene 10	0.0112	0.9036	0.0208	0.9047	0.0000	0.0000	0.9000

Table 1. Data results for some scenes. N_{br} is the number of scene SIFT features, FP: number of false positives; FPAF: number of false positives after the filter.

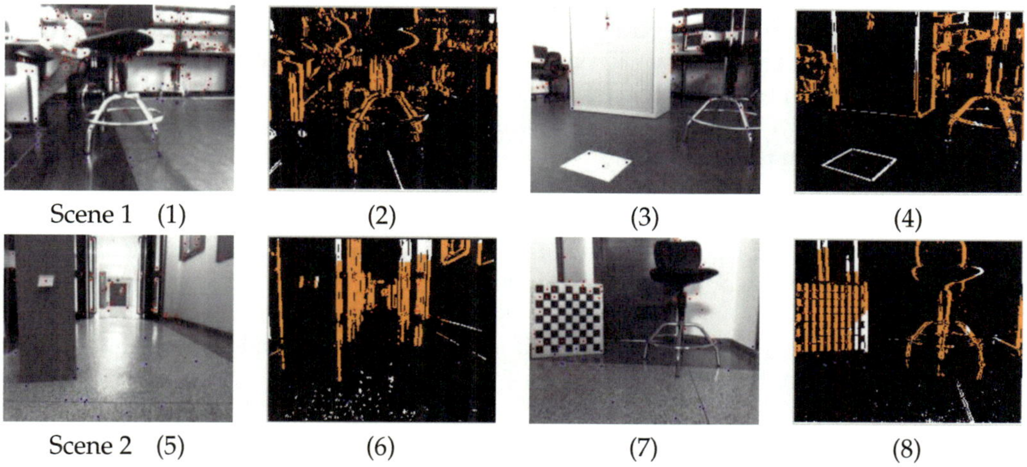

Fig. 11. (1), (3), (5), (7): Undistorted second frame of different pairs of consecutive images of Scenes 1, and 2. (2), (4), (6), (8): Obstacle contours.

Figure 11 shows four examples of the obstacle contour discrimination algorithm applied over images of a sequence recorded by the mobile robot during the autonomous navigation phase in two different scenarios. Pictures (1), (3), (5) and (7) are the second frame of four different pairs of consecutive images. Pictures (2), (4), (6) and (8) show the corresponding edge map with the obstacle profiles highlighted in orange. Note how the paper in picture (3) has not been detected as an obstacle since all features lying on it were classified as ground points, as well as, although picture (5) shows a very high inter-reflection on the ground and a very granulated texture on the floor tiles, only real obstacle boundaries have survived.

Figures 12, 13, 14 and 15 show some examples of the complete navigation algorithm tested on the moving robot. Missions consisted of navigating through several environments with some special characteristics, avoiding the obstacles, including columns and walls. The navigation algorithm was run with a variable β and the filtering process, and with all the same settings reported at the beginning of this section. Pictures (1), (2), (3) and (4) in all four figures show the second frame of some pairs of consecutive images recorded and processed during the navigation through scenarios 1, 2, 3. Every image was taken before the robot had to turn to avoid the frontal obstacles; obstacle points are shown in red and ground points in blue. Figure 12 (scenario 1) shows a room full of obstacles with regular and irregular shape. This scene presents shadows and inter-reflections. Figure 13 (scenario 2) corresponds to a corridor with a very high textured floor, columns, walls, inter-reflections and some specularities. Figures 14 and 15 (scenario 3) present bad illumination conditions, important inter-reflections and specularities on the floor, and some image regions (white walls, shelves and lockers) have homogeneous intensities and/or textures, resulting in few distinctive features and poorly edged obstacles which can complicate its detection. Pictures (5), (6), (7) and (8) in all four figures show the vertical contours (in orange) comprising obstacle points. As shown, obstacle contours were differentiated from the rest of the edges. Range and angle of the computed world points with respect to the camera coordinates were estimated using equations (16). Those obstacle-to-ground contact points closer than 1′5m were highlighted in pink.

Histograms (9), (10), (11) and (12) in figures 12, 13, 14 and 15 account for the number of obstacle-to-ground contact points detected in each polar direction. Therefore, they turn out

to be local occupancy maps in a bird's-eye view of a semicircular floor portion with a radius of 1'5m. These maps show the world polar coordinates, with respect to the camera position (which is in the center of the semicircle), of those obstacle points in contact with the floor. The grid gives a qualitative idea of which part of the robot vicinity is occupied by obstacles and the proximity of them to the robot.
The algorithm analyzes next the polar histograms and defines the direction of the center of the widest obstacle-free polar zone as the next steering direction (shown in green). The experiments performed suggest a certain level of robustness against textured floors, bad illumination conditions, shadows or inter-reflections, and deals with scenes comprising significantly different planes. In all scenes, features were well classified with success rates greater than 90% , obstacle profiles were correctly detected and the robot navigated through the free space avoiding all obstacles.
Figure 16 shows in plots (1), (2), (3) and (4) the trajectories followed by the robot during the navigation through the environments of experiments 1, 2, 3 and 4 displayed in figures 12, 13, 14 and 15. The blue circle denotes the starting point and the red circle denotes the end point.

7. Conclusions

Reactive visual-based navigation solutions that build or use local occupancy maps representing the area that surrounds the robot and visual sonar-based solutions are sensitive to floor and obstacle textures, homogeneity in the color intensity distribution, edges or lighting conditions. The construction of local maps is a suitable way to clearly identify the presence and position of obstacles and thus to determine the direction to follow. But it is not essential to determine or to identify exact obstacle shapes, dimensions, colors or textures. In this chapter, a new navigation strategy including obstacle detection and avoidance has been presented. The algorithm shows a certain robustness to the presence of shadows, inter-reflections, specularities or textured floors, overcomes scenes with multiple planes and uses only a certain number of image points. The complete strategy starts with a novel image feature classifier that distinguishes with a success rate greater that 90% between obstacle features from features lying on the ground. The detection of points that belong to obstacles permits: a) discriminating the obstacle boundaries from the rest of edges, and b) the detection of obstacle-to-ground contact points.
By computing the world coordinates of those obstacle-to-ground contact points detected in the image, the system builds a radial qualitative model of the robot vicinity. Range and angle information are quantitatively and accurately computed to create a qualitative occupancy map. Navigation decisions are taken next on the basis of qualitative criteria. What is reflected in these maps is not the total area that the obstacle occupies or its exact shape or identification, but it is an evidence of the presence of *something* that has to be avoided in a determined direction and at a defined distance.
The experimental setup consisted of different scenarios with different characteristics, different obstacles, different illumination conditions and different floor textures. In all cases the mobile robot was able to navigate through the free space avoiding all obstacles, walls and columns.

8. Future Work

The proposed strategy can be applied as an obstacle detection and avoidance module in more complex robot systems, like programmed missions for exploration of unknown environments, map-building tasks, or even, for example, as a guiding robot. The algorithm depicted does not

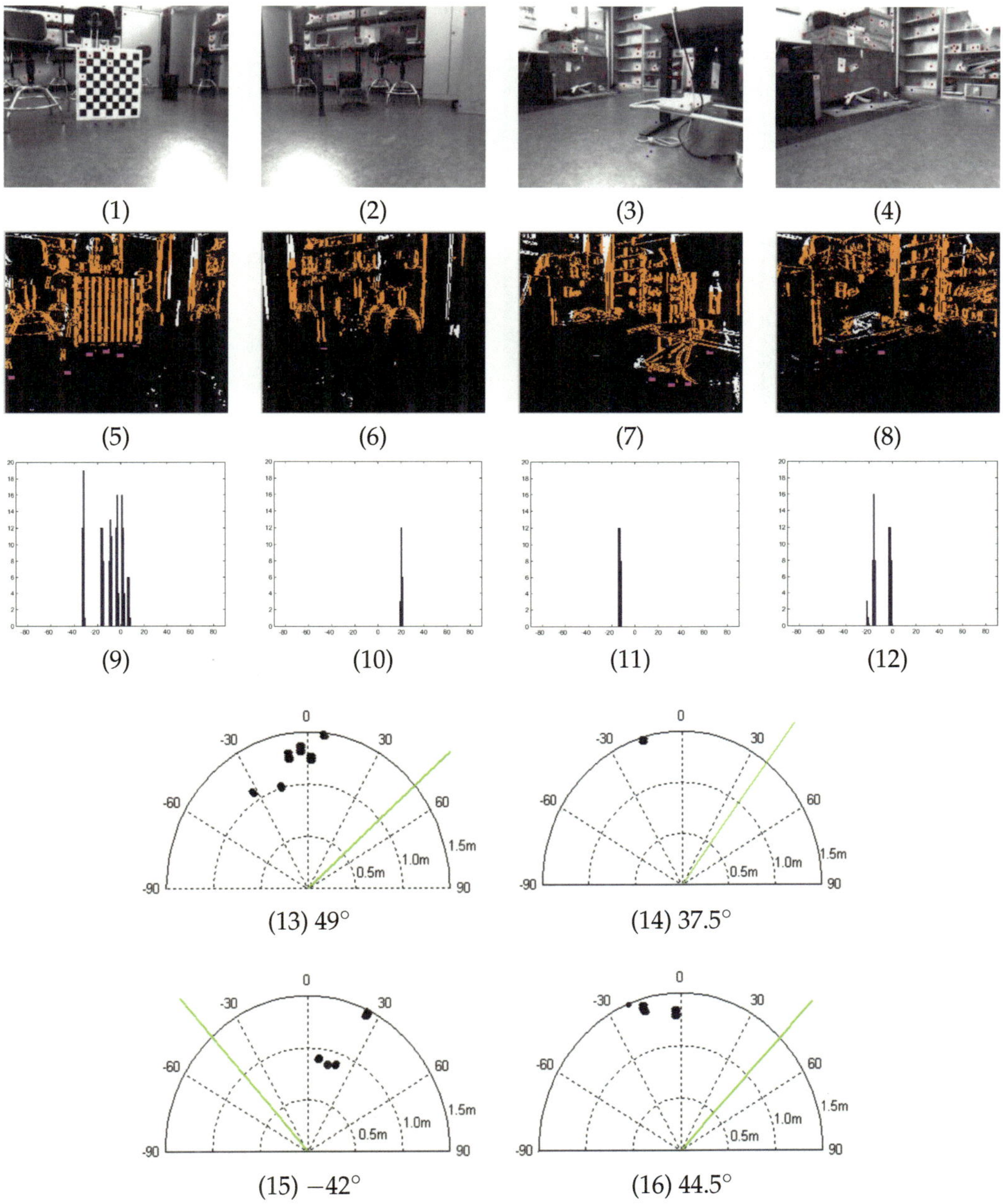

Fig. 12. Scenario 1. Experiment 1: (1), (2), (3) and (4), undistorted second frames; (5), (6), (7) and (8), corresponding edge maps with obstacle borders highlighted in orange. (9), (10), (11), (12), histograms of obstacle-to-ground contact points for each polar direction between -90° and 90°. (13), (14), (15) and (16), local occupancy map with the resulting steering vector, for images (1), (2), (3) and (4) respectively.

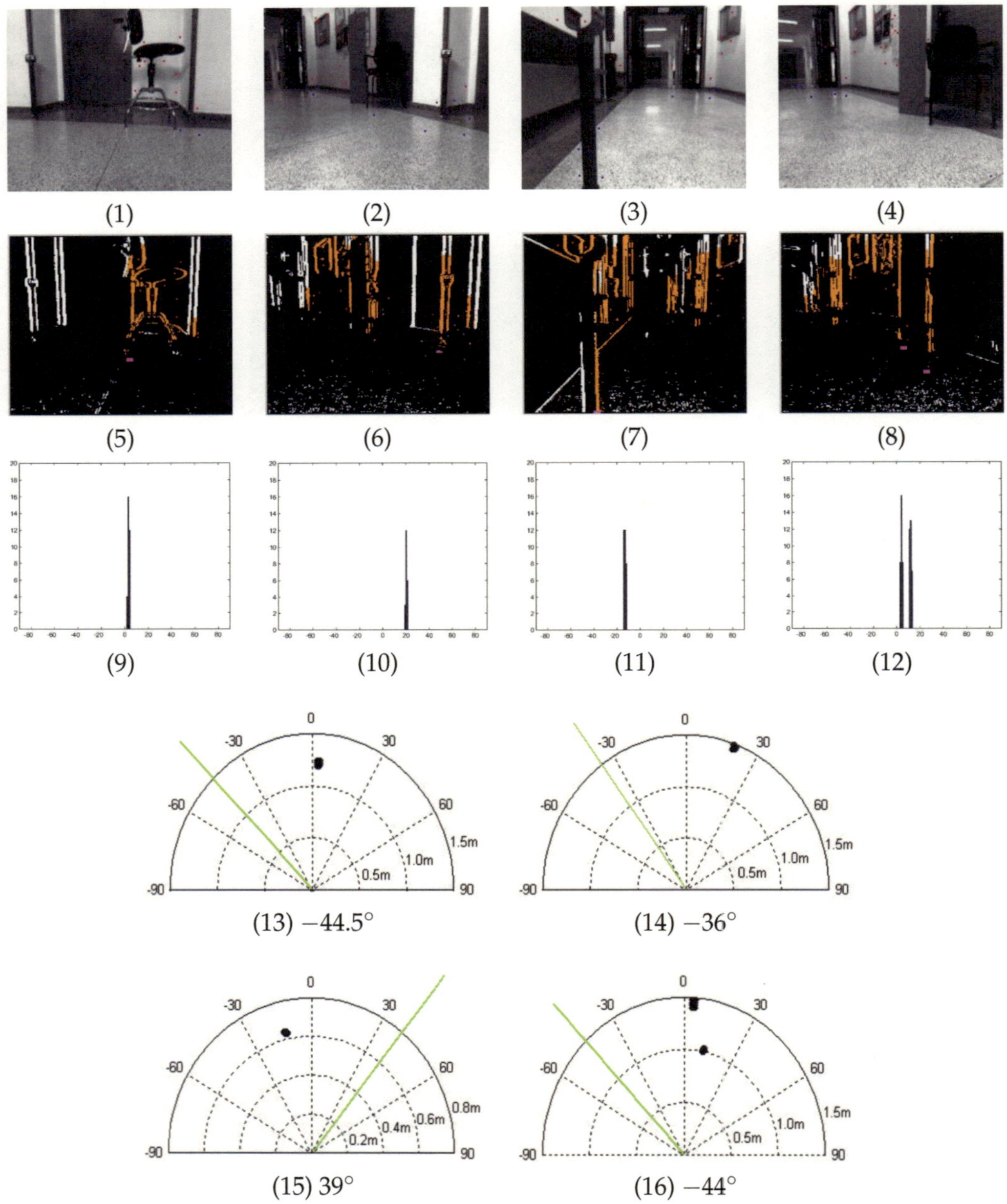

Fig. 13. Scenario 2. Experiment 2: floor with a very granulated texture. (1), (2), (3), (4), undistorted second frames; (5), (6), (7) and (8), corresponding edge maps with obstacle borders highlighted in orange; (9), (10), (11), (12), histograms of obstacle-to-ground contact points for each polar direction between −90° and 90°; (13), (14), (15) and (16), local occupancy map with the resulting steering vector, for images (1), (2), (3) and (4), respectively.

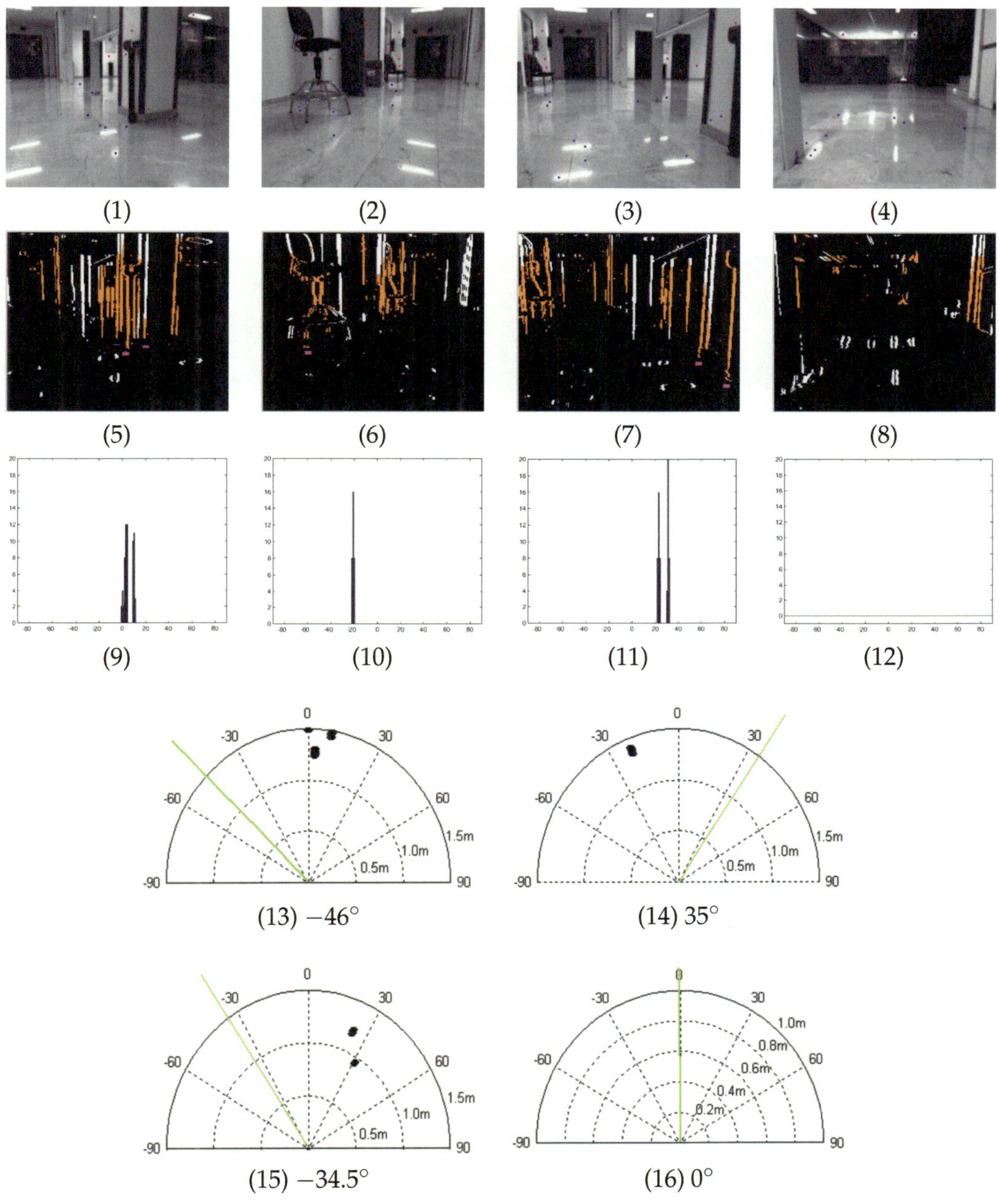

Fig. 14. Scenario 3. Experiment 3: some inter-reflections and bad illumination conditions. (1), (2), (3) and (4), undistorted second frames; (5), (6), (7) and (8), corresponding edge maps with obstacle borders highlighted in orange; (9), (10), (11) and (12) histograms of obstacle-to-ground contact points for each polar direction between −90° and 90°; (13), (14), (15) and (16), local occupancy map with the resulting steering vector, for images (1), (2), (3) and (4) respectively.

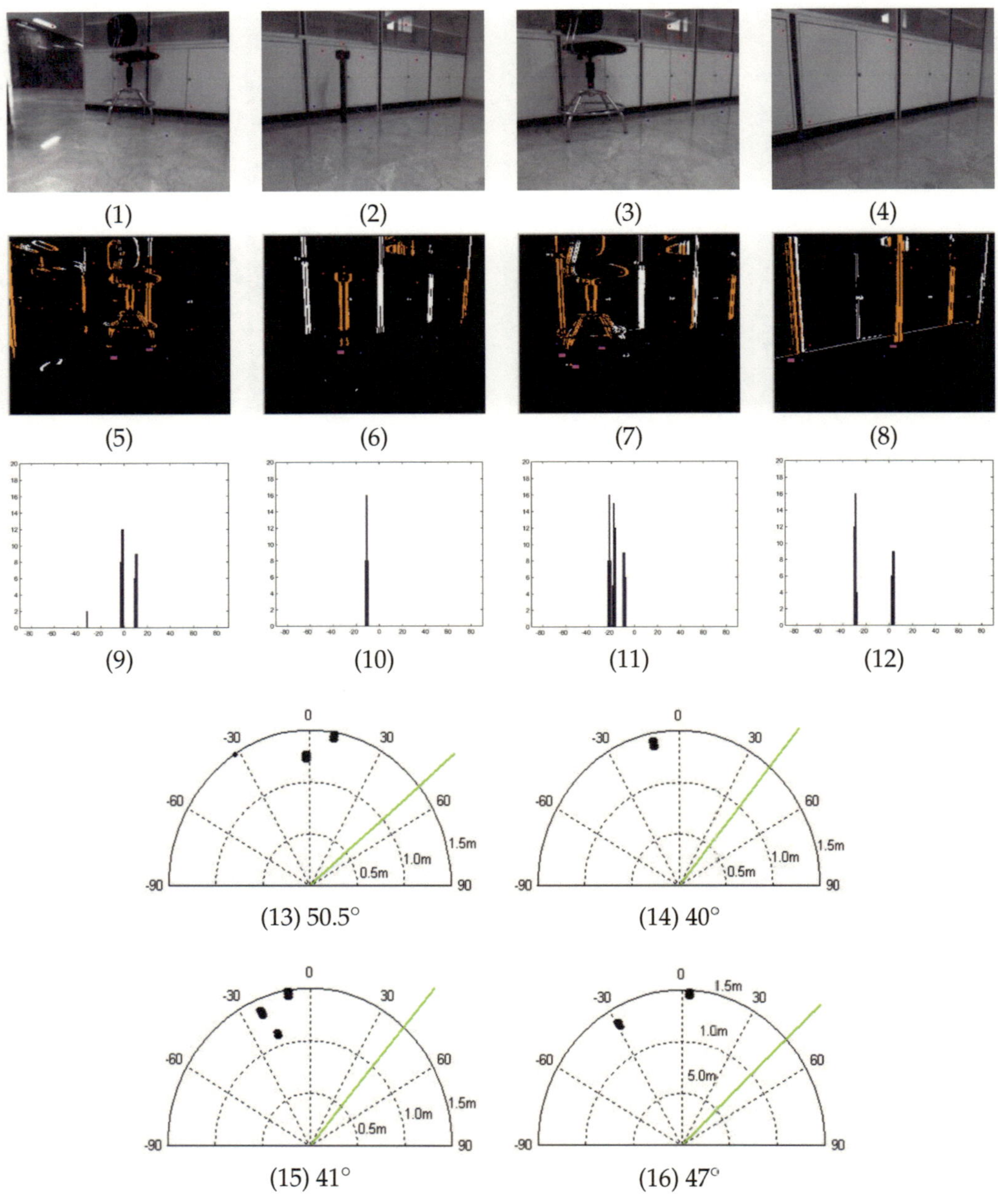

Fig. 15. Scenario 3. Experiment 4: few distinctive points, few borders, some inter-reflections and bad illumination conditions.(1), (2), (3), (4), undistorted second frames; (5), (6), (7) and (8), corresponding edge maps with obstacle borders highlighted in orange; (9), (10), (11), (12), histograms of obstacle-to-ground contact points for each polar direction between $-90°$ and $90°$. (13), (14), (15) and (16), local occupancy map with the resulting steering vector, for images (1), (2), (3) and (4) respectively.

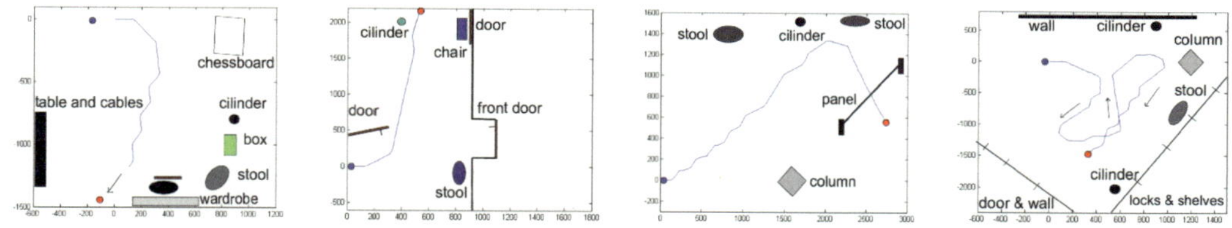

(1) (2) (3) (4)

Fig. 16. (1), (2), (3) and (4), robot trajectories for tests of figures 12, 13, 14 and 15, respectively.

restrict the method used for feature detection and tracking. Depending on this method, the number of detected features can change, features can be detected in different image points, their classification can change and the algorithm time of execution can also be different. To explore different choices for detecting and tracking features becomes necessary to optimize our algorithm in terms of: a) number of necessary features, b) their location in the image, and c) time of execution

9. References

Badal, S., Ravela, S., Draper, B. & Hanson, A. (1994). A practical obstacle detection and avoidance system, *Proceedings of 2nd IEEE Workshop on Applications of Computer Vision*, Sarasota FL USA, pp. 97–104.

Batavia, P., Pomerleau, D. & Thorpe, C. E. (1997). Overtaking vehicle detection using implicit optical flow, *IEEE Conference on Intelligent Transportation System*, Boston, MA, USA, pp. 729–734.

Bertozzi, M. & Broggi, A. (1998). Gold: a parallel real-time stereo vision system for generic obstacle and lane detection, *IEEE Transactions on Image Processing* **7**(1): 62–81.

Bonin, F., Ortiz, A. & Oliver, G. (2008). Visual navigation for mobile robots: a survey, *Journal of Intelligent and Robotic Systems* **Vol. 53**(No. 3): 263–296.

Borenstein, J. & Koren, I. (1991). The vector field histogram - fast obstacle avoidance for mobile robots, *Journal of Robotics and Automation* **7**(3): 278–288.

Bowyer, K., Kranenburg, C. & Dougherty, S. (2001). Edge detector evaluation using empirical roc curves, *Computer Vision and Image Understanding* **84**(1): 77–103.

Canny, J. (1986). A computational approach to edge detection, *IEEE Transactions on Pattern Analysis and Machine Intelligence* **8**(6): 679 – 698.

Choi, Y. & Oh, S. (2005). Visual sonar based localization using particle attraction and scattering, *Proceedings of IEEE International Conference on Mechatronics and Automation*, Niagara Falls, Canada, pp. 449–454.

Duda, R. & Hart, P. (1973). *Pattern Classification and Scene Analysis*, John Wiley and Sons Publisher, USA.

Fasola, J., Rybski, P. & Veloso, M. (2005). Fast goal navigation with obstacle avoidance using a dynamic local visual model, *Proceedings of the SBAI'05 VII Brazilian Symposium of Artificial Intelligence*, Ao Luiz, Brasil.

Goldberg, S., Maimone, M. & Matthies, L. (2002). Stereo vision and rover navigation software for planetary exploration, *Proceedings of IEEE Aerospace Conference*, Big Sky, Montana, USA, pp. 2025–2036.

Hanley, J. A. & McNeil, B. (1982). The meaning and use of the area under a receiver operating charateristic (ROC) curve, *Radiology* **143**(1): 381–395.

Harris, C. & Stephens, M. (1988). Combined corner and edge detector, *Proceedings of the Fourth Alvey Vision Conference*, Manchester, UK, pp. 147–151.

Hartley, R. & Zisserman, A. (2003). *Multiple View Geometry in Computer Vision*, Cambridge University Press, ISBN: 0521623049, Cambridge, UK.

Horswill, I. (1994). Collision avoidance by segmentation, *Proceedings of IEEE International Conference on Intelligent Robots and Systems (IROS)*, Munich ,Germany, pp. 902–909.

Lenser, S. & Veloso, M. (2003). Visual sonar: Fast obstacle avoidance using monocular vision, *Proceedings of IEEE International Conference on Intelligent Robots and Systems (IROS)*, Pittsburgh, PA, USA, pp. 886–891.

Lowe, D. (2004). Distinctive image features from scale-invariant keypoints, *International Journal of Computer Vision* **Vol. 60**(No. 2): 91–110.

Ma, G., Park, S., Müller-Schneiders, S., Ioffe, A. & Kummert, A. (2007). Vision-based pedestrian detection - reliable pedestrian candidate detection by combining ipm and a 1d profile, *Proceedings of the IEEE Intelligent Transportation Systems Conference*, Seattle, WA, USA, pp. 137–142.

Mallot, H., Buelthoff, H., Little, J. & Bohrer, S. (1991). Inverse perspective mapping simplifies optical flow computation and obstacle detection, *Biomedical and Life Sciences, Computer Science and Engineering* **64**(3): 177–185.

Martin, M. C. (2006). Evolving visual sonar: Depth from monocular images, *Pattern Recognition Letters* **27**(11): 1174–1180.

Mikolajczyk, K. & Schmid, C. (2005). A performance evaluation of local descriptors, *IEEE TPAMI* **27**(10): 1615–1630.

Rabie, T., Auda, G., El-Rabbany, A., Shalaby, A. & Abdulhai, B. (2001). Active-vision-based traffic surveillance and control, *Proceedings of the Vision Interface Annual Conference*, Ottawa, Canada, pp. 87–93.

Rodrigo, R., Zouqi, M., Chen, Z. & Samarabandu, J. (2009). Robust and efficient feature tracking for indoor navigation, *IEEE Transactions on Systems, Man and Cybernetics* **Vol. 39**(No. 3): 658–671.

Saeedi, P., Lawrence, P. & Lowe, D. (2006). Vision-based 3-d trajectory tracking for unknown environments, *IEEE Transactions on Robotics* **22**(1): 119–136.

Shi, J. & Tomasi, C. (1994). Good features to track, *Proceedings of the IEEE IntŠl Conference on Computer Vision and Pattern Recognition (CVPR)*, pp. 593–600.

Shu, Y. & Tan, Z. (2004). Vision-based lane detection in autonomous vehicle, *Proceedings of the Congress on Intelligent Control and Automation*, Xi'an Jiaotong, China, pp. 5258–5260.

Simond, N. & Parent, M. (2007). Obstacle detection from ipm and super-homography, *Proceedings of IEEE International Conference on Intelligent Robots and Systems (IROS)*, California, Sant Diego, USA, pp. 4283–4288.

Stephen, S., Lowe, D. & Little, J. (2005). Vision-based global localization and mapping for mobile robots, *IEEE Transactions on Robotics* **Vol. 21**(No. 3): 364–375.

Zhou, J. & Li, B. (2006). Homography-based ground detection for a mobile robot platform using a single camera, *Proceedings of the IEEE Int'l Conference on Robotics and Automation (ICRA)*, Arizona, Tempe, USA, pp. 4100–4101.

6

Vision-based Navigation Using an Associative Memory

Mateus Mendes
ESTGOH, Polytechnic Institute of Coimbra
Institute of Systems and Robotics, University of Coimbra
Portugal

1. Introduction

One of the most challenging long-term goals of Robotics is to build robots with human-like intelligence and capabilities. Although the human brain and body are by no means perfect, they are the primary model for roboticists and robot users. Therefore, it is only natural that robots of the future share many key characteristics with humans. Among these characteristics, reliance on visual information and the use of an associative memory are two of the most important.

The information is stored in our brain in sequences of snapshots that we can later retrieve full or in part, starting at any random point. A single cue suffices to remind us of a past experience, such as our last holidays. Starting from this cue we can relive the most remarkable moments of the holidays, skipping from one snapshot to another. Our work is inspired by these ideas. Our robot is a small platform that is guided solely by visual information, which is stored in a Sparse Distributed Memory (SDM).

The SDM is a kind of associative memory proposed in the 1980s by Kanerva (1988). The underlying idea is the mapping of a huge binary memory onto a smaller set of physical locations, so-called *hard locations*. Every datum is stored distributed by a set of hard locations, and retrieved by *averaging* those locations. Kanerva proves that such a memory, for high dimensional binary vectors, exhibits properties similar to the human memory, such as ability to work with sequences, tolerance to incomplete and noisy data, and learning and forgetting in a *natural* way.

We used a SDM to navigate a robot, in order to test some of the theories in practice and assess the performance of the system. Navigation is based on images, and has two modes: one learning mode, in which the robot is manually guided and captures images to store for future reference; and an autonomous mode, in which it uses its previous knowledge to navigate autonomously, following any sequence previously learnt, either to the end or until it gets lost or interrupted.

We soon came to the conclusion that the way information is encoded into the memory influences the performance of the system. The SDM is prepared to work with random data, but robot sensorial information is hardly well distributed random data. Thus, we implemented four variations of the model, that deal with four different encoding methods. The performance of those variations was then assessed and compared.

Section 2 briefly describes some theories of what intelligence is. Section 3 describes the SDM. Section 4 presents an overview of various robot navigation techniques. In sections 5 and 6 the hardware and software implementation are described. In section 7 we describe the encoding problem and how it can be solved. Finally, in section 8 we describe some tests we performed and the results obtained, before drawing some conclusions in section 9.

2. Human and machine Intelligence

The biggest problem one faces when researching towards building *intelligent machines* is that of understanding what is intelligence. There are essentially three problems researchers have to face: 1) What is intelligence; 2) How can it be tested or measured; and 3) How can it be artificially simulated. We're not deeply concerned about these points in this study, but the very definition of intelligence deserves some attention, for it is the basis of this work—after all, the goal is to build a system able to perform intelligent vision-based navigation.

2.1 Definitions of intelligence

Until very recently, the most solid ground on this subject was a series of sparse and informal writings from psychologists and researchers from related areas—and though there seems to be a fairly large common ground, the boundaries of the concept are still very cloudy and roughly defined.

Moreover, it is in general accepted that there are several different "intelligences", responsible for several different abilities, such as linguistic, musical, logical-mathematical, spacial and other abilities. However, in many cases individuals' performance levels in all these different fields are strongly correlated. Spearman (1927) calls this positive correlation the *g*-factor. The *g*-factor shall, therefore, be a general measure of intelligence. The other intelligences are mostly specialisations of the general one, in function of the experience of the individual.

2.1.1 Gottfredson definition

Gottfredson (1997)[1] published an interesting and fairly complete review of the mainstream opinion in the field . Gottfredson wrote a summary of her personal definition of intelligence, and submitted it to half a dozen "leaders in the field" for review. The document was improved and then submitted to 131 experts in the field, who were then invited to endorse it and/or comment on it. 100 experts responded: 52 endorsed the document; 48 didn't endorse it for various reasons. Of those who didn't, only 7 stated that it did not represent the mainstream opinion about intelligence. Therefore, it is reasonable to assume that a representative number of experts agree with this very definition of intelligence:

> Intelligence is a very general mental capability that, among other things, involves the ability to reason, plan, solve problems, think abstractly, comprehend complex ideas, learn quickly and learn from experience. It is not merely book learning, a narrow academic skill, or test-taking smarts. Rather, it reflects a broader and deeper capability for comprehending our surroundings—"catching on,", "making sense" of things, or "figuring out" what to do.

It is our understanding that Gottfredson emphasises some key aspects: **problem solving**, **learning** and **understanding**. It should be noted that there's little consideration with the performance of the intelligent agent. At most, that is part of the "problem solving" assessment.

[1] The reference Gottfredson (1997) states the article was first published in the *Wall Street Journal*, December 13, 1994.

On the contrary, this definition strongly depends on the ability to "understand". However, there's no definition of what is "understanding", meaning that this definition of intelligence is of little use for engineers in the task of building intelligent machines.

2.1.2 Legg's formal definition

Legg & Hutter (2007) also present a thorough compilation of interesting definitions, both from psychologists and AI researchers. And they end up with a shorter and very pragmatic definition:

> Intelligence measures an agent's ability to achieve goals in a wide range of environments.

This very definition has the merit of being much shorter and clearer from the point of view of an engineer, as it is very pragmatic. Legg starts from this informal definition towards a more formal one, and proposes what is probably one of the first formal definitions of intelligence. According to Legg, an intelligent agent is the one who is able to perform *actions* that change the surrounding *environment* in which he exists, assess the *rewards* he receives and thus *learn* how to behave and profit from his actions. It must incorporate, therefore, some kind of reinforcement learning.

In a formal sense, the following variables and concepts can be defined:

o observation of the environment
a agent's action
r reward received from the environment
π an agent
μ an environment
E the space of all environments

The agent π is defined as a probability measure or its current action, given its complete history: $\pi(a_k|o_1r_1...o_{k-1}r_{k-1}), \forall \ \ k \in \mathbf{N}$.

The environment μ is defined as a probability function of its history: $\mu(o_kr_k|o_1r_1a_1....o_{k-1})$

Legg also imposes the condition that the total reward is bounded to 1, to make the sum of all the rewards received in all the environments finite:

$$V_\mu^\pi := E \sum_{i=1}^{\infty} r_i \leq 1 \tag{1}$$

One important point to consider when evaluating the performance of the agent is also the complexity of the environment μ. On this point, Legg considers the Kolmogorov complexity, or the length of the shortest program that computes μ:

$$K(\mu) = \min_p\{l(p) : \mathcal{U}(p) = \mu\} \tag{2}$$

where $\mathcal{U}$ is the universal Turing Machine.

Additionally, each environment, in this case, is described by a string of binary values. As each binary value has two possible states, it must reduce the probability of the environment by $1/2$. Therefore, according to Legg, the probability of each environment must be well described by the *algorithmic probability distribution* over the space of environments: $2^{-K(\mu)}$.

From these assumptions and definitions, Legg proposes the following measure for the universal intelligence of an agent μ:

$$Y(\pi) = \sum_{\mu \in E} 2^{-K(\mu)} V_{\mu}^{\pi} \quad (3)$$

The intelligence Y of an agent π is, therefore, a measure of the sum of the rewards it is able to receive in all the environments—a formal definition that is according to the informal ones described before. Unfortunately, the interest of this definition up to this point is most from a theoretical point of view, as this equation is not computable. It is, nonetheless, an interesting approach to formalise intelligence. And it is still interesting from a practical point of view, as a general demonstration that intelligent agents need to be versatile to perform well in a wide range of environments, as well as profit from past experience.

2.1.3 Discussion

So far, we have presented two mainstream definitions of Intelligence:

1. Gottfredson's definition of intelligence as an ability to learn, understand and solve problems;
2. Legg's formal definition of intelligence as a measure of success in an environment.

These definitions are not incompatible, but if the first is to be accepted as the standard, we need an additional definition of what is understanding. Searle (1980) proposed an interesting thought experiment which shows that performance is different from understanding. Imagine Searle in a room where he is asked some questions in Chinese. Searle knows nothing of Chinese, but he has a book with all the possible questions and the correct answers, all in Chinese. For every question, Searle searches the book and sends the correct answer. Therefore, Searle gives the correct answer 100 % of the times, without even knowing a single word of the language he's manipulating.

Anyway, the definitions seem to agree that successfully solving problems in a variety of environments is key to intelligence. Dobrev (2005) goes even further, proposing that an agent that correctly solves 70 % of the problems (i.e., takes the correct decision 7 out of every 10 times), should be considered an intelligent agent.

2.2 The brain as a memory system

From above, intelligence is solving problems and learning. But how does the brain do it? That is currently an active and open area of research. However, current evidence seems to point that the brain works more as a sophisticated memory than a high speed processing unit.

2.2.1 On the brain

The study of the brain functions *one by one* is a very complex task. There are too many brain functions, too many brain regions and too many connections between them. Additionally, although there're noticeable physical differences between brain regions, those differences are only but small. Based on these observations, V. Mountcastle (1978) proposed that *all* the brain might be performing basically the same algorithm, the result being different only depending on the inputs. Even the physical differences could be a result of the brain wiring connections. Although this may seem an unrealistic proposal at first sight, many scientists currently endorse Mountcastle's theory, as it can't be proven wrong and explains phenomena which would be harder to explain assuming the brain is an enormous conglomerate of specialised neurons. One important observation is probably the fact that the brain is not static—it adapts to its environment and changes when necessary. People who are born deaf process visual information in areas where other people usually perform auditory functions. Some people who have special brain areas damaged can have other parts of the brain processing information which is usually processed in the damaged area in healthy people. Even more convincing, neuroscientists have surgically rewired the brains of newborn ferrets, so that their eyes could send signals to the areas of cortex that should process auditory information. In result, the ferrets developed visual pathways in the auditory portions of their brains (Hawkins & Blakeslee (2004)).

The brain is able to process large quantities of information up to a high level of abstraction. How those huge amounts of information are processed is still a *mystery*. The *misery* is yet more intriguing as we find out that the brain performs incredibly *complicated* tasks at an incredibly fast speed. It is known neurons take about 5 ms to fire and reset. This means that our brain operates at about 200 Hz—a frequency fairly below any average modern computer. One possible explanation for this awesome behaviour is that the brain performs many tasks in parallel. Many neurons working at the same time would contribute to the overall final result. This explanation, though, is not satisfactory for all the problems the brain seems able to solve in fractions of seconds. Harnish (2002) proposes the 100 steps thought experiment to prove this. The brain takes about 1/10th of a second to perform tasks such as language understanding or visual recognition. Considering that neurons take about 1/1000 of a second to send a signal, this means that, on average, those tasks cannot take more than 100 serial steps. On the other hand, a computer would need to perform billions of steps to attempt to solve the same problem. Therefore, it is theorised, the brain must not work as a linear computer. It must be operating like a vast amount of multi-dimensional computers working in parallel.

2.2.2 Intelligence as memory

The theory of the brain working as a massive parallel super-computer, though attractive, is not likely to explain all the phenomena. This arises from the observation that many actions the human brain seems to perform in just fractions of a second cannot be done in parallel, for some steps of the overall process depend on the result of previous steps. An example from Hawkins & Blakeslee (2004) is the apparently simple task of catching a ball moving at some speed. The brain needs to process visual information to identify the ball, its speed and direction, and compute the motor information needed to move all the muscles which have to be stimulated in order to catch the ball. And more intriguing, the brain has to be repeating all those steps several times in a short time interval for better accuracy, while at the same time controlling basic impulses such as breathing and keeping a stable stance and equilibrium. To build a robot able to perform this apparently simple task is a nightmare, if not at all impossible, no matter how many processors can be used. The most difficult part of the problem is that motor information cannot be processed while sensory information is not available. No matter how many processors are used, there is always a number of steps which cannot be performed in parallel. A simple analogy, also from J. Hawkins, is that if one wants to carry one hundred stone blocks across a desert and it takes a million steps to cross the desert, one may hire one hundred workers to only cross the desert once, but it will, nonetheless, take one million steps to get the job done.

Based on the one-hundred step rule, J. Hawkins proposes that the human brain must not be a computer, but a memory system. It doesn't compute solutions, but retrieves them based on analogies with learnt experiences from past situations. That also explains why practice and experience lead us closer to perfection—our *database* of cases, problems and solutions is

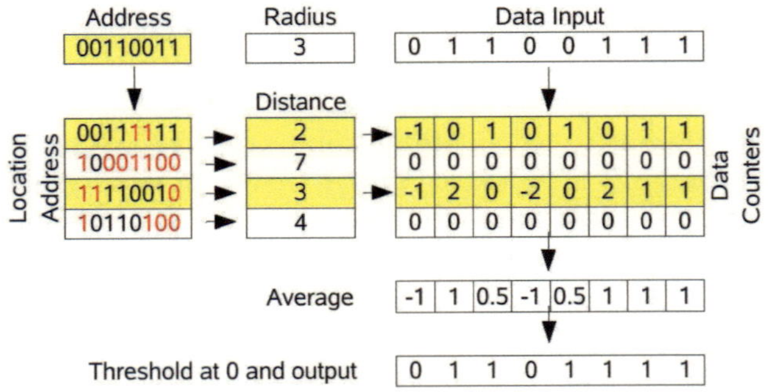

Fig. 1. One model of a SDM.

enriched, allowing us to retrieve better solutions to problems similar to the ones we've already captured.
Even before Hawkins' memory model, other researchers proposed models which somehow try to mimic human characteristics. Willshaw et al. (1969) and Hopfield (1982) propose two neural network models which are very interesting. A more promising proposal, however, was that of Pentti Kanerva. Kanerva (1988) proposes a complete model for the system, and not just a network model.

3. The Sparse Distributed Memory

Back in the 1980s, Pentti Kanerva advocated the same principle stated above: intelligence is probably the result of using a sophisticated memory and a little processing. Based on this assumption, Kanerva proposed the Sparse Distributed Memory model, a kind of associative memory based on the properties of high-dimensional binary spaces.
Kanerva's proposal is based on four basic ideas: the space 2^n, for $100 < n < 10^5$, exhibits properties which are similar to our intuitive notions of relationships between the concepts; neurons with n inputs can be used as address decoders of a random-access memory; unifying principle: data stored in the memory can be used as addresses to the same memory; and time can be traced in the memory as a function of where the data are stored. Kanerva presents thorough demonstrations of how those properties are guaranteed by the SDM. Therefore, we will only focus on the implementation details. Figure 1 shows a model of a SDM. The main modules are an array of addresses, an array of bit counters, a third module that computes the average of the bits of the active addresses, and a thresholder.
"Address" is the reference address where the datum is to be stored or read from. In conventional memories, this reference would activate a single location. In a SDM, it will activate all the addresses in a given access radius, which is predefined. Kanerva proposes that the Hamming distance, that is the number of bits in which two binary vectors are different, is used as the measure of distance between the addresses. In consequence of this, all the locations that differ less than a predefined number of bits from the reference address (within the radius distance, as shown in Figure 1), are selected for the read or write operation.
Writing is done by incrementing or decrementing the bit counters at the selected addresses. Data are stored in arrays of counters, one counter for every bit of every location. To store 0 at a given position, the corresponding counter is decremented. To store 1, it is incremented. The counters may, therefore, store either a positive or a negative value.

Reading is done by summing the values of all the counters columnwise and thresholding at a predefined value. If the value of the sum is below the threshold, the bit is zero, otherwise it is one. For a memory where the counters are incremented or decremented one by one, 0 is a good threshold value.

Initially, all the bit counters must be set to zero, for the memory stores no data. The bits of the address locations should be set randomly, so that the addresses would be uniformely distributed in the addressing space.

One drawback of SDMs becomes now clear: while in traditional memories we only need one bit per bit, in a SDM every bit requires a counter. Nonetheless, every counter stores more than one bit at a time, making the solution not so expensive as it might seem. Kanerva calculates that such a memory should be able to store about 0.1 bits per bit, although other authors state to have achieved higher ratios Keeler (1988).

There's no guarantee that the data retrieved is exactly the same that was written. It should be, providing that the hard locations are correctly distributed over the binary space and the memory has not reached saturation.

4. Robot navigation and mapping

To successfully navigate a robot, it must have some basic knowledge of the environment, or accurate exploring capacities. This means that the problems of navigation and mapping are closely related. Several approaches have been tried to overcome these problems, but they are still subject to heavy research. It is accepted (see e.g. Kuipers & Levitt (1988)) that robust mapping and navigation means that performance must be excellent when resources are plentiful and degradation graceful when resources are limited.

View based methods, most of the times, rely on the use of sequences of images, which confer the robot the ability to follow learnt paths. Topological maps may or may not be built. This is according to the human behaviour, for it is known that humans rely on sequences of images to navigate, and use higher level maps only for long distances or unknown areas.

However, despite the importance of vision for humans, view based methods are not among the most popular between researchers. One reason for this is that vision usually requires huge processing power. Other approaches include the use of Voronoi Diagrams and Potential Fields methods. Navigating through the use of View Sequences is not as common as other major approaches, but it's becoming increasingly popular as good quality cameras and fast processors become cheaper.

4.1 Some popular mapping and navigation methods

One popular approach is indeed very simplistic: the occupancy grid (OG). The grid is simply a matrix, where each element means the presence or absence of an obstacle. The robot must be able to position itself in the grid by scanning its surroundings and/or knowing its past history. Then it can move from one grid cell to another empty cell, updating the map accordingly. This method is often combined with a Potential Field algorithm. The robot's goal is to reach the centre of the potential field, to where it is being attracted. Every pixel in the matrix contains a number, representing the power of the potential field. The higher the potential, the closer the robot is to its goal. The robot must then try to find the path by following the positive gradient of the potential values. The disadvantages of the OG are obvious: huge memory requirements, and difficulty in scaling to large environments.

Another navigation method is the Voronoi Diagram (VD). The VD is a geometric structure which represents distance information of a set of points or objects. Each point in the VD is equidistant to two or more points. While moving, the robot must sense the objects and walls and incrementally create the diagram. Its goal is to always be in the centre. It must then move between objects and walls, thus avoiding collisions.

Topological maps overcome many of the drawbacks of the grid-based methods. They consist of more sophisticated representations, which neglect details of the environment. The robot builds a graph of the routes available for the robot to travel. Then, algorithms such as Dijskstra (1959) or A* can be used to compute the possible paths and possibly choose the best alternative. Using these models, there is no need to record information of all the path that the robot follows. Instead, the robot only stores information about the points at which decisions are made.

Kuipers & Levitt (1988) proposes a semantic hierarchy of the descriptions of the interaction with the environment, consisting of four hierarchical levels:

1. *Sensorimotor*—This is the lower level of the hierarchy, represented by the sensor input and actuator output data.
2. *Procedural*—These are procedures the robot learns to accomplish particular instances of place finding or route following tasks. These procedures are acquired in terms of sensorimotor primitives, such as control strategies to cross a boundary defined by two landmarks. The basic element of procedural behaviours are represented in a production-like schema, $< goal, situation, action, result >$. The interpretation of the production is "When attempting to reach goal $goal$, if the current view is $situation$, perform action $action$ and expect the result to be $result$. At this level, the robot is able to perform basic navigation tasks and path planning.
3. *Topological*—While at the procedural level the environment is described in terms of the egocentric sensorimotor experience of the robot, at the topological level the world is described in terms of relations between other entities. A description of the environment is possible in terms of fixed entities, such as places, paths and landmarks, linked by topological relations, such as connectivity, containment and order. At this level, it is possible to perform navigation tasks and route planning more efficiently than at the procedural level. However, there is no information on the cost of alternative paths. In topological terms, it is only possible to describe actions such as "turn" or "travel", but there is no associated description of the magnitude required for the action.
4. *Metric*—This level adds to the topological level metric information, such as distance and angle information. At this level the robot has all the information it needs to plan routes and choose the quickest or shortest alternative path. It is possible to compute accurately the length of a path, as well as the number and magnitude of the turns that the robot has to perform.

Kuipers proposes three models which are based on the idea of a four levels semantic hierarchy: the Tour model, the Qualnav simulator and the NX Robot. All these models have been tested in software simulation Kuipers & Levitt (1988), to validate the four levels hierarchy described. The Tour model is a computational model of a robot more suitable for environments that have approximate network-like structures, such as urban environments or the interior of large buildings with corridors and walls. The Tour model robot is expected to explore the world and find places and paths that can be followed, in order to build a topological map with metric information of the environment. At the sensorimotor level, Tour has available a sequence of views and actions. At the procedural level, it has procedures built from the sensorimotor schemas. This means that Tour is expected to grab a sequence of views $V_0, ...V_n$, and for each view V_j, it must perform action A_j. At the topological level, Tour builds place-path networks, boundary relations, regions and skeletal networks. At the metric level, Tour keeps information about local geometry of places and paths. This confers it the ability to perform actions where the action can be $Travel(\delta)$ to move forward or backward, and $Turn(\alpha)$ to change direction. Kuipers simulated robots obtain the topological models without great difficulty, in the simulation environment. In a virtual environment, sensorimotor readings can be assumed to be correct. Kuipers used these readings to feed the topological level of the semantic hierarchy and build the topological representation of the environment. In the real world, however, sensorial readings are subject to a multitude of interferences that make the task of building a topological map much more difficult than in a controlled environment. Variable amounts of noise from the sensors, scenario changes and other phenomena interfere with the performance of the system and make the mapping task a very challenging one. Many authors implemented topological navigation, based on Kuipers' simulated models, although the practical problems have to be addressed to achieve a robust navigation model.

4.2 View based navigation

Many approaches consist of teaching the robot some sequence of images and then make it follow the same path by capturing an image, retrieve the closest image from its memory and execute the same motion that is associated with it.
View sequence navigation is extremely attractive, for it is very simple to implement, and a single sensor, i.e., the camera, provides a lot of information. Humans are able to navigate quite well based only on visual information. But robots are usually guided with many other sensors, such as sonars, infrared or other distance sensors. Those sensors provide additional information that has to be processed in real time, and the robots usually have to develop internal models of the world based on this sensorial information. "Teach and follow", is a much simpler and biologically inspired approach for basic navigation purpose. The disadvantage is that images have to be grabbed and stored at regular intervals during learning, and matched against a large database of images during the autonomous run. Good resolution images take a lot of storage space and processing time. To overcome this problem, some authors choose to extract some features from the images, in order to save processing needs in real time.
One possible approach for navigation based on a view sequence is that of using landmarks. Those landmarks may be artificially placed on the scene (a barcode or data matrix, for example), or selected from the actual images or the real scene in runtime. Selecting a few landmarks which are easy to identify, the navigation task is greatly facilitated. Rasmussen & Hager (1996) follow such an approach. They store panoramic images at regular intervals during learning, and select salient *markers* from them. *Markers* are characteristics considered invariant over time, such as colour, shape or texture. By sticking to these *markers*, the system saves considerable processing power, for there is no need to process the whole image to detect the best match.

4.2.1 Matsumoto's approach

Matsumoto et al. (1999; 2000) propose a vision-based approach for robot navigation, based on the concept of a "view-sequence" and a look-up table of controlling commands. Their approach requires a learning stage, during which the robot must be guided. While being guided, the robot memorises a sequence of views automatically. While autonomously running, the robot performs automatic localisation and obstacle detection, taking action in real-time.

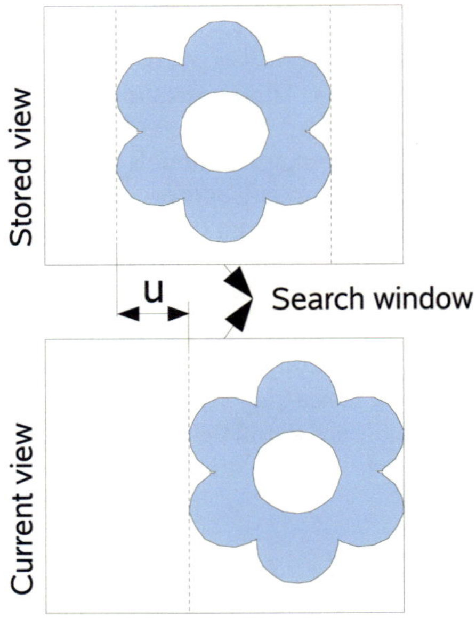

Fig. 2. Matching of two images, using a search window.

Localisation is calculated based on the similarity of two views: one stored during the learning stage and another grabbed in real-time. The robot tries to find matching areas between those two images, and calculates the distance between them in order to infer *how far* it is from the correct path. That distance is then used to extract stored motor controls from a table, thus guiding the robot through the same path it has been taught before.

To calculate the drift in each moment, Matsumoto uses a block matching process, as Figure 2 illustrates. A search window taken from the memorised image is matched against an equivalent window in the current view, calculating the horizontal displacement that results in the smallest error e. Considering two images I_1 and I_2, Matsumoto defines the matching error between them as:

$$e(u) = \sum_{x=s}^{w-s} \sum_{y=0}^{h} |I_1(x,y) - I_2(x+u,y)| \tag{4}$$

(w,h) are the width and height of the image, in pixels. u is the offset, or horizontal displacement of the search window s. $I_i(x,y)$ is the brightness intensity of pixel (x,y) of image i. And the error that is of interest for us is the minimum $e(u)$, defined as follows:

$$e = min(e(u)), -s \leq u < s \tag{5}$$

If the robot is following a previously learnt image sequence, its view in each moment must match some stored image. If there is a horizontal drift, then e will be minimum for some horizontal displacement $u \neq 0$. Equation 4 is just the sum or the errors between the pixels in the image, for some value u of the horizontal search range. Equation 5 determines the horizontal displacement u that gives the minimum error e.

Matsumoto uses 32×32 images, a search window 16×32 and a horizontal search range of 8 pixels, so that $-8 \leq u < 8$. The original images, captured by the robot, are 480×480, but

the author claims that there is no significant loss of essential information when the images are subsampled up to the 32×32 thumbnails that are being used.
In a later stage of the same work, Matsumoto et al. (2003) equipped the robot to use omniview images. Omniview images represent all the surroundings of the robot. This is achieved through the use of a spherical mirror, that is placed above the robot and reflects the scenario 360° wide onto a conventional camera. Omniviews are neither easy to recognise for humans, who have a narrow field of view, nor to process using conventional image processing algorithms. However, they allow the robots to overcome the limitation of the narrow field of view of traditional cameras. One camera can be used to sense all the directions at the same time. Forward and backward motion and collision avoidance may be planned using the same single sensor. To facilitate image processing, the omniview image can then be transformed into a cylindrical image that represents the surroundings of the robot. This cylindrical image can then be processed as if it was a common image, although it is necessary to pay attention to the fact that it represents a field of view of 360°. Its left and right borders are actually images of the back of the robot, while the middle of the image represents its front.
Matsumoto extended the navigation algorithms and sequence representations. Junctions, such as corridor intersections, were detected, based on the optical flow differences. Assuming the optical flow is just caused by the motion of the robot, closer objects generate larger optical flows in the image. This simple principle makes it possible to detect junctions and construct a topological map of the building. The images were stored with additional information of neighbouring images, so that it was possible to follow a corridor and, at the appropriate junction, skip to another. Route planning was done using the Dijskstra (1959) algorithm, so that the shortest path was followed. Matsumoto's approach, however, has the disadvantages of being too computationally intensive and suitable only for indoors navigation.

4.2.2 Ishiguro's approach

Ishiguro & Tsuji (1996) used an approach slightly different from Matsumoto. Ishiguro uses omni-directional views, but in order to speed up processing, the images are replaced by their Fourier transforms. The omni-directional views are periodic along the azimuth axis. Thus, the Fourier transform is applied to each row of an image, and the image is then replaced by the set of magnitude and phase Fourier coefficients. This technique reduces both the memory and the computational requirements.
In order model the geometry of the environment, Ishiguro defines a set of observation points. From each observation point, the robot captures a view I_i of the environment. Then it compares this view with all the views I_j that it has learnt before, computing a measure of similarity, using the formula:

$$Sim(I_i, I_j) = \sum_{y=0}^{l-1} \sum_{k=0}^{m-1} |F_{iy}(k) - F_{jy}(k)| \tag{6}$$

where $F_{iy}(k)$ and $F_{jy}(k)$ are the Fourier coefficients of the frequency k of the row y of images I_i and I_j. The similarity is interpreted as a measure of the distance—the larger the similarity measure, the farther apart the images must be. The relation holds up to a threshold value. Above this threshold, the similarity measure is meaningless, meaning that the images are probably unrelated at all.
Based on these ideas, Ishiguro proposes a navigation strategy. To start, the agent explores the unknown environment, capturing and storing images at a number of reference points. These images are then processed and organised according to the similarities computed, leading to

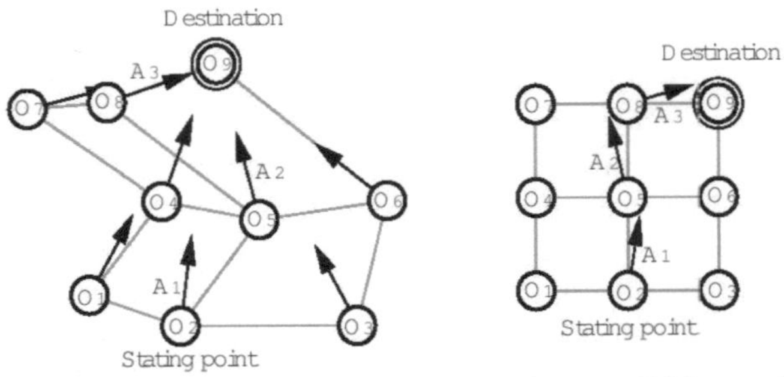

Fig. 3. Geometry of a recovered and real environment. Source: Ishiguro & Tsuji (1996).

a geometrical representation that must describe the environment accurately in terms of paths that can be followed, as illustrated in Figure 3. The robot is then able to navigate from one reference point to another, choosing the shortest path according to the perceived distance between images.

4.2.3 The T-Net

One related work is the Target Network (T-Net), implemented by Ishiguro et al. (1995). A T-Net is similar to the topological mapping model, but it relies on some key "feature points", paths and intersections between these paths, as shown in Figure 4. Ishiguro uses a robot with a panoramic vision system. The robot travels along the paths by tracking the feature points of those paths, which are their starting and ending points. The angular relations between the paths are also calculated, based on the panoramic views. As the robot moves, it picks candidates for intersections between paths and explores the environment to verify if the intersections are possible. If the intersections are possible, they are stored, as passage points between different paths. The T-Net is, therefore, constituted by the set of feature points, paths and intersections, thus being a solid basis for quick and efficient route planning and navigation.
Similarity between the images of the feature points is computed by a special algorithm, known as the Sequential Similarity Detection Algorithm (SSDA). However, to make tracking of the features points possible, it is necessary that the images input to the SSDA algorithm do not present significant changes in size. Ishiguro solves this problem using cameras with zoom. The magnification factor is decreased as the robot approaches the feature point and increased as it moves away from it.
However robust, navigation based on a T-Net is clearly a messy and expensive approach, for it requires expensive hardware (a mobile robot with at least two cameras, although Ishiguro reports to have used four) and a lot of computer power to process the images and compute the intersections between paths in real time. Besides, it is not clear how the feature points have to be defined.

4.2.4 Other view-based approaches

Jones et al. (1997) also attempted view-based navigation, in an approach very similar to Matsumoto's idea described above. The images used in his system are not panoramic, but low resolution wide angle images. Correlation between the images is computed using a method of Zero mean Normalised Cross Correlation (ZNCC). The trajectory of the robot is adjusted in order to maximise the correlation between the images grabbed by the robot and the ones

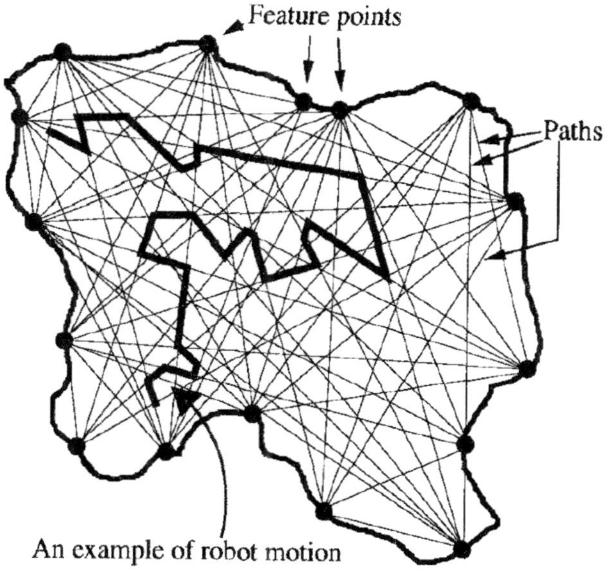

Fig. 4. Feature points and paths of a T-Net. Source: Ishiguro et al. (1995).

stored in the database. Odometric information is also used to correct the estimated position of the robot.

Winters & Santos-Victor (1999) use yet another different approach. The authors also propose a view based navigation method, based on omni-directional images. The images are compressed using Principal Component Analysis (PCA), thus producing a low dimensional eigenspace. The eigenvalues of the images are projected into the eigenspace and connected by a linear interpolation model. This forms a manifold in the eigenspace, which represents the path that the robot must follow. The manifold is a kind of topological map of the environment. The robot is then guided with the goal of minimising the angle between the path followed and the desired path.

Winter and Santos-Victor approach is in many aspects similar to Franz et al. (1998)'s approach, although the latter do not use compressed images. The manifold is constituted by the images themselves. To save computational requirements, only images that are relevant to the navigation task are stored, which means that only "snapshot images" taken at decision points are retained. The authors also consider the problem of similar views, which is solved using the past history of the robot, assuming that the robot moves continuously in the navigation space. Table 1 summarises the approaches that have been described above, and Table 2 compares the described mapping methods.

4.3 Previous work using SDMs

4.3.1 Rao and Fuentes Goal-Directed navigation

Rao & Fuentes (1998) were probably the first to use a SDM in the robotics domain. They used a SDM to store perception (sensorial) information, which was later used to navigate the robot. Rao and Fuentes' model was a hierarchical system, inspired by Brooks (1986) subsumption architecture, in which the lower levels were responsible for lower level tasks, such as collision

Approach	Images	Landmarks	Compression	Similarity mode
Matsumoto	omniview	intersections	–	block match
Iconic memory	omniview	user defined points	Fourier trans.	Fourier coef.
T-net	4 cameras	beg. & end of paths	–	SSDA
Stephen Jones	wide angle	–	–	ZNCC
Winters	omniview	–	PCA	eigenvalues
Franz	omniview	intersections	–	neural net

Table 1. Summary of the analysed view-based navigation approaches.

Method	Sensor requirements	Memory requirements	Processing requirements	Scalability
Occupancy Grids	various	huge	high	low
Voronoi Diagrams	various	large	large	medium
Topological Maps	various	low	low	good
View Sequence	camera	large	large	good
Landmark based	landmark	low	low	low

Table 2. Summary of the analysed mapping approaches.

detection and obstacle avoidance. At this level the behaviour of the system was essentially reactive, and a simple hill-climbing learning algorithm was implemented.

The SDM used was implemented as a Neural Network, as shown in Figure 5. This Neural Network is used at the upper level, to provide goal-directed navigation. It was trained by the user, who manually guided the robot through the desired path, during a learning stage. While in the learning mode, the sensorial information from optical sensors (Perception) was recorded and stored into the SDM, along with the motor control vectors. During the autonomous run, similar perceptions (readings from the optical sensors), are expected to retrieve the correct actions (motor commands), making the system follow the same path by using this information, thus repeating the same trajectory. The authors report simulation results only, and they mention nothing about drift corrections or other error control strategies.

The SDM used in this system was also a variant of the original Kanerva's proposal. The initial addresses are picked at random, as Kanerva suggests, and represent the first layer of the Neural Network. This means that before operation, the weights w of the neural connections are assigned random values. But, contrary to the original idea, in this implementation the values

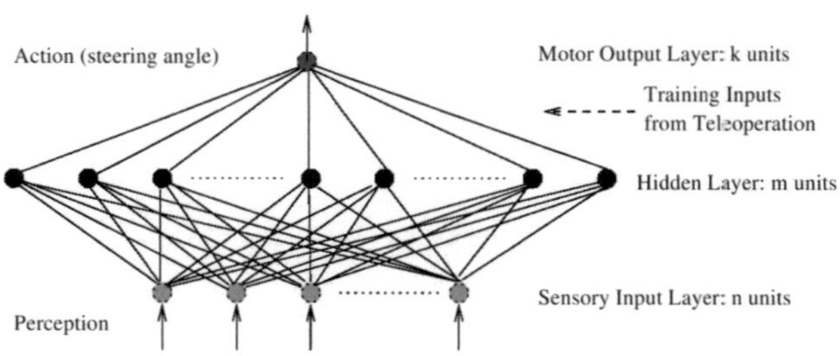

Fig. 5. Rao and Fuentes implementation of a SDM.

of these neurons can be changed, adjusting the addresses towards the most active regions of the address space. Rao and Fuentes call this implementation a "Self-Organizing SDM".
Learning in this memory, both for the address and the data spaces, occurs using a soft competitive learning rule. For each perception (input) vector p, at time t, the Euclidian distance between p and the corresponding neural weight w_j is computed: $d_j = \| w_j^t - p \|$. Then, the weight vector is adjusted as follows:

$$w_j^{t+1} \leftarrow w_j^t + g_j(t) \cdot P_t(d_j) \cdot (p - w_j^t) \tag{7}$$

P is the equivalent of the probability of the prototype vector w_j winning the current competition for perception p, which, for m neurons in a layer, is computed as follows:

$$P_t(d_j) = \frac{e^{\frac{-d_j^2}{\lambda_j(t)}}}{\sum_{i=1}^{m} e^{\frac{-d_j^2}{\lambda_j(t)}}} \tag{8}$$

$\lambda_j(t)$ is the equivalent of the "temperature" of the system, thus representing its susceptibility to change. The temperature is higher at the beginning and lowers as the system stabilises over time. $g_j(t)$ is also a stabiliser parameter, given by:

$$g_j(t) = \frac{1}{n_j(t)}, where \quad n_j(t+1) = n_j(t) + P_t(d_j) \tag{9}$$

4.3.2 Watanabe et al AGV

Watanabe et al. (2001) also applied a SDM in robotics, though just for the small task of scene recognition in a factory environment. The goal is to build intelligent vehicles that can move around autonomously—Autonomously Guided Vehicles (AGV)—in industrial environments. Those vehicles are usually required to run the same routes in a repetitive manner, transporting tools or other materials, from one point to another of the production line. But under normal circumstances it is required that they must be able to identify small changes in the environment, such as the presense of other AGVs, people, tools or other entities that may get into the route of the AGV. Even in the presence of those obstacles, they must avoid collision with them and successfully complete their goals.
Watanabe et al. use a Q-learning technique to teach the robots the paths they must perform, as well as learn the behaviour to negotiate with other AGVs in the environment. Scene recognition is performed based on the use of a SDM. The SDM is, therefore, used as a mere pattern recognition tool.
The factory plan is input to the AGV in the form of an occupancy grid. When moving, for each grid position, the system computes in real time the correct motion to execute, in function of its goal. But if the scene its sensorial readings at its current position differ from the expected sensorial readings, which are stored in the SDM, then an obstacle is probably in the way of the AGV. In this case, the system has to replan its trajectory and find an alternative way to bypass the obstacle and still make its way to the target point.
To the best of our knowledge, the authors report simulation results only, for a virtual AGV that can sense obstacles around itself, capture the scenes to store into the SDM, and knows every time its current location, as well as its goal location. The SDM used was implemented as a Neural Network.

Fig. 6. Robot used.

5. Experimental Platform

We used a SDM to navigate a robot, in order to test some of the theories in practice and assess the performance of the system. The robot used was a Surveyor[2] SRV-1, a small robot with tank-style treads and differential drive via two precision DC gearmotors (see Figure 6). Among other features, it has a built in digital video camera with 640x480 resolution, four infrared sensors and a Zigbee 802.15.4 radio communication module. This robot was controlled in real time from a laptop with an Intel 1.8 GHz Pentium IV processor and 1 Gb RAM.
The overall software architecture is as shown in Figure 7. It contains three basic modules:

1. The SDM, where the information is stored.
2. The Focus (following Kanerva's terminology), where the navigation algorithms are run.
3. A low level layer, responsible for interfacing the hardware and some tasks such as motor control, collision avoidance and image equalisation.

Navigation is based on vision, and has two modes: one learning mode, in which the robot is manually guided and captures images to store for future reference; and an autonomous mode, in which it uses its previous knowledge to navigate autonomously, following any sequence previously learnt, either to the end or until it gets lost (when it doesn't recognise the current view).
Level 1 is working as a finite state machine with two states: one where it executes all the orders from above, and the other where it is blocked awaiting orders. The robot is normally operating in the first state. When an image is out of focus or the infrared proximity detectors detect an obstacle close to the robot, Lizard stops an autonomous run and waits until further order is received from the user. In historical terms, Level 1 can be considered as inspired by the first level of competence of the Brooks' subsumption architecture (Brooks (1986)). In biological terms, it can be considered as inspired by the "primitive brain", which controls basic body functions such as breathing and other instinctive behaviours. This layer is also responsible for

[2] http://www.surveyor.com.

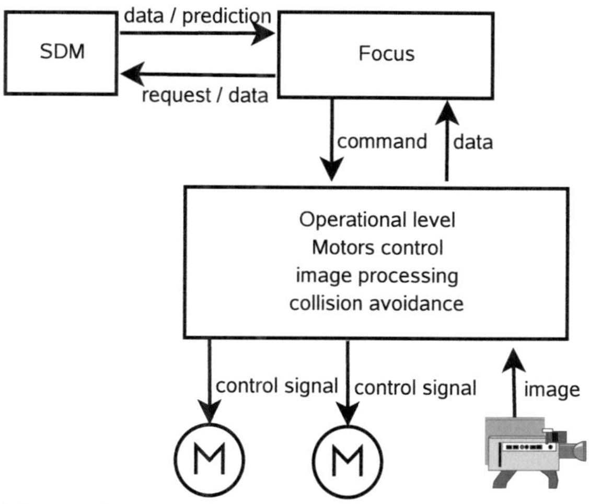

Fig. 7. Architecture of the implemented software.

Image resolution	Image bytes	Overhead	Total bytes	Total bits
80 × 64	5120	13	5133	41064

Table 3. Summary of the dimensions of the input vector.

converting the images to 8 bit grayscale and equalise the brightness to improve quality and comparability.

Navigation using a view sequence is based on the proposal of Matsumoto et al. (2000). This approach requires a learning stage, during which the robot must be manually guided. While being guided, the robot memorises a sequence of views automatically. While autonomously running, the robot performs automatic image based localisation and obstacle detection, taking action in real-time.

Localisation is accomplished with basis on the similarity of two views: one stored during the learning stage and another grabbed in real-time. During autonomous navigation, the robot tries to find matching areas between those two images, and calculates the horizontal distance between them in order to infer *how far* it is from the correct path. That distance is then used to correct eventual drifts, until the error is smaller than 5 pixels or cannot be made smaller after 5 iterations.

6. Our implementations of the SDM

In our implementation, input and output vectors consist of arrays of bytes, meaning that each individual value must fit in the range [0, 255]. Every individual value is, therefore, suitable to store the graylevel value of an image pixel or an 8-bit integer.

The composition of the input vectors is as summarised in Table 3 and Equation 10:

$$x_i = < im_i, seq\_id, i, timestamp, motion > \qquad (10)$$

where im_i is the last image. *seq_id* is an auto-incremented, 4-byte integer, unique for each sequence. It is used to identify which sequence the vector belongs to. i is an auto-incremented, 4-byte integer, unique for every vector in the sequence. It is used to quickly identify every

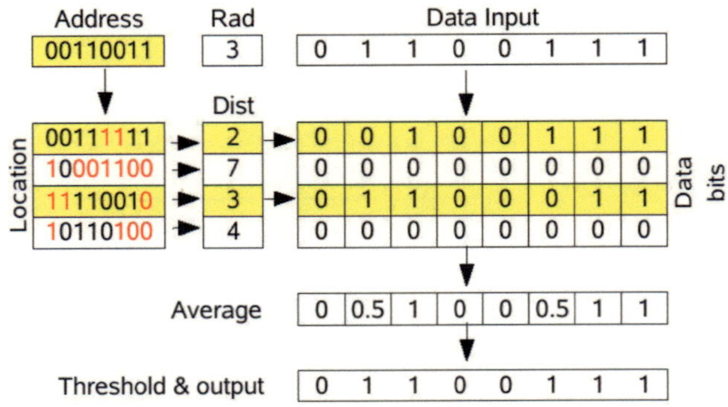

Fig. 8. Bitwise SDM, not using bit counters.

image in the sequence. *timestamp* is a 4-byte integer, storing Unix timestamp. It is read from the operating system, but not being used so far for navigation purposes. *motion* is a single character, identifying the type of movement the robot was performing when the image was grabbed.

We are using Portable Gray Map (PGM) images, in which each pixel is an 8-bit integer, representing a gray level between 0 (black) and 255 (white). Resolution is 80x64, implying that the image alone needs $80 \times 64 = 5120$ bytes The overhead information comprises 13 additional bytes, meaning the input vector contains 5133 bytes.

The memory is used to store vectors as explained, but addressing is done using just the part of the vector corresponding to one image. During the autonomous run, the robot will predict im_i from im_{i-1}. Therefore, the address is im_{i-1}, not the whole vector. The remainder bits could be set at random, as Kanerva suggests. According to the SDM theory, 20 % of the bits correct and the remainder bits set at random should suffice to retrieve the right datum with a probability of 0.6. But it was considered preferable to set up the software so that it is able to calculate similarity between just part of two vectors, ignoring the remainder bits. This saves computational power and reduces the probability of false positives being detected. Since we're not using the *overhead* to address, the tolerance to noise increases a little bit, resulting in less possible errors during normal operation.

Another difference in our implementation, relative to Kanerva's proposal, is that we don't fill the virtual space placing hard locations randomly in the addressing space in the beginning of the operation. Instead, we use Ratitch et al's Randomised Reallocation algorithm Ratitch & Precup (2004): start with an empty memory, and allocate new hard locations when there's a new datum which cannot be stored in enough existing locations. The new locations are allocated *randomly* in the neighbourhood of the new datum address.

6.1 Bitwise implementation

Kanerva's model has a small handicap: the arrays of counters are hard to implement in practice and require a lot of processing, which increases the processing time. Furber et al. (2004) claim their results show that the memory's performance is not significantly affected if a single bit is used to store one bit, instead of a bit counter, under normal circumstances. For real time operation, this simplification greatly reduces the need for processing power and memory size. In our case, the original model was not implemented, and the system's performance was ac-

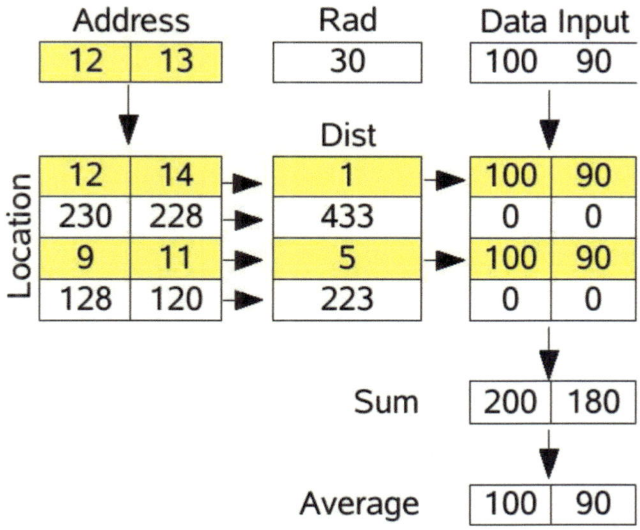

Fig. 9. Arithmetic SDM, which works with byte integers.

ceptable using this implementation where the bit counters are replaced by a single bit each, as shown in Figure 8.

Writing in this model is simply to replace the old datum with the new datum. Additionally, since we're not using bit counters and our data can only be 0 or 1, when reading, the average value of the hard locations can only be a real number in the interval $[0, 1]$. Therefore, the threshold for bitwise operation is at 0.5.

6.2 Arithmetic implementation

Although the bitwise implementation works, we also implemented another version of the SDM, inspired by Ratitch & Precup (2004). In this variation of the model, the bits are grouped as byte integers, as shown in Figure 9. Addressing is done using an arithmetic distance, instead of the Hamming distance, and writing is done by applying to each byte value the following equation:

$$h_t^k = h_{t-1}^k + \alpha \cdot (x^k - h_{t-1}^k), \quad \alpha \in \mathbb{R} \wedge 0 \leq \alpha \leq 1 \tag{11}$$

h_t^k is the kth 8-bit integer of the hard location, at time t. x^k is the corresponding integer in the input vector x and α the learning rate. $\alpha = 0$ means to keep the previous values unchanged. $\alpha = 1$ implies that the previous value of the hard location is overwritten (one-shot learning). In practice, $\alpha = 1$ is a good compromise, and that's the value being used.

6.3 Determination of the access radius

To calibrate the system, it is necessary to previously estimate noise levels. We consider noise the distance between two consecutive pictures taken without any environmental change (i.e., the lighting and scenario are the same).

To make navigation a little more robust, a dynamic algorithm was implemented, to automatically adjust the system to the noise level before learning. Once the system is turned on, the robot captures three consecutive images and computes the differences between the first and

the second, and between the second and the third. The average of the two values is taken as a good approximation to the actual noise level.
As proposed in Mendes et al. (2007), to make sure the images are retrieved from the memory when following the sequence, the access radius is set as a function of the noise level. It is set to the average value of the noise increased 40 % for bitwise operation, and 70 % for arithmetic operation.

7. The encoding problem

In Natural Binary Code (NBC), the value of each bit depends on its position. 0001_2 (1_{10}) is different from 1000_2 (8_{10}), although the number of ones and zeros in each number is exactly the same. The Arithmetic Distance (AD) between those numbers is $8 - 1 = 7$, and the Hamming Distance (HD) is 2. If we consider the numbers 0111_2 (7_{10}) and 1000_2 (8_{10}), the AD is 1 and the HD is 4.
These examples show that the HD is not proportional to the AD. There are some *undesirable transitions*, i.e., situations where the HD decreases and the AD increases, as shown in Table 4. However, sensorial data is usually encoded using the natural binary code and is hardly random. This means that the data might not be appropriate to make the most of the SDM. Additionally, the number of ones can increase and decrease as the represented value of the number grows. `0100` contains less ones than `0011`, but its binary value is twice the value of `0011`. This characteristic means that the Hamming Distance (HD) is not proportional to the binary difference of the numbers.

	000	001	010	011	100	101	110	111
000	0	1	1	2	1	2	2	3
001		0	2	1	2	1	3	2
010			0	1	2	3	1	2
011				0	3	2	2	1
100					0	1	1	2
101						0	2	1
110							0	1
111								0

Table 4. Hamming distances for 3-bit numbers.

Table 4 shows the HDs between all the 3-bit binary numbers. As it shows, this distance is not proportional to the Arithmetic Distance (AD). The HD sometimes even decreases when the arithmetic difference increases. One example is the case of `001` to `010`, where the AD is 1 and the HD is 2. And if we compare `001` to `011`, the AD increases to 2 and the HD decreases to 1. In total, there are 9 undesirable situations in the table, where the HD decreases while it should increase or, at least, maintain its previous value. In the case of PGM images, they are encoded using the natural binary code, which takes advantage of the position of the bits to represent different values. But the HD does not consider positional values. The performance of the SDM, therefore, might be affected because of these different criteria being used to encode the information and to process it inside the memory.
These characteristics of the NBC and the HD may be neglectable when operating with random data, but in the specific problem of storing and retrieving graylevel images, they may pose serious problems. Suppose, for instance, two different copies, im_i and im_j, of the same image. Let's assume a given pixel P has graylevel 127 (`01111111`) in im_i. But due to noise,

	000	001	011	010	110	111	101	100
000	0	1	2	1	2	3	2	1
001		0	1	2	3	2	1	2
011			0	1	2	1	2	3
010				0	1	2	3	2
110					0	1	2	1
111						0	1	2
101							0	1
100								0

Table 5. Hamming distances for 3-bit Gray Code.

	000	001	010	100	101	111	011	110
000	0	1	1	1	2	3	2	2
001		0	2	2	1	2	1	3
010			0	2	3	2	1	1
100				0	1	2	3	1
101					0	1	2	2
111						0	1	1
011							0	2
110								0

Table 6. Hamming distances for a 3-bit optimised code.

P has graylevel 128 (`10000000`) in im_j. Although the value is *almost* the same, the Hamming distance between the value of *P* in each image is the maximum it can be—8 bits.
A solution to this problem could rely on the use of the Gray Code (GC), where only one bit changes at a time as the numbers increase. This would ensure that transitions such as the one from 7 to 8 have only a difference of one, while in NBC all the bits differ.
The GC, however, also exhibits many undesirable transitions, as Table 5 shows. It may solve some particular problems of adjacent bytes, but it's not a general solution. Besides, it is circular, meaning that a white image can easily be confused with a black image.
Another approach is simply to sort the bytes in a more convenient way, so that the HD becomes proportional to the AD—or, at least, does not exhibit so many undesirable transitions. This sorting can be accomplished by trying different permutations of the numbers and computing the matrix of Hamming distances. For 3-bit numbers, there are 8 different numbers and $8! = 40,320$ permutations. This can easily be computed using a modern personal computer, in a reasonable amount of time. After an exhaustive search, different sortings are found, but none of them ideal. Table 6 shows a different sorting, better than the NBC shown in Table 4. This code shows only 7 undesirable transitions, while the NBC contains 9. Therefore, it should perform better with the SDM. It should also be mentioned that there are several sortings with similar performance. There are 2,783 other sortings that also have seven undesirable transitions. The one shown is the first that our software found. In our case, we are looking for the best code to compute the similarity distance between images. If those images are equalised, then the distribution of all the brightness values is such that all the values are approximately equally probable. This means that it is irrelevant which sorting is chosen, among those with the same number of undesirable transitions. Yet another approach is to use a Sum-Code (SC). As previously written, using 256 graylevels it's not possible to find a suitable binary code with minimum undesirable transitions, so that one can take advantage of the representativity of the NBC and the properties of the SDM. The only way to avoid undesirable transitions at all is to reduce the number of different gray levels to the number of bits + 1 and use a kind of

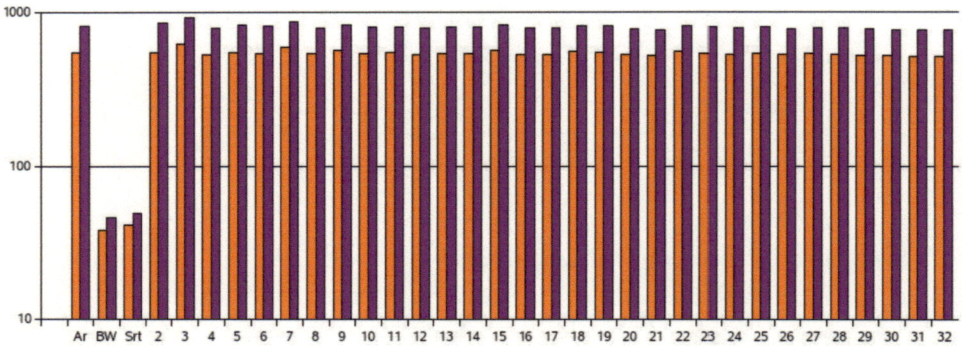

Fig. 10. Error increments. Light colour: to the second best image. Darker: to the average.

0	0000
1	0001
2	0011
3	0111
4	1111

Table 7. Code to represent 5 graylevels.

sum-code. Therefore, using 4 bits we can only use 5 different gray levels, as shown in Table 7. Using 8 bits, we can use 9 gray levels and so on. This is the only way to work with a Hamming distance that is proportional to the arithmetic distance.
The disadvantage of this approach, however, is obvious: either the quality of the image is much poorer, or the dimension of the stored vectors has to be extended to accommodate additional bits. In Mendes et al. (2009) this encoding problem is discussed in more detail.

8. Tests and Results

Different tests were performed in order to assess the behaviour of the system using each of the approaches described in the previous sections. The results were obtained using a sequence of 55 images. The images were equalised, and the memory was loaded with a single copy of each.

8.1 Results

Table 8 shows the average of 30 operations. The tests were performed using the arithmetic distance; using the NBC and the Hamming distance (8 bits, 256 graylevels, represented using the natural binary code); using the the Hamming distance and a partially optimised sorting of the bytes; and bitwise modes in which the graylevels were reduced to the number of bits + 1. We tested using from 1 to 32 bits, which means from 2 to 33 graylevels, in order to experimentally get a better insight on how the number of bits and graylevels might influence the performance of the system.
The table shows the distance (error in similarity) from the input image to the closest image in the SDM; the distance to the second closest image; and the average of the distances to all the images. It also shows, in percentage, the increase from the closest prediction to the second and to the average—this is a measure of how *successful* the memory is in separating the desired datum from the pool of information in the SDM. We also show the average processing time for each method. Processing time is only the memory prediction time, it does not include the

image capture and transmission times. The clock is started as soon as the command is issued to the SDM and stopped as soon as the prediction result is returned.
For clarity, chart 10 shows, using a logarithmic scale, the increments of the distance from the closest image to the second closest one (lighter colour) and to the average of all the images (darker colour).

	Dist. to best	Dist. to 2nd	inc. (%)	Dist. to Average	inc. (%)	Time (ms)
Ar.	18282	118892	550.32	166406.53	810.22	241.29
NBC	6653	9186	38.07	9724.80	46.17	231.35
Sort.	6507	9181	41.09	9720.56	49.39	240.45
B2	101	653	546.53	961.25	851.73	979.31
B3	144	1034	618.06	1465.57	917.76	983.02
B4	232	1459	528.88	2069.46	792.01	964.34
B5	291	1893	550.52	2689.06	824.08	970.88
B6	365	2349	543.56	3308.30	806.38	974.53
B7	412	2849	591.50	3964.05	862.15	963.56
B8	517	3312	540.62	4605.01	790.72	968.84
B9	569	3791	566.26	5257.01	823.90	996.56
B10	654	4214	544.34	5897.50	801.76	981.74
B11	724	4706	550.00	6546.08	804.15	968.81
B12	810	5142	534.81	7183.31	786.83	969.92
B13	871	5608	543.86	7817.77	797.56	971.62
B14	944	6084	544.49	8469.16	797.16	983.49
B15	986	6555	564.81	9126.96	825.66	992.54
B16	1098	6963	534.15	9750.75	788.05	977.52
B17	1180	7487	534.49	10424.05	783.39	967.14
B18	1208	7938	557.12	11040.56	813.95	965.06
B19	1290	8410	551.94	11729.28	809.25	968.77
B20	1406	8843	528.95	12377.95	780.37	975.30
B21	1498	9298	520.69	13015.70	768.87	996.89
B22	1494	9794	555.56	13680.24	815.68	978.63
B23	1591	10230	542.99	14290.35	798.20	968.75
B24	1687	10679	533.02	14934.10	785.25	977.01
B25	1744	11178	540.94	15616.34	795.43	971.71
B26	1850	11646	529.51	16277.14	779.85	974.81
B27	1898	12086	536.78	16880.55	789.39	999.59
B28	1988	12533	530.43	17558.76	783.24	965.80
B29	2083	13000	524.10	18178.87	772.73	965.99
B30	2175	13512	521.24	18878.92	768.00	968.89
B31	2263	13936	515.82	19489.28	761.21	981.75
B32	2336	14433	517.85	20163.64	763.17	967.21
B33	2372	14900	528.16	20796.13	776.73	1012.32

Table 8. Experimental results using different metrics.

Some results are also plotted in charts 10 and 11. The first shows, using a logarithmic scale, the increments of the distance from the closest image to the second closest one (lighter colour)

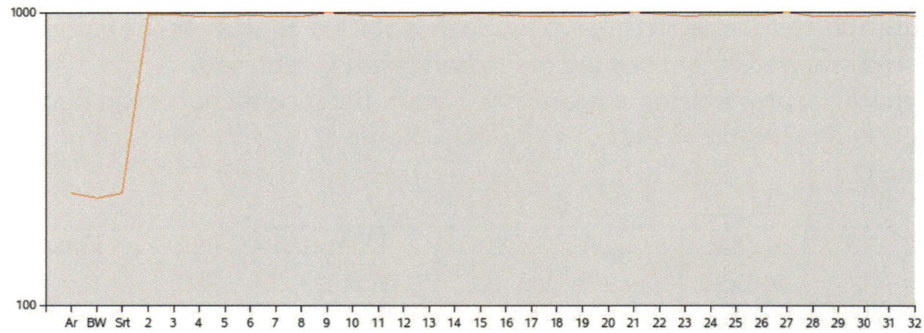

Fig. 11. Processing time.

and to the average of all the images (darker colour). The second chart shows the processing time, again using a logarithmic scale.

8.2 Analysis of the results

It can be confirmed that the bitwise mode using the NBC seems to be remarkably worse than the other methods, which seem to show similar results. Sorting the bytes results in a small, but not significant, improvement. Another interesting point is that the number of graylevels seems to have little impact on the selectivity of the image, for images of this size and resolution.

The processing time exhibits a great variation, due to the fact that the tests were run on a computer using Linux (OpenSuSE 10.2), a *best effort* operating system. Even with the number of processes running down to the minimum, there were very disparate processing times. For better precision and real time operation, a real time operating system would be recommended. The average processing times for the arithmetic and bitwise mode are about 240 ms for the complete cycle to fetch the closest matching image. Using the NBC with the HD, the time is a little shorter, and using a different sorting of the bytes the time increased a little. This was expectable, since the only variation in this method was implemented using an indexed table, where each position held the sorted byte. Therefore, to compute the similarity between two pixels, two accesses had to be done to the indexed table, which considerably increases the total memory access time. A more efficient approach would be to make the conversion as soon as the images were grabbed from the camera. This is undesirable in our case, though, as we're also testing other approaches.

As for the other approaches using different graylevels, the processing times are all similar and about 4 times larger than the time of processing one image using the arithmetic mode. The reason for this is that, again, an indexed table is used to address the binary code used. And in this case there's the additional workload of processing the conversion into the desired number of gray values. In a production system, obviously, the conversion would only need to be done once, just as the images were grabbed from the camera.

9. Conclusions

To the best of our knowledge, this is the first time a robot has actually been guided by a system with a SDM at its helm. Our implementation consisted in guiding the robot using a view sequence stored in the SDM.

The first problem noticed was that of encoding the information, because sensorial information is hardly random, as the SDM theory considers. Thus, our tests used four different operational

modes: one based upon the natural binary code; another based on an optimised code; a third one based on an arithmetic mode; and the last using a sum-code.
In the original SDM model Kanerva proposes that the Hamming distance be used to compute the similarity between two memory items. Unfortunately, this method exhibits a poor performance if the data are not random. The NBC with the Hamming distance shows the worst performance. By sorting some bytes the performance is slightly improved. If the bits are grouped as bytes and an arithmetic distance is used, the memory shows an excellent performance, but this can fade some characteristics of the original model, which is based on the properties of a binary space. If the number of graylevels is reduced and a sum-code is used, the performance is close to that of the arithmetic mode and the characteristics of the memory must still hold..
Although our work was performed using images as data, our results should still be valid for all non-random data, as is usually the case of robotic sensorial data.
Future work includes the study of the impact of using different encoding methods on the performance of the SDM itself, in order to infer which characteristics shall still hold or fade.
Implemented in software the SDM is very computer intensive and storage can be as low as 0.1 bits per bit. However, it is a viable and interesting model, making it possible to implement models and behaviours similar to the human brain, based on pattern recognition, such as the case of navigation based on visual sequences.

10. References

Brooks, R. A. (1986). A robust layered control system for a mobile robot, *IEEE Journal of Robotics and Automation* **2**(1).

Dijskstra, E. W. (1959). A note on two problems in connexion with graphs, *Numerische Mathematik* **1**(1): 269–271.

Dobrev, D. (2005). Formal definition of artificial intelligence, *Information Theories and Applications* **12**(3): 277–285.

Franz, M. O., SchÃűlkopf, B., Mallot, H. A., BÃijlthoff, H. H. & Olkopf, B. S. (1998). Learning view graphs for robot navigation, *Autonomous Robots* **5**(1): 111–125.

Furber, S. B., Bainbridge, J., Cumpstey, J. M. & Temple, S. (2004). Sparse distributed memory using *n*-of-*m* codes., *Neural Networks* **17**(10): 1437–1451.

Gottfredson, L. S. (1997). Mainstream science on intelligence: An editorial with 52 signatories, history and bibliography, *Intelligence* **24**(1): 13–23.

Harnish, R. M. (2002). *Minds, brains, computers: an historical introduction to the foundations of cognitive science*, Wiley-Blackwell.

Hawkins, J. & Blakeslee, S. (2004). *On Intelligence*, Times Books, New York.

Hopfield, J. J. (1982). Neural networks and physical systems with emergent collective computational abilities., *Proceedings of the National Academy of Science*, Vol. 79, pp. 2554–2558.

Ishiguro, H., Miyashita, T. & Tsuji, S. (1995). T-net for navigating a vision-guided robot in real world, *ICRA*, pp. 1068–1074.

Ishiguro, H. & Tsuji, S. (1996). Image-based memory of environment, *in Proc. IEEE/RSJ Int. Conf. Intelligent Robots and Systems*, pp. 634–639.

Jones, S. D., Andresen, C. & Crawley, J. L. (1997). Appearance based processes for visual navigation, *Proceedings of the IEEE International Conference on Intelligent Robots and Systems*, Grenoble, France.

Kanerva, P. (1988). *Sparse Distributed Memory*, MIT Press, Cambridge.

Keeler, J. D. (1988). Comparison between kanerva's sdm and hopfield-type neural networks, *Cognitive Science* **12**(3): 299–329.
URL: *http://dx.doi.org/10.1016/0364-0213(88)90026-2*

Kuipers, B. J. & Levitt, T. S. (1988). Navigation and mapping in large-scale space, *International Journal of Artificial Intelligence* **9**(2): 25–43.

Legg, S. & Hutter, M. (2007). Universal intelligence: A definition of machine intelligence, *Minds and Machines* **17**(4): 391–444. http://www.vetta.org/about-me/publications/.

Matsumoto, Y., Ikeda, K., Inaba, M. & Inoue, H. (1999). Exploration and map acquisition for view-based navigation in corridor environment, *Proceedings of the International Conference on Field and Service Robotics*, pp. 341–346.

Matsumoto, Y., Inaba, M. & Inoue, H. (2000). View-based approach to robot navigation, *Proceedings of 2000 IEEE/RSJ International Conference on Intelligent Robots and Systems (IROS 2000).*

Matsumoto, Y., Inaba, M. & Inoue, H. (2003). View-based navigation using an omniview sequence in a corridor environment, *Machine Vision and Applications.*

Mendes, M., Coimbra, A. P. & Crisóstomo, M. (2007). AI and memory: Studies towards equipping a robot with a sparse distributed memory, *Proceedings of the IEEE International Conference on Robotics and Biomimetics*, Sanya, China.

Mendes, M., Crisóstomo, M. & Coimbra, A. P. (2009). Assessing a sparse distributed memory using different encoding methods, *Proceedings of the 2009 International Conference of Computational Intelligence and Intelligent Systems*, London, UK.

Mountcastle, V. (1978). An organizing principle for cerebral function: the unit model and the distributed system, *in* G. M. Edelman & V. Mountcastle (eds), *The mindful brain*, MIT Press, Cambridge, Mass.

Rao, R. & Fuentes, O. (1998). Hierarchical learning of navigational behaviors in an autonomous robot using a predictive sparse distributed memory, *Machine Learning* **31**(1-3): 87–113.

Rasmussen, C. & Hager, G. D. (1996). Robot navigation using image sequences, *In Proc. AAAI*, pp. 938–943.

Ratitch, B. & Precup, D. (2004). Sparse distributed memories for on-line value-based reinforcement learning., *ECML.*

Searle, J. (1980). Minds, brains, and programs, *Behavioral and Brain Sciences* (3): 417–424.

Spearman, C. E. (1927). *The abilities of man, their nature and measurement*, Macmillan, New York.

Watanabe, M., Furukawa, M. & Kakazu, Y. (2001). Intelligent agv driving toward an autonomous decentralized manufacturing system, *Robotics and computer-integrated manufacturing* **17**(1-2): 57–64.
URL: *citeseer.ist.psu.edu/274654.html*

Willshaw, D. J., Buneman, O. P. & Longuet-Higgins, H. C. (1969). Non-holographic associative memory, *Nature* **222**(5197): 960–962.

Winters, N. & Santos-Victor, J. (1999). Mobile robot navigation using omni-directional vision, *In Proc. 3rd Irish Machine Vision and Image Processing Conference (IMVIP'99)*, pp. 151–166.

7

Vision Based Robotic Navigation: Application to Orthopedic Surgery

P. Gamage[1], S. Q. Xie[1], P. Delmas[1] and W. L. Xu[2]
[1]*The University of Auckland,* [2]*Massey University*
New Zealand

1. Introduction

Vision guided medical technologies are currently emerging that will influence the way in which orthopedic procedures are diagnosed, planned, simulated, and performed. Medical robotics is one such field that has benefited through the recent advances in the fields of medical imaging and computer vision (Miyamoto, Sugiura et al. 2003).
The orthopedic specialty presents several opportunities to the application of vision guided robotic technology. Radiographic imaging technologies such as c-arm fluoroscopy, X-ray and CT (Computed Tomography) can be used as medical imaging modalities for bony anatomy. The latter is of considerable interest as it enables the building of 3D bone models pre-operatively which permits pose estimation during operative procedures. Moreover, unlike soft tissue, the procedures that involve the manipulation of bones are able to withstand an applied force from tools (robotics) without significant deformation. This has lead to the development of orthopedic robotic technologies including several for femur fracture realignment (Joskowicz L, Milgrom C et al. 1998; Graham and Xie 2007; Westphal R, Winkelbach S et al. 2007).
Our work focuses on femur fracture orthopedics with an emphasis on a procedure for fracture reduction called closed intramedullary nailing. The procedure initially requires the alignment of the proximal and distal segments of the bone followed by the insertion of a nail into the medullary cavity of the long bone, typically inserted minimally invasively through the proximal part of the femur. Finally lateral locking screws are placed to hold the nail in place. Intramedullary nailing is performed for cases of femur shaft fractures which are commonly caused by high-energy injury mechanisms (e.g. traffic accidents or heavy falls). Statistics gathered by (Westphal, Winkelbach et al. 2007) indicate an approximate femur fracture incidence rate of 37 per 100,000 persons per year, and thus it is a frequently encountered injury. In 2004, 3200 patients with fractures of the thigh bone have been counted in New Zealand (Cure-Research 2004). These figures include fractures in the proximal (hip side) femur as well as the shaft (the middle, diaphyseal) region.
Intra-operative fluoroscopy is the imaging modality utilized for visualizing underlying bone and surgical tool positions in femur fracture orthopedic procedures. Fluoroscopic image guidance of robotic systems can be divided into two categories: 1) open loop calibrated guidance 2) closed loop un-calibrated guidance. Open loop calibrated guidance methods

compute the robot's spatial localization with respect to the camera coordinate system by imaging a target with known geometry. The desired robot pose is then specified, either automatically or manually, in the camera coordinate system and the robot is aligned accordingly. Since the internal camera parameters are required for robot pose estimation, the c-arm must be calibrated. Closed loop un-calibrated methods guide the robot to the desired pose based solely on the acquired images. The desired target pose is specified, either automatically or manually, in the image coordinate system. The robot pose is then updated continuously according to the images, until the desired pose is attained.
We have opted for closed loop guidance due to the reduction in pre-operative imaging that is required. The main difference in requirement between the open and closed loop systems is in the definition of the robot target pose. Closed loop methodologies require the 3D volumetric model to be registered to the intra-operative situation using a 2D-3D registration technique. This defines the robot target pose intra-operatively. The focus of the chapter is placed on new methods and technologies for performing the aforementioned 2D-3D registration. The chapter will discuss the developed algorithms to recognize the object to be manipulated by matching image features to a geometrical model of the object and computing its position and orientation (pose) relative to the robot coordinate system. This absolute pose and cartesian-space information is used to move the robot to the desired pose.
Apart from fracture reduction, hip and knee arthroplasties and several spinal procedures are currently seen as potential areas of orthopedics benefited by intra-operative 3D pose estimation, through a 2D-3D registration process. Literature work that conduct tracking of fractured bone segments through intra-operative 2D-3D registration can be is seen in (Joskowicz L, Milgrom C et al. 1998; Westphal R, Winkelbach S et al. 2007; Gamage, Xie et al. 2008). Intra-operative pose estimation techniques could further be used during spinal orthopedic procedures such as reinforcement of falling vertebra and pedicle screw placement (Penny 1999; Zollei 2001; Tomaževic, Likar et al. 2003). Furthermore, in hip arthroplasty, the positioning and implanting of the acetabular cup into the pelvic bone can also be aided through intra-operative pose estimation (LaRose, Cassenti et al. 2000; Hüfner, Meller et al. 2005). Several other (non orthopedic) areas for the use of intra-operative pose-estimation has been identified as radiotherapy (Bollet, Mcnair et al. 2003) and endovascular treatments (Zollei 2001; Tomaževic 2002).
The pose estimation work conducted by the authors is motivated by a recent study conducted on femur fracture reduction, which demonstrated a shift towards 3D visualization modalities. It confirmed that computer-aided systems significantly improve the accuracy of orthopedic procedures by augmenting the current 2D image guidance with interactive display of 3D bone models (Joskowicz L, Milgrom C et al. 1998). Research indicates that the positioning errors and complications that are seen in 18% of femur fracture cases and the misalignments created would be reduced with the introduction of an interactive display of 3D bone models into the fracture reduction process (Joskowicz L, Milgrom C et al. 1998).
This chapter is divided into three main sections. The first section documents the current state-of-the-art research in pose estimation associated with orthopedic IGS systems. Section two presents the proposed methodology in full detail. Section three provides the results of the tests conducted.

2. Literature Review

Several methodologies that tackle the problem of intra-operative registration of bony anatomy in orthopedic surgery appear in literature. The schemes developed by (Joskowicz L, Milgrom C et al. 1998; Westphal R, Winkelbach S et al. 2007) track the bone fragments in real-time by means of an optical tracking system using a set of infrared markers. Thus to track the position of the distal and proximal bone fragments, the surgeon implants fiduciary markers into the bone segments. These physical tracking methodologies are accurate. However the implanting of the optical trackers on the bone is an arduous task for the surgeon/technician who already deals with a narrow field of view with the present system. Another drawback of such systems is the guidance inaccuracies caused due to movement, deformation and changes in anatomy since the time of initial imaging. Furthermore optical tracking requires a direct line of sight between the LED assembly on the patient and the external sensor assembly. This is a cumbersome requirement in a crowded operating theatre. Moreover, this would also introduce new training and process requirements that would limit the performance of the surgery. These difficulties hinder the widespread introduction of fiducial marker based intra-operative tracking into orthopedic procedures.

Several other studies have performed image based registration between intra-operative x-ray/fluoroscopic images and the pre-operative 3D CT data of the anatomy of interest. These methodologies can be grouped as feature based registration techniques (Besl and McKay. 1992; Taylor, Mittelstadt et al. 1994; Lavallee, Szeliski et al. 1995; Livyatan, Yaniv et al. 2003; Tomaževic, Likar et al. 2003) or as intensity based registration techniques (Penney, Batchelor et al. 2001; Zollei, Grimson et al. 2001; Rohlfing and Maurer 2002).

Feature based approaches rely on the presence and identification of natural landmarks in the input datasets in order to determine the best alignment. Feature based techniques can be again subdivided into either point based or surface based techniques depending on the type of 3D data utilized. Feature point based methodologies identify corresponding landmark points on the 2D image and 3D volume (Taylor, Mittelstadt et al. 1994). These key feature points can be defined manually or through some automatic feature identification process. In this scenario the 2D-3D registration is concerned with minimizing the distance between the two point sets after the 3D landmark points are projected onto the 2D plane. Surface based (Besl and McKay. 1992; Lavallee, Szeliski et al. 1995; Livyatan, Yaniv et al. 2003; Tomaževic, Likar et al. 2003) feature registration approaches utilize the outer surfaces of an object of interest (extracted from a 3D model), and contours that outline the object on one or more 2D images. Registration is concerned with finding the object pose that minimizes the distance between surface and the contour. One way to achieve this minimum is by extending 3D projection lines from points on the contour in the 2D image to a point representing the X-ray source. Then the distance to be minimized can be represented as the Euclidean distance between a projection line and the nearest point on the 3D surface (Lavallee, Szeliski et al. 1995). Another methodology is to project 3D surface points onto the 2D plane and then attempt to minimize the distance between the contour of the projected image and the initial 2D contour. The work done by (Lavallee, Szeliski et al. 1995; Livyatan, Yaniv et al. 2003; Tomaževic, Likar et al. 2003) has presented another methodology where projections of the volumetric data gradients are computed and compared with X-ray image gradients. The volumetric data pose is adjusted to minimize this gradient difference.

Intensity based measures operate on the pixel or voxel intensities directly. They calculate various statistics using the raw intensity values of the inputs which are then compared in

the images to be aligned (Penney, Weese et al. 1998). The matching can be restricted to regions of interest (ROIs) in the image, such as regions around bone surfaces in CT and fluoroscopic images, or the entire acquired image. Intensity based registration consists, generating digitally reconstructed radiographs (DRRs) for each pose, measuring the pose difference by comparing the DRRs with the fluoroscopic images through a similarity measure, and finally computing a pose that minimizes that difference. The calculation of a DRR by numerical summation of CT image intensities along projection rays involves high computation cost and is thus time consuming. Number of methods have been proposed that simplify and consequently speeds up the calculation of DRRs, without losing information that is needed for registration (LaRose, Bayouth et al. 2000). The similarity measure performed between the DRR and the acquired radiograph is important as it dictates the success of the optimization process. Work has been done by Penny et al. (Penney, Weese et al. 1998) where several similarity measures for registration of 3D CT and 2D X-ray images were tested providing some insight to the possible choice of an adequate similarly measure. Though the number of points to be registered is much greater than in the case of the feature-based methods, the key characteristic of intensity-based registration is that it does not require segmentation and feature extraction, thus reducing the influence of outliers and increasing robustness.
Due to the timeliness exhibited by feature based registration methodologies the intra-operative pose estimation framework proposed in this chapter has made use of this technique. Although related registration methodologies have been developed in the past, there remain significant challenges as these methodologies have not yet been introduced into fractured bone segment pose estimation. The anatomy based intra-operative pose estimation framework proposed in this chapter is motivated by these limitations.

3. Methods

Fig. 1 illustrates the proposed framework and conveys how the 2D-3D registration algorithm is used intra-operatively along with the pre-operatively reconstructed 3D fractured bone model. The 2D-3D registration framework can be split into two distinct phases: 1) Frontal and lateral pose estimation 2) Axial pose estimation. Since the registration is performed through images acquired from the frontal and lateral viewpoints, registration in these planes will be performed highly accurately through the first phase of the 2D-3D registration process. The axial alignment, which is critical as it has a high impact on functional biomechanics of the leg, will be conducted in the second phase. The intra-operative 2D-3D registration framework discussed is independent of how the patient-specific 3D data is acquired. The proceeding sections will discuss the required processing of the fluoroscopic images to extract the features of interest, CT dataset segmentation for patient-specific model creation, followed by the 2D-3D registration algorithm.

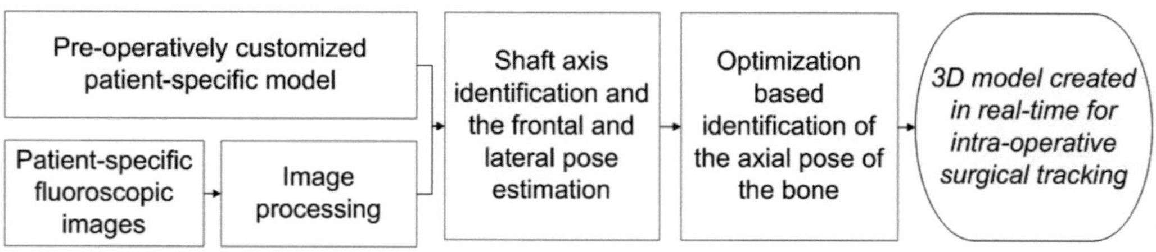

Fig. 1. The main process steps of the proposed framework.

3.1 Acquisition Geometry and Calibration of Fluoroscopic Images

In this chapter the fluoroscopic image acquisition is described through a pinhole camera model (Tsai 1987), that represents mapping from a 3D scene onto a 2D image (Fig. 2).

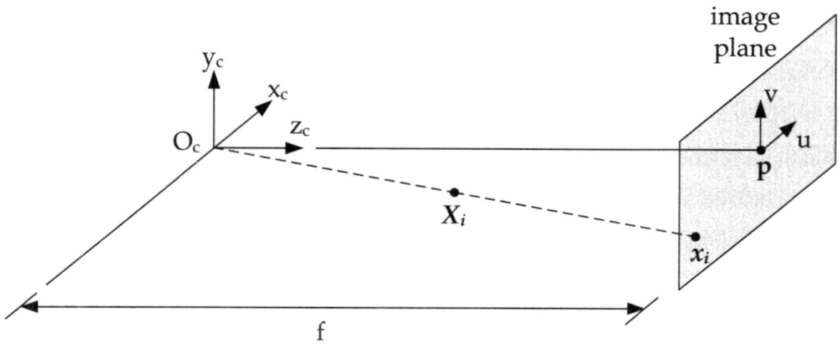

Fig. 2. Pinhole camera model showing camera centre (O_c), principal point (p), focal length (f), 3D point (X) and its image projection (x).

The X-ray center of projection is defined as O_c and the imaging plane is located at z_c = focal length (f). The ray from the center of projection to the image plane is called the principal axis, and the principal point (p) is the point at which the light that passes through the image is perpendicular to the imaging plane. The pinhole camera model dictates that 3D object points X_i map onto the imaging plane through the intersection of rays that originate from the centre of projection and pass through X_i. Simple geometry shows that the image coordinates (u,v) are related to the object coordinates (x_o,y_o,z_o), of point Xi, through Equation (1).

$$u_i = \frac{f}{z_o} x_o \text{ and } v_i = \frac{f}{z_o} y_o \tag{1}$$

The relationship between the coordinates of a 2D image pixel, and its corresponding 3D object point can be expressed through Equation (2) below.

$$x = MX \text{ where } M = K[R \mid t] \tag{2}$$

Here the 3x4 projection matrix M, relates any 3D point $X = (x_o, y_o, z_o, 1)^T$ to its corresponding projection $x = (u,v,1)^T$ in the acquired image. The intrinsic projection parameters of the X-ray tube (focal length and principal point coordinates), are represented through K, and the extrinsic parameters (rotation and translation of the acquisition system in a world coordinate system) through $[R \mid t]$. The intrinsic projection parameter matrix can be defined through Equation (3). Here (u_o,v_o) denote the coordinates of the principal point. The pixel sizes along the u and v axes is denoted by pix_u and pix_v respectively.

$$K = \begin{bmatrix} \frac{f}{pix_u} & 0 & u_o & 0 \\ 0 & \frac{f}{pix_v} & v_o & 0 \\ 0 & 0 & 1 & 0 \end{bmatrix} \tag{3}$$

The camera calibration methodology is not an integral part of this chapter. The intrinsic camera calibration method simply relies on the technique described in (Tsai 1987) where a set of coplanar points visible on the image, are used to compute the camera parameters. We utilized a radio-opaque board with spherical metal markers applied to it on both sides. The respective positions of the markers on the fluoroscopic images are identified through segmentation. In order to obtain the intrinsic parameters, a set of views of the calibration board at different poses is used. First the parameters are approximated by a closed-form solution which disregards lens distortion. Then the reprojection error is minimized using gradient descent yielding the final values for the intrinsic parameters.
The extrinsic parameters relating to the rotation R and translation T of the acquisition system are computed for different c-arm orientations. The c-arm orientation is described by two anatomical angles, cranio-caudal(a) and right/left anterior (β) and a translational adjustment between the source and the imaging object (Source to Image Distance, or SID). The SID and the a/β angles are measured in real time by sensors (Fig. 3). The extrinsic parameters of the c-arm are modeled as a function of a and β angles (Equation 4). Here, R_o is the rotational matrix describing the initial ($a=0$ and $\beta=0$) local camera frame with respect to the global coordinate frame. T_o is the initial ($a=0$ and $\beta=0$) translation of the center of projection in global reference frame coordinates. R_{ai} is the rotational transformation due to rotation of a_i about the resulting alpha axis. $R_{\beta i}$ is the rotational transformation due to rotation of β_i about the constant beta axis. It is assumed that both axes are orthogonal and intersect.

$$\begin{aligned} R &= R_o^{\ T} R_{\beta 2} R_{\alpha 2} R_{\beta 1}^{\ T} R_{\alpha 1}^{\ T} \\ T &= R_o^{\ T} (R_{\beta 2} R_{\alpha 2} - R_{\beta 1} R_{\alpha 1}) T_0 \end{aligned} \tag{4}$$

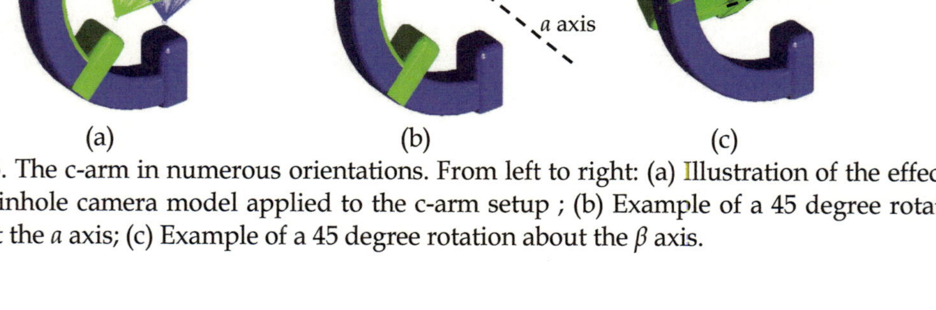

Fig. 3. The c-arm in numerous orientations. From left to right: (a) Illustration of the effect of the pinhole camera model applied to the c-arm setup ; (b) Example of a 45 degree rotation about the a axis; (c) Example of a 45 degree rotation about the β axis.

3.2 Fluoroscopic Image Processing

Image processing is performed on the fluoroscopic images to extract the necessary feature information for the 2D-3D registration process. The processing performed can be separated into two stages: segmentation (edge extraction) and key morphological feature extraction (femur shafts).

The main objective of the edge extraction technique is to identify object boundaries with sufficient continuity to be successfully employed in the proceeding pose estimation. Many of the classic first (Roberts, Prewitt, Sobel) and second (LOG) derivative based edge segmentation methodologies extract isolated edge pixels and do not provide continuous edge contours. The proposed edge extraction technique attempts to link sets of potential edge pixels to create continuous boundaries. It employs two tactics to achieve this: thresholding with hysteresis and edge relaxation.

Firstly, adaptive (local) hysteresis based thresholding is performed on the gradient image where the two threshold values are set to be the 50th and 75th percentile of gradient magnitude values in the local window. Adaptive thresholding adjusts the threshold level according to the intensity statistics of a local region. This technique is employed typically with X-ray/fluoroscopic images to counter the illumination gradients present on the radiographs.

Secondly, edge relaxation is performed through a region growing exercise. This region growing is conducted on the intermediate pixels (pixels that fall between the 50th and 75th percentile of gradient magnitude values) to ensure sufficient continuity of the edge contour. Edge relaxation involves the recursive re-labeling of intermediate pixels with one or more neighboring edge pixels, utilizing an eight neighboring connectivity scheme. In-order to be reclassified as a foreground edge pixel the difference of the magnitude and orientation of the intervening pixel with the surrounding edge pixels will be checked and has to be within a user specified tolerance level. Following the edge relaxation a small component elimination morphological operation is performed to remove all connected pixel components with too few pixels. This is a noise elimination step that will remove any misidentified edge contour pixels.

Following the edge extraction, further image processing is conducted to identify the femur edges that form the outer diameter of the shaft. A classical Hough transform is used to isolate these feature lines within the segmented fluoroscopic image. The classical Hough transform requires that the desired features be specified in some parametric form, and hence is ideal to be used for the detection of regular shapes such as lines. The main advantage of the Hough transform technique is that it is tolerant of gaps in feature boundary descriptions and is thus unaffected by slight image occlusions (Beutel, Kundel et al. 2000).

Once potential lines have been identified through the Hough transform they will be paired and classified as an outer edge or noise (Fig. 4). This classification is performed by utilizing data gathered by (Noble, Alexander et al. 1988) on the mean and variance of femur shaft cross sectional anthropometry. Thus line pairs that fall within a certain range (mean ± standard deviation) of the anthropometric measurements will be classified as a pair representing the outer diameter of the shaft. The edge contour image that will result following the segmentation and the extracted feature lines will provide the required input to the 2D-3D registration process as will be discussed in the proceeding section.

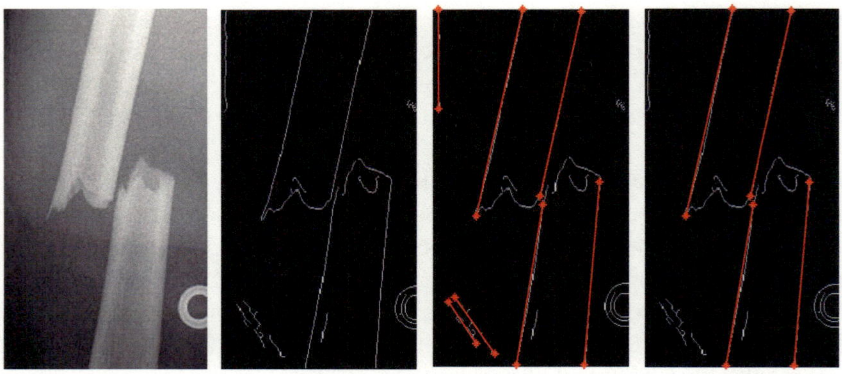

Fig. 4. An example of the segmentation and feature extraction operations that are performed on the radiographic images. From left to right: (a) Original image; (b) Segmented Image: Edge Extraction; (c) Feature lines identified through the Hough transform; (d) Paired shaft lines.

3.3 Extraction of Anatomical Surface Model

The patient-specific 3D anatomical bony structures required for the intra-operative registration are pre-operatively extracted from CT data. Bony anatomies appear as high intensity regions in the CT slice images. Reconstruction of 3D models from CT volumes consists of a two-step process. Firstly, an image slice segmentation is required for the extraction of the outer contours of the anatomical structures, and secondly, 3D reconstruction is performed by utilizing a surface triangulation technique such as the marching cubes algorithm (Kim, Kim et al. 2004; Momi, Motyl et al. 2005). Femoral contour extraction is a difficult process due to the variation in the bone intensity and the lack of a distinct joint space. The interior structure of the femur contains trabecular bone with a shell of cortical bone. The image intensity varies between these two bone structure types. Furthermore, weakly defined joint space around the femoral head and the pelvic bone also adds to the complexity of the contour extraction process.

Several techniques that appear in literature were considered to perform the segmentation and contour extraction. Atlas based segmentation techniques merge image segmentation with image registration (Beutel, Kundel et al. 2000). However, fractured bone segmentation is not possible through this technique. Region growing approaches can segment whole skeletal structures, but cannot separate individual bones (Beutel, Kundel et al. 2000). Thus a Level-Set based segmentation technique was developed to provide adequate flexibility to segment fractured bones while ensuring the ability to extract only femoral bone fragments of interest. Level-Set methods have been widely used in the fields of fluid mechanics and material sciences for some time and have recently been applied within the field of machine vision for segmentation problems (Li, Xu et al. 2005).

The principal idea behind level set methods is the definition of a static, evenly spaced mesh in an image or volume space. The values at each point on the mesh relate to the proximity of the mesh point to an evolving curve or surface with the level set of zero defining the location of the curve or surface. Mesh points contained within the evolving surface are given negative values and mesh points outside the surface are given positive values. An evolving speed function for the movement of the curve or surface is defined and mesh values are updated (from an initial value) using a discrete time finite element update as described in Equation 5. Let the moving interface be $\Gamma(t) t \in [0,1]$ and the level set function as $\phi(x) = \pm d$. Where d is the distance between the point **x** and $\Gamma(t)$, and the plus/minus sign is chosen depending on whether the point is outside/ inside the interface.

$$\phi_{t+1} + F|\nabla \phi_t| = 0 \tag{5}$$

In the above equation, F is the speed of the interface point along its normal direction. The moving interface evolves under the effect of F. It expands when F is positive, while it contracts when F is negative. When F is equal to zero, the interface stops and gives the segmentation result. The method implemented is a 3D level set which forms a single unconstrained 2D surface in 3D space. The formulation of the speed function is given in equation below. The speed function F controls the deformation of the interface.

$$F(x,y) = (F_0 \nabla \phi_{x,y} + F_c(x',y') \nabla \phi_{x',y'}) e^{-F_i(x',y')} \tag{6}$$

In the above equation $F(x,y)$ is the force at mesh point (x,y) and (x',y') is the nearest point on the zero level set to (x,y). F_o is the Advection Force term, F_c the Curvature Force term and F_i the Image Force term based on the Gaussian derivative filters.

The image force term F_i is based on a 1D Gaussian derivative filter orientated in the normal direction of the zero level set surface at the point of interest (x_0, y_0).

This filter is preferable over a simple edge detection such as a Sobel or Canny edge detector as its increased range means that less defined edges may be detected.

Level set methods have a high computational cost as the nearest point on the zero level set must be found for each mesh point. Narrow-band extensions to level set methods lower the computational cost of the algorithms by only updating the mesh in an area local to the zero level set. These methods require the mesh to be reinitialized every few time steps as the zero level set approaches the mesh points that have not been updated. This re-initialization is in itself computationally expensive, however the overall computational cost over time was reduced substantially using this method.

The narrow band update method was used in the implementation with a band range of 5 in plane voxel widths. It is useful to note that mesh values may be used to determine how close to the level set the mesh point is and whether it is inside or outside the level set, based on the sign. A relatively large time step is used in out implementation as smaller time steps do not appear to affect the final result and increase the computational cost. The Advection Force is set to unity.

Following the segmentation, a 3D triangulated surface may be formed from the mesh by iso-surfacing with the value zero using the 'Marching Cubes' algorithm (Kim, Kim et al. 2004; Momi, Motyl et al. 2005). This algorithm is based on examining each 8 adjacent points in the mesh and determining the triangulation required.

3.4 Pose Estimation

The proposed pose estimation framework employs the set of 2D fluoroscopic images and the 3D anatomical surface model, and identifies the transformation of the model so that its projections on the anterior and lateral planes match the acquired fluoroscopic images. This registration can be treated as determining the equivalent affine transformation which includes a set of translational (T_x, T_y, T_z), and rotational (R_x, R_y, R_z) parameters where the x, y and z axes are aligned with the frontal, lateral and axial axes of the bone segment. As illustrated in Fig. 5 the 2D-3D registration between a 2D projection image and 3D model is concerned with determination of the transformation T2D/3D such that the 3D to 2D projection fulfils the conditions defined above. The image to physical space registration (*T*) can be described as finding the geometrical transformation that determines the position of the imaged anatomy in the world coordinate system.

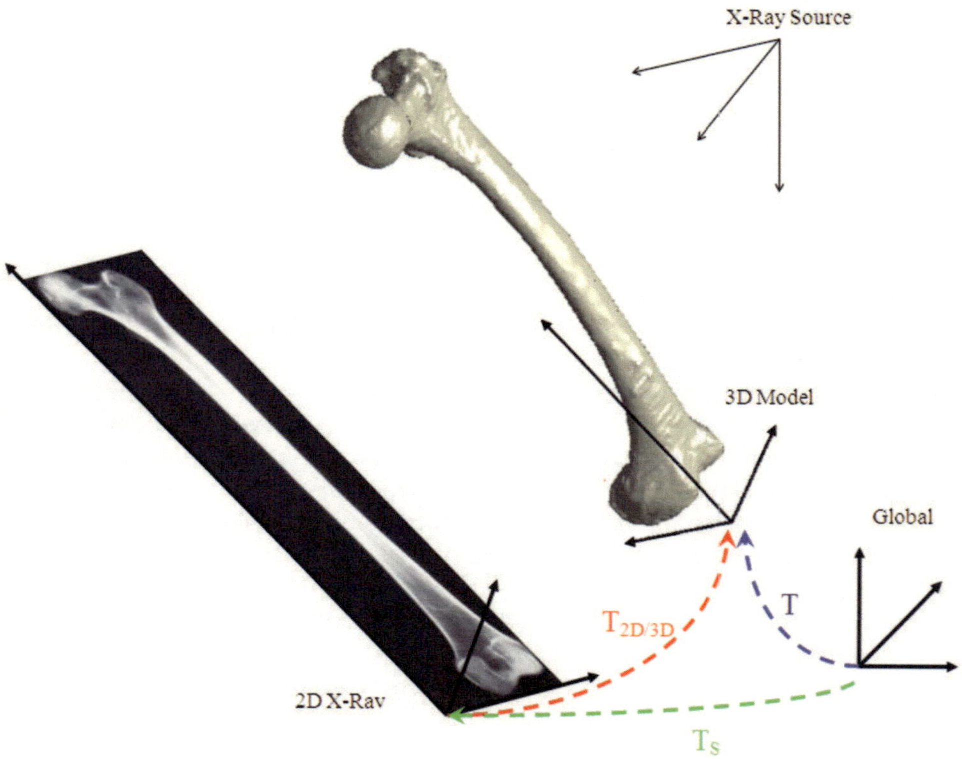

Fig. 5. 2D-3D registration ($T_{2D/3D}$) and 3D image to physical space registration (T). A pin-hole projection model is used here for illustrative purposes.

The frontal and lateral alignment is driven by the outer shaft lines identified through the fluoroscopic image processing. The inputs required for this alignment are the two 2D gradient directional vectors of the shaft in the frontal and lateral planes as well as two arbitrary points that lie anywhere on the mid shaft axis in those planes.

Firstly the mid shaft line is calculated by averaging the start and end points of the outer shaft lines in each plane (from which the required directional vectors and the arbitrary points are extracted). This mid shaft line is then projected perpendicular to the plane. The intersection of these perpendicular projections from the frontal and lateral planes will form the axis of rotations for a particular segment (Fig. 6). The gradient information of the mid shaft line is utilized to calculate the normal vectors of these projected planes by obtaining the cross product between the direction vectors of the mid shaft lines and the imaging plane normals. These normal vectors, $n_{frontal}$ and $n_{lateral}$ and the arbitrary points identified on the lines ($P_{frontal}$ and $P_{lateral}$) are used in Equation (7) to solve for the vector line equation of the shaft axis of rotation in 3D. This is accomplished by identifying a point that lie on the 3D axis of rotation (P_{axis}) as well as the direction vector of the axis (M_{axis}) as seen in Equation (7).

$$P_{axis} = \left(pinv(A)\right)\begin{bmatrix} n_{frontal}{}^{T} P_{frontal} \\ n_{lateral}{}^{T} P_{lateral} \end{bmatrix}, \quad M_{axis} = Null(A)$$
$$where \quad A = \begin{bmatrix} n_{frontal}{}^{T} \\ n_{lateral}{}^{T} \end{bmatrix} \tag{7}$$

Once the axis of rotation is identified for the target images, the model axis of rotation can then be aligned with it utilizing Equation (8). Here ${}^{model}T_{global}$ and ${}^{target}T_{global}$ are homogeneous transformation matrices which relate the local coordinate frames of the bone segments to a global coordinate frame. The z-axis of these local frames coincide with the axial rotation axis of the bone segments, while their origins are anchored on the corresponding feature points in the model and target bones. The final alignment transformation between the model and the target is then expressed as, ${}^{model}T_{target}$.

$${}^{model}T_{target} = {}^{model}T_{global}\left[{}^{target}T_{global}\right]^{-1}$$
$${}^{model}T_{target} = {}^{model}T_{global}\,{}^{global}T_{target} \tag{8}$$

It should be noted however that the axial alignment of the coordinate frames with respect to the bones may not be identical in both the model and the target. As a result, even after the application of the transformation obtained in Equation (8), a final adjustment of the axial rotation is still required to complete the pose estimation process. This axial alignment process is discussed in the proceeding section. Fig. 6 illustrates the various notations involved in the axis of rotation identification process. Fig. 7(a)/(b) illustrates the axial alignment process.

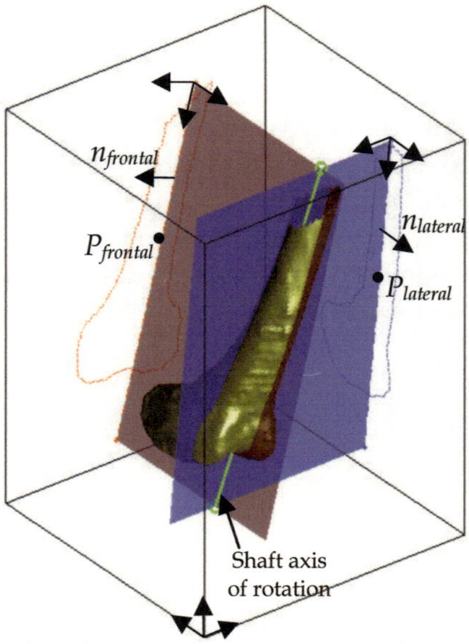

Fig. 6. The notations involved in the axis of rotation identification process for the frontal and lateral alignment.

Following the anterior and lateral pose estimation the axial rotational and translational alignment is conducted through an optimization based framework. The objective functions (similarity measure) proposed for this task is the summation of the Euclidean distance between each surface boundary contour point of the projections from the 3D surface model and the corresponding closest point on the edge contour identified on the fluoroscopic image. Fig. 7(b) illustrates the objective function for variations of angular axial rotations (R_z direction). The objective function posed through the similarity measure that is proposed can be classified as Nonlinear, Continuous, Unconstrained and Deterministic. Arguably the problem can be classified as a constrained optimization problem with constraints imposed on the possible transformations. However, these constraints will not play an essential role in the optimization and will only serve as general safety limitations and hence were excluded from the optimization process. Many algorithms for nonlinear optimization problems seek only a local solution, and do not always identify the global optima. The logical methodology to ensure the global convergence is to ensure that the problem is one of convex programming. For a convex function, global optimality is guaranteed by local optimality. The current objective function shown in Fig. 7(b) has the required convex shape (in the proximity of the optima). The simplex Nelder-Mead method (Lagarias, Reeds et al. 1998) was utilized to solve this multivariable optimization problem. The optimization process is run under two conditions that ensure successful convergence and timeliness. Firstly, a multi-resolution framework is employed that involves first searching for the solution from a highly sub-sampled projected contour and then refining the solution through a series of reductions to the sub-sampling. Secondly a variable step size based implementation is employed where the rotation and transformation steps start with large sizes and iteratively lessens in size as the algorithm nears its optimal solution.

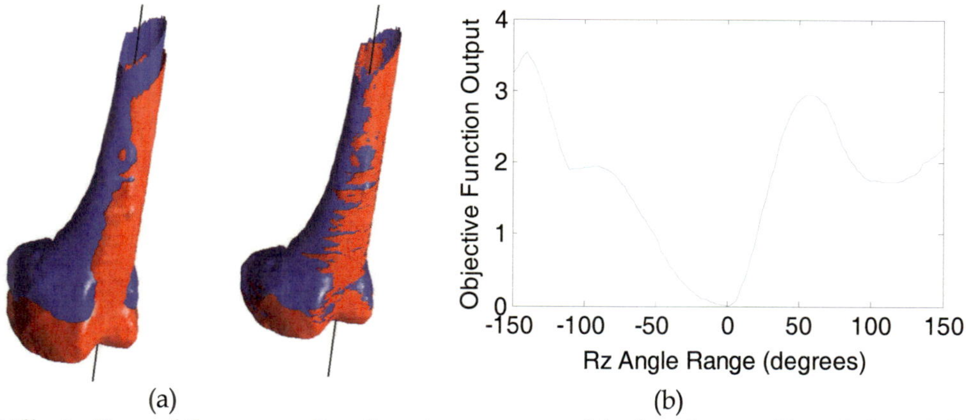

Fig. 7. Illustrations of the pose estimation stages proposed in this chapter. From left to right: (a) The axial alignment process, where the images show the before and after illustrations of aligning the model and target bones axially; (b) The objective function output for variation in the axial (R_z) direction. The registration used anterior and lateral target images acquired at the neutral position of R_z being set to zero.

4. Results

To test the pose estimation capabilities of the 2D-3D registration algorithm and the effectiveness of the proposed similarity measure (objective function) several phantom studies were conducted.

The first study involved a synthetically broken CT data set from which pairs of fluoroscopic images were acquired in the frontal and lateral planes. This acquisition was repeated for a series of poses of the CT data. Through this synthetic CT volume movements the authors were able to obtain highly realistic fluoroscopic images that were analogous to those obtained clinically on human subjects (Fig. 8). These acquired fluoroscopic images were next utilized in the testing phase where the 2D-3D registration was performed with a prebuilt 3D surface model of the fracture region. This 3D model was acquired from the CT data set and was initialized manually. Fig. 8 illustrates a few qualitative results of the tests performed. Moreover, Table 1 indicates the absolute average difference between the actual and identified rotations/translations through the 2D-3D registration process.

Digitally Reconstructed Radiographs (DRRs) simulating the fluoroscopic images were created from the CT dataset utilizing ray-casting. This technique initially constructed rays between points on the imaging plane and the imaging source and then the individual intensity values of the DRR images were computed by summing up the attenuation coefficients associated with each voxel along a particular ray in the CT data.

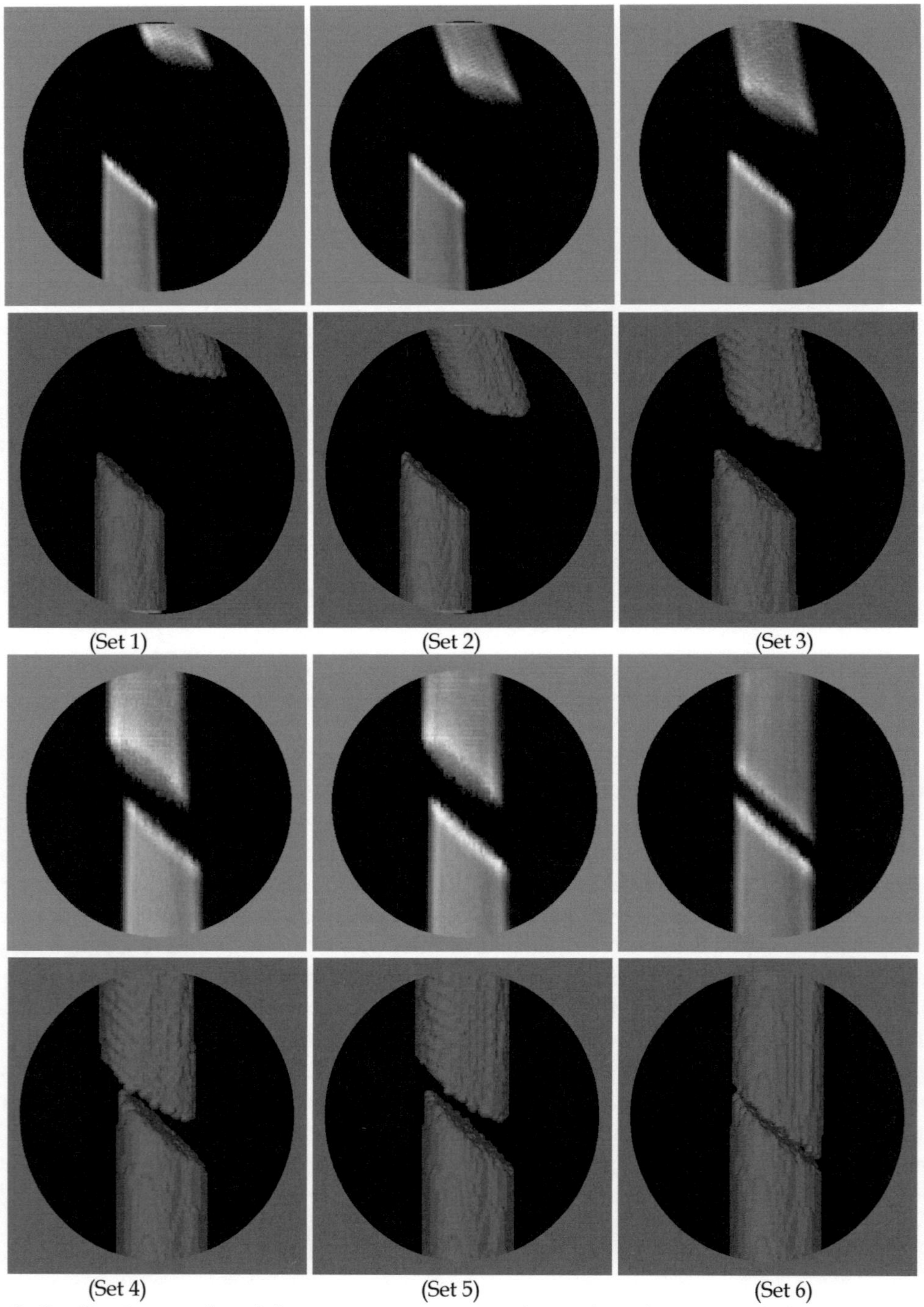

Fig. 8. Qualitative results of the pose estimation performed on the series of phantom fracture reduction fluoroscopic images (Study 1). Each set of paired images represents a pose that was estimated through the 2D-3D Registration algorithm. The top image of each set is the frontal fluoroscopic image generated while the bottom is the registered 3D bone fragments overlaid on the fluoroscopic images.

The results in Table 1 convey that the registration was performed at sub-degree and sub-mm accuracy and with highly robust repeatability. This is in line with the accuracy requirements for image guidance required during present orthopedic femur fracture reduction procedures.

The second study was performed with a distal fragment of an artificially fractured plastic bone (Fig. 9). The fragment was attached to a Stewart platform and moved through a series of rotations in the Rx, Ry and Rz direction. Fluoroscopic imaging was emulated through a USB camera mounted on a rotary arm (similar to a fluoroscopy c-arm). Even though the effects of variation of X-ray absorption in tissues such as muscle, fat, and skin cannot be simulated with this test setup, effort was made to closely match the actual clinical process steps undertaken. The proposed pose estimation technique was applied to this test setup and 20 iterations of the same test were conducted (Fig. 10). The average absolute mean R_x error was 0.567 degrees, R_y error was 0.487 degrees and the R_z error was 0.604 degrees. The standard deviation of errors was 0.098 degrees. The results further convey that the registration can be performed at sub-degree accuracy.

Pose Iteration	Rotational Registration Average Error (Degrees)	Translational Registration Average Error (mm)
1	0.965	1.056
2	0.710	0.981
3	0.862	1.198
4	0.997	0.912
5	1.069	0.896
6	1.159	1.287

Table 1. 2D-3D registration results for Study 1.

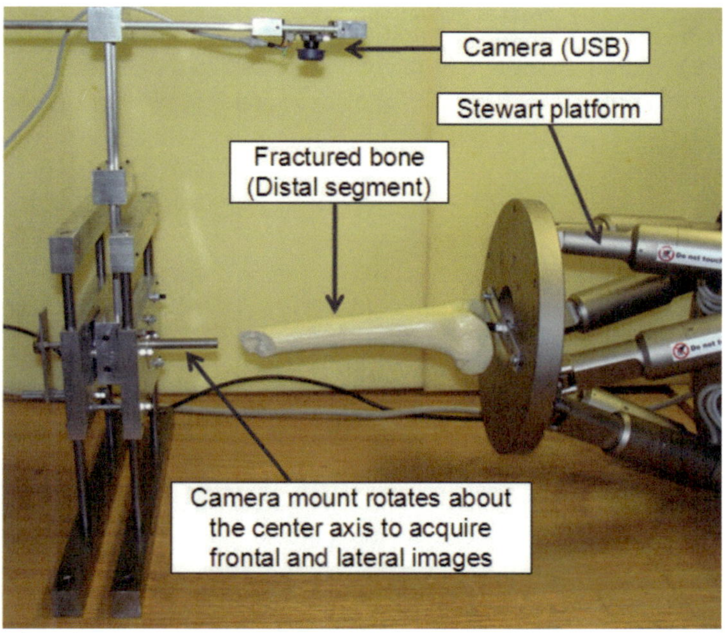

Fig. 9. The test rig setup.

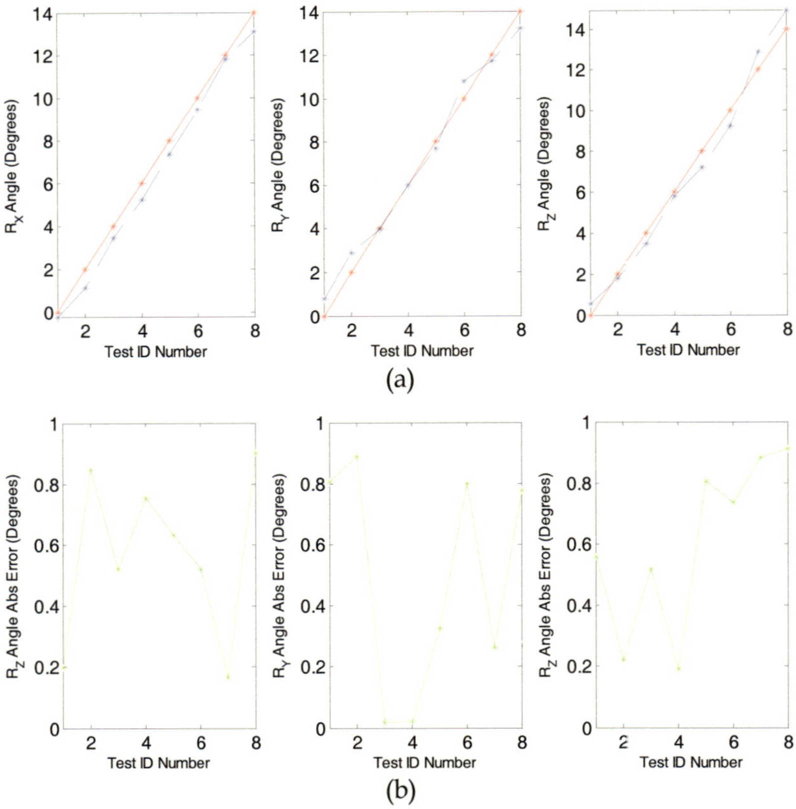

Fig. 10. Results obtained with the Stewart platform tests. From top to bottom: (a) Results obtained in the frontal (R_x) lateral (R_y) and axial (R_z) directions. The red lines indicate the rotation of the Stewart platform, while the blue lines indicate the identified rotation in the R_x, R_y and R_z directions respectively; (b) The corresponding absolute registration error in degrees.

5. Conclusion

The results indicate that the pose estimation framework discussed in this chapter is able to identify the orientation of femur shaft fracture segments in 3D with acceptable accuracies, from 2D orthogonal views. The registration was performed at sub-degree accuracy with successful repeatability. Future testing will be conducted by the authors with the aid of actual intra-operatively obtained fluoroscopic images. The authors are also exploring techniques to further augment the pose estimation performed through the 2D-3D registration. One such measure includes skin based markers that may be employed to identify the axial misalignment between the proximal and distal segments. This axial alignment has been identified as one of the vital requirements for clinically successful fracture reduction surgery.

6. References

Besl, P. J. and N. D. McKay. (1992). "A method for registration of 3-D shapes." IEEE Transactions on pattern analysis and machine intelligence **14**(2): 239-256.

Beutel, J., H. L. Kundel, et al., Eds. (2000). Handbook of Medical Imaging. Bellingham, SPIE Press.

Bollet, M. A., H. A. Mcnair, et al. (2003). "Can Digitally Reconstructed Radiographs (DRRS) Replace Simulation Films in Prostate Cancer Conformal Radiotheraphy?" Int. J. Radiation Oncology Biol. Phys **57**(4): 1122–1130.

Cure-Research. (2004). "http://www.cureresearch.com/f/fractured_femur/stats-country.htm." Fracture Statistics.

Gamage, P., S. Q. Xie, et al. (2008). Intra-Operative 3D Pose Estimation of Fractured Bone Segments for Image Guided Orthopedic Surgery. IEEE International Conference on Robotics and Biomimetics. Bangkok, IEEE.

Graham, A. E. and S. Q. Xie (2007). Robotic Long Bone Fracture Reduction. Medical Robotics. V. Bozovic, i-Tech Education and Publishing: 85-102.

Hüfner, T., R. Meller, et al. (2005). "The role of navigation in knee surgery and evaluation of three-dimensional knee kinematics." Oper. Tech. Orthop. **15**: 64–69.

Joskowicz L, Milgrom C, et al. (1998). "FRACAS: A System for Computer-Aided Image-Guided Long Bone Fracture Surgery." Comp Aid Surg: 271–288.

Kim, Y. H., J. K. Kim, et al. (2004). "Three-dimensional reconstruction of human femur using consecutive computer tomography images and simulated implantation system." Med. Eng. Technol **28**: 205–210.

Lagarias, J. C., J. A. Reeds, et al. (1998). "Convergence Properties of the Nelder-Mead Simplex Method in Low Dimensions." SIAM Journal of Optimization **9**(1): 112-147.

LaRose, D., J. Bayouth, et al. (2000). Transgraph: Interactive intensity-based 2D/3D registration of X-ray and CT data. Proceedings of SPIE - The International Society for Optical Engineering, Society of Photo-Optical Instrumentation Engineers.

LaRose, D., L. Cassenti, et al. (2000). Postoperative measurements of acetabular Cup Position Using X-Ray/CT registration. MICCAI.

Lavallee, S., R. Szeliski, et al. (1995). Anatomy-Based Registration of Three Dimensional Medical Images, Range Images, X-Ray Projections, and Three Dimensional Models Using Octree-Splines. Computer-integrated surgery, technology and clinical applications. R. H. Taylor: 115-144.

Li, C., C. Xu, et al. (2005). Level Set Evolution Without Re-initialization: A New Variational Formulation. Proceedings of the 2005 IEEE Computer Society Conference on Computer Vision and Pattern Recognition (CVPR'05).

Livyatan, H., Z. Yaniv, et al. (2003). "Gradient-Based 2-D/3-D Rigid Registration of Fluoroscopic X-Ray to CT." IEEE Transactions on Medical Imaging **22**(11): 1395-1406.

Miyamoto, S., M. Sugiura, et al. (2003). "Development of Minimally Invasive Surgery Systems." Hitachi Review **52** (4): 189-195.

Momi, E. D., B. Motyl, et al. (2005). Hip joint anatomy virtual and stereolithographic reconstruction for preoperative planning of total hip replacement. Proceedings of CARS 2005 International Congress Series Elsevier

Noble, P. C., J. W. Alexander, et al. (1988). "The Anatomic Basis of Femoral Component Design." Clinical Orthopaedics and Related Research **235**: 148-165.

Penney, G. P., P. G. Batchelor, et al. (2001). "Validation of a 2D to 3D registration algorithm for aligning preoperative CT images and intraoperative fluoroscopy images." Med. Phys. **28**(6).

Penney, G. P., J. Weese, et al. (1998). "A Comparison of Similarity Measures for Use in 2D-3D Medical Image Registration " IEEE Transactions on Medical Imaging **17**(4): 586-595.

Penny, G. P. (1999). Registration of Tomographic Images to X-ray Projections for Use in Image Guided Interventions. London, University of London. **PhD**.

Rohlfing, T. and C. R. Maurer (2002). A novel image similarity measure for registration of 3-D MR images and X-ray projection images. Medical Image Computing and Computer Assisted Intervention Conf.

Taylor, R. H., B. D. Mittelstadt, et al. (1994). "An image-directed robotic system for precise orthopedic surgery." IEEE Trans. Robot. Automat. **10**: 261–275.

Tomaževic, D. (2002). 2D-3D Registration of Medical Images. Faculty of Electrical Engineering. Ljubljana, University of Ljubljana.

Tomaževic, D., B. Likar, et al. (2003). "3-D/2-D Registration of CT and MR to X-Ray Images." IEEE Transactions on Medical Imaging **22**: 1407 - 1416.

Tsai, R. (1987). "A versatile camera calibration technique for high-accuracy 3D machine vision metrology using off-the-shelf TV cameras and lenses." IEEE Journal in Robotics and Automation **RA-3**(4): 323-344.

Westphal R, Winkelbach S, et al. (2007). Telemanipulated Long Bone Fracture Reduction.

Westphal, R., S. Winkelbach, et al. (2007). Telemanipulated Long Bone Fracture Reduction.

Zollei, L. (2001). 2D-3D Rigid-Body Registration of X-Ray Fluoroscopy and CT Images. Electrical Engineering and Computer Science. Massachusetts, Massachusetts Institute of Technology. **Masters**.

Zollei, L., W. E. L. Grimson, et al. (2001). 2D-3D rigid registration of X-ray fluoroscopy and CT images using mutual information and sparsely sampled histogram estimators. IEEE Computer Vision and Pattern Recognition Conf.

8

Navigation and Control of Mobile Robot Using Sensor Fusion

Yong Liu
CareFusion
United States of America

1. Introduction

Mobile robot, especially wheeled mobile robot, with its simple mechanical structure and inherent agility, has attracted significant attentions for dynamic environment applications in the last two decades (Pin et al. 1994 and Purwin 2006).
A general mobile robot Guidance, Navigation and Control (GNC) system is illustrated in the following figure. The main function of guidance system is to generate a feasible trajectory command, usually in multiple dimension of freedom (DOF) to achieve a robot task. The objective of control system is to drive the mobile robot following the commanded trajectory with acceptable tracking errors and stability margin. The function of robot navigation system is to provide accurate position, velocity and/or orientation information for the control system and guidance system. A stable and accurate navigation system is the bridge between the guidance system and control system of mobile robots, which ultimately determines the robot performance.

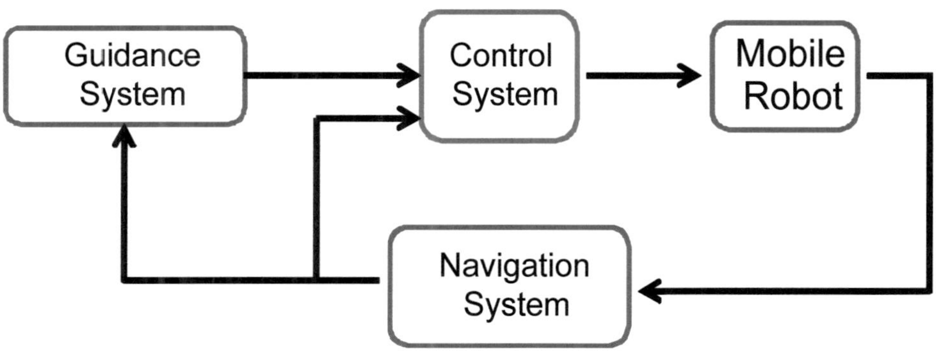

Fig. 1. Mobile Robot GNC System

2. Mobile Robot Navigation System

Mobile robot navigation system, also known as robot positioning system, is to measure the robot's position and/or orientation. On mobile robot, many different sensors and navigation system structures are available (Borenstein et al. 1996).

In mobile robot navigation systems, onboard navigation sensors based on dead-reckoning are widely installed. This type of sensors include various odometry encoder, and inertial navigation system, such as accelerometer and gyroscope. These sensors measure the robot translational and rotational velocity or acceleration rates. By integrating sensor measurements, the position and orientation of mobile robot are estimated, which is known as dead-reckoning. Onboard navigation sensors are usually low-cost with high bandwidth and high sampling rate. Dead-reckoning method is well known suitable for short-term navigation. The advantages of these onboard sensors is that they are totally self-contained. The recent advance on inertial navigation system makes most onboard sensors attractive and affordable. However, the onboard sensors usually have inevitable accumulated errors due to the nature of dead-reckoning process. Onboard sensors require an external reference for continuous calibration.
Many mobile robots are also installed with external absolute position sensors. These sensors include cameras, global positioning system (GPS), infrared radar, active Beacons and artificial landmark recognition. They sense the absolute position and orientation of the robot without drifting. The external sensors are usually working at low bandwidth and sampling rate. The built-in signal processing of these sensors may introduce delay and outlier measurements. If using merely external positioning sensor, the delay and failures of signal processing may lead to a deteriorated performance of robot control system. In mobile robot, vision system is a typical external positioning sensor. By using image processing algorithm, a vision system is able to detect the position or velocity of a mobile robot.
Sensor fusion is a useful technique to combines both types of positioning sensors to provide fast measurement without drifting (Goel et al. 1999).
The main technical challenge of sensor fusion on mobile robot is that robot kinematics is a nonlinear process; therefore the traditional Kalman filter based technique has to be adapted to address the nonlinearity in the system. The sensor fusion system also has to eliminate potential outlier measurement from external sensor and compensate for the different sampling rate between external sensors and onboard sensors.
When using a sensor fusion technique in mobile robot navigation, it should be noted that the fusion process and control system dynamics interact. Additional theoretical analysis and practical consideration should be taken to ensure the stability of the overall navigation and control system.

3. Sensor Fusion for Robot Navigation and Control

3.1 Robot Kinematics and Navigation Equation

Mobile robot dynamics are usually described in two coordinate frames: the body frame {B} and the world frame {W}. The body frame is fixed on the moving robot, usually with the origin at the center of mass. The world frame is fixed on the field. Figure 2 illustrate the the relationship of the two frames.
The kinematics of the robot is given by a coordinate transformation from the body frame {B}to the world frame {W}

$$\begin{bmatrix} \dot{x} \\ \dot{y} \\ \dot{\Psi} \end{bmatrix} = \begin{bmatrix} \cos\Psi(t) & -\sin\Psi(t) & 0 \\ \sin\Psi(t) & \cos\Psi(t) & 0 \\ 0 & 0 & 1 \end{bmatrix} \begin{bmatrix} u \\ v \\ r \end{bmatrix} \tag{1}$$

where x and y denote the robot location in {W}, Ψ denotes the robot orientation in {W}, u and v are the robot translational velocity in {B}, and r is the robot rotation angular velocity in {B}. Velocity u, v and r are also called body rate.

In order to formulate the robot navigation system with sensor fusion, the robot kinematics (1) are first approximated by using forward Euler method

$$\begin{bmatrix} x_k \\ y_k \\ \Psi_k \end{bmatrix} = \begin{bmatrix} x_{k-1} \\ y_{k-1} \\ \Psi_{k-1} \end{bmatrix} + \begin{bmatrix} \cos\Psi_{k-1} \cdot T & -\sin\Psi_{k-1} \cdot T & 0 \\ \sin\Psi_{k-1} \cdot T & \cos\Psi_{k-1} \cdot T & 0 \\ 0 & 0 & T \end{bmatrix} \begin{bmatrix} u_{k-1} \\ v_{k-1} \\ r_{k-1} \end{bmatrix} \tag{2}$$

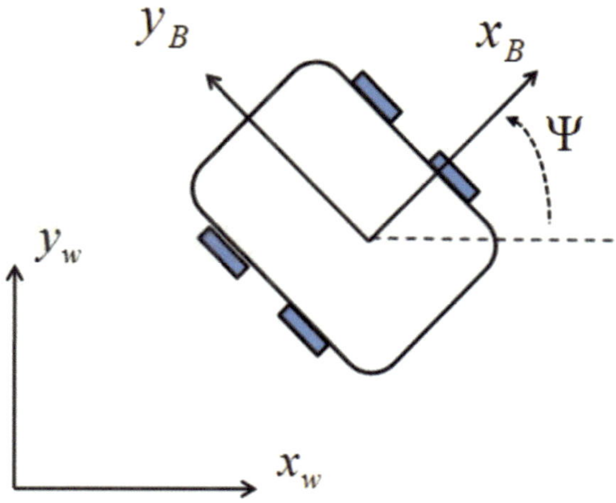

(a) World frame$\{W\}$ (b) Body frame$\{B\}$

Fig. 2. Mobile Robot Coordinate Frames

where T is the sampling time and k denotes the sampling tick. Equation (2) is a first order approximation of robot kinematics. In this Chapter, it is called navigation equation. The navigation system analysis and design are based on Equation (2). It should be noted that higher order approximation is also available and the sensor fusion method described in this chapter can be applied with minor changes.

In this chapter, without loss of generality, it is assuming that the body rate measurement is from onboard sensors; and the robot position and orientation is from an external absolute positioning sensor, such as a vision system. By defining $\begin{bmatrix} \hat{u}_k & \hat{v}_k & \hat{r}_k \end{bmatrix}^T$ as the body rate measurement, $\begin{bmatrix} w_{1k} & w_{2k} & w_{3k} \end{bmatrix}^T$ as the body rate measurement noise,the body rate measurement model is described as

$$\begin{bmatrix} \hat{u}_k & \hat{v}_k & \hat{r}_k \end{bmatrix}^T = \begin{bmatrix} u_k & v_k & r_k \end{bmatrix}^T + [w_{1,k}, w_{2,k}, w_{3,k}]^T \tag{3}$$

By defining $\begin{bmatrix} z_{1,k} & z_{2,k} & z_{3,k} \end{bmatrix}^T$ as position and orientation measurements by external absolute position sensor, and $\begin{bmatrix} d_{1,k} & d_{2,k} & d_{3,k} \end{bmatrix}^T$ as vision system measurement noise, the vision system measurement model is described as

$$\begin{bmatrix} z_{1,k} \\ z_{2,k} \\ z_{3,k} \end{bmatrix} = \begin{bmatrix} x_k \\ y_k \\ \Psi_k \end{bmatrix} + \begin{bmatrix} d_{1,k} \\ d_{2,k} \\ d_{3,k} \end{bmatrix} \tag{4}$$

Both $\begin{bmatrix} w_{1,k} & w_{2,k} & w_{3,k} \end{bmatrix}^T$ and $\begin{bmatrix} d_{1,k} & d_{2,k} & d_{3,k} \end{bmatrix}^T$ are assumed to be zero-mean white noise with normal distribution, such that

$$p\left(\begin{bmatrix} w_{1,k} & w_{2,k} & w_{3,k} \end{bmatrix}^T\right) \sim N\left(0, Q_k\right)$$
$$p\left(\begin{bmatrix} d_{1,k} & d_{2,k} & d_{3,k} \end{bmatrix}^T\right) \sim N\left(0, R_k\right)$$

where $Q_k \in \mathbb{R}^{3\times3}$ is the body rate measurement noise covariance, and $R_k \in \mathbb{R}^{3\times3}$ is the vision system observation noise covariance.

3.2 Kalman Filter and Its Variations

Kalman filter is an optimal filter design for a class of discrete-time linear stochastic system (Kalman 1960 and Welch et al. 2001). Kalman filter and its various adapted formulas are widely employed in sensor fusion (Hall et al. 2004). The standard Kalman filter is for linear dynamic system with Gaussian noise distribution. In this subsection, the Kalman filter algorithm is briefly reviewed to facilitate deriving the mobile robot sensor fusion filter algorithm. A general discrete-time linear stochastic system is described as

$$X_k = AX_{k-1} + BU_{k-1} + w_{k-1} \tag{5}$$

where $X \in \mathbb{R}^n$ is the system state and $w \in \mathbb{R}^n$ is the process noise. The goal of Kalman filter is to estimate the best X_k by a noisy measurement $Z \in \mathbb{R}^m$, where

$$Z_k = HX_k + d_k \tag{6}$$

d_k represents the measurement noise. The process noise and measurement are usually assumed independent, white with normal distribution

$$p\left(w\right) \sim N\left(0, Q\right)$$
$$p\left(d\right) \sim N\left(0, R\right)$$

The Kalman filter consists of two steps: prediction and correction
(1) Prediction

$$\begin{aligned} \hat{X}_k^- &= A\hat{X}_{k-1} + BU_{k-1} \\ P_k^- &= AP_{k-1}A^T + Q \end{aligned} \tag{7}$$

(2) Correction

$$\begin{aligned} K_k &= P_k^- H^T \left(HP_k^- H^T + R\right)^{-1} \\ \hat{X}_k &= \hat{X}_k^- + K_k\left(z_k - H\hat{X}_k^-\right) \\ P_k &= \left(I - K_k H\right) P_k^- \end{aligned} \tag{8}$$

In the above formula, $\hat{X}_k^-$ is referred as a priori estimate of the true state X_k and $\hat{X}_k$ is referred as a posteriori estimate.
For nonlinear systems, the process matrices A, B and H are not constant. In practice, they are usually derived by linearizing the nonlinear model along some nominal trajectories, which results in time-varying matrices. Techniques such as linearized Kalman filter, extended Kalman filter, unscented Kalman filter and Particle filter have been developed and applied successfully in many practical applications(Brown et al. 1996). Both linearized Kalman filter and extended Kalman filter (EKF) extend standard Kalman filter by linearizing the original nonlinear system (Brown et al. 1996). In a linearzed Kalman filter, linearization is along a predefined trajectory.

The disadvantage of linearized Kalman filter is that the dynamic system state may diverge from the predefined trajectory over time. Linearized Kalman filter is usually used in short-time mission. In EKF, the linearization is about the state estimation. Thus there is a danger that error propagation and filter divergence may occur. To overcome such a disadvantage, unscented Kalman filter (UKF) and particle filters (PFs) are developed. In UKF, the state distribution is approximated by Gaussian Random Variable (GRV) and is represented using a set of carefully chosen sample points (Richard et al. 1983). Particle filters (PFs) are a group of optimal and suboptimal Bayesian estimation algorithms for nonlinear and non Gaussian system (Arulampalam et al. 2001). PFs employ sequential Monte Carlo methods based on particle representations of state probability densities. UKF and PFs require much larger computational power to implement, compared to linearized Kalman filter and EKF.

3.3 Nonlinear Kalman Filter for Mobile Robot Navigation and Control System

In this subsection, the sensor fusion for mobile robot is illustrated using the framework of nonlinear Kalman filter.

First, the navigation equation of mobile robot is rewritten in the canonical formular for Kalman Filter.

$$\begin{bmatrix} x_k \\ y_k \\ \Psi_k \end{bmatrix} = \begin{bmatrix} cos(\Psi_{k-1}) \cdot T & -sin(\Psi_{k-1}) \cdot T & 0 \\ sin(\Psi_{k-1}) \cdot T & cos(\Psi_{k-1}) \cdot T & 0 \\ 0 & 0 & 1 \cdot T \end{bmatrix} \begin{bmatrix} u_{k-1} \\ v_{k-1} \\ r_{k-1} \end{bmatrix} + \begin{bmatrix} x_{k-1} \\ y_{k-1} \\ \Psi_{k-1} \end{bmatrix} + \begin{bmatrix} cos(\Psi_{k-1}) \cdot T & -sin(\Psi_{k-1}) \cdot T & 0 \\ sin(\Psi_{k-1}) \cdot T & cos(\Psi_{k-1}) \cdot T & 0 \\ 0 & 0 & 1 \cdot T \end{bmatrix} \begin{bmatrix} w_{1,k-1} \\ w_{2,k-1} \\ w_{3,k-1} \end{bmatrix} \tag{9}$$

The external sensor observation is represented by

$$\begin{bmatrix} z_{1,k} \\ z_{2,k} \\ z_{3,k} \end{bmatrix} = H_k \cdot \begin{bmatrix} x_k \\ y_k \\ \Psi_k \end{bmatrix} + \begin{bmatrix} d_{1,k} \\ d_{2,k} \\ d_{3,k} \end{bmatrix}, \text{ where } H_k = \begin{bmatrix} 1 & 0 & 0 \\ 0 & 1 & 0 \\ 0 & 0 & 1 \end{bmatrix} \tag{10}$$

The sensor fusion for mobile robot navigation is to calculate an optimal estimate of $\begin{bmatrix} x_k & y_k & \Psi_k \end{bmatrix}^T$,from the onboard measurement $\begin{bmatrix} \hat{u}_k & \hat{v}_k & \hat{r}_k \end{bmatrix}^T$ and external sensor reading $\begin{bmatrix} z_{1,k} & z_{2,k} & z_{3,k} \end{bmatrix}^T$. It should be noted that equation (9) is a linear process if either the robot is stationary or does not rotate. In either cases, standard linear Kalman filter can be applied. For multiple DOF motion, equation (9) is a nonlinear process.

Define $\begin{bmatrix} \hat{x}_k & \hat{y}_k & \hat{\Psi}_k \end{bmatrix}^T$ as estimated robot location, then the projected robot location using onboard sensor measurement is

$$\begin{bmatrix} x_k^- \\ y_k^- \\ \Psi_k^- \end{bmatrix} = \begin{bmatrix} cos(\hat{\Psi}_{k-1}) \cdot T & -sin(\hat{\Psi}_{k-1}) \cdot T & 0 \\ sin(\hat{\Psi}_{k-1}) \cdot T & cos(\hat{\Psi}_{k-1}) \cdot T & 0 \\ 0 & 0 & 1 \cdot T \end{bmatrix} \begin{bmatrix} \hat{u}_{k-1} \\ \hat{v}_{k-1} \\ \hat{r}_{k-1} \end{bmatrix} + \begin{bmatrix} \hat{x}_{k-1} \\ \hat{y}_{k-1} \\ \hat{\Psi}_{k-1} \end{bmatrix} \tag{11}$$

where $\begin{bmatrix} x_k^- & y_k^- & \Psi_k^- \end{bmatrix}$is the location a priori prediction from on-board sensor.

Then the predicted external sensor observation is

$$\begin{bmatrix} z_{1,k}^- \\ z_{2,k}^- \\ z_{3,k}^- \end{bmatrix} = H_k \cdot \begin{bmatrix} x_k^- \\ y_k^- \\ \Psi_k^- \end{bmatrix} = \begin{bmatrix} x_k^- \\ y_k^- \\ \Psi_k^- \end{bmatrix} \tag{12}$$

Define prediction error and observation error as

$$\begin{bmatrix} e_{x_k} \\ e_{y_k} \\ e_{\Psi_k} \end{bmatrix} = \begin{bmatrix} x_k^- \\ y_k^- \\ \Psi_k^- \end{bmatrix} - \begin{bmatrix} x_k \\ y_k \\ \Psi_k \end{bmatrix} \tag{13}$$

$$\begin{bmatrix} e_{z_{1,k}} \\ e_{z_{2,k}} \\ e_{z_{3,k}} \end{bmatrix} = \begin{bmatrix} z_{1,k}^- \\ z_{2,k}^- \\ z_{3,k}^- \end{bmatrix} - \begin{bmatrix} z_{1,k} \\ z_{2,k} \\ z_{3,k} \end{bmatrix} \tag{14}$$

By linearizing equation (11) and along $\begin{bmatrix} x_k & y_k & \Psi_k \end{bmatrix}^T$, the prediction error dynamics are

$$\begin{bmatrix} e_{x_k} \\ e_{y_k} \\ e_{\Psi_k} \end{bmatrix} = \begin{bmatrix} 1 & 0 & -\sin(\overline{\Psi}_{k-1}) \cdot \overline{u}_{k-1} \cdot T - \cos(\overline{\Psi}_{k-1}) \cdot \overline{v}_{k-1} \cdot T \\ 0 & 1 & \cos(\overline{\Psi}_{k-1}) \cdot \overline{u}_{k-1} \cdot T - \sin(\overline{\Psi}_{k-1}) \cdot \overline{v}_{k-1} \cdot T \\ 0 & 0 & 1 \end{bmatrix} \cdot \left(\begin{bmatrix} \hat{x}_{k-1} \\ \hat{y}_{k-1} \\ \hat{\Psi}_{k-1} \end{bmatrix} - \begin{bmatrix} x_{k\text{-}1} \\ y_{k\text{-}1} \\ \Psi_{k\text{-}1} \end{bmatrix} \right)$$
$$+ \begin{bmatrix} cos(\Psi_{k-1}) \cdot T & -sin(\Psi_{k-1}) \cdot T & 0 \\ sin(\Psi_{k-1}) \cdot T & cos(\Psi_{k-1}) \cdot T & 0 \\ 0 & 0 & 1 \cdot T \end{bmatrix} \cdot \begin{bmatrix} w_{1,k-1} \\ w_{2,k-1} \\ w_{3,k-1} \end{bmatrix} \tag{15}$$

The observation error is

$$\begin{bmatrix} e_{z_{1,k}} \\ e_{z_{2,k}} \\ e_{z_{3,k}} \end{bmatrix} = H_k \cdot \begin{bmatrix} e_{x_k} \\ e_{y_k} \\ e_{\Psi_k} \end{bmatrix} + \begin{bmatrix} d_{1,k} \\ d_{2,k} \\ d_{3,k} \end{bmatrix} \tag{16}$$

Equation (15) and (16) are linear. However, in Equation (15), the real position $[x_{k-1}\, y_{k-1}\, \Psi_{k-1}]^T$ are unknown. One option is to employ extended Kalman filter, in which the $[x_{k-1}\, y_{k-1} \Psi_{k-1}]^T$ in Equation (15) is replaced by the filter estimate $\begin{bmatrix} \hat{x}_k & \hat{y}_k & \hat{\Psi}_k \end{bmatrix}^T$. Note that the filter output $\begin{bmatrix} \hat{x}_k & \hat{y}_k & \hat{\Psi}_k \end{bmatrix}^T$ is fed back to the process, which renders the filter process into a nonlinear process. It is well known that such a structure may introduce instability. The convergence of extended Kalman filter has been recently proven for a class of nonlinear systems given a small initial estimation error (Krener, 2003). In (Chenavier, 1992), experimental result were demonstrated for mobile robot location sensor fusion based on EKF.

In mobile robot GNC system, the navigation system is coupled with control system. Therefore, additional concerns have to be taken to guarantee the stability of the coupled system. Kalman filter in Navigation system, in certain degree, can be considered as an observer for the control system. Therefore, observer design theory can be used to analyze the interaction and stability of both systems. In general, the navigation system is required to converge faster than the control system.

Another option is to integrate the navigation system and control system together (Liu, et al. 2007). The structure of integrated approach is similar to linearized Kalman filter, as shown in Figure 3.

In this structure, the nominal system trajectory generated by the control system is used to linearize Equation (15). The nominal trajectory is essentially the filtered position and orientation commands. The filter dynamics are a time-varying linear system instead of a nonlinear system. The integrated control and navigation structure is motivated by TLC observer design (Huang et al. 2003). The stability of the coupled control system and navigation system can be analyzed within the framework of trajectory linearization observer design using linear time-varying system theory. In this structure, the controller drives the robot to follow the nominal trajectory (command). Thus the divergence problem in the linearized Kalman filter is alleviated. The stability of the filter and controller are guaranteed locally around the commanded trajectory. The system stability is guaranteed given a small initial tracking error and a small initial filter observation error. One advantage of such a structure is the computational efficiency.

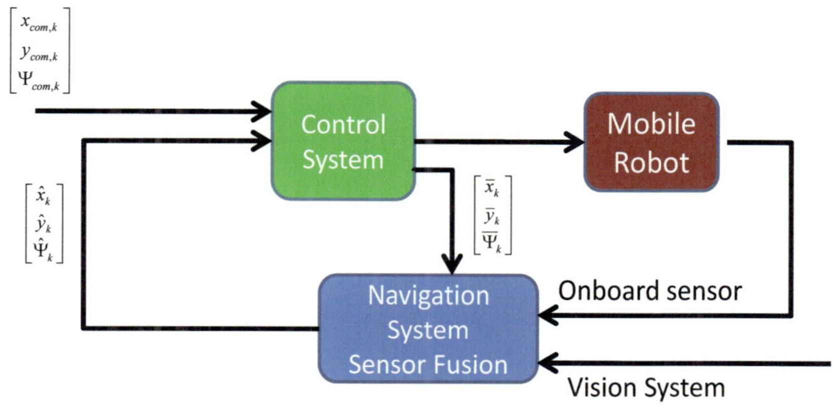

Fig. 3. Integrated navigation and control system for mobile robot

The overall navigation and control system algorithm is illustrated below

Step 1:

Read robot command trajectory $\begin{bmatrix} x_{com,k} & y_{com,k} & \Psi_{com,k} \end{bmatrix}^T$ and calculate the nominal trajectory $\begin{bmatrix} \bar{x}_k & \bar{y}_k & \bar{\Psi}_k \end{bmatrix}^T$

Read onboard sensor measurement and estimate robot position and orientation

$$\begin{bmatrix} x_k^- \\ y_k^- \\ \Psi_k^- \end{bmatrix} = \begin{bmatrix} \hat{x}_{k-1} \\ \hat{y}_{k-1} \\ \hat{\Psi}_{k-1} \end{bmatrix} + \begin{bmatrix} \cos(\hat{\Psi}_{k-1}) \cdot T & -\sin(\hat{\Psi}_{k-1}) \cdot T & 0 \\ \sin(\hat{\Psi}_{k-1}) \cdot T & \cos(\hat{\Psi}_{k-1}) \cdot T & 0 \\ 0 & 0 & 1 \cdot T \end{bmatrix} \begin{bmatrix} \hat{u}_{k-1} \\ \hat{v}_{k-1} \\ \hat{r}_{k-1} \end{bmatrix} \tag{17}$$

Calculate the time-varying matrices

$$A_k = \begin{bmatrix} 1 & 0 & -\sin(\bar{\Psi}_{k-1}) \cdot \bar{u}_{k-1} \cdot T - \cos(\bar{\Psi}_{k-1}) \cdot \bar{v}_{k-1} \cdot T \\ 0 & 1 & \cos(\bar{\Psi}_{k-1}) \cdot \bar{u}_{k-1} \cdot T - \sin(\bar{\Psi}_{k-1}) \cdot \bar{v}_{k-1} \cdot T \\ 0 & 0 & 1 \end{bmatrix}$$

$$W_k = \begin{bmatrix} \cos(\hat{\Psi}_{k-1}) \cdot T & -\sin(\hat{\Psi}_{k-1}) \cdot T & 0 \\ \sin(\hat{\Psi}_{k-1}) \cdot T & \cos(\hat{\Psi}_{k-1}) \cdot T & 0 \\ 0 & 0 & 1 \cdot T \end{bmatrix}$$

Step 2: Calculate the prediction covariance matrix and predicted external sensor observation

$$P_k^- = A_k \cdot P_{k-1} \cdot A_k^T + W_k \cdot Q_{k-1} \cdot W_k^T$$

$$\begin{bmatrix} z_{1,k}^- \\ z_{2,k}^- \\ z_{3,k}^- \end{bmatrix} = \begin{bmatrix} x_k^- \\ y_k^- \\ \Psi_k^- \end{bmatrix} \tag{18}$$

Step 3: Correction with valid external sensor data.
Read sensor measurement $\begin{bmatrix} z_{1,k} & z_{2,k} & z_{3,k} \end{bmatrix}^T$
Calculate correction matrix and update prediction error covariance matrix

$$K_k = P_k^- \left(P_k^- + R\right)^{-1} \tag{19}$$
$$P_k = (I - K_k)\, P_k^-$$

where R_k is the external measurement noise covariance. Then a posteriori position estimate is

$$\begin{bmatrix} \hat{x}_k \\ \hat{y}_k \\ \hat{\Psi}_k \end{bmatrix} = \begin{bmatrix} x_k^- \\ y_k^- \\ \Psi_k^- \end{bmatrix} + K_k \left(\begin{bmatrix} z_{1,k} \\ z_{2,k} \\ z_{3,k} \end{bmatrix} - \begin{bmatrix} z_{1,k}^- \\ z_{2,k}^- \\ z_{3,k}^- \end{bmatrix} \right) \tag{20}$$

Goto Step 1.

3.4 Implementation for Mobile Robot Navigation System

(a) Eliminate outlier measurement
The actual external sensor, such as a vision system, may encounter errors in signal processing or communication error. These inevitable errors usually result in measurement with significant large error. These errors are difficult to predict. If these outlier measurements are input into the sensor fusion filter, the filter response has large estimate error, which may cause instability of navigation and control systems. In order to improve the stability of navigation system, gating, is employed to eliminate the outlier vision measurement.
Gating is used in sensor fusion to remove most unlikely observation-to-track pairings (Brown et al. 1996). In mobile robot navigation system, rectangular gate has good performance and is simple to implement. Rectangular gate removes the most unlikely observation.
Rectangular Gating is defined as the following

$$|e_{z_{1,k}}| \le 3\sqrt{\sigma_{R(i)}^2 + \sigma_{P(i)}^2}, i = 1,2,3 \tag{21}$$

where $\sigma_{R(i)}^2$ is the diagonal element of the external sensor noise covariance R, and $\sigma_{P_k(i)}^2$ is the appropriate diagonal element of the prediction covariance P_k^-. If all innovation residues satisfy the above gating inequality, the external sensor data is considered as valid, and will be used in filter correction. Otherwise, the external sensor data is determined as invalid.
(b) Synchronization between external and onboard sensor
In the mobile robot navigation system, the onboard sensor usually has higher bandwidth and faster sampling time than the external positioning sensor. The sensor fusion algorithm described above is executed at the onboard sensor sampling rate. When the external sensor data is not available due to the slow update rate or the sensor data is considered as an outlier, the sensor fusion filter is executed without correction. Step 3 in the filter is reduced as

$$\left[\hat{x}_k \quad \hat{y}_k \quad \hat{\Psi}_k\right]^T = \left[x_k^- \quad y_k^- \quad \Psi_k^-\right]^T \tag{22}$$

$$P_k = P_k^- \tag{23}$$

4. An Example of Mobile Robot Navigation and Control

4.1 Introduction of Omni-directional Mobile Robot and Navigation System

(a) Introduction of Omni-directional mobile robot.

An omni-directional mobile robot is a type of holonomic robot. It has inherent agility which makes it suitable for dynamic environment applications (Purwin 2006). One interesting application is Robocup competition in which mobile robots compete in soccer-like games. In this section, an example of navigation system of omni-directional robot is illustrated. The robot mechanical configuration is shown in Figure 4.

The three omni-directional wheels are driven by electrical motors individually. An Optical encoder are installed on each motor shaft.

(b) Introduction of Navigation System

In the sample system, a roof camera senses the position and the orientation of robots by image processing. The vision system communicates with the robot control system via a serial port. The vision system identified position and orientation are in the camera frame. A second-order polynomials is used to map the camera frame to world frame.

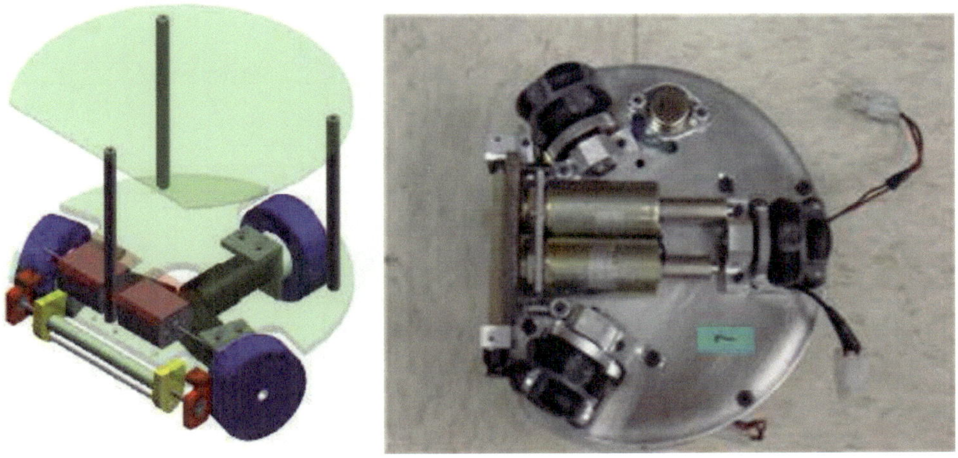

Fig. 4. Omni-directional mobile robot

In the illustrated sample system, the robot control system is a dual-loop trajectory linearization control (TLC) system (Liu et al. 2008). The illustrated sample system has the most important features for a general mobile robot navigation and control system. The objective of mobile robot control system is to track a feasible trajectory, which requires an accurate and fast position/orientation measurement. The robot and orientation can be estimated by odometry, which has accumulated error. The overhead camera has accurate but slow measurements. The overhead camera can only capture as high as 60 fps and the period to process each frame varies randomly. The vision system may also lose frames or misidentify objects on the field. The asynchronous serial communication has randomly mismatched data frame, which results in incorrect vision data.

4.2 Omni-directional Mobile Robot Navigation Performance

Omni-directional mobile robot navigation system following sensor fusion is developed using the approach in section 3. In this subsection, several test results are demonstrated. It can be seen that the sensor fusion improves the navigation system accuracy and overall robot tracking peformance.

(a) Square Trajectory with Fixed Orientation

In this test, the robot command trajectory is a square curve with a fixed orientation. The actual robot trajectory was plotted on the field of play by an attached pen. The robot trajectory is also plotted by recorded experiment data. Two experiments were performed and compared. One used only the onboard encoder data, the other used navigation system with sensor fusion. Controller tracking performances using both methods are shown in Figure 5 (a) and (b). In both cases, the tracking error is very small relative to the given measurement. The actual robot tracking performance is determined by the navigation system. Figure 6 (a) and (b) are photos of actual robot trajectories drawn by the attached pen. From these two photos, it can be seen that by using sensor fusion, the robot drew a correct square curve with good repeatability in two rounds; while using encoder alone, the robot was totally disoriented with an accumulated error. Figure 7 and 8 show the Kalman filter performance and gating decision. Figure 7 shows that vision system generated many outlier measurements, while the sensor fusion with gating is able reject the wrong vision data and provide stable and accurate reading. In Figure 8, 1 means acceptance of the vision data, 0 means rejection of the vision data. Experiment using vision system alone was also conducted. The disturbance induced by vision system failure destabilized the robot very soon.

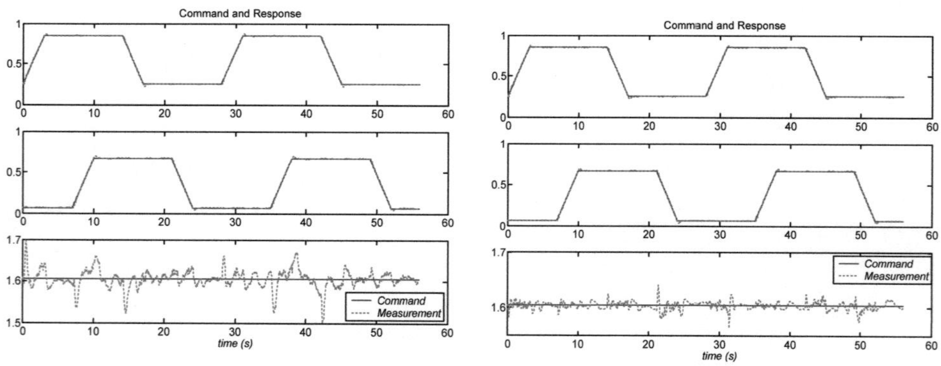

(a) Using Sensor Fusion (b) Using Onboard Sensor

Fig. 5. Square Trajectory Tracking Performance using Sensor Fusion

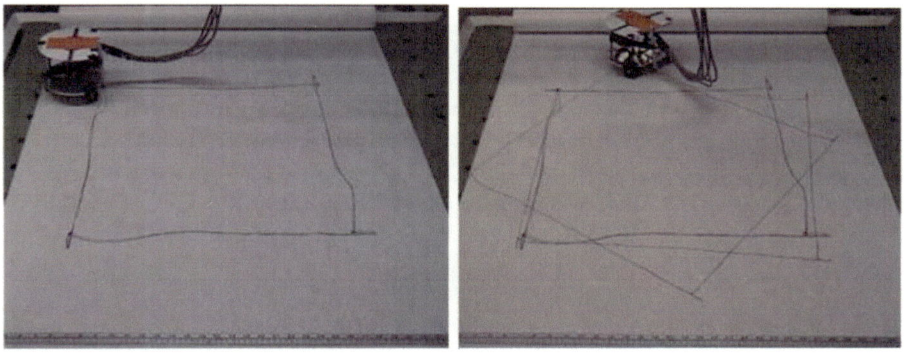

(a) Using Sensor Fusion (b) Using Onboard Sensor

Fig. 6. Trajectory for Square Trajectory Command

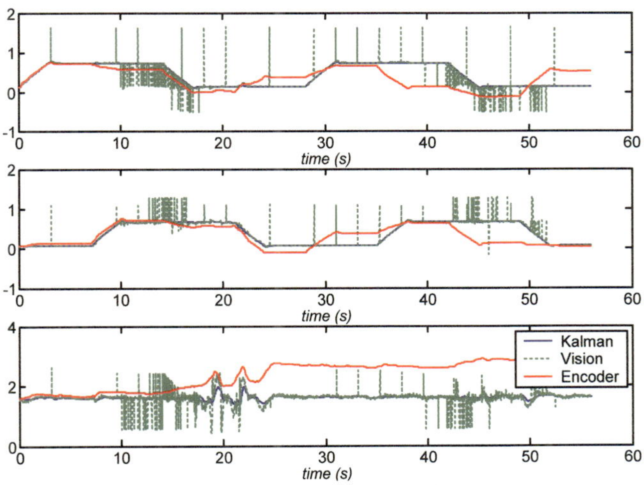

Fig. 7. Square Trajectory Sensor Fusion Kalman Filter Performance

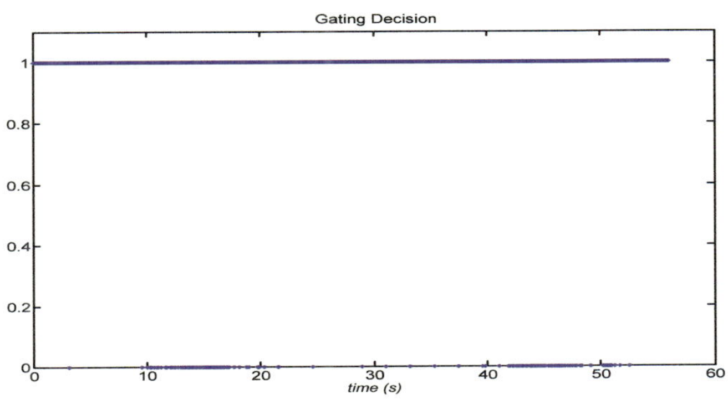

Fig. 8. Square Trajectory Sensor Fusion Gating Decision

(b) Circular trajectory with rotation

In this test, the robot was commanded to accelerate from the initial position, and draw a circle of 0.25 m radius at an angular rate of 1 rad/s. The robot orientation is commanded to change between ± 1 rad. In this test, the robot nonlinear dynamics are stimulated. In Figure 9, the robot controller showed accurate tracking performance. Figure 10 illustrates the navigation system performance. It should be noted that the navigation system performance is similar to test (a) though the robot's motion is nonlinear due to the rotation.

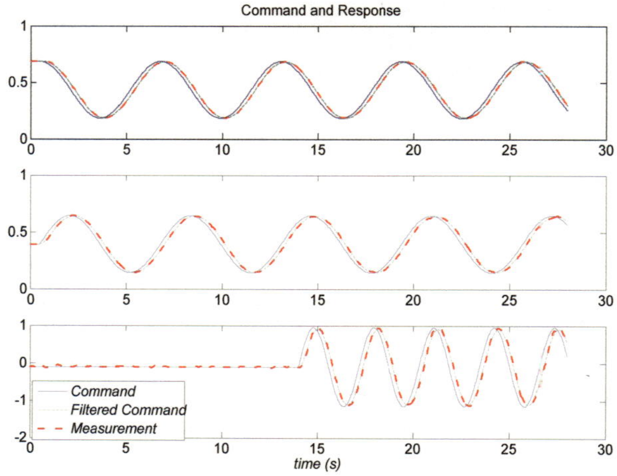

Fig. 9. Circular Trajectory Tracking Performance using Sensor Fusion

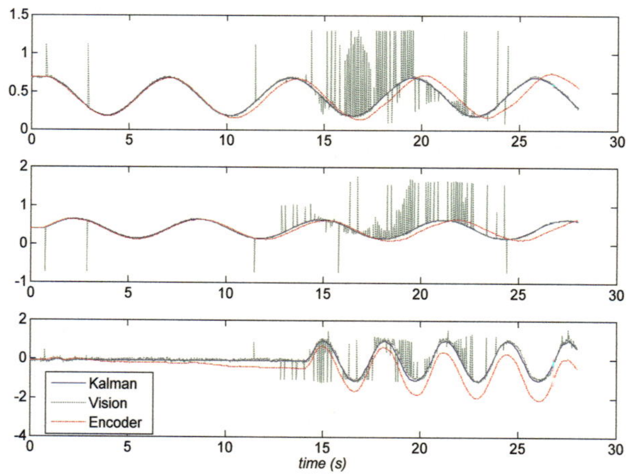

Fig. 10. Circular Trajectory Sensor Fusion Performance

(c) Rose Curve

In this test, the robot is commanded to draw a rose curve generated by a function: $r = a\sin(n\theta)$, where r and θ are the radius and the rotation angle in polar coordinate, and n is an integer determining the number of petals. The robot orientation was fixed. Figure 11 is the result for $n = 4$. Figure 11 (a) and (b) are pictures of robot trajectory using sensor fusion and onboard encoder alone respectively. The robot trajectory shifted significantly when using the onboard sensor alone. As the result, the trajectory plotted when using encoder only is much lighter than the one using sensor fusion. Figure 12 is the recorded data for test with sensor fusion navigation. From this figure, it is clear without vision system correction, the onboard encoder reading slowly drifts away.

(a) Using Sensor Fusion (b) Using Onboard Sensor

Fig. 11. Actual Robot Trajectory for Rose Curve

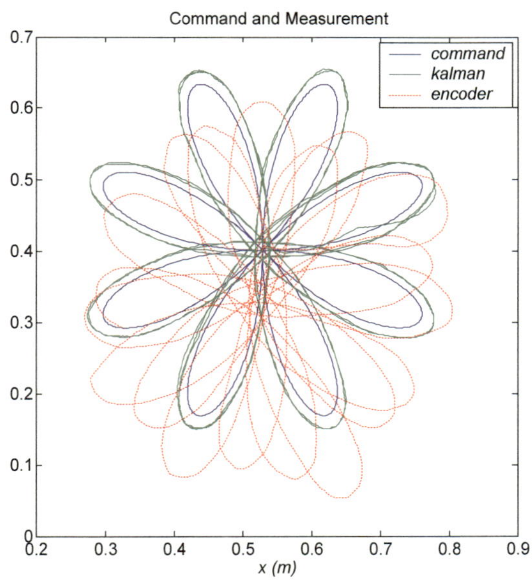

Fig. 12. Robot Tracking Performance Using Sensor Fusion

5. References

Arulampalam, S.; Maskell, S. ; Gordon, N. J.; Clapp, T. (2001). A Tutorial on Particle Filters for On-line Non-linear/Non-Gaussian Bayesian Tracking, *IEEE Transactions of Signal Processing*, Vol. 50, No.2, pp. (174-188), 2001, ISSN 1053-587X.

Brown, R. G.; Hwang, P. Y.C. (1996). *Introduction to random signals and applied Kalman filtering : with MATLAB exercises and solutions*, 3rd ed, ISBN ISBN: 978-0-471-12839-7, Wiley, New York.

Borenstein, J., Everett H. R.; Feng, L. (1996). *Sensors and Methods for Mobile Robot Positioning, The University of Michgan*, 1996.

Chenavier, F.; Crowley, J. (1992), Position Estimation for a Mobile Robot Using Vision and Odometry, *1992 IEEE International Conference on Robotics and Automation*, pp. 2588-2593, Nice, France, 1992.

Goel, P.; Roumeliotis, S. I.; Sukhatme, G. S. (1999). Robust localization using relative and absolute position estimates, *Proceedings of the IEEE/RSJ International Conference on Intelligent Robots and Systems (1999)*, pp. 1134-1140, ISBN: 0-7803-5184-3, Kyongju, South Korea.

Hall, D. L.; McMullen , S. A. H. (2004). *Mathematical Techniques in MultiSensor Data Fusion*, 2nd ed., ISBN 1580533353, Artech House, Boston, MA.

Huang, R.; Mickle, M. C. and Zhu, J. J. (2003), Nonlinear Time-varying Observer Design Using Trajectory Linearization, *Proceedings of the 2003 American Control Conference*. v 6, , p 4772-4778, ISBN: 0-7803-7896-2, Denver, CO, 2003.

Kalman, R. E. (1960), *Transactions of the ASME- Journal of Basic Engineering*, 82(series D): 35-45, 1960.

Krener, A.J. (2003), The convergence of the extended Kalman filter, *Directions in mathematical systems theory and optimization, (Lect. Notes in Control and Information Sciences).*, pp. 173-182, Springer, ISBN: 3540000658,Berlin, 2003.

Liu, Y.; Williams II, R. L.;Zhu, J. J. (2007). Integrated Control and Navigation for Omni-directional Mobile Robot Based on Trajectory Linearization, *Proceedings of the 2007 American Control Conference*, pp. 3053-3058, New York, NY, July 2007, ISSN:0921-8890.

Liu, Y.; Williams II, R.; Zhu J. J.; Wu, J. (2008). Omni-Directional Mobile Robot Controller Based on Trajectory Linearization, *Robotics and Autonomous Systems*, vol. 56, no. 5, pp. 461-479, DOI :10.1016/j.robot.2007.08.007 , 2008, ISSN: 0921-8890.

Purwin, O; D'Andrea, R (2006). Trajectory Generation and Control for Four Wheeled Omnidirectional vehicles, *Robotics and Automation Systems*, vol. 54, pp. 13-22, ISSN: 0921-8890.

Pin, F.G.; Killough, S. M; (1994). A new family of omnidirectional and holonomic wheeled platforms for mobile robots, *IEEE Trans. Robotics Automat.*, vol. 10, no. 2, 1994, pp.480-489, ISSN: 1042-296X.

Richard, J.; Sigpurwalla, N. D.(1983). Understanding the Kalman Filter, *The American Statistician*, May 1983, pp. ,Vol. 37, No. 2.

Welch, G.; Bishop, G.(2001), *An Introduction to Kalman Filter*, ACM, INC, 2001

9

Visual Navigation for Mobile Robots

Nils Axel Andersen, Jens Christian Andersen,
Enis Bayramoğlu and Ole Ravn
Technical University of Denmark, Department of Electrical Engineering
Denmark

1. Introduction

Looking at the number of living creatures using vision as their main sensor one should expect that vision also would be the first choice for mobile robots considering nice features as low price, low power, non contact and high potential information contents. Unfortunately it has proven much more difficult to extract the information from vision than expected and still no commercial robot relies on vision as its main sensor.

In spite of this several successful methods have been developed. This chapter presents a number of visual methods that has been experimentally verified: artificial visual landmarks, corridor following using vanishing point, and road following using terrain classification based on data fusion of laser scanner and vision.

2. Artificial visual landmarks

In well structured environments (both indoor and outdoor) a mobile robot is able to navigate a reasonable distance based on odometry and inertial measurements. However to keep the navigation error bounded absolute position measurements are needed. These can be provided by visual landmarks. Landmark navigation is based on the assumption that the robot from recognizing a landmark can get a localization reference.

The landmark could be artificial and placed to be recognized by the robot, i.e. for indoor applications a method is to place unique landmarks on the ceiling and let a robot camera look for these landmarks, and further place the landmarks at so short intervals that the robot could navigate from one landmark to the next with sufficient accuracy to be able to find the next landmark.

The landmark itself could be at a known position, or just act as a unique reference position so that any ambiguity or accumulating errors could be resolved or reduced when recognizing the landmark. The initial position of the robot could be resolved by recognition of a unique artificial landmark. This landmark could refer to an entry in the robot database with knowledge of that specific area. One or more landmarks could be placed close to a recharging station that requires specifically accurate navigation.

Artificial visual landmarks have been studied by several researchers. Kabuka and Arenas (1987) study a standard pattern and present a thorough error analysis using simulation. Lin and Tummala (1997) describe a system based of simple geometrical patterns using a

Modified Elliptical Hough Transform for detecting the landmark and its properties. Bais and Sablating (2006) present a landmark based system used for soccer robots.

2.1 Design of an artificial landmark

The landmark must be easy to recognize and distinguish from other items normally occurring in the environment of the mobile robot. It should be detectable at different distances and at different angles. One of the easy and stable detectable shapes are checkerboard corners, they are scale invariant, and to some extent viewing angle invariant. The landmark should be simple to reproduce, and thus printable on a sheet of paper would be preferable. The final design was selected with a double checkerboard frame and a central area for a unique code as shown in Fig. 1.

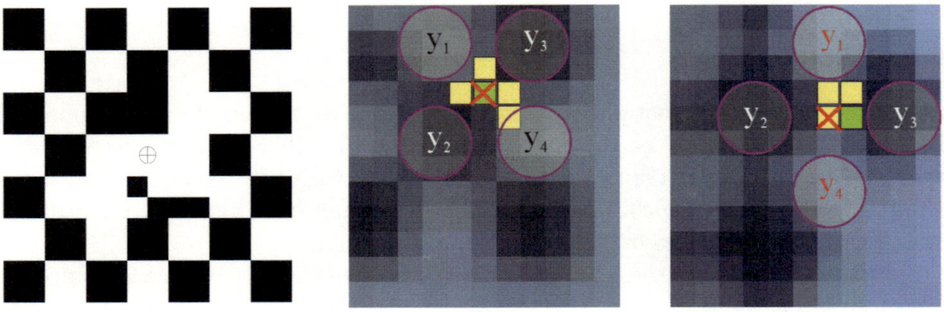

(a) (b) (c)

Fig. 1. The landmark in (a) consists of a checkerboard frame and a central code. The camera view of the lower left part is shown in (b) and (c). The corner filter uses four 3 x 3 pixel areas to detect a corner at the centre position.

The centre code holds 9 square areas; each can be filled with a 4 bit code. Two of the top left squares are used as orientation marks to make it possible to decide the orientation of the landmark. This leaves 7 squares for codes. A few code combinations can be confused with the orientation mark and must thus be avoided, leaving some 24 usable bits except for 2^{16} unusable code combinations, or in total 16711680 code possibilities.

A smaller frame with just 4 squares in the centre would be sufficient in most cases, with one corner as orientation mark, and at maximum 3 bits used in the remaining a total of 9 bits or 512 codes would be available.

The landmark in Fig. 1(a) has two black bits set in each of the two least significant squares -- bottom right inside the frame -- corresponding to the value $9C_{hex}$ or 156 decimal.

2.2 Detection of a landmark

The landmark is detected in four steps: corner detection, frame detection, code detection and frame localization, each of these steps are described in the following.

2.2.1 Detection of corners

The corner detection is done by performing a comparison of four areas in the image expected to match two black areas and two white areas. The full image is first filtered using a 3 x 3pixel Gaussian kernel with σ =0.95. This yields the central pixel a weight *G(r,c)* of about as much as the sum of weights of the remaining 8 pixels. A set of corner pixels C_1 is found using equation **(1)**

$$\begin{aligned}
&a = (r,c) \in C_1 \\
&\textit{if} \;\; (y_1 - y_2 > k_c \wedge y_1 - y_3 > k_c \wedge y_4 - y_2 > k_c \wedge y_4 - y_3 > k_c) \\
&\textit{where} \\
&y_1 = G(r-2, c-2) \\
&y_2 = G(r+2, c-2) \\
&y_3 = G(r-2, c+2) \\
&y_4 = G(r+2, c+2) \\
&k_c = \tfrac{1}{3}(\max(y_1, y_2, y_3, y_4) - \min(y_1, y_2, y_3, y_4)) + k_{\min} \\
&w = y_1 + y_4 - y_2, y_3
\end{aligned} \tag{1}$$

An intensity difference is required from all bright pixels to all black pixels. This difference must be greater than a threshold k_c which proportional with the intensity difference from the brightest to the darkest pixel and includes a fixed minimum threshold k_{min}= 7 out of 256 intensity levels. This ensures that a landmark in both bright areas and darker areas is detectable.

This filter will detect a corner that is bright in the upper-left and lower-right part. The set of intensity-reversed corners C_2 is found in the same way by exchanging the calculation of the for pixel differences.

The landmark may however be observed at different orientations depending on the positioning of the landmark and the camera. By adding a guard band of one pixel between the 4 corner areas, the filter will be relatively insensitive to viewing angle rotation of the landmark relative to the camera, the corner detection sensitivity will be reduced as the angle increases, and at 45 degrees the sensitivity will be zero. To be able to detect landmarks at any rotation angle a second set of filter masks (rotated 45 degrees) is added as shown in Fig. 1 (c), using the same filter function as above giving two more sets of corner pixels C_3 and C_4

The corner pixels in {C_1, C_2 , C_3 and C_4 }are then enumerated individually using 8-connectivity into the total set of corner groups H_n. The centre of each corner group $h_n(H_n)$ is found as shown in equation **(2)**

$$h_n(H_n) = \frac{1}{\sum_{i \in H_n} w_i} \sum_{i \in H_n} a_i w_i \tag{2}$$

where the accuracy improvement by using the intensity weight w_i from equation 1 is neither quantified nor optimized. In Fig. 1 (b) and (c) the detected corner pixels are shown as bright colored squares, where dark green marks the pixel closest to found corner position.

2.2.2 Detection of frames

The corner positions have to match with the frame of the landmark, i.e. from a frame corner there should be two sets of 6 corners each describing a straight line following a frame edge, and further the corners should have almost the same separation.

Fig. 2 shows an example with three landmarks -- rotated at different angles. The original image is shown faintly in the background. The corner pixels are color coded, each color corresponds to one of the four filters.

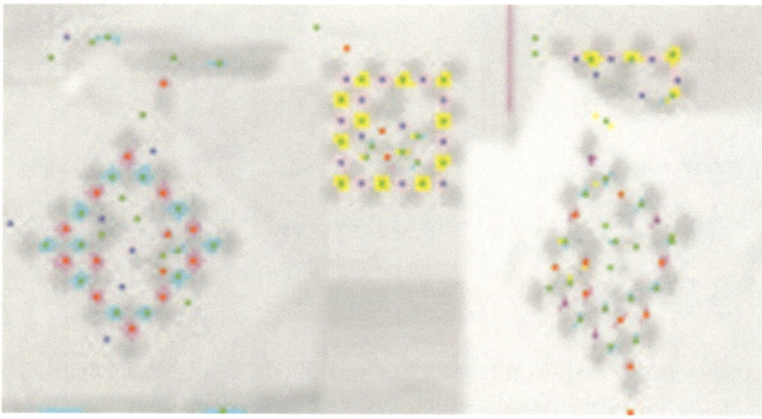

Fig. 2. The corner pixels from three landmarks are shown. The different colors correspond to the four used corner filters.

From all corner positions the up to eight closest neighbors are found within a maximum distance - of $\frac{1}{5}$ image height -- allowing a landmark to fill the whole image.

A frame edge corner set f_j is therefore described as six corners on an approximately straight line fulfilling the requirements in equation (3)

$$f_j = \left\langle \begin{matrix} \{h_i\} \\ i \in [1,2,...,6] \\ h_i \in h_n \end{matrix} \middle| \begin{matrix} v_2 = h_2 - h_1 \\ \hat{h}_2 = h_2 \\ \hat{h}_{i+1} = \hat{h}_i + v_i \\ v_{i+1} = v_i + k_g(h_i - \hat{h}_i) \\ |h_i - \hat{h}_i| < k_{\lim}|v_i| \\ i \in [2,5] \end{matrix} \right\rangle \tag{3}$$

where $k_{\lim} = 0.37$ and $k_g = 0.5$.

A frame corner should be the end point of at least two frame edges. In this way a full frame F is a set of four frame edges as described in (4) with the corners in each edge ordered as described in frame conditions

$$F = \left\langle \{f_1, f_2, f_3, f_4\} \middle| \begin{array}{l} F_{n,m} = h_m \in f \\ F_{1,1} = F_{2,1} \\ F_{2,6} = F_{3,1} \\ F_{1,6} = F_{4,1} \\ v_n = F_{n,6} - F_{n,1} \\ \left|v_1 - v_3\right| =< k_p \left|v_1\right| \\ \left|v_2 - v_4\right| =< k_p \left|v_2\right| \end{array} \right\rangle \tag{4}$$

where the frame is described counter-clockwise, so that f_1 is the topmost edge and f_2 is the leftmost edge. The edges of a frame should in pairs be approximately parallel and of equal lengths, i.e. $f1$ parallel to f_3 and f_2 parallel to f_4 with the limits $k_p = 0.5$.
The six corners h_1 to h_6 are fitted to a straight line, and the crossing of this line with the line from one of the adjacent edges is used as the true frame corner. The frame can then alternatively be described by these four frame corners, describing the frame counter-clockwise with h'1 as the topmost corner

$$F = \{h_1', h_2', h_3', h_4'\} \tag{5}$$

2.2.3 Detection of code

The code in the landmark requires detection of black and white areas in the centre of the frame, and each of the code bits cover an area of only a quarter of the blocks in the frame. The intensity level that separates a black bit from a white bit must further be determined.
The size of the code bits are selected so that the probability of detection for the frame and the code vanishes at about the same distance. At the distance where the frame is detected with a 95% probability, the code is correctly detected with a probability of about 95% (of the instances where the frame is detected).A frame grid is constructed by dividing the distance between two adjacent corners on every frame edge in two. The corners are projected to the fitted line edge, but the distance between the corners are not equalized.
The correct distance between the corners may change over the frame if the landmark is seen in perspective, but this effect is mostly significant if part of the landmark is very close to the camera, and being close to the camera the code detection is usually easy, as a high number of pixels are available for each code bit.
At longer distances all cells in the grid will be very close to the same size, and here the grid accuracy is more important for code recognition. A minor improvement in code detection may therefore be obtainable if the grid spacing along the edges was made equal.

Fig. 3. shows an example of some detected landmarks. The code grid is painted in green and includes the inner part of the frame blocks as well as the code area itself.
All pixels inside the green area are evaluated as belonging to one of the cells, and the average intensity of the pixels inside the cell is used to estimate its value.

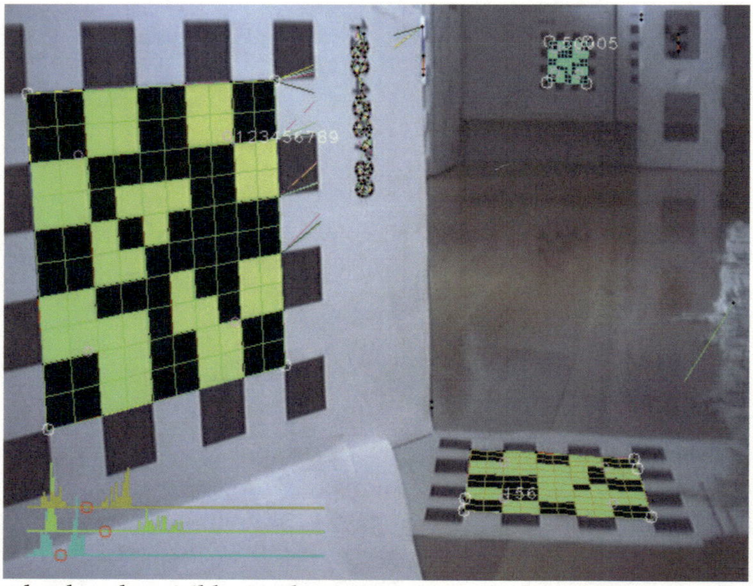

Fig. 3. Three landmarks visible in the same scene to demonstrate the limitations. All landmarks have a frame width of 17.5cm. The near is at 0.46m and the far at 3.2m, the one on the floor is tilted 79^0. The image resolution is 640 x 480 pixels.

Half of the cells covering the frame blocks are always white, the other half black. The average intensity for these cells is used as a threshold value when classifying bits as black or white in the code area.
The histograms in the bottom left corner of Fig. 3 show the distribution of intensity values for each of the three detected landmarks. Left is black, right is white on the histogram line.
The histogram color should match the grid color painted on top of the landmark.
The two all black code areas for the orientation mark are located, and the code values in the remaining code area are ordered accordingly. The two FF_{hex} squares mark the top left corner of the code area, and in this orientation the four bits in each block are coded as follows:

1	2
3	4

The ordering of the code blocks from the most significant to the least significant is located as follows:

*	*	1
2	3	4
5	6	7

The code in the large landmark in Fig. 3 is therefore $75BCD15_{hex}$, or in decimal 123456789.

2.2.4 Position estimation

The landmark position relative to the camera can be estimated when the size of the landmark is known and the camera geometry is assumed to be available. The landmark corner positions are known with a relatively high accuracy, as these are averaged from the line fitting of the frame edge. The perspective described by the positioning of the landmark corners should therefore allow a reasonably accurate estimate of the orientation too. The landmark position and orientation is estimated using a least square parameter estimation method. From the frame extraction algorithm above the position in the image of the frame corners are known $h'_i = (h_r, h_c)$. The position of the corners on the landmark surface is known from the landmark design as four coordinate pairs. The coordinates on the landmark are selected as being seen in the same way as a robot, that is x being forward (in front of the landmark), z being up, and when looking in the direction of x (from behind the landmark) y is to the left. When looking at the landmark on a wall, then z is up and y is right.
The centre of the landmark is taken as the reference position, i.e. the top right frame corner has the frame coordinate $B = [0, b_y, b_z]^T$ with positive values for both b_y and b_z.
A landmark may be at any position $g_t = [x,y,z]^T$ relative to the robot and rotated following the normal convention: first turned κ around the vertical z-axis with positive being counter-clockwise, then tilted Φ around the y-axis with positive being a down tilt and finally roll Ω around the x-axis with positive being a roll to the right.
When a point on the landmark surface $B = (0, b_y, b_z)$ is being seen at the 3D position $A = [a_x, a_y, a_z, 1]^T$ in robot coordinates, then A and B are related with the landmarks orientation and position (x,y,z,Ω, Φ,κ) (also in robot coordinates) as in (6)

$$\begin{bmatrix} 0 \\ b_y w \\ b_z w \\ w \end{bmatrix} = R_\Omega R_\Phi R_\kappa T A \tag{6}$$

where $R_\Omega, R_\Phi, R_\kappa$ are rotation matrices in homogeneous coordinates and T is a translation matrix as shown below:

$$R_\Omega = \begin{bmatrix} 1 & 0 & 0 & 0 \\ 0 & \cos(\Omega) & \sin(\Omega) & 0 \\ 0 & -\sin(\Omega) & \cos(\Omega) & 0 \\ 0 & 0 & 0 & 1 \end{bmatrix} \tag{7}$$

$$R_\Phi = \begin{bmatrix} \cos(\Phi) & 0 & -\sin(\Phi) & 0 \\ 0 & 1 & 0 & 0 \\ \sin(\Phi) & 0 & \cos(\Phi) & 0 \\ 0 & 0 & 0 & 1 \end{bmatrix} \tag{8}$$

$$R_{\kappa} = \begin{bmatrix} \cos(\kappa) & \sin(\kappa) & 0 & 0 \\ -\sin(\kappa) & \cos(\kappa) & 0 & 0 \\ 0 & 0 & 1 & 0 \\ 0 & 0 & 0 & 1 \end{bmatrix} \tag{9}$$

$$T = \begin{bmatrix} 1 & 0 & 0 & -x \\ 0 & 1 & 0 & -y \\ 0 & 0 & 1 & -z \\ 0 & 0 & 0 & 1 \end{bmatrix} \tag{10}$$

The conversion between image coordinates and the 3D position A of the point on the landmark are -- except for lens distortion -- as defined in (11)

$$\begin{bmatrix} h_r w \\ h_c w \\ w \end{bmatrix} = \begin{bmatrix} -1 & 0 & h_x \\ 0 & 1 & h_y \\ 0 & 0 & 1 \end{bmatrix} \begin{bmatrix} 0 & 0 & 1 & 0 \\ 0 & -1 & 0 & 0 \\ \frac{1}{c} & 0 & 0 & 0 \end{bmatrix} \begin{bmatrix} a_x \\ a_y \\ a_z \\ 1 \end{bmatrix} \tag{11}$$

$$I = bPA$$

where $I = [h_r\ w,\ h_c\ w,\ w]^T$ holds the row h_r and column h_c of the corresponding pixel position of $A = [a_x, a_y, a_z, 1]^T$ in the image.

The b-matrix offsets the position to get positive row and column values by adding the (optical) image centre (h_x, h_y)and changing the direction of the row axis to get down as positive. P-matrix adds the perspective by scaling the row and column values by 1/c into w proportional to the distance from the camera a_x. The a_y direction corresponds to columns in the image with changed sign, and the height a_z corresponds to image rows.

When the camera is positioned at the centre of the robot coordinates, then the two equations (11) and (6) can be combined as shown in (12)

$$\begin{bmatrix} h_r w \\ h_c w \\ w \end{bmatrix} = bPT^{-1} R_{\kappa}^T R_{\Phi}^T R_{\Omega}^T \begin{bmatrix} 0 \\ b_y \\ b_z \\ 1 \end{bmatrix} \tag{12}$$

The right side of this equation can be evaluated to three functions of the unknown $v=[x,y,z,\Omega, \Phi,\kappa]^T$ and the known position (b_y, b_z) as

$$\begin{bmatrix} h_r w \\ h_c w \\ w \end{bmatrix} = \begin{bmatrix} f_r(x, y, z, \Omega, \Phi, \kappa, b_y, b_z) \\ f_c(x, y, z, \Omega, \Phi, \kappa, b_y, b_z) \\ f_w(x, y, z, \Omega, \Phi, \kappa, b_y, b_z) \end{bmatrix} \tag{13}$$

The last w equation can be inserted into the first two as in (14) where the six unknowns are replaced by the vector v

$$\begin{bmatrix} h_r f_w(v,b_y,b_z) - f_r(v,b_y,b_z) \\ h_c f_w(v,b_y,b_z) - f_c(v,b_y,b_z) \end{bmatrix} = \begin{bmatrix} 0 \\ 0 \end{bmatrix} \tag{14}$$

To solve for the six unknowns at least six equations are needed, so the four corners of the landmark frame yield eight equations by substituting b_y, b_z, h_r and h_c in (14) with the values from the remaining three corners. The problem may then be solvable. The eight functions on the left side of (14) should now all evaluate to zero with the correct value of the six unknowns

$$F = 0 \tag{15}$$

As the functions are nonlinear the six unknown parameters are estimated using Newton's iteration method. With an initial guess of the ^v the equations will (probably) not be zero, but assuming that the errors are small and the equations are approximately linear at the guessed position, the error can be compensated for by a linear adjustment Δv as shown in (16)

$$F(\hat{v}) + J(\hat{v}) + \Delta v = 0 \tag{16}$$

where $F(\hat{v})$ is the value of the eight equations evaluated with the guessed set of parameters $\hat{v}$ and $J(\hat{v})$ is the Jacobian F with respect to the unknowns in v taken at $\hat{v}$, finally Δv is the adjustment to the guess needed to get the required zero result.

A better guess of v would therefore be $\hat{v}_2$ as shown in (17)

$$\hat{v}_2 = \hat{v} + \Delta v \tag{17}$$

The estimated adjustment Δv is found by solving (16) as:

$$\Delta v = -(J^T J)^{-1} J^T F \tag{18}$$

Equations (16), (17) and (18) are then repeated, setting $\hat{v} = \hat{v}_2$ for the next iteration, until the estimated parameters have converged sufficiently. The pixel position in the image is adjusted for radial lens error prior to insertion into the functions in F

The iteration is terminated when the parameter change Δv_n in iteration n is significantly small according to the stop criteria in (19)

$$stop\,criteria{:}\Delta v_n = \left[\hat{x},\hat{y},\hat{z},\hat{\Omega},\hat{\Phi},\hat{\kappa}\right] \left| \begin{array}{l} |\hat{x},\hat{y},\hat{z}| < P_{\inf} \wedge \\ |\hat{\Omega},\hat{\Phi},\hat{\kappa}| < R_{\inf} \end{array} \right. \tag{19}$$

When looking at a landmark that is tilted slightly forward or backward it may be difficult to see the difference, this could indicate local optimum that could trap the parameter estimation.

Fig. 4 shows the pixel error as a function of a combination of turn (κ) and tilt (Φ). This shows the correct value for these parameters ($\Phi=5^0$) and ($\kappa=22^0$) but also a local minimum at about ($\Phi=-13^0$) and ($\kappa=25^0$)

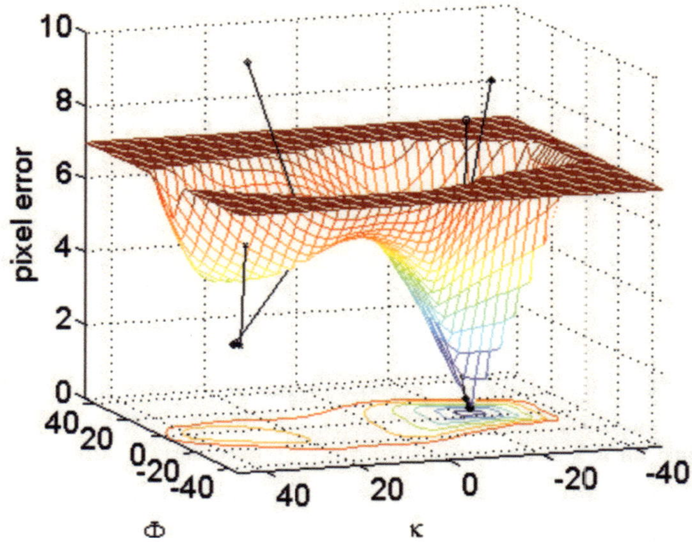

Fig. 4. Parameter estimation for the position and orientation of a landmark has (often) local minimum. The pixel error is shown as a function of turn of turn (κ) and tilt (Φ) of the landmark (limited to a maximum error of seven pixels).

The rotation (Ω) of the landmark will have four equally accurate solutions, as there is no discrimination of the four frame corners. But the position of the code index is known and is used to get the correct Ω -value. The position has a local minimum at the same distance behind the camera, but this is easily avoided by selecting an initial guess in front of the camera (a positive x-value). To avoid the (κ,Φ) local minimum, four initial positions in the four quadrants in the κ Φ–coordinate system are tested, and after a few iterations the parameter set with the least pixel error is continued to get a final estimate. The iteration error progress is shown in Fig. 4 as four black lines, of which two ends in the local minimum at with a minimum pixel error of 2.5 pixels, compared to 0.12 pixels at the global minimum in $\Phi=5.0^0$ and $\kappa=-22.8^0$.

2.3 Experimental results with artificial visual landmarks

Three experiments have been carried out to evaluate the performance of the landmark system in navigation of mobile robots. The first test investigates the repeatability of the position estimates by taking several readings from the same position with different viewing angle. The second test deals with the robustness of the landmark code reading function performing hundreds of code readings from different positions and the third experiment uses the landmarks to navigate a mobile robot between different positions showing that the drift of odometry may be compensated by landmark position readings. In all three experiments the used camera is a Philips USB-web camera with a focal length of 1050 pixels. The used image resolution is 640 X 320 pixels.

2.3.1 Relative estimation accuracy

In this experiment the repeatability of the position measurement is tested. The camera is placed 2.2 m from the landmark and the landmark is placed with four different viewing angles. At each viewing angle 100 measurements are taken. As seen in Table 1 the estimation accuracy of a landmark position is dependent on the viewing angle of the landmark.

Viewing angle κ	Position $\sigma_{\lvert x,y \rvert}$	Orientation σ_{Ω} (roll)	Orientation σ_{Φ} (tilt)	Orientation σ_{κ} (turn)	Block pixels	N samples
0^0	1.7 mm	0.04^0	1.55^0	0.61^0	11.9	100
10^0	1.3 mm	0.06^0	0.72^0	0.27^0	11.7	100
30^0	2.2 mm	0.12^0	0.21^0	0.12^0	10.3	100
60^0	2.5 mm	0.10^0	0.11^0	0.06^0	5.9	24

Table 1. Relative estimation accuracy of 100 position requests of a landmark at 2.2 m at different turn angles of the landmark.

The position estimation error in (x, y) is about 0.2 cm and is partially correlated with an estimation error in the landmark orientation; typically a small tilt combined with a slight turn makes the landmark seem slightly smaller and thus further away.
When the turn angle is zero (landmark is facing the camera) the relative estimation error in roll σ_{Ω} is uncorrelated with the other errors and thus small, at larger turn angles the roll error increases and the error value is now correlated with the other estimated parameters.
The obtainable absolute position accuracy is dependent on the mounting accuracy of the camera, the focal length of the lens and the accuracy of the estimated lens (radial) errors. With the used USB camera an absolute position accuracy of less than 5 cm and an angle accuracy of less than 5^0 is obtained within the camera coverage area.
When a landmark is viewed with a rotation of 22.5^0 -- just in between the two sets of corner filters ($C_{1,2}$ and $C_{3,4}$) -- the sensitivity is slightly reduced. This reduces the distance at which the landmark can be detected.
The number of pixels needed for each of the squares in the frame to be able to detect the landmark is shown in Table 2 as 'block pixels'.

Orientation of grid	pd= 0.5 Pixels	meter	pd= 0.95 Pixels	meter
0.00^0	3.8	3.4	3.9	3.3
22.5^0	4.6	2.8	4.8	2.7
45.0^0	4.2	3.1	4.3	3.0

Table 2. Number of pixels needed for each frame block to detect landmarks at different rotation angles relative to camera. The distance in meters corresponds to a focal length of 525 pixels (image size of 320 x 240 pixels)

When the probability of detection (pd) is about 0.95 the landmark code is evaluated correctly with a probability of about 0.95 too (for the detected landmarks). Stable landmark detection requires that each of the blocks in the landmark frame should be covered by at least five pixels. When the landmark is not at the distance with the optimal focus the detection distance will decrease further.

2.3.2 Landmark code reader test

To test the landmark code reader performance an experiment with a small mobile robot (see Fig. 5) has been done.

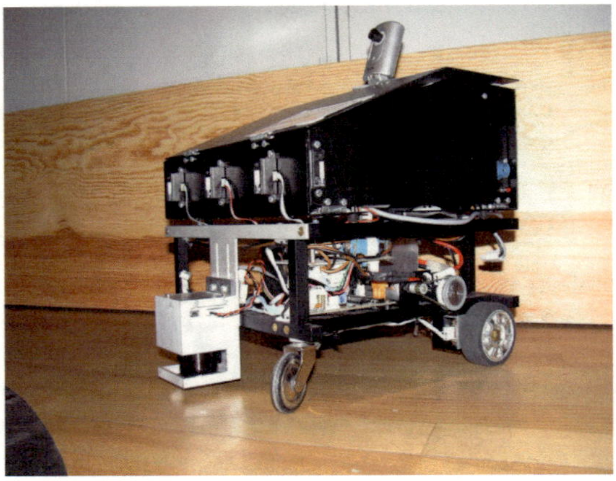

Fig. 5. Mobile robot used for experiments.

Two landmarks have been put on the wall beside two office doors. The distance between the two landmarks is approximately 8 meters. A black tape stripe is put in the middle of the corridor and the mobile robot is programmed to run between the two landmarks following the black tape stripe. At each landmark the robot turns 90 degrees and faces towards the landmark at a distance of approximately 1.5 meters. The code of the landmark is read by the robot and compared to the expected code. In one experiment the mobile robot goes back and fro 100 times which is about the maximum allowed by the battery capacity. In each experiment the number of reading errors is registered. The experiment has been carried out more than ten times indicating a robust system as more than 2000 errorless readings are made.

2.3.3 Landmark navigation test

In this experiment the same mobile robot (Fig. 5) is program to drive between two points using odometry. One point is placed 1 meter in front of a landmark the other is placed at a distance of 3 m from the landmark. When the robot is at the one-meter point facing the landmark the odometry is corrected using the measured position of the landmark. This means that the landmark measurement is used to compensate for the drift of odometry coordinates. Each time the robot is at the one-meter point its position is measured. In the experiment the robot drives between the two points 100 times. The measurements show that the one-meter position of the robot stays within a circle with radius of 10 cm which means that the use of landmark position measurements is able to compensate for drift in odometry coordinates if the distance between landmarks is sufficiently small. The exact maximum distance depends on the odometry accuracy of the given robot.

3. Corridor following

Office buildings and hospitals are often dominated by long corridors so being able to drive along a corridor solves a great part of the navigation problem in these buildings. A method that uses a Hough transform with a novel discretization method to extract lines along the corridor and find the vanishing point from these is presented (Bayramoğlu. et al.,2009) Fusion of odometry data and vanishing point estimates using extended Kalman filter methods have lead to a robust visual navigation method for corridors. Experiments have shown that the robot is able to go along the corridor with lateral errors less than 3-4 cm and orientation errors less than 1-2 degrees.

3.1 Visual Pose Estimation

The low-level processing of the images consists of the detection of edge pixels and the extraction of lines from those edge pixels. The resulting lines are then classified to find a parallel set that constitutes the lines along the corners. The corresponding vanishing point, i.e., the point where the corner lines meet, is used for the classification. The classified lines are finally matched to the known width and height of the corridor to estimate the orientation and the lateral position.

3.1.1 Low-level Processing

Two feature detectors are used in consequence to prepare the data for higher level processing. First, a Canny edge detector (Canny, 1986) is used. Canny edge detector is a non-linear filter that marks pixels with a high intensity change, combined with other criteria, as edge pixels. The result is an edge image with the detected edge pixels colored white on a black background.

Lines are then extracted from the edge image using a segmented Hough transform method. The procedure starts by segmenting the image into 10x10 sub-images to increase the speed of the following steps. Line segments are extracted from these sub-images using a modified version of the Hough transform (Duda and Hart, 1972). The idea of the Hough transform is to evaluate every possible line through the image by the number of edge pixels along the line. The lines with highest support are admitted. These line segments are then traced through the image to be combined with other collinear line segments. Fig. 6. illustrates these steps.

(a) (b) (c)

Fig. 6. Steps of the low level image processing. (a) The original image taken with the robot's camera. (b) Edge image obtained from the Canny edge detector (c) Extracted lines superimposed on the original image.

3.1.2 Vanishing Point Extraction

Lines, that are parallel in 3D space, converge to a point (possibly at infinity) when their perspective projection is taken on an image. This point is called the vanishing point of that set of lines, and equivalently of their direction.

The vanishing point is useful in two ways; first, it can be used to eliminate lines that are not along its corresponding direction, since such lines are unlikely to pass through it on the image. Second, its image coordinates only depend on the camera orientation with respect to its corresponding direction; therefore, it gives a simple expression for the orientation.

The vanishing point of the corridor direction is expected to be found near the intersection of many lines. In order to find it, an intersection point for every combination of two image lines is calculated as a candidate. If there are *N* corridor lines among *M* lines in the image, there will be a cluster of *N(N+1)/2* candidates around the vanishing point as opposed to *M(M+1)/2* total candidates. This cluster is isolated from the vast number of faulty candidates by iteratively removing the furthest one from the overall center of gravity. This procedure makes use of the density of the desired cluster to discard the numerous but scattered faulty candidates. After removing most of the lines, the center of gravity of the remaining few candidates gives a good estimate of the vanishing point. Refer to Fig. 7 for the illustration of these steps.

Fig. 7. The illustration of the vanishing point extraction. The extracted lines are shown in red, the vanishing point candidates are shown in blue and the green cross at the center is the detected vanishing point.

3.1.3 Estimation of the Orientation

The image coordinates of the vanishing point is a function of, first, its corresponding direction in the scene, and second, the camera orientation. If the direction is given in the real corridor frame by the vector $\vec{v}$, then we can call its representation in the image frame $\vec{v}^{\,i}(\theta,\alpha,\beta)$ and it is a function of the orientation parameters θ,α,β. The image coordinates of the vanishing point are then given by;

$$x_{vp} = \frac{v_x^i}{v_z^i}, y_{vp} = \frac{v_y^i}{v_z^i} \tag{20}$$

In order to derive an expression for the orientation parameters, they are defined as follows; θ is the orientation of the mobile robot, it is the angular deviation of the front of the mobile robot from the direction of the corridor measured counter-clockwise. In the assumed setup the camera is able to rotate up or down. α is the angle of deviation of the camera from the horizon and it increases as the camera looks down. β is included for completeness and it is the camera orientation in the camera z axis, and is always equal to 0. With these definitions for the parameters the following expressions are obtained for θ, α :

$$\begin{aligned} \alpha &= \arctan\left(\frac{y_{vp} - c_y}{f'}\right) \\ \theta &= -\arctan\left(\frac{(x_{vp} - c_x)\cos\alpha}{f'}\right) \end{aligned} \tag{21}$$

Here, c_x and c_y are the image coordinates of the image center, usually half the image resolution in each direction. f' is the camera focal length in pixels.

3.1.4 Line Matching

Those image lines that are found to pass very close to the vanishing point are labeled to be along the direction of the corridor. The labelled lines need to be assigned to either of the corners, (or the line at the center of the floor for the particular corridor used in the experiments). The location of a classified line with respect to the vanishing point restricts which corner it could belong to. If the line in the image is to the upper left of the vanishing point, for instance, it can only correspond to the upper left corner if it is a correct line. The center line on the floor creates a confusion for the lower lines, each lower line is matched also to the center line to resolve this. At this point, pairs of matched image lines and real lines are obtained.

3.1.5 Estimation of the Lateral Position

Assume that the image lines are expressed in the image coordinates with the Cartesian line equation given in Eq. (22). a, b and c are the parameters defining the line and they are calculated during line extraction. Each image line - real line pair gives a constraint for the camera lateral position as given in Eq. (23).

$$ax + by = c \tag{22}$$

$$\begin{aligned} &a\left(\left(-f'\cos\theta - c_x\cos\alpha\sin\theta\right)y_d + c_x\sin\alpha z_d\right) + \\ &b\left(\left(-f'\sin\alpha\sin\theta - c_y\cos\alpha\sin\theta\right)y_d + \left(-f'\cos\alpha + c_y\sin\alpha\right)z_d\right) = c\left(-\cos\alpha\sin\theta y_d + \sin\alpha z_d\right) \end{aligned} \tag{23}$$

Here, $y_d = \left(y_{camera} - y_{line}\right)$ is the lateral distance between the real line and the camera and $z_d = \left(z_{camera} - z_{line}\right)$ is the height difference between the camera and the real line. y and z directions are defined as the axes of a right-handed coordinate frame when x points along the corridor and z points up.

The only unknown in Eq. ((23)) is the camera lateral position, therefore each matched line pair returns an estimate for it. A minority of these estimates are incorrect as the line matching step occasionally matches wrong pairs. As in the vanishing point estimation, a dense cluster of estimates are expected around the correct value. The same method of iterative furthest point removal is followed to find the correct value. To increase the robustness further, while calculating the center, the estimates are weighted according to their likelihoods based on the prior estimate.

3.2 Fusion with Dead Reckoning

The pure visual pose estimation method described so far returns a value for the orientation and the lateral position in an absolute frame. However, a single instance of such a measurement contains a considerable amount of error, especially in position (10-15 cm). The sampling rate is also low (5 fps) due to the required processing time. These problems are alleviated by fusing the visual measurements with dead reckoning, which has a high sampling rate and very high accuracy for short distances.

Probabilistic error models for both dead reckoning and visual pose estimation are required, in order to apply Bayesian fusion. The error model chosen for the dead reckoning is described by Kleeman, 2003. It is a distance driven error model where the sources of error are the uncertainty on the effective wheel separation and distances traveled by each wheel. The amount of uncertainty is assumed to be proportional to the distance traveled for a particular sample. A simple uncorrelated Gaussian white noise is assumed for the visual measurements.

An extended Kalman filter(EKF) is used to perform the fusion. The time update step of the EKF is the familiar dead reckoning pose update with the mentioned distance driven error model. The update is performed for every wheel encoder sample until a visual measurement arrives. The measurement update step of the EKF is applied when it arrives. The assumed measurement model is given as follows:

$$\begin{bmatrix} \theta_v(k) \\ y_v(k) \end{bmatrix} = \begin{bmatrix} 1 & 0 & 0 \\ 0 & 0 & 1 \end{bmatrix} \begin{bmatrix} \theta(k) \\ x(k) \\ y(k) \end{bmatrix} + \vec{v}(k) \tag{24}$$

Where $\vec{v}(k)$ is an uncorrelated Gaussian white noise with a covariance matrix calculated empirically.

3.3 Observed Performance

The performance of the method is evaluated by comparing its measurements with the actual robot pose. The visual pose estimation is calculated to be accurate within 1-2 degrees of error in the orientation. Since it is hard to measure the robot orientation to this accuracy, the performance is evaluated based on the error in the lateral position.

Single frame visual estimation is evaluated for performance first. Fig. 8 contains four interesting cases. In Fig. 8 (a), part of the corridor is obscured by a person and a door, but the estimation is not effected at all with an error of 2.5cm. Fig. 8 (b) displays a case where only the left wall is visible, but the method still succeeds with an error of 0.2cm. Fig. 8 (c) shows an extreme case. Even though the end of the corridor is not visible, the algorithm performs well with an error of 0.9cm. Fig. 8 (d) shows a weakness of the method. The image has no particular difficulty, but the measurement has 11.8cm error. The final case occurs rarely but it suggests the use of a higher standard deviation for the assumed measured error.

The second step is the evaluation of the performance after fusion with dead reckoning. The navigation task is moving backwards and forwards at the center of the corridor. Fig. 9 contains three sets of data plotted together. The red curve is the overall pose estimation after sensor fusion. The green dots are the visual estimations alone. Finally, the blue curve is a collection of absolute measurements taken with a ruler. The error is observed to remain below 3cm in this experiment.

(a) Only two corners are detected

(b) The view is partially blocked

(c) Moving towards the wall

(d) This case has high error

Fig. 8. Images with special properties illustrating the strengths and the weaknesses of the pure visual estimation. (a), (b) and (c) illustrate difficult cases successfully measured while (d) show a case with a convenient image with a high measurement error.

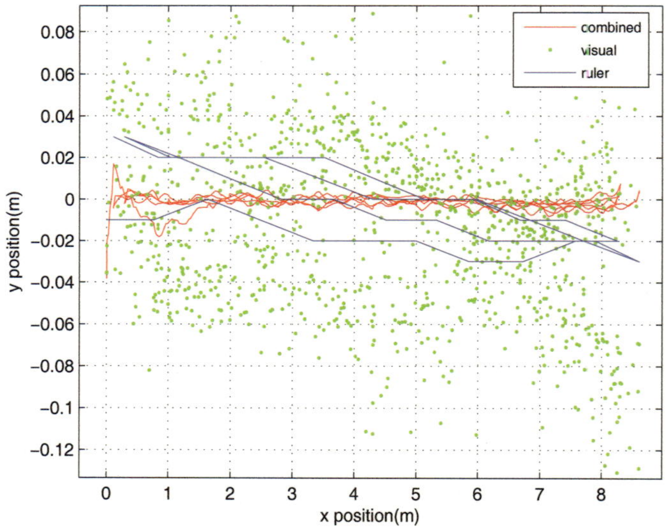

Fig. 9. Position data from various sources for system performance illustration.

4. Laser and vision based road following

Many semi structured environments with gravel paths and asphalt roads exist e.g. public parks. A method for navigating in such environments is presented. A slightly tilted laser scanner is used for classification of the area in front of the vehicle into traversable and non-traversable segments and to detect relevant obstacles within the coverage area. The laser is supplemented with a vision sensor capable of finding the outline of the traversable road beyond the laser scanner range (Fig. 10). The detected features - traversable segments, obstacles and road outline- are then fused into a feature map directly used for path decisions. The method has been experimentally verified by several 3 km runs in a nature park having both gravel roads and asphalt roads.

Fig. 10. The robot with laser scanner measurements and camera coverage

4.1 Related work

Current work in the area tends to focus on using 3D laser scanners or a combination of 3D laser scanners and vision. Using 3D laser scanner solutions has been proposed by Vandapel et al. (2004) by transforming point clouds into linear features, surfaces, and scatter. These were classified by using a Bayesian filter based on a manually classified training set.

Identification of navigable terrain using a 3D laser scanner by checking if all height measurements in the vicinity of a range reading had less than a few centimeters deviation is described in Montemerlo & Thrun (2004)

An algorithm that distinguished compressible grass (which is traversable) from obstacles such as rocks using spatial coherence techniques with an omni-directional single line laser is described in (Macedo et. al.,2000).

A method for detection and tracking the vertical edges of the curbstones bordering the road, using a 2D laser scanner, described in Wijesoma et. Al. (2004) is a way of indirect road detection.

Detection of borders or obstacles using laser scanners is often used both indoors and in populated outdoor environments, and is the favored method when the purpose includes map building, as in Guivant et al. (2001) and Klöör et al. (1993).

Detection of nontraversasble terrain shapes like steps using laser scanner for planetary exploration is described in Henriksen & Krotkov (1997)

The DARPA Grand Challenge 2004 race demonstrated the difficulties in employing road following and obstacle avoidance for autonomous vehicles (Urmson et. al, 2004).

This situation seems to be improved in the 2005 version of the race, where five autonomous vehicles completed the 212~km planned route. The winning team from Stanford perceived the environment through four laser range finders, a radar system, and a monocular vision system. Other teams, like the gray team Trepagnier et al. (2005) also use laser scanners as the main sensor for traversability sensing supplemented by (stereo) vision.

The solution of the winning team in 2005 is described in (Thrun et al., 2006); a 2D laser scanner detects traversable road based on the vertical distance between measurements, this solution is combined with vision and radar for longer range detections.

4.2 Terrain classification from laser scanner

A slightly tilted laser obtains scans in front of the robot (Fig. 10). The assumption is that the terrain seen by the laser scanner can be divided into three different classes $C = \{C_t\ (traversable), C_n (not\ traversable), C_{\varnothing} (invalid\ data)\}$ and that this can be done by mapping function $M_{CF} : F \rightarrow C$. Here F is a set of features extracted from single laserscans:

$F = \{H_h\ rawheight, F_\sigma\ roughness, F_z\ \ stepsize, F_c\ curvature, F_t\ slope, F_w\ width\}$

The roughness of data in a 2D laser scan is defined as the square root of the local vatiance of the distance to reflections along the scan. A roughness value is calculated as deviation from a fitted line for measurements converging approx. a wheel base distance (0.45 m), to emphasize terrain variation with a spatial period shorter than this distance. The roughness feature function F_σ divides the measurements into groups based on this roughness value, these groups are then combined and filtered based on the remaining feature functions. Each of these functions increases the probability that the measurements are correctly classified. The method is described in detail in (Andersen et al.,2006b)

An example of the obtained classification is shown in Fig. 11 where a narrow gravelled road is crossed by a horse track. The road and the horse track are first divided into a number of roughness groups as shown in Fig. 2b, these are then filtered down to three traversable segments, one for the road (in the middle) and one each side from the horse track.

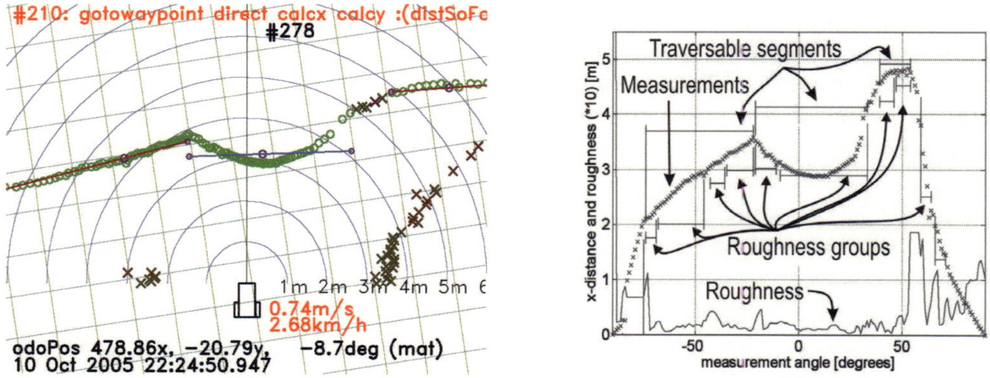

(a) (b)

Fig. 11. Data from a graveled road crossed by a horse track

The laser scanner measurements are shown in (a) as circles (traversable) and crosses (not traversable), the rough grass on the road edges before the horse track is just visible left and right of the robot. The road is the area with the high profile (about 15 cm higher at the center). On both side are relative flat areas from the horse track. The segmentation into roughness groups and traversable segments are shown in (b).

4.3 Road outline from vision

As seen on Fig. 10 the laserscan overlaps the camera image.The method (Andersen et al.,2006a) estimates the outline of the road by analyzing the image, based on a seed area in the image classified as traversable by the laserscanner. The main features describing the road are its homogeneity. But there may be variation in the visual expression due to e.g. shadows, sunlight, specular reflections, surface granularity, flaws, partially wet or dry surface and minor obstacles like leaves.

The road detection is therefore based on two features: the chromaticity $\mathbf{C}$ and the intensity gradient ∇I. The chromaticity is colour stripped from intensity as shown in Eq. (25) based on a RGB image.

$$\mathbf{c} = \begin{bmatrix} c_{\text{red}} \\ c_{\text{green}} \end{bmatrix} = \begin{bmatrix} r/(r+g+b) \\ g/(r+g+b) \end{bmatrix} \tag{25}$$

Each pixel $H_{i,j}$ is classified into class R = {road, not road} based on these features. The R_{road} classification is defined as

$$\mathrm{R}_{\mathrm{road}}(H_{i,j}) = \left\{ H_{i,j} \left| \begin{array}{l} P_c(\mathbf{C}(H_{i,j})) + \\ P_e(\nabla I(H_{i,j})) \\ > K_{\mathrm{limit}} \end{array} \right. \right\} \tag{26}$$

where $P_c(\cdot)$ Eq. (27) is a probability function the based on the Mahalanobi distance of the chromaticity relative to the seed area. $P_e(\cdot)$ Eq. (28) is based on the intensity gradient, calculated using a Sobel operator. The Sobel kernel size is selected as appropriate for the position in the image, i.e. the lower in the image the larger the kernel (3x3 at the top and 5x5 pixels at the bottom for the used 320 X 240 image resolution).

$$P_c(i,j) = \left(1 + w_c(i)(\mathbf{c}_{i,j} - \bar{\mathbf{c}}_w)^T \mathbf{Q}^{-1} (\mathbf{c}_{i,j} - \bar{\mathbf{c}}_w)\right)^{-1} \tag{27}$$

$$P_e(i,j) = \left(1 + w_e \left[\left| \frac{\partial I(i,j)}{\partial i} \right|^2 + \left| \frac{\partial I(i,j)}{\partial j} \right|^2 \right] \right)^{-1} \tag{28}$$

$\mathbf{Q}$ is the chromaticity covariance for the seed area. The $w_c(i)$ and w_e are weight factors. An example of the capabilities of the filter functions is shown in Fig. 12. Only the pixels at the road contour are evaluated, i.e. from the seed area pixels are tested towards the image edge or road border, the road border is then followed back to the seed area.

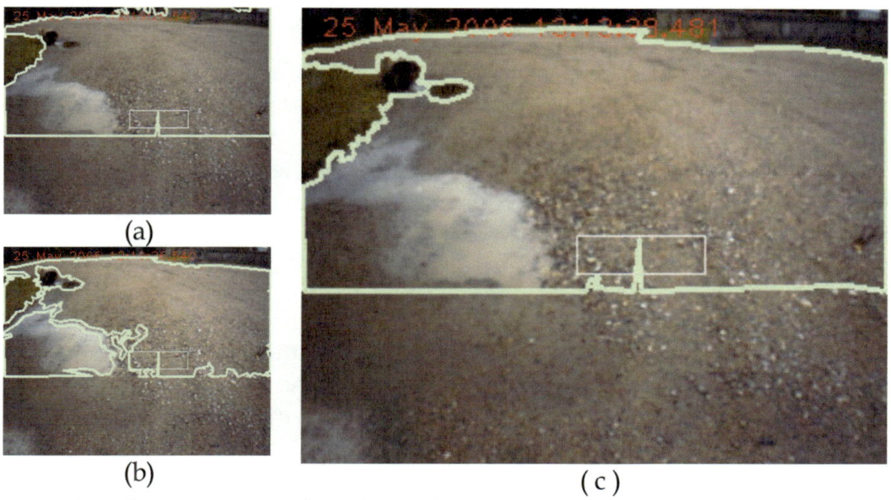

Fig. 12. Road outline extraction based on chromaticity (a), on gradient detection (b) and combined (c). In the top left corner there is a stone fence, this is not distinguished from the gravel road surface using the chromaticity filter in (a). The gradient filter (b) makes a border to the pit (bottom left). The combined filter (c) outlines the traversable area as desired. The seed area classified by the laser scanner is shown as a (thin) rectangle. The part of the image below the seed area is not analyzed.

4.4 Fusion of laser and vision data

A feature map representation is adapted for sensor fusion and navigation planning. The detected features are the traversable segments from the laser scanner covering ranges up to about 2.5 m in front of the robot, the vision based road outline from about 2 m and forward, and the obstacles detected from the laser scanner data.

Each traversable segment s_j^k extracted by the laserscanner in the most recent scan k is correlated with traversable segments from previous scans s^{k-i}, forming a set of traversable corridors B as shown in Eq. (29) correlation exists if the segments overlap with more than a robot width.

$$B_i = \{S_{a^0}^{k}, S_{a^1}^{k-1}, S_{a^2}^{k-2}, \cdots, S_{a^N}^{k-N}\} \quad (29)$$

where S_a^{k-i} is the a th traversable segment found in scan $k-i$.

This corridor of traversable segments gets extended beyond the range of the laserscanner using the road outline from the vision sensor. Intersection lines S^{k+v} (perpendicular to the current robot heading) at increasing intervals are used to extend the laser scanner corridors, as shown in Eq. (30)

$$B_i = \{S_{b^1}^{v1}, S_{b^2}^{v2}, \cdots, S_{b^M}^{vM}, S_{a^0}^{k}, S_{a^1}^{k-1}, S_{a^2}^{k-2}, \cdots, S_{a^N}^{k-N}\} \quad (30)$$

where S_b^{vn} is the b th intersection segment of intersection line n inside the estimated road utline. See example in Fig. 15

A number of such corridors may exist, e.g. left and right of obstacles, left and right in road forks or as a result of erroneous classification from the laser scanner or form the vision. A navigation route is planned along each of these corrodors considering the obstacles, current navigation objectives and the robot dynamics. The best route is qualified using a number of parameters including corridor statistics. If the vision is unable to estimate a usable road outline then the laser scanner data is used only.

4.5 Experimental results

The method is tested primarily on several runs of a 3 km route in a national park. The navigation is guided by a script specifying how to follow the roads and for how long. At the junctions the script guides the robot in an approximate direction until the next road is found. GPS is used sparsely to determine when a road section is about to end. Fig. 13 shows the road width detection from two road sections, a homogene asphalt road (a) and a 4 m wide gravelled road (b). The weather conditions were overcast with mild showers. The road width is estimated based on the available data EQ.(30) at time of manoeuvre decision. The vision based road width estimate is in the plane of the robot base, and as the road is mostly convex curved, the road width in the projected plane is narrower than in reality.

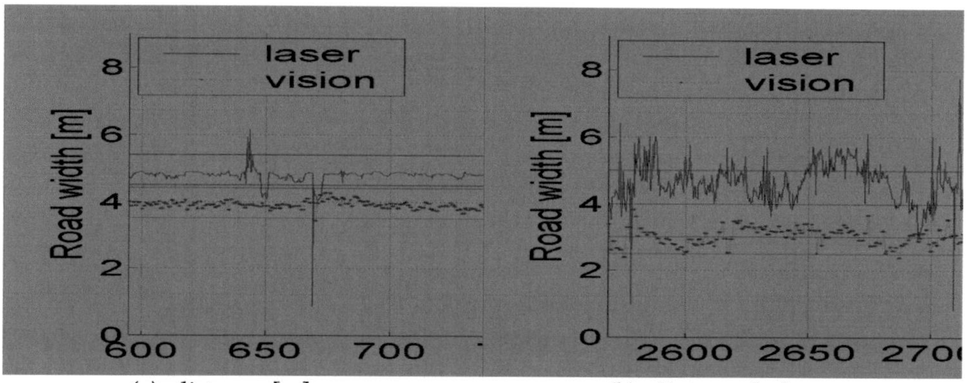

(a) distance [m] (b) distance [m]

Fig. 13. Road width estimation based on laser scanner (upper (red) curve) and vision based (dotted blue). A section from a 4.9 m wide asphalt road (a), and a $\approx$4 m wide gravelled road (b). The vision based road width is estimated in the plane of the robot base, and as the road is (convex) curved, the estimated road width is narrower. The asphalt road (a) is easy for both the laser scanner and the vision sensor. The gravelled road (b) is detected with a higher uncertainty, especially by the laser scanner.

The road width estimate and the road width stability can be taken as a performance measure of the vision and laser scanner sensors. The road width estimates are summarized in Table 3 for the laser scanner and vision sensor respectively. The laser scanner based estimate shows the correct road width in most cases, with a tendency to include the road shoulder at times, especially for the gravelled road where the roughness difference between the road and the road shoulder is limited

	true	laser based				vision based				Fig.
Road segment	width [m]	mean	σ	failed	N	mean	σ	failed	N	ref
Asphalt gray/wet	4.9	4.8	0.19	0%	1000	3.9	0.11	0%	291	Fig. 13a
Graveled gray/wet	4	4.7	0.62	0%	1000	3.1	0.30	1%	276	Fig. 13b
Asphalt gray/wet	3--4	3.5	0.63	0%	890	2.8	0.36	2%	224	
Asphalt sun/shade	3--4	3.3	0.46	0%	482	2.8	0.53	16%	79	

Table 3. Road width estimate summary from the data shown in Fig. 4. On the asphalt roads the laser scanner based estimate are with good precision, on the gravelled road the flat road shoulder widens the average road width estimate and makes the width estimate uncertain (higher σ). The last two rows are from the same road segment but in different weather conditions. N is the number of measurements.

The vision part shows a narrower road width estimate, as expected. Additionally the vision tends to estimate a to narrow road in case of shadows. The last two rows in Table 3 are from

a road segment that is partially below large trees, and here the road outline estimates failed in 16% of the measurements on the day with sunshine, compared to just 2% in gray and wet weather condition.
The vision based road outline detector does not cope well with focused shadow lines as shown in Fig. 14b and c, nor with painted road markings as in Fig. 14d. Unfocused shadows as in Fig. 14a are handled reasonably well.Wet and dry parts of the road are much less of a problem for the road outline detector as shown in Fig. 14d.

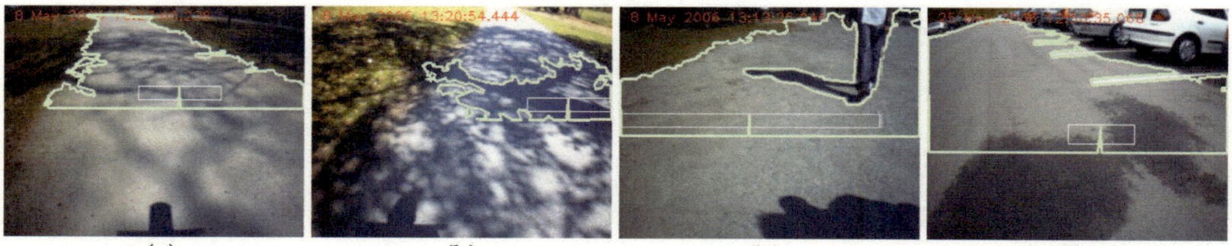

(a) (b) (c) (d)

Fig. 14. Shadows and road markings at the limits of the vision sensor capabilities. Unfocused shadows like in (a) are handled reasonably well, but if the shadows are more focused as in (b) the result is of little or no use. Hard shadows as in (c) and road markings as the white markings in a parking lot in (d) are handled as obstacles.

When the road outline is limited by obstacles as in the situation shown in Fig. 15a, the route possibilities in the feature map (Fig. 15b) will be limited correspondingly, and the result is an obstacle avoidance route initiated at an early stage. The pedestrian can follow the robot intentions as soon as the obstacle avoidance route is initiated, and thus limit potential conflict situations.

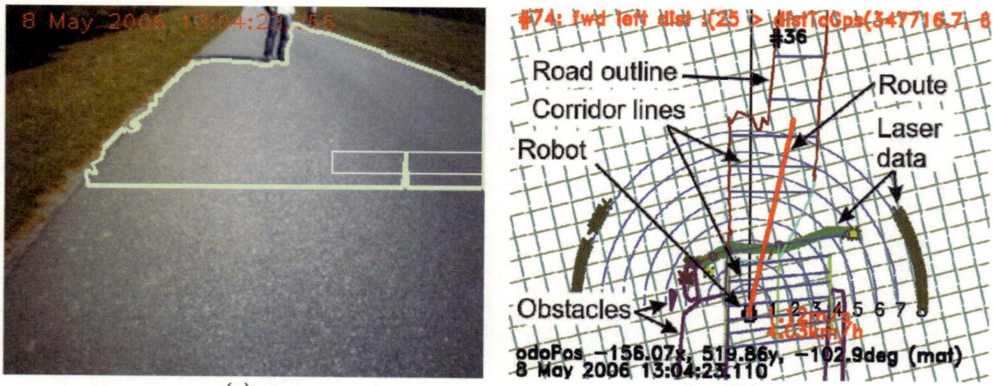

(a) (b)

Fig. 15. The pedestrian (and his shadow) is reducing the road outline (a) and an obstacle avoidance route is planned (as shown in (b)) long before the obstacle is seen by the laser scanner.

5. Conclusion

Three methods for support of visual navigation have been presented: Artificial visual landmarks, corridor following using vanishing point, and road following using terrain classification based on data fusion of laser scanner and vision. All the methods have been verified experimentally so that their usefulness in real systems is demonstrated. It has been shown that a combination of artificial landmarks and odometry will be able to limit the navigation error to a given level if the landmarks are placed with a sufficiently small distance. Using both landmarks and corridor following the same navigation accuracy may be obtained with much fewer landmarks thus enhancing the usability of the system.
The results for terrain classification show that fusing data from laser and vision gives a good foundation for path and road-following for outdoor robots. This may be used for service robots that are operating in e.g. public parks and gardens.

6. References

Andersen, J. C..; Blas M. R.; Ravn, O.; Andersen, N. A.; Blanke, M.(2006a). Traversable terrain classification for autonomous robots using single 2D laser scans. *Integrated Computer-aided engineering,* Vol.13, No.3,pp. 223-232, ISSN 1069-2509

Andersen J. C.(2006b). *Mobile Robot Navigation. ,PhD. Thesis* , Technical University of Denmark, ISBN 87-91184-64-9, Kgs. Lyngby Denmark

Andersen, J. C..; Andersen, N. A.; Ravn O.(2008). Vision Assisted Laser Navigation for Autonomous Robot *Experimental Robotics,* Star 39, Khatib,O.; Kumar, V. & Rus D. (Eds.), pp. 111-120,Springer-Verlag Berlin Heidelberg

Bais, A & Sablatnig R. (2006) Landmark based global self-localization of mobile soccer robots, In: COMPUTER VISION-ACCV 2006,PT II, Lecture Notes In Computer Sc ience,, pp. 842-851, Springer-Verlag Berlin, ISBN 3-540-31244-7, Berlin Germany

Bayramoğlu, E.; Andersen,N.A.; Poulsen, N.K.; Andersen, J. C.; Ravn, O. (2009). Mobile Robot Navigation in a Corridor Using Visual Odometry. Procedings of 14th Int. Conf. In Advanced Robotics, id. 58, June 22-26, 2009, Munich, Germany

Canny, J. (1986) A computational approach to edge detection. *IEEE Transactions on Pattern Analysis and Machine Intelligence,* 8:679--98, 1986.

Duda ,R.O. & Hart, P.E.(1972). Use of the Hough transformation to detect lines and curves in pictures. *Commun. ACM,* 15(1):11--15, 1972.

Guivant, J. E., Masson, F. R. & Nebot, E. M. (2001), Optimization of the simultaneous localization and map-building algorithm for real-time implementation, *IEEE Trans. on Robotics and Automation,* 17 (3),pp. 242–257, The University of Sidney, Australia.

Henriksen, L. & Krotkov, E. (1997), Natural terrain hazard detection with a laser rangefinder, *IEEE International Conference on Robotics and Automation,* Vol. 2, pp. 968--973.

Kabuka, M.& Arenas, A. (1987). Position verification of a mobile robot using standard pattern. *Journal of Robotics and Automation,* Vol.3, No.6,pp. 505-516, ISSN 1042296x

Kleeman, L.(2003). Advanced sonar and odometry error modeling for simultaneous localisation and map building. *IEEE/RSJ International Conference on Intelligent Robots and Systems,* 1:699--704, 2003.

Klöör, P.L., Lundquist, P., Ohlsson, P., Nygårds, J. & Wernersson, A. (1993), Change detection in natural scenes using laser range measurements from a mobile robot, *Proceedings of 1st IFACInternational Workshop on Intelligent Autonomous Vehicles*, IFAC, University of Southampton, pp. 71--76.

Lin, C.C. & Tummala, R. L.. (1997). Mobile robot navigation using artificial landmarks. *Journal of Robotic Systems,* Vol.14, No.2,pp. 93-106, ISSN 0741-2223

Macedo,J.; Matthies, L.; & Manduchi, R.(2000). Ladar.based discriminations of grass from obstacles for autonomous navigation. *Experimental Robotics VII,* Proceedings ISER 2000, Waikiki, Hawaii, Springer ,pp. 111-120

Trepagnier, P. G., Kinney, P. M., Nagel, J. E., Doner, M. T. & Pearce (2005), *Team gray techical paper*, Technical report, Gray & Company Inc.

Urmson, C., Anhalt, J., Clark, M., Galatali, T., Gonzalez, J. P.,Gutierrez, A., Harbaugh, S., Johnson-Roberson, M., Kato, H., Koon, P. L., Peterson, K., Smith, B.K., Spiker, S., Tryzelaar, E. & Whittaker, W. R.L. (2004), High speed navigation of unrehearsed terrain: Red team technology for grand challenge 2004, *Technical Report CMU-RI-TR-04-37*, Robotics Institute, Carnegie Mellon University, Pittsburgh, PA.

Vandapel, N., Huber, D., Kapuria, A. & Hebert, M. (2004), Natural terrain classification using 3-d ladar data, *Robotics and Automation Proceedings. ICRA '04. 2004 IEEE International Conference on'*, IEEE, pp. 5117--5122.

Wijesoma, W., Kodagoda, K. & Balasuriya, A. (2004), `Road-boundary detection and tracking using ladar sensing, *Robotics and Automation, IEEE Transactions on*, pp. 456-464.

Thrun, S., Montemerlo, M., Dahlkamp, H., Stavens, D., Aron, A., Diebel, J., Fong, P., Gale, J., Halpenny, M., Hoffmann, G., Lau, K., Oakley, C.,Palatucci, M., Pratt, V. & Pascal,S. (2006), Stanley: The robot that won the DARPA grand challenge, *http://cs.stanford.edu/group/roadrunner*

10

Interactive object learning and recognition with multiclass support vector machines

Aleš Ude
Jožef Stefan Institute,
Slovenia
ATR Computational Neuroscience Laboratories,
Japan

1. Introduction

A robot vision system can be called humanoid if it possesses an oculomotor system similar to human eyes and if it is capable to simultaneously acquire and process images of varying resolution. Designers of a number of humanoid robots attempted to mimic the foveated structure of the human eye. Foveation is useful because, firstly, it enables the robot to monitor and explore its surroundings in images of low resolution, thereby increasing the efficiency of the search process, and secondly, it makes it possible to simultaneously extract additional information – once the area of interest is determined – from higher resolution foveal images that contain more detail. There are several visual tasks that can benefit from foveated vision. One of the most prominent among them is object recognition. General object recognition on a humanoid robot is difficult because it requires the robot to detect objects in dynamic environments and to control the eye gaze to get the objects into the fovea and to keep them there. Once these tasks are accomplished, the robot can determine the identity of the object by processing foveal views.

Approaches proposed to mimic the foveated structure of biological vision systems include the use of two cameras per eye (Atkeson et al., 2000; Breazeal et al., 2001; Kozima & Yano, 2001; Scassellati, 1998) (Cog, DB, Infanoid, Kismet, respectively), i. e. a narrow-angle foveal camera and a wide-angle camera for peripheral vision; lenses with space-variant resolution (Rougeaux & Kuniyoshi, 1998) (humanoid head ESCHeR), i. e. a very high definition area in the fovea and a coarse resolution in the periphery; and space-variant log-polar sensors with retina-like distribution of photo-receptors (Sandini & Metta, 2003) (Babybot). It is also possible to implement log-polar sensors by transforming standard images into log-polar ones (Engel et al., 1994), but this approach requires the use of high definition cameras to get the benefit of varying resolution. Systems with zoom lenses have some of the advantages of foveated vision, but cannot simultaneously acquire wide angle and high resolution images.

Our work follows the first approach (see Fig. 1) and explores the advantage of foveated vision for object recognition over standard approaches, which use equal resolution across the visual field. While log-polar sensors are a closer match to biology, we note that using two cameras per eye can be advantageous because cameras with standard chips can be utilized. This makes it possible to equip a humanoid robot with miniature cameras (lipstick size and

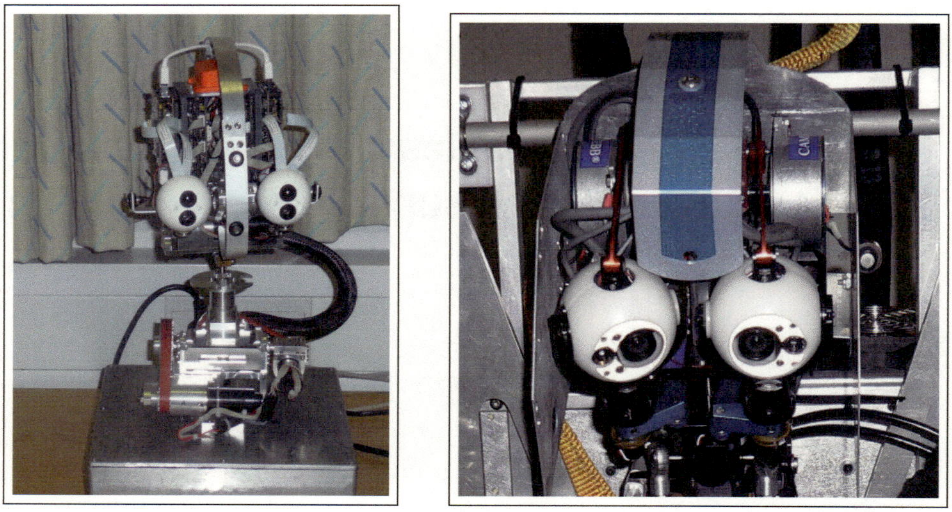

Fig. 1. Two humanoid heads with foveated vision. The left head was constructed by University of Karlsruhe for JSI (Asfour et al., 2008), while the right one is part of a humanoid robot designed by SARCOS and ATR (Cheng et al., 2007). Foveation is implemented by using two cameras in each eye. On the left head, the narrow-angle cameras, which provide foveal vision, are mounted above the wide-angle cameras, which are used for peripheral vision. The right head has foveal cameral on the outer sides of peripheral cameras.

smaller), which facilitates the mechanical design of the eye and improves its motion capabilities.

Studies on oculomotor control in humanoid robots include vestibulo-ocular and optokinetic reflex, smooth pursuit, saccades, and vergence control (Manzotti et al., 2001; Panerai et al., 2000; Rougeaux & Kuniyoshi, 1998; Shibata et al., 2001). On the image processing side, researchers studied humanoid vision for visual attention (Breazeal et al., 2001; Vijayakumar et al., 2001), segmentation (Fitzpatrick, 2003), and tracking (Metta et al., 2004; Rougeaux & Kuniyoshi, 1998). The utilization of foveation for object recognition was not of major concern in these papers. In our earlier work we demonstrated how foveation (Ude et al., 2003) can be used for object recognition. Our initial system employed LoG (Laplacian of the Gaussian) filters at a single, manually selected scale and principal component analysis to represent objects. Two other systems that utilized foveation for object recognition are described in (Arsenio, 2004), who are mainly concerned with using multi-modal cues for recognition, and (Björkman & Kragic, 2004), who present a complete system. In this chapter we focus on the analysis of benefits of foveated vision for recognition.

1.1 Summary of the Approach

On a humanoid robot, foveal vision can be utilized as follows: the robot relies on peripheral vision to search for interesting areas in visual scenes. The attention system reports about salient regions and triggers saccadic eye movements. After the saccade, the robot starts pursuing the area of interest, thus keeping it visible in the high-resolution foveal region of the eyes, assisted by peripheral vision if foveal tracking fails. Finally, high-resolution foveal vision provides the

humanoid with a more detailed description of the detected image areas, upon which it can make a decision about the identity of the object.
Since humanoids operate in dynamic environments and use active vision to monitor the external world, it is necessary that the detection and tracking algorithms are all realized in real-time. To this end, some ground knowledge is normally assumed such as for example color and shape probability distributions of the objects of interest. A suitable detection and tracking algorithm based on such assumptions is described in (Ude et al., 2001), where the details can be found. For the purpose of this chapter it is important to note that in this way we can estimate the location and extent of the object in the image. An important current research topics is how to extract image regions that contain objects without assuming prior knowledge about the objects of interest (Ude et al., 2008).
To support foveal vision we developed a control system whose primary goal is to maintain the visibility of the object based on 2-D information from peripheral views. The developed system attempts to maintain the visibility of the object in foveal views of both eyes simultaneously. The secondary goal of the system is to enhance the appearance of the humanoid through mimicking aspects of human movement: human eyes follow object movement, but without head and body movement have a limited range; thus, the robot's control system supports its eye movements through head and body movements. The details can be found in (Ude et al., 2006).
In the rest of this chapter we describe an approach to object learning and recognition that utilizes the results of these susbsytems to achieve recognition in foveal views.

2. Object Representation

Early approaches to object recognition in static images were implemented predominantly around the 3-D reconstruction paradigm of (Marr & Nishihara, 1978), but many of the more recent recognition systems make use of viewpoint-dependent models (Longuet-Higgins, 1990; Poggio & Edelman, 1990; Sinha & Poggio, 1996). View-based strategies are receiving increasing attention because it has been recognized that 3-D reconstruction is difficult in practice (mainly due to difficulties in segmentation). There is also psychophysical evidence that supports view-based techniques(Tarr & Bülthoff, 1998).

2.1 Normalization through Affine Warping

In view-based systems objects are represented by a number of images (or features extracted from 2-D images) taken from different viewpoints. These model images are compared to test images acquired by the robot. However, since both a humanoid robot and objects can move in space, objects appear in images at different positions, orientations and scales. It is obviously not feasible to learn all possible views due to time and memory limitations. The number of required views can, however, be reduced by normalizing the subimages that contain objects of interest to images of fixed size.
This reduction can be accomplished by utilizing the results of the tracker. Our tracker estimates the shape of the tracked object using second order statistics of pixels that are probabilistically classified as "blob pixels" (Ude et al., 2001). From the second order statistics we can estimate the planar object orientation and the extent of the object along its major and minor axes. In other words, we can estimate the ellipse enclosing the object pixels. As the lengths of both axes can differ significantly, each object image is normalized along the principal axis directions instead of image coordinate axes and we apply a different scaling factor along each of these directions. By aligning the object's axes with the coordinate axes, we also achieve

Fig. 2. Example images of eight objects. Scaling and planar rotations are accounted for by affine warping using the results of visual tracking.

invariance against planar rotations, thus reducing the number of views that need to be stored to represent an object because rotations around the optical axis result in the same example images. The results of the normalization process are shown in Fig. 2 and 3.

Normalization along the principal axes is implemented by applying the following transformations: (1) translate the blob so that its center is aligned with the origin of the image, (2) rotate the blob so that its principal directions are aligned with the coordinate axes, (3) scale the blob so that its major and minor axis are as long as the sides of a predefined window, (4) translate the blob so that its center is aligned with the center of the new window. The resulting mapping in homogeneous coordinates is given by the following affine transformation:

$$\boldsymbol{A} = \begin{bmatrix} 1 & 0 & \frac{w_x}{2} \\ 0 & 1 & \frac{w_y}{2} \\ 0 & 0 & 1 \end{bmatrix} \begin{bmatrix} \frac{w_x}{2a} & 0 & 0 \\ 0 & \frac{w_y}{2b} & 0 \\ 0 & 0 & 1 \end{bmatrix} \begin{bmatrix} \boldsymbol{R}(\theta)^T & 0 \\ 0 & 1 \end{bmatrix} \begin{bmatrix} 1 & 0 & -u \\ 0 & 1 & -v \\ 0 & 0 & 1 \end{bmatrix} = \begin{bmatrix} a_{11} & a_{12} & a_{13} \\ a_{21} & a_{22} & a_{23} \\ 0 & 0 & 1 \end{bmatrix}, \tag{1}$$

where $\boldsymbol{u} = [u, v]^T$ and θ are the position and orientation of the blob, a and b are the half lengths of its major and minor axis, and w_x and w_y are the predefined width and height of the window onto which we map the window containing the blob.

The process of geometrically transforming the input image by the affine mapping given in Eq. (1) is known as *affine warping*. Since matrix $\boldsymbol{A}$ is invertible, we implemented affine warping by parsing through the pixels of the output window, which is smaller than the input window, and by applying the inverse mapping $\boldsymbol{A}^{-1}$ to each of the pixels in this window. The associated color intensities at these positions are estimated either by a nearest neighbor or cubic interpolation.

2.2 Gabor Jets

Early view-based approaches used raw grayscale images as input to the selected classifier, e. g. principal component analysis (Turk & Pentland, 1991). This kind of approaches turned out to be fairly successful as long as the amount of noise in the images is small and the illumination conditions do not change. To achieve robustness against brightness changes, it is necessary to compute an improved, illumination insensitive characterization of the local image structure. Some of the more recent recognition systems therefore apply a bank of illumination-insensitive filters to the original images before starting the recognition process. We follow the biologically motivated approach of (Wiskott et al., 1997), who proposed to apply a bank of Gabor filters to the incoming images containing objects of interest. Gabor filters are known to be good edge detectors and are therefore robust against varying brightness. They have limited support both in space and frequency domain and have a certain amount of robustness against translation, distortion, rotation, and scaling (Wiskott et al., 1997).

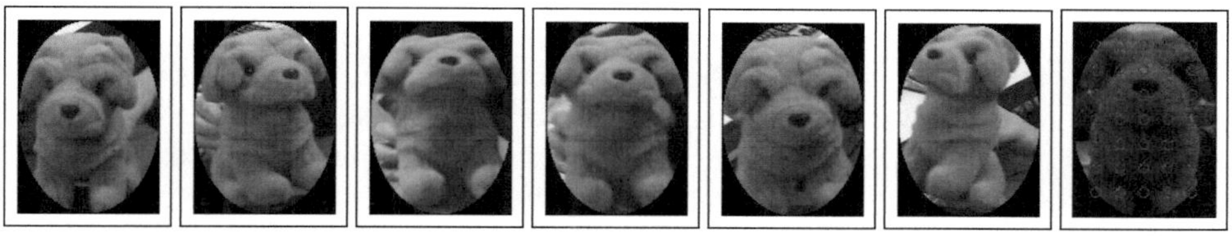

Fig. 3. Training images for one of the objects used in statistical experiments. To take care of rotations in depth, we must collect a sufficient amount of typical viewpoints. The rightmost image shows a regular pixel grid at which feature vectors are calculated. The actual grid was denser than the depicted one.

Complex Gabor kernels are defined by

$$\Phi_{\mu,\nu}(\boldsymbol{x}) = \frac{\|\boldsymbol{k}_{\mu,\nu}\|^2}{\sigma^2} \cdot \exp\left(-\frac{\|\boldsymbol{k}_{\mu,\nu}\|^2\|\boldsymbol{x}\|^2}{2\sigma^2}\right) \cdot \left(\exp\left(i\boldsymbol{k}_{\mu,\nu}^T\boldsymbol{x}\right) - \exp\left(-\frac{\sigma^2}{2}\right)\right), \quad (2)$$

where $\boldsymbol{k}_{\mu,\nu} = k_\nu[\cos(\phi_\mu), sin(\phi_\mu)]^T$. Gabor jet at pixel $\boldsymbol{x}$ is defined as a set of complex coefficients $\{J_j^{\boldsymbol{x}}\}$ obtained by convolving the image with a number of Gabor kernels at this pixel. Gabor kernels are selected so that they sample a number of different wavelengths k_ν and orientations ϕ_μ. (Wiskott et al., 1997) proposed to use $k_\nu = 2^{-\frac{\nu+2}{2}}$, $\nu = 0,\ldots,4$, and $\phi_\mu = \mu\frac{\pi}{8}$, $\mu = 0,\ldots,7$, but this depends both on the size of the incoming images and the image structure. They showed that the similarity between the jets can be measured by

$$S\left(\{J_i^{\boldsymbol{x}}\},\{J_i^{\boldsymbol{y}}\}\right) = \frac{\boldsymbol{a}_{\boldsymbol{x}}^T * \boldsymbol{a}_{\boldsymbol{y}}}{\|\boldsymbol{a}_{\boldsymbol{x}}\|\|\boldsymbol{a}_{\boldsymbol{y}}\|}, \quad (3)$$

where $\boldsymbol{a}_{\boldsymbol{x}} = [|J_1^{\boldsymbol{x}}|,\ldots,|J_s^{\boldsymbol{x}}|]^T$ and s is the number of complex Gabor kernels. This is based on the fact that the magnitudes of complex coefficients vary slowly with the position of the jet in the image.

We use Gabor jets to generate feature vectors for recognition. To reduce the dimensionality of these feature vectors, we did not make use of all jets. Ideally, one would calculate the jets only at important local features. We did not attempt to extract local features because it is often difficult to extract them in a stable manner. Instead, we decided to build the feature vectors from Gabor jets positioned on a regular grid of pixels (the selected grid size was 5×5). Normalized jets $\{a_j^{\boldsymbol{x}}/\|\boldsymbol{a}^{\boldsymbol{x}}\|\}_{j=1}^n$ calculated on this grid and belonging to the ellipse enclosing the object like in Fig. 3 were finally utilized to build feature vectors.

It is important to note that we first scale the object images to a fixed size and then apply Gabor filters. In this way we ensure that the size of local structure in the acquired images does not change and consequently we do not need to change the frequencies k_ν of the applied filters.

2.3 Training

Our goal is to learn a three-dimensional representation for each object of interest. To achieve this, it is necessary to show the objects to the humanoid from all relevant viewing directions. In computer vision this is normally achieved by accurate turntables that enable the collection of images from regularly distributed viewpoints. However, this solution is not practical for autonomous robots that need to seamlessly acquire new knowledge in natural environments. On the other hand, learning in human environments can effectively be supported by human-robot interaction. We therefore explored whether it is possible to reliably learn 3-D descriptions from images collected while a human teacher moves the object in front of the robot. Using the previously described attention, tracking, and smooth pursuit systems, the robot acquires foveal images of the object in motion and collects feature vectors based on Gabor jets from many different viewpoints (see Figure 3 and 2). In the next section we present our approach to object recognition using Gabor jets, followed by experimental results that show that such collections of feature vectors are sufficient for 3-D object recognition.

3. Recognition with Support Vector Machines

Support vector machines (SVMs) are a relatively new classification system rooted in the statistical learning theory. They are considered as state of the art classifiers because they deliver high performance in real-world applications. To distinguish between two different classes, a support vector machine draws the (optimal) separating hyperplane between training data points belonging to the two classes. The hyperplane is optimal in the sense that it separates the largest fraction of points from each class, while maximizing the distance from either class to the hyperplane. First approaches that utilized SVMs for object recognition applied the basic method that deals with a two-class classification problem. In the context of object recognition, a binary tree strategy (Guo et al., 2001; Pontil & Verri, 1998) was proposed to solve the multi-class problem. While this approach provides a simple and powerful classification framework, it cannot capture correlations between the different classes since it breaks a multi-class problem into multiple independent binary problems (Crammer & Singer, 2001). In addition, the result is not independent of how the candidate objects are paired. There were attempts to generalize SVMs to multi-class problems, but practical implementation have started to emerge only recently. Here we follow the generalization proposed in (Crammer & Singer, 2001), which is briefly described in Section 3.1. To improve classification results we utilized nonlinear variant of support vector machines with a specially designed kernel function that exploits the properties of Gabor jets. We made use of the implementation described in (Joachims, 1999; Tsochantaridis et al., 2004).

3.1 Nonlinear Multiclass Support Vector Machines

Multi-class classification addresses the problem of finding a function defined from an input space $\Psi \subset \mathcal{R}^n$ onto a set of classes $\Omega = \{1, \ldots, m\}$. Let $\boldsymbol{S} = \{(\boldsymbol{x}_1, y_1), \ldots, (\boldsymbol{x}_n, y_n)\}$, $\boldsymbol{x}_i \in \Psi$, $y_i \in \Omega$, be a set of n training samples. We look for a function $\boldsymbol{H} : \Psi \rightarrow \Omega$ so that $\boldsymbol{H}(\boldsymbol{x}_i) = y_i$. (Crammer & Singer, 2001)[1] proposed to search for $\boldsymbol{H}$ among linear classifiers of the form

$$\boldsymbol{H}_{\boldsymbol{M},\boldsymbol{b}}(\boldsymbol{x}) = \arg\max_{r \in \Omega} \{\boldsymbol{M}_r * \boldsymbol{x} + b_r\}, \tag{4}$$

where $\boldsymbol{b} = [b_1, \ldots, b_k]^T$, $\boldsymbol{M} \in \mathcal{R}^{m \times n}$ is a matrix of size $m \times n$ and $\boldsymbol{M}_r$ is the r-th row of $\boldsymbol{M}$. Standard two-class SVMs result in classifiers $\boldsymbol{H} = (\boldsymbol{w}, b)$ that predict the label of a data point $\boldsymbol{x}$ as 1 if $\boldsymbol{w} * \boldsymbol{x} + b \geq 0$ and 2 otherwise. They can be expressed in the above form by taking a matrix $\boldsymbol{M}$ with rows $\boldsymbol{M}_1 = \boldsymbol{w}$, $\boldsymbol{M}_2 = -\boldsymbol{w}$, and $b_1 = b$, $b_2 = -b$.

---

[1] The bias parameters b_r were omitted in (Crammer & Singer, 2001) to simplify the optimization problem. Here we keep them in the interest of clarity of presentation.

The following error function can be used to to evaluate the performance of a multi-class predictor of form (4)

$$\frac{1}{n}\sum_{i=1}^{n}\left(\max_{r\in\Omega}\left\{\boldsymbol{M}_r * \boldsymbol{x}_i + b_r + 1 - \delta_{y_i,r}\right\} - \boldsymbol{M}_{y_i} * \boldsymbol{x}_i - b_{y_i}\right). \tag{5}$$

Here $\delta_{y_i,r} = 1$ if $y_i = r$ and 0 otherwise. The above criterion function is always greater or equal zero and has its minimum at zero if for each data point $\boldsymbol{x}_i$ the value $\boldsymbol{M}_r * \boldsymbol{x}_i + b_r$ is larger by at least 1 for the correct label than for all other labels. In this case, the sample S is called linearly separable and it satisfies the constraints

$$\boldsymbol{M}_{y_i} * \boldsymbol{x}_i + b_{y_i} + \delta_{y_i,r} - \boldsymbol{M}_r * \boldsymbol{x}_i - b_r \geq 1, \ \forall\, i, r. \tag{6}$$

Obviously, any $(\boldsymbol{M}, \boldsymbol{b})$ satisfying these conditions results in a decision function that classifies all samples correctly.
To generalize support vector learning to non-separable problems, slack variables $\xi_i \geq 0$ need to be introduced. In this case, constraints (6) become

$$\boldsymbol{M}_{y_i} * \boldsymbol{x}_i + b_{y_i} + \delta_{y_i,r} - \boldsymbol{M}_r * \boldsymbol{x}_i - b_r \geq 1 - \xi_i, \ \forall\, i, r. \tag{7}$$

(Crammer & Singer, 2001) showed that optimal multi-class support vector machine can be calculated by solving a quadratic programming optimization problem:

$$\min_{\boldsymbol{M},\boldsymbol{b},\boldsymbol{\xi}} \frac{1}{2}\beta\left(\sum_{r=1}^{m}\sum_{i=1}^{n} M_{ri}^2 + \sum_{r=1}^{m} b_r^2\right) + \sum_{i=1}^{n}\xi_i \tag{8}$$

$$\text{subject to :} \quad \begin{array}{l} \boldsymbol{M}_{y_i} * \boldsymbol{x}_i + b_{y_i} + \delta_{y_i,r} - \boldsymbol{M}_r * \boldsymbol{x}_i - b_r \geq 1 - \xi_i \\ \xi_i \geq 0, \forall\, i, r \end{array}$$

Here $\boldsymbol{\xi}_i \geq 0$ are the slack variables that need to be introduced to solve non-separable problems. This constrained quadratic optimization problem is convex and can therefore be solved efficiently. Note that in optimization problem (8) the data points appear only in inner products $\boldsymbol{M}_j * \boldsymbol{x}_i$. Furthermore, the same authors proved that the rows of the optimal classifier matrix $\boldsymbol{M}$ are given by

$$\boldsymbol{M}_r^T = \sum_{i=1}^{n} \tau_{ir}\boldsymbol{x}_i, \ \tau_{i,r} \geq 0, \ r = 1, \ldots, m, \tag{9}$$

and the corresponding decision function can be written as

$$\boldsymbol{H}_{\boldsymbol{M},\boldsymbol{b}}(\boldsymbol{x}) = \arg\max_{r\in\Omega}\left\{\sum_{i=1}^{n} \tau_{i,r}\boldsymbol{x}_i^T * \boldsymbol{x} + b_r\right\}. \tag{10}$$

Here the data points appear only in inner products $\boldsymbol{x}_i^T * \boldsymbol{x}$. Lets assume now that the data points were transformed with a nonlinear mapping Φ, which maps the data into a possibly higher dimensional feature space. The optimal hyperplane can then be constructed in this space and the scalar products $\boldsymbol{x} * \boldsymbol{y}$ are replaced by $\Phi(\boldsymbol{x}) * \Phi(\boldsymbol{y})$. The main idea is to find a feature space in which it is easier to separate the classes than in the original data space.

The nonlinear mappings of interest are those that allow for an efficient calculation of high-dimensional inner products via kernel functions

$$\mathrm{K}(\boldsymbol{x}, \boldsymbol{y}) = \Phi(\boldsymbol{x}) * \Phi(\boldsymbol{y}). \tag{11}$$

To find the optimal multi-class support vector machine in a higher dimensional feature space, we need to solve a constrained quadratic optimization problem in which inner products $\Phi(\boldsymbol{x}_i) * \Phi(\boldsymbol{x}_j)$ are replaced with the kernel function $\mathrm{K}(\boldsymbol{x}_i, \boldsymbol{x}_j)$. The decision function (10) becomes

$$\boldsymbol{H}_{\boldsymbol{M},\boldsymbol{b}}(\boldsymbol{x}) = \arg\max_{r \in \Omega} \left\{ \sum_{i=1}^{n} \tau_{i,r} \mathrm{K}(\boldsymbol{x}_i, \boldsymbol{x}) + b_r \right\}. \tag{12}$$

The convergence of the optimization algorithm can be guaranteed for all kernel functions K that allow the construction of nonlinear mapping Φ such that (11) holds. The condition for this is given by the Mercer's theorem (Burges, 1998).

3.2 Kernel Functions for Gabor Jets

The similarity measure for Gabor jets (3) provides a good starting point to define a suitable decision function. Let $\boldsymbol{X}_G$ be the set of all grid points within two normalized images at which Gabor jets are calculated and let $J_{\boldsymbol{X}_G}$ and $L_{\boldsymbol{X}_G}$ be the Gabor jets calculated in two different images, but on the same grid points. Based on (3), we define the following kernel function

$$\mathrm{K}_G(J_{\boldsymbol{X}_G}, L_{\boldsymbol{X}_G}) = \exp\left(-\rho_1 \frac{1}{M} \sum_{\boldsymbol{x} \in \boldsymbol{X}_G} \left(1 - \frac{\boldsymbol{a}_{\boldsymbol{x}}^T * \boldsymbol{b}_{\boldsymbol{x}}}{\|\boldsymbol{a}_{\boldsymbol{x}}\| \|\boldsymbol{b}_{\boldsymbol{x}}\|}\right)\right), \tag{13}$$

where M is the number of grid points in $\boldsymbol{X}_G$. This function satisfies the Mercer's condition (Burges, 1998) and can thus be used for support vector learning.

Kernel function (13) assumes that the set of grid points $\boldsymbol{X}_G$ does not change from image to image. (Wallraven et al., 2003) showed that it is possible to define kernel functions using local feature detectors computed on sets of image points that vary from image to image. They designed kernel functions defined on feature vectors of variable lengths and with different ordering of features. While feature order is not a problem for our system due to the affine warping procedure, it would be advantageous to exclude some of the grid points because due to noise some of the points in the warped images do not belong to the object, even after clipping the parts outside of the enclosing ellipse. We can, however, use the results of the tracking/segmentation to exclude such points from the calculation. For each pixel, our tracker (Ude et al., 2001) can estimate the probability whether or not this pixel belong to the tracked object. We can thus define the set $\boldsymbol{X}_G$ on each image to include only points for which these probabilities are greater than a pre-specified threshold. Let $\boldsymbol{X}_G^1$ and $\boldsymbol{X}_G^2$ be two sets of grid points with tracking probabilities greater than a pre-specified threshold. We can define a new kernel function

$$\mathrm{K}'_G(J_{\boldsymbol{X}_G^1}, L_{\boldsymbol{X}_G^2}) = \boldsymbol{K}_G(J_{\boldsymbol{X}_G^1 \cap \boldsymbol{X}_G^2}, L_{\boldsymbol{X}_G^1 \cap \boldsymbol{X}_G^2}) \cdot \exp\left(-\rho_1 \frac{1}{M} \left(\sum_{\boldsymbol{x} \in \boldsymbol{X}_G^1 \cup \boldsymbol{X}_G^2 - \boldsymbol{X}_G^1 \cap \boldsymbol{X}_G^2} 2 \right)\right) \tag{14}$$

where M is the number of grid points in $\boldsymbol{X}_G^1 \cup \boldsymbol{X}_G^2$. We add the penalty of 2 for grid points that are not classified as object points only in one of both images because this is the highest possible value for one term in the criterion function (13). The reasoning for this is that if a pixel does not belong to the object, the Gabor jets calculated at this point are meaningless. We should therefore add the highest possible penalty for the function of type (3). While this kernel function assumes that the ordering of grid points is the same in both images, it is much less computationally expensive than the more general functions proposed in (Wallraven et al., 2003). This is important both for faster training and for real-time recognition.

4. Experimental results

We used a set of ten objects to test the performance of the recognition system on a humanoid robot (6 teddy bears, two toy dogs, a coffee mug, and a face). For each object we recorded two or more movies using a video stream coming from the robot's foveal cameras. In each of the recording sessions the experimenter attempted to show one of the objects to the robot from all relevant viewing directions. One movie per object was used to construct the SVM classifier, while one of the other movies served as input to test the classifiers. Thus the support vector machine was trained to distinguish between 10 classes. Each movie was one minute long and we used at most 4 images per second (out of 30) for training. Since slightly more than first ten seconds of the movies were needed to initialize the tracker, we had at most 208 training images per object. For testing we used 10 images per second, which resulted in 487 test images per object. Except for the results of Table 4, all the percentages presented here were calculated using the classification results obtained from 4870 test images. Three types of classifiers were used to test the performance of foveated recognition. The first one was a nonlinear multi-class support vector machine based on kernel functions K_G and K'_G from Eq. (13) and (14), respectively. It is denoted as SVM nonlinear in Table 1 - 6. Gabor jets were calculated at 8 different orientations and 5 different scales and the grid size was 5 pixels in both directions. The filters were scaled appropriately when using lower resolution images. The second classifier we tested was a more standard linear multi-class SVM using the same feature vectors. It is denoted by SVM linear in the tables. The third classifier was the nearest neighbor classifier (NNC) that used the similarity measure (3) – summed over all grid points – to calculate the nearest neighbor based on the same Gabor jets as input data.
Results in Tables 1 - 3 demonstrate that foveation is useful for recognition. Kernel function (14) was used here. The classification results clearly become worse with the decreasing resolution. In fact, the data of Table 3 had to be calculated differently because we could not estimate the planar orientation accurately enough for affine warping, which made the normalization procedure fail. This resulted in significantly worse classification results. To calculate the results of Table 3, we sampled the Gabor jets on the images of size 160×120 with a 20 sampling grid, which resulted in the same number of grid points as when image resolution is reduced from

Fig. 4. Images taken under different lighting conditions

Training views per object	SVM nonlinear	SVM linear	NNC
208	97.6 %	96.8 %	95.9 %
104	96.7 %	95.3 %	93.7 %
52	95.1 %	94.0 %	91.5 %
26	91.9 %	89.9 %	86.7 %

Table 1. Correct classification rate (image resolution 120 $\times$ 160 pixels)

Training views per object	SVM nonlinear	SVM linear	NNC
208	94.2 %	94.4 %	89.3 %
104	92.4 %	91.1 %	87.3 %
52	90.7 %	89.7 %	84.4 %
26	86.7 %	84.5 %	79.2 %

Table 2. Correct classification rate (image resolution 60 $\times$ 80 pixels)

Training views per object	SVM nonlinear	SVM linear	NNC
208	91.0 %	89.6 %	84.7 %
104	87.2 %	85.8 %	81.5 %
52	82.4 %	81.1 %	77.8 %
26	77.1 %	75.5 %	72.1 %

Table 3. Correct classification rate (image resolution 30 $\times$ 40 pixels)

160 $\times$ 120 to 40 $\times$ 30 and the grid size is kept the same. The recognition rate dropped even with such data. Our results also show that we can collect enough training data even without using accurate turntables to systematically collect the images. While based on these results it is not possible to say what is the maximum number of objects that can be recognized using the proposed approach, we note that the method produced similar recognition rates when only subsets of objects were used for training and classification.

We also tested the performance of the system on data captured under changed lighting condition (see Fig. 4) and on noise corrupted data (see Fig. 5, two objects – a teddy bear and a toy dog – were used in this experiment). The classification performance for these two objects on original images was a bit higher than the combined performance, but this was purely coincidental and we did not intentionally select these two object to test the varying brightness condition. For classification we used the same SVMs as in Tables 1-3. While the performance decreased slightly on darker images, the results show that the method still performs well in such conditions. This is due to the properties of Gabor jets and due to the normalization of jets given by the similarity function (3). Our experiments showed that the classification rate drops significantly if one of the standard kernel functions, e. g. a linear kernel, is used for the support vector learning.

Unlike in other tables, the results of Table 5 and 6 were calculated using SVMs based on kernel function K_G from Eq. (13), thus not taking into account the segmentation results. The

Fig. 5. Images degraded with white Gaussian noise (std. dev. = 10)

segmentation results were not used for the nearest neighbor classification either. Comparing Tables 5 and 6 we can say that SVMs are robust against noise as well. The results of Table 6 can be directly compared to Table 2, the only difference being in the use of segmentation results. While both types of SVMs performed well in this case, the performance of the nearest neighbor classification dropped significantly when all the data from the enclosing ellipse was used. This shows that unlike nearest neighbor classification, SVMs can cope well with outliers. Nevertheless, it is still advantageous to use the kernel function that can include the segmentation results because such an approach reduces the amount of data that needs to be considered to calculate SVMs, hence resulting in faster computation times. We expect that differences between the two types of kernel functions would become more significant for objects that cannot be accurately enclosed within an ellipse.

The presented results cannot be directly compared to the results on standard databases for benchmarking object recognition algorithms because here the training sets are much less complete. Some of the classification errors are caused by the lack of training data rather than by a deficient classification approach. Unlike many approaches from the computer vision literature that avoid the problem of finding objects, we tested the system on images obtained through a realistic object tracking and segmentation procedure. Only such data is relevant for foveated object recognition because without some kind of object detection procedure it is not possible to direct the fovea towards the objects of interest.

5. Conclusions

Using foveation control, our system can learn truly three-dimensional object representations just by collecting the data while the demonstrator attempts to show the objects from all relevant viewing directions. Our experimental results demonstrate that this statistical approach

Image resolution	normal	dark	very dark
120×160	99.5 %	97.7 %	97.9 %
60×80	96.7 %	93.5 %	95.0 %
30×40	93.6 %	89.3 %	88.2 %

Table 4. Correct classification rate for images with varying lighting conditions (see Fig. 4). Only two object were tested in this case (the database still contained ten objects) and nonlinear SVMs calculated based on 208 views per training objects were used.

Training views per object	SVM	NNC
208	91.5 %	79.8 %
104	90.7 %	74.5 %
52	90.5 %	68.0 %
26	87.1 %	60.3 %

Table 5. Correct classification rate for noise degraded images (see Fig. 5). The image resolution was 60 × 80 and segmentation results were not used. Nonlinear SVMs were used in this experiment.

Training views per object	SVM	NNC
208	94.4 %	75.8 %
104	93.1 %	69.2 %
52	91.4 %	60.3 %
26	88.1 %	53.6 %

Table 6. Correct classification rate without noise degradation. The image resolution was 60 × 80 and segmentation results were not used. Nonlinear SVMs were used in this experiment.

is sufficient for object learning and that it is not necessary to use specially designed turntables to accurately collect the views from all relevant viewing directions. Our experimental results prove (see Tab. 1 - 3) that higher resolution images provided by foveation control significantly improve the classification rates of object recognition. In addition, previous approaches that employed support vector machines for object recognition used binary SVMs combined with decision trees (Guo et al., 2001; Pontil & Verri, 1998; Wallraven et al., 2003) to solve the multi-class recognition problem. We proposed a new recognition system that makes use of multi-class nonlinear SVMs to solve the multi-class recognition problem. We also developed a new kernel function based on the Gabor jet similarity measure that can utilize the results of bottom-up segmentation. Experimental results show high recognition rates in realistic test environments.

6. References

Arsenio, A. M. (2004). Object recognition from multiple percepts, *Proc. IEEE-RAS/RSJ Int. Conf. Humanoid Robots (Humanoids 2004)*, Los Angeles, California, USA.

Asfour, T., Azad, P., Welke, K., Ude, A. & Dillmann, R. (2008). The Karlsruhe humanoid head, *Proc. IEEE-RAS/RSJ Int. Conf. Humanoid Robots (Humanoids 2008)*, Daejeon, Korea. To appear.

Atkeson, C. G., Hale, J., Pollick, F., Riley, M., Kotosaka, S. Schaal, S., Shibata, T., Tevatia, G., Ude, A., Vijayakumar, S. & Kawato, M. (2000). Using humanoid robots to study human behavior, *IEEE Intelligent Systems* **15**(4): 46–56.

Björkman, M. & Kragic, D. (2004). Combination of foveal and peripheral vision for object recognition and pose estimation, *Proc. 2004 IEEE Int. Conf. Robotics and Automation*, New Orleans, Louisiana, pp. 5135–5140.

Breazeal, C., Edsinger, A., Fitzpatrick, P. & Scassellati, B. (2001). Social constraints on animate vision, *IEEE Trans. Systems, Man, and Cybernetics* **31**(5): 443–452.

Burges, C. J. C. (1998). A tutorial on support vector machines for pattern recognition, *Data Min. Knowl. Discov.* **2**(2): 121–167.

Cheng, G., Hyon, S.-H., Morimoto, J., Ude, A., Hale, J. G., Colvin, G., Scroggin, W. & Jacobsen, S. C. (2007). CB: a humanoid research platform for exploring neuroscience, *Advanced Robotics* **21**(10): 1097–1114.

Crammer, K. & Singer, Y. (2001). On the algorithmic implementation of multiclass kernel-based vector machines, *Journal of Machine Learning Research* **2**: 265–292.

Engel, G., Greve, D. N., Lubin, J. M. & Schwartz, E. L. (1994). Space-variant active vision and visually guided robotics: Design and construction of a high-peformance miniature vehicle, *Proc. 12th IAPR Int. Conf. Pattern Recognition. Vol. 2 - Conf. B: Computer Vision & Image Processing*, Jerusalem, Israel, pp. 487 – 490.

Fitzpatrick, P. (2003). First contact: an active vision approach to segmentation, *Proc. 2003 IEEE/RSJ Int. Conf. Intelligent Robots and Systems*, Las Vegas, Nevada, pp. 2161–2166.

Guo, G., Li, S. Z. & Chan, K. L. (2001). Support vector machines for face recognition, *Image and Vision Computing* **19**(9-10): 631–638.

Joachims, T. (1999). Making large-scale support vector machine learning practical, *in* B. Schölkopf, C. J. C. Burges & A. J. Smola (eds), *Advances in Kernel Methods - Support Vector Learning*, MIT Press, Cambridge, MA.

Kozima, H. & Yano, H. (2001). A robot that learns to communicate with human caregivers, *Proc. Int. Workshop on Epigenetic Robotics*, Lund, Sweden.

Longuet-Higgins, H. C. (1990). Recognizing three dimensions, *Nature* **343**: 214–215.

Manzotti, R., Gasteratos, A., Metta, G. & Sandini, G. (2001). Disparity estimation on log-polar images and vergence control, *Computer Vision and Image Understanding* **83**(2): 97–117.

Marr, D. & Nishihara, H. K. (1978). Representation and recognition of the spatial organization of three-dimensional shapes, *Proc. R. Soc. of London, B* **200**: 269–294.

Metta, G., Gasteratos, A. & Sandini, G. (2004). Learning to track colored objects with log-polar vision, *Mechatronics* **14**: 989–1006.

Panerai, F., Metta, G. & Sandini, G. (2000). Visuo-inertial stabilization in space-variant binocular systems, *Robotics and Autonomous Systems* **30**(1-2): 195–214.

Poggio, T. & Edelman, S. (1990). A network that learns to recognize three-dimensional objects, *Nature* **343**: 263–266.

Pontil, M. & Verri, A. (1998). Support vector machines for 3D object recognition, *IEEE Trans. Pattern Anal. Machine Intell.* **20**(6): 637–646.

Rougeaux, S. & Kuniyoshi, Y. (1998). Robust tracking by a humanoid vision system, *Proc. IAPR First Int. Workshop on Humanoid and Friendly Robotics*, Tsukuba, Japan.

Sandini, G. & Metta, G. (2003). Retina-like sensors: motivations, technology and applications, *in* F. G. Barth, J. A. C. Humphrey & T. W. Secomb (eds), *Sensors and Sensing in Biology and Engineering*, Springer-Verlag, Wien-New York.

Scassellati, B. (1998). Eye finding via face detection for a foveated, active vision system, *Proc. Fifteenth Nat. Conf. Artifficial Intelligence (AAAI '98)*, Madison, Wisconsin, pp. 969–976.

Shibata, T., Vijayakumar, S., Jörg Conradt, J. & Schaal, S. (2001). Biomimetic oculomotor control, *Adaptive Behavior* **9**(3/4): 189–208.

Sinha, P. & Poggio, T. (1996). Role of learning in three-dimensional form perception, *Nature* **384**: 460–463.

Tarr, M. J. & Bülthoff, H. H. (1998). Image-based object recognition in man, monkey, and machine, *Cognition* **67**(1-2): 1–20.

Tsochantaridis, I., Hofmann, T., Joachims, T. & Altun, Y. (2004). Support vector machine learning for interdependent and structured output spaces, *Proc. Twenty-first Int. Conf. Machine Learning*, Banff, Alberta, Canada. Article No. 104.

Turk, M. & Pentland, A. (1991). Eigenfaces for recognition, *Journal of Cognitive Neuroscience* **3**(1): 71–86.

Ude, A., Atkeson, C. G. & Cheng, G. (2003). Combining peripheral and foveal humanoid vision to detect, pursue, recognize and act, *Proc. 2003 IEEE/RSJ Int. Conf. Intelligent Robots and Systems*, Las Vegas, Nevada, pp. 2173–2178.

Ude, A., Gaskett, C. & Cheng, G. (2006). Foveated vision systems with two cameras per eye, *Proc. IEEE Int. Conf. Robotics and Automation*, Orlando, Florida, pp. 3457–3462.

Ude, A., Omrčen, D. & Cheng, G. (2008). Making object learning and recognition an active process, *International Journal of Humanoid Robotics* **5**(2).

Ude, A., Shibata, T. & Atkeson, C. G. (2001). Real-time visual system for interaction with a humanoid robot, *Robotics and Autonomous Systems* **37**(2-3): 115–125.

Vijayakumar, S., Conradt, J., Shibata, T. & Schaal, S. (2001). Overt visual attention for a humanoid robot, *Proc. 2001 IEEE/RSJ Int. Conf. on Intelligent Robots and Systems*, Maui, Hawaii, USA, pp. 2332–2337.

Wallraven, C., Caputo, B. & Graf, A. (2003). Recognition with local feature: the kernel recipe, *Proc. Ninth IEEE Int. Conf. Computer Vision*, Nice, France, pp. 257–264.

Wiskott, L., Fellous, J.-M., Krüger, N. & von der Malsburg, C. (1997). Face recognition by elastic bunch graph matching, *IEEE Trans. Pattern Anal. Machine Intell.* **19**(7): 775–779.

11

Recognizing Human Gait Types

Preben Fihl and Thomas B. Moeslund
Aalborg University
Denmark

1. Introduction

Everyday people will observe, analyze, and interpret the motion and actions of the people surrounding them. This is a source of very valuable information about not only what each person is doing but also things like their intentions, their attitude towards the observer, situations they perceive as dangerous or interesting, etc. In open spaces where people are moving around the type of motion will be an important cue for a lot of this information. More specifically, the human gait has been actively investigated in different research areas for this reason. Within psychology the expression and perception of emotions through styles of motions has been investigated by e.g. (Montepare et al., 1987) and the question of how people infer intention from actions has been studied within neuroscience by e.g. (Blakemore & Decety, 2001). In biomechanics (Alexander, 2002) describes how the choice of different gait types (walking and running) are based on the minimizing of energy consumption in muscles and (Whittle, 2001) describes how gait analysis can be used within clinical diagnostics to diagnose a number of diseases.

A lot of the information that is embedded in the gait can be extracted by simply observing a person. Systems that operate around people can benefit greatly from such observations. This fact has driven much research within robotics and computer vision to focus on analysis of human gait with a number of different applications as the aim.

Robots that move and work around humans will be very dependant on their ability to observe people and to interact with humans in an efficient way and the ability to recognize basic human activities is furthermore necessary. Methods for recognizing human gestures to enable natural human-robot interaction has been presented in e.g. (Yang et al., 2006; Meisner et al., 2009; Waldherr et al., 2000). Natural human-robot interaction also requires the robot to behave in a way that is in accordance with the social rules of humans. A method for adapting the robot behavior according to the motion of people is presented in (Svenstrup et al., 2009). Since the human gait is a very distinctive type of motion it can be used in many contexts to detect the presence of people, e.g. from surveillance cameras (Cutler & Davis, 2000; Ran et al., 2007; Viola et al., 2005). Gait as a biometric measure has also received much attention because it is non-intrusive (Collins et al., 2002; Liu & Sarkar, 2006; Veeraraghavan et al., 2005; Wang et al., 2004; Yam et al., 2002). Finally, there has been considerable interest in the computer vision community in the classification of gait types or, more generally, of different types of human action (Blank et al., 2005; Dollár et al., 2005; Schüldt et al., 2004). The research in human action recognition is applicable in a number of areas besides human-robot interaction, e.g. in advanced user interfaces, annotation of video data, intelligent vehicles, and automatic surveillance.

An interesting and challenging area of human gait type recognition is motion in open spaces like town squares, courtyards, or train stations where one of the main human activities is that of gait, i.e. people are walking, jogging, or running. The movements of people in such spaces are however rarely constrained so seen from a camera this will result in challenges like changing direction of motion, significant changes in the scale of people, varying speeds of motion, and often also dynamics backgrounds. This chapter will show how to build a gait type classification system that can handle a number of the challenges that a real life scenario imposes on such a gait classification system. i.e. a general system which is *invariant* to camera frame rate and calibration, view point, moving speeds, scale change, and non-linear paths of motion.

Much research concerned with gait attempts to extract features related to the person specific style of gait whereas this work is concerned with the three general types of gait (walking, jogging and running) and it is therefore more related to the action recognition research than the research on the use of gait in personal identification.

Systems that are invariant to one or more of the factors listed above have been presented in the literature, but so far none has considered all these factors simultaneously. (Masoud & Papanikolopoulos, 2003) presents good results on classification of different types of human motion but the system is limited to motion parallel to the image plane. (Robertson & Reid, 2005) describes a method for behavior understanding by combining actions into human behavior. The method handles rather unconstrained scenes but uses the moving speed of people to classify the action being performed. The moving speed cannot be used for gait-type classification. A person jogging along could easily be moving slower than another person walking fast and human observers distinguishing jogging from running do typically not use the speed as a feature. Furthermore, estimation of speed would require scene knowledge that is not always accessible. (Blank et al., 2005) uses space-time shapes to recognize actions independently of speed. The method is robust to different viewpoints but cannot cope with non-linear paths created by changes in direction of movement. Other state-of-the-art approaches are mentioned in section 8 along with a comparison of results.

Current approaches to action classification and gait-type classification consider two or three distinct gait classes, e.g. (Masoud & Papanikolopoulos, 2003; Robertson & Reid, 2005) who consider walking and running, or (Blank et al., 2005; Dollár et al., 2005; Schüldt et al., 2004) who consider walking, jogging, and running. However, this distinct classification is not always possible, not even to human observers, and we therefore extend the gait analysis with a more appropriate gait continuum description. Considering gait as a continuum seems intuitive correct for jogging and running, and including walking in such a continuum makes it possible to apply a single descriptor for the whole range of gait types. In this chapter we present a formal description of a gait continuum based on a visual recognizable physical feature instead of e.g. a mixture of probabilities of walking, jogging, and running.

1.1 Gait type description based on the Duty-factor

The work presented in this chapter describe the major gait types in a unified gait continuum using the *duty-factor* which is a well established property of gait adopted from the biomechanics literature (Alexander, 2002). To enhance the precision in estimation of the duty-factor we use an effective gait type classifier to reduce the solution space and then calculate the duty-factor within this subspace. The following section will elaborate and motivate our approach.

A current trend in computer vision approaches that deal with analysis of human movement is to use massive amounts of training data, which means spending a lot of time on extracting and annotating the data and temporally aligning the training sequences. To circumvent these problems an alternative approach can be applied in which computer graphics models are used to generate training data. The advantages of this are very fast training plus the ability to easily generate training data from new viewpoints by changing the camera angle.

In classifying gait types it is not necessary to record a person's exact pose, and silhouettes are therefore sufficient as inputs. Silhouette based methods have been used with success in the area of human identification by gait (Collins et al., 2002; Liu & Sarkar, 2006; Wang et al., 2004). The goal in human identification is to extract features that describe the personal variation in gait patterns. The features used are often chosen so that they are invariant to the walking speed and in (Yam et al., 2002) the same set of features even describe the personal variation in gait patterns of people no matter whether they are walking or running. Inspired by the ability of the silhouette based approaches to describe details in gait, we propose a similar method. Our goal is however quite different from human identification since we want to allow personal variation and describe the different gait types through the duty-factor.

A silhouette based approach does not need a completely realistic looking computer graphics model as long as the shape is correct and the 3D rendering software Poser[1], which has a build-in Walk Designer, can be used to animate human gaits.

To sum up, our approach offers the following three main contributions.

1. The methods applied are chosen and developed to allow for classification in an unconstrained environment. This results in a system that is invariant to more factors than other approaches, i.e. invariant in regard to camera frame rate and calibration, viewpoint, moving speeds, scale change, and non-linear paths of motion.
2. The use of the computer graphics model decouples the training set completely from the test set. Usually methods are tested on data similar to the training set, whereas we train on computer-generated images and test on video data from several different data sets. This is a more challenging task and it makes the system more independent of the type of input data and therefore increases the applicability of the system.
3. The gait continuum is based on a well-established physical property of gait. The duty-factor allows us to describe the whole range of gait types with a single parameter and to extract information that is not dependant on the partially subjective notion of jogging and running.

The remainder of this chapter will first give a thorough introduction of the duty-factor and show its descriptive power. Next, the gait classification frame work will be described in detail. The framework is shown in Fig. 1. The human silhouette is first extracted (section 3) and represented efficiently (section 4). We then compare the silhouette with computer graphics silhouettes (section 6) from a database (section 5). The results of the comparison are calculated for an entire sequence and the gait type and duty-factor of that sequence is

---

[1] Poser version 6.0.3.140 was used for this work. Currently distributed by Smith Micro Software, Inc.

extracted (section 7). Results are presented in section 8 and section 9 contains a discussion of these results. Sections 10 to 12 present solutions to some of the additional challenges that arise when the gait classification system is applied in an online system with multiple cameras, real-time demands, and maintenance of silhouette quality over long time. Section 13 concludes the chapter.

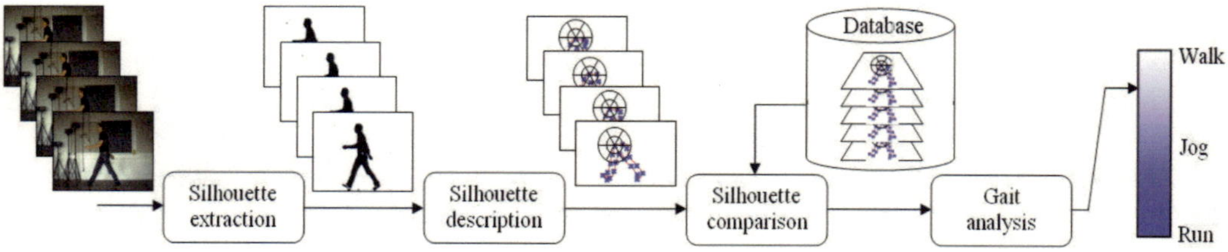

Fig. 1. An overview of the approach. The main contributions of the method presented here are the computer generated silhouette database, the gait analysis resulting in a gait continuum, and the ability to handle unconstrained environments achieved by the methods applied throughout the system. The gait analysis is further detailed in Fig. 7.

2. The Duty-Factor

When a human wants to move fast he/she will run. Running is not simply walking done fast and the different types of gaits are in fact different actions. This is true for vertebrates in general. For example, birds and bats have two distinct flying actions and horses have three different types of gaits. Which action to apply to obtain a certain speed is determined by minimizing some physiological property. For example, turtles seem to optimize with respect to muscle power, horses and humans with respect to oxygen consumption and other animals by minimizing metabolic power. Furthermore, physiological research has shown that the optimal action changes discontinuously with changing speed. (Alexander, 1989)
From a computer vision point of view the question is now if *one* (recognizable) descriptor exist, which can represent the continuum of gait. For bipedal locomotion in general, the *duty-factor* can do exactly this. The duty-factor is defined as "*the fraction of the duration of a stride for which each foot remains on the ground*" (Alexander, 2002). Fig. 2. illustrates the duty-factor in a walk cycle and a run cycle.
To illustrate the power of this descriptor we have manually estimated the duty-factor in 138 video sequences containing humans walking, jogging, or running, see Fig. 3. These sequences come from 4 different sources and contain many different individuals entering and exiting at different angles. Some not even following a straight line (see example frames in Fig. 10).
Fig. 3. shows a very clear separation between walking and jogging/running which is in accordance with the fact that those types of gait are in fact different ways of moving. Jogging and running however, cannot be separated as clearly and there is a gradual transition from one gait type to the other. In fact, the classification of jogging and running is dependent on the observer when considering movements in the transition phase and there exists no clear definition of what separates jogging from running.

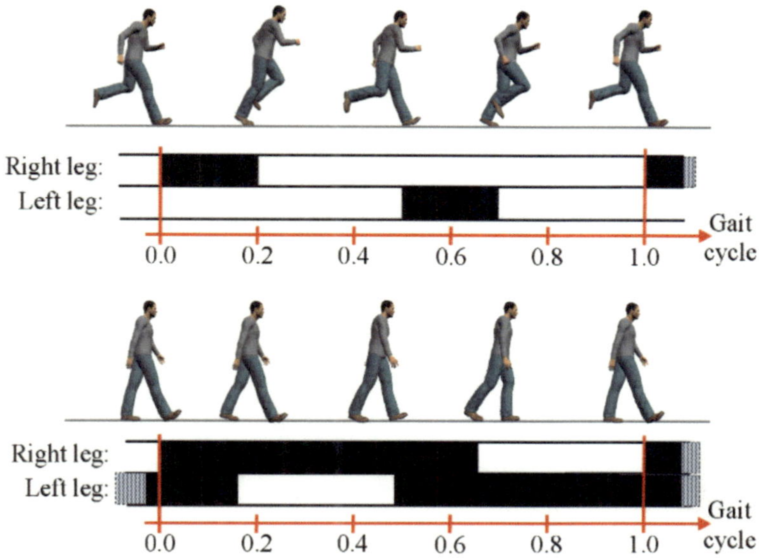

Fig. 2. Illustration of the duty-factor. The duration of a gait cycle where each foot is on the ground is marked with the black areas. The duty-factor for the depicted run cycle (top) is 0.2 and 0.65 for the depicted walk cycle (bottom).

This problem is apparent in the classification of the sequences used in Fig.3. Each sequence is either classified by us or comes from a data set where it has been labeled by others. By having more people classify the same sequences it turns out that the classification of some sequences is ambiguous which illustrates the subjectivity in evaluation of jogging and running[2]. (Patron & Reid, 2007) reports classification results from 300 video sequences of people walking, jogging, and running. The sequences are classified by several people resulting in classification rates of 100% for walking, 98% for jogging, and only 81% for running, which illustrates the inherent difficulty in distinguishing the two gait types.

With these results in mind we will not attempt to do a traditional classification of walking, jogging, and running which in reality has doubtful ground truth data. Rather, we will use the duty-factor to describe jogging and running as a continuum. This explicitly handles the ambiguity of jogging and running since a video sequence that some people will classify as jogging and other people will classify as running simply map to a point on the continuum described by the duty-factor. This point will not have a precise interpretation in terms of jogging and running but the duty-factor will be precise.

As stated earlier walking and jogging/running are two different ways of moving. However, to get a unified description for all types of gait that are usually performed by people in open spaces we also apply the duty-factor to walking and get a single descriptor for the whole gait continuum.

---

[2] The problem of ambiguous classification will be clear when watching for example video sequences from the KTH data set (Schüldt et al., 2004), e.g. person 4 jogging in scenario 2 versus person 2 running in scenario 2.

Even though jogging and running are considered as one gait type in the context of the duty-factor they still have a visual distinction to some extend. This visual distinction is used with some success in the current approaches which classify gait into walking, jogging, and running. We acknowledge the results obtained by this type of approaches and we also propose a new method to classify gait into walking, jogging, and running. In our approach however, this is only an intermediate step to optimize the estimation of the duty-factor which we believe to be the best way of describing gait.

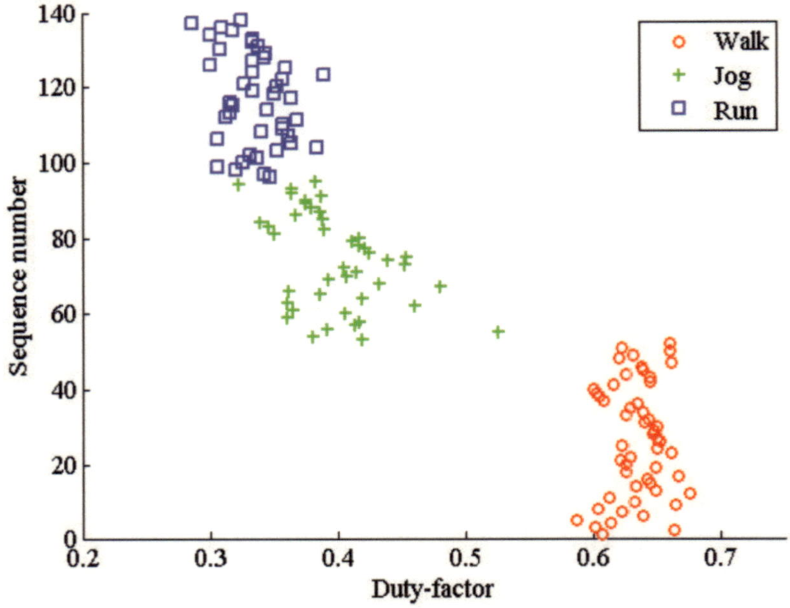

Fig. 3. The manually annotated duty-factor and gait type for 138 different sequences. Note that the sole purpose of the y-axis is to spread out the data.

3. Silhouette extraction

The first step in the gait analysis framework is to extract silhouettes from the incoming video sequences. For this purpose we do foreground segmentation using the Codebook background subtraction method as described in (Fihl et al., 2006) and (Kim et al., 2005). This method has been shown to be robust in handling both foreground camouflage and shadows. This is achieved by separating intensity and chromaticity in the background model. Moreover, the background model is multi modal and multi layered which allows it to model moving backgrounds such as tree branches and objects that become part of the background after staying stationary for a period of time. To maintain good background subtraction quality over time it is essential to update the background model and (Fihl et al., 2006) describes two different update mechanisms to handle rapid and gradual changes respectively. By using this robust background subtraction method we can use a diverse set of input sequences from both indoor and outdoor scenes.

4. Silhouette description

When a person is moving around in an unconstrained scene his or her arms will not necessarily swing in a typical "gait" manner; the person may be making other gestures, such as waving, or he/she might be carrying an object. To circumvent the variability and complexity of such scenarios we choose to classify the gait solely on the silhouette of the legs. Furthermore, (Liu et al., 2004) shows that identification of people on the basis of gait, using the silhouette of legs alone, works just as well as identification based on the silhouette of the entire body.

To extract the silhouette of the legs we find the height of the silhouette of the entire person and use the bottom 50% as the leg silhouette. Without loss of generality this approach avoids errors from the swinging hands below the hips, although it may not be strictly correct from an anatomic point of view. To reduce noise along the contour we apply morphological operations to the silhouette. Some leg configurations cause holes in the silhouette, for example running seen from a non-side view in Fig. 5. (c). Such holes are descriptive for the silhouette and we include the contour of these holes in the silhouette description.

To allow recognition of gait types across different scales we use shape contexts and tangent orientations (Belongie et al., 2002) to describe the leg silhouettes. n points are sampled from the contour of the leg silhouette and for each point we determine the shape context and the tangent orientation at that point, see Fig. 4. With K bins in the log-polar histogram of the shape context we get an n x (K+1) matrix describing each silhouette. Scale invariance is achieved with shape contexts by normalizing the size of the histograms according to the mean distance between all point pairs on the contour. Specifically, the normalizing constant q used for the radial distances of the histograms is defined as follows:

$$q = \frac{1}{n^2} \sum_{i=1}^{n} \sum_{j=1}^{n} | p_i - p_j | \quad (1)$$

where n is the number of points p sampled from the contour.

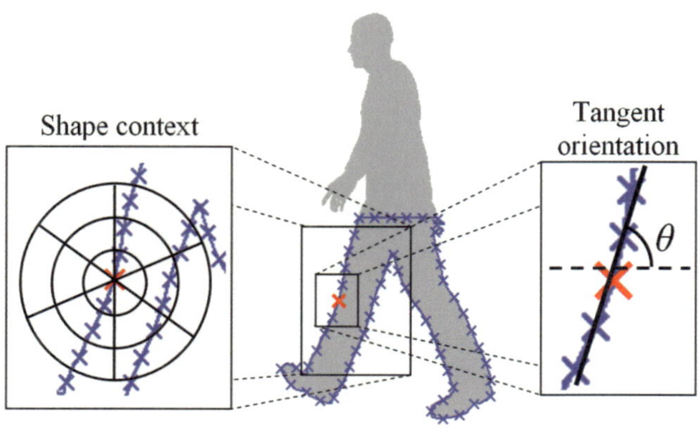

Fig. 4. Illustration of the silhouette description. The crosses illustrate the points sampled from the silhouette. Shape contexts and tangent orientations are used to describe the silhouette.

5. Silhouette database

To represent our training data we create a database of human silhouettes performing one cycle of each of the main gait types: walking, jogging, and running. To make our method invariant to changes in viewpoint we generate database silhouettes from three different camera angles. With 3D-rendering software this is an easy and very rapid process that does not require us to capture new real life data for statistical analysis. The database contains silhouettes of the human model seen from a side view and from cameras rotated 30 degrees to both sides. The combination of the robust silhouette description and three camera angles enable the method to handle diverse moving directions and oblique viewing angles. Specifically, database silhouettes can be matched with silhouettes of people moving at angles of at least ±45 degrees with respect to the viewing direction. People moving around in open spaces will often change direction while in the camera's field of view (creating non-linear paths of motion), thus we cannot make assumptions about the direction of movement. To handle this variability each new input silhouette is matched to database silhouettes taken from all camera angles. Fig. 10, row 1 shows a sequence with a non-linear motion path where the first frame will match database silhouettes from a viewpoint of -30 degrees and the last frame will match database silhouettes from a viewpoint of 30 degrees. The silhouettes generated are represented as described in section 4. We generate T silhouettes of a gait cycle for each of the three gait types. This is repeated for the three viewpoints, i.e. $T \cdot 3 \cdot 3$ silhouettes in total. Fig. 5 shows examples of the generated silhouettes.
Each silhouette in the database is annotated with the number of feet in contact with the ground which is the basis of the duty-factor calculation.
To analyze the content of the database with respect to the ability to describe gait we created an Isomap embedding (Tenenbaum et al., 2000) of the shape context description of the silhouettes. Based on the cyclic nature of gait and the great resemblance between gait types we expect that gait information can be described by some low dimensional manifold. Fig. 6. shows the 2-dimensional embedding of our database with silhouettes described by shape contexts and tangent orientations and using the costs resulting from the Hungarian method (described in section 6) as distances between silhouettes.

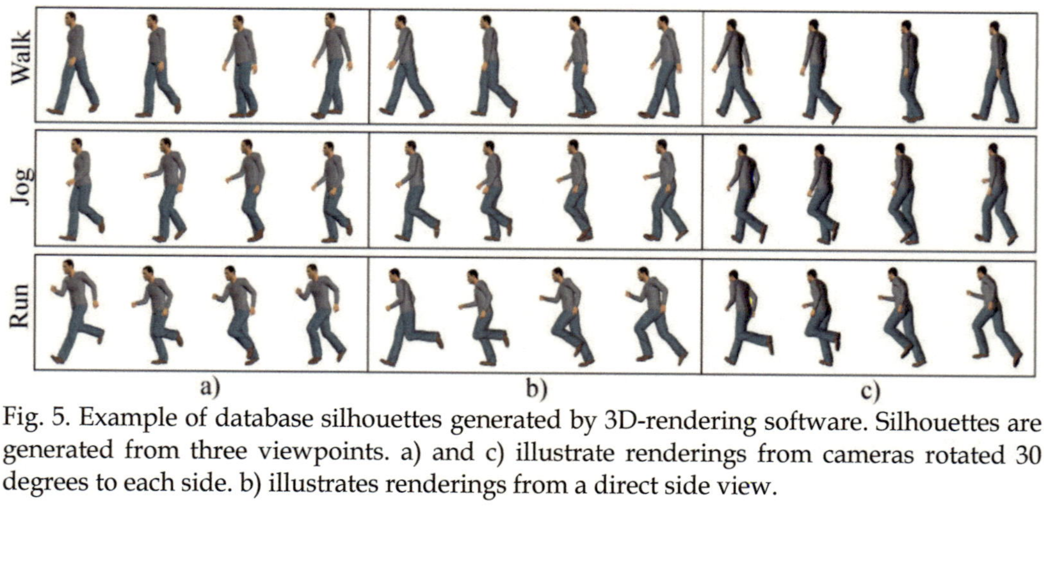

Fig. 5. Example of database silhouettes generated by 3D-rendering software. Silhouettes are generated from three viewpoints. a) and c) illustrate renderings from cameras rotated 30 degrees to each side. b) illustrates renderings from a direct side view.

According to figure 6 we can conclude that the first two intrinsic parameters of the database represent 1) the total distance between both feet and the ground and 2) the horizontal distance between the feet. This reasonable 2-dimensional representation of the database silhouettes shows that our description of the silhouettes and our silhouette comparison metric does capture the underlying manifold of gait silhouettes in a precise manner. Hence, gait type analysis based on our silhouette description and comparison seems promising

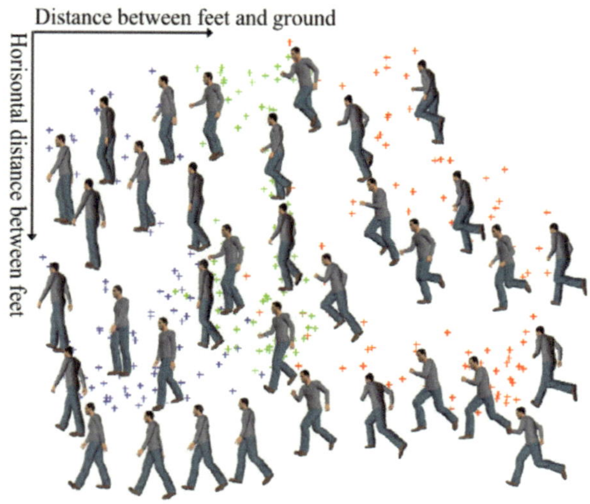

Fig. 6. Illustration of the ISOMAP embedding and a representative subset of the database silhouettes.

6. Silhouette comparison

To find the best match between an input silhouette and database silhouettes we follow the method of (Belongie et al., 2002). We calculate the cost of matching a sampled point on the input silhouette with a sampled point on a database silhouette using the χ^2 test statistics. The cost of matching the shape contexts of point p_i on one silhouette and point p_j on the other silhouette is denoted $c_{i,j}$. The normalized shape contexts at points p_i and p_j are denoted $h_i(k)$ and $h_j(k)$ respectively with k as the bin number, $k=\{1,2,...,K\}$. The χ^2 test statistics is given as:

$$c_{i,j} = \frac{1}{2}\sum_{k=1}^{K}\frac{[h_i(k)-h_j(k)]^2}{h_i(k)+h_j(k)} \quad (2)$$

The normalized shape contexts gives $c_{i,j} \in [0;1]$.
The difference in tangent orientation $\varphi_{i,j}$ between points p_i and p_j is normalized and added to $c_{i,j}$ ($\varphi_{i,j} \in [0;1]$). This gives the final cost $C_{i,j}$ of matching the two points:

$$C_{i,j} = a \cdot c_{i,j} + b \cdot \varphi_{i,j} \quad (3)$$

where a and b are weights. Experiments have shown that $\varphi_{i,j}$ effectively discriminates points that are quite dissimilar whereas $c_{i,j}$ expresses more detailed differences which should have a high impact on the final cost only when tangent orientations are alike. According to this observation we weight the difference in tangent orientation $\varphi_{i,j}$ higher than shape context distances $c_{i,j}$. Preliminary experiments show that the method is not too sensitive to the choice of these weights but a ratio of 1 to 3 yields good results, i.e. a=1 and b=3.

The costs of matching all point pairs between the two silhouettes are calculated. The Hungarian method (Papadimitriou & Steiglitz, 1998) is used to solve the square assignment problem of identifying which one-to-one mapping between the two point sets that minimizes the total cost. All point pairs are included in the cost minimization, i.e. the ordering of the points is not considered. This is because points sampled from a silhouette with holes will have a very different ordering compared to points sampled from a silhouette without holes but with similar leg configuration, see row three of Fig. 5. (c) (second and third image) for an example.

By finding the best one-to-one mapping between the input silhouette and each of the database silhouettes we can now identify the best match in the whole database as the database silhouette involving the lowest total cost.

7. Gait analysis

The gait analysis consists of two steps. First we do classification into one of the three gait types, i.e. walking, jogging, or running. Next we calculate the duty-factor D based on the silhouettes from the classified gait type. This is done to maximize the likelihood of a correct duty-factor estimation. Fig. 7. illustrates the steps involved in the gait type analysis. Note that the silhouette extraction, silhouette description, and silhouette comparison all process a single input frame at a time whereas the gait analysis is based on a sequence of input frames.

To get a robust classification of the gait type in the first step we combine three different types of information. We calculate an *action error* E for each action and two associated weights: *action likelihood* α and *temporal consistency* β. The following subsections describe the gait analysis in detail starting with the action error and the two associated weights followed by the duty-factor calculation.

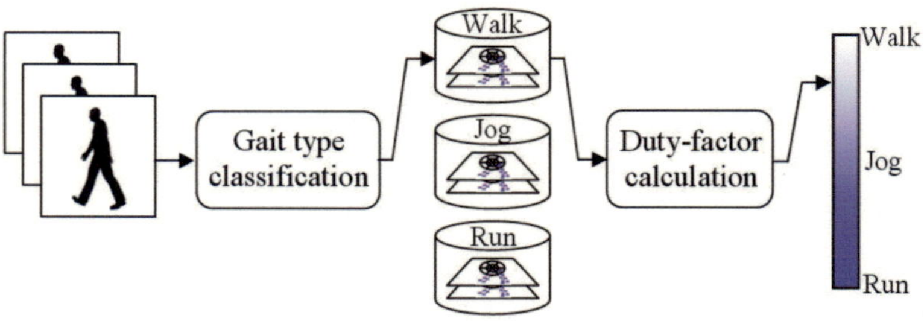

Fig. 7. An overview of the gait analysis. The figure shows the details of the block "Gait analysis" in Fig. 1. The output of the silhouette comparison is a set of database silhouettes matched to the input sequence. In the gait type classification these database silhouettes are classified as a gait type which defines a part of the database to be used for the duty-factor calculation.

7.1 Action Error

The output of the silhouette comparison is a set of distances between the input silhouette and each of the database silhouettes. These distances express the difference or error between two silhouettes. Fig. 8. illustrates the output of the silhouette comparison. The database silhouettes are divided into three groups corresponding to walking, jogging, and running, respectively. We accumulate the errors of the best matches within each group of database silhouettes. These accumulated errors constitute the *action error E* and corresponds to the difference between the action being performed in the input video and each of the three actions in the database, see Fig. 9.

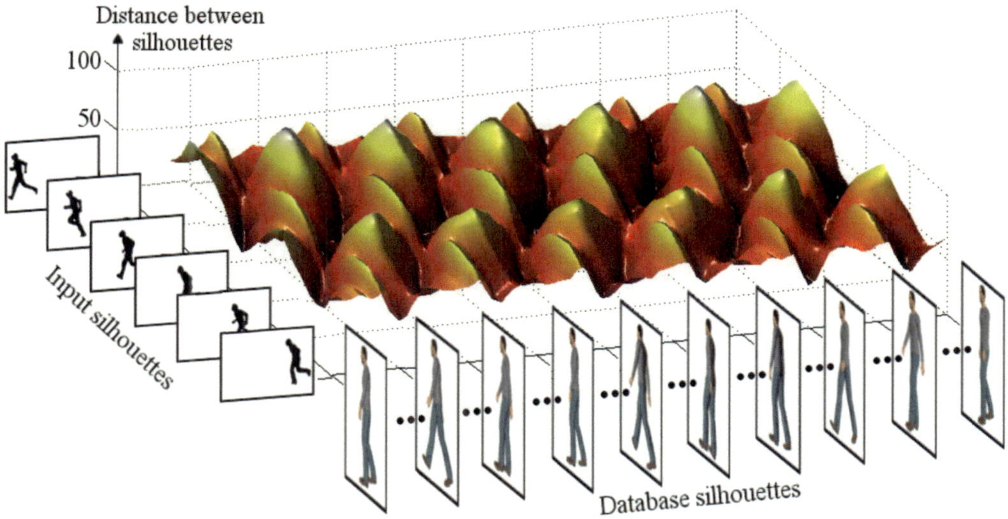

Fig. 8. Illustration of the silhouette comparison output. The distances between each input silhouette and the database silhouettes of each gait type are found (shown for walking only). 90 database silhouettes are used per gait type, i.e. T=30.

7.2 Action Likelihood

When silhouettes of people are extracted in difficult scenarios and at low resolutions the silhouettes can be noisy. This may result in large errors between the input silhouette and a database silhouette, even though the actual pose of the person is very similar to that of the database silhouette. At the same time, small errors may be found between noisy input silhouettes and database silhouettes with quite different body configurations (somewhat random matches). To minimize the effect of the latter inaccuracies we weight the action error by the likelihood of that action. The action likelihood of action *a* is given as the percentage of input silhouettes that match action *a* better than the other actions.

Since we use the minimum action error the actual weight applied is one minus the action likelihood:

$$\alpha_a = 1 - \frac{n_a}{N} \tag{4}$$

where n_a is the number of input silhouettes in a sequence with the best overall match to a silhouette from action *a*, and *N* is the total number of input silhouettes in that video sequence.

This weight will penalize actions that have only a few overall best matches, but with small errors, and will benefit actions that have many overall best matches, e.g. the running action in Fig. 9.

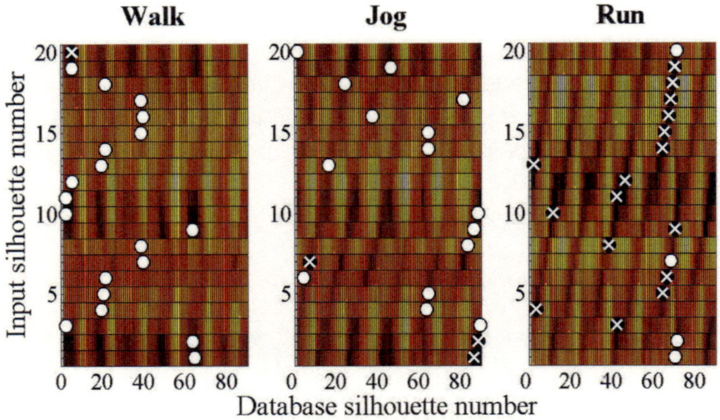

Fig. 9. The output of the silhouette comparison of Fig. 8. is shown in 2D for all gait types (dark colors illustrate small errors and bright colors illustrate large errors). For each input silhouette the best match among silhouettes of the same action is marked with a white dot and the best overall match is marked with a white cross. The shown example should be interpreted as follows: the silhouette in the first input frame is closest to walking silhouette number 64, to jogging silhouette number 86, and to running silhouette number 70. These distances are used when calculating the action error. When all database silhouettes are considered together, the first input silhouette is closest to jogging silhouette number 86. This is used in the calculation of the two weights.

7.3 Temporal Consistency

When considering only the overall best matches we can find sub-sequences of the input video where all the best matches are of the same action *and* in the right order with respect to a gait cycle. This is illustrated in Fig. 9. where the running action has great temporal consistency (silhouette numbers 14-19). The database silhouettes are ordered in accordance with a gait cycle. Hence, the straight line between the overall best matches for input silhouettes 14 to 19 shows that each new input silhouette matches the database silhouette that corresponds to the next body configuration of the running gait cycle.

Sub-sequences with correct temporal ordering of the overall best matches increase our confidence that the action identified is the true action. The temporal consistency describes the length of these sub-sequences. Again, since we use the minimum action error we apply one minus the temporal consistency as the weight β_a:

$$\beta_a = 1 - \frac{m_a}{N} \tag{5}$$

where m_a is the number of input silhouettes in a sequence in which the best overall match has correct temporal ordering within action *a*, and *N* is the total number of input silhouettes in that video sequence.

Our definition of temporal consistency is rather strict when you consider the great variation in input silhouettes caused by the unconstrained nature of the input. A strict definition of temporal consistency allows us to weight it more highly than action likelihood, i.e. we apply a scaling factor w to β to increase the importance of temporal consistency in relation to action likelihood:

$$\beta_a = 1 - w\frac{m_a}{N} \tag{6}$$

7.4 Gait-type classification

The final classifier for the gait type utilizes both the action likelihood and the temporal consistency as weights on the action error. This yields:

$$Action = \arg\min_a (E_a \cdot \alpha_a \cdot \beta_a) \tag{7}$$

where E_a is the action error, α_a is the action likelihood, β_a is the weighted temporal consistency.

7.5 Duty-Factor Calculation

As stated earlier the duty-factor is defined as the fraction of the duration of a stride for which each foot remains on the ground. Following this definition we need to identify the duration of a stride and for how long each foot is in contact with the ground.

A stride is defined as one complete gait cycle and consists of two steps. A stride can be identified as the motion from a left foot takeoff (the foot leaves the ground) and until the next left foot takeoff (see Fig. 2. for an illustration). Accordingly a step can be identified as the motion from a left foot takeoff to the next right foot takeoff. Given this definition of a step it is natural to identify steps in the video sequence by use of the silhouette width. From a side view the silhouette width of a walking person will oscillate in a periodic manner with peaks corresponding to silhouettes with the feet furthest apart. The interval between two peaks will (to a close approximation) define one step (Collins et al., 2002). This also holds for jogging and running and can furthermore be applied to situations with people moving diagonally with respect to the viewing direction. By extracting the silhouette width from each frame of a video sequence we can identify each step (peaks in silhouette width) and hence determine the mean duration of a stride t_s in that sequence.

For how long each foot remains on the ground can be estimated by looking at the database silhouettes that have been matched to a sequence. We do not attempt to estimate ground contact directly in the input videos which would require assumptions about the ground plane and camera calibrations. For a system intended to work in unconstrained open scenes such requirements will be a limitation to the system. In stead of estimating the feet's ground contact in the input sequence we infer the ground contact from the database silhouettes that are matched to that sequence. Since each database silhouette is annotated with the number of feet supported on the ground this is a simple lookup in the database. The ground support estimation is based solely on silhouettes from the gait type found in the gait-type classification which maximize the likelihood of a correct estimate of the ground support.

The total ground support G of both feet for a video sequence is the sum of ground support of all the matched database silhouettes within the specific gait type.

To get the ground support for each foot we assume a normal moving pattern (not limping, dragging one leg, etc.) so the left and right foot have equal ground support and the mean ground support g for each foot during one stride is $G/(2n_s)$, where n_s is the number of strides in the sequence. The duty-factor D is now given as $D=g/t_s$. In summary we have

$$Duty\text{-}factor\ D = \frac{G}{2 \cdot n_s \cdot t_s} \tag{8}$$

where G is the total ground support, n_s is the number of strides, and t_s is the mean duration of a stride in the sequence.

The manual labeled data of Fig. 3. allows us to further enhance the precision of the duty-factor description. It can be seen from Fig. 3. that the duty-factor for running is in the interval [0.28;0.39] and jogging is in the interval [0.34;0.53]. This can not be guarantied to be true for all possible executions of running and jogging but the great diversity in the manually labeled data allows us to use these intervals in the duty-factor estimation. Since walking clearly separates from jogging and running and since no lower limit is needed for running we infer the following constraints on the duty factor of running and jogging:

$$\begin{aligned} D_{running} &\in [0;0.39] \\ D_{jogging} &\in [0.34;0.53] \end{aligned} \tag{9}$$

We apply these bounds as a post-processing step. If the duty-factor of a sequence lies outside one of the appropriate bounds then the duty-factor will be assigned the value of the exceeded bound.

8. Results

To emphasize the contributions of our two-step gait analysis we present results on both steps individually and on the gait continuum achieved by combining the two steps.

A number of recent papers have reported good results on the classification of gait types (often in the context of human action classification). To compare our method to these results and to show that the gait type classification is a solid base for the duty-factor calculation we have tested this first step of the gait analysis on its own. After this comparison we test the duty-factor description with respect to the ground truth data shown in Fig. 3., both on its own and in combination with the gait type classification.

The tests are conducted on a large and diverse data set. We have compiled 138 video sequences from 4 different data sets. The data sets cover indoor and outdoor video, different moving directions with respect to the camera (up to ±45 degrees from the viewing direction), non-linear paths, different camera elevations and tilt angles, different video resolutions, and varying silhouette heights (from 41 pixels to 454 pixels). Fig. 10. shows example frames from the input videos. Ground truth gait types were adopted from the data sets when available and manually assigned by us otherwise.

For the silhouette description the number of sampled points n was 100 and the number of bins in the shape contexts K was 60. 30 silhouettes were used for each gait cycle, i.e., T=30. The temporal consistency was weighted by a factor of four determined through quantitative experiments, i.e. w=4.

8.1 Gait-type classification

When testing only the first step of the gait analysis we achieve an overall recognition rate of 87.1%. Table 1 shows the classification results in a confusion matrix.

	Walk	Jog	Run
Walk	96.2	3.8	0.0
Jog	0.0	65.9	34.1
Run	0.0	2.6	97.4

Table 1. Confusion matrix for the gait type classification results.

The matching percentages in Table 1 cannot directly be compared to the results of others since we have included samples from different data sets to obtain more diversity. However, 87 of the sequences originate from the KTH data set (Schüldt et al., 2004) and a loose comparison is possible on this subset of our test sequences. In Table 2 we list the matching results of different methods working on the KTH data set.

Methods	Classification results in %			
	Total	Walk	Jog	Run
Kim & Cipolla (2009)*	92.3	99	90	88
Our method	92.0	100.0	80.6	96.3
Li et al. (2008)*	89.0	88	89	90
Laptev et al. (2008)*	89.3	99	89	80
Patron & Reid (2007)	84.3	98	79	76
Schüldt et al. (2004)	75.0	83.3	60.4	54.9

Table 2. Best reported classification results on the KTH data set. The matching results of our method are based on the 87 KTH sequences included in our test set. * indicate that the method work on all actions of the KTH data set.

The KTH data set remains one of the largest data sets of human actions in terms of number of test subjects, repetitions, and scenarios and many papers have been published with results on this data set, especially within the last two years. A number of different test setups have been used which makes a direct comparison impossible and we therefore merely list a few of the best results to show the general level of recognition rates. We acknowledge that the KTH data set contains three additional actions (boxing, hand waving, and hand clapping) and that some of the listed results include these. However, for the results reported in the literature the gait actions are in general not confused with the three hand actions. The results can therefore be taken as indicators of the ability of the methods to classify gait actions exclusively.

Another part of our test set is taken from the Weizmann data set (Blank et al., 2005). They classify nine different human actions including walking and running but not jogging. They achieve a near perfect recognition rate for running and walking and others also report 100% correct recognitions on this data set, e.g. (Patron et al., 2008). To compare our results to this we remove the jogging silhouettes from the database and leave out the jogging sequences

from the test set. In this walking/running classification we achieve an overall recognition rate of 98.9% which is slightly lower. Note however that the data sets we are testing on include sequences with varying moving directions where the results in (Blank et al., 2005) and (Patron et al., 2008) are based on side view sequences.
In summary, the recognition results of our gait-type classification provides a very good basis for the estimation of the duty-factor.

Fig. 10. Samples from the 4 different data sets used in the test together with the extracted silhouettes of the legs used in the database comparison, and the best matching silhouette from the database. Top left: data from our own data set. Bottom left: data from the Weizmann data set (Blank et al., 2005). Top right: data from the CMU data set obtained from mocap.cs.cmu.edu. The CMU database was created with funding from NSF EIA-0196217. Bottom right: data from the KTH data set (Schüldt et al., 2004).

8.2 Duty-factor

To test our duty-factor description we estimate it automatically in the test sequences. To show the effect of our combined gait analysis we first present results for the duty-factor estimated without the preceding gait-type classification to allow for a direct comparison.
Fig. 11. shows the resulting duty-factors when the gait type classification is not used to limit the database silhouettes to just one gait type. Fig. 12. shows the estimated duty-factors with our two-step gait analysis scheme. The estimate of the duty-factor is significantly improved by utilizing the classification results of the gait type classification. The mean error for the estimate is 0.050 with a standard deviation of 0.045.

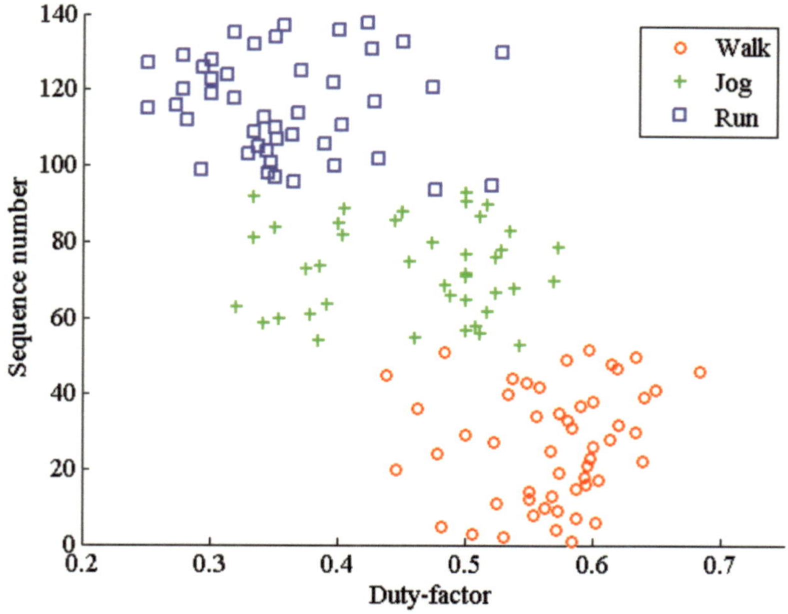

Fig. 11. The automatically estimated duty-factor from the 138 test sequences without the use of the gait type classification. The y-axis solely spreads out the data.

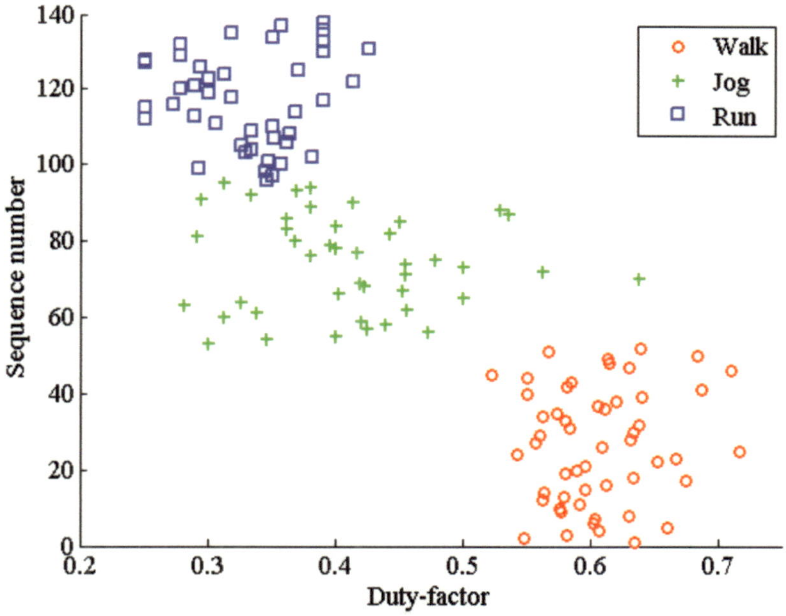

Fig. 12. The automatically estimated duty-factor from the 138 test sequences when the gait type classification has been used to limit the database to just one gait type. The y-axis solely spreads out the data.

9. Discussion

When comparing the results of the estimated duty-factor (Fig. 12.) with the ground truth data (Fig. 3.) it is clear that the overall tendency of the duty-factor is reproduced with the automatic estimation. The estimated duty-factor has greater variability mainly due to small inaccuracies in the silhouette matching. A precise estimate of the duty-factor requires a precise detection of when the foot actually touches the ground. However, this detection is difficult because silhouettes of the human model are quite similar just before and after the foot touches the ground. Inaccuracies in the segmentation of the silhouettes in the input video can make for additional ambiguity in the matching.

The difficulty in estimating the precise moment of ground contact leads to considerations on alternative measures of a gait continuum, e.g. the Froude number (Alexander, 1989) that is based on walking speed and the length of the legs. However, such measures requires information about camera calibration and the ground plane which is not always accessible with video from unconstrained environments. The processing steps involved in our system and the silhouette database all contributes to the overall goal of creating a system that is invariant to usual challenges in video from unconstrained scenes and a system that can be applied in diverse setups without requiring additional calibrations.

The misclassifications of the three-class classifier also affect the accuracy of the estimated duty-factor. The duty-factor of the four jogging sequences misclassified as walking disrupt the perfect separation of walking and jogging/running expected from the manually annotated data. All correctly classified sequences however maintain this perfect separation.

To test wether the presented gait classification framework provides the kind of invariance that is required for unconstrained scenes we have analyzed the classification errors in Table 1. This analysis shows no significant correlation between the classification errors and the camera viewpoint (pan and tilt), the size and quality of the silhouettes extracted, the image resolution, the linearity of the path, and the amount of scale change. Furthermore, we also evaluated the effect of the number of frames (number of gait cycles) in the sequences and found that our method classifies gait types correctly even when there are only a few cycles in the sequence. This analysis is detailed in Table 3 which shows the result of looking at a subset of the test sequences containing a specific video characteristic.

Video characteristic		Percentage of	Percentage of
Non-side view		43	41
Small silhouettes	(1)	58	59
Low resolution images	(2)	63	65
Non linear path		3	0
Significant scale change	(3)	41	41
Less than 2 strides		43	41

Table 3. The table shows how different video characteristics effect the classification errors, e.g. 43% of the sequences have a non-side view and these sequences account for 41% of the errors. The results are based on 138 test sequences out of which 17 sequences were erroneously classified. Notes: (1): Mean silhouette height of less than 90 pixels. (2): Image resolution of 160x120 or smaller. (3): Scale change larger than 20% of the mean silhouette height during the sequence.

A number of the sequences in Table 3 have more than one of the listed characteristics (e.g. small silhouettes in low resolution images) so the error percentages are somewhat correlated. It should also be noted that the gait type classification results in only 17 errors which gives a relatively small number of sequences for this analysis. However, the number of errors in each subset corresponds directly to the number of sequences in that subset which is a strong indication that our method is indeed invariant to the main factors relevant for gait classification.

The majority of the errors in Table 1 occur simply because the gait type of jogging resembles that of running which supports the need for a gait continuum.

10. Multi Camera Setup

The system has been designed to be invariant towards the major challenges in a realistic real-world setup. Regarding invariance to view point, we have achieved this for gait classification of people moving at an angle of up to ±45 degrees with respect to the view direction. The single-view system can however easily be extended to a multi-view system with synchronized cameras which can allow for gait classification of people moving at completely arbitrary directions. A multi-view system must analyze the gait based on each stride rather than a complete video sequence since people may change both moving direction and type of gait during a sequence.

The direction of movement can be determined in each view by tracking the people and analyzing the tracking data. Tracking is done as described in (Fihl et al., 2006). If the direction of movement is outside the ±45 degree interval then that view can be excluded. The duration of a stride can be determined as described in section 2 from the view where the moving direction is closest to a direct side-view. The gait classification results of the remaining views can be combined into a multi-view classification system by extending equations 7 and 8 into the following and doing the calculations based on the last stride in stead of the whole sequence.

$$Action = \arg\min_{a}\left(\sum_{V} E_a \cdot \alpha_a \cdot \beta_a\right) \tag{10}$$

$$D = \frac{1}{n_V} \cdot \sum_{V} D_V \tag{11}$$

where V is the collection of views with acceptable moving directions, E_a is the action error, α_a is the action likelihood, β_a is the temporal consistency, D is the duty-factor, n_V is the number of views, and D_v is the duty-factor from view v.

Fig. 13. illustrates a two-camera setup where the gait classification is based on either one of the cameras or a combination of both cameras.

11. Real Time Performance

The full potential of the gait analysis framework can only be achieved with real-time performance. Non-real-time processing can be applied for annotation of video data but for e.g. human-robot interaction, automated video surveillance, and intelligent vehicles real-time performance is necessary.

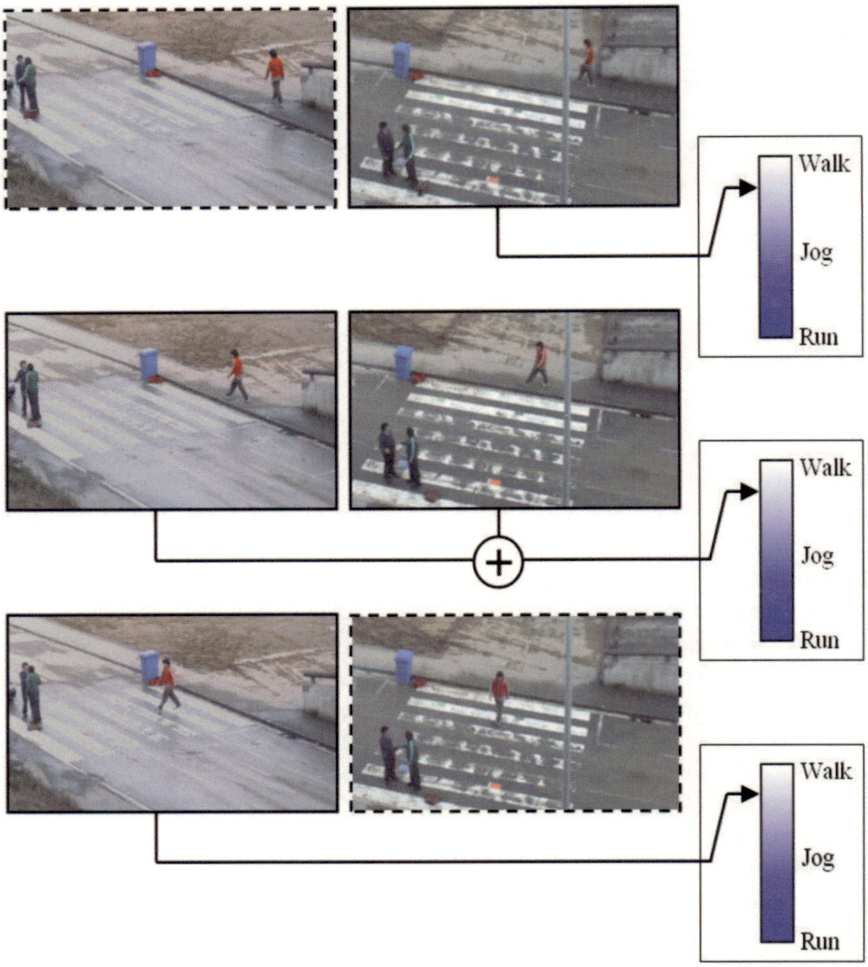

Fig. 13. A two-camera setup. The figure shows three sets of synchronized frames from two cameras. The multi-camera gait classification enables the system to do classification based on either one view (top and bottom frames) or a combination of both views (middle frame).

Real-time performance can be achieved with an optimized implementation and minor changes in the method. The extraction of the contour of the silhouettes is limited to the outermost contour. Disregarding the inner contours (see Fig. 14.) gave a decrease in processing time but also a small decrease in classification results due to the loss of details in some silhouettes.

Fig. 14. Left: the input silhouette. Middle: the outermost contour extracted in the real time system. Right: the contour extracted in the original system.

The most time consuming task of the gait classification is the matching of the input silhouette to the database silhouettes both represented in terms of Shape Contexts. By decreasing the number of points sampled around the contour from 100 points to 20 points and by decreasing the number of bins in the Shape Contexts from 60 to 40 the processing time is significantly improved while still maintaining most of the descriptive power of the method.

With these changes the gait classification system is running at 12-15 frames per second on a standard desktop computer with a 2GHz dual core processor and 2GB of RAM. This however also means a decrease in the classification power of the system. When looking at the gait type classification a recognition rate of 83.3% is achieved with the real-time setup compared to 87.1% with the original setup. The precision of the duty-factor estimation also decreases slightly. This decrease in recognition rate is considered to be acceptable compared to the increased applicability of a real-time system.

12. Online parameter tuning of segmentation

The silhouette extraction based on the Codebook background subtraction is a critical component in the system. Noise in the extracted silhouettes has a direct impact on the classification results. Illumination and weather conditions can change rapidly in unconstrained open spaces so to ensure the performance of the background subtraction in a system receiving live input directly from a camera we have developed a method for online tuning of the segmentation.

The performance of the Codebook background subtraction method is essentially controlled by three parameters; two controlling the allowed variation in illumination and one controlling the allowed variation in chromaticity. The method is designed to handle shadows so with a reasonable parameter setup the Codebook method will accept relatively large variations in illumination to account for shadows that are cast on the background. However, changes in lighting conditions in outdoor scenes also have an effect on the chromaticity level which is not directly modeled in the method. Because of this, the parameter that controls the allowed variation in chromaticity σ is the most important parameter to adjust online (i.e. fixed parameters for the illumination variation will handle changing lighting conditions well, whereas a fixed parameter for the chromaticity variation will not).

To find the optimal setting for σ at runtime we define a quality measure to evaluate a specific value of σ and by testing a small set of relevant values for each input frame we adjust σ by optimizing this quality measure.

The quality measure is based on the difference between the edges of the segmentation and the edges of the input image. An edge background model is acquired simultaneously with the Codebook background model which allows the system to classify detected edges in a new input frame as either foreground or background edges. The map of foreground edges has too much noise to be used for segmentation itself but works well when used to compare the quality of different foreground segmentations of the same frame. The quality score Q is defined as follows:

$$Q = \frac{\sum E_{fg} \cdot E_{seg}}{\sum E_{seg}} \tag{12}$$

where E_{fg} are the foreground edges and E_{seg} are the edges of the foreground mask from the background subtraction. So the quality score describes the fraction of edges from the foreground mask that corresponds to foreground edges from the input image.
The background subtraction is repeated a number of times on each input frame with varying values of σ and the quality score is calculated after each repetition. The segmentation that results in the highest quality score is used as the final segmentation. Fig. 15. and Fig. 16. show example images of this process.

Fig. 15. Left: the input image. Middle: the background edge model. Right: the foreground edges.

Fig. 16. Three segmentation results with varying values of σ. Left: σ -value too low. Middle: optimal σ -value. Right: σ -value too high.

The repetitive segmentation of each frame slows the silhouette extraction of the gait classification system down but by only testing a few values of σ for each frame real time performance can still be achieved. The first frames of a new input sequence will be tested with up to 30 values of σ covering a large interval (typically [1:30]) to initialize the segmentation whereas later frames will be tested with only four to six values of σ in the range ±2 of the σ -value from the previous frame.

13. Conclusion

The gait type of people that move around in open spaces is an important property to recognize in a number of applications, e.g. automated video surveillance and human-robot interaction. The classical description of gait as three distinct types is not always adequate and this chapter has presented a method for describing gait types with a gait continuum which effectively extends and unites the notion of running, jogging, and walking as the three gait types. The method is *not* based on statistical analysis of training data but rather on a general gait motion model synthesized using a computer graphics human model. This makes training (from different views) very easy and separates the training and test data completely. The method is designed to handle challenges that arise in an unconstrained scene and the method has been evaluated on different data sets containing all the important factors which such a method should be able to handle.The method performs well (both in its own right and in comparison to related methods) and it is concluded that the method can be characterized as an *invariant* method for gait description.

The method is further developed to allow video input from multiple cameras. The method can achieve real-time performance and a method for online adjustment of the background subtraction method ensures the quality of the silhouette extraction for scenes with rapid changing illumination conditions.

The quality of the foreground segmentation is important for the precision of the gait classification and duty-factor estimation. The segmentation quality could be improved in the future by extending the color based segmentation of the Codebook method with edge information directly in the segmentation process and furthermore including region based information. This would especially be an advantage in scenes with poor illumination or with video from low quality cameras.

The general motion model used to generate training data effectively represents the basic characteristics of the three gait types, i.e. the characteristics that are independent of person-specific variations. Gait may very well be the type of actions that are most easily described by a single prototypical execution but an interesting area for future work could be the extension of this approach to other actions like waving, boxing, and kicking.

The link between the duty-factor and the biomechanical properties of gait could also be an interesting area for future work. By applying the system in a more constrained setup it would possible to get camera calibrations and ground plane information that could increase the precision of the duty-factor estimation to a level were it may be used to analyze the performance of running athletes.

14. Acknowledgment

This work was supported by the EU project HERMES (FP6 IST-027110) and the BigBrother project (Danish Agency for Science, Technology, and Innovation, CVMT, 2007-2010).

15. References

Alexander, R. (1989). Optimization and Gaits in the Locomotion of Vertebrates, *Physiological Reviews* **69**(4): 1199 - 1227.

Alexander, R. (2002). Energetics and Optimization of Human Walking and Running: The 2000 Raymond Pearl Memorial Lecture, *American Journal of Human Biology* **14**(5): 641 - 648.

Belongie, S., Malik, J. & Puzicha, J. (2002). Shape Matching and Object Recognition Using Shape Contexts, *IEEE Transactions on Pattern Analysis and Machine Intelligence* **24**(4): 509–522.

Blakemore, S.-J. & Decety, J. (2001). From the Perception of Action to the Understanding of Intention, *Nature Reviews Neuroscience* **2**(8): 561–567.

Blank, M., Gorelick, L., Shechtman, E., Irani, M. & Basri, R. (2005). Actions as Space-Time Shapes, *ICCV '05: Proceedings of the Tenth IEEE International Conference on Computer Vision*, IEEE Computer Society, Washington, DC, USA, pp. 1395–1402.

Collins, R., Gross, R. & Shi, J. (2002). Silhouette-Based Human Identification from Body Shape and Gait, *FGR '02: Proceedings of the Fifth IEEE International Conference on Automatic Face and Gesture Recognition*, IEEE Computer Society, Washington, DC, USA, pp. 351–356.

Cutler, R. & Davis, L. S. (2000). Robust Real-Time Periodic Motion Detection, Analysis, and Applications, *IEEE Transactions on Pattern Analysis and Machine Intelligence* **22**(8): 781–796.

Dollár, P., Rabaud, V., Cottrell, G. & Belongie, S. (2005). Behavior Recognition via Sparse Spatio-Temporal Features, *2nd Joint IEEE International Workshop on Visual Surveillance and Performance Evaluation of Tracking and Surveillance.*

Fihl, P., Corlin, R., Park, S., Moeslund, T. & Trivedi,M. (2006). Tracking of Individuals in Very Long Video Sequences, *International Symposium on Visual Computing*, Lake Tahoe, Nevada, USA.

Kim, K., Chalidabhongse, T., Harwood, D. & Davis, L. (2005). Real-time Foreground-Background Segmentation using Codebook Model, *Real-time Imaging* **11**(3): 167–256.

Kim, T.-K. & Cipolla, R. (2009). Canonical Correlation Analysis of Video Volume Tensors for Action Categorization and Detection, *IEEE Transactions on Pattern Analysis and Machine Intelligence* **31**(8): 1415–1428.

Laptev, I., Marszalek, M., Schmid, C. & Rozenfeld, B. (2008). Learning Realistic Human Actions from Movies, *CVPR 2008: IEEE Conference on Computer Vision and Pattern Recognition*, Alaska, USA.

Li, Z., Fu, Y., Huang, T. & Yan, S. (2008). Real-time Human Action Recognition by Luminance Field Trajectory Analysis, *MM '08: Proceeding of the 16th ACM international conference on Multimedia*, ACM, New York, NY, USA, pp. 671–676.

Liu, Z., Malave, L., Osuntugun, A., Sudhakar, P. & Sarkar, S. (2004). Towards Understanding the Limits of Gait Recognition, *International Symposium on Defense and Security*, Orlando, Florida, USA.

Liu, Z. & Sarkar, S. (2006). Improved Gait Recognition by Gait Dynamics Normalization, *IEEE Transactions on Pattern Analysis and Machine Intelligence* **28**(6): 863 - 876.

Masoud, O. & Papanikolopoulos, N. (2003). A Method for Human Action Recognition, *Image and Vision Computing* **21**(8): 729 - 743.

Meisner, E. M., Ábanovic, S., Isler, V., Caporeal, L. C. R. & Trinkle, J. (2009). ShadowPlay: a Generative Model for Nonverbal Human-robot Interaction, *HRI '09: Proceedings of the 4th ACM/IEEE International Conference on Human Robot Interaction.*

Montepare, J. M., Goldstein, S. B. & Clausen, A. (1987). The Identification of Emotions from Gait Information, *Journal of Nonverbal Behavior* **11**(1): 33–42.

Papadimitriou, C. & Steiglitz, K. (1998). *Combinatorial Optimization: Algorithms and Complexity*, Courier Dover Publications, Mineola, NY, USA.

Patron, A. & Reid, I. (2007). A Probabilistic Framework for Recognizing Similar Actions using Spatio-Temporal Features, *18th British Machine Vision Conference.*

Patron, A., Sommerlade, E. & Reid, I. (2008). Action recognition using shared motion parts, *Proceedings of the Eighth International Workshop on Visual Surveillance 2008.*

Ran, Y., Weiss, I., Zheng, Q. & Davis, L. S. (2007). Pedestrian Detection via Periodic Motion Analysis, *International Journal of Computer Vision* **71**(2): 143 - 160.

Robertson, N. & Reid, I. (2005). Behaviour Understanding in Video: A Combined Method, *10th IEEE International Conference on Computer Vision*, pp. 808–814.

Schüldt, C., Laptev, I. & Caputo, B. (2004). Recognizing Human Actions: a Local SVM Approach, *ICPR '04: Proceedings of the 17th International Conference on Pattern Recognition*, IEEE Computer Society, pp. 32–36.

Svenstrup, M., Tranberg, S., Andersen, H. & Bak, T. (2009). Pose Estimation and Adaptive Robot Behaviour for Human-Robot Interaction, *International Conference on Robotics and Automation*, Kobe, Japan.

Tenenbaum, J., de Silva, V. & Langford, J. (2000). A Global Geometric Framework for Nonlinear Dimensionality Reduction, *Science* **290**(5500): 2319 - 2323.

Veeraraghavan, A., Roy-Chowdhury, A. & Chellappa, R. (2005). Matching Shape Sequences in Video with Applications in HumanMovement Analysis, *IEEE Transactions on Pattern Analysis and Machine Intelligence* **27**(12): 1896 - 1909.

Viola, P., Jones, M. J. & Snow, D. (2005). Detecting Pedestrians Using Patterns of Motion and Appearance, *International Journal of Computer Vision* **63**(2): 153 - 161.

Waldherr, S., Romero, R. & Thrun, S. (2000). A Gesture Based Interface for Human-Robot Interaction, *Autonomous Robots* **9**(2): 151–173.

Wang, L., Tan, T. N., Ning, H. Z. & Hu, W. M. (2004). Fusion of Static and Dynamic Body Biometrics for Gait Recognition, *IEEE Transactions on Circuits and Systems for Video Technology* **14**(2): 149–158.

Whittle, M.W. (2001). *Gait Analysis, an Introduction*, Butterworth-Heinemann Ltd.

Yam, C., Nixon, M. & Carter, J. (2002). On the Relationship of Human Walking and Running: Automatic Person Identification by Gait, *International Conference on Pattern Recognition*.

Yang, H.-D., Park, A.-Y.& Lee, S.-W. (2006). Human-Robot Interaction by Whole Body Gesture Spotting and Recognition, *International Conference on Pattern Recognition*.

12

Environment Recognition System for Biped Robot Walking Using Vision Based Sensor Fusion

Tae-Koo Kang, Hee-Jun Song and Gwi-Tae Park
Korea University
Korea

1. Introduction

Biped walking robots are in general composed of two open kinematical chains called legs, which are connected to a main body and two contacting points to the ground, foot. There can be additional components, but this is the basic structure to identify a biped walking robot. Since biped walking robots have to have functions of mimicking human movements such as walking, or even running, they are typically complex in design, having numerous degrees of freedom (DOF) and usually include many serial links usually over 20. Therefore, it is not easy to analyze and plan the motion by using conventional robotics theories. However, there exist control techniques capable of producing a walking motion with long-term efforts from many researches. The researches on biped walking motion planning and controlling can be largely classified into three categories, 'walking pattern generation', 'motion control' and currently being researched 'whole-body control'.

Walking pattern generation means to analyze the dynamics of a biped walking robot and plan its moving trajectory for every joint. A biped walking can be divided into two steps, double support phase, when two feet are contacted to the ground and single support phase, when one of them are in the air. Then it is possible to plan the moving trajectory for the foot and hip in single support phase by using simple function generation algorithm such as polynomial interpolation method. With the trajectories of hip and foot, trajectories for other joints, mainly knee joints, can be acquired by calculating the inverse dynamics between the joints(Craig, 1989)(Huang et al., 2001)(Shih et al., 1993). In recent years, novel trajectory generation methods using artificial intelligence algorithms such as Artificial Neural Networks and Genetic Algorithms are vigorously being researched(Kim et al., 2005)(Endo et al., 2003).

In motion control and whole body control, it is the main issue how to maintain the stability of biped walking robot while walking or doing other motions. Biped robot walking can be divided into two groups, static walking and dynamic walking, by the characteristics of walking. In the static walking motion, the motion of a robot is designed for the center of gravity (COG) on the floor never to leaves the support polygon. So the robot can stop its motion in any moment and not fall down. However, fast link motions are not possible with static walking since the dynamic couplings could affect the static equilibrium. In contrast to static walking, a dynamic walking is realized when the ZMP never leaves the supporting polygon(Kim et al., 2005). The concept of ZMP is considering other forces applied to a robot as well as the gravitational forces. Therefore, the motion of robot depends on the whole dynamics, and consequently this analysis makes the motion of robot more efficient, smoother and faster. The concept of whole body control is to analyze the stability of the robot considering the dynamics of not only leg parts but also other links such as waist and arms. In the aspect of whole body control, it is very important to control the robot on-line while biped walking could be realized in most cases in case of motion control of only lower parts. In recent years, there have been numerous researches on whole body control, including conventional control methods as well as novel methods such as artificial intelligence techniques(Yamaguchi et al., 1999)(Nishiwaki et al. 2004).

As mentioned above, there have been numerous achievements of biped robot walking. However, most of them have been achieved with predetermined terrain conditions, mostly flat surfaces. Therefore, it is needed to develop biped robot walking algorithms capable of walking in unknown environments and it should be researched to develop the methods of recognizing the surrounding environments of robot by using vision system or other sensors.

Sensors are a necessity not only for biped walking robot but also for any moving autonomous machines. Without sensors a robot would be restricted to performing proper tasks. In biped walking robot realizations, sensors are mainly used for two purposes, checking internal states or external states of robots.

Internal states of a biped walking robot generally stand for the stability of walking and they are expressed by ZMP stability criteria in many cases. In real cases, the stability is possibly evaluated by using force sensing registers, inclinometers or gyro sensors. By utilizing those sensors, a robot can be controlled on-line to stabilize its posture using feedbacks from sensors(Kim et al., 2005)(Zheng & Shen, 1990)(Farkas & Asada, 2005). External states represent the surrounding environments and walking conditions of a robot. They can be obtained by using distance sensors such as ultrasonic sensors or Infrared sensors and vision cameras. Those sensors are mostly used for recognizing objects to handle them or obstacles to avoid them. Unlike wheeled robots, biped walking robots have the advantage of moving over obstacles. However, in the case of moving over an obstacle, it is critically important to attain the precise information of obstacles as much as possible since the robot should contact with the obstacle by calculating the appropriate motion trajectories to the obstacle. Unfortunately, there have been not many outcomes on this topic, dynamic motion trajectory generation. Still, the researches on biped robot walking are limited within the range of walking algorithm and stability. In addition, it is critically needed to use vision cameras to obtain precise information about surrounding environment, and the techniques of vision systems such as pinhole camera model or background subtraction, etc. do not work well with cameras on the neck of a biped walking robot since the camera consistently keeps swaying because of the high disturbances of robot walking. Therefore, most of the biped walking robots uses high-priced stereo vision system to have the depth information(Gerecke et al., 2002)(Michel et al., 2005). It is an important issue to develop efficient vision processing algorithm with a single vision camera to popularize humanoids in real world.

There still remain problems in developing biped walking robots. To progress biped walking robots to the level of humanoids, technologies in robot intelligence are in need to be more developed as well as robot motion analysis and control. The currently being developed biped walking robots including the most powerful robots at present such as ASIMO and

HUBO, etc. have problems that they cannot be operated in unknown environments. Therefore, those robots are not possible to replace the entire human works with the current level of technology. Considering the developing speed of artificial intelligence, it seems not possible to build robots with a similar level of intelligence to the one of human beings. However, it would be possible to make a robot to mimic the behaviors of human beings by using an appropriate level of preprogrammed intelligence, communication with human beings and environment recognition system. In addition, it is extremely urgent to reduce the price of biped walking robots to an affordable level for ordinary people. It is remarkably important to build a system for recognizing surrounding environments of robot and making appropriate decisions against the change of environments. In addition, a real humanoid must have the function of self-decision making as well as executing tasks given by users.

To work or to carry out a given task in an unknown environment, a biped walking robot must recognize and react to its surrounding environments. For the purpose, a robot should detect an object and track it to deal with the object. The most common method for detecting a moving object in an image is background subtraction in the literatures of vision systems(Li et al., 2004). In recent years, color-based object tracking methods which use the characteristics of objects represented by color histograms have been widely used in wheeled and biped walking robot researches(Fieguth & Terzopoulos, 1997). However, those are not appropriate methods for biped walking robots since the whole background moves with the target object when a robot walks unlike the cases of using fixed cameras. Moreover, it is needed to have the predetermined color information of target object to use color-based methods. In this chapter, a method for object detection and tracking using modified optical flow algorithm is proposed. The optical flow is a method of detecting the flow of lights between time series images and it provides the information of distribution of direction and velocities in an image(Lee, 1980). Even though, the optical flow method provides motion information, it is still not proper because all the points in images move in case of biped robot walking. To overcome this problem, a modified method of the optical flow using K-means clustering algorithm is proposed and realized. The proposed system generates the optical flow field for input images and eliminates the most common motion components considering their velocities and directions by K-means clustering, which probably belong to the background. In such way, a foreground moving object can be efficiently detected and tracked.

In addition to the object detection and tracking, the function of object recognition is very important for a biped walking robot to appropriately react to its environment conditions. In this chapter, the method of object recognition is developed to make a robot to be provided proper information to climb up and down or avoid obstacles. Unlike the tracking process of moving object, those obstacles do not move. Consequently it is not possible to detect them by the same method for moving object detection. A cascade of boosted classifier (Adaboost) is used to detect obstacles. Also, those obstacles can be categorized into a couple of groups such as walls, stairs or slopes. A hierarchical Support Vector Machines (SVM) is proposed in this chapter to classify obstacles into each category. The information from the recognition system is combined with the data obtained from other sensors to determine the current state of a robot and the total information of the obstacle so as for the robot to move around or up.

The system mentioned above have been realized and verified by experiments conducted with a biped walking robot. With the system, it is expected to build a biped walking robot capable of

efficiently moving by adapting its environment with low cost by using proposed vision system methods with a single CCD camera with sensors instead of a stereo vision system.
This chapter is organized as follows. In chapter 2, the proposed environment recognition system is introduced. More specifically, the concepts of object tracking system and obstacle recognition system for a biped walking robot are illustrated. This chapter also gives examples which utilize the proposed system. In chapter 3, the results of experiments focusing on verifying the performances of the proposed system is given. They are object tracking tests and obstacle avoiding/climbing tests using the whole proposed system. Chapter 4 concludes the paper by presenting the contributions of this paper and the recommendations for future works.

2. Environment Recognition System

2.1 Overall System Structure

The overall system is constructed as illustrated in Fig. 1. The system largely consists of two parts, a biped walking robot and a Host PC. Those are connected with a Blue-Tooth wireless communication module using RS-232C. Since the realization of a biped walking robot which autonomously moves in an unknown environment as well as executes assigned tasks by a user is the main purpose of the system, the robot is equipped with several kinds of sensors gather the information of the surrounding environments. Consequently, the robot is basically designed to move autonomously without any control from the user by recognizing the environment using sensors. For instance, the robot can control its posture stability by itself, by using gyro sensors and actuators in the waist joints.

Fig. 1. Overall system architecture

In applications of biped walking robot, dynamical motion trajectory generation is more desirable than walking with a pre-determined walking motion. However, a robot must recognize its surrounding environment in advance to dynamically generate the motion trajectory. For the purpose, it is needed to develop a system of recognizing a robot's

environment and it must be one of the fundamental conditions for more developed biped walking robot. In this chapter, environment conditions for a biped walking robot are classified into three categories: even surface, moving object and obstacles in a broad sense.
Fig. 2 shows the environment recognition system built for the biped walking robot. As shown in Fig. 2, this system is composed of two parts: moving object tracking and obstacle recognition. The moving object detecting system shown in the left of the bottom window detects and tracks a moving object by using modified optical flow method. Unlike the usual method for object detection in vision system is background subtraction, the modified optical flow method is proposed due to the always non-stationary background so that the background subtraction method detects the whole region of input image as foreground(Fieguth & Terzopoulos, 1997)(Denavit & Hartenbeg, 1955)(Beauchmin & Barron, 1995). The proposed method is illustrated in more detail in chapter 2.2.
The window in the right of the bottom in Fig. 2 shows the obstacle recognition system. The possible obstacles recognized and classified with this system are obstacles which a biped walking robot can climb up and the other obstacles which it cannot climb up but should avoid. The former are again classified into stairs or slopes. For the purpose, the recognition system detects the region of an obstacle by using a cascade of boosted classifier (Adaboost) and extracts the most important features in the selected region by using Principle Component Analysis (PCA). Then the features go into a hierarchical Support Vector Machine to determine what the obstacle is. The final decision is made with other data such as distance to the obstacle from ultrasonic and infrared sensors. The more detailed descriptions are given in chapter 2.3. The environment recognition system provides not only the information of existence of objects and obstacles, but also the details of them. For instance, when the system detects a stairs in front of the robot, it estimates the distance to the stairs, the height and width of a stair so that the robot can calculate the corresponding motion trajectory to climb the stairs.

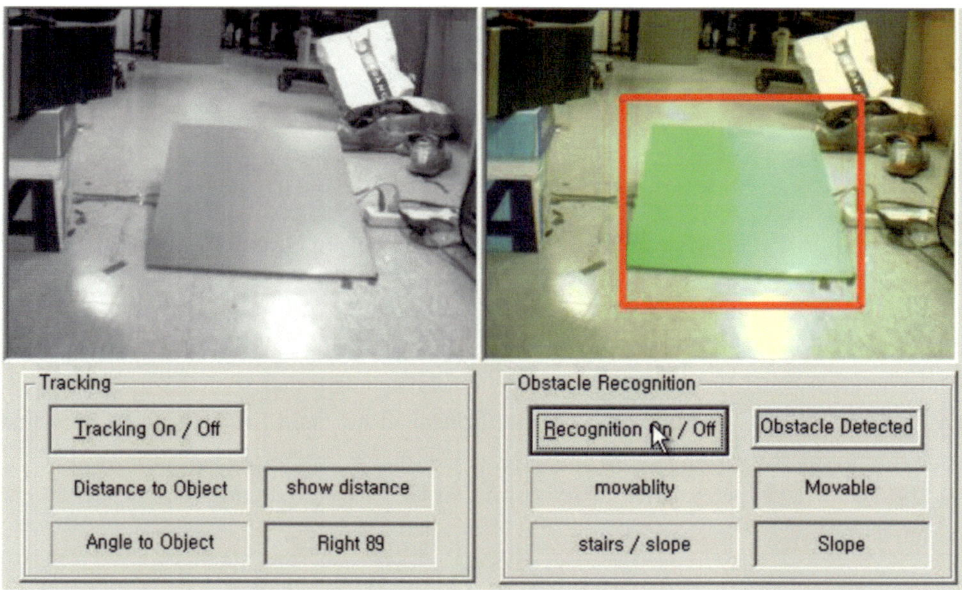

Fig. 2. Environment recognition system

2.2 Moving Object Detection Using Modified Optical Flow

2.2.1 Optical Flow Concept

An optical flow represents the apparent velocities of movement of brightness patterns in an image. The optical flow can arise from relative motion of objects and the viewer(Denavit & Hartenbeg, 1955)(Gibson, 1966)(Tomasi & Kanade, 1991). It provides the information about the changes of motion between images in time. Consequently, the optical flow method has the advantages of extracting moving objects in images, no matter what the object is. How to obtain an optical flow from a series of images in time is illustrated in the following.

Let $I(x,y,t)$ be the image brightness that changes in time to provide an image sequence. Two main assumptions can be made:

- Brightness $I(x,y,t)$ smoothly depends on coordinates (x,y) in greater part of the image.
- Brightness of every point of a moving or static object does not change in time

Let us suppose that an object moves in an image. By using Taylor series, the displacement after time dt can be expressed as,

$$I(x+dx,y+dy,t+dt)=I(x,y,t)+\frac{\partial I}{\partial x}dx+\frac{\partial I}{\partial y}dy+\frac{\partial I}{\partial t}dt+\cdots \quad (1)$$

when dt is small enough. Then, according to the second assumption,

$$I(x+dx,y+dy,t+dt)=I(x,y,t) \quad (2)$$

and therefore,

$$\frac{\partial I}{\partial x}dx+\frac{\partial I}{\partial y}dy+\frac{\partial I}{\partial t}dt+\cdots=0 \quad (3)$$

Let us define the components of an optical flow field as,

$$\frac{dx}{dt}=u \quad \text{and} \quad \frac{dy}{dt}=v \quad (4)$$

Substituting (4) in the equation (3), the optical flow constraint equation is obtained,

$$-\frac{\partial I}{\partial t}=\frac{\partial I}{\partial x}u+\frac{\partial I}{\partial y}v \quad (5)$$

where, u and v are components of the optical flow field in x and y coordinates, respectively. Now the problem is to solve the derivative equation of (5).

Since, the vector u is perpendicular to v, and so is x to y, the constraint equation can be rewritten as,

$$(I_x,I_y)\cdot(u,v)=-I_t \quad (6)$$

where, I_x, I_y and I_t are the partial derivatives of I, corresponding to each subscript. Consequently, the component of an image velocity in the direction of the image intensity gradient of a point in the image is,

$$(u,v) = \frac{-I_t}{\sqrt{I_x^2 + I_y^2}} \tag{7}$$

However, the solution to (7) cannot be directly obtained since it has more than one solution. There have been a couple of methods to solve the optical flow constraint equation by obtaining more constraints. An example of calculating an optical flow field for a rotating sphere is given in Fig. 3.

In the case of real applications, a method of feature selection based on a model of affine changes is preceded to calculating the optical flow of images, since it is computationally very expensive to apply the optical flow to every point in the images(Shi & Tomasi, 1994).

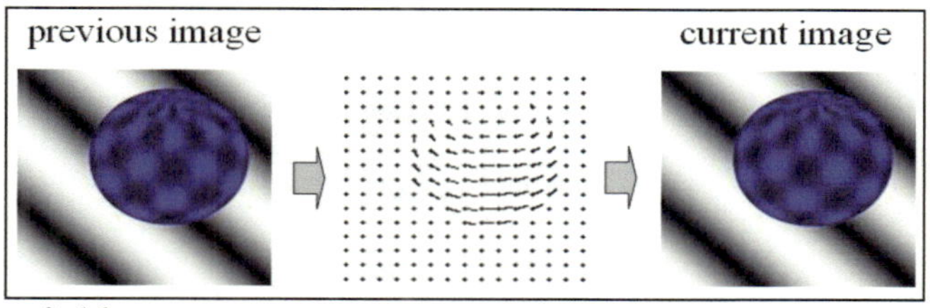

Fig. 3. Optical flow field

2.2.2 Modified Optical Flow for Non-stationary Background

The optical flow is an efficient algorithm for extracting moving components or tracking moving objects in images. However, the original optical flow method is not applicable in case of biped walking robot. Because the whole image varies so that all the points in an image have the optical flow components of velocities and directions. Therefore, moving objects as well as background are considered that they are moving in such case. To resolve this problem, a modification of the optical flow method is proposed to eliminate background components by using K-means clustering.

Fig. 4 represents the generated optical flow fields with a fixed camera and a moving camera, respectively. Even in case of a fixed camera, there are some extracted features to be tracked. However, it can be empirically known that the components of a moving object and ones of background are possibly classified into different groups. Therefore, in case that an object is moving in an image, the whole set of extracted motion features from the optical flow field can be classified into two groups. However, a problem still remains, that is, how to determine which group consists of the object. To overcome this problem, it is assumed that the features in a moving object have a larger distribution than ones in the background.

This might be a sound assumption since a moving object usually has various components as seen in Fig. 4, while the motion of background is almost only translational in a short time. To divide the features of each group, K-means algorithm is applied to the set in the feature space(MacQueen, 1967)(Gonzalez & Woods, 2002). In addition, it would not be necessary to divide the object and the background in case of non-moving object. Therefore, the distance between the centers belonging to each group is calculated and it is considered as one group when the distance is small enough.

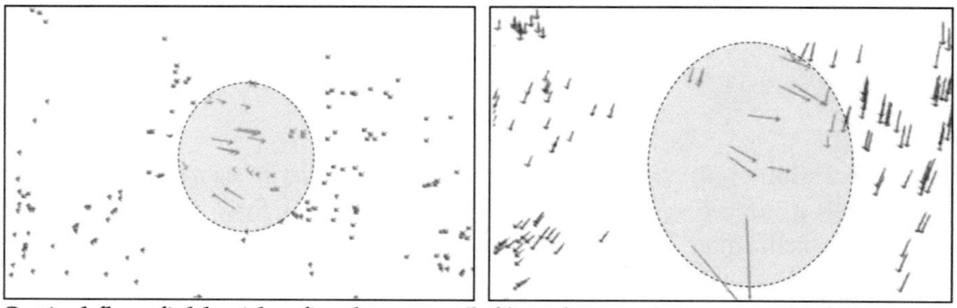

Fig. 4. Optical flow field with a fixed camera (left) and a moving camera(right)

2.2.3 Moving object detecting system

The detailed description of the procedure is given in the following:

1. Extract the good features to track.
2. Calculate the optical flow field and the set of components.

$$S = \{u_k, v_k\} \qquad k = 1,2,...,n \tag{8}$$

3. For the selected components, generate a feature space denoted as S', consisting of the components of velocities and directions.

$$S = \{u_k, v_k\} \quad \Rightarrow \quad S' = \{r_k, \theta_k\} \tag{9}$$

4. Divide the set into two clusters by using K-means clustering.

$$S' = \{S'_1, S'_2\} = \{(r_l, \theta_l), (r_m, \theta_m)\}$$
$$\text{where } l = 1,2,...,n_1,\ m = 1,2,...,n_2 \text{ and } n = n_1 + n_2 \tag{10}$$

5. Calculate the standard deviation of each cluster.

$$\sigma_k = \sqrt{E((S'_k - E(S'_k))^2)} = \sqrt{E(S'^2_k) - (E(S'_k))^2} \qquad k = 1,2 \tag{11}$$

6. Eliminate the features in the background.

$$k = \max(\sigma_1, \sigma_2) \qquad k = 1,2$$
$$S' = \{S'_1, S'_2\} \quad \Rightarrow \quad S' = \{S'_k\} \tag{12}$$

7. Determine if a moving object actually exist in the image by calculating the distance between the centers of each cluster. If it is smaller than a threshold value, consider the two clusters as one cluster.
8. For the features in the selected cluster, calculate the center of gravity. It represents the center of the moving object.

$$S' \quad \Rightarrow \quad S(x,y,t)$$
$$R = \frac{1}{N}\sum_{1}^{n} S(x,y) \qquad n\text{: number of selected features} \tag{13}$$

By using the proposed method, moving objects in images can be detected and tracked in most cases. Fig. 5 illustrates the whole procedure of the object tracking system.

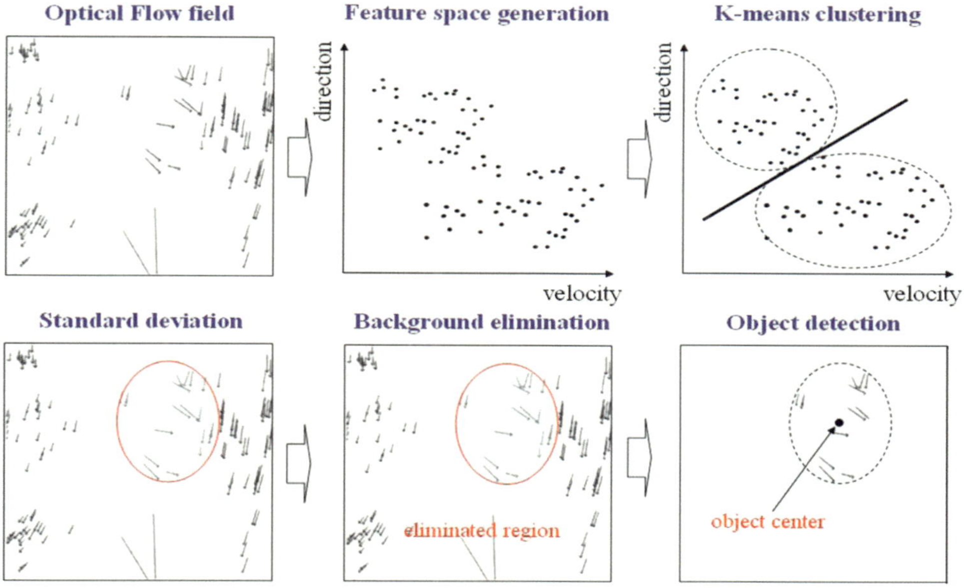

Fig. 5. Moving object detecting system

2.3 Obstacle Recognition Using Hierarchical Support Vector Machines

2.3.1 Proposed Obstacle Recognition System

The whole procedure of obstacle recognition system is illustrated in Fig. 6. As stated in previous chapters in chapter 2.1, the obstacle recognition system classifies an obstacle which a robot faces while walking and determines the details of the obstacle so that the robot is enabled to autonomously determine its behavior and generate the appropriate trajectory. This must be a mandatory system to realize humanoid robots since the current walking robots are only possible to walk in pre-programmed known environments.

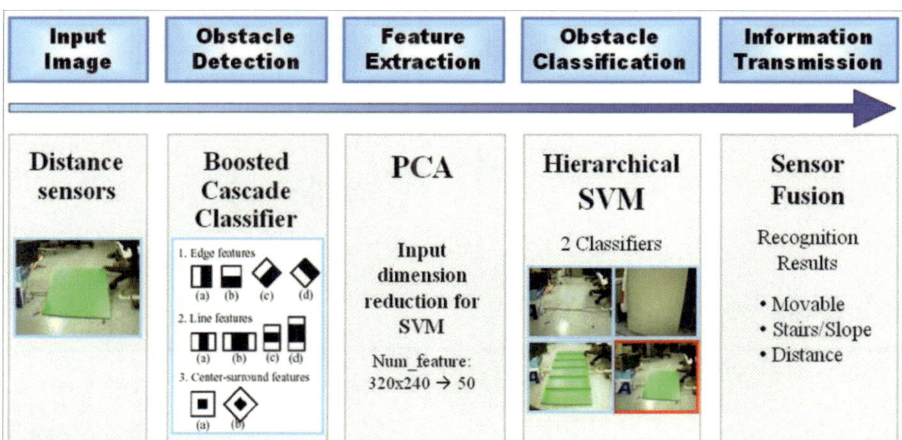

Fig. 6. Obstacle recognition system

2.3.2 Obstacle Detection : A Cascade of Boosted Classifier

To recognize an object in an image obtained from the camera of a biped walking robot, it is needed to use an algorithm capable of functioning a classifier. In this chapter, a hierarchical Support Vector Machine is applied for classifying objects. However, the image ROI (region of interest) specified by the SVM classifier generally does not correctly match to the input images, there is a need of using an algorithm which sets the image ROI for the classifier. In this chapter, those algorithms of recognition using a cascade of boosted classifier and classification using *a* hierarchical SVM are used to detect(recognize) and classify obstacles in front of a biped walking robot. For the purpose, a cascade of boosted classifier is applied to input images to specify the ROI in advance to the SVM classifier(Viola & Jones, 2001)(Lienhart & Maydt, 2002).

Given example images $(x_1, y_1), \ldots, (x_n, y_n)$

where $y_i = 0,\ 1$ for negative and positive examples repectively.

Initialize weights $w_{1,i} = \frac{1}{2m}, \frac{1}{2l}$ for $y_i = 0,\ 1$ respectively,

where m and l are the number of negatives and positives respectively.

For $t = 1, \ldots, T$:

1. Normalize the weights,

$$w_{t,i} \leftarrow \frac{w_{t,i}}{\sum_{j=1}^{n} w_{t,j}}$$

so that w_t is a probability distribution.

2. For each feature, j, train a classfier h_j which is restricted to using a single feature.

The error is evaluated with respect to w_l, $\varepsilon_j = \sum_i w_i \left| h_j(x_i) - y_i \right|$.

3. Choose the classfier, h_t, with the lowest error ε_t.
4. Update the weights :

$$w_{l+1,i} = w_{t,i} \beta_t^{1-e_i}$$

where $e_i = 0$ if example x_i is classified correctly, $e_i = 1$ otherwise, $\beta_t = \frac{\varepsilon_t}{1-\varepsilon_t}$.

The final strong classifier is :

$$h(x) = \begin{cases} 1 & \sum_{t=1}^{T} \alpha_t h_t(x) \geq \frac{1}{2} \sum_{t=1}^{T} \alpha_t \\ 0 & \text{otherwise} \end{cases}$$

where $\alpha_t = \log \frac{1}{\beta_t}$

Fig. 7. Adaboost algorithm

The basic scheme of a cascade of boosted classifier, as known as Adaboost or general boosting algorithm, is to combine multiple weak classifiers into a more powerful decision

rule for classification(Schapire, 1999). The boosted classifier is realized with a number of simple Haar filters by applying Adaboost algorithm to make the weak classifier consisting of those Haar filters to be strong. The brief algorithm of Adaboost is introduced in Fig. 7.
The algorithm performs a sequence of training rounds, and at each round a new classifier is trained. Initially, each training vector has an associated weight that encodes its importance in the learning algorithm. The training set is classified according to the decision rule of the current step, and then the weights are modified according to the classification results. This process is repeated building each time classifiers more focused on the most difficult examples. The result is a set of classifiers which combined achieve higher classification ratios.

In the boosted classifier used in the proposed obstacle detecting system, a set of Haar filters as features are used to train the classifiers. A weak classifier is not capable of detecting a rotated or translated input image. However, once a boosted classifier is generated, it is able to adaptively detect the obstacles even when they are rotated or translated. The concept of a boosted classifier and the boosted classifier used for detecting a stairs are given in Fig. 8.
Consequently, the ROI from input image is obtained as a result of using the generated cascade of boosted classifier and a feature extraction process is performed to reduce the dimensionality of input images in advance to applying the ROI to the main classifier, a hierarchical SVM.

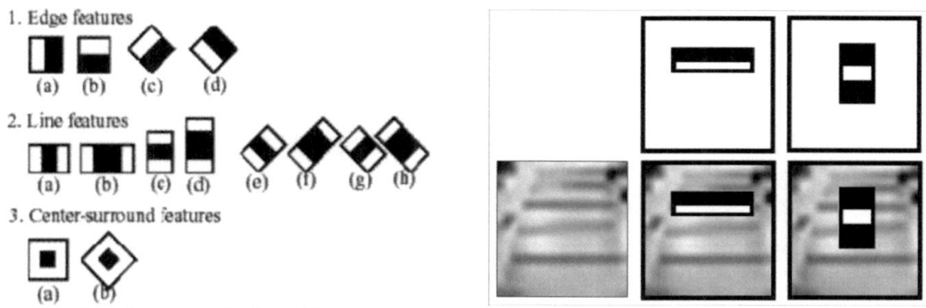

Fig. 8. A cascade of boosted classifier

2.3.3 Feature Extraction : Principle Component Analysis

Principle Component Analysis (PCA) is known as a useful technique to extract dominant features or reduce the dimensionality of large data sets in image processing and data mining and can also be used to find signals in noisy data in signal processing. In some cases, the dimension of the input is too large, but the components in the input are highly correlated (redundant), PCA is useful to reduce the dimension of the input. PCA has three representative effects: (1) it orthogonalizes the components of the input vectors so that they are uncorrelated with each other, (2) it orders the resulting orthogonal components (principal components) so that those with the largest variation come first, and (3) it eliminates those components that contribute the least to the variation in the data set. Since the results derived from PCA are orthogonal to each other, there is much less redundancies in the resulting data(Jolliffe, 1986).
As shown in Fig. 9, two input dataset having different dimension, 50 and 25 are generated to be modeled by SVM. First, the whole input data (320 x 240) from input images are

transformed by PCA. Then the generated arrays having the trends of the original data (number of samples x 50 or number of samples x 25) are extracted. Hence, the finally resulting arrays contain 50 or 25 dimensional data containing the principal information of the original input image. These arrays are split into training and test dataset, which used to train and test using SVM.

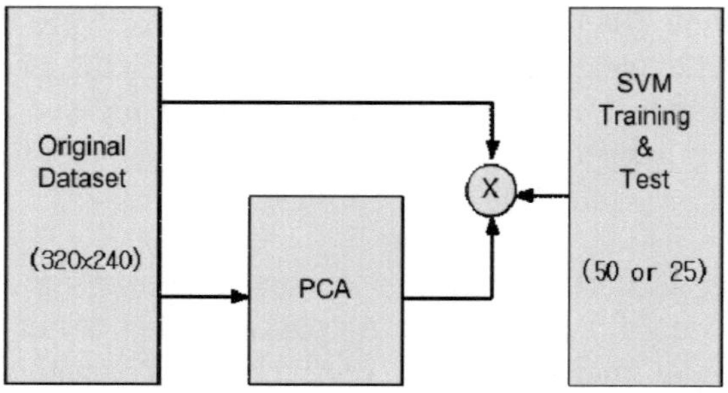

Fig. 9. Principle Component Analysis

2.3.4 Obstacle Recognition : Hierarchical Support Vector Machines

To recognize and classify the obstacles which a biped walking robot faces while walking, a hierarchical Support Vector Machine (SVM) is implemented to construct an efficient classifier. SVM is a learning tool originated in modern statistical learning theory. SVM can be used for a variety of applications and it is considered as a powerful classifier in the field of vision processing. The formulation of SVM learning is based on the principle of structural risk minimization. Instead of minimizing an objective function based on the training samples, such as mean square error (MSE), the SVM attempts to minimize a bound on the generalization error (i.e., the error made by the learning machine on test data not used during training). As a result, an SVM tends to perform well when applied to data outside the training set. Indeed, it has been reported that SVM-based approaches are able to significantly outperform competing methods in many applications(Burges, 1998)(Muller et al., 2001)(Wernick, 1991). SVM achieves this advantage by focusing on the training examples that are most difficult to classify. These "borderline" training examples are called support vectors(Vapnik, 1995)(Cortes & Vapnik, 1995). The procedure how SVM classifies features in a feature space is described in the following.

Given a set of linear separating training samples $(x_i, y_i)_{1 \le i \le N}, x_i \in R^d, y_i \in \{-1,1\}$ is the class label which x_i belongs to. The general form of linear classification function is $g(x) = w \cdot x + b$ which corresponds to a separating hyperplane $w \cdot x + b = 0$. It is possible to normalize $g(x)$ to satisfy $|g(x)| \ge 1$ for all x_i, so that the distance from the closest point to the hyperplane is $1/\|w\|$. Among the separating hyperplanes, the one for which the distance to the closest point is maximal and that is called optimal separating hyperplane. Since the distance to the closest point is $1/\|w\|$, finding the optimal separating hyperplane amounts to minimizing $\|w\|$ and the objective function is,

$$\begin{aligned} &\min \phi(w) = \frac{1}{2}\|w\|^2 = \frac{1}{2}(w \cdot w) \\ &\textit{Subject to:} \\ &y_i(w \cdot x_i + b) \geq 1, \qquad i = 1,\ldots,N \end{aligned} \tag{14}$$

If the N non-negative Lagrangian multipliers associated with constraints in (16) are denoted with $(\alpha_1,\cdots,\alpha_N)$, the optimal separating hyperplane can be constructed by solving a constrained quadratic programming problem. The solution w has an expansion $w = \sum_i \alpha_i y_i x_i$ in terms of a subset of training patterns, support vectors. Support vectors lie on the margin. Thus, the classification function written as,

$$f(x) = sign\left(\sum_i \alpha_i y_i x_i \cdot x + b\right) \tag{15}$$

When the data is not linearly separable, on the one hand, SVM introduces slack variables and a penalty factor such that the objective function can be modified as,

$$\phi(w,) = \frac{1}{2}(w \cdot w) + C\left(\sum_1^N \varsigma_i\right) \tag{16}$$

On the other hand, the input data can be mapped through some nonlinear mapping into a high-dimensional feature space in which the optimal separating hyperplane is constructed. Thus the dot production can be represented by $k(x,y) := (\phi(x) \cdot \phi(y))$ when the kernel k satisfy Mercer's condition. [42] Finally, the classification function can be obtained as,

$$f(x) = sign\left(\sum_i \alpha_i y_i \cdot k(x_i \cdot x) + b\right) \tag{17}$$

Because SVM can be analyzed theoretically using concepts from the statistical learning theory, it has particular advantages when applied to problems with limited training samples in the high-dimensional space. Consequently, SVM can achieve a good performance when applied to real problem. Fig. 10 illustrates the concept of SVM classification with a linear kernel.

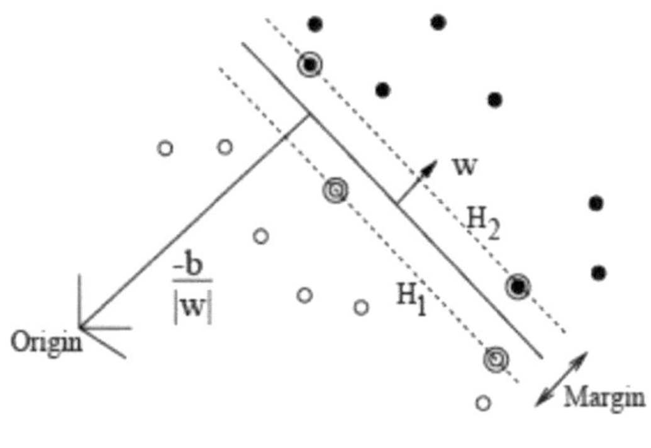

Fig. 10. SVM classification

However, as seen in Fig. 10, the original concept of SVM is not applicable to the case of obstacle recognition for biped walking robot, because there are more than two kinds of obstacles to be classified. When a robot is walking, it could face infinite kinds of obstacles in its surrounding environments. In this chapter, obstacles are categorized largely into two groups, obstacles which a biped walking robot can climb up and ones which should be avoided. In addition, the former group can be classified into two groups again, slope and stairs, since the walking characteristics of them are quite different. Consequently, there exist at least four kinds of obstacles including an even surface. The use of the original SVM is not appropriate in this case. Therefore, in this chapter a hierarchical SVM is proposed to classify a variety of obstacles, more than two kinds.
The structure of the proposed hierarchical SVM is depicted in Fig. 11.

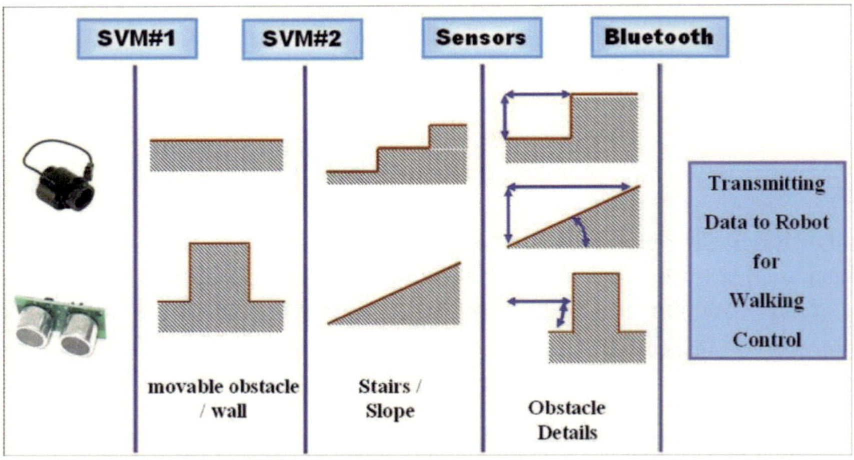

Fig. 11. Proposed hierarchical SVM structure

When an obstacle is detected by the vision camera and ultrasonic sensors installed in the robot, the input image is processed by the procedures stated in chapter 2.3.2 and 2.3.3 in advance to being applied to SVM classifier. In the classification process, a SVM classifier trained to classify even surfaces and walls is applied to the extracted features of the input image at the first stage. It determines whether the robot can climb up the obstacle or not, and returns the possibility of climbing up to the robot by using Blue-Tooth communication. Then the robot modifies its motion trajectory in a way of avoiding in case of walls or other un-climbable obstacles. If the obstacle is classified as climbable by the first SVM classifier, the features are applied to the SVM second classifier. It classifies the object into the categories of stairs or a slope. Then the recognition system determines the more detailed information such as the height and width of a stair and the inclining degree of a slope, according to the information obtained from infrared sensors. Also, the determined result is transmitted to the robot and the robot generates a corresponding trajectory to the obstacle.

3. Experiments and Analysis

3.1 Experiments for the Moving Object Detection

3.1.1 Experimental Conditions

The conditions for experiments to evaluate the performance of the proposed moving object detection / tracking system is as following.

- Experiments have been largely conducted in 2 camera conditions with a fixed camera and a camera installed on the neck of the walking robot. Since the tracking system is originally designed to be robust in case that a robot does biped walking, it is expected that the performance of moving camera cases is almost similar or little lower than the one of fixed camera.
- The number of clusters in K-means clustering is set to 2. This is because it is meaningless for the walking robot to track more than 2 objects and follow them. Obviously, the tracking system can separately detect and track any number of objects by setting the correspondent number of clusters.
- The modified optical flow algorithm has 200 / 300 / 400 of features to track. As the number of tracking features becomes larger, the tracking system can be expected to be more susceptible while it might have more noises which lower the accuracy of the system.

3.1.2 Experimental Results and Analysis

The proposed tracking algorithm is evaluated with real-time video streams. There are 10 video streams of human moving used for the test and each video stream consists of 100 frames. Fig. 12 shows the optical flow fields in case of fixed camera and moving camera.

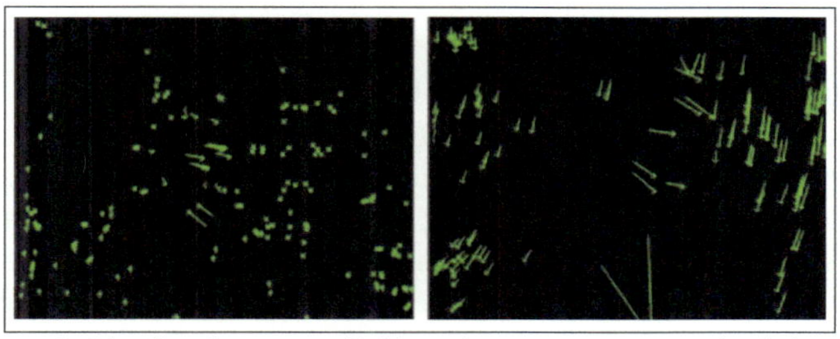

Fig. 12. Optical flow fields: fixed camera (left) and moving camera (right)

As shown in Fig. 12, the vectors in the optical flow field do not have noticeable intensities in the background region in case of a fixed camera used. In addition, it is easily seen that the number of features in the moving object region is much smaller than the one in the background region as expected. In contrast, the optical flow vectors generated by a camera mounted on the walking robot show different patterns. The vectors belonging to the background region have much larger intensities with similar directions in this case while the vectors in the object region do not have much difference from the case of fixed camera.

In both cases, the moving object regions are clearly recognized since they show remarkably different tendencies in the intensity and direction of vector elements. In the left window of Fig. 13 and Fig. 14, final results of processing the modified optical flow method are presented. The centers of moving human are marked with colored circles.

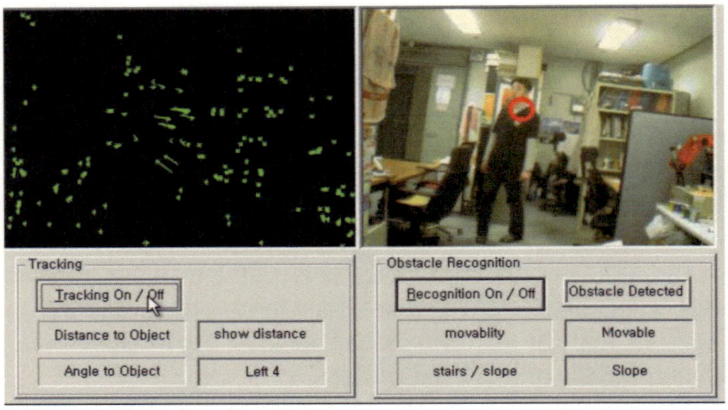

Fig. 13. Object tracking with a fixed camera

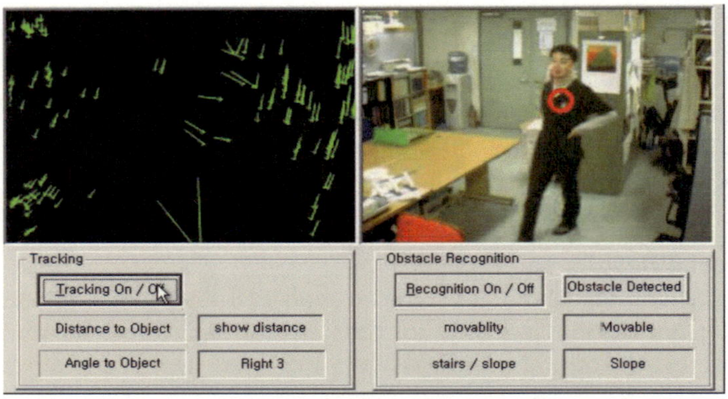

Fig. 14. Object tracking with a camera installed in a biped walking robot

From Fig. 13 and Fig. 14, it can be known that the proposed method effectively detects moving objects in both cases of fixed camera and moving camera. The evaluation of tracking accuracy is given in Table 1. The test results indicate the number of frames which the proposed algorithm correctly detects moving object out of 1000 frames. From the results of performance tests above, it can be noticed that the proposed algorithm shows little better performance in case of fixed camera, however there is no distinguishable difference and the algorithm shows approximately 90% of accuracies in both cases.
Considering the proposed algorithm is performed in every frame so that there is no possibility of being affected by occlusions or losing objects while tracking. In addition, the average processing time is 20.9 ms and the camera carries out to send images at the speed of 30 frames per second. Therefore, the proposed algorithm can be concluded to be effective for moving object tracking system in biped robot walking.

camera	num_features	processing time (ms)	tracking accuracy (%)
fixed	200	18.2	91.78
	300	21.2	93.14
	400	23.3	92.52
moving	200	17.8	85.38
	300	21.4	88.43
	400	23.2	87.59
average		20.9	89.81

Table 1. Moving object detection / tracking accuracy test results

3.2 Experiments for the Obstacle Recognition

3.2.1 Experimental Conditions

The experimental conditions for the obstacle recognition system are given in the following.

- Cascade of Boosted Classifier (Adaboost): Adaboost detects the region of interest from the input image. The output image sizes after Adaboost are set to have 25x25 pixels and 30x30 pixels. For the learning of Adaboost, 500 of wall images, 500 of slope images, 500 of stairs images and 1000 of negative images are used. Those input images are taken by rotationally and horizontally moving the obstacles. Adaboost is set to have 140 patterns (small classifiers) in 14 stages after the learning.
- Principle Component Analysis (PCA): PCA uses the images after Adaboost which have 25x25 or 50x50 pixels. Therefore the input data dimension to PCA is 625 or 2500. To reduce the dimensionality of input data for hierarchical SVM, the 625 or 2500 data dimension is reduced to have 25 or 50 principle components after PCA processing.
- Hierarchical Support Vector Machine (SVM): In this stage, 2 SVM classifiers are serially connected to classify movable or not movable obstacle (wall or not) with the first classifier, then the second classifier classifies whether the movable obstacle is a slope or stairs. For the input data, the principle components having 25 or 50 dimension are used from the PCA processing. The classification accuracy is evaluated by using different kernels such as linear, polynomial and radial basis function (RBF) kernels.

3.2.2 Experimental Results and Analysis

The proposed obstacle recognition system is evaluated by applying 10 of 10 second video streams at the speed of 30 frames per second in each test category. (3000 frames in total) Table 2 gives the experimental result of the proposed system. The classification accuracy is measured by calculating the ratio of correct classification for the 3000 input images.

Adaboost Ada_win_size	PCA num_PC	SVM SVM_kernel	accuracy (%)			Processing time (ms)
			wall	slope	stairs	
25x25	25	linear	80.1	83.1	92.9	22.38
		polynomial	85.2	83.4	95.5	22.76
		RBF	88.1	87.2	97.6	23.21
	50	linear	85.1	84.2	93.4	23.35
		polynomial	86.2	85.9	95.7	24.12
		RBF	87.3	86.2	97.8	24.06
30x30	25	linear	84.1	84.1	93.1	23.78
		polynomial	86.1	85.9	95.5	24.35
		RBF	87.6	86.6	97.8	24.89
	50	linear	84.9	84.6	94.1	24.43
		polynomial	86.8	87.2	95.9	25.32
		RBF	88.4	86.7	98.1	25.47
average			85.83	85.43	95.62	22.16

Table 2. Obstacle recognition performance test results

From the evaluation in Table 2, the proposed obstacle recognition algorithm shows appropriate processing time, approximately 22 ms and it is enough to be carried out in real time with camera at the transmission speed of 30 frames per second. The results of accuracy tests show differences by the types of obstacles. In case of wall and slope, the region detection accuracy by Adaboost is relatively high, however they also have high false alarm rate so that the total accuracies of both cases are about 85 %, which is not satisfactory. On the contrary, the classification accuracy of stairs is approximately 10% higher than the ones of other obstacles. In addition, cases with larger window size, larger number of principle components and RBF kernel show little better results for the cases of all types of obstacles but it is not that remarkable difference since the difference is just within 5-7%.

The evaluation results can be understood that stairs have the most distinguishable features while wall and slope are similar in shape, hence the classification of wall and slope is disturbed because of the high false alarm rate caused by misclassification between wall and slope. However, this algorithm is only required to be executed every few frames since this only functions to fire the autonomous walking trajectory generation procedure of the walking robot. The proposed obstacle recognition algorithm is available to be used for biped robot walking.

Fig. 15 shows the obstacle recognition for a wall, stairs, a slope, and corresponding actual robot walking. The left window indicates the region detected by Adaboost algorithm and it is marked with a rectangle in the right window. The information window in the bottom of the right window shows the classification results.

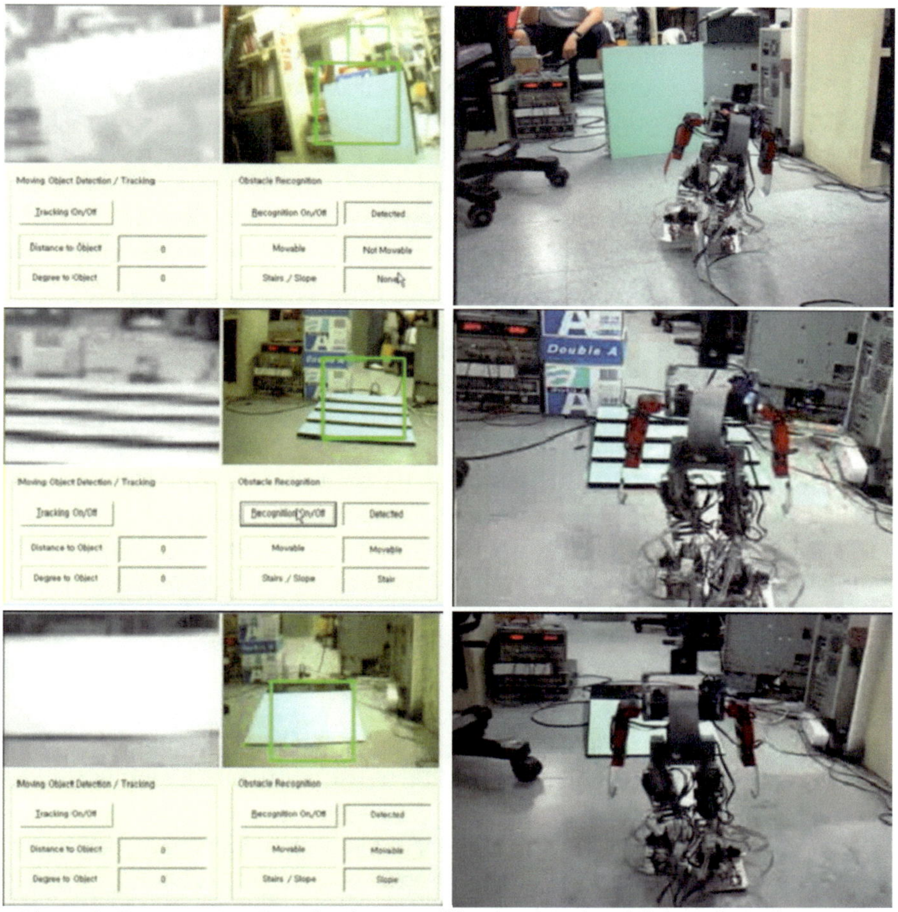

Fig. 15. Obstacle Recognition Results for a wall(top), stairs(middle), a slope(bottom)

4. Conclusion

This chapter presents the systems of environment recognition system and human robot interaction system for biped walking robot. For the realization of humanoid robot, they are the mandatory conditions to make a robot autonomously recognize its surrounding environment and adaptively walk by generating its motion trajectories. Therefore, this chapter has the meaning of developing aid technologies for biped robot walking control. The environment recognition system is realized by combining sensory data obtained from a walking robot including image data taken by a single camera. The problems in developing vision system in biped walking robot operated in a real world are derived from the fact that the condition for the vision system of a biped walking robot quite differs from the one of a fixed camera or a camera mounted on a wheeled robot. With a biped walking robot in real world, the commonly used vision analysis methods such as background subtraction or color-based object detection methods are not applicable since the camera always sways and it cannot be previously known what color the object has. To overcome these problems, object tracking system by using modified optical flow method and obstacle recognition system by using a hierarchical Support Vector Machines are proposed in this chapter. Those systems are realized and verified their effectiveness with a number of experiments by implementing them into a biped walking robot. Also, the results are presented and analyzed.

In conclusion, the systems proposed in this chapter are significantly useful in the sense that they are the characterized systems highly focused on and applicable to real-world biped walking robot. There still remain more researches to be done. They are as following:

- Because the vision system used in the proposed system totally depends on the Host PC, there is a need of developing a stand-alone vision system which works in a biped walking robot system itself.
- By using a stereo vision system, more detailed and accurate information in 3-dimension can be obtained. However, a vision system using stereo vision system costs a lot more than a single vision system in computation and money. Therefore, a way of developing more reasonable stereo vision system for biped walking robot must be developed to popularize high performance robots.
- Biped walking robot in the future should be connected to a massive network to be operated in a ubiquitous environment. Therefore, fundamental technologies for networked humanoid robot should be developed. At present, a realization of a robot connected to a TCP/IP based network such as internet could be realized.

5. References

Craig J.J.; (1989). *Introduction to Robotics Mechanics and Control,* Silma Inc..

Huang, Q., Yokoi K., Kajita S., Kaneko K., Arai H., Koyachi N. & Tanie K. (2001). Planning walking patterns for a biped robot. IEEE Trans. on Robotics and Automation, Vol. 17, No. 3 pp.280-289.

Shih C. L., Gruver W. A. & Lee T.T. (1993). Inverse kinematics and inverse dynamics for control of a biped walking machine, Journal of Robot Systems, Vol. 10, No. 4, pp. 531-555.

Kim D., Seo S. J. & Park G. T. (2005). Zero-moment Point Trajectory Modeling of a Biped Walking Robot Using an Adaptive Neuro-fuzzy System, Proceedings of IEE Control Theory Appl., Vol. 152, No. 4, pp. 441-426, 2005.

Endo K., Maeno T. & Kitano H. (2003). Co-evolution of Morphology and Walking Pattern of Biped Humanoid Robot Using Evolutionary Computation - Evolutionary Designing Method and its Evaluation, Proceedings of IEEE Intl. Conf. on Intelligent Robots and Systems, pp.340-345, Las Vegas, USA, 2003.

Yamaguchi J., Soga E., Inoue S., & Takanishi A. (1999). Development of a Bipedal Humanoid Robot-Control Method of Whole Body Cooperative Biped Walking, Proceedings of IEEE International Conference on Robotics & Automation, pp.368-374, 1999.

Nishiwaki K., Kuga M., Kagami S., Inaba M., & Inoue H. (2004). Whole-body Cooperative Balanced Motion Generation for Reaching, Proceedings of IEEE Humanoid 2004, pp.672-689, 2004.

Zheng Y. & Shen J. (1990). Gait Synthesis for the SD-2 Biped Robot to Climb Sloped Surface, IEEE Trans. Robot Automation, Vol. 6, No. 1. pp. 86-96.

Mayer N. M., Farkas F. & Asada M. (2005). Balanced walking and rapid movements in a biped robot by using a symmetric rotor and a brake, Proceedings of Intl. Conference on Mechatronics and Automation, Vol. 1, pp. 345-350, 2005.

Gerecke M., Albert A & Gerth W. (2002). Vision Guided Biped Walking - Trajectories an Communication, Proceedings of the Fifth Intl. Conference on Climbing an Walking Robots and their Supporting Technologies, pp. 155-162, Paris, France, 2002.

Michel P., Chestnutt J., Kuffner J., & Kanade T. (2005). Vision-Guided Humanoid Footstep Planning for Dynamic Environments, Proceedings of 5th IEEE-RAS Intl. Conference on Humanoid Robots, pp13-18, 2005.

Li L., Huang W., Gu I. Y. & Tian Q. (2004). Statistical Modeling of Complex Backgrounds for Foreground Object Detection, IEEE Trans. Image Processing, Vol. 13, No. 11, pp. 1459-1472.

Fieguth P. & Terzopoulos D. (1997). Color-based Tracking of Heads and Other Mobile Objects at Video Frame Rates, Proceedings of IEEE Conference on Computer Vision and Pattern Recognition, pp. 21-27, 1997.

Lee D. N. (1980). The Optic Flow Field: The Foundation of Vision, Philosophical Transactions of the Royal Society of London, Series B, Biological Sciences, Vol. 290, No. 1038, pp. 169-178.

Denavit J., Hartenbeg R. S. (1955). A Kinematics Notation for Lower-Pair Mechanisms Based on Matrices, ASME Journal of Applied Mechanics, pp. 215-221.

Beauchemin S. S. & Barron J. L. (1995). The Computation of Optical Flow, ACM Computing Surveys, Vol. 27, No. 3. pp.433-467.

Gibson J. J.; (1996). The Senses Considered As Perceptual Systems, Houghton Mifflin, Boston.

Tomasi C. & Kanade T. (1991). Detection and Tracking of Point Features, Carnegie Mellon University Technical Report CMU-CS-91-132, 1991.

Shi J. & Tomasi C. (1994). Good Features to Track, Proceedings of IEEE Conference on Computer Vision and Pattern Recognition, pp. 593-600, 1994.

MacQueen J. B. (1967). Some Methods for classification and Analysis of Multivariate Observations, Proceedings of 5th Berkeley Symposium on Mathematical Statistics and Probability, Vol. 1, pp. 281-297, 1967.

Gonzalez R. C. & Woods R. E. (2002). Digital Image Processing (2nd Edition), Prentice Hall.

Viola P. & Jones M. (2001). Rapid object detection using a boosted cascade of simple features, Proceedings of IEEE Conference on Computer Vision and Pattern Recognition, Vol. 1, pp. 511-518, 2001.

Lienhart R. & Maydt J. (2002). An Extended Set of Haar-like Features for Rapid Object Detection, Proceedings of IEEE Intl. Conference on Image Processing, Vol. 1, pp. 900-903, 2002.

Schapire R. E. (1999). A Brief Introduction to Boosting, Proceedings of Intl. Joint Conference on Artificial Intelligent, pp. 1401-1406, 1999.

Jolliffe I. T. (1986). Principal Component Analysis, Springer-Verlag, New-York, 1986.

Burges C. J. (1998). A Tutorial on Support Vector Machines for Pattern Recognition, Knowledge Discovery and Data Mining, Vol. 2, pp. 121-167.

Muller K. R., Mika S., Ratsch G., Tsuda K. & Scholkopf B. (2001). An Introduction to Kernel-Based Learning Algorithms, IEEE Trans. Neural Networks, Vol. 12, pp. 181-201.

Wernick M. N. (1991). Pattern Classification by Convex Analysis, Journal of Opt. Soc. Amer. A, Vol. 12, pp. 1874-1880, 1991.

Vapnik V. (1995). The Nature of Statistical Learning Theory, Springer-Verlag, New-York.

Cortes C., & Vapnik V. (1995). Support Vector Networks, Machine Learning, Vol. 20. pp. 273-297.

13

Non Contact 2D and 3D Shape Recognition by Vision System for Robotic Prehension

Bikash Bepari, Ranjit Ray and Subhasis Bhaumik
Haldia Institute of Technology, Haldia, India
Central Mechanical Engineering Research Institute, Durgapur, India
Bengal Engineering and Science University, Shibpur, Howrah, India

1. Introduction

The increasing demand for robotic applications in today's manufacturing environment motivates the scientists towards the design of dexterous end-effectors, which can cope with a wide variety of tasks. The human hand can serve as a model for a robotic hand for prehension, which interacts with the environment with more than twenty-seven degrees of freedom (dof^s). The articulation and accommodation of the human hand in terms of dexterity, stability, tactile and /or nontactile sensation, stiffness, weight to grip force ratio, resistance to slip, and adaptability provide clear direction for active research in dexterous manipulation by the robot.

Robotic hands, which have been developed over past three decades, sometimes on adhoc basis to accomplish a predefined task. In robotic prehension, perhaps the choice of grip to ensure stable grasp has become the main hurdles to confront with. Since the inception of development of robotic hand, this has been revealed from thorough research that, more emphasis has been given on the electro-mechanical considerations than on the stability of the grasp, that too under vision assistance. This leads to an effort to develope new algorithms for stable grasp irrespective of its shape.

Prehension combines the choice of grip and the act of grasping including its control. A desire, internally or externally generated, triggers responses in the memory and the eyes; the hand instantaneously takes a position over the object, grips it and manipulates the task. The process of prehension is controlled by feedback loops with the position and the force of the fingers as shown in Fig.1. The eye is basically a sensor, whereas the brain is the central processing unit, which sends signal to the different muscles and tendons to act accordingly to actuate the hands for manipulation. Choosing a grip is an important step in the process of prehension. The block diagram in Fig. 2 illustrates the relationship between the different activities included in prehension. This can be simulated by using a vision system on a robot and a processor with feedback loop to manipulate the tasks by an appropriate gripper in the similar pattern of eye-memory analysis as shown in Fig. 3.

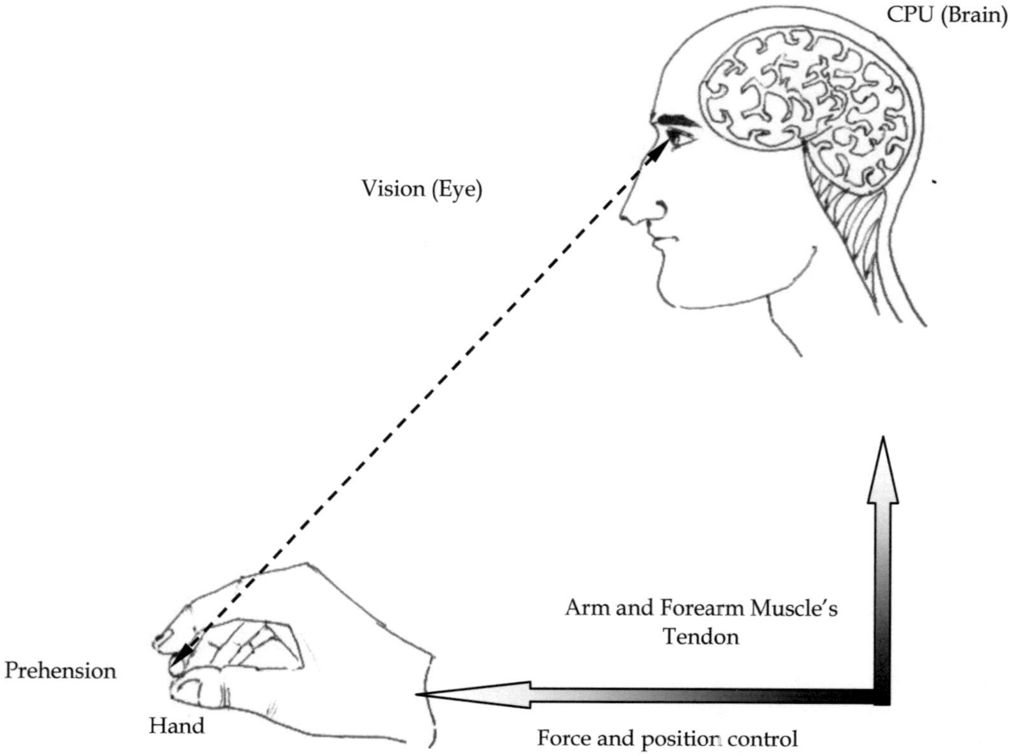

Fig. 1. The eye -memory integration-based human prehension

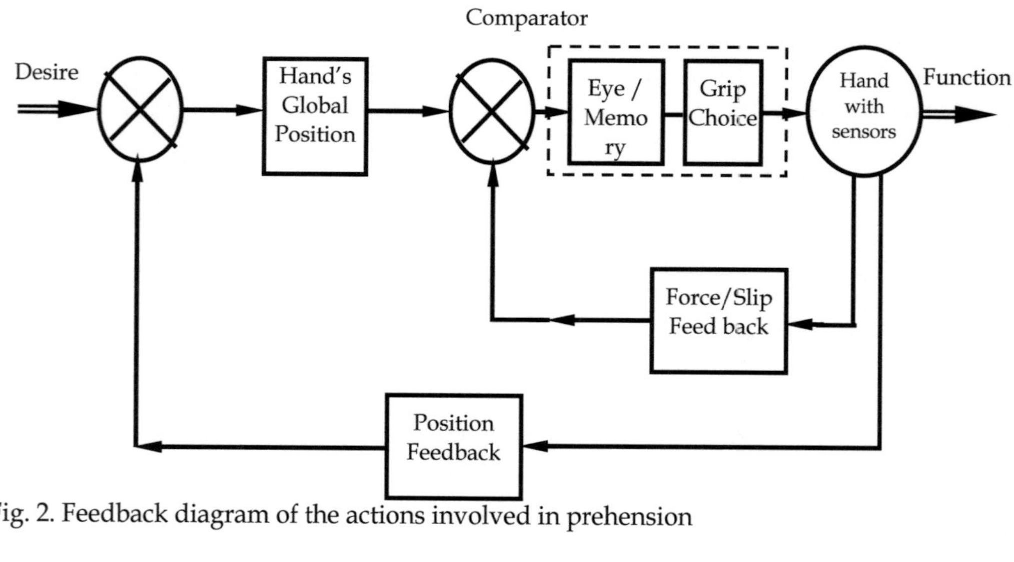

Fig. 2. Feedback diagram of the actions involved in prehension

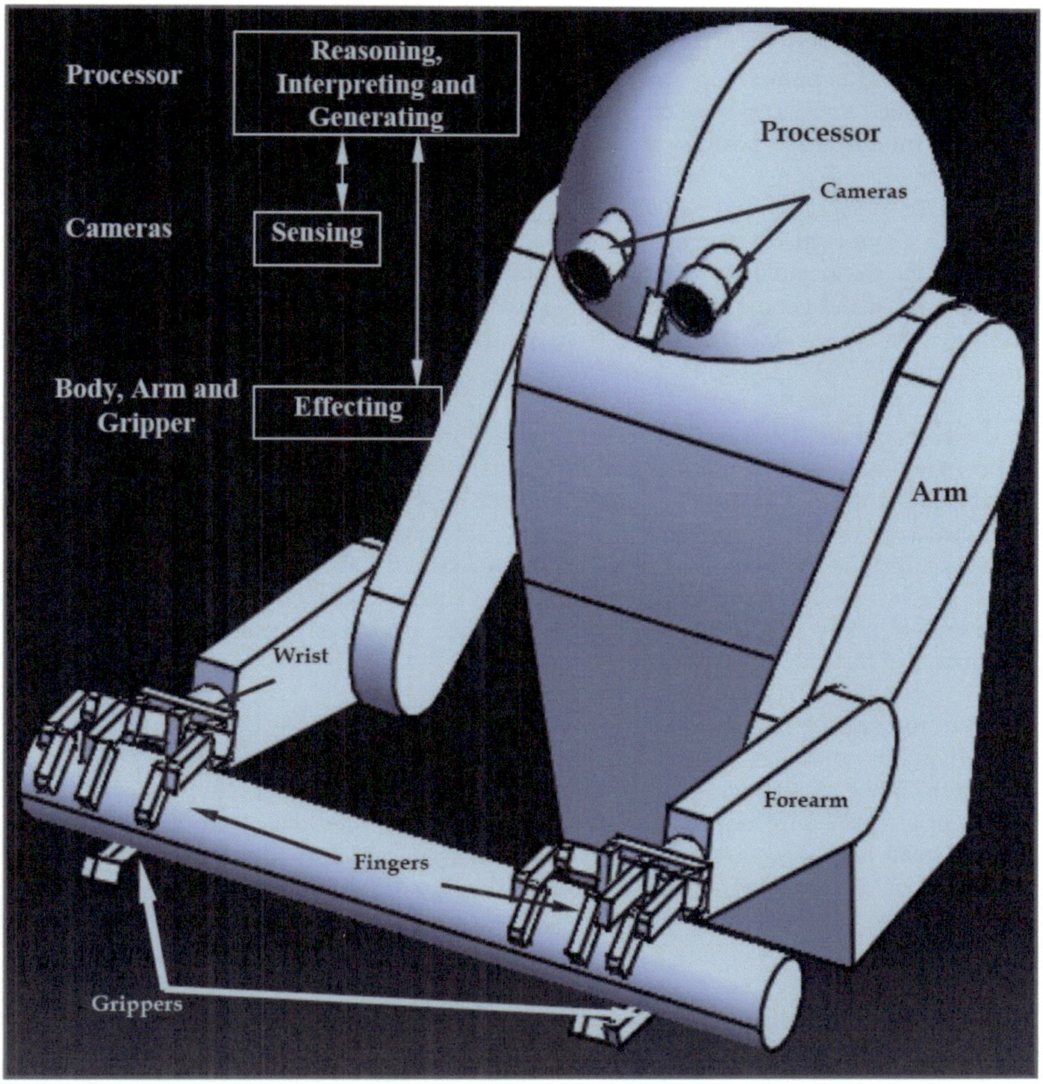

Fig. 3. Simulation of the robotic prehension

The concept of replication of the attributes of human morphology, sensory system and neurological apparatus alongwith the behavior leads to a notion of embodiment - this in turn over time is refined, as the brain and physiology change. If the grasping modes are critically examined between a child and an adult, a distinguishable difference may be observed between the two. The presense of simultaneous path planning and preshaping differentiates the latter one from the former.

The essential goal of the present work was to ensure the stability of a grasp under visual guidance from a set of self generating alternatives by means of logical ability to impart adroitness to the system (robotic hand).

2. Survey of Previous Research

As a step towards prehension through vision assistance in robotic system, Geisler (Geisler, 1982) described a vision system consisting of a TV camera, digital image storage and a mini computer for shape and position recognition of industrial parts.

Marr (Marr, 1982) described 3-D vision as a 3-D object reconstruction task. The description of the 3D shape is to be generated in a co-ordinate system independent of the viewer. He ensures that the complexity of the 3-D vision task dictates a sequence of steps refining descriptions of the geometry of the visible surfaces. The requirements are to find out the pixels of the image, then to move from pixels to surface delineation, then to surface orientation and finally to a full 3-D description.

Faugeras (Faugeras, 1993) established a simple technique for single camera calibration from a known scene. A set of '**n**' non-co-planar points lies in the 3-D world and the corresponding 2-D image points are known. The correspondence between a 3-D scene and 2-D image point provides an equation. The solution so obtained, solves an over-determined system of linear equations. But the main disadvantage of this approach is that the scene must be known, for which special calibration objects are often used. Camera calibration can also be done from an unknown scene. At least two views are needed, and it is assumed that the intrinsic parameters of the camera do not change.

Different researchers like (Horaud et al., 1995), (Hartley, 1994) and (Pajdha & Hlavac, 1999) worked on this approach. Horaud considered both rotational and translational motion of the camera from one view to another. Hartley restricted the camera motion to pure rotation and Pajdha et al. used pure translational motion of camera to get linear solution. Sonka et al. (Sonka, 1998) discussed on the basic principle of stereo vision (with lateral camera model) consisting of three steps: a) Camera calibration, b) Establishing point correspondence between pairs of points from the left and the right image and c) Reconstruction of 3D coordinates of the points in the scene.

David Nitzan (Nitzan, 1988) used a suitable technique to obtain the range details for use in robot vision. The methodology followed in his work is, image formation, matching, camera calibration and determination of range or depth. Identifying the corresponding points in two images that are projections of the same entity is the key problem in 3D vision. There are different matching techniques for finding the corresponding points.

Victor et al. (Victor & Gunasekaran, 1993) used correlation formula in their work on stereovision technique. They determined the three-dimensional position of an object. Using the correlation formula they have computed the distance of a point on an object from camera and have shown that the computed distance from camera is almost equal to the actual distance from camera.

Lee et al. (Lee et al., 1994) used perspective transformation procedure for mapping a 3-D scene onto an image plane. It has also been shown that the missing depth information can be obtained by using stereoscopic imaging techniques. They derived an equation for finding the depth information using 3-D geometry. The most difficult task in using the equation for obtaining the depth information is to actually find two corresponding points in different images of the same scene. Since, these points are generally in the same vicinity, a frequently used approach is to select a point within a small region in one of the image views and then attempt to find the best matching region in the other view by using correlation techniques. The geometry of a 3-D scene can be found if it is known which point from one image corresponds to a point in the second image. This correspondence problem can be reduced by using several constraints.

Klette et al. (Klette et al., 1996) proposed a list of constraints like uniqueness constraint, photometric compatibility constraint, and geometric similarity constraint etc that are commonly used to provide insight into the correspondence problem. They illustrated this approach with a simple algorithm called block matching. The basic idea of this algorithm is that all pixels in the window (called a block) have the same disparity, meaning that one and only one disparity is computed for each block.

But later on Nishihara (Nishihara, 1984)noted that such point-wise correlators are very heavy on processing time in arriving at a correspondence. He proposed another relevant approach to match large patches at a large scale, and then refine the quality of the match by reducing the scale using the coarser information to initialize the finger-grained match.

Pollard et al. (Pollard et al., 1981) developed the PMF algorithm using the feature-based correspondence method. This method use points or set of points those are striking and easy to find, such as pixels on edges, lines or corners. They proceed by assuming that a set of feature points [detected edges] has been extracted from each image by some internal operator. The output is a correspondence between pairs of such points.

Tarabanis et al. (Tarabanis & Tsai, 1991) described the next view planning method as follows: "Given the information about the environment as well as the information about that the vision system has to accomplish (i.e. detection of certain object features, object recognition, scene reconstruction, object manipulation), develop strategies to automatically determine sensor parameter values that achieve this task with a certain degree of satisfaction".

Maver et al. (Maver & Bajcsy, 1993) proposed an NVP (Next View Planning) algorithm for an acquisition system consisting of a light stripe range scanner and a turntable. They represent the unseen portions of the viewing volume as 2½-D polygons. The polygon boundaries are used to determine the visibility of unseen portions from all the next views. The view, which can see the largest area unseen up to that point, is selected as the next best view.

Connolly (Connolly, 1985) used an octree to represent the viewing volume. An octree node close to the scanned surface was labeled to be seen, a node between the sensor and this surface as empty and the remaining nodes as unseen. Next best view was chosen from a sphere surrounding the object.

Szeliski (Szeliski, 1993) first created a low-resolution octree model quickly and then refined this model iteratively, by intersecting each new silhouette with the already existing model. Niem (Niem, 1994) uses pillar-like volume elements instead of an octree for the model representation.

Whaite et al. (Whaite & Ferrie, 1994) used the range data sensed to build a parametric approximate model of the object. But this approach does not check for occlusions and does not work well with complex objects because of limitations of a parametric model.

Pito (Pito, 1999) used a range scanner, which moves on a cylindrical path around the object. The next best view is chosen as the position of the scanner, which samples as many void patches as possible while resampling at least a certain amount of the current model.

Liska (Liska, 1999) used a system consisting of two lasers projecting a plane onto the viewing volume and a turntable. The next position of the turntable is computed based on information from the current and the preceding scan.

Sablating et al. (Sablating et al., 2003; Lacquaniti & Caminiti, 1998). described the basic shape from Silhouette method used to perform the 3-D model reconstruction. They experimented with both synthetic and real data.

Lacquaniti et al. (Lacquaniti & Caminiti, 1998) reviewed anatomical and neurophysical data processing of a human in eye-memory during grasping. They also established the different mapping techniques for ocular and arm co-ordination in a common reference plane.

Desai (Desai, 1998) in his thesis addressed the problem of motion planning for cooperative robotic systems. They solved the dynamic motion-planning problem for a system of cooperating robots in the presence of geometric and kinematic constraints with the aid of eye memory co ordination.

Metta et al. (Metta & Fitzpatrick, 2002) highlighted the sensory representations used by the brain during reaching, grasping and object recognition. According to them a robot can familiarize itself with the objects in its environment by acting upon them. They developed an environment that allows for a very natural developmental of visual competence for eye-memory prehension.

Barnesand et al. (Barnesand & Liu, 2004)developed a philosophical and psycho-physiological basis for embodied perception and a framework for conceptual embodiment of vision-guided robots. They argued that categorization is important in all stages of robot vision. Further, classical computer vision is not suitable for this categorization; however, through conceptual embodiment active perception can be erected.

Kragic et al. (Kragic & Christensen, 2003) considered typical manipulation tasks in terms of a service robot framework. Given a task at hand, such as "pick up the cup from the dinner table", they presented a number of different visual systems required to accomplish the task. A standard robot platform with a PUMA560 on the top is used for experimental evaluation.

The classical approach-align-grasp idea was used to design a manipulation system (Bhaumik et al., 2003). Both visual and tactile feedback was used to accomplish the given task. In terms of image processing, they started by a recognition system, which provides a 2-D estimate of the object position in the image. Thereafter, a 2-D tracking system was presented and used to maintain the object in the field of view during an approach stage. For the alignment stage, two systems are available. The first is a model based tracking system that estimates the complete pose/velocity of the object. The second system was based on corner matching and estimates homography (matching of periphery) between two images. In terms of tactile feedback, they presented a grasping system that performs power grasps. The main objective was to compensate for minor errors in object's position/orientation estimate caused by the vision system.

Nakabo et al. (Nakabo et al., 2002) considered real-world applications of robot control with visual servoing; both 3-D information and a high feedback rate is required. They developed a 3-D target tracking system with two high-speed vision systems called Column Parallel Vision (CPV) systems. To obtain 3-D information, such as position, orientation and shape parameters of the target object, a feature-based algorithm has been introduced using moment feature values extracted from vision systems for a spherical object model.

3. Objective

In the present investigation, an attempt has been made to enable a four-fingered robotic hand consisting of the index finger, middle finger, ring finger and the thumb to ensure stable grasp. The coordinated movement of the fingertips were thoroughly analyzed to preshape the fingers during trajectory planning in order to reduce task execution time. Since the displacement of the motor was coordinated with the motion of the fingertips, the corelation between these two parameters was readily available thorugh CAD simulation using Visual Nastran 4D (MSC. VisualNastrun 4D, 2001).

The primary objectives of the present investigation are:

a) analysis of the object shapes and dimensions using 2D image processing techniques and vision based preshaping of the finger's pose depending on the basis of prehension,

b) hierarchical control strategies under vision guidance for slip feedback,

c) experimentation on the hand for intelligent grasping,

4. Brief Description of the Setup for Prehension

4.1 Kinematics of the Hand

The newly developed hand uses a direct linkage mechanism to transfer motions. From Fig.4 it is clear that the crank is given the prime motion, which ultimately presses the push link-1 to turn the middle link about the proximal joint. As the middle link starts rotating, it turns the distal link simultaneously, because the distal link, middle link and push link-2 form a crossed four bar linkage mechanism. The simultaneous movement of the links ultimately stops when the lock pin comes in contact with the proximal link. The proximal link is kept in contact with the stay under the action of a torsional spring. As the lock pin comes in contact with the proximal link, it ultimately restricts all the relative motions between the links of the finger and at that position the whole finger moves as an integrated part. The crank is coupled to a small axle on which a worm wheel is mounted and the worm is directly coupled to a motor by coupling as shown in Fig.5.

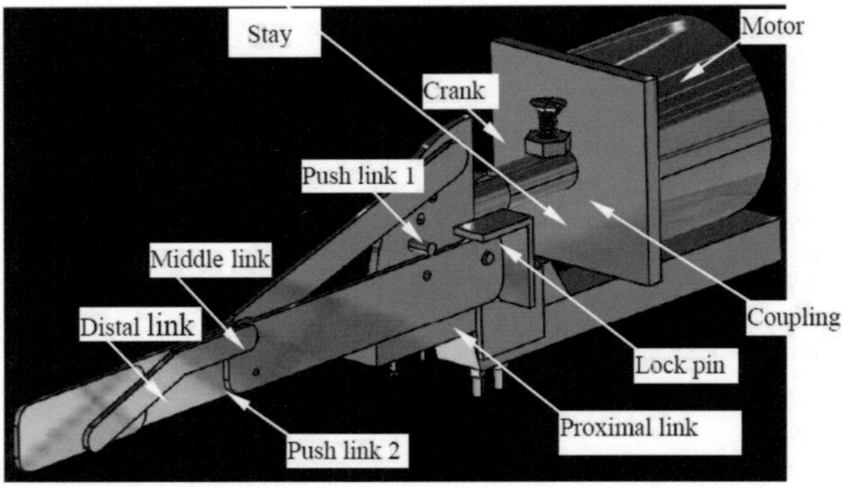

Fig. 4. The kinematic linkages for the robot hand

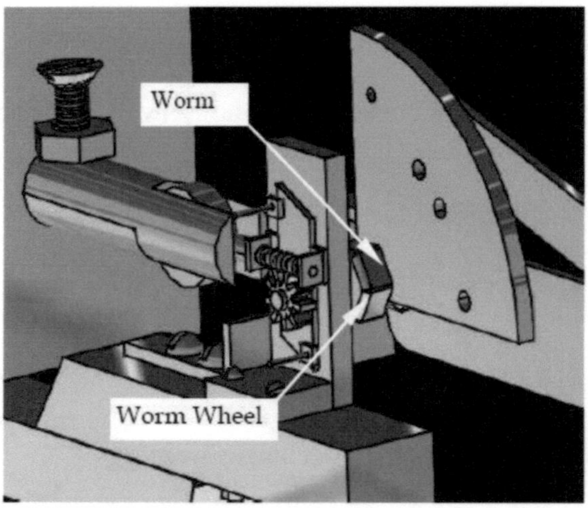

Fig. 5. The worm worm-wheel mechanism for actuation of the fingers

4.2 Description of the Mechanical System

The robotic hand consists of four fingers namely thumb, index, middle and ring fingers. Besides, there is a palm to accommodate the fingers alongwith the individual drive systems for actuation. The base, column and the swiveling arm were constructed in this system for supporting the hand to perform the experiments on grasping. The design of the base, column and swiveling arm were evolved from the absence of a suitable robot.

The base is mild steel flat on which the column is mounted. On the free end of the column, a provision (hinge) has been made to accommodate the swiveling arm adaptor. The CAD model of the setup has been shown in Fig.6.

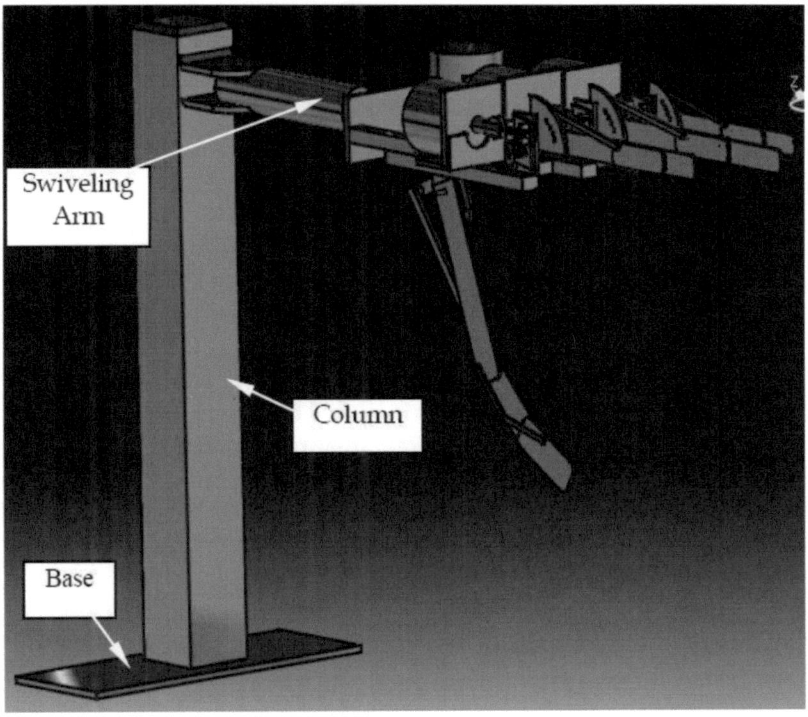

Fig. 6. The assembled CAD Model of the robot hand

4.3 Vision System

The specification of the camera is as follows:

a.	Effective picture element	:	752 (H) × 582 (V)
b.	Horizontal frequency	:	15.625 KHz ± 1%
c.	Vertical Frequency	:	50Hz ± 1%
d.	Power requirements	:	12v DC ± 1%
e.	Dimension	:	44(W) × 29 (H) × 57.5(D) mm
f.	Weight	:	110 gm

A two-channel PC based image-grabbing card was used to acquire the image data through the camera. Sherlock ™ (Sherlock) is a window based machine vision environment specifically intended to simplify development and deployment of high performance alignment, gauging inspection, assembly verification, and machine guidance tasks. This was used to detect all the peripheral pixels of the object being grasped after thresholding and calibration. The dimensional attributes are solely dependant on the calibration. After calibration a database was made for all the peripheral pixels. The camera alongwith the mounting device has been shown in Fig.7.

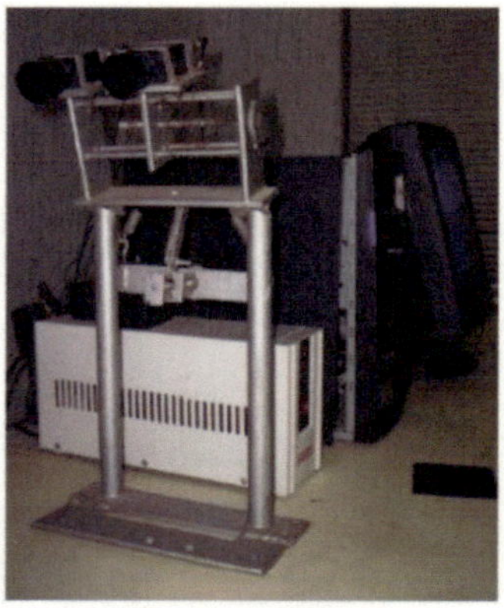

Fig. 7. The Camera alongwith the mounting device

5. Fingertip Trajectories and Acquisition of Pre-shape Values

To determine the trajectories of the fingers in space, points on the distal palmer tip were chosen for each of the fingers and during simulation the locus of those points were traced. The instantaneous crank positions were also taken simultaneously. As the fingers flex, the coordinate abscissa (X) value either increases or decreases depending on the position of the origin as the current system. Since the incremental values for coordinate (X) are correlated with the angular movement of the crank, during preshape of the fingers, proper actuation can be made as shown in Fig.8. Once the vision based sensory feedback values are known, the motors may be actuated to perform the required amount of incremental movements.

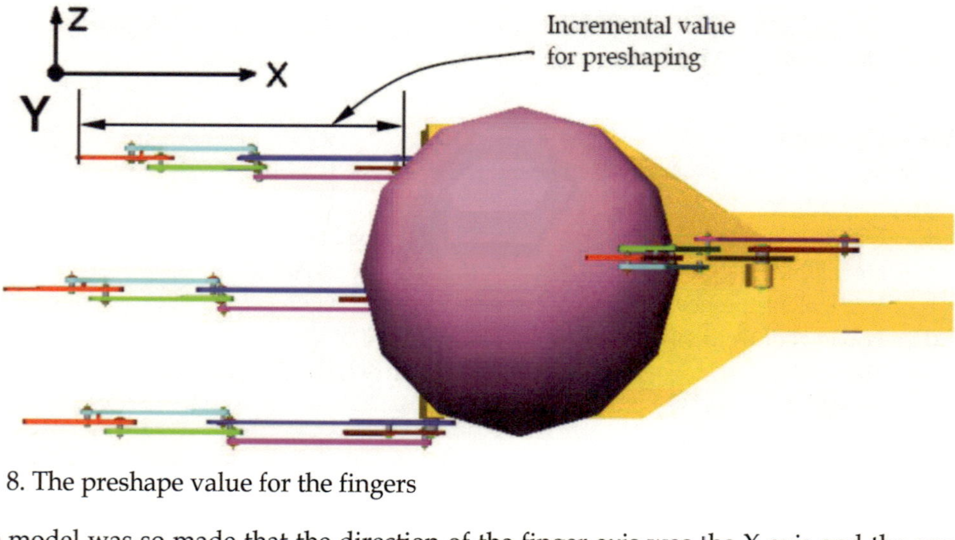

Fig. 8. The preshape value for the fingers

The model was so made that the direction of the finger axis was the X-axis and the gravity direction was the Y direction. Figure 9 shows the trajectories for different fingers. The correlations of the incremental values in preshaping direction and the corresponding crank movement have been shown in Fig.10, Fig.11, Fig.12 and Fig.13. The R^2 values in the curves imply the correlation constant and as the value tends to 1 (one) implies a good correlation of the curve fitting.

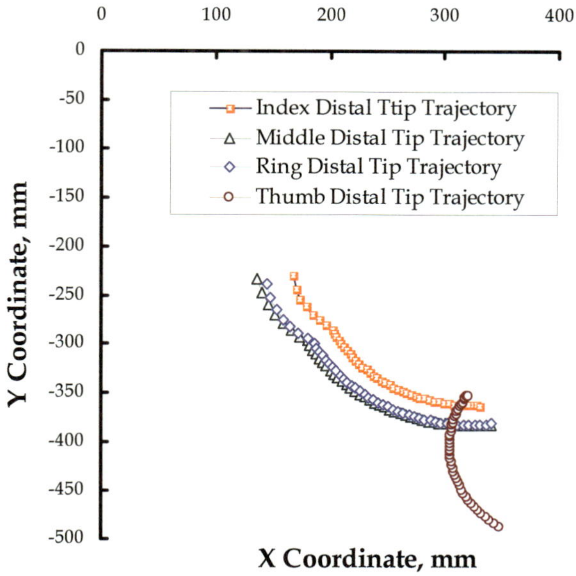

Fig. 9. The trajectories of the fingertips of the fingers

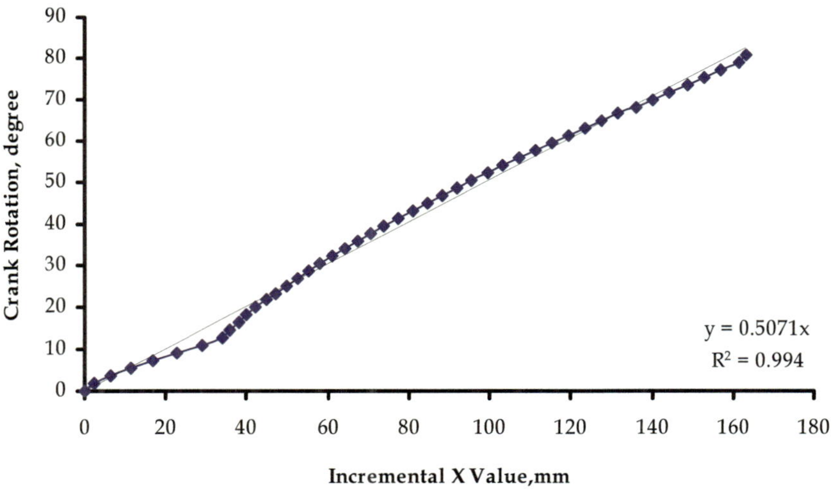

Fig. 10. Preshape value vs. crank rotation angle plot for index finger

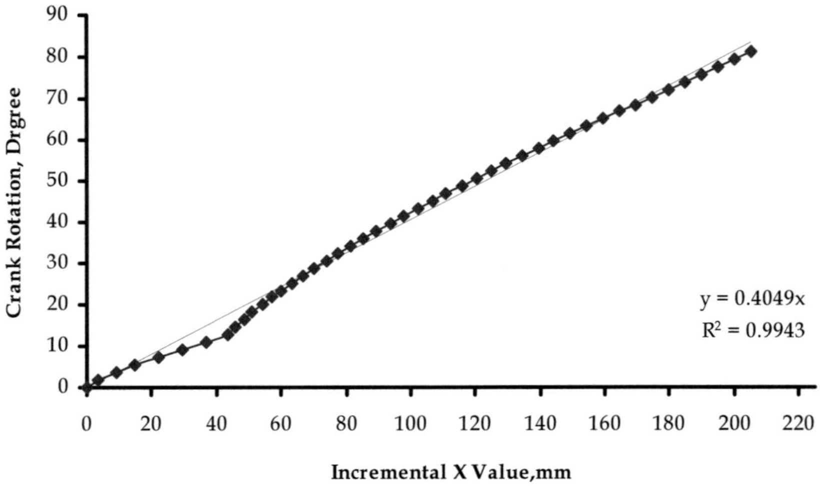

Fig. 11. Preshape value vs. crank rotation angle plot for middle finger

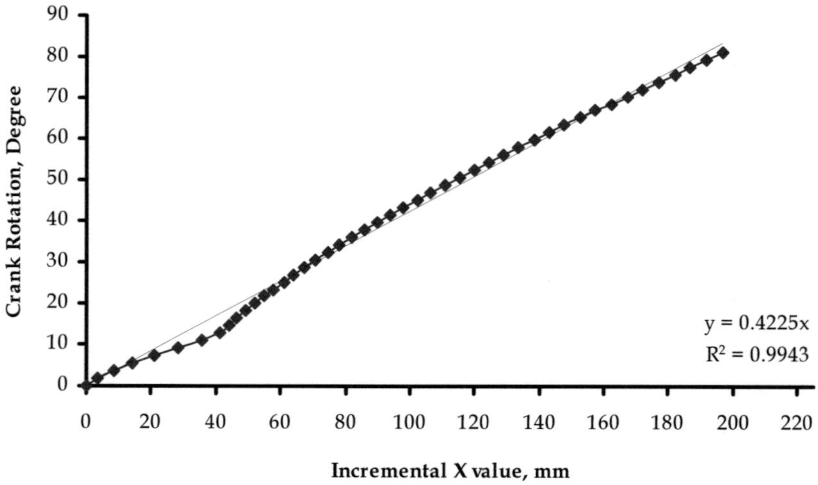

Fig. 12. Preshape value vs. crank rotation angle plot for ring finger

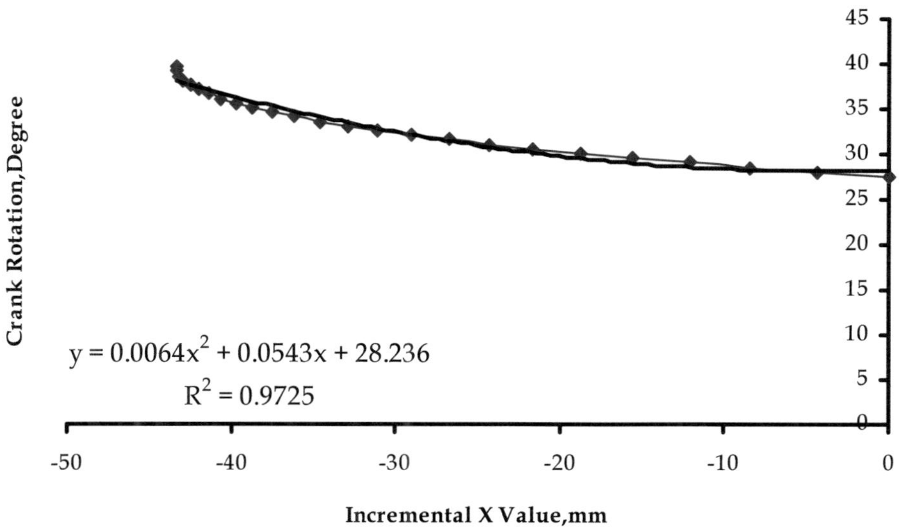

Fig. 13. Plot showing preshape value vs. crank rotation angle for thumb

6. Control Hierarchy and Vision Assistance

The control architecture is a three level hierarchy, which consists of the following blocks:

6.1 A computer with CCD Camera i.e. Master Computer–I

The computer at the top level of hierarchy gives the object shape information to the next level computer to actuate the motors for preshaping through the slave i.e. the microcontroller motherboard.

6.2 The Master Computer-II

The second level computer acting in master mode communicates with the micro-controller motherboard that acts as slave through the serial port, RS 232.

6.3 Controller Mother Board with Micro Controller Chip (AT89C52)

The main function of micro-controller motherboard is to behave like that of a Data Acquisition System (DAS) and thus helps the master by providing the required data from different sensors. Evaluating the controller mode equation through software, the master downloads the firing angle information and motor direction information in to the micro-controller chip (AT89C52), which in turn sends these signals to the drive circuitry. Figure 14 represents the realistic view for the three-generation controller. Figure 15 depicts the overall control architecture used in this scheme.

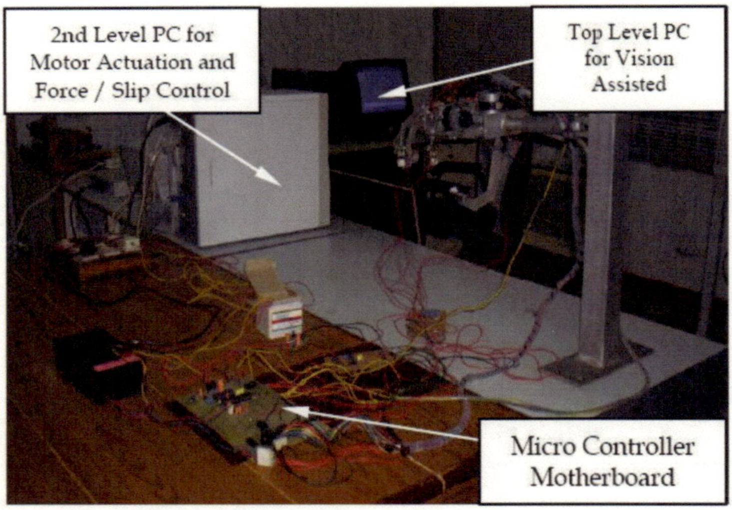

Fig. 14. Prehension system with three level hierarchy

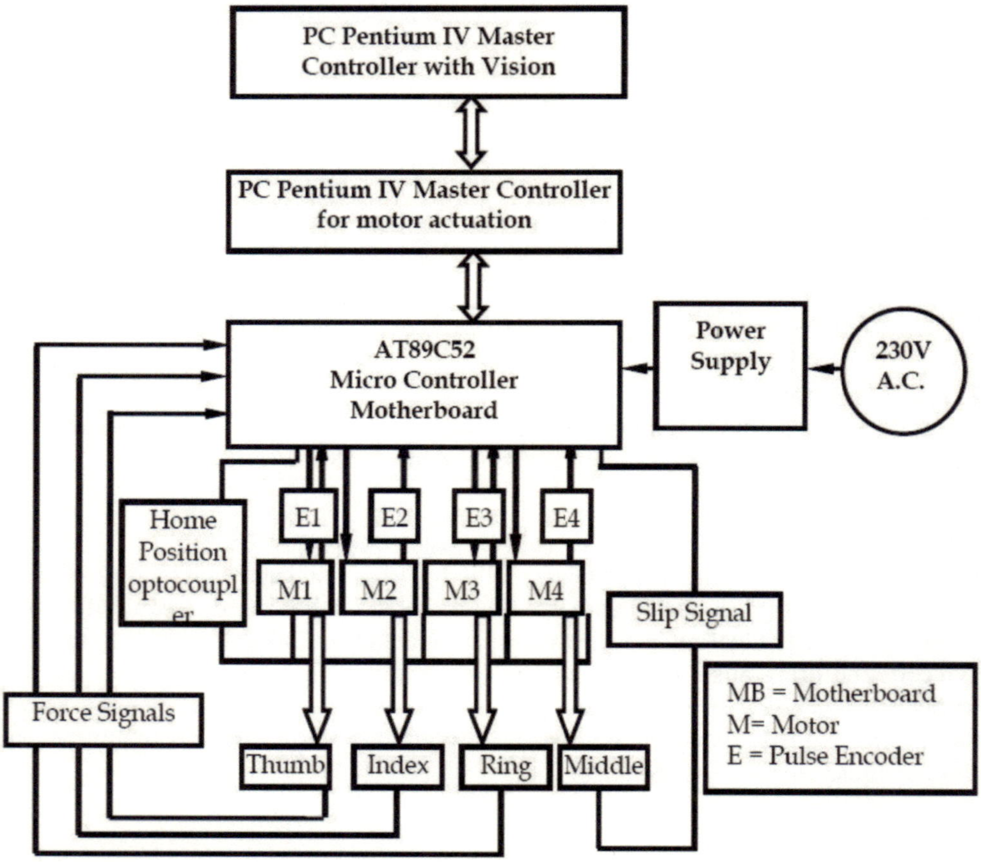

Fig. 15. The three level hierarchy of control system

6.4 Actuation of Motors under Vision Assistance

The motors are acting as actuators for finger motion as the finger positions are determined by the motor position. The vision assistance helps the fingers to preshape to a particular distance so that the fingertips are a few units apart from the object. As soon as the fingers touch the object, the force sensor reads the current value of the force exerted by all the fingers. The incremental step is given to all the motors as 7.2° i.e. four counts.

The control strategy is divided into three steps:

a) The object shape information can be had by CCD camera to generate the amount of preshape (i.e. the pulse count by which the motor will rotate to encompass the job). The initial set value for the position comes from the vision assistance. The scheme has been depicted in Fig.16.

b) Secondly it is to generate a database for grasping force exerted by individual finger for grasping different materials under no slip condition. The amount of slip is then fed back to the computer and the computer through microcontroller sends signal to the motors via motor drive card to move forward. The total control strategy to generate the database of force at no slip condition has been shown in Fig.16.

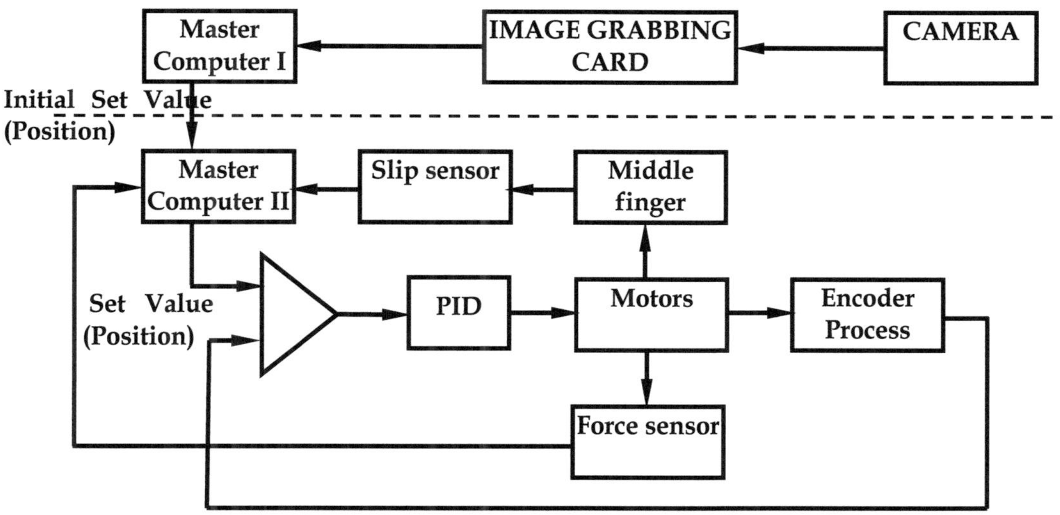

Fig. 16. The vision based preshaping and slip feedback

Then the values of the grasping forces at which slip stops is feed to the controller i.e. the grasping force exerted by the individual fingers for different objects. Once the set value is reached then the controller simultaneously checks whether there is any slip or not. If till now the fingers are not capable to grip, then the set values are dynamically increased to a maximum of 10% of the initial set values with an increment of 1%. Beyond which the system will declare that the process is out of range.

This process approaches towards adaptive control. The schematic diagram of force control has been shown in Fig.17. The microcontroller motherboard is connected to the computer by RS-232 serial port. But position forward scheme does not imply that there will always be a force signal, rather the fingertips are to be in contact with the object at first, only then the force signals can be achieved.

In order to control the grasp position of the gripper for holding an object securely the motor should achieve the desired set position smoothly without any overshoot and undershoot obviously with negligible offset error. This set position corresponds to the stable grasp position. To control the gripping force required for an object, a PID closed loop feedback control scheme is adopted. The initial set value for position comes from the vision data and the motors rotate to preshape the objects dimension and to see whether the gripper is in contact with the object or not. If the gripper is not in contact with the object then the motor moves forward till all the fingers come in contact with the job. If the contact exists, then the PID controller sets the current process value plus four counts as set value and checks whether there is any slip or not. Now if there is a slip, the set value is increased by another four counts until no slip condition is reached and the master computer–II saves all the optimum grasping value in the database. The flow chart has been depicted in Fig.18.

In the second scheme i.e. the force control scheme, the initial set values for force comes from the database of the master computer. Feed forward signal are given to the motors for wrapping the object. This process continues till the desired set values for all the fingers are reached. Then it is ensured whether there is any slip or not after reaching to the set position. If till now there is any slip then the set value will be set as process value plus 1% of the set value until slippage stops and gripper holds the object securely. Each fingertip contains electrical strain gauge type force sensing elements for the measurement of the forces. The control flowchart scheme has been shown in Fig.19.

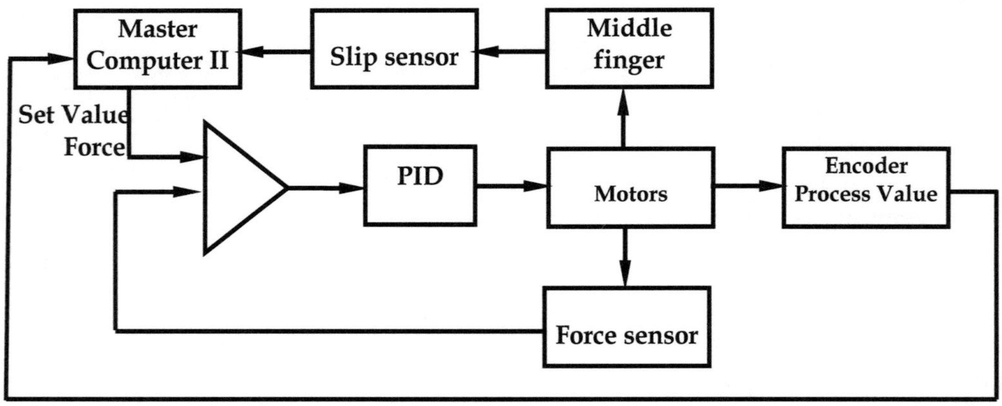

Fig. 17. The force feedback for stable grasp

The main advantage of this composite control, PID mode is that the integral mode eliminates the offset error produced by proportional mode and the overshoot and undershoot of the controlled output is minimized by derivative action through its anticipatory property. The overall effect is that the output-controlled variable achieves the desired value without much cycling. Critically damping condition has been implemented in the present work. The control software has got the feature to set the set value manually or automatically (from the database). The gain values can also be set from the software as shown in Fig.20.

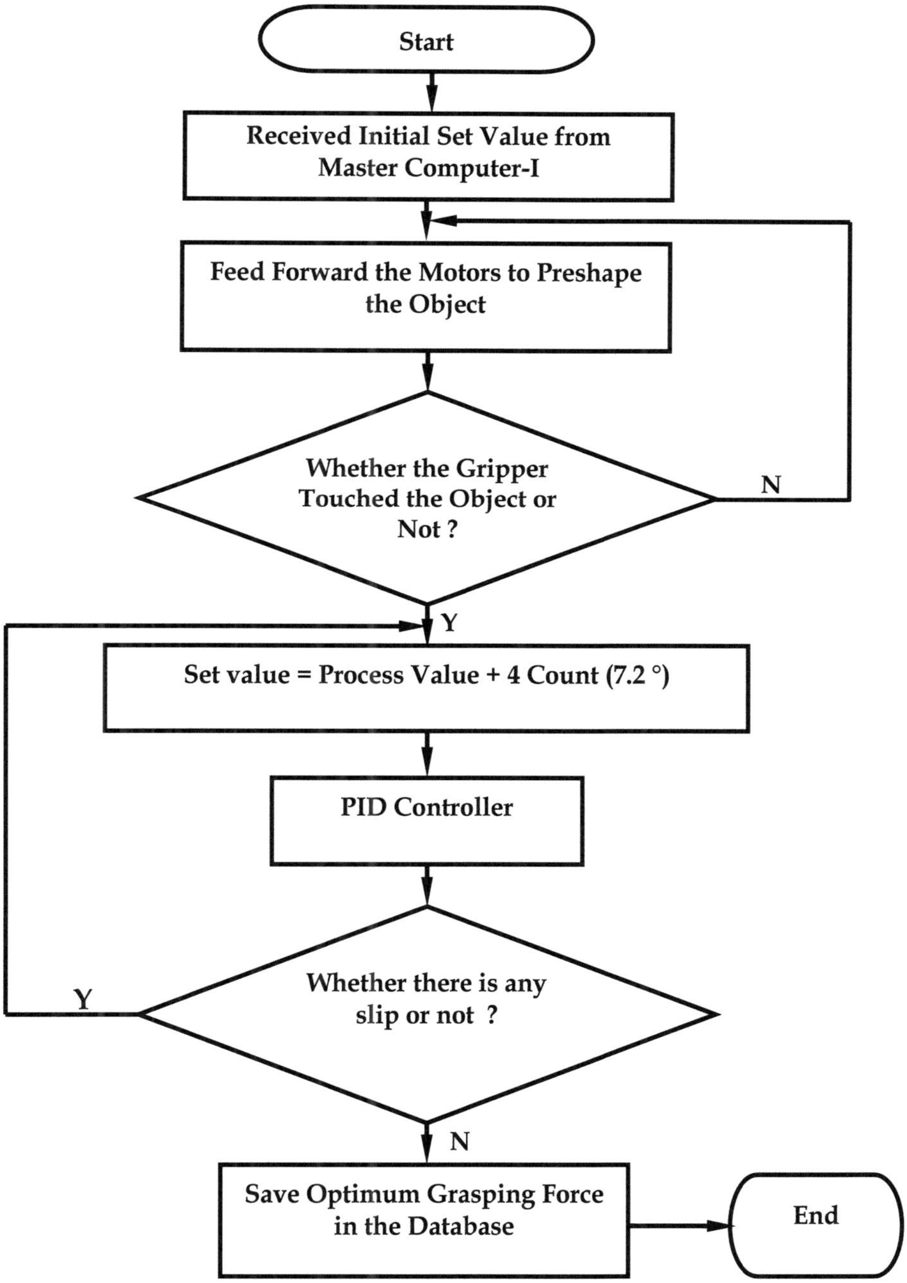

Fig. 18. The flowchart depicting vision assisted preshape and slip feedback

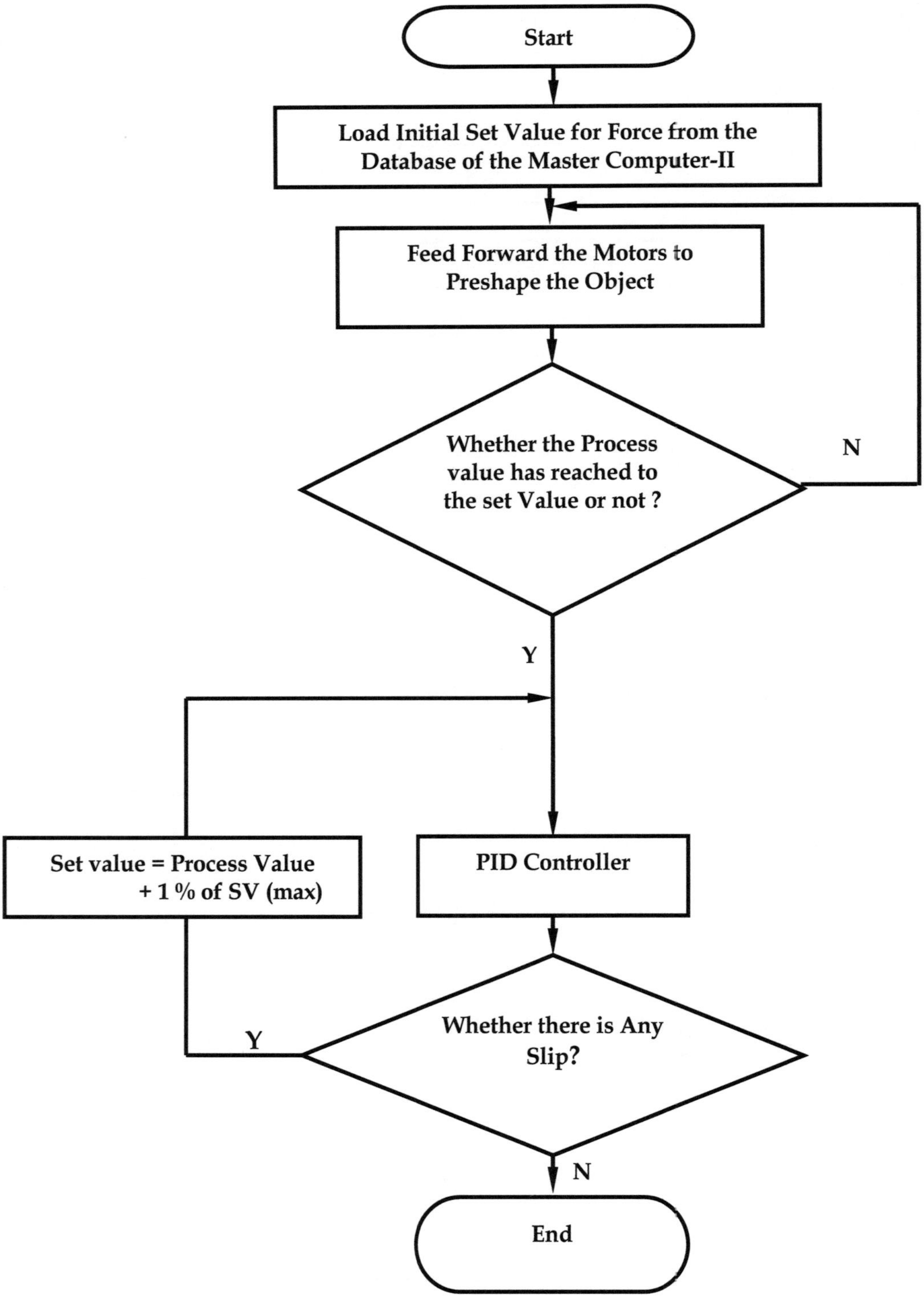

Fig. 19. The flowchart showing force feedback

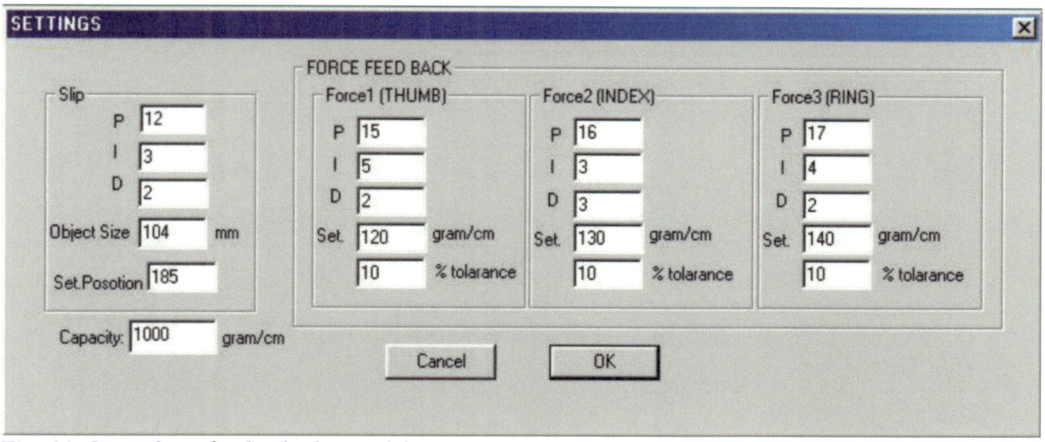

Fig. 20. Set values for both slip and force

A CCD camera has been used to generate the information about the object shape. The home position of the fingers before grasping is known. A logic has been developed to find out the movements of the corresponding motors of the fingers in terms of P1 and P2 as shown in Fig 21.

In article 5 the correlation between the motor position and incremental preshape value has already been found out form the correlation equations indicated in Figs 10, 11, 12 and 13. The Master Computer-II acquires the dimension from the Master Computer-I and calculates the preshape. In the software a provision has been made to input either the object size data obtained from the visual information incorporate user input data for the geometry of the primitive encompassing the object. The data for object size has been illustrated in Fig.22.

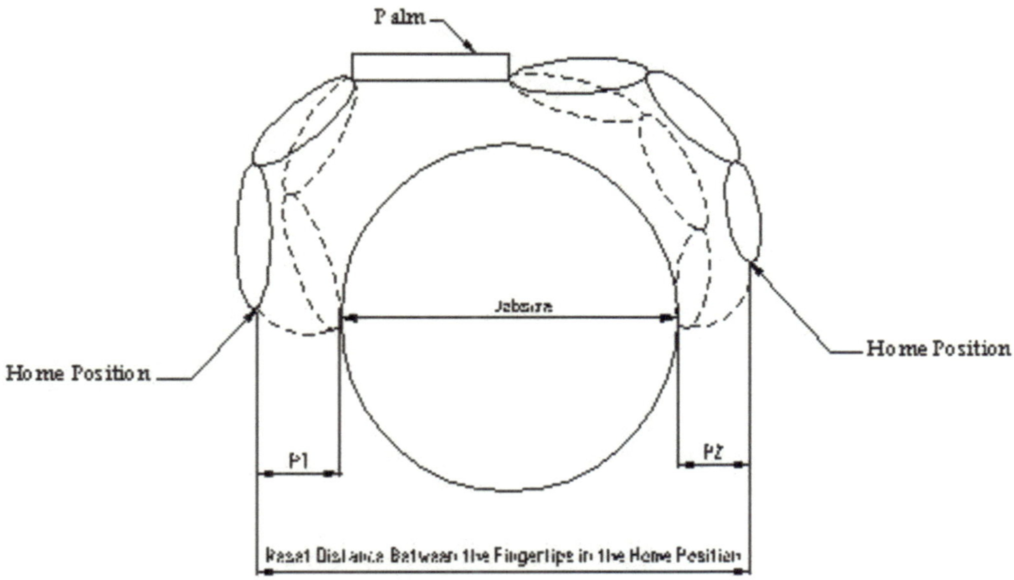

Fig. 21. The preshape calculation for the fingers

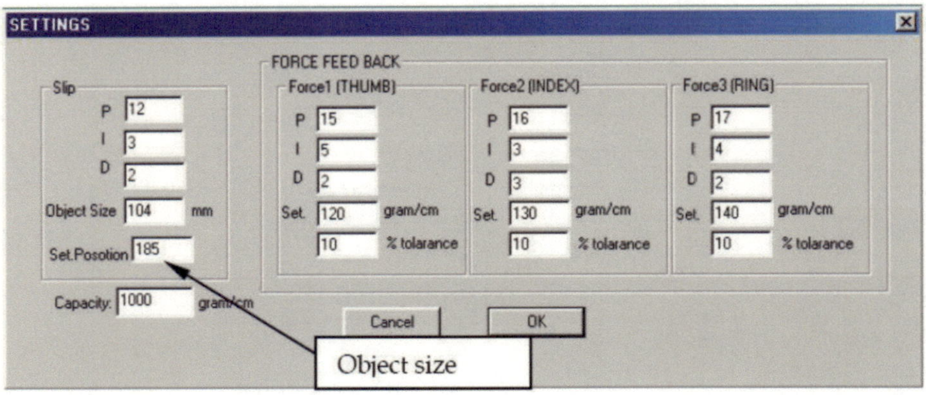

Fig. 22. The provision for incorporation of the object size

7. Grasp Stability Analysis through Vision

7.1 Logic for Stable Grasp

When an object is held through a robot hand, to maintain stability it becomes very important that the line of action of the force exerted by the finger tip should lie within the cone of friction shown in Fig.23. As it is well known that the cone of friction is again a function of the coefficient of friction. For this reason it has been checked that, whether the line of action of the forces are lying with the cone of friction or not.

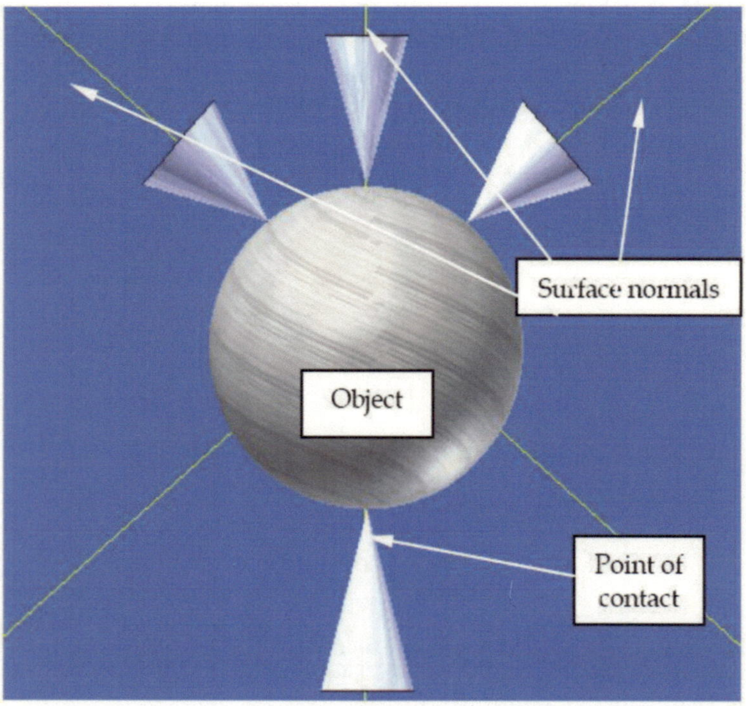

Fig. 23. The relative position of the fingertips with respect to the object

7.2 Interpolation of Cubic Spline to form the mathematical Silhouette

In order to find out instantaneous normal on the silhouette a piece-wise cubic spline was interpolated amongst the peripheral points. The logic for cubic spline is as follows:

For a set of data (had from silhouette) points it is necessary to inculcate the mode of connectivity and order of joining of the points-this in turn yield the idea about continuity when a piecewise polynomial curve come in the design scenario. By continuity we mean the index of smoothness at the juncture of two pieces of a curve. Theoretically a continuous curve means, within the boundary of the independent variable the dependent variables are fully predictive. At the same time polynomial of degree N, has a continuity of derivatives of order (N-1). Parametric cubic splines are used to interpolate two given data, not to design free form curves as Bezier and β-Spline curves do. The Hermite form of Cubic Spline is determined by defining positions and tangent vectors at the data points. Therefore, four conditions are required to determine the co-efficients of the parametric Cubic Spline curve. When these are the positions of the two end points and the two tangent vectors at the points, a hermite cubic spline results.

The parametric equation of the Cubic Spline segment is given by,

$$P(u) = \sum_{i=1}^{3} C_i u^i, \qquad 0 \le u \le 1 \tag{1}$$

Where u is the parameter and C_i is the polynomial co-efficient.
The equation 1 can be written in an expanded form as

$$P(u)=C_3u^3 + C_2u^2 + C_1u + C_0 \tag{2}$$

This equation can also be written in a matrix form as

$$P(u)=U^TC \tag{3}$$

Where, $U=[u^3 \quad u^2 \quad u \quad 1]^T$ and $C=[C_3 \quad C_2 \quad C_1 \quad C_0]^T$
The tangent vector to the curve at any point is given by

$$P'(u)=\sum_{0}^{3} C_i i u^{i-1} \qquad 0 \le u \le 1 \tag{4}$$

The co-efficients are to be replaced by the geometry of the spline. In order to eliminate the co-efficients two end points P(0) and P(1) (as shown in the adjoining Fig.24) and the two end tangents P′(0) and P′(1) are to be given .

$$P(0) = C_0, \tag{5}$$

$$P'(0)=C_1 \tag{6}$$

$$P(1)= C_3 + C_2 + C_1 + C_0 \tag{7}$$

$$P'(1)= 3C_3 + 2C_2 + C_1 \tag{8}$$

Where, P (0) = Coordinates of the first point at t = 0
P (1) = Coordinates of the last point at t = 1
P′ (0) = Values of the slopes in x, y, z directions at t = 0
P′ (1) = Values of the slopes in x, y, z directions at t = 1

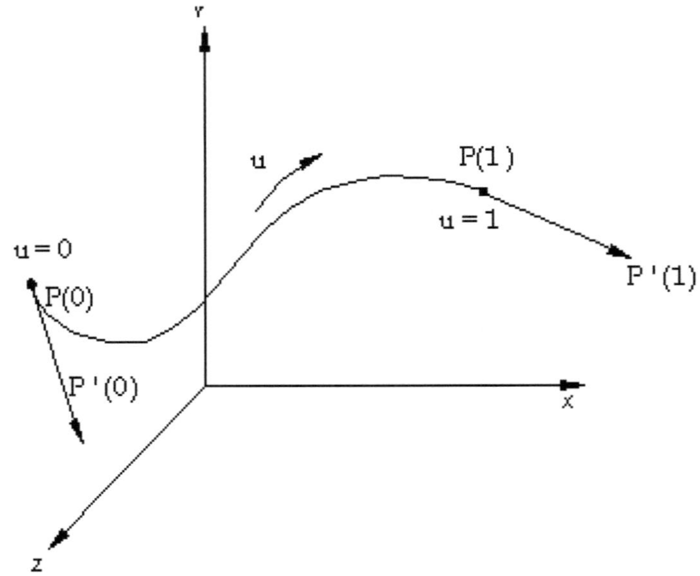

Fig. 24. Parametric representation of cubic spline

The solution of the four simultaneous equations written above for the coefficients, results the following equations

$$C_0 = P(0) \tag{9}$$

$$C_1 = P'(0) \tag{10}$$

$$C_2 = 3[P(1) - P(0)] - 2[P'(0) - P'(1)] \tag{11}$$

$$C_3 = 2[(P(0) - P(1)] + P'(0) + P'(1) \tag{12}$$

Now substituting these values of the coefficients into the equation 2, we get

$$P(u) = (2u^3 - 3u^2 + 1)P_0 + (-2u^3 + 3u^2)P_1 + (u^3 - 2u^2 + u)P'_0 + (u^3 - u^2)P'_1, \qquad 0 \le u \le 1 \tag{13}$$

Differentiating equation 13 the tangent vector can be obtained,

$$P'(u) = (6u2 - 6u)P0 + (-6u^2 + 6u)P_1 + (3u^2 - 4u + 1)P'_o + (3u^2 - 2u)P'_1 \qquad 0 \le u \le 1 \tag{14}$$

The functions of u in the equation 13 and 14 are called blending functions.

Equation 13 can be written in the matrix form as,

$$P(u) = U^T[M_H]V, \qquad 0 \le u \le 1 \tag{15}$$

Where, $[M_H]$ is the Hermite matrix and V is the geometry (or boundary conditions) vectors. Both are given by

$$[M_H]=\begin{bmatrix} 2 & -2 & 1 & 1 \\ -3 & 3 & -2 & -1 \\ 0 & 0 & 1 & 0 \\ 1 & 0 & 0 & 0 \end{bmatrix} \tag{16}$$

$$V=\begin{bmatrix} P_0 & P_1 & P'_0 & P'_1 \end{bmatrix}^T \tag{17}$$

Comparing eq^n 3 and eq^n 15, we can see that,

$$C=[M_H]V \text{ or } V=[M_H]^{-1}C \tag{18}$$

Now eq^n 13 shows that a cubic spline curve can be represented by its two endpoints and two tangent vectors. The curve passes through the end points (u=0 and 1) and from these above equations; it can be shown that, changing the end points or the tangent vectors, the shape of the curve can be controlled.

7.3 Algorithm for Stable Grasp

A suitable algorithm has been developed for thresholding and edge detection (Bepari, 2006; Datta & Ray, 2007). After finding out the silhouette, a virtual hand is utilized for grasping the periphery of the object. At every instance the object rotates by an angle of 1° and the angle between line of action of the force exerted by the finger and the instantaneous surface normal at that point of contacts are stored for optimization purpose. If this angle is less than that of the cone of friction of the work-hand pair, then the mapping is accepted otherwise rejected.

The said procedure iterates until the optimized grasp is obtained. The object snap, threshold figure and the optimal grasp have been shown in Fig.25. The contact property can be changed by changing the co-efficient of friction. The software has been developed by using VISUAL BASIC. Another constraint during design of stable grasp is the maximum distance between object's centre of gravity and hand's centre of gravity shown in the same figure and the absolute values of the coordinates of the two said points may be selected for stable orientation.

The methodology for stable grasp is as follows:

i. Snap of the object (in the plane of grasp or from the direction normal to the grasping plane),

ii. Generate the binary image,

iii. Calibrate the image,

iv. Generate edge detected boundary points using band-thresolding,

v. Cubic spline polynomials are interpolated,

vi. Input user input data (the translation zone of the end effector i.e. the starting coordinate and end coordinate enclosing a rectangle, co efficient of friction, μ, step angle, translational step),

vii. Specify the line of action of the force of the fingertips i.e. the plane of finger actuation,

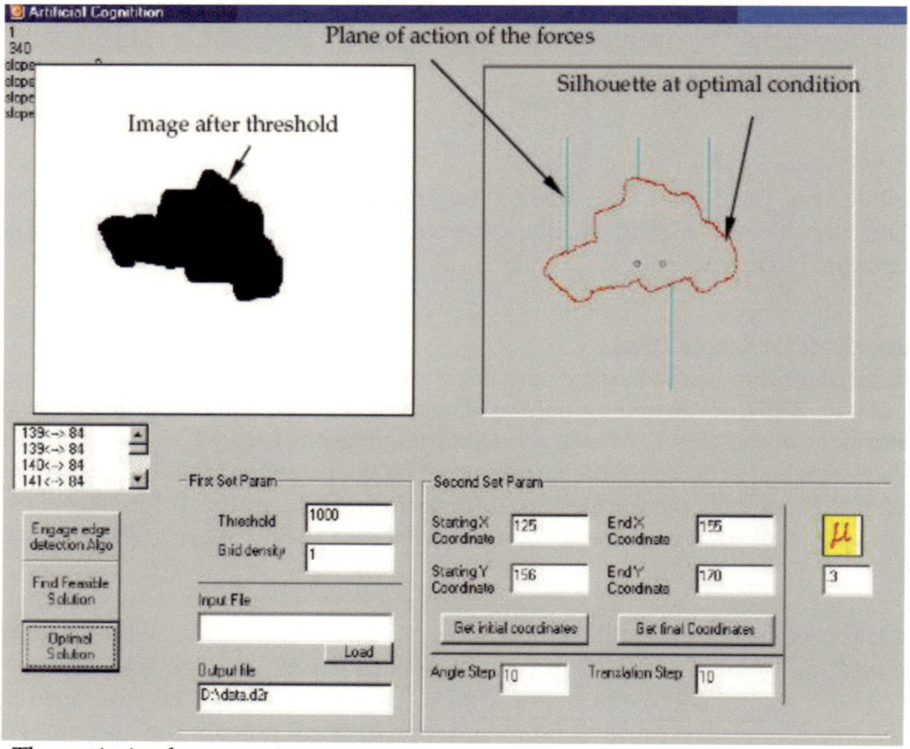

Fig. 25. The optimized grasp orientation

viii. Generate the feasible solution,

a. Simultaneously rotate and translate the boundary points,

b. At each step of rotation the entire finger plane intersects at points with the profile of the object are found,

c. Corresponding surface normal is found,

d. The angles between the normal at those points and the line of action of the force are calculated.

e. Since μ is given it is checked whether the angle of the cone of friction is less than $\tan^{-1}(\mu)$ or not,

f. If it is less than $\tan^{-1}(\mu)$ for all the fingers then angle of each finger and the coordinates of the figure are stored in a database as a feasible solution,

g. The optimal solution is found where summation of all the four angle of the cone of friction is minimum,

h. The process will continue till it reaches to the end coordinate from starting coordinate.

ix. End of securing for the stable grasp condition.

8. 3D Shape Recognition

The acquisition system consists of a stepper motor on which the object is mounted, one CCD camera and a frame grabber card. The frame grabber card is connected to the PC. The camera is fixed while the object mounted on the stepper motor can rotate around vertical axis with one degree of freedom. The minimal rotation angle of the stepper motor is 13.85° and in this way a total number of 26 images were taken. The photographic view of the image acquisition system is shown below in Fig.26.

Fig. 26. Photographic view of the imagecquisition system

These images are then calibrated and processed through image processing software (Sherlock-32 (Sherlock)). The peripheral points are found out from the calibrated images after thresholding and a database has been made to store the peripheral points of each of the twenty six calibrated images. By CATIA these peripheral points have been employed to regenerate the virtual object, which can be rotated with six degrees of freedom during pattern matching. The first image with the corresponding database points are shown in Fig.27.

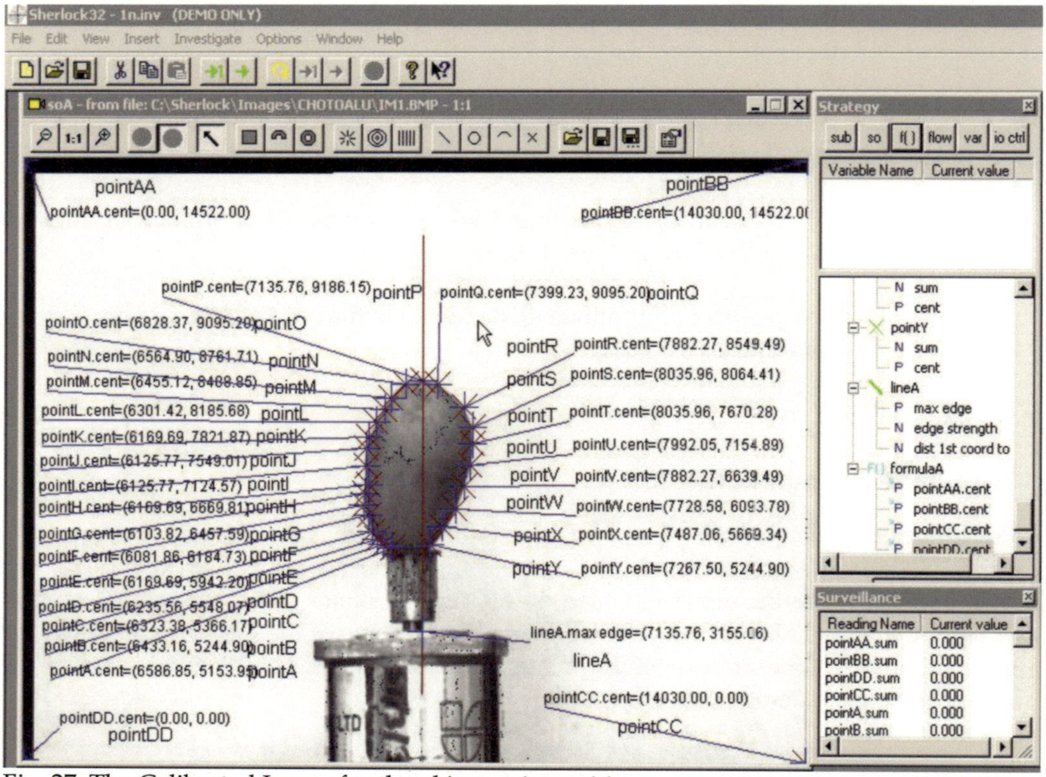

Fig. 27. The Calibrated Image for the object at 1st position

The Wire Frame Model of the Object in CATIA is shown in Fig.28. The Online 3-D modeling in CATIA has been shown in Fig.29 and the virtual 3-D synthetic models of the object after rendering in CATIA as viewed from different perspectives are shown in Fig.30 below.

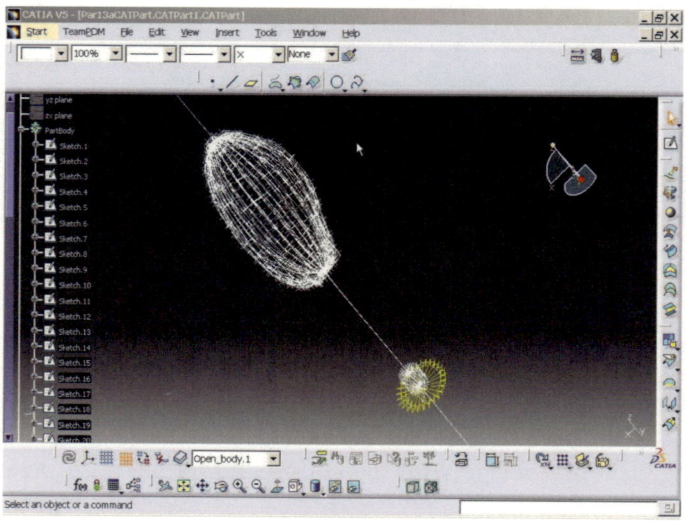

Fig. 28.Wire frame model of the object in CATIA

Fig. 29. Online 3-D modeling in CATIA

Fig. 30. 3-D synthetic models of the object after rendering in CATIA as viewed from different perspectives

9. Conclusion

From the study of the presion of the robotic hand, the following general conclusions may be drawn:

a) Object shapes and dimensions have been analyzed through PC-based 2D image processing technique and the information about the object shape has been incorporated in the three-tier hierarchy of the control system for determining the preshape of the fingers during manipulation.

b) A CCD camera has been employed to grab the image of the object to be gripped and a vision-based algorithm has been developed for analyzing the stable grasp positions and orientations.

c) It has been found that the vision assistance can minimize the down time for grasping an object in a pre-defined manner by preshaping the fingers.

10. Future Scope

a) In the present setup the hand was so developed that the fingers only ensured planar grasp, though for real time grasping the spatial considerations are to be taken of.

b) A single CCD camera has been employed for generation of images which resulted in acquisition of dimension of the object in a plane. In order to have the the 3D shape information it would have been better to use another camera at 90°.

c) 3-D shape information havs given a better idea about the object and its grasping strategies. The algorithm, which has been developed for 2-D, may be extended for 3-D grasp.

11. References

Geisler, W. (1982). A Vision System for Shape and Position Recognition of Industrial Parts, *Proceedings of International Conference on Robot Vision and Sensory Controls*, Stuttgart, November 1982, Germany

Marr, D. (1982). *Vision-A Computational Investigation into the Human Representation and Processing of Visual Information*, W. H. Freeman, San Francisco, 1982

Faugeras, O. D. (1993). *Three-Dimensional Computer Vision: A Geometric Viewpoint*, MIT Press, ISBN 0-262-06158-9, Cambridge, MA

Horaud, R.; Mohr, R.; Dornaika, F. & Boufama, B. (1995). The Advantage of Mounting a Camera in a Robot Arm, *Proceedings of the Europe-China Workshop on Modelling and Invariant for Computer Vision*, pp: 206-213, Xian, 1995, China

Hartley, R. I. (1994). Self-Calibration from Multiple Views with a Rotating Camera, *3rd European Conference on Computer Vision*, pp. 471-478, Springer-Verlag, Stockholm, Sweden

Pajdha, T. & Hlavac, V. (1999). Camera Calibration and Euclidean Reconstruction from Known Translations, *Conference on Computer Vision and Applied Geometry*, Nordfjordeid, 1st-7th August 1995, Norway

Sonka, M.; Hlavac, V. & Boyle, R. (1998). *Image Processing, Analysis, and Machine Vision*, PWS Publishing, ISBN 053495393X

Nitzan, D. (1988). Three-Dimensional Vision Structure for Robot Applications, *IEEE Transactions on Pattern Analysis and Machine Intelligence*, Vol. 10, No. 3, 1988, pp. 291-309

Victor, A. & Gunasekaran, S. (1993). Range Determination of Objects Using Stereo Vision, *Proceedings of INCARF*, pp. 381-387, December, 1993, New Delhi, India

Lee, C. S. G.; Fu, K. S. & Gonzalez, R. C. (1994). *Robotics - Control, Sensing, Vision and Intelligence*, Mc-Graw Hill Publication Company, ISBN 0070226253, New York, USA

Klette, R.; Koschan, A. & Schluns, K. (1996). *Computer Vision-Raumliche Information Aus Digitalen Bildern*, Friedr, Vieweg & Sohn, Braunschweig 1996

Nishihara, H. K. (1984). Practical Real-Time Imaging Stereo Matcher, *Optical Engineering*, Vol. 23, No 5, 1984,pp. 536-545

Pollard, S. B.; J. Mayhew, E. W. & Frisby, J. P. (1981). PMF: A Stereo Correspondence Algorithm Using a Disparity Gradient Limit, *Perception*, Vol. 14, pp. 449-470, 1981

Tarabanis, K. A. &Tsai, R. Y. (1991). Computing Viewpoints that Satisfy Optical Constraints, *Proceedings of IEEE Conference on Computer Vision and Pattern Recognition*, pp: 152-158,Maui, , June, 1991, Hawaii

Maver, J. & Bajcsy, R. (1993). Occlusions as a Guide for Planning the Next View, *IEEE Transactions on Pattern Analysis and Machines Intelligence*, Vol. 15, No. 5, May 1993, pp. 417-432

Connolly, C. (1985). The Determination of Next Best Views, *Proceedings of IEEE International Conference on Robotics and Automation*, pp. 432-435, Durham, March, 1985, England

Szeliski, R. (1993). Rapid Octree Construction from Image Sequences, *CVGIP: Image Understanding*, Vol. 58, No. 1, July 1993, pp. 23-32

Niem, W. (1994). Robust and Fast Modeling of 3D Natural Objects from Multiple Views, *Image and Video Processing II, Proceedings of SPIE*, pp. 388-397, San Jose, February, 1994, CA

Whaite, P. & Ferrie, F. P. (1994). Autonomous Exploration: Driven by Uncertainty, *Proceedings of IEEE Conference on Computer Vision and Pattern Recognition*, pp. 339-346, Seattle, June, 1994, Washington

Pito, R. (1999). A Solution to the Next Best View Problem for Automated Surface Acquisition, *IEEE Transactions on Pattern Analysis and Machine Intelligence*, Vol. 21, No. 10, October 1999, pp. 1016-1030

Liska, C. (1999). Das Adaptive Lichtschnittverfahren cur Oberflachenkonstruktion mittels Laserlicht, *Master's thesis, Vienna University of Technology, Institute of Computer Aided Automation, Pattern Recognition and Image Processing Group*, Vienna, Austria, 1999.

Sablating, R.; Tosovic, S. & Kampel, M.(2003). Next View Planning for Shape from Silhouette, Computer Vision - CVWW'03, pp. 77–82, Valtice, February, 2003, Czech Republic

Lacquaniti, F. & Caminiti, R. (1998). Visuo-motor Transformations for Arm Reaching, *European Journal Of Neuroscience*, Vol. 10, pp. 195-203, 1998.

Desai, J. P. (1998). Motion Planning and Control of Cooperative Robotic Systems, *Ph. D. Dissertation in Mechanical Engineering and Applied Mechanics, University of Pennsylvania*, 1998.

Metta, G. & Fitzpatrick, P. (2002). Early Integration of Vision and Manipulation. *Giorgio Metta, LIRA-Lab, DIST – University of Genova, Viale Causa, 13 – I-16145*, Genova, Italy, 25th October, 2002.

Barnesand, N. & Liu, Z. Q. (2004). Embodied Categorization for Vision-Guided Mobile Robots, *Pattern Recognition*, Vol. 37, No. 2, February 2004, pp. 299-312

Kragic, D. & Christensen, H. I. (2003). A. Framework for Visual Servoing. In: *Computer Vision Systems*, J.L. Crowley et al. (Eds.), pp. 345–354, Springer-Verlag Berlin Heidelberg, ISBN 978-3-540-00921-4, LNCS 2626

Bhaumik, S., Barai, N. C. and Ray, R. (2003). Vision Control Mobile Manipulator, *Manufacturing Technology Today, A Journal of Central Manufacturing Technology Institute*, Bangalore, Vol. 3, No. 5, pp. 12-16

Nakabo, Y.; Ishii, I. & Ishikawa, M. (2002). 3D Tracking Using Two High-Speed Vision Systems, Proceedings of International Conference on Intelligent Robots and Systems, pp.360-365, Lausanne, October 2002, Switzerland

MSC. VisualNastrun 4D 2001 R2, MSC Software Corporation, 2 Mc Arthur Place, Santa Ana, California 92707 USA

Bepari. B. (2006); Computer Aided Design and Construction of an Anthropomorphic Multiple Degrees of Freedom Robot Hand. *Ph. D. Thesis*, Jadavpur University, Kolkata, India

S. Datta and R. Ray (2007), AMR Vision System for Perception and Job Identification in a Manufacturing Environment. In: *Vision Systems: Applications*, Goro Obinata and Ashish Dutta (Ed), ISBN 978-3-902613-01-1, pp. 519-540, I-Tech, Vienna, Austria, June, 2007

Sherlock TM, CORECO Imaging, 6969 Trans Canada Highway, Suite 142, St. Laurent, Quebec, http://www.imaging.com

14

Image Stabilization in Active Robot Vision

Angelos Amanatiadis[1], Antonios Gasteratos[1],
Stelios Papadakis[2] and Vassilis Kaburlasos[2]
[1]*Democritus University of Thrace*
[2]*Technological Educational Institution of Kavala*
Greece

1. Introduction

Recent demands in sophisticated mobile robots require many semi-autonomous or even autonomous operations, such as decision making, simultaneous localization and mapping, motion tracking and risk assessment, while operating in dynamic environments. Most of these capabilities depend highly on the quality of the input from the cameras mounted on the mobile platforms and require fast processing times and responses. However, quality in robot vision systems is not given only by the quantitative features such as the resolution of the cameras, the frame rate or the sensor gain, but also by the qualitative features such as sequences free of unwanted movement, fast and good image pre-processing algorithms and real-time response. A robot having optimal quantitative features for its vision system cannot achieve the finest performance when the qualitative features are not met. Image stabilization is one of the most important qualitative features for a mobile robot vision system, since it removes the unwanted motion from the frame sequences captured from the cameras. This image sequence enhancement is necessary in order to improve the performance of the subsequently complicated image processing algorithms that will be executed.

Many image processing applications require stabilized sequences for input while other present substantially better performance when processing stabilized sequences. Intelligent transportation systems equipped with vision systems use digital image stabilization for substantial reduction of the algorithm computational burden and complexity (Tyan et al. (2004)), (Jin et al. (2000)). Video communication systems with sophisticated compression codecs integrate image stabilization for improved computational and performance efficiency (Amanatiadis & Andreadis (2008)), (Chen et al. (2007)). Furthermore, unwanted motion is removed from medical images via stabilization schemes (Zoroofi et al. (1995)). Motion tracking and video surveillance applications achieve better qualitative results when cooperating with dedicated stabilization systems (Censi et al. (1999)), (Marcenaro et al. (2001)), as shown in Fig. 1.

Several robot stabilization system implementations that use visual and inertial information have been reported. An image stabilization system which compensates the walking oscillations of a biped robot is described in (Kurazume & Hirose (2000)). A vision and inertial cooperation for stabilization have been also presented in (Lobo & Dias (2003)) using a fusion model for the vertical reference provided by the inertial sensor and vanishing points from images. A visuo-inertial stabilization for space variant binocular systems has been also developed in (Panerai et al. (2000)), where an inertial device measures angular velocities and linear accelerations, while image geometry facilitates the computation of first-order motion parameters. In

(a)

(b) (c) (d)

Fig. 1. Performance of automatic license plate recognition system: a) sample frame, b) processed frame only by zooming algorithm, c) processed frame only by stabilization algorithm, d) processed frame by both stabilization and zooming algorithms.

(Zufferey & Floreano (2006)), course stabilization and collision avoidance is achieved using a bioinspired model of optic flow and inertial information applied to autonomous flying robots.

2. Image Stabilization

Image stabilization schemes can be classified into three major categories. The optical image stabilizer employs a prism assembly that moves opposite to the shaking of camera for stabilization (Cardani (2006)), (Tokyo (1993)). A two axis gyroscope is used to measure the movement of the camera, and a microcontroller directs that signal to small linear motors that move the image sensor, compensating for the camera motion. Other designs move a lens somewhere in the optical chain within the camera. The electronic image stabilizer compensates the image sequence by employing motion sensors to detect the camera movement for compensation (Oshima et al. (1989)), (Kinugasa et al. (1990)). Gyroscopes are still used to detect the jitter, but instead of altering the direction of the prism, the image is simply shifted in software by a certain number of pixels. Both electronic and optical image stabilizers are hardware dependent and require built-in devices such as inertial sensors and servo motors. The digital image

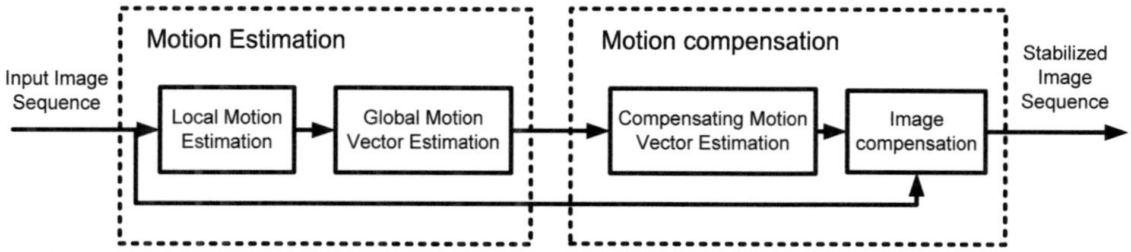

Fig. 2. Typical architecture of an image stabilization technique.

stabilizer (DIS) does not need any mechanical or optical devices since the image compensation is made through image processing algorithms. This attribute makes it suitable for low cost electronics (Ko et al. (1999)), (Vella et al. (2002)), (Xu & Lin (2006)), (Pan & Ngo (2005)). The DIS comprises two processing units: the motion estimation unit and the motion compensation unit. The purpose of motion estimation unit is to estimate reliably the global camera movement through the local motion estimation vectors of the acquired image sequence. The effectiveness of a DIS is closely tied with the accuracy of detecting the local motion vectors, in order to produce the right global motion vector. Following motion estimation, the motion compensation unit generates the compensating motion vector and shifts the current picking window according to the compensating motion vector to obtain a smoother image sequence. Motion compensation can take up 10% of the total computation of a digital stabilizer (Chen et al. (2007)). Various algorithms have been developed to estimate the local motion vectors, such as representative point matching (Vella et al. (2002)), edge pattern matching (Paik et al. (1992)), block matching (Xu & Lin (2006)) and bit plane matching (Ko et al. (1999)). All the previous algorithms, despite their high accuracy and reliability, are strictly constrained to regular conditions exhibiting high sensitivity to various irregular conditions such as moving objects, intentional panning, sequences acquired in low signal-to-noise ratio or zooming. For moving objects, solutions have been proposed such as in (Erturk (2003)). For sequences acquired in low signal-to-noise ratio, a blind DIS with the use of genetic algorithms is proposed in (Nait-Ali (2007)). Intentional panning has also been greatly improved using background estimation (Hsu et al. (2005)). For zooming, CMOS digital image stabilization schemes have been proposed in (Cho et al. (2007)) and (Cho & Hong (2007)). However, due to the fact that they are based on the distortion effect caused by the rolling shuttering mechanism of the CMOS sensor, they are effective only in CMOS sensors.

A typical architecture of a DIS is shown in Fig. 2. The motion estimation unit computes the motion between two consecutive frames. This is achieved firstly by the local motion estimation subunit, which estimates the local motion vectors within frame regions. Secondly, the global motion estimation unit determines the global motion vectors by processing the previously estimated local motion vectors. Following the motion estimation unit, the motion compensation unit firstly, generates the compensating motion vector and secondly, shifts the current picking window according to the compensating motion vector to obtain a free of high frequency image sequence but still keep the global ego-motion of the sequence.

3. Active robot vision

The term active vision is used to describe vision systems, where the cameras do not stand still to observe the scene in a passive manner, but, by means of actuation mechanisms, they can aim towards the point of interest. The most common active stereo vision systems comprise

a pair cameras horizontally aligned (Gasteratos et al. (2002)), (Samson et al. (2006)). In these systems the movement of the stereo rig is done by means of 2 degrees of freedom: one for the horizontal movement (pan) and the other for the vertical one (tilt); moreover each of the cameras obeys to an independent pan movement (vergence), which raises the total degrees of freedom of the system to four. To these apparatuses are often incorporated other sensors, such as gyros, accelerometers or acoustical ones (Lungarella et al. (2003)). The integration of other than visual sensors on an active stereo head is used as a supplementary source of information from the environment. They are utilized in additional feedback loops, in order to increase the system robustness. Such an application is the utilization of gyros for image stabilization and gaze control (Panerai et al. (2003)).
When a robot with a vision system moves around its environment undesirable position fluctuations in its visual field might occur, due to its locomotion. It is apparent that such fluctuation degrades the robot's visual functions and, thus, it is critical to avoid them, by stabilizing the images. In biological systems this is avoided owing to Vestibulo-Ocular Reflex (VOR), which derives from the brain and governs compensatory eye movements. However, in a tele-operated robot there is not any mean to wire the operator's brain with the actuators on the robot head. In this case a local control loop should be applied, that replicates the VOR on the tele-operated head. Figure 3 depicts a rough block diagram of the closed-loop control scheme for the pan dof, which incorporates a look-ahead control loop for the external horizontal disturbance. The look-ahead control strategy is utilized to predict the image fluctuations due to abrupt disturbances on the stereo head. The horizontal component of the disturbance applied on the head is measured by the inertial sensor. This signal is then fed into the look-ahead controller, which produces a control signal for the controller of the pan degree of freedom (G_c). The controller G_c is a standard PID controller $(G_c = K_p + \frac{K_i}{s} - K_d \times s)$, which produces a counteracting order to the actuator that moves the pan (G_p). This way the rotational component of the horizontal disturbance is suppressed. At the final stage, the horizontal retinal slippage is computed on two sequential image frames using a differential technique. This is used as a feedback signal in a closed-loop that fine-tunes the image stabilization. An identical local control loop is utilized for vertical disturbance and the tilt (having the same PID parameters). Images are stabilized in two axes in this manner, and the operator's suffering from fast image changes is compensated.

4. Evaluation measures

Evaluation procedures for image stabilization algorithms and architectures are presented in (Engelsberg & Schmidt (1999)), (Morimoto & Chellappa (1998)) and (Balakirsky & Chellappa (1996)). In robot vision the factors that are more important in the image stabilization schemes are the accuracy of the system in terms of image quality and the displacement range in terms of pixels or degrees per second. The quality of a stabilized sequence can be measured with the help of the interframe transformation fidelity which is defined as the PSNR between two consecutive stabilized frames, which is given by:

$$ITF = \frac{1}{N-1} \sum_{k=1}^{N-1} PSNR(I_k, I_{k+1}) \tag{1}$$

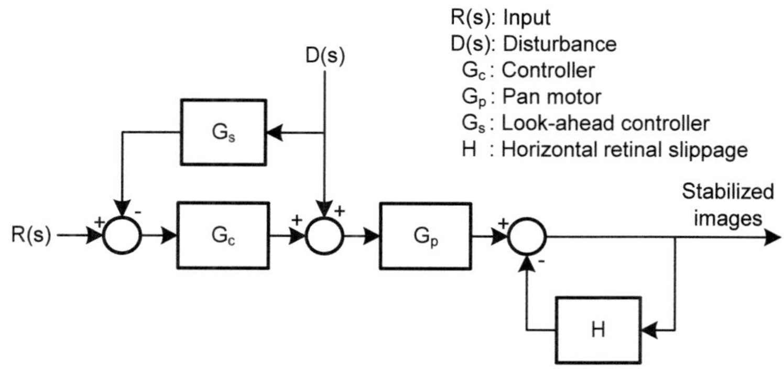

Fig. 3. Control scheme for compensation of the horizontal disturbances. The inertial sensors are used for a look-ahead mechanism, which directly measures the disturbance and provides a negative input to the controller. The horizontal component of the optic flow measured in both cameras is used as feedback to the system.

with N the number of frames of the sequence. The PSNR between two consecutive frame I_k and I_{k+1} is given by:

$$PSNR(I_k, I_{k+1}) = 20 \times log_{10} \left(\frac{MAX_I}{RMSE(I_k, I_{k+1})} \right) \quad (2)$$

5. Case study

A rotational and translational image stabilization system for a pan and tilt active stereo camera head will be presented. The system is designed to fit into mobile rover platforms allowing the architecture to be modular and the whole system expandable. Special attention was paid to the real-time constraints, particularly for the control part of the system. The stabilization system as shown in Fig. 4, consists of a stereo vision head (Gasteratos & Sandini (2001)), two high resolution digital cameras, a DSP inertial sensor, four actuators and controllers and two processing units. Pan and tilt compensation is achieved though mechanical servoing while vertical and horizontal compensation is achieved by frame shifting through a digital frame stabilization algorithm. A key feature is the real-time servo control system, written in C, using Open Source Software which includes a Linux-based Real-Time Operating System, a Universal Serial Bus to RS-232 serial driver, CAN bus drivers and an open source network communication protocol for the communication between the two processing units.

5.1 Hardware Architecture

The system functions can be separated into information processing and motion control. Information processing includes the gyrosensor output and the image processing. However, image processing presents a high computational burden and recourses while it demands the full usage of certain instruction sets of a modern microprocessor. In contrast, motion control requires the operation system to be able to execute real-time tasks. This demand for high multimedia performance and real-time motion control has forced us to adopt a computer structure consisting of a computer with Windows operating system for the image processing and a computer with RT-Linux operating system for the control tasks. The computers are connected to each other by a high speed network protocol for synchronization and frame compensation

Fig. 4. The stereo head vision system. The modules shown here are: the stereo vision head with the fixed actuators, the two digital cameras, the inertial sensor and the four controllers.

purposes. This inter-host communication protocol between the computers uses a higher level abstraction, built on top of sockets, meeting the requirements for low latency. The interfaces used are CAN bus for the controllers (Tindell et al. (1994)), USB 2.0 for the cameras a USB 1.0 to serial output for the inertial sensor. The drivers for the interfaces connected to the RT-Linux computer are open source under the General Public License.

In order to fully utilize the advantages and precision of the modern digital servo drives a fine tuning process (Astrom & Hagglund (1995)) for the pan and tilt PID controllers was carried out. The tuning was orientated for position control and due to the different inertia load seen on the motor shaft of the pan and tilt axis the integral, derivative and proportional band values were set to different values for each axis respectively. In order to determine the internal camera geometric and optical characteristics, camera calibration was necessary. A variety of methods have been reported in the bibliography. The method we used is described in (Bouget (2001)) using its available C Open Source code. The method is a non self-calibrating thus, we used a projected chessboard pattern to estimate the camera intrinsics and plane poses. Finally, the calibration results were used to rectify the images taken from cameras in order to have the best results in the subsequent image processing algorithms.

5.2 Software Architecture

Key feature for the implementation of the real-time control is the operating system we used. Since critical applications such as control, need low response times, OCERA operating system (OCERA project home page (2008)) was chosen. OCERA is an Open Source project which provides an integrated execution environment for embedded real-time applications. It is based on components and incorporates the latest techniques for building embedded systems. OCERA architecture is designed to develop hybrid systems with hard and soft real-time activities as shown in Fig. 5. In this case, we allocated the critical task of control at the RTLinux level and the less critical tasks, such as inertial data filtering, at the Linux level. The interface for both kinds of activities is a POSIX based interface.

For motion estimation, the rectified frames are processed with an optic flow method in order to extract the global motion translation vector for the motion compensation. The affine model

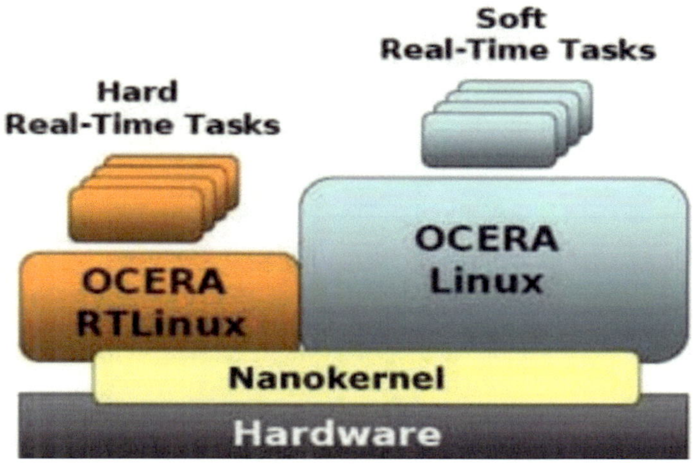

Fig. 5. The chosen operating system combines the use of two kernels, Linux and RTLinux-GPL to provide support for critical tasks (RTLinux-GPL executive) and soft real-time applications (Linux kernel).

of the optic flow that was used is described in (Koenderink & van Doorn (1991)) for the basis of frame translation, using a single camera input. For motion compensation process, the estimation method in (Hsu et al. (2005)) was selected, in order to remove the undesired shaking motion and simultaneously maintain the ego-motion of the stereo head.
The digital inertial sensor consists of a compact sensor package, which includes accelerometers and gyros to measure accelerations and angular rates. The errors in the force measurements introduced by accelerometers and the errors in the measurement of angular change in orientation with respect to the inertial space introduced by gyroscopes are two fundamental error sources which affect the error behavior of the rotational stabilization. Furthermore, inertial measurements are corrupted by additive noise (Ovaska & Valiviita (1998)). The Kalman filter (Welch & Bishop (2001)), (Trucco & Verri (1998)) was used which is a form of optimal estimator, characterized by recursive evaluation using an estimated internal model of the dynamics of the system. The filtering is implemented on the RT-Linux computer where the inertial sensor is attached. Finally, the optimized filter outputs of pan and tilt are the subsequent feedback to the controllers for opposite movement of the pan and tilt axis, respectively.
The concurrency and parallelism was considered in the programming of the robotic system by using a multi-thread model. The motor run time models are not using the *wait.until.done*() function, while a change in the operator's field of view indicates that the previous movement should not be completed but a new motion position command should be addressed. Simultaneous and non-synchronized accesses to the same resources, such as servo motors, is a critical aspect since both stabilization and head tracking movement are performed at the same time, as shown in Fig. 6. Thus, a priority scheduling feedback loop (Locke (1992)) was implemented. The priority feedback scheduler is implemented as an additional real-time periodic task. The inputs are the measured response times of the control tasks and the inputs from both sensors. Priority was given to head posing tracker since we were interested firstly in giving the operator the desired view and then an optimized view by mechanical stabilization.
The RT-Linux kernel keeps track of the real time tasks execution cycles, thus allowing to recover a precise measure of the control tasks execution times from the scheduling regulator. As

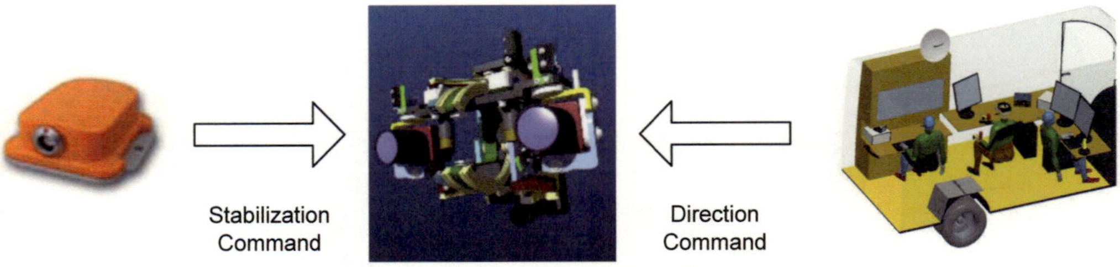

Fig. 6. Concurrent movement commands are applied to the same axis.

the feedback scheduler is a simple feedback algorithm running at a slow rate, its computing cost is quite low. The software programming infrastructure considered the shared resources and critical sections in order to guarantee the expandability and flexibility of the stereo vision system. The critical sections were easily implemented since the protected operations were limited. However, special attention was paid since critical sections can disable system interrupts and can impact the responsiveness of the operating system.

5.3 Algorithm Implementation

5.3.1 Kalman Filtering

Discrete Kalman filter computes the best estimate of the systems's state at t_k, $\bar{x}$, taking into account the state estimated by the system model at t_{k-1} and the measurement, z_k, taken at t_k. The Kalman filter equations are characterized by the state covariance matrices, P_k and $P_k^{'}$, and the gain matrix, K_k. $P_k^{'}$ is the covariance matrix of the k-th state estimate

$$\bar{x}_k^{'} = \Phi_{k-1}\bar{x}_{k-1} \tag{3}$$

predicted by the filter immediately before obtaining the measurement z_k, where Φ_{k-1} is a time dependent $n \times n$ matrix called state transition matrix. P_k is the covariance matrix of the k-th state estimate, $\bar{x}_k$ computed by the filter after integrating the measurement, z_k, with the prediction, $\bar{x}_k^{'}$. The covariance matrices are a quantitative model of the uncertainty of $x_k^{'}$ and x_k. Finally, K_k establishes the relative importance of the prediction, $\bar{x}_k^{'}$, and the state measurement, $\bar{x}_k$. Let Q_k and R_k be the covariance matrices of the white, zero-mean, Gaussian system and measurement noise respectively. The Kalman filter equations are

$$P_k^{'} = \Phi_{k-1}P_{k-1}\Phi_{k-1}^{\top} + Q_{k-1} \tag{4}$$

$$K_k = P_k^{'}H_k^{\top}(H_kP_k^{'}H_k^{\top} + R_k)^{-1} \tag{5}$$

$$\bar{x}_k = \Phi_{k-1}\bar{x}_{k-1} + K_k(z_k - H_k\Phi_{k-1}\bar{x}_{k-1}) \tag{6}$$

$$P_k = (I - K_k)P_k^{'}(I - K_k)^{\top} + K_kR_kK_k^{\top} \tag{7}$$

Using (4) to (7), we estimate the state and its covariance recursively. Initial estimates of the covariance matrix P_0 and of the state, $\bar{x}_0$, were set to 0 and 1 respectively (Welch & Bishop (2001)). First, $P_k^{'}$ is estimated according to (4). Second, the gain of the Kalman filter is computed by (5), before reading the new inertial measurements. Third, the optimal state estimate at time t_k, $\bar{x}_k$, is formed by (6), which integrates the state predicted by the system model ($\Phi_{k-1}\bar{x}_{k-1}$) with the discrepancy of prediction and observation ($z_k - H_k\Phi_{k-1}\bar{x}_{k-1}$) in a sum weighted by the gain matrix, K_k. Finally, the new state covariance matrix, P_k, is evaluated through (7). In our

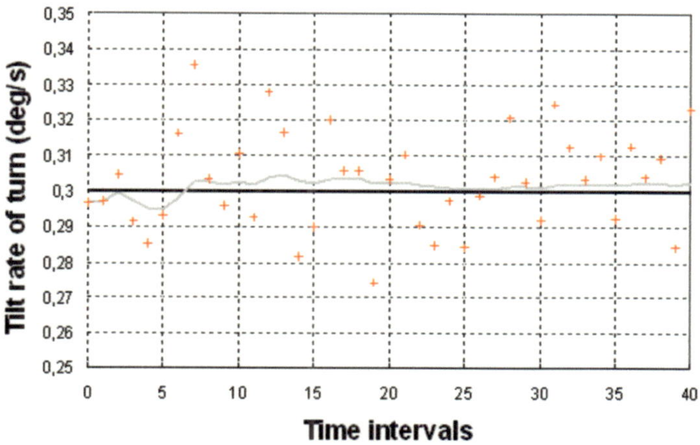

Fig. 7. Sample data during the experiment session. The input reference is $0.3deg/ses$ (black line), the output of the inertial sensor (crosses) and the filtered Kalman output (gray line).

inertial sensor, the calibrated rate of turn noise density is $0.1units/\sqrt{Hz}$ with units in deg/s. Operating in $40Hz$ bandwidth, the noise is $0.015deg/s$. An experiment was carried out to quantify the filtering behavior of the system in real-time. We applied a recursive motion profile to the tilt axis with constant velocity of $0.3deg/sec$. During the experiment the following parameters were stored to estimate the overall performance: (i) the velocity stimulus input reference (ii) position angle of the controlled tilt servo encoder, (iii) output of the inertial sensor and (iv) the Kalman filter output. Figure 7 shows the sample data recorded during the test session. As it can seen the Kalman filtered output is close to the input reference by estimating the process state at a time interval and obtaining feedback in the form of the noisy inertial sensor measurement.

5.3.2 Optic Flow and Motion Compensation

Techniques for estimating the motion field are divided in two major classes: differential techniques (Horn & Schunck (1981)) and matching techniques (Barron et al. (1994)). A widely used differential algorithm (Lucas & Kanade (1981)) that gives good results was chosen for implementation. Given the assumptions of the image brightness constancy equation yields a good approximation of the normal component of the motion filed and that motion field is well approximated by a constant vector field within any small patch of the image plane, for each point p_i within a small, $n \times n$ patch, Q, we derive

$$(\nabla E)^{\top}\mathbf{v} + E_t = 0 \tag{8}$$

where spatial and temporal derivatives of the image brightness are computed at $\mathbf{p}_1, \mathbf{p}_2, \ldots, \mathbf{p}_{N^2}$, with $E = E(x, y, t)$ the image brightness and $\mathbf{v}$, the motion filed. Therefore, the optical flow can be estimated within Q as the constant vector, $\bar{\mathbf{v}}$, that minimizes the functional

$$\Psi[\mathbf{v}] = \sum_{\mathbf{p}_i \in Q} [(\nabla E)^{\top}\mathbf{v} + E_t]^2 \tag{9}$$

The solution to this least squares problem can be found by solving the linear system

$$A^{\top}A\mathbf{v} = A^{\top}\mathbf{b} \tag{10}$$

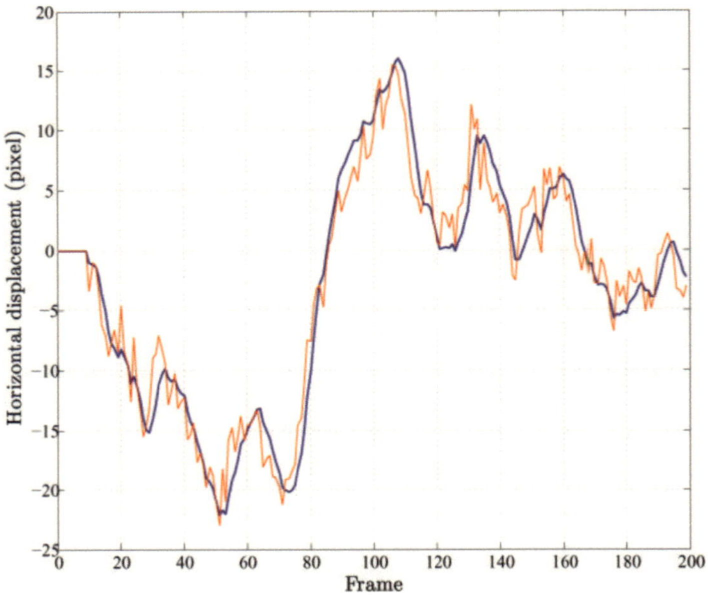

Fig. 8. Horizontal frame sample data during the experiment session. The input before stabilization (red line) and the output after stabilization (blue line) is demonstrated.

The i-th row of the $N^2 \times 2$ matrix A is the spatial image gradient evaluated at point $\mathbf{p}_i$

$$A = [\nabla E(\mathbf{p}_1), \nabla E(\mathbf{p}_2), \ldots, \nabla E(\mathbf{p}_{N\times N})]^\top \tag{11}$$

and $\mathbf{b}$ is the N^2-dimensional vector of the partial temporal derivatives of the image brightness, evaluated at $\mathbf{p}_1, \mathbf{p}_2 \ldots \mathbf{p}_{N^2}$, after a sign change

$$\mathbf{b} = -[E_t(\mathbf{p}_1), E_t(\mathbf{p}_2), \ldots, E_t(\mathbf{p}_{N\times N})]^\top \tag{12}$$

Finally, the optic flow $\bar{\mathbf{v}}$ at the center of patch Q can be obtained as

$$\bar{\mathbf{v}} = (A^\top A)^{-1} A^\top \mathbf{b} \tag{13}$$

Furthermore, we applied to each captured rectified image a Gaussian filter with a standard deviation of $\sigma_s = 1.5$. The filtering was both spatial and temporal in order to attenuate noise in the estimation of the spatial image gradient and prevent aliasing in the time domain. The patch used is 5×5 pixels and three consecutive frames are the temporal dimension. The algorithm is applied for each patch and only the optic flow for the pixel at the center of the patch is computed, generating a sparse motion field with high performance speed of $10 frames/sec$ for 320×240 image resolution.

The Global Motion Vector (GMV) is represented by the arithmetic mean of the local motion vectors in each of the patches and can be potentially effective when subtracting the ego-motion commands of the stereo head which are available through the servo encoders. Subsequently, the compensation motion vector estimation is used to generate the Compensating Motion Vectors (CMVs) for removing the undesired shaking motion but still keeping the steady motion

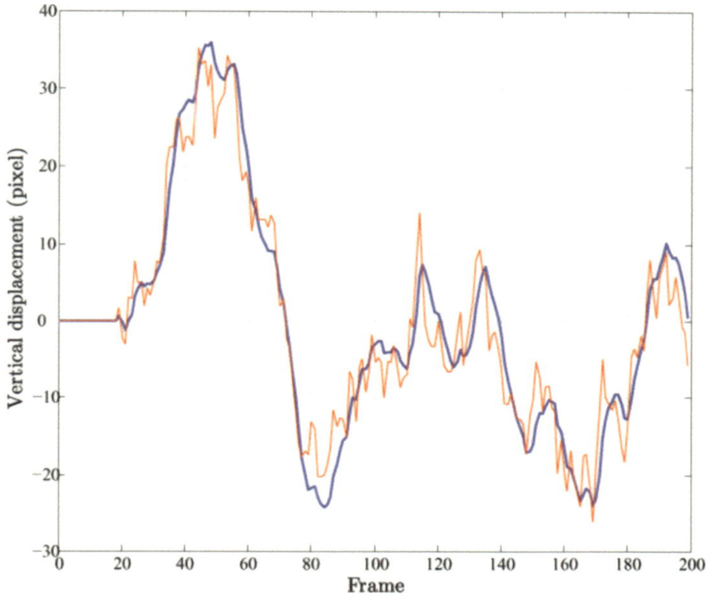

Fig. 9. Vertical frame sample data during the experiment session. The input before stabilization (red line) and the output after stabilization (blue line) is demonstrated.

of the image. The compensation motion vector estimation for the final frame shifting is given by (Paik et al. (1992))

$$\begin{aligned} CMV(t) = {} & k\,(CMV(t-1)) \\ & + (a\,GMV(t) + (1-a)\,GMV(t-1)) \end{aligned} \tag{14}$$

where t represents the frame number, $0 \leq a \leq 1$ and k is a proportional factor for designating the weight between current frame stabilization and ego-motion. Finally, frame shifting is applied when both horizontal and vertical CMVs are determined.

5.4 System Performance

Due to the fact that rotational stabilization process runs on the RT-Linux computer we have succeeded its real-time operation. Thus, stabilization can be considered as two separate processes that operate independently, since the frame sequences captured from the camera have been already rotationally stabilized by the mechanical servoing. The horizontal and vertical stabilization experiments are demonstrated in Fig. 8 and Fig. 9, respectively. The results show a frame sequence free of high frequency fluctuations, maintaining though, the ego-motion of the trajectory. The overall system is capable of processing 320×240 pixel image sequences at approximately $10\,frames/sec$, with a maximum acceleration of $4\,deg/sec^2$.

6. Conclusion

In this chapter, we covered all the crucial features of image stabilization in active robot vision systems. The topics included real-time servo control approaches for the electronic image stabilization, image processing algorithms for the digital image stabilization, evaluation measures, and robot control architectures for hard and soft real-time processes. A case study of an active robot vision image stabilization scheme was also presented, consisting of a four degrees of freedom robotic head, two high resolution digital cameras, a DSP inertial sensor, four actuators and controllers and one processing unit. Pan and tilt compensation was achieved through mechanical servoing while vertical and horizontal compensation was achieved by frame shifting through a digital frame stabilization algorithm. key feature was the real-time servo control system, written in C, using Open Source Software which includes a Linux-based Real-Time Operating System, a Universal Serial Bus to RS-232 serial driver, CAN bus drivers and an open source network communication protocol for the communication between the two processing units.

7. References

Amanatiadis, A. & Andreadis, I. (2008). An integrated architecture for adaptive image stabilization in zooming operation, *IEEE Trans. Consum. Electron.* **54**(2): 600–608.

Astrom, K. & Hagglund, T. (1995). *PID controllers: Theory, Design and Tuning*, Instrument Society of America, Research Triangle Park.

Balakirsky, S. & Chellappa, R. (1996). Performance characterization of image stabilization algorithms, *Proc. Int. Conf. Image Process.*, Vol. 1, pp. 413–416.

Barron, J., Fleet, D. & Beauchemin, S. (1994). Performance of optical flow techniques, *International Journal of Computer Vision* **12**(1): 43–77.

Bouget, J. (2001). Camera calibration toolbox for Matlab, *California Institute of Technology, http//www.vision.caltech.edu* .

Cardani, B. (2006). Optical image stabilization for digital cameras, *IEEE Control Syst. Mag.* **26**(2): 21–22.

Censi, A., Fusiello, A. & Roberto, V. (1999). Image stabilization by features tracking, *Proc. Int. Conf. Image Analysis and Process.*, pp. 665–667.

Chen, H., Liang, C., Peng, Y. & Chang, H. (2007). Integration of digital stabilizer with video codec for digital video cameras, *IEEE Trans. Circuits Syst. Video Technol.* **17**(7): 801–813.

Cho, W. & Hong, K. (2007). Affine motion based CMOS distortion analysis and CMOS digital image stabilization, *IEEE Trans. Consum. Electron.* **53**(3): 833–841.

Cho, W., Kim, D. & Hong, K. (2007). CMOS digital image stabilization, *IEEE Trans. Consum. Electron.* **53**(3): 979–986.

Engelsberg, A. & Schmidt, G. (1999). A comparative review of digital image stabilising algorithms for mobile video communications, *IEEE Trans. Consum. Electron.* **45**(3): 591–597.

Erturk, S. (2003). Digital image stabilization with sub-image phase correlation based global motion estimation, *IEEE Trans. Consum. Electron.* **49**(4): 1320–1325.

Gasteratos, A., Beltran, C., Metta, G. & Sandini, G. (2002). PRONTO: a system for mobile robot navigation via CAD-model guidance, *Microprocessors and Microsystems* **26**(1): 17–26.

Gasteratos, A. & Sandini, G. (2001). On the accuracy of the Eurohead, *Lira-lab technical report, LIRA-TR* **2**.

Horn, B. & Schunck, B. (1981). Determining optical flow, *Artificial Intelligence* **17**(1-3): 185–203.

Hsu, S., Liang, S. & Lin, C. (2005). A robust digital image stabilization technique based on inverse triangle method and background detection, *IEEE Trans. Consum. Electron.* **51**(2): 335–345.

Jin, J., Zhu, Z. & Xu, G. (2000). A stable vision system for moving vehicles, *IEEE Trans. on Intelligent Transportation Systems* **1**(1): 32–39.

Kinugasa, T., Yamamoto, N., Komatsu, H., Takase, S. & Imaide, T. (1990). Electronic image stabilizer for video camera use, *IEEE Trans. Consum. Electron.* **36**(3): 520–525.

Ko, S., Lee, S., Jeon, S. & Kang, E. (1999). Fast digital image stabilizer based on gray-coded bit-plane matching, *IEEE Trans. Consum. Electron.* **45**(3): 598–603.

Koenderink, J. & van Doorn, A. (1991). Affine structure from motion, *Journal of the Optical Society of America* **8**(2): 377–385.

Kurazume, R. & Hirose, S. (2000). Development of image stabilization system for remote operation of walking robots, *Proc. IEEE Int. Conf. on Robotics and Automation*, Vol. 2, pp. 1856–1861.

Lobo, J. & Dias, J. (2003). Vision and inertial sensor cooperation using gravity as a vertical reference, *IEEE Trans. Pattern Anal. Mach. Intell.* **25**(12): 1597–1608.

Locke, C. (1992). Software architecture for hard real-time applications: Cyclic executives vs. fixed priority executives, *Real-Time Systems* **4**(1): 37–53.

Lucas, B. & Kanade, T. (1981). An iterative image registration technique with an application to stereo vision, *Proc. DARPA Image Understanding Workshop*, Vol. 121, p. 130.

Lungarella, M., Metta, G., Pfeifer, R. & Sandini, G. (2003). Developmental robotics: a survey, *Connection Science* **15**(4): 151–190.

Marcenaro, L., Vernazza, G. & Regazzoni, C. (2001). Image stabilization algorithms for video-surveillance applications, *Proc. Int. Conf. Image Process.*, Vol. 1, pp. 349–352.

Morimoto, C. & Chellappa, R. (1998). Evaluation of image stabilization algorithms, *Proc. Int. Conf. Acoust., Speech, Signal Process.*, Vol. 5, pp. 2789–2792.

Nait-Ali, A. (2007). Genetic algorithms for blind digital image stabilization under very low SNR, *IEEE Trans. Consum. Electron.* **53**(3): 857–863.

OCERA project home page (2008). *http//www.ocera.org* .

Oshima, M., Hayashi, T., Fujioka, S., Inaji, T., Mitani, H., Kajino, J., Ikeda, K. & Komoda, K. (1989). VHS camcorder with electronic image stabilizer, *IEEE Trans. Consum. Electron.* **35**(4): 749–758.

Ovaska, S. & Valiviita, S. (1998). Angular acceleration measurement: A review, *IEEE Trans. Instrum. Meas.* **47**(5): 1211–1217.

Paik, J., Park, Y., Kim, D. & Co, S. (1992). An adaptive motion decision system for digital image stabilizer based on edge pattern matching, *IEEE Trans. Consum. Electron.* **38**(3): 607–616.

Pan, Z. & Ngo, C. (2005). Selective object stabilization for home video consumers, *IEEE Trans. Consum. Electron.* **51**(4): 1074–1084.

Panerai, F., Metta, G. & Sandini, G. (2000). Visuo-inertial stabilization in space-variant binocular systems, *Robotics and Autonomous Systems* **30**(1-2): 195–214.

Panerai, F., Metta, G. & Sandini, G. (2003). Learning visual stabilization reflexes in robots with moving eyes, *Neurocomputing* **48**: 323–338.

Samson, E., Laurendeau, D., Parizeau, M., Comtois, S., Allan, J. & Gosselin, C. (2006). The agile stereo pair for active vision, *Machine Vision and Applications* **17**(1): 32–50.

Tindell, K., Hansson, H. & Wellings, A. (1994). Analysing real-time communications: Controller area network (CAN), *Proc. 15 th Real-Time Systems Symposium*, Citeseer, pp. 259–263.

Tokyo, J. (1993). Control techniques for optical image stabilizing system, *IEEE Trans. Consum. Electron.* **39**(3): 461–466.

Trucco, E. & Verri, A. (1998). *Introductory Techniques for 3-D Computer Vision*, Prentice Hall PTR Upper Saddle River, NJ, USA.

Tyan, Y., Liao, S. & Chen, H. (2004). Video stabilization for a camcorder mounted on a moving vehicle, *IEEE Trans. on Vehicular Technology* **53**(6): 1636–1648.

Vella, F., Castorina, A., Mancuso, M. & Messina, G. (2002). Digital image stabilization by adaptive block motion vectors filtering, *IEEE Trans. Consum. Electron.* **48**(3): 796–801.

Welch, G. & Bishop, G. (2001). An introduction to the Kalman filter, *ACM SIGGRAPH 2001 Course Notes* .

Xu, L. & Lin, X. (2006). Digital image stabilization based on circular block matching, *IEEE Trans. Consum. Electron.* **52**(2): 566–574.

Zoroofi, R., Sato, Y., Tamura, S. & Naito, H. (1995). An improved method for MRI artifact correction due to translational motion in the imaging plane, *IEEE Trans. on Medical Imaging* **14**(3): 471–479.

Zufferey, J. & Floreano, D. (2006). Fly-inspired visual steering of an ultralight indoor aircraft, *IEEE Trans. Robot. Autom.* **22**(1): 137–146.

15

Real-time Stereo Vision Applications

Christos Georgoulas, Georgios Ch. Sirakoulis and Ioannis Andreadis
Laboratory of Electronics, Democritus University of Thrace
Xanthi, Greece

1. Introduction

Depth perception is one of the important tasks of a computer vision system. Stereo correspondence by calculating the distance of various points in a scene relative to the position of a camera allows the performance of complex tasks, such as depth measurements and environment reconstruction (Jain et al., 1995). The most common approach for extracting depth information from intensity images is by means of a stereo camera setup. The point-by-point matching between the two images from the stereo setup derives the depth images, or the so called disparity maps, (Faugeras, 1993). The computational demanding task of matching can be reduced to a one dimensional search, only by accurately rectified stereo pairs in which horizontal scan lines reside on the same epipolar plane, as shown in Figure 1. By definition, the epipolar plane is defined by the point P and the two camera optical centers O_L and O_R. This plane PO_LO_R intersects the two image planes at lines EP_1 and EP_2, which are called epipolar lines . Line EP_1 is passing through two points: E_L and P_L, and line EP_2 is passing through E_R and P_R respectively. E_L and E_R are called epipolar points and are the intersection points of the baseline O_LO_R with each of the image planes. The computational significance for matching different views is that for a point in the first image, its corresponding point in the second image must lie on the epipolar line, and thus the search space for a correspondence is reduced from 2 dimensions to 1 dimension. This is called the epipolar constraint. The difference on the horizontal coordinates of points P_L and P_R is the disparity. The disparity map consists of all disparity values of the image. Having extracted the disparity map, problems such as 3D reconstruction, positioning, mobile robot navigation, obstacle avoidance, etc, can be dealt with in a more efficient way (Murray & Jennings, 1997; Murray & Little, 2000).

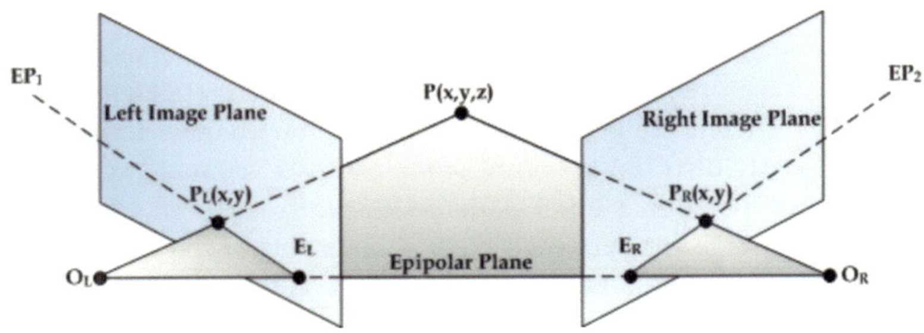

Fig. 1. Geometry of epipolar plane

Detecting conjugate pairs in stereo images is a challenging research problem known as the correspondence problem, i.e. to find for each point in the left image, the corresponding point in the right one (Barnard & Thompson, 1980). To determine a conjugate pair, it is necessary to measure the similarity of the points. The point to be matched should be distinctly different from its surrounding pixels. In order to minimise the number of false correspondences in the image pair, several constraints have been imposed. The uniqueness constraint (Marr & Poggio, 1979) requires that a given pixel from one image cannot correspond to more than one pixel on the other image. In the presence of occluded regions within the scene, it may be impossible at all to find a corresponding point. The ordering constraint (Baker & Binford, 1981) requires that if a pixel is located to the left of another pixel in image, i.e. left image, the corresponding pixels in right image must be ordered in the same manner, and vice versa, i.e. ordering of pixels is preserved across the images. The ordering constraint may be violated if an object in the scene is located much closer to the camera than the background, and one pixel corresponds to a point on the object while the other pixel corresponds to a point in the background. Finally , the continuity constraint (Marr & Poggio, 1979), which is valid only for scenarios in which smooth surfaces are reconstructed, requires that the disparity map should vary smoothly almost everywhere in the image. This constraint may be violated at depth discontinuities in the scene.

Three broad classes of techniques have been used for stereo matching: area-based (Di Stefano et al., 2004; Scharstein & Szelinski, 2002), feature-based (Venkateswar & Chellappa, 1995; Dhond & Aggarwal, 1989), and phase-based (Fleet et al., 1991; Fleet, 1994). Area-based algorithms use local pixel intensities as a distance measure and they produce dense disparity maps, i.e. process the whole area of the images. An important drawback of area-based techniques is the fact that uniform depth across a correlation window is assumed, which leads to false correspondences near object edges, especially when dealing with large windows. A compact framework was introduced by (Hirschmuller, 2001), where instead of using a large window several smaller neighbouring windows are used. Only the ones that contribute to the overall similarity measure in a consistent manner are taken into account. A left-right consistency check is imposed to invalidate uncertain correspondences. Accurate depth values at object borders are determined by splitting the corresponding correlation windows into two parts, and separately searching on both sides of the object border for the optimum similarity measure. These improvements of the classical area-based approach are demonstrated by (Hirschmuller, 2001) and in more detail by (Hirschmuller et al., 2002) to significantly improve the overall performance of three-dimensional reconstruction.

On the other hand, feature-based algorithms rely on certain points of interest. These points are selected according to appropriate feature detectors. They are more stable towards changes in contrast and ambient lighting, since they represent geometric properties of a scene. Feature-based stereo techniques allow for simple comparisons between attributes of the features being matched, and are hence faster than area-based matching methods. The major limitation of all feature-based techniques is that they cannot generate dense disparity maps, and hence they often need to be used in conjunction with other techniques. Because of the sparse and irregularly distributed nature of the features, the matching results should be augmented by an interpolation step if a dense disparity map of the scene is desired. Additionally, an extra stage for extensive feature detection in the two images is needed, which will increase the computational cost. Thus feature-based methods are not suitable for real-time applications.

In phase-based techniques the disparity is defined as the shift necessary to align the phase value of band-pass filtered versions of two images. In (Fleet et al., 1991) it is shown that phase-based methods are robust when there are smooth lighting variations between stereo images. It also shows that phase is predominantly linear, and hence reliable approximations to disparity can be extracted from phase displacement.
Real-time stereo vision techniques capable of addressing the stereo vision matching problem, producing disparity maps in real-time speeds, are presented in this chapter. While these techniques are based on many different approaches to detect similarities between image regions, all of them present real-time characteristics along with increased accuracy on the computed disparity map.

2. Real-Time Stereo Vision Implementations

Numerous applications require real-time extraction of 3D information. Many researchers have been focused in finding the optimum selection of tools and algorithms to obtain efficient results. The main characteristics of a real-time stereo vision implementation are the produced accuracy of the extracted disparity map, versus the frame rate throughput of such a system. There is always a trade off between disparity map accuracy and speed. Most of the applications require also a dense output. Software-based techniques cannot easily handle such requirements due to the serial behaviour. Real-time dense disparity output requires a significant amount of computational resources. Software-based techniques cannot easily handle such requirements due to the serial operation. Increasing the image size of the stereo pair, or the disparity levels range, can result in a dramatic reduction on the operating throughput. Thus, most of the recent research on real-time stereo vision techniques is oriented towards the use of a dedicated hardware platform. Hardware devices offer the use of parallelism, pipelining and many more design techniques, which result in efficient overall operation in image processing, presenting considerably better results compared to serial software-based solutions.

2.1 SAD-based Implementations

SAD-based implementations are the most favourable area-based techniques in real-time stereo vision, since they can be straightforwardly implemented in hardware. The calculations required in terms of design units are simple, since only summations and absolute values are performed. Parallel design units can be utilized in order to handle various disparity ranges, in order to reduce the computational time required. Area-based methods techniques involve window based operation, where small image windows are directly compared along corresponding epipolar lines according to a pixel-based similarity measure. Common similarity measures are the cross-correlation coefficient, the sum of absolute differences, or the sum of squared differences (Franke & Joos, 2000). Evaluations of various techniques using similarity measures are given by (Scharstein & Szelinski 2002; Hirscmuller & Scharstein, 2007). The mathematical formula of the SAD similarity measures is presented below:

$$SAD(i,j,d) = \sum_{\mu=-w}^{w} \sum_{\nu=-w}^{w} \left| I_l(i+\mu, j+\nu) - I_r(i+\mu, j-d+\nu) \right| \tag{1}$$

where I_l and I_r denote the left and right image pixel grayscale values, d is the disparity range, w is the window size and i, j are the coordinates (rows, columns) of the center pixel of the working window for which the similarity measures are computed. Once the SAD is computed for all pixels and for all disparity values, a similarity accumulator has been constructed for each pixel, which indicates the most likely disparity. In order to compute the disparity map a search in the SAD for all disparity values, (d_{min} up to d_{max}), is performed for every pixel. At the disparity range, (d_{min} up to d_{max}), where the SAD is minimum for a pixel, this value is given as the corresponding pixel value for disparity map:

$$D(i,j) = \underset{d \in [d_{\min}, d_{\max}]}{\arg\min} \; SAD(i,j,d) \tag{2}$$

The FPGA based architecture along with an off-the-self PCI board by (Niitsuma & Maruyama, 2005), uses an SAD-based technique to efficiently calculate optical flow. Dense vector maps can be generated by the proposed system at 840 frames per second for a 320x240, and at 30 frames per second for a 640x480 pixels stereo image pair correspondingly. A matching window of 7x7 pixels is used by the area-based technique, along with a maximum disparity range of 121 levels.

The stereo matching architecture presented by (Ambrosch et al., 2009) presents a cost-efficient hardware pipelined implementation of a real-time stereo vision using an optimised technique of the SAD computation. Disparity maps are calculated using 450x375 input images and a disparity range of up to 100 pixels at a rate of nearly 600 frames per second. Their results show that the device resource usage increases exponentially when increasing the desired frame rate. On the other hand, increasing the block size leads to a more linear increase of consumed logic elements due to their SAD optimized implementation.

Another implementation that uses a modified version of the SAD computation is the one presented by (Lee et al., 2005). Various versions of SAD algorithms are synthesized by the authors to determine resource requirements and performance. By decomposing a SAD correlator into column and row SAD calculator using buffers, a saving of around 50% is obtained in terms of resource usage of the FPGA device. Additionally, by using different shapes of matching windows, rather than rectangular ones, they reduced storage requirements without the expense of quality. Disparity maps at the rate of 122 frames per second are produced, for an image pair of 320x240 pixels spatial resolution, with 64 levels of disparity.

The FPGA based architecture presented in (Arias-Estrada & Xicotencatl, 2001) is able to produce dense disparity maps in real time. The architecture implements a local algorithm based on the SAD, aggregated in fixed windows. Parallel processing of the input data is performed by the proposed design architecture. An extension to the basic architecture is also proposed in order to compute disparity maps on more than 2 images. This method can process 320x240 pixels image pairs with 16 disparity levels at speeds reaching 71 frames per second.

A technique based on adaptive window aggregation method in conjunction with SAD is used in (Roh et al., 2004). It can process images of size up to 1024x1024 pixels with 32 disparity levels at 47 frames per second. The implemented window-based algorithms present low FPGA resource usage, along with noticeable performance in disparity map quality.

In (Niitsuma & Maruyama, 2004), a compact system for real-time detection of moving objects is proposed. Realization of optical flow computation and stereo vision by area-based matching on a single FPGA is addressed. By combining those features, moving objects as well as distances to the objects, can be efficiently detected. Disparity map computation at a

rate of 30 frames per second, for 640x480 pixels images, with 27 disparity levels, is achieved by the proposed system.
Finally, a slightly more complex implementation than the previous ones is proposed in (Hariyama et al., 2005). It is based on the SAD using adaptive sized windows. The proposed method iteratively refines the matching results by hierarchically reducing the window size. The results obtained by the proposed method are 10% better than that of the fixed-window method. The architecture is fully parallel and as a result all the pixels and all the windows are processed simultaneously. The speed for 64x64 pixel images with 8 bit grayscale precision and 64 disparity levels is 30 frames per second.
The SAD-based hardware implemented stereo vision implementations discussed above are summarized in Table 1 below.

Author	Frame rate (fps)	Image Size (pixels)	Disparity Range	Window Size (pixels)
Niitsuma & Maruyama ,2005	840	320×240	121	7×7
Ambrosch et al., 2009	599	450×375	100	9×9
Lee et al., 2005	122	320×240	64	16×16
Arias-Estrada & Xicotencatl, 2001	71	320×240	16	7×7
Roh et al., 2004	47	1024x1024	32	16×16
Niitsuma & Maruyama ,2004	30	640×480	27	7×7
Hariyama et al., 2005	30	64×64	64	8×8

Table 1. SAD-based Hardware Implementations

2.2 Phase-based Implementations

New techniques for stereo disparity estimation have been exhibited, in which disparity is expressed in terms of phase differences in the output of local, band-pass filters applied to the left and right views (Jenkin & Jepson, 1988; Sanger, 1988; Langley et al., 1990). The main advantage of such approaches is that the disparity estimates are obtained with sub-pixel accuracy, without requiring explicit sub-pixel signal reconstruction or sub-pixel feature detection and localization. The measurements may be used directly, or iteratively as predictions for further, more accurate, estimates. Because there are no restrictions to specific values of phase (i.e. zeros) that must first be detected and localized, the density of measurements is also expected to be high. Additionally the computations may be implemented efficiently in parallel (Fleet et al. 1991). Hardware implementation of such algorithms turned out to be much faster than software-based ones.
The PARTS reconfigurable computer (Woodfill & Herzen, 1991), consists of a 4x4 array of mesh-connected FPGAs. A phase algorithm based on the census transform, which mainly consists of bitwise comparisons and additions, is proposed. The algorithm reaches 42 frames per second for 320x240 pixels image pair, with 24 levels of disparity.
The method in (Masrani & MacClean, 2006), uses the so-called Local Weighted Phase-Correlation (LWPC), which combines the robustness of wavelet-based phase-difference methods with the basic control strategy of phase-correlation methods. Four FPGAs are used to perform image rectification and left-right consistency check to improve the quality of the produced disparity map. Real-time speeds reaching 30 frames per second for an image pair with 640x480 pixels with 128 levels of disparity. LWPC is also used in (Darabiha et al., 2006).

Again four FPGAs are used for the hardware implementation of the algorithm, reaching 30 frames per second for a 256x360 pixels image pair with 20 disparity levels.
The phase-based hardware implementations are presented in Table 2 below.

Author	Frame rate (fps)	Image Size (pixels)	Disparity Range
Woodfill & Herzen, 1991	42	320×240	24
Masrani & MacClean, 2006	30	640×480	128
Darabiha et al., 2006	30	256×360	20

Table 2. Phase-based Hardware Implementations

2.3 Disparity Map Refinement

The resulting disparity images are usually heavily corrupted. This type of random noise is introduced during the disparity value assignment stage. The disparity value assigned to some pixels does not correspond to the appropriate value. Hence, in a given window, some pixels might have been assigned with the correct disparity value and some others not. This can be considered as a type of random noise in the given window. Various standard filtering techniques, such as mean, median, Gaussian can not provide efficient refinement (Murino et al., 2001). Typical low-pass filters result in loss of detail and do not present adequate false matchings removal. Adaptive filtering is also unsuccessful, presenting similar results.

2.3.1 CA Filtering

Filtering using a cellular automata (CA) approach presents better noise removal with detail preservation and extremely easy, simple and parallel hardware implementation (Popovici & Popovici, 2002; Rosin, 2005).
Regarding CA, these are dynamical systems, where space and time are discrete and interactions are local and they can easily handle complicated boundary and initial conditions (Von Neumann, 1966; Wolfram, 1983). Following, a more formal definition of a CA will be presented (Chopard & Droz, 1998). In general, a CA requires:

1. a regular lattice of cells covering a portion of a d-dimensional space;
2. a set $\mathbf{C}(\vec{r},t)=\{C_1(\vec{r},t), C_2(\vec{r},t), \ldots, C_m(\vec{r},t)\}$ of variables attached to each site $\vec{r}$ of the lattice giving the local state of each cell at the time $t = 0, 1, 2, \ldots$;
3. a Rule $\boldsymbol{R}=\{R_1, R_2, \ldots, R_m\}$ which specifies the time evolution of the states $\mathbf{C}(\vec{r},t)$ in the following way:

$$C_j(\vec{r},t+1)=R_j\left(\mathbf{C}(\vec{r},t), \mathbf{C}(\vec{r}+\vec{\delta}_1,t), \mathbf{C}(\vec{r}+\vec{\delta}_2,t), \ldots, \mathbf{C}(\vec{r}+\vec{\delta}_q,t)\right) \qquad (3)$$

where $\vec{r}+\vec{\delta}_k$ designate the cells belonging to a given neighborhood of cell $\vec{r}$.
In the above definition, the Rule R is identical for all sites, and it is applied simultaneously to each of them, leading to a synchronous dynamics.
CA have been applied successfully to several image processing applications (Alvarez et al., 2005; Rosin, 2006; Lafe, 2000). CA are one of the computational structures best suited for a VLSI realization (Pries et al., 1986; Sirakoulis, 2004; Sirakoulis et al., 2003). Furthermore, the

CA approach is consistent with the modern notion of unified space-time. In computer science, space corresponds to memory and time to processing unit. In CA, memory (CA cell state) and processing unit (CA local Rule) are inseparably related to a CA cell (Toffoli & Margolus, 1987).

According to the disparity value range, every disparity map image is decomposed into a set of d images, where d is the range of the disparity values, a technique similar to, the so-called 'threshold decomposition'. Hence for a given image pair with i.e. 16 levels of disparity, 16 binary images are created, where C_1 image has logic ones on every pixel that has value 1 in the disparity map, and logic zeros elsewhere. C_2 image has ones on every pixel that has value 2 in the disparity map, and zeros elsewhere, and so on. The CA rules are applied separately on each C_d binary image and the resulting disparity map is further recomposed by the following formula:

$$D(i,j) = \sum C_d(i,j) \cdot d, \qquad d \in [d_{\min}, d_{\max}] \tag{4}$$

The CA rules can be selected in such way that they produce the maximum possible performance within the given operating windows. The main effect of this filtering is the rejection of a great portion of incorrect matches.

2.3.2 Occlusion and false matching detection

Occluded areas can also introduce false matches in the disparity map computation. There are three main classes of algorithms for handling occlusions: 1) methods that detect occlusions (Chang et al, 1991; Fua, 1993), 2) methods that reduce sensitivity to occlusions (Bhat & Nayar, 1998; Sara & Bajcsy, 1997), and 3) methods that model the occlusion geometry (Belhumeur, 1996; Birchfield & Tomasi, 1998). Considering the first class, left-right consistency checking may also be used to detect occlusion boundaries. Computing two disparity maps, one based on the correspondence from the left image to the right image, and the other based on the correspondence from the right image to the left image, inconsistent disparities are assumed to represent occluded regions in the scene. Left-right consistency checking is also known as the "two-views constraint". This technique is well suited to remove false correspondences caused by occluded areas within a scene (Fua, 1993). Due to its simplicity and overall good performance, this technique was implemented in many real-time stereo vision systems (Faugeras et al., 1993; Konolige, 1997; Matthies et al., 1995).

Using the left-right consistency checking, valid disparity values are considered, only those that are consistent in both disparity maps, i.e. those that do not lie within occluded areas. A pixel that lies within an occluded area will have different disparity value in the left disparity map, from its consistent pixel in the right disparity map. For example, a non-occluded pixel in the left disparity image must have a unique pixel with equally assigned disparity value in the right disparity map according to the following equations:

$$D_{\text{left-right}}(i,j) = D_{\text{right-left}}(i,j-d), \; (d = D_{\text{left-right}}(i,j)) \tag{5}$$

$$D_{\text{right-left}}(i,j) = D_{\text{left-right}}(i,j+d), \; (d = D_{\text{right-left}}(i,j)) \tag{6}$$

The same applies, for false matched points not exclusively due to occlusions, but due to textureless areas or sensor parameter variations. These points are assigned with a false disparity value during the disparity map assignment stage described by equation (2), since there might be more than one minimum SAD value for a given pixel, which leads to false disparity value assignment for that pixel. Thus, the disparity value assigned to some pixels does not correspond to the appropriate correct value. Performing this consistency check, the occluded pixel along with the false matched points within the scene can be derived.

3. Hardware Realization

Most of the real-time stereo vision techniques implementation relies on the use of an FPGA device. FPGAs provide with high processing rates, which is ideal for speed demanding applications. On the other hand, they offer high density designs with low cost demands, shorter time-to-market benefits, which enable them in many hardware-based system realizations. Compared to an ASIC device, their main advantage is the much lower level of NRE (Non-Recurring Engineering) costs, typically associated with ASIC design. Additionally, FPGAs provide extensive reconfigurability, since they can be rewired in the field to fix bugs, and much simpler design methodology compared to ASIC devices. Compared to a processor, their main advantage is the higher processing rate. This is due to the fact that FPGAs can customize the resources' allocation to meet the needs of a specific application, whereas processors have fixed functional units.

3.1 SAD-based Disparity Computation with CA post-filtering

The work by (Georgoulas et al., 2008), presents a hardware-efficient real-time disparity map computation system. A modified version of the SAD-based technique is imposed, using an adaptive window size for the disparity map computation. A CA filter is introduced to refine false correspondences, while preserving the quality and detail of the disparity map. The presented hardware provides very good processing speed at the expense of accuracy, with very good scalability in terms of disparity levels.

CA are discrete dynamical systems that can deal efficiently with image enhancement operations such as noise filtering (Haykin, 2001). More specifically, the reasons why CA filter can be ideally implemented by VLSI techniques are: (1) the CA generating rules have the property of native parallel processing; (2) the proposed 2-D CA cell structure with programmable additive rules is easily implemented by using AND/OR gates.

In area-based algorithms the search is performed over a window centered on a pixel. However, a major issue is that small windows produce very noisy results, especially for low textured areas, whereas large windows fail to preserve image edges and fine detail. Thus, it is beneficial to estimate a measure of local variation, in terms of pixel grayscale value, over the image using variable sized windows, in order to obtain more efficient disparity map evaluation. The measure of a pixel local variation in a support window is a simple statistic of the intensity differences between neighboring pixels in the window.

This first step consists of calculating the local variation of image windows for the reference (left) image. Local variation (LV) is calculated according to the following formula:

$$LV(p) = \sum_{i=1}^{N}\sum_{j=1}^{N}\left|I(i,j) - \mu\right| \quad , where\ \mu = average\ grayscale\ value\ of\ image\ window \tag{7}$$

where the local variation for a given window central pixel p is calculated according to the neighboring pixel grayscale values. *N* is the selected square window size, in this case, 2 or 5. In the case of a 2x2 window the local variation is calculated for the upper left pixel. Initially the local variation over a window of 2x2 pixels is calculated and points with smaller local variation than a certain threshold value are marked for further processing. The local variation over a 5x5 range is computed for the marked points and is then compared to a second threshold. Windows presenting smaller variation than the second threshold are marked for larger area processing. To obtain optimum results various thresholds configurations can be manually selected.

The overall architecture is realised on a single FPGA device of the Stratix II family of Altera devices, with a maximum operating frequency of 256 MHz. Real time disparity maps are extracted at a rate of 275 frames per second for a 640x480 pixels resolution image pair with 80 levels of disparity. The hardware architecture is depicted in Figure 2. The module operates in a parallel-pipelined manner. The serpentine memory block is used to temporarily store the pixel grayscale values during the processing of the image. The serpentine memory block is used to increase processing speed. As the working windows move over the image, overlapping pixels exist between adjacent windows. The serpentine memory architecture is used to temporarily store overlapping pixels in order to reduce the clock cycles needed to load image pixels into the module (Gasteratos et al., 2006). CA filtering design is most efficient when implemented in hardware, due to the highly parallel independent processing. CA can be designed in a parallel structure, which results in real-time processing speeds.

For a disparity range of 80 and a maximum working window of 7x7, on the first scanline of the image, after an initial latency period of 602 clock cycles, where the set of registers for the right image requires to store 80 overlapping 7x7 working windows, (49+7*79=602), output is given every 7 clock cycles. Every time the working window moves to the next scanline, after an initial latency of 7 clock cycles which are the only new pixels due to window overlapping with the previous scanline, output is given once every clock cycle. By using an FPGA device operating at 256MHz for the CA-based approach, a 1Mpixel disparity map can be extracted in 11.77 msec, i.e. 85 frames per second. The relationship between the number of frames processed per second and the processed image width, assuming square images and a disparity range of 80 is presented in Figure 3.

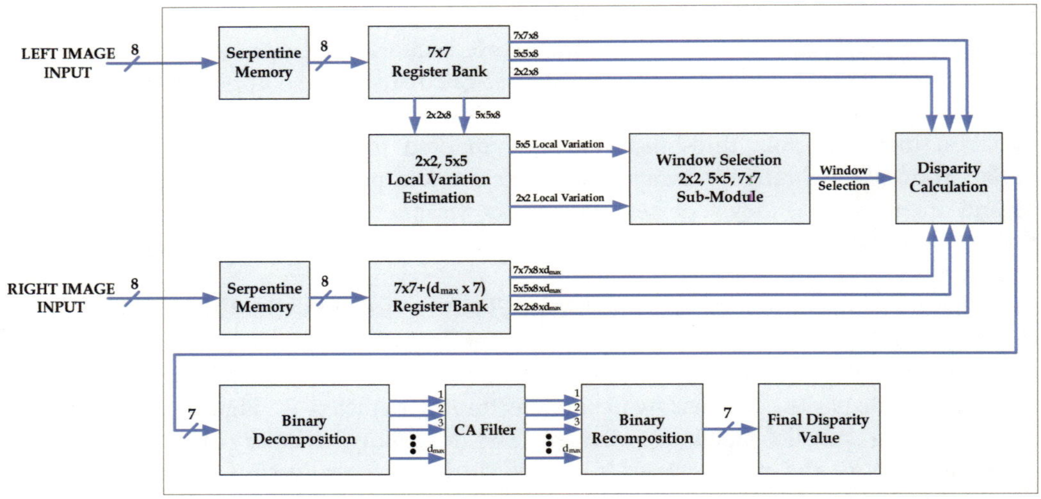

Fig. 2. FPGA Design (Georgoulas et al., 2008)

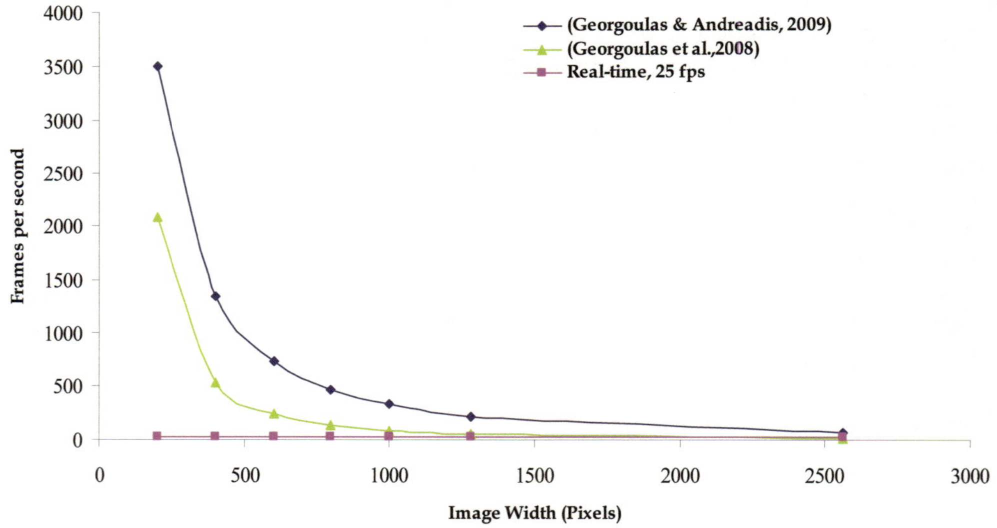

Fig. 3. Frame rate output versus image width

3.2 Occlusion-aware Disparity Computation

In (Georgoulas & Andreadis, 2009) a SAD window based technique using full color RGB images as well as an occlusion detection approach to remove false matchings are employed. The architecture is based on fully parallel-pipelined blocks in order to achieve maximum processing speed. Depending on the required operating disparity range the module can be parameterized, to adapt to the given configuration, in order to obtain efficient throughput rate. Both from qualitative and quantitative terms, concerning the quality of the produced disparity map and the frame rate output of the module, a highly efficient method dealing with the stereo correspondence problem is presented.

The overall architecture is realised on a single FPGA device of the Stratix IV family of Altera devices, with a maximum operating frequency of 511 MHz. Real-time speeds rated up to 768 frames per second for a 640x480 pixel resolution image pair with 80 disparity levels, are achieved, which enable the proposed module for real stereo vision applications. The relationship between the number of frames processed per second and the processed image size assuming square images, for an operating range of 80 disparity levels, is presented in Figure 3. The hardware architecture is shown in Figure 4.

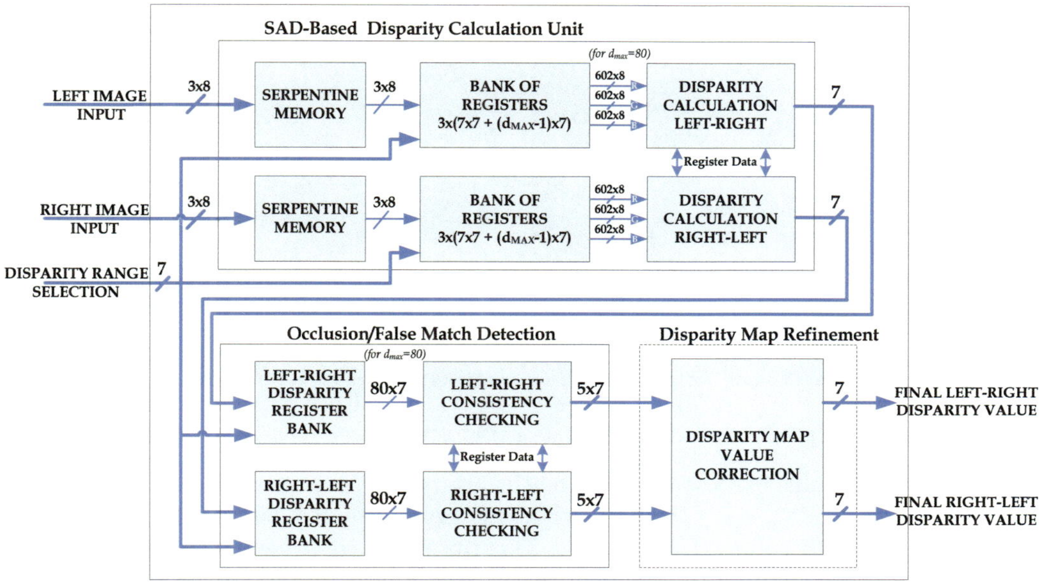

Fig. 4. FPGA Design (Georgoulas & Andreadis, 2009)

3.3 FPGA device specifications

The architectures by (Georgoulas et al., 2008; Georgoulas & Andreadis, 2009) have been implemented using Quartus II schematic editor by Altera. Both approaches have been then simulated to prove functionality, and once tested, finally mapped on FPGA devices.
The analytical specifications of the target devices are given in Table 3. As it can be found out, space efficiency while maintaining high operating frequencies, is achieved.

Author	Device	Total Registers	Total ALUTs (%)	Total LABs (%)	Total Pins (%)
Georgoulas et al., 2008	Altera EP2S180F1 020C3	5,208	59 (84,307/143,520)	83 (7,484/8,970)	3 (25/743)
Georgoulas & Andreadis, 2009	Altera EP4SGX290 HF35C2	15,442	59 (143,653/244,160)	74 (9,036/12,208)	10 (70/660)

Table 3. Specifications of target devices

4. Experimental Results

In (Georgoulas et al., 2008) the disparity map is computed using an adaptive technique where the support window for each pixel is selected according to the local variation over it. This technique enables less false correspondences during the matching process while preserving high image detail in regions with low texture and among edges. The post filtering step comprising the CA filter enables satisfactory filtering of any false reconstructions in the image, while preserving all the necessary details that comprise the disparity map depth values. The resulting disparity maps are presented in Figure 5.

(a) (b)

Fig. 5. Resulting disparity map for (a) Corridor (b) Cones image pair, respectively

Considering the occlusion-based approach satisfactory improvement in the accuracy of the resulting disparity maps is obtained, while preserving all the necessary details of the disparity map depth values. The resulting disparity maps are presented in Figure 6 along with original image pairs for (a) Tsukuba and (b) Cones.

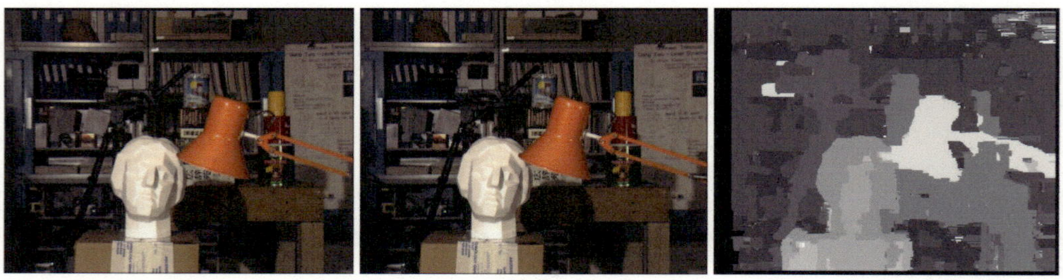

(a)

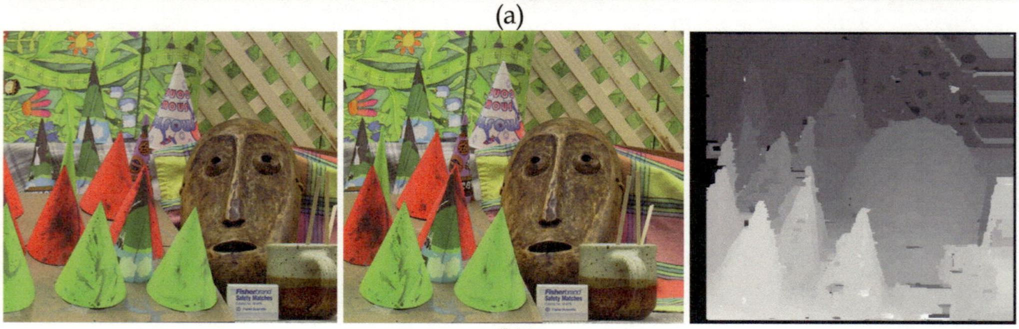

(b)

Fig. 6. Resulting disparity map for (a) Tsukuba (b) Cones image pair, respectively

Quantitative results under various configurations can be seen in Table 4. The Cov (coverage) term, shown in Table 4, states the percentage of the image total pixels, for which a disparity value has been assigned. The Acc (accuracy) term states the ratio of the pixels given a correct disparity value (as compared with the ground truth) to the total assigned pixels.

Approach		Tsukuba		Cones		Teddy	
		Acc(%)	Cov(%)	Acc(%)	Cov(%)	Acc(%)	Cov(%)
Georgoulas et al., 2008	Initial Disparity Map	55	88	48	65	90	49
	Refined Disparity Map	88	51	72	56	93	47
Georgoulas & Andreadis, 2009	Initial Disparity Map	94	77	99	80	98	77
	Refined Disparity Map	95	91	94	93	92	95

Table 4. Quantitative results of the proposed module under various configurations

5. Conclusions

The stereo correspondence problem comprises an active wide range of research. Many efforts have been made towards efficient solutions to address the various issues of stereo matching. As the improvements in computational resources steadily increase, the demand for real-time applications is getting compulsory. This chapter focuses on the latest improvements in the area of real-time stereo vision.

Area-based techniques prove to be more appropriate, handling the stereo correspondence problem aiming at real-time speeds. Their straightforward implementation in hardware enables them suitable in numerous applications such as high-speed tracking and mobile robots, object recognition and navigation, biometrics, vision-guided robotics, three-dimensional modelling and many more. Phase-based techniques also allow for efficient realization of such systems, requiring though slightly more complex design methodologies.

Additionally, it must be noted that there are many other stereo vision techniques that were not covered by this work, due to the fact that they are mainly targeted in software-based platforms presenting higher processing times, not suitable for real-time operations.

FPGA implementations handling the stereo matching problem can be a promising alternative towards real-time speeds. Their uniqueness relies on their architecture and the design methodologies available. Parallel-pipelined processing is able to present great computational capabilities, providing with proper scalability opposed to the serial behaviour of most software-based techniques. On the other hand considering their significantly small volume, low cost, and extensive reconfigurability, they can be oriented towards embedded applications where space and power are significant concerns.

6. References

Alvarez, G.; Hernández Encinas, A.; Hernández Encinas, L.; Martín del Rey, A. (2005). A secure scheme to share secret color images, *Computer Physics Communications*, Vol. 173, No. 1-2, (December 2005) 9-16, ISSN :0010-4655.

Ambrosch, K.; Humenberger,M.; Kubinger, W.; Steininger, A. (2009). SAD-Based Stereo Matching Using FPGAs, In : *Embedded Computer Vision : Advances in Pattern Recognition*, (Ed., Branislav Kisacanin, Shuvra S. Bhattacharyya, Sek Chai), pp 121-138, Springer London, ISBN:978-1-84800-303-3.

Arias-Estrada, M. ; Xicotencatl, J.M. (2001). Multiple stereo matching using an extended architecture. *Proceedings of the 11th International Conference on Field-Programmable Logic and Applications*, pp. 203-212, ISBN:3-540-42499-7, Belfast Northern Ireland, August 2001, Springer, London.

Baker, H. H.; Binford, T. O. (1981). Depth from Edge and Intensity Based Stereo. *Proceedings of the 7th International Joint Conference on Artificial Intelligence*, pp. 631–636, Vancouver, Canada, August 1981, William Caufmann, Canada.

Barnard, S.T.; Thompson, W.B. (1980). Disparity analysis of images, *IEEE Transactions on Pattern Analysis and Machine Intelligence*, Vol. 2, No. 4, (July 1980) 333–340, ISSN: 0162-8828.

Belhumeur, P.N. (1996). A Bayesian Approach to Binocular Stereopsis. *International Journal of Computer Vision*, Vol. 19, No. 3, (1996) 237-260, ISSN:0920-5691.

Bhat, D.N.; Nayar, S.K. (1998). Ordinal Measures for Image Correspondence. *IEEE Transactions on Pattern Analysis and Machine Intelligence*, Vol. 20, No. 4, (April 1998) pp. 415-423, ISSN:0162-8828.

Birchfield, S.; Tomasi, C. (1998). Depth Discontinuities by Pixel-to- Pixel Stereo. *Proceedings of the 6th IEEE International Conference on Computer Vision*, pp. 1073-1080, ISBN: 8173192219, Bombay, India, January 1998, Narosa Pub. House, New Delhi.

Chang, C.; Chatterjee, S.; Kube, P.R. (1991). On an Analysis of Static Occlusion in Stereo Vision. *Proceedings of IEEE Conference on Computer Vision and Pattern Recognition*, pp. 722-723, ISBN:0-8186-2148-6, Maui, USA, June 1991.

Chopard, B.; Droz, M. (1998). *Cellular Automata Modeling of Physical Systems*, Cambridge University Press, ISBN-13:9780521673457, ISBN-10:0521673453, Cambridge.

Darabiha, A. ; Maclean, J.W. ; Rose, J. (2006): Reconfigurable hardware implementation of a phase-correlation stereo algorithm. *Machine Vision and Applications*, Vol. 17, No. 2, (March 2006) 116–132, ISSN:0932-8092.

Dhond, U. R.; Aggarwal, J. K. (1989). Structure from Stereo - A Review, *IEEE Transactions on Systems, Man, and Cybernetics*, Vol. 19, No. 6, (November/December 1989) 1489-1510, ISSN:0018-9472.

Di Stefano, L.; Marchionni, M.; Mattoccia, S. (2004). A fast area-based stereo matching algorithm, *Proceedings of the 15th International Conference on Vision Interface*, pp. 983-1005, Calgary Canada, October 2004,

Faugeras, O. (1993). *Three Dimensional Computer Vision: a geometric viewpoint*, MIT Press, ASIN:B000OQHWZG, Cambridge, MA.

Faugeras, O. ; Vieville, T.; Theron, E. ; Vuillemin, J. ; Hotz, B. ; Zhang, Z. ; Moll, L. ; Bertin, P. ; Mathieu, H. ; Fua, P. ; Berry G. ; Proy, C. (1993b). Real-time correlation-based stereo: algorithm, implementations and application. *Technical Report RR 2013*, INRIA, 1993.

Fleet, D.J. (1994). Disparity from local weighted phase-correlation, *Proceedings of the IEEE International Conference on Systems, Man, and Cybernetics,* pp. 48-54, ISBN:0-7803-2129-4 1994, October 1994, San Antonio, TX, USA.

Fleet, D.J.; Jepson, A.D. ; Jepson, M. (1991). Phase-based disparity measurement, *CVGIP: Image Understanding,* Vol. 53, No. 2, (March 1991) 198-210, ISSN:1049-9660.

Franke, U.; Joos, A. (2000). Real-time Stereo Vision for Urban Traffic Scene Understanding, *Proceedings of the IEEE Intelligent Vehicles Symposium,* pp. 273-278, ISBN: 0-7803-6363-9, Deaborn, MI, October 2000.

Fua, P. (1993). A Parallel Stereo Algorithm that Produces Dense Depth Maps and Preserves Image Features. *Machine Vision and* Applications, Vol. 6, No. 1, (December 1993) 35-49, ISSN :0932-8092.

Gasteratos, I.; Gasteratos, A.; Andreadis, I. (2006). An Algorithm for Adaptive Mean Filtering and Its Hardware Implementation, *Journal of VLSI Signal Processing,* Vol. 44, No. 1-2, (August 2006) 63-78, ISSN:0922-5773.

Georgoulas, C.; Andreadis, I. (2009). A real-time occlusion aware hardware structure for disparity map computation. *Proceedings of the 15th International Conference on Image Analysis and Processing,* In press, Salerno, Italy, September 2009, Salerno, Italy, Springer, Germany.

Georgoulas, C.; Kotoulas, L.; Sirakoulis, G.; Andreadis, I.; Gasteratos, A. (2008). Real-Time Disparity Map Computation Module. *Journal of Microprocessors & Microsystems,* Vol. 32, No. 3, (May 2008) 159-170. ISSN:0141-9331.

Hariyama, M.; Sasaki, H.; Kameyama, M. (2005). Architecture of a stereo matching VLSI processor based on hierarchically parallel memory access. *IEICE Transactions on Information and Systems,* Vol. E88-D, No. 7, (2005) 1486–1491, ISSN: 1745-1361.

Haykin, S. (2001). *Adaptive Filter Theory,* forth edition, Prentice-Hall, ISBN:0-13-090126-1, Englewood Cliffs, NJ.

Hirschmueller, H. (2001). Improvements in real-time correlation-based stereo vision. *Procedings of the IEEE Workshop on Stereo and Multi-Baseline Vision,* pp. 141, ISBN:0-7695-1327-1, Kauai, Hawaii, December 2001.

Hirschmuller H.; Scharstein, D. (2007). Evaluation of cost functions for stereo matching. *Proceedings of the International Conference on Computer Vision and Pattern Recognition,* volume 1, pp. 1–8, ISBN: 1-4244-1180-7, Minneapolis, MN, June 2007.

Hirschmuller, H.; Innocent, P.; Garibaldi, J. (2002). Real-Time Correlation-Based Stereo Vision with Reduced Border Errors. *International Journal of Computer Vision,* Vol. 47, No. 1-3, (April 2002) 229-246, ISSN: 0920-5691.

Jain, R.; Kasturi, R.; Schunck, B.G. (1995). *Machine Vision,* first edition, McGraw-Hill, ISBN:0-07-032018-7, New York.

Jenkin, M. ; Jepson, A.D. (1988): The measurements of binocular disparity, In: *Computational Processes in Human Vision,* (Ed.) Z. Pylyshyn, Ablex Publ. New Jersey.

Konolige, K. (1997). Small vision systems: Hardware and implementation. Proceeding of the 8th International Symposium on Robotics Research, pp. 203-212, Hayama, Japan, Springer, London.

Lafe, O. (2000). *Cellular Automata Transforms: Theory and Applications in Multimedia Compression, Encryption and Modeling,* Kluwer Academic Publishers, Norwell, MA.

Langley, K. ; Atherton, T.J. ; Wilson, R.G. ; Larcombe, M.H.E. (1990). Vertical and horizontal disparities from phase. *Proceeding of the 1st European Conference on Computer Vision*, pp. 315-325, Antibes, 1990, Springer-Verlag.

Lee, Su.; Yi, J.; Kim, J. (2005). Real-time stereo vision on a reconfigurable system, *Lecture Notes in Computer Science : Embedded Computer Systems*, 299–307, Springer, ISBN:978-3-540-26969-4.

Marr, D.; Poggio, T. (1979). A Computational Theory of Human Stereo Vision. *Proceedings of Royal Society of London. Series B, Biological Sciences*, pp. 301–328, May 1979, London.

Masrani, D.K.; MacLean, W.J. (2006). A real-time large disparity range stereo-system using FPGAs, *Proceedings of the IEEE International Conference on Computer Vision Systems*, pp. 13-13, ISBN:0-7695-2506-7, New York, USA, January 2006, (2006).

Matthies, L.; Kelly, A.; Litwin, T. ; Tharp, G. (1995). Obstacle detection for unmanned ground vehicles: A progress report. *Proceedings of the Intelligent Vehicles '95 Symposium*, ISBN:0-7803-2983-X, pp. 66-71, Detroit, MI, USA, September 1995.

Murino, V.; Castellani, U.; Fusiello, A. (2001). Disparity Map Restoration by Integration of Confidence in Markov Random Fields Models, *Proceedings of the IEEE International Conference on Image Processing*, ISBN:0-7803-6725-1, pp. 29-32, Thessaloniki, Greece, October 2001.

Murray, D.; Jennings, C. (1997). Stereo vision based mapping for a mobile robot, *Proceedings of the IEEE International Conference on Robotics and Automation*, 1997, ISBN:0-7803-3612-7, pp. 1694-1699, Albuquerque, NM, USA, April 1997.

Murray, D.; Little, J.J. (2000). Using real-time stereo vision for mobile robot navigation, *Journal of Autonomous Robots*, Vol. 8, No. 2, (April 2000) 161-171, ISSN:0929-5593.

Niitsuma, H.; Maruyama, T. (2004). Real-time detection of moving objects, In: *Lecture Notes in Computer Science : Field Programmable Logic and Applications*, 1155–1157, Springer, ISBN:978-3-540-22989-6.

Niitsuma, H.; Maruyama, T. (2005). High-speed computation of the optical flow, In: *Lecture Notes in Computer Science : Image Analysis and Processing*, 287–295, Springer, ISBN:978-3-540-28869-5.

Popovici, A.; Popovici, D. (2002). Cellular automata in image processing, *Proceedings of the 15th International Symposium on Mathematical Theory of Networks and Systems*, 6 pages, Indiana, USA, August 2002.

Pries, W.; McLeod, R.D.; Thanailakis, A.; Card, H.C. (1986). Group properties of cellular automata and VLSI applications, *IEEE Transaction on Computers*, Vol. C-35, No. 12, (December 1986) 1013-1024, ISSN :0018-9340.

Roh, C.; Ha, T.; Kim, S.; Kim, J. (2004). Symmetrical dense disparity estimation: algorithms and FPGAs implementation. *Proceedings of the IEEE International Symposium on Consumer Electronics*, pp. 452-456, ISBN:0-7803-8527-6, Reading, UK, September 2004.

Rosin, P.L. (2005). Training cellular automata for image processing, *Proceedings of the 14th Scandinavian Conference on Image Analysis*, ISBN:0302-9743, pp. 195-204, Joensuu, Finland, June 2005, Springer.

Rosin, P.L. (2006). Training Cellular Automata for Image Processing, *IEEE Transactions on Image Processing*, Vol. 15, No. 7, (July 2006) 2076-2087, ISSN:1057-7149.

Sanger, T. (1988). Stereo disparity computation using Gabor filters. *Journal of Biological Cybernetics*, Vol 59, No. 6, (October 1988) 405-418, ISSN:0340-1200.

Sara, R.; Bajcsy, R. (1997). On Occluding Contour Artifacts in Stereo Vision. *Proceedings of Computer Vision and Pattern Recognition*, ISBN:0-8186-7822-4, pp. 852-857, San Huan, Puerto Rico, June 1997.

Scharstein, D.; Szeliski, R. (2002). A Taxonomy and Evaluation of Dense Two-Frame Stereo Correspondence Algorithms, *International Journal of Computer Vision*, Vol. 47, No. 1, (April 2002) 7–42, ISSN:0920-5691.

Sirakoulis, G.Ch. (2004). A TCAD system for VLSI implementation of the CVD process using VHDL. *Integration, the VLSI Journal*, Vol. 37, No. 1, (February 2004) 63-81, ISSN:0167-9260.

Sirakoulis, G.Ch.; Karafyllidis, I.; Thanailakis, A. (2003). A CAD system for the construction and VLSI implementation of Cellular Automata algorithms using VHDL. *Microprocessors and Microsystems*, Vol. 27, No. 8, (September 2003) 381-396, ISSN:0141-9331.

Toffoli, T.; Margolus, N. (1987). *Cellular Automata Machines: A New Environment for Modeling*, MIT Press, Cambridge, MA.

Venkateswar, V.; Chellappa, R. (1995). Hierarchical Stereo and Motion Correspondence Using Feature Groupings, *International Journal of Computer Vision*, Vol. 15, No. 3, (July 1995) 245-269, ISSN:0920-5691

Von Neumann, J. (1966). *Theory of Self-Reproducing Automata*, University of Illinois Press, Urbana.

Wolfram, S. (1993). Statistical Mechanics of Cellular Automata, *Journal of Review of Modern Physics*, Vol. 55, No. 3, (July 1983) 601-644.

Woodfill, J.; Von Herzen, B. (1997). Real-time stereo vision on the PARTS reconfigurable computer, *Proceedings of the 5th IEEE Symposium on FPGAs Custom Computing Machines*, ISBN:0-8186-8159-4, Napa Valley, CA, USA, April 1997.

16

Robot vision using 3D TOF systems

Stephan Hussmann and Torsten Edeler
Westcoast University of Applied Sciences
Germany

1. Introduction

Consistent 3D imaging of robot surroundings is extremely useful for aiding navigation, and a lot of research effort has been applied to propose good solutions to this challenge. In principle there are three main methods used to acquire 3D information using vision-based systems: structure from motion (SfM) and stereo vision (SV) systems, laser range scanners (LRS) and time-of-flight (TOF) cameras.

SfM and SV systems usually rely on establishing correspondences between two images taken simultaneously (Faugeras, 1993), or taken by one camera at different times and places (Oliensis, 2000). Stereo cameras introduce physical restrictions on the robot due to the need for camera separation. Further, stereo cameras depend on texture matching from both camera images for range estimation. This produces a rather sparse and unevenly distributed data set. Due to the allocation problem dynamic tracking of objects is not an easy task (Hussmann & Liepert, 2009). SfM techniques must deal with correspondence, and also uncertainty about the position at which each image is taken, and dynamic changes that may occur in the time between the two images.

LRSs deliver one scanning line of accurate distance measurements often used for navigation tasks (Nuechter et al., 2003). LRSs measure distances at a coarse grid across the range sensor field-of-view, also providing sparse data sets. The major disadvantage of LRS systems is the use of mechanical components and that they do not deliver 3D range data at one image capture. In dynamical scenes the range data has to be corrected due to the laser scan process. They also do not deliver any intensity or colour information of the objects. Some researchers have mounted both LRS and camera on the same robot, and integrated the data to give both image and range information (Ho & Jarvis, 2008).

TOF cameras (Blanc et al., 2004 ; Schwarte et al., 1997) combine the advantage of active range sensors and camera based approaches as they provide a 2D image of intensity and exact (not estimated) distance values in real-time for each pixel. No data integration is needed since range and intensity measurements are made at each pixel. Compared to SV systems TOF cameras can deal with prominent parts of rooms such as walls, floors, and ceilings even if they are not structured. In addition to the 3D point cloud, contour and flow detection in the image plane yields motion information that can be used for applications such as car or person tracking (Hussmann et al., 2008). Compared to an LRS all range data are captured at one time between different object sample points. In conclusion it can be said

that TOF cameras are the most suitable 3D imaging systems for robot vision as they are able to deliver 3D dynamic information of objects.
Because of the enormous progress in TOF-vision systems, nowadays 3D matrix cameras can be manufactured und be used for many application such as robotic, automotive, industrial, medical and multimedia applications. Due to the increasing demand of safety requirements in the automotive industry it can be assumed that the TOF-camera market will grow and the unit price of these systems in the mass production will drop down to ca. 100 € (Hussmann & Hess, 2006).
For all application areas new accurate and fast algorithms for 3D object recognition and classification are needed. As now commercial 3D-TOF cameras are available at a reasonable price the number of research projects is expected to increase significantly. One early example of using a TOF-camera based on the Photonic-Mixer-Devices (PMD)-Technology for 3D object recognition in TOF data sets are presented in (Hess et al., 2003). In this paper the transition from a general model of the system to specific applications such as intelligent airbag control and robot assistance in surgery are demonstrated. A more current example in using a PMD-TOF camera on a robot system, highlighting the advantages of TOF- compared to SV-vision systems, is reported in (Hussmann & Liepert, 2009).
This book chapter is structured as follows. In Section II we derive the basics of PMD TOF vision systems and expose the issues which motivate a new approach for robot vision systems. In Section III one exemplary robot application demonstrates the advantage of 3D-TOF vision systems based on the PMD-technology over the other vision-based systems. Concluding remarks will summarize the paper.

2. Basics of PMD TOF vision systems

2.1 Operating principle

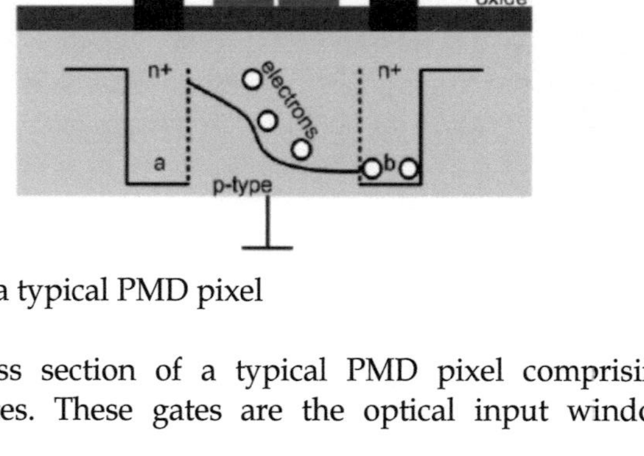

Fig. 1. Cross section of a typical PMD pixel

Fig. 1 shows the cross section of a typical PMD pixel comprising two symmetrical, transparent photo gates. These gates are the optical input window for the receiving modulated optical echo P_{opt}. They are isolated from the p-doped substrate by a SiO_2 - or Si_3N_4 – isolation layer (channel stop) and bounded on the left and right side by n^+ - diffusion readout gates. The photo gates are controlled by the modulation voltage u_m and the offset voltage U_0. The schematic potential distribution in the p-doped substrate between the photo gates is shown in Fig. 1 for a negative modulation voltage u_m.

A PMD pixel may be understood as a modulation controlled photo charge distributer (photonic mixer). In principle the PMD pixel works like a seesaw for electrons while controlling its motion by means of polarity and slope of the seesaw. If no modulated light is received the photo generated charges symmetrically drift to both readout gates *a* and *b*. If modulated light is received the photo generated charges drift only to readout gate *b*, when the modulated light and the modulation voltage have a phase difference of 180° (see Fig. 1). If the phase difference is 0° the photo generated charges drift only to readout gate *a*.

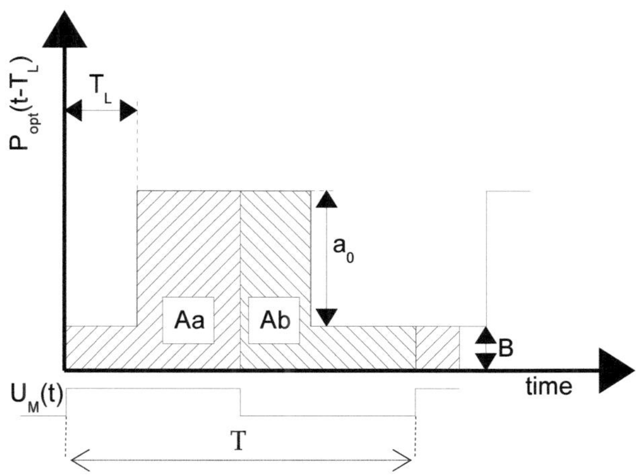

Fig. 2. Correlation process between the received optical echo P_{opt} and the modulation voltage u_m for one single modulation period

The readout gates *a* and *b* are each connected to an integration capacitor. Hence the corresponding voltages U_a and U_b can be expressed as a correlation function between the optical echo $P_{opt}(t-T_L)$ and the modulation voltage $u_m(t)$ over the integration time T_{int}. State of the art is to use continuous wave (CW) modulation with square waves for TOF cameras with a typical modulation frequency of 20 MHz. Hence the modulation voltage can be easily generated digitally with a high accuracy and stability using programmable logic devices (PLDs) such as complex programmable logic devices (CPLD) or field programmable gate arrays (FPGA) (Hussmann et al., 2008).

Fig. 2 illustrates the correlation process for one single modulation period *T* for the two square waves $P_{opt}(t-T_L)$ and $u_m(t)$. The modulation voltage $u_m(t)$ is defined as follows:

$$u_m(t) = \begin{cases} 1, & \text{for } 0 \le t - N \cdot T \le T/2 \\ 0, & \text{for } T/2 < t - N \cdot T \le T \end{cases}, \qquad N = 0,1,2... \tag{1}$$

T_L is the 'time-of-flight' time for the light (camera-object-camera), B is the received unmodulated background light and a_0 is the amplitude of the received modulated light. U_a and U_b are then proportional to the areas A_a and A_b as shown in Fig. 2. If the complete integration time T_{int} (corresponds to several hundreds or thousands of periods) has taken into account, U_a and U_b can be written as:

$$U_a(T_L) = K \cdot \int_0^{T_{\text{int}}} P_{opt}(t - T_L) \cdot u_m(t) dt = K \cdot \frac{T_{\text{int}}}{T} \cdot A_a(T_L) \tag{2}$$

and

$$U_b(T_L) = K \cdot \int_0^{T_{\text{int}}} P_{opt}(t - T_L) \cdot u_m(t - T/2) dt = K \cdot \frac{T_{\text{int}}}{T} \cdot A_b(T_L) \tag{3}$$

The conversion gain K converts the received optical energy into a voltage. The integration time T_{int} does not have to be necessarily a multiple of the single period time T as the number of periods integrated over the integration time is in the range of hundreds to thousands. Looking at Fig. 2 it can be noticed that U_a and U_b are always a positive voltage. To remove the influence of the background light the difference of ΔU_{ab} has to be determined:

$$\Delta U_{ab}(T_L) = U_a - U_b = K \cdot \frac{T_{\text{int}}}{T} \cdot \left(A_a(T_L) - A_b(T_L) \right) \tag{4}$$

ΔU_{ab} relates to the distance value of a PMD pixel. The sum of U_a and U_b corresponds to all received and converted photons. Hence this sum is equivalent to the grey level value of standard CCD/CMOS video cameras:

$$\Sigma U_{ab} = U_a + U_b = K \cdot \frac{T_{\text{int}}}{T} \cdot (A_a + A_b) = K \cdot \int_0^{T_{\text{int}}} P_{opt}(t - T_L) dt \tag{5}$$

Equation (4) and (5) demonstrate the advantage of the PMD technology compared to other range measurement systems such as SV systems or LRS. The PMD pixel is a TOF vision system with inherent suppression of uncorrelated light signals such as sun light or other modulated light disturbances. More advantages of a PMD TOF vision system are the acquisition of the grey level and range data in each pixel without high computational cost and any moving components as well as the monocular setup.

2.2 Range image calculation

As mention in the last section the range value corresponds to ΔU_{ab}. First the 'time-of-flight' time for the light T_L has to be determined. Two different solutions for equation (4) are needed to find T_L. Looking at Fig. 2 a mathematical description for U_a and U_b can be derived. Two cases have to be taken into account to determine the mathematical description. U_{a1} and U_{b1} are as follows for the first case ($0 \le T_L < T/2$):

$$U_{a1}(T_L) = K \cdot \frac{T_{\text{int}}}{T} \cdot \left[B \cdot \frac{T}{2} + a_0 \cdot \left(\frac{T}{2} - T_L \right) \right] \quad \text{for } 0 \le T_L < T/2 \tag{6}$$

and

$$U_{b1}(T_L) = K \cdot \frac{T_{\text{int}}}{T} \cdot \left[B \cdot \frac{T}{2} + a_0 \cdot T_L \right] \quad \text{for } 0 \le T_L < T/2 \tag{7}$$

Now the ΔU_{ab1} can be calculated:

$$\Delta U_{ab1}(T_L) = K \cdot \frac{T_{\text{int}}}{T} \cdot a_0 \cdot \left[\frac{T}{2} - 2T_L \right] \quad \text{for } 0 \le T_L < T/2 \tag{8}$$

U_{a2} and U_{b2} are as follows for the second case ($T/2 \le T_L \le T$):

$$U_{a2}(T_L) = K \cdot \frac{T_{\text{int}}}{T} \cdot \left[B \cdot \frac{T}{2} + a_0 \cdot \left(T_L - \frac{T}{2} \right) \right] \quad \text{for } T/2 \le T_L \le T \tag{9}$$

and

$$U_{b2}(T_L) = K \cdot \frac{T_{\text{int}}}{T} \cdot \left[B \cdot \frac{T}{2} + a_0 \cdot (T - T_L) \right] \quad \text{for } T/2 \le T_L \le T \tag{10}$$

The corresponding ΔU_{ab2} is then:

$$\Delta U_{ab2}(T_L) = K \cdot \frac{T_{\text{int}}}{T} \cdot a_0 \cdot \left[-\frac{3}{2}T + 2T_L \right] \quad \text{for } T/2 \le T_L \le T \tag{11}$$

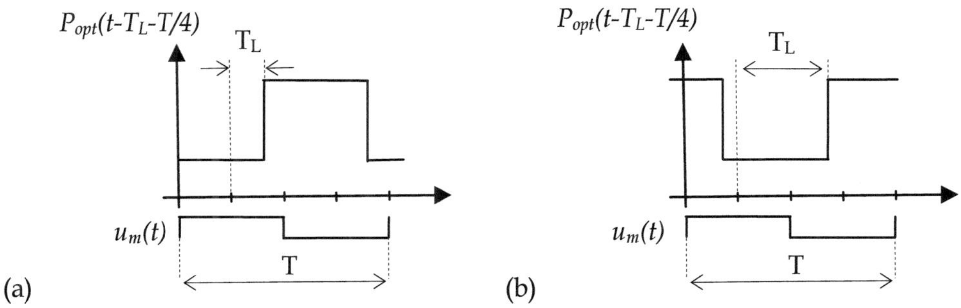

Fig. 3. Correlation process between the shifted optical echo and the modulation voltage for one single modulation period for (a) $0 \le T_L < T/4$ as well as $3T/4 < T_L \le T$ and (b) $T/4 \le T_L \le 3T/4$

To get another solution for ΔU_{ab} the optical echo $P_{opt}(t\text{-}T_L)$ is shifted by $T/4$. Three cases have to be taken into account to determine a mathematical description for U_a and U_b as shown in Fig. 3. $U_{a1}(T_L\text{-}T/4)$ and $U_{b1}(T_L\text{-}T/4)$ are as follows for the first case ($0 \le T_L < T/4$):

$$U_{a1}(T_L - T/4) = K \cdot \frac{T_{\text{int}}}{T} \cdot \left[B \cdot \frac{T}{2} + a_0 \cdot \left(\frac{T}{4} - T_L \right) \right] \quad \text{for } 0 \le T_L < T/4 \tag{12}$$

and

$$U_{b1}(T_L - T/4) = K \cdot \frac{T_{\text{int}}}{T} \cdot \left[B \cdot \frac{T}{2} + a_0 \cdot \left(\frac{T}{4} + T_L \right) \right] \quad \text{for } 0 \le T_L < T/4 \tag{13}$$

The corresponding $\Delta U_{ab1}(T_L\text{-}T/4)$ is then:

$$\Delta U_{ab1}(T_L - T/4) = -K \cdot \frac{T_{\text{int}}}{T} \cdot a_0 \cdot 2T_L \quad \text{for } 0 \le T_L < T/4 \tag{14}$$

$U_{a2}(T_L\text{-}T/4)$ and $U_{b2}(T_L\text{-}T/4)$ are as follows for the second case ($T/4 \le T_L \le 3T/4$):

$$U_{a2}(T_L - T/4) = K \cdot \frac{T_{\text{int}}}{T} \cdot \left[B \cdot \frac{T}{2} + a_0 \cdot \left(T_L - \frac{T}{4} \right) \right] \quad \text{for } T/4 \le T_L \le 3T/4 \tag{15}$$

and

$$U_{b2}(T_L - T/4) = K \cdot \frac{T_{\text{int}}}{T} \cdot \left[B \cdot \frac{T}{2} + a_0 \cdot \left(\frac{3}{4}T - T_L \right) \right] \quad \text{for } T/4 \le T_L \le 3T/4 \tag{16}$$

The corresponding $\Delta U_{ab2}(T_L\text{-}T/4)$ is then:

$$\Delta U_{ab2}(T_L - T/4) = K \cdot \frac{T_{\text{int}}}{T} \cdot a_0 \cdot \left[2T_L - T \right] \quad \text{for } T/4 \le T_L \le 3T/4 \tag{17}$$

$U_{a3}(T_L\text{-}T/4)$ and $U_{b3}(T_L\text{-}T/4)$ are as follows for the third case ($3T/4 < T_L \le T$):

$$U_{a3}(T_L - T/4) = K \cdot \frac{T_{\text{int}}}{T} \cdot \left[B \cdot \frac{T}{2} + a_0 \cdot \left(\frac{5T}{4} - T_L \right) \right] \quad \text{for } 3T/4 < T_L \le T \tag{18}$$

and

$$U_{b3}(T_L - T/4) = K \cdot \frac{T_{\text{int}}}{T} \cdot \left[B \cdot \frac{T}{2} + a_0 \cdot \left(T_L - \frac{3}{4}T \right) \right] \quad \text{for } 3T/4 < T_L \le T \tag{19}$$

The corresponding $\Delta U_{ab3}(T_L\text{-}T/4)$ is then:

$$\Delta U_{ab3}(T_L - T/4) = K \cdot \frac{T_{\text{int}}}{T} \cdot a_0 \cdot [2T - 2T_L] \qquad \text{for } 3T/4 < T_L \leq T \tag{20}$$

Now all equations are derived which are needed to calculate T_L. By dividing equation (8) by equation (14) T_L can be calculated as follows for $0 \leq T_L < T/4$:

$$T_L = \frac{T}{4} \cdot \frac{\Delta U_{ab1}(T_L - T/4)}{\Delta U_{ab1}(T_L - T/4) - \Delta U_{ab1}(T_L)} \qquad \text{for } 0 \leq T_L < T/4 \tag{21}$$

By dividing equation (8) by equation (17) T_L can be calculated as follows for $T/4 \leq T_L < T/2$:

$$T_L = \frac{T}{4} \cdot \frac{\Delta U_{ab2}(T_L - T/4) + 2\Delta U_{ab1}(T_L)}{\Delta U_{ab2}(T_L - T/4) + \Delta U_{ab1}(T_L)} \qquad \text{for } T/4 \leq T_L < T/2 \tag{22}$$

By dividing equation (11) by equation (17) T_L can be calculated as follows for $T/2 \leq T_L < 3T/4$:

$$T_L = \frac{T}{4} \cdot \frac{2\Delta U_{ab2}(T_L) - 3\Delta U_{ab2}(T_L - T/4)}{\Delta U_{ab2}(T_L) - \Delta U_{ab2}(T_L - T/4)} \qquad \text{for } T/2 \leq T_L < 3T/4 \tag{23}$$

By dividing equation (11) by equation (20) T_L can be calculated as follows for $3T/4 \leq T_L \leq T$:

$$T_L = \frac{T}{4} \cdot \frac{4\Delta U_{ab2}(T_L) + 3\Delta U_{ab3}(T_L - T/4)}{\Delta U_{ab2}(T_L) + \Delta U_{ab3}(T_L - T/4)} \qquad \text{for } 3T/4 \leq T_L \leq T \tag{24}$$

Looking at equation (21) - (24) it can be seen that T_L depends only on the difference voltage ΔU_{ab}. The range value R can now be calculated by taken into account the modulation frequency f_{mod} and the physical constant for the speed of light c ($3 \cdot 10^8$ m/s).

$$R = \frac{c}{2 \cdot f_{\text{mod}}} \cdot \left(\frac{\omega T_L}{2\pi} \right) \tag{25}$$

It has to be noticed that the range calculation is only valid for ideal square waves. Due to the low-pass characteristic of the IR-LEDs used for the illumination unit, the square waves' harmonics are attenuated for larger frequencies. This results in an optical output that gradually looks sinusoidal for frequencies larger than 5-10 MHz. If this has to taken into account the range calculation has to be derived in a different way as shown in (Hussmann et al., 2008).

2.3 Amplitude and grey level image calculation

By subtracting equation (14) from equation (8) the modulation amplitude a_0 can be determined for $0 \le T_L < T/4$:

$$a_0 = \frac{2}{K \cdot T_{\text{int}}} \cdot \left(\Delta U_{ab1}(T_L) - \Delta U_{ab1}(T_L - T/4)\right) \tag{26}$$

By adding equation (17) and equation (8) the modulation amplitude a_0 is as follows for $T/4 \le T_L < T/2$:

$$a_0 = -\frac{2}{K \cdot T_{\text{int}}} \cdot \left(\Delta U_{ab1}(T_L) + \Delta U_{ab2}(T_L - T/4)\right) \tag{27}$$

By subtracting equation (17) from equation (11) the modulation amplitude a_0 is as follows for $T/2 \le T_L < 3T/4$:

$$a_0 = \frac{2}{K \cdot T_{\text{int}}} \cdot \left(\Delta U_{ab2}(T_L - T/4) - \Delta U_{ab2}(T_L)\right) \tag{28}$$

By adding equation (20) and equation (11) the modulation amplitude a_0 is as follows for $3T/4 \le T_L \le T$:

$$a_0 = \frac{2}{K \cdot T_{\text{int}}} \cdot \left(\Delta U_{ab2}(T_L) + \Delta U_{ab3}(T_L - T/4)\right) \tag{29}$$

The gray level value of the PMD pixel, which is equivalent to the grey level value of standard CCD/CMOS video cameras, can be calculated by adding U_a and U_b as mentioned in section 2.1. It does not matter if equation (6) and (7) or equation (9) and (10) or equation (12) and (13) or equation (15) and (16) or equation (18) and (19) is used. The sum is always the same:

$$\Sigma U_{ab} = B \cdot T + \frac{T}{2} a_0 \tag{30}$$

The background light B can also easily be calculated using equation (26) - (30). By inserting equation (26) in equation (30) the background light B is for $0 \le T_L < T/4$:

$$B = \frac{\Sigma U_{ab}}{T} + \frac{\Delta U_{ab1}(T_L - T/4) - \Delta U_{ab1}(T_L)}{K \cdot T_{\text{int}}} \tag{31}$$

By inserting equation (27) in equation (30) the background light B is for $T/4 \le T_L < T/2$:

$$B = \frac{\Sigma U_{ab}}{T} + \frac{\Delta U_{ab2}(T_L - T/4) + \Delta U_{ab1}(T_L)}{K \cdot T_{\text{int}}} \tag{32}$$

By inserting equation (28) in equation (30) the background light B is for $T/2 \le T_L < 3T/4$:

$$B = \frac{\Sigma U_{ab}}{T} + \frac{\Delta U_{ab2}(T_L) - \Delta U_{ab2}(T_L - T/4)}{K \cdot T_{\text{int}}} \tag{33}$$

By inserting equation (29) in equation (30) the background light B is for $3T/4 \le T_L \le T$:

$$B = \frac{\Sigma U_{ab}}{T} - \frac{\Delta U_{ab2}(T_L) + \Delta U_{ab3}(T_L - T/4)}{K \cdot T_{\text{int}}} \tag{34}$$

Again equation (26) - (29) demonstrate the advantage of the PMD technology compared to other range measurement systems such as SV systems or LRS. Using the amplitude image uncorrelated light signals such as sun light or other modulated light sources are suppressed. Still the grey level image (ΣU_{ab}), which is normally used in 2D image processing applications with standard video cameras, is available. Hence standard 2D-Image processing algorithms can be used. The additional range values can lead to a superior solution for a given application based on 3D-TOF systems as demonstrated in the next section.

3. Robot application

3.1 Experimental setup

To demonstrate the advantage of using 3D-TOF vision systems for robot applications compared to the other vision-based systems, the following laboratory setup has been chosen. The setup, shown in Fig. 4, demonstrates a real world problem on a smaller scale. A container ship has to be loaded in such a way that the containers use minimum storage area. A 3D-TOF camera (PMD[vision]® 19k) is mounted on top of the robot system, delivering the range data of the measure objects (containers) for the robot system (Kuka KR3). The robot system has a repeatability accuracy of ± 0.05 mm. A PC converts these range values in 3D space coordinates of the robot system and sends the range values, the centre of gravity (COG) values and rotation angle of the objects to the Kuka Robot. Subsequently the Kuka robot picks up the containers and places them optimally on the ship.

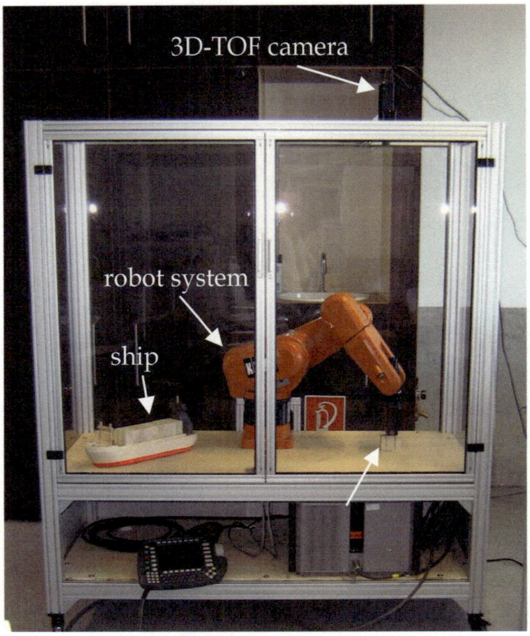

Fig. 4. Laboratory setup

3.2 System calibration

The 3D space coordinates of the measure objects are calculated using standard image segmentation and shape description methods. Before determining the 3D space coordinates, an x, y and z-calibration of the range values of the 3D-TOF camera must be realized. For the x- and y-calibration the calibration technique proposed by Tsai is used (Tsai, 1987). For the z-calibration a linear calibration technique with respect to the background and the upper limit of the measuring range is used.

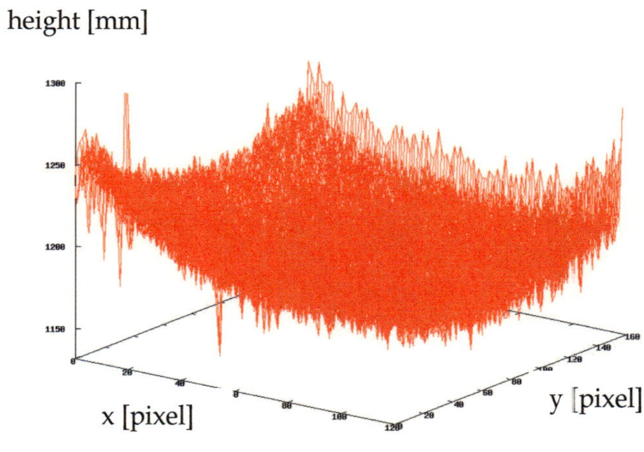

Fig. 5. Range image of a planar surface

Fig. 5. shows the range image of a planar surface. Due to the opening angle of the optics the outer pixel have a longer optical path therefore the range measurements are larger compared to the centre pixels. To correct this effect a background image is captured which is always subtracted from a taken range image. Hence for the range calibration first a range image of the background R_B is taken. This range image is taken at the beginning of the measuring range. In our application the wooden platform of the laboratory setup without the measure objects. Subsequently another range image R_x is taken at the end of the measuring range x. The corrected range value R_{cor} can then be calculated as follows:

$$R_{cor} = \frac{R - R_B}{R_x - R_B} \cdot x \tag{35}$$

It has to be noticed that the measuring range in this application is very small (around 10 cm). A more sophisticated calibration method has to be used for longer measuring ranges.

3.3 Image segmentation and object analysis algorithms

A 4-connected chain code algorithm is used to extract the measure objects. Chain codes can also be used to calculate certain boundary features such as object perimeter, width and height (Pitas, 2000). In this application the chain codes are used to segment the objects in the range image of the 3D-TOF camera and to place a surrounding rectangle. The compression advantage is not applied because the object boundary coordinates are needed for determining the surrounding rectangle. Once each measure object is segmented by its surrounding rectangle in the range image, the content of the rectangle is binaries into background and object.

Fig. 6 shows a screenshot of the developed graphical user interface (GUI) of the robot application. In the upper left corner the range image of the background R_B is shown. It can be clearly seen that the range measurements of the outer pixel are larger compared to the centre pixels (a brighter colour means a smaller range value). Beside the background range image is the grey level image of the scene. A segmentation of the objects is difficult as the objects have the same grey level values as the background (wooden objects on a wooden platform). The grey level histogram in the lower right corner in Fig. 6 illustrates this circumstance. The object grey level values can not be separated from the background grey level values.

The image beside the grey level image shows the uncorrected range image of the scene. Again it can be noticed that the range measurements of the outer pixel are larger compared to the centre pixels. The last image in the row (upper right corner) shows the result of the subtraction (range image - background range image). The objects can now easily be detected in the range image. Applying the image segmentation and object analysis algorithms leads to the last image shown in the lower right corner. All objects are segmented by their surrounding rectangles and can be separately chosen by the software. The COG is illustrated by the blue cross and the rotation angle by the white dotted line.

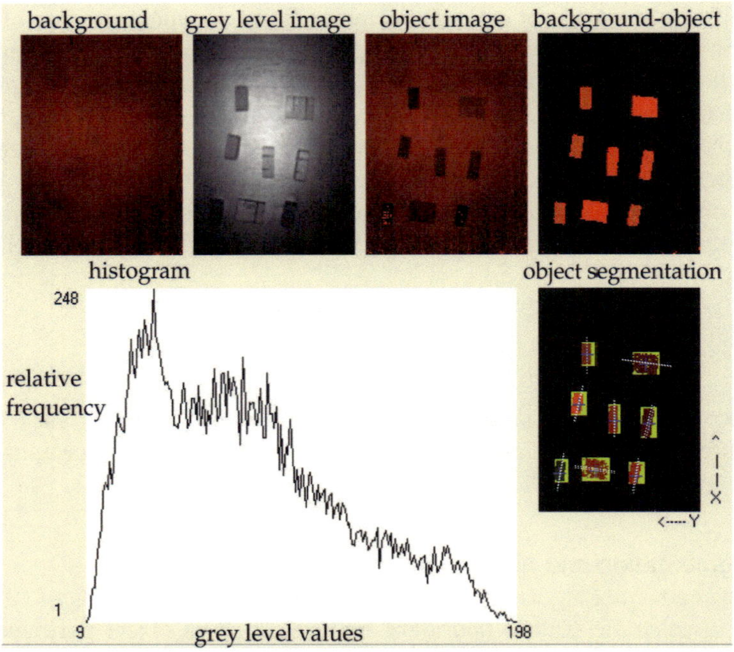

Fig. 6. Screen shot of the robot application GUI showing the grey level histogram

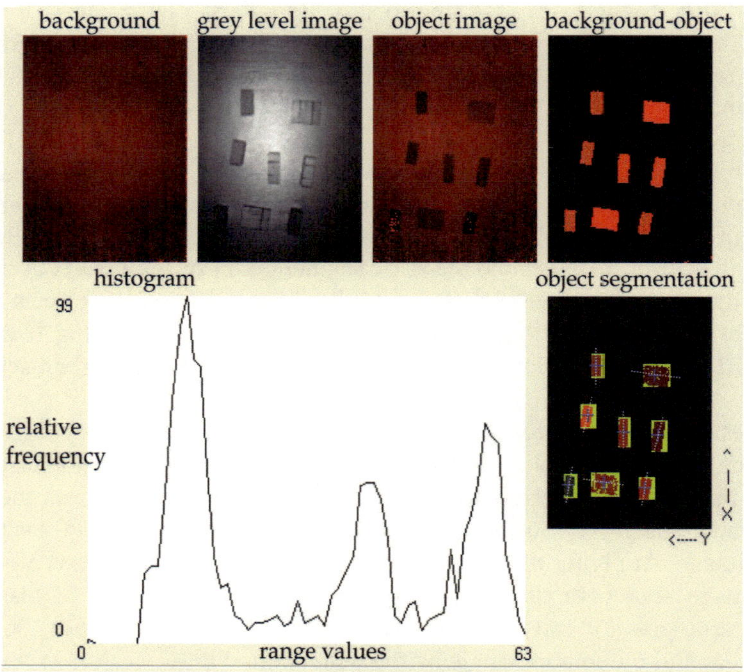

Fig. 7. Screen shot of the robot application GUI showing the range histogram

The only difference between Fig. 6 and Fig. 7 is the image in the lower left corner. The image shows the histogram of the range image. In comparison to the grey level histogram a segmentation of the object are now obvious. The three peaks illustrate the three different object heights (wooden block standing, on the side and on the other side). Fig. 6 and Fig. 7 make it clear that TOF vision system are superior in scenes with equal grey level values compared to the other vision based systems for robot applications. The object segmentation and analysis can be realized without complex image algorithms.
Subsequently the (x, y, z)-coordinates of the COG and the rotation angle of the objects are sent to the robot system. A more detailed algorithm description can be found in (Hussmann & Liepert, 2009). The Kuka K3 has now all required position data to pick up the containers correctly and place them on the ship

3.4 Experimental results

The experimental results show that the proposed TOF vision systems cannot only be used for long range measurements up to 7.5 m but also for near range measurements up to 1.2 m. The accuracy and repeatability of the system is applicable for industrial applications. The robot could pick up all measure objects correctly and placed them on the ship. Even when objects with different heights are placed in random positions on the table, the robot vision system worked fine. A more detailed description of the experimental results can be found in (Hussmann & Liepert, 2009).

4. Conclusion

In this chapter we highlighted the advantages of the PMD technology for robot vision compared to other range measurement systems such as SV systems or LRS. The equations needed for the design of such a system are derived and demonstrate the simplicity of the extraction of the range information. A PMD camera delivers absolute geometrical dimensions of objects without depending on the object surface, - distance, -rotation and – illumination. Hence PMD TOF vision systems are rotation-, translation- and illumination invariant.
The major advantage of the PMD technology is the delivery of an evenly distributed range and intensity images because each pixel calculates a range and intensity value. The PMD technology has an inherent suppression of uncorrelated light signals such as sun light or other modulated light disturbances. However if those light sources saturate the sensor, the range information is lost. More advantages of a PMD technology are the acquisition of the intensity and range data in each pixel without high computational cost and any moving components as well as the monocular setup. All these advantages lead to a compact and economical design of 3D TOF vision system with a high frame rate. This vision system can not only be used for robot applications but also for many other applications such as automotive, industrial, medical and multimedia applications.
In this chapter experimental results of a PMD TOF vision system for a typical robot application are presented. The range data image of the 3D-TOF camera allows a correct segmentation of objects with equal gray level values. In such images, SV systems have difficulties to find corresponding image coordinates and therefore complex algorithms have to be used to get a correct object segmentation. The described application in this paper has demonstrated that a 3D-TOF robot vision system segments successfully objects with the

same gray level values as the background (wooden objects on a wooden platform). Furthermore it has been shown that the range data of the 3D-TOF camera is independent on the reflection coefficient of the measured objects. The reflection coefficient influences the received modulation amplitude and the modulation amplitude has no effect on the range measurement. The experimental results demonstrate that the accuracy and repeatability of the 3D-TOF robot vision system is applicable for industrial applications.

5. References

Blanc, N., Oggier, T., Gruener, G., Weingarten, J., Codourey, A. & Seitz, P. (2004). Miniaturized smart cameras for 3D-imaging in real-time, *Proc. of the IEEE Sensors*, vol.1, pp. 471-4

Faugeras, O. (1993). *Three-Dimensional Computer Vision: A Geometric Viewpoint*, MIT Press, Cambridge, Massachusetts

Hess, H., Albrecht, M., Grothof, M., Hussmann, S., Oikonomidis, N. & Schwarte, R. (2003). 3D object recognition in TOF data sets, *Proc. SPIE*, vol. 5086, pp. 221-228

Ho, N. & Jarvis, R. (2008). Towards a Platform Independent Real-Time Panoramic Vision Based Localisation System, *Proc. of the Australasian Conference on Robotics and Automation*, Canberra

Hussmann, S. & Hess, H. (2006). Dreidimensionale Umwelterfassung, *Trade Journal: "Elektronik automotive"*, WEKA Publisher House, Issue 8, ISSN 1614-0125, pp. 55-59

Hussmann, S., Ringbeck, T. & Hagebeuker, B. (2008). A performance review of 3D TOF vision systems in comparison to stereo vision systems, In: *Stereo Vision* (Online book publication), I-Tech Education and Publishing, Vienna, Austria, ch. 7, ISBN 978-953-7619-22-0, pp. 103-120

Hussmann, S. & Liepert, T. (2009). 3D-TOF Robot Vision System, *IEEE Trans. on Instrumentation and Measurement*, 58(1), pp.141-146

Lange, R. & Seitz, P. (2001). Solid-state time-of-flight range camera, *IEEE Journal of Quantum Electronics*, vol. 37, no. 3, pp. 390–397

Nuechter, A., Surmann, H. & Hertzberg, J. (2003). Automatic model refinement for 3D reconstruction with mobile robots, *Proc. of the 4th IEEE Intl. Conference on Recent Advances in 3D Digital Imaging and Modeling*, pp. 394–401

Oliensis, J. (2000). A Critique of Structure-from-Motion Algorithms, *Computer Vision and Image Understanding*, 80(2), pp. 172-214

Pitas, I. (2000). *Digital Image Processing Algorithms and Applications*, John Wiley & Sons, ISBN-0-471-37739-2

Ringbeck, T. & Hagebeuker, B. (2007). A 3D Time of flight camera for object detection, *Proc. of the 8th Conf. On Optical 3-D Measurement Techniques*, Zürich, Online-publication: (http://www.pmdtec.com/inhalt/download/documents/070513Paper-PMD.pdf)

Schwarte, R., Xu, Z., Heinol, H., Olk, J., Klein, R., Buxbaum, B., Fischer H. & Schulte, J. (1997). New electro-optical mixing and correlating sensor: facilities and applications of the photonic mixer device (PMD), *Proc. SPIE, vol. 3100*, pp. 245-53

Tsai, R. Y. (1987). A versatile Camera Calibration Technique for High-Accuracy 3D Machine Vision Metrology Using Off-the-Shelf TV Cameras and Lenses, *IEEE Journal of Robotics and Automation*, RA-3(4), pp. 323-44

17

Calibration of Non-SVP Hyperbolic Catadioptric Robotic Vision Systems

Bernardo Cunha, José Azevedo and Nuno Lau
ATRI-IEETA/DETI, Universidade de Aveiro
Portugal

1. Introduction

RoboCup (http://www.robocup.org) is an international worldwide initiative that aims to promote research and development in mobile robotics and related areas. Robotic soccer is one of the proposed problems since it represents a challenge of high complexity, in which fully autonomous robots cooperate in order to achieve a common goal (win the game). Within Robocup soccer competitions, the Middle-Size League proposes a challenge where two teams of five fast robots, measuring up to 80cm and weighting up to 40Kg, play soccer in a 18x12m field in a semi-structured, highly dynamic environment. This challenge requires a real time perception of the overall environment in order to allow self localization, mate and opponent localization and, of course, determination of the ball position and movement vector. This, in practice, determines that adopting an omni-directional vision system, as the main sensorial element of the robot, although not mandatory, has significant advantages over other solutions such as standard panoramic vision systems. A common solution found in robots from most teams of this competition, as well as in robots for other autonomous mobile robot applications, is based on a catadioptric omni-directional vision system composed of a regular video camera pointed at a hyperbolic mirror - or any other mirror obtained from a solid of revolution (e.g. ellipsoidal convex mirror). This is the case, just to name a few, of those teams described in (Zivkovic & Booij, 2006), (Wolf, 2003), (Menegatti et al, 2001, 2004) and (Lima et al, 2001).
This type of setup ensures an integrated perception of all major target objects in the robots surrounding area, allowing a higher degree of maneuverability at the cost of higher resolution degradation with growing distances away from the robot (Baker & Nayar, 1999) when compared to non-isotropic setups. For most practical applications, as is the case of the RoboCup competition, this setup requires the translation of the planar field of view, at the camera sensor plane, into real world coordinates at the ground plane, using the robot as the center of this system. In order to simplify this non-linear transformation, most practical solutions adopted in real robots choose to create a mechanical geometric setup that ensures a symmetrical solution for the problem by means of single viewpoint (SVP) approach (Zivkovic & Booij, 2006), (Wolf, 2003) and (Lima et al, 2001). This, on the other hand, calls for a precise alignment of the four major points comprising the vision setup: the mirror focus, the mirror apex, the lens focus and the center of the image sensor. Furthermore, it also

demands the sensor plane to be both parallel to the ground field and normal to the mirror axis of revolution, and the mirror foci to be coincident with the effective viewpoint and the camera pinhole (Benosman & Kang, 2001). Although tempting, this approach requires a precision mechanical setup and generally precludes the use of low cost video cameras, due to the commonly found problem of translational and angular misalignment between the image sensor and the lens plane and focus. In these cameras the lens is, most of the times, attached to a low stability plastic mechanical system that further adds to this problem. Furthermore, the game itself, where robots sometimes crash against each other, or where the ball can violently be shot against other robots (sometimes striking the vision sub-system), tends to mechanically misalign this system over time.

In this chapter we describe a general solution to calculate the robot centered distances map on non-SVP catadioptric setups, exploring a back-propagation ray-tracing approach and the mathematical properties of the mirror surface as explained by (Blinn,J.F. , 1977) and (Foley et al, 1995). This solution effectively compensates for the misalignments that may result either from a simple mechanical setup or from the use of low cost video cameras. Therefore, precise mechanical alignment and high quality cameras are no longer pre-requisites to obtain useful distance maps of the ground floor, reducing significantly the overall cost of the robot and providing a fast method for misalignment compensation over time.

The method described in this chapter can also extract most of the required parameters from the acquired image itself, allowing it to be used for self-calibration purposes. Results from this technique applied in the robots of the CAMBADA team (Cooperative Autonomous Mobile robots with Advanced Distributed Architecture) are presented, showing the effectiveness of the solution.

This first section of the chapter provides the introduction. Section 2 presents the related work on calibration of catadioptric vision systems, including both SVP and non-SVP setups. The next section describes the characteristics of the vision system used by the CAMBADA team. Section 4 discusses, in a constructive manner, the developed calibration methodologies. Two visual feedback tools that can be used to further trim the vision system parameters, in a semi-automated solution, are presented in section 5. Finally, section 6 concludes the chapter.

2. Related work

A significant amount of work exists referring to the development of methods for calibration of catadioptric camera systems. A very complete calibration method survey is presented by (Scaramussas, D., 2008), including auto-calibration by means of laser range finder and cross-matching between laser and camera images. However, most of the proposed calibration methods assume the single view point system. This is the case of (Kang, 2000) who proposed a self-calibration method for a catadioptric camera system that consists of a paraboloidal mirror and an orthographic lens by using the mirror boundary on the image. It assumes, however, that this boundary is a circle, restricting the possible mirror posture in the system. (Barreto and Araujo, 2002) also proposed a method for central catadioptric camera calibration based on lines as geometrical invariants. (Geyer and Daniilidis, 2002) proposed a method of calibration to estimate intrinsic parameters of a catadioptric camera system that consists of a paraboloidal mirror and an orthographic lens. These calibration methods, however, are only for para-catadioptric cameras, configurations which have a unique effective viewpoint and in which the reflective surface is a parabolic mirror that, together with the camera, induces an orthographic projection. (Ying and Hu, 2003) proposed a central catadioptric camera calibration method that uses images of lines or images of spheres as geometric invariants. (Micusik and Pajdla, 2004) also proposed another method for para-catadioptric camera self calibration from point correspondences in two views based on the epipolar constraint. (Micusik, B. and Pajdla, T., 2006) present a calibration method based on matching points in different perspective images. Outliers are excluded by the use of RANSAC. Although this paper discusses the application to real world systems the presented solution is valid for SVP orthographic solutions only. As previously stated, all these methods are effective only for central catadioptric cameras, assuming the SVP restriction.

Less work has been done on calibration methods for non-SVP catadioptric cameras. (Aliaga, 2001) proposed a paracatadioptric camera calibration method which relaxes the assumption of the perfect orthographic placement and projection. (Stelow et al, 2001) proposed a model for the relation between the mirror and camera which integrates translation and rotation of the mirror. The accuracy of this method, while estimating parameters, depends on the initial values, due to nonlinear optimization, and produces poor results. (Micusik and Pajdla, 2004) also proposed an auto-calibration and 3D reconstruction method by using a mirror boundary and an epipolar geometry approach. In this method, they also assume that the mirror boundary in the image is a circle. These methods are effective while compensating for minor mirror misalignments. (Mashita et al, 2006) also proposed a calibration method for a catadioptric camera system that they claim can estimate all degrees of freedom of mirror posture. This method assumes five degrees of freedom for the mirror, and uses the mirror boundary to determine the elliptic pattern on the image. It also proposes a selection method for finding the best solution, since the method produces more than one. This approach does not, however, consider the effect of the non normal restriction between the mirror axes of revolution and the plane of reference of the robot (in our application, the floor). It also depends significantly on the image resolution and contrast (either in luminance or chrominance) for an effective and precise evaluation of the mirror elliptic pattern in the image. (Voigtländer et al, 2007) present a method using piecewise linear functions in polar coordinates. They determine 12 support vectors for 45 different directions based on a calibration pattern placed on the ground.

3. The framework

In the following discussion the specific vision setup used in the CAMBADA team of robots will be assumed (Fig. 1). This can be generalized for other configurations, including the use of different types of mirrors, as long as their surface can be described by an analytical expression.

The setup comprises a catadioptric vision module mounted on top of a mechanical structure, and lies between 60cm and 80cm above the ground. It includes a low cost Fire-I Point Grey FL2-08S2C video camera with a 4mm focal distance inexpensive lens. This camera uses a 1/3" CCD sensor providing a resolution of 1032x776 pixels. The camera is set to acquire images with a 640x480 pixel size, at an acquisition rate of 30 frames/second. The main characteristics of the sensor, including pixel size, can be depicted in Fig. 2.

The mirror, used in the CAMBADA robot setup, has a hyperbolic surface, described by the following equation:

$$\frac{y^2}{1000} - \frac{\left(x^2 + z^2\right)}{1000} = 1 \ \ (\text{mm}) \ . \tag{1}$$

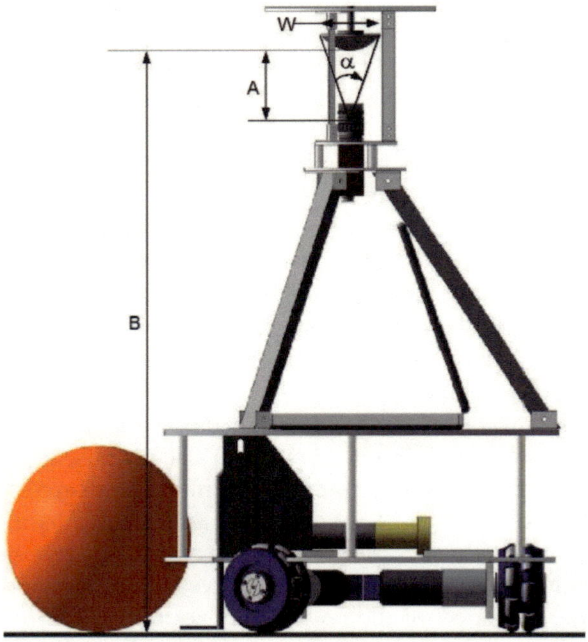

Fig. 1. The robot setup with the top catadioptric vision system.

where y is mirror axis of revolution and z is the axis parallel to a line that connects the robot center to its front. The mirror maximum radius is 35mm and the mirror depth, obtained from its equation, is 15.55mm. Height from the mirror apex to the ground plane is roughly 680mm, while distance from the mirror apex to the lens focus is approximately 110mm.

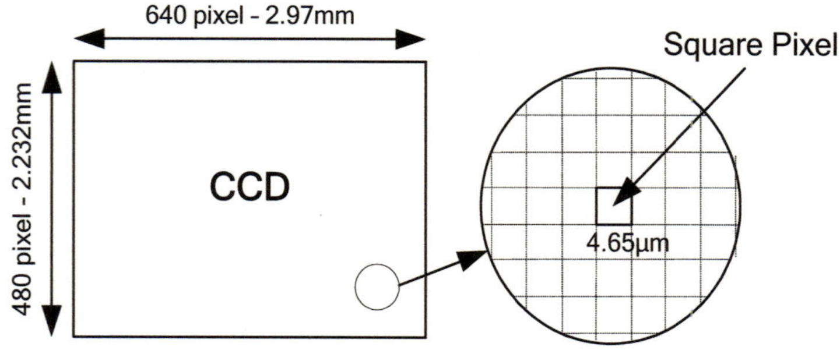

Fig. 2. The Point Grey camera CCD main characteristics, in 640x480 acquisition mode.

Some simplifications will also be used in regard with the diffraction part of the setup. The used lens has a narrow field of view and must be able to be focused at a short distance. This, together with the depth of the mirror, implies a reduced depth of field and therefore an associated defocus blur problem (Baker & Nayar, 1999). Fortunately, since spatial resolution of the acquired mirror image decreases significantly as distance to the seen object gets higher, this problem has a low impact in the solution when compared with the low-resolution problem itself. The focus plane is adjusted to be slightly behind the mirror apex so that objects in the vicinity of the robot are well defined, as this is the area where precise measurements, namely the distance to the ball, is actually relevant.

A narrow field of view, on the other hand, also reduces achromaticity aberration and radial distortion introduced by the lens. Camera/lenses calibration procedures are a well-known problem and are widely described in the literature (Zhang, 2000) and (Hartley & Zisserman, 2004). The setup has been tested with both 4mm and 6mm inexpensive lenses. The second requires a bigger distance between the camera and the mirror, increasing the overall volume of the catadioptric system. It also produces a narrower field of view when compared with the 4mm lens, reducing de radial distortion. The 4mm lens produces a more compact mechanical solution at the expense of greater radial distortion and smaller depth of field.

For compensating for radial distortion, a chess-board like black and white pattern is placed in front of the camera while removing the mirror (Fig. 3). The mirror support is used to place this pattern.

Fig. 3. The chess-board pattern seen by the Point Grey camera with a 4mm (left) and a 6mm (right) lenses respectively.

Automatic determination of pattern interception points in the image is followed by generation of the coefficients of a third order polynomial equation of the form

$$C(\theta) = k_0 + k_1\theta + k_2\theta^2 + k_3\theta^3 \ . \qquad (2)$$

where $C(\theta)$ is the additive correction factor applied to the angle of any ray vector exiting the lens relative to the lens central plane (Fig. 4). The third order term is usually enough to model medium to large field of view lenses.

Coefficients are calculated using an iterative method that minimizes the co-variance of the two functions in the discrete domain.

The polynomial function is used both to determine the focal distance at the center of the image and to correct the diffraction angle produced by the lens. With the tested lenses the actual focal distance for the 4mm lens, obtained by this method, is 4.56mm while, for the 6mm lens, the actual focal distance is 6.77mm.
Polynomial coefficients K_0, K_1, K_2 and K_3, calculated for the two tested lenses, are respectively [0, 0, 0.001, .0045] and [0, 0, 0.0002, 0.00075].

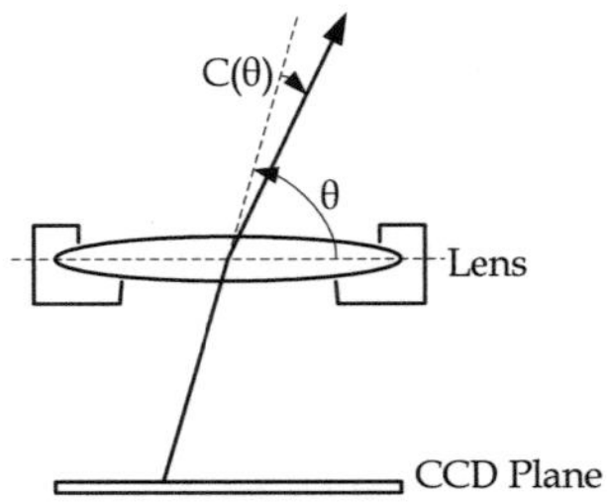

Fig. 4. Correction of radial distortion as a function of θ.

Using this method we will also assume that the pinhole model can provide an accurate enough approach for our practical setup, therefore disregarding any other distortion of the lens.

4.Discussion

Instead of elaborating on the general problem from the beginning, we will start by applying some restrictions to it that will simplify the initial solution. Later on, these restrictions will be relaxed in order to find a general solution.

4.1 Initial approach

Let's start by assuming a restricted setup as depicted in Fig. 5.
Assumptions applied to this setup are as follows:

- The origin of the coordinate system is coincident with the camera pinhole through which all light rays will pass;
- i, j and k are unit vectors along axis X, Y and Z, respectively;
- The Y axis is parallel to the mirror axis of revolution and normal to the ground plane;
- CCD major axis is parallel to the X system axis;
- CCD plane is parallel to the XZ plane;
- Mirror foci do not necessarily lie on the Y system axis;
- The vector that connects the robot center to its front is parallel and has the same direction as the positive system Z axis;
- Distances from the lens focus to the CCD plane and from the mirror apex to the XZ plane are htf and mtf respectively and can be readily available from the setup and from manufacturer data;
- Point $Pm(m_{cx}, 0, m_{cz})$ is the intersection point of the mirror axis of revolution with the XZ plane;
- Distance unit used throughout this discussion will be the millimeter.

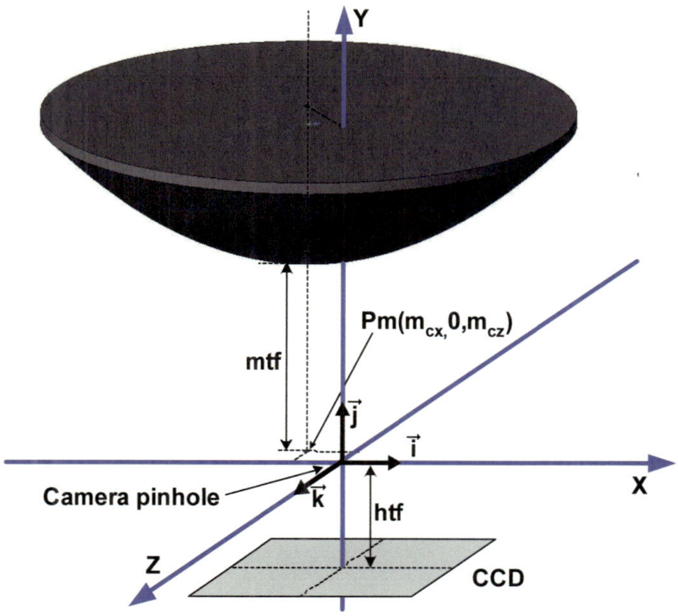

Fig. 5. The restricted setup with its coordinate system axis (***X, Y, Z***), mirror and CCD. The axis origin is coincident with the camera pinhole. Note: objects are not drawn to scale.

Given equation (1) and mapping it into the defined coordinate system, we can rewrite the mirror equation as

$$y = \sqrt{1000 + (x - m_{cx})^2 + (z - m_{cz})^2} + K_{off} \; . \tag{3}$$

where

$$k_{off} = mtf - \sqrt{1000} \; . \tag{4}$$

Let's now assume a randomly selected CCD pixel ($\boldsymbol{X_x, X_z}$), at point $\boldsymbol{Pp(p_{cx}, -htf, p_{cz})}$, as shown in Fig. 6, knowing that

$$\frac{p_{cx}}{X_x} = \frac{p_{cz}}{X_z} = \frac{4.65 \times 10^{-3}}{1} \; . \tag{5}$$

The back propagation ray that starts at point $\boldsymbol{Pp(p_{cx}, -htf, p_{cz})}$ and crosses the origin, after correction for the radial distortion, may or may not intersect the mirror surface. This can be easily evaluated from the ray vector equation, solving $\boldsymbol{P_i(x(y), y, z(y))}$ for $\boldsymbol{y=mtf+md}$, where ***md*** is the mirror depth. If the vector module $|P_bP_i|$ is greater than the mirror maximum radius then the ray will not intersect the mirror and the selected pixel will not contribute to the distance map.

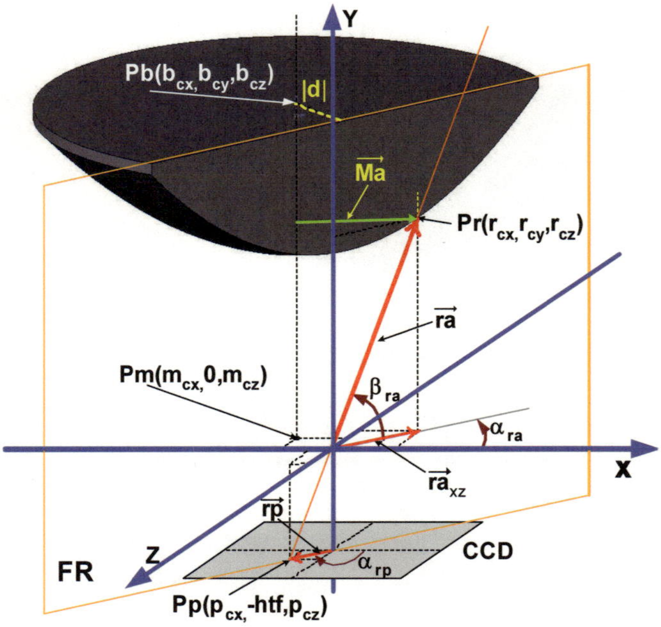

Fig. 6. A random pixel in the CCD sensor plane is the start point for the back propagation ray. This ray and the ***Y*** axis form a plane, ***FR***, that intersects vertically the mirror solid. ***Pr*** is the intersection point between ***ra*** and the mirror surface.

Assuming now that this particular ray will intersect the mirror surface, we can then come to the conclusion that the plane ***FR***, normal to ***XZ*** and containing this line, will cut the mirror parallel to its axis of revolution. This plane can be defined by equation

$$z = x\tan(\alpha_{ra}) \ . \tag{6}$$

The line containing position vector **ra,** assumed to lie on plane defined by eq. 6, can be expressed as a function of ***X*** as

$$y = x\tan(\beta_{ra})/\cos(\alpha_{ra}) \ . \tag{7}$$

where

$$\alpha_{ra} = \tan^{-1}\left(\frac{p_{cz}}{p_{cx}}\right) + pi \qquad \beta_{ra} = \tan^{-1}\left(\frac{htf}{\sqrt{p_{cx}{}^2 + p_{cz}{}^2}}\right) . \tag{8}$$

Substituting (6) and (7) into (3) we get the equation of the line of intersection between the mirror surface and plane ***FR***, The intersection point, ***Pr***, which belong both to **ra** and to the mirror surface, can then be determined from the equality

$$\frac{x\tan(\beta_{ra})}{\cos(\alpha_{ra})} = \sqrt{1000 + (x - m_{cx})^2 + (x\tan(\alpha_{ra}) - m_{cz})^2} + K_{off} \ . \tag{9}$$

Equation (9) can, on the other hand, be transformed into a quadratic equation of the form

$$ax^2 + bx + c = 0 \tag{10}$$

where

$$a = \left(1 + k_{tn}^{\ 2} - k_{tc}^{\ 2}\right). \tag{11}$$

$$b = 2\left(k_{tc}k_{off} - k_{tn}m_{cz} - m_{cx}\right) \cdot \tag{12}$$

$$c = 1000 + m_{cz}^{\ 2} + m_{cx}^{\ 2} - K_{off}^{\ 2} \cdot \tag{13}$$

and

$$k_{tc} = \frac{\tan(\beta_{ra})}{\cos(\alpha_{ra})} \qquad k_{tn} = \tan(\alpha_{ra}). \tag{14}$$

Assuming that we have already determined that there is a valid intersection point, this equation will have two solutions: one for the physical mirror surface, and other for the symmetrical virtual one. Given the current coordinate system, the one with the higher y value will correspond to the intersection point ***Pr***.

Having found ***Pr***, we can now consider the plane ***FN*** (Fig. 7) defined by ***Pr*** and by the mirror axis of revolution.

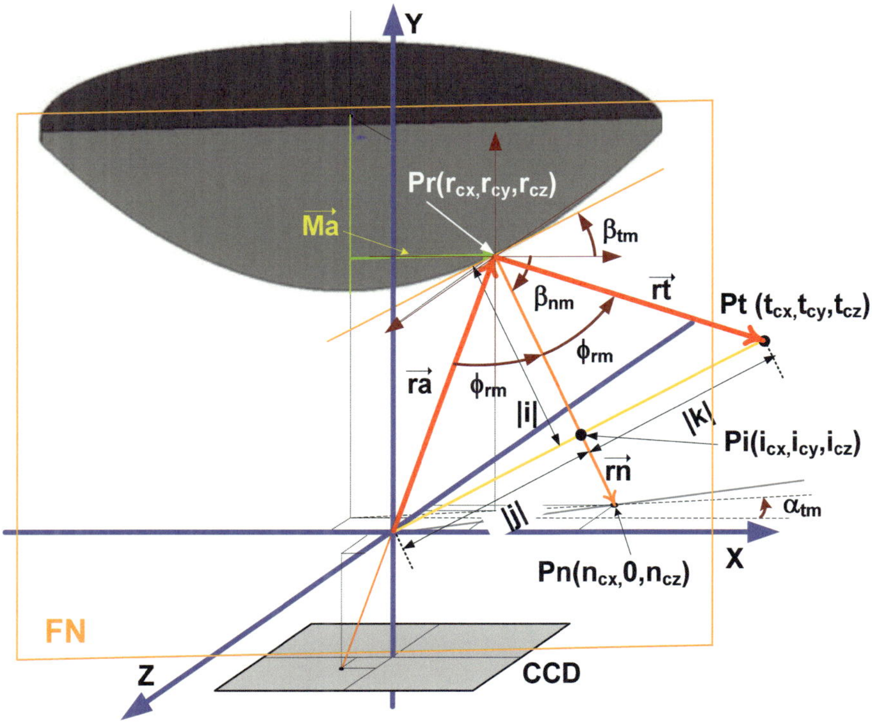

Fig. 7. Determining the normal to the mirror surface at point ***Pr*** and the equation for the reflected ray.

In this plane, we can obtain the angle of the normal to the mirror surface at point ***Pr*** by equating the derivative of the hyperbolic function at that point, as a function of ***|Ma|***

$$\frac{\partial h}{d\left|\overrightarrow{M_a}\right|} = \frac{\left|\overrightarrow{M_a}\right|}{\sqrt{1000 + \left|\overrightarrow{M_a}\right|^2}} \qquad \beta_{tm} = \tan^{-1}\left(\frac{\left|\overrightarrow{M_a}\right|}{\sqrt{1000 + \left|\overrightarrow{M_a}\right|^2}}\right) - \pi/2 . \tag{15}$$

This normal line intercepts the ***XZ*** plane at point ***Pn***

$$Pn = \left\{ r_{cx} - r_{cy}\frac{\cos(\alpha_{nm})}{\tan(\beta_{nm})}, 0, r_{cz} - r_{cy}\frac{\sin(\alpha_{nm})}{\tan(\beta_{nm})} \right\} . \tag{16}$$

where

$$\alpha_{nm} = \tan^{-1}\left(\frac{r_{cz} - m_{cz}}{r_{cx} - m_{cx}}\right) . \tag{17}$$

The angle between the incident ray and the normal at the incidence point can be obtained from the dot product between the two vectors, -***ra*** and ***rn***. Solving for ϕ_{rm}:

$$\phi_{rm} = \cos^{-1}\left(\frac{r_{cx}(r_{cx} - n_{cx}) + r_{cy}(r_{cy} - n_{cy}) + r_{cz}(r_{cz} - n_{cz})}{\left|\overrightarrow{ra}\right|\left|\overrightarrow{rn}\right|}\right) . \tag{18}$$

The reflection ray vector, ***rt***, (Fig. 8) starts at point ***Pr*** and lies on a line going through point ***Pt*** where

$$Pt = \{t_{cx}, t_{cy}, t_{cz}\} = \{2i_{cx}, 2i_{cy}, 2i_{cz}\} . \tag{19}$$

$$\left|\overrightarrow{ri}\right| = \left|\overrightarrow{ra}\right|\cos(\phi_{rm}) \quad \text{and} \quad i_{cx} = r_{cx} + \left|\overrightarrow{ri}\right|\cos(\beta_{nm})\cos(\alpha_{nm}) . \tag{20}$$

$$i_{cy} = r_{cy} + \left|\overrightarrow{ri}\right|\sin(\beta_{nm}) . \tag{21}$$

$$i_{cz} = r_{cz} + \left|\overrightarrow{ri}\right|\cos(\beta_{nm})\sin(\alpha_{nm}) . \tag{22}$$

Its line equation will therefore be

$$P = (r_{cx}\vec{i} + r_{cy}\vec{j} + r_{cz}\vec{k}) + u((t_{cx} - r_{cx})\vec{i} + (t_{cy} - r_{cy})\vec{j} + (t_{cz} - r_{cz})\vec{k}) . \tag{23}$$

Note that if $(t_{cz}\text{-}r_{cz})$ is equal or greater than zero, the reflected ray will be above the horizon and will not intersect the ground. Otherwise, the point ***Pg*** can be obtained from the mirror to ground height ***hmf***, and from the ground plane and ***rt*** line equations (23), which, evaluating for ***u*** (23), gives

$$u = \frac{(mtf - hmf) - r_{cy}}{t_{cy} - r_{cy}} \tag{24}$$

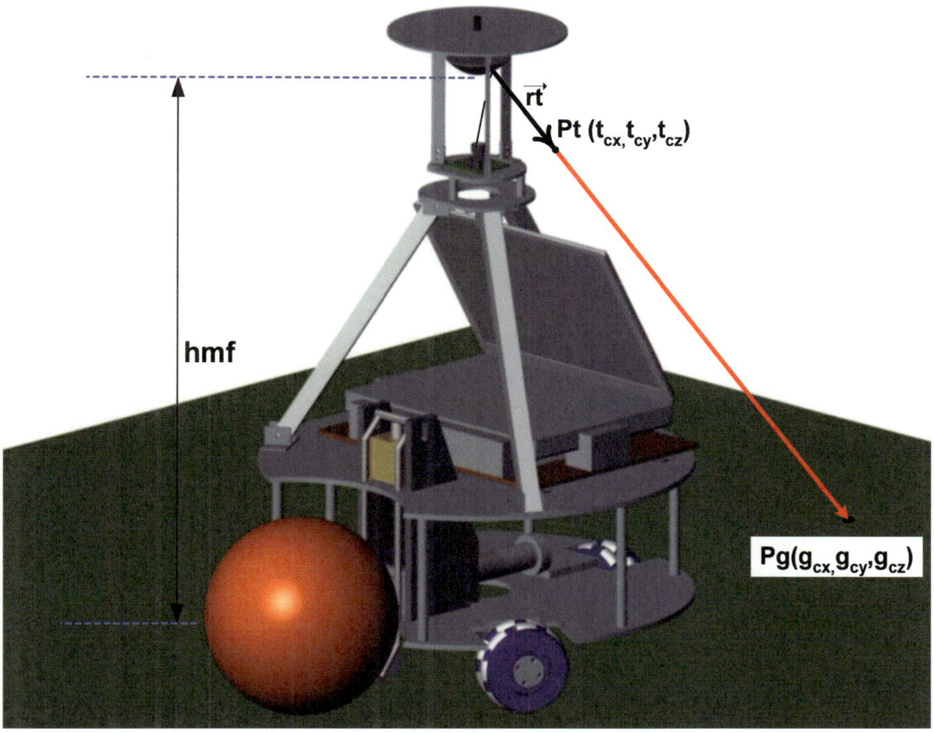

Fig. 8. (**Pg**) will be the point on the ground plane for the back-propagation ray.

4.2 Generalization

The previous discussion was constrained to a set of restrictions that would not normally be easy to comply to in a practical setup. In particular, the following misalignment factors would normally be found in a real robot using low cost cameras:

- The CCD plane may be not perfectly parallel to the ***XZ*** plane;
- The CCD minor axis may not be correctly aligned with the vector that connects the robot center to its front.
- The mirror axis of rotation may not be normal to the ground plane;

The first of these factors results from the mirror axis of rotation being not normal to the CCD plane. We will remain in the same coordinate system and keep the assumptions that its origin is at the camera pinhole, and that the mirror axis of rotation is parallel to the ***Y*** axis.
The second of the misalignment factors, which results from a camera or CCD rotation in relation with the robot structure, can also be integrated as a rotation angle around the ***Y*** axis.
To generalize the solution for these two correction factors, we will start by performing a temporary shift of the coordinate system origin to point ***(0, -htf, 0)***. We will also assume a CCD center point translation offset given by (***-dx, 0, -dy***) and three rotation angles applied to the sensor: γ, ρ and θ, around the ***Y'***, ***X'*** and ***Z'*** axis respectively (Fig. 9).

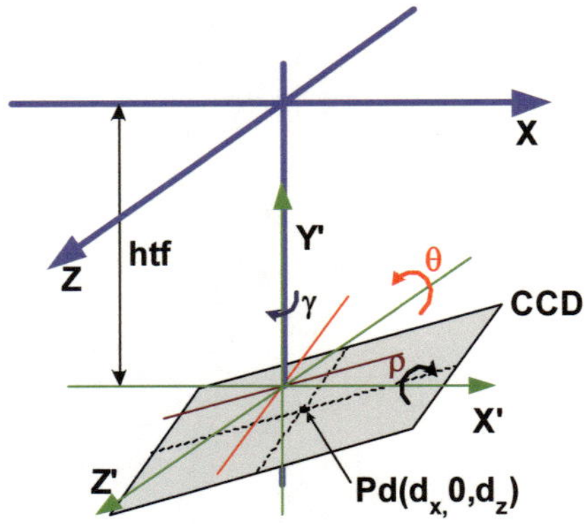

Fig. 9. New temporary coordinate system [***X'***,***Y'***,***Z'***] with origin at point (***0***, ***-htf***, ***0***). γ, ρ and θ, are rotation angles around the ***Y'***, ***X'*** and ***Z'*** axis. ***Pd*** is the new offset CCD center.

These four geometrical transformations upon the original ***Pp*** pixel point can be obtained from the composition of the four homogeneous transformation matrices, resulting from their product

$$R_x(\rho)\bullet R_y(\gamma)\bullet R_z(\theta)\bullet T=\begin{bmatrix} t1_{\rho\gamma\theta} & t2_{\rho\gamma\theta} & t3_{\rho\gamma} & d_x \\ t1_{\rho\theta} & t2_{\rho\theta} & t3_{\rho} & 0 \\ t1_{\rho\gamma\theta} & t2_{\rho\gamma\theta} & t3_{\rho\gamma} & d_z \\ 0 & 0 & 0 & 1 \end{bmatrix} \tag{25}$$

The new start point ***Pp'***(p'_{cx}, p'_{cy}, p'_{cz}), already translated to the original coordinate system, can therefore be obtained from the following three equations:

$$p'_{cx}=p_{cx}(\cos(\gamma)\cos(\theta)+\sin(\rho)\sin(\gamma)\sin(\theta))+p_{cz}(\sin(\gamma)\cos(\rho))+d_x \tag{26}$$

$$p'_{cy}=p_{cx}(\cos(\rho)\sin(\theta)+p_{cz}\sin(\rho)-htf \tag{27}$$

$$p'_{cz}=p_{cx}(-\sin(\gamma)\cos(\theta)+\sin(\rho)\cos(\gamma)\sin(\theta))+p_{cz}(\cos(\gamma)\cos(\rho))+d_z \tag{28}$$

Analysis of the remaining problem can now follow from (5) substituting ***Pp'*** for ***Pp***.
Finally we can also deal with the third misalignment - resulting from the mirror axis of revolution not being normal to the ground - pretty much in the same way. We just have to temporarily shift the coordinate system origin to the point (***0***, ***mtf-hmf***, ***0***), assume the original floor plane equation defined by its normal vector ***j*** and perform a similar geometrical transformation to this vector. This time, however, only rotation angles ρ and θ need to be applied. The new unit vector ***g***, will result as

$$g_{cx}=-\sin(\theta) \tag{29}$$

$$g_{cy}=\cos(\rho)\cos(\theta)-mtf+hmf \tag{30}$$

$$g_{cz}=\sin(\rho)\cos(\theta) \tag{31}$$

The rotated ground plane can therefore be expressed in Cartesian form as

$$g_{cx}X + g_{cy}Y + g_{cz}Z = g_{cy}(mtf - hmf) \tag{32}$$

Replacing the ***rt*** line equation (23) for the ***X***, ***Y*** and ***Z*** variables into (32), the intersection point can be found as a function of ***u***. Note that we still have to check if ***rt*** is parallel to the ground plane - which can be done by means of the ***rt*** and g dot product. This cartesian product can also be used to check if the angle between ***rt*** and g is obtuse, in which case the reflected ray will be above the horizon line.

4.3 Obtaining the model parameters

A method for fully automatic calculation of the model parameters, based only on the image of the soccer field, is still under development, with very promising results. Currently, most of the parameters can either be obtained automatically from the acquired image or measured directly from the setup itself. This is the case of the ground plane rotation relative to the mirror base, the distance between the mirror apex and the ground plane and the diameter of the mirror base. The first two values do not need to be numerically very precise since final results are still constrained by spatial resolution at the sensor level. A 10mm precision in the mirror to ground distance, for instance, will held an error within 60% of resolution imprecision and less than 0.2% of the real measured distance for any point in the ground plane. A 1 degree precision in the measurement of the ground plane rotation relative to the mirror base provides similar results with an error less than 0.16% of the real measured distance for any point in the ground plane.
Other parameters can be extracted from algorithmic analysis of the image or from a mixed approach. Consider, for instance, the thin lens law

$$f = \frac{g}{1 + G/B} \, . \tag{33}$$

where f is the lens focal distance, g is the lens to focal plane distance and ***G/B*** is the magnification factor. ***G/B*** is readily available from the diameter of the mirror outer rim in the sensor image; f can be obtained from the procedure described in section 3, while the actual pixel size is also defined by the sensor manufacturers. Since the magnification factor is also the ratio of distances between the lens focus and both the focus plane and the sensor plane, the g value can also be easily obtained from the known size of the mirror base and the mirror diameter size on the image.
The main image features used in this automatic extraction are the mirror outer rim diameter - assumed to be a circle -, the center of the mirror image and the center of the lens image.

5. Support visual tools and results

A set of software tools that support the procedure of distance map calibration for the CAMBADA robots, have been developed by the team. Although the misalignment parameters can actually be obtained from a set of features in the acquired image, the resulting map can still present minor distortions. This is due to the fact that spatial resolution on the mirror image greatly degrades with distance - around 2cm/pixel at 1m, 5cm/pixel at 3m and 25cm/pixel at 5m. Since parameter extraction depends on feature recognition on the image, degradation of resolution actually places a bound on feature extraction fidelity. Therefore, apart from the basic application that provides the automatic extraction of the relevant image features and parameters, and in order to allow further trimming of these parameters, two simple image feedback tools have also been developed.

The base application treats the acquired image from any selected frame of the video stream. It starts by determining the mirror outer rim in the image, which, as can be seen in Fig. 10 may not be completely shown or centered in the acquired image. This feature extraction is obtained by analyzing 6 independent octants of the circle, starting at the image center line, and followed by a radial analysis of both luminance and chrominance radial derivative. All detected points belonging to the rim are further validated by a space window segmentation based on the first iteration guess of the mirror center coordinates and radius value, therefore excluding outliers. The third iteration produces the final values for the rim diameter and center point.

Fig. 10. Automatic extraction of main image features, while robot is standing at the center of a MSL middle field circle.

This first application also determines the lens center point in the image. To help this process, the lens outer body is painted white. Difference between mirror and lens center coordinates provides a first rough guess of the offset values between mirror axis and lens axis. This application also determines the robot body outer line and the robot heading, together with the limits, in the image, of the three vertical posts that support the mirror structure. These features are used for the generation of a mask image that invalidates all the pixels that are not relevant for real time image analysis.

Based on the parameters extracted from the first application and on those obtained from manufacturer data and from the correction procedure described in section 3, a second application calculates the pixel distance mapping on the ground plane, using the approach described in sections 4.1 and 4.2 (Fig. 11).

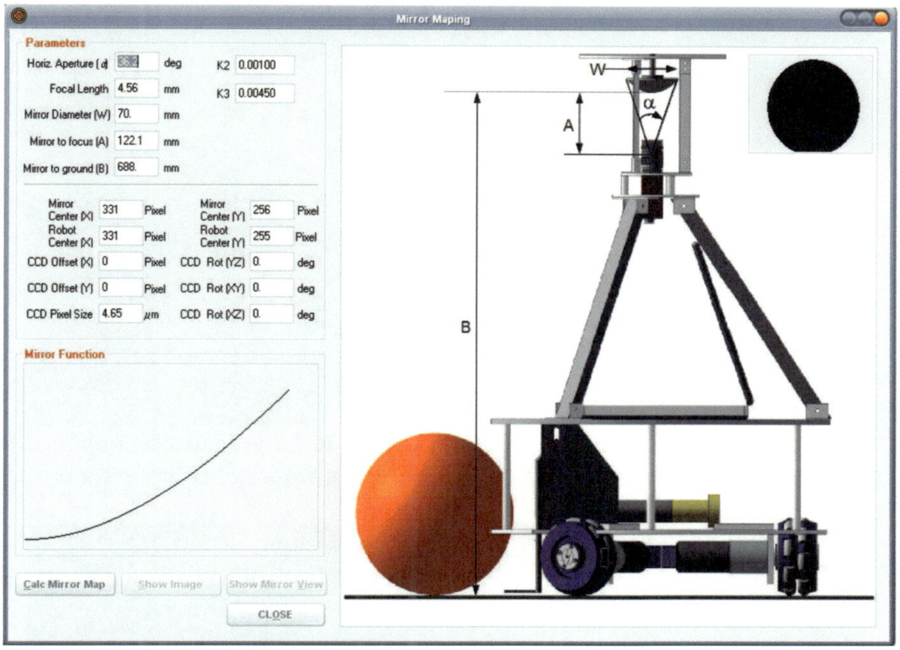

Fig. 11. Obtaining the pixel distance mapping on the ground plane; application interface.

All parameters can be manually corrected, if needed. The result is a matrix distance map, where each pixel coordinates serve as the line and column index and the distance values for each pixel are provided in both cartesian and polar coordinates referenced to the robot center. Since robot center and camera lens center may not be completely aligned, extraction of robot contour and center, performed by the first application, is also used to calculate the translation geometrical operation necessary to change the coordinate system origin from the center of the lens to the center of the robot.

Based on the generated distances maps, a third application constructs a bird's eye view of the omni-directional image, which is actually a reverse mapping of the acquired image into the real world distance map. The resulting image, depending on the zoom factor used, can result in a sparse image where, depending on the distance to the robot center, neighbor pixels in the CCD are actually several pixels apart in the resulting reconstruction. To increase legibility, empty pixels are filled with a luminance and chrominance value that is obtained by a weighted average of the values of the nearest four pixels as a function to the distance to each one of them. The result is a plane vision from above, allowing visual check of line parallelism and circular asymmetries (Fig. 12).

Finally, the last application generates a visual grid, with 0.5m distances between both lines and columns, which is superimposed on the original image. This provides an immediate visual clue for the need of possible further distance correction (Fig. 13).

Since the mid-field circle, used in this particular example setup, has exactly an outer diameter of 1m, incorrect distance map generation will be emphasized by grid and circle misalignment. This also provides a clear and simple visual clue of the parameters that need further correction, as well as the sign and direction of the needed correction.

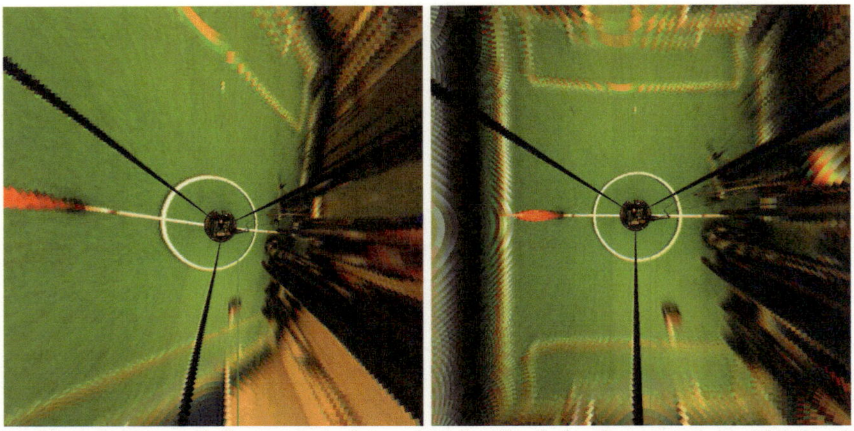

Fig. 12. Bird's eye view of the acquired image. On the left, the map was obtained with all misalignment parameters set to zero. On the right, after semi-automatic correction.

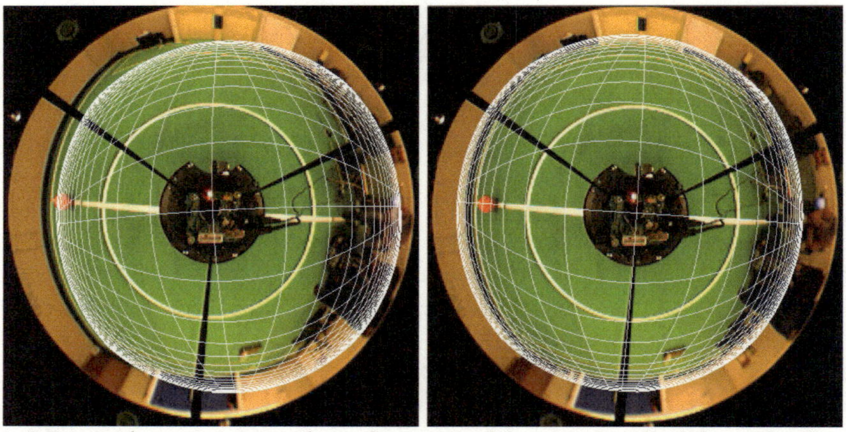

Fig. 13. A 0.5m grid, superimposed on the original image. On the left, with all correction parameters set to zero. On the right, the same grid after geometrical parameter extraction.

Furthermore, this tool provides on-line measurement feedback, both in cartesian and polar form, for any point in the image, by pointing at it with the mouse. Practical measurements performed at the team soccer field have shown really interesting results. Comparison between real distance values measured at more than 20 different field locations and the values taken from the generated map have shown errors always bellow twice the image spatial resolution. That is, the distance map has a precision that is better than +-1.5 cm at 1m, +-4cm at 2m and around +-20cm at 5m distances. These results are perfectly within the required bounds for the robot major tasks, namely object localization and self-localization on the field. The calibration procedure and map generation will take less than 5 seconds in full automatic mode, and normally less than one minute if further trimming is necessary.

6. Conclusions

Use of low cost cameras in a general-purpose omni-directional catadioptric vision system, without the aid of any precision adjustment mechanism, will normally preclude the use of a SVP approach. To overcome this limitation, this chapter explores a back propagation ray tracing geometrical algorithm (*"bird's eye view"*) to obtain the ground plane distance map in the CAMBADA soccer robotic team. Taking into account the intrinsic combined spatial resolution of mirror and image sensor, the method provides viable and useful results that can actually be used in practical robotic applications. Although targeted at the Robocup MSL particular application, several other scenarios where mobile robots have to navigate in a non-structured or semi-structured environments can take advantage from this approach. This method is supported by a set of image analysis algorithms that can effectively extract the parameters needed to obtain a distance map with an error within the resolution bounds. Further trimming of these parameters can be manually and interactively performed, in case of need, with the support of a set of visual feedback tools that provide the user with an intuitive solution for analysis of the obtained results. This approach has proven to be very effective both from the spatial precision and time efficiency point of view. The CAMBADA team participates regularly in the Robocup International competition in the Middle Size League, where it ranked first in the 2008 edition, held in Suzhou, China, and third in the 2009 edition, held in Graz, Austria.

7. Acknowledgments

This work was partially supported by project ACORD, Adaptive Coordination of Robotic Teams, FCT/PTDC/EIA/70695/2006.

8. References

Aliaga, D. G., (2001), Accurate catadioptric calibration for realtime pose estimation of room-size environments, *Proceedings Of IEEE International Conference on Computer Vision*, pp. I: 127–134

Baker,S., Nayar, S. K. (1999). A theory of single-viewpoint catadioptric image formation. *International Journal of Computer Vision*, Volume 35, no. 2, pp 175–196.

Barreto, J. P. and Araujo, H. (2002), Geometric Properties of Central Catadioptric Line Images, *Proceedings of European Conference on Computer Vision*, Volume 4, pp. 237–251

Benosman,R., Kang., S.B. (Eds.) (2001). *Panoramic Vision - Sensors, Theory, and Applications*, Springer, ISBN: 978-0-387-95111-9

Blinn,J.F. (1977). A Homogeneous Formulation for Lines in 3D Space, *ACM SIGGRAPH Computer Graphics* , Volume 11, Issue 2, pp 237-241, ISSN:0097-8930

E. Menegatti F. Nori E. Pagello C. Pellizzari D. Spagnoli. (2001). Designing an omnidirectional vision system for a goalkeeper robot, In: *RoboCup-2001: Robot Soccer World Cup V*, A. Birk S. Coradeschi and P. Lima, (Ed.), pp 78–87, Springer, LNAI, 2377 , ISBN-13: 978-3540439127

Fabrizio, J. , Torel, J. and BenosmanR. (2002), Calibration of Panoramic Catadioptric Sensors made Easier, *Proceedings Of the Third Workshop on Omnidirectional Vision*, pp. 45–52

Foley, J.D., van Dam, A., Feiner,S.K., Hughes,J.F. (1995). *Computer Graphics: Principles and Practice in C,* Addison-Wesley Professional; 2 edition, ISBN-10: 0201848406

Geyer, C. and Daniilidis, K. , (2002), Paracatadioptric camera calibration. *IEEE Transations on Pattern Analysis and Machine Intelligence,* Volume 24, 5, pp. 687–695

Hartley, R., Zisserman, A. (2004). *Multiple View Geometry in Computer Vision.* Cambridge University Press, Second Edition, ISBN: 0521540518

Juergen Wolf (2003). Omnidirectional vision system for mobile robot localization in the Robocup environment, In: *Master's thesis,* Graz, University of Technology.

Kang, S. B. (2000), Catadioptric self-calibration, *Proceedings of IEEE Conference on Computer Vision and Pattern Recognition,* Volume 1, pp. 201–207

Lima, P., Bonarini1,A., Machado,C., Marchese1,F., Marques,C., Ribeiro,F., Sorrenti1,D. (2001). Omni-directional catadioptric vision for soccer robots. *Robotics and Autonomous Systems,* Volume 36, Issues 2-3 , 31, pp 87-102.

Mashita, T., Iwai, Y., Yachida. M. (2006), Calibration Method for Misaligned Catadioptric Camera, *IEICE - Transactions on Information and Systems archive,* Volume E89-D , Issue 7, pp. 1984-1993, ISSN:0916-8532

Menegatti, E. Pretto, A. Pagello, E. (2004). Testing omnidirectional vision-based Monte Carlo localization under occlusion, *Proceedings of the IEEE/RSJ Int. Conference on Intelligent Robots and Systems,* Volume 3, pp 2487- 2494

Micusik, B. and Pajdla, T. (2004), Para-catadioptric camera autocalibration from epipolar geometry, *Proceedings of Asian Conferenceon Computer Vision,* Volume 2, pp. 748–753

Micusik, B. and Pajdla, T. (2004), Autocalibration & 3D Reconstruction with Non-central Catadioptric Cameras, *Proceedings of IEEE Conference on Computer Vision and Pattern Recognition,* Volume 1, pp. 58–65

Micusik, B. and Pajdla, T. (2006), Para-catadioptric Camera Auto-Calibration from Epipolar Geometry, *IEICE - Transactions on Information and Systems archive,* Vol. E89-D , Issue 7, pp. 1984-1993, ISSN:0916-8532

Scaramussas, D., (2008), Omnidirectional Vision: From Calibration to Robot Motion Estimation, *Phd Thesis,* Roland Siegwart (ETH Zurich, thesis director), Università di Perugia, Italy

Stelow, D., Mishler, J., Koes, D. and Singh, S. (2001), Precise omnidirectional camera calibration, *Proceedings of IEEE Conference on Computer Vision and Pattern Recognition,* Volume 1, pp. 689–694

Voigtländer, A., Lange, S. , Lauer, M. and Riedmiller, M. (2007), Real-time 3D Ball Recognition using Perspective and Catadioptric Cameras, *Online Proceedings of the 3rd European Conference on Mobile Robots (ECMR)*

Ying, X. and Hu, Z. (2003), Catadioptric Camera Calibration Using Geometric Invariants, *Proceedings of IEEE International Conference on Computer Vision,* pp. 1351–1358

Zhang, Z. (2000), A Flexible New Technique for Camera Calibration. *IEEE Transactions on Pattern Analysis and Machine Intelligence,* vol. 22, no. 11, pp. 1330-1334, ISSN:0162-8828

Zivkovic, Z., Booij, O. (2006). How did we built our hyperbolic mirror omni-directional camera - practical issues and basic geometry, In: *IAS technical report IAS-UVA-05-04,* Intelligent Systems Laboratory Amsterdam, University of Amsterdam

18

Computational Modeling, Visualization, and Control of 2-D and 3-D Grasping under Rolling Contacts

Suguru Arimoto[1,2], Morio Yoshida[2], and Masahiro Sekimoto[1]
[1]*Ritsumeikan University and* [2]*RIKEN-TRI Collaboration Center*
Japan

Abstract
This chapter presents a computational methodology for modeling 2-dimensional grasping of a 2-D object by a pair of multi-joint robot fingers under rolling contact constraints. Rolling contact constraints are expressed in a geometric interpretation of motion expressed with the aid of arclength parameters of the fingertips and object contours with an arbitrary geometry. Motions of grasping and object manipulation are expressed by orbits that are a solution to the Euler-Lagrange equation of motion of the fingers/object system together with a set of first-order differential equations that update arclength parameters. This methodology is then extended to mathematical modeling of 3-dimensional grasping of an object with an arbitrary shape.
Based upon the mathematical model of 2-D grasping, a computational scheme for construction of numerical simulators of motion under rolling contacts with an arbitrary geometry is presented, together with preliminary simulation results.
The chapter is composed of the following three parts.

Part 1 Modeling and Control of 2-D Grasping under Rolling Contacts between Arbitrary Smooth Contours
Authors: S. Arimoto and M. Yoshida

Part 2 Simulation of 2-D Grasping under Physical Interaction of Rolling between Arbitrary Smooth Contour Curves
Authors: M. Yoshida and S. Arimoto

Part 3 Modeling of 3-D Grasping under Rolling Contacts between Arbitrary Smooth Surfaces
Authors: S. Arimoto, M. Sekimoto, and M. Yoshida

1. Modeling and Control of 2-D Grasping under Rolling Contacts between Arbitrary Smooth Contours

1.1 Introduction

Modeling and control of dynamics of 2-dimensional object grasping by using a pair of multi-joint robot fingers are investigated under rolling contact constraints and an arbitrary geometry of the object and fingertips. First, modeling of rolling motion between 2-D rigid objects with an arbitrary shape is treated under the assumption that the two contour curves coincide at the contact point and share the same tangent. The rolling contact constraints induce an Euler equation of motion parametrized by a pair of arclength parameters and constrained onto the kernel space as an orthogonal complement to the image space spanned from all the constraint gradients. Further, it is shown that all the Pfaffian forms of the constraints are integrable in the sense of Frobenius and therefore the rolling contacts are regarded as a holonomic constraint. The Euler-Lagrange equation of motion of the overall fingers/object system is derived together with a couple of first-order differential equations that express evolution of contact points in terms of quantities of the second fundamental form. A control signal called "blind grasping" is defined and shown to be effective in stabilization of grasping without using the details of object shape and parameters or external sensing.

1.2 Modeling of 2-D Grasping by Euler-Lagrange Equation

Very recently, a complete model of 2-dimensional grasping of a rigid object with arbitrary shape by a pair of robot fingers with arbitrarily given fingertip shapes (see Fig. 1) is presented based upon the differential-geometric assumptions of rolling contacts [Arimoto et al., 2009a]. The assumptions are summarized as follows:
1) Two contact points on the contour curves must coincide at a single common point without mutual penetration, and
2) the two contours must have the same tangent at the common contact point.

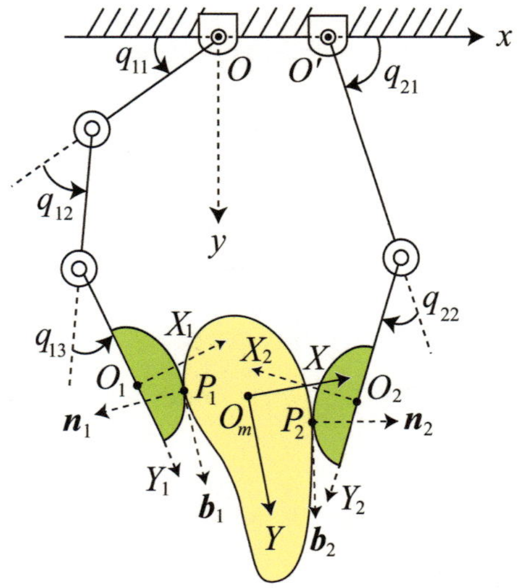

Fig. 1. A pair of two-dimensional robot fingers with a curved fingertip makes rolling contact with a rigid object with a curved contour.

As pointed out in the previous papers [Arimoto et al., 2009a] [Arimoto et al., 2009b], these two conditions as a whole are equivalent to Nomizu's relation [Nomizu, 1978] concerning tangent vectors at the contact point and normals to the common tangent. As a result, a set of Euler-Lagrange's equations of motion of the overall fingers/object system is presented in the

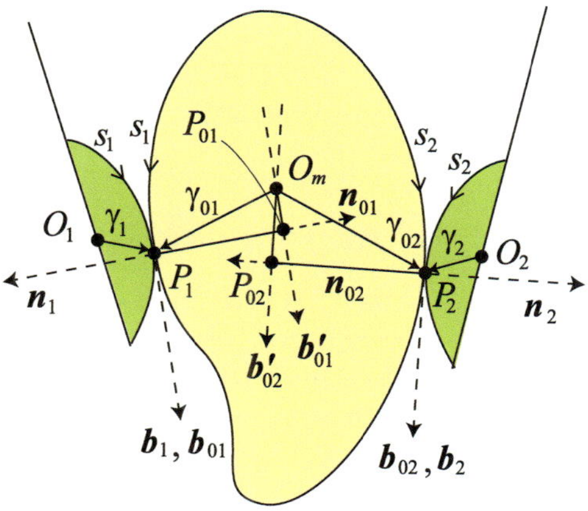

Fig. 2. Definitions of tangent vectors $\boldsymbol{b}_i$, $\boldsymbol{b}_{0i}$ and normals $\boldsymbol{n}_i$ and $\boldsymbol{n}_{0i}$ at contact points P_i for $i = 1, 2$.

following forms:

$$M\ddot{\boldsymbol{x}} - \sum_{i=1,2} (f_i \bar{\boldsymbol{n}}_{0i} + \lambda_i \bar{\boldsymbol{b}}_{0i}) = 0 \tag{1}$$

$$I\ddot{\theta} + \sum_{i=1,2} (-1)^i \{f_i(\boldsymbol{b}_{0i}^{\mathrm{T}} \gamma_{0i}) - \lambda_i(\boldsymbol{n}_{0i}^{\mathrm{T}} \gamma_{0i}) = 0 \tag{2}$$

$$G_i(q_i)\ddot{q}_i + \left\{\frac{1}{2}\dot{G}_i(q_i) + S_i(q_i, \dot{q}_i)\right\}\dot{q}_i + f_i\{J_i^{\mathrm{T}}(q_i)\bar{\boldsymbol{n}}_{0i} - (-1)^i(\boldsymbol{b}_i^{\mathrm{T}}\gamma_i)\boldsymbol{e}_i\}$$
$$+\lambda_i\left\{J_i^{\mathrm{T}}(q_i)\bar{\boldsymbol{b}}_{0i} - (-1)^i(\boldsymbol{n}_i^{\mathrm{T}}\gamma_i)\boldsymbol{e}_i\right\} = u_i, \quad i = 1, 2 \tag{3}$$

where q_i denotes the joint vector as $q_1 = (q_{11}, q_{12}, q_{13})^{\mathrm{T}}$ and $q_2 = (q_{21}, q_{22})^{\mathrm{T}}$, $\dot{\theta}$ denotes the angular velocity of rotation of the object around the object mass center O_m expressed by position vector $\boldsymbol{x} = (x, y)^{\mathrm{T}}$ in terms of the inertial frame coordinates O-xy. Equation (1) expresses the translational motion of the object with mass M and (2) its rotational motion with inertia moment I around the mass center O_m. At the contact point P_i, $\boldsymbol{b}_i$ denotes the unit tangent vector expressed in local coordinates of O_i-X_iY_i fixed to the fingertip of finger i ($i = 1, 2$) as shown in Fig. 1, and $\boldsymbol{n}_i$ denotes the unit normal to the tangent expressed in terms of O_i-X_iY_i. Similarly, $\boldsymbol{b}_{0i}$ and $\boldsymbol{n}_{0i}$ are the unit tangent and normal at P_i expressed in terms of local coordinates O_m-XY fixed to the object. All these unit vectors are determined uniquely from the assumptions 1) and 2) on the rolling contact constraints at each contact point P_i dependently on each corresponding value s_i of arclength parameter for $i = 1, 2$ as shown in Fig. 2. Equation (3) denotes joint motions of finger i with the inertia matrix $G_i(q_i)$ for $i = 1, 2$ and $\boldsymbol{e}_1 = (1, 1, 1)^{\mathrm{T}}$ and $\boldsymbol{e}_2 = (1, 1)^{\mathrm{T}}$. All position vectors γ_i and γ_{0i} for $i = 1, 2$ are defined as in Fig. 2 and expressed in their corresponding local coordinates, respectively. Both the unit vectors $\bar{\boldsymbol{b}}_{0i}$ and $\bar{\boldsymbol{n}}_{0i}$ are expressed in the inertial frame coordinates as follows:

$$\bar{\boldsymbol{b}}_{0i} = \Pi_0 \boldsymbol{b}_{0i}, \quad \bar{\boldsymbol{n}}_{0i} = \Pi_0 \boldsymbol{n}_{0i}, \quad \Pi_0 = (\boldsymbol{r}_X, \boldsymbol{r}_Y) \tag{4}$$

where $\Pi_0 \in SO(2)$ and $\boldsymbol{r}_X$ and $\boldsymbol{r}_Y$ denote the unit vectors of X- and Y-axes of the object in terms of the frame coordinates O-xy. In the equations of (1) to (3), f_i and λ_i are Lagrange's multipliers that correspond to the following rolling contact constraints respectively:

$$\begin{cases} Q_{bi} = (\boldsymbol{r}_i - \boldsymbol{r}_m)^{\mathrm{T}}\bar{\boldsymbol{b}}_{0i} + \boldsymbol{b}_i^{\mathrm{T}}\gamma_i - \boldsymbol{b}_{0i}^{\mathrm{T}}\gamma_{0i} = 0, \quad i = 1,2 & (5) \\ Q_{ni} = (\boldsymbol{r}_i - \boldsymbol{r}_m)^{\mathrm{T}}\bar{\boldsymbol{n}}_{0i} - \boldsymbol{n}_i^{\mathrm{T}}\gamma_i - \boldsymbol{n}_{0i}^{\mathrm{T}}\gamma_{0i} = 0, \quad i = 1,2 & (6) \end{cases}$$

where $\boldsymbol{r}_i$ denotes the position vector of the fingertip center O_i expressed in terms of the frame coordinates O-xy and $\boldsymbol{r}_m$ the position vector of O_m in terms of O-xy. In parallel with Euler-Lagrange's equations (1) to (3), arclength parameters s_i $(i = 1,2)$ should be governed by the following formulae of the first order differential equation :

$$\{\kappa_{0i}(s_i) + \kappa_i(s_i)\}\frac{\mathrm{d}s_i}{\mathrm{d}t} = (-1)^i(\dot{\theta} - \dot{p}_i), \quad i = 1,2 \tag{7}$$

where $\kappa_i(s_i)$ denotes the curvature of the fingertip contour for $i = 1,2$ and $\kappa_{0i}(s_i)$ the curvature of the object contour at contact point P_i corresponding to length parameter s_i for $i = 1,2$. Throughout the paper we use $(\dot{\ })$ for denoting the differentiation of the content of bracket ( ) in time t as $\dot{\theta} = \mathrm{d}\theta/\mathrm{d}t$ in (7) and $(')$ for that of ( ) in length parameter s_i as illustrated by $\gamma_i'(s_i) = \mathrm{d}\gamma_i(s_i)/\mathrm{d}s_i$. As discussed in the previous papers, we have

$$\boldsymbol{b}_i(s_i) = \gamma_i'(s_i)\left(= \frac{\mathrm{d}\gamma_i(s_i)}{\mathrm{d}s_i}\right), \quad \boldsymbol{b}_{0i}(s_i) = \gamma_{0i}'(s_i), \quad i = 1,2 \tag{8}$$

and

$$\boldsymbol{n}_i(s_i) = \kappa_i(s_i)\boldsymbol{b}_i'(s_i), \quad \boldsymbol{n}_{0i}(s_i) = \boldsymbol{b}_{0i}'(s_i), \quad i = 1,2 \tag{9}$$

and further

$$\boldsymbol{b}_i(s_i) = -\kappa_i(s_i)\boldsymbol{n}_i'(s_i), \quad \boldsymbol{b}_{0i}(s_i) = -\kappa_{0i}(s_i)\boldsymbol{n}_{0i}'(s_i), \quad i = 1,2 \tag{10}$$

It is well known as in text books on differential geometry of curves and surfaces (for example, see [Gray et al., 2006]) that equations (9) and (10) constitute Frenet-Serre's formulae for the fingertip contour curves and object contours. Note that all equations of (1) to (3) are characterized by length parameters s_i for $i = 1,2$ through unit vectors $\boldsymbol{n}_{0i}$, $\boldsymbol{b}_{0i}$, $\boldsymbol{b}_i$, and $\boldsymbol{n}_i$, and vectors γ_{0i} and γ_i expressed in each local coordinates, but quantities of the second fundamental form of contour curves, that is, $\kappa_i(s_i)$ and $\kappa_0(s_i)$ for $i = 1,2$, do not enter into equations (1) to (3). It is shown that the set of Euler-Lagrange equations of motion (1) to (3) can be derived by applying the variational principle to the Lagrangian of the system

$$L(X; s_1, s_2) = K(X, \dot{X}) - \sum_{i=1,2}(f_i Q_{ni} + \lambda_i Q_{bi}) \tag{11}$$

where X denotes the position state vector defined as

$$X = (x, y, \theta, q_1^{\mathrm{T}}, q_2^{\mathrm{T}})^{\mathrm{T}} \tag{12}$$

and

$$K(X, \dot{X}) = \frac{M}{2}(\dot{x}^2 + \dot{y}^2) + \frac{I}{2}\dot{\theta}^2 + \sum_{i=1,2}\frac{1}{2}\dot{q}_i^{\mathrm{T}}G_i(q_i)\dot{q}_i \tag{13}$$

Note that $K(X, \dot{X})$ is independent of the shape parameters s_1 and s_2 but Q_{ni} and Q_{bi} defined by (5) and (6) are dependent on s_i for $i = 1, 2$ respectively. The variational principle is written in the following form:

$$\int_{t_0}^{t_1} \left\{ \delta L + u_1^{\mathrm{T}} \delta q_1 + u_2^{\mathrm{T}} \delta q_2 \right\} \mathrm{d}t = 0 \tag{14}$$

From this it follows that

$$G(X)\ddot{X} + \left(\frac{1}{2}\dot{G}(X) + S(X, \dot{X}) \right) \dot{X} + \sum_{i=1,2} \left(f_i \frac{\partial}{\partial X} Q_{ni} + \lambda_i \frac{\partial}{\partial X} Q_{bi} \right) = B \begin{pmatrix} u_1 \\ u_2 \end{pmatrix} \tag{15}$$

where $G(X) = \mathrm{diag}(M, M, I, G_1(q_1), G_2(q_2))$, $S(X, \dot{X})$ is a skew-symmetric matrix, and B denotes the 8×5 constant matrix defined as $B^{\mathrm{T}} = (0_{3\times5}, I_5)$, $0_{3\times5}$ signifies the 3×5 zero matrix, and I_5 the 5×5 identity matrix.

1.3 Fingers-Thumb Opposable Control Signals

In order to design adequate control signals for a pair of multi-joint fingers like the one shown in Fig. 1, we suppose that the kinematics of both the robot fingers are known and measurement data of joint angles and angular velocities are available in real-time but the geometry of an object to be grasped is unknown and the location of its mass center together with its inclination angle can not be measured or sensed. This supposition is reasonable because the structure of robot fingers is fixed for any object but the object to be grasped is changeable from time to time. This standpoint is coincident to the start point of Riemannian geometry that, if the robot (both the robot fingers) has its own internal world, then the robot kinematics based upon quantities of the first fundamental form like $\gamma_i(s_i)$ and $\boldsymbol{b}_i(s_i)$ together with q_i and $\dot{q}_i$ must be accessible because these data are intrinsic to the robot's internal world. However, any quantities of the second fundamental form like $\kappa_i(s_i)$ $(i = 1, 2)$ can not be determined from the robot's intrinsic world. By the same season, we assume that the positions of finger centers O_1 and O_2 denoted by $\boldsymbol{r}_1$ and $\boldsymbol{r}_2$ are accessible from the intrinsic robot world and further the Jacobian matrices defined by $J_i(q_i) = \partial \boldsymbol{r}_i / \partial q_i$ for $i = 1, 2$ are also assumed to be intrinsic, that is, real-time computable. Thus, let us now consider a class of control signals defined by the following form

$$u_i = -c_i \dot{q}_i + (-1)^i \beta J_i^{\mathrm{T}}(q_i)(\boldsymbol{r}_1 - \boldsymbol{r}_2) - \alpha_i \hat{N}_i \boldsymbol{e}_i, \quad i = 1, 2 \tag{16}$$

where β stands for a position feedback gain common for $i = 1, 2$ with physical unit [N/m], α_i is also a positive constant common for $i = 1, 2$, $\hat{N}_i$ is defined as

$$\hat{N}_i = \boldsymbol{e}_i^{\mathrm{T}} \{ q_i(t) - q_i(0) \} = p_i(t) - p_i(0), \quad i = 1, 2 \tag{17}$$

and c_i denotes a positive constant for joint damping for $i = 1, 2$. The first term of the right hand side of (16) stands for damping shaping, the second term plays a role of fingers-thumb opposition, and the last term adjusts possibly some abundunt motion of rotation of the object through contacts. Note that the sum of inner products of u_i and $\dot{q}_i$ for $i = 1, 2$ is given by the equation

$$\sum_{i=1,2} \dot{q}_i^{\mathrm{T}} u_i = -\frac{\mathrm{d}}{\mathrm{d}t} \left\{ \frac{\beta}{2} \|\boldsymbol{r}_1 - \boldsymbol{r}_2\|^2 + \sum_{i=1,2} \frac{\alpha_i}{2} \hat{N}_i^2 \right\} - \sum_{i=1,2} c_i \|\dot{q}_i\|^2 \tag{18}$$

Substitution of control signals of (16) into (3) yields

$$G_i\ddot{q}_i + \left\{\frac{1}{2}\dot{G}_i + S_i\right\}\dot{q}_i + c_i\dot{q}_i - (-1)^i\beta J_i^{\mathrm{T}}(\boldsymbol{r}_1 - \boldsymbol{r}_2) + \alpha_i\hat{N}_i\boldsymbol{e}_i$$
$$+ f_i\left\{J_i^{\mathrm{T}}\bar{\boldsymbol{n}}_{0i} - (-1)^i(\boldsymbol{b}_i^{\mathrm{T}}\gamma_i)\boldsymbol{e}_i\right\} + \lambda_i\left\{J_i^{\mathrm{T}}\bar{\boldsymbol{b}}_{0i} - (-1)^i(\boldsymbol{n}_i^{\mathrm{T}}\gamma_i)\boldsymbol{e}_i\right\} = 0, \quad i = 1,2 \tag{19}$$

Hence, the overall closed-loop dynamics is composed of the set of Euler-Lagrange's equations of (1), (2), and (19) that are subject to four algebraic constraints of (5) and (6) and the pair of the first-order differential equations of (7) that governs the update law of arclength parameters s_1 and s_2. It should be also remarked that, according to (18), the sum of inner products of (1) and $\dot{\boldsymbol{x}}$, (2) and $\dot{\theta}$, and (19) and $\dot{q}_i$ for $i = 1,2$ yields the energy relation

$$\frac{\mathrm{d}}{\mathrm{d}t}E(X,\dot{X}) = -\sum_{i=1,2} c_i\|\dot{q}_i\|^2 \tag{20}$$

where

$$E(X,\dot{X}) = K(X,\dot{X}) + P(X) \tag{21}$$
$$P(X) = \frac{\beta}{2}\|\boldsymbol{r}_1 - \boldsymbol{r}_2\|^2 + \sum_{i=1,2}\frac{\alpha_i}{2}\hat{N}_i^2 \tag{22}$$

and $K(X,\dot{X})$ is the total kinetic energy defined by (13) and $P(X)$ is called the artificial potential energy that is a scalar function depending on only q_1 and q_2. It is important to note that the closed-loop dynamics of (1), (2), and (19) can be written into the general form, correspondingly to (15),

$$G(X)\ddot{X} + \left\{\frac{1}{2}\dot{G}(X) + S(X,\dot{X}) + C\right\}\dot{X} + \frac{\partial P(X)}{\partial X}$$
$$+ \sum_{i=1,2}\left(f_i\frac{\partial}{\partial X}Q_{ni} + \lambda_i\frac{\partial}{\partial X}Q_{bi}\right) = 0 \tag{23}$$

where $C = \mathrm{diag}(0_2, 0, c_1 I_3, c_2 I_2)$. This can be also obtained by applying the principle of variation to the Lagrangian

$$L = K(X,\dot{X}) - P(X) - \sum_{i=1,2}(f_i Q_{ni} + \lambda_i Q_{bi}) \tag{24}$$

1.4 Necessary Conditions for Design of Fingertip Shape

It has been known [Arimoto, 2008] that, in a simple case of "ball-plate" pinching, a solution to the closed-loop dynamics corresponding to (23) under some holonomic constraints of rolling contacts converge to a steady (equilibrium) state that minimizes the potential $P(X)$ under the constraints. However, a stabilization problem of control signals like (16) still remains unsolved or rather has not yet been tackled not only in a general setup of arbitrary geometry like the situation shown in Fig. 1 but also in a little more simple case that the object to be grasped is a parallelepiped but the fingertip shapes are arbitrary. In this paper, we will tackle this simple problem and show that minimization of such an artifically introduced potential can lead to stable grasping under some good design of fingertip shapes (see Fig. 3).

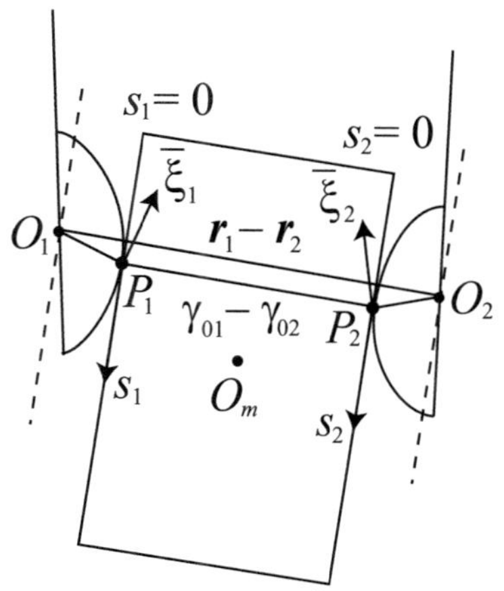

Fig. 3. Minimization of the squared norm $\|r_1 - r_2\|^2$ over rolling motions is attained when the straight line $\overline{P_1P_2}$ connecting the two contact points becomes parallel to the vector $(r_1 - r_2)$, that is, $\overline{O_1O_2}$ becomes parallel to $\overline{P_1P_2}$.

First, we remark that, since the first term of $P(X)$ in (22) in the squared norm of the vector $\overrightarrow{O_2O_1}$ times $\beta/2$, it must be a function only dependent on length parameters s_1 and s_2. Then, it will be shown that minimization of the squared norm $\|r_1 - r_2\|^2$ over rolling contact motions is attained when the straight line $\overline{P_1P_2}$ connecting the two contact points becomes parallel to the vector $(r_1 - r_2)$. That is, $U(X)$ $(= (\beta/2)\|r_1 - r_2\|^2)$ is minimized when $\overline{O_1O_2}$ becomes parallel to $\overline{P_1P_2}$. To show this directly from the set of Euler-Lagrange's equations (1), (2), and (19) seems difficult even in this case. Instead, we remark that $(r_1 - r_2)$ can be expressed in terms of length parameters s_i for $i = 1, 2$ as follows:

$$r_1 - r_2 = -\Pi_1\gamma_1 + \Pi_2\gamma_2 + \Pi_0(\gamma_{01} - \gamma_{02}) \tag{25}$$

where $\Pi_i \in SO(2)$ denotes the rotational matrix of O_i-X_iY_i to be expressed in the frame coordinates O-xy. Since the object is rectangular, all b_{0i} and n_{0i} for $i = 1, 2$ are invariant under the change of s_i for $i = 1, 2$. Therefore, as seen from Fig. 3, if the object width is denoted by l_w and zero points of s_1 and s_2 are set as shown in Fig. 3, then it is possible to write (25) as follows:

$$r_1 - r_2 = (s_1 - s_2)\bar{b}_{01} + (-b_1^{\mathrm{T}}\gamma_1 + b_2^{\mathrm{T}}\gamma_2)\bar{b}_{01} - l_w\bar{n}_{01} + (n_1^{\mathrm{T}}\gamma_1 + n_2^{\mathrm{T}}\gamma_2)\bar{n}_{01} \tag{26}$$

Since $\bar{b}_{01} \perp \bar{n}_{01}$, $U(X)$ can be expressed as

$$\begin{aligned} U(X) &= \frac{\beta}{2}\|r_1 - r_2\|^2 = \frac{\beta}{2}\left\{d^2(s_1, s_2) + l^2(s_1, s_2)\right\} \\ &= U(s_1, s_2) \end{aligned} \tag{27}$$

where

$$d(s_1, s_2) = s_1 - s_2 - b_1^{\mathrm{T}}\gamma_1 + b_2^{\mathrm{T}}\gamma_2 \tag{28}$$

$$l(s_1, s_2) = -l_w + (n_1^{\mathrm{T}}\gamma_1 + n_2^{\mathrm{T}}\gamma_2) \tag{29}$$

Note that the artificial potential $U(X)$ can be regarded as a scalar function defined in terms of length parameters s_1 and s_2. When minimization of $U(s_1, s_2)$ over some parameter intervals

$s_i \in I_i = (a_i, b_i)$ is considered for $i = 1,2$, it is important to note that the vector $(\boldsymbol{r}_1 - \boldsymbol{r}_2)$ is originally subject to the constraint

$$V(s_1, s_2) = (\boldsymbol{r}_1 - \boldsymbol{r}_2)^{\mathrm{T}}\bar{\boldsymbol{n}}_{01} - \boldsymbol{n}_1^{\mathrm{T}}\gamma_1 - \boldsymbol{n}_2^{\mathrm{T}}\gamma_2 - \boldsymbol{n}_{01}^{\mathrm{T}}\gamma_{01} - \boldsymbol{n}_{02}^{\mathrm{T}}\gamma_{02} = 0 \tag{30}$$

which is obtained by subtraction of Q_{n2} from Q_{n1} defined in (5) and (6). Hence, by introducing a Lagrange multiplier η, minimization of the function

$$W(s_1, s_2; \eta) = U(s_1, s_2) + \eta V(s_1, s_2) \tag{31}$$

must be equivalent to that of $U(X)$. Then it follows that

$$\frac{\partial W}{\partial s_i} = (-1)^i \beta \kappa_i (\boldsymbol{r}_1 - \boldsymbol{r}_2)^{\mathrm{T}} \bar{\boldsymbol{\xi}}_i + \eta \kappa_i \boldsymbol{b}_i^{\mathrm{T}} \gamma_i, \quad i = 1,2 \tag{32}$$

where we define, for abbreviation,

$$\bar{\boldsymbol{\xi}}_i = (\boldsymbol{n}_i^{\mathrm{T}}\gamma_i)\bar{\boldsymbol{b}}_{0i} + (\boldsymbol{b}_i^{\mathrm{T}}\gamma_i)\bar{\boldsymbol{n}}_{0i}, \quad i = 1,2 \tag{33}$$

The derivation of this equation is discussed in [Arimoto et al. 2009c]. At this stage, we remark that the vectors $\bar{\boldsymbol{\xi}}_i$ for $i = 1,2$ appear at contact points P_1 and P_2 as indicated in Fig. 3. Evidently from the right hand side of (32), if we set

$$\eta = \beta(\boldsymbol{r}_1 - \boldsymbol{r}_2)^{\mathrm{T}}\bar{\boldsymbol{n}}_{01} \quad \left(= -\beta(\boldsymbol{r}_1 - \boldsymbol{r}_2)^{\mathrm{T}}\bar{\boldsymbol{n}}_{02}\right) \tag{34}$$

and at the same time

$$(\boldsymbol{r}_1 - \boldsymbol{r}_2)^{\mathrm{T}}\bar{\boldsymbol{b}}_{0i} = 0, \qquad i = 1,2 \tag{35}$$

then (32) implies

$$\frac{\partial W}{\partial s_i} = 0, \qquad i = 1,2 \tag{36}$$

In view of the geometrical meaning of (35) that the vector $\overrightarrow{O_2O_1} \perp \bar{\boldsymbol{b}}_{0i}$, when $\boldsymbol{r}_1 - \boldsymbol{r}_2$ becomes perpendicular to $\boldsymbol{b}_{0i}$ from some starting posture by rolling contact motion, s_i for $i = 1,2$ must have the same value s^* and $\boldsymbol{b}_1^{\mathrm{T}}\gamma_1 = \boldsymbol{b}_2^{\mathrm{T}}\gamma_2$. That is, satisfaction of the conditions

$$s_1 = s_2 = s^*, \quad \boldsymbol{b}_1^{\mathrm{T}}\gamma_1 = \boldsymbol{b}_2^{\mathrm{T}}\gamma_2 \tag{37}$$

is equivalent to that $\overrightarrow{O_2O_1}$ becomes parallel to $\overrightarrow{P_2P_1}$ as shown in Fig. 3. Under (37),

$$\left.\frac{\partial W}{\partial s_i}\right|_{s_i = s^*} = 0, \qquad i = 1,2 \tag{38}$$

Finally, it is important to check the positivity of the Hessian matrix $H = (\partial^2 U / \partial s_i \partial s_j)$. Bearing in mind the form of (32) together with (34), we obtain [Arimoto et al. 2009c]

$$\begin{aligned} \left.\frac{\partial^2 U}{\partial s_i \partial s_i}\right|_{s_i = s^*} &= \kappa_i (-1)^i \beta (\boldsymbol{r}_1 - \boldsymbol{r}_2)^{\mathrm{T}} \bar{\boldsymbol{n}}_{0i} (\kappa_i \boldsymbol{n}_i^{\mathrm{T}}\gamma_i + \boldsymbol{b}_i^{\mathrm{T}}\gamma_i') \\ &= -\beta l(s_1, s_2)\kappa_i^2 \left(\frac{1}{\kappa_i} + \boldsymbol{n}_i^{\mathrm{T}}\gamma_i\right), \qquad i = 1,2 \end{aligned} \tag{39}$$

and

$$\left.\frac{\partial^2 U}{\partial s_1 \partial s_2}\right|_{s_i=s^*} = 0 \tag{40}$$

where $l(s_1, s_2)$ is defined by (29). Since $l(s_1, s_2) < 0$ from the geometrical meaning of the situation shown in Fig. 3, it is possible to conclude that the potential function $U(s_1, s_2)$ is minimized at the posture satisfying (37) provided that

$$\frac{1}{\kappa_i(s_i)} > -\boldsymbol{n}_i^{\mathrm{T}}(s_i)\gamma_i(s_i), \qquad i = 1, 2 \tag{41}$$

for all s_i belonging to $(s^* - \delta_i, s^* + \delta_i)$ with some $\delta_i > 0$ for $i = 1, 2$.
Geometric and physical meanings of the condition of (41) will be discussed more in detail in a future paper [Arimoto et al., 2009c].

1.5 Derichlet-Lagrange Stability for Pinching a Rectangular Object

In this section, we show that, when the line connecting the contact points P_1 and P_2 becomes parallel to the line $\overline{O_1O_2}$ as shown in Fig. 3, P(X) is minimized under the constraint of equalities (5) and (6) and at the same time any solution to the set of closed-loop dynamics (1), (2), and (19) under rolling constraints (5) and (6) converges asymptotically to such an equilibrium posture, provided that the solution trajectory starts in a neighborhood of the equilibrium state. To do this, define

$$\begin{cases} \Delta f_i = f_i + \beta l(s_1, s_2) & (42) \\ \Delta\lambda_i = \lambda_i - (-1)^i \beta d(s_1, s_2) & (43) \end{cases}$$

and note that

$$-(-1)^i \beta J_i^{\mathrm{T}}(\boldsymbol{r}_1 - \boldsymbol{r}_2) = \beta J_i^{\mathrm{T}} \left\{ l\bar{\boldsymbol{n}}_{0i} - (-1)^i d\bar{\boldsymbol{b}}_{0i} \right\}, \qquad i = 1, 2 \tag{44}$$

Substituting (44) into (19) and referring to (42) and (43) yield

$$G_i\ddot{q}_i + \left\{\frac{1}{2}\dot{G}_i + S_i\right\}\dot{q}_i + c_i\dot{q}_i + \Delta f_i \left\{J_i^{\mathrm{T}}\bar{\boldsymbol{n}}_{0i} - (-1)^i(\boldsymbol{b}_i^{\mathrm{T}}\gamma_i)\boldsymbol{e}_i\right\}$$
$$+\Delta\lambda_i\left\{J_i^{\mathrm{T}}\bar{\boldsymbol{b}}_{0i} - (-1)^i(\boldsymbol{n}_i^{\mathrm{T}}\gamma_i)\boldsymbol{e}_i\right\} + \Delta N_i\boldsymbol{e}_i = 0, \qquad i = 1, 2 \tag{45}$$

where

$$\Delta N_i = \beta\left\{(-1)^i l(\boldsymbol{b}_i^{\mathrm{T}}\gamma_i) - d(\boldsymbol{n}_i^{\mathrm{T}}\gamma_i)\right\} + \alpha_i\left\{p_i - p_i(0)\right\}, \qquad i = 1, 2 \tag{46}$$

On the other hand, (1) and (2) can be rewritten into the forms:

$$M\ddot{\boldsymbol{x}} - \Delta f_1\bar{\boldsymbol{n}}_{01} - \Delta f_2\bar{\boldsymbol{n}}_{02} - \Delta\lambda_1\bar{\boldsymbol{b}}_{01} - \Delta\lambda_2\bar{\boldsymbol{b}}_{02} = 0 \tag{47}$$

$$I\ddot{\theta} - \Delta f_1(\boldsymbol{b}_{01}^{\mathrm{T}}\gamma_{01}) + \Delta f_2(\boldsymbol{b}_{02}^{\mathrm{T}}\gamma_{02}) + \Delta\lambda_1(\boldsymbol{n}_{01}^{\mathrm{T}}\gamma_{01}) - \Delta\lambda_2(\boldsymbol{n}_{02}^{\mathrm{T}}\gamma_{02}) + S_N = 0 \tag{48}$$

where

$$S_N = \beta l(\boldsymbol{b}_{01}^{\mathrm{T}}\gamma_{01} - \boldsymbol{b}_{02}^{\mathrm{T}}\gamma_{02}) - \beta d(\boldsymbol{n}_{01}^{\mathrm{T}}\gamma_{01} + \boldsymbol{n}_{02}^{\mathrm{T}}\gamma_{02}) = \beta\{(s_1 - s_2)l + l_w d\} \tag{49}$$

Now it is possible to show that the set of equations (47) to (49) together with (7) can be regarded as a set of Euler-Lagrange equations obtained by applying the variational principle to the Lagrangian

$$L = K(X, \dot{X}) - U(s_1, s_2) + \sum_{i=1,2} (\Delta f_i Q_{ni} + \Delta\lambda_i Q_{bi}) \tag{50}$$

in which the external forces of damping $c_i \dot{q}_i$ for $i = 1,2$ through finger joints are taken into account. In fact, from (27) to (29) it follows that

$$\begin{aligned}
\frac{dU(s_1,s_2)}{dt} &= \sum_{i=1,2} \frac{dU_i}{ds_i}\frac{ds_i}{dt} = \sum_{i=1,2} (-1)^i \beta \left\{ (\boldsymbol{n}_i^{\mathrm{T}}\gamma_i)d - (-1)^i(\boldsymbol{b}_i^{\mathrm{T}}\gamma_i)l \right\} \kappa_i \frac{ds_i}{dt} \\
&= \sum_{i=1,2} \beta \left\{ (\boldsymbol{n}_i^{\mathrm{T}}\gamma_i)d - (-1)^i(\boldsymbol{b}_i^{\mathrm{T}}\gamma_i)l \right\} (\dot{\theta} - \dot{p}_i) \qquad (51) \\
&= \beta \left\{ \boldsymbol{n}_1^{\mathrm{T}}\gamma_1 + \boldsymbol{n}_2^{\mathrm{T}}\gamma_2)d + (\boldsymbol{b}_1^{\mathrm{T}}\gamma_1 - \boldsymbol{b}_2^{\mathrm{T}}\gamma_2)l \right\} \dot{\theta} + \sum_{i=1,2} \beta N_i \dot{p}_i \qquad (52)
\end{aligned}$$

where N_i is defined as

$$N_i = (-1)^i(\boldsymbol{b}_i^{\mathrm{T}}\gamma_i)l - (\boldsymbol{n}_i^{\mathrm{T}}\gamma_i)d \tag{53}$$

By using (28) and (29), (52) can be written as

$$\begin{aligned}
\frac{dU(s_1,s_2)}{dt} &= \beta \{(l + l_w)d + (s_1 - s_2 - d)l\} \dot{\theta} + \sum_{i=1,2} \beta N_i \dot{p}_i \\
&= S_N \dot{\theta} + \sum_{i=1,2} \beta N_i \boldsymbol{e}_i^{\mathrm{T}} \dot{q}_i \qquad (54)
\end{aligned}$$

Thus, we conclude that from (46) the variation of P takes the form

$$\begin{aligned}
dP &= d\left[U + \sum \frac{\alpha_i}{2} \{p_i - p_i(0)\}^2 \right] \\
&= S_N d\theta + \sum_{i=1,2} [\beta N_i + \alpha_i \{p_i - p_i(0)\}] dp_i \\
&= S_N d\theta + \sum_{i=1,2} \Delta N_i \boldsymbol{e}_i^{\mathrm{T}} dq_i \qquad (55)
\end{aligned}$$

The last term of the left hand side of (48) comes directly from the first term of the right hand side of (55) in the variational form of the potential $P(X, s_1, s_2)$. The last term $\Delta N_i \boldsymbol{e}_i$ also comes directly from the last term of (55). Thus, it is possible to prove that, if the posture of the fingers-object system satisfying the condition that $\overline{O_1O_2}$ is parallel to $\overline{P_1P_2}$ as shown in Fig. 3 is an isolated equilibrium state, then the posture must be asymptotically stable because the system is fully dissipated (see [Arimoto, 2010]), no matter how the system is holonomically constrained. If both the fingers are of single degrees-of-freedom, then the total degrees-of-freedom of the system becomes single and therefore the equilibrium state is isolated. In a case of redundant degrees-of-freedom system like the setup illustrated in Fig. 1, it is necessary to extend the so-called Dirichlet-Lagrange stability theorem (see [Arimoto et al., 2009c] and [Arimoto, 2010a]) to a system with redundancy in degree-of-freedom together with holonomic constraints. Such an extension of the theorem is possible as already discussed in a special class of robot control problems (see [Arimoto, 2007]), but the details are too mathematically sophysticated and therefore will be discussed in a future paper.

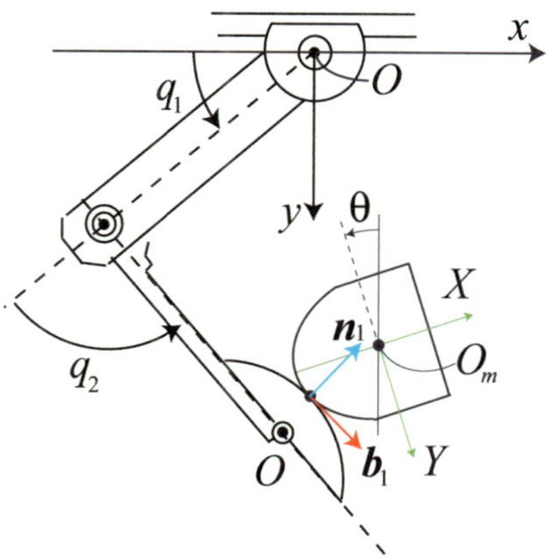

Fig. 4. Robot finger pinching an object pivoted at a fixed point O_m.

1.6 Conclusions

Modeling and control of precision prehension of 2-D objects by a pair of planar robot fingers with an arbitrary fingertip geometry are discussed. Stability of a control signal based upon the fingers-thumb opposition is analyzed by extending the Dirichlet-Lagrange stability theorem in a case that the object has parallel flat surfaces.

To find an effective control scheme that stabilizes grasping of an object with an arbitrary geometry remains unsolved, even in the case of 2-D grasping.

2. Simulation of 2-D Grasping under Physical Interaction of Rolling between Arbitrary Smooth Contour Curves

2.1 Introduction

Numerical simulation of motions of a rolling contact between two 2-dimensional (2-D) rigid bodies with an arbitrary smooth contour is carried out by using an extended constraint stabilization method (CSM), in order to testify the physical validity of the Euler-Lagrange equation of rolling contact motion. To gain a physical insight into the problem, a simpler control problem is treated in relation to stabilization of a rotational motion of a rigid body pivoted around a fixed point in a horizontal plane by using a planar robot with two joints. A CSM is applied extensively to the derived Euler-Lagrange equation that is characterized by an arclength parameter, that is commonly used to specify the contact position on the object contour and the fingertip contour. In parallel to the Euler-Lagrange equation, a first-order differential equation of the arclength parameter must be integrated simultaneously in order to update the position of the rolling contact (see [Yoshida et al., 2009a and 2009b]).

2.2 A Testbed Problem of Stabilization for Rolling Contact Motion

In order to gain a physical and intuitive insight into a rolling contact phenomenon between two rigid bodies in a horizontal plane, a simple mechanical setup depicted in Fig. 4 is considered. The robot finger has two joints and its fingertip is shaped by an arbitrary smooth contour curve. The object pivots around the fixed point O_m $(= (x, y))$ and has a contour with an arbitrary geometry. It is assumed that motion of the overall fingers-object system is restricted to the horizontal plane and therefore the effect of gravity is ignored. Denote the joint vector of

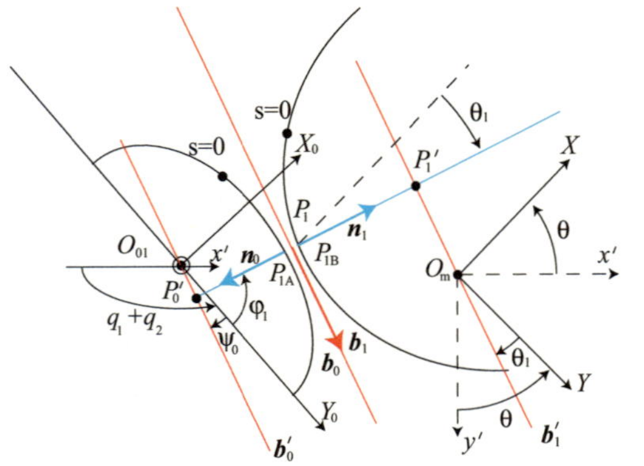

Fig. 5. Geometrical relationship between local coordinates O_m-XY and O_{01}-X_0Y_0.

finger joint angles by $q = (q_1, q_2)^{\mathrm{T}}$ and the orientation angle of the object by θ. As shown in Fig. 4, O-xy expresses the inertial frame, O_m-XY the local coordinates attached to the object, and O_{01}-X_1Y_1 the local coordinates of the fingertip as shown in Fig. 5. Suppose that the object contour is described by a curve $\gamma(s) = (X(s), Y(s))^{\mathrm{T}}$ with the aid of the arclength parameter s as shown in Fig. 4 and Fig. 5. At the same time, define the unit tangent $\boldsymbol{b}_1(s)$ and the unit normal $\boldsymbol{n}_1(s)$ at the contact point P_{1B} as shown in Fig. 5. Similarly, define $\boldsymbol{b}_0(s)$ and $\boldsymbol{n}_0(s)$ at the contact point P_{1A} on the contour curve $\gamma_0(s) = (X_0(s), Y_0(s))$ of the fingertip. Since we assume that the two contact points P_{1A} and P_{1B} must coincide at a single common point P_1 without mutual penetration and the two contours share the same tangent at the contact point, $\boldsymbol{n}_0 = -\boldsymbol{n}_1$ and $\boldsymbol{b}_0 = \boldsymbol{b}_1$ as seen in Fig. 5. If we define angles $\theta_1(s)$ and $\psi_0(s)$ by

$$\theta_1(s) = \arctan\{X'(s)/Y'(s)\} \tag{56}$$

$$\psi_0(s) = \arctan\{X_0'(s)/Y_0'(s)\} \tag{57}$$

then unit tangents and normals can be expressed as

$$\boldsymbol{b}_1 = \begin{pmatrix} \sin(\theta+\theta_1) \\ \cos(\theta+\theta_1) \end{pmatrix}, \quad \boldsymbol{b}_0 = \begin{pmatrix} -\cos(q_1+q_2+\psi_0) \\ \sin(q_1+q_2+\psi_0) \end{pmatrix} \tag{58}$$

$$\boldsymbol{n}_1 = \begin{pmatrix} \cos(\theta+\theta_1) \\ -\sin(\theta+\theta_1) \end{pmatrix}, \quad \boldsymbol{n}_0 = -\begin{pmatrix} \sin(q_1+q_2+\psi_0) \\ \cos(q_1+q_2+\psi_0) \end{pmatrix} \tag{59}$$

where we denote the derivative of $X(s)$ in s by $X'(s)$ $(= \mathrm{d}X(s)/\mathrm{d}s)$ and similarly the derivatives of $Y(s)$, $X_0(s)$, and $Y_0(s)$ by $Y'(s)$, $X_0'(s)$, and $Y_0'(s)$. Further, it is important to introduce the following four quantities that can be determined from the local fingertip and object geometries (see Fig. 6):

$$l_{b0}(s) = X_0(s)\sin\psi_0 + Y_0(s)\cos\psi_0 \tag{60}$$

$$l_{b1}(s) = -X(s)\sin\theta_1 - Y(s)\cos\theta_1 \tag{61}$$

$$l_{n0}(s) = X_0(s)\cos\psi_0 - Y_0(s)\sin\psi_0 \tag{62}$$

$$l_{n1}(s) = -X(s)\cos\theta_1 + Y(s)\sin\theta_1 \tag{63}$$

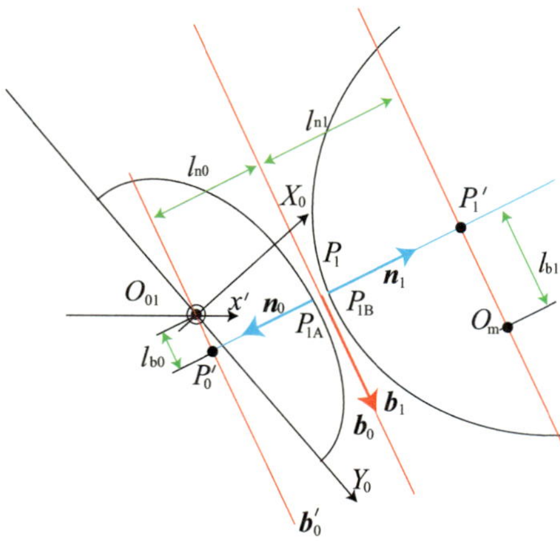

Fig. 6. Geometrical relationship of l_{n0}, l_{n1}, l_{b0}, and l_{b1}.

As discussed in detail by [Arimoto et al., 2009a], the rolling contact constraint is composed of the two algebraic equations:

$$R = (x_{01} - x)\sin(\theta + \theta_1) + (y_{01} - y)\cos(\theta + \theta_1) + l_{b0}(s) + l_{b1}(s) = 0 \quad (64)$$

$$Q = (x_{01} - x)\cos(\theta + \theta_1) - (y_{01} - y)\sin(\theta + \theta_1) + l_{n0}(s) + l_{n1}(s) = 0 \quad (65)$$

Note that these two equalities express the geometrical relations described in the following ways (see Fig. 6):

$$\overline{P_0'P_1'} = l_{no} + l_{n1} \quad (66)$$

$$\overline{O_m P_1'} + \overline{P_0' O_{01}} = l_{b0} + l_{b1} \quad (67)$$

Further, from the definition of directional derivatives of $\boldsymbol{b}_0$ and $\boldsymbol{b}_1$ that coincide at the contact point, the arclength parameter should be updated through the following first-order differential equation [Arimoto et al., 2009a]:

$$\{\kappa_0(s) + \kappa_1(s)\}\frac{\mathrm{d}s}{\mathrm{d}t} = (\dot{q}_1 + \dot{q}_2 - \dot{\theta}) \quad (68)$$

where $\kappa_0(s)$ denotes the curvature of the fingertip contour curve and $\kappa_1(s)$ that of the object contour. These quantities can be calculated from the quantities of the second fundamental form as follows:

$$\kappa_0(s) = -X_0''(s)Y_0(s) + X_0'(s)Y_0''(s) \quad (69)$$

$$\kappa_1(s) = X''(s)Y'(s) - X'(s)Y''(s) \quad (70)$$

The total kinetic energy of the system is given by the form

$$K = \frac{1}{2}\dot{q}^{\mathrm{T}}G(q)\dot{q} + \frac{1}{2}I\dot{\theta}^2 \quad (71)$$

where $G(q)$ stands for the inertia matrix of the finger and I for the inertia moment of the object rigid body around the pivotal axis at O_m. Then, by applying the variational principle for the Lagrangian

$$L = K - fQ - \lambda R \quad (72)$$

the following Euler-Lagrange equation is obtained [Arimoto et al., 2009a]:

$$I\ddot{\theta} + f l_{b1} - \lambda l_{n1} = 0 \tag{73}$$

$$G(q)\ddot{q} + \left\{\frac{1}{2}\dot{G}(q) + S(q,\dot{q})\right\}\dot{q} + f\{J_{01}^{\mathrm{T}}(q)\boldsymbol{n}_1 + l_{b0}\boldsymbol{e}\} + \lambda\{J_{01}^{\mathrm{T}}(q)\boldsymbol{b}_1 - l_{n0}\boldsymbol{e}\} = u \tag{74}$$

where $\boldsymbol{e} = (1,1)^{\mathrm{T}}$ and f and λ signify Lagrange's multipliers corresponding to constraints $Q = 0$ and $R = 0$ respectively. Finally, we introduce the control signal

$$u = -c\dot{q} - \frac{f_d}{r} J_{01}^{\mathrm{T}}(q) \begin{pmatrix} x_{01} - x \\ y_{01} - y \end{pmatrix} \tag{75}$$

where c stands for a positive damping constant and f_d/r a positive constant with the physical dimension [N/m]. It should be noted [Arimoto et al., 2009a] that by substituting u of (75) into (74) and rewriting (73) and (74), we obtain the closed-loop dynamics of the system described by

$$I\ddot{\theta} + \Delta f \frac{\partial Q}{\partial \theta} + \Delta\lambda \frac{\partial R}{\partial \theta} + \frac{f_d}{r} N_1 = 0 \tag{76}$$

$$G(q)\ddot{q} + \left\{\frac{1}{2}\dot{G} + S\right\} c\dot{q} + \Delta f \frac{\partial Q}{\partial q} + \Delta\lambda \frac{\partial R}{\partial q} - \frac{f_d}{r} N_1 \boldsymbol{e} = 0 \tag{77}$$

where

$$\begin{cases} \Delta f = f + \dfrac{f_d}{r} Q_1, \quad \Delta\lambda = \lambda + \dfrac{f_d}{r} R_1 \\ N_1 = l_{b0} Q_1 - l_{n0} R_1 = -l_{b0} l_{n1} + l_{n0} l_{b1} \end{cases} \tag{78}$$

and

$$Q_1 = -l_{n0}(s) - l_{n1}(s), \quad R_1 = l_{b0}(s) + l_{b1}(s) \tag{79}$$

2.3 Numerical Simulation

We carry out numerical simulations in order to verify the validity of the derived mathematical model and the effectiveness of the control signal. The physical parameters of the overall system are given in Table 1 and the control input parameters are in Table 2. As an object with an arbitrary geometry, the contour carve $\gamma(s) = (X(s), Y(s))$ is given by a function described by

$$X(s) = -0.03 + \frac{\sqrt{1 + 4 \times 50^2 \times (s - 3.363 \times 10^{-3})^2}}{2 \times 50} \tag{80}$$

$$Y(s) = \frac{A\sinh(2 \times 50 \times (2 - 3.363 \times 10^{-3}))}{2 \times 50} \tag{81}$$

The fingertip contour curve is given by a function described as

$$X_0(s) = 0.035 - \frac{\sqrt{1 + 4 \times 20^2 \times s}}{2 \times 20} \tag{82}$$

$$Y_0(s) = \frac{A\sinh(2 \times 20 \times s)}{2 \times 20} \tag{83}$$

l_{11}	length	0.065 [m]
l_{12}	length	0.065 [m]
m_{11}	weight	0.045 [kg]
m_{12}	weight	0.040 [kg]
I	object inertia moment	6.6178×10^{-6} [kgm^2]

Table 1. Physical parameters of the fingers and object.

f_d	internal force	0.500 [N]
c	damping coefficient	0.006 [Nms]
r	constant value	0.010 [m]
γ_{f1}	CSM gain	1500
$\gamma_{\lambda 1}$	CSM gain	3000
ω_{f1}	CSM gain	225.0×10^4
$\omega_{\lambda 1}$	CSM gain	900.0×10^4

Table 2. Parameters of control signals & CSM gains.

Both the contour curves are depicted in Fig. 7. The pair of the second-order differentia equations (73) and (74) together with (75) and the other pair of holonomic constraints expressed by (64) and (65) are combined into a CSM form by introducing a pair of CSM gains γ_{f1} and ω_{f1} and another pair of $\gamma_{\lambda 1}$ and $\omega_{\lambda 1}$ that are given in Table 2. In the CSM form, the derivative of length parameter s in t is required, which is obtained by the update equation of the length parameter shown in (68). As discussed in the recent paper [Arimoto et al., 2009b], the equilibrium sate is realized when the line $\overline{O_{01}O_m}$ meets the contact point P_1. In other words, the artificial potential $U(s) = \frac{f_d}{2r}\{(l_{b1} + l_{b0})^2 + (l_{n0} + l_{n1})^2\}$ is minimized at the position satisfying $N_1 = 0$, that is, the line $\overline{O_{01}O_m}$ meets the contact point P_1.

We show the initial pose of the system and another pose of the system after 3.0 [s] in Fig. 8. The initial pose is obtained by solving the inverse kinematics problem and the initial angular velocities $\dot{q}_i$ $(i = 1, 2)$ and $\dot{\theta}$ are set zero in this simulation. The trasient responses of all physical variables are shown in Figs. 9 to 17. As seen from Fig. 11, N_1 tends to zero as t increases and, in parallel to this fact, the value of the artificial potential $U(s)$ tends to its minimum as t increases as shown in Fig. 18. As predicted from Fig. 8 (b), the system's position tends to converge to the posture at which the line connecting the fingertip center O and the object center O_m meets the contact point P_1.

2.4 Conclusions

A preliminary result of numerical simulation of control of rolling contact motions between two 2-D rigid bodies with an arbitrary contour curve is presented. In this note, the two contour curves are given in an analytically well-defined form. Nevertheless, to construct a numerical simulator for the purpose of its preactical use, it is necessary to design another numerical simulator that can calculate numerical quantities of the second fundamental form when the concerned contour curves are given by a set of numerical data points. Then, the problem for finding a unique contact point between the two contour curves without penetration becomes crucial in the design of such a practically useful simulator.

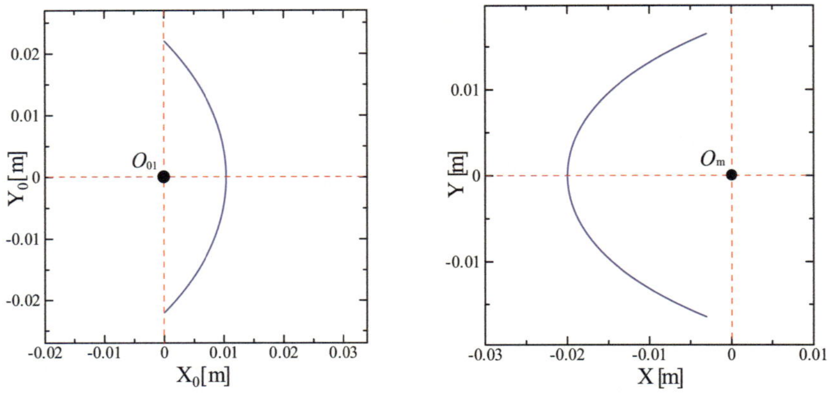

(a) The curve of the fingertip's contour (b) The curve of the object's contour

Fig. 7. The local coordinates of the fingertip and the object.

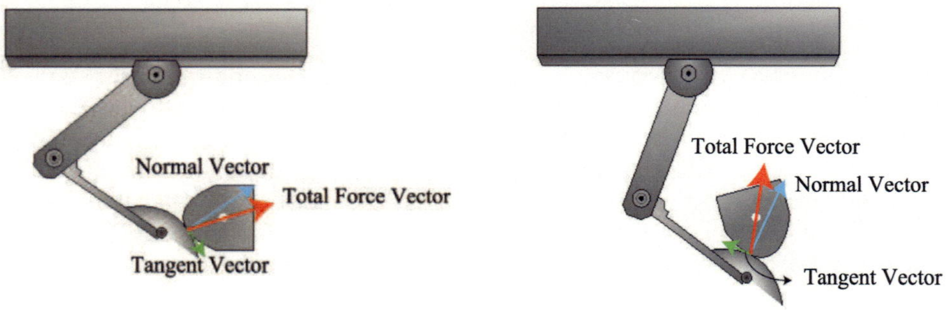

(a) Initial pose (b) After 3 seconds

Fig. 8. Motion of pinching a 2-D object with arbitrary shape.

3. Modeling of 3-D Grasping under Rolling Contacts between Arbitrary Smooth Surfaces

3.1 Introduction

A possible extension of modeling and control of 2-D (2-dimensional) grasping of a rigid object by means of a pair of planar robot fingers to 3-D grasping under rolling contacts is discussed, under the circumstance of an arbitrary geometry of surfaces of the robot fingertips and a given 3-D rigid object.

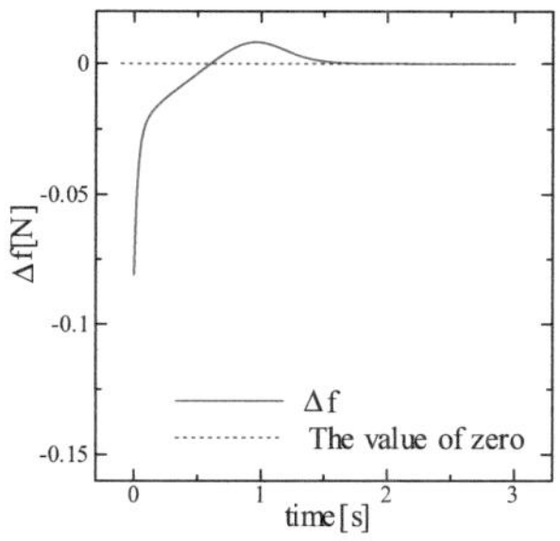

Fig. 9. Δf

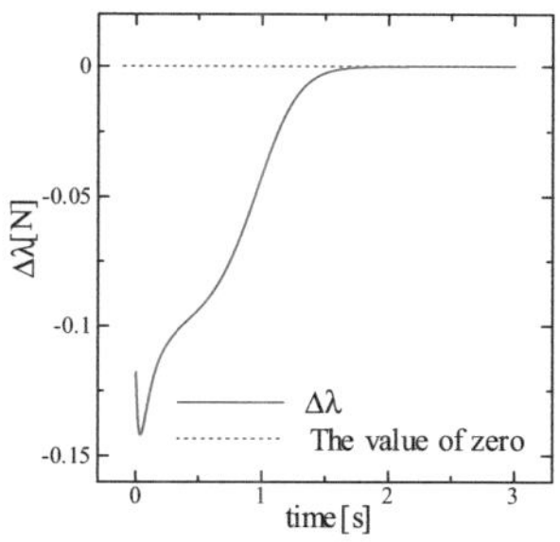

Fig. 10. $\Delta\lambda$

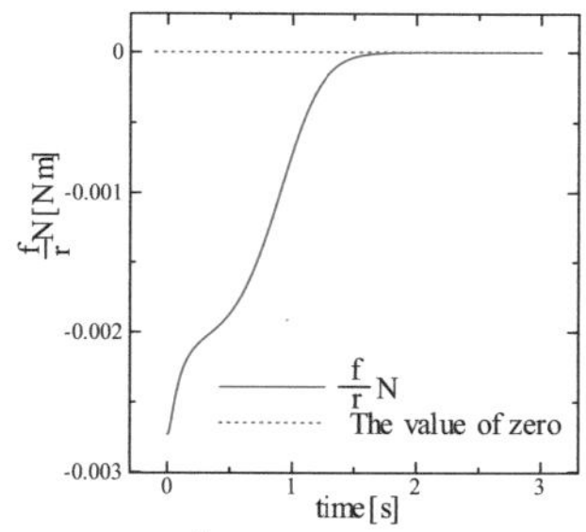

Fig. 11. $\frac{f_d}{r}N_1$

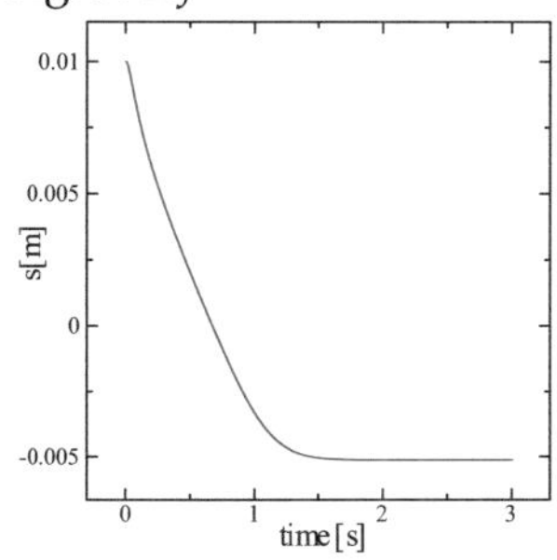

Fig. 12. s

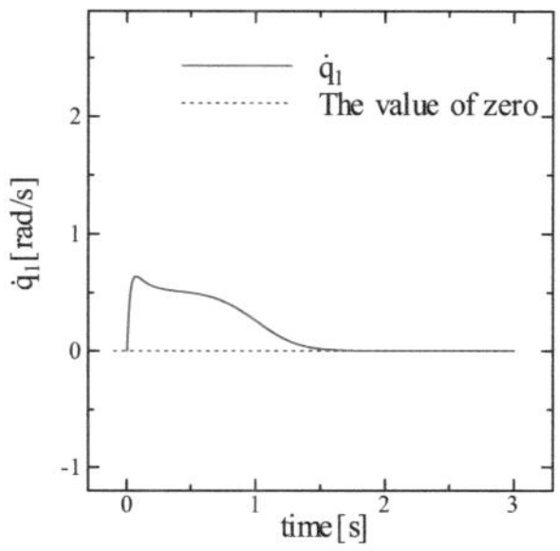

Fig. 13. $\dot{q}_1$

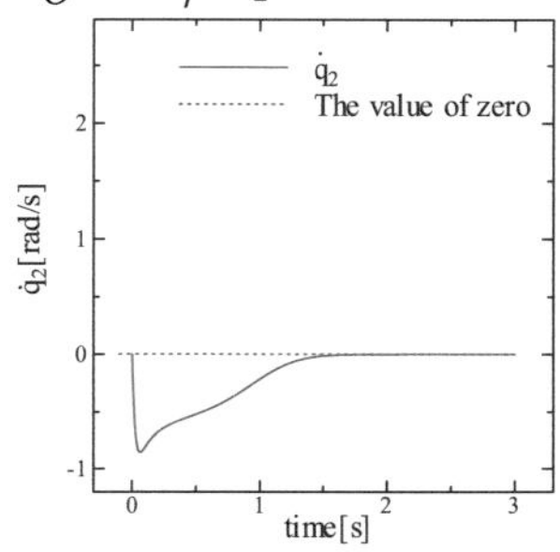

Fig. 14. $\dot{q}_2$

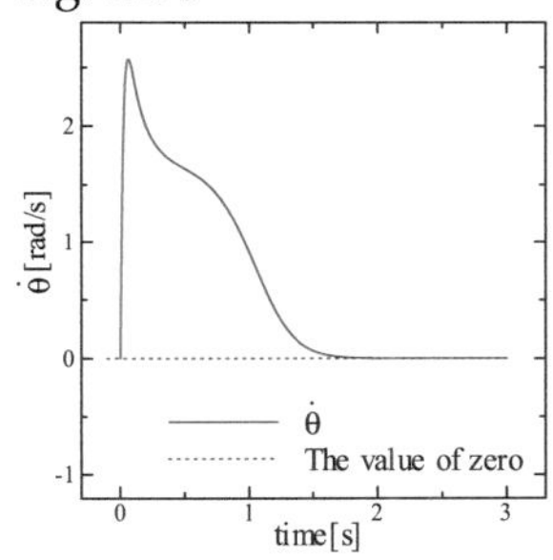

Fig. 15. $\dot{\theta}$

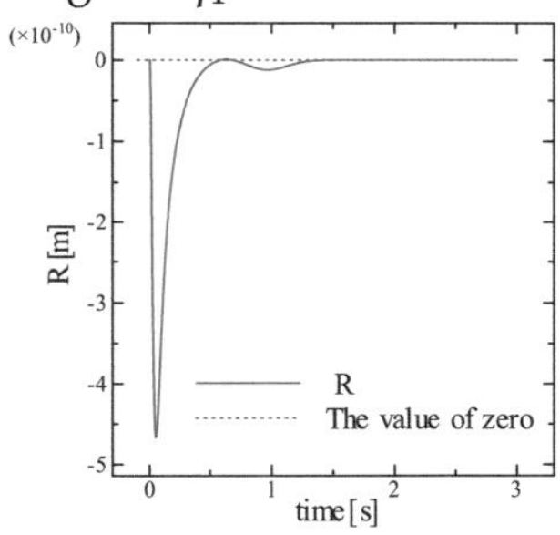

Fig. 16. R

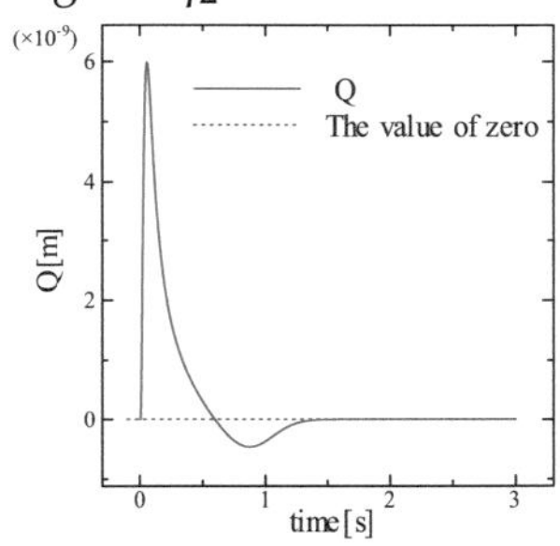

Fig. 17. Q

3.2 Mathematical Modeling of 3-D Grasping under Rolling Contacts

Very recently in the previous papers [Arimoto et al., 2009a and 2009b], a complete set of Euler-Lagrange equations of motion of 2-dimensional grasping under rolling contact constraints is given in a wrench space form from the standpoint of a new definition of rolling contact constraints. The rolling contact between two rigid bodies with smooth surfaces is now interpreted as a condition that the contact points coincide at a single point and share a common tangent at the contact point. This standpoint was first proposed in differential geometry by Nomizu [Nomizu, 1978], that reflects in a two-dimensional case a well-known theorem on curves that, given two smooth planar curves with the same curvature along their arclengths respectively, the one can coincide with another by a homogeneous transformation. The recent works [Arimoto et al., 2009a and 2009b] show that such a mathematical observation can be extended more to the dynamics and control of physical interaction between 2-D rigid bodies with an arbitrary geometry.

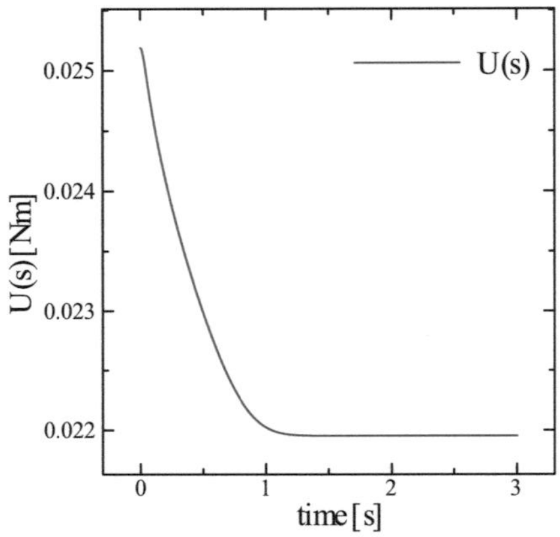

Fig. 18. Transient responses of the value of $U(s(t))$.

This note is concerned with a certain possibility of extending this standpoint to the problem of modeling and control of 3-D grasping under rolling contact constraints (see Fig. 19). Fortunately, it is also well-known in geometry of curves and surfaces that, given two smooth curves in the 3-D Enclidean space characterized by the common arclength parameters, the curves can coincide by finding an adequate homogeneous transformation if and only if the curves have the same curvature and torsion along their arclength parameters. Again in the work [Nomizu, 1978], Nomizu showed a mathematical model of rolling an n-D submanifold M on another n-D submanifold N in a Euclidean space and obtained a kinematic interpretation of the second fundamental form. Thus, we observe that, even in the case of 3-D motion of rolling contacts, each locus of points of the contact between the two surfaces can be characterized by a curve $\gamma_i(s)$ lying on each corresponding surface S_i (see Fig. 20). Thus, a rolling contact as a physical interaction of a rigid object with a rigid fingertip is interpreted by the following two conditions:

A-1) Given a curve $\gamma_1(s_1)$ as a locus of points of the contact on S_1 and another curve $\gamma_0(s_0)$ as a locus of contact points on S_0, the two curves coincide at contact point P_1 and share the same tangent plane at P_1 (see Fig. 20).

A-2) During any continuation of rolling contact, the two curves $\gamma_0(s_0)$ and $\gamma_1(s_1)$ can be described in terms of the same length parameter s in such a way that $s_0 = s + c_0$ and $s_1 = s + c_1$, where c_0 and c_1 are constant.

The details of derivation of the Euler-Lagrange equation of grasping motion of the fingers-object system will be presented in the paper [Arimoto, 2010b].

3.3 Computational Backgrounds for Design of a Numerical Simulator

In the case of 3-D grasping, the core of a numerical simulator for numerically evaluating the loci of contact points between the rigid bodies must be an algorithmic tool for determining the unique contact point together with finding the common tangent and the normal to the tangent between the two surfaces whose data are given as a huge amount of data points. A common contact point should be uniquely determined from the set of data points without penetrating through each other, in conjunction with finding the common tangent and normal at the contact point. Numerical evaluation of the normal curvatures along the loci $\gamma_i(s)$ on the surfaces is also indispensable for contruction of a numerical simulator. Once the numerical data of all

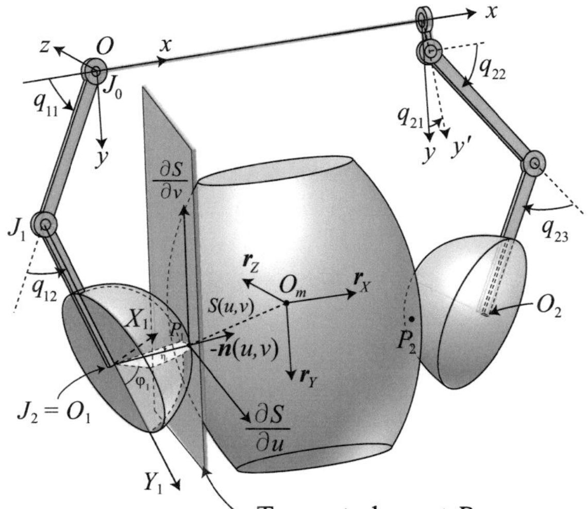

Fig. 19. A pair of robot fingers is grasping a rigid object with arbitrary smooth surfaces. The inertial frame is denoted by the coordinates O-xyz and the body coordinates are expressed by O_m-XYZ with body-fixed unit vectors $\boldsymbol{r}_X$, $\boldsymbol{r}_Y$, and $\boldsymbol{r}_Z$.

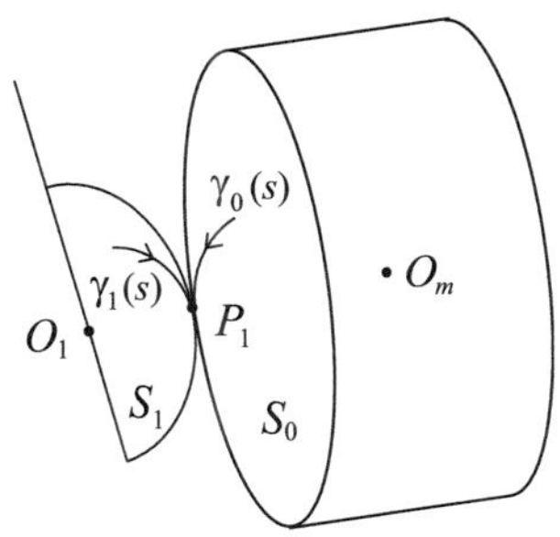

Fig. 20. A locus of points of contact on the left hand fingerend surface S_1 is denoted by $\gamma_1(s)$ and that on the object surface by $\gamma_0(s)$. If there does not arise any slipping, both loci can be traced by the common length parameter s.

the loci $\gamma_i(s)$ are calculated through the Euler-Lagrange equation, all the geometrical data of motion of the robot fingers and the object can be recovered from the kinematics and the equalities of rolling contact constraints. Then, visualization is a matter of course of computer graphics of curves and surfaces.

4. References

Arimoto, S.; Yoshida, M.; Sekimoto, M; Tahara, K. (2009a). Modeling and control of 2-D grasping of an object with arbitrary shape under rolling contact, *SICE J. of Control, Measurement and System Integration*, Vol. 2, No. 6, pp. 379-386

Arimoto, S.; Yoshida, M.; Sekimoto, M.; Tahara, K. (2009b). A Riemannian-geometry approach for control of robotic systems under constraints, *SICE J. of Control, Measurement and System Integration*, Vol. 2, No. 2, pp. 107–116

Nomizu, K. (1978). *Kinematics and differential geometry of submanifolds – Rolling a ball with a prescribed locus of contact –*, Tohoku Math. Journ., Vol. 30, pp. 623–637

Gray, A.; Abbena, E.; Salamon, S. (2006). *Modern Differential Geometry of Curves and Surfaces with Mathematica*, Chapman & Hall/CRC, Boca Raton, Florida, USA

Arimoto, S. (2008). *Control Theory of Multi-fingered Hands: A Modelling and Analytical-Mechanics Approach for Dexterity and Intelligence*, Springer, London, Great Britain

Arimoto, S.; Yoshida, M.; Sekimoto, M.; Bae, J.-H. (2009c). A Riemannian-geometric approach for intelligent control of multi-fingered hands, submitted to *Advanced Robotics* in August 2009 and accepted for publication in October 2009

Arimoto, S. (2010a). Derichlet-Lagrange stability for redundant mechanical systems under constraints: A Riemannian geometric approach for Bernstein's problem of degrees-of-freedom, to be submitted to *SICE J. of Control, Measurement and System Integration*

Arimoto, S. (2007). A differential-geometric approach for 2D and 3D object grasping and manipulation, *Annual Review in Control*, Vol. 31, No. 2, pp. 189–209

Yoshida, M.; Arimoto, S.; Tahara, K. (2009a). Manipulation of 2D object with arbitrary shape by robot finger under rolling constraint, *Proc. of the ICROS-SICE Int. Conf. 2009*, Fukuoka, Japan, August 18-21, pp. 695–699

Yoshida, M.; Arimoto, S.; Tahara, K. (2009b). Pinching 2D object with arbitrary shape by two robot fingers under rolling constraints, to be published in *Proc. of the IROS 2009*, Saint Louis, USA, Oct. 11-15, pp. 1805-1810

Arimoto, S. (2010b). Dynamics of grasping a rigid object with arbitrary smooth surfaces under rolling contacts, *SICE J. of Control, Measurement and System Integration*, to be published in Vol. 3

19

Towards Real Time Data Reduction and Feature Abstraction for Robotics Vision

Rafael B. Gomes, Renato Q. Gardiman, Luiz E. C. Leite,
Bruno M. Carvalho and Luiz M. G. Gonçalves
Universidade Federal do Rio Grande do Norte
DCA-CT-UFRN, Campus Universitário, Lagoa Nova, 59.076-200, Natal, RN
Brazil

1. Introduction

We introduce an approach to accelerate low-level vision in robotics applications, including its formalisms and algorithms. We depict in detail image the processing and computer vision techniques that provide data reduction and feature abstraction from input data, also including algorithms and implementations done in a real robot platform. Our model shows to be helpful in the development of behaviorally active mechanisms for integration of multi-modal sensory features. In the current version, the algorithm allows our system to achieve real-time processing running in a conventional 2.0 GHz Intel processor. This processing rate allows our robotics platform to perform tasks involving control of attention, as the tracking of objects, and recognition.

This proposed solution support complex, behaviorally cooperative, active sensory systems as well as different types of tasks including bottom-up and top-down aspects of attention control. Besides being more general, we used features from visual data here to validate the proposed sketch. Our final goal is to develop an active, real-time running vision system able to select regions of interest in its surround and to foveate (verge) robotic cameras on the selected regions, as necessary. This can be performed physically or by software only (by moving the fovea region inside a view of a scene).

Our system is also able to keep attention on the same region as necessary, for example, to recognize or manipulate an object, and to eventually shift its focus of attention to another region as a task has been finished. A nice contribution done over our approach to feature reduction and abstraction is the construction of a moving fovea implemented in software that can be used in situations where avoiding to move the robot resources (cameras) works better. On the top of our model, based on reduced data and on a current functional state of the robot, attention strategies could be further developed to decide, on-line, where is the most relevant place to pay attention. Recognition tasks could also be successfully done based on the features in this perceptual buffer. These tasks in conjunction with tracking experiments, including motion calculation, validate the proposed model and its use for data reduction and abstraction of features. As a result, the robot can use this low level module to make control decisions, based on the information contained in its perceptual state and on the current task being executed, selecting the right actions in response to environmental stimuli.

The developed technique is implemented in a built stereo head robot operated by a PC with a 2.0 GHz processor. This head operates on the top of a Pioneer AT robot with an embedded PC with real-time operating system. This computer is linked to the stereo head PC by a dedicated bus, thus allowing both to run different tasks (perception and control). The robot computer provides control of the robotic devices, as taking navigation decisions according to the goal and sensors readings. It is also responsible for moving the head devices. On its way, the stereo head computer provides the computing demands for the visual information given by the stereo head, including image pre-processing and feature acquisition, as motion and depth. Our approach is currently implemented and running inside the stereo head computer. Here, besides better formalizing the proposed approach for reduction of information from the images, we also describe shortly the stereo head project.

2. Related works

Stereo images can be used in artificial vision systems when a unique image does not provide enough information of the observed scene. Depth (or disparity) calculation (Ballard & Brown, 1982; Horn, 1986; Marr & Poggio, 1979; Trucco & Verri, 1998) is such kind of data that is essential to tasks involving 3D modeling that a robot can use, for example, when acting in 3D spaces. By using two (or more) cameras, by triangulation, it is possible to extract the 3D position of an object in the world, so manipulating it would be easier. However, the computational overloading demanded by the use of stereo techniques sometimes difficult their use in real-time systems Gonçalves et al. (2000); Huber & Kortenkamp (1995); Marr (1982); Nishihara (1984). This extra load is mostly caused by the matching phase, which is considered to be the constriction of a stereo vision system.

Over the last decade, several algorithms have been implemented in order to enhance precision or to reduce complexity of the stereo reconstruction problem (Fleet et al., 1997; Gonçalves & Oliveira, 1998; Oliveira et al., 2001; Theimer & Mallot, 1994; Zitnick & Kanade, 2000). Resulting features from stereo process can be used for robot controlling (Gonçalves et al., 2000; Matsumoto et al., 1997; Murray & Little, 2000) that we are interested here between several other applications. We remark that depth recovering is not the only purpose of using stereo vision in robots. Several other applications can use visual features as invariant (statistical moments), intensity, texture, edges, motion, wavelets, and Gaussians. Extracting all kind of features from full resolution images is a computationally expensive process, mainly if real time is a need. So, using some approach for data reduction is a good strategy. Most methods aim to reduce data based on the use of the classical pyramidal structure (Uhr, 1972). In this way, the scale space theory (Lindeberg, n.d.; Witkin, 1983) can be used towards accelerating visual processing, generally on a coarse to fine approach. Several works use this approach based on multi-resolution (Itti et al., 1998; Sandon, 1990; 1991; Tsotsos et al., 1995) for allowing vision tasks to be executed in computers. Other variants, as the Laplacian pyramid (Burt, 1988), have been also integrated as a tool for visual processing, mainly in attention tasks (Tsotos, 1987; Tsotsos, 1987). Besides we do not rely on this kind of structure but a more compact one that can be derived from it, some study about them would help to better understanding our model.

Another key issue is related to feature extraction. The use of multi-features for vision is a problem well studied so far but not completely solved yet. Treisman (Treisman, 1985; 1986) provides an enhanced description of a previous model (Treisman, 1964) for low-level perception, with the existence of two phases in low-level visual processing: a parallel feature extraction and a sequential processing of selected regions. Tsotsos (Tsotsos et al., 1995) depicts

an interesting approach to visual attention based on selective tuning. A problem with multi-feature extraction is that the amount of visual features can grow very fast depending on the task needs. With that, it can also grow the amount of processing necessary to recover them. So using full resolution images can make processing time grows up.
In our setup, the cameras offer a video stream at about 20 frames per second. For our real-time machine vision system to work properly, it should be able to make all image operations (mainly convolutions) besides other attention and recognition routines at most in 50 milliseconds. So to reduce the impact of image processing load, we propose the concept of multi-resolution (MR) retina, a dry structure that used a reduced set of small images. As we show in our experiments, by using this MR retina, our system is able to execute the processing pipeline including all routines in about 3 milliseconds (that includes calculation of stereo disparity, motion, and several other features).
Because of a drastic reduction on the amount of data that is sent to the vision system, our robot is able to react very fast to visual signals. In other words, the system can release more resources to other routines and give real-time responses to environmental stimuli, effectively. The results show the efficiency of our method compared to other traditional ways of doing stereo vision if using full resolution images.

3. The stereo head

A stereo head is basically a robotic device composed by an electronic-mechanical apparatus with motors responsible for moving two (or more) cameras, thus able to point the cameras towards a given target for video stream capture. Several architectures and also built stereo systems can be found in the literature (A.Goshtasby & W.Gruver, 1992; D.Lee & I.Kweon, 2000; Garcia et al., 1999; Nickels et al., 2003; S.Nene & S.Nayar, 1998; TRACLabs, 2004; Truong et al., 2000; Urquhart & Siebert, 1992; W.Teoh & Zhang, 1984). Here, we use two video cameras that allow capture of two different images from the same scene. The images are used as basis for feature extraction, mainly a disparity map calculation for extracting depth information from the imaged environment. A stereo should provide some angle mobility and precision to the cameras in order to minimize the error when calculate the depth making the whole system more efficient. As said previously, the aim of using stereo vision is to recover three-dimensional geometry of a scene from disparity maps obtained from two or more images of that scene, by way of computational processes and without reduction of data this is complex. Our proposed technique helps solving this problem. It has been used by our built stereo head that is shown in Figure 1 to reduce sensory data. Besides using analogic cameras, tests were also successfully performed using conventional PCs with two web cameras connected to them. Structures Multiresolution (MR) and Multifeatures (MF) used here represent the mapping of topological and spatial indexes from the sensors to multiple attention or recognition features.
Our stereo head has five degrees of freedom. One of them is responsible for vertical axis rotation of the whole system (*pan* movement, similar to a neck movement as a "not" with our head). Other two degrees of freedom rotate each camera horizontally (*tilt* movement, similar to look up and look down). The last two degrees of freedom rotate each camera in its vertical axis, and together converge or diverge the sight of stereo head. Each camera can point up or down independently. Human vision system does not have this behavior, mainly because we are not trained for that despite we are able to make the movement.

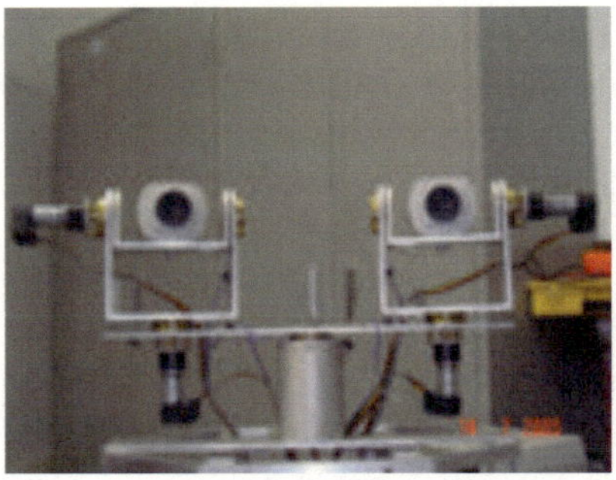

Fig. 1. UFRN Stereo Head platform with 5 mechanical degrees of freedom

The stereo head operate in two distinct behaviors, in the first, both cameras center the sight in the same object, so in this case we will use stereo algorithm. But the second behavior each camera can move independently and deal with different situations.

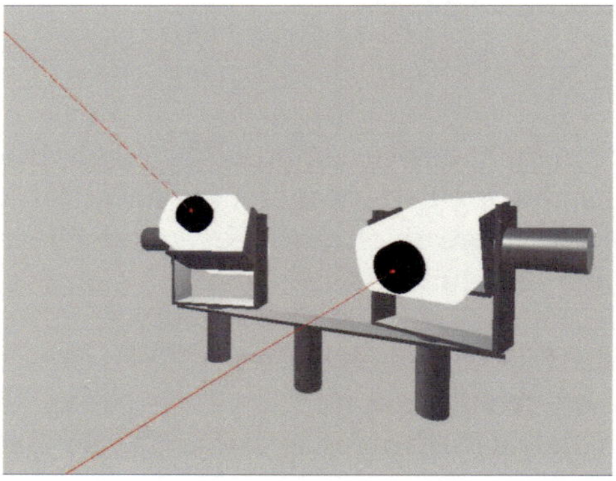

Fig. 2. Illustration of stereo head simulator operating in independent mode.

Figure 2 illustrates the robotic head operating in *Independent Mode* with each camera focusing a distinct object. Figure 3 illustrates it operating in *Dependent Mode*. The images captured are high correlated because the two cameras are pointing to the same object. This is essential for running stereo algorithms. This initial setup, in simulation, is done to test the correct working of the kinematic model developed for stereo head, seen next.

3.1 Physically modeling the head

Figure 4 shows an isometric view of the stereo head. The two cameras are fixed on the top of a *U* structure. A motor responsible for neck rotation (rotation around main vertical axis) is fixed on the basis of the head (neck). The motors responsible for rotation around vertical axis of each camera are fixed on the upper side of the basis of the *U* structure. Finally, motors responsible for the horizontal rotation of each camera are fixed beside the *U* structure, moving together with the camera. This structure is built with light metals like aluminum and stainless steel giving to the system a low weight structure generating a low angular inertial momentum to the joint motors. With this design, the motors are positioned at each axis center of mass, so efforts done by the motors are minimized and it is possible to use more precise and less power motors.

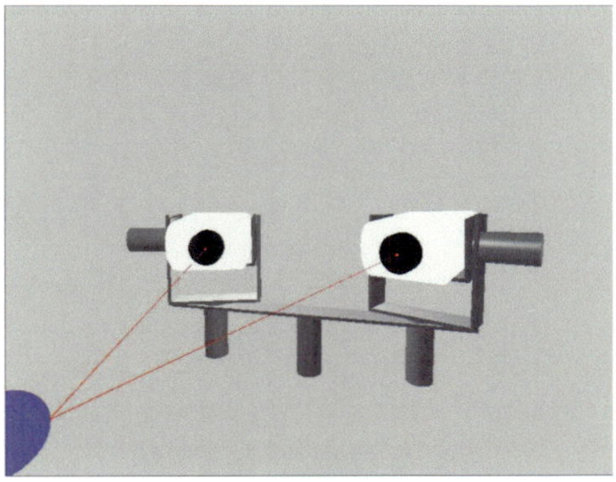

Fig. 3. Illustration of stereo head simulator operating in dependent mode.

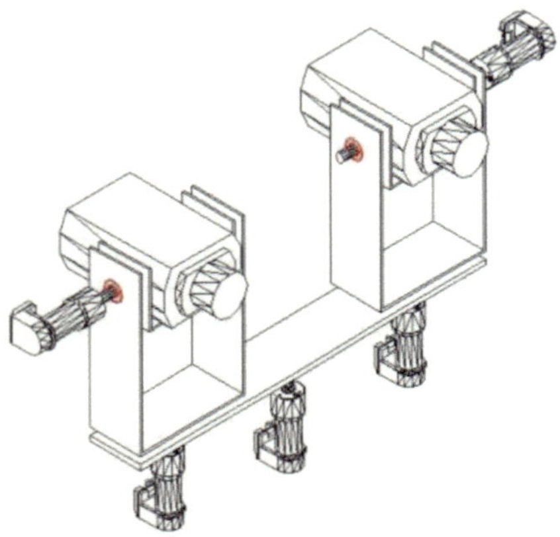

Fig. 4. Isometric view of the Stereo Head

3.2 Kinematics of the stereo head

In the adopted kinematics model, the stereo head structure is described as a chain of rigid bodies called *links*, interconnected by joints (see Figure 5). One extremity of the chain is fixed on the basis of the stereo head, which is on the top of our robot, and the cameras are fixed on two end joints. So each camera position is given by two rotational joints plus the rotational joint of the basis.

From current joint values (angles) it is possible to calculate the position and orientation of the cameras, allowing the mapping of the scene captured by the cameras to a specific point of view. Direct kinematics uses homogeneous transforms that relate neighbor links in the chain. On agreement with the parameters obtained by Denavit-Hartenberg method (Abdel-Malek & Othman, 1999) and due to the symmetry of stereo head, the matrix for calculating direct kinematics for one of the cameras is quite similar to the other. At the end, the model for determining position and orientation for each camera uses two matrices only. The Denavit-Hartenberg parameters are shown below, in Table 1.

The link transformation matrices, from the first to the last one, are given by:

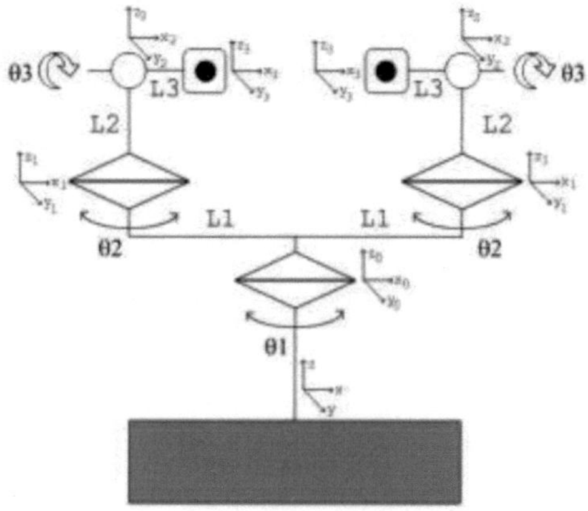

Fig. 5. Kinematics model of the robotic stereo head, L1=12cm, L2=12cm, L3=6cm.

i	$a_i - 1$	$\alpha_i - 1$	d_i	θ_i
1	0	0	0	$\theta1 + \theta2$
2	L_1	0	0	0
3	0	$\theta3$	L_2	0
4	L_3	0	0	0

Table 1. Denavit-Hartenberg parameters for modeling the direct kinematics of the stereo head

$$T_1^0 = \begin{bmatrix} cos(\theta1+\theta2) & -sin(\theta1+\theta2) & 0 & 0 \\ sin(\theta1+\theta2) & cos(\theta1+\theta2) & 0 & 0 \\ 0 & 0 & 1 & 0 \\ 0 & 0 & 0 & 1 \end{bmatrix},$$

$$T_2^1 = \begin{bmatrix} 1 & 0 & 0 & L_1 \\ 0 & 1 & 0 & 0 \\ 0 & 0 & 1 & 0 \\ 0 & 0 & 0 & 1 \end{bmatrix},$$

$$T_3^2 = \begin{bmatrix} 1 & 0 & 0 & 0 \\ 0 & cos(\theta3) & -sin(\theta3) & 0 \\ 0 & sin(\theta3) & cos(\theta3) & L2 \\ 0 & 0 & 0 & 1 \end{bmatrix},$$

$$T_4^0 = \begin{bmatrix} 1 & 0 & 0 & L_3 \\ 0 & 1 & 0 & 0 \\ 0 & 0 & 1 & 0 \\ 0 & 0 & 0 & 1 \end{bmatrix}$$

By composing the link transforms, the direct kinematics matrix is obtained as:

$$T_4^0 = \begin{bmatrix} c_{12} & -c_3 s_{12} & s_{12}^2 & L_1 L_3 c_{12}^2 \\ s_{12} & c_{12}^2 & -s_3 c_{12} & L_1 L_3 s_{12}^2 \\ 0 & s_3 & c_3 & L_2 \\ 0 & 0 & 0 & 1 \end{bmatrix}$$

where $c_{12} = cos(\theta1 + \theta2)$, $s_{12} = sin(\theta1 + \theta2)$, $c_3 = cos(\theta3)$, $s_3 = sin(\theta3)$.

3.3 Head control

The control of the head motors is done by microcontrollers all interconnected by a CAM bus. Each motor that is responsible for a joint movement has its own microcontroller. A module operating in software is responsible for coordinating the composed movement of all joints according to a profile of the angular velocities received from each motor. In order to do this, it is necessary to correct drive the five joint's motors and to perform the calibration of the set before it starts operating. The head control software determines the signal position by calculating the error between the desired position and de actual position given by the encoders. With this approach, the second embedded computer, which is responsible for the image processing, has only this task. This solution makes the two tasks (head's motors control and high level control) faster. This is also a fundamental factor for the functioning of the system in real time.

4. The proposed solution

Figure 6 shows a diagram with the logical components of the visual system. Basically, the acquisition system is composed by two cameras and two video capture cards, which convert analog signals received from each camera into a digital buffer in the memory system. The next stage is the pre-processing functions that create various small images, in multiresolution, all with the same size in a schema inspired by the biological retina. The central region of the captured image that has the maximum of resolution, called fovea, is represented in one of the small images (say the last level image). Then, growing to the periphery of the captured image, the other small images are created by down-sampling bigger regions, increasing in sizes on the captured image, but with decreasing degrees of resolution according to the augmentation of the distance to the fovea. This process is made for both images and, thus, feature extraction techniques can be applied on them, including stereo disparity, motion and other features as intensity and Gaussian derivatives. This set of characteristic maps are extracted to feed higher level processes like attention, recognition, and navigation.

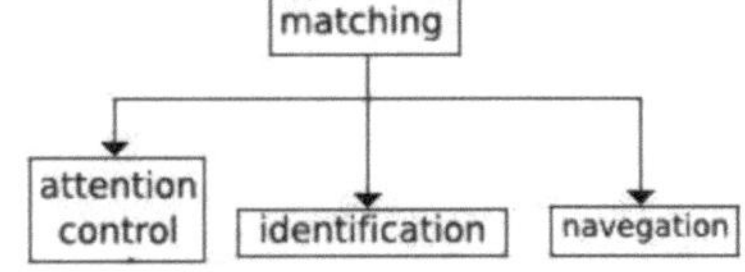

Fig. 6. Stereo vision stages

4.1 Reduction of resolution

Performing stereo processing in full resolution images usually requires great power of processing and a considerable time. This is due to the nature of the algorithms used and also to the huge amount of data that a pair of large images have. Such restrictions make the task of doing real-time stereo vision difficult to execute. Data reduction is a key issue for decreasing the elapsed time for processing the two stereo images. The system evidenced here proposes to make this reduction by breaking an image with full resolution (say 1024×768 pixels) into several small images (say 5 images with 32 × 24 pixels) that represent all together the original image in different resolutions. This resulting structure is called a multiresolution retina (MR) that is composed of images with multiple levels of resolution. Application of this technique can be observed in Figure 7.

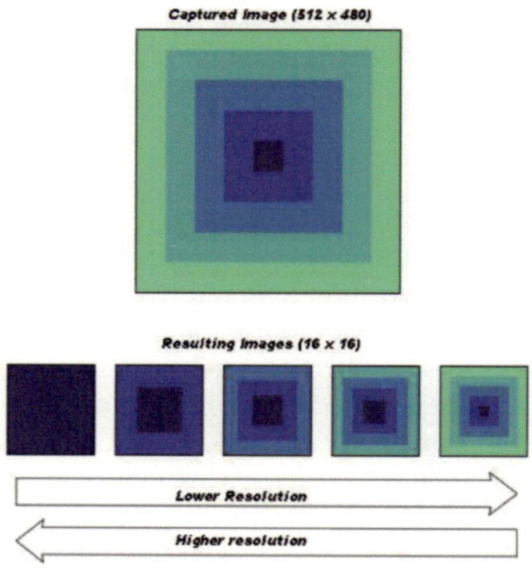

Fig. 7. Building multiresolution images

As it can be seen, the image with higher resolution corresponds to the central area of the acquired image (equivalent to the fovea) and the image with lower resolution represents a large portion of the acquired image (peripheral vision). In the level of best resolution, the reduced image is simply constructed by directly extracting the central region of the acquired image. For the other levels of resolution, a different method is used. In these cases, each reduced image is formed by a pixel sampling process combined with a mean operation over the neighborhood of a pixel with a given position.

This process is done by applying a filter mask with dimensions **h**×**h** in the interest region at intervals of **h** pixels in horizontal direction and **h** pixels in vertical direction. In the first sampling, the mask is applied to pixel **P1**, in the next sampling it will take the pixel **P2**, which is horizontally far by **h** pixels from **P1** and so on, until a total of image height × image width (say 32 × 24) pixels is obtained forming the resulting reduced image. The interval *h* is chosen accordingly, of course. To speedup this process while avoiding unexpected noise effects in the construction of the reduced images, a simple average is taken between the target pixel (**P(x,y)**) and the horizontal neighborhood pixels (**P(x + subh, y)** and **P(x - subh, y)**) and vertical neighborhood too (**P(x, y - subh)** and **P(x, y + subh**), where **subh** is the value of dimension **h** divided by 3. In the case where **h** is not multiple of 3, it should be taken the first multiple above it. With this, it is guaranteed that **subh** is an integer value. The implementation of this procedure is presented in the Algorithm 1.

Algorithm 1 Multi-resolution algorithm

```
Input: Image Im, Level N, Size DI, Size DJ;
Output: SubImage SubIm;

Calculate h;
Calculate subh;

for i = 0;i + +;i < DI do
   for j = 0;j + +;j < DJ do
      SubIm(i,j) = (Im(i*h, j*h) +
                    Im(i*h + subh, j*h) +
                    Im(i*h - subh, j*h) +
                    Im(i*h, j*h + subh) +
                    Im(i*h, j*h - subh)) / 5;
   end for
end for
```

5. Feature extraction (images filtering)

To allow extraction of information from the captured images, a pre-processing phase should be done before other higher level processes as stereo matching, recognition and classification of objects in the scene, attention control tasks (Gonçalves et al., 1999), and navigation of a moving robot. The use of image processing techniques (Gonzales & Woods, 2000) allows to extract visual information for different purposes. In our case, we want enough visual information in order to provide navigation capability and to execute tasks like object manipulation that involves recognition and visual attention.

5.1 Gaussian filtering

The use of smoothing filters is very common in the pre-processing stage and is employed mainly for noise reduction that can mix up the image in next stages. Among the most common smoothing filters are the Gaussian filters, that can be described by the formula shown in Equation 1.

$$G(x,y) = \frac{1}{2\pi\sigma^2} e^{-\frac{x^2+y^2}{2\sigma^2}} \tag{1}$$

The mask 3×3 of Gaussian filter used in this work can be seen in Table 2.

$\frac{1}{16}$

1	2	1
2	4	2
1	2	1

Table 2. Gaussian filtering

5.2 Sharpening spatial filters

Extraction of edges is fundamental for construction of feature descriptors to be used, for example, in identification and recognition of objects in the scene. The most usual method to perform this task is generally based on the gradient operator. The magnitude of the gradient of an image $f(x,y)$, at the position (x,y), is given by Equation 2. We implemented the Gaussian gradient as an option for treatment of high frequency noises at the same time that it detects edges.

$$\nabla f = mag(\nabla \mathbf{f}) = \left[\left(\frac{\partial f}{\partial x} \right)^2 + \left(\frac{\partial f}{\partial y} \right) \right]^{1/2} \tag{2}$$

For determining the direction of the resultant gradient vector at a pixel (x,y), we use Equation 3 that returns the value of the angle relative to the **x** axis.

$$\alpha(x,y) = \tan^{-1} \left(\frac{G_y}{G_x} \right) \tag{3}$$

So, for the implementation of gradient filter, we have chosen the Sobel operator because it incorporates the effect of smoothing to the partial differentiation processes giving better results. Tables 3 and 4 show the masks used for calculating the gradient in directions **x** and **y**, respectively.

-1	-2	-1
0	0	0
1	2	1

Table 3. Gradient filter in direction **x**

-1	0	-1
-2	0	-2
-1	0	-1

Table 4. Gradient filter in direction **y**

5.3 Applying the Laplacian filter

The Laplacian of an image is defined as been the second-order derivative of the image. When applied to an image, this function is defined by equation 4. Often used together with gradient filters, this filter helps out some segmentation tasks in an image, and can also be used for texture detection. Here again, we implemented also the option of blurring together with Laplacian, in other words, the use the Laplacian of Gaussian filter in order to allow the reduction of high frequency noise.

$$\nabla^2 f = \frac{\partial^2 f}{\partial x^2} + \frac{\partial^2 f}{\partial y^2} \tag{4}$$

The mask used to implement the Laplacian of Gaussian filter is shown in Table 5.

0	-1	0
-1	4	-1
0	-1	0

Table 5. Laplacian Filter

5.4 Motion detection

Motion detection plays an important role in navigation and attention control subsystem, making the robot able to detect changes in the environment. The variation between an image **I** in a given instance of time **t** and an image captured in a moment before **t**$-$**1** is given by the equation 5, which has a simple implementation.

$$Motion = \Delta I = I(t) - I(t-1) \tag{5}$$

In the same way, to reduce errors, *motion* images can be computed by applying a Gaussian equation in the above "difference" retina representation, which is given by Equation 6, where $g_d^{(1)}$ represents the Gaussian first derivatives.

$$M_{d=x,y} = g_d^{(1)} * [\Delta I] \tag{6}$$

In fact, the above equation implements the smoothed derivatives (in x and y directions) of the difference between frames, that can be used to further approximate motion field.

5.5 Calculation of stereo disparity

The bottle-neck for calculation of a disparity map is the matching process, that is, given a pixel in the left image, the problem is to determine its corresponding pixel in the right image, such that both are projections of the same point in the 3D scene. This process most often involves the determination of correlation scores between many pixels in both images, that is in practice implemented by doing several convolution operations (Horn, 1986; Hubber & Kortenkamp, 1995; Marr, 1982; Nishihara, 1984). As using convolution in full images is expensive, this is one more reason for using reduced images. Besides a small image is used, we also use one level to predict disparity for the next one. Disparity is computed for images acquired from both cameras, in both ways, that is, from left to right and from right to left. We measure similarities with normalized cross correlations, approximated by a simple correlation coefficient. The correlation between two signals x and y with n values is computed by Equation 7, below.

$$r_{x,y} = \frac{n\sum(x_i y_i) - \sum(x_i)\sum(y_i)}{\sqrt{n\sum(x_i^2) - (\sum x_i)^2}\sqrt{n\sum(y_i^2) - (\sum y_i)^2}}. \tag{7}$$

6. Results

Initial tests for the methodology used for reduction of resolution were made using a system that captures a single frame per turn. In this first case, images of 294×294 pixels wide are acquired from two cameras using frame grabbers. Reduction process takes 244 micro-seconds for each image, thus approximately 0.5 ms for the stereo cameras. We note that this processing can be done in the interval window while other image pair is being acquired. The whole process of feature extraction takes 2.6 ms, without stereo disparity calculation that takes other 2.9 ms. The result is some 5.5 ms, for each reduced MR image, against 47 ms if using each of the full captured images. Disparity computation using original images takes 1.6 seconds, what is impracticable to do in real time. These and other results can be seen in Table 6 that shows times taken in a PC with a 2.4 Ghz processor. Overall, a gain of 1800% in processing time could be observed from using original images to reduced ones.

When using images with 352 × 288, from a web camera, times grow up a little due to image acquisition, but yet allowing real time processing. Table 7 shows the times for this experiment. Four images of 32 × 32 are generated and its features calculated. Filtering process indicated

Phase	Multiresolution (μs)	Original (μs)
Multiresolution	244	–
Gaussian	584	10480
Gradient	1169	21020
Laplacian	579	10506
Motion	62	5355
Stereo (3x3)	2916	1653555
Stereo (5x5)	5081	3053555
Total w/ st	**2638**	**47361**

Table 6. Results obtained in PC implementation

on the Table involves gradient in x and y, gradient magnitude plus a threshold, Gaussian, Gaussian gradient in x and y, Gaussian gradient magnitude plus a threshold, and the Laplacian of Gaussian. We note that copying to memory can be avoided. Also, if the capture gets implemented as a thread, it would enhance performance, taking off waiting time.

Phase	Multiresolution (ms)
Acquiring	21.8
Memory copy	1.5
Multiresolution	1.2
Filtering	3.6
Stereo	2.9
Total (without acq.)	9.2

Table 7. Results obtained using web cameras

As a rate of about 20 frames per second is enough for our needs and the process of acquisition of new frame can be executed in parallel with the graphics processing, it can be seen that the time available for graphics processing plus the time employed for intelligence of the robot can easily be under 50 ms. That is, Table 6 has proven that an overall time of 11 ms, for both cameras including filtering and disparity calculation in both ways, is enough to the pre-processing necessary. So it remains about 39 ms to other high level processes eventually involving robot intelligence. Compared with the time necessary for processing over the original image, it is notable a gain of 1800%, which undersigns the viability of our acquisition rate.
In order to visually illustrate the results of our method, Figure 8 shows a fully acquired (original) image and Figure 9 shows the resulting multiresolution images constructed by using our algorithm.
Figures 10 to 14 show resulting images of the feature extraction processes for the image presented at Figure 8.
As an interesting application of our implementation, an experiment was performed to test a moving fovea approach (Gomes et al., 2008). In this case, a hand holding a ball appears in front the camera mount and the system should track it without moving resources, in principle, by only changing the position of the fovea in the current viewing position by software. If the ball tends to leave the visual field during the tracking, that is, the fovea center is at the image boundary, the system suggests the camera mount to make a movement, putting the ball inside the image limits again. Figure 15 shows the system performing the tracking of the ball. By

Fig. 8. Original image

Fig. 9. Multiresolution representation

Fig. 10. Gaussian filter

Fig. 11. Gradient filter in X direction

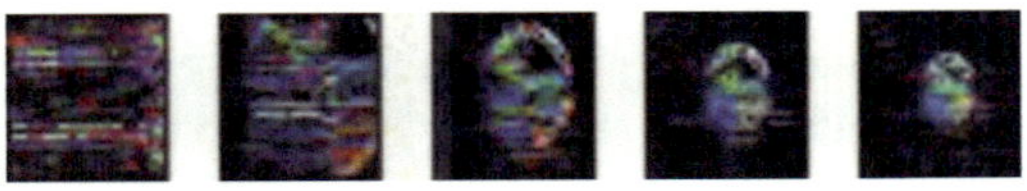

Fig. 12. Gradient filter in Y direction

Fig. 13. Laplacian filter

Fig. 14. Detection of motion

using the moving fovea, it is possible to disengage attention from one position and to engage it to another position from a frame to another. If using our stereo head robot, even using the default MRMF approach (fovea in the image center), this task could take some 500 because it needs a motion of the cameras. Of course, even with the moving fovea, when it gets the image periphery a physical motion is necessary. Then the robot has to eventually wait for this task to be completed in order to acquire other pair of frames.

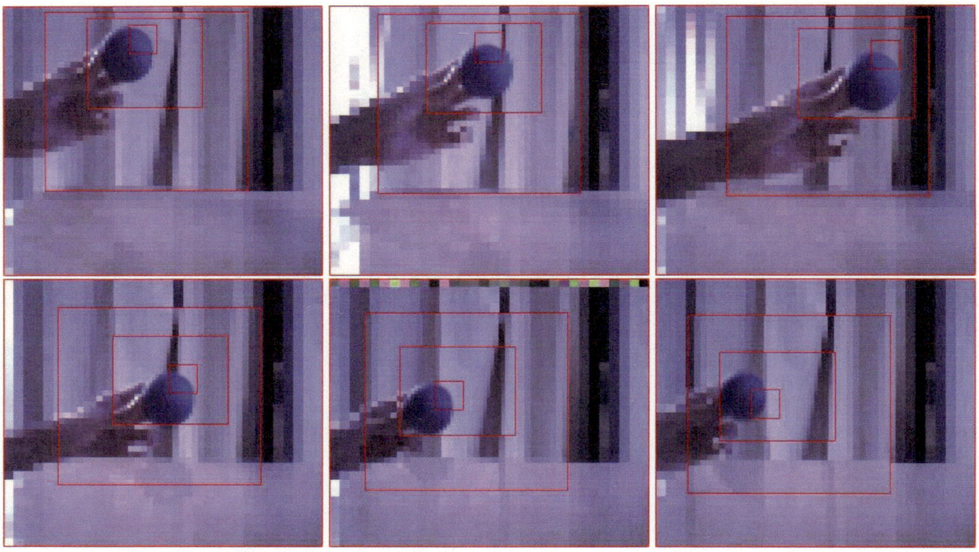

Fig. 15. Tracking a ball using a moving fovea.

As a last experiment with this implementation, two objects, a tennis ball and a domino, were presented in several positions to the system. About 35 images were taken for each one, on-line. Then, the above model was applied to all of them and the BPNN was then trained with 1300 epochs, using the processed input data. Then, the same objects were presented again to the cameras and the activation calculated in the net. It was taken 79 different samples for the ball, from which 8 were classified as domino (domino < 0.5 and ball < 0.1), 5 were classified as probable domino ($0.2 <$ domino < 0.4 and ball < 0.1), 10 were not classified ($0.2 <$ ball and domino < 0.3), and 56 were classified as ball (ball > 0.5 and domino < 0.1). For the domino, it was taken 78 samples, from which 6 were classified as ball (ball > 0.6 and domino < 0.1), 6 were not classified ($0.2 <$ ball and domino < 0.3), 5 were classified as probable domino ($0.2 <$ domino < 0.4 and ball < 0.1), and 62 were classified as domino (domino > 0.4 and ball < 0.1). This results in about 70% of positive identification for the ball and about 85% for the domino.

7. Conclusions and Perspectives

We have built useful mechanisms involving data reduction and feature abstraction that could be integrated and tested in attention control and recognition behaviors. To do that, the first step is data reduction. By using an efficient down-sampling schema, a structure derived from the classical pyramid, however much more compact, is constructed in real-time (2.7 ms in a PC 2.0 GHz). Then computer vision techniques, as shape from stereo, shape from motion, and other feature extraction processes are applied in order to obtain the desired features (each single filter costs about 500 μs). By using this model, tested behaviors have accomplished real-time performance mainly due to the data reduction (about 1800% of gain) and abstraction of features performed. A moving fovea representation could be implemented on the top of this low-level vision model, allowing tasks as overt attention to be done in real-time, that can be applied to accelerate some tasks. So the main contribution of this work is the schema for data reduction and feature abstraction. Besides, other experiments involving attention and recog-

nition, with novel approaches were also done. So we believe that the main result obtained was the definition of a methodology that can be applied to different types of tasks involving attention and recognition, without needs of strong adaptation, just by changing weight tuning strategies and thus the set of features on the robot platforms. So, high-level processes can rely on this methodology, in order to accomplish other tasks, as navigation or object manipulation for example. Main results of this work show the efficiency of the proposed method and how it can be used to accelerate high level algorithms inside a vision system.
Besides using only visual data in this work, similar strategies can be applied to a more general system involving other kind of sensory information, to provide a more discriminative feature set. We believe that the low level abilities of data reduction and feature abstraction are the basis not only for experiments described here, but also for other more complex tasks involved in robot cognition. This model was inspired by the biological model in the sense that the more precise resolution levels are located in the center of the image. In this way, the less resolution levels can be used for example to detect motion or features to be used in navigation tasks (mainly bottom-up stimuli) and the finer levels of resolution can be applied to tasks involving recognition as reading or object manipulation. A search task can use a combination of one or more levels. Of course, in this case, a moving fovea does play an important role, avoiding the head of performing motions, only if necessary.

8. Acknowledgments

We thanks Brazilian Research Sponsoring Agency CNPQ the financial supports given to Luiz Gonçalves, Rafael Gomes, Bruno Carvalho and Renato Gardiman.

9. References

Abdel-Malek, K. & Othman, S. (1999). Multiple sweeping using the denavit-hartenberg representation method.

A.Goshtasby & W.Gruver (1992). Design of a single-lens stereo camera system, *Design of a Single-Lens Stereo Camera System*, Pattern Recognition.

Ballard, D. H. & Brown, C. M. (1982). *Computer Vision*, Prentice-Hall, Englewood Cliffs, NJ.

Burt, P. (1988). Smart sensing within a pyramid vision machine, *Proceedings of the IEEE* **76**(8): 1006–1015.

D.Lee & I.Kweon (2000). A novel stereo camera system by a bipirism, *A Novel Stereo Camera System by a Bipirism*, IEEE Journal of Robotics and Automation.

Fleet, D. J., Wagner, H. & Heeger, D. J. (1997). Neural encoding of binocular disparity: Energy models, position shifts and phase shifts, *Technical report*, Personal Notes.

Garcia, L. M., Oliveira, A. A. & A.Grupen, R. (1999). A framework for attention and object categorization using a stereo head robot, *A framework for Attention and Object Categorization Using a Stereo Head Robot*.

Gomes, R. B., Carvalho, B. M. & Gonçalves, L. M. G. (2008). Real time vision for robotics using a moving fovea approach with multi resolution., *Proceedings of Internacional Conference on Robotics and Automation*.

Gonçalves, L. M. G., Giraldi, G. A., Oliveira, A. A. F. & Grupen, R. A. (1999). Learning policies for attentional control, *IEEE International Symposium on Computational Intelligence in Robotics ans Automation*.

Gonçalves, L. M. G., Grupen, R. A., Oliveira, A. A., Wheeler, D. & Fagg, A. (2000). Tracing patterns and attention: Humanoid robot cognition, *The Intelligent Systems and their Applications* **15**(4): 70–77.

Gonçalves, L. M. G. & Oliveira, A. A. F. (1998). Pipeline stereo matching in binary images, *XI International Conference on Computer Graphics and Image Processing (SIBGRAPI'98)* pp. 426–433.

Gonzales, R. C. & Woods, R. E. (2000). *Processamento de Imagens Digitais*, Edgard Blücher Ltda.

Horn, B. K. P. (1986). *Robot Vision*, MIT Press.

Hubber, E. & Kortenkamp, D. (1995). Using stereo vision to pursue moving agents with a mobile robot, *proceedings on Robotics and Automation* .

Huber, E. & Kortenkamp, D. (1995). Using stereo vision to pursue moving agents with a mobile robot, *IEEE Conference on Robotics and Automation*.

Itti, L., Koch, C. & Niebur, E. (1998). A model of saliency-based visual attention for rapid scene analysis, *IEEE Transactions on Patten Analysis and Machine Intelligence* **20**(11): 1254–1259.

Lindeberg, T. (n.d.). Scale-space theory in computer vision, *Kluwer Academic Publishers* .

Marr, D. (1982). *Vision – A Computational Investigation into the Human Representation and Processing of Visual Information*, The MIT Press, Cambridge, MA.

Marr, D. & Poggio, T. (1979). A computational theory of human stereo vision, *Proc. of the Royal Society of London*, Vol. 204, pp. 301–328.

Matsumoto, Y., Shibata, T., Sakai, K., Inaba, M. & Inoue, H. (1997). Real-time color stereo vision system for a mobile robot based on field multiplexing, *Proc. of IEEE Int. Conf. on Robotics and Automation* .

Murray, D. & Little, J. (2000). Using real-time stereo vision for mobile robot navigation, *Autonomous Robots* .

Nickels, K., Divin, C., Frederick, J., Powell, L., Soontornvat, C. & Graham, J. (2003). Design of a low-power motion tracking system, *Design of a low-power motion tracking system*, The 11th International Conferece on Advanced Robotics.

Nishihara, K. (1984). Practical real-time stereo matcher, *Ai lab technical report, optical engeneering*, Massachusetts Institute of Technology.

Oliveira, A. A. F., Gonçalves, L. M. G. & Matias, I. d. O. (2001). Enhancing the volumetric approach to stereo matching., *Brazilian Symposium on Computer Graphics and Image Processing*, pp. 218–225.

Sandon, P. (1990). Simulating visual attention., *Journal of Cognitive Neuroscience* **2**: 213–231.

Sandon, P. A. (1991). Logarithmic search in a winner-take-all network, *IEEE Joint Conference on Neural Networks* pp. 454–459.

S.Nene & S.Nayar (1998). Stereo with mirrors, *Stereo with Mirrors*, In Proceedings International Conference Computer Vision.

Theimer, W. M. & Mallot, H. A. (1994). Phase-based binocular vergence control and depth reconstruction using active vision, *Computer Vision, Graphics, and Image Processing: Image Understanding* **60**(3): 343–358.

TRACLabs (2004). Introduncing biclops, *Introduncing biclops*, http://www.traclabs.com/tracbiclops.htm.

Treisman, A. (1964). Selective attention in man, *British Medical Bulletin* .

Treisman, A. (1985). Preattentive processing in vision, *Computer Graphics and Image Processing* (31): 156–177.

Treisman, A. (1986). Features and objects in visual processing, *Scientific American* **255**(5).

Trucco, E. & Verri, A. (1998). *Introductory Techniques for 3D Computer Vision*, Prentice Hall.

Truong, H., Abdallah, S., Rougenaux, S. & Zelinsky, A. (2000). A novel mechanism for stereo active vision, *A Novel Mechanism for Stereo Active Vision*.

Tsotos, J. K. (1987). A complexity level analysis of vision, *in* I. Press (ed.), *Proceedings of International Conference on Computer Vision: Human and Machine Vision Workshop*, Vol. 1.

Tsotsos, J., Culhane, S., Wai, W., Lai, Y., Davis, N. & Nuflo, F. (1995). Modeling visual attention via selective tuning, *Artificial Intelligence Magazine* **78**(1-2): 507–547.

Tsotsos, J. K. (1987). Knowledge organization and its role in representation and interpretation for time-varying data: the alven system, pp. 498–514.

Uhr, L. (1972). Layered 'recognition cone' networks that preprocess, classify and describe, *IEEE Transactions on Computers*, pp. 758–768.

Urquhart, C. W. & Siebert, J. (1992). Development of a precision active stereo system, *Development of a Precision Active Stereo System*, The Turing Institute Limited.

Witkin, A. P. (1983). Scale-space filtering, *Proc. 8th International Joint Conference on Artificial Intelligence* **1**(1): 1019–1022.

W.Teoh & Zhang, X. (1984). An inexpensive stereo-scopic vision system for robots, *An inexpensive stereo-scopic vision system for robots*, In Proceeedings IEEE International Conference Robotics and Automation.

Zitnick, C. L. & Kanade, T. (2000). A cooperative algorithm for stereo matching and occlusion detection, *Transactions on Pattern Analysis and Machine Intelligence* **22**(7): 675–684.

LSCIC Pre coder for Image and Video Compression

[1]Muhammad Kamran, [2]Shi Feng and [2]Wang YiZhuo
[1]*Department of Electrical Engineering, University of Engineering and Technology, Lahore-54890, Pakistan*
[2]*Department of Computer Science and Engineering, Beijing Institute of Technology, Beijing-100081, China*

1. Introduction

Image and video compression schemes are implemented for the optimum reconstruction of image with respect to speed and quality. LSCIC (Layered Scalable Concurrent Image Compression) pre coder is introduced here to utilize best available resources to obtain reasonable good image or video even at low band width of the system. This pre coder will make the layers of input data whether video or image and after synchronization send it to the output of pre coder on two different layers at the same time. Prior to understand image compression issue it is more important to become familiar with different image standard formats under usage for certain application. Mainly they include JPEG, GIF, and TIFF etc. Image compression scenario is the main entity to be included in the dissertation as per our project requirement. A new idea for scalable concurrent image compression is introduced which gives superior image reconstruction performance as compare to existing techniques. The verification can be done by calculating gray level and PSNR of reconstructed image. The bit stream is required to be compressed for image data transfer if the main system requirement is the memory saving and fast transformation with little sacrifice in the quality of image for lossy compression scheme. A valuable study is accomplished by K Shen, 1997 for parallel implementation of image and video compression. It is suggested that an ideal algorithm should have a low compressed data rate, high visual quality of the decoded image/video and low computational complexity. In hardware approaches special parallel architectures can be design to accelerate computation suggested by R. J. Gove(1994) and Shinji Komori (1988) et al. Parallel video compression algorithms can be implemented using either hardware or software approaches as proved by V. Bhaskaran (1995). These techniques provided the guidelines to deal with digital image compression schemes fro speed and complexity point of view. For video compression, motion estimation phenomenan has its own importance and different techniques are already presented to have motion estimation to get good quality image. Decoding is considered as first step of compression followed by encoding at receiving end of image and reconstruction side. Intermediate step in data/image and video compression is the transform. Different transform techniques have been used depending upon application.

2. LSCIC Architecture

In order to describe complete working of LSCIC image/video compression pre coder, different steps are defined starting with the elaboration of LSCIC architecture. Fig .1 is architecture initially considered followed by Fig.2 which an optimal modified design.

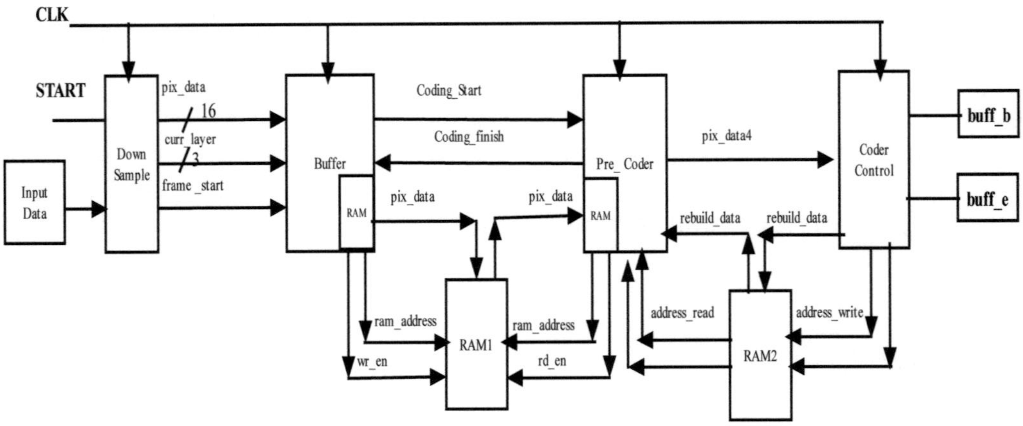

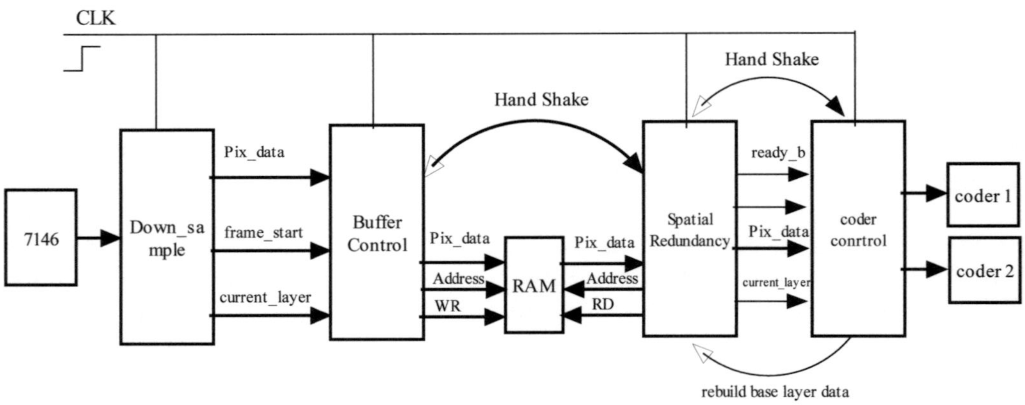

Fig. 1. and Fig. 2. Initially proposed and modified pre coder design

Initially proposed design is quite complicated which includes 16 frames RAM with lot of handshaking signals. It was investigated later on that the design can be simplified by proposing a PING PONG RAM and reducing handshaking signals.

Fig. 2. represents LSCIC pre coder architecture. This pre coder is comprised of 5 modules which are integrated after complete verification of design with respect to their operation.

3. LSCIC Phase-I

LSCIC architecture is divided into two sub phases for the design and testing convenience and also to be become acquainted with hurdles encountered during algorithmic design and architecture implementation.

LSCIC phase-I addresses a problem of large data to be processed through RAM in proposed design. As image data is large in size and randomly extracted from image, the requirement of system is to place and temporarily hold the data in large size RAM prior to its transmission to next module for further processing. RAM with conventional design is not able to complete simulation process in desired time and unwanted delay is introduced. Prior to realize the design it is important to circumvent this problem of large data handling and inclusion of huge hardware components in design.

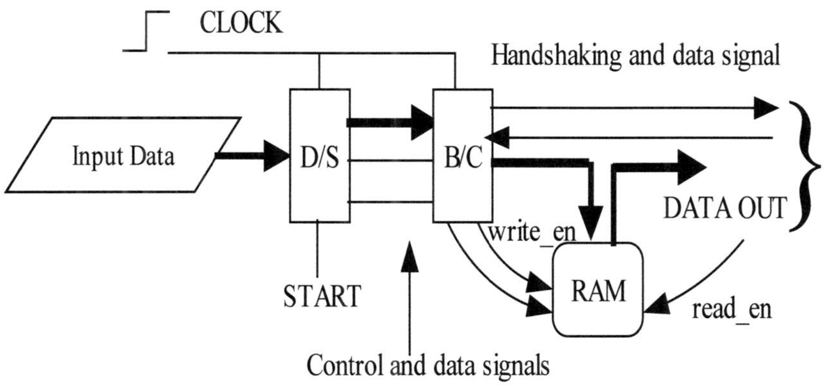

Fig. 3. (Phase-I) Module 1, Module 2 and RAM unit for Data pixel recognition

Figure 3 is the phase-I of LSCIC pre coder describing operation of first 3 units of proposed design with all inevitable control and data signals. It mainly emphasizes the issue to include large RAM unit into design with all constraints with ample solution. Directional bold arrows represent the data path while thin lines indicate the control and hand shaking signals.

3.1 LSCIC Phase-I (Circuit operation) and Mathematical Model

For image compression process, designed circuit will perform different useful tasks. One of them is to get output data concurrently from two independent channels and secondly, circuit may be adaptive to different band widths to capture reasonably good quality image. For MPEG applications, if load on the network is changing causing variations in the system band width may cause video disturbance. The resulting design can handle the situation and provides good compression even when net work is over loaded. After obtaining the solution of large input data for the simulation through external file, next step is to place it for certain operation like down sampling, buffering and proper recognition of pixels.

First module works to "Down Sample" image data to give four image layers B1, E2, E3, E1 initially and fifth layer B2 is extracted afterwards from one of the available enhanced layers E1, E2 or E3. This multilayer scenario, as discussed before is called Multi description scheme as each layer describes its own characteristics and behavior. All layers are of same size except B2 which is ¼ of the size of any other pixel layer. These layers are required to be placed in PING PONG RAM to make one frame with a unique starting address.

The design was initially proposed with a RAM placed after down sample and Buffer control module with 16 frames. But after careful investigation, it has been concluded that only two frames are sufficient in address RAM for data handling on the bases of concurrent writing and reading data process, CWCR. This characteristic of CWCR made it to work as PING PONG RAM i.e. concurrent Read and Write operation.
It is suggested that design should be made for complete data processing with minimum possible time. The RAM discussed above is designed for the purpose of data storage with 12 address lines and 4096 unique addresses which gives output with considerable long time delay and sticks to infinite time when synthesis of design is carried out. This problem during behavioral design implementation is well addressed in this chapter and results are obtained by incorporating the co-design methodology which causes simulation to be completed in reasonable short time. According to proposed design which is extendable to large scale, one pixel is comprised of 16 bits and there are 256X128 pixels in one layer. As there are 5 layers in each frame, a large data is to be handled and placed properly in designed RAM prior to coder operation proposed by Kamran and Shi in 2006. The READ operation is kept fast as compare to WRITE in order to keep the stability of circuit high. High stability means, during transmission of data in given unit, minimum data loss is observed and almost all pixels reached the receiving end. Prior to proposing pseudo code of phase-I of LSCIC pre processor design, it is regarded as more important to describe mathematical model to get preliminary information about different signals and sequences of operation.
For the verification of proposed algorithm, a mathematical model is presented to clarify the pixels processing with respect to timing and control signals. The design of LSCIC phase-I is described comprehensively by adding all required signals along with data flow path. As described earlier, given model explains the operations of first three modules with mathematical notations explaining the design operating sequence.
Figure 4 gives mathematical representation of all input and processing signals with components encountered in LSCIC-phase-I architecture. Image is characterized as one dimension column matrix containing pixels, P_1 to P_n. Logic value of "Start" signal decides whether pixels are required to be transmitted or not. Down sample module will divide the image into number of layers with addresses decided by a special control signal "Current Layer". It is 3 bit signal needed to represent addresses of 5 possible image pixel layers formed in module 1(4 initial and one extracted layers after wards). Buffer control just controls the sequence of pixel stream and generates WRITE address in RAM to store pixel information. The objectives of design are described as under in two steps;

(1) Question was to generate large data automatically, instead of doing manual labor which wastes considerable design simulation time.

(2) Secondly, the problem of large size component inclusion fails the synthesis operation, which ultimately causes the failure of design.

Explaining the mathematical model of Figure 4, it is mentioned that input video/image data is sent to the down sample module, which divides this data initially into 4 layers. 5th layer b2 is extracted from 'e1' whose size is ¼ of the size of e1. Buffer control module just calculates the addresses of layers to be placed into specific locations in RAM. RAM is designed such that READ process is faster as compare to WRITE for more efficient data handling. Despite of all these observations, input signal "START" should be kept high for all operations to be processed.

$\partial \rightarrow \mathrm{Re}\, presents\ Downsample\, \mathrm{Pr}\, ocess;$

$\alpha \rightarrow Denotes\ addresses\ in\ RAM\ for\ Different\ layers;$

$$Video\ Input\ data = \begin{bmatrix} p_0 \\ p_1 \\ \cdots \\ p_n \end{bmatrix} \quad ; \quad Start(Signal) = \{0,1\}$$

$1 - \underline{D / Sample(\partial(Video\_data); b1, e2, e3, e1 \,\&\, b2);}$

$b1, e2, e3 \,\&\, e1 \quad \in Video\ Input\ data \quad ;$

$\Rightarrow \partial(Video\_data) \rightarrow b1, e2, e3 \,\&\, e1(All\ same\ number\ of\ pixels)$

$\Rightarrow b2(Extracted\ layer) = \partial(e1)$

$Size\ of \quad b2 = (size\ of\ any\ layer) / 4;$

$\underline{2 - Buffer\_Control(\partial(Video(b1, e2, e3 \,\&\, e1), Coding\_finish; (\alpha(RAM\_address), wr\_en, Coding\_start)}$

$\alpha 1 \rightarrow address\ for \quad b1,$

$\alpha 2 \rightarrow address\ for \quad e2,$

$\alpha 3 \rightarrow address\ for \quad e3,$

$\alpha 4 \rightarrow address\ for \quad e1,$

$\alpha 5 \rightarrow address\ for \quad b2,$

$All\ adresses\ are\ generated\ when\ \mathrm{coding\_finish}\ is\ high;$

$Followed\ by\ Coding\_start = '1';$

$\underline{3 - RAM(write / read, Pixel\_data\_in, \alpha; pixel\_data\_out)}$

$Number\ of\ Frames = 2;$

$Each\ frame\ contains\ all\ layers(b1, e2, e3, e1 \,\&\, b2);$

$Condition:$

$Speed\ of\ Write\ operation \quad < \quad Speed\ of\ \mathrm{Re}\, ad$

Fig. 4. Mathematical Model description of Phase-I

To attain the first objective of LSCIC phase-I that is automatic data transfer for simulation which can be accomplished by creating an external data "*.dat" file giving rise to hardware/software co design approach. This idea is quite successful for simulation, but synthesis does not allow such external file additions into design as synthesis tool does not have option to add such files in design by Kamran. After proposing solution of first constraint in design by adding external data file to verify simulation, second point was concentrated to find the way to add large size hardware components like, RAM, ROM, Buffers, Multipliers etc., in design. It is advised for designers, if overall digital system is a big scenario and some hardware component as described above is a part of it, IP core is recommended to be placed. It will cause fast simulation, synthesis and verification of design on behavioral and on circuit level with minimum time. For the purpose of LSCIC-Phase-I verification, IP core RAM is used. The procedure to append RAM into design is given below;

Single port RAM is selected with the maximum capacity of 32768 pixels location for 30,000 gates device under operation. While appending the core into design, designer should have to get the core component and port map information from automatically generated *.vho file. Figure 5 represents block diagram of CORE RAM wrapped in VHDL source file. Component and port map is copied from *.vho and paste them in *.vhd RAM file should present in the project. Lastly in wrapper file we make connections of core signals and wrapper inputs and outputs. This combination of *.vhd and *.vhofile describing components becomes IP CORE which becomes part of design instead of module placed with the help of conventional VHDL code. It is to be noted here that data transfer is successfully achieved during our research by conventional RAM design but it costs more time as compare to IP Core.

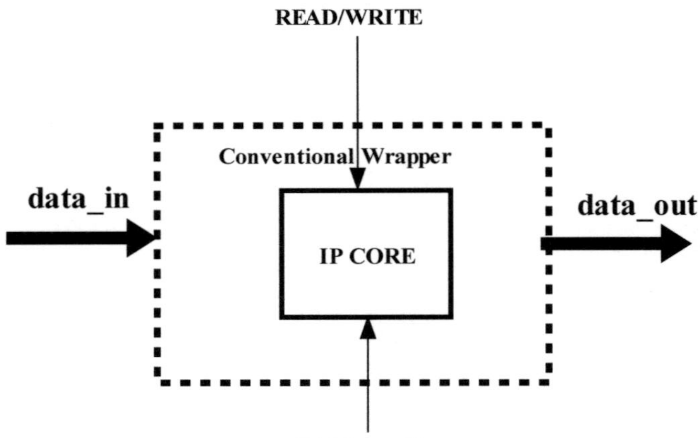

Fig. 5. IP CORE Wrapped in VHDL Source File

Following is the pseudo code description of appending IP RAM into conventional VHDL RAM design;

Code Description
    Defining IEEE library
Entity ur_ram is
    Entity portion to define our wrapper file of RAM
Architecture Behavioral of ur_ram is
    Component first_ram
            IP Core is acting as component of ur_ram.
    End component;
        Define all component parameters as signal
      begin
        u1: first_ram
            port map (Generated core)
        Assigning the core signals to the wrapper file signals to act as complete unit.
End Behavioral;

3.2 LSCIC-Phase-I (Results)

Last portion of LSCIC phase-I is to present results after successful simulation and synthesis. Figure 6 gives the simulation results after completion of PINGPONG RAM processing. It is important to note that same data is used throughout the testing of different aspects and characteristics of LSCIC pre coder.

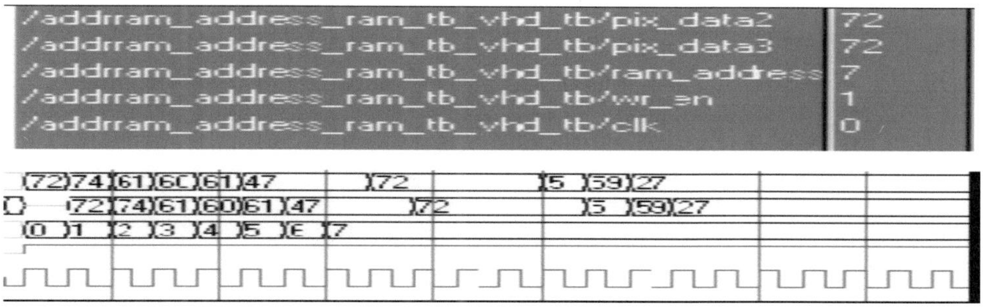

Fig. 6. RAM IP CORE operation

Figure 7. provides the results after joining first two defined modules DOWN SAMPLE and BUFFER CONTROL in proposed design.

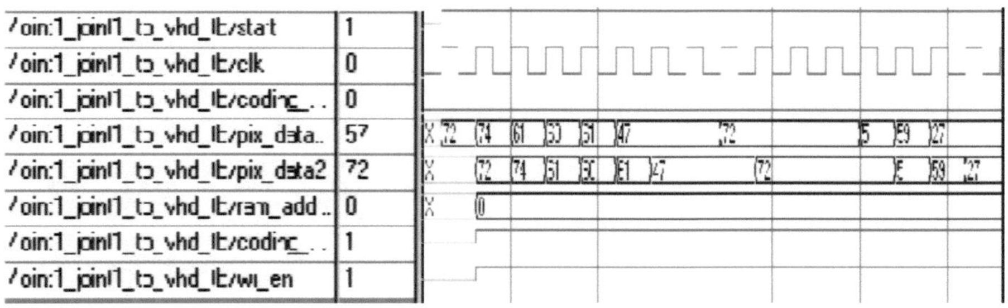

Fig. 7. Simulation Results of DOWN SAMPLE and BUFFER CONTROL connection

After acquiring the pixel data from BUFFER CONTROL, RAM comes in action and picks the pixels one by one into their respective addresses defined by Current-layer signal to perform WRITE operation. The two simulation results show complete coordination of data with 0% loss of data pixel till RAM module. But during post simulation it is found that some anonymous pixels due to circuit constraints are introduced but they seldom affect the quality of image. The relation between expected final result and experimental result is shown in Figure 8.

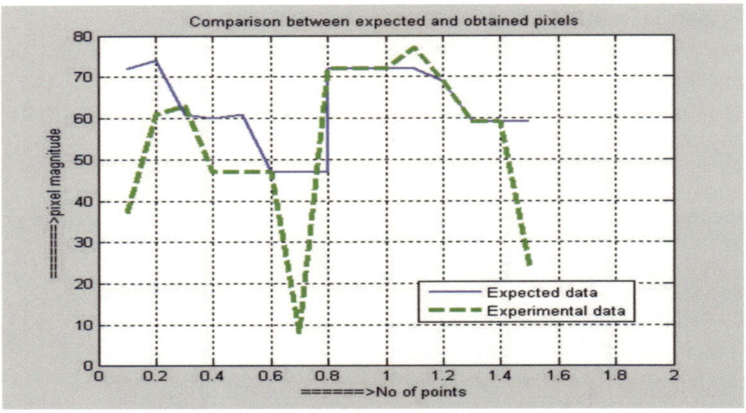

Fig. 8. Comparison of experimental and expected data results

4. Resource Allocation Results

After simulation and synthesis results, it is feasible to include hardware resource allocation results which design occupies on selected FPGA. For proposed design verification, Spartan 2-E, xc2s300e-6fg456 with 30,000 gates internally is utilized. Table 1 gives final module resource utilization information on target FPGA proved by Kamran 2006. It is already proved by Shinji Komori, in 1988 that for data driven processors, elastic pipelined causes high processing rate and smooth data stream concurrently. Our design is also meant to get concurrent data for processing for fast and efficient operation.

Logic Utilization	Used	Available	Utilization
Number of Slices	1372	3072	44%
Number of Slice Flip Flops	1379	6144	22%
Number of 4 input LUTs	2489	6144	40%
Number of bonded IOBs	49	329	14%
Number of TBUFs	7	3072	0%
Number of BRAMs	1	16	6%
Number of GCLKs	1	4	25%

Table 1. LSCIC (Stage 4) Resource Allocation Table

Table 1 provides the estimated device utilization summary of all modules implemented. Similarly data is collected for other subtasks and evaluation of resource utilization is made to become acquainted with the module complexity. Table 2 is the comparison of all sub modules with respect to resource utilization. It is required to be mentioned that stage 1 is comprised of down sample and buffer control module combination, stage 2 is formed by integrating stage 1 and RAM, stage 3 is organized by joining stage 2 and spatial redundancy module while stage 4 represents LSCIC pre coder by combining stage 3 and coder control module which causes the concurrent data to be extracted for coder and compression process. Figure 9 gives the graph for the resource utilization versus module addition in the design. This graph also provides us the information about the complexity of the module, i.e., more complex the module is, more utilization of slices, flip flops and other resources available on destination FPGA device is found. Moreover, it gives negligible difference between %age resources utilization in stage 1 and stage 2 as these two stages are approximately equally complex in configuration.

Logic Utilization	Stage-4	Stage-3	Stage-2	Stage-1
Slices	44%	25%	4%	3%
Slice F/F	22%	12%	2%	2%
4 Input LUT	40%	23%	2%	2%
Bonded IOB's	14%	16%	10%	12%

Table 2. Resource Utilization comparison between different stages

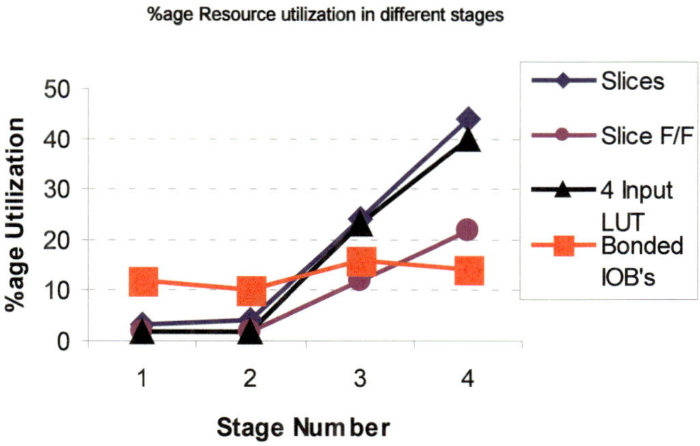

Fig. 9. Graphical Representation of Resource Utilization in different stages

5. Conclusion

The given LSCIC image and video compression is found quite amazing with respect to compression ratio and quality of reconstructed image. LSCIC is also adaptive with respect to band width variations. More experiments are being arranged for video reconstruction using wavelet transform with LSCIC pre coder.

6. References

Ke Shen (1997). "A study of real time and rate scalable image and video compression", PhD Thesis, Purdue University, pp. 8-9, USA, December 1997

Muhammad Kamran, Suhail Aftab Qureshi, Shi Feng and A. S. Malik," Task Partitioning-An Efficient Pipelined Digital Design Scheme", Proceedings of IEEE ICEE2007, April 11-12, 2007, 147~156

Muhammad Kamran, Shi Feng and Abdul Fattah Chandio, "Hardware Component Inclusion, Synthesis and Realization in Digital Design", Mehran University Research Journal of Engineering and Technology, July 2006, vol.25 issue 3, 223~230

R. J. Gove," The MVP: a highly-integrated video compression chip", Proceedings of IEEE Data Compression Conference, March 28-31, 1994, 215~224

Shinji Komori, Hidehiro Takata, Toshiyuki Tamura, Fumiyasu Asai, Takio Ohno, Osamu Tomisawa, Tetsuo Yamasaki, Kenji Shima, Katsuhiko Asada and Hiroaki Terada, "An Elastic Pipeline Mechanism by Self Timed Circuits", IEEE Journal of Solid State Circuits, February 1988, vol. 23, issue 1, 111~117

S. M. Akramullah, I. Ahmad, and M. Liou, "A data-parallel approach for real time Mpeg-2 video encoding", Journal of Parallel and Distributed Computing, vol. 30, issue 2, November 1995, 129~146

V.Bhaskaran and K. Konstantindies, "Image and Video Compression standards algorithms and architectures", Massachusetts, Kluwer Academic Publishers, 1995

21

The robotic visual information processing system based on wavelet transformation and photoelectric hybrid

DAI Shi-jie and HUANG-He
School of Mechanical Engineering, Hebei University of Technology, Tianjin 300130, China; Dshj70@163.com.

1. Introduction

There are mainly two outstanding characteristics for the developing trend of robotics: on one hand, the robotic application fields expand gradually and robotic species increase day by day; on the other hand, the robotic performance improves constantly, gradually developing towards intellectualization.

To make robots have intelligence and reactions to environmental changes, first of all, robots should have the abilities of environmental perception, so using sensors to collect environmental information is the first step for robotic intellectualization; secondly, the significant embodiment of robotic intellectualization is how to deal with the environmental information gained by sensors comprehensively. Therefore, sensors and their information processing systems complement each other, offering decision-making basis to robotic intelligent work[1]. So the intelligent feature of intelligent robots is its interactive ability with external environment, where the visual, tactile, approaching and force sense have great significance, especially the visual sense which is deemed to be the most important one. Sensor-based robotic intelligent engineering has become a significant direction and research focus[2-5].

Vision is one of the most important senses for human being. Over 70% information obtained from external environment for human is done by vision, so visual information processing is one of the core tasks for current information researches. Human eyes collect massive information from their environment, and then according to knowledge or experience, the cerebrum fulfills the processing work such as machining and reasoning so as to recognize and understand surrounding environment. Likewise, robotic vision is to install visual sensors for robots, simulating human vision, collecting information from image or image sequence and recognizing the configuration and movement of objective world so as to help robots fulfill lots of difficult tasks[6]. In industry, robots can auto-install parts automatically[7], recognize accessories, track welding seams[8-11], cut material willingly, and so on; in business, they can be utilized to patrol, track and alarm automatically[12-17]; in the aspect of remote sensing, they can be used to survey, map and draw voluntarily. The visual devices of mobile robots could not only recognize indoor or outdoor scenery, carry out path tracking and autonomous navigation, and fulfill tasks such as moving dangerous materials, detecting field rearward situation of enemy, sweeping landmine in enemy areas, and so on[18-24], but also automatically watch military targets, judge and track moving targets. Therefore, without visual systems, it is hard for robots to response to surrounding environment in an intelligent and sweet way.

In general, robotic vision means industrial visual systems operating together with robots, and its several basic issues include image filtering, edge feature extraction, workpiece pose determination, and so on. By means of introducing visual systems into robots, the operational performance of robots is extended greatly, which makes robots have a better adaptability to complete tasks. Besides satisfying low price, robotic visual systems should also meet demands such as good discrimination abilities towards tasks, real-time performance, reliability, universality, and so on. In recent years, the studies on robotic vision have become a research focus in robotic field, and many different solutions to improve the performance of visual systems are proposed in succession[25-26]. Of course, these solutions unavoidably require a higher demand on visual system and data processing ability on computers, especially real-time performance which is called more difficulties.

An important characteristic of robotic visual system is that its information data amount is large, and it demands a high processing rate to meet real-time controlling. Although the operation speed of resent computers has been very high, the information transmission and processing rate still can not satisfy the robotic real-time perceptual system. So processing rate is a bottleneck of robotic visual system urgently needing to be resolved based on practical purpose. At present, many researches are devoting into this problem, whose methods mainly include perfecting computer program, adopting parallel processing technology based on Transputer or optical information processing technology to improve image processing rate.

1.1 Design of robotic visual system based on photoelectric hybrid

Image feature extraction is one of the research emphases in robotic visual fields. People used to utilize various software algorithms to do this. Recently, along with the improvement of computer performance and the present of high performance algorithm, the processing rate of image feature extraction is raised greatly, but it still can not meet the real-time demand. For this reason, the photoelectric hybrid method is designed to realize robotic visual system.

Optical information processing indicates using optical methods to realize various transformations or treatments to the input information. Optical image information can be treated by optical methods. According to mathematics, the function of optical lens to luminous beam can be seemed as one kind of Fourier transformation. A serious of Fourier transformation theorems all have their correspondences in optical diffraction phenomena. The function of Fourier transformation is to separate the mixed information of images in frequency domain in order to treat it in spatial frequency spectrum, that is the basic principle of optical information processing. According to cohence between time and space of the using illuminant, optical information processing can be divided into coherent optical information processing, incoherent optical information processing and white light optical information processing. Coherent optical information processing is commonly used, because its processing abilities are more flexible and varied than incoherent optical information processing.

Making full use of optical functions such as large-capacity, fast response and parallel processing, two-dimensional optical processing get widely used. However, it has some inherent defects: firstly, a pure optical processing is hard to program. Although a pure optical system to complete certain tasks can be designed, it can not be used in some situations needing flexibility; secondly, optical system based on Fourier transformation is a simulation system, so it can not reach high precise; moreover, optical system can not make judgment, but some electronic system can do this. Even the simplest judgment is based on the comparison between output value and storage value, which can not realize without electronics.

In addition, the weakness of the optical system just stresses the advantages of the electronic system, for example, accuracy, controllability and programmability are all the characteristics of digital computers. Therefore, the idea that combining the optical system to the electronic system is very natural. By means of this approach, the optical quick processing and parallelism is widely used.

1.2 Hybrid optical signal processing system

Optical spectrum analysis systems, optical filtering systems and other optics-related systems have in common that they all perform two-dimensional processing at the same time and have simple structures. However, compared with computer data processing system, there are two drawbacks with them: Firstly, low accuracy, which is determined by the quality of optical system, especially by the photosensitive materials used to manufacture the filters; secondly, poor flexibility. Once the image types change, it is necessary to make their corresponding filters, and it is better to make them in the same device to get a better effect. The speed of current computer processing system is low and two-dimensional images contain a large amount of information, so it is necessary to get a high-speed and large-capacity computer to meet these requirements. But even with such advanced computer, it still can not meet the needs of real-time control. Therefore, when two methods combine, both of them can learn from each other and supplement each other. According to the characteristic of optical fast property, the image can be preprocessed to get a low accuracy one with little information. With this input, the computer capacity and its processing time can be greatly reduced, thus the requirements of real-time systems are met.

With the development of national economy, scientific technology and national defense construction, information processing capacity and speed have been put forward higher and higher requirements. Because of optical information processing and optical computing with faster processing speed, large flow information and many other features, it has become an important research field in modern optical systems.

These characteristics of optical information processing system are attributed to its use of light (light waves) as information carriers. First of all, just as other electromagnetic waves, the light waves also have a number of physical parameters, such as amplitude, phase, frequency, polarization state, and so on, and they can be modulated to carry information. Then, light has high frequency up to $3.9\text{-}7.5\times10^{14}$Hz in the visible light range, which allows the transmitted signals to have great bandwidth. In addition, the light has a very short wavelength and fast spreading speed in the range of 400-760nm among the visible light range, together with the principle of independent propagation of light wave, it can transfer two-dimensional information distributed in the same plane to another surface with high resolution capacity via optical system, so as to provide conditions for two-dimensional "parallel" processing.

Making full use of the optical large capacity and parallel processing capabilities, two-dimensional optical processing has gained a wide range of applications. The particular interesting applications are the processing of the image correlation in pattern recognition, image subtraction used in robotic vision and digital processing adopted in optical computing. Although optical correlator based on the general holographic filtering technique has already put forward for a long time, the concept of programmability in optical signal processing is introduced recently. Owing to the latest developments of perfect spatial light modulator and the photorefractive crystal, various real-time hybrid optical signal processing system (microcomputer-based optical processor) can be established.

The first way to realize microcomputer-based optical processors is to use 4*f* (*f* denotes focal length) optical processing devices, the importation and spatial filter of which are produced by the programmable Spatial Light Modulator (SLM), as shown in fig.1. Programmable complex conjugate Fourier transform of the reference pattern is generated by microcomputer on SLM2. Consequently, CCD detector array can be used to detect the cross correlation between importation and reference pattern, then the detected signals can give a feedback to the microcomputer used for display and judgment. It is evident that if there is enough Spatial Bandwidth Product (SBP) and resolution for SLM to show the plural spatial filter generated by computer, a programmable real-time optical signal processors can be realization in 4f structures.

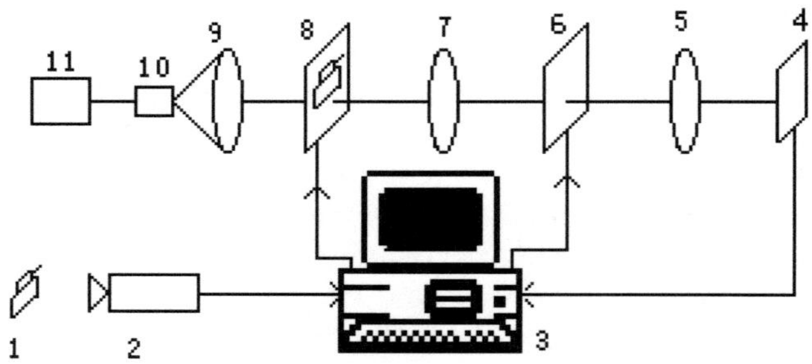

1. Object; 2.CCD camera; 3. Microcomputer; 4. CCD detector array; 5. Fourier transform lensL2; 6.SLM2; 7. Fourier transform lensL1; 8.SLM1; 9. Collimating lens; 10. Pinhole filter; 11.lasers

Fig. 1. Optical processor based on computer

The second way to realize the mixed optical processors is to apply the structure of joint Fourier transform, the importation and spatial impulse response of which can be displayed in the input Spatial Light Modulator namely SLM1, as shown in fig. 2. For example, programmable spatial reference functions and importation can be produced side-by-side, so the Joint-transform Power spectrums (JTPS) can be detected by CCD1. Then, JTPS is displayed on SLM2, and the cross correlation between importation and reference function can be obtained in the back focal plane of the Fourier transform lens FTL2. From the above, it is easy to educe that real-time mixed optical processor can be achieved with joint transform structures.

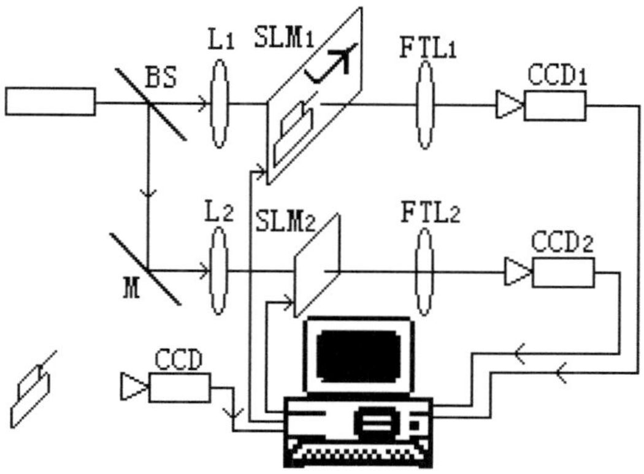

1. BS---Beam Splitter; 2. L---Collimating Lens; 3. FTL---Fourier Transform Lens
Fig. 2. Joint transform processor based on computer

Although hybrid optical structure functions of the 4*f* system and joint transform system are basically same, they have an important difference, that is the integrated spatial filter (such as Fourier holograms) has nothing to do with the input signal, but the joint power spectrum displayed on the SLM2 (such as joint transform filter) is related with the input signal. Therefore, non-linear filtering can be used in the 4*f* system, but in general not in joint transform system, which would leads to undesirable consequences (e.g., false alarm and low noise ratio of the output).

1.3 The optical realization of Fourier transform

Fourier transform is one of the most important mathematical tools among numerous scientific fields (in particular, signal processing, image processing, quantum physics, and so on). From a practical point of view, when one considers the Fourier analysis, it usually refers to (integral) Fourier transform and Fourier series.

1.3.1 Fourier transform

At first, look at the state in one-dimensional situation, suppose a signal as $g(x)$, and its Fourier transform can be defined as:

$$G(f) = \int_{-\infty}^{\infty} g(x) \exp(-ifx) dx \tag{1}$$

Where, $G(f)$ is called as Fourier transform or frequency spectrum of $g(x)$. If $g(x)$ denotes a physical quantity in a certain spatial domain, $G(f)$ is the representation of this physical quantity in the frequency domain. Its inverse transform is defined as:

$$g(x) = \int_{-\infty}^{\infty} G(f) \exp(ifx) df \tag{2}$$

In (1), the content of the component with the frequency f in $g(x)$ is $G(f)$, x is a time or space variable, and $G(f)$ denotes the component content of time frequency or spatial frequency. Equation (1) indicates that $G(f)$ is the integral of the product of $g(x)$ and $e^{-j2\pi fx}$ which denotes the index function of the simple harmonic motion or the plane wave, ranging from $-\infty$ to $+\infty$. Equation (2) indicates that $g(x)$ can be decomposed into a linear superposition of a series of simple harmonic motion or plane waves, while $G(f)$ is the weight function in the superposition computing.

Then, look at the state in two-dimensional situation, suppose a signal as $g(x,y)$, and its Fourier transform can be defined as:

$$G(u,v) = \int_{-\infty}^{\infty}\int g(x,y)\exp[-i2\pi(ux+vy)]dxdy \tag{3}$$

The inverse transformation of (3) is :

$$g(x,y) = \int_{-\infty}^{\infty}\int G(u,v)\exp[i2\pi(ux+vy)]dudv \tag{4}$$

The existence conditions of the transformation are as follows:

1. $g(x,y)$ is absolutely integrable in the whole plane;
2. In the whole plane, $g(x,y)$ only has a finite number of discontinuous points, and in any finite region only with a finite number of extremum;
3. There is no infinite discontinuous point with $g(x,y)$.

The conditions mentioned above are not necessary. In fact, "physical reality" is the sufficient condition for transformation. But for most of the optical system, the function expressions of signals are two-dimensional. For optical Fourier transform, x and y are spatial variables, but u and v are spatial frequency variables.

1.3.2 Optical Fourier transform and $4f$ optical system

Known from information optics, far-field diffraction has characteristics of Fourier transform. As the back focal planes of thin lens or lens group are equivalent to ∞, it can be educed that any optical system having positive focal length should have the function of Fourier transform.

In coherent optical processing system, what the system transfers and processes is the distribution information of complex amplitude of optical images, and in general the system meets the principle of superposition to complex amplitude distribution.

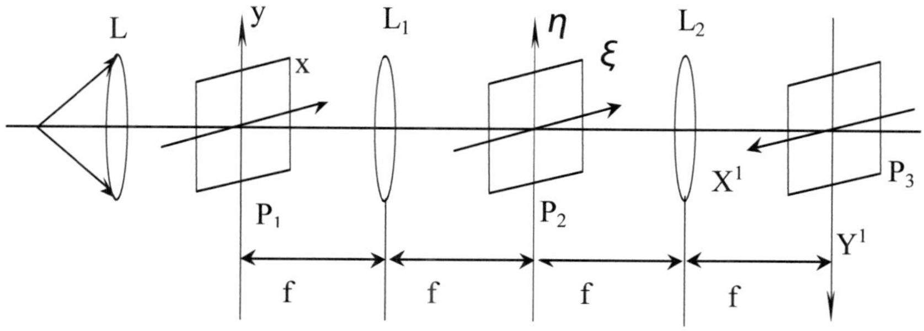

Fig. 3. Optical filter system

In physical optics, the Abbe - Porter experimental system is a coherent optical processing system: using all kinds of spatial filters to change the spectrums of objects and images so as to change the structures of images, that is to make optical processing for the input information (optical information). Seen from geometrical optics, the $4f$ optical system is an imaging system with two confocal lenses and its magnification is -1. In general, the $4f$ optical system (also known as dual-lens system) as shown in fig. 3 is often used to carry on coherent optical processing: the output plane (x', y') is overlapped with the front focal plane of FTL1, the input plane (x, y) is overlapped with the back focal plane of FTL2, and spectrum plane is located in the coincidence position of the back focal plane of FTL1 and the front focal plane of FTL2. Irradiate the object with collimating coherent light, and its frequency spectrum will appear in the frequency plane, that is, when the input plane is located in the front focal plane of Fourier transform lens FTL1, the accurate Fourier transform of the object function $\widetilde{E}(x, y)$ can be get from the back focal plane of FTL1:

$$\widetilde{E}(u,v) = \iint_{-\infty}^{\infty} \widetilde{E}(x,y)\exp[-i2\pi(\xi x + \eta y)]dxdy \tag{5}$$

Where $u = \lambda f \xi$, $\upsilon = \lambda f \eta$ ---coordinates of the back focal plane of FTL1.
Because the back focal plane of FTL1 is overlapped with the front focal plane of Fourier transform lens FTL2, the Fourier transform of the spectral function $\widetilde{E}(x', y')$ can be get from the back focal plane of FTL2:

$$\widetilde{E}(x',y') = \iint_{-\infty}^{\infty} \widetilde{E}(u,v)\exp[-i2\pi(\xi' u, \eta' v)]dudv \tag{6}$$

Where $x' = \lambda f \xi'$, $y' = \lambda f \eta'$ ---coordinates of the back focal plane of FTL2.

Therefore, (5) is substituted into (6), and the result is shown as follows:

$$\widetilde{E}'(x',y') = \iint_{-\infty}^{\infty} \widetilde{E}(x,y)\delta(x+x',y+y')dxdy = \widetilde{E}(x',y') \tag{7}$$

This equation shows that after twice Fourier transform, the final output image function of the object function $\widetilde{E}(x,y)$ is same as its input image function, only being a reversed image.

Coherent optical information processing is normally carried out in the frequency domain, that is, using various spatial filters to change the spectrum in the spectrum plane so as to change the output image to achieve the purpose of image processing. This kind of operation which changes the spectrum components is entitled "Spatial Frequency Filtering", and "Spatial Filtering" for short.

Based on the assumption that complex amplitude transmission coefficient of spatial filter is $\widetilde{t}\left(\frac{u}{\lambda f},\frac{v}{\lambda f}\right)$, the spectrum function passing through the spatial filter is:

$$\widetilde{E}'\left(\frac{u}{\lambda f},\frac{v}{\lambda f}\right) = \widetilde{E}\left(\frac{u}{\lambda f},\frac{v}{\lambda f}\right)\widetilde{t}\left(\frac{u}{\lambda f},\frac{v}{\lambda f}\right) \tag{8}$$

Neglecting the aperture effect of lenses, $\widetilde{E}'\left(\frac{u}{\lambda f},\frac{v}{\lambda f}\right)$ is the spectrum of image, but $\widetilde{E}\left(\frac{u}{\lambda f},\frac{v}{\lambda f}\right)$ is the spectrum of input object (image). The object-image relationship in the frequency domain depends on the complex amplitude transmission coefficient $\widetilde{t}\left(\frac{u}{\lambda f},\frac{v}{\lambda f}\right)$ of the spatial filter. From a standpoint of transfer function, the complex amplitude transmission coefficient of the spatial filter is the coherent transfer function of system, and in optical information processing system, it is the filter function. Therefore, loading what kind of filter function in the spectrum plane is the key to achieve the ultimate image processing. Thus, if the spectrum of the wavelet function is added to the public focal plane of two lenses, the frequency composition of object information can be changed, namely changing the object information. Then, after the inverse transform of the second lens, image of the treated object is obtained.

From inputting object to spectrum, it is the process of decomposition of various frequency components; from spectrum to outputting object, it is the process of re-synthesis of various frequency components. Due to the restriction of finite size pupil in the spectrum plane, frequency components which is re-synthesized in the image plane has lost high frequency components beyond the cut-off frequency of system, so the $4f$ coherent imaging system is essentially a low-pass filtering system.

1.4 Robotic visual system realization based on photoelectronic hybrid

According to the above analysis, it is known that if there are proper filters placed in the public focal plane of the *4f* system, the image information can be improved. Therefore, if a suitable wavelet filter can be designed and placed in this plane, the features of the image information is able to extract out, which will significantly reduce the image information collected into computers, so that the workload of computer software will be also greatly reduced to enhance the real-time performance of robot vision. Based on this principle, and fully taking into account the high parallel and high-capacity characteristics of the optical information processing, the robotic visual system is designed as shown in fig. 4.

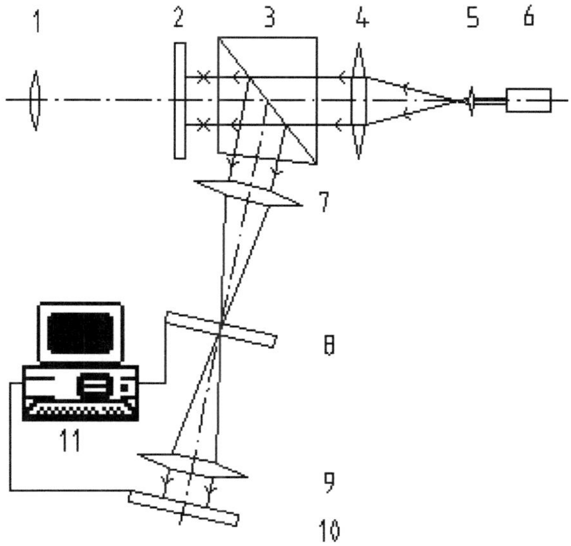

1.Imaging objective lens (L1); 2. OA-SLM; 3. Polarization splitter prism; 4.Collimating lens; 5. Collimating lens; 6. Semiconductor laser; 7.FTL_1; 8.EASLM; 9. FTL_2; 10.CCD; 11.Computer
Fig. 4. Optical-electronical hybrid implementation visual system

Through lens (L1), external target (object) is imaged in the optical addressing spatial light modulator (OA-SLM) which is equal to an imaging negative, and then is read out by collimating coherent light to realize conversion from the non-coherent light to coherent light. The process is as follows: by collimating lens, the laser produced by lasers is transformed into parallel light irradiating into the polarization prism, and then the prism refracts polarized light to OA-SLM. The read-out light of OA-SLM goes back along the original route, then incidents into the first Fourier lens (FTL1) through the polarization prism. After the optical Fourier transform, the spectrum of object information is obtained in the back focal plane of FTL1. Place electrical addressing spatial light modulator (EA-SLM) in spectrum plane, and load spectrum of filter function for EA-SLM via computer, then the EA-SLM will become a spatial filter. In this way, after going through EALSM, object information passes through spatial filtering and its spectrum has changed. That is, it completes the product with the read-out image spectrum. If a suitable filter function is chosen, an appropriate spatial filter will be created, and it will be able to achieve a good filtering effect. Because EASLM is also located in the front focal plane of FTL2, after affected by the second Fourier lens (FTL2), object information completes the inverse Fourier transform and transits back to the spatial domain from the frequency domain. In this way, the image information collected by CCD is the information passing through spatial filtering, namely the information extracted object features, so its amount will greatly reduced. Then, input this simplified information into computer system. The workload of computer software is also greatly decreased, and its runtime is shorten greatly, so its real-time performance is enhanced greatly.

Known from the above analysis, the innovation of this proposed visual system is to do spatial filtering for object information by adopting filters, and then to extract object features so as to reduce the workload of computer software, as optical information processing speed is the speed of light, so that it can enhance the real-time performance of vision.

1.5 The optical devices of the photoelectric hybrid-based robotic visual system

The designed photoelectric hybrid-based robotic visual system is composed of object reader, 4*f* optical system and computer coding electrical addressing spatial light modulator. The devices mainly include coherent light collimator, optical addressing spatial light modulator, polarization splitter prism, Fourier transform lenses, electrical addressing spatial light modulator, and so on.

1.5.1 The object reading device

As shown in fig.5, the main parts of the object reading device consist of spatial light modulator, polarization splitter prism, coherent light collimator, illuminant of writing light, illuminant of reading light, and so on.

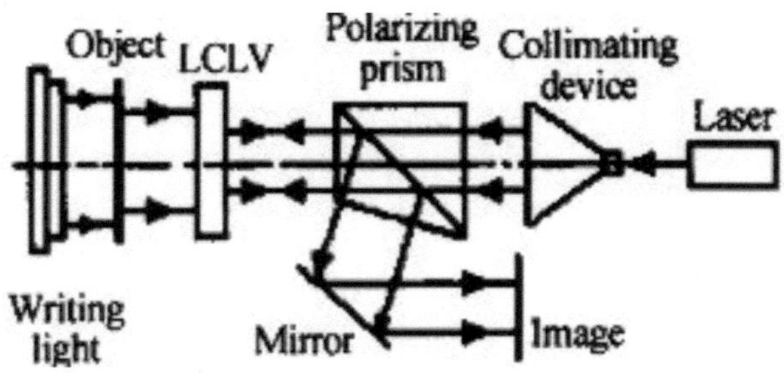

Fig. 5. Object reading principle of visual system

Under the irradiation of writing light (white light), the object images in OA-SLM. As reading light, collimating coherent light is reflected after irradiating in OA-SLM. In this way, the object information is coupled to the reflected beam, that is, the reflected beam has carried the object information. Then, the reflected light is reflected by polarization splitter prism to read the object image.

2. The design of coherent light collimator

Taking into account that the visual system should reliable and durable and its structure should compact, DL230382033 type low current, heat-resistant semiconductor laser is selected as illuminant of writing light. Its wavelength λ is 635 nm, output power is 10mW, and the working environment temperature is range from $-10^{\circ}C$ to $+50^{\circ}C$. As the semiconductor laser beam is astigmatic elliptical Gaussian beam, after going through extender lens, the low-frequency part of this Gaussian beam is located in the vicinity of optical axis, while the high-frequency component is far away from the optical axis. To this end, an aperture diaphragm is placed in the back focal plane of the extender lens L1 (as shown in fig. 6), in order to filter out high-frequency component and high-frequency interference noise, so as to improve the quality of coherent light beam.

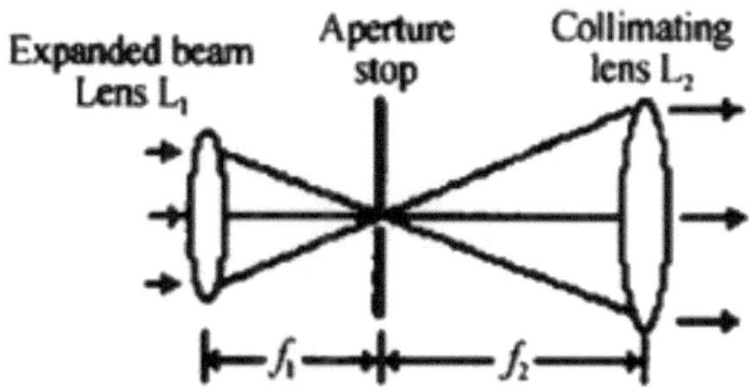

Fig. 6. Generation of collimated light beam

There is an average divergence angle for laser beams due to the width of the waist of Gaussian beam. Considering the influence of divergence angle to the area of focused spot, an aperture diaphragm with d = 15μm is selected by calculating. As shown in fig. 6, the proportion relation between the corresponding edges of the similar triangles is:

$$f_1/f_2 = DL1/DL2$$

Where, f_1 and f_2 respectively denote the focal lengths of extender lens and collimating lens; DL1 and DL2 respectively represent the light-passing diameters of extender lens and collimating lens.

Hence, it can be computed that the focal length of collimating lens f_2 is 190 mm, and the diameter of collimating light spot is 32mm. The two in fig. 8 respectively represent experimental results of the beams in distance of 500mm and 1000mm from the collimator. The collimation degree of collimator is 0.4%, reaching the desired design effect.

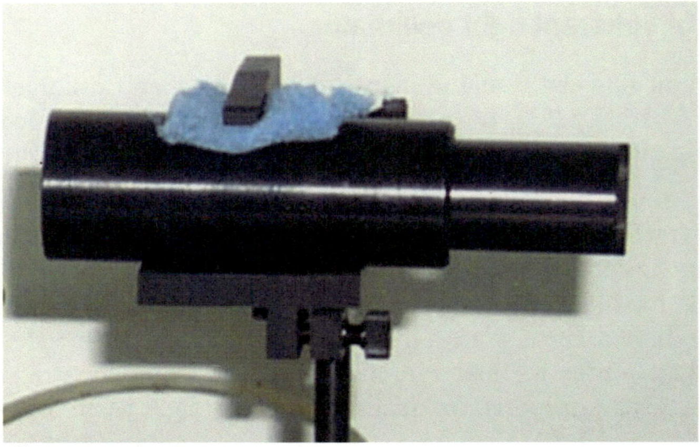

Fig. 7. Photo of collimating device

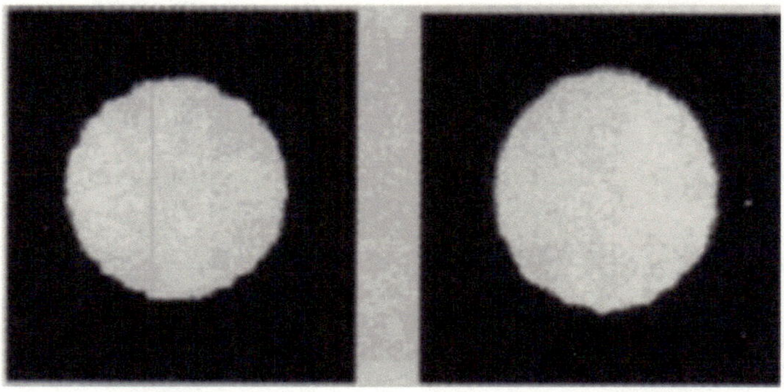

Distance $l = 500$ mm Distance $l = 1000$ mm

Fig. 8. Experiment results of collimated light beam

3. Optical addressing spatial light modulator (OA-SLM)

Optical addressing spatial light modulator (OA-SLM), namely Liquid Crystal Light Valve (LCLV), under the control of illuminant signal, it can modulate light wave, and write the information recorded by source signals into incident coherent light wave. The main performance parameters of LCLV are shown in Table 1. The photo of OA-SLM is shown in Fig. 9.

Size of image plane	$45 \times 45\ mm^2$	gray level	7-8
lowest energy of writing light	6.3 $\mu W / cm^2$	spatial resolution	55 Lp / mm
exposure dose of the threshold	3.7 Erg / cm^2	responding time	30-40 ms
lowest energy of reading light	4.0 $\mu W / cm^2$	contrast gradient	150

Table 1. The main performance parameters of LCLV

Fig. 9. Photo of O-SLM

4. Real-time reading of object image

By the experiment of object reading device, intensity of writing light, the distance between liquid crystal light valve and polarization splitting prism, as well as working voltage and frequency of liquid crystal light valve all have obvious influence on reading light.

Firstly, intensity of reading light and writing light is non-simple corresponding, curves of input and output is campaniform. In upward section, with increase of writing light intensity, reading light intensity monotonously increased, and the output of liquid crystal light valve was positive image, as shown in fig. 10(a). In descent segment, with increase of writing light, reading light intensity monotonously decreased, and the output of liquid crystal light valve was inverse image, as shown in fig. 10(b).

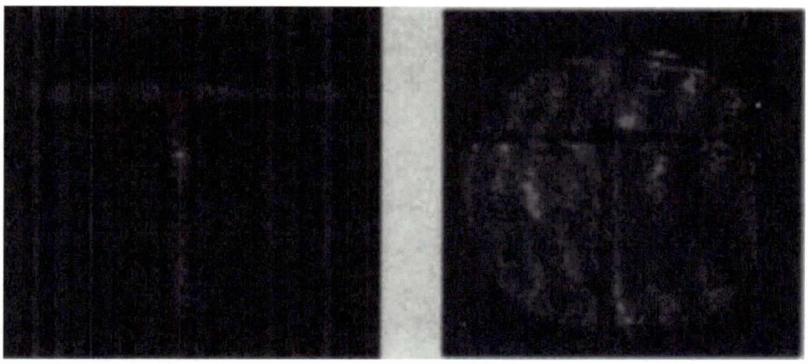

(a) Positive image (b) Inverse image

Fig. 10. Experiment results of reading light

Secondly, orthogonal experiment between working voltage and working frequency was done, and the results showed that when working frequency was about 3.3 *kHz*, the output was best, working frequency influence scope was $2.7kHz \leq f \leq 3.5\ kHz$. In certain working frequency, when voltage was 3.2*v* or 5.2*v*, clear object information can be obtained. Compared to original image, the reading object information had some noise, but the obtained image was clear.

4.1 Fourier Transform Lenses of optical system

The design characteristics of Fourier Transform Lens of 4*f* system is : its requirements are that every point of front focal plane give off light through lens focus a point of rear focal plane accurately, a point of front focal plane give off light through lens is mutual parallel, and two conjugate surfaces must have sinusoidal conditions.

Fourier transform lenses are used in the conditions of homochromatism. If one lens is needed to adapt to several wavelength light, the method is to increase color difference of axial direction, and different wavelength use different focal plane. In addition, focal length of Fourier transform Lens is longer, if focal length is large enough, it can scatter all levels spectrum, and introduce reference light easily. Meanwhile, numbers of lenses should decrease as less as possible to reduce coherent light noise.

As Focal length of Fourier transform Lens is longer, to shorten structure size of system, symmetry distance-based Fourier transform Lens structure is adopted.

5. The optical parameters determination of Fourier lens

Double long-distance Fourier transform lens can shorten the distance between pre- focus and post-focus so as to reduce the structure size of the optical processing system. In addition, because variables of this Fourier lens to eliminate aberration are more, it is benefit to enlarge pore sizes and field of view.

Because Fourier transform lens computes the complex amplitude of object function, in order to ensure sufficient computing precision, its aberration is need to be strictly corrected. The wave aberration is usually controlled within the diffraction limit, namely ($1/4$ to $1/10$) λ. Therefore, as long as system variables are enough, adopting Fourier transform lens with symmetry structures is beneficial. Thus, in order to adapt to the photoelectric hybrid-based robotic visual system, the double long-distance structure is selected.

The main optical parameters of Fourier transform lens are focal length f, the object plane, the working size of spectrum plane, and so on. According to the requirements of 4*f* coherent processing system, the specific conditions of actual devices are as follows: coherent working wavelength λ is $635nm$, and the maximum diameter of lighting parallel beam is about $25mm$ which is determined by the light-passing diameter of polarization splitter prism, and limits the object plane size as a window function $W(x,y)$. In the spectrum plane, a computer-controlled Thin Film Transistor Liquid Crystal Displays (TFT-LCD) is adopted as a spatial filter, so the size of TFT-LCD determines the size of the spectrum plane. In the object plane, OA-SLM is used as an input device, and its spatial resolution limits the highest spatial frequency of object function image. According to the formula $u = \lambda f_1 \zeta, v = \lambda f_1 \eta$, when the highest spatial frequency ζ_m (or η_m) of the object and the maximum size $2u_m$ (or $2v_m$) of spectrum plane are known, the focal length of the Fourier transform lens FTL1 can be determined:

$$f_1 = \frac{u_m}{\lambda \zeta_m} \quad \text{or} \quad f_1 = \frac{v_m}{\lambda \eta_m} \tag{9}$$

Similarly, for FTL2, its spectrum plane size is same as that of FTL1, and its image plane size is determined by the receiver (CCD), so the focal length of the Fourier transform lens FTL2 should meet the following relationship:

$$f_2 = f_1 \frac{W'}{W} = f_1 \ \beta \tag{10}$$

Where $\beta = \dfrac{f_2}{f_1} = \dfrac{W'}{W}$ —linear magnification of 4f imaging system.

In photoelectric hybrid-based robotic visual system, the main working parameters of the selected devices are as follows:

1. Optical Addressing Spatial Light Modulator (OA-SLM)

Its spatial frequency is $\mu_{1\max} = 40lp/mm$, and the light-passing diameter is $40mm$.

2. Thin Film Transistor Liquid Crystal Displays (TFT-LCD)

SVGA1 produced in British CRL company is introduced, and its spatial frequency is $\mu_{2\max} = 30lp/mm$; the size of Liquid Crystal Display is $28.48mm(W) \times 20.16mm(H)$.

3. CCD: its camera element is $1/2$ inch, and the resolution is 600 lines.

4. Polarization splitter prism: the working area is $\phi 25mm$.

Based on these data, optical parameters of FTL1 and FTL2 are as shown in Table 2.

Fourier Transform Lens	focal length	image (object) plane size	spectrum plane size
FTL1	381mm	25mm	25mm
FTL2	252mm	25mm	25mm

Table 2. Optical parameters of FTL1 and FTL2

Affected by pixel size of EA-SLM of loading spatial filter and array structure, a number of images will overlapped in the output plane of the processing system. In order to separate these images, the input object plane size should be reduced to meet the following relationship:

$$W_e = \lambda \gamma_F f_1 \tag{11}$$

Where, W_e —Limited working size of the object plane;

γ_F —Spatial resolution of filter.

According to formula (10) and (11), limited sizes of object plane and image plane can be obtained, and they respectively are $W_L = 7.25mm$, $W_L' = 9.7mm$. However, in order to make optical elements have good generality, they are still designed in accordance with Table 2.

6. Comprehensive evaluation of optical design result and image quality of Fourier lenses

According to the demand of design, the structures of the designed Fourier transform lenses and optical parameters are shown as fig. 11, fig. 12, table 3 and table 4 respectively. Their geometric aberration, wave aberration and optical modulation transfer function curves are shown as fig. 13, 14, 15 and 16. Two Fourier transform lenses are shown as fig. 17 and fig. 18.

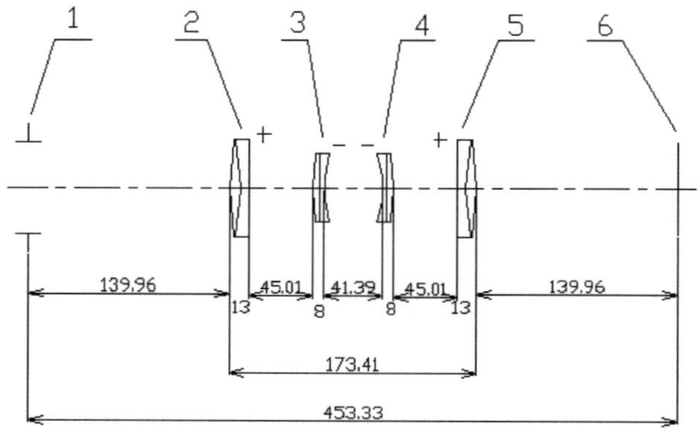

Fig. 11. Optical system of FTL1 (Unit: mm)

focal length f	381.01	relative aperture D/f	1/15.24
object distance L_F	-140.05	object plane, spectrum plane diameter D	25
spectral plane distance L'_F	140.05	coherent wavelength λ	635nm
cylinder length L	180.25	maximum wave aberration W	0. 088λ
distance between two focus D	460.35	disposable highest spatial frequency v	51.6lp/mm

Table 3. Main optical parameters of FTL1 system (Unit: mm)

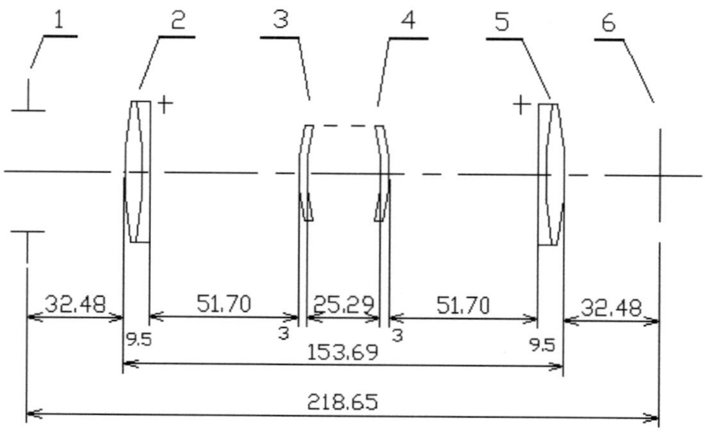

Fig. 12. Optical system of FTL2 (Unit: mm)

focal length f	252.01	relative aperture D/f	1/10.1
object distance L_F	-32.48	object plane, spectrum plane diameter D	25
spectral plane distance L'_F	32.48	coherent wavelength λ	635nm
cylinder length L	153.69	maximum wave aberration W	0.1λ
distance of two focus D	218.65	disposable highest spatial frequency v	78.1p/mm

Table 4. Main optical parameters of FTL2 system (Unit: mm)

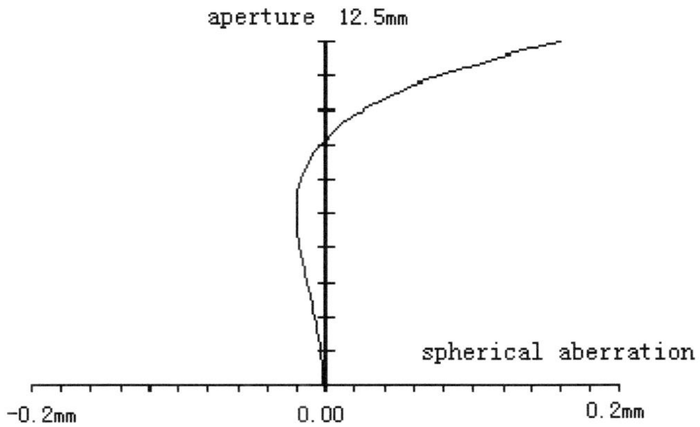

Fig. 13. Spherical aberration of FTl

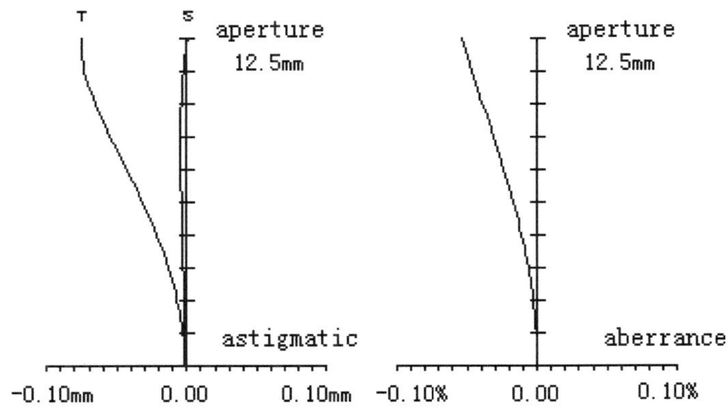

Fig. 14. Astigmatism and distortion of FTL

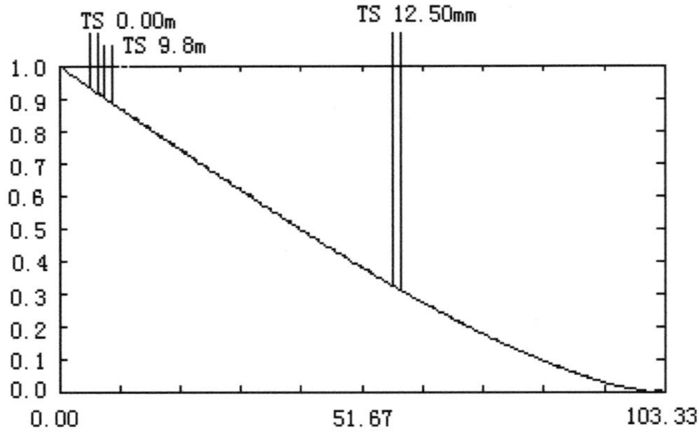

Fig. 15. Modulated transfer function of FTL

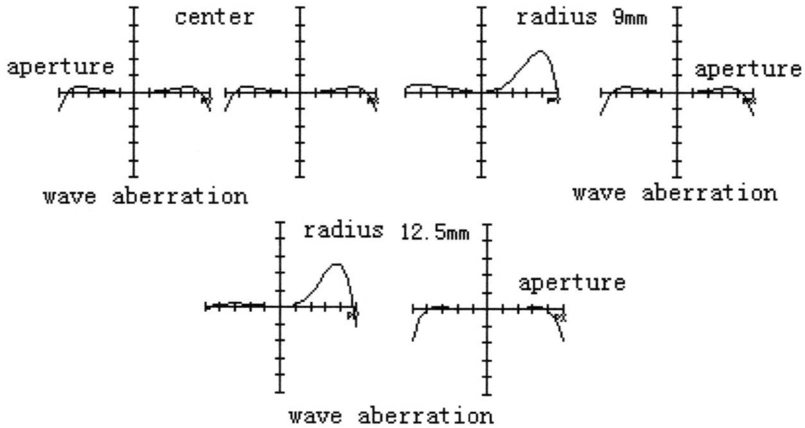

Fig. 16. Optical path difference of FTL

Known from the above, transfer function of both Fourier transform lenses are completely same as diffraction-limited transfer function, and the wave aberration is controlled within the wavelength of $1/10$ in the whole field range. This shows that both Fourier transform lenses are excellent, and the design is successful.

Fig. 17. Photo of Fourier transform lens

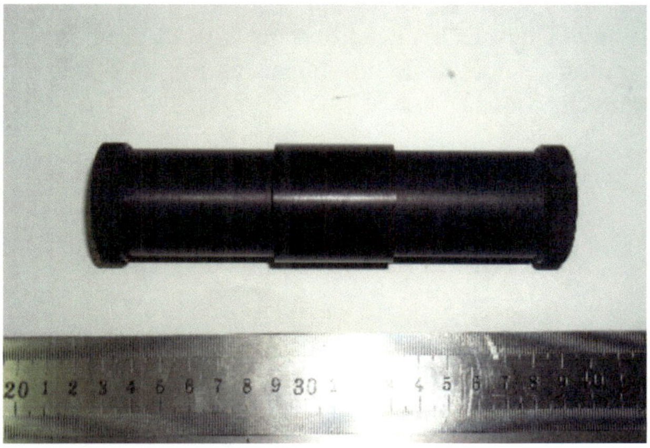

Fig. 18. Photo of Fourier inverse transform lens

6.1 Loading and experiment of wavelet filter

Adding wavelet filter in spectrum plane can change spectrum to process image. So, SVGA1 electrical addressing spatial light modulator produced in British CRL Company is introduced as loading platform of wavelet filter. The wavelet filter is added to electrical addressing spatial light modulator through computer programming method to realize photoelectric hybrid system of image information.

7. Electrical Addressing Spatial Light Modulator (EA-SLM)

The input signal of electrical addressing spatial light modulator, type SVGA1, is electrical, the electrical signal is time series, and transported into the pixels of spatial light modulator (SLM) successively with serial addressing mode. The modulator is mainly composed of a driver card and a Liquid Crystal Device (LCD), the card is supported by 12V power supply and connected to PC by parallel interface, the LCD connects to drive card through a special flat cable with a 30 pins plug, and its spatial resolution is $\mu, \mu_{\max} = 30Lp/mm$.

On the inner face of the two substrates of LCD, there are orthogonal grating transparent poles printed by Photo lithography. The liquid crystal layer is packaged between the substrates. The horizontal grids printed on the front surface are scanning poles, and the vertical grids printed on the back surface are signal poles. If neglecting the lag of liquid crystal responding to external electrical field, for the pixel at the crossing point of scanning pole and signal pole, the transmittance of pixel is depended on the voltage between the two poles. Thus, the scanning pole and signal pole divide the LCD into pixel elements of matrix form that is Thin Film Transistors (TFT) array. These TFT and electrical pole arrays can be observed by microscope in strong light. The material of liquid crystal is light-electrical, and responds to voltage applied. The pixel transmittance, namely pixel gray, is controlled by voltage of scanning pole and signal pole.

The pixel array of type SVGA1 light modulator is showed in fig. 19(a). There are 800 pixels in the width direction, 600 pixels in the height direction, and the length of span is 33 μm. Every pixel is a controllable unit with 24μm(Height)× 26μm(Width). LCD is very different from analog display unit, such as pixel and signal having no single valued relation. Although signals received by electrical addressing spatial light modulator is analog, the transmittance responding to voltage is non-linear, as fig. 19(b),and this nonlinear can be compensated by countermeasour.

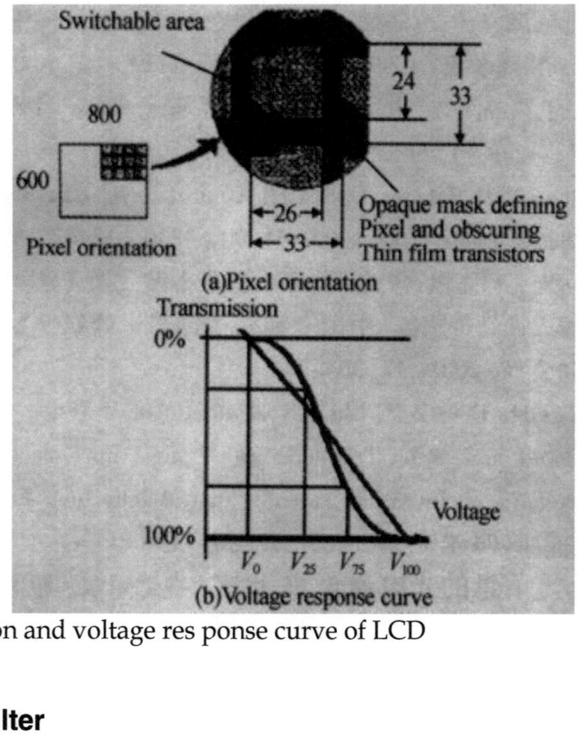

Fig. 19. Pixel orientati on and voltage res ponse curve of LCD

8. Optical wavelet filter

There are various kinds of wavelet function, including Morlet wavelet, Haar wavelet, Mexican-hat wavelet, Spline wavelet and Daubechies wavelet. In practical engineering, Haar wavelet and Mexican-hat wavelet have got widely used. Here, using computer programming, optical wavelet filter is constructed in electrical addressing spatial light modulator.

1. Optical Haar wavelet filter
One-dimensional Haar wavelet is a bipolar step-type function, and there are three forms of the two-dimensional combination, including horizontal edge wavelet, vertical edge wavelet and angular Haar wavelet. The important characteristic of Haar wavelet is its orthogonal nature. So it is commonly used in corner feature extraction of binary image function.
Two-dimensional Haar wavelet function can be expressed as:

$$\psi(x,y) = rect(x \pm 0.5, y \pm 0.5) - rect(x \pm 0.5, y \mp 0.5)$$

It is staggeredly consisted of two pairs of bipolar two-dimensional rectangular function. Obviously, Haar wavelet function is not continuous, and its combinations in different forms have good effects when extracting the corner features of images. When optical Haar wavelet filter is constructed based on computer programming method, the Haar wavelet function should be sampled at first; and then sample points are Fourier transformed; finally, Haar wavelet function spectrum is obtained. As long as the sample points are enough, the needed optical Haar wavelet filter 1 will be designed. Fig. 20 is the Haar wavelet spectrum when sample point numbers are 100. Seen from Fig. 20, Haar wavelet spectrum obtained by computer programming is more normative than that of physical methods, and flexible to operate.

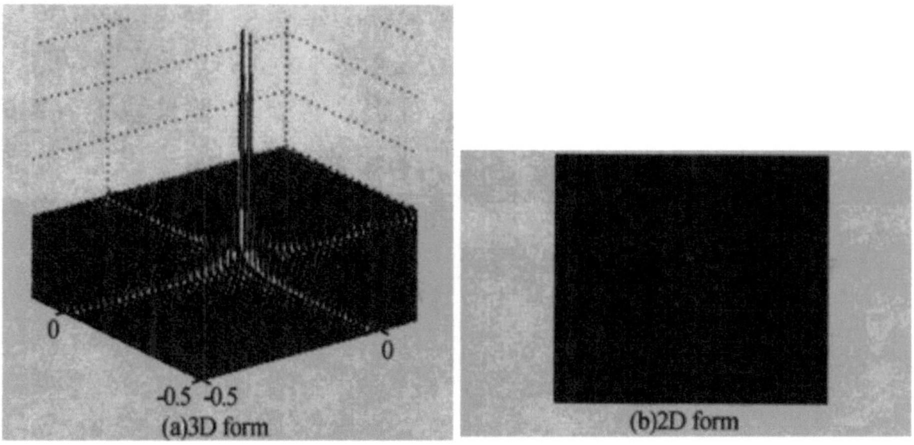

Fig. 20. Frequency spectrum of Haar wavelet when sample points are 100

Dual-cross optical Haar wavelet filter can be constructed by further graying the spectrogram of Haar wavelet function.

2. Optical Mexican-hat wavelet filter
The forms of two-dimensional Mexican-hat wavelet in spatial domain and frequency domain respectively are:

$$h(x,y) = [1-(x^2+y^2)]\exp(-\frac{x^2+y^2}{2}) \tag{12}$$

$$H(u,v) = 4\pi^2\sigma^2(u^2 + v^2)\exp[-2\pi^2\sigma^2(u^2 + v^2)] \quad (13)$$

Equation (12) and (13) are both real-even functions, and their morphologies are shown as Fig. 21 (a). In optical system, Mexican-hat wavelet is often approximated as ring-band filters in frequency domain, which constitutes the wavelet filter as shown in Fig. 21 (b).

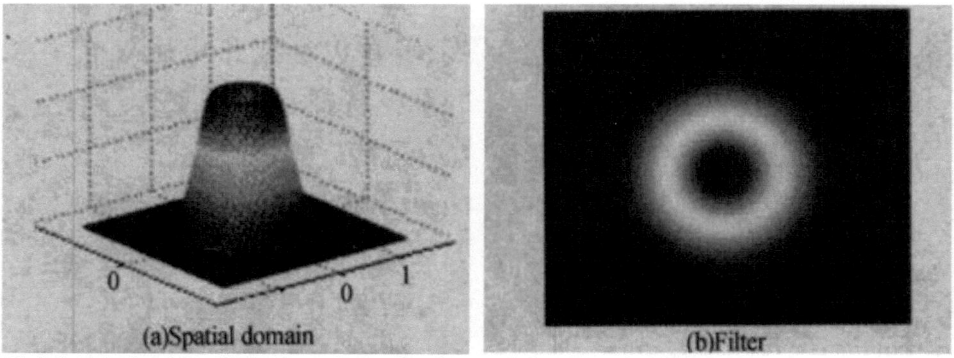

Fig. 21. Morphologies of Mexican-hat wavelet and the wavelet filter

8.1 The noise processing of optical addressing spatial light modulator (OA-SLM)

In the designed system, incoherent images are transformed into coherent images by Optical Addressing Spatial Light Modulator (OA-SLM) in the speed of light; however, the resolution of OA-SLM can not be comparable with the wavelength of light, so it inevitably introduces pseudo-frequency when segmenting the objective images in special domain, and then there is Quantization Noise generated when quantizing the image energy.

Therefore, during image processing, to remove interference noise is an important issue which must be settled. Here, according to the parameters of OA-SLM in the proposed system, prepositive antialiasing filter was designed.

9. Sampling theory

The frequency of light wave is above 1014Hz, but the highest resolution of present OA-SLM is $60lp/\text{mm}$, which can be considered as that sampling continuous image by spatial light modulator. Sampling processing is for every T seconds sampling the analog signal x (t), and the time t is discretized into the unit of sampling interval T, t = nT, n = 0,1,2,3 ......For this reason, plenty of pseudo high-frequency composition is inevitably introduced in the frequency domain which are regular, that is, each frequency composition is the periodic ($f_s = 1/T$) reproduction of the original signal in the whole frequency axis. Taking the sinusoidal signal $x(t) = \exp(2\pi jft)$ of a single frequency f for example, before the sampling, its frequency is f. But after sampling, it is $x(nT) = \exp(2\pi fnT)$, that means copying the original frequency periodically with intervals of f_s and it can be expressed as $f' = f + mf_s$, $m = 0,\pm1,\pm2,\pm3\ldots$. As a result, there will be much more confusion added to

the original signal, and with the introduction of pseudo-frequency, in order to avoid interference, it must satisfy the sampling theorem.
Spatial sampling of spatial light modulator is similar to the above processing. It simples the spatial continuous image $f(x, y)$. The resolution of OA-SLM is 35lp/mm, so the sampling frequency $f_s = 35$ kHz, and then deduced from $f_s \geq 2f_{\max}$, the maximum frequency is $f_{\max} = 17.5$ kHz, namely the spatial frequency to process images is up to 17.5kHz.

10. Design of antialiasing pre-filters

For sampling signal under the ideal condition and meeting sampling theory, the signal must be filtered by antialiasing pre-filters, cut-off frequency $f_{\max}$ of pre-filters is at least $f_s/2$, spectrum replication induced by sampling process is shown as fig. 22.

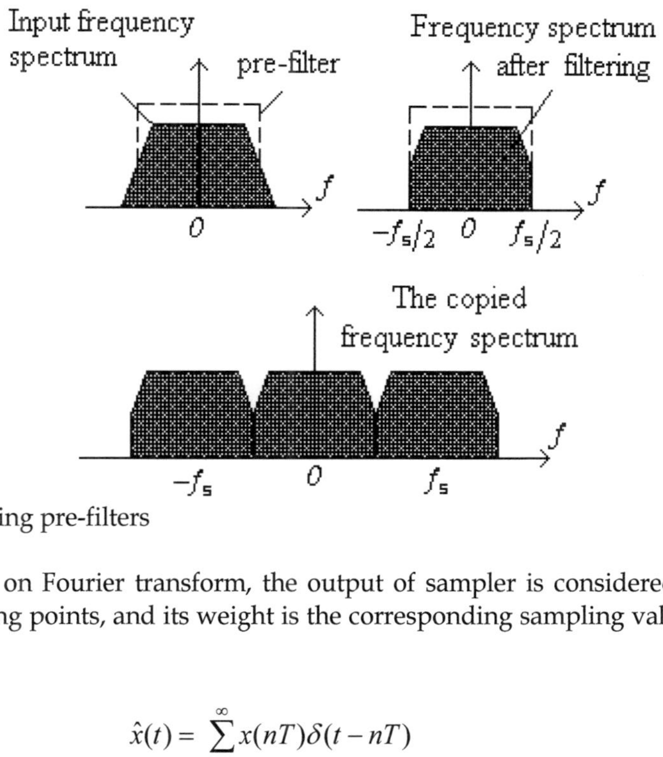

Fig. 22. Antialiasing pre-filters

Analyzed based on Fourier transform, the output of sampler is considered composing by pulses of sampling points, and its weight is the corresponding sampling value, so, sampling signal is:

$$\hat{x}(t) = \sum_{n=-\infty}^{\infty} x(nT)\delta(t - nT) \tag{14}$$

Its spectrum is:

$$\hat{X}(f) = \int_{-\infty}^{\infty} \hat{x}(t)\exp(-2\pi jft)dt = \frac{1}{T}\sum_{m=-\infty}^{\infty} X(f - mf_s) \tag{15}$$

From the above equations, spectrum replication can be known.

Perfect filters are shown as fig. 22, which have got rid of stimulant input signals exceed $|f_s/2|$.But in fact, antialiasing pre-filters is not ideal, and it can't completely filtrate all frequency which is bigger than $|f_s/2|$, so it introduce aliasing necessarily. To solve this problem, it can design rational pre-filters to reach concessional bound in engineering.

Actual antialiasing pre-filters are shown as fig. 23, and $[-f_{pass}, f_{pass}]$ is important frequency range, which must be within $[-f_{pass}, f_{pass}]$. In optics system, Fresnel diffraction (far-field diffraction) can be used for filtrate antialiasing. As locating before spectrum, it also called antialiasing pre-filters.

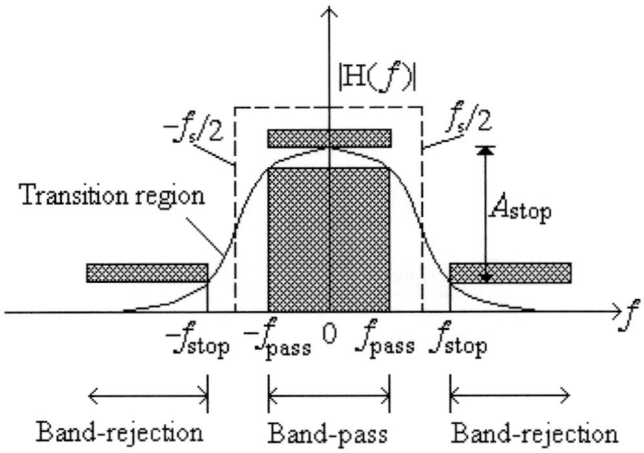

Fig. 23. The practical antialiasing lowpass pre-filter

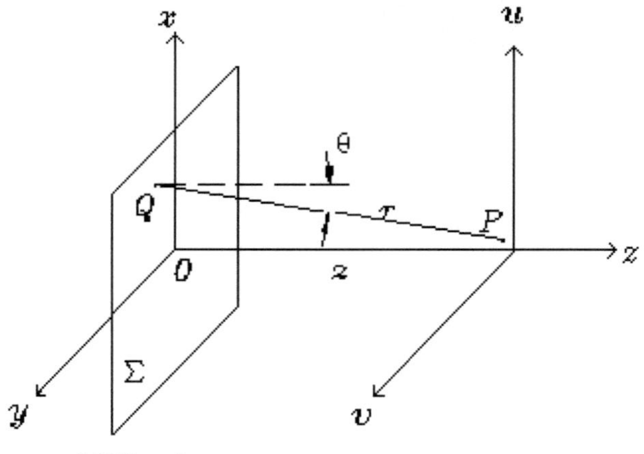

Fig. 24. The sketch map of diffraction

This system use laser as lamp-house, so it analyzes diffraction which cast monochrome plane wave to a hatch $\sum$ as shown in fig. 24. Let hatch plane is xy plane, transforming plane is uv plane, x、y axis parallels u、v axis respectively.

If coordinates of Q is (x, y) and coordinates of P is (u, v), distance r between these two points is:

$$r = \sqrt{z^2 + (u-x)^2 + (v-y)^2} \quad (16)$$

If distance between watching plane and hole is bigger than the dimension of the hole, and only considering that field angle is not big field of diffraction hole in the transforming plan (paraxial nearby), $\cos\theta \approx 1$ (error is less than 5% when θ is lower than 18°).
r can be expressed as follows:

$$r = z[1 + (\frac{u-x}{z})^2 + (\frac{v-y}{z})^2]^{1/2} \quad (17)$$

$(\frac{u-x}{z})^2 + (\frac{v-y}{z})^2 << 1$, via making binomial theorem on radical of above formula, the following relationship can be obtained:

$$r = z\{1 + \frac{1}{2}(\frac{u-x}{z})^2 + \frac{1}{2}(\frac{v-y}{z})^2 - \frac{1}{8}[(\frac{u-x}{z})^2 + (\frac{v-y}{z})^2]^2 + ...\} \quad (18)$$

Omiting over quadratic term, then it can get:

$$r = z[1 + \frac{1}{2}(\frac{u-x}{z})^2 + \frac{1}{2}(\frac{v-y}{z})^2] \quad (19)$$

Substituting (19) to $\exp(ikr)$, it can get:

$$\exp(ikr) = e^{ikr} \cdot e^{\frac{ik}{2z}[u-x)^2 + (v-y)^2]} \quad (20)$$

Therefore, from the Kirchhoff diffraction formula:

$$\widetilde{E}(p) = \frac{1}{i\lambda r} \times \frac{1+\cos\theta}{2} \iint_{\Sigma} \widetilde{E}(Q)\exp(ikr)d\sigma \quad (21)$$

The following relationship can be obtained:

$$\widetilde{E}(u,v) = \frac{e^{ikz}}{i\lambda z} \iint_{\Sigma} \widetilde{E}(x,y)\exp\{\frac{ik}{2z}[(u-x)^2 + (v-y)^2]\}dxdy \quad (22)$$

Where, the integral interval is aperture Σ, when beyond Σ, the complex amplitude $\widetilde{E}(x,y) = 0$.

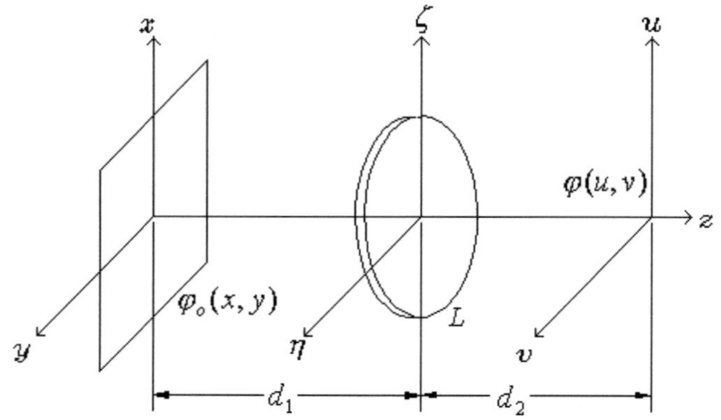

Fig. 25. The transform effect of lens

In the optical wavelet transform system, as fig. 25, the input plane xy locates in d_1 where is front of the lens L, and output planar uv locates in d_2 where is behind of lens L. Suppose the transmission of light wave between d_1 and d_2 meets the Fresnel approximation condition, then the lens' anterior surface field $\varphi_l(x, y)$ can be expressed as:

$$\varphi_l(x,y)=\frac{e^{ikd_1}}{i\lambda d_1}\int\int_{-\infty}^{\infty}\varphi_o(x,y)\cdot\exp\{i\frac{k}{2d_1}[(\zeta-x)^2+(\eta-y)^2]\}dxdy \tag{23}$$

Phase transform effect of lens is as follows:

$$\varphi_l^{'}(\zeta,\eta)=t_l\cdot\varphi_l=\frac{1}{f}e^{-ikf}\cdot\exp[i\frac{k}{2f}(\zeta^2+\eta^2)]\varphi_l(x,y) \tag{24}$$

Where, the constant phase term $\exp(ik\Delta)$ is omitted.
Using the Fresnel approximation formula again, the field of output planar (u,v) can be got:

$$\varphi(u,v)=\frac{e^{ikd_2}}{i\lambda d_2}\int\int_{-\infty}^{\infty}\varphi_l^{'}(\zeta,\eta)\cdot\exp\{i\frac{k}{2d_2}[(u-\zeta)^2+(v-\eta)^2]\}d\zeta d\eta \tag{25}$$

Substituting equation (23) and (24) into (25), the following relationship can be got:

$$\varphi(u,v)=-\frac{1}{\lambda^2 d_1 d_2 f}e^{ik(d_1+d_2-f)}\cdot e^{[i\frac{k}{2d_2}(u^2+v^2)]}\times\int\int_{-\infty}^{\infty}\varphi_o(x,y)\cdot\exp[i\frac{k}{2d_1}(x^2+y^2)]\Lambda(x,y)dxdy \tag{26}$$

where：

$$\Lambda(x,y)=\int\int_{-\infty}^{\infty}\exp\{i\frac{k}{2}[(\frac{1}{d_1}+\frac{1}{d_2}-\frac{1}{f})(\zeta^2+\eta^2)-2(\frac{x}{d_1}+\frac{u}{d_2})\zeta-2(\frac{y}{d_1}+\frac{v}{d_2})\eta]\}d\zeta d\eta$$

Define $d_1 = d_2 = f$, then:

$$\varphi(u,v) = \frac{e^{ikf}}{i\lambda f^2} \int_{-\infty}^{\infty}\int \varphi_o(u,v) \cdot \exp[-i\frac{2\pi}{\lambda f}(xu + yv)]dxdy \qquad (27)$$

Then, restrict Σ as rectangular opening with the length and width b and a separately. Define the origin coordinates at the center of the rectangular opening, and suppose $l = \frac{u}{f}$, $m = \frac{v}{f}$, let $C = \frac{e^{ikf}}{i\lambda f^2}\varphi_o(u,v)$, so (27) can be transformed as:

$$\varphi(u,v) = C \int_{-\frac{b}{2}}^{\frac{b}{2}} \exp(-ik(lx + my)dxdy$$

$$= C \cdot ab \cdot \frac{\sin\frac{klb}{2}}{\frac{klb}{2}} \cdot \frac{\sin\frac{kla}{2}}{\frac{kla}{2}} \qquad (28)$$

Let $\alpha = \frac{klb}{2}$, $\beta = \frac{kla}{2}$,then light intensity of point P is:

$$I = I_0(\frac{\sin\alpha}{\alpha})^2 \cdot (\frac{\sin\beta}{\beta})^2 \qquad (29)$$

Where, I_0 is light intensity of point P_0 on the optical axis.

Then, analyze the distribution of light intensity in one-dimensional space, and take y axis for example, then $I = I_0(\frac{\sin\beta}{\beta})^2$. Obviously, when $\beta = 0$, $I = I_0$, so the P_0 point has the maximum intensity, and when $\beta = \pm\pi, \pm 2\pi, \pm 3\pi ...$, $I = 0$, the points corresponding to the values are dark.

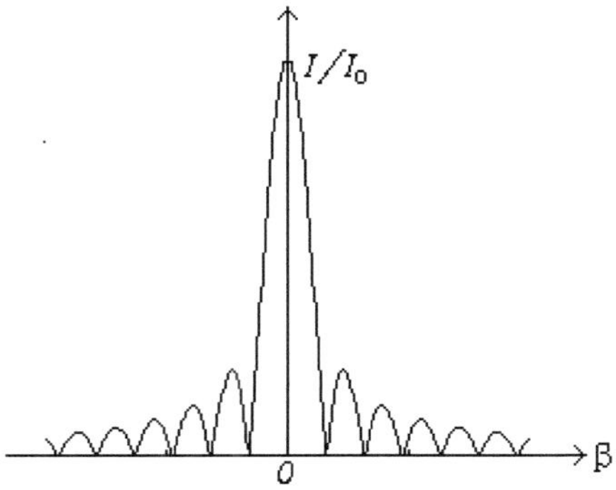

Fig. 26. The optical intension diffraction

Between the two minimum values of intensity, there is a second maximum value. These positions of maximum values can be obtained from following formula:

$$\frac{d}{d\beta}\left(\frac{\sin\beta}{\beta}\right)^2 = 0 \text{, that is } tg\beta = \beta \tag{30}$$

From fig. 26, it can be seen that suitable a and b can make the maximum intensity as prepositive removing aliasing filter. According the above analysis, a and b are both equal to $14mm$.

10.1 Experiment result

On the optical experimental platform, the experimental devices of the visual system based on wavelet transformation and photoelectric hybrid is constructed, as shown in fig. 27. In order to verify the correctness of system scheme, it adopted different types and factors optical wavelet function filter in the experiment, and operated graphic feature extraction experiment for corresponding target. Fig. 28 shows the graphic edge feature extracted form targets typing L using Mexican-hat wavelet filter.

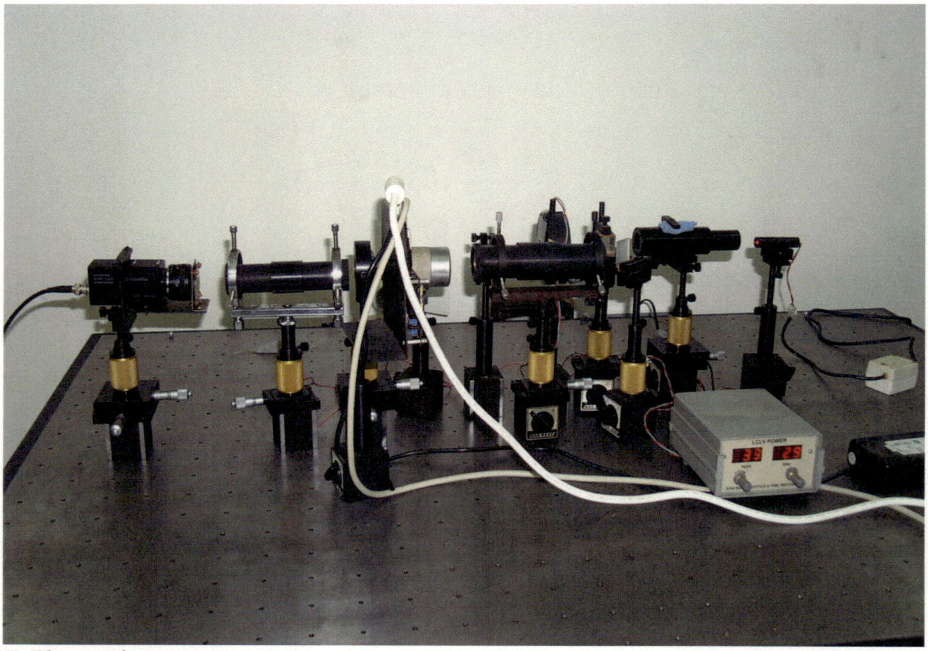

Fig. 27. Photo of experiment system

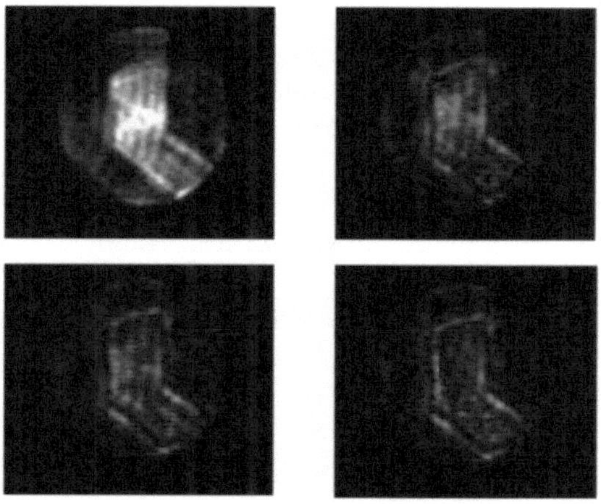

Fig. 28. Results of L-shape objective image feature extracting

11. References

1. J. Z. Sasiadek. Sensor fusion. Annual Reviews in Control. 2002, 26(2): 203-228
2. Nic Fleming. Interview: Robotic futures. The New Scientist. 2009, 203: 28-29
3. Amir A.F. Nassiraei, Kazuo Ishii. Concept of Intelligent Mechanical Design for Autonomous Mobile Robots. Journal of Bionic Engineering, Volume 4, Issue 4, December 2007, Pages 217-226
4. H.R.Nicholls,M.H.Lee. A Survey of Robot Tactile Sensing Technology. The Int. J, of Robotics Research. 1989, 8(3): 3-30
5. CAI Zixing. Advances in intelligent robots: Trends and gaming. Robot. 1996, 8(4): 248-252
6. Nguyen, Minh-Chinh. Vision-based Intelligent Robots. Proceeding of SPIE-The International Society for Optical Engineering. 2000, 4080: 41-47
7. Waurzyniak, Patrick. Robot Vision Guides Assembly. Manufacturing Engineering. 1999, 123(3): 42-46
8. Rhee Sehun, Lee Chang Hee. Automatic Teaching of Welding Robot for Free-formed Seam Using Laser Vision Sensor. Optics and Lasers in Engineering. 1999, 31(3): 173-182
9. Ferretti, Marc. Vision Sensors Give Eyes to the Welding Robot. Welding Journal. 1999, 78(7): 51-52
10. Meguro Shin-ichi, Muto Shin-yo, Katayama Atsushi. New Arc Welding Robot System Equipped with Laser Vision Sensor and Spatial Path Generation Scheme. NTT R&D. 1998, 47(7): 819-824
11. Uota, Koichi. Servo Robot's Laser Vision System for Welding. Sumitomo Metals. 1997, 49(3): 73-78
12. Wira P., Kihl H.. Robot Vision Tracking with a Hierarchical CMAC Controller. International Conference on Knowledge-Based Intelligent Electronic Systems. 2000, : 271-274

13. Zanela Andrea, Taraglio Sergio. Cellular Neural Network Stereo Vision System for Autonomous Robot Navigation. Proceedings of the IEEE International Workshop on Cellular Neural Networks and Their Applications. 2000, : 117-122.
14. Graf, Birgit. Small Robot Agents with On-board Vision and Local Intelligence. Advanced Robotics. 2000, 14(1):51-64
15. Deguchi, Koichiro. Direct Interpretation of Dynamic Images with Camera and Object Motions for Vision Guided Robot Control. International Journal of Computer Vision. 2000, 37(1): 7-20
16. Bonarini Andrea, Aliverti Paolo, Lucioni Michele. Omnidirectional Vision Sensor for Fast Tracking for Mobile Robots. IEEE Transactions on Instrumentation and Measurement. 2000, 49(3): 509-512
17. Okhotsimsky D.E., Platonov A.K., et al.. Vision System for Automatic Capturing a Moving Object by the Robot Manipulator. IEEE International Conference on Intelligent Robots and Systems. 1998, 2: 1073-1079
18. Abe Yasunori et al. Vision Based Navigation System for Autonomous Mobile Robot. JSME International Journal. Series C: Mechanical System, Machine Elements and Manufacturing. 2000, 43(2): 408-414
19. Murray Don, Little James J. Using Real-time Stereo Vision for Mobile Robot Navigation. Autonomous Robots. 2000, 8(2): 161-171
20. Shim Hyun-Sik, et al.. Design of Action Level in a Hybrid Control Structure for Vision Based Soccer Robot System. IEEE International Conference on Intelligent Robots and Systems. 1999, Oct.: 1406-1411
21. Cannata, Giorgio, et al.. On Perceptual Advantages of Active Robot Vision. Journal of Robotic Systems. 1999, 16(3): 163-183
22. Nygards, Jonas, Wernersson, Ake. On Covariances for Fusing Laser Rangers and Vision with Sensors Onboard a Moving Robot IEEE International Conference on Intelligent Robots and Systems. 1998, Oct.: 1053-1059
23. Nakamura, T., et al.. Development of a Cheap On-board Vision Mobile Robot for Robotic Soccer Research. IEEE International Conference on Intelligent Robots and Systems. 1998, Oct.: 431-436
24. Aufrere R. A Dynamic Vision Algorithm to Locate a Vehical on a Nonstructured Road. The International Journal of Robotics Research. 2000, 19(5):411-423
25. Vilesoma SW, Rolfe D F H, Richards R J, Eye-to-hand ,Coordination for Vision-guided Robot Control Applications. The Int. J of Robotics Research, 1993, 12(1): 65-78
26. Hen W Z, Korde U A, Skaar S B, Position Control Exteriments Using Vision. The Int. J. of Robotics Research, 1994, 13(3): 199-208

22

Direct visual servoing of planar manipulators using moments of planar targets

Eusebio Bugarin and Rafael Kelly
Centro de Investigación Científica y de Educación Superior de Ensenada
Mexico

1. Introduction

Visual servoing is a control strategy that uses a vision system with one or more cameras to establish the movement of a robotic system (Hutchinson et al., 1996) and emerges as a good alternative to close the control loop between the robot and its environment. Vision is a non-contact method that can relax the setup on an industrial robot and can give more characteristic of autonomy to advanced robots, which operate in adverse ambient or execute service tasks. Depending on the place where the cameras are located, visual servoing is classified by the fixed-camera and camera-in-hand configurations.
This chapter addresses the regulation of a planar manipulator by the visual servoing strategy in fixed-camera configuration. To simplify the problem, it is considered that the camera optical axis is perpendicular to the robot motion plane. The specification of the robot motion by the visual servoing strategy must be established trough image features obtained from target objects in the scene or robot workspace. However, most of the developed theory in this area is based on the use of target objects with simple geometry like points, lines, cylinders or spheres (local features); or in more complex target objects but simplifying them to simple geometric objects trough image processing techniques (Collewet & Chaumette, 2000; Benhimane & Malis, 2006). On the other hand, image moments represent global features of an arbitrary target object projected in image plane. The main objective of this chapter is to extend the use of simple target objects toward the use of a more complex target objects in the direct visual servoing of manipulators. Particularly, the target object will be a planar object with arbitrary shape and the image features will be computed trough image moments combinations of this planar target.
The direct visual servoing term refers to the class of visual servo-controllers where the visual feedback is converted to joint torques instead to joint or Cartesian velocities; it does mean that the full nonlinear dynamic model of the robot is considered in the control analysis (Hager, 1997). The first explicit solution to the direct visual servoing problem is due to Miyazaki & Masutani (1990). We can find similar works in Espiau et al. (1992) and Kelly et al. (2000) where the problem is approached for a 6 degrees of freedom (6 d.o.f.) manipulator in camera-in-hand configuration. In Kelly (1996); Zergeroglu et al., (1999); Fang et al., (2002); Cheah et al., (2007); and Wang et al. (2008) we can see works that consider the dynamic

model of the manipulator in the control analysis and the robustness against to parametric uncertainties of the vision system.

The definition of image moments as image features for the visual servoing was expressed rigorously in Bien et al. (1993); although image moment combinations like the area, the orientation and the centroid were used to control 4 d.o.f. of a manipulator in an approximated manner. The analytic form of the time variation for the image moments was developed first in Tu & Fu (1995) and later in Chaumette (2004). This time variation for the image moments is expressed in terms of a matrix named image Jacobian (due to the image moments) which is essential for the design of a visual servoing scheme (Espiau et al., 1992; Hutchinson et al., 1996). This image Jacobian depends on the target object and the vision system 3D parameters.

In Chaumette (2004) is addressed a visual servo-control for the regulation of a 6 d.o.f. manipulator in camera-in-hand configuration by means of 6 image features that are based on combinations of image moments of a planar target with arbitrary shape; and in Tahri & Chamette (2005) is continued the later work with 6 image features based on image moments invariants to uncoupling the manipulator degrees of liberty and to achieve a better convergence domain with an adequate robot trajectory. It is worth noticing that these works do not belong to the direct visual servoing scheme because they just consider the cinematic model in the control analysis.

Specifically, in this chapter the controller is designed under the transpose Jacobian structure (Takegaki & Arimoto, 1981) and the robotic system stability and parametric robustness are analyzed in the Lyapunov sense. Also, we propose an alternative method for the determination of the time variation of the image moments based on the transformation of moments.

This chapter is organized as follows. Section 2 presents some definitions and the transformation between the two-dimensional Cartesian moments of a planar object and their corresponding image moments. Section 3 describes the formulation of the control problem. The design of the visual servo-controller is developed in Section 4 together with a robustness analysis. Section 5 proposes the selection of acceptable image features. To corroborate the performance of a robotic system with the designed controller, Section 6 presents some simulation data. Finally, the concluding remarks are exposed in Section 7.

2. Transformation of moments

2.1 Definitions

Consider a dense planar object $\mathcal{O}_S$ placed on the plane $S_1 - S_2$ of a frame $\Sigma_S = \{S_1, S_2, S_3\}$, also consider that the object is compound by a set of closed contours; then the two-dimensional Cartesian moments ${}^S m_{ij}$ of $\mathcal{O}_S$ (respect to Σ_S), of order $i + j$ ($i, j \in \{0, 1, 2, \ldots\}$), are defined as (Prokop & Reeves, 1992)

$$ {}^S m_{ij} = \iint_{\mathcal{O}_S} S_1^i S_2^j f(S_1, S_2) dS_1 dS_2 \tag{1} $$

where $f(S_1, S_2)$ is the density distribution function of $\mathcal{O}_S$.

A special class of moments are determined placing the object $\mathcal{O}_S$ such that its centroid $S_g = [S_{g_1} \ \ S_{g_2}]^T = [{}^S m_{10}/{}^S m_{00} \ \ {}^S m_{01}/{}^S m_{00}]^T$ matches with the origin of the plane $S_1 - S_2$, these moments are called Cartesian centered moments ${}^S\mu_{ij}$ of the object $\mathcal{O}_S$; which are computed by

$$ {}^S\mu_{ij} = \iint_{\mathcal{O}_S} [S_1 - S_{g_1}]^i [S_2 - S_{g_2}]^j f(S_1, S_2) dS_1 dS_2 \qquad (2) $$

where $f(S_1, S_2)$ is the density distribution function of $\mathcal{O}_S$.

There exist the next relations between the regular moments and the centered moments:

$$ \begin{aligned} {}^S\mu_{ij} &= \sum_{k=0}^{i}\sum_{l=0}^{j} \binom{i}{k}\binom{j}{l} [-S_{g_1}]^{i-k} [-S_{g_2}]^{j-l} \, {}^S m_{kl} \\ {}^S m_{kl} &= \sum_{m=0}^{k}\sum_{n=0}^{l} \binom{k}{m}\binom{l}{n} S_{g_1}^{\,k-m} S_{g_2}^{\,l-n} \, {}^S\mu_{mn} \end{aligned} \qquad (3) $$

where

$$ \binom{i}{k} = \frac{i!}{k!(i-k)!}. $$

2.2 The transformation

In this subsection is detailed the transformation between the two-dimensional Cartesian moments of a planar object with arbitrary shape $\mathcal{O}_O$ (respect to a plane $O_1 - O_2$) and the image moments computed from the projection of this object $\mathcal{O}_O$ over $\mathcal{O}_y$ in the image plane $y_1 - y_2$. The used camera model corresponds to the thin lens model one and it is considered that the camera optical axis is perpendicular to the object plane.

Figure 1 shows a view of the object perpendicular to the camera optical axis. Notice that it has been placed several Cartesian frames: the object frame Σ_O attached, precisely, to the object; the world frame Σ_W fixed somewhere in the scene or workspace; the camera frame Σ_C; and the image plane $y_1 - y_2$. The variable θ denotes the orientation of the object frame respect to the world frame, ψ represents also the orientation of the object frame but now respect to the image plane and ϕ is the rotation of the camera frame respect to W_3; in such a way that $\theta = \psi + \phi$.

A point $x_O = [x_{O_1} \ \ x_{O_2} \ \ x_{O_3}]^T$ in the object, respect to Σ_O, can be transformed to Σ_W by means of

where the vector $O_W^O \in \Re^3$ denotes the position of the origin of Σ_O respect to Σ_W and

$$ x_W = R_W^O(\theta) x_O + O_W^O \qquad (4) $$

represents the rotation matrix of the frame Σ_O respect to Σ_W.

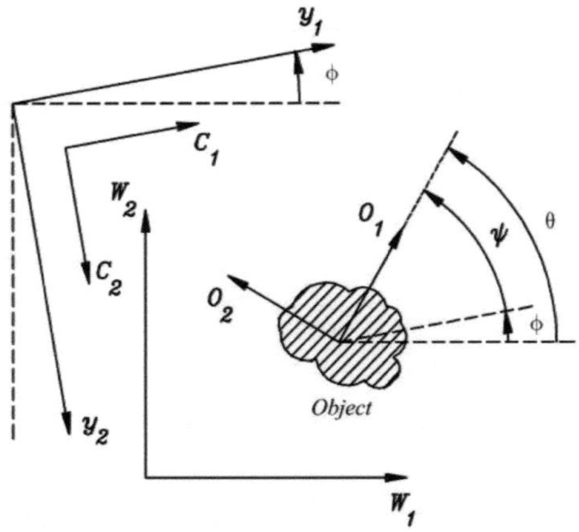

Fig. 1. View of the object perpendicular to the camera optical axis

$$R_W^O(\theta) = \begin{bmatrix} \cos(\theta) & -\sin(\theta) & 0 \\ \sin(\theta) & \cos(\theta) & 0 \\ 0 & 0 & 1 \end{bmatrix}$$

In its turn, the vector $x_W = [x_{W_1} \;\; x_{W_2} \;\; x_{W_3}]^T$ can be transformed to camera frame coordinates through

$$x_C = R_W^{C\,T}(\phi)\left[x_W - O_W^C\right] \tag{5}$$

where $O_W^C \in \Re^3$ is the position vector of Σ_C origin respect to Σ_W and

$$R_W^C(\phi) = \begin{bmatrix} \cos(\phi) & \sin(\phi) & 0 \\ \sin(\phi) & -\cos(\phi) & 0 \\ 0 & 0 & -1 \end{bmatrix} \tag{6}$$

is the rotation matrix of the camera frame respect to Σ_W.

For this particular case, the components of the vector x_C, after the substitution of (4) in (5) and simplifying, are

$$\begin{aligned} x_{C_1} &= \cos(\psi)x_{O_1} - \sin(\psi)x_{O_2} + c_1 \\ x_{C_2} &= -\sin(\psi)x_{O_1} - \cos(\psi)x_{O_2} + c_2 \\ x_{C_3} &= -[O_{W_3}^O - O_{W_3}^C] \end{aligned} \tag{7}$$

where

$$\begin{aligned} c_1 &= \cos(\phi)[O_{W_1}^O - O_{W_1}^C] + \sin(\phi)[O_{W_2}^O - O_{W_2}^C] \\ c_2 &= \sin(\phi)[O_{W_1}^O - O_{W_1}^C] - \cos(\phi)[O_{W_2}^O - O_{W_2}^C]. \end{aligned}$$

In this way, the mapping of a point x_O in the object (respect to Σ_O) to the image plane is obtained through the coordinate transformations (4) and (5) and the next thin lens camera model (Hutchinson et al., 1996; Kelly, 1996):

$$y = \begin{bmatrix} y_1 \\ y_2 \end{bmatrix} = \frac{\alpha\lambda}{x_{C_3} - \lambda}\begin{bmatrix} x_{C_1} \\ x_{C_2} \end{bmatrix} + \begin{bmatrix} u_0 \\ v_0 \end{bmatrix}$$

where α is a conversion factor from meters to pixels, λ is the focal length of the lens, the vector $[u_0 \quad v_0]^T$ denotes the image center and $x_C = [x_{C_1} \quad x_{C_2} \quad x_{C_3}]^T$ is the position vector of the point x_O respect to the camera frame; which is expressed in (7).

Observe that the depth x_{C_3} of all the points in the $O_1 - O_2$ plane is the same for this adopted camera configuration. For the sake of notation, define

$$\gamma = \frac{\alpha\lambda}{x_{C_3} - \lambda},$$

which, therefore, is a constant. Hence, the imaging model, for the adopted camera configuration, can be expressed as

$$y = \gamma \begin{bmatrix} x_{C_1} \\ x_{C_2} \end{bmatrix} + \begin{bmatrix} u_0 \\ v_0 \end{bmatrix}. \tag{8}$$

Now, according to (1), the two-dimensional Cartesian moments ${}^O m_{ij}$ of the object $\mathcal{O}_O$ respect to $O_1 - O_2$ are computed through

$${}^O m_{ij} = \iint_{\mathcal{O}_O} x_{O_1}^i x_{O_2}^j \, dO_1 dO_2 \tag{9}$$

where, in this case, $f(O_1, O_2) = 1$ for a point x_O in $\mathcal{O}_O$ and null elsewhere. And the image moments ${}^y m_{ij}$ of the object $\mathcal{O}_y$ respect to the image plane $y_1 - y_2$ in a binarized image $f(y_1, y_2)$ are defined as

$${}^y m_{ij} = \iint_{\mathcal{O}_y} y_1^i y_2^j \, dy_1 dy_2 \tag{10}$$

where $f(y_1, y_2) = 1$ for a point $y = [y_1 \quad y_2]^T$ inside the object $\mathcal{O}_y$ and null elsewhere.

The purpose is to find the relation between the Cartesian moments of the object and their respective image moments. To this end, consider the following theorem for the change of variables with multiple integrals (Swokowski, 1988).

Theorem 1. If $S_1 = g(U_1, U_2)$ and $S_2 = h(U_1, U_2)$ is a coordinate transformation from Σ_U to Σ_S, then

$$\iint_{\mathcal{O}_S} f(S_1, S_2) dS_1 dS_2 = \pm \iint_{\mathcal{O}_U} f(g(U_1, U_2), h(U_1, U_2)) \left| \frac{\partial(S_1, S_2)}{\partial(U_1, U_2)} \right| dU_1 dU_2$$

where $\mathcal{O}_U$ is the object respect to Σ_U, $\mathcal{O}_S$ is the transformed object from Σ_U to Σ_S and

$$\left| \frac{\partial(S_1, S_2)}{\partial(U_1, U_2)} \right| = \left\| \begin{bmatrix} \frac{\partial S_1}{\partial U_1} & \frac{\partial S_1}{\partial U_2} \\ \frac{\partial S_2}{\partial U_1} & \frac{\partial S_2}{\partial U_2} \end{bmatrix} \right\|$$

is the determinant of the transformation Jacobian.

It is chosen the positive or the negative sign depending on the fact that, if when a point $[U_1 \ \ U_2]^T$ in the frontier of $\mathcal{O}_U$ travels in the positive sense ($\mathcal{O}_U$ always remains at the left side), the corresponding point $[S_1 \ \ S_2]^T$ in $\mathcal{O}_S$ travels in the positive or the negative sense, respectively.

Therefore, following Theorem 1 and using (7)-(10), we have that

$$\begin{aligned} {}^y m_{ij} &= \gamma^2 \iint_{\mathcal{O}_O} [\gamma x_{C_1} + u_0]^i [\gamma x_{C_2} + v_0]^j dO_1 dO_2 \\ &= \gamma^2 \iint_{\mathcal{O}_O} [\gamma \cos(\psi) x_{O_1} - \gamma \sin(\psi) x_{O_2} + \gamma c_1 + u_0]^i \cdot \\ &\qquad [-\gamma \sin(\psi) x_{O_1} - \gamma \cos(\psi) x_{O_2} + \gamma c_2 + v_0]^j dO_1 dO_2 \end{aligned} \tag{11}$$

where the determinant of the transformation Jacobian is

$$\left| \frac{\partial(y_1, y_2)}{\partial(O_1, O_2)} \right| = \left\| \begin{bmatrix} -\gamma \sin(\psi) & -\gamma \cos(\psi) \\ -\gamma \cos(\psi) & \gamma \sin(\psi) \end{bmatrix} \right\| = -\gamma^2.$$

Note that it has been selected the negative sign in the application of the theorem because the axis C_3 of the camera frame and the O_3 axis of the object frame point in opposite directions and this provokes a negative sense in the motion of a point in the object frontier.

According to the multinomial theorem and the distributive law for multiple sums (Graham et al., 1989), (11) can be expressed as

$$
\begin{aligned}
{}^{y}m_{ij} &= \gamma^2 \iint_{\mathcal{O}_O} \left| \sum_{k_1,k_2,k_3} \frac{i!}{k_1!k_2!k_3!} [\gamma \cos(\psi) x_{O_1}]^{k_1} [-\gamma \sin(\psi) x_{O_2}]^{k_2} [\gamma c_1 + u_0]^{k_3} \right| \cdot \\
&\qquad \left| \sum_{l_1,l_2,l_3} \frac{j!}{l_1!l_2!l_3!} [-\gamma \sin(\psi) x_{O_1}]^{l_1} [-\gamma \cos(\psi) x_{O_2}]^{l_2} [\gamma c_2 + v_0]^{l_3} \right| dO_1 dO_2 \\
&= \gamma^2 \sum_{k_1,k_2,k_3} \sum_{l_1,l_2,l_3} \frac{i!}{k_1!k_2!k_3!} \frac{j!}{l_1!l_2!l_3!} [\gamma \cos(\psi)]^{k_1} [-\gamma \sin(\psi)]^{k_2} [\gamma c_1 + u_0]^{k_3} \cdot \\
&\qquad [-\gamma \sin(\psi)]^{l_1} [-\gamma \cos(\psi)]^{l_2} [\gamma c_2 + v_0]^{l_3} \iint_{\mathcal{O}_O} x_{O_1}^{k_1+l_1} x_{O_2}^{k_2+l_2} dO_1 dO_2 \\
&= \gamma^2 \sum_{k_1,k_2,k_3} \sum_{l_1,l_2,l_3} \frac{i!}{k_1!k_2!k_3!} \frac{j!}{l_1!l_2!l_3!} [\gamma \cos(\psi)]^{k_1} [-\gamma \sin(\psi)]^{k_2} [\gamma c_1 + u_0]^{k_3} \cdot \\
&\qquad [-\gamma \sin(\psi)]^{l_1} [-\gamma \cos(\psi)]^{l_2} [\gamma c_2 + v_0]^{l_3} \, {}^{O}m_{k_1+l_1, k_2+l_2}
\end{aligned}
\tag{12}
$$

where k_1, k_2, k_3, l_1, l_2 and l_3 are nonnegative integers such that $k_1 + k_2 + k_3 = i$ and $l_1 + l_2 + l_3 = j$. Notice that in the last step it has been used (9).

In this way, it is shown that by means of (12) the image moments of a planar object with arbitrary shape, in the adopted camera configuration, can be computed from the previous knowledge of the Cartesian moments of this object respect to its plane of definition. Though, it may be necessary to know camera parameters and the posture of the object frame Σ_O respect to the camera frame Σ_C.

Particularly, the object centroid in image plane y_g is related to the corresponding centroid in the object plane $x_{gO} = [x_{gO_1} \quad x_{gO_2}]^T$ by

$$
\begin{aligned}
y_g &= \begin{bmatrix} y_{g_1} \\ y_{g_2} \end{bmatrix} \\
&= \gamma \begin{bmatrix} \cos(\psi) & -\sin(\psi) \\ -\sin(\psi) & -\cos(\psi) \end{bmatrix} x_{gO} + \begin{bmatrix} \gamma c_1 + u_0 \\ \gamma c_2 + v_0 \end{bmatrix}.
\end{aligned}
\tag{13}
$$

Following similar arguments we can find the next relation for the centered moments:

$$
\begin{aligned}
{}^{y}\mu_{ij} = \gamma^2 \sum_{k_1,k_2} \sum_{l_1,l_2} \frac{i!}{k_1!k_2!} \frac{j!}{l_1!l_2!} [\gamma \cos(\psi)]^{k_1} [-\gamma \sin(\psi)]^{k_2} \cdot \\
[-\gamma \sin(\psi)]^{l_1} [-\gamma \cos(\psi)]^{l_2} \, {}^{O}\mu_{k_1+l_1, k_2+l_2}
\end{aligned}
\tag{14}
$$

where k_1, k_2, l_1 and l_2 are nonnegative integers such that $k_1 + k_2 = i$ and $l_1 + l_2 = j$.

3. Formulation

Consider a planar manipulator of n d.o.f. with the next dynamic model (Sciavicco & Siciliano, 2000):

$$M(q)\ddot{q} + C(q,\dot{q})\dot{q} + g(q) = \tau \tag{15}$$

where $q \in \Re^n$ is the vector of joint displacements, $\tau \in \Re^n$ is the vector of applied joint torques, $M(q) \in \Re^{n\times n}$ is the symmetric and positive definite inertia matrix, $C(q,\dot{q}) \in \Re^{n\times n}$ is the matrix associated with the centrifugal and Coriolis torques, and $g(q) \in \Re^n$ is the vector of the gravitational torques.

Two important properties of the dynamics of a manipulator are as follows (Spong & Vidyasagar, 1989):

Property 1. The matrix $C(q,\dot{q})$ and the time derivative $\dot{M}(q)$ of the inertia matrix satisfy

$$\dot{q}^T\left[\frac{1}{2}\dot{M}(q) - C(q,\dot{q})\right]\dot{q} = 0, \quad \forall q,\dot{q} \in \Re^n .$$

Property 2. The matrix $C(q,\dot{q})$ satisfies

$$C(q,0) = 0, \quad \forall q \in \Re^n .$$

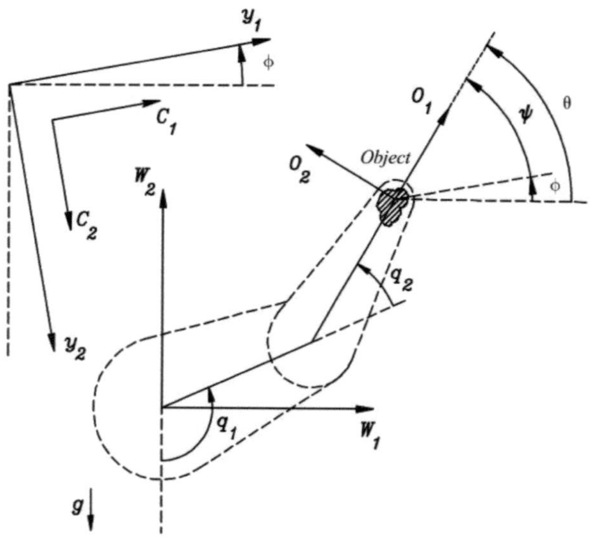

Fig. 2. View of the planar manipulator in fixed-camera configuration

Now, consider also a fixed camera observing the manipulator with a planar target object of arbitrary shape attached in its end-effector. Figure 2 presents a view of this robotic system. Also, in this figure, it can be observed the world frame Σ_W in the manipulator base, the camera frame Σ_C fixed somewhere in such a way that the planar target object can always be projected in the image plane $y_1 - y_2$, and the object frame Σ_O attached to the manipulator

end-effector where the target object is located. Notice that it is used the imaging model (8) where the camera optical axis is perpendicular to the manipulator motion plane; in this way the planes $W_1 - W_2$, $O_1 - O_2$, $C_1 - C_2$, and $y_1 - y_2$ are parallel (this keep relation with the system already described in the previous section). The angle ϕ denotes the rotation of the camera frame respect to W_3, θ is the orientation of the plane $O_1 - O_2$ respect to W_1 and $\psi = \theta - \phi$ is the orientation of the plane $O_1 - O_2$ in the image plane. The position of the manipulator end-effector respect to Σ_W is expressed trough the vector $O_W^O \in \Re^3$ because the frame Σ_O is attached to the end-effector.
Observe that if the planar manipulator is rotational, that is, with only revolute joints, then $\theta = \sum_{i=1}^{n} q_i - \pi/2$ and $\psi = \sum_{i=1}^{n} q_i - \pi/2 - \phi$. Otherwise, just the revolute joints would contribute to the sum. If such contribution is denoted by Σ_{q_r}, then

$$\theta = \Sigma_{q_r} - \pi/2 \text{ and } \psi = \Sigma_{q_r} - \pi/2 - \phi.$$

Now define an image feature vector $s \in \Re^r$ ($r \geq m$, where m is the dimension of the operational space) in function of the image moments ${}^y m_{ij}$ of the projection in the image plane of the target object. It is worth noticing that also the centered image moments ${}^y \mu_{ij}$ can be used since there exist the relation (3). According to (12) and (14) the image moments are in function of the variables ψ and O_W^O, which in their turn are in function of the vector of joint displacements q; this means that

$$\begin{aligned} s &= s({}^y m_{ij}(q)) \\ &= s(q). \end{aligned}$$

Thus, the time variation of the image feature vector $\dot{s}$ can be determined by

$$\begin{aligned} \dot{s} &= \frac{\partial s(q)}{\partial q} \dot{q} \\ &= J_s(q, {}^y m_{ij}) \dot{q} \end{aligned}$$

where

$$J_s(q, {}^y m_{ij}) = \frac{\partial s(q)}{\partial q}.$$

If the next factorization for the image feature vector s is valid:

$$s = \gamma A(\phi) f(q), \tag{16}$$

with $A(\phi) \in \Re^{r \times r}$ an orthogonal and constant matrix, then

$$\begin{aligned} \dot{s} &= \gamma A(\phi) \frac{\partial f(q)}{\partial q} \dot{q} \\ &= \gamma A(\phi) J(q, {}^y m_{ij}) \dot{q} \end{aligned} \tag{17}$$

where

$$J(q, {}^y m_{ij}) = \frac{\partial f(q)}{\partial q}. \tag{18}$$

On the other hand, denote with $s_d \in \Re^r$ the desired vector of image features which is supposed constant. Also, it is supposed that there exist at least one vector of joint displacements q_d, unknown but isolated, where the manipulator end-effector satisfies s_d. One way to establish such a reference s_d is by means of the teach-by-showing strategy (Weiss et al., 1987).
Finally, define the error vector of image features $\tilde{s}$ as

$$\tilde{s} = s_d - s.$$

If $s = \gamma A(\phi) f(q)$, then

$$\tilde{s} = \gamma A(\phi)[f(q_d) - f(q)]. \tag{19}$$

In short, the control problem is to design a control law for the system just described such that determines the torques τ to move the manipulator in such a way that the image feature vector s reaches the constant desired image feature vector s_d established previously; that is, the control objective is to drive asymptotically to zero the image feature error vector $\tilde{s}$, which is expressed by

$$\lim_{t \to \infty} \tilde{s}(t) = 0. \tag{20}$$

4. Control design

The designed controller corresponds to the transpose Jacobian structure, which was originally introduced by Takegaki & Arimoto (1981) and applied to the direct visual servoing in the case of punctual image features in Kelly (1996). Assuming that the image feature vector meets $s = \gamma A(\phi) f(q)$, which is described in (16); the controller is expressed by

$$\tau = J(q, {}^y m_{ij})^T K_p A(\phi)^T \tilde{s} - K_v \dot{q} + g(q) \tag{21}$$

where $K_p \in \Re^{r \times r}$ is a symmetric and positive definite matrix called proportional gain and $K_v \in \Re^{n \times n}$ is another symmetric and positive definite matrix named derivative gain.
It is worth noticing that the controller needs the measures of the joint positions q and the joint velocities $\dot{q}$, the knowledge of the gravitational torques vector $g(q)$ and the computation of the Jacobian $J(q, {}^y m_{ij})$. This Jacobian, depending on the selection of the image feature vector s, requires the direct measure in the image plane of certain image moments and the previous knowledge of some 3D parameters from the target object, the camera and the manipulator. However, it is no necessary to solve the inverse kinematics of the robotic system.
The closed-loop system corresponds to a nonlinear autonomous differential equation and it is obtained substituting in the manipulator dynamic model (15) the controller (21):

$$M(q)\ddot{q} + C(q, \dot{q})\dot{q} = J(q, {}^y m_{ij})^T K_p A(\phi)^T \tilde{s} - K_v \dot{q};$$

which, in terms of the state vector $[q^T \;\; \dot{q}^T]^T \in \Re^{2n}$, it is expressed by means of

$$\frac{d}{dt}\begin{bmatrix} q \\ \dot{q} \end{bmatrix} = \begin{bmatrix} \dot{q} \\ M(q)^{-1}\left[J(q, {}^y m_{ij})^T K_p A(\phi)^T \tilde{s} - K_v \dot{q} - C(q, \dot{q})\dot{q}\right] \end{bmatrix}. \tag{22}$$

The equilibrium points of the closed-loop system (22) satisfy

$$\begin{bmatrix} q \\ \dot{q} \end{bmatrix} = \begin{bmatrix} q_e \\ 0 \end{bmatrix}$$

where $q_e \in \Re^n$ is the solution of

$$J(q, {}^y m_{ij})^T K_p A(\phi)^T \tilde{s}(q) = 0.$$

Suppose that the Jacobian $J(q, {}^y m_{ij})$ is continuously differentiable with respect to each element of q and that it is of full range in $q = q_d$; then the equilibrium

$$\begin{bmatrix} q \\ \dot{q} \end{bmatrix} = \begin{bmatrix} q_d \\ 0 \end{bmatrix}$$

is a isolated equilibrium of (22), since it is also supposed that $s(q) = 0$ has isolated solution in $q = q_d$.
The stability analysis will be held trough the direct method of Lyapunov (see Vidyasagar (1993) for example). In this way, consider the next Lyapunov function candidate:

$$V(q_d - q, \dot{q}) = \frac{1}{2}\dot{q}^T M(q)\dot{q} + \frac{1}{2}\gamma[f(q_d) - f(q)]^T K_p [f(q_d) - f(q)], \tag{23}$$

which is a locally definite positive function because in the first term, $M(q) = M(q)^T > 0$; and in the second term $\gamma > 0$, $K_p = K_p^T > 0$ by design and it is supposed that $s(q) = \gamma A(\phi)[f(q_d) - f(q)] = 0$ has an isolated solution in $q = q_d$. Notice that (19) is used.
The time derivative of (23) yields

$$\dot{V}(q_d - q, \dot{q}) = \dot{q}^T M(q)\ddot{q} + \frac{1}{2}\dot{q}^T \dot{M}(q)\dot{q} + \gamma[\dot{f}(q_d) - \dot{f}(q)]^T K_p [f(q_d) - f(q)]. \tag{24}$$

Notice that $\dot{f}(q_d) = 0$ and, according to (18), $\dot{f}(q) = J(q, {}^y m_{ij})\dot{q}$; in this way, substituting the later and the closed-loop system (22) in (24), (23) can be simplified to

$$\dot{V}(q_d - q, \dot{q}) = \dot{q}^T\left[J(q, {}^y m_{ij})^T K_p A(\phi)^T \tilde{s} - \gamma J(q, {}^y m_{ij})^T K_p [f(q_d) - f(q)] - K_v \dot{q}\right] + \dot{q}^T\left[\frac{1}{2}\dot{M}(q) - C(q, \dot{q})\right]\dot{q}$$

Now, by means of Property 1 of the manipulator dynamic model and the fact that related with (19): $f(q_d) - f(q) = \frac{1}{\gamma} A(\phi)^T \tilde{s}$, since $A(\phi)$ is an orthogonal matrix; the time derivative of (23) finally yields

$$\dot{V}(q_d - q, \dot{q}) = -\dot{q}^T K_v \dot{q}\,.$$

And, because $K_v = K_v^T > 0$ by design, then $\dot{V}(q_d - q, q)$ is a globally negative semidefinite function. Therefore, according to the direct Lyapunov method, the equilibrium

$$\begin{bmatrix} q \\ \dot{q} \end{bmatrix} = \begin{bmatrix} q_d \\ 0 \end{bmatrix}$$

of the closed-loop system (22) is a stable equilibrium.

As mentioned, the closed-loop system is an autonomous one, hence it can be studied the asymptotic stability of the equilibrium by LaSalle's theorem (see Vidyasagar (1993) for example). For this purpose, in the region

$$\Omega = \left\{ \begin{bmatrix} q \\ \dot{q} \end{bmatrix} : \dot{V}(q_d - q, \dot{q}) = 0 \right\},$$

it is obtained the invariant set over the close-loop system (22) as $\dot{q} = 0$ and $q \in \Re^n : J(q, {}^y m_{ij})^T K_p A(\phi)^T \tilde{s}(q) = 0$. And according to the assumptions imposed on $J(q, {}^y m_{ij})$ and $\tilde{s}(q)$, the later is satisfied in $q = q_d$. Hence, by LaSalle's theorem it is demonstrated that the equilibrium point

$$\begin{bmatrix} q \\ \dot{q} \end{bmatrix} = \begin{bmatrix} q_d \\ 0 \end{bmatrix}$$

is asymptotically stable, it means that $\lim_{t \to \infty} [q_d - q(t)] = 0$ and $\lim_{t \to \infty} \dot{q}(t) = 0$ provided that $q_d - q(0)$ and $\dot{q}(0)$ are sufficiently small. Now, since $q_d - q = 0$ implies that $f(q_d) - f(q) = 0$, then, according to (20), $f(q_d) - f(q) = 0$ is true if and only if $\tilde{s} = 0$; therefore, the control objective (21) is satisfied.

4.1 Robustness analysis

Based on the results found in Kelly (1996), here it is analyzed the robustness of the controller (21) against uncertainties in 3D parameters of the target object and the camera. To this end, it will be used the first Lyapunov method instead of the direct Lyapunov method (see Vidyasagar (1993) for example).

Basically, it will be analyzed the uncertainty to ϕ and to parameters in the Jacobian $J(q, {}^y m_{ij})$; therefore there will be only an estimate $\hat{\phi}$ of the angle ϕ and an estimate $\hat{J}(q, {}^y m_{ij})$ of the Jacobian $J(q, {}^y m_{ij})$. This modifies the control law (21) to the next:

$$\tau = \hat{J}(q, {}^y m_{ij})^T K_p A(\hat{\phi})^T \tilde{s} - K_v \dot{q} + g(q). \tag{25}$$

The closed-loop system with (25) as control law in terms of the state vector $[\tilde{q}^T \;\; \dot{q}^T]^T$, where $\tilde{q} = q_d - q$, can be written as

$$\frac{d}{dt}\begin{bmatrix}\tilde{q}\\ \dot{q}\end{bmatrix} = \begin{bmatrix} -\dot{q} \\ M(q)^{-1}\left[\hat{J}(q, {}^y m_{ij})^T K_p A(\hat{\phi})^T \tilde{s} - K_v \dot{q} - C(q,\dot{q})\dot{q}\right]\end{bmatrix}, \tag{26}$$

which is an autonomous system with the origin as an equilibrium point.
To linearize the system (26), it will be applied the next lemma (Kelly, 1996):
Lemma 1: Consider the nonlinear system

$$\dot{x} = D(x)x + E(x)h(x) \tag{27}$$

where $x \in \Re^n$, $D(x)$ and $E(x)$ are $n \times n$ nonlinear functions of x and $h(x)$ is a $n \times 1$ nonlinear function of x. Suppose that $h(0) = 0$, hence $x = 0 \in \Re^n$ is an equilibrium point of system (27). Then, the linearized system of (27) around the equilibrium point $x = 0$ is given by

$$\dot{z} = \left[D(0) + E(0)\frac{\partial h}{\partial x}(0)\right] z \tag{28}$$

where $z \in \Re^n$.
Following Lemma 1, defining $x = [\tilde{q}^T \;\; \dot{q}^T]^T$ and using Property 2 of the manipulator dynamic model; the system (26) linearized around the origin results

$$\dot{z} = \begin{bmatrix} 0 & -I \\ \gamma M(q_d)^{-1} \hat{J}(q_d, {}^y m_{ij}{}^*)^T K_p A(\hat{\phi})^T A(\phi) J(q_d, {}^y m_{ij}{}^*) & -M(q_d)^{-1} K_v \end{bmatrix} z \tag{29}$$

where ${}^y m_{ij}{}^*$ is ${}^y m_{ij}$ evaluated in $q = q_d$ and I is the identity matrix.
Now, define the error matrix of the Jacobian estimation $\tilde{J}(q, {}^y m_{ij})$ as

$$\tilde{J}(q, {}^y m_{ij}) = \hat{J}(q, {}^y m_{ij}) - J(q, {}^y m_{ij}), \tag{30}$$

and the error of angle estimation $\tilde{\phi}$ as

$$\tilde{\phi} = \hat{\phi} - \phi.$$

In what follows, to simplify the development, it will be considered a 2 d.o.f. manipulator (nonredundant) with the dimension of the image feature space equal to the dimension of the operational space, that is, $n = m = r = 2$. Also, it will be considered $K_p = k_p I \in \Re^{2\times 2}$ (with $k_p > 0$) and $A(\phi) \in \Re^{2\times 2}$ an elementary rotation matrix (see Sciavicco & Siciliano (2000) for example), so that

$$\begin{aligned} A(\hat{\phi})^T A(\phi) &= A(\tilde{\phi})^T = A(-\tilde{\phi}) \\ \frac{A(\tilde{\phi})^T - A(\tilde{\phi})}{2} &= \sin(\tilde{\phi}) I_{a_2} \\ \frac{A(\tilde{\phi})^T + A(\tilde{\phi})}{2} &= \cos(\tilde{\phi}) I_2 \end{aligned} \tag{31}$$

where I_{a_2} is a 2×2 skew symmetric matrix with unitary norm and I_2 is the 2×2 identity matrix. The last equation implies that if $\cos(\tilde{\phi}) > 0$ then $A(\tilde{\phi}) > 0$.
Observing that $z = [z_1^T \;\; z_2^T]^T$, (29) can be rewritten as

$$\frac{d}{dt}\begin{bmatrix} z_1 \\ z_2 \end{bmatrix} = \begin{bmatrix} 0 & -I \\ M(q_d)^{-1}[F+G] & -M(q_d)^{-1}K_v \end{bmatrix}\begin{bmatrix} z_1 \\ z_2 \end{bmatrix} \tag{32}$$

where

$$F = \gamma k_p J(q_d, {}^y m_{ij}{}^*)^T A(\hat{\phi})^T J(q_d, {}^y m_{ij}{}^*) \tag{33}$$

and

$$G = \gamma k_p \tilde{J}(q_d, {}^y m_{ij}{}^*)^T A(\tilde{\phi})^T J(q_d, {}^y m_{ij}{}^*). \tag{34}$$

The stability analysis of (32) will be held trough the next Lyapunov function candidate proposed in Kelly (1996):

$$V(z_1, z_2) = \frac{1}{2}[\varepsilon z_1 - z_2]^T M(q_d)[\varepsilon z_1 - z_2] + \frac{1}{2} z_1^T [F + \varepsilon K_v - \varepsilon^2 M(q_d)] z_1 \tag{35}$$

where[1]

$$\varepsilon = \frac{\lambda_m\{K_v\}}{2\lambda_M\{M(q_d)\}}$$

[1]The notations $\lambda_m\{A\}$ and $\lambda_M\{A\}$ indicate the smallest and largest eigenvalues of a matrix A, respectively.

is a positive constant, since both K_v and $M(q_d)$ are symmetric and positive definite matrices. This also means that $\lambda_m\{K_v\} > \varepsilon\lambda_M\{M(q_d)\}$, which implies that the matrix $K_v - \varepsilon M(q_d)$ is positive definite. Finally, suppose that $A(\tilde{\phi}) > 0$, if this is the case then the matrix F will be positive definite (due to the full range assumption for $J(q_d, {}^y m_{ij})$). Hence, the Lyapunov function candidate, under the previous implications, is globally positive definite function.
The time derivative of the Lyapunov function candidate (35) along the trajectories of the system (32) after some algebraic manipulations, results (eliminating the obvious arguments for simplicity)

$$\begin{aligned}\dot{V} = &-\gamma k_p \varepsilon z_1^T \left[\frac{\hat{J}^T A(\tilde{\phi})^T \hat{J} + \hat{J}^T A(\tilde{\phi})\hat{J}}{2}\right] z_1 + \gamma k_p \varepsilon z_1^T \hat{J}^T A(\tilde{\phi})^T \tilde{J} z_1 - \\ &z_2^T [K_v - \varepsilon M(q_d)] z_2 + \gamma k_p z_2^T \left[\tilde{J}^T A(\tilde{\phi})^T [\hat{J} - \tilde{J}]\right] z_1 - \\ &\frac{1}{2}\gamma k_p z_1^T \left[[\hat{J} - \tilde{J}]^T A(\tilde{\phi})^T [\hat{J} - \tilde{J}] - [\hat{J} - \tilde{J}]^T A(\tilde{\phi}) [\hat{J} - \tilde{J}]\right] z_2.\end{aligned} \tag{36}$$

Observe that for any matrix $N \in \Re^{2\times 2}$, the following is true:

$$N^T I_{a_2} N = \det\{N\} I_{a_2}.$$

According to the above and considering (31), (36) satisfies

$$\begin{aligned}\dot{V} \le &-\gamma k_p \varepsilon \lambda_m \{\cos(\tilde{\phi})\hat{J}^T \hat{J}\} \|z_1\|^2 + \gamma k_p \varepsilon \left\|\hat{J}\right\| \left\|\tilde{J}\right\| \|z_1\|^2 - \\ &\lambda_m\{K_v\}\|z_2\|^2 + \varepsilon \lambda_M\{M\}\|z_2\|^2 + \gamma k_p \left\|\hat{J}\right\| \left\|\tilde{J}\right\| \|z_1\|\|z_2\| + \gamma k_p \left\|\tilde{J}\right\|^2 \|z_1\|\|z_2\| + \\ &\gamma k_p \,|\sin(\tilde{\phi})|\left[|\det\{\hat{J}\}| + 2\left\|\hat{J}\right\|\left\|\tilde{J}\right\| + |\det\{\tilde{J}\}|\right]\|z_1\|\|z_2\| \\ \le &-\begin{bmatrix}\|z_1\| & \|z_2\|\end{bmatrix}\begin{bmatrix} v_{11} & v_{12} \\ v_{21} & v_{22}\end{bmatrix}\begin{bmatrix}\|z_1\| \\ \|z_2\|\end{bmatrix}\end{aligned}$$

where

$$\begin{aligned} v_{11} &= \gamma k_p \varepsilon \lambda_m \{\cos(\tilde{\phi})\hat{J}^T \hat{J}\} - \gamma k_p \varepsilon \left\|\hat{J}\right\|\left\|\tilde{J}\right\| \\ v_{12} &= v_{21} = -\frac{1}{2}\gamma k_p \left[\left\|\hat{J}\right\|\left\|\tilde{J}\right\| + \left\|\tilde{J}\right\|^2 + |\sin(\tilde{\phi})|\left[|\det\{\hat{J}\}| + 2\left\|\hat{J}\right\|\left\|\tilde{J}\right\| + |\det\{\tilde{J}\}|\right]\right] \\ v_{22} &= \frac{1}{2}\lambda_m\{K_v\}.\end{aligned}$$

Consequently, the time derivative of the Lyapunov function candidate is negative definite if $v_{11} > 0$ and if $v_{11}v_{22} - v_{12}^2 > 0$. This leads to next inequalities:

$$\left\|\tilde{J}\right\| < \cos(\tilde{\phi})\frac{\lambda_m\{\hat{J}^T\hat{J}\}}{\left\|\hat{J}\right\|} \tag{37}$$

$$\lambda_m^2\{K_v\} > \frac{\gamma k_p \lambda_M\{M\}\left[\left\|\hat{J}\right\|\left\|\tilde{J}\right\| + \left\|\tilde{J}\right\|^2 + |\sin(\tilde{\phi})|\left[|\det\{\hat{J}\}| + 2\left\|\hat{J}\right\|\left\|\tilde{J}\right\| + |\det\{\tilde{J}\}|\right]\right]^2}{\cos(\tilde{\phi})\lambda_m\{\hat{J}^T\hat{J}\} - \left\|\hat{J}\right\|\left\|\tilde{J}\right\|}. \quad (38)$$

The assumption $A(\tilde{\phi}) > 0$ implies that $\cos(\tilde{\phi}) > 0$. In conclusion, if the inequality (37) is satisfied, then the inequality (38) indicates that there will be a symmetric and positive definite matrix K_v sufficiently large such that the equilibrium point $[z_1^T \ z_2^T]^T = 0 \in \Re^4$ of the linearized system (32) be asymptotically stable. This means, according to the first Lyapunov method, that the equilibrium point $[\tilde{q}^T \ \dot{q}^T]^T = 0 \in \Re^4$ of the original closed-loop system (26) is asymptotically stable and by the implications at the end of the previous subsection, then it is guaranteed the fulfillment of the control objective (20).

5. Selection of image features

In this section will be described two image feature vectors that are in function of image moments and that satisfy the requirements of the controllers (21) and (25). The first one is the object centroid in the image plane and the second one is a combination of image moments of order two.

5.1 Centroid

Equation (13) represents the mapping of the centroid x_{g_O} of the target object (respect to Σ_O) located on the manipulator end-effector (see Figure 2) to the image plane. Note that $\psi = \Sigma_{q_r} - \pi/2 - \phi$ and both c_1 and c_2 come from (7); also note that their time derivatives are expressed by

$$\begin{aligned} \dot{\psi} &= \dot{\Sigma}_{q_r} \\ \dot{c}_1 &= \cos(\phi)\dot{O}_{W_1}^O + \sin(\phi)\dot{O}_{W_2}^O \\ \dot{c}_2 &= \sin(\phi)\dot{O}_{W_1}^O - \cos(\phi)\dot{O}_{W_2}^O. \end{aligned} \quad (39)$$

Now, since it is a planar manipulator, the linear and angular velocities (respect to Σ_W) denoted by v_W and w_W, respectively; can be expressed as

$$\begin{bmatrix} v_W \\ w_W \end{bmatrix} = \begin{bmatrix} \dot{O}_{W_1}^O & \dot{O}_{W_2}^O & 0 & 0 & 0 & \dot{\psi} \end{bmatrix}^T = J_{G_W}(q)\dot{q}$$

where $J_{G_W}(q)$ is the geometric Jacobian of the manipulator; or simplifying

$$\begin{bmatrix} \dot{O}_{W_1}^O \\ \dot{O}_{W_2}^O \\ \dot{\psi} \end{bmatrix} = J_{G_{126W}}(q)\dot{q} \quad (40)$$

where $J_{G_{126W}}(q)$ are the rows 1, 2 and 6 of the geometric Jacobian $J_{G_W}(q)$. Consequently, the time derivative of (13) can be written as

$$\dot{y}_g = \gamma \underbrace{\begin{bmatrix} \cos(\phi) & -\sin(\phi) \\ \sin(\phi) & \cos(\phi) \end{bmatrix}}_{A(\phi)} \underbrace{\begin{bmatrix} 1 & 0 & c_3(q, x_{g_O}) \\ 0 & -1 & -c_4(q, x_{g_O}) \end{bmatrix} J_{G_{126W}}(q)}_{J(q, {}^y m_{ij})} \dot{q}$$
$$= \gamma A(\phi) J(q, {}^y m_{ij}) \dot{q}$$

where

$$\begin{aligned} c_3(q, x_{g_O}) &= \cos(\Sigma_{q_r}) x_{g_{O_1}} - \sin(\Sigma_{q_r}) x_{g_{O_2}} \\ c_4(q, x_{g_O}) &= \sin(\Sigma_{q_r}) x_{g_{O_1}} + \cos(\Sigma_{q_r}) x_{g_{O_2}}; \end{aligned} \tag{41}$$

that is, the centroid y_g, which depends on the image moments of order one, fulfills the requirement of (16) and can be used in the controllers (21) or (25). It is worth noticing that the Jacobian $J(q, {}^y m_{ij})$ depends on x_{g_O}, which is a 3D parameter of the target object; on the geometric Jacobian of the manipulator $J_{G_{126W}}(q)$; and on the measures of the joint displacements q. If the centroid of the target object x_{g_O} coincides with the origin of the frame Σ_O, then we have the same robotic system as in Kelly (1996).

5.2 Image features in function of image moments of order two

Next, it is described an image feature vector in function of the image moments or order two that fulfills the requirements of the controllers (21) and (25). In this sense, it is necessary to compute the time variation of the image moments of order two.
Thus, from (49), (39) and (40):

$$\begin{aligned} {}^y\dot{m}_{11} = \gamma \begin{bmatrix} \cos(\phi) & -\sin(\phi) \end{bmatrix} \begin{bmatrix} {}^y m_{01} & -{}^y m_{10} \\ -{}^y m_{10} & -{}^y m_{01} \end{bmatrix} \begin{bmatrix} 1 & 0 & c_3(q, x_{g_O}) \\ 0 & 1 & c_4(q, x_{g_O}) \end{bmatrix} J_{G_{126W}}(q)\dot{q} + \\ \begin{bmatrix} 0 & 0 & {}^y\mu_{02} - {}^y\mu_{20} \end{bmatrix} J_{G_{126W}}(q)\dot{q}. \end{aligned} \tag{42}$$

Now, consider $s_{aux} = \frac{1}{2}[{}^y m_{02} - {}^y m_{20}]$, in such a way that from (49), (39) and (40), $\dot{s}_{aux}$ results

$$\begin{aligned} \dot{s}_{aux} = \gamma \begin{bmatrix} \sin(\phi) & \cos(\phi) \end{bmatrix} \begin{bmatrix} {}^y m_{01} & -{}^y m_{10} \\ -{}^y m_{10} & -{}^y m_{01} \end{bmatrix} \begin{bmatrix} 1 & 0 & c_3(q, x_{g_O}) \\ 0 & 1 & c_4(q, x_{g_O}) \end{bmatrix} J_{G_{126W}}(q)\dot{q} - \\ \begin{bmatrix} 0 & 0 & 2\,{}^y\mu_{11} \end{bmatrix} J_{G_{126W}}(q)\dot{q}. \end{aligned} \tag{43}$$

The time variation of the centered image moments can be computed from (50), (39) and (40), yielding

$$
\begin{aligned}
{}^{y}\dot{\mu}_{11} &= \begin{bmatrix} 0 & 0 & {}^{y}\mu_{02} - {}^{y}\mu_{20} \end{bmatrix} J_{G_{126W}}(q)\dot{q} \\
{}^{y}\dot{\mu}_{20} &= \begin{bmatrix} 0 & 0 & {}^{y}\mu_{11} \end{bmatrix} J_{G_{126W}}(q)\dot{q} \\
{}^{y}\dot{\mu}_{02} &= \begin{bmatrix} 0 & 0 & -{}^{y}\mu_{11} \end{bmatrix} J_{G_{126W}}(q)\dot{q}.
\end{aligned} \tag{44}
$$

The proposed image feature vector in function of image moments of order two s_{m_2} is expressed as

$$
s_{m_2} = \begin{bmatrix} {}^{y}m_{11} - {}^{y}\mu_{11} \\ \frac{1}{2}[{}^{y}m_{02} - {}^{y}m_{20}] + {}^{y}\mu_{20} - {}^{y}\mu_{02} \end{bmatrix},
$$

which from (42)-(44) has the next time derivative:

$$
\begin{aligned}
\dot{s}_{m_2} &= \gamma \underbrace{\begin{bmatrix} \cos(\phi) & -\sin(\phi) \\ \sin(\phi) & \cos(\phi) \end{bmatrix}}_{A(\phi)} \underbrace{\begin{bmatrix} {}^{y}m_{01} & -{}^{y}m_{10} \\ -{}^{y}m_{10} & -{}^{y}m_{01} \end{bmatrix} \begin{bmatrix} 1 & 0 & c_3(q, x_{g_O}) \\ 0 & 1 & c_4(q, x_{g_O}) \end{bmatrix} J_{G_{126W}}(q)\dot{q}}_{J(q, {}^{y}m_{ij})} \\
&= \gamma A(\phi) J(q, {}^{y}m_{ij})\dot{q},
\end{aligned} \tag{45}
$$

therefore s_{m_2} is another image feature vector that fulfills the conditions of the controllers (21) and (25).
Notice that

$$
s'_{m_2} = {}^{y}m_{00}^{p} \begin{bmatrix} {}^{y}m_{11} - {}^{y}\mu_{11} \\ \frac{1}{2}[{}^{y}m_{02} - {}^{y}m_{20}] + {}^{y}\mu_{20} - {}^{y}\mu_{02} \end{bmatrix} \tag{46}
$$

where $p \in \Re$ is a constant, with time derivative

$$
\begin{aligned}
\dot{s}'_{m_2} &= \gamma \underbrace{\begin{bmatrix} \cos(\phi) & -\sin(\phi) \\ \sin(\phi) & \cos(\phi) \end{bmatrix}}_{A(\phi)} \underbrace{{}^{y}m_{00}^{p} \begin{bmatrix} {}^{y}m_{01} & -{}^{y}m_{10} \\ -{}^{y}m_{10} & -{}^{y}m_{01} \end{bmatrix} \begin{bmatrix} 1 & 0 & c_3(q, x_{g_O}) \\ 0 & 1 & c_4(q, x_{g_O}) \end{bmatrix} J_{G_{126W}}(q)\dot{q}}_{J(q, {}^{y}m_{ij})} \\
&= \gamma A(\phi) J(q, {}^{y}m_{ij})\dot{q},
\end{aligned}
$$

is another acceptable image feature vector (since ${}^{y}m_{00}$ is constant in the configuration of the robotic system considered).

6. Simulations

To illustrate the performance of the direct visual servoing just described, it will be presented simulations using the model of a 2 d.o.f. manipulator that is in the Robotics Laboratory of CICESE. A scheme of such manipulator can be seen in Figure 3.

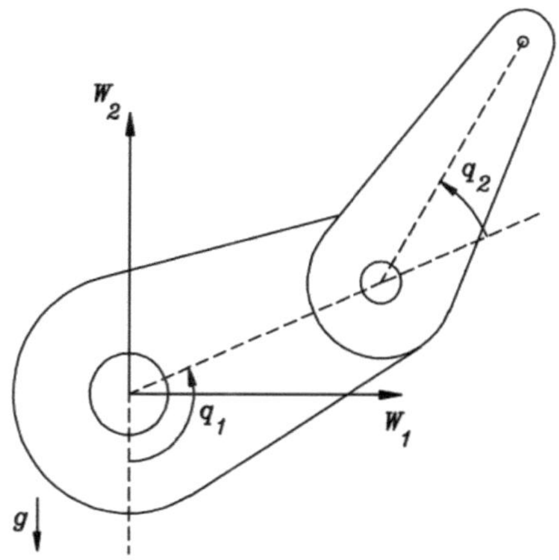

Fig. 3. Scheme of the manipulator

Respect to its dynamic model (15), their elements are expressed by

$$M(q) = \begin{bmatrix} 0.3353 + 0.0244\cos(q_2) & 0.0127 + 0.0122\cos(q_2) \\ 0.0127 + 0.0122\cos(q_2) & 0.0127 \end{bmatrix} [\text{Nm sec}^2/\text{rad}]$$

$$C(q,\dot{q}) = \begin{bmatrix} -0.0122\sin(q_2)\dot{q}_2 & -0.0122\sin(q_2)\dot{q}_1 - 0.0122\sin(q_2)\dot{q}_2 \\ 0.0122\sin(q_2)\dot{q}_1 & 0 \end{bmatrix} [\text{Nm sec/rad}] \quad (47)$$

$$g(q) = \begin{bmatrix} 11.5081\sin(q_1) + 0.4596\sin(q_1 + q_2) \\ 0.4596\sin(q_1 + q_2) \end{bmatrix} [\text{Nm}].$$

Description	Notation	Value	Units
Conversion factor ([m] to [pixels])	α	72000	pixels/m
Focal length of the lens	λ	0.0075	m
Image center	$[u_0 \;\; v_0]^T$	$[160 \;\; 120]^T$	pixels
Camera frame position	O_W^C	$[0 \;\; 0 \;\; 3]^T$	m
Camera frame orientation	ϕ	$10\pi/180$	rad

Table 1. Camera parameters

Now, its geometric Jacobian $J_{G_{126W}}(q)$ is

$$J_{G_{126W}}(q) = \begin{bmatrix} l[\cos(q_1) + \cos(q_1 + q_2)] & l\cos(q_1 + q_2) \\ l[\sin(q_1) + \sin(q_1 + q_2)] & l\sin(q_1 + q_2) \\ 1 & 1 \end{bmatrix} \tag{48}$$

where $l = 0.26$ [m].

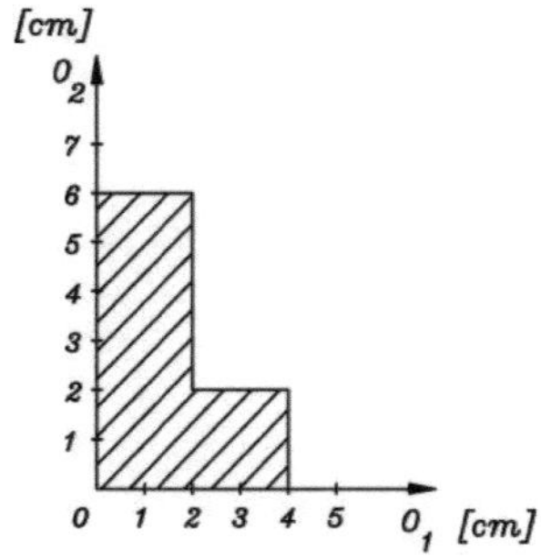

Fig. 4. The planar target object

Table 1 presents the intrinsic and extrinsic camera parameters, which correspond to the adopted camera configuration. Note that there are eight camera parameters, however, the controller only needs a estimation of the parameter ϕ.

Figure 4 shows the planar target object which has a relative complex shape to facilitate the simulations, but the target can be a more sophisticated planar object like a photography for example. The two-dimensional Cartesian moments of this target object to order two, respect to the plane $O_1 - O_2$, are concentrated in Table 2.

Moment	Value	Units
${}^{O}m_{00}$	1.6×10^{-3}	m^2
${}^{O}m_{10}$	2.4×10^{-5}	m^3
${}^{O}m_{01}$	4×10^{-5}	m^3
x_{g_O}	$[1.5 \;\; 2.5]^T \times10^{-2}$	m
${}^{O}m_{11}$	4.8×10^{-7}	m^4
${}^{O}m_{20}$	5.3333×10^{-7}	m^4
${}^{O}m_{02}$	1.4933×10^{-6}	m^4
${}^{O}\mu_{11}$	-1.2×10^{-7}	m^4
${}^{O}\mu_{20}$	1.7333×10^{-7}	m^4
${}^{O}\mu_{02}$	4.9333×10^{-7}	m^4

Table 2. Two-dimensional Cartesian moments of the target object respect to $O_1 - O_2$

Respect to the 3D parameters of the target object, the controller only needs a estimation of the object centroid x_{g_O}.
The image feature vector selected corresponds to (46) with $p = -1$, denote with s_a this image feature vector expressed with

$$s_a = \frac{1}{{}^y m_{00}} \begin{bmatrix} {}^y m_{11} - {}^y \mu_{11} \\ \frac{1}{2}[{}^y m_{02} - {}^y m_{20}] + {}^y \mu_{20} - {}^y \mu_{02} \end{bmatrix},$$

with Jacobian $J(q, {}^y m_{ij})$ described by

$$J(q, {}^y m_{ij}) = \begin{vmatrix} y_{g_2} & -y_{g_1} \\ -y_{g_1} & -y_{g_2} \end{vmatrix} \begin{bmatrix} 1 & 0 & c_3(q, x_{g_O}) \\ 0 & 1 & c_4(q, x_{g_O}) \end{bmatrix} J_{G_{126W}}(q).$$

The initial condition is the manipulator at rest with position vector $q(0) = 0$ [rad]. By means of the teach-by-showing method it is computed the desired image feature vector s_{a_d} on the desired manipulator configuration, such that $q_d = [45\pi/180 \;\; 90\pi/180]^T$ [rad], obtaining

$$s_{a_d} = \begin{bmatrix} 2.8408 \\ -1.7333 \end{bmatrix} \times 10^4 \;\; [\text{pixels}^2].$$

The controller (25) was tuned with the gains:

$$K_p = 4I_2 \times 10^{-6} \quad \text{and} \quad K_v = 0.8 I_2;$$

but with the next estimations:

$$\hat{\phi} = 0.5\phi$$
$$\hat{x}_{g_{O_1}} = 0.5 x_{g_{O_1}}$$
$$\hat{x}_{g_{O2}} = 0.5 x_{g_{O2}}$$
$$\hat{l} = 0.95 l.$$

This satisfies the inequalities (37) and (38), since

$$\|\tilde{J}\| < \cos(\tilde{\phi}) \frac{\lambda_m\{\hat{J}^T \hat{J}\}}{\|\hat{J}\|}$$

$$7.8242 < 15.8702$$

$$\lambda_m^2\{K_v\} > \frac{\gamma k_p \lambda_M\{M\}\left[\|\hat{J}\|\|\tilde{J}\| + \|\tilde{J}\|^2 + |\sin(\tilde{\phi})| \left[|\det\{\hat{J}\}| + 2\|\hat{J}\|\|\tilde{J}\| + |\det\{\tilde{J}\}|\right]\right]^2}{\cos(\tilde{\phi})\lambda_m\{\hat{J}^T \hat{J}\} - \|\hat{J}\|\|\tilde{J}\|}$$

$$0.6400 > 0.5524.$$

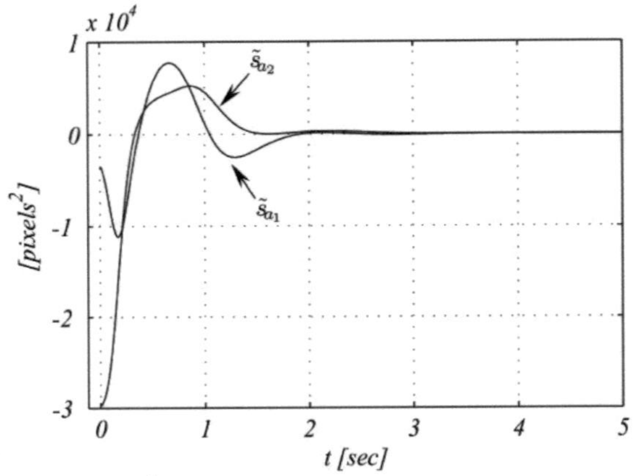

Fig. 5. Evolving respect to time of $\tilde{s}_a$

Observe trough figures 5 and 6 that the performance of the robotic system is satisfactory. The error image feature vector is practically null in about 3 [sec], as can be seen in Figure 5; this shows that the control objective is reached. Likewise, the trace of the centroid y_g of the target object is reported in Figure 6 together with 3 snapshot of the manipulator and the target object configuration at the initial condition when $t = 0$ [sec], when $t = 0.2$ [sec] and when the simulation ends at $t = 5$ [sec].

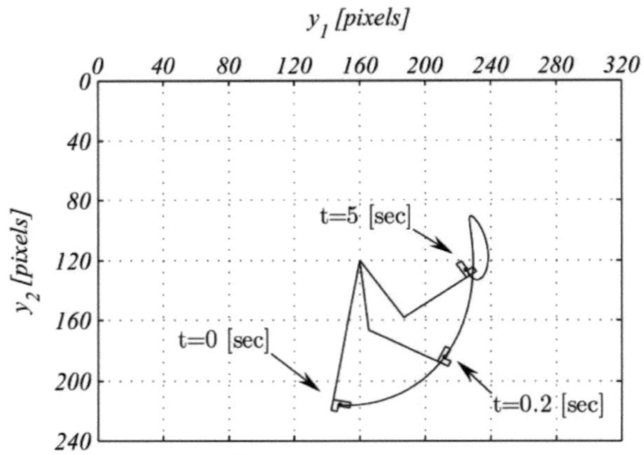

Fig. 6. Trace of the target object centroid y_g

7. Conclusions

In this chapter is designed a direct visual servo control for planar manipulators in fixed-camera configuration, with the camera optical axis perpendicular to the robot motion plane. The target is a planar object with arbitrary shape, that is, it can be of complex geometry. It has been proposed a global image feature vector in function of the image moments of such a target object; and in base on the transformation of moments it is computed the time variation of this global image features. This represents an alternative development compared to the one described in Chaumette (2004).

The designed controller corresponds to the transpose Jacobian structure and, by means of the Lyapunov theory, it is demonstrated that the controller is robust against uncertainties in 3D parameters of the target object, the camera and the geometric Jacobian of the manipulator. Finally, simulations are presented to validate the fulfillment of the control objective.

8. Appendix

In this appendix is developed the analytic form of the time variation for the regular and centered image moments with the configuration of the system detailed in Section 2.

8.1 Regular image moments

The time variation of the regular image moments ${}^{y}\dot{m}_{ij}$ can be computed by the time derivative of (12), therefore

$$ {}^{y}\dot{m}_{ij} = a_1 + a_2 + a_3 + a_4 + a_5 + a_6 $$

where

$$ a_1 = \gamma^2 \sum_{k_1,k_2,k_3} \sum_{l_1,l_2,l_3} \frac{i!}{k_1!k_2!k_3!} \frac{j!}{l_1!l_2!l_3!} k_1[\gamma\cos(\psi)]^{k_1-1}[-\gamma\sin(\psi)]^{k_2}[\gamma c_1 + u_0]^{k_3} \cdot \\ [-\gamma\sin(\psi)]^{l_1}[-\gamma\cos(\psi)]^{l_2}[\gamma c_2 + v_0]^{l_3} {}^{O}m_{k_1+l_1,k_2+l_2}[-\gamma\sin(\psi)]\dot{\psi} $$

$$ a_2 = \gamma^2 \sum_{k_1,k_2,k_3} \sum_{l_1,l_2,l_3} \frac{i!}{k_1!k_2!k_3!} \frac{j!}{l_1!l_2!l_3!} [\gamma\cos(\psi)]^{k_1} k_2[-\gamma\sin(\psi)]^{k_2-1}[\gamma c_1 + u_0]^{k_3} \cdot \\ [-\gamma\sin(\psi)]^{l_1}[-\gamma\cos(\psi)]^{l_2}[\gamma c_2 + v_0]^{l_3} {}^{O}m_{k_1+l_1,k_2+l_2}[-\gamma\cos(\psi)]\dot{\psi} $$

$$ a_3 = \gamma^2 \sum_{k_1,k_2,k_3} \sum_{l_1,l_2,l_3} \frac{i!}{k_1!k_2!k_3!} \frac{j!}{l_1!l_2!l_3!} [\gamma\cos(\psi)]^{k_1}[-\gamma\sin(\psi)]^{k_2} k_3[\gamma c_1 + u_0]^{k_3-1} \cdot \\ [-\gamma\sin(\psi)]^{l_1}[-\gamma\cos(\psi)]^{l_2}[\gamma c_2 + v_0]^{l_3} {}^{O}m_{k_1+l_1,k_2+l_2}[\gamma\dot{c}_1] $$

$$ a_4 = \gamma^2 \sum_{k_1,k_2,k_3} \sum_{l_1,l_2,l_3} \frac{i!}{k_1!k_2!k_3!} \frac{j!}{l_1!l_2!l_3!} [\gamma\cos(\psi)]^{k_1}[-\gamma\sin(\psi)]^{k_2}[\gamma c_1 + u_0]^{k_3} \cdot \\ l_1[-\gamma\sin(\psi)]^{l_1-1}[-\gamma\cos(\psi)]^{l_2}[\gamma c_2 + v_0]^{l_3} {}^{O}m_{k_1+l_1,k_2+l_2}[-\gamma\cos(\psi)]\dot{\psi} $$

$$ a_5 = \gamma^2 \sum_{k_1,k_2,k_3} \sum_{l_1,l_2,l_3} \frac{i!}{k_1!k_2!k_3!} \frac{j!}{l_1!l_2!l_3!} [\gamma\cos(\psi)]^{k_1}[-\gamma\sin(\psi)]^{k_2}[\gamma c_1 + u_0]^{k_3} \cdot \\ [-\gamma\sin(\psi)]^{l_1} l_2[-\gamma\cos(\psi)]^{l_2-1}[\gamma c_2 + v_0]^{l_3} {}^{O}m_{k_1+l_1,k_2+l_2}[\gamma\sin(\psi)]\dot{\psi} $$

$$ a_6 = \gamma^2 \sum_{k_1,k_2,k_3} \sum_{l_1,l_2,l_3} \frac{i!}{k_1!k_2!k_3!} \frac{j!}{l_1!l_2!l_3!} [\gamma\cos(\psi)]^{k_1}[-\gamma\sin(\psi)]^{k_2}[\gamma c_1 + u_0]^{k_3} \cdot \\ [-\gamma\sin(\psi)]^{l_1}[-\gamma\cos(\psi)]^{l_2} l_3[\gamma c_2 + v_0]^{l_3-1} {}^{O}m_{k_1+l_1,k_2+l_2}[\gamma\dot{c}_2] $$

and k_1, k_2, k_3, l_1, l_2 and l_3 are nonnegative integers such that $k_1 + k_2 + k_3 = i$ and $l_1 + l_2 + l_3 = j$.

Simplifying,

$$a_3 = i\gamma^y m_{i-1,j}\dot{c}_1$$

$$a_6 = j\gamma^y m_{i,j-1}\dot{c}_2$$

$$a_1 + a_2 = i\left[{}^y m_{i-1,j+1} - [\gamma c_2 + v_0]^y m_{i-1,j}\right]\dot{\psi}$$

$$a_4 + a_5 = j\left[-{}^y m_{i+1,j-1} + [\gamma c_1 + u_0]^y m_{i,j-1}\right]\dot{\psi}.$$

Finally,

$$\begin{aligned} {}^y\dot{m}_{ij} = {} & i\gamma^y m_{i-1,j}\dot{c}_1 + j\gamma^y m_{i,j-1}\dot{c}_2 + i\left[{}^y m_{i-1,j+1} - [\gamma c_2 + v_0]^y m_{i-1,j}\right]\dot{\psi} + \\ & j\left[-{}^y m_{i+1,j-1} + [\gamma c_1 + u_0]^y m_{i,j-1}\right]\dot{\psi}. \end{aligned} \tag{49}$$

8.2 Centered image moments

The time variation of the centered image moments ${}^y\dot{\mu}_{ij}$ can be computed by the time derivative of (14), hence

$${}^y\dot{\mu}_{ij} = b_1 + b_2 + b_3 + b_4$$

where

$$\begin{aligned} b_1 = {} & \gamma^2 \sum_{k_1,k_2}\sum_{l_1,l_2} \frac{i!}{k_1!k_2!}\frac{j!}{l_1!l_2!} k_1[\gamma\cos(\psi)]^{k_1-1}[-\gamma\sin(\psi)]^{k_2} \cdot \\ & [-\gamma\sin(\psi)]^{l_1}[-\gamma\cos(\psi)]^{l_2}{}^O\mu_{k_1+l_1,k_2+l_2}[-\gamma\sin(\psi)]\dot{\psi} \end{aligned}$$

$$\begin{aligned} b_2 = {} & \gamma^2 \sum_{k_1,k_2}\sum_{l_1,l_2} \frac{i!}{k_1!k_2!}\frac{j!}{l_1!l_2!} [\gamma\cos(\psi)]^{k_1} k_2[-\gamma\sin(\psi)]^{k_2-1} \cdot \\ & [-\gamma\sin(\psi)]^{l_1}[-\gamma\cos(\psi)]^{l_2}{}^O\mu_{k_1+l_1,k_2+l_2}[-\gamma\cos(\psi)]\dot{\psi} \end{aligned}$$

$$\begin{aligned} b_3 = {} & \gamma^2 \sum_{k_1,k_2}\sum_{l_1,l_2} \frac{i!}{k_1!k_2!}\frac{j!}{l_1!l_2!} [\gamma\cos(\psi)]^{k_1}[-\gamma\sin(\psi)]^{k_2} \cdot \\ & l_1[-\gamma\sin(\psi)]^{l_1-1}[-\gamma\cos(\psi)]^{l_2}{}^O\mu_{k_1+l_1,k_2+l_2}[-\gamma\cos(\psi)]\dot{\psi} \end{aligned}$$

$$\begin{aligned} b_4 = {} & \gamma^2 \sum_{k_1,k_2}\sum_{l_1,l_2} \frac{i!}{k_1!k_2!}\frac{j!}{l_1!l_2!} [\gamma\cos(\psi)]^{k_1}[-\gamma\sin(\psi)]^{k_2} \cdot \\ & [-\gamma\sin(\psi)]^{l_1} l_2[-\gamma\cos(\psi)]^{l_2-1}{}^O\mu_{k_1+l_1,k_2+l_2}[\gamma\sin(\psi)]\dot{\psi} \end{aligned}$$

and k_1, k_2, l_1, and l_2 are nonnegative integers such that $k_1 + k_2 = i$ and $l_1 + l_2 = j$. Simplifying,

$$b_1 + b_2 = i\,{}^y\mu_{i-1,j+1}\dot{\psi}$$

$$b_3 + b_4 = -j^y\mu_{i+1,j-1}\dot{\psi}.$$

Finally,

$${}^y\dot{\mu}_{ij} = [i^y\mu_{i-1,j+1} - j^y\mu_{i+1,j-1}]\dot{\psi}. \tag{50}$$

9. References

Bien, Z.; Jang, W. & Park, J. (1993). Characterization and use of feature-Jacobian matrix for visual servoing. *Visual servoing*. K. Hashimoto, Ed. Singapore: World Scientific, pp. 317--363.

Benhimane, S. & Malis, E. (2006). Homography-based 2D visual servoing. *IEEE International Conference on Robotics and Automation*. Orlando, Florida. 2397--2402.

Chaumette, F. (2004). Image moments: A general and useful set of features for visual servoing. *IEEE Transactions on Robotics*. 20(4): 713--723.

Cheah, C. C.; Liu, C. & Slotine, J. J. E. (2007). Adaptive vision based tracking control of robots with uncertainty in depth information. *IEEE International Conference on Robotics and Automation*. Roma, Italy. 2817--2822.

Collewet, C. & Chaumette, F. (2000). A contour approach for image-based control on objects with complex shape. *IEEE/RSJ Int. Conf. on Intelligent Robots and Systems*. 751--756.

Espiau, B.; Chaumette, F. & Rives, P. (1992). A new approach to visual servoing in robotics. *IEEE Transactions on Robotics and Automation*. 8(3): 313--326.

Fang, Y.; Behal, A.; Dixon, W. E.; & Dawson, D. M. (2002). Adaptive 2.5D visual servoing of kinematically redundant robot manipulators. *IEEE Conference on Decision and Control*. Las Vegas, NV. 2860--2865.

Graham, R. L.; Knuth, D. E. & Patashnik, O. (1989). *Concrete Mathematics*. Addison-Wesley Publishing Company. New York. 625 pp.

Hager, G. D. (1997). A modular system for robust positioning using feedback from stereo vision. *IEEE Transactions on Robotics y Automation*. 13(4): 582--595.

Hutchinson, S.; Hager, G. & Corke, P. (1996). A tutorial on visual servoing. *IEEE Transactions on Robotics and Automation*. 12(5): 651--670.

Kelly, R. (1996). Robust asymptotically stable visual servoing of planar robots. *IEEE Transactions on Robotics and Automation*. 12(5): 759--766.

Kelly, R.; Carelli, R.; Nasisi, O.; Kuchen., B. & Reyes, F. (2000). Stable visual servoing of camera-in-hand robotic systems. *IEEE/ASME Trans. on Mechatronics*. 5(1): 39--48.

Miyazaki, F. & Masutani, Y. (1990). Robustness of sensory feedback control based on imperfect Jacobian. *Robotics Research: The Fifth International Symposium*. H. Miura and S. Arimoto, Eds. Cambridge, MA: MIT Press, pp. 201--208.

Prokop, R. J. & Reeves, A. P. (1992). A survey of moments based techniques for unoccluded object representation. *Graphical Models and Image Processing*. 54(5): 438--460.

Sciavicco, L. & Siciliano, B. (2000). *Modeling and Control of Robot Manipulators*. Springer--Verlag. London. 378 pp.

Spong, M. W. & Vidyasagar, M. (1989). *Robot Dynamics and Control*. John Wiley and Sons, New York, NY. 352 pp.

Swokowski, E. W. (1988). *Cálculo con Geometría Analítica*. Grupo Editorial Iberoamérica. Segunda Edición. México. 1097 pp.

Tahri, O. & Chaumette, F. (2005). Point-based and region-based image moments for servoing of planar objects. *IEEE Transactions on Robotics*. 21(6): 1116--1127.

Takegaki, M. & Arimoto, S. (1981). A new feedback method for dynamic control of manipulators. *ASME, Transactions, Journal of Dynamic Systems, Measurement and Control*. 103:119--125.

Tu, H. & Fu, L. C. (1995). Application of image moment flow of a RPP to 6 DOF visual tracking. *Conference on Decision and Control*. New Orleans, LA. 3757--3758.

Vidyasagar, M. (1993). *Nonlinear Systems Analysis*. Prentice Hall. Second edition. New Jersey, USA. 498 pp.

Wang, H. Y.; Liu, H. & Zhou, D. (2008). Adaptive visual servoing using point and line features with an uncalibrated eye-in-hand camera. *IEEE Transactions on Robotics*. 24(4): 843--857.

Weiss, L. E.; Sanderson, A. C. & Neuman, C. P. (1987). Dynamic sensor-based control of robots with visual feedback. *IEEE Journal of Robotics and Autom.* RA-3(5): 404--417.

Zergeroglu, E.; Dawson, D.; de Queiroz, M. & Behal, A. (1999). Vision-based non-linear tracking controllers with uncertain robot-camera parameters. *IEEE/ASME International Conference on Advanced Intelligent Mechatronics*. Atlanta, GA. 854--859.

Industrial robot manipulator guarding using artificial vision

Fevery Brecht[1], Wyns Bart[1], Boullart Luc[1]
Llata García José Ramón[2] and Torre Ferrero Carlos[2]
[1]*Ghent University*
Belgium
[2] *University of Cantabria*
Spain

1. Introduction

Since a long time, the public opinion on robotics is that humans and robots work together, side by side, sharing and interacting in a common space (Oestreicher & Eklundh, 2006). However, until recently reality was quite different. Robots were introduced in the work place in the sixties as very effective, but simple-minded workers. For a long time, there was a lack of concern for safety and for human-robot interaction. Therefore industrial robots have been far too dangerous to share the workspace with humans. It is only since the nineties that academics and researchers from industry started to investigate the possibilities of implementing intelligent security systems in the robot's operating system in order to allow for this human-robot interaction in the future. In this chapter an artificial vision based security system for safeguarding an industrial robot is introduced.

As in many electromechanical devices also robots suffer from malfunctioning of machinery e.g. electrical potential drops, falling parts, pressurized fluids, etc. But more important are risks specific to robots and that occur during execution of a robot movement, such as a collision or undesired manipulator acceleration. These events can happen because of human errors, control errors, unauthorized access to the workspace, mechanical failures or improper work cell installation. As mentioned in (Hirschfeld et al., 1993) the robot users in the greatest danger for a nearby robot are by far the operators and maintenance workers, since they spend a lot of time in the robot's presence.

Main safety methods employed in industrial robots can be divided in two categories, that is, passive protection and active protection. Passive protection or passive safety refers to safety devices that improve the human safety without changing the robot's behaviour. Passive safety is static and simple to design; therefore it is very reliable but easily bypassed. Examples of these devices are visual devices such as warning lights, warning signs, boundary chains and painted boundaries, also physical devices such as fences, barriers and robot cages. On the other hand, active protection or active safety systems refer to safety devices that modify the robot's behaviour, or the environment, in order to avoid dangerous situations. In fact, they sense and react to changes in the cell's environment. The most popular examples of active safety devices are laser curtains, pressure mats, interlocked gates, ultrasonic or infrared barriers, capacitance devices, etc. All these sensorial elements try to detect undesired presence in the work cell of the robot. When a presence is detected the robot is stopped through an emergency stop and by cutting the power. In order to reactivate the robot national and international standard regulations require both removing the presence and deliberative reactivating the robot (ISO 10218-1, 2006). All these safety devices try to enforce segregation between robots and humans. It is on this philosophy that the earliest technical literature on the topic of robotic safety is based (Bixby, 1991; Graham, 1991; Dhillon, 1991) as well as the robotics safety regulations and standards (ANSI/RIA, 1986).

However, this philosophy is getting old and even impossible to fulfil because in many cases, such as teaching, trouble-shooting, repairs and maintenance, operators have to work inside the robot work cell (OSHA, 2006). For this reason, new safety systems have been developed and, nowadays, robot safety equipment also includes a wide range of additional subsystems such as emergency robot braking, work cell limitation, load limitation, motor and voltage monitoring, deadman function and, of course, an emergency stop system, in case the robot needs to be stopped immediately.

However, safety still is subject to discussion and the situation is changing radically because new applications such as assisted industrial manipulation, collaborative assembly, domestic work, entertainment, rehabilitation or medical applications, etc. ask for a larger interaction between human and robot. In all of these cases, robot and human, or robot with other robots, have to work together, sharing the same physical environment. Therefore, a new safety paradigm is needed where an active security/safety system (ASSYS) gets the control of the industrial robot in order to analyse the possibility of collision with the detected object, human or robot and, if this is the case, to generate a new alternative trajectory. In this way, the ASSYS is able to adapt the robot behaviour to the actual situation of a dynamical environment in real-time. It is clearly much more useful for human-robot interaction and for robots collaborating compared to previous safety systems.

In order to obtain a proper ASSYS, three key issues must be fulfilled. Firstly, three-dimensional perception of the dynamical environment is needed. A flexible solution is to use a camera-based vision system to obtain a global view on the robot's work cell. However, it is important to obtain a good synchronisation among all the cameras and to keep in mind that the image processing time must be very small compared with the robot and environment dynamics. Secondly, an alternative path planner is constructed. Nowadays, several options, such as artificial intelligence techniques, servoing control techniques, optimization, etc. are being analyzed. Finally, a fast communication system for moving data among cameras, processing system and robot controller is also needed.

The goal of this chapter is to introduce an ASSYS, based on artificial vision. A set of ceiling-mounted, static cameras is used to build a three-dimensional representation of the environment and to detect obstacles in the robot's work cell. With a stereoscopic reconstruction algorithm, the obstacle's location and dimensions are obtained. This ASSYS includes an artificial intelligence decision taking process. It is based on fuzzy logic and it is used for calculating an alternative path to the desired workspace point but avoiding the detected obstacle. This is one of the principal contributions of this paper because the robot keeps doing its task although dynamic obstacles are present in the workspace.

This chapter is organized as follows. Initially, an ASSYS literature overview is carried out in section 2, introducing different solutions and the most interesting existing technologies for vision-based ASSYS. Next, a detailed explanation on the stereoscopic 3D vision system used in this ASSYS is given. In section 4, the artificial intelligence system based on fuzzy logic, used for calculating the alternative trajectory is presented. Then, the experimental setup (section 5) and the results (section 6) obtained for the proposed ASSYS are discussed. Finally, in section 7 conclusions are summarized and future improvements are proposed.

2. Literature overview

As stated in the introduction, active security systems are formed by many different subsystems all closely working together to guarantee human safety. Among the most important and critical subsystems is the sensor system. Using sensory equipment the robot senses the environment looking for objects (static or dynamic, human or not) blocking the path of its normal pre-programmed trajectory. Without question a sensor system is a fundamental component based on which the manipulator will make his next move in case of a possible collision. Given the scope of this contribution, this section will mainly focus on sensor systems, more specifically on vision techniques.

Sophisticated solutions for sensing the work cell exist, like laser curtains, light barriers, scanner or safety mats, etc. often hardwired to a safety PLC (programmable logic controller) for fast intervention in case of problems. See (Ogorodnikova, 2006) for a technical overview of current safeguarding systems. (Novak & Feddema, 1992; Feddema & Novak, 1994) used capacitance sensors as artificial sensor skin for collision avoidance. In (Llata et al., 1998) a set of ultrasonic sensors, located near the end effector is used for detecting the local environment of the robot's grip. In (Yu & Gupta, 1999) a wrist-mounted laser scanner was used for a similar purpose. All of these approaches are based on local information only. Therefore, only surroundings to the current robot position can be examined. Then, using local information only local path planning is possible. So obstacles farther away from the robot arm (out of the reach of the sensor system) cannot be detected.

A more flexible solution is to use a vision system mounted in such a way that a good overview of the work cell is obtained. A camera network based human-robot coexistence system was already proposed in (Baerveldt, 1992) in the early nineties. He used computer vision to obtain the location of the operator. Robot and operator communicated through speech allowing a fast and safe intervention when needed. (Noborio & Nishino, 2001) used a wrist-mounted camera for path planning. Unfortunately an important prerequisite was that the image taken by the camera has to be known within the target configuration. Also, only local information is gathered because of the position of the camera on the wrist.

Several techniques exist to obtain a global view on the robot's work cell. Backprojection is a widely used technique to reconstruct an object by collating multiple camera images of the work cell. Eckert (2000) used this method for accurately reconstructing a single object in 3D space, including texture information giving a very realistic view of the object. In case of an ASSYS such a high level of detail is not necessary and more attention should be given to the object's contours. Noborio & Urakawa (1999) used backprojection in the context of robotics with multiple objects. They used colour cameras and were able to separate objects having sufficiently different colours only. In (Ebert & Henrich, 2001) a look-up-table-based sensor fusion algorithm for performing image-based collision tests based on backprojection into configuration space was presented. They use reference images for detecting human operators and other obstacles. Their approach was not very optimized with regard to computation time and memory requirements. This work was further extended and applied in several other contributions (Ebert & Henrich, 2002; Gecks & Henrich, 2005). The former contribution presented a method for avoiding collisions based on difference images. Part of this method uses epipolar lines for resolving unknown and error pixels in the images. They also developed a technique to filter out the robot arm, possibly occluding an object.

The image difference method was applied to a pick-and-place application several stationary gray scale cameras to safeguard operators moving into the work cell (Gecks & Henrich, 2005). For the method to work properly objects had to be substantially different from the background pixels. In (Kuhn et al., 2006) the authors extended the same method to secure guided robot motion. Velocity of the manipulator was decreased when a human operator came too close to the arm.

A combination of both local and global sensors can be found in the MEPHISTO system (Steinhaus et al., 1999). Laser scanners were mounted on the robots (local information) and a couple of colour cameras were surveying the robot's work cell to acquire global information.

They also apply reference images that are updated at run-time. The difference between the reference image and the current image is mapped in the form of a polygonal region. MEPHISTO also provides a distributed redundant environment model allowing straightforward local path planning and reducing communication transmission problems.

Panoramic cameras (fisheye) are used in (Cervera et al., 2008). According to the authors the 360° field of view can seriously simplify safety issues for a robot arm moving in close proximity to human beings. The proposed technique tracks both manipulator and human based on a combination of an adaptive background model at pixel level and an improved classification at frame level filtering global illumination. Although this technique was used in the context of visual servoing it clearly shows that also in that area of research safety is an important concern.

A safety system also using a network of cameras in an on-line manner was presented in (D. Ebert et al., 2005). A specialized tracking-vision-chip was designed obtaining a cycle time of more than 500Hz using only a small 8-bit microcontroller for the vision-chip. Unfortunately, the robot was immediately stopped when a human entered the work cell.

Additional reviews on safety and computer vision for use in industrial settings can be found in (Piggin 2005;Wöhler, 2009).

In the future robots will increasingly become part of everyday life (Weng et al., 2009). Safety already is an important issue in industrial robotics dealing with heavy payloads and fast execution. But many authors also realize that safety is becoming an important issue in service robots (Oestreicher & Eklundh, 2006; Burghart et al., 2007; Burghart et al., 2005) or even toys. ASSYS, although designed for industrial purposes, could hence also be (partially) reused in this context as well. Service robots are intended for close interaction with humans and hence all actions performed by such a robot should never harm the human they assist. An example of this can already be found in (Ohta & Amano, 2008). Both authors propose a technique predicting the collision of a human with surrounding objects, using a physical simulator and a stereo vision system. Based on the input data from the vision system, the physical simulator tries to model the object's speed and direction and estimates when and

where the object could collide with the human. This estimate is then used to warn the human in case the object will come to close.
It is important to note that in many of the contributions discussed above, the robot is halted upon detection of an object or human. The combination of both an alternative path planning algorithm and a robust and general system for object detection, in a real-time framework is far from easy to realize. This is probably because of a lot of technical insight from many different research disciplines is needed in order to build a high performing ASSYS. The approach in this contribution aims at constructing such an ASSYS, including alternative trajectory planning, camera vision and real-time performance using fairly simple (standard) hardware equipment.

3. Camera vision

3.1 Stereoscopic vision

Stereoscopic vision is based on the differences that arise when a single object is observed from two different points of view. The three-dimensional position of a point in space can then be calculated by means of the positional difference, known as disparity, of its projections onto two image planes. These two images can be acquired by two cameras, by one single camera moving between two known positions or even one fixed camera and object turning (Torre Ferrero et al., 2005).
All methods based on stereo vision involve two fundamental steps. A first one is finding point correspondences and the second one is a 3D coordinate calculation. For the point correspondence step characteristic points must be located in both images and subsequently matched in pairs. Each pair contains the projections of a single identical point in the 3D space onto two different images. This problem is critical, since it has a high computational cost and it represents the main source of errors in 3D reconstruction. This is the reason why many approaches have been proposed for trying to solve it in the most efficient way (Scharstein & Szeliski, 2002). These algorithms use geometric restrictions in order to simplify the problem and almost all define a global energy function that is minimized for finding the disparities of corresponding points. In our vision system, corner pixels are detected as the characteristic image points, see section 3.3.1 for the employed detection algorithm.
On the other hand, 3D coordinates calculation is a quite simple task when compared to finding point correspondence. However this calculation can only be computed once the matching points are available and, in addition, it requires an accurate calibration of the cameras. According to the camera model used for this calibration, the 3D position of the point in space can be determined as the intersection of the two projection lines corresponding to each pair of image points that were matched.

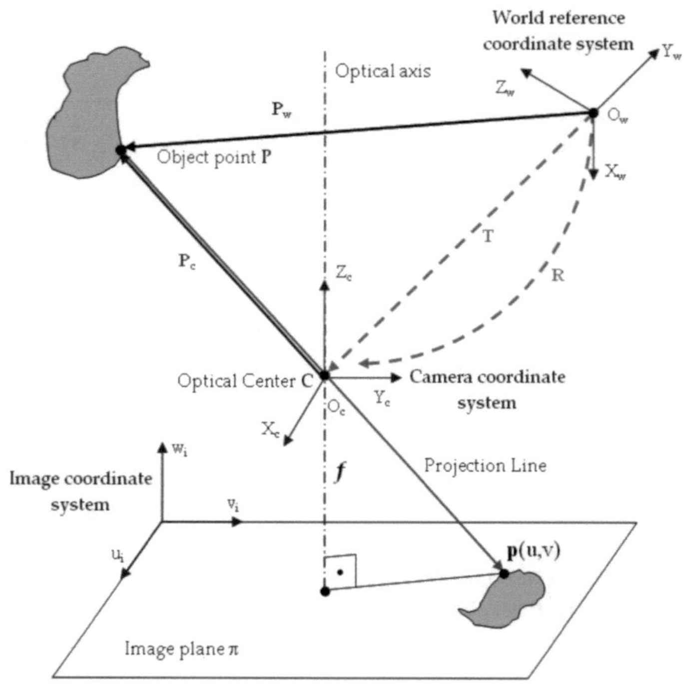

Fig. 1. The pinhole projection model

3.1.1 Camera model

In this work we have used the perspective camera model. According to this model, called the pinhole projection model, each point P in the object space is projected by a straight line through the optical center into the image plane (see Fig. 1.). A key parameter in this pinhole model is the focal distance *f*, which displays the perpendicular distance between the optical center and the image plane. The projection of the 3D point P is projected into the image plane in the image point p with pixel coordinates (u, v).

The world reference system $O_wX_wY_wZ_w$, shown in Fig. 1, will be attached by the calibration method to one of the images of the calibration pattern. This coordinate system will be made coincident with the reference coordinate system of the robot, to which the robot controller refers all tool center point positions and end effector orientations.

Based on coordinate transformations we can now compose a direct transformation between the world reference coordinate system and the image coordinate system. Knowing that P_w can be transformed to the camera coordinate system $O_cX_cY_cZ_c$ by applying a rotation and a translation (see Fig. 1.) and considering how the pinhole model projects the points into the image plane, the following transformation is obtained:

$$\widetilde{p} = \left[K \cdot R \quad | \; K \cdot T \right] \cdot \begin{bmatrix} P_w \\ 1 \end{bmatrix} = M \cdot \widetilde{P}_w \tag{1}$$

where $\widetilde{P}_w$ and $\widetilde{p}$ are both expressed in homogeneous coordinates.

M, known as the projection matrix of the camera system, allows projecting any arbitrary object point in the reference system into the image plane. It is composed of both intrinsic and extrinsic camera parameters: the first 3x3 matrix describes a rotation and the right 3x1 column vector represents a translation. The matrix **K**, known as the calibration matrix of the camera, contains the intrinsic parameters that describe, without taking into account projection errors due to lens distortion, how object points expressed in the camera reference system are projected into the image plane. These parameters describe a specific camera and are independent of the camera's position and orientation in space. On the other hand, the extrinsic parameters (rotation matrix R and translation vector T) depend on the camera's position and orientation in space, since they describe the relationship between the chosen world reference coordinate system and the camera reference system.
The presented pinhole projection model is only an approximation of a real camera model since distortion of image coordinates, due to imperfect lens manufacturing and camera assembly, is not taken into account. When higher accuracy is required, a more comprehensive camera model can be used that describes the systematical distortions of image coordinates. These lens distortions cause the actual image point to be displaced both radially and tangentially in the image plane. In their paper on camera calibration, Heikkilä & Silvén (1997) proposed an approximation of both radial and tangential distortions that was used in this project. The set of camera parameters that have been presented describes the mapping between 3D reference coordinates and 2D image coordinates.
Calibration of our camera system is done using a software camera calibration toolbox that is based on the calibration principles introduced by (Heikkilä & Silvén, 1997). For an exhaustive review of calibration methods (Salvi et al., 2002) can be consulted.

3.1.2 3D Reconstruction from matching points

The problem of reconstructing three-dimensional positions is known as the inverse mapping. To successfully execute an inverse mapping, the pixel coordinates of two corresponding image points must be known. Since the pixel coordinates tend to be distorted due to lens imperfections, in a first step of the inverse mapping, these coordinates will have to be undistorted.
Since the expressions for the distorted pixel coordinates are fifth order nonlinear polynomials, there is no explicit analytic solution to the inverse mapping when both radial and tangential distortion components are considered. Heikkilä & Silvén (1997) present an implicit method to recover the undistorted pixel coordinates, given the distorted coordinates and the camera intrinsic parameters obtained from the calibration process.
Once the pixel coordinates of corresponding image points are corrected, the calculation of 3D position can be performed. A general case of image projection into an image plane is presented in Fig. 2. The same object point P is projected into the left and right image planes. These two camera systems are respectively described by their projection matrices $\mathbf{M}_l$ and $\mathbf{M}_r$. The optical centers of both projection schemes are depicted as C_l and C_r, while the projections of P in both image planes are p_l and p_r.

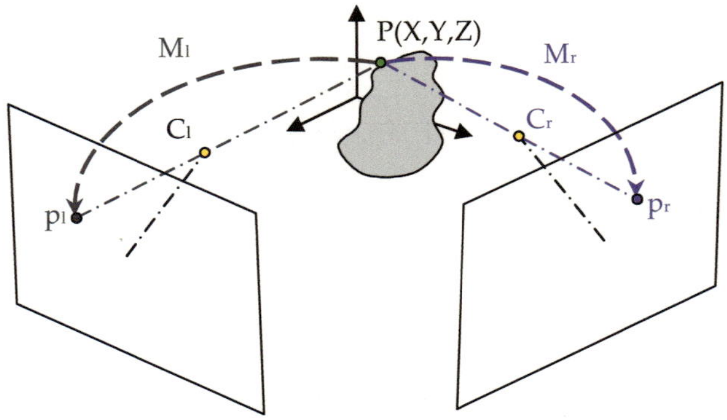

Fig. 2. Object point projection in two image planes

Given the pixel coordinates of p_l and p_r, (u_l,v_l) and (u_r,v_r) , the homogeneous coordinates of the 3D point can be calculated by solving the following equation:

$$\begin{bmatrix} u_l \cdot m_{3l} - m_{1l} \\ v_l \cdot m_{3l} - m_{2l} \\ u_r \cdot m_{3r} - m_{1r} \\ v_r \cdot m_{3r} - m_{2r} \end{bmatrix} \cdot \widetilde{P} = A \cdot \widetilde{P} = 0 \tag{2}$$

where m_{kl} and m_{kr} (k=1, 2, 3) are the rows of matrices $\boldsymbol{M_l}$ and $\boldsymbol{M_r}$ respectively.
The solution $\widetilde{P}$ of (2) is the one that minimizes the squared distance norm $\left\| A \cdot \widetilde{P} \right\|^2$. The solution to this minimization problem can be identified as the unit norm eigenvector of the matrix $\left(A^T \cdot A\right)$, that corresponds to its smallest eigenvalue. Dividing the first three coordinates by the scaling factor, Euclidean 3D coordinates of the point P are obtained.

3.2 Geometry of a stereo pair

Before any 3D position can be reconstructed, the correspondence of characteristic image points has to be searched for in all images involved in the reconstruction process. Typically, geometrical restrictions in the considered image planes will be used since they simplify the correspondence (Hartley & Zisserman, 2004). We will focus on epipolar lines, given that they can considerably reduce the time needed to find correspondences in the images.
Often used in combination with epipolar lines, specific detection methods are employed to identify objects that have certain characteristics. E.g. an object that is constituted of clearly separated surfaces will be easy to detect using edge detection methods. Because separated surfaces are illuminated in a different way, regions with different colour intensity will be displayed in the object's image.

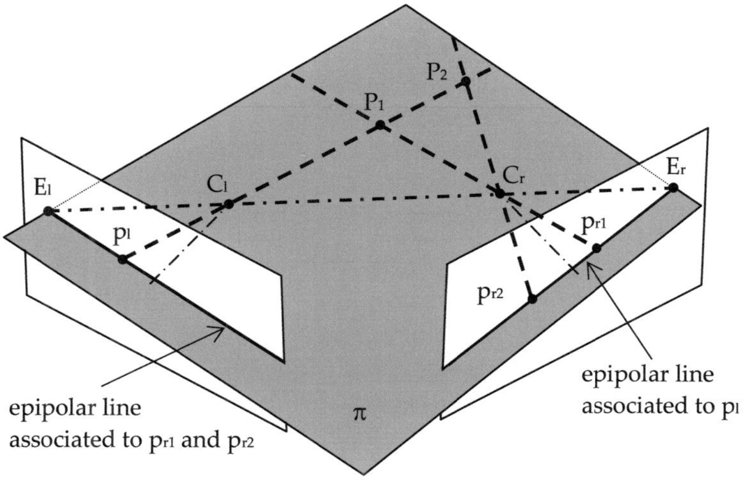

Fig. 3. Epipolar geometry

3.2.1 Epipolar Geometry

As can be seen in Fig. 3, P_1 and P_2 have the same projection p_l in the left image plane since they share the projection line C_lp_l. The projection in the right image of the set of points in space that lie on that projection line is known as the epipolar line associated to the image point p_l. In a similar way, the conjugate epipolar line in the left image plane can be constructed. The plane π formed by P_l and the optical centers C_l and C_r is denominated as the epipolar plane since it intersects with the image planes along both epipolar lines. All other points in space have associated epipolar planes that also contain the line C_lC_r. This causes all epipolar lines for each image plane to intersect in the same point. These special points, denoted as E_l and E_r in Fig. 3., are denominated epipoles.

Thanks to the geometric restriction of epipolar lines, the search for the correspondence of a point in the left image reduces to a straight line in the right image. In order to use them in the design of a vision system, it will be necessary to obtain the equations of the epipolar lines. As can be seen in Fig. 3, a point P in the 3D space can be represented with respect to each of two camera coordinate systems. Since the extrinsic parameters, known through the calibration procedure, allow transforming each camera frame into the reference frame, it is also possible to transform one camera frame into the other.

Let us denominate the rotation matrix of this transformation as $\mathbf{R_c}$ and the translation vector as $\mathbf{T_c}$. Then, if the epipolar geometry of the stereo pair is known, there exists a matrix that defines the relation between an image point, expressed in pixel coordinates, and its associated epipolar line in the conjugate image. This matrix, called fundamental matrix, can be obtained by using the following expression:

$$F = \left(K_l^{-1}\right)^T \cdot R_c \cdot S(T_c) \cdot K_r^{-1} \tag{3}$$

where $\mathbf{K_l}$ and $\mathbf{K_r}$ are the calibration matrices of left and right camera respectively and $S(T_c)$ is obtained as follows:

$$S(T_c) = \begin{bmatrix} 0 & -t_z & t_y \\ t_z & 0 & -t_x \\ t_y & t_x & 0 \end{bmatrix}, \text{ with } T_c = \begin{bmatrix} t_x \\ t_y \\ t_z \end{bmatrix} \tag{4}$$

Given an image point $\widetilde{p}_l$ in the left image, expressed in homogeneous pixel coordinates, the parameter vector s_r of its associated epipolar line can be obtained as,

$$s_r = F \cdot \widetilde{p}_l \tag{5}$$

Therefore, all the points that lie on the epipolar line in the right image plane must satisfy the following equation,

$$\widetilde{p}_r^{\,T} \cdot s_r = 0 \tag{6}$$

In an equivalent way, the equation of the epipolar line in the left image associated to the projection p_r in the right image can be obtained by changing the subscripts.

3.2.2 Trinocular algorithm based on epipolar lines

Applying the epipolar restriction to a pair of images only restricts the candidate corresponding pixels in the conjugate image to a set of points along a line. Adding a third camera view will make it possible to solve the pixel correspondence problem in a unique way (Ayache & Lustman, 1991). Other algorithms using multi-view reconstruction are compared and evaluated by (Seitz et al., 2006).

The explanation of the designed method will focus on the pixel p_l that lies in the left image plane I_l, and that is the projection of the object point P through the optical center C_l (Fig. 4). The actual corresponding projections in the right and central image plane I_r and I_c with optical centers C_r and C_c are denoted p_r and p_c respectively.

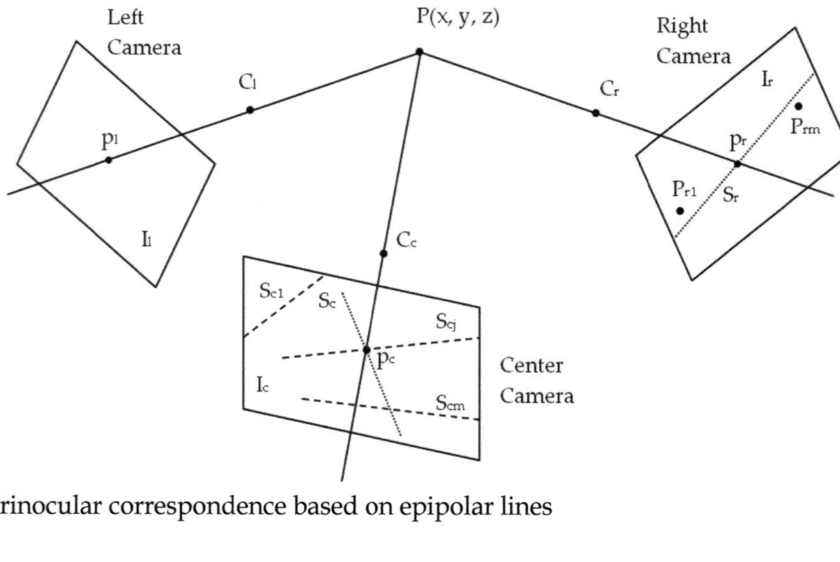

Fig. 4. Trinocular correspondence based on epipolar lines

Knowing the intrinsic and extrinsic parameters of the camera triplet, the epipolar lines corresponding to the projection p_l of P in the left image can be constructed in the right and central image plane. These epipolar lines are denoted S_r and S_c for right and central image plane respectively. In the right image plane we now consider the pixels that have been previously detected as characteristic ones (e.g. corner pixels) and select those that lie on the epipolar line S_r or sufficiently close to it. A set of so called *candidate pixels* arises in the image plane I_r and they are denoted in Fig. 4 as P_{ri}, i=1...m.
In the central image plane we can now construct the epipolar lines that correspond to the pixels P_{ri}. This set of epipolar lines is denoted as $\{S_{ci}, i=1...m\}$. The correct pixel correspondence is now found by intersecting S_c with the epipolar lines of the set $\{S_{ci}\}$ and selecting the central image pixel that lies on the intersection of S_c and a line S_{cj} in the set $\{S_{ci}\}$. Once this pixel is detected, the unique corresponding pixel triplet $\{p_l, p_c, p_r\}$ is found.
In practice, correspondent pixels will never lie perfectly on the intersection of the epipolar lines constructed in the third image. Therefore, we have to define what pixel distance can be considered as sufficiently small to conclude a pixel correspondence. Furthermore, extra attention has to be paid to the noise effect in images, which tends to promote the detection of untrue characteristic pixels.
In the ideal case, no pixel correspondence will be detected for an untrue characteristic pixel, because it hasn't been detected in the other images and its epipolar line doesn't come close to one of the true or untrue characteristic pixels in the other images. When the algorithm does detect a correspondence that originates from one or more untrue characteristic pixels, a matched triplet is obtained. However, the algorithm can be taught to only look within the boundaries of the visible world coordinate frame and to discard the untrue correspondence after reconstructing its 3D location. This is possible because it is more probable that the resulting 3D point will lie far from the 3D workspace in which the object is supposed to be detected.

3.3 Parallelepiped object detection

An important step in the overall vision method is the identification of an object in a camera image. A priori knowledge about the object's colour and shape is therefore often used to detect obstacles in the robot's workspace as quickly as possible. For example the detection of a table is easier compared to a human because of its rectangular surfaces which allows edge and corner detection. In this research, we worked with a foam obstacle of parallelepiped structure. Here, we will explain how such objects are detected and reconstructed.

3.3.1 Observation of parallelepiped structures

As will be explained in section 5.1, images from all three cameras are continuously (each 50 milliseconds) extracted and stored in the control software. The obstacle of parallelepiped form is detected in one of those images (for time-saving) by first converting the image into binary form. Subsequently, the program searches for contours of squared form. Because a square has equal sides the relation between its area and its perimeter reduces to:

$$\frac{perimeter^2}{area} = \frac{(4a)^2}{a^2} = 16 \tag{7}$$

In an image of binary form, the perimeter and area of closed contours can be calculated at low computational costs. Shadow effects can cause the real object shapes to be slightly deformed. This may result in deviations of the contour's area and perimeter. To incorporate for this, a lower and upper threshold have to be set, e.g. 14 as lower and 18 as upper threshold. Of course, other solutions to quickly detect the presence of an obstacle exist. Detection based on the object's colour is a common alternative approach.

When an obstacle is detected, images are taken out of the video stream of the same camera until the obstacle is motionless. Motion of the obstacle is easily checked by subtracting two subsequent image matrices. As soon as the obstacle is motionless, images are drawn out of the video stream of all three cameras and saved for further processing.

3.3.2 Detection of corner pixels and object reconstruction

The 3D reconstruction of the foam obstacle is then started by looking for corners in the three images. An edge detector is applied to detect edges and contours within the image. The curvature of identified contours along their lengths is computed using a curvature scale space corner detector (He & Yung, 2004). Local maxima of the curvature are considered as corner candidates. After discarding rounded corners and corners due to boundary noise and details, the true image corners remain. We typically reconstruct the 3D location of the obstacle's four upper corners. Because the curvature maxima calculation consumes a lot of computaton time, it is good practice to restrict the search window in the images. By again applying the square detecting criterion, this window can be placed around the top of the parallellepiped obstacle to reduce the search area from an original 640x480 matrix to e.g. a 320x240 matrix. Once characteristic points –true and also false object corners due to image noise or nearby objects– are detected, the epipolar lines algorithm introduced in section 3.2.2 is applied to determine the corresponding corners.

Summarizing, starting with the images returned by the obstacle detection procedure, the following steps are undertaken:

1. Application of a corner detection function to detect corner candidates in all three images as described in (He & Yung, 2004);
2. For every assumed corner pixel in the first image, execution of the following steps (see section 3.2 for a detailed explanation):
   a. Construction of the associated epipolar lines in images two and three;
   b. Search for corner pixels in the second image that lie close to the epipolar line;
   c. Construction in the third image of the epipolar lines that correspond to pixels found in (b);
   d. Calculation of intersections between epipolar lines;
   e. Detection of corner pixels in the third image that lie sufficiently close to the calculated intersections;
   f. Formation of triplets of pixel correspondences;
3. Application of inverse camera projection model to undo pixel distortions of all pixel correspondences (as described in section 3.1.1);
4. Reconstruction of 3D positions using the obtained pixel correspondences;
5. Elimination of false pixel correspondences by discarding of 3D positions that lie outside the expected 3D range of the obstacle;
6. Ordering the 3D positions to a structured set that describes the location of the obstacle in the robot's workspace.

4. Adding robot intelligence

A motion planning algorithm that guarantees a collision-free path for robot movement is an important step when integrating both humans and robots (or multiple robots) in a single work cell. In this section we will introduce a fuzzy logic based technique to solve the obstacle avoidance problem.

Fuzzy logic controllers (FLC) are a useful tool to transform linguistic control strategies based on expertise into an automated control strategy and are very popular in robotics (Surdhar & White, 2003; Kumar & Garg, 2005; Cojbašic & Nikolic, 2008; Alavandar & Nigam, 2008; Hitam, 2001; Ghalia & Alouani, 1995). The basic idea is to assign linguistic labels to physical properties. The process that converts a numerical value into a linguistic description is the fuzzification process. Using a rule base that simulates human reasoning in decision taking, a number of linguistic control actions is computed and subsequently defuzzified or converted to numerical control actions. In what follows each step of this process will be briefly described. For more information and a detailed introduction on fuzzy controllers, please consult (Cordon et al., 2001; Driankow et al., 1996).

As main reasons for implementing an obstacle avoidance strategy based on fuzzy logic we indicate that a fuzzy algorithm and its rule base can be constructed relatively easily and in an intuitive, experimental way. It is easier to encode human expert knowledge in the FLC without the necessity of precise mathematical modelling. Furthermore, the fuzzy operators that are used to link the inputs of the fuzzy system to its output can be chosen as basic operators such as sum, product, min and max.

4.1 Fuzzy avoidance strategy

A fuzzy rule base that simulates human reasoning and that contains two types of actuating forces was designed. An attracting force proportional to the 1D distance differences between actual tool center point coordinates and target location coordinates causes the FLC to output distance increments towards the goal location. A repelling force describing the distance to the obstacle's side planes deactivates the attracting force and invokes specific avoidance actions that have to be undertaken by the robot's end effector to avoid collision with the obstacle. The idea of implementing repelling and attracting forces for the design of a fuzzy rule base is based on (Zavlangas & Tzafestas, 2000). The authors describe a 1D fuzzy logic controller that outputs increments and decrements for the robot axes' angles.

Different from (Zavlangas & Tzafestas, 2000), we construct 3D safety zones around the obstacle, based on the distance differences between the tool center point and the obstacle's sides. When the robot's tool center point enters one of these safety zones around the obstacle, two types of avoidance actions are undertaken. Rotational actions guarantee the end effector's orthogonal position to the obstacle's side and translational actions assure accurate collision avoidance as depicted in Fig. 5.

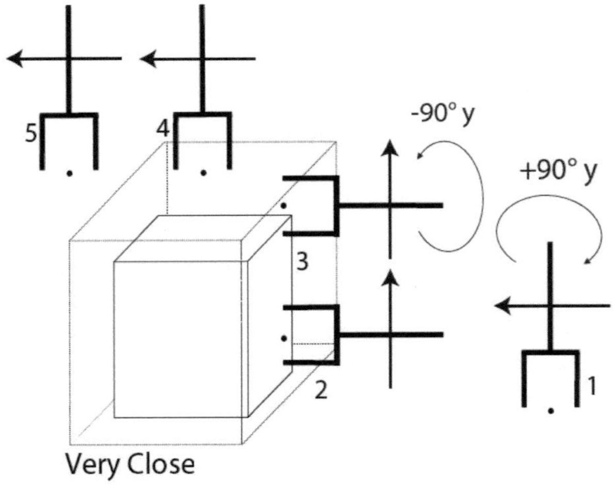

Fig. 5. A graphical example of the robot's end effector, tool center point (denoted by the black dot) , and the target behaviour of the robot arm using a fuzzy avoidance strategy.

4.2 Inputs to the fuzzy logic controller

Two inputs are fed into the FLC. The first, related to the attracting force, describes a 1D distance difference between the actual tool center point and the target location, while the second input, related to the repelling force, indicates if the tool center point is near to one of the obstacle's sides. A singleton fuzzificator is used to fuzzify both inputs.

The distance to the target location can be described in linguistic terms as e.g. *close* or *far*. For a given distance, each of the linguistic labels will be true with a certain value in the range [0, 1]. This value will be determined by the membership function (MF) of the specified linguistic distance label. Figure 6 illustrates the MFs of the labels that describe the distance difference between the tool center point and the target location. MFs of triangular and open trapezoidal form were chosen because they are easy to implement and require short evaluation times. The triangular in the middle represents the MF for contact with the obstacle.

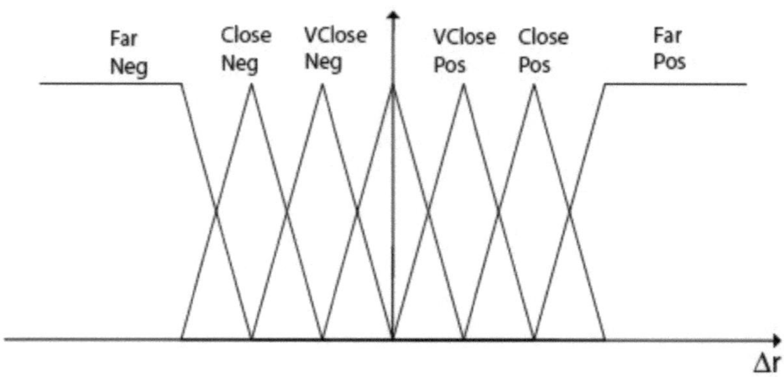

Fig. 6. Membership functions for fuzzy sets of attracting force

The second FLC input is related to the repelling force. To understand how these FLC inputs originate, we give the following example (see Fig. 7). Suppose the robot's tool center point is *very close to the positive x side* of the obstacle. This means it is very close to the border of the obstacle measured along the positive x direction, and it must be *within the y and z range* of the obstacle. This conditional statement is translated into fuzzy logic mathematics by multiplying the value of the 1D MF for being close to positive x side with the values of similar MFs for being *within y and z range*. This way, three-variable MFs are formed to evaluate what the designer of the rule base can interpret as *volumetric* linguistic labels.

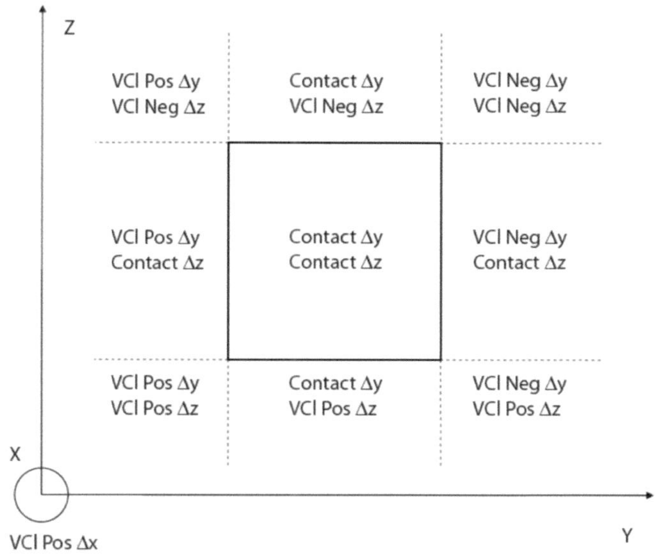

Fig. 7. Construction of label *very close positive x*.

Storing these volumetric linguistic labels in a database that is evaluated at every position along the alternative trajectory, virtual safety zones around the obstacle can be constructed as shown in Fig. 5. Analogously, zones *close* and *not close*, and an outer region *far*, complementary to the inner zones, can be constructed.

4.3 Design of a rule base

An important task of the FLC is the deactivation of the attracting force when the repelling force is triggered. The FLC designer has to implement this condition when constructing the logical rules for approaching the target location.

For the rules related to the repelling force, we can state that the designer of the rule base is free to choose the direction, magnitude and orientation of the avoidance actions. We decided to undertake an avoidance action in positive z direction when the tool center point is (very) close to the (negative or positive) x or y side of the obstacle.

The avoidance action is chosen intelligently by taking the shortest path between the tool center point's current position and the target location.

As soon as the tool center point enters the safety zone (not close), a rotation of -90° or +90° around the appropriate axis of a fixed coordinate system needs to be undertaken, to prevent the end effector from hitting the obstacle (see Fig. 5).

To resolve the fuzzy intersection operator we used a T-norm of the product type. In the aggregation of rule consequents an S-norm for the fuzzy union operator was chosen. We implemented the maximum operator for this S-norm.

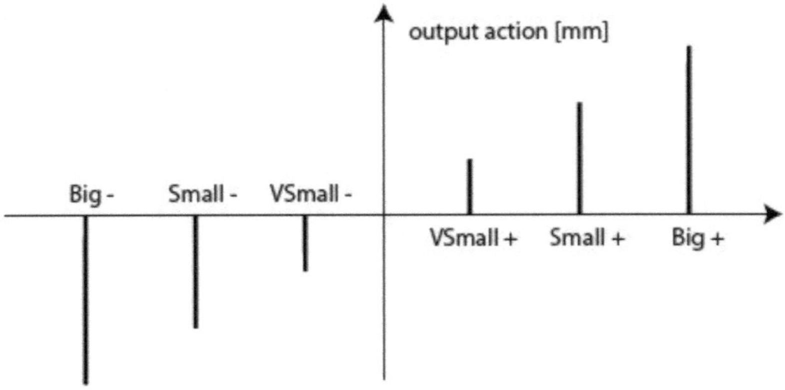

Fig. 8. Fuzzy output functions. The label "big" corresponds to 30mm, "small" to 5mm and "very small" to 3mm.

4.4 Outputs of the fuzzy logic controller

Fuzzy outputs of the Sugeno singleton type were used for defuzzification. Depending on the output of a rule, a specific value can be assigned to the considered system output. Output functions for positional actions are depicted in Fig. 8. The designer of the FLC is free to determine the size of the output actions.

Given an initial and target position and an obstacle's location supplied by the vision system, the FLC outputs a set of positional and rotational commands that guarantees collision-free motion towards the final location. An example of such a command can be [+50, 0, -50, +90°, 0°] in which the first three numbers indicate distance increments in millimeter of x, y and z coordinates of the tool center point and the last two numbers indicate the rotation angles of the tool center point with respect to the fixed coordinate system.

5. Experimental setup

Before the manipulator can move along an alternative trajectory upon appearance of an object, some choices with regard to camera setup and communication between the different components of the active security system have to be made. This is described in this section.

5.1 Camera setup

As can be intuitively understood, a two-dimensional camera image no longer contains the three-dimensional information that fully describes an object in space, because the image has lost the profundity information. However, once the corresponding image points have been detected in a pair or a triplet of images, the profundity information can be calculated. Therefore, a triplet of network cameras (type AXIS 205) was installed to watch the robot's

workspace. The cameras were positioned in a triangular pattern and mounted on the ceiling above the robot's workspace. Camera images (sized 480 x 640 x 3 bytes in Red Green Blue image space) are obtained by sending an image request signal to their IP address over a Local Area Network (LAN). More details on the LAN's setup are given in 5.2. After installation, every camera is calibrated according to (Heikkilä and Silvén, 1997) as explained in section 3.1.1.
Storing and transferring images (i.e. a matrix of dimension 480x640x3 bytes) between various components of the ASSYS is time-consuming. Many image acquisition software routines set up a connection between the pc and the camera, each time a function call is made. After the picture has been saved, this connection is closed again. Opening and closing each time an image is requested is a waste of computation time. Experiments in the TEISA lab showed that this delay sometimes takes up to 0.5 seconds. Faster picture storage is possible through maintaining the connection pc - camera open as long as new images are processed. This was implemented by C. Torre Ferrero using the ActiveX component of the AXIS camera software making it possible to view motion JPEG video streams. Using the ActiveX components, subsequent picture images are stored in processing times never exceeding 80 milliseconds.

5.2 Real-time communication network

Fast access to the network cameras and communication of an alternative trajectory is very important for safety reasons. To obtain correct pixel correspondences, we need a picture frame of each one of the three cameras, ideally taken at the very same moment in time. When registering moving objects, the smallest time interval between grabbing the three picture frames, will lead to incorrect pixel correspondences and therefore incorrect 3D position calculations. Also, robotic control applications often have cycle times of typically tens of milliseconds. When operational data needs to be exchanged between a robot and an operator's pc, the speed and the guarantee of data transmission is very important.
For many years, Ethernet was banned as a communication medium in industry, because data packages that are sent by devices connected to a same local area network can collide. Due to the network's media access control protocol (CSMA/CD) retransmission is non-deterministic and offers no guarantees with respect to time. Nowadays, fast Ethernet switches can be used to isolate network devices into their own collision domain, hereby eliminating the chance for collision and loss of data packages. Ethernet switches together with the development of fast Ethernet (100Mbps) and gigabit Ethernet (1Gbps) have made Ethernet popular as a real-time communication medium in industrial settings (Decotignie, 2005; Piggin & Brandt 2006). In this application, five devices are connected to a single fast Ethernet switch (100Mbps): the three Axis network cameras, the robot controller and the pc from which control actions are monitored.
On top of Ethernet the Transmission Control Protocol (TCP) is used. TCP supports error recovery and assures the correct order of data packages received. This is, however, time consuming due to the exchange of supplementary control information, such as sending acknowledgements, retransmission if errors occurred, etc. This makes the TCP protocol less suitable for time critical applications. However, together with fast Ethernet, a limited number of devices connected to a dedicated switch (no in-between routers) and short cable lengths, the overhead of TCP is negligible and better reliability was obtained. The robot manipulator provides TCP connection-oriented communication options, such as socket messaging (combination of IP address and TCP port number), which makes it easy to program.

5.3 The FANUC ArcMate 100iB

All robot experiments were performed on a FANUC Robot Arc Mate 100iB (Fig. 9). This is an industrial robot with six rotational axes and with a circular range of 1800mm.
A multitasking active security application was programmed in the KAREL programming language, and compiled off-line using WinOLPC+ software. A motion task executes a normal operation trajectory until a condition handler is triggered by the detection signal that was received through an Ethernet socket by a concurrently running communication task. When this condition handler is triggered, robot motion is halted and the current position of the tool center point is sent to the operator's pc, where the FLC calculates the first sequence of alternative positions and sends them back over the opened socket connection to the communication task. An interrupt routine for motion along the alternative path is then invoked in the motion task and the communication task completes reading of subsequent alternative positions and rotational configurations. Coordination between the motion task and the communication task was realized by the use of semaphores.
During practical testing, a moving object is simulated by dragging the parallelepiped foam obstacle into the robot's workspace using a rope. This object is also shown in Fig. 9. Remark that the object remains static after entering the manipulator's workspace because the algorithm is not yet programmed in a dynamic way. Once the obstacle stands still the obstacle reconstruction routine using stereoscopic techniques starts. From this moment on, no new images are processed in the software.

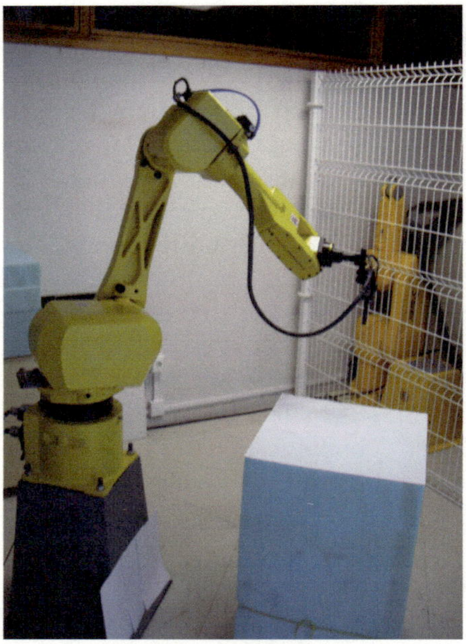

Fig. 9. The FANUC Arc Mate 100iB. The parallelepiped foam obstacle is shown in the bottom right corner.

6. Results and discussion

The artificial vision system, the fuzzy logic controller and the robot control application were tested both separately as well as in an integrated way. In this section the results from these tests are briefly described. We also discuss some issues that could be improved further.

6.1 Evaluation of the vision system

We will first discuss the experimentally obtained upper bounds of execution times of the vision subsystem. The processing times are given in table 1. The steps of the vision system algorithm that involve corner detection are rather time consuming as expected. Mainly mathematical operations such as pixel correspondence search and 3D reconstructions are less time consuming.

Image processing task	Upper time limit [milliseconds]
Detect moving object	220
Total picture package time	350
Corner detection in 3 images	2500
Find pixel correspondence	16
Reconstruct 3D positions	16

Table 1. Time consumption of image processing tasks. The total picture package time is the time needed to store the images of all three pictures as soon as an object has been detected by one of the cameras.

Given the basic equipment used, the obtained processing times are acceptable. If the robot moves at a reasonable speed, the presence of an obstacle can be signalled fast enough (after 220msec upon transmission of the images) to avoid a collision between the robot's end effector and the obstacle. It is also encouraging to see that transmission of three images (large quantity of data) over the LAN doesn't take that much time. If camera images need to be available at a higher time rate, cameras equipped with frame grabbers can always be installed for future projects.

The corner detection process is extremely time-consuming, which can be understood taking into account the exhaustive curvature calculation procedure that is used in this algorithm. The robot is paused during this calculation procedure. Once the robot has received the first alternative position calculated by the FLC, it will start moving again.

The obstacle is dragged into the robot's workspace when the robot arm is close to the leftmost or rightmost point of its regular trajectory. The parallelepiped shape in Fig. 10 depicts the result of the vision system after reconstruction. Absence of the robot arm in the central zone of the workspace is necessary for correct obstacle detection because the robot arm would deform the binary image of the obstacle's squared contour. Further development of the vision system is therefore needed to distinguish the robot arm from the obstacle, e.g. by colour identification or marker on the robot arm, in order to be able to signal obstacle presence in all operational situations. However, if the robot arm is occulting one of the obstacle's upper corners in one of the three images, performing an accurate reconstruction of the obstacle's 3D location is still possible, since a free view on three of the four upper corners in all images is sufficient for the reconstruction.

6.2 Real-time performance of the switched Ethernet communication

Times to execute socket communication actions were measured using built-in timing routines of the controller software and the KAREL system. The upper bounds of the most important actions are stated in table 2. In KAREL, the result of the timing routines is dependent on a system variable that indicates the step size with which the timer is incremented. For the Arc Mate 100iB this system variable has a minimum setting of 4 milliseconds. Hence, execution times marked with a (*) need to be interpreted as times smaller then the counting step of the timer feature. So these times are not equal to zero but surely smaller than 4msec.

Before the ASSYS can start constructing the alternative trajectory, the actual position of the tool center point needs to be sent from the robot controller to the FLC, which runs in Matlab. For this data exchange a simple client socket application written in Perl based on (Holzner, 2001) was used. This Perl script (Client.pl) gives a good impression of the time needed to perform communication actions. Client.pl is called from Matlab and establishes a connection with the robot controller that acts as the server, receives the actual position of the tool center point and is closed again in the KAREL program. It therefore incorporates time to connect, disconnect and send data.

Matlab socket action	**Upper bound [msec]**
Misconnect	0 (*)
Mssend	0 (*)
perl('Client.pl')	160
Msclose	0 (*)
KAREL socket action	
MSG_DISCO('S3', Status)	0 (*)
MSG_CONNECT('S3', Status)	0 (*)
WRITE ComFile(tcp_x)	0 (*)
READ 110 bytes in input buffer	240

Table 2. Socket communication times for Matlab and KAREL actions. tcp_x is an integer variable containing the x coordinate of the tool center point. Similar operations are needed to transfer the y and z coordinate. S3 is the name tag assigned to the server socket.

Once a first package of alternative positions and rotational actions is received, the robot axes' motors start accelerating immediately and motion continues until the specified location is reached. In the mean time subsequent commands generated by the FLC arrive at the robot's socket and are processed without any observable delay in the movement of the manipulator arm.

In this particular situation we found no justifiable need for dedicated hardware, for example as is used in (Janssen & Büttner, 2004). Connecting a limited number of devices to a fast Ethernet switch (thereby avoiding collisions) on a reserved part of the LAN network, and covering only short distances (all equipment is situated close to each other) provide an adequate and cost-effective solution.

6.3 Evaluation of the ASSYS

For the ASSYS to work properly, the designer of the FLC has to choose the step size (in millimeters) of translational commands. This was done in a rather experimental way trying to find an optimal mix between the number of motion commands on the one hand and accuracy of the resulting ASSYS' avoidance behaviour on the other hand. In this contribution a step size of 50 millimeters was used. However, a thorough study can be performed making a trade-off between small increments and thus larger calculation times and larger robot processing times or large distance increments and thus smaller calculation times and robot processing times. This last option implicates however that the safety zones around the obstacle need to be bigger and that longer trajectories have to be completed by the end effector before it reaches the target location. Figure 10 depicts the result of the ASSYS.

An important manipulator characteristic is the processing time needed by the robot's operating system to handle new motion instructions. Robot constructor FANUC provides a motion clause that allows the program execution to continue after launching a motion instruction. In this way, a continuous transition between two separate motion commands is possible. The FLC outputs a long sequence of alternative positions to reach a desired goal state thereby avoiding collision. With distance increments of 50 millimeters, the FLC typically outputs a sequence of about 40 alternative positions. Nevertheless, we chose to keep the number of motion commands as limited as possible and decided to only send every fourth alternative position as an effective motion instruction to the robot. Given the fact that alternative positions are situated close to each other (see Fig. 10, blue crosses), this strategy still results in accurate obstacle avoidance and in smooth, continuous robot motion.

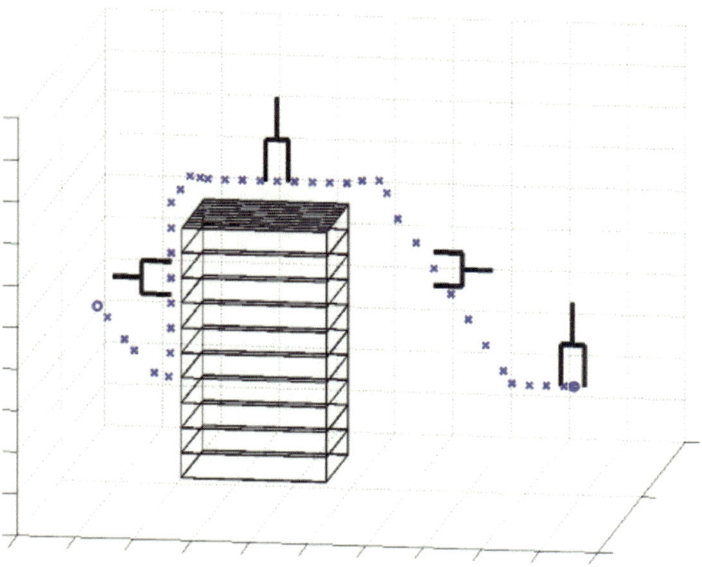

Fig. 10. A graphical example of the alternative trajectory around the reconstructed parallelliped obstacle

The robot application in KAREL was implemented in a non-cyclic way; upon reaching the goal position, program execution is aborted. In an industrial environment it would be desirable that robot motion continues when a safe location (where no collision with the obstacle is possible) is reached. This can be easily implemented by running the obstacle detection routine again. This routine would then tell if the obstacle is still present or not and make sure the robot executes an alternative path (in case a new obstacle is blocking the robot's path) or the regular, predetermined path in case of a free workspace.
The FLC only takes the tool center point's position as an input. Collision of the robot's arm is prevented by rotating the end effector by +90° or -90° when it enters the safety zone *not close*. For the majority of practically executable robot trajectories, this precautionary action has proven to be sufficient. In general situations, the distance to the obstacle of extra points on the robot's arm will have to be monitored to guarantee safer motion. Also, the rotation over 90° is not entirely independent of the shape of the object.

7. Conclusion

In this contribution the design of an active security system for an industrial FANUC manipulator was introduced. Stereo vision techniques were used to design a vision method that can identify and localize obstacles of certain predefined shape in the robot's workspace. A fuzzy logic controller was successfully applied for the design of a 3D obstacle avoidance strategy. With some help from a fairly simple communication system, alternative path positions and rotational configurations could be transferred to the robot's system at a time-critical rate. Although experiments showed good performance of the ASSYS, there still are quite a few issues that have to be solved before using this system in a real-life environment.
Basic methods for object recognition were employed. In future work, advanced identification methods can be used, e.g. to distinguish the robot's end effector from foreign objects and to design an approach that isn't based on a-priori knowledge on the obstacle's shape. So far, only static objects are supported. In an advanced stadium, detection criteria for human operators can also be elaborated.
In the current setting, the time needed to calculate the characteristic positions of a parallelepiped obstacle was rather high, in some cases up to 2.5 seconds. A better technique can be developed for detecting obstacle corners.
As mentioned at the end of the previous chapter, a more automated KAREL application can be designed in which robot motion continues when the final position of the alternative path is reached. For this application, a more thorough interaction between the KAREL communication task and the vision system would be required to signal the presence or the absence of an obstacle in the robot's work space. Subsequently, the decision to return to the normal robot task or to follow a new alternative path has to be undertaken.
For industrial settings, where small robot motion execution times are very important, a trade-off study between more commands because of smaller step sizes, and less commands with larger step sizes is an interesting topic. More specifically, a time efficient and distance optimal path construction algorithm can be designed.

8. References

Alavandar, S. & Nigam, M. J. (2008). Neuro-fuzzy based approach for inverse kinematics solution of industrial robot manipulators. *International journal of Computers, Communications & Control*, 3, 3, 224-234, 1841-9836

ANSI/RIA R15, 06-1986. Robot and Robot Systems-Safety Requirements. *American National Standards Institute*. New York, 1986.

Ayache, N. & Lustman, F. (1991). Trinocular stereo vision for robotics. *IEEE Transactions on Pattern Analysis and Machine Intelligence*, 13, 1, 73-85, ISSN:0162-8828

Baerveldt, A.-J. (1992). Cooperation between Man and Robot : Interface and Safety, *Proceedings of the IEEE international workshop on robot and human communication*, pp. 183-187, 0-7803-0753-4, Tokyo, Japan, September 1992, IEEE Press.

Bicchi, A.; Peshkin, M.A. & Colgate, J.E. (2008). Safety for Physical Human–Robot Interaction, In: *Springer Handbook of Robotics*, Siciliano, B. & Khatib, O. (Eds.), pp. 1335-1348, Springer, 978-3-540-23957-4, Berlin-Heidelberg, Germany

Bixby, K. (1991). Proactive safety design and implementation criteria, *Proceedings of National Robot Safety Conference*

Burghart, C.; Holzapfel, H.; Haeussling, R. & Breuer, S. (2007). Coding interaction patterns between human and receptionist robot, *Proceedings of the 7th IEEE-RAS Conference on Humanoid Robots*, pp. 454-460, Pittsburgh, PA, November 2007

Burghart, C.; Mikut, R.; Stiefelhagen, R.; Asfour, T.; Holzapfel, H.; Steinhaus, P. & Ruediger Dillmann (2005). A Cognitive Architecture for a Humanoid Robot: A First Approach, *Proceedings of 5th IEEE-RAS International Conference on Humanoid Robots*, pp. 357-362, Tsukuba, Japan, December 2005, IEEE Press

Cervera, E.; Garcia-Aracil, N.; Martínez, E.; Nomdedeu, L. & del Pobil, A.P. (2008). Safety for a robot arm moving amidst humans by using panoramic vision, *Proceedings of the IEEE International Conference on Robotics and Automation*, pp. 2183-2188, 978-1-4244-1646-2, Pasadena, CA, USA, May 2008, IEEE Press

Cojbašic, Ž. M. & Nikolic, V. D. (2008). Hybrid industrial robot motion control. *Automatic Control and Robotics*, 7, 1, pp. 99 - 110

Cordon, O.; Herrera, F.; Hoffmann, F. & Magdalena, L. (2001). Genetic Fuzzy Systems. Evolutionary tuning and learning of fuzzy knowledge bases, In *Advances in Fuzzy Systems: Applications and Theory*

Decotignie, J. D. (2005). Ethernet-based real-time and industrial communications. *Proceedings of the IEEE*, 93, 6, June 2005, 1102-1117, 0018-9219.

Dhillon, B.S. (1991). *Robot Reliability and Safety*, Springer-Verlag, 038-7-975-357, New York, USA

Driankow, D.; Hellendoorn, H. & Reinfrank, M. (1996). *An introduction to fuzzy control - Second edition*, Springer-Verlag

Ebert, D. & Heinrich, D. (2001). Safe human-robot-cooperation: problem analysis, system concept and fast sensor fusion, *Proceedings of the international conference on Multisensor Fusion and Integration for Intelligent Systems*, pp. 239- 244, ISBN: 3-00-008260-3, Kongresshaus Baden-Baden, Germany, August 2001

Ebert, D. & Henrich, D. (2002). Safe Human-Robot-Cooperation: image-based collision detection for industrial robots, *Proceedings of the IEEE/RSJ International conference on intelligent robots and systems*, pp. 1826-1831, Lausanne, France, October 2002, IEEE Press

Ebert, D.; Komuro, T.; Namiki, A. & Ishikawa, M. (2005). Safe human-robot-coexistence: emergency-stop using a high-speed vision-chip, *Proceedings of the IEEE/RSJ International Conference on In Intelligent Robots and Systems*, pp. 2923-2928, Edmonton, Alberta, Canada, August 2005, IEEE Press.

Eckert, G. (2000). Automatic Shape Reconstruction of Rigid 3-D Objects from Multiple Calibrated Images, *Proceedings of the European Signal Processing Conference*, pp. 2105-2108, 952-15-0443-9, Tampere, Finland, September 2000, TTKK-Paino, Tampere, FINLAND.

Feddema, J.T. & Novak, J.L. (1994). Whole arm obstacle avoidance for teleoperated robots, *Proceedings of the IEEE International Conference on Robotics and Automation*, pp. 3303-3309 vol.4, 0-8186-5330-2, San Diego, CA, USA, May 1994, IEEE Press

Gecks, T. & Henrich, D. (2005). Human-robot corporation: safe pick-and-place operations, *Proceedings of the IEEE International Workshop on Robots and Human Interactive Communication*, pp. 549-554, ISBN, Nashville, Tennesse, USA, August 2005, IEEE Press

Ghalia, M.B. & Alouani, A. T. (1995). A robust trajectory tracking control of industrial robot manipulators using fuzzy logic. *Proceedings of the 27th Southeastern Symposium on System Theory*, 268

Graham, J.H. (1991). *Safety, Reliability and Human Factors in Robotics Systems*, John Wiley & Sons, Inc., 0442002807, New York, USA.

Hartley, R. I. & Zisserman, A. (2004). *Multiple View Geometry in Computer Vision*, Cambridge University Press, ISBN: 0521540518, Cambridge, UK.

He, X. C. & Yung, N. H. C. (2004). Curvature scale space corner detector with adaptive threshold and dynamic region of support, Proceedings of the 17th International Conference on Pattern Recognition - Volume 2, pp.791-794, 0-7695-2128-2, Cambridge, UK, August 2004

Heinzmann, J. & Zelinsky, A. (1999). Building Human-Friendly Robot Systems, *Proceedings of the International Symposium of Robotics Research*, pp. 9-12, Salt Lake City (UT), USA, October 1999

Hirschfeld, R.A.; Aghazadeh, F. & Chapleski, R.C. (1993). Survey of Robot Safety in Industry. *The International Journal of Human Factors in Manufacturing*, 3, 4, pp. 369-379, 1045-2699/93/040369-11. John Wiley & Sons, Inc.

Hitam, M.S. (2001). Fuzzy logic control of an industrial robot. *Proceedings of Joint 9th IFSA World Congress and 20th NAFIPS International Conference*, 257-262 vol. 1, July 2001

Holzner, S. (2001). *Perl Black Book, Second Edition*, Paraglyph Press, 978-1-932-11110-1, USA

Heikkilä, J. & Silvén, O. (1997). A Four-step Camera Calibration Procedure with Implicit Image Correction. *Proceedings of the 1997 Conference on Computer Vision and Pattern Recognition*, 1106--1112, 0-8186-7822-4

ISO 10218-1:2006(E). Robot for Industrial Environments, Safety requirements, Part1: Robot. *International Organization for Standardization*. Switzerland, 2006.

Janssen, D.; Büttner, H. (2004). Real-time Ethernet: the EtherCAT solution. *Computing & Control Engineering Journal*, 15, pp. 16-21

Kuhn, S.; Gecks, T. & Henrich, D. (2006). Velocity control for safe robot guidance based on fused vision and force/torque data, *Proceedings of the IEEE International Conference on Multisensor Fusion and Integration for Intelligent Systems*, pp. 485-492, Heidelberg, Germany, September 2006

Kumar, M. & Garg, D. P. (2005). Neuro-fuzzy control applied to multiple cooperating robots. *Industrial Robot: An International Journal*, 32, 3, 234 - 239

Llata, J.R.; Sarabia, E.G.; Arce, J. & Oria, J.P. (1998). Fuzzy controller for obstacle avoidance in robotic manipulators using ultrasonic sensors, *Proceedings of the 5th International Workshop on Advanced Motion Control*, pp. 647-652, 9780780344846, Coimbra, Portugal, June 1998

Noborio, H. & Urakawa, K. (1999). Three or more dimensional sensor-based path planning algorithm HD-I, *Proceedings of the IEEE/RSI Int. Conf. on Intelligent Robots and Systems vol. 3*, pp. 1699-1706, October 1999, IEEE Press

Noborio, H. & Nishino, Y. (2001). Image-Based Path-Planning Algorithm on the Joint Space, *Proceedings of the 2001 IEEE International Conference on Robotics and Automation*, pp. 1180-1187 vol. 2, 0-7803-6576-3, Seoul, Korea, May 2001

Novak, J.L. & Feddema, J.T. (1992). A capacitance-based proximity sensor for whole arm obstacle avoidance, *Proceedings of the IEEE International conference on Robotics and Automation*, pp. 1307-1314 vol. 2, 0-8186-2720-4, Nice, France, May 1992

Oestreicher, L. & Eklundh, K. S. (2006). User Expectations on Human-Robot Cooperation, *Proceedings of the 15th IEEE International Symposium on Robot and Human Interactive Communication*, pp. 91-96, ISBN, Hatfield, UK, September 2006

Ogorodnikova, O. (2006). Human-Robot Interaction. Safety problems, *Proceedings of the 15th International Workshop on Robotics in Alpe-Adria-Danube Region*, pp. 63-68, Balatonfüred, Hungary, June, 2006

Ohta, A. & Amano, N. (2008). Collision prediction using physical simulator and stereo vision system for human support robot, *Proceedings of the international conference on instrumentation, control and information technology*, pp. 2286-2290, The University Electro-Communications, August 2008, Chofu, Tokyo, Japan

OSHA (2006). Industrial Robots and Robot System Safety. In *United states department of labor, occupational safety & health administration technical manual*, Section IV, Chapter 4.

Piggin, R. (2005). Developments in industrial robotic safety. *Industrial robot*, 32, 4, pp. 303-311, 0143-991X.

Piggin, R. & Brandt, D. (2006). Wireless ethernet for industrial applications. *Assembly Automation*, 26, 3, 205-215.

Salvi, J.; Armangu, X. & Batlle, J. (2002). A Comparative Review of Camera Calibrating Methods with Accuracy Evaluation. *Pattern Recognition*, 35, 7, pp. 1617-1635, ISSN: 0031-3203.

Scharstein, D. & Szeliski, R. (2002). A taxonomy and evaluation of dense two-frame stereo correspondence algorithms. *International Journal of Computer Vision*, 47, 7-42, ISSN:0920-5691.

Seitz, S. M.; Curless, B.; Diebel, J.; Scharstein, D. & Szeliski, R. (2006). A Comparison and Evaluation of Multi-View Stereo Reconstruction Algorithms, *Proceedings of the IEEE Computer Society Conference on Computer Vision and Pattern Recognition*, pp. 519-528, (vol. 1) ISBN: 0-7695-2597-0, New York, USA, June 2006, IEEE Press.

Steinhaus, P.; Ehrenmann, M. & Dillmann R. (1999). MEPHISTO: A modular and existensible path planning system using observation, In: *Lecture Notes in Computer Science 1542*, EDITOR (Ed.), pp. 361-375, Springer-Verlag, 3-540-65459-3, London, UK

Surdhar, J. S. & White A. S. (2003). A parallel fuzzy-controlled flexible manipulator using optical tip feedback. *Robotics and Computer-Integrated Manufacturing*, 19, 3, June 2003, 273-282

Torre-Ferrero, C.; Llata García, J. & González Saro, A. (2005). Monocular 3d reconstruction by applying a clustering algorithm to the Hough parameter space, *Proceedings of the 7th IASTED International Conference on Control and Applications*, pp. 82-87, 0-88986-502-7, Cancun, Mexico, May 2005, Acta Press

Yu, Y. & Gupta, K. (1999). Sensor-based roadmaps for motion planning for articulated robots in unknown environments: some experiments with an eye-in-hand system, *Proceedings of IEEE/RSJ International Conference on Intelligent Robots and Systems*, pp. 1707-1714, ISBN, Kyongju, South Korea, October 1999, IEEE Press

Weng, Y.-H.; Chen, C.-H. & Sun, C.-T. (2009). Toward the human-robot co-existence society: on safety intelligence for Next Generation Robots. Accepted for publication in *International Journal of Social Robotics*, 1875-4791 (Print) 1875-4805 (Online)

Wöhler, C. (2009). Applications to Safe Human–Robot Interaction, In *3D Computer Vision: efficient methods and applications*, Wöhler, C. (Ed.), pp. 277-301, Springer, 978-3-642-01731-5 (Print) 978-3-642-01732-2 (Online), Berlin Heidelberg

Zavlangas, P. G. & Tzafestas, S. G. (2000). Industrial robot navigation and obstacle avoidance employing fuzzy logic. *Journal of Intelligent and Robotic Systems*, 27, 1-2, January 2000, 85-97, 0921-0296

24

Remote Robot Vision Control of a Flexible Manufacturing Cell

Silvia Anton, Florin Daniel Anton and Theodor Borangiu
University Politehnica of Bucharest
Romania

1. Introduction

In a robotized flexible manufacturing cell, robot (-vision) controllers are masters over local workstations or cells, because robot manipulators connect two important material flows: the *processing* flow and the *transportation* flow. One solution to integrate these two flows with on-line *quality control* in the manufacturing module, further networked with the design and planning modules, is to adopt a unified feature-based description of parts and assemblies, technological operations, geometric & surface quality control, grasping and manipulating (Tomas Balibrea, *et al.*, 1997).

The chapter presents a system which can be used to unify, control and observe the cell's devices (in particular each robot-vision system) from a remote location for control and learning purposes, using an advanced web interface.

The system is a software product designed to support multiple remote connections with a number of Adept Technology robot-vision controllers, either located in a local network, or via Internet. Additionally the platform allows users to run remote robot vision sessions and to develop and execute robot-vision programs, being a versatile tool for remote student training (Anton et al., 2006; Borangiu et al., 2006).

The system has multiple functions:

Observing *locally* the *foreground* of robot workplaces (processing area, storage, conveyor belt, part buffer, pallet) using multiple area cameras - stationary or mobile, arm mounted, and *globally* the robot *workstation;*

Set up of the *operating environment* (lighting pattern, virtual camera configuration, feature selection for material flow description) and learning the *model parameters* for scene description, part recognition and measuring, part grasping and gripper fingerprints for collision avoidance;

Editing, debugging and downloading application data and programs.

Remote shared control of multiple robot systems from a central point and event-driven supervision of robot actions including reaction and emergency routines launching;

Access via a Lotus Domino-based messaging and collaboration portal to a team workspace addressing hands-on team training and authenticated e-learning in the areas of computer aided design, planning, control and quality inspection for networked manufacturing workstations/cells (Brooks et al., 2004; Harris et al., 2004).

2. The Structure of the System

The strong impact of the project is in stimulating the cooperation between different networked areas of an enterprise.

2.1 Technical Background

The task is to build a system that provides access to public information for a wider audience and at the same time supports collaboration between registered members, provides safe access to protected contents and enables the publication and editing of contents. The system can be accessed from a great variety of places. Therefore great care was taken to also ensure optimal use in case of lower bandwidth and poorer quality hardware. The high level of security and availability are key components. This was ensured by the selection of high quality technical devices and the well-planned loading. As the portal must be prepared for a growing number of users, the tool must be highly scalable. It needs to integrate contents and services and provide access for document repositories. User groups must be able to access personalised contents.

A first step to install a framework is to create the infrastructure that is necessary for the safe operation and use of the portal (Fig. 1).

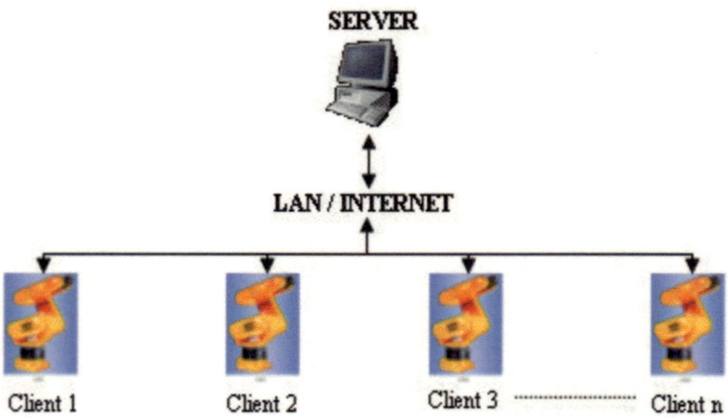

Fig. 1. The connexion between the server application and Adept controllers

High-level availability must be guaranteed. The system must be scalable according to loadness and requirements. The use of NLBS (Network Load Balancing System) provides a solution for an even load of the network. The portal user interface need to be customized, templates must be created and uploaded. The authorisations and user groups must be defined.

2.2 The Communication structure and protocol

The application was built to remotely command and supervise robot systems that can be located into an industrial LAN or Internet. The materials flow is supervised locally for each station and the results are sent to the server application which stores them into a data base.

The server uses the TCP/IP protocol to establish the connexion with the clients, the communication being achieved using messages and confirmations (Borangiu, 1996). The length of one message cannot be more than 128 bytes; this limit is imposed by the operating system of Adept controllers. The message has two parts: the header of the message (two bytes), and the body (0 to 126 bytes) (Fig. 2).

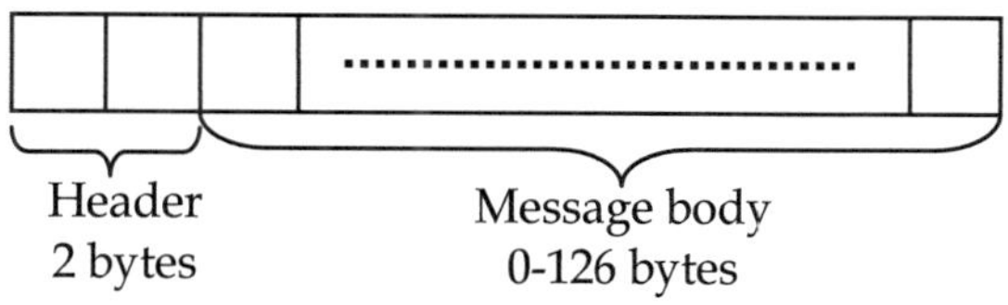

Fig. 2. The message structure

The header represents the type of the message and specifies the way in which the body of the message will be utilised. For example the headers can be:

1. Headers sent from the server:
   - '/C' - message containing a monitor command; the message is processed by the client as an instruction that will be executed immediately, and the result will be sent to the server;
   - '/T' - message containing a variable and signal list; the variables and signals must be supervised and if a modification is detected the server must be informed;
   - '/E' - message which mark the end of a program;
   - '/S' - the message contains monitor commands requiring a special execution mechanism;
2. Headers sent from the clients:
   - '/M' - message to be displayed on the server terminal (this message can be a user message, a error message, or a message generated by a instruction or a command;
   - '/A' - ACK message;
   - '/V' - Vision ACK message (the client tell the server that the image was acquired, and is ready to be loaded to the server;

As a safety measure, but at the same time to ease the use of the application, the clients which will be connected to the configuration of the server must be specified. A client is added by specifying the IP address, and the associated name (see section 7).

The system is composed by the following applications (Fig. 3):

The **Server Application (SA)**: Remote visual control and monitoring of multiple robot controllers from mobile and stationary matrix cameras.

- *Visual control*: the Server Application supports almost all V+ and AdeptVision program instructions and monitor commands. The robot training and control is interactive - menu-driven and acknowledged by image display in a VISION window. Some of the main functions available in this window are: choice of the physical and virtual cameras and of the image buffers; selecting the display mode and resolution; histogram and average curve contrast analysis; selection of switches and parameters for virtual camera construction; display of vision system status; training and planning multiple ObjectFinder models for recognition and locating (AVI & GVR); learning fingerprint models for collision-free grasping; editing, saving, loading and running V+ programs.
- *Monitoring*: a Monitoring/Treatment scheme can be defined for each Client/Station (the latter can be selected from a drop-down list of robot controllers connected to the server, by adding/removing them from the Client window). For each client a list of events and controller variables to be monitored according to a user-definable timing and precedence,

and reacted at by user-definable actions/sequences can be specified in an Automatic Treatment Window.

- *Communication management*: the Server Application manages the communication with the robot controllers and the observation cameras, transfers real-time images from the cameras observing the robot workplace and production environment, reports status information, stores in a database and displays images taken by the robot camera via its controller. Finally, the SA outputs commands which are received from the eClients or acknowledges task execution.

The **eClients Applications (eCA)**: Java applications running in web browsers. They provide portal services and the connection of networked production agents: image data and RV program / report management; real-time robot control and cell / workplace observation. The eCA are composed by two applications:

- one application which has the function of retrieving the images from the observation cameras (AXIS 214 PTZ) and display them in real-time and also gives the user the possibility to change the orientation and zoom factor of the cameras.
- the second application is a VNC client.

The VNC viewer (Java client) is a web teleoperation application which can be executed into a web browser. The application connects to the Domino web server which makes a secure connection using a TCP/IP tunnel with a server having a private IP address, which cannot be accessed from internet but only using the Domino server.

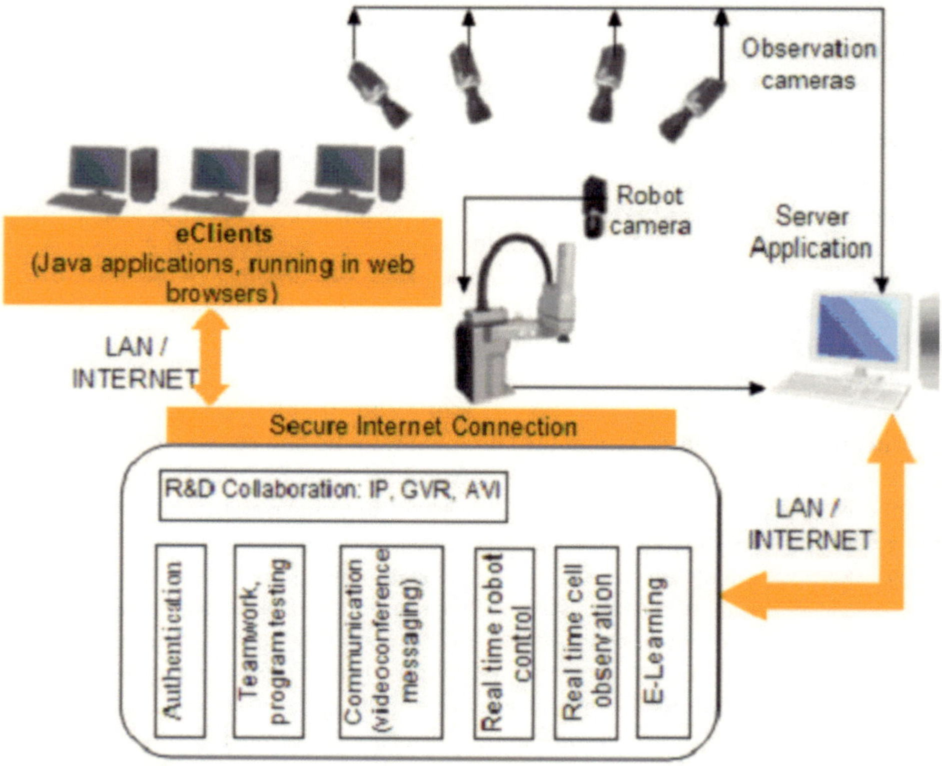

Fig. 3. The System Structure

The private IP machine has a VNC server that exports the display, and also the teleoperation application (see Fig. 4). Using the exported display the user can view and use the application as when the application runs on his own computer. The access is made using a username and a password, process managed by the Domino server.

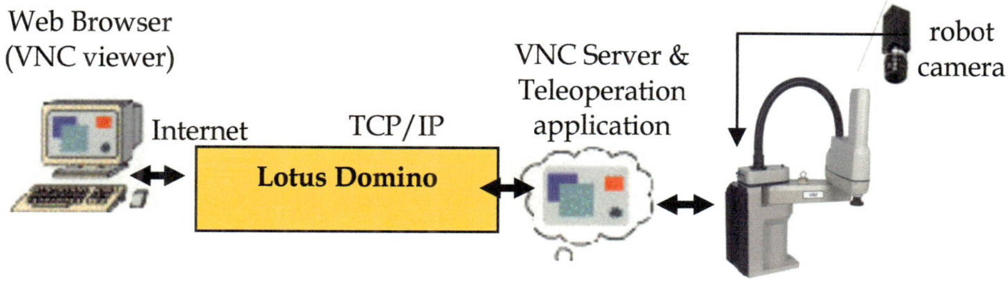

Fig. 4. The VNC communication

The access to the eClient application is granted based on the Domino defined ACL's (Access Control Lists), such that in order to connect to the application the user must specify a user name and a password. There were defined two classes of privileges:

A **user class** where the operator can observe images acquired from the observation web cameras and images from the VISION system taken by multiple area cameras; he can also view the commands issued by the trainer and watch the results of the commands;

A **trainer class** where the operator is authorized to issue commands for every connected robot system, upload, download and modify programs. The trainer can also take pictures from an individual camera and use the specific vision tools to process that image. The observation cameras can also be moved and positioned in the desired location by the trainer. The trainer can give full or partial permissions to users for program testing purposes.

For team training and application development, the system allows accessing related documents, presentations and multimedia materials, Web conferencing, instant messaging and teamwork support for efficient and security-oriented creation and use of group workspaces (students / trainers, researchers).

The Server and eClients Applications run on IBM PC workstations on which IBM Lotus software offerings are customized and integrated with other applications in a virtual training and research laboratory across geographical boundaries.

Lotus-oriented solutions have been considered for transferring messages, status reports, data and video camera images, interpreting them and accessing databases created by all partners. The final objective of the platform is to develop an E-Learning component allowing students to access and download technical documentation, create, test, debug and run RV and AVI programs, attend real-time laboratory demonstrations, and check their skills in proposed exercises.

Thus, IBM Lotus software unifies all three Application modules, providing the necessary management and interconnecting tools for distributed industrial controllers, and the collaborative tools with back-end relational databases for team training and research.

3. Some Functions of the System

In the following paragraph some functions of the system will be detailed accompanying a usage example.
To start up the system each robot controller must connect to the SA application; this operation is accomplished by a small V+ program which is running under the 27th AdeptWindows operating system task, and verifies continuously the connectivity. After at least one controller is connected the system is functional and users can connect and work remotely.
To have access to the system, a user must have a username and a valid password to enter in the system. First the user must access the portal site using a java aware browser (like Internet Explorer, Opera, Firefox, with the JRE installed). After entering the correct username and password, the user is allowed in the system and has access to a menu driven interface which allows him to interact with the system (see Fig. 5).

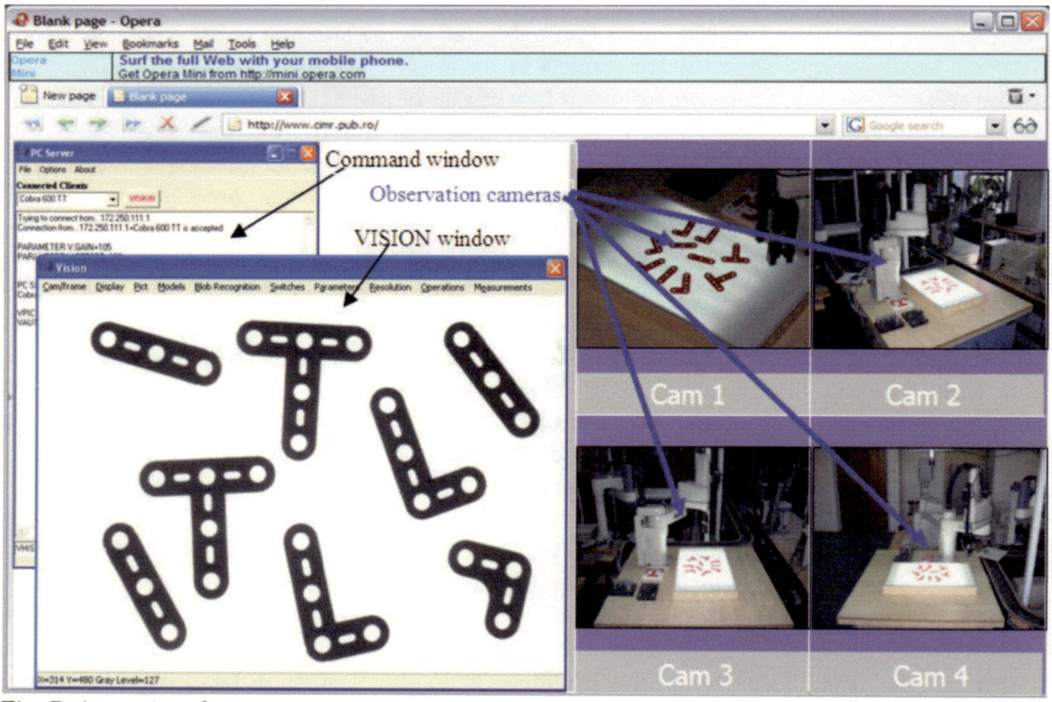

Fig. 5. Accessing the system

The teleoperation application is composed by two windows:
A command window (Fig. 6.) where the user can select the robot system which he want to control and issue commands from the command line or activate the vision window.
The robot stations are commanded using the command line and the menus. When a client is connected, the IP address is checked and if the client is accepted, the name attached to the IP address is added to a drop down list from which the user can select what client he wishes to command. When a client who has a video camera attached the VISION button is enabled and if it is pressed the VISION Window will open.

Using that interface the user can select the robot system which he want to control and issue commands from the command line or activate the vision window.
From the VISION window, vision commands can be issued by selecting the wanted actions from the menus.

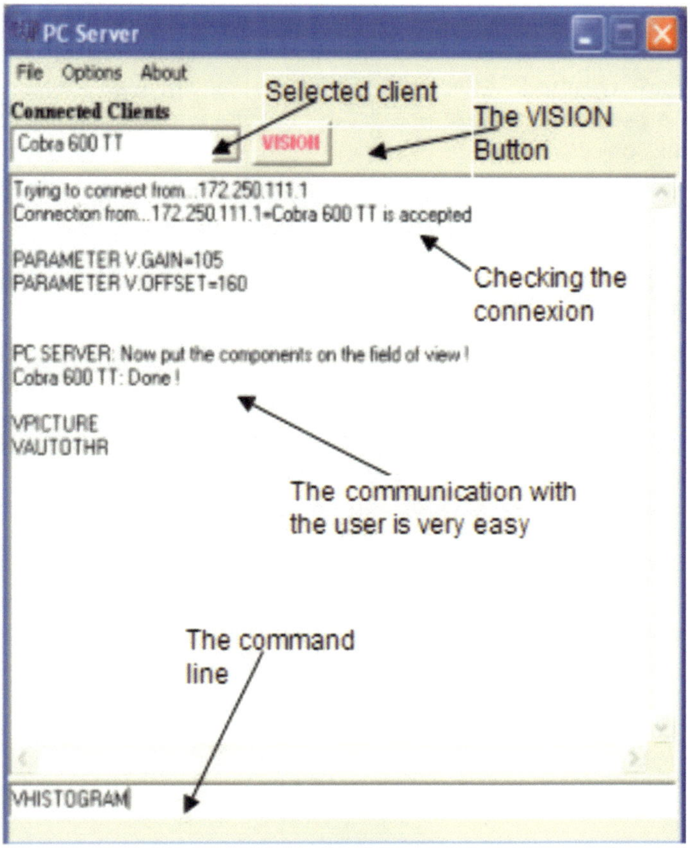

Fig. 6. Command line interface

The most important functions are:
- selecting the physical and virtual cameras, and the virtual image buffers;
- selecting the display mode and the resolution;
- image acquisition;
- issuing primary operations (histogram, thresholding, etc.);
- displaying the vision system status;
  training models;
- switches and parameters configuration for virtual camera set-up.

The advantage of the Vision window is that all commands can be issued using menus, but also the fact that the image acquired by the camera and sent to the server can now be accessed at pixel level. Another major advantage is that the training of the part recognition and grasping models become a single-step process during which a unique window is used for parameters and constraints specification.

The vision window gives the user the possibility to select the physical, and virtual camera to work, gives a set of visual tools to establish the acquisition parameters to obtain a proper image for the application, apply filters, measure objects, or train and recognize object models.
In order to execute vision programs the user must setup the vision parameters in such way that the system will "see" the objects with the best image quality. The system have specialized functions to establish those parameters automatically or, manually if some special settings are required. After setting the parameters and loading the calibration camera-robot, the user can measure objects, apply filters, apply morphological operators, train and recognize objects.
The client application can acquire full or partial images via the VGETPIC V+ operation and send them to the server (Adept Technology, 2001).
Captured image can be processed via the menus (filtering, binarization, convolution, morphing, etc.), saved into a common format and sent to a specialized image processing application. After processing, the image can be sent back to the client and integrated to the image processing board using the VPUTPIC operation, for further use (an application using this mechanism is in course to be developed, and consists in a new part identifying algorithm based on skeleton computation and matching.
A basic approach to representing the structural shape of a manufactured part is to reduce it to a graph. This reduction was carried out by obtaining the *skeleton of the region* via a thinning (also called skeletonizing) algorithm.
The *medial axis transformation* (MAT) of a region R with boundary B is defined as follows: for each point *p* in R, find its closest point in B. If *p* has more than one such neighbour, it is said to belong to the MAT (*skeleton*) of R. The results of the medial axis transformation depend on the particular distance metrics that is selected. The MAT is sensitive to local distortions of the contour and small 'bumps' can give rise to extraneous skeletal lines. Fig. 7 illustrates the MAT of a metallic part having a 'bump'.

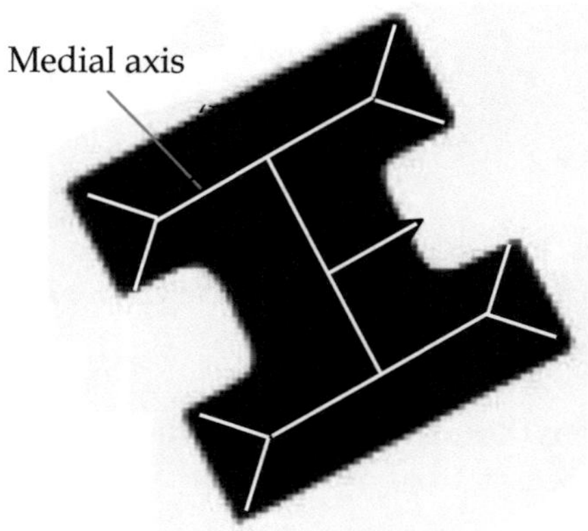

Fig. 7. Medial axis transform (MAT) of a 'T'-shaped part with a lateral 'bump'

An algorithm producing the medial axis representation of a region with improved computational efficiency was chosen based on *thinning* methods that iteratively delete edge points of a region subject to the constraints that deletion of these points: (i) does not remove

end points; (ii) does not break connectedness; (iii) does not cause excessive erosion of the region (Borangiu, 2004), (Borangiu et al., 2005).
Binary region points were assumed to have value 1 and background points to have value 0. Successive passes of two basic steps were applied to the contour points of the given region, where a contour point is any pixel of value 1 and having at least one 8-neighbour valued 0. Fig. 8 shows the definition adopted for the 8-neighbourhood.

p_9	p_2	p_3
p_8	p_1	p_4
p_7	p_6	p_5

0	1	1
0	p_1	0
1	1	0

Fig. 8. Definition (left) and example (right) of the 8 neighbourhood for blob thinning

<u>STEP 1</u>. A contour point p is flagged for deletion if the following conditions hold:

$$\begin{array}{ll} 1.1 & 2 \le N(p_1) \le 6\,; \\ 1.2 & S(p_1) = 1\,; \\ 1.3 & p_2 \cdot p_4 \cdot p_6 = 0\,; \\ 1.4 & p_4 \cdot p_6 \cdot p_8 = 0\,, \end{array} \qquad (1)$$

where $N(p_1)$ is the number of nonzero neighbours of p_1, i.e. $N(p_1) = \sum_{i=2}^{9} p_i$, and $S(p_1)$ is the number of $0 \rightarrow 1$ transitions in the ordered sequence of the bits $p_2, p_3, ..., p_8, p_9$. For the example in Figure 7, $N(p_1) = 4$ and $S(p_1) = 2$.
Step 1 is applied to every contour point in the binary region of interest. If one or more of conditions $(1.1) - (1.4)$ are violated, the value of the respective point is not changed. However, the point is not deleted until *all* contour points have been processed, which prevents changing the structure of the data during execution of the algorithm. After applying step 1 to all border points, those which were flagged are deleted (changed to 0).
<u>STEP 2</u>. A contour point p is flagged for deletion if the following conditions hold:

$$\begin{array}{ll} 2.1 & 2 \le N(p_1) \le 6\,; \\ 2.2 & S(p_1) = 1\,; \\ 2.3 & p_2 \cdot p_4 \cdot p_8 = 0\,; \\ 2.4 & p_2 \cdot p_6 \cdot p_8 = 0\,. \end{array} \qquad (2)$$

Step 2 is applied to data resulting from step 1 in exactly the same manner. After step 2 has been applied to all border points, those that were flagged are deleted (changed from 1 to 0). Thus one iteration of the thinning algorithm consists of:

1. Applying step 1 to flag contour points for deletion.
2. Deleting the point flagged in step 1.

3. Applying step 2 to flag the remaining contour points for deletion.
4. Deleting the points flagged in step 2.

This basic cycle is applied iteratively until no further points were deleted, at which time the algorithm terminates yielding the skeleton of the region.

Such types of applications for which the complexity of the computation is very high were developed on a powerful IBM xSeries server instead of the robot vision controller.

The skeleton computation is included in the measurements category (Borangiu, *et al.*, 2005) which include also signature analysis, polar and linear offset signatures which are computed, and stored to be used in other applications (see sections 4, 5 and 6).

An important feature of the system is the mechanism of training object models and multiple grasping positions related to each model in order to accomplish a collision free grasping position on the runtime.

The training of object models can be done in two wais:

- first is the standard ObjectFinder model, which is computed by the vision board included in the system. The procedure to train such a model requires a set of steps which have been compacted in a single form in the application.
- the second way is to store a set of object features into a structure which characterize each model (Fig. 9.) (Borangiu, 2004).

After the models are trained and stored the user can write applications using the trained models, and/or can learn also grasping positions in order to manipulate the objects (Fig. 10).

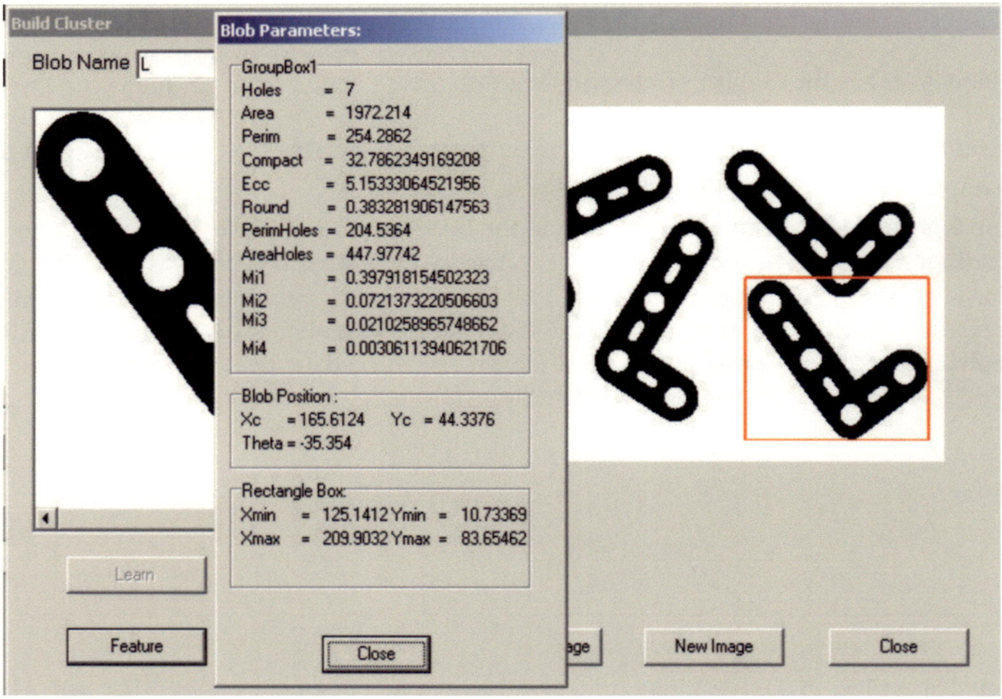

Fig. 9. Building a cluster

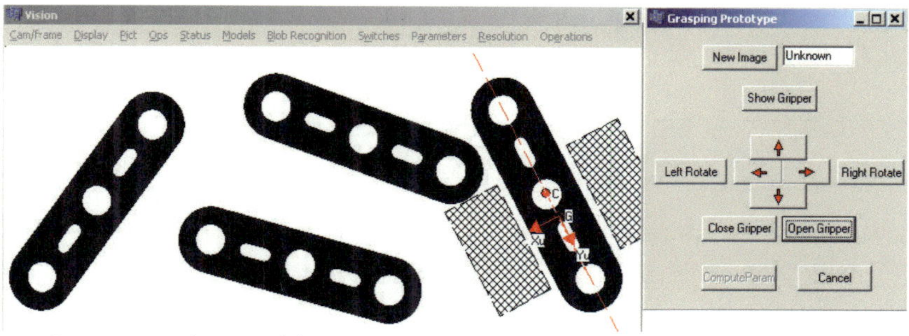

Fig. 10. Learning a grasping position

4. Internal Descriptors of a Region – Scalar Features

Part measurement and recognition are basic functions in merged Guidance Vision for Robots (GVR) and Automated Visual Inspection (AVI) tasks. Internal features describe a region in terms of its internal characteristics (the pixels comprising the body). An internal representation is selected either for the recognition of simple shapes based on sets of *standard intrinsic features* (number of holes, area, perimeter, compactness, eccentricity, invariant moments, etc) or when the primary interest is on reflectivity properties of the object's surface or by statistical, structural or spectral approaches).

Internal scalar transform techniques generate shape descriptors based on the region shape.

One of the most frequently used methods is that of moments. The *standard moments* m_{pq} of order $(p+q)$ of an image intensity function $f(x,y)$ are:

$$m_{pq} = \int_{-\infty}^{\infty}\int_{-\infty}^{\infty} x^p y^q f(x,y)dxdy \quad p,q = 0,1,2,... \tag{3}$$

A uniqueness theorem states that if $f(x,y)$ is piecewise continuous and has nonzero values only in a finite part of the x_{vis}, y_{vis} plane, moments of all order exist and the moment sequence (m_{pq}) is uniquely determined by $f(x,y)$. Conversely, (m_{pq}) uniquely determines $f(x,y)$.

In the discrete domain of digital images, equation (3) is transformed and the sum is carried out over the entire sub-image within which the shape of interest lies, to get the standard moments of $(p+q)$ order of an object O:

$$m_{pq}(O) = \sum_{X=0}^{N_x}\sum_{Y=0}^{N_y} X^p Y^q f_O(X,Y) \quad p,q = 0,1,2,... \tag{4}$$

where:

- $m_{pq}(O)$ is the moment of $(p+q)$ order of object O;
- X,Y are the x,y coordinates of the analysed pixel of object O;

- $f_O(X,Y) = \begin{cases} 0, & \text{pixel not belonging to object } O \\ 1, & \text{pixel belonging to object } O \end{cases}$
- N_x, N_y are the maximum values respectively for the X,Y image coordinates, e.g. $N_x = 640, N_y = 480$.

However, because these moments are computed on the basis of the absolute position of the shape, they will vary for a given shape O depending on its location. To overcome this drawback, one can use the *central moments* of order $(p + q)$:

$$\mu_{pq}(O) = \sum_{X=0}^{N_x} \sum_{Y=0}^{N_y} (X - \overline{X})^p (Y - \overline{Y})^q f_O(X,Y) \quad p,q = 0,1,2,... \tag{5}$$

where $\overline{X} = m_{10} / m_{00}, \overline{Y} = m_{01} / m_{00}$ are the coordinates of the shape's centroid. Thus, these moments take the centroid of the shape as their reference point and hence are position-invariant.

For binary images of objects O, m_{00} is simply computed as the sum of all pixels within the shape. Assuming that a pixel is one unit area then m_{00} is equivalent to the area of the shape expressed in raw pixels.

If the binary image of the object was coded using the run-length coding technique, let us consider that $r_{i,k}$ is the kth run of the ith line and that the first run in each row is a run of zeros. If there are m_i runs on the ith line, and a total of M lines in the image, the area can be computed as the sum of the run lengths corresponding to ones in the image:

$$Area(O) = m_{00}(O) = \sum_{i=1}^{M} \sum_{k=1}^{m_i/2} r_{i,2k} \tag{6}$$

Note that the sum is over the even runs only.

Similarly, m_{10} and m_{01} are effectively obtained respectively by the summation of all the *x*-coordinates and *y*-coordinates of pixels in the shape.

The central moments up to order three are given as expressed in (7):

$$\begin{aligned}
&\mu_{00} = m_{00} \quad \mu_{11} = m_{11} - \overline{Y} m_{10} \\
&\mu_{10} = 0 \quad \mu_{30} = m_{30} - 3\overline{X} m_{20} + 2\overline{X}^2 m_{10} \\
&\mu_{01} = 0 \quad \mu_{03} = m_{03} - 3\overline{Y} m_{02} + 2\overline{Y}^2 m_{01} \\
&\mu_{20} = m_{20} - \overline{X} m_{10} \quad \mu_{12} = m_{12} - 2\overline{Y} m_{11} - \overline{X} m_{02} + 2\overline{Y}^2 m_{10} \\
&\mu_{02} = m_{02} - \overline{Y} m_{01} \quad \mu_{21} = m_{21} - 2\overline{X} m_{11} - \overline{Y} m_{20} + 2\overline{X}^2 m_{01}
\end{aligned} \tag{7}$$

The central moments can be normalized, defining a set of normalized central moments, η_{pq}, and having the expression $\eta_{pq}(O) = \mu_{pq}(O) / \mu_{00}(O)^k$, where $k = (p+q)/2+1,\ p+q = 2, 3, \ldots$.

Moment invariants are preferred for shape description as they generate values which are invariant to translation, rotation, and scale changes. Equation (8) describes a set of seven *invariant moments* which are derived from the second and third normalized central moments.

Shape descriptors based on moment invariants convey significant information for simple objects but fail to do so for complicated ones. Since we are dealing with internal scalar transform descriptors, it would seem that these moments can only be generated from the entire region. However, they can also be generated from the boundary of the object by exploiting the theorems of Stoke or Green, both of which relate the integral over an area to an integral around its contour (Ams, 2002).

$$
\begin{aligned}
\phi_1 &= \eta_{20} + \eta_{02} \\
\phi_2 &= (\eta_{20} - \eta_{02})^2 + 4\eta_{11}^{\ 2} \\
\phi_3 &= (\eta_{30} - 3\eta_{12})^2 + (3\eta_{21} - \eta_{03})^2 \\
\phi_4 &= (\eta_{30} + \eta_{12})^2 + (\eta_{21} + \eta_{03})^2 \\
\phi_5 &= (\eta_{30} - 3\eta_{12})(\eta_{30} + \eta_{12})[(\eta_{30} + \eta_{12})^2 - 3(\eta_{21} + \eta_{03})^2] + \\
&\quad (3\eta_{21} - \eta_{03})(\eta_{21} + \eta_{03})[3(\eta_{30} + \eta_{12})^2 - (\eta_{21} + \eta_{03})^2] \\
\phi_6 &= (\eta_{20} - \eta_{02})[(\eta_{30} + \eta_{12}) - (\eta_{21} + \eta_{03})^2] + \\
&\quad 4\eta_{11}(\eta_{30} + \eta_{12})(\eta_{21} + \eta_{03}) \\
\phi_7 &= (3\eta_{21} - \eta_{03})(\eta_{30} + \eta_{12})[(\eta_{30} + \eta_{12})^2 - 3(\eta_{21} + \eta_{03})^2] - \\
&\quad (3\eta_{12} - \eta_{30})(\eta_{21} + \eta_{03})[3(\eta_{30} + \eta_{12})^2 - (\eta_{21} + \eta_{03})^2]
\end{aligned}
\tag{8}
$$

The simplest internal scalar feature of a region to be identified in robot-vision tasks is its *area*, defined as the number of pixels contained within its boundary. *Compactness* and *roundness* can also be considered as scalar region descriptors, as their formulae contain the blob's area. Compactness is a dimensionless feature and thus is invariant to scale changes.

The *principal axes* of a region are the eigenvectors of the covariance matrix obtained by using the pixels within the region as random variables.

One solution adopted frequently to overcome this difficulty is to use as an internal scalar transform descriptor the ratio of the large to the small eigenvalue. Other simple internal scalar descriptors based on the region's area are:

- The *ratio of the areas of the original blob to that of its convex hull.*
- The *ratio of the area of the original blob to that of its circumcircle.*
- The *ratio of the area of the original shape to the area of the minimal bounding rectangle*. This is a measure of rectangularity and is maximized for perfectly rectangular shapes.
- The *ratio of the area of the original blob to the square of the total limb-length of its skeleton.*

Topological properties are used for global descriptions of regions. Such properties are not affected by any deformation (e.g. stretching). Note that, as stretching affects distances, topological properties do not depend on the notion of distance or any properties implicitly

based on the concept of distance measure. A widely used topological descriptor is the *number of holes in the region,* which is not affected by stretching or rotation transformations (Fogel, 1994; Ghosh, 1988).
The number of holes H and connected components C in a region can be used to define another topological feature - the *Euler number E* of a region:

$$E = C - H \tag{9}$$

Recall that a connected component of a set is a subset of maximal size such that any two of its points can be joined by a connected curve lying entirely within the subset. Fig. 11 exemplifies the above defined topological descriptors for the blob image of a carburettor flange:

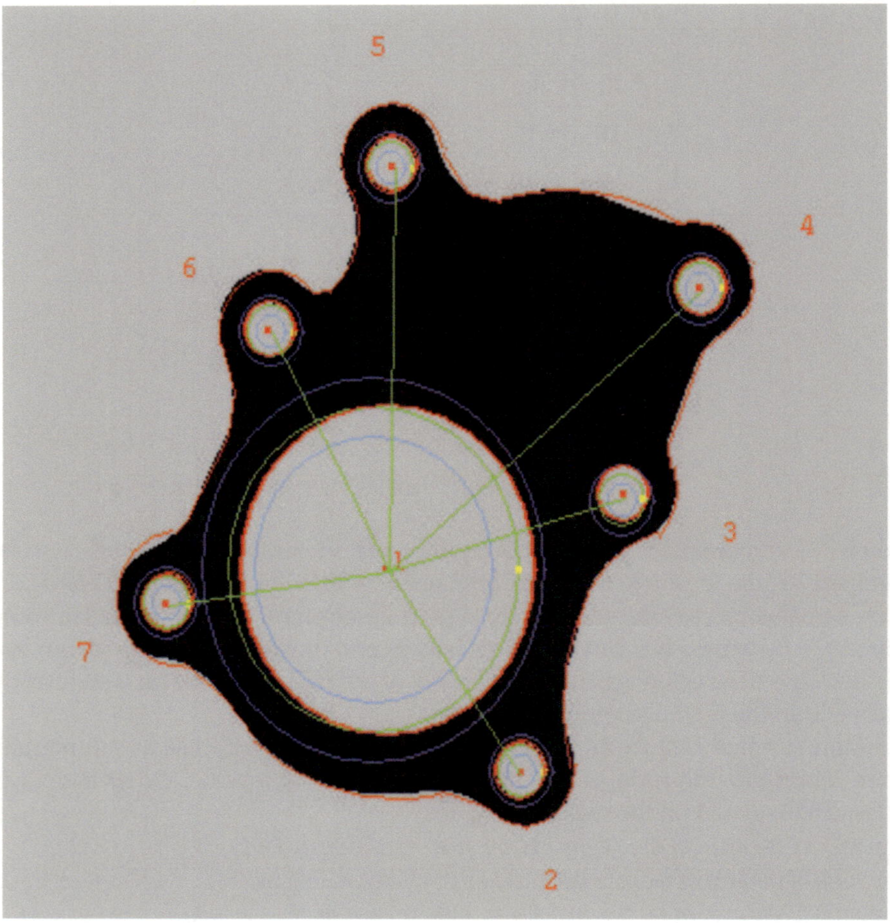

Fig. 11. Topological descriptors of a region: number of holes, $H = 7$, number of connected components, $C = 1$, and Euler number, $E = -6$.

5. Space Domain Descriptors of Boundaries: The Signatures

External space domain features describe the spatial organization of the object's boundary. One frequently used technique is the use of syntactic descriptors of *boundary primitives*, e.g. atomic edges (lines and arcs), and corners. Thus, the list of shape descriptors (or string of primitive shapes) must follow given rules: the *shape syntax* or grammar.
Signatures are 1-D functional representations of boundaries and may be generated in various ways, for example as polar radii signatures or linear offset signatures. Regardless of how a signature is generated, however, the main idea approached in the present research devoted to real-time visual analysis of parts handled by robots is to reduce the boundary representation to a 1-D function, which is easier to describe than the original 2-D boundary (Borangiu and Calin, 1996; Camps, et al., 1991).
A *polar radii signature,* encoding the distance from the shape centroid to the shape boundary as a function of angle θ, is shown in Fig. 12.

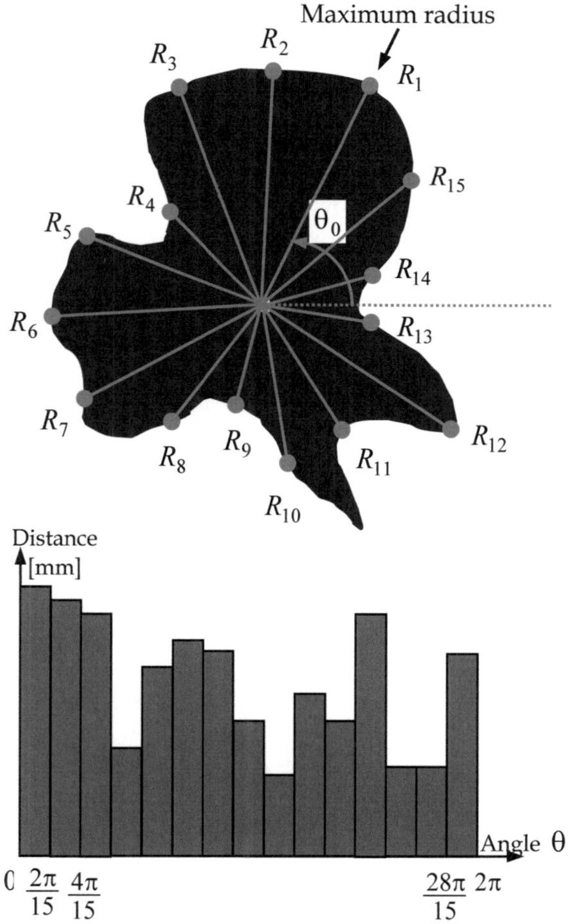

Fig. 12. Angular radii signature of a shape. A 15-element vector $[R_1, R_2,..., R_{15}]$ is defined, where $R_i, i = 1,...,15$ is the distance from the centroid to the edge of the blob, measured at an angle of $(\theta_0 + 24i)$ degrees, and θ_0 is the orientation derived from the greatest radius, R_1

Such polar radii signatures are invariant to translation, but they do depend on rotation and scaling. To rend such signatures invariant to rotation, there must be found a method to select the same starting point to generate the signature, regardless of the shape's orientation. One possibility is to choose the starting point as the point on the boundary farthest from the blob's centroid, but only if this point is unique and independent of rotational aberrations for each class of objects of interest. Another solution is to select the starting point on the axis of least inertia farthest from the centroid. This method requires more computation, but is more rugged because the direction of the major eigen axis is determined from the covariance matrix, which is based on all boundary points.

Based on the assumption of uniformity in scaling with respect to both axes and that sampling is taken at equal intervals of θ, changes in size of a shape result in changes in the amplitude values of the corresponding signature. One simple way to normalize for the result is to scale all functions so that they span the same range of values, e.g. $[0,1]$. The advantage of this method is simplicity, but the potential drawback is that scaling of the entire function depends on only two values: the minimum and the maximum. If the shapes are noisy, this dependence can be a source of error from one object class instance to the other.

A more robust approach is to divide each sample by the variance of the signature, assuming that the variance is greater than a residual value and hence does not create computational difficulties. Use of the variance yields a variable scaling factor that is inversely proportional to changes in the shape's size.

A linear offset signature, encoding the distance from the axis of least inertia to the shape boundary as a function of distance *d*, is also a space descriptor of the contour. The shape in Fig. 13 has contour segments parallel to its major eigen axis.

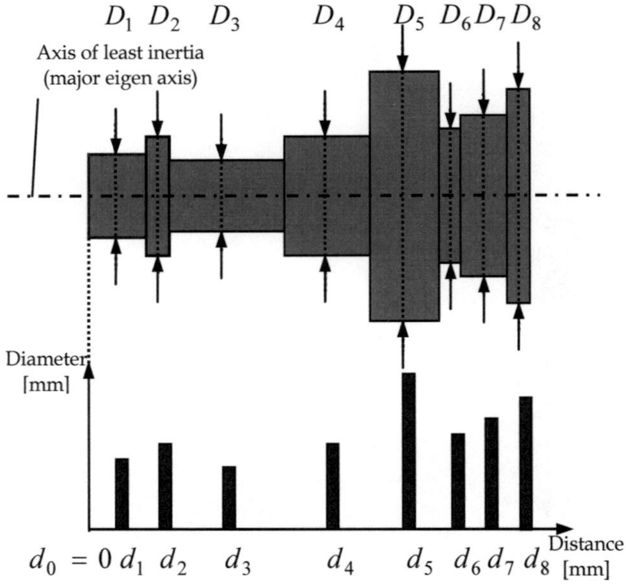

Fig. 13. Linear offset signature of a lathe-turned shape. An 8-element vector $[D_1, D_2, ..., D_8]$ is defined, where D_i, $i = 1,...,8$ is the twice the distance from the minimum inertia axis to the edge of the blob, measured respectively at $d_i, i = 1,...,8$ mm from the "small lateral" edge of the shape

It can be observed that in this case sampling is not taken at equal intervals of d, i.e. $d_i - d_{i-1} \neq \text{const}, \; i = 1,...,8$.

External space domain descriptors based on signatures are generally simple, and require reduced storage capability.

More complex space domain descriptors are often based on the Fourier series expansion of a periodic function derived from the boundary. For example, the boundary could be traversed at the angle plotted between a line tangent to the boundary and a reference line as a function of position along the boundary.

Consider, for example, the shape depicted in Fig. 14. The rotation angle θ of the tangent at the boundary of the object varies between 0 and 2π radians as the boundary is traversed. In particular, θ will vary with the distance s around the perimeter and can be expressed as a function, $\theta(s)$, called *slope of the boundary.*

Fig. 14. The slope is obtained by rotation of tangent to the boundary of the shape

If L is the length of the boundary of the shape, $\theta(0) = 0$ and $\theta(L) = -2\pi$. However, the function $\theta(s)$ is not periodic, and consequently it cannot be expressed in terms of a Fourier series expansion. An alternative formulation, suggested by Zhan and Roskies (1972), defines a new function, $\phi(t)$:

$$\phi(t) = \theta(\frac{Lt}{2\pi}) + t \tag{10}$$

Now, $\phi(0) = \phi(2\pi) = 0$, and the function $\phi(t)$ is invariant to scaling, translation and rotation of the shape; hence, the low-order coefficients of its Fourier expansion can be used as features for translation, rotation, and scaling in shape recognition.

A variation of this approach is to use the so-called *slope density function* as a signature. This function is simply a histogram of tangent-angle values. As a histogram is a measure of concentration of values, the slope density function highlights sections of the boundary with constant tangent angles (straight or nearly straight segments) and has deep valleys in sections producing rapidly varying angles (corners or sharp inflexions).

The *curvature* is defined as the rate of change of the slope. In general, obtaining reliable measures of curvature at a point in a digital boundary is difficult because the boundaries tend to be locally "ragged". A solution consists into using the difference between the slopes of adjacent atomic boundary segments (e.g. represented as straight lines) as a descriptor of curvature at the point of intersection of the segments.

6. Experimental Results for Signature Analysis

The reported research was directed towards integrating a set of efficient, high-speed vision tools: *Windows Region of Interest* (WROI), point-, line-, and arc *finders*, and linear and circular *rulers* into an algorithm of interactive signature analysis of classes of mechanical parts tracked by robots in a flexible production line. To check the geometry and identify parts using the signature, you must follow the steps:

1. Train an object

   The object must represent very well its class - it must be "perfect". The object is placed in the plane of view and then the program which computes the signature is executed; the position and orientation of the object is changed and the procedure is repeated for a few times.

   The user must specify for the first sample the starting point, the distances between each ruler and the length of each ruler. For the example in Fig. 15 of a **linear offset signature**, one can see that the distances between rulers (measurements) are user definable.

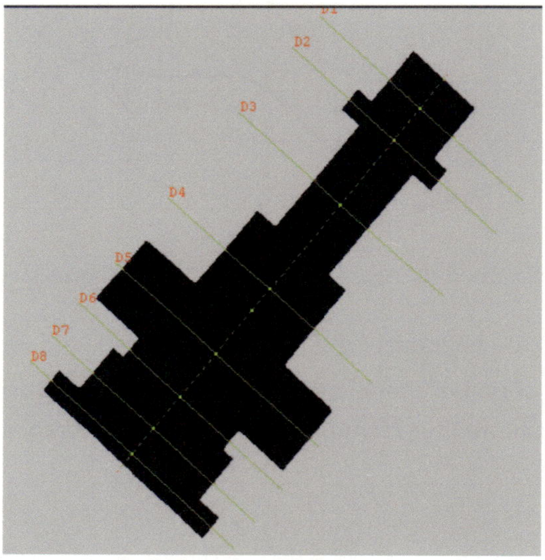

Fig. 15 The linear offset signature of a lathe-turned shape

   If we want to compute a **polar signature** the user must specify the starting point and the angle between each measure.

   During the training session, the user can mark some edges (linear or circular) of particular interest that will be further searched and analysed in the recognition phase. For example if we want to verify if a linear edge is inclined at a certain angle with respect to the part's Minimal Inertia Axis (MIA), the start and the end point of this edge will be marked with the mouse of the IBM PC terminal of the robot-vision system. In a similar way, if a circular edge must be selected, we will mark the start point, the end point and a third point on that arc-shaped edge.

   The program computes one type of signature according to the object's class. The class is automatically defined by the program from the numerical values of a computed set of

standard scalar internal descriptors: compactness, eccentricity, roundness, invariant moments, number of bays, a.o.
After the training the object has associated a class, a signature, a name and two parameters: the tolerance and the percentage of verification.

2. Setting the parameters used for recognition
   - The *tolerance*: each measure of the recognized object must be into a range: (original measure ± the tolerance value). The tolerance can be modified anytime by the user and will be applied at run time by the application program.
   - The *percentage of verification*: specifies how many measures can be out of range (100% - every measure must be in the range, 50% - the maximum number of rulers that can be out of range is ½ of the total number). The default value of the percentage of verification proposed by the application is 95%.
3. The recognition stage
   The sequence of operations used for measuring and recognition of mechanical parts includes: taking a picture, computation of the class to which the object in the WROI belongs, and finally applying the associated set of vision tools to evaluate the particular signature for all trained objects of this class.
   The design of the signature analysis program has been performed using specific vision tools on an Adept Cobra 600 TT robot, equipped with a GP-MF602 Panasonic camera and AVI vision processor.
   The length measurements were computed using linear rulers (VRULERI), and checking for the presence of linear and circular edges was based respectively on the finder tools VFIND.ARC and VFIND.LINE (Adept, 2001).

The pseudo-code below summarizes the principle of the interactive learning during the training stage and the real time computation process during the recognition stage.

i) Training

1. *Picture acquisition*
2. *Selecting the object class* (from the computed values of internal descriptors: compactness, roundness,...)
3. *Suggesting the type of signature analysis*:
   Linear Offset Signature (LOF)
   specify the starting point and the linear offsets
   Polar Signature (PS)
   specify the starting point and the incremental angle
4. *Specify the particular edges to be verified*
5. *Improve the measurements?*
   Compute repeatedly only the signature (the position of the object is changed every time)
   Update the mean value of the signature.
6. *Compute the recognition parameters* (tolerance, percentage of verification) and *name* the learned model.
7. *Display the results and terminate the training sequence.*

ii) Run time measurement and recognition

1. *Picture acquisition*
2. *Identifying the object class* (using the compactness, roundness,... descriptors)
3. *Computing the associated signature analysis* for each class model trained.
4. *Checking the signature against its trained value,* and inspecting the particular edges (if any) using finder and ruler tools
5. *Returning the results* to the AVI program or GVR robot motion planner (the name of the recognized object, or void).
6. *Updating the reports* about inspected and/or manipulated (assembled) parts; sequence terminated.

Fig. 16 and Table 1 show the results obtained for a polar signature of a leaf-shaped object.

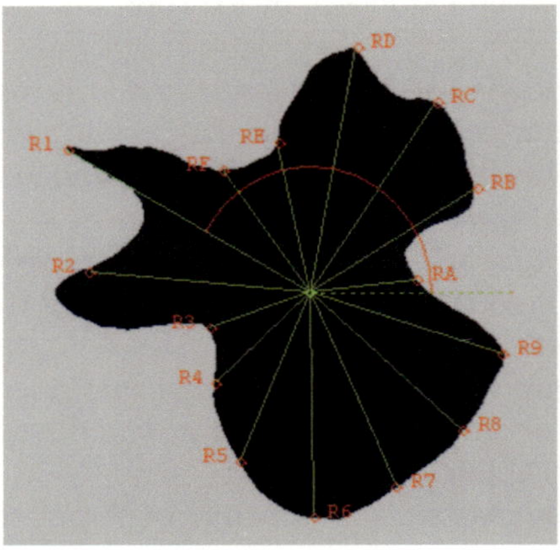

Fig. 16. Computing the polar signature of a blob

Parameter	Min value (min)	Max value (max)	Mean value (*avg*)	Dispersion (*disp*)	Number of ruler tools used
*R*1	68.48	70.46	68.23	1.98	1
*R*2	56.59	58.44	57.02	1.85	1
*R*3	26.68	28.42	27.41	1.74	1
*R*4	32.24	34.03	33.76	1.52	1
*R*5	44.82	45.92	45.42	1.10	1
*R*6	54.07	55.92	54.83	1.85	1
*R*7	51.52	52.76	52.05	1.24	1
*R*8	50.39	51.62	50.98	1.23	1
*R*9	49.15	51.18	49.67	2.03	1
RA	25.41	26.98	26.22	1.57	1
RB	47.41	48.68	47.91	1.27	1
RC	53.71	55.30	54,64	1.59	1
RD	57.79	59.51	58.61	1.72	1
RE	35.69	37.39	36.80	1.70	1
RF	35.42	36.72	36.17	1.30	1

Table 1. Statistical results for the polar radii signature of the leaf-shaped object

The dispersion was calculated for each parameter $P_i, i = 1,...,10$ as: $disp(P_i) = max(P_i) - min(P_i)$, and is expressed in the same units as the parameter (millimetres or degrees). The min/max values are: $min = min(P_i)$, $max = max(P_i)$. The expression of the mean value is: $avg = \frac{1}{10}\sum_i P_i$.

7. The Supervising Function

The server application is capable to command and supervise multiple client stations (Fig. 17). The material flow is supervised using the client stations and the status from each station is recorded into a data base.

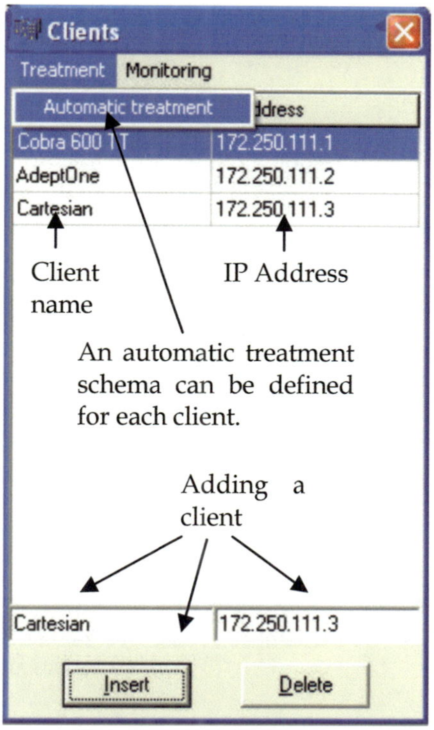

Fig. 17. Automatic treatment

For the supervising function a variable and signals list is attached to each client (Fig. 18). The variables and signals are verified by the clients using a chosen strategy, and if a modification occurs, the client sends to the server a message with the state modification. Supervising can be based on a predefined timing or permanent.

If the status of a signal or variable is changed the server analyse the situation and take a measure to treat the event, so each client has a list of conditions or events that are associated with a set of actions to be executed (Fig. 19). This feature removes much more from the human intervention, the appropriate measures being taken by a software supervisor.

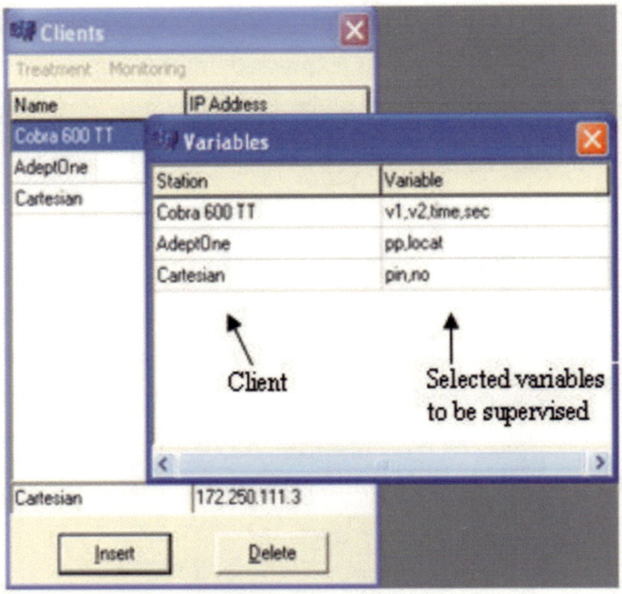

Fig. 18. Selecting the variables and the signals to be supervised

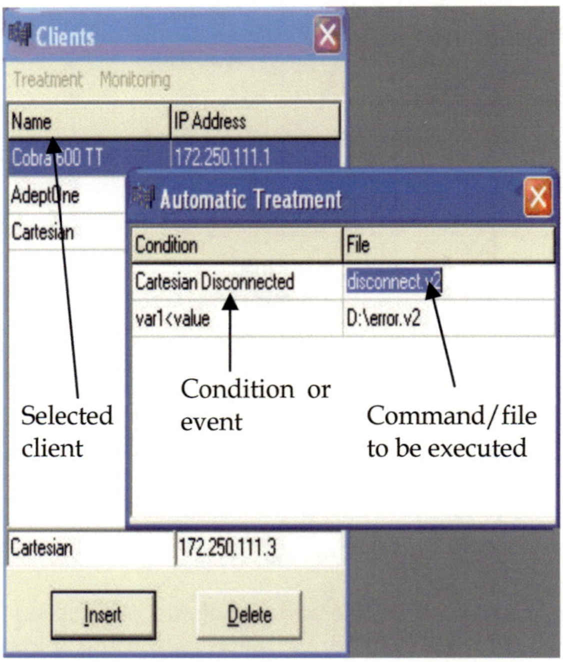

Fig. 19. Selecting the events and the actions to be automatically taken

When the *supervise* mode is selected, the server sends to the client (using a message with header '/T') the variable list to be supervised and the time interval when the client must verify the status of the variables (in the case when the supervise mode is periodical).

The events which trigger response actions can be produced by reaction programs run by the controller (REACTI or REACTE type) or by special user commands from the terminal. The list of actions contains direct commands for the robot (ABORT, KILL 0, DETACH, etc) and program execution commands (EXECUTE, CALL).

8. Conclusions

The project was finished at the end of 2008 as part of the PRIC research program (Shared Research and Training Resources).
The research project provide a communication and collaboration portal solution for linking the existing pilot platform with multiple V+ industrial robot-vision controllers from Adept Technology located in four University Labs from Romania (Bucharest, Craiova, Iasi and Galati). This allow teachers to train their student using robots and expensive devices which they do not dispose, and allow students to practice their skills using specialised labs without geographical barriers, and even from home. Also the portal will allow team training and research due to the messaging feature introduced by Domino.
The fault tolerance solution presented in this paper is worth to be considered in environments where the production structure has the possibility to reconfigure, and where the manufacturing must assure a continuous production flow at batch level (job shop flow).
The spatial layout and configuring of robots must be done such that one robot will be able to take the functions of another robot in case of failure. If this involves common workspaces, programming must be made with much care using robot synchronizations and monitoring continuously the current position of the manipulator.
The advantages of the proposed solution are that the structure provides a high availability robotized work structure with an insignificant downtime due to the automated monitoring and treatment function.
In some situations the solution could be considered as a fault tolerant system due to the fact that even if a robot controller failed, the production can continue in normal conditions by triggering and treating each event using customized functions.
The project can be accessed at: http://pric.cimr.pub.ro.

9. References

Adept Technology Inc., (2001). *AdeptVision Reference Guide Version 14.0 Part Number 00964-03000,* San Jose, Technical Publications.

Ams, E. (2002). Eine für alles ?, *Computer & Automation*, No. **5**, pp. 22-25.

Anton F., D., Borangiu, Th., Tunaru, S., Dogar, A., and S. Gheorghiu. (2006). Remote Monitoring and Control of a Robotized Fault Tolerant Workcell, *Proc. of the 12th IFAC Sympos. on Information Control Problems in Manufacturing INCOM'06*, Elsevier.

Borangiu, TH. and L. Calin (1996). Task Oriented Programming of Adaptive Robots and Integration in Fault-Tolerant Manufacturing Systems, *Proc. of the Int. Conf. on Industrial Informatics, Section 4 Robotics, Lille*, pp. 221-226.

Borangiu, Th., (2004). Intelligent Image Processing in Robotics and Manufacturing, Romanian Academy Press, Bucharest.

Borangiu, Th., F.D. Anton, S. Tunaru and N.-A. Ivanescu, (2005). Integrated Vision Tools And Signature Analysis For Part Measurement And Recognition In Robotic Tasks, IFAC World Congress, Prague.

Borangiu, Th., Anton F., D., Tunaru, S., and A. Dogar. (2006). A Holonic Fault Tolerant Manufacturing Platform with Multiple Robots, Proc. of *15th Int. Workshop on Robotics in Alpe-Adria-Danube Region RAAD 2006.*

Brooks, K., R. Dhaliwal, K. O'Donnell, E. Stanton, K. Sumner and S. Van Herzele, (2004). *Lotus Domino 6.5.1 and Extended Products Integration Guide,* IBM RedBooks.

Camps, O.I., L.G. Shapiro and R.M. Harlick (1991). PREMIO: An overview, Proc. IEEE Workshop on Directions in Automated CAD-Based Vision, pp. 11-21.

Fogel, D.B. (1994). Evolutionary Computation: Toward a New Philosophy of Machine Intelligence, IEEE Press, New York.

Ghosh, P. (1988). A mathematical model foe shape description using Minkowski operators, *Computer Vision Graphics Image Processing,* **44**, pp. 239-269.

Harris, N., Armingaud, F., Belardi, M., Hunt, C., Lima, M., Malchisky Jr., W., Ruibal, J., R. and J. Taylor, (2004). *Linux Handbook: A guide to IBM Linux Solutions and Resources,* IBM Int. Technical Support Organization, 2nd Edition.

Tomas Balibrea, L.M., L.A. Gonzales Contreras and M. Manu (1997). *Object Oriented Model of an Open Communication Architecture for Flexible Manufacturing Control,* Computer Science 1333 - Computer Aided System Theory, pp. 292-300, EUROCAST '97, Berlin.

Zhan, C.T. and R.Z. Roskies (1972). Fourier descriptors for plane closed curves, *IEEE Trans. Computers,* Vol. **C-21**, pp. 269-281.

Network-based Vision Guidance of Robot for Remote Quality Control

Yongjin (James) Kwon[1], Richard Chiou[2], Bill Tseng[3] and Teresa Wu[4]
[1]*Industrial and Information Systems Engineering*
Ajou University
Suwon, South Korea, 443-749
[2]*Applied Engineering Technology*
Drexel University
Philadelphia, PA 19104, USA
[3]*Industrial Engineering*
The University of Texas at El Paso
El Paso, TX 79968, USA
[4]*Industrial Engineering*
Arizona State University
Tempe, AZ 85287, USA

1. Introduction

A current trend for manufacturing industry is shorter product life cycle, remote monitoring/control/diagnosis, product miniaturization, high precision, zero-defect manufacturing and information-integrated distributed production systems for enhanced efficiency and product quality (Cohen, 1997; Bennis et al., 2005; Goldin et al., 1998; Goldin et al., 1999; Kwon et al., 2004). In tomorrow's factory, design, manufacturing, quality, and business functions will be fully integrated with the information management network (SME, 2001; Center for Intelligent Maintenance Systems, 2005). This new paradigm is coined with the term, e-manufacturing. In short, "e-manufacturing is a system methodology that enables the manufacturing operations to successfully integrate with the functional objectives of an enterprise through the use of Internet, tether-free (wireless, web, etc.) and predictive technologies" (Koc et al., 2002; Lee, 2003). In fact, the US Integrated Circuit (IC) chip fabrication industries routinely perform remote maintenance and monitoring of production equipment installed in other countries (Iung, 2003; Rooks, 2003). For about the past decades, semiconductor manufacturing industry prognosticators have been predicting that larger wafers will eventually lead the wafer fabrication facilities to become fully automated and that the factories will be operated "lights out", i.e., with no humans in the factory. Those predictions have now become a reality. Intel's wafer fabrication facilities in Chandler, Arizona, USA, are now controlled remotely and humans only go inside the facility to fix the problems. All operators and supervisors now work in a control room, load/unload wafers through commands issued over an Intranet. Within the e-manufacturing paradigm, e-quality for manufacture (EQM) is a holistic approach to designing and embedding efficient quality control functions into the network-integrated production systems. Though strong emphasis has been given to the application of network-based technologies into comprehensive quality control, challenges remain as to how to improve the overall operational efficiency and how to improve the quality of the product being remotely manufactured. Commensurate with the trends, the authors designed and implemented a network-controllable production system to explore the use of various components including robots, machine vision systems, programmable logic controllers, and sensor networks to address EQM issues (see Fig. 1).

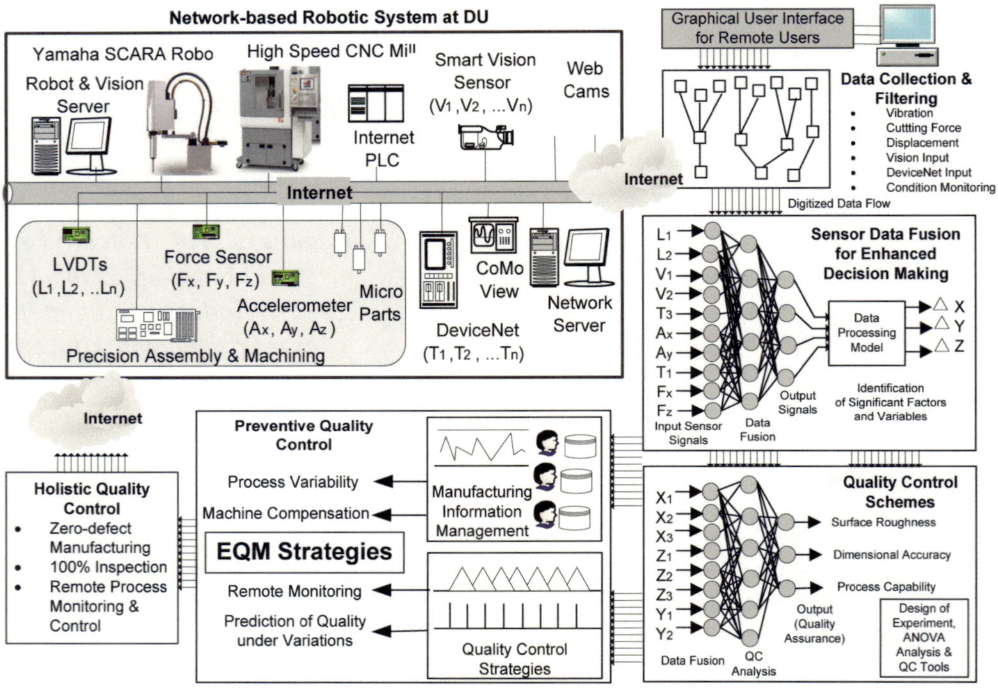

Fig. 1. The proposed concept of EQM within the framework of network-based robotic system developed at Drexel University (DU)

Each component in the system has the access to the network and can be monitored and controlled from a remote site. Such circumstance presents unprecedented benefits to the current production environment for more efficient process control and faster response to any changes. The prototype system implemented enables this research, that is, improving the remote quality control by tackling one of the most common problems in vision-based robotic control (i.e., difficulties associates with vision calibration and subsequent robotic control based on vision input). The machine vision system, robot, and control algorithms are integrated over the network in the form of Application Control Interface (ACI), which effectively controls the motion of robot. Two machine vision systems track moving objects on a conveyor, and send the *x*, *y*, *z* coordinate information to the ACI algorithm that better estimates the position of moving objects with system motion information (speed, acceleration, etc.). Specifically, the vision cameras capture 2D images (top and side views of part) and combine to get the 3D information of object position. The position accuracy is affected by the distance of parts to the image plane within the camera field of view. The data, such as image processing time and moving speed of the conveyor, can be combined to approximate the position. The study presented in this paper illustrates the benefits of combining e-manufacturing with information-integrated remote quality control techniques. Such concept (i.e., the combination of EQM and e-manufacturing) is novel, and it is based on the prediction that the industry will need an integrated approach to further enhance its production efficiency and to reduce operational costs. Therefore, this study manifests the future direction of e-quality integrated, networked production system, which is becoming a mainstay of global manufacturing corporations.

2. Review of Related Literature

2.1 Technical challenges in network-based systems integrated with EQM

E-manufacturing allows geographically separated users to have their designs evaluated and eventually produced over the network. Using a web browser, a remote operator can program and monitor the production equipment and its motions with visual feedback via the network in real-time. EQM may represent many different concepts in automated production environment, such as 100%, sensor-based online inspection of manufactured goods, network-based process control, rule-based automatic process adjustment, and remote, real-time monitoring of part quality. Industrial automation processes, primarily for pick-and-place operations involving robots, use various sensors to detect the movement of product on a conveyor and guide the robot for subsequent operations. Such system requires precise calibration of each sensors and tracking devices, usually resulting in a very complex and time consuming setup. In Bone and Capson's study (2003), automotive components were assembled using a vision guided robot without the use of conventional fixtures and jigs, which saved the time and cost of production operations. In the study, a host computer was connected through the LAN (local area network) to control the robot, vision system, robot gripper, system control architecture, etc. The coordinates of workcell devices were measured by the vision sensor and the information was transmitted to the robot over the LAN. The loss rate and temporal communication delays commonly occurring in the Internet have been clearly outlined in the study. The same was true in Lal and Onwubolu (2008), where the customized, three tiered web-based manufacturing system was developed. For hardware, a three-axis computer numerically controlled drilling machine was remotely operated and the results showed that a remote user's submission job time was largely dependent on the bandwidth. In fact, the communication time delay problem has been the active research topic since the 1960s, and abundant study materials exist in dealing with delay related problems (Brady & Tarn, 2000). However, the communication linkage between the operator and remote devices are limited by the bandwidth, thus, time-varying delays can only be reduced to some extent. Even a small delay can seriously degrade the intuition of remote operators. Therefore, Brady and Tarn (2000) developed a predictive display system to provide intuitive visual feedback to the operators. Existing industry practices, e.g., network-based factory and office automation usually require a three-layer architecture of information communication, including device-connection layer, equipment-control layer, and information-management layer. The time and cost encountered for setting up the layered communication system prohibits the broader applications. As a result, Ethernet technologies (e.g., Fast Ethernet and Ethernet Switch) are becoming a mainstay of factory automation networking to replace the traditional industrial networks (Hung et al., 2004). Development of web-based manufacturing system is also abundant in literature, mainly dealing with the integration architecture between devices, equipment, servers, and information networks in distributed shop floor manufacturing environment (Wang & Nace, 2009; Kang et al., 2007; Xu et al., 2005; Wang et al., 2004; Lu & Yih, 2001; Smith & Wright, 1996). Lal and Onwubolu (2007) developed a framework for three-tiered web-based manufacturing system to address the critical issues in handling the data loss and out-of-order delivery of data, including coordinating multi-user access, susceptibility to temporal communication delays, and online security problems. The study well illustrated the problems in Internet-based tele-operation of manufacturing systems. The same problems have been well outlined in Luo et al. (2003), which predicted that the use of Internet in terms of controlling remote robots will ever increase due to its convenience. However, despite the numerous studies conducted by many field experts, solving the delay related problems of the Internet would remain as a challenging task for many years (Wang et al., 2004).

2.2 Calibration for vision-guided robotics in EQM

Technical complications in vision-guided robotics stem from the challenges in how to attain precise alignment of image planes with robot axes, and the calibration of image coordinates against corresponding robot coordinates, which involve expensive measuring instruments and lengthy derivation of complex mathematical relationships (Emilio et al., 2002; Emilio et al., 2003; Bozma & Yal-cin, 2002; Maurício et al., 2001; Mattone et al., 2000; Wilson et al., 2000). Generally speaking, robot calibration refers to the procedure during start-up for establishing the point of reference for each joint, from which all subsequent points are based, or the procedure for measuring and determining robot pose errors to enable the robot controller to compensate for positioning errors (Greenway, 2000; Review of techniques, 1998; Robot calibration, 1998). The latter is a critical process when (1) robots are newly installed and their performance characteristics are unknown, (2) the weight of end-of-arm tooling changes significantly, (3) robots are mounted on a different fixture, and (4) there is a need for robot performance analysis. To position a robot at a desired location with a certain orientation, a chain of homogeneous transformation matrixes that contain the joint and link values mathematically model the geometry and configuration of the robot mechanism. This kinematic modeling, which is stored in a robot controller, assumes the robot mechanism is perfect, hence no deviations are considered between the calculated trajectories and the actual robot coordinates (Greenway, 2000; Review of techniques, 1998). In addressing kinematic modeling, robot calibration research has three main objectives related to robot errors: (1) robot error parameter modeling, (2) a measurement system for collecting pose error measurements, and (3) parameter identification algorithms. Despite extensive research efforts, most calibration systems require complicated mathematical modeling and expensive measuring devices, both of which entail special training, lengthy setups and substantial downtime costs on companies (Greenway, 2000; Robot calibration, 1998; Review of techniques, 1998). Even after errors are mathematically modeled, calibration becomes susceptible to slight changes in setup. Consequently, only a few calibration methods have been practical, simple, economical and quick enough for use with industrial robots (Maurício et al., 2001; Albada et al., 1994; Emilio et al., 2003; Hidalgo & Brunn, 1998; Janocha

& Diewald, 1995; Lin & Lu, 1997; Meng & Zhuang, 2001; Meng & Zhuang, 2007; Young & Pickin, 2000). Another compounding factor is introduced when a robot's position is controlled via a machine vision system. The transformation of camera pixel coordinates into corresponding robot coordinate points requires not only a precise alignment between the robot and vision systems' primary axes, while maintaining a fixed camera focal length, but also a precise mapping between the camera field of view and the robot workspace bounded by the field of view. Slight discrepancies in alignment and boundary delineation usually result in robot positioning errors, which are further inflated by other factors, such as lens distortion effects and inconsistent lighting conditions. Indeed, visual tracking has been the interests of industry and academia for many years, and still an active area of research (Bozma & Yal-cin, 2002). These studies commonly investigate the optimal way of detecting the moving object, separating them from the background, and efficiently extracting information from the images for subsequent operations (Cheng & Jafari , 2008; Bouganis & Shanahan, 2007; Lee et al., 2007; Golnabi & Asadpour, 2007; Tsai et al., 2006; Ling et al., 2005; Stewart, 1999; Yao, 1998). Note vision related studies suffer from technical difficulties in lighting irregularities, optical distortions, calibration, overlapped parts, inseparable features in the image, variations in settings, etc. Even though many years of efforts have been dedicated to the vision research, finding an optimal solution is highly application dependent and no universal model exists in motion tracking.

3. System Setup

At Drexel University, the network-based robotic systems have been under development in the last five years. The aim is to develop robotic, vision, and micro machining systems integrated with sensor networks, which can be accessed and controlled through the Internet. Each equipment has own IP address for network-based data transfer and communication. Some of the constituents include micro/macro-scale robots (Yamaha SCARA YK-150X, YK-220X & YK-250X), a high speed computer numerical control micro milling machine with an Ethernet card (Haas Office Mini CNC Mill), a micro force transducer (Kistler Co.), ultra precision linear variable displacement sensors (LVDTs), Internet programmable logic controllers (DeviceNet Allen Bradley PLCs), a SmartCube network vacuum controller (Festo Co.) for robot end-effector, network computer vision systems (DVT Co.), and a CoMo View remote monitor/controller (Kistler Co.), D-Link DCS-5300 web cameras, network cameras, a BNT 200 video server, and web servers. The SmartImage vision system from DVT Company is Internet-based and self-contained with a lens, a LED ring lighting unit, FrameWork software, and an A/D converter. The camera can be accessed over the network through its IP/Gateway addresses. Any image processing, inspection and quality check can be performed remotely and instant updates on system parameters are possible. The camera contains a communication board with eight I/O ports, which can be hardwired for sending and receiving 24-V signals based on inspection criteria (i.e., Fail, Pass, and Warning). Also, descriptive statistics can be sent over the network in the form of text string using a data link module. The two SmartImage Sensors used are DVT 540 (monochrome) and 542C (color). The first one is a gray-scale CCD camera with a pixel resolution of 640 x 480 and the CCD size being 4.8 x 3.6 mm. This camera is used to provide the height of the moving object for robot's Z-axis control. The 542C camera has a pixel resolution of 640 x 480 with a CCD size of 3.2 x 2.4mm. The 542C is used to find the exact center location of moving objects on a conveyor and is placed horizontally above the conveyor in the X & Y plane. A Kistler CoMo View Monitor has connectivity with sensors, including a high sensitivity force transducer for micro-scale assembly force monitoring and a LVDT for dimensional accuracy check with one micron repeatability. The CoMo View Monitor contains a web server function with a variety of process monitoring and control menus, enabling Internet-based sensor networks for process control. The Yamaha YK 250X SCARA (selective compliance assembly robot arm) robot is specifically configured to have a high accuracy along the horizontal directions in the form of swing arm motions (Groover 2001). This renders the robot particularly suitable for pick and place or assembly operations. The robot has the repeatability along horizontal planes of +/- 0.01 mm (+/- 0.0004-in.). For part handling, a variable speed Dorner 6100 conveyor system is connected with robot's I/O device ports in order to synchronize the conveyor with the motion of robot (Fig. 2).

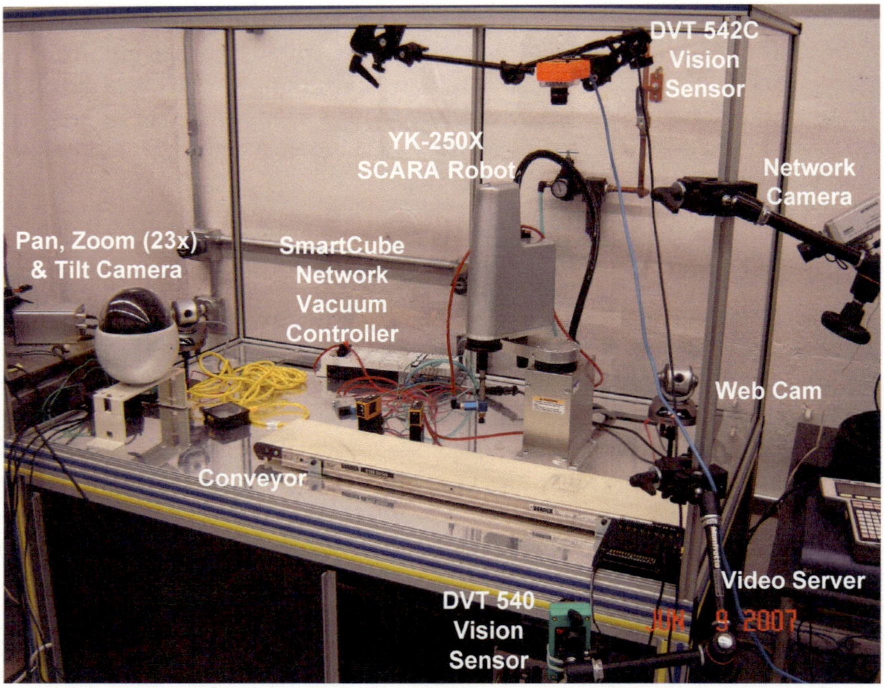

Fig. 2. Experimental setup for network-based, vision-guided robotic system for EQM

The robot's RCX 40 controller is equipped with an onboard Ethernet card, an optional device for connecting the robot controller over the Internet. The communications protocol utilizes TCP/IP (Transmission Control Protocol/Internet Protocol), which is a standard Internet Protocol. PCs with Internet access can exchange data with the robot controller using Telnet, which is a client-server protocol, based on a reliable connection-oriented transport. One drawback to this approach is the lack of auditory/visual communications between the robot and the remotely situated operators. To counter this problem, the Telnet procedure has been included in the Java codes to develop an Application Control Interface (ACI), including windows for the robot control, data, machine vision, and web cameras (Fig. 3).

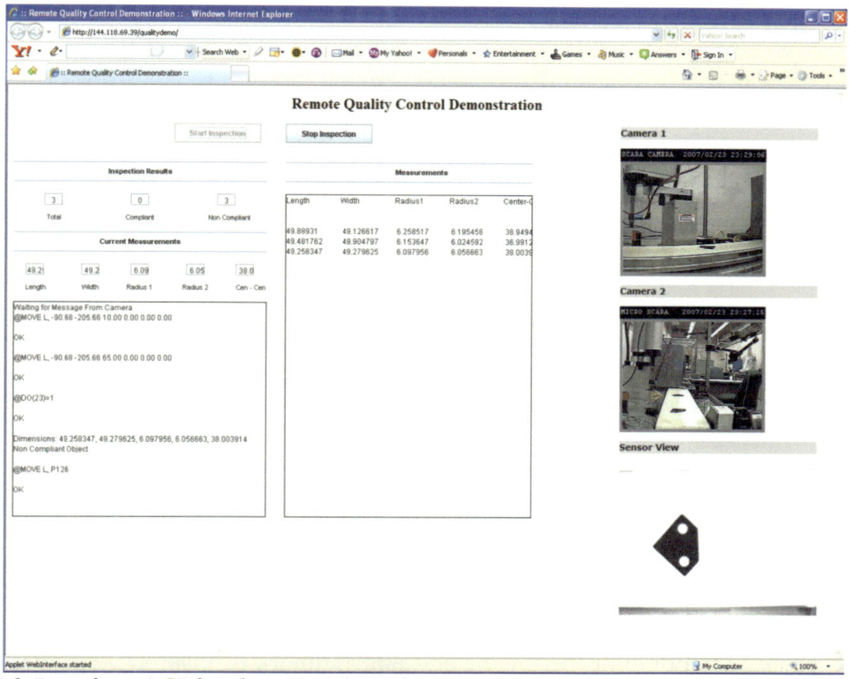

Fig. 3. Web Interface ACI for the remote quality experiment

The basic workings are as follows. The user first tells the ACI to connect to the robot controller. The connection between the application and the robot controller is established by the utilization of Winsock control on port 23 and other control functions that communicate through IP addresses. The robot follows a Telnet type connection sequence. Once connected, the ACI automatically sends the robot to a starting position. The ACI then starts the conveyor belt, which is activated by a digital output from the robot controller. The user establishes a contact with the DVT cameras using DataLink control, and the live images are displayed with the help of DVTSID control. When an object is detected by the ObjectFind SoftSensor in the camera, the x and y coordinates of the object are passed to the ACI from the DVT 542C SmartImage Sensor. The z-coordinate, which is the height of the object, is also passed to the ACI. The robot then moves to the appropriate location, picks up the object and places it in a predefined location, off from the conveyor. The whole process then starts again. The ACI improves not only the visualization of robot operations in the form of an intuitive interface, but also provides enhanced controllability to the operators. The ACI can verify the robot coordinate points, once the robot has been driven to the vision guided locations. The ACI monitors the current robot position, and calculates the shortest approach as the vision sends the part coordinates to the robot. In addition to the web camera, for a high degree of visual and auditory communications, three fixed focus network cameras and one PZT (pan, zoom, and tilt) camera with 23 x optical zoom are connected with a BNT 200 video server, through which remotely located operators can observe the robot operations over the secure web site. This enhanced realism in the simulated environment guarantees the higher reliability of the performance and confidence about the remote operation of the system (Bertoni et al., 2003).

4. Calibration of Vision System

Vision calibration for robotic guidance refers to the procedure for transforming image coordinates into robot Cartesian coordinates (Gonzalez-Galvan et al., 2003; Motta et al., 2001). This procedure is different than the robot calibration, which describes (1) the procedure during start-up for establishing the point of reference for each joint, from which all subsequent points are based, or (2) the procedure for measuring and determining robot pose errors to enable the robot's controllers to compensate for the errors (Bryan, 2000; Review of techniques, 1998; Robot calibration, 1998). Vision calibration is a critical process when (1) robots are newly installed, (2) camera optics and focal length have changed significantly, (3) robots are mounted on a different fixture, and (4) there is a need for vision guidance. To position a robot at a desired location, pixel coordinates from the camera have to be converted into corresponding robot coordinates, which are prone to many technical errors. The difficulties stem from the facts that (1) lens distortion effects, (2) misalignment between image planes and robot axes, and (3) inherent uncertainties related to the defining of image plane boundaries within the robot work space. Precise mathematical mapping of those inaccuracies are generally impractical and computationally extensive to quantify (Amavasai et al., 2005; Andreff et al., 2004; Connolly, 2005; Connolly, 2007). Most calibration procedures require complicated mathematical modeling and expensive measuring devices, both of which entail special training and lengthy setups, hence imposing substantial downtime costs on companies (Bryan, 2000; Robot calibration, 1998; Review of techniques, 1998). Even after mathematical modeling, calibration becomes susceptible to slight changes in setup. Consequently, only a few calibration methods have been practical, simple, economical and quick enough for use with industrial robots (Abderrahim & Whittaker, 2000; Hosek & Bleigh, 2002; Meng & Zhuang, 2001; Meng & Zhuang, 2007; Pena-Cabrera et al., 2005; Perks, 2006; Young & Pickin, 2000; Zhang & Goldberg, 2005; Zhang et al., 2006).

In this context, the methodology developed in this study emulates production environment without the use of highly complicated mathematical calibrations. The image captured by the camera and the robot working space directly over the conveyor are considered as two horizontal planes. Two planes are considered parallel, hence any point on the image plane (denoted as a_i and b_i) can be mapped into the robot coordinates. By operating individual values of a_i and b_i with the scale factors (S_x and S_y), the image coordinates (pixel coordinates) can be translated into the robot coordinates using the following functional relationship (Wilson et al., 2000):

$$f: \mathbf{P}_\mathrm{i} \triangleq \mathbf{R}_\mathrm{i} + \mathbf{S}_\mathrm{i} \cdot \mathbf{v}_\mathrm{i} + \boldsymbol{\varepsilon}_\mathrm{i} \quad (1)$$

where $\mathbf{P}_\mathrm{i}$ = the robot state vector at time i, $\mathbf{R}_\mathrm{i}$ = the robot coordinate vector at the origin of the image plane, $\mathbf{S}_\mathrm{i}$ = the scale vector with 2 x 2 block of the form $\begin{bmatrix} S_x & 0 \\ 0 & S_y \end{bmatrix}$, $\mathbf{v}_\mathrm{i} = [a_i, b_i]^\mathrm{T} - [a_0, b_0]^\mathrm{T}$, a_o and b_o = the image coordinate zero, and $\boldsymbol{\varepsilon}_\mathrm{i}$ = a zero mean Gaussian error vector due to coordinate mapping. The robot state vector assumes a form:

$$\mathbf{P_i}=\left[\mathbf{x},\dot{\mathbf{x}},\mathbf{y},\dot{\mathbf{y}},\mathbf{z},\dot{\mathbf{z}},\alpha,\dot{\alpha},\beta,\dot{\beta},\gamma,\dot{\gamma}\right]^{\mathrm{T}} \simeq [x_i, y_i, z_i]^{\mathrm{T}} \tag{2}$$

where x, y, z = the translated robot coordinates (mm) from the pixel or image coordinates, α, β, γ = the relative orientation described by roll, pitch, and yaw angles, and $\dot{\mathbf{x}}, \dot{\mathbf{y}}, \dot{\mathbf{z}}, \dot{\alpha}, \dot{\beta}, \dot{\gamma}$ = the relative velocities. Considering the work area as a 2D surface, the scale factors for each axis can be represented as:

$$S_x = \sqrt{\frac{(x_1 - x_r)^2 + (y_1 - y_r)^2}{(a_1 - a_0)^2 + (b_1 - b_0)^2}};\ S_y = \sqrt{\frac{(x_2 - x_r)^2 + (y_2 - y_r)^2}{(a_2 - a_0)^2 + (b_2 - b_0)^2}} \tag{3}$$

The goal is to minimize the transformation error caused by lens distortion and other minor misalignments between the planes:

$$\Theta_{\mathrm{min}} \le \varepsilon_i(\mathbf{x}, \mathbf{y}) \approx \max[(\hat{\mathbf{P}}_i(\mathbf{x}) - \mathbf{P}_i(\mathbf{x})), (\hat{\mathbf{P}}_i(\mathbf{y}) - \mathbf{P}_i(\mathbf{y}))] \le \Theta_{\mathrm{max}} \tag{4}$$

where $\mathbf{P_i}$ = the true location, $\hat{\mathbf{P}}_i$ = the observed robot position over the networks, and Θ_{min} & Θ_{max} = the preset limits for the magnitude of errors in accordance with the focal length. Vision calibration was conducted by dividing the region captured by the camera into a 4 x 4 grid, and applying separate scaling factors for a better accuracy (Fig. 4). The division of image plane into equally spaced blocks increases the accuracy of the system by countering the problems in (High-Accuracy Positioning System User's Guide, 2004): (1) the image plane cannot be perfectly aligned with the robot coordinate axes, which is the case in most industrial applications, (2) the perfect alignment requires a host of expensive measuring instruments and a lengthy setup, and (3) the imperfections caused by optics and image distortion. Initially, it was tried with the calibration grid from Edmund Optics Company, which has 1 micron accuracy for solid circles on a precision grid. The circles were, however, too small for the camera at the focal length. Sixteen, solid-circle grid was designed with AutoCAD software and printed on a white paper. The diameter of circle is equivalent to the diameter of the robot end-effector (i.e., vacuum suction adaptor), of which radius being 10.97mm. Once the grid is positioned, the robot end-effector was positioned directly over each circle, and corresponding robot coordinates were recorded from the robot controller. This reading was compared with the image coordinates. For that purpose, the center of each circle was detected first. The center point is defined as:

$$Ctr_x = K^{-1} \cdot \sum_{k=1}^{K} \left[Xe_k - Xs_k\right] \cdot 2^{-1}; Ctr_y = G^{-1} \cdot \sum_{g=1}^{g} \left[Ye_g - Ys_g\right] \cdot 2^{-1} \tag{5}$$

where *K and G* = the total numbers of pixel rows and columns in the object, respectively, *Xe* = the x coordinate point for the left most pixel in row *k*, *Xs* = the x coordinate point for the right most pixel in row *k*, *Ye* = the y coordinate point for a bottom pixel in column *g*, and *Ys* = the y coordinate point for a top pixel in column *g*.

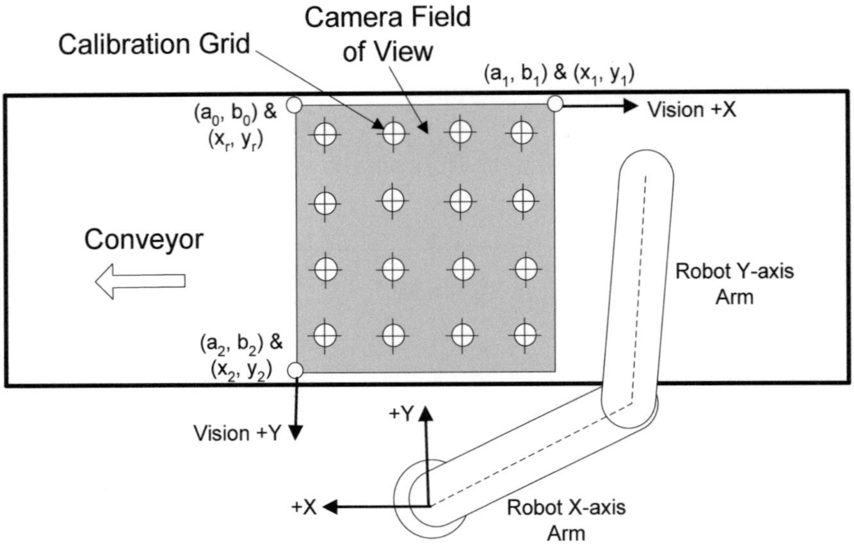

Fig. 4. Schematic of vision calibration grid

The scale factors consider the robot Cartesian coordinates at every intersection of the grid lines. Any point detected within the image plane will be scaled with respect to the increment in the grid from the origin. Let $P(a_i, b_i)$ be the center point of the moving object detected, then the following equations translate it into:

$$x_i = x_r + \sum_{n=1}^{p-1} S_{x,n} \cdot \left|a_n - a_{n-1}\right| + S_{x,p}\left[a_i - a_{p-1}\right] + \varepsilon_x;$$
$$y_i = y_r + \sum_{m=1}^{q-1} S_{y,m} \cdot \left|b_m - b_{m-1}\right| + S_{y,q}\left[b_i - b_{q-1}\right] + \varepsilon_y \quad (6)$$

where n = the number of columns, m = the number of rows, *p and q* = the number of grids from the origin where $P(a_i, b_i)$ is located, and ε_x & ε_y = imprecision involved in scaling. In order to capture the moving objects on a conveyor, a series of images is taken at a fixed rate and the time interval between each frame is calculated. The algorithms in the ACI automatically detect the center of moving object and translate that into robot coordinates. The speed of the object is defined as:

$$\upsilon_P(mm/s) = \left\|\mathbf{u} - \mathbf{v}\right\| \cdot t_f^{-1} = \left[(Ctr_{x,f} - Ctr_{x,f-1})^2 + (Ctr_{y,f} - Ctr_{y,f-1})^2\right]^{1/2} \cdot t_f^{-1} \quad (7)$$

where $\mathbf{u} = (Ctr_{x,f}, Ctr_{y,f})$, the center point of the object at frame no. *f*, $\mathbf{v} = (Ctr_{x,f-1}, Ctr_{y,f-1})$, the center point of the object at frame no. *f-1*, and t_f= the time taken for a part to travel from frame no. *f-1* to frame no. *f*. The time includes not only the part travel between consecutive image frames, but also the lapse for part detection, A/D conversion, image processing, mapping, and data transfer from the camera to a PC. The detection of the moving object, image processing, and calculation of center point are done within the vision system, and the only data transmitted out of the vision system over the networks are the x and y pixel coordinates. Tests showed no delays in receiving the data over the Internet. The request is sent to the DVT camera by using the syntax: "*object.Connect remoteHost, remotePort.*" The remoteHost is the IP address assigned to the DVT camera and the default remote port is 3246. The DVT DataLink Control is used for the passing of the data from the DVT Smart Image Sensor to the Java application. The data is stored in the string and which is transferred synchronously to the application. DataLink is a built-in tool used to send data out of the system and even receive a limited number of commands from another device. This tool is product-specific, that is, every product has its own DataLink that can be configured depending on the inspection and the SoftSensors being used. DataLink consists of a number of ASCII strings that are created based on information from the SoftSensors: "*<ControlName>.Connect2 (strIPAddress as String, iPort as Integer).*" This is the syntax to connect to the DVT DataLink control.

The speed of the robot as provided by the manufacturer ranges from integer value 1 to 100 as a percentage of the maximum speed (4000 mm/s). The ACI calculates the speed of the moving objects, then adjusts the robot speed. Once a part is detected, a future coordinate point where the part to be picked up, is determined by the ACI. This information is automatically transmitted to the robot controller, and the robot moves to pick up at the designated location. Therefore, the robot travel time to reach the future coordinate must coincide with the time taken by the part to reach the same coordinate. The reach time t_r (ms) is defined in the form of:

$$t_r = \left[\sum_{f=2}^{h} \|\mathbf{u}-\mathbf{v}\| \right] \cdot \left[\|\mathbf{u}-\mathbf{v}\| \cdot t_f^{\ -1} \right]^{-1} = \left[(x_i - x_r)^2 + (y_i - y_r)^2 \right]^{1/2} \cdot \upsilon_r^{-1} \tag{8}$$

where f = the frame number, indicating the first frame from which the vision system detects the center of moving object, h = the frame number at a pick up location, x_i & y_i = the coordinate of the pick up location, and υ_r = the robot speed (mm/s). The discrepancy between the vision generated pick up location and the actual robot coordinate was measured using the following equation:

$$Error(mm) = \left[(Ctr_{x,f} - x_i)^2 + (Ctr_{y,f} - y_i)^2 \right]^{1/2} \tag{9}$$

5. Empirical Verification

To simulate the industrial applications, two different sets of moving speed (20 & 30 mm/s) were used for conveyor, while varying the part heights (65, 55, & 42 mm). To facilitate the testing of robot positioning accuracy, round objects were CNC machined out of aluminum, and its diameter was made intentionally identical to that of a vacuum adaptor. Parts surface was painted matt black in order to accentuate the contrast against the background. Parts were randomly placed on the conveyor and the ACI was initiated to track and guide the robot. The first 12 parts are 65-mm high, then 55 mm, followed by 42-mm parts. Each 36 data points were tested under two speed settings. The height or the z-axis of the object is calculated with the DVT 540 camera, which is kept parallel to the z-axis and perpendicular to the x-y plane. For x-y coordinates, the DVT 540C camera is positioned above the conveyor, parallel to the robot x and y axes. To facilitate the part pick-up, the robot z-coordinate was set intentionally lower (by 1-mm) than the detected part height from the camera. The vacuum adaptor is made out of compliant rubber material, compressible to provide a better seal between the adaptor and the part surface. Figures 5 and 6 illustrate the errors in x & y plane as well as along the z-direction. Figure 5 shows a slight increase in the magnitude of errors as the part height decreases, while in Figure 6, the error is more evident due to height variation. Such circumstance can be speculated for a number of reasons: (1) possible errors while calibrating image coordinates with robot coordinates; (2) pronounced lens distortional effect; and (3) potential network delay in data transfer.

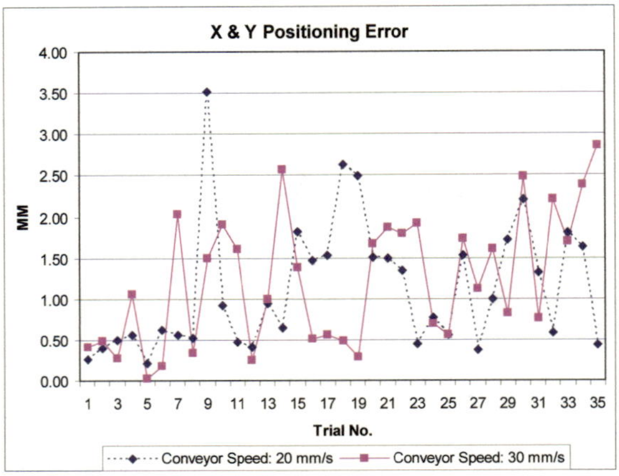

Fig. 5. Errors in X & Y-coordinates (First Trial)

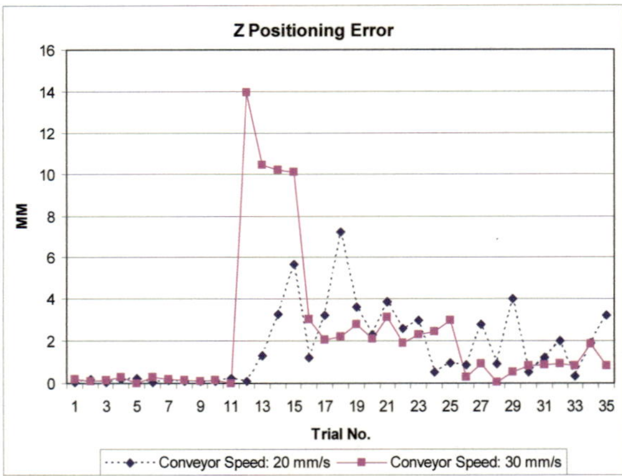

Fig. 6. Errors in Z-coordinates (First Trial)

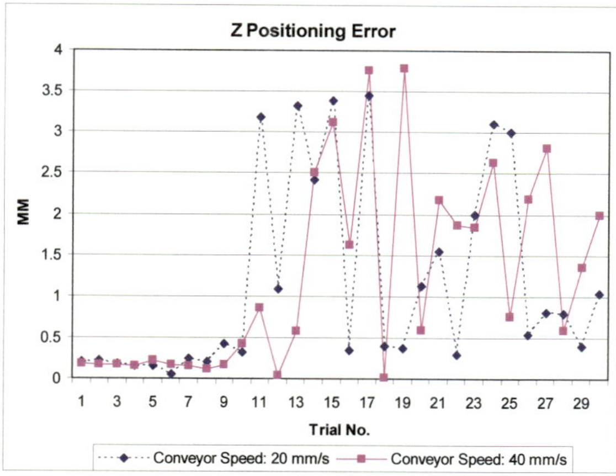

Fig. 7. Errors in Z-coordinates (Second Trial)

To test the speculation, the second set of experiments was conducted. This time, the conveyor speed was increased to 40 mm/sec, in order to observe any speed related fluctuations. The errors in x and y directions show the similar pattern as the first trial. The z directional errors also display a very similar pattern, however, all data points fall below the 4-mm error line (Fig. 7). This indicates that the system acts more stable, compared to the first trial. By observing the two graphs along z direction, it can be stated that the lens distortion effect is more serious in the 540 camera. Other factor might be contributed to the initial location of parts on a conveyor. Based on where the parts are positioned, it can be further from the 540 camera or quite close to the camera lens. Such situation will obviously affect the calibration, and resulted in the larger errors.

6. Experiment on Remote Quality Control

For quality control tasks, the computer vision system is initially trained to learn the profile of the object. The training is done using FrameWork software, which is the firmware of the vision system. Pattern matching techniques are then applied by the firmware to detect the presence of the similar objects under different orientations. Once trained, the camera makes live measurement on the objects passing on the conveyor. Once the object is detected, measurements are made automatically by the vision system. Each inspection and measurement task is defined through soft-sensors (i.e., user defined image processing and analysis algorithms). Figure 8 shows 5 soft-sensors for detecting the object, and extracting its length, width, radii and a center-to-center distance. The 'WorkPiece' is an ObjectFinder soft-sensor, defined by the rectangular box as shown in Fig. 8, which is trained to detect the shape and position of the product. At the core of this system is the Java-based software that integrates all the hardware components and provides the user with an unified view of the system in terms of quality control operation, information exchange (text and video), decision functions, and robot operations. The software is implemented as three separate entities: scripts on the hardware (e.g., vision sensor, robot, and web-cams), the application server and the applet-based client interface. Though the vision camera can be set to detect and measure the objects using the firmware, the task of formatting the measurements and communicating it to the server is done through the built-in Java-based scripting tool. Two scripts are defined for this purpose. Inter script communication between these two script happens by setting and clearing status flags in the common memory registers. The first script, called the inspection script, is executed after each snapshot.

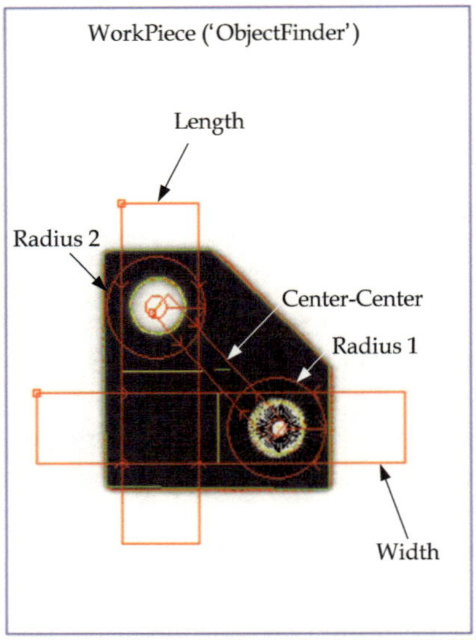

Overall Result	PASS	
SoftSensor	Result	< Output Value
WorkPiece	PASS	# Objects=1, X=318, Y=265, Angle=0
Width	PASS	D=146.00 Pixels, Angle=0.00deg.
Length	PASS	D=142.53 Pixels, Angle=0.66deg.
Radius1	PASS	Radius = 15.27 Pixels
Radius2	PASS	Radius = 17.23 Pixels
CenterCenter	PASS	D=72.79 Pixels, Angle=0.00deg.

Fig. 8. Configuration of vision soft-sensors for quality measurement

The inspection script checks if an object has been detected after each snapshot and informs the main script of the outcome. If an object is detected, the background script informs this to the robot, which stops the conveyor momentarily. Once an acknowledgement is received from the application server that the belt is halted, the main script sets the 'ready for measurements' flag. The inspection script reads this flag after the next snapshot and makes the necessary measurements. It passes them on to the main script by setting the 'measurement ready' flag and writing the measured values to pre-known register locations. The main script reads these values, parses them to the required format and transmits it to the application server. Once an acknowledgement is received from the application server, it goes back on the detection mode and waits for the next object. The second script, called the main script, runs constantly in the background. It is responsible for establishing and maintaining communications with the application server. It uses the standard Java style *Socket()* function to open an TCP connection to the application server on a dedicated port. Once the connection is established, it exchanges information on this connection with the application server through the *send()* and *recv()* functions. The main program starts by waiting for a TCP connection on a predetermined port from a browser through the *ServerSocket()* class object. Since the end user has to activate the inspection process, this is deemed as the appropriate entry point into the program. Once a connection is accepted through the accept() method, an object of *BrowserSession* class, which is a class designed to handle all the browser communication is initialized with this new connection. This newly initialized object is then used as a parameter to initialize an object of the *Operations* class. The *Operations* class is designed to handle the communications with the computer vision camera and the robot. The *Operations* object implements the Java *Runnable* system class - therefore being able to run as a thread. A thread is a mini-program within a program that can execute in parallel with other threads. The reason behind assigning the browser communications to a separate class and the robot-camera operations to another class should be evident from the way the system is organized. The browser forms the client part of the operation, while the robot and camera constitute the server side of the system, hence this division. Once the initialization of the objects is done, a new thread is started with the newly initialized *Operations* object and the thread is started. This effectively establishes the required connections between the entities in the system and starts operation. The *BrowserSession* class encapsulates all operations pertaining to the communications with the browser. The class provides a *WriteMessage()* method through which information is sent to the browser. The main workhorse of this system is the *Operations* class. It is initialized with an instant of the *BrowserSession* class as an input, which effectively gives it access to the connection with the browser. It then utilizes the *TelnetWrapper* class for communicating with the Telnet daemon on the robot. This class emulates a Telnet client in Java for communications with the robot. An instance of the *Operations* class, once run as a thread, starts of with opening a connection and initializing the robot.

The next step is to establish connection with the camera, through a TCP/IP socket on a pre-assigned port. Once connected, it continuously waits for messages from the camera that include measurements, object position and other status messages. It processes this incoming measurement information to decide on the quality of the product. Once a decision is made, it instructs the robot to perform the necessary action on the inspected object. Figure 3 shows a screen capture of the web-based end-user interface. The applet does not execute any task upon loading. The user initiates the inspection procedure by clicking on the 'Start Inspection' button. Once clicked, it attempts to establish a connection with the application server. Successful establishment of connection also starts the inspection process at the other end as explained earlier. There are several fields in the applet that gives a live analysis of the ongoing inspection process such as a number of objects inspected, a number of compliant objects, current dimension and cumulative measurement history. The browser interface also includes two web camera views and the computer vision sensor's inspection view that show the robotic operation. The web cameras are equipped with an embedded web server, which capture a stream of images over the Internet using the HTTP protocol. The system is tested using the sample objects, of which geometry is shown in Fig. 9.

Six key dimensions: length (L), width (W), diameters of the two circles (D_1, D_2), horizontal center-center distance between the circles (CC_L), and vertical center-center distance between the circles (CC_W) are shown in Fig. 9. These pieces are machined with a +/- 0.25 mm tolerance limit. Pieces whose dimensions lay outside this range are rejected. Twenty five pieces are made, with a few purposely machined out of tolerance limits on each dimension. Several pieces from each type are mixed up and fed through the conveyor belt for inspection. The specifications for the different test pieces used for testing are shown in Table 1. Although this object does not pose any serious measurement challenge, it presents a moderate complexity for the requirement of our work. Since we concentrate mostly on 2-D measurement, the work-piece thickness is limited to less than 1 mm. Otherwise, a higher thickness would result in problems due to shadows, unless a telecentric lens is used. Shadows would trick the camera to see the object as being elongated on some sides and lead to wrong measurements under the current lighting configuration.

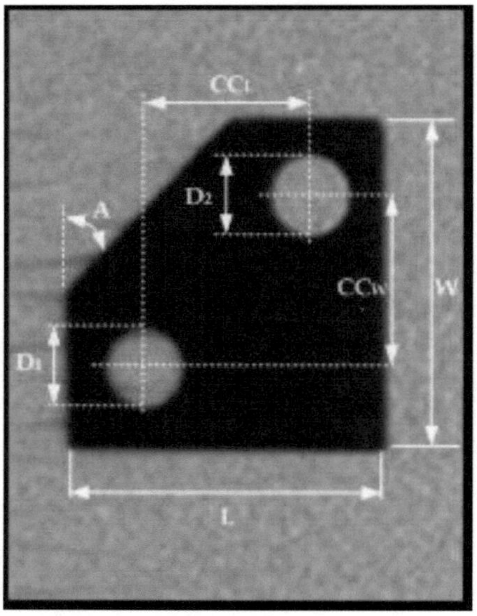

Fig. 9. Test piece geometry

Type	L	W	D_1	D_2	CC_L	CC_W	A(angle)	Remarks
1	50	50	12	12	26	26	45	Correct Dimensions
2	52	50	12	12	26	26	45	Wrong Length
3	50	52	12	12	26	26	45	Wrong Width
4	50	50	14	12	26	26	45	Wrong Radius
5	50	50	12	14	26	26	45	Wrong Radius
6	50	50	12	12	28	26	45	Wrong Center-to-Center Horizontal Distance
7	50	50	12	12	26	28	45	Wrong Center-to-Center Vertical Distance
8	50	50	12	12	26	26	47	Wrong Slope

Table 1. Workpiece specifications (all units are in mm except the angular dimensions (degrees))

The camera extracts the first 4 features and the center-to-center distance between the circles. The center-to-center distance is measured instead of the last two quantities (i.e., CC_W and CC_L) since they can be jointly quantified by the center-to-center distance, CC_D. However, this requires us to develop a tolerance limit, based on which object has to be classified. The tolerance limit for CC_D is determined using the root sum of squares (RSS) approach. CC_D, CC_W, and CC_L have a simple geometrical relationship given by:

$$CC_D = \left[CC_W^2 + CC_L^2\right]^{1/2} \tag{10}$$

Since this is a non linear relationship, the non linear RSS extension is employed. The variance of CC_D is defined as:

$$Var(CC_D) = \left[\partial(CC_D) \big/ \partial(CC_W)\right]^2 \cdot Var(CC_W) + \left[\partial(CC_D) \big/ \partial(CC_L)\right]^2 \cdot Var(CC_L) \tag{11}$$

where ∂ = the partial derivative operator, and Var () = the variance of the dimensions. For six sigma quality control, the standard deviation would correspond to the full tolerance limit, hence the following relationship holds:

$$Var(CC_X) = Tol(CC_X) \tag{12}$$

where X corresponds to either D,W or L, and Tol() = corresponding tolerance limits. Hence Equation (12) can be written as:

$$Tol(CC_D) = \left[\left(\frac{\partial(CC_D)}{\partial(CC_W)}\right)^2 \cdot Tol^2(CC_W) + \left(\frac{\partial(CC_D)}{\partial(CC_L)}\right)^2 \cdot Tol^2(CC_L)\right]^{1/2} \tag{13}$$

Differentiation Equation 11 with respect to CC_L and CC_W yields:

$$\frac{\partial(CC_D)}{\partial(CC_L)} = -CC_L \cdot \left[CC_W^2 + CC_L^2\right]^{-0.5}; \frac{\partial(CC_D)}{\partial(CC_W)} = -CC_W \cdot \left[CC_W^2 + CC_L^2\right]^{-0.5} \tag{14}$$

When substituted in (13) results in:

$$Tol(CC_D) = \left[\frac{CC_W^2}{CC_W^2 + CC_L^2} \cdot Tol^2(CC_W) + \frac{CC_L^2}{CC_W^2 + CC_L^2} \cdot Tol^2(CC_L)\right]^{1/2} \tag{15}$$

We substitute the following numerical values from the design specifications: CC_W = 26 mm, CC_L = 26 mm, and +/- 0.25 mm for Tol(CC_W) and Tol(CC_L), then test for a tolerance limit on five dimensions (L, W, D_1, D_2 and CC_D) for quality compliance. The corresponding process control chart during a trial run is given in Fig.10. The CL line corresponds to the mean value, which is calculated to be 36.8 mm. Therefore, the upper control limit (UCL) and lower control limit (LCL) lines correspond to 0.25 mm above and below the mean value. The 4 offsets outside the limits represent the non-compliant objects (Types 6 & 7) that are intentionally mixed up with the compliant ones. Otherwise, it can be seen that the center to center distance measurements follow the expected statistical behavior with a 0.25 mm tolerance limit.

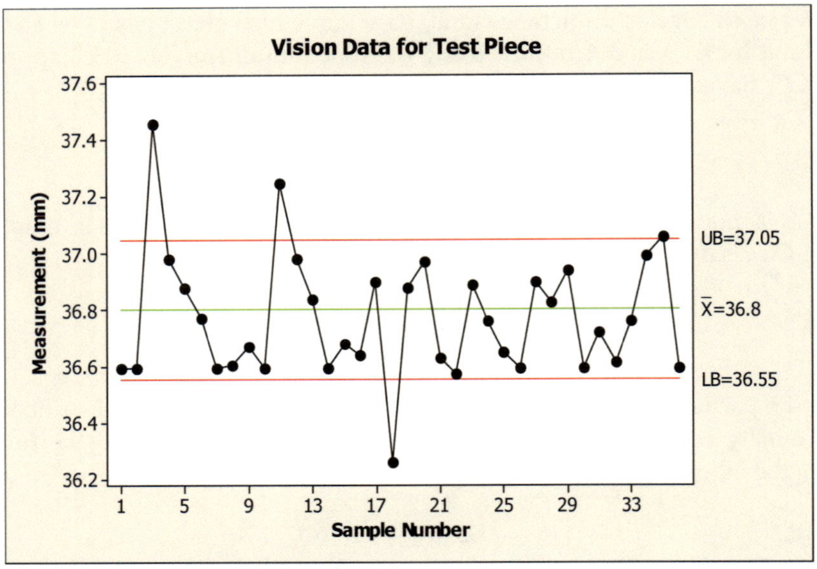

Fig. 10. Statistical process control chart for CC_D

7. Conclusions

This work successfully demonstrates a concept of EQM through the implementation of web-based quality control. A computer vision system measures the dimensions of products on the conveyor belt and reports it to an application server, which activates an appropriate action for the robot. Various image processing and analysis algorithms have been integrated with the ACI for remote quality inspection. Operators can remotely adjust the inspection routine in the case of process changes, such as lighting conditions, part variations, and quality criteria. In the event of changes in moving speed of conveyor or the part spacing, the inspection speed and the inspection region should be adjusted accordingly. The changes are necessary due to varying exposure time of passing parts on a conveyor and the time should be sufficient for the vision system to complete the intended quality control functions. This conforms to the changing environment to ensure the seamless transition between different production settings. One of the most problematic troubles associated with the vision system is the ambient lighting. Sometimes, a precise control of lighting is difficult and consequently, inspection routines may become ineffective. To counter such problem, the parameter settings, such as delay after trigger, exposure time, digitizing time, use of integrated illumination, use of anti-blooming filter, reflectance calibration, field of view balance, product sensor gain, and image area to acquire can be reset remotely. This capability provides less delay in production due to subtle or unexpected changes, which has a great potential, since engineers can access and control the equipment anytime, from anywhere.

8. References

Abderrahim, M. & Whittaker, A. R. (2000). "Kinematic model identification of industrial manipulators," *Journal of Robotics and Computer-Integrated Manufacturing*, Vol.16, pp. 1-8.

Albada, G.D.V., Lagerberg, J.M. & Visser, A. (1994). "Eye in hand robot calibration," *Journal of Industrial Robot*, Vol. 21, No. 6, pp. 14-17.

Amavasai, B. P., Caparrelli, F. & Selvan, A. (2005). "Machine vision methods for autonomous micro-robotic systems," *Kybernetes*, Vol. 34 No. 9/10, pp. 1421-1439.

Andreff, N., Renaud, P., Martinet, P. & Pierrot, F. (2004). "Vision-based kinematic calibration of an H4 parallel mechanism: practical accuracies," *Journal of Industrial Robot*, Vol. 31, No. 3, pp. 273–283.

Bennis, F., Castagliola, P. & Pino, L. (2005). "Statistical Analysis of Geometrical Tolerances: A Case Study," *Journal of Quality Engineering*, Vol. 17, No. 3, pp. 419 - 427.

Bone, M. G. & Capson, D. (2003). "Vision-guided fixtureless assembly of automotive components," *Robotics and Computer Integrated Manufacturing*, Vol. 19, pp. 79-87.

Bouganis, A. & Shanahan, M. (2007). "A vision-based intelligent system for packing 2-D irregular shapes," *IEEE Transactions on Automation Science and Engineering*, Vol. 4, No. 3, pp. 382-394.

Bozma, H.I. & Yal-cin, H. (2002). "Visual processing and classification of items on a moving conveyor: a selective perception approach," *Robotics and Computer Integrated Manufacturing*, Vol. 18, pp. 125-133.

Brady, K & Tarn, T-J. (2000). "Internet based manufacturing technology: Intelligent remote teleoperation," *Proceedings of the 2000 IEEE/RSJ International Conference on Intelligent Robots and Systems*, pp. 843-848.

Center for Intelligent Maintenance Systems, 2005, URL: http://wumrc.engin.umich.edu/ims/?page=home.

Cheng, Y. & Jafari, M.A. (2008). "Vision-Based Online Process Control in Manufacturing Applications," IEEE Transactions on Automation Science and Engineering, Vol. 5, No. 1, pp. 140 - 153.

Cohen, A. (1997). *Simulation Based Design*, DARPA Plus-Up Workshop on SBD Alpha Release, (DARPA/TTO Program).

Connolly, C. (2005). "Vision enabled robotics," *Journal of Industrial Robot*, Vol. 32, No. 6, pp. 456-459.

Connolly, C. (2007). "A new integrated robot vision system from FANUC Robotics," *Journal of Industrial Robot*, Vol. 34, No. 2, pp. 103-106.

Goldin, D., Venneri, S. & Noor, A. (1998). "New Frontiers in Engineering," *Mechanical Engineering*, Vol. 120, No. 2, pp. 63-69.

Goldin, D., Venneri, S. & Noor, A. (1999). "Ready For the Future?" *Mechanical Engineering*, Vol. 121, No. 11, pp. 61-70.

Golnabi, H. & Asadpour, A. (2007). "Design and application of industrial machine vision systems," *Robotics and Computer Integrated Manufacturing*, Vol. 23, pp. 630-637.

González-Galván, E.J., Cruz-Ramírez, S.R., Seelinger, M.J. & Cervantes-Sánchez, J.J. (2003). "An efficient multi-camera, multi-target scheme for the three-dimensional control of robots using uncalibrated vision," *Journal of Robotics and Computer-integrated manufacturing*, Vol. 19, No. 5, pp. 387-400.

Gonzalez-Galvana, E.J., Pazos-Floresa, F, Skaarb, S.B. & Cardenas-Galindo, A. (2002). "Camera pan/tilt to eliminate the workspace-size/pixel-resolution tradeoff with camera–space manipulation," *Journal of Robotics and Computer Integrated Manufacturing*, Vol. 18, No. 2, pp. 95-104.

Greenway, B. (2000). "Robot accuracy," *Journal of Industrial Robot*, Vol. 27, No. 4, pp. 257-265.

Groover, M.P. (2001). *Automation, Production Systems and Computer Integrated Manufacturing*, 2/e, Prentice Hall, Inc., NJ.

Hidalgo, F. & Brunn, P. (1998). "Robot metrology and calibration systems - a market review," *Journal of Industrial Robot*, Vol. 25, No. 1, pp. 42-47.

High-Accuracy Positioning System User's Guide, Version 2.0, Adept Technology, Inc., 2004, URL: http://www.adept.com/.

Hosek, M., & Bleigh, T. (2002). "Brooks automation expands control capability of precision industrial robots," *Journal of Industrial Robot*, Vol. 29, No. 4, pp. 334-348.

Hung, M-H, Tsai, J., Cheng, F-T & Yang, H-C, (2004). "Development of an Ethernet Equipment Integration Framework for Factory Automation," *Journal of Robotics and Computer-Integrated Manufacturing*, Vol. 20, No. 5, pp. 369-383.

Janocha, H. & Diewald, B. (1995). "ICAROS: over-all-calibration of industrial robots," *Journal of Industrial Robot*, Vol. 22, No. 3, pp. 15-20.

Iung, B. (2003). "From remote maintenance to MAS-based e-maintenance of an industrial process," *Journal of Intelligent Manufacturing*, Vol. 14, No. 1, pp. 59-82.

Kang, Y.G., Wang, Z., Li, R. & Jiang, C. (2007). "A fixture design system for networked manufacturing," *International Journal of Computer Integrated Manufacturing*, Vol. 20, No. 2, pp. 143-159.

Koc, M., Ni, M.J. & Lee, J. (2002). "Introduction of e-manufacturing," *Proceedings of the International Conference on Frontiers on Design and Manufacturing*, Dalian, China.

Kwon, Y., Wu, T & Ochoa, J. (2004). "SMWA: A CAD-based decision support system for the efficient design of welding," *Journal of Concurrent Engineering: Research and Applications*, Vol. 12, No. 4, pp. 295-304.

Lal, S.P. & Onwubolu, G.C. (2008). "E-manufacturing system: from design to performance evaluation," *International Journal of Internet Manufacturing and Services*, Vol. 1, No. 4, pp. 323-344.

Lal, S.P. & Onwubolu, G.C. (2007). "Three tiered web-based manufacturing system-Part 1: System development," *Robotics and Computer-Integrated Manufacturing*, Vol. 23, pp. 138-151.

Lee, K-M, Li, Q. & Daley, W. (2007). "Effects of classification methods on color-based feature detection with food processing applications," *IEEE Transactions on Automation Science and Engineering*, Vol. 4, No. 1, pp. 40-51.

Lee, J. (2003). "E-manufacturing—fundamental, tools, and transformation," *Journal of Robotics and Computer-Integrated Manufacturing*, Vol. 19, No. 6, pp. 501-507.

Lin, G.C.I. & Lu, T-F (1997). "Vision and force/torque sensing for calibration of industrial robots," *Journal of Industrial Robot*, Vol. 24, No. 6, pp. 440-445.

Ling, D.S.H., Hsu, H-Y, Lin, G.C.I. & Lee, S-H (2005). "Enhanced image-based coordinate measurement using a super-resolution method," *Robotics and Computer-Integrated Manufacturing*, Vol. 21, pp. 579-588.

Luo, R.C., Su, K.L., Shen, S.H. & Tsai, K.H. (2003). "Networked intelligent robots through the Internet: issues and opportunities," *Proceedings of the IEEE*, Vol. 91, No. 3, pp. 371-382.

Lu, T-P & Yih, Y. (2001). "An agent-based production control framework for multi-line collaborative manufacturing," *International Journal of Production Research*, Vol. 39, No. 10, pp. 2155-2176.

Mattone, R., Campagiorni, G. & Galati, F. (2000). "Sorting of items on a moving conveyor belt. Part 1: a technique for detecting and classifying objects," *Journal of Robotics and Computer Integrated Manufact*uring, Vol. 16, pp. 73-80.

Maurício, J, Motta, S.T., de Carvalho, G.C. & McMaster, R.S. (2001). "Robot calibration using a 3D vision-based measurement system with a single camera," *Journal of Robotics and Computer-integrated manufacturing*, Vol. 17, No. 6, pp. 487-497.

Meng, Y. & Zhuang, H. (2001). "Self-calibration of camera-equipped robot manipulators," *Journal of Robotics Research*, Vol. 20, No. 11, pp. 909-921.

Meng, Y. & Zhuang, H. (2007). "Autonomous robot calibration using vision technology," *Journal of Robotics and Computer-Integrated Manufacturing*, Vol. 23, pp. 436–446.

Pena-Cabrera, M., Lopez-Juarez, I., Rios-Cabrera, R. & Corona-Castuera, J. (2005). "Machine vision approach for robotic assembly," *Assembly Automation*, Vol. 25, No. 3, pp. 204–216.

Perks, A. (2006). "Advanced vision guided robotics provide "future-proof" flexible automation," *Assembly Automation*, Vol. 26, No. 3, pp. 216–220.

Review of techniques, Robotics and Automation Research at UWA, December 1998, URL: http://www.mech.uwa.edu.au/jpt/CalibrationPages/Menu1.htm.

Robot calibration, Robotics and Automation Research at UWA, December 1998, URL: http://www.mech.uwa.edu.au/jpt/calibration.html.

Rooks, B. (2003). "Machine tending in the modern age," *International Journal of Industrial Robot*, Vol. 30, No. 4, pp. 313-318.

SME Manufacturing Engineering - Tomorrow's Factory: Manufacturing Industry Takes First Steps Toward Implementing Collaborative E-Manufacturing Systems, pp. 43-60, Nov. 2001.

Smith, C.S. & Wright, P.K. (1996). "CyberCut: A World Wide Web based design-to-fabrication tool," *Journal of Manufacturing Systems*, Vol. 15, No. 6, pp. 432-442.

Stewart, C.V. (1999). "Robust parameter estimation in computer vision," *SIAM Review*, Society for Industrial and Applied Mathematics, Vol. 41, No. 3, pp. 513-537.

Tsai, M.J., Hwung, J.H., Lu, T-F & Hsu, H-Y, (2006). "Recognition of quadratic surface of revolution using a robotic vision system," *Robotics and Computer-Integrated Manufacturing*, Vol. 22, pp. 134-143.

Wilson, W.J., Hulls, C.C. & Janabi-Sharifi, F. (2000). "Chapter 13. Robust image processing and position-based visual servoing," appeared in "*Robust Vision for Vision-Based Control of Motion*, edited by Markus Vincze and Gregory D. Hager," IEEE Press, 3 Park Avenue, 17th Floor, New York, NY.

Wang, L., Orban, P., Cunningham, A. & Lang, S. (2004). "Remote real-time CNC machining for web-based manufacturing," *Robotics and Computer-Integrated Manufacturing*, Vol. 20, pp. 563-571.

Wang, L., Shen, W. & Lang, S. (2004). "Wise-ShopFloor: a Web-based and sensor-driven e-Shop Floor," *ASME Journal of Computing and Information Science in Engineering*, Vol. 4, pp. 56-60.

Wang, L. & Nace, A. (2009). "A sensor-driven approach to Web-based machining," *Journal of Intelligent Manufacturing*, Vol. 20, No. 1, pp. 1-14.

Xu, Y., Song, R.,Korba, L., Wang, L., Shen, W. & Lang, S. (2005). "Distributed device networks with security constraints," *IEEE Transactions on Industrial Informatics*, Vol. 1, No. 4, pp. 217-225.

Yao, J. (1998). "A New Method for Passive Location Estimation from Image Sequence Using Adaptive Extended Kalman Filter," *Proceedings of ICSP '98*, pp. 1002-1005.

Young, K. & Pickin, C.G. (2000). "Accuracy assessment of the modern industrial robot," *Journal of Industrial Robot*, Vol. 27, No. 6, pp. 427-436.

Zhang, M. T. & Goldberg, K. (2005). "Fixture-based industrial robot calibration for silicon wafer handling," *Journal of Industrial Robot*, Vol. 32, No. 1, pp. 43-48.

Zhang, M., Tao, W., Fisher, W. & Tarn, T.-J. (2006). "An industrial solution to automatic robot calibration and workpiece pose estimation for semiconductor and gene-chip microarray fabrication," *Journal of Industrial Robot*, Vol. 33, No. 2, pp. 88-96.

Robot Vision in Industrial Assembly and Quality Control Processes

Niko Herakovic
University of Ljubljana, Slovenia

1. Introduction

In modern industrial assembly and quality control processes, that provide one of the crucial factors for the competitiveness of industry in general, there is a strong need for advanced robot-based object detection and recognition, object grasping and for the capability to perform assembling operations in non-structured environments with randomly positioned objects. Vision-based robotic assembly and quality control systems, that have been a topic of continued research interest for almost four decades, have now matured to a point where they can be effectively applied to advanced robot-based assembly and quality control tasks. This chapter will give an overview of research work related to the field of automated vision systems for assembly and quality control processes.

The nowadays' economy is more concentrated on producing customized products, however, and much less focused on mass manufacturing. In such an economy the need is far more dependent on ease of use, higher degrees of adaptation including assembling operations and control processes in non-structured environments with diversified and randomly positioned objects that enable small runs of made-to-order products. Automating a manual visual inspection process through a robot vision environment can create faster cycle times and level rates of throughput. Also robots will be ubiquitous in the industrial assembly of the future (table 1) and will support mass customization in smaller factories, where production runs are short, lot sizes small and products are modular in configuration and highly variable in features (Kellett, 2009).

Robots in Manufacturing	Today	Future
Production mode	Mass production	Mass Customization
Production runs	Long	Short
Lot sizes	Large	Small
Product configurations	Non-modular	Modular
Product features	Limited variety	Highly variable

Table 1. Robots in Manufacturing: Today Versus the Future (Kellett, 2009)

As advanced robotic systems are becoming more popular and widespread in many industrial assembly settings, the need for reliable operation with the least possible amount of downtime is a common, expected demand. Traditional assembly robots are programmed to pick up a part from the exact same location every time and if the part is even slightly out of the place, the robot will fail to pick that part. Significant advantages can be realized when these robots are coupled with vision systems. Modern robot vision configurations with advanced recognition systems are used more often in later time to adjust the coordinates from where the robot expected to find the object to where it actually is located. This can be achieved with using only a single camera, multiple cameras or different combination systems. Cameras, computer and software work together with the robot to adjust the robot's position, allowing retrieval of the part. One of the examples in this direction is the continued improvements to 3D robot vision. The advances in 3D vision have made robots adept at recognizing a changing environment and adapting to it. This flexibility has allowed robots to work on projects that lack precise consistency, something that was very difficult for a robot to do in the past. Nowadays, robotic vision research is expanding into many new areas. Robots can now pick variously shaped objects from an indexing conveyor, eliminating the need for part designated in-feed systems and machines (figure 1). Research in this area has even made it feasible to pick from a box for certain part configurations (Christe, 2009).

Fig. 1. Vision Guided Robotic Flexible Feeding (Christe, 2009)

Many current vision systems require extensive support from trained experts and are less reliable due to their complexity. This is the main reason why a fundamental step change to simplify the programming and mechanical complexity of robotic guidance applications is necessary. An innovative vision scheme is only half the battle. Mechanical reliability also plays an important role.

Implementation of robot vision in assembly and quality control processes is a multilayer problem and demands therefore expert knowledge, experiences, innovations and most often a problem specific solution. Usually, the procedure of the planning and development of a process of an assembly, inspection and measurement equipment using machine vision is split into precise determination of tasks and goals like detection, recognition, grasping, handling, measurement, fault detection, etc. and into machine vision component selection and working conditions determination like camera, computer, lenses and optics, illumination, position determination, etc. With regard to the automatic assembly part handling, robotic handling and assembly systems offer good prospects for the rationalization and flexibilisation of assembly and quality control processes.

Fig. 2. Vision equipped robot in a bin picking application (Brumson, 2009)

Machine vision will certainly help take robot based assembly to the next level, and machine vision will probably be a part of the next generation safety solution. Off-the-shelf products already offer work cell protection based on 360-degree vision technology, and more robot controllers now come with built-in machine vision capability. Very frequently used operation in industrial assembly, a random part bin picking (figure 2), will probably benefit from such advancements, as will other complex tasks too (Brian, 2008).

2. Industrial assembly

Industrial assembly is a part of the production process (figure 3) and can be defined as an ordered sequence of physical handling tasks in which discrete parts and components are brought together and joined or mated to form a specified configuration. Assembly is a production process operation that provides a crucial factor for the competitiveness of industry in general. It is surprising, that such an important manufacturing process, that can take up to 30% of the manufacturing cost of an end product (Rowland & Lee, 1995), is still mainly performed by hand. Manual assembly becomes expensive, if high levels of quality are to be achieved, because it involves highly skilled human laborers. Also much verification and inspection is needed to compensate for potential human insufficiencies. Manual assembly is often difficult, tedious and time consuming.

Fig. 3. Assembly as part of the production process (Rampersad, 1994)

For this reason it is often difficult for companies to follow market demands, when their assembly is mainly based on manual assembly processes. This becomes even truer, as the market requires products which satisfy high expectations in the areas of quality, price and delivery time. The key word in achieving this goal is the continuous refinement of product and production. Assembly is often the weakest point in the whole production process, because this activity takes up a substantial part of the total production costs and the throughput time (figure 4). The main reasons for this fact are the increasing labour costs, product variety and the decreasing product quantity.

Taking into consideration all these facts, together with constant price cuts for robots and overall turnkey systems in assembly and especially with continually improving performance of robots and machine vision systems, it is possible to understand the reasons for considerable grow of the area of robot-based assembly in the world in the last few years Robotic assembly offers good perspectives also in small and medium sized batch production (Handelsman, 2006; Kellett, 2009; Christe, 2009; Rowland & Lee, 1995; Rampersad, 1994).

Assembly, as a part of production systems, involves handling of parts and subassemblies, which have mostly been manufactured at different times and possibly even in separate locations (Nof et al., 1997). Assembly tasks thus result from the requirement to join certain individual parts, subassemblies and substances such as lubricants and adhesives into final assemblies of higher complexity in a given quantity and within a given time period.

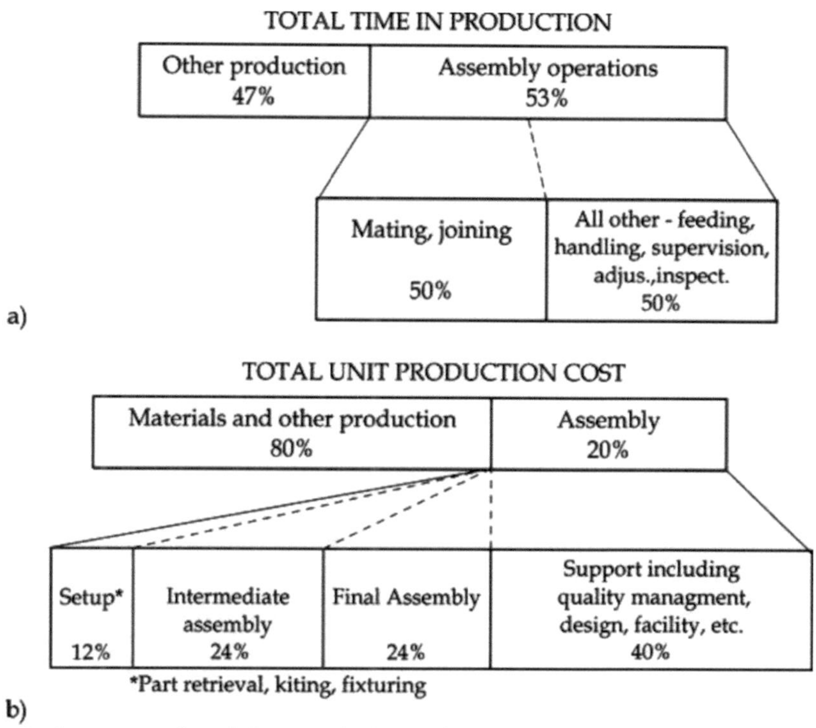

Fig. 4. Typical average breakdown of a) production time and b) production costs of industrial products (Nof et al. 1997)

A typical assembly cell, which exact configuration may vary, will comprise of computer-controlled devices (robots, grippers, etc.), components and fixtures that can functionally accomplish or support one or all of the following tasks (Cecil et al., 2007):

- grasping of an organized/randomly positioned target part from a belt or a bin,
- manipulation and placement/assembly of parts,
- part and object recognition before, during and after assembly,
- quality control and inspection,
- planning and control of the actuators and grippers to accomplish the physical assembly.

Industrial robots nowadays can perform assembly and material handling jobs with very high speed and impressively high precision. However, compared to human operators, robots are hampered by their lack of sensory perception and their need for advanced sensorial capabilities in order to achieve more sophisticated tasks in a non-structured environment (King et al., 1988; Peňa-Cabera et al., 2005). In assembly processes, computer vision is often required to provide data to the applied robot systems in order to allow reliable grasping of objects and performing assembly tasks. Using a vision system for assembly often involves several challenges especially in the areas of data aquisition, coordinate transformation, invariant object recognition with vision systems as well as for the configuration and integration of vision systems into the robot environment.

3. Computer and robot vision

Robot vision is concerned with the sensing of vision data and its interpretation by a computer and thus serves as a versatile robotic sensor. There is a growing demand requiring more complex and faster image processing capabilities in order to allow the implementation of vision systems into sophisticated industrial applications, like advanced assembly automation is.

Robot or machine vision is the application of computer vision to industry and manufacturing, mainly in robots. As computer vision is mainly focused on machine-based image processing, robot vision most often requires also digital input/output devices and computer networks to control other manufacturing equipment such as robotic arms (Davies, 2005). Specific advantages of robot vision systems include precision, consistency, cost effectiveness and flexibility.

Because of its primary mission, a computer vision is a part of a research discipline called artificial intelligence. Many methods, like neural networks and machine learning, developed in the field of artificial intelligence are used in computer vision. Computer vision is also linked with other research disciplines like neurophysiology, psychophysics, physics, computer graphics, digital signal processing etc. (Solina, 2006).

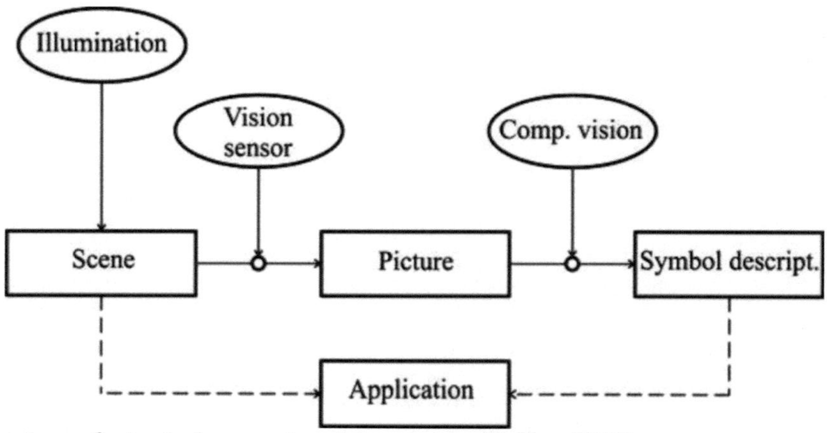

Fig. 5. Structure of a typical computer vision system (Solina, 2006)

Nevertheless, there are many research works being performed in this direction. In many cases in the area of assembly processes, especially in bin picking, a robot must perceive its 3-D environment to be effective. Jet recovering 3-D information and describing it still remains the subject of fundamental research. Some research works (Gupta & Knopf, 1993; Hou et al., 2007; Shapiro & Stockman, 2001) are dealing with artificial vision systems based on the neural morphology of the biological human vision system, aiming to design computational neural structures and artificial vision systems following neural paradigms, mathematical models and computational architectures (Neuro –Vision Systems). Basic components of the computer vision system are presented in figure 5. Appearance of a 3-D scene depends mostly on illumination, position and the direction of the vision sensor.

In a robot vision system, a variety of components are included. The systems layout mainly depends on factors like the environment, the application and the budget. Nevertheless, there are several common ingredients to all vision systems. A typical robot or machine vision system for assembly tasks consists of several of the following components (Davies, 2005; Griot, 2009; Batchelor, 2006; Batchelor & Whelan, 2002):

- one or more digital or analogue cameras (black-and-white or colour) with suitable optics for acquiring images,
- a camera interface for digitizing images (frame grabber) - depends on the application,
- a processor (often a PC or embedded processor, such as a DSP) - when processors and frame grabbers are integrated into the camera itself, such cameras are called »smart cameras«,
- input/Output hardware or communication links,
- optics - lenses to focus the desired field of view onto the image sensor,
- light source (LED, fluorescent or halogen lamps etc.),
- a program to process images and detect relevant features,
- a synchronizing sensor for part detection to trigger image acquisition and processing,
- actuators to sort or reject the processed parts.

Analog systems with classical frame grabbers have become well established in the marketplace and are built into many machines nowadays. The change from analog to digital technologies in the industrial image-processing sector causes that the classical frame grabber appears to be increasingly headed out to pasture. This is because digital communications interfaces such as Gigabit Ethernet, USB and FireWire allow for adequate camera-based solutions without image-capture cards (Leumann, 2009). The classical frame grabber is nowadays usually implemented in new projects primarily when a very short and calculable latency period plays a role in transmission of image data, such as for use with line scanning cameras or for implementation of high-speed cameras. They require data bandwidth from 25 to 70 megabytes per second, which exceeds the bit-serial standards such as USB 2.0, FireWire and Gigabit Ethernet. Additionally, the CameraLink Standard can achieve data-transfer rates up to 680 Mbps. So the classical frame grabber as plug-in card will have to support the CameraLink Standard for a long time to come.

Digital technology has some significant advantages in comparison to the analog one:

- digital image-processing systems allow significantly better image quality,
- up to 12-bit dynamic range,
- the camera's parameters can be set using software,
- the camera's availability, as well as its properties, can be maintained remotely,
- upgrading the camera in the field is easily achieved etc.

The most commonly used vision sensors in robot-based assembly are nowadays black-and-white (or colour for some applications) CCD (charge-coupled device) cameras. 2D-vision systems consist of standard industrial CCD cameras used to take images that are processed by the robot to make decisions on how parts should be handled. Such systems are appropriate for parts, which are laying flat on a belt or in a bin with separator sheets.

For parts that can stack upon each other or that may shift from side to side as the parts stack up or when parts are oriented randomly in a bin, depth estimation for a vision system is necessary. For depth estimation most commonly stereo vision systems are used. For such applications 3-D vision systems have to be applied to get a range image and the orientation of a part in 3D-space. Different laser sensors in conjunction with 2-D cameras, sensors with structured light and stereo cameras, together with different algorithms, can provide 3-D information (Baba et al., 2004; Thorsley et al., 2004; Schraft & Ledermann, 2003). Even though these systems work well, stereo vision systems can provide inaccurate depth estimations, especially in cases with texture-less regions of images or in situations with insufficient illumination of the scene. Most of all, stereo vision is fundamentally limited by the baseline distance between the two cameras, which tends to provide inaccurate depth estimations, as the distances considered are getting large.

Different research approaches are addressing the depth estimation problem by using monocular visual cues, such as texture variations and gradients, defocus, colour etc. With applying a Markov Random Field learning algorithm to capture some of these monocular cues and with incorporating them into a stereo vision system, a significantly better accuracy in depth estimation is obtained than it is possible using either monocular or stereo cues alone (Saxena et al., 2007 a; Saxena et al., 2007 b).

Some other papers treat monocular 3-D vision and object pose estimation in a robot assembly environment. The approach described by L. P. Ray (Ray, 1990) is based on the estimation of the three dimensional position and orientation of objects from one or more monocular images on the prerequisite that the identities of the objects are known and that the three dimensional geometrical models are available. The main weakness of these solutions is the fact, which they fail to achieve the real time performance, necessary in many assembly applications. A solution of this problem is proposed by (Winkler et al., 1997). In this research approach a feature map strategy for the real time 3-D object pose estimation from single 2-D perspective views is presented. Based on the neural network and the systematic training of the Kohonen's self-organizing feature map, the method satisfies the accuracy requirements of object pose estimation in more than 90% of all considered cases.

With the intention to achieve an economic and flexible automatic assembly system working with a SCARA-robot, operating in a random environment, some research activities present the use of simple 2-D CCD cameras in conjunction with additional force sensors and embedded fuzzy sliding mode controllers (Scharstein & Szelinski, 2002). The experimental results prove that the robotic motion control performance is good enough for executing the investigated assembly tasks.

The paper of Sharstein and Szelinski offers a very good overview of stereo vision systems and algorithms, developed by different researchers over the past few decades. In their work the authors present the taxonomy of dense, two-frame stereo methods, compare existing stereo methods and present experiments evaluating the performance of many different variants.

In robotic assembly, vision sensors have a different role than - for example - in mobile robots, where the tasks usually involve exploration of the environment. A robotic assembly cell represents a relatively well ordered environment and is part of an integrated manufacturing process, rather than operating in isolation. This facilitates the fulfillment of some of the major requirements for effective robot assembly. This is especially helpful for applications where expensive and complex machine vision systems should be avoided. The application of vision systems in robot-based assembly systems can be simplified, when products and components are designed for a robot-based assembly and if parts are fed to the system with a relatively accurate position and orientation (Boothroyd, 2005).

The slightly asymmetrical screwed part (figure 6) would not present significant problems in manual handling and insertion, whereas for automatic handling, an expensive vision system would be needed to recognize its orientation. In fact, it can be said that one of the possible benefits of introducing automation in the assembly of a product is, that it forces a reconsideration of its design, which might not only facilitate the part recognition but might also be used to implement other cost-saving or quality-related improvements (e.g. Poka-Yoke design).

Fig. 6. Design change to simplify automatic feeding and orientation (Boothroyd, 2005)

The major role of vision sensors in a robot assembly cell is to compare reality with expectations and to evaluate discrepancies. Essentially this means detecting presence or absence of correct parts and measuring to allow for the detection of component tolerances and positioning errors during relevant stages of assembly.

On one hand, many industrial assembly applications are successfully being handled nowadays using computer vision and robots, especially in robot-based assembly cells. However, for these applications objects have a simple (2D) shape and/or are organized in a structured manner. On the other hand, a general so-called »Bin-picking«, where the objects have a 3-D shape and are randomly organized in a box, still remains a problem. Despite of many research works, that offer special solutions and improvements in the overcoming the bin-picking problem (Schraft & Ledermann, 2003; Kirkegaard, 2005; Kirkegaard & Moeslud, 2006; Hema et. al., 2007), the oldest challenge in robotics remains still unsolved.

4. Object recognition

In robot assembly, a vision recognition system aims to mimic the human sense of vision and must be capable of perceiving and detecting assembly parts as good as the humans can. Three-dimensional object recognition entails representation of a 3-D object, identification of the object from its image, estimation of its position and orientation and registration of multiple views of the object for automatic model construction. Important stages in the design and development of a recognition system are presented in figure 7.

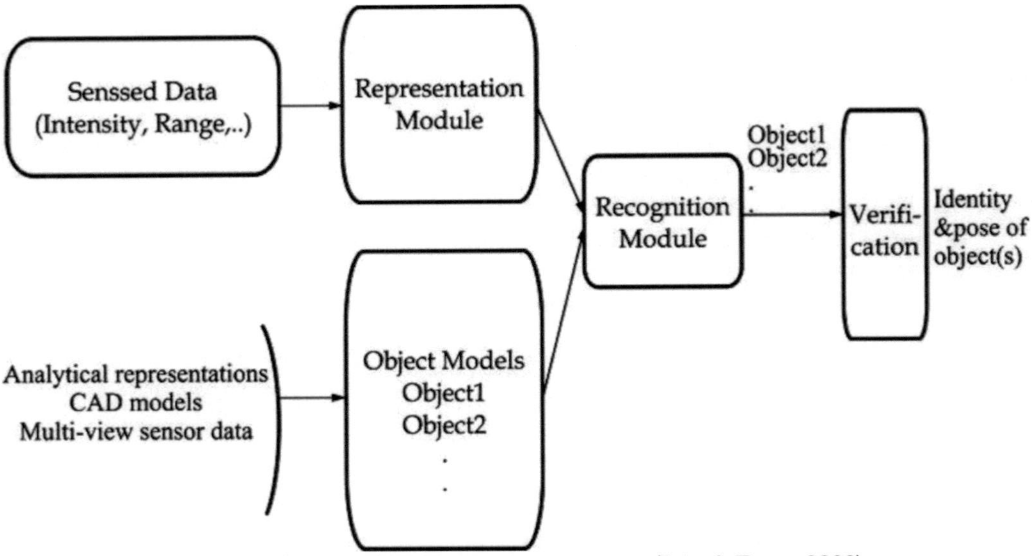

Fig. 7. Key components of a 3-D object recognition system (Jain & Dora, 2000)

A typical approach for handling the object recognition tasks using traditional image processing and computer vision methods usually consists of five steps (Kirkegaard, 2005; Jain & Dora, 2000; Pope, 1994; Faugeras, 1993; Yli-Yaasaki & Ade, 1996):

- Detection or pre-processing – is the low level signal processing which extracts information from the scene and represents it as some form of primitive symbols (Motai & Kosaka, 2004; Pope & Lowe, 2000; Pope & Lowe 1996; Roth et al., 2002; Vujovic et al., 2007).
- Grouping or segmentation – is based on the low level symbols, the primitive features are grouped into higher order features, which give more information for the selection and matching in the next steps (Lowe, 1987; Balslev & Eriksen, 2002).
- Indexing or feature extraction – selecting from the stable object features the most likely model from a library of models (model base) and finding a way of quickly comparing a set of features with a model, avoiding a search through all models. As a critical component, a stable, representative feature extraction system should be developed to extract key features for a specific problem domain in the feature extraction stage. The result of feature extraction is normally a feature vector (Kirkegaard, 2005). There is usually one of two methods of representation applied:
  - appearance-based approach – information about appearance of the object is used (Pope, 1994; Balslev & Eriksen, 2002),
  - model-based methods – information about geometrical features, type and spatial relations of the object is used (Motai & Kosaka, 2004; Lowe, 1987).
- Matching or classification – finding the best fitting between the scene features and the model features and solving the localization problem. In this stage, a classifier system uses extracted key features to distinguish the classes of the objects of interest. The algorithms

or methods for these stages are generally domain dependent, particularly when using traditional image processing and computer vision techniques. Learning paradigms such as neural networks or genetic programming approaches have usually been applied to the matching or classification stage Kirkegaard, 2005).
- Verification - verifying the estimated identity and location of an object (Kirkegaard, 2005, Pope & Lowe, 1996).

To facilitate the task of identification and localization, a description of each object to be recognized is available to the computer and can be used. These descriptions can either be model-based or appearance-based, or a combination of both.

Based on the dimensionality of their spatial description, various types of object recognition problems can be stated (Antrade-Ceto & Kak, 2000):
- recognition of a 2-D object from a single 2-D image,
- recognition of a 3-D object from a single 2-D image,
- recognition of a 3-D object from a single 3-D image (a range map),
- recognition of a 2-D or 3-D object from multiple 2-D images taken from different viewpoints, etc.

In the past decades, much progress has been made in the research of recognizing 2-D objects in single 2-D images and in recognizing 3-D objects in range maps. A considerable progress has also been made in the recognition of 2-D or 3-D objects using multiple 2-D images, as in binocular or stereo vision. However, today object recognition remains largely unsolved and is still a very active field of research.

The data of assembly parts is usually obtained by a CCD camera, giving intensity data or by laser line scanning which gives a range or depth map. From this data, features have to be extracted for object recognition, which involves the matching of image features from either range or intensity data, against a previous internal representation of the object (a model).

Certain features like curvatures are independent of the view point for the object. After inspection of respective signs of an object curvature using different approaches, it is possible to define the local surface area as being one of eight fundamental primitive types: peak, pit, ridge, valley, saddle ridge, saddle valley, minimal and flat. Different algorithms have been proposed to extract curvatures from an object (Fischler & Bolles, 1986; Rosin & West, 1995, Cox et al., 1993). The difficulty of these approaches is that extracted curvatures are highly dependent on the selected starting points and the order of the edge linking. Some other approaches (Alter & Basri, 1998) propose dynamic programming and relaxation to avoid such problems. In this case the edges are organized as nodes of a graph and linked to each other through graphs.

Other common features, which are extracted from objects are edges, planar regions etc. Edge detection is a very important step in low level image processing and can be used in measurement of a distance from the obstacle. In (Vujovic et al., 2007) a new approach is proposed, which promises much faster edge detection capabilities as previously known edge detectors can provide.

Many different approaches and methods have been developed or tackled in the field of object detection and recognition by different researchers in the past years. A quite detailed survey of previous work has been treated by (Jain & Dora, 2000) and (Antrade-Ceto & Kak, 2000). The authors discuss the recognition problems, methodologies and algorithms like object shape complexity, size of object model database, learning, individual and generic object categories, non-rigidity of objects, occlusion and viewpoint-dependency, object representations and recognition strategies (image sensors, models, matching strategies) and 3-D free form object recognition.

A very important field of research in object recognition is represented by the area of learning/adaptive algorithms. One of the major advantages of a learning system is the ability to learn/extract the useful features from the training data set and to apply these features to the test data. Some authors (Roth et al., 2002) use a PAC (Probably Approximately Correct) model for their learning strategies. In this research, authors quantify success relatively to the distribution of the observed objects, without making assumptions on the distribution. In (Pope & Lowe, 1996) authors model the appearance of an object using multiple views, including a training stage, in which the system learns to extract the models characteristics from training images and recognizes objects with it. The model uses probability distributions to characterize the significance, position, intrinsic measurements of various discrete features of appearance and also describes topological relations among features. A matching procedure, combining qualities of both iterative alignment and graph matching uses feature uncertainty information recorded by the model to guide the search for a match between model and image.

In recent years, since the late 1980s, neural and genetic learning paradigms (neural networks, genetic paradigms and genetic programming) have attracted attention as very promising methods of solving automatic target recognition and detection problems. In particular, neural and genetic systems offer potentially powerful learning and adaptive abilities and are very suitable for automatic object recognition in real time (Winkler et al., 1997, Klobucar et al., 2007).

In general, the currently available computer vision systems for object recognition are still not as adaptive and universal as biological systems are. Successful commercial systems of computer vision are usually designed to solve well defined and/or specific tasks. For solving tasks computer vision systems often combine multiple standard strategies or even apply strategies that have been developed individually for a specific application (Forsyth & Ponce, 2002).

In robot-based assembly production processes, there is very often a need for grasping and manipulating of complex objects. Most of the robot vision systems require the complete knowledge of both, the shape and the position of the assembly parts. Due to the fact that vision systems are often specifically adapted to the individual 2D-shapes and the individual way the parts are fed to the system, a change of the produced parts usually requires a time consuming adaptation of the overall system. This could represent a cost problem especially for small series. With respect to the before mentioned aspects, there is a need for efficient robots with advanced machine vision capabilities that allow the recognition of complex, and randomly organized parts, lying on a conveyor belt or in a bin, with little or no prior knowledge about the pose and geometry of the parts. Especially the so called bin-picking problem - the picking of randomly organized 3-D parts in a bin - has not yet been solved in a general manner, primarily due to severe occlusion problems.

Many researchers are dealing with this basic problem, which represents one of the remaining obstacles to a widespread introduction of vision systems to robot-based assembly. In searching for appropriate solutions, the above mentioned methodologies and algorithms for object detection and recognition are applied. In (Boughorbel et al., 2003; Goldfeder et al., 2007) range maps have been applied for the reconstruction of objects using super quadric representations and decomposition trees. Based on laser scanners for 3-D object detection a model based approach in combination with CAD models (Schraft & Ledermann, 2003; Kristensen et al., 2001) or Harmonic Shape Context features (Kirkegaard, 2005; Kirkegaard & Moeslund, 2006), which are invariant to translation, scale and 3-D rotation, have been applied. Also some research has been done applying stereo vision together with a set of two neural networks (which are then compared with each other) namely the Radial Basis Function nets and Simple Feed forward nets (Hema et al., 2007). An algorithm for segmentation of partially occluded bin objects and the location of the topmost object is proposed. The experimental results have shown that the proposed algorithm might be appropriate for many bin picking applications if special attention is paid to the lighting situation. The results of the above mentioned research in bin-picking are very promising but the research is still more or less in research stage. Even though that grasping is not optimal and for some object not feasible, all contributions show an improved accuracy and efficiency in bin picking and sorting.

5. Applications of robot vision in control processes

Introduction of robot vision control to an assembly process initially demands a clarification of the purpose of the application, which is usually not just a problem of measuring one or more product parameters in a very short time, but also fault detection, usually detected in manual assembly by operators, based on an appropriate sample.

In many assembly processes, the control process is still undertaken by the operators. They are capable of making an estimation and judgment about the accuracy and shape faults of a product or part using their acquired skills for quick and accurate decisions based on the human vision system. These tasks are usually complex and the accuracy and speed depend on the operator's psychological and physical condition. The consequences are unreliable results and a very serious possibility of overlooking faults. The reliability of human decisions is also reduced by the monotony of the task and by tiredness (Herakovic, 2007a).

Today's robot vision and identification systems are more and more reliable and robust, and therefore convenient for industrial applications and are becoming indispensable to the assembly or disassembly process (Braggins, 2006; Ostojic et al., 2008). Control systems, based on robot vision, are capable of maintaining a control process even more efficiently than a human if the conditions for an appropriate use of the technical benefits of robot vision are ensured (West, 2006, West, 2009).

A robot vision system, which is used in an industrial environment for tasks such as inspection, measurement and fault detection, has to be a robust and very reliable system. For this reason, the development of measurement equipment using robot vision has to follow a fixed procedure (Trdic, 2000; Skvarc, 2000). Usually, the procedure is split into a precise determination of tasks (measuring, fault detection) and goals, into the robot vision selection and working conditions (illumination and position determination), component selection of the robot vision (camera, computer, lenses and optics), and finally, the development of an automatic robot handling system for the parts.

5.1 Fault detection and dimension control

When using a robot vision system for fault detection and dimension control, lighting is always a critical component and should be treated as one of the first steps of component selection. The effectiveness of an illuminating source in an inspection and fault detection process is determined by the direction at which light strikes an object and the direction of the reflected light into, or away from the camera. Suitable illumination covers the required field of view, creates a consistently measurable degree of contrast and does not cause reflected glare. Different light types are required to provide successful illumination for the broad range of products being inspected by automated systems (Merva, 2009).

Let us take an example of a robot vision application in quality control processes during the electromotor (EM) stator assembly. To get the optimal conditions for the effective robot vision quality control, some experimental research efforts of the robot vision tasks determination and especially of the influence of lighting on the fault detection and dimension control of electromotor (EM) stator are considered (Herakovic, 2007 b).

In control process, final product quality control is in fact an inspection of parts and of final product in technical and visual manner. The challenge is greater when the product is composed of parts, produced by an unstable process. The EM stator, assembled from thin metal plates, represents such an example (figure 8). The assembling process is performed by a well known special forming machine. High accuracy and no visible faults on the EM stator are demanded so the 100 percent control process should be guaranteed by the robot vision. Assembly process is followed by painting and drying, and in both processes inaccuracy and fault can occur. The control process involves:

- EM stator height measuring,
- slot width measuring,
- spherity or so called had-shape control
- position and rotation of claw,
- painting quality - uniformity,
- slot occurrence on the roll outside,
- plate derivation and
- randomly, the inside and outside diameters of EM stator have to be measured.

Fig. 8. EM stator assembled from thin metal plates

Mechanical defects on the inside and outside of EM stator, as a result of non-adequate assembly process, are shown in the figures 9a and b. Such defects are slot occurrences between plate (inside or outside) and broken EM stator.

a) b)

Fig. 9. Slots inside and outside (a, b) and broken EM stator (b)

Figure 10a shows mechanical damages, such as ruptured and derivate plats (can occur in performing the manual control by mechanical caliber). The derivations of plates inside of the EM stator are usually effected by assembly process (figure 10 b). The appearance of varnish or paint on the EM stator also means a false product (figure 10 b).

a) b)

Fig. 10. Moved and derivate plates (a, b) and paint rest (b)

Manual control process of the above described critical places of the EM stator has been recognized as not reliable enough and is even a source of new damages of the finished product. The control process is also a bottleneck in the assembly process. In such a case the automation of the inspection and measuring of the EM stator can be the optimal solution for a reliable quality assurance.

The analysis of necessary conditions for the robot vision application in final quality control of the EM stator package can give very satisfying results through the experimental approach related to the technique and the type of illumination, which can guarantee a reliable robot vision quality control. For each critical area of the EM stator, the conditions which can influence the successful machine vision fault detection should be examined in grater detail. In the presented research this has been done by using the variation of influential parameters like the position of the camera and light source (Burns, 1999), type of the camera lenses (Jenny, 2000) and above all by the variation of the angle of the stator position regarding to the camera and the light source position. In the research the Sony XC-ST50-CE camera has been used.

Each critical area of the controlled stator demands a specific experimental setup, which must allow the analysis of all variations of different parameter influencees on the quality of the robot vision control of the stator. The aim of all presented experimental setups is to assure satisfactory quality of the detection of as many faults as possible, with a minimum number of handling operations of the stator and with the least possible changes of the type and sort of lighting and camera lenses.

Figure 11a represents an experimental setup for the analysis of the impact of a direct general-purpose different colour illumination (low angle ring illuminator) and the impact of different colour backgrounds on a depth control (for the reason of the light reflection), contrast and on a detection of visual defects of the EM stator. It is supposed that different background and illumination colours are more suitable for the visibility of some surface defects like remains of varnish and mechanical damages.

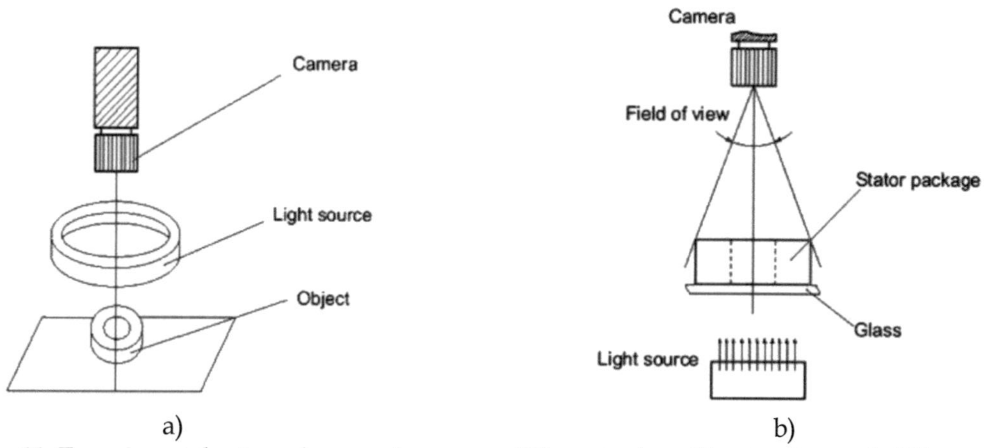

Fig. 11. Experimental setup: a) general-purpose different colour illumination and different colour background; b) backlight illumination

Experimental setup with the backlight illumination (figure 11b) enables the analysis of parameters like the rapture of the stator plates, dimensions of the stator slots, general stator dimensions etc. The presented experimental setup is suitable for the reliable detection of the many of before mentioned parameters only with the use of appropriate camera lenses (conventional, telecentric etc.). In this case the type of lighting is not so important for the quality of detection.

For the detection of some parameters like mechanical damages on the outer stator circumference and slot occurrence as well as plate derivation and shifting on the inner stator circumference, the experimental setups presented in figure 12 are convenient. Also in this case the reliability of the detection of before mentioned parameters depends on the use of appropriate camera lenses; however, the type of lighting is decisive for the quality of detection this time.

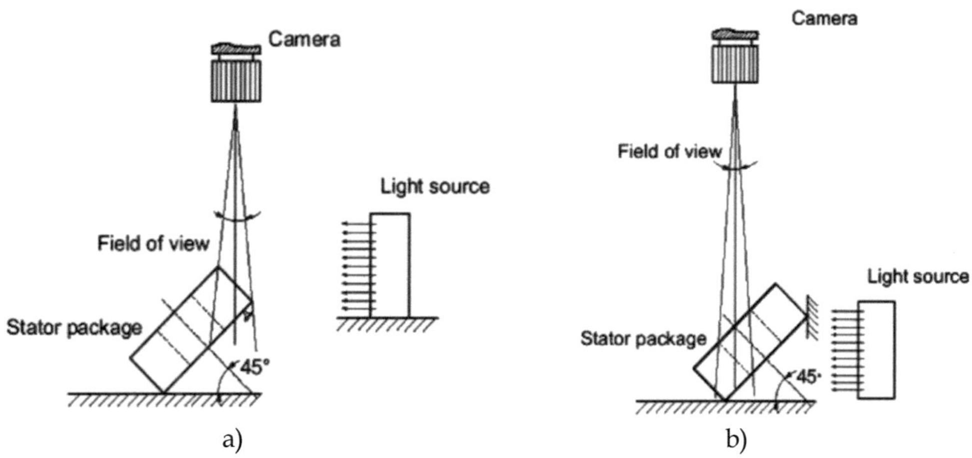

Fig. 12. Fault detection on a) outer stator circumference and b) inner stator circumference

As it is evident from the figure 12, one of the key parameters for the satisfactory quality detection of the stator faults is beside the camera lenses and lighting, also the angle of the stator inclination and the distance of the camera from the observed field. It is necessary to reach the best possible sharpness of the stator on the screen. The incline of the stator demands also the best possible depth sharpness, which is theoretically better when the incline of the object is bigger.

Using the experimental setup in figure 13a, an exact determination of spherity, height/width, parallelism and perpendicularity of the stator package is possible. The quality of the detection depends mainly on the type of lenses used and a little bit less on the type and the colour of the illumination.

In the case of the EM stator the inclination is limited with its geometry. The maximal theoretic inclination angle of the stator is 60° as shown in figure 13b. If the inclination angle is bigger, the upper edge of the stator covers over the lower edge of the inner circumference and the camera filed of view can not cover the whole lower half of the inner circumference of the stator. For this reason more detailed experimental analysis of the influence of the stator inclination angle on the quality of the fault detection must be carried out with the consideration of the optimal distance of the camera from the observed object to get the largest possible filed of view at a time.

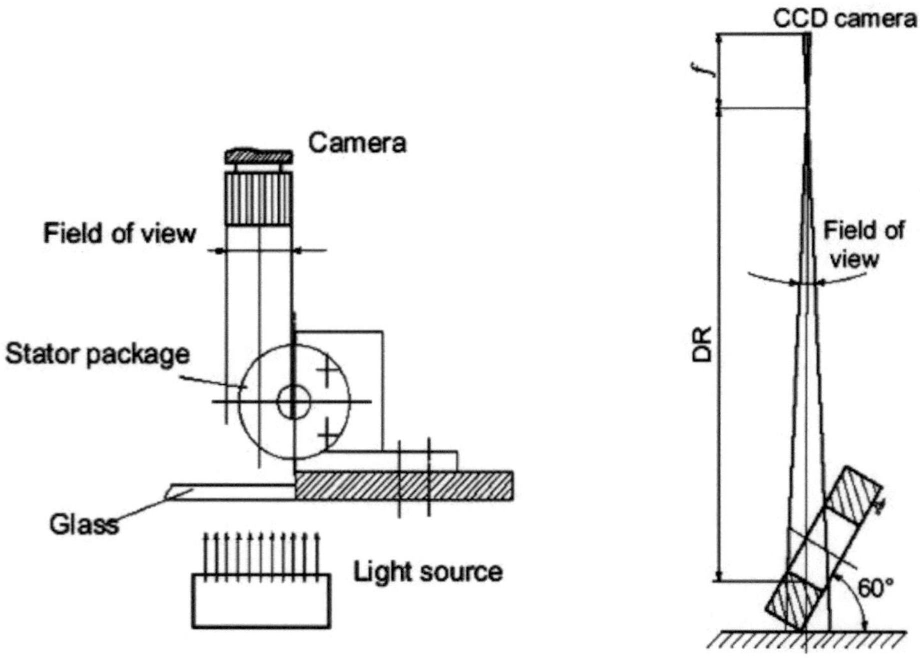

a) b)

Fig. 13. a) Spherity and dimension control; b) Maximal stator inclination angle

5.2 Experimental results

With the results obtained from the above presented experimental research work it is possible to identify necessary conditions regarding the technique and the type of illumination as well as the inclination angle of the stator package to get the desired results with the robot vision quality control of the dimensions, mechanical damages and visual look of the EM stator.

Figure 14 shows the influence of the stator inclination angle on the fault detection quality. The increase of the inclination angle brings on better detection quality mainly of both edges of the inner stator circumference.

a)

b)

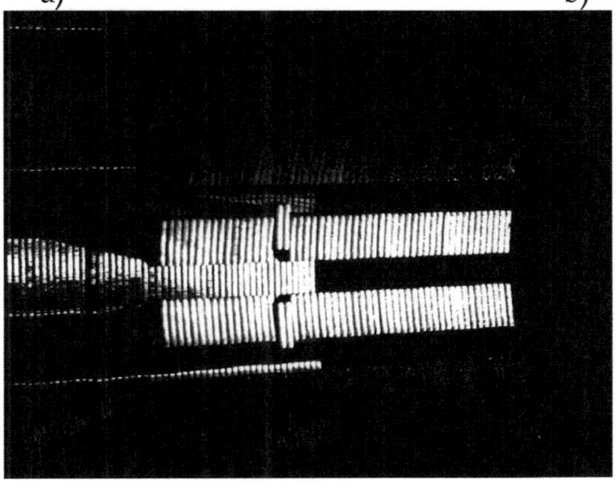

c)

Fig. 14. Impact of the stator inclination angle a) 30°, b) 45° in c) 55°

However, the increase of the inclination angle causes the difference in the distance between the lighting source on one side and the upper and lower edge respectively of the observed segment on the other side. It has for consequence a non homogeneous illumination of the stator and herewith unreliable fault detection, as shown in figure 15.

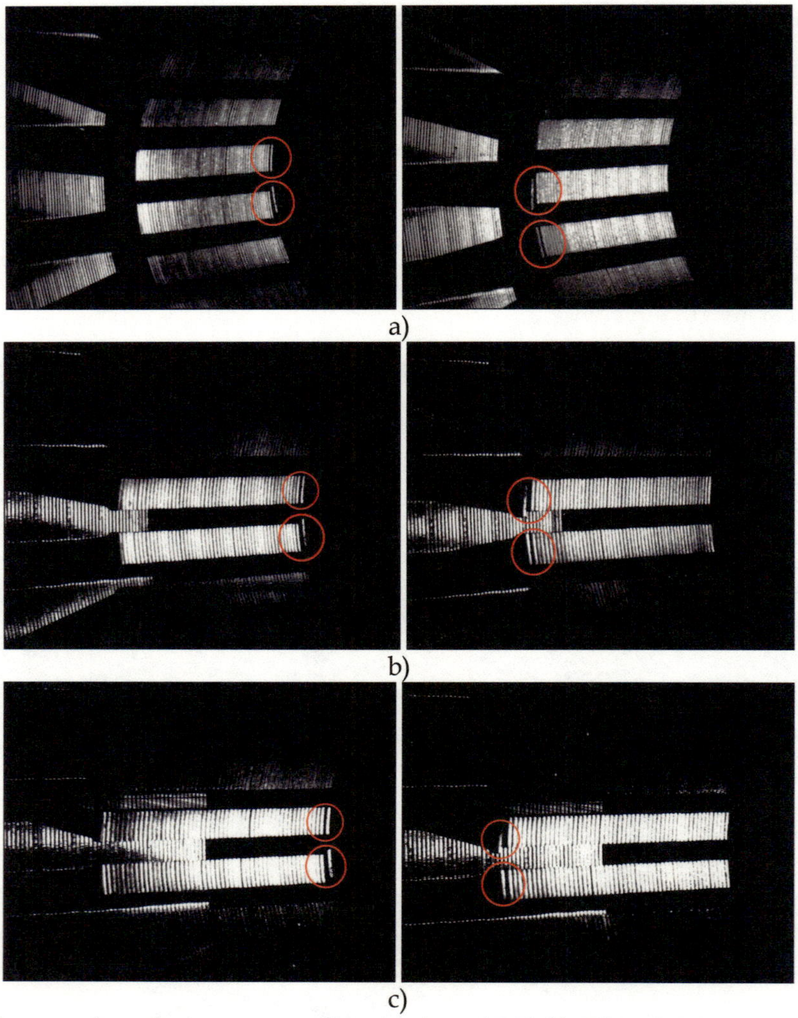

Fig. 15. Influence of non homogeneous illumination: a) 30°, b) 45° in c) 55°

Fig. 16. Front surface defects – varnish accumulation

One of the experimental results, using a low angle ring illuminator (figure 11a) with different colour lighting and different background colours, is presented in figure 16. In this case a black background colour was applied. Bright areas of the stator represent surface defects as a consequence of varnish accumulation or nonuniformity of varnish on the surface. The method is appropriate for the control of the front surfaces regarding the detection of the varnish nonuniformity.

The best results of the control of one of the most important dimension parameters of the stator, of the slot width, are possible with the back light illumination method (figure 11b) and with the use of a telecentric lenses. Figure 17 shows one of the experimental results, where it is obvious that the use of a telecentric lens (figure 17a) eliminates the negative effect of the depth, a parallax, which appears with the conventional lens (figure 17b).

The stator appears on the screen as 2D picture in ground plan with clear and sharp edges. This fact assures the 100 % control of the slot width along the whole depth of the stator package. With this method also the 100 % control of the inner and outer diameter of the stator package is possible.

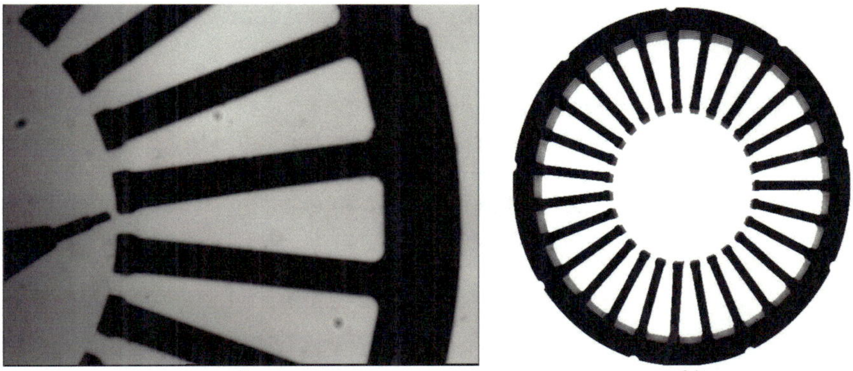

a) b)

Fig. 17. Control of the slot width with: a) telecentric and b) conventional lens

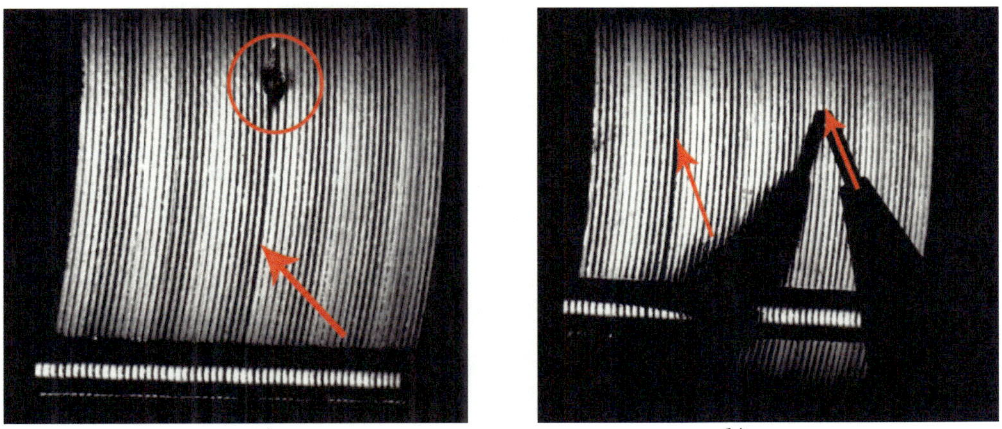

a) b)

Fig. 18. Mechanical damages (a) and slots (b) on the outer stator circumference

Results of the experimental detection of the mechanical damages of outer and inner stator circumference with the experimental setup from the figure 12 are presented in figures 18 and 19, where a mechanical damage (figure 18a) and slots between the stator plates on outer circumference (figure 18b) are very well visible. Slots and plate derivations on the inner stator circumference are clearly visible in the figure 19.

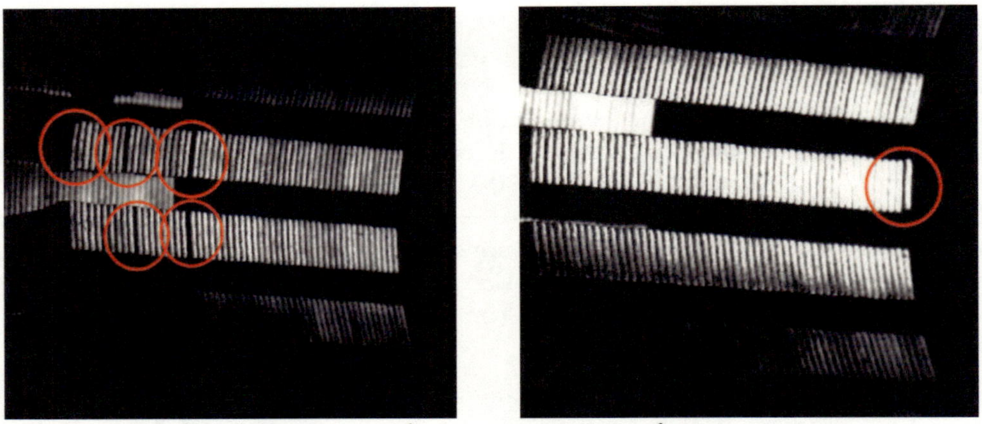

Fig. 19. Slots and plate derivations on the inner stator circumference

Results of the detection of spherity, height/width, parallelism and perpendicularity of the stator package are shown in figure 20. In figure 20a an example of (non)spherity and the height/width of the stator is visible. An example of successful detection of parallelism and perpendicularity of the stator package is shown in figure 20b. In both cases a satisfactory result is achieved only with a telecentric lens.

a) b)

Fig. 20. Successful detection of: a) (non)spherity, the height and b) parallelism and perpendicularity.

The results of the experimental analysis of conditions for a successful replacement of manual (done by workers) quality control of EM stator packages by a robot vision control can enable better efficiency and accuracy of the stator quality control process through the unlimited time period, independently of different subjective and objective disturbances. At the same time the machine vision control can help with the humanization of the pretentious labour filed.

5.3 Algorithm development for a diameter and roundness measurement of a welded ring

Another assembly application, where an intelligent measuring control system with integrated robot vision for enabling the solving of complex assembly and quality control tasks with high accuracy and speed is needed, is the welding of a metal ring. The welding process must satisfy high quality standards and expectations because the diameter of the welded ring D_N must reach the accuracy ±0.05 mm with the repeatability ±0.01 mm and at the same time the roundness of the welded ring O_V must reach the accuracy ±0.25mm with the repeatability ±0.05mm (figure 21). The ring is shown as black points and the minimum (*Dmin*) and maximum (*Dmax*) diameters are shown as two thinner red hatched curves. The difference between the maximum and minimum diameters is an indication of the roundness of the ring (*Ov*). A high level of accuracy and repeatability for the measurement, demands the introduction of a 100-percent control process. The quality-control procedure for a welded ring must involve a visual observation of the inner surface of the welded ring, checking the inner and the outer diameter as well as the roundness of the welded ring.

The application of robot vision in a quality-control procedure for a welded ring is a very complex and purpose-specific task which demands a great amount of expert knowledge, experiences and innovations. Besides the previously described approaches and conditions for an effective robot vision application, the development of the mathematical algorithm, which enables the use of robot vision for the diameter and the roundness measurement of welded rings is one of the major challenges in this case. Even greater challenge represents the demand, that the measuring system must satisfy all the demands for the successful implementation in industrial application.

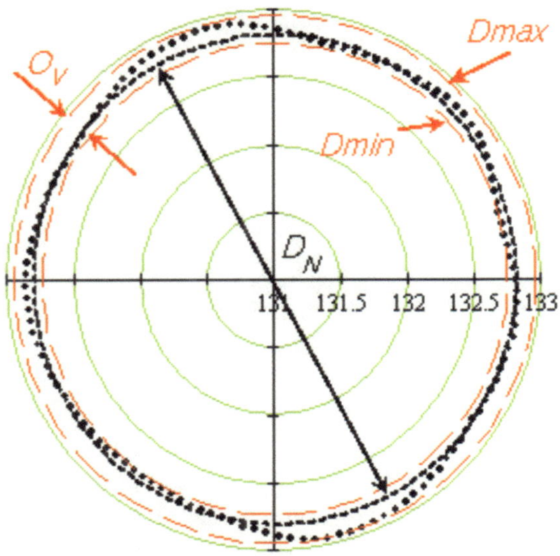

Fig. 21. Graphical representation of the measuring values, ring curve

In the past few years there have been developments of mathematical algorithms for each measurement procedure in the robot vision control process, which is a multilayer problem for every new application of robot vision. A robot vision system which is used in an industrial environment for tasks such as inspection, measurement, and fault detection, has to be a robust and very reliable system. For that reason, the development of measurement equipment using robot vision has to follow a fixed procedure (Skvarc, 2000; Trdic, 2000). Usually, the procedure is split into a precise determination of tasks (measuring, fault detection) and goals, into the robot vision and working conditions selection (illumination and position determination), component selection of the machine vision (camera, computer, lenses and optics), and, finally, the development of an automatic robot handling system for the parts.

Main idea of the control procedure is the non-contact control method using robot vision, which involves cameras and laser diodes mounted on a solid holder and a rotating table, presented in figure 22 (Petrisic, 2008).

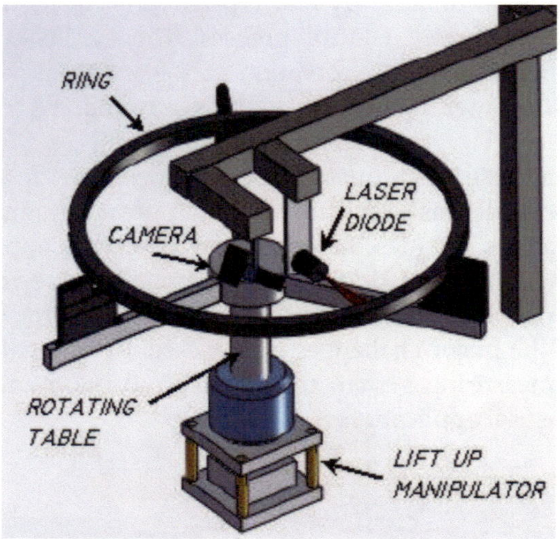

Fig. 22. Measuring system configuration

The ring is placed on the table, which is rotating during the measuring process. The laser path (the vertical lighting line on the inner surface of the ring) is observed with a camera (Pauli, 2001; Redford, 1986). A lift-up manipulator is used when the ring is put on and off the table. The heart of the process is the FDS Imaging Vision software with the integrated numerical program VBA (Visual Basic for Application). After choosing laser triangulation method (Demeyere, 2006) as the measuring process, it is important to analyze a mathematical description of the ring's trajectory and to develop the main algorithm for the eccentric placement elimination. The final step is the development of the proper mathematical algorithm, which is then integrated into the VBA program (Simic et al., 2009).

Measuring the surface of a complex relief by using the laser triangulation method is a well-known and often-used process. The laser path and the correctly oriented camera are shown in figure 23a. Moving the laser path and the camera together along the surface makes it possible to measure the relief. This principle is used also in our case for measuring the shape (the diameter and roundness) of the welded ring (figure 23b).

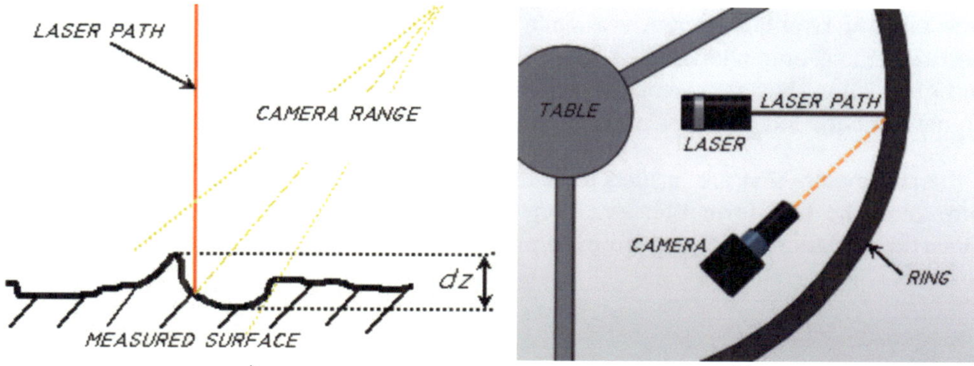

a) b)

Fig. 23. a) Surface measurement using laser triangulation; b) Laser triangulation method, ring movement

The measuring configuration consists of a single camera and a single laser diode, which are then mounted in the fixed holder. The welded ring is placed – but not fixed – on the rotating table without centering it. The laser path is directed to the inside of the ring's surface, so it is possible to get moving the vertical lighting lines by moving the ring edge along the laser's path. This laser line is observed using a CCD camera, which has to be set up correctly. A *30* to *60* degree angle between the camera (optical axis) and the laser path is needed to achieve the optimum conditions (Hecht, 1987; Gruen, 2001).

When the welded ring is rotating, the observing line or point moves along the laser path, and what we see on the camera screen is shown in figures 24 a and b.

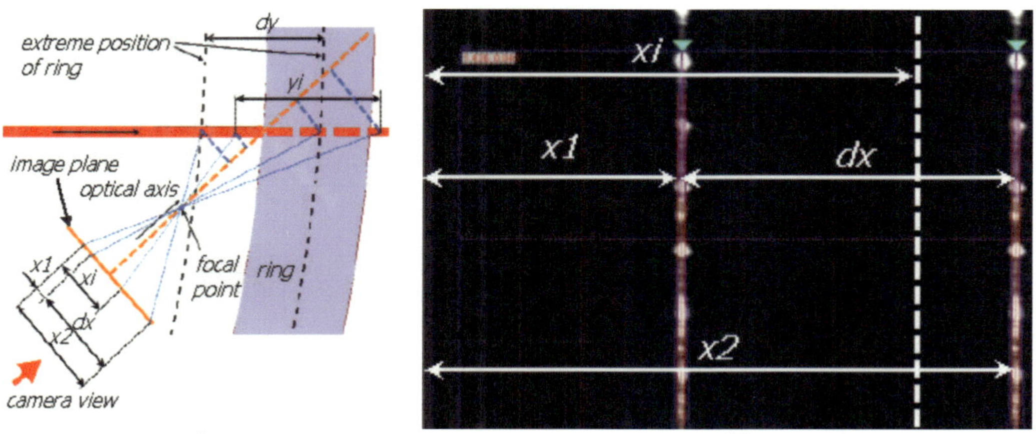

a) b)

Fig. 24. a) Principle of the laser triangulation method; b) Camera view, calibration on the camera screen, FDS Imaging software interface

During a single turn of the ring, one hundred photos are taken (the camera grabs one image for every 3.6 degrees of rotation). The whole camera process can be referred to as image processing. The camera image, presented on the main display of the computer, is shown in figure 24b. The laser line, shown as a white vertical line, is moving right and left. For a better presentation and understanding of the problem, two white lines are sketched on the screen (see figure 24b). They represent the extreme right and left positions of the laser line (the extreme right and left positions of the welded ring) while the ring is rotating.

All the parameters that are needed for a triangulation-method calculation are presented in figure 24a. The transformation equation for the presented triangulation method, which defines the deviation of the ring from the previously defined parameters, is given by eq. (1):

$$y_i = (x_i - x_1) \cdot k \tag{1}$$

On the basis of eq. (1) it is possible to calculate the movement of a ring y_i by knowing the parameters x_i (the actual movement of the laser line), x_1 (the extreme left position of the laser line, used for the scale calibration) and the transformation factor k, known as the scale factor, which can be calculated by using eq. (2) (see figure 24a).

$$k = \frac{dy}{dx} \tag{2}$$

Theoretical and mathematical descriptions of the measuring-point trajectory are treated in detail by Simic (Simic et al., 2009). It is important to emphasize that the measuring system, which is described in figure 22, needs to be ideal, which means:

- the axis of the rotating table is ideal, i.e., it is without any oscillations during the rotation,
- the welded ring and the rotating table are treated as a rigid body.

When an industrial measuring principle is set as the final goal, it is clear that it is impossible to place the welded ring exactly on the rotating axle. For this reason the movement of the measuring point for the ideal circular ring has to be especially considered, where the centre of the ring is placed outside the rotating axle, which represents the origin of the (x, y) global coordinate system (see figure 25a). When the ring is rotating, the centre of the ring moves along the centre trajectory, as shown in figure 25b.

For this case the laser line's movement on the ring is described by eq. (3), where $R_i(\alpha)$ represents the variable diameter of the ring, depending on the rotating angle α. Figure 25c presents the results of the points $R_i(\alpha)$, calculated using eq. (3).

$$R_i(\alpha) = E \cdot \cos\alpha_i + \sqrt{R_v^{\,2} - (E \cdot \sin\alpha_i)^2} \tag{3}$$

using the parameters: E… the eccentricity of ring [mm], $R_{V...}$ the radius of ring [mm], a …the angle of rotation [°]

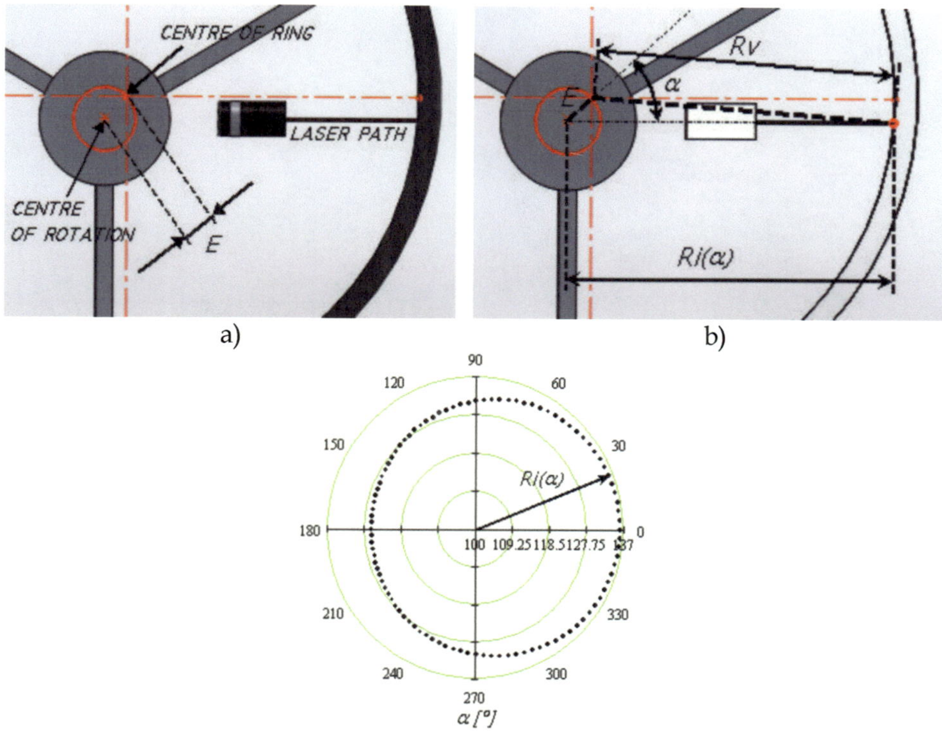

c)

Fig. 25. a) Ideal circular ring centered outside the rotating axle - influence on the value of the diameter; b) Trigonometric representation of the ring projection; c) Sketched ring points $R_i(\alpha)$

It is also necessary to consider carefully the influence of the eccentric position of the laser path on the diameter value, as it is shown in figures 26 a and b. A critical situation only occurs when the position of the laser is changed during the measuring process or the rotation of the ring. Otherwise, this problem can be eliminated by the software correction of the ring's radius (radius calibration).

If the position of the laser diodes is changed by a distance $\pm z$, the diameter value can be calculated using eq. (4). A comparison between the calculated values of the diameter $R_i(\alpha)$ and $R_z(\alpha)$ and the dependence on the rotating angle α are shown in figure 26c. It is also necessary to consider the influence of the system vibration during the measuring process (Simic et al., 2009).

$$R_z(\alpha) = E \cdot \cos\alpha_i + \sqrt{R_v^{\,2} - (E \cdot \sin\alpha_i - z)^2} \tag{4}$$

where the parameters are as follows:

E… the eccentricity of ring [mm]
R_V… the radius of the ring [mm]
α_i… the angle of rotation [°]
z…the eccentricity of the laser path [mm]

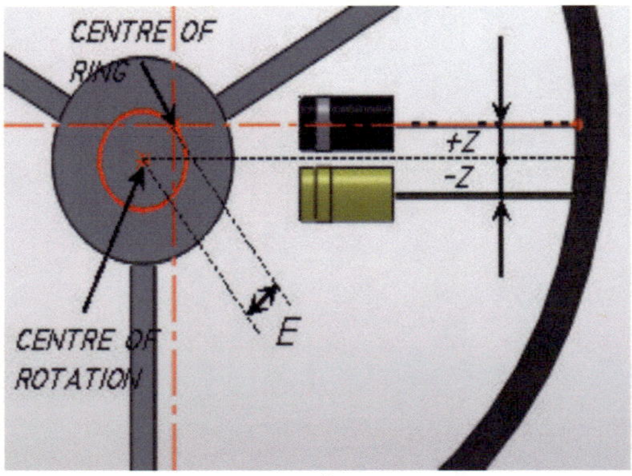

a)

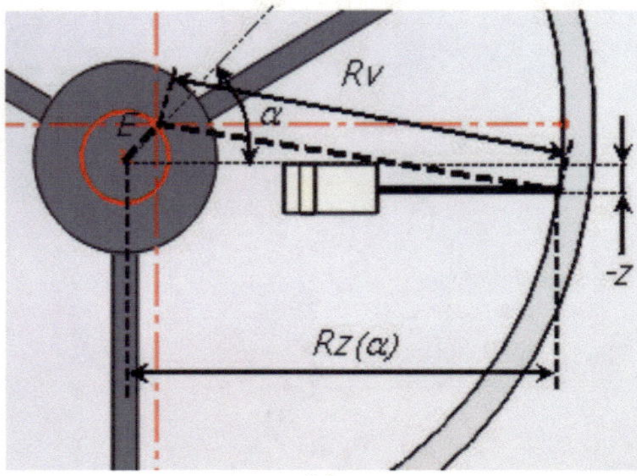

b)

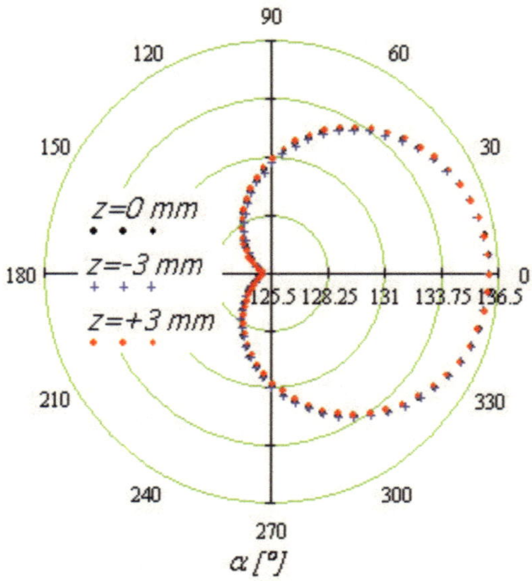

c)

Fig. 26. a) Eccentric position of the laser - influence on the diameter value; b) Graphical analysis of the ring projection; c) Comparison between the $R_i(\alpha)$ and the $R_z(\alpha)$

One of the possibilities to eliminate the eccentric displacement of the ring is to calculate the area and the centre of this area, which is generated by measuring the points that are subsequently connected by lines to generate a polygon. From knowing the size and the centre point of the area and with further optimization of the mathematical algorithm, it is possible to eliminate the eccentric displacement of the ring on the rotating table (Simic et al., 2009).

By considering the optimized mathematical algorithm, experimental verifications and industrial demands, it is possible to apply the robot vision system for the quality control of the diameter and roundness measurement of the welded ring. The results and graphical explanation of the ring diameter and the ring roundness are presented in figures 27a and b. The calculated average radius or diameter is shown as a full curve in figure 27a and the measuring points, transformed into the origin are shown as the hatched curve, as shown in the same figure. The black points in figure 27b represent the real ring shape, while the average diameter curve represents the x axis of the graph (full black line). The difference between the full and hatched curves (O) is given by eq. (5), and is calculated for every single point of the ring circumference at the given angle α:

$$O(\alpha) = R_{vi} - R\_avg \tag{5}$$

The minimum (O_{min}) and the maximum (O_{max}) differences between these two curves are used to calculate the roundness of the ring, O_v (Zhao & Chen, 2005) – equations 6 and 7.

$$\begin{aligned} O_{\min}(\alpha) &= \min(R_{vi} - R\_avg) \\ O_{\max}(\alpha) &= \max(R_{vi} - R\_avg) \end{aligned} \tag{6}$$

$$Ov = |O_{\min}(\alpha)| + |O_{\max}(\alpha)| \tag{7}$$

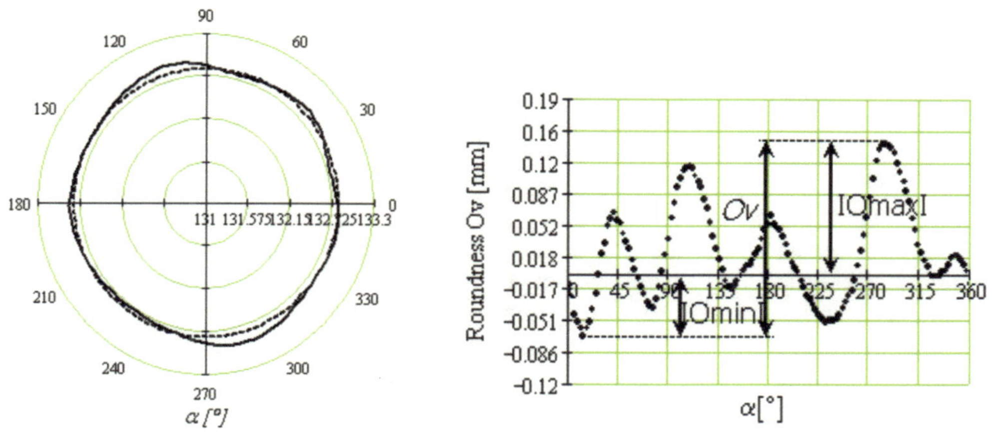

a) b)

Fig. 27. Results: a) Average and ring diameter curves; b) Roundness of the ring depending on the rotation angle α[°] (Simic et al., 2009)

6. Conclusion

The application of robot vision in robot assembly and control processes provides immense potential and challenges, at the same time, for both research and industrial applications, as can be seen by the recent developments summarized in this chapter. It can easily be perceived that the next generation of assembly technology will include versatile robot vision systems with a high level of versatility and robustness. The chapter provides a brief overview of the most recent research efforts in the area of machine vision in assembly and control processes. Various approaches and issues relating assembly, robot assembly, robot vision and object recognition including the bin picking problem are addressed.

In the first part of the chapter, a general overview and the state-of-the art of the robot vision implementation in the filed of assembly and quality control processes is given, considering robot vision with its advantages and disadvantages and the structure of a typical robot vision system with its basic components description. Some methods, most commonly used in the robot vision, are briefly described and some recognition principles of objects as well as the depth estimation techniques are presented, discussed and some researches are introduced.

In the second part of the chapter, object recognition in assembly and quality control processes is discussed. In this regard all key components of an object recognition system are presented and discussed more in detail by giving an overview of different research works and published papers considering various algorithms for effective object recognition. Also the bin-picking problem with randomly organized 3-D parts in a bin is treated.

In the third or last part of the chapter the implementation of robot vision in control processes is discussed more in detail by considering handling, measurement, fault detection etc. of objects in laboratory and in industrial environment. Additionally, some examples of algorithm development and its practical implementation supported with research results are presented and discussed.

The impact of the illumination on the accuracy of the quality control using the robot vision in the case of the EM stator package assembly process is presented more in detail. Some experimental methods of the identification of conditions and lighting techniques are presented, which decisively influence the practical introduction of the robot vision in the process of quality control in the EM stator assembly. The experimental results prove that the reliable replacement of the manual quality control with the robot vision control in the assembly of the EM stator depends decisively on the right choice of the techniques and the type of illumination of the object. The chapter ends with the presentation and discussion of the results of the research work, focused on the development of a mathematical-numerical algorithm for a modern robot-vision measuring system. A robot-vision experimental system for the ring-diameter and ring-roundness measurements is presented.

7. References

Alter, T., Basri, R. (1998). Extracting salient curves from images: An analysis of the saliency network, *International Journal of Computer Vision*, Volume 27, Issue 1 (March 1998), pp. 51 - 69, ISSN:0920-5691

Antrade-Cetto, J. & Kak, A.C. (2000). Object Recognition, *Wiley Encyclopedia of Electrical Engineering*, J.G. Webster ed., John Wiley & Sons, Sup. 1, 2000, pp. 449-470

Baba, M., Narita, D. & Ohtani, K. (2004). A New Method of Measuring the 3-D Shape and Surface Reflectance of an Object Using a Laser Rangefinder, *Proceedings of Instrumentation and Measurement Technology Conference IMTC 2004*, Corno, Italy, 2004

Balslev, I. & Eriksen R.D. (2002). From belt picking to bin picking, *Proceedings of SPIE – The International Society for Optical Engineering*, 4902:616–623, 2002

Batchelor, B.G. & Whelan, P.F. (2002). Intelligent Vision Systems for Industry, e-book, ivsi@cs.cf.ac.uk, 2002

Batchelor, B.G. (2006). Natural and artificial vision, *Cardiff University*, http://bruce.cs.cf.ac.uk/index

Boothroyd, G. (2005). Assembly Automation and Product Design, *CRC Press*, 2005

Boughorbel, F., Zhang, Y., Kang, S., Chidambaram, U., Abidi, B., Koschan, A. & Abidi, M. (2003). Laser ranging and video imaging for bin picking, *Assembly Automation*, Vol. 23, No. 1, 2003, pp. 53-59

Braggins, D. (2006). Vision today for assembly automation, *Assembly Automation* 2, 6/2 (2006), pp. 181 - 183.

Brian, H. (2008). What's Next for Robotics, *Robotic Industries Association*, www.robotics.org, October 2008

Brumson, B. (2009). Seeing and Moving: A Preview of the 2009 International Robot, Vision and Motion Control Show, www.robotics.org, April 2009

Burns, R. A. (1999). Machine vision lighting Techniques for electronics assembly, *RVSI Northeast Robotics, http://www.machinevisiononline.org/public/articles/RVSI_LightingforMachineVision.pdf*

Cecil, J., Powell, D. & Vasquez, D. (2007). Assembly and manipulation of micro devices - A state of the art survey, *Robotics and Computer Integrated Manufacturing*, 23 (2007), pp. 580-588, www.elsevier.com

Christe, B. (2009). Robotic Application Research: Past, Present, & Future, www.robotics.org, July 2009

Cox, I., Rehg, J. & Hingorani, S. (1993). A bayesian multiple-hypothesis approach to edge grouping and contour segmentation, *IJCV 1993*, 11(1): pp. 5-24

Davies, E.R. (2005). Machine vision: Theory. Algorithms. Practicalities., *Elsevier/Morgan Kaufman Publishers*, ISBN 0-12-206093-8

Faugeras, O. (1993). Three-Dimensional Computer Vision - A Geometric Viewpoint, *The MIT Press*, 1993,

Fischler, M. & Bolles, R. (1986). Perceptual organization and curve partitioning, *PAMI 1986*, 8(1): pp. 100-105

Forsyth, D.A. & Ponce, J. (2002). Computer Vision: A Modern Approach, *Prentice Hall*, 2002

Goldfeder, C., Allen, P.K., Lackner, C. & Pelossof, R. (2007). Grasp planning via decomposition trees, *IEEE ICRA* - International Conference on Robotics and Automation, Rome, 2007

Griot, M. (2009) Machine vision, www.mellesgriot.com/products/machinevision/, July 2009

Gruen, A. (2001). Calibration and orientation of cameras in computer vision, *Springer*, Berlin, 2001

Guichard, F. & Tarel J.P. (1999). Curve Finder Perceptual Gruping and a Kalman Like Fitting, *Proceedings of the 7th IEEE International Conference on Computer Vision*, Kerkyra, Greece, September 1999, pp 1003–1008

Gupta, M.M. & Knopf, G. (1993). Neuro-Vision Systems: A Tutorial, a selected reprint, *IEEE Press*, Volume IEEE, Neural networks Council Sponsor, New York, 1993

Handelsman, M. (2006). Vision, tactile sensing simplify many tasks, www.industrialcontroldesignline.com

Hecht, E. (1987). Optics, *Addison-Wesley*, 2001

Hema, C.R., Paulraj, M.P., Nagarajan, R. & Sazali Y. (2007). Segmentation and Location Computation of Bin Objects, *International Journal of Advanced Robotic Systems*, Vol 4., No. 1 (2007), pp. 57-62

Herakovic, N. (2007) a. Computer and Machine Vision in Robot-based Assembly, *Journal of Mechanical Engineering*, Vol. 53, Nr. 12, 12/2007, pp. 858-871, ISSN 0039-2480

Herakovic, N. (2007) b. An experimental analysis of the conditions for machine vision quality control for FEM stator assembly, *Ventil,* Vol. 13, Nr. 5, Oct. 2007, pp. 324-329, ISSN 1318-7279

Hou. Z.-G., Song, K.-Y., Gupta, M. & Tan, M. (2007). Neural Units with Higher-Order Synaptic Operations for Robotic Image Processing Applications, *Springer*, Soft Computing, 2007, Vol. 11, Nr. 3, pp. 221-228

http://bruce.cs.cf.ac.uk/index

Huang, S.-J. & Tsai, J.-P. (2005). Robotic automatic assembly system for random operating condition,
International Journal of Advanced Manufacturing Technology, 27 (2005), pp. 334-344, ISBN 0-262-06158-9

Jain, A.K. & Dora C. (2000). 3D object recognition: Representation, *Statistics and Computing,* 10 (2000), pp. 167-182

Jenny, R. (2000). Fundamentals of optics–An Introduction for Beginners, *Journal of Computer Vision*, 40(2) 2000, pp. 142-167

Kellett, P. (2009). Roadmap to the Future, www.robotics.org, August 2009

King, F.G., Puskorius, G.V., Yuan, F., Meier, R.C., Jeyabalan, V. & Feldkamp, L.A. (1988). Vision guided robots for automated assembly, IEEE, *Proceedings of International Conference on Robotics and Automation*, Volume 3, 1988, pp. 1611 - 1616

Kirkegaard, J. & Moeslund, T.B. (2006). Bin-Picking based on Harmonic Shape Contexts and Graph-Based Matching, *The 18th International Conference on Patern Recognition (ICPR'06)*, 2006 IEEE

Kirkegaard, J. (2005). Pose Estimation of Randomly Organized Stator Housings using Structured Light and Harmonic Shape Context, *Master Thesis*, Aalborg University, Denmark, 2005

Klobucar, R., Pacnik, G. & Safaric, R. (2007). Uncalibrated visual servo control for 2 DOF parallel manipulator

Kristensen, S., Estable, S., Kossow, M. & Broesel, R. (2001). Bin-picking with a solid state range camera, *Robotics and Autonomous Systems,* 35 (2001), pp. 143-151

Leumann, M. (2009). Trends in Industrial Image Processing, *Vision & sensors,* www.visionsensorsmag.com, March 2009

Lowe, D.G. (1987). Three-Dimensional Object Recognition from Single Two-Dimensional Images, *Artificial Intelligence*, 31, 3(1987), pp. 355-395

Merva, J.J. (2009). What Every Machine Vision User Should Know About Lighting, www.machinevisiononline.org, July 2009

Motai, Y. & Kosaka, A. (2004). Concatenate Feature Extraction for Robust 3D Elliptic object Localization, *Symposium on Applied Computing,* ACM 2004, Cyprus, 2004

Nof, S. Y., Wilhelm, W. E. & Warnecke, H-J. (1997). Industrial Assembly, *Chapman & Hall,* ISBN 0 412 55770 3

Ostojic, G.; Lazarevic, M.; Stankovski, S.; Cosic, I. & Radosavljevic, Z. (2008). Radio Frequency Identification Technology Application in Disassembly Systems, *Journal of Mechanical Engineering*, Vol. 54, Nr. 11, pp. 759-767.

Pauli, J. (2001). Learning - Based Robot Vision, *Springer*, 2001

Peña-Cabrera, M., Lopez-Juarez, I, Rios-Cabrera, R. & Corona-Castuera J. (2005). Machine vision approach for robotic assembly, *Assembly Automation*, 25/3 (2005), pp. 204-216

Petrisic, J., Suhadolnik, A. & Kosel F., (2008). Object length and area calculations on the digital image, *Proceedings of 12th International Research/Expert Conference Trends in the Development of Machinery and Associated Technology TMT 2008*, Istanbul, Turkey, 26-30 August, 2008.

Pope, A. (1994). Learning Object recognition Models from Images, *Ph.D. research Proposal*, University of British Columbia

Pope, A.R. & Lowe D.G. (1996). Learning appearance models for object recognition, *Proceedings of International Workshop on Object Representation for Computer Vision*, Springer, Berlin, 1996, pp. 201-219

Pope, A.R. & Lowe D.G. (2000). Probabilistic Models of Appearance for 3-D Object Recognition, *International Journal of Computer Vision*, Volume 40, Number 2, November 2000 , pp. 149-167(19)

Rampersad, H. K. (1994). Integrated and Simultaneous design for Robotic Assembly, *John Wiley & Sons*, England, ISBN 0 471 95018 1

Ray, L.P. (1990). Monocular 3D Vision for a Robot Assembly, *International Conference on Systems Engineering, IEEE*, 1990

Redford, A. H. (1986). Robots in assembly, *Open University Press*, 1986, ISBN: 033515400X

Rosin, P. & West, G. (1995). Nonparametric segmentation of curves into various representations, *PAMI 1995*, 17(12): pp. 1140-1153

Roth, D., Yang, M.-H. & Ahuja N. (2002). Learning to recognize Objects, *Neural Computation 14/2002*

Rowland, J. J. & Lee, M. H. (1995). Intelligent assembly systems, *World Scientific*, ISBN 981022494X

Saxena, A, Chung, S.H. & Ng, A.Y., (2007) a. 3-D Depth reconstruction from a Single Still Image, *International Journal of Computer Vision (IJCV)*, Aug. 2007

Saxena, A, Schulte, J. & Ng, A.Y., (2007) b. Depth Estimation using Monocular and Stereo Cues, *Proceedings of 20th International Joint Conference on Artificial Intelligence (IJCAI)*, 2007

Scharstein, D. & Szelinski, R. (2002). A Taxonomy and Evaluation of Dense Two-Frame Stereo Correspondence Algorithms, *International Journal of Computer Vision*, 47(1/2/3) 2002, pp. 7-42

Schraft, R.D., Ledermann, T. (2003). Intelligent picking of chaotically stored objects, *Assembly Automation*, Vol.23, Nr. 1, 2003, pp. 38-42

Shapiro, L.G. & Stockman, G.C. (2001). Computer Vision, *Prentice Hall*, 2001

Sharma, R. & Srinivasa, N. (1996). A framework for robot control with active vision using neural network based spatial representation, *Proceedings of the 1996 IEEE International Conference on Robotics and Automation*, Mineapolis, 1996

Simic, M., Trdic, F., Skvarc, J. & Herakovic, N. (2009).Diameter and roundness measurement principle of the welded ring in the control process using the robot vision, *Proceedings of 18th International Workshop on Robotics in Alpe- Adria-Danube Region – RAAD 09*, ISSN 2066-4745, Brasov, May 2009

Skvarc, J. (2000). Solving an industrial problems using the machine vision as an universal appliance, FDS Research company, 2000

Solina, F. (2006). Racunalniski vid nekdaj in danes, *Proceedings of the conference ROSUS 2006 Maribor*, pp. 3-12 , Maribor, 2006 (in Slovene language)

Thorsley, M., Okouneva, G. & Karpynczyk J. (2004). Stereo Vision Algorithm for Robotic Assembly Operations, *Proceedings of First Canadian Conference on Computer and Robot Vision (CRV 2004)*

Trdic, F. (2000). Vision Technologies and Neuro Inspectors Training Course, FDS Research company, 2000

Trucco, E. & Verri, A. (1998). Introductory Techniques for 3-D Computer Vision, *Prentice Hall*, 1998

Vujovic, I., Petrovic I. & Kezic D. (2007). Wavelet-Based Edge Detection for Robot Vision Applications, *Proceedings of 16th International Workshop on Robotics in Alpe-Adria-Danube Region – RAAD 2007*, Ljubljana, 2007

West, P. (2006). A Roadmap for building a Machine Vision System, *Automated Vision System*, http://www.imagenation.com/pdf/roadmap.pdf

West, P.C. (2009). Choosing the Right Vision Technology, *Vision & Sensors*, June 2009, http://www.visionsensorsmag.com/Articles/

Winkler, S., Wunsch, P. & Hirzinger, G. (1997). A Feature Map Approach to Real-Time 3-D Object Pose estimation from Single 2-D Perspective Views, *Proceedings of 19. DAGM Symposium*, 1997

with neural network, *Proceedings of 16th International Workshop on Robotics in Alpe-Adria-Danube Region – RAAD 2007*, Ljubljana

Yli-Jaaski, A. & Ade, F. (1996). Grouping symmetrical structures for object segmentation and description, *Computer Vision and Image Understanding*, 63(3) 1996, pp. 399-417

Zhao, J. W. & Chen, G. Q. (2005). Roundness error assessment, *Institute of physics Publishing*, 13/2005

27

Testing Stereoscopic Vision in Robot Teleguide

Salvatore Livatino [1], Giovanni Muscato[2] and Christina Koeffel [3]
[1]*Engineering and Technology, University of Hertfordshire*
[2]*Ingegneria Elettrica Elettronica e Sistemi, University of Catania*
[3]*Center for Usability Research and Engineering*
[1]*United Kingdom,* [2] *Italy,* [3]*Austria*

1. Abstract

The aim of this chapter is to provide a focused guideline on how to test virtual reality (VR) systems used in robot teleoperation. The guideline is demonstrated based on a real experiment. The goal of this experiment is to test the characteristics and the advantages of a telerobotic system based on video transmission and stereoscopic viewing. The experimentation design follows a systematic approach that relies on identification of a number of key parameters and a usability evaluation designed according them. Two different 3D visualization facilities are considered for evaluating performance on systems with different characteristics, cost and application context. The results of the experiments are expected to provide insight into stereoscopic robot teleguide, and to understand on what system, and to what extent, is stereo vision beneficial.

2. Introduction

Robot telerobotion is typically related to survey and intervention in inaccessible, unknown, or hazardous environments. Despite of the latest generation of robotic systems possesing a high level of autonomy, remotely directed robot intervention is still typically human-driven. Humans are irreplaceable in tasks that require high-accuracy or deep environment cognition. The latter is typically needed to resolve situations with high unpredictability, where fast decision making and comprehension is required.

Robot teleoperation systems typically rely on 2D displays. These systems suffer from many limitations. Among them are misjudgement of self-motion and spatial localization, limited comprehension of remote ambient layout, object size and shape, etc. The above limitations may lead to unwanted collisions during navigation and long training periods for an operator.

An advantageous alternative to traditional 2D (monoscopic) visualization systems is represented by the use of a stereoscopic viewing. In the literature we can find works demonstrating that stereoscopic visualization may provide a user with higher sense of presence in remote environments because of higher depth perception, leading to higher

comprehension of distance, as well as aspects related to it, e.g. ambient layout, obstacles perception, and manoeuvre accuracy.
The aim of the proposed testing activity is to test stereoscopic vision on mobile robot teleguide. The experimentation is run in an indoor workspace. This represents a challenging setup for our testing because indoor ambient layouts, typically man-made, are simple and emphasize monocular depth cues such as perspective, texture gradient, etc., so they diminish the advantage of binocular stereo.
This chapter provides a brief introduction to stereo vision in video-based robot teleoperation. The next section (Section 3) presents the design of the proposed experiment. Then, the guideline together with its application to the experiment is presented (Section 4), followed by an analysis of the results (Section 5). Some final remarks conclude the chapter (Section 6).

2.1 Video Images in Robot Teleoperation

Performance in robot teleoperation can be improved by enhancing the user's sense of presence in remote environments (telepresence). Vision being the dominant human sensor modality, large attention has been paid by researchers and developers to the visualization aspect.
The use of visual sensors in Telerobotics has become very common because video images provide very rich and high contrasted information. Therefore, they are largely used in tasks that need accurate observation and intervention.
The rich information provided by a camera may require a large bandwidth to be transmitted at interactive rates. This often represents a challenge in transmission to distant locations or when the employed medium has limited communication capabilities.
Several video compression techniques have been developed which may reduce or solve the transmission delay problem. In case of stereo images, the information to be transmitted is larger (double, in principle). However, this can greatly be reduced, e.g. based on redundant information in stereo images, while specific networks for streaming video have been proposed, (Ferre' et al., 2005).
The bandwidth constraint may lead to transmission delays and this may affect interaction performance, e.g. response speed and accuracy. (Corde et al., 2002) claims that a delay of more than 1 sec. leads to eminent decrease of performance.

2.2 Stereoscopic Viewing

Stereoscopic visualization can play a major role towards increasing the user's involvement and immersion, because of the increased level of depth awareness. This is expected to give more accurate action performance and environment comprehension.
Stereoscopy improves: comprehension and appreciation of presented visual input, perception of structure in visually complex scenes, spatial localization, motion judgement, concentration on different depth planes, and perception of surface materials.
Most of the benefits of stereo viewing may affect robot teleguide because stereopsis enhances: perception of relative locations of objects in the observed remote worlds [3], impression of telepresence and of 3D layout (Bocker et al., 1995) , ability to skilfully manipulate a remote environment (Ferre' et al., 2005), response time and accuracy when operating in dangerous environments, etc.

The main drawback of stereoscopic viewing, which has yet prevented its large application, is that users may have to make some sacrifices, (Sexton et al., 1999). A stereo image may be hard to "get right" at first attempt, hardware may cause crosstalk, misalignment, image distortion (due to lens, displays, projectors), and all this may cause eye strain, double images perception, depth distortion, look around distortion (typical for head-tracked displays).

3. Testing Stereoscopic Teleguide

The testing of the proposed stereoscopic teleguide is organized by having a robot operating on a factory like scenario created in the Robitcs lab at the DIEES department of the University of Catania, Italy, and a user driving it sitting at the Medialogy lab at the Aalborg University in Copenhagen, Denmark. The two sites are approximately 3,000 km apart. Figure 1 shows a representation of the local-remote system interaction.

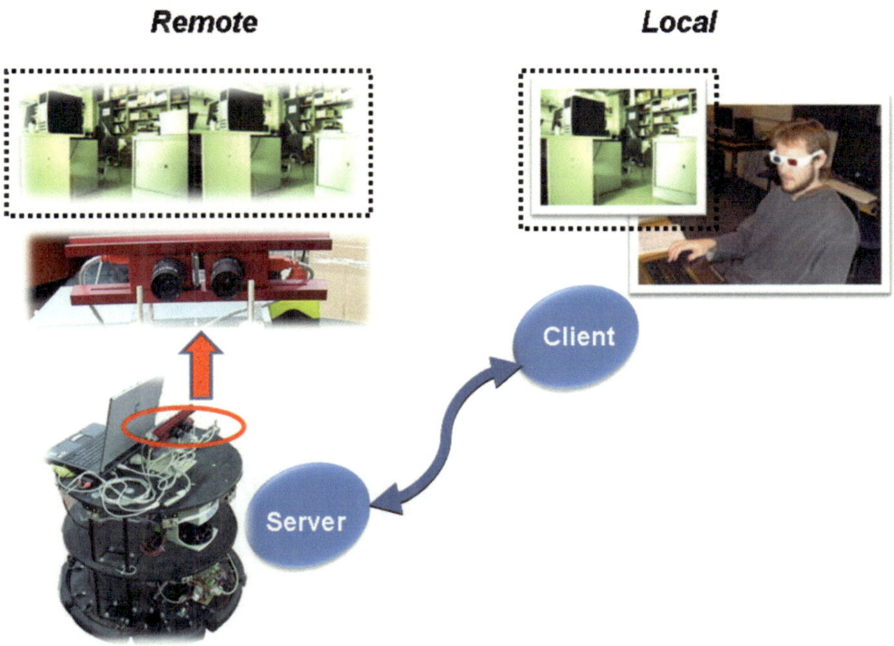

Fig. 1. A representation of the local-remote system interaction. The mobile robot on the figure left-hand side is located at the Robotcs lab at the DIEES department of the University of Catania, Italy. The user (tele-) driving the mobile robot, shown in the right-hand side, is sitting at the Medialogy lab of the Aalborg University, Copenhagen, Denmark. The two sites are approximately 3,000 km apart.

The stereoscopic testing is delimitated to two different visual displays and stereo approaches.

The visual displays are very different in size and type of technology. They are presented in the following points:

- **Wall**. A Wall display is typically composed by a projector and a screen with a size up to several meters.
- **Laptop**. A Laptop display uses LCD technology and it has a relatively small display size, typically up to 19 inches with high resolution.

The proposed stereoscopic approaches are very different in cost and performance. They are presented in the following points:

- **Polarized Filters**. The Polarized Filters nicely reproduce colours, have nearly no crosstalk, and they are very comfortable to a viewer. However, they require a complex and expensive setup and the system is less portable.
- **Coloured Anaglyph.** The Colored Anaglyph is cheap, easy to produce and very portable. However, it has poor colour reproduction and it often generates crosstalk which affects precision and viewing comfort.

The wall display uses Polarized Filters, therefore we call it Polarized Wall. The display's dimension is 2x2 meters. It is capable of providing high user involvement, 3D impression and comfort, suitable for training purposes or for tasks requiring accurate manoeuvring and long operational sessions.

For the Laptop system we use Coloured Anaglyph, therefore we call this setup Anaglyph Laptop. The display diagonal is 15 inches. This results on having stereo on a portable system, which is suitable for tasks requiring a user to be close to mobile robot operational environments. Furthermore the hardware is available at low-cost.

The figure 2 shows the visualization systems used in our investigation.

Fig. 2. The visualization systems used in our tests. The Wall (left) and the Laptop (right).

We have restricted our experimental conditions to indoor environments and a "factory-like" scenario. The stereo camera system follows the objectives of having a realistic observation. It is intended to appear close to the observation obtained when looking at the environment with our own eyes. Therefore, the stereo cameras pair should have a baseline close to the one typical for human eye distance. The same baseline should also satisfy the condition of showing effective left-right image separation for an expected average distance to visualized objects of about 2 meters.

A compromise setting is estimated for the camera parameters. The camera system sits on the top of the robot with a height of 95 cm, it looks 25 deg. downwards (tilt angle) and it has a baseline of 7 cm. Our stereo camera system has been designed based on the directions given in the literature.

It is important for the experiment that all trials are run under the same conditions.

4. Evaluation Guidelines

This section describes the proposed set of directives for the usability evaluation of stereoscopic vision in robot teleoperation. Usability describes how effectively and efficiently a user is able to fulfil tasks using a system. Especially in the field of VR the user's experience should also be taken into account. The following paragraphs will be addressing main issues when conducting usability evaluations of VR systems. Nevertheless also user experience related problems will be briefly described.

The following paragraphs are divided into sub-sections addressing specific aspects. The content of the description is based on selected literature in the field of VR and stereo viewing that the authors have investigated.

The test designer is left with some freedom of choice depending on:

- The guideline specific aspects
- Application context
- Available time
- Pre-determined objective

To support the designer's decision in making a choice, the guideline often directly refers to the results of our investigation in specific aspects in terms of percentage of literature works.

4.1 Test Plan

When forming the idea of conducting an evaluation, a test plan should be created. This document contains in principle every kind of knowledge necessary for the usability study. It serves as the basic document for communication to other people that might be involved in the user study (e.g. second test monitor).

Using the test plan, every involved person knows the main principles and ideas behind the evaluation. Therefore open questions and misunderstandings can be clarified. Furthermore, the test plan describes the resources needed and gives an overview of the milestones already accomplished. A properly formulated test plan for user studies in the field of VR should contain the following items:

- **Purpose**: The purpose describes the research question and the main problems treated as well as the current state of the art of the project.

- **Problem statement/test objectives**: The problem statement treats the main issues and questions connected to the evaluation, e.g. the questions derived from the hypothesis.
- **User profile**: The user profile describes the target group and the participants to be acquired for the study.
- **Test design**: The test design includes decisions about the entire session of the usability study, such as the evaluation method, e.g. if doing a between or within subjects evaluation. Furthermore the test design specifically describes each single step during the user study, starting from the arrival of the participants until the time they leave.
- **Task list**: The task list describes every task and sub-task that the participants will be asked to accomplish and on which VR device tasks are accomplished.
- **Test environment/equipment**: This section elaborates the test environment and equipment used in the test, e.g. VR devices and rooms needed.
- **Test monitor role**: The description of the test monitor role includes information about the test monitor and possible spectators.
- **Evaluation measures**: The evaluation measures should be described on a list enumerating all data collected during the user study (data logging, questionnaires, etc.).
- **Report contents and presentation**: This section gives a short preview on the data contained in the final test report and the presentation of the results obtained during the user study.

4.2 Research Question

Before starting to build a setup for an evaluation, the research question for the usability study needs to be formulated. A general research question defining the purpose of the entire project should already exist; nevertheless a specific research question should be formulated for the special purpose of the evaluation. This defines the main subject of the study.
It is very important to create a strong and valid research question that summarizes the goal of the evaluation in only one sentence/paragraph.
It is essential that the purpose of the entire project as well as the evaluation is clear to everybody on the project/evaluation team. Additionally, the research question should help to formulate the hypothesis we want the project to be tested against.

To formulate the research question we start from the problem statement, which in our case study has two hypotheses. They are:

- Users performing tasks employing stereo visualization perform better than users performing the same tasks employing mono visualization.
- The same task is not performed with the same efficiency and accuracy on different VR facilities.

The research question can be synthesized as in the following points.

- **Mono versus Stereo**. What are the main characteristics and advantages of using stereoscopic visualization in mobile robot teleguide in terms of navigation skills and remote environment comprehension?
- **Anaglyph Laptop versus Polarized Wall**. How may the characteristics and advantages associated to stereoscopic viewing vary for different approaches of stereo and display systems?

4.3 Ethics

Since user tests are conducted with humans, it is essential to assure that there will be no harm to the participants and that their personal rights are maintained, (Burdea & Coiffet, 2003). Users' mental and physical health must not be at risk and they need to be informed about potential hazards. Furthermore, users have to be able to stop whenever they feel uncomfortable and desire the test to end.

Certain universities or research centers dispose of an ethical department that administrates all studies and evaluations conducted involving humans. In this case, the researchers have to apply to this committee and do have to obey certain rules. If the institution where the evaluation is supposed to take place does not dispose of such a department, ethical considerations have to be taken into account as well. Especially when there is no board reviewing the studies, one has to make sure that all ethical concerns are respected. Furthermore also legal considerations of the country where the study is planned should be reviewed.

Virtual reality applications offer many possible risks to the participants of a user study, e.g. in cases when new devices are invented and tested or when existing devices have not entirely been tested for health risks. Additional hazards can appear through the use of e.g. head mounted displays, laser diodes, etc. Different mechanical devices in use, such as haptic tools can endanger the participants' health when applied incorrectly, this also includes stereoscopic viewers. Side-effects such as the occurrence of cybersickness need attention when using VR systems depending, e.g. on the type of stereoscopic approach and display size. They might even require a participant to stop the test.

4.4 Evaluation Method

At the very beginning of each user study it is important to choose and define the appropriate evaluation methods applicable to the setup to be tested. According to J. Nielsen these are: performance measures, thinking aloud, questionnaires, interviews, logging actual use and user feedback. These evaluation methods can also be applied in a combined version. Depending on the time when the evaluation takes place and the kind of data collected, one can distinguish between formative and summative user studies. Formative usability evaluations usually take place several times during the development cycle of a product to collect data of prototypes. Typically summative evaluations are applied at the end of a project, for example, to compare different products. Formative user studies are rare in VR. When comparing two or more different VR devices/applications (summative evaluation), one can decide whether to use a within or between subjects design. Between subjects studies are more common in VR. A statistical analysis conducted in (Koeffel, 2008) has shown that a total of 61% of user studies in VR were designed as between subjects studies.

In our experiments different types of VR devices were compared against each other, therefore the study is designed as summative evaluation. Because of the limited number of participants and the difficulty of finding equally skilled participants, a within subjects design was preferred over a between subjects design. Therefore each participant fulfilled the same amount of tasks on all available VR devices.

The study includes quantitative and qualitative evaluations. The following evaluation measures were collected through robot sensors and calculated for the following quantitative evaluation measures:

- **Collision Rate**. The Collision Number divided by the Completion Time. It provides information about obstacle detection and avoidance which is independent from user speed. This is the most relevant measurement as it provides explicit information about driving accuracy.
- **Collision Number**. The number of collisions registered during a trial. It may provide information about obstacle detection and avoidance.
- **Obstacle Distance**. The mean of minimum distance to obstacles along the path followed during a trial. It provides information about obstacle detection and avoidance.
- **Completion Time**. The time employed to complete the navigation trial. It provides information about user's environment comprehension. This parameter may also show user's confidence, (sometime a false confidence). The knowledge of the completion time is needed to estimate the Collision Rate.
- **Path Length**. The length of the robot journey. It may provide information about drive efficiency and obstacle detection.
- **Mean Speed**. The mean speed of each trial. It may show user's confidence.

The following evaluation measures were collected through questionnaires and calculated for the following qualitative evaluation measures:

- **Depth Impression**. The extent of perceived depth when observing different objects.
- **Suitability to Application**. The adequacy of the system and stereo approach to the specific task.
- **Viewing Comfort**. The eye strain and general body reaction.
- **Level of Realism**. The realism of the visual feedback including objects dimension and general appearance.
- **Sense of Presence**. The perceived sense of presence and isolation from surrounding space.

During the evaluation of the data, the questions were grouped into five categories corresponding to the five qualitative judgement categories, in order to be able to compare the results in each area. The 7 scale semantic differentials were used for the answer of questionnaires.

4.5 Setup

In our recommendations the setup is distinguished into the testing environment and the technological setup.

- **Testing environment**
  Evaluations conducted by students and academic researchers usually take place in the facilities of universities or research centers. In some cases these institutions dispose of their own usability labs for conducting evaluations, but in most of the cases the evaluations occur in computer labs or classrooms. Since classrooms are not always comfortable (and hard to find relaxing), while it is required that the participants feel at ease, it is very important to create a comfortable environment. It has to be avoided the presence of people that are not involved in the project, the presence of those running

around hectically and preparing the evaluation, and other distractions such as loud noises.
It is generally important not to give the participants unnecessary information about the project or to bias the results by telling the users some weaknesses or previous results. If the user study requires a test monitor logging data while the participants perform the testing, it is fundamental that he/she respects the participants' privacy by not sitting too close to them. Furthermore, any kind of stress and emotional pressure has to be kept away from the participants in order not to influence the results.

- **Technological setup**
  Student and research evaluations often base on an already finished project (summative evaluations), referring to the hardware and/or the software. Therefore the technological setup might already be given. Considering the different VR setups, it is very important to assure that all needed devices are at the test monitors' disposal on the day(s) of the usability study. Furthermore it is very important to test if the application, the software, and the data logging, are well functioning. Since VR devices and applications are still considered to be "new technology" they are sometimes unstable and tend not to work all the time. Hence, it is crucial to organize and reserve technical facilities and rooms, and to inspect the functionalities of the project to be tested.

4.6 Participants

Several fundamental elements of evaluations are related to participants. Before recruiting volunteers, it is very important to investigate the target population of the user study. Therefore users with the desired attributes such as age, gender, education, experience with VR, computer experience, gaming experience, visual abilities, etc. can be selected. Generally, it is advisable to test user groups with a great internal variance. Users should be recruited from different age groups, gender and experience. A careful selection of participants should also be according to expected system users. In any case, main users' characteristics such as average age, gender, experience, etc., should clearly be stated.
Based on authors' experience the men participating in user studies in the field of VR are twice as many as women. This could be acceptable in case of men being the main users of a VR product.
Concerning the number of participants, it mainly depends on the kind of user study conducted (i.e. formative or summative evaluation, between or within subjects design, etc.). Generally, usability experts (Faulkner, 2000; Nielsen, 1993; Nielsen & Mack, 1994; Rubin, 1994) hold that 2 to 4 participants suffice for conducting a representative pilot study, and 5 to 20 participants suffice for conducting a formal user study. Nevertheless, more recent approaches on evaluations in the field of VR have suggested testing a higher number of participants in order to obtain meaningful results.
A number of approximately 23 participants is suggested for within subject designs and 32 for between subject designs. In case of pilot studies, a minimum number of 6 participants is proposed. These figures are based on our literature analysis.
Participants are typically volunteers and/or they do not receive any financial compensation. Nevertheless, it is highly recommended to hand the participants a small token of appreciation after finishing the user study.

Twelve subjects take part in the described evaluation study. They are tested among students or staff members of the university. The target population is composed of participants with varying background and have none or medium experience with VR devices. The age of the participants ranged between 23 and 40, with an average of 25.8

4.7 Forms

Forms are different documents that are handed to the participants during the course of a user study. Concerning the forms given to the participants, this guideline conforms to the traditional approaches introduced in (Nielsen, 1993; Rubin, 1994) and the results of the statistical analysis of relevant literature in (Koeffel, 2008). Therefore we recommend the use of the following forms:

- **Information sheet:** The information sheet (also called test script) provides an overview of the entire testing process. This form should be handed to the participants at the very beginning before the actual testing, and it should contain information about: the title of the project, names and contact information, introduction to the project, duration of the study, tasks to be completed, and the possibility to withdraw from the study at any time. In 5 out of the 18 studies investigated, the participants have reported to have received written or displayed information before the testing process.
- **Consent form:** The consent form states that the researchers are allowed to use and publish the data collected during the user study. This may also include pictures or videos taken during experiments. It is a reassurance for the participants that their data will not be used for any other purpose than the one explained in the consent form and/or in the information sheet. For the researcher this form is a legal reassurance that he/she is allowed to use and publish the obtained data.
- **Questionnaires:** Generally questionnaires should contain the information required by the research question which is not possible to be collected automatically through data logging and performance measures. Therefore, mostly subjective qualitative data is collected using questionnaires. Special issues should be treated in questionnaires in order to emphasize the conclusion and the results of the data collection. Questionnaires can provide answers about personal feelings or preferences. We distinguish among: screening, pre-test, device, post-test, background, presence, simulator sickness, and the EVE-experience questionnaire.
- **Task scenarios:** It might be necessary to provide participants with a task scenario (describing each step in detail) for each task he/she should complete. This allows every participant to gain the same amount of information. Furthermore it clarifies the knowledge necessary to complete a given task.
- **Data collection forms:** Experience has shown that it is not always sufficient to auto-log data using software. Sometimes it is necessary that the test monitor writes down notes or information during a task session. This can be additional information such as time or estimates expressed by participants.
- **Thank you form:** In addition to the possible personal gratification that participants may receive by taking part in a user study, a thank you letter should also be handed to them. This is important in order to formally thank the participants and tell them where to find further information about the progress of the project, e.g. published papers.

The forms should be adapted to the needs of the user study. Generally we suggest the employment of semantic differentials as answering options.

In our experiments we provide a page as information sheet and consent form. We use questionnaires in our qualitative evaluation. We have a number of questions for gather users' background information, including their experience and gaming abilities (e.g. hours per week). We have then a questionnaire for each of the five proposed qualitative evaluation measures, (depth impression, suitability to application, viewing comfort, level of realism, sense of presence), and users' overall impression after the user study. The questions are designed to get answers for the research questions.
As example, the questionnaire for the level-of-realism parameter included the following questions: "How realistic is the environment layout?", "How realistic are the visualized objects size and shape?", "How natural was the driving?", "What mark would you give as general level of realism?". The questionnaire also included user's suggestion for improvement and general remarks. A conclusive comparative questionnaire was provided at the end of each experiment.
We conform to the traditional approaches in terms of forms and questionnaires, with few additions (Livatino et al., 2007). We use a seven scale semantic differential for answering the questions. In particular the possible values range between -3 and +3, with -3 is for the worst and +3 for the best result.
We provide our users with a task scenario page that contains information about the workspace they tele-explore. We do not use data collection forms in our quantitative evaluation. A thank you letter is provided at the end of user trials together with sweets and drinks.

4.8 Procedure

The test procedure is part of the test design and it very much depends on the specific subject and application context. The procedure should be carefully designed in order to provide meaningful data.
In our experiment four steps are performed. First, an introductory phase that includes a practice drive. Then, each participant is asked to teledrive the robot (remotely located) toward a final location while avoiding collisions. The drive is performed on both the proposed facilities (wall and laptop), using both stereo and mono viewing conditions. This results in four navigation trials per participant.
The participants are eventually asked to complete predesigned questionnaires. Practice sessions are administrated before testing. A debriefing phase ends the test session.

The figure 3 right-hand side shows images from our test sessions: the top-right image shows our forms and stereoscopic goggles ready before testing; the middle image shows test users filling in the questionnaires.

4.9 Schedule

It is essential to estimate the overall completion time per participant and to prepare a schedule showing the sequence of participants and their assigned tasks. In particular, the schedule should include: timing of the single tasks, overall completion time, the sequence of the tasks per participant, possible breaks, time needed for introduction and debriefing, room locations, etc.

The studies analyzed indicate an overall completion time per participant that ranges from 23 to 240 minutes with an average completion time of 45 minutes. This time includes the time from when a participant arrived at the testing facility until the time he/she left.

In the field of VR it is very important to keep the single task sessions as well as the overall completion time as short as possible. A maximum of 30 minutes per task is recommended by Bowman et al. (Bowman et al., 2002). Too long sessions might cause exhaustion of the participants and side effects such as cyber-sickness, which could negatively affect the results. It is important to counterbalance the sequence of the single tasks in order to avoid learning effects and biasing of the results.

In our experiments the test trials runs during several days. The average execution time is per participant is 40 min. Each participant executes the same number of tasks under the same conditions. Participants are assisted by a test monitor and a technician during the entire test session. We turn special attention on the counterbalancing of the tasks, therefore the participant tasks and facilities are given according to a predetermined schedule. The sequence during the entire user study is designed to avoid fatigue and learning effects.

4.10 Test Monitor and Spectators

The role of each person present during the user study has to be predefined. Especially the test monitor should be well instructed and capable to serve his/her purpose.

The test monitor is present during all parts of the usability study and interacts with the participants. If possible somebody who has ground knowledge in usability (especially evaluations) should be employed as test monitor. In case that there is no expert in usability available, the person in the role of test monitor should acquire basic knowledge in this area. The test monitor should be able to comfortably interact with the participants, which requires an open and friendly personality (i.e. a "people-person"). It is also important that the test monitor does not get too close to the participants physically as well as mentally, to give them some privacy.

In case other people than the test monitor and the participant, are present during a test session, e.g. technical staff, VR project development team, spectators, etc., they should be introduced to participants at the beginning and the roles of the spectators need to be defined clearly. Generally, the number of spectators during a testing session should be kept small since they tend to make the users nervous. If not part of the research question, spectators should avoid talking during task sessions. This is especially crucial for VR applications, since distractions such as loud noises might disturb the sense of presence.

Since VR systems are still considered new technology and unstable, it might happen that the participant gets frustrated because something is not working properly or it is very difficult to accomplish. In such a case, the test monitor should not judge the participant or the system by expressing that e.g. "this error always occurs" or otherwise by negatively influencing the user. The test monitor should encourage the participant to go on as long as possible.

The figure 3 images bottom-right and top-left show test monitors interacting with users during the introduction to the test and forms (bottom-right) and assisting the user during robot teleguide (top-left).

4.11 Pilot Study

It is generally recommended to perform a pilot study before testing a project in a formal user study. The pilot study should be conducted in the same way as the formal study and each participant should be treated as if he/she were in the formal study (including the forms to be used).

The pilot study is useful for removing errors from the project/setup, debug the test design, debug the experimental design, detect biased questions in the questionnaires, refine the questionnaires and detect the overall time necessary per participant. Furthermore, rooms and technical facilities should be tested of their functionality.

A minimum number of 6 participants is suggested. In general, the more participants are tested, the more indicative the results are.

The pilot study is essential in case of problems that may not be predicted and only occur during the study.

4.12 Formal Study

In an ideal case, a pilot study has been conducted before the formal study and the results of the pilot study have been taken into account when planning and conducting the formal study. If required, additional tests could be conducted at the very beginning of the study in order to categorize the participants. Furthermore, a practice session should be administrated for all testing activities which need a test-user to become acquainted with system commands and behavior. In the literature that we have reviewed, an average of 4.1 tasks is accomplished per participant in practice sessions.

In order to avoid negative side effects (such as motion sickness) and fatigue, long enough breaks should be held between the single task sessions.

The figure 3 left-hand side (middle and bottom image) shows some moments of our formal study with test-users teleguiding the robot on different facilities and working on the questionnaires. An assistant is also monitoring the robot platform at the remote site.

Fig. 3. Some moment of our usability evaluation.

The right-hand side, top and middle images, show our forms ready before the testing together with stereoscopic goggles, and test-users filling in the questionnaires.
The bottom-right and top-left images show test monitors interacting with users during the introduction to the test and forms, or assisting the users during robot teleguide.
The left-hand side, middle and bottom images, show some moments of our usability study with test-users teleguiding the robot on the different facilities.
The image in the center of the figure shows our robot at the remote site together with an assistant that monitors its actions.

5. Results and Presentation

Another important part of conducting usability studies is the processing and evaluation of the collected data. The processing of the results can be very complex and time consuming since most of the time a lot of data is collected. Therefore it is recommended to employ statistical tools. The most frequently used are: mean, median, frequency distribution, Bonferroni, standard deviation, t-test, and ANOVA (Analysis of Variance).
For the graphical display of the gained data, frequency distributions (in form of histograms) are very popular (83% of the cases in our investigation). Their main purpose is to display error rates and time.

As inferential statistics the analysis of variance (ANOVA) is used the most to detect the statistical significance of test results. The ANOVA is a common method of separating the effects of multiple investigation factors (independent variables) on evaluation measures (dependent variables). The ANOVA examines which factors have a significant influence on a dependent variable by comparing the variance within a factor to the variance between factors, (Wanger et al. 1992).

A one-way ANOVA is to be used to estimate the effect of one factor (independent variable) on one of the evaluation measure. A two-way ANOVA is to be used to estimate the effect of two factors (independent variables) on one evaluation measures. According to the literature it is hard to analyze more than two factors using an ANOVA.

In case the effect of a factor is to be estimated on more than one evaluation measure, a multivariate ANOVA (MANOVA) should be applied. A MANOVA is an extension of the ANOVA that reports for multiple dependent variables.

The results of ANOVAs should be displayed in tables, while bar graphs are mostly used to display descriptive statistics.

The researcher may decide to expose statistically significant results only, as well as display results of the descriptive statistics only when those show meaningful trends. A different approach could be to present all data regardless their meaning, to give a reader a complete overview of all the experimental findings. A middle-ground popular approach is to expose all statistical output synthesized on tables and then only comment on text most meaningful findings. This gives readers the opportunity to discover specific data relations and trends on their own, while keeping a concise and to-the-point text description. A result analysis and conclusions may be included along the exposition of results if these are of brief content. It is instead advisable to include an extra section dedicated to the result analysis if the authors wish to elaborate and thoroughly discuss the experimental output.

In our experiments the collected evaluation measures were analyzed through inferential and descriptive statistics and the results were graphically represented by diagrams.

We measure statistical significance of results by estimating a two-way ANOVA. This is applied to measure the effect of the two dependent variables: stereo–mono and laptop–wall.

We set the P value to 0.05 to determine whether the result is judged statistically significant.

We additional measure mean, standard deviation, and percentage of improvement, to observe general trends and specific tendencies.

We present all the results in tables (excluding the percentage of improvement), and report and comment on text only most meaningful findings and specific trends observation. On text we also add some conclusions based on our result analysis.

The figures 5 and 6 show the descriptive statistics and the table 1 the inferential statistics. The results are presented on text commented according to the proposed research questions.

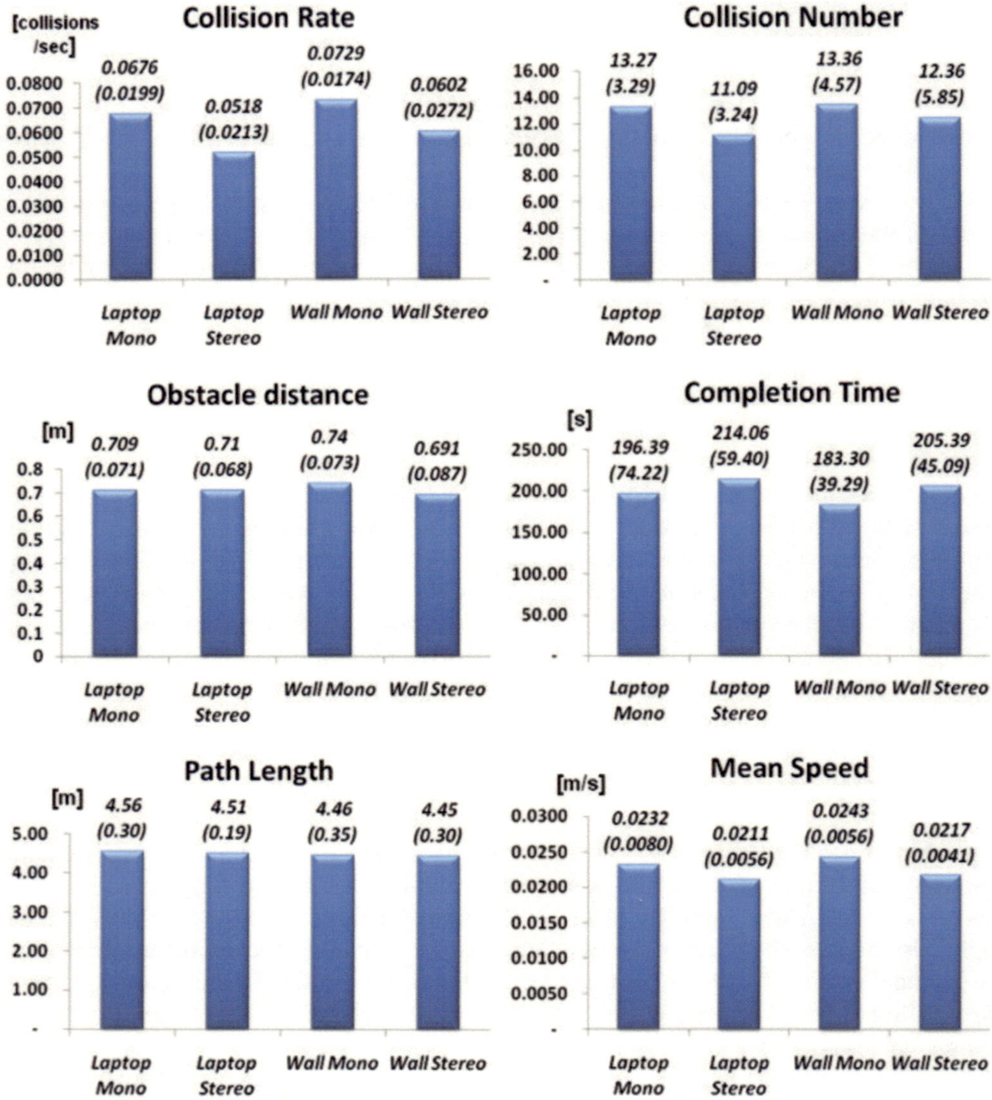

Fig. 5. Bar graphs illustrating mean values and standard deviation (in brackets) for the quantitative variables.

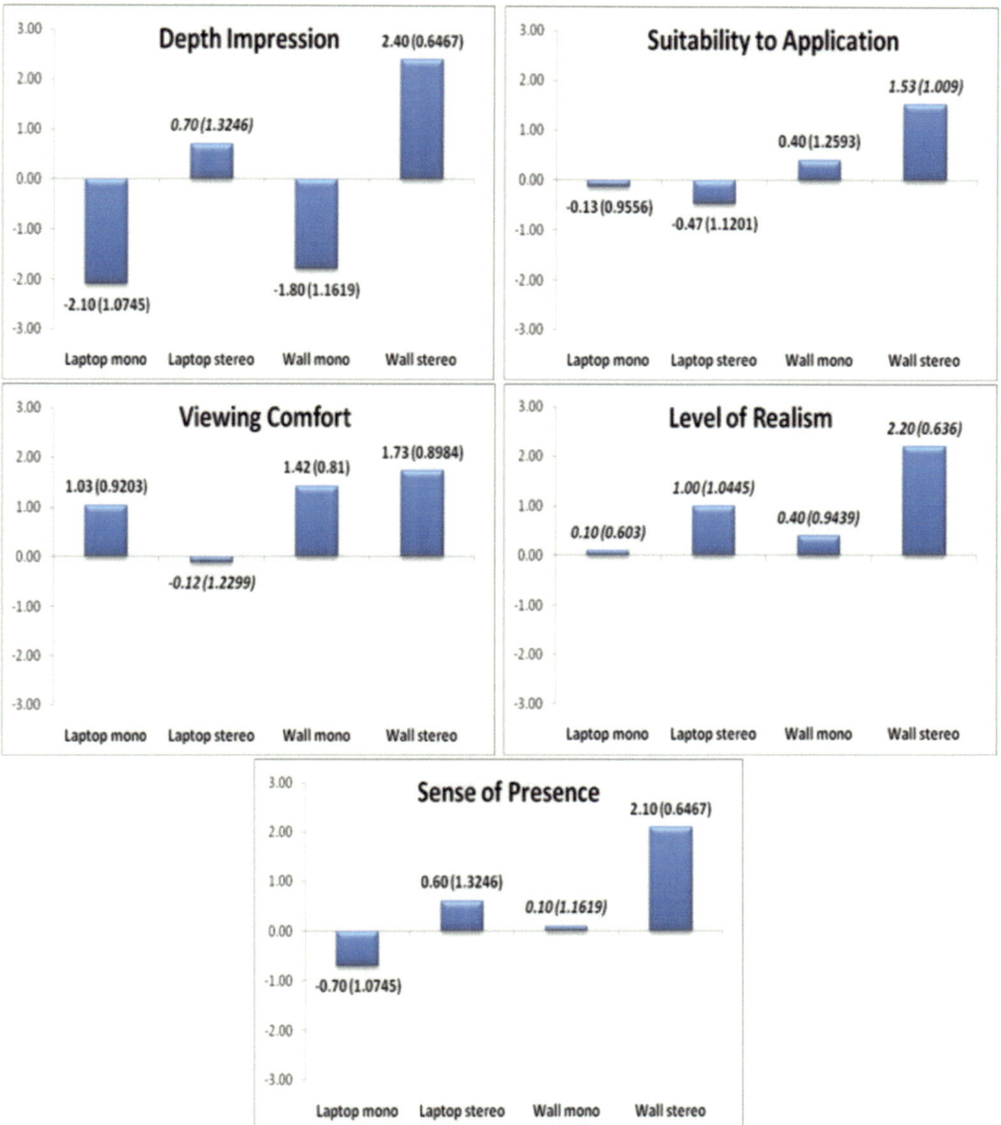

Fig. 6. Bar graphs illustrating mean values and standard deviation (in brackets) for the qualitative variables. The qualitative data were gathered through questionnaires, where the participants provided their opinions by assigning values that ranged between +3 (best performance) and -3 (worst performance).

Collision Rate					Collision Number				
	SS	df	F	p		SS	df	F	p
Mono-Stereo	**0.00228**	**1**	**5.83**	**0.0204**	Mono-Stereo	**27.841**	**1**	**1.57**	**0.2181**
Laptop-Wall	**0.00338**	**1**	**8.65**	**0.0054**	Laptop-Wall	**59.114**	**1**	**3.32**	**0.0757**
Interaction	**0.00017**	**1**	**0.45**	**0.5076**	Interaction	**2.75**	**1**	**0.15**	**0.6962**
Error	**0.01561**	**40**			Error	**711.273**	**40**		
Obstacle distance					**Completion Time**				
	SS	df	F	p		SS	df	F	p
Mono-Stereo	**6359**	**1**	**1.28**	**0.2638**	Mono-Stereo	**4348.3**	**1**	**1.4**	**0.2435**
Laptop-Wall	**37757.9**	**1**	**7.63**	**0.0086**	Laptop-Wall	**2992.9**	**1**	**0.96**	**0.332**
Interaction	**124.9**	**1**	**0.03**	**0.8746**	Interaction	**373.2**	**1**	**0.12**	**0.7306**
Error	**198013**	**40**			Error	**124120.4**	**40**		
Path Length					**Mean Speed**				
	SS	df	F	p		SS	df	F	p
Mono-Stereo	**0.00445**	**1**	**0.05**	**0.8164**	Mono-Stereo	**0.0001**	**1**	**3.04**	**0.0891**
Laptop-Wall	**0.14136**	**1**	**1.73**	**0.1954**	Laptop-Wall	**0.00007**	**1**	**2.18**	**0.1473**
Interaction	**0.00123**	**1**	**0.02**	**0.9029**	Interaction	**0.00001**	**1**	**0.35**	**0.5553**
Error	**3.26154**	**40**			Error	**0.00154**	**40**		
Depth Impression					**Suitability to Application**				
	SS	df	F	p		SS	df	F	p
Mono-Stereo	**75.142**	**1**	**51.86**	**0**	Mono-Stereo	**1.3359**	**1**	**0.78**	**0.3824**
Laptop-Wall	**2.506**	**1**	**1.73**	**0.196**	Laptop-Wall	**0.1237**	**1**	**0.07**	**0.7895**
Interaction	**0.96**	**1**	**0.66**	**0.4204**	Interaction	**0.1237**	**1**	**0.07**	**0.7895**
Error	**57.955**	**40**			Error	**68.5051**	**40**		
Viewing Comfort					**Level of Realism**				
	SS	df	F	p		SS	df	F	p
Mono-Stereo	**2.1976**	**1**	**1.63**	**0.2091**	Mono-Stereo	**19.1136**	**1**	**23.79**	**0**
Laptop-Wall	**3.1824**	**1**	**2.36**	**0.1323**	Laptop-Wall	**1.4545**	**1**	**1.81**	**0.186**
Interaction	**0.1067**	**1**	**0.08**	**0.7799**	Interaction	**0.2045**	**1**	**0.25**	**0.6166**
Error	**53.9293**	**40**			Error	**32.1364**	**40**		

Sense of Presence				
	SS	df	F	p
Mono-Stereo	**75.142**	**1**	**51.86**	**0**
Laptop-Wall	**2.506**	**1**	**1.73**	**0.196**
Interaction	**0.96**	**1**	**0.66**	**0.4204**
Error	**57.955**	**40**		

Table 1. The results of two-way ANOVA for the quantitative and qualitative measurements. Rows show values for the independent variables (stereo–mono, laptop–wall), their interaction, and error. Columns show the sum of squares (SS), the degrees of freedom (DoF), the F statistic, and the P value.

5.1 Mono-Stereo

- **Collision Rate and Number:** Under stereoscopic visualization the users perform significantly better in terms of collision rate. The ANOVA shows the main effect of stereo viewing on the number of collisions per time unit: F=5.83 and P=0.0204. The improvement when comparing mean values is 20.3%. Both collision rate and collision number are higher in case of monoscopic visualization in most of the users' trials. The diagram in Figure 7 shows the collision number for a typical user in both the facilities. This supports the expectation, based on the literature, that the higher sense of depth provided by stereo viewing may improve driving accuracy.
- **Obstacle distance**: There is no relevant difference in the mean of minimum distance to obstacles between mono- and stereo driving. The result from the ANOVA is not significant, and the improvement when comparing mean values is only 3.3%.
- **Completion time**: There is no significant difference in completion time. Nevertheless, we have observed that the time spent for a trial is greater in stereo visualization in 77% of the trials. The test participants have commented that the greater depth impression and sense of presence provided by stereoscopic viewing make a user spending a longer time in looking around the environment and avoid collisions.
- **Path length**: There is no significant difference in path length. Nevertheless, the user shows different behaviors under mono- and stereo conditions. Under stereo-viewing conditions, the path is typically more accurate and well balanced.
- **Mean speed**: The results for the mean speed show a clear tendency in reducing speed in case of stereo viewing. The ANOVA shows a tendency to be significant (F=3.04, P=0.0891). In general, a slower mean speed is the result of a longer time spent to drive through the environment.
- **Depth impression**: All users had no doubts that depth impression was higher in case of stereo visualization. The result from ANOVA shows the main effect of stereo viewing: F=51.86 and P=0.0. This result is expected and agrees with the literature.
- **Suitability to application**: There is no significant difference in terms of adequacy of the stereo approach and display to the specific task. Nevertheless, we notice an improvement of 74% on mean values in the case of polarized stereo (anaglyph stereo penalizes the final result).
- **Viewing comfort**: There is no significant difference in viewing comfort between stereo and mono visualization, which contradicts the general assumption of stereo viewing being painful compared with mono. Stereo viewing is considered even more comfortable than mono in the polarized wall. The higher sense of comfort of the wall system is claimed to be gained by a stronger depth impression obtained in stereo. Our conclusion is that the low discomfort of polarized filters is underestimated as an effect of the strong depth enhancement provided in the polarized wall.
- **Level of realism**: All users find stereo visualization closer to how we naturally see the real world. The result from the ANOVA shows the main effect of stereo viewing: F=23.79 and P=0.0. The mean values show an improvement of 84%.
- **Sense of presence**: All users believe that stereo visualization enhances the presence in the observed remote environment. The ANOVA has F=51.86 and P=0.0. The improvement in mean values is 97%.

5.2 Laptop versus Wall

- **Collision**: Users perform significantly better in the laptop system in terms of collision rate. The ANOVA has F=8.65 and P=0.0054, and the improvement when comparing mean values is 10.3%. The collision number ANOVA shows a tendency to be significant (F=3.32, P=0.0757). The effect of stereoscopic visualization compared with the monoscopic one is analogous on both facilities.
- **Obstacle distance**: When sitting in front of the laptop system, users perform significantly better compared with the wall in terms of mean of minimum distance to obstacles. The ANOVA has F=7.63 and P=0.0086.
- **Completion time**: There is no significant difference between the two systems. Nevertheless, a faster performance is noted in larger screens. Most of the participants argued that the faster performance is due to the higher sense of presence given by the larger screen. The higher presence enhances driver's confidence. Therefore, smaller time is employed to complete a trial.
- **Path length**: There is almost no difference between the two systems in terms of path length.
- **Mean speed**: There is no significant difference in mean speed between the two systems. The higher mean speed is typically detected on the wall. The large screen requires users to employ their peripheral vision, which allows for spending less time looking around and explains the wall better performance. The mean values show the same patterns on both facilities.
- **Depth impression**: There is no significant difference between the two facilities. This confirms that the role played by the stereoscopic visualization is more relevant than the change of facilities. The improvement when driving in stereo is 76% on the laptop and 78% on the wall. It may surprise the reader that most users claim a very high 3-D impression with laptop stereo. Confirmation that perceived depth impression can be high in small screens is found in the work of Jones et al. (Jones et al., 2001), which shows how the range of depth tolerated before the loss of stereo fusion can be quite large on a desktop. In our case, the range of perceived depth in the laptop stereo typically corresponds a larger workspace portion than in large screens systems (in other words, the same workspace portion corresponds to a wider range of perceived depth for large screens), but we typically lose stereo after 5–7 m.
- **Suitability to application**: There is no significant difference between the two systems; however, we can observe that users believe that a large visualization screen is more suitable to the mobile robot teleguide. This goes along with Demiralp et al. considerations (Demiralp et al. 2006), telling that looking-out tasks (i.e., where the user views the world from inside–out as in our case), require users to use their peripheral vision more than in looking-in tasks (e.g., small-object manipulation). A large screen presents the environment characteristics closer to their real dimension, which enforces adequacy of this display to the application. The polarized wall in stereo is considered the most suitable for teledriving tasks, which makes this facility very suitable for training activities. On the other side, the laptop stereo is considered inadequate for long teledriving tasks because of the fatigue an operator is exposed to. The laptop system remains nevertheless most suitable as a low-cost and portable facility.

- **Viewing comfort**: There is no significant difference between the two systems; however, the mean bar graph and typical users' comments show that a higher comfort is perceived in case of a polarized wall. This result is expected, and it confirms the benefit of front projection and polarized filters that provide limited eye strain and cross talk, and great color reproduction. The passive anaglyph technology (laptop stereo) strongly affects viewing comfort, and it calls for high brightness to mitigate viewer discomfort. The mean values show an opposite tendency between the two facilities in terms of stereo versus mono.
- **Level of realism**: The mean level of realism is higher in case of the wall system, with a mean improvement of 58%. This is claimed due to the possibility given by large screens to represent objects with a scale close to real. The realism is higher under stereo viewing on both facilities.
- **Sense of presence**: The mean sense of presence is higher in case of the wall system, with a mean improvement of 40%. The large screen involves user's peripheral vision more than the small screen, which strongly affects sense of presence. The presence is higher under stereo visualization on both facilities.

6. Conclusion

The present chapter introduced a guideline for usability evaluation of VR applications with focus on robot teleoperation. The need for an effort in this direction was underlined in many literature works and was believed relevant by the authors being human-computer interaction a subject area in great expansion with an increasing need for user studies and usability evaluations. The proposed work targets researchers and students who are not experts in the field of evaluation and usability in general. The guideline is therefore designed to represent a simple set of directives (a handbook) which would assist users drawing up plans and conducting pilot and formal studies.

The guideline was applied to a real experiment while it was introduced. The goal was to facilitate the reader's understanding and the guideline actual use. The experiment involved mobile robot teleguide based on visual sensor and stereoscopic visualization. The test involved two different 3D visualization facilities to evaluate performance on systems with different characteristics, cost and application context.

The results of the experiments were illustrated in tables and described after key parameters proposed in the usability study.

The results were evaluated according to the proposed research question. This involved two factors: monoscopic versus stereoscopic visualization and laptop system versus wall system. The two factors were evaluated against different quantitative variables (collision rate, collision number, obstacle distance, completion time, path length, mean speed) and qualitative variables (depth impression, suitability to application, viewing comfort, level of realism, sense of presence). The result of the evaluation on the stereo-mono factor indicated that 3-D visual feedback leads to fewer collisions than 2-D feedback and is therefore recommended for future applications. The number of collisions per time unit was significantly smaller when driving in stereo on both the proposed visualization systems. A statistically significant improvement of performance of 3-D visual feedback was also

detected for the variables such as depth impression, level of realism, and sense of presence. The other variable did not lead to significant results on this factor.
The results of the evaluation on the laptop-wall factor indicated significantly better performance on the laptop in terms of the mean of minimum distance to obstacles. No statistically significant results were obtained for the other variables. The interaction between the two factors was not statistically significant.
The results therefore provide insight on the characteristics and the advantages of using stereoscopic teleguide.

7. References

Bocker M., Runde D., & Muhlback L., "On the reproduction of motion parallax in videocommunications," in *Proc. 39th Human Factors Society*, 1995, pp. 198–202.

Bowman, D.A., Gabbard, J.L. & Hix, D. (2002). A survey of usability evaluation in virtual environments: classification and comparison of methods. In *Presence: Teleoperation inVirtual Environments*, 11(4):404-424

Burdea, G.C., & Coiffet, P. (2003). *Virtual Reality Technology*, John Wiley & Sons, Inc., 2ndedition, ISBN 978-0471360896

Corde L. J., Caringnan C. R., Sullivan B. R., Akin D. L., Hunt T., and Cohen R., "Effects of time delay on telerobotic control of neural buoyancy," in *Proc. IEEE. Int. Conf. Robotics and Automation*, Washigton, USA, 2002, pp. 2874-2879.

Demiralp, C., Jackson, C.D., Karelitz, D.B., Zhang, S. & Laidlaw, D.H. (2006). CAVE andfishtank virtual-reality displays: A qualitative and quantitative comparison. *In proc. Of IEEE Transactions on Visualization and Computer Graphics*, vol. 12, no. 3, (May/June, 2006). pp. 323-330.

Faulkner, X. (2000). Usability engineering. Palgrave Macmillan, ISBN 978-0333773215

Fink, P.W., Foo, P.S. & Warren W.H.(2007). Obstacle avoidance during walking in real andvirtual environments. *ACM Transaction of Applied Perception.*, 4(1):2

Ferre M., Aracil R., & Navas M, "Stereoscopic video images for telerobotic applications," *J. Robot. Syst.*, vol. 22, no. 3, pp. 131–146, 2005.

Jones G., Lee D., Holliman N., & Ezra D., "Controlling perceived depth in stereoscopic images," in *Proc. SPIE*, 2001, vol. 4297, pp. 422–436.

Koeffel, C. (2008). Handbook for evaluation studies in vr for non-experts, *Tech.Rep.* Medialogy, Aalborg University, Denmark, 2008.

Livatino, S. & Koeffel, C. (2007), Handbook for evaluation studies in virtual reality. *In proc. Of VECIMS '07: IEEE Int. Conference in Virtual Environments, Human-Computer Interface and Measurement Systems,*, Ostuni, Italy, 2007

Nielsen, J. (1993). *Usability engineering*, Morgan Kaufmann, ISBN 978-0125184069

Nielsen, J., & Mack R.L. (1994). *Usability Inspection Methods*, John Wiley & Sons, New York,USA, May 1994, ISBN 978-0471018773

Rubin, J. (1994). *Handbook of Usability Testing: How to Plan, Design, and Conduct Effective Tests.*

Sexton I, & Surman P., "Stereoscopic and autostereoscopic display systems," *IEEE Signal Process.* Mag., vol. 16, no. 3, pp. 85–89, 1999.

Wanger, L.R., Ferweda J.A., Greenberg, D.P. (1992). Perceiving spatial reletionships in computer generated images. *In Proc. of IEEE Computer Graphics and Animation.*

28

Embedded System for Biometric Identification

Ahmad Nasir Che Rosli
Universiti Malaysia Perlis
Malaysia

1. Introduction

Biometrics refers to automatic identification of a person based on his or her physiological or behavioral characteristics which provide a reliable and secure user authentication for the increased security requirements of our personal information compared to traditional identification methods such as passwords and PINs (Jain et al., 2000). Organizations are looking to automate identity authentication systems to improve customer satisfaction and operating efficiency as well as to save critical resources due to the fact that identity fraud in welfare disbursements, credit card transactions, cellular phone calls, and ATM withdrawals totals over $6 billion each year (Jain et al., 1998). Furthermore, as people become more connected electronically, the ability to achieve a highly accurate automatic personal identification system is substantially more critical. Enormous change has occurred in the world of embedded systems driven by the advancement on the integrated circuit technology and the availability of open source. This has opened new challenges and development of advanced embedded system. This scenario is manifested in the appearance of sophisticated new products such as PDAs and cell phones and by the continual increase in the amount of resources that can be packed into a small form factor which requires significant high end skills and knowledge. More people are gearing up to acquire advanced skills and knowledge to keep abreast of the technologies to build advanced embedded system using available Single Board Computer (SBC) with 32 bit architectures.

The newer generation of embedded systems can capitalize on embedding a full-featured operating system such as GNU/Linux OS. This facilitate embedded system with a wide selection of capabilities from which to choose inclusive of all the standard IO and built in wireless Internet connectivity by providing TCP/IP stack. Only a few years ago, embedded operating systems were typically found only at the high end of the embedded system spectrum (Richard, 2004). One of the strengths of GNU/Linux OS is that it supports many processor architectures, thus enabling engineers to choose from varieties of processors available in the market. GNU/Linux OS is therefore seen as the obvious candidate for various embedded applications. More embedded system companies development comes with SDK which consists of open source GNU C compiler. This chapter demonstrates the idea of using an embedded system for biometric identification from hardware and software perspective.

2. Biometric Identification

Biometrics is the measurement of biological data (Jain et al., 1998). The term biometrics is commonly used today to refer to the science of identifying people using physiological features (Ratha et al., 2001). Since many physiological and behavioral characteristics are distinctive to each individual, biometrics provides a more reliable and capable system of authentication than the traditional authentication systems. Human physiological or behavioral characteristics that can be used as biometric characteristics are universality, distinctiveness, permanence and collectability (Jain et al., 2000, 2004; Garcia et al., 2003). A biometric system is essentially a pattern recognition system that operates by acquiring biometric data from an individual, extracting a feature set from the acquired data, and comparing this feature set against the template set in the database (Jain et al., 2004). A practical biometric system should meet the specified recognition accuracy, speed, and resource requirements, be harmless to the users, be accepted by the intended population, and be sufficiently robust to various fraudulent methods and attack on the system. A biometric system can operate either in *verification* mode or *identification* mode depending on the application context.

In the verification mode, the system validates a person's identity by comparing the captured biometric data with her own biometric template(s) stored system database such as via a PIN (Personal Identification Number), a user name, a smart card, etc., and the system conducts a one-to one comparison to determine whether the claim is true or not. In the identification mode, the system recognizes an individual by searching the templates of all the users in the database for a match. Therefore, the system conducts a one-to-many comparison to establish an individual's identity without the subject having to claim an identity. The verification problem may be formally posed as follows: given an input feature vector X_Q (extracted from the biometric data) and a claimed identity I, determine if (I, X_Q) belongs to class w_1 or w_2, where w_1 indicates that the claim is true (a genuine user) and w_2 indicates that the claim is false (an impostor). Typically, X_Q is matched against X_I, the biometric template corresponding to user I, to determine its category. Thus,

$$(I, X_Q) \in \begin{cases} w_1 & \text{if } S(X_Q, X_I) \geq t, \\ w_2 & \text{otherwise} \end{cases} \quad (1)$$

where S is the function that measures the similarity between feature vectors X_Q and X_I, and t is a predefined threshold. The value $S(X_Q, X_I)$ is termed as a similarity or matching score between the biometric measurements of the user and the claimed identity. Therefore, every claimed identity is classified into w_1 or w_2 based on the variables X_Q, I, X_I and t, and the function S. Note that biometric measurements (e.g., fingerprints) of the same individual taken at different times are almost never identical. This is the reason for introducing the threshold t. The identification problem, on the other hand, may be stated as follows: given an input feature vector X_Q, determine the identity I_k, $k \in \{1, 2 \ldots N, N+1\}$. Here $I_1, I_2, \ldots, I_N$ are the identities enrolled in the system and I_{N+1} indicates the reject case where no suitable identity can be determined for the user. Hence,

$$X_Q \in \begin{cases} I_k & \text{if } \max_k \{S(X_Q, X_{I_k})\} \geq t, \; k = 1, 2, \ldots, N, \\ I_{N+1} & \text{otherwise} \end{cases} \quad (2)$$

where X_{I_k} is the biometric template corresponding to identity I_k, and t is a predefined threshold.

A biometric system is designed using the following four main modules: sensor module, feature extraction module, matcher module and system database module. The sensor module captures the biometric data of an individual such as a camera to capture a person face image for face biometric. The feature extraction module is a very important process where the acquired biometric data is processed to extract a set of salient or discriminatory features. An example is where the position and orientation of face image are extracted in the feature extraction module of a face-based biometric system. The matcher module ensures that the features during recognition are compared against the stored templates to generate matching scores. For example, in the matching module of a face-based biometric system, the number of matching minutiae between the input and the template face images is determined and a matching score is reported. The matcher module also encapsulates a decision making module in which a user's claimed identity is confirmed (verification) or a user's identity is established (identification) based on the matching score.

The system database module is used by the biometric system to store the biometric templates of the enrolled users. The enrollment module is responsible for enrolling individuals into the biometric system database. During the enrollment phase, the biometric characteristic of an individual is first scanned by a biometric reader to produce a digital representation (feature values) of the characteristic. The data captured during the enrollment process may or may not be supervised by a human depending on the application. A quality check is generally performed to ensure that the acquired sample can be reliably processed by successive stages. In order to facilitate matching, the input digital representation is further processed by a feature extractor to generate a compact but expressive representation called a template. Depending on the application, the template may be stored in the central database of the biometric system or be recorded on a smart card issued to the individual. Usually, multiple templates of an individual are stored to account for variations observed in the biometric trait and the templates in the database may be updated over time.

3. Comparison of Biometric Technologies

A number of biometric characteristics exist and are in use in various applications. Each biometric has its strengths and weaknesses, and the choice depends on the application. No single biometric is expected to effectively meet the requirements of all the applications. In other words, no biometric is "optimal". The match between a specific biometric and an application is determined depending upon the operational mode of the application and the properties of the biometric characteristic. Any human physiological or behavioral characteristic can be used as a biometric characteristic as long as it satisfies the requirements such as *universality* where each person posseses a characteristic; *distinctiveness* i.e. any two persons should be sufficiently different in term of the characteristic; *permanence,* where the characteristic should neither change nor be alterable; *collectability,* the characteristic is easily quantifiable; *performance,* which refers to the achievable recognition accuracy and speed, the robustness, as well as its resource requirements and operational or environmental factors that affect its accuracy and speed; *acceptability* or the extent people are willing to accept for a particular biometric identifier in their daily lives; and *circumvention,* which reflects how easily the system can be fooled using fraudulent methods.

Biometric Identifier	**Universality**	**Distinctiveness**	**Permanence**	**Collectability**	**Performance**	**Acceptability**	**Circumvention**
DNA	H	H	H	L	H	L	L
Ear	M	M	H	M	M	H	M
Face	H	L	M	H	L	H	H
Facial Thermogram	H	H	L	H	M	H	L
Fingerprint	M	H	H	M	H	M	M
Gait	M	L	L	H	L	H	M
Hand Geometry	M	M	M	H	M	M	M
Hand Vein	M	M	M	M	M	M	L
Iris	H	H	H	M	H	L	L
Keystroke	L	L	L	M	L	M	M
Odor	H	H	H	L	L	M	L
Palmprint	M	H	H	M	H	M	M
Retina	H	H	M	L	H	L	L
Signature	L	L	L	H	L	H	H
Voice	M	L	L	M	L	H	H

Table 1. Comparison of various biometric technologies based on the perception of the authors (Jain et al., 2000, 2004; Garcia et al., 2003). H-high, M-medium, L-low.

A brief comparison of various biometric techniques based on the seven factors is provided in Table 1. The applicability of a specific biometric technique depends heavily on the requirements of the application domain. No single technique can outperform all the others in all operational environments. In this sense, each biometric technique is admissible and there is no optimal biometric characteristic. For example, it is well known that both the fingerprint-based techniques are more accurate than the voice-based technique. However, in a tele-banking application, the voice-based technique may be preferred since it can be integrated seamlessly into the existing telephone system. Biometric-based systems also have some limitations that may have adverse implications for the security of a system. While some of the limitations of biometrics can be overcome with the evolution of biometric technology and a careful system design, it is important to understand that foolproof personal recognition systems simply do not exist and perhaps, never will. Security is a risk management strategy that identifies, controls, eliminates, or minimizes uncertain events that may adversely affect system resources and information assets. The security level of a system

depends on the requirements (threat model) of an application and the cost-benefit analysis. The properly implemented biometric systems are effective deterrents to perpetrators.
There are a number of privacy concerns raised on the use of biometrics. A sound tradeoff between security and privacy may be necessary; collective accountability/acceptability standards can only be enforced through common legislation. Biometrics provides tools to enforce accountable logs of system transactions and to protect an individual's right to privacy. As biometric technology matures, there will be an increasing interaction among the market, technology, and the applications. This interaction will be influenced by the added value of the technology, user acceptance, and the credibility of the service provider. It is too early to predict where and how biometric technology would evolve and get embedded in which applications. But it is certain that biometric-based recognition will have a profound influence on the way we conduct our daily business.

4. Face Recognition

Face recognition is an important research problem spanning numerous fields and disciplines and one of the most successful applications of image analysis and understanding. This is due to numerous practical applications such as bankcard identification, access control, Mug shots searching, security monitoring, and surveillance system. Face recognition is a fundamental human behaviors that is essential for effective communications and interactions among people (Tolba et al., 2005). A formal method of classifying faces was first proposed by Galton (1888). The author proposed collecting facial profiles as curves, finding their norm, and then classifying other profiles by their deviations from the norm. This classification is multi-modal, i.e. resulting in a vector of independent measures that could be compared with other vectors in a database. Progress has advanced to the point that face recognition systems are being demonstrated in real-world settings (Zaho, 1999). The rapid development of face recognition is due to a combination of factors--active development of algorithms, the availability of large databases of facial images, and a method for evaluating the performance of face recognition algorithms.

Face recognition is a biometric identification technology which uses automated methods to verify or recognize the identity of a person based on his/her physiological characteristics. A general statement of the problem of face recognition system can be classified as a process to identify or verify one or more persons in the static images or video images of a scene by comparing with faces stored in database (Zhao et al., 2003). Available collateral information such as race, age, gender, facial expression, or speech may be used in narrowing the search (enhancing recognition). Face recognition starts with the detection of face patterns in sometimes cluttered scenes, proceeds by normalizing the face images to account for geometrical and illumination changes, possibly using information about the location and appearance of facial landmarks, identifies the faces using appropriate classification algorithms, and post processes the results using model-based schemes and logistic feedback (Chellappa et al., 1995). In identification problems, the input to the system is an unknown face, and the system reports back the determined identity from a database of known individuals, whereas in verification problems, the system needs to confirm or reject the claimed identity of the input face.

All face recognition algorithms consist of two major parts (Tolba et al., 2005): (1) face detection and normalization; and (2) face identification. Algorithms that consist of both parts are referred to as fully automatic algorithms and those that consist of only the second part are called partially automatic algorithms. Partially automatic algorithms are given a facial image and the coordinates of the center of the eyes. Fully automatic algorithms are only given facial images. Face recognition has recently received significant attention, especially during the past few years (Zhao et al., 2003), which is shown by the emergence of face recognition conferences such as the International Conference on Audio and Video-Based Authentication (AVBPA) since 1997 and the International Conference on Automatic Face and Gesture Recognition (AFGR) since 1995, systematic empirical evaluations of face recognition technique (FRT), including the FERET (Phillips et al., 1998), (Phillips et al., 2000),(Rizvi et al., 1998), FRVT 2000 (Blackburn et al., 2001), FRVT 2002 (Phillips et al., 2003) and XM2VTS (Messer et al., 1999) protocols, and many commercially available systems.

5. Hardware Platforms for Embedded Systems

An embedded system has been around for over a decade and enormous change has occurred since then. In the early embedded system application, limitations in component choice resulted in functional limitations. Most embedded systems were run with relatively simple 8-bit microcontrollers. Until recently, the vast majority of these embedded systems used 8- and 16-bit microprocessors, requiring little in the way of sophisticated software development tools, including an Operating System (OS). But the breaking of the $5 threshold for 32-bit processors is now driving an explosion in high-volume embedded applications (Stepner et al., 1999). A new trend towards integrating a full system on- a-chip (SOC) promises a further dramatic expansion for 32- and 64-bit embedded applications. The traditional small, narrowly focused embedded systems retain their significant presence, but these newer arrivals can capitalize on embedding a full-featured operating system, especially Linux OS (Badlishah et al., 2006a). These embedded systems are ubiquitously used to capture, store, manipulate, and access data of a sensitive nature (e.g. personal appliances such as cell phones, PDAs, smart card, portable storage devices), or perform safety-critical functions (e.g. automotive and aviation electronics, medical appliances) (Aaraj et al., 2006).

The integration of embedded computing is a hard task and it is difficult to integrate in both software and hardware. A strong effort by the scientific and industrial community has taken place to overcome this complex issue by splitting up the complex system in different smaller parts with very specific purposes. Ramamritham and Arya (2003) define that embedded applications are characterized by a number of issues: control, sequencing, signal processing and resource management. Tan et al. (2003) describe how energy consumption has become a major focus in embedded systems research and there has been a move from hardware-oriented low energy design techniques to energy-efficient embedded software design. It is known that the Operating System (OS) has a significant impact on the system energy consumption.

Al-Ali et al. (2003) propose a small system for measuring blood pressure and other variables in a patient monitoring device. Kroll et al. (2003) show the use of more complex solution for medical imaging by using Java on embedded systems in order to incorporate cryptographic algorithms specified in the DICOM standard1. Lamberti and Demartini (2003) propose a design and development of low-cost homecare architecture for remote patient telemetry based on Java software and an embedded computer. The researchers prove the concept by using new approaches like Personal Digital Assistants and WAP enabled GSM/GPRS mobile phones for real-time monitoring of ECGs. In experimental nuclear science there is a high presence of embedded systems research for instrumentation (Deb et al., 2000; Dufey et al., 2000; Fryer, 1998; Gori et al., 1999). In other application, as reviewed in Baber and Baumann (2002), human interaction with embedded technology (in the wearable sense) is considered. In this paper, the authors opine that the Human-Computer Interaction (HCI) will move away from the desktop to be merged into the rest of daily activities.

Product	Manufacturer	Operating System	Processor	Key Features
Psion Series 5 (Handheld)	Psion PLC, London	EPOC32	ARM 7100	Touch-typable keyboard, long battery life
Palm III (Palm device)	3Com Corp., Santa Clara, Claif	Palm OS	Motorola 68328	Longest battery life, very lightweight
Communicator 9110 (Smart Phone)	Nokia Mobile Phones, Espoo, Finland	GEOS 3.0	AMD 486	Portable Digital GSM
IS630 screen phone (Smart Phone)	Philips Consumer Communications LP, Murray Hill, N.J.	Inferno / Personal-Java	Digital Strong ARM 1100	Desktop Unit, IR Keyboard, color display, two PCCard slots, 28.8kbps modem
ICES (In car System)	Visteon Automotive Systems (a Ford Motor enterprise), Dearborn, Mich.	Windows CE 2.0	Intel Pentium	Voice recognition and text-to-speech capability, traffic conditions, navigation, cell phone, rear-seat movies...

Table 2. Information appliances (Comerford, 1998)

Some requirements of an embedded system are different to those which are required for a desktop computer--the system has to be responsive, a considerable design effort is given to system testability (doing a proper debug can be difficult without display or keyboard), there are strong reliability and stability requirements and memory space is limited. On the other hand, special tools are required to program these devices, power considerations are sometimes critical, but high throughput may be needed. And they have always a cost oriented design. An embedded system is considered a computer system hidden inside another product with other goals that being a general purpose computer system. Microprocessor-based cores like Intel x86 family are slowly migrating to embedded systems and are becoming cost-competitive against the alternatives already existent in the market. This fact is provoking dramatic changes in our society as cleverer and faster embedded computer systems are reaching consumer market. These devices are changing the way in which we communicate with each other (mobile telephony) via the addition of high efficiency audio-video encoding/decoding algorithms. These algorithms can be implemented in cheap (and complex) telephone terminals that optimize bandwidth in such a way that is cost effective enough to sell personal video communication at consumer market.

Perera et al. (2003) show that hardware platforms used at research level and even present market are really varied but there is a clear evolution towards high end profile µProcessors for portable and embedded computing. A study on information appliances is found in Table 2 where it is remarkable that microprocessors from x86 architecture like AMD 486 that were formerly used as the CPU of a desktop computer some years ago are now used as embedded processors in devices like Communicator 9110 from Nokia. This has caused manufacturers to provide the market with different kinds of embedded appliances that are actually full computers (in the sense of CPU, Data Storage Support, Memory, Serial & Parallel ports, Network devices, Data acquisition, etc.). Recently even some companies have begun manufacturing systems based on the so called system-on-chip (SoC from now on), where all CPU peripherals are not included in a chip-set mounted on the same printed circuit board but integrated in the same dice. The migration from 8- to 16- to 32-bit devices is helping the addition of more advanced technologies into consumer markets. From a pattern recognition view this can be noticed in handwriting recognition in PDAs, voice/speech recognition, biometric systems for security, and others. These techniques can be applied into industrial market as well.

6. Image Acquisition and Processing in Embedded Device

A variety of smart camera architecture designed in academia and industry exists today as stated in Bramberger et al (2006) and Wolf et al. (2002). Fleck et al. (2007) suggested that all smart cameras system is the combination of a sensor, an embedded processing unit and a connection, which is nowadays often a network unit. The embedded processing unit can be classified in DSPs, general purpose processors, FPGAs, and a combination thereof. More people are doing research on Linux running embedded on the smart camera. There exist several projects which also focus on the integration of image acquisition and image processing in a single embedded device. Fleck and Straßer (2005) present a particle filter algorithm for tracking objects in the field of view of a single camera. They used a commercially available camera which comprised a CCD image sensor, a Xilinx FPGA for low-level image processing and a Motorola PowerPC CPU. They also implemented a multi-camera tracking (Fleck and Straßer ,2006) using the particle filter tracking algorithm. However, in this work, the handover between cameras is managed by a central server node. Cao et al. (2005) proposed an image sensor mote architecture, in which an FPGA connects to a VGA (640x 480 pixels) CMOS imager to carry out image acquisition and compression. An ARM7 microcontroller processes image further and communicates to neighbouring motes via an ultra-low-power-transceiver.

Rahimi et al. (2005) suggested another powerful image sensor mote, which combines Agilent Technologies' Cyclops with Crossbow's Mica2 mote. Cyclops was developed as an add-on CIF (320x240 pixel) CMOS camera module board, which hosts an on-board 8-bit microcontroller and 64 Kbytes of static and 512 Kbytes of flash memory for pixel-level processing and storage. Oliveira et al. (2006) presented a smart camera mote architecture that uses an FPGA as its central processing unit, a VGA CMOS imager, and 10 Mbytes of static and 64 Mbytes of flash memory to perform early vision. Downes et al. (2006) introduced mote architecture with minimal component count, which deploys an ARM7 microcontroller as its core, 2 Mbytes flash memory, and a 2.4 GHz IEEE 802.15.4 radio. Velipasalar et al. (2006) described a PC based decentralized multi-camera system for multi-object tracking using a peer-to-peer infrastructure. Each camera identifies moving objects and follows their track. When a new object is identified, the camera issues a labelling request containing a description of the object. If the object is known by another camera, it replies the label of the object; otherwise a new label is assigned which results in a consistent labelling over multiple cameras. Rowe et al. (2005) promoted a low cost embedded vision system. The aim of this project was the development of a small camera with integrated image processing. Due to the limited memory and computing resources, only low-level image processing like threshold and filtering were possible. The image processing algorithm could not be modified during runtime because it was integrated into the processor's firmware.

Agent systems have also been used as a form of abstraction in multi-camera applications. Remagnino et al. (2001) described the usage of agents in visual surveillance systems. An agent based framework is used to accomplish scene understanding. Abreu et al. (2000) presented Monitorix, a video-based multi-agent traffic surveillance system based on PCs. Agents are used as representatives in different layers of abstraction. Quaritsch et al. (2006) presented a decentralized solution for tracking objects across multiple embedded smart cameras that combine video sensing, processing and communication on a single embedded device which is equipped with a multi-processor computation and communication infrastructure. Each object of interest has a corresponding tracking instance which is represented by a mobile agent. Hengstler and Aghajan (2006) introduced energy-efficient smart camera mote architecture with intelligent surveillance. This is a low-resolution stereo vision system continuously determines position, range, and size of moving object entering its field of view. Kleihorst et al. (2006) introduce a wireless smart camera based on a SIMD video-analysis processor and an 8051 microcontroller as a local host. Williams et al. (2006) described the design and implementation of two distributed smart camera applications i.e. a fall detector and an object finder. Fleck et al. (2007) propose network-enabled smart cameras for probabilistic tracking. The smart cameras' tracking results are embedded in an integrated 3D environment as live textures and can be viewed from arbitrary perspectives.

7. Single Board Computer (SBC)

Single Board Computers (SBCs) have changed dramatically over the years. Early microcomputer typically consisted of circuit board which implemented the central processing unit (CPU), memory, disk controllers and serial/parallel port functions. These microcomputers are used for data acquisition, process control, and R&D projects, but are generally too bulky to be used as the intelligence embedded within devices (LinuxDevices, n.d.). Advancement in the density, complexity and capability of the silicon improved the choice and selection methodology for SBCs. Today, software, board size, and time-to-market are the key decision factors in addition to just the power and speed of the CPU. Historically, the initial SBC structure was a simple extension of the common bus architecture used by the microprocessor. It had an onboard local bus and off-board expansion bus. Early SBCs could only support a minimum number of functions on a single board. Therefore, initial SBC specification standards focused on memory and I/O expansion by means of multiple boards connected via a backplane bus or mezzanine. However, as the SBC market has evolved and matured, the backplane bus importance has diminished.

The first industrial microprocessor based SBC standard was Intel's Multibus I introduced in the late 70's (Robert, n.d.). It was optimized for Intel's 80xx processor family. In the early 1980's integrated circuit (IC) technology had advanced to where functions that occupied entire circuit boards could be crammed into single "large-scale integrated" (LSI) logic chips (Badlishah, 2006a). The result of the semiconductor advances was that it was possible to increase the functional density on the boards while decreasing cost and increasing reliability. Instead of a system requiring multiple boards, a complete microcomputer system is implemented on a single board. Three technical developments will impact the use of single board computers in industrial automation in the near term. They are flat panel display technology, network-based computing, and Linux. There are a wide range of architectures that are being used to develop an embedded system. In general, embedded systems can be divided into three classes i.e. Small Scale Embedded Systems, Medium Scale Embedded Systems and Sophisticated Embedded Systems (Badlishah et al., 2006b). Small scale embedded systems have a less hardware and software complexities. They are designed with a single 8- or 16-bit micro-controller and involve board level design. Examples: 8051, 68HC05. Medium scale embedded systems have both hardware and software complexities. They are designed with a single or few 16- or 32-bit micro-controller or Reduced Instructions Set Computer (RISCs). Sophisticated embedded systems have an enormous hardware and software complexities. Besides they may need scalable processor or configurable processor. The TCP/IP stacking and network driver are also implemented in the hardware. Examples: PowerPC, ARM7 and Intel 80960CA.

Generally there are four categories of embedded systems which are stand-alone embedded systems, real-time embedded systems, networked appliances and mobile devices. Table 3 lists a few of the embedded system built using different architectures (Richard, n.d.). There are a number of reasons developers should choose to use SBC for development such as speed development, low development cost, increasing clock speed and availability of GNU/Linux(Badlishah et al., 2006a). An embedded system designed from scratch requires that boards be designed, fabricated, and debugged. The software must be tested and debugged on the target system. In addition, high speed buses like PCI take more design effort to get it right; instead, SBC boards had someone else did the job of making it works. Embedded systems based on SBC require no costly board design/fabrication/debug cycles. Standard PC Tools are usually used for software development, eliminating the need to purchase emulators. As product development cycles get shorter, there is an incentive to buy proven, off-the-shelf components. Another factor is the increasing clock speed of the hardware which passes to GHz range. Due to the GNU/Linux free kernel that is available for most of CPU architecture, it makes the application development much easier. Even the source code of some of the applications is in the Internet.

Product	Platform (Microprocessor)
Vendo V-MAX 720 vending machine	8-bit Motorola 68HC11
Sonicare Plus toothbrush:	8-bit Zilog Z8
Miele dishwashers	8-bit Motorola 68HC05
NASA's Mars Sojourner Rover	8-bit Intel 80C85
Garmin StreetPilot GPS Receiver	16-bit
Palm Vx handheld	32-bit Motorola Dragonball EZ
Motorola i1000plus iDEN Multi-Service Digital Phone	Motorola 32-bit MCORE
Rio 800 MP3 Player	32-bit RISC
RCA RC5400P DVD player	32-bit RISC
Sony Aibo ERS-110 Robotic Dog	64-bit MIPS RIS

Table 3. Embedded System with different hardware platform (Richard, n.d.)

Some embedded designs can still be accomplished using processor with clock rates in the low MHz range. However, as clock rates go up and the development costs follow, more companies concentrate their effort on the hardware and software that makes their product unique. Off-the-Shelf CPUs, Ethernet boards, and similar components parts are treated as commodity parts, which they are. So why assign an engineer to spend three months developing a board that looks and works like a hundred other identical designs? Single Board Computer (SBC) is one type of embedded system technology widely used for recent years. SBC can perform specific tasks like computer as it has a processor, RAM, hard disk and OS or languages. Many applications have been developed for current and future technology as described in (Dan, 2003; Wiencke, 2006; Wood, 2006).

8. System Overview

This research focus on the development and implementation of embedded system for biometric identification based on iris detection using SBC and GNU/Linux which enables the replacement of traditional techniques of authentication system for security such as smart card reader system. This system uses *Face Reader* to acquire face image and performs the image preprocessing process to extract a facial features of a person's face for biometric identification purposes. The approach proposed was the use of an embedded system (SBC) for controlling the external devices such as Universal Serial Bus (USB) web camera, LCD panel and matrix keypad and connectivity. The control was executed via ANSI-C software coded on top of an open source operating system (GNU/Linux).

The software code is portable to a desktop system for integration with other software components such as biometric identification software. Only changes in acquisition devices such camera and keypad module is required in order to perform the task. The software code is portable to a small embedded system without the need of the specific SBC or without the use of SBC based system. The software works in any platform where Linux kernel has been ported. The software code is written regardless any limitation of the hardware platform such as slow processing speed and low image quality captured by the camera.

9. Hardware Design

Face Reader hardware design is composed of a SBC as the main component. Other components such as the Universal Serial Bus (USB) webcam, LCD panel, Compact Flash Card, PCMCIA Wireless Network Card and matrix keypad are attached to the SBC. Figure 1(a) shows the necessary components used for the proposed system. The integration and configuration of the hardware components constituted a physical model of a *Face Reader*. Figure 1(b) shows the illustration of a *Face Reader* model. *Face Reader* is responsible for testing initialization and image capturing processes. It is a compact SBC unit with a USB webcam mounted on top of it. The LCD Panel provides the mechanism of input prompting, system status information display and processing results. It is used to communicate with users. The keypad, which is mounted in front of the unit, is used by the user to key in their user ID or presses the instructed key by referring to the LCD. Getting the system to function appropriately involves the installation of appropriate device driver module to the operating system (OS) by considering the version of Linux kernel and libraries on board.

(a) (b)

Fig. 1. a) *Face Reader* components; b) Physical Model for *Face Reader*

The face image database and biometric identification software are embedded in the SBC; thus the recognition and verification of face images for small database system is performed on the board itself. For a large database system, external high speed PC server is used as a database to store face images and biometric identification software. The high speed PC server receives images and user ID send through network protocol (TCP/IP) and interface by *Face Reader*. Results from biometric identification is sent through a network to the *Face Reader* to be displayed through LCD panel. In order to accomplish the task (recognition and verification) by using the biometric identification algorithm, high speed processor PC Server based on GNU/Linux is chosen.

9.1 TS5500 SBC

The compatibility of an embedded system refers to the element of the processor, memory, I/O maps and BIOS. Memory for this model is dependant on the capacity of compact flash used within range from 32 MB - 1GB. SBC model from Technologic Systems, Inc is boot from IDE compact flash, DiskOnChip or On-board flash drive. TS5500 SBC (Figure 2) are compatible with several embedded OS with x86-based operating system. They are TSLinux, DOS, Windows CE, Net BSD, MicroCommander, SMX, QNX, Phar Lap, MicroC/OS II and eRTOS. The most popular OS used with this x86 models are DOS and TSLinux. This model has three COM ports and COM 2 is used to be a monitor for SBC using null modem. A serial port is connected from the board at COM 2 to serial port at computer localhost. To enable the console at localhost to function well, a minicom should be installed first. Linux has provided a package that contains minicom. A default baud rate should be changed from 9600 to 115200. At the same time, the correct serial port that has been connected from localhost must be set at minicom configuration. The board is equipped with TSLinux 3.07a that has been preinstalled by Technologic Systems, Inc company before shipping. TS Linux is one type of embedded OS that is created by Technologic Systems, Inc and has many similarities like normal Linux features especially in filesystem but in small size.

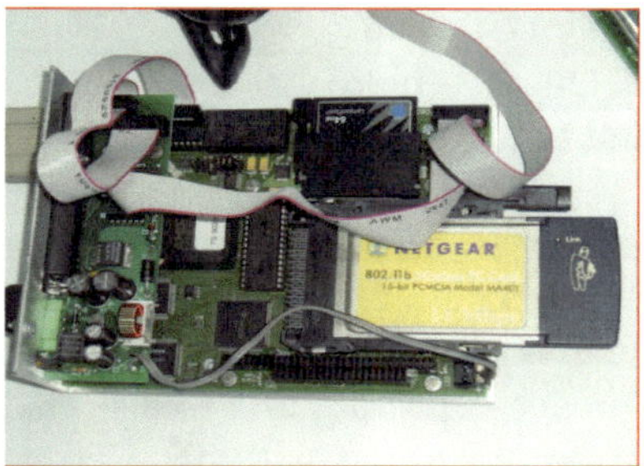

Fig. 2. TS5500 SBC

Network support is one important feature for latest SBC technology. TS5500 has one RJ45 port and support standard network by using Telnet and file transfer protocol (FTP). But it does not support Secure Shell (SSH) function. Furthermore, the Secure CoPy (SCP) is allowed by this model by activating the dropbear function provided by TS Linux. The network point provides two LEDs to represent an active connection, and active data flow. On the other hand, PCMCIA is also reliable using 802.11 standard for wireless network. 5 Volt voltages are provided by and external power supply adapter connected to a standard 240V AC outlet. At the back of the unit is a reset button for reseting the unit to the factory defaults setting. The board comes with an AMD Elan 520 (equivalent to an Intel x86) processor that runs at 133MHz as well as 64 MB of RAM, a 2 MB flash disk, a Disk On Chip socket, and a PC/104 bus. It also has a Type 1 Compact Flash card reader, USB, PCMCIA a 10/100Base-T Ethernet interface, 40 Digital I/O lines and an alphanumeric LCD interface. The board requires 5V DC power at 800mA.

9.2 Development of Webcam Device Driver

The USB Webcam plays an important role in this project. The webcam is mounted on top of the *Face Reader* and attached to the SBC. This webcam is used for capturing face image which is then pre-processed and extracted for face facial recognition. Selecting the appropriate USB Webcam to integrate with the board requires a lot of testing and configuration. Most of the USB webcam is manufactured to comply with the Window environment; this means the manufacturer does not provide any supported driver for this webcam to work in Linux operating system. In this project, a few USB webcam models (Table 4) which are available in the market are chosen and tested for their compatibility with Linux operating system. This is done by utilizing the availability of open source and driver in Linux community. Results show that only two webcam can be configured and integrated with Linux operating system. Besides the availability of the Linux device driver for specific webcam model, Linux kernels version is also an important issue in configuring and integrating the webcam with Linux operating system.

	Webcam Model	**Linux Device Driver (V4L)**
1	Creative Webcam Instant	Not Available
2	Logitech QuickCam Communicate STX/USB	spca500-20050101
3	Logitech QuickCam Express- USB	Not Available
4	Logitech QuickCam Chat	Not Available
5	Philip CU 2006	Not Available
6	Logitech QuickCam Pro 4000	pwc-8.8 & usb-pwcx-8.2.2

Table 4. Webcam Model and Linux V4L Device Driver

The integration and configuration of the webcam with TS Linux OS includes the testing which is done for Logitech QuickCam Communicate STX/USB and Logitech QuickCam Pro 4000 webcams. This testing is divided into a few features i.e. webcam workability in different kernel versions, image capturing and image readability. The testing is to find a suitable webcam that can be integrated with TS 5500 embedded PC. Besides TS Linux (kernel 2.4.23-25.ts), testing is also done in different platforms i.e. RedHat 8.1 (kernel 2.4.18-14), RedHat 7.3 (kernel 2.4.18-3), RedHat 7.3 (kernel 2.4.20) and RedHat 7.3 (kernel 2.4.23-25.ts). The selection of the USB Webcam Logitech QuickCam Pro 4000 for this project is based on results of the testing as shown in Table 5 and Table 6.

USB Web Camera	Logitech QuickCam Communicate STX		
Driver	spca500-20050101		
Features	Camera detected	Image capture	Image readability
RedHat8.1(kernel 2.4.18-14)	yes	Yes	yes
RedHat7.3(kernel 2.4.18-3)	-	-	-
RedHat7.3(kernel 2.4.20)	-	-	-
RedHat 7.3 (kernel 2.4.23-25.ts)	no	No	no
TS Linux (kernel 2.4.23-25.ts)	no	No	no

Table 5. Logitech QuickCam Communicate STX Webcam Configured with Different Linux Kernel

The TS 5500 SBC is installed with TS Linux version 3.07a with 2.4.23-25.ts kernel. Logitech Quickcam Pro 4000 web camera driver works in fresh kernel 2.4.20 and works well with the Philips web camera drivers modules i.e. PWC core modules (pwc-8.8.tar.gz) and PWCX decompressor modules (pwcx-8.2.2.tar.gz).

USB Web Camera	Logitech Quickcam Pro 4000		
Driver	pwc-8.8 & usb-pwcx-8.2.2		
Features	Camera detected	Image capture	Image readability
RedHat8.1 (kernel 2.4.18-14)	no	No	no
RedHat7.3 (kernel 2.4.18-3)	no	No	no
RedHat7.3 (kernel 2.4.20)	yes	Yes	yes
RedHat 7.3 (kernel 2.4.23-25.ts)	yes	Yes	yes
TS Linux (kernel 2.4.23-25.ts)	yes	Yes	yes

Table 6. Logitech QuickCam Pro 4000 Webcam Configured with Different Linux Kernel

9.3 Development of LCD Panel and Keypad Device Driver

Technologic Systems provide the documentation to integrate the SBC with Lumex LCD Panel by using LCDproc i.e. Linux LCD display driver. LCDproc is a piece of software that displays real-time system information from Linux box on a LCD. The server supports several serial devices and some devices connected to the LPT port. Various clients are available that display things like CPU load, system load, memory usage, uptime, and a lot more. LCDproc is consists of two parts: LCDd and user clients. LCDd is the deamon that interacts with the LCD display. User clients tell the deamon what to display on the LCD display. LCDd must be installed and running on the 32 bit embedded PC. The client need not install on the embedded PC or host itself because LCDd listens on a network interface.

The TS 5500 SBC support a matrix keypad provided by Technologic Systems. The matrix keypad code uses 8 digital I/O lines as row outputs and column inputs to scan a 4x4 keypad. The square wave output function of the real time clock is used as a pacing clock to generate interrupts on IRQ8. The interrupt service routine calls the keypad scans routine and provides debounce timing. The kernel module for the matrix keypad is ts_keypad.o, and exports the device node /dev/SBC/TSKeypad. When the device node is opened, the driver begins its keypad scan routine, storing key-presses into a buffer. When the device node is read from, if any key-presses were made, they a sent back to the user.

10. Software Development

BIOI^{2}D software is developed on embedded GNU/Linux OS and SBC. The SBC is pre-installed with TS-Linux kernel 2.24.23. The selection of GNU/Linux OS is to utilize the availability of open source resources such as GCC compiler, libraries, kernels and drivers in developing and implementing this system. The *Face Reader* is designed to operate in real-time mode, which requires the face identification and recognition software to identify a person face, and pre-process the image. BIOI^{2}D software system can operate in two (2) modes i.e. stand-alone and network mode. In stand-alone mode, all of the process in done on the *Face Reader* itself, while in network mode, server perform the biometric identification process using face image send by *Face Reader* through TCP/IP network protocol. BIOI^{2}D software design is structured in five (5) modules i.e. User Interface, Image Acquisition, Image Preprocessing, Network and Biometric Identification. All software relies on an embedded version of the Linux OS and tailored with GNU C utilities. User interface module incorporates the development of a system control program and the integration of LCD panel and matrix keypad to the SBC. The development of image acquisition module or the camera module involves the usage of open source Video4Linux (V4L) Application Programming Interface (API). Image is captured using YUV420P format and before the image is saved it is converted into greyscale format because image preprocessing algorithm and face recognition algorithm is functions only in greyscale format.

In image preprocessing module, image preprocessing algorithms are used to perform initial processing that performs primary data reduction and analysis task easier. The objective of image preprocessing module is to preprocess face image by converting the image to grayscale, removing the image background, improving image appearance and scale down the image. The output image is use by face recognition software for recognition purposes. Network mode involves client-server applications. Network module is developed by using socket API, which enable the communication between processes over the Internet, within the LAN or on single PC. The *sendfile* system call provides an efficient mechanism for copying data from one PC to another. In this mode, the client program sends the face image file and user ID variable to the server. The server performs face recognition and sending back the result to the client. Biometric identification module incorporates face recognition algorithm based on iris detection for identification and verification. Recognition system is based on template matching and the process is performed one-to-one matching (direct matching) by using user ID.

10.1 Image Pre-processing

The Face Reader is design to operate in real-time mode, which requires the face identification and recognition software to identify the person face from the captured image. The preprocessing algorithms are used to perform initial processing that makes the primary data reduction and analysis task easier. This include operations related to extracting regions of interest, performing basic algebraic operations on images, enhancing specific image features, and reducing data in both resolution and brightness. Face image is captured in color format and the image is with complex background. The objective of image preprocessing module is to preprocess face image by converting the image to grayscale, removing the image background, improving image appearance and scale down the image. The image preprocessing technique performs are the color space conversion, motion analysis technique, grayscale modification and image scaling. The output image is use by face recognition software for recognition purposes. Color space conversion is the process of changing one type of color-encoded signal into another. Face image is captured in YUV420P format. The conversion process implemented is converting from YUV420P to RGB and from RGB to Grayscale. In first conversion, source data is converted from the YUV420P color space to the RGB color model. A YUV image is then converted to a gamma-corrected RGB image. This function will returns the R, G, B component values that are equivalent to the color represented by the YUV420P values. . For RGB to grayscale conversion, it is clear that black grayscale is equal in value only to the RGB grayscale. The conversion formulas are:

$$R = Y + 1.593*(V-128) \quad (3)$$
$$G = Y - 0.390*(U-128) - 0.515*(V-128) \quad (4)$$
$$B = Y + 2.015*(U-128) \quad (5)$$

The formula for conversion from RGB to Grayscale is as below:

$$\text{Grayscale intensity} = 0.2990R + 0.5870G + 0.1140B \quad (6)$$

Motion analysis is connected with real-time analysis. It is used to obtain comprehensive information about moving and static objects present in the scene. The input to a motion analysis system is a temporal image sequence, with a corresponding increase in the amount of processed data. For motion detection, it registers any detected motion and usually by using a single static camera. The software perform four steps to detect and analyze movement in image sequence i.e. frame differencing, threshold, noise removal and morphological filtering. Frame differencing operation is used to find the difference between the current image and the background image. If the difference between the pixel values is greater than constant value fixed, the movement has been significant and the pixel is set to black otherwise if the change is less than this threshold, the pixel is set to white. This image now indicates if something has moved and where the movement is located. To remove the noise, the program scans the threshold image with a 3 x 3 frame and removes all black pixels which are isolated in a white area. If the center pixel of the 3 x 3 frame is black and less than three of the pixels in the frame are black, the algorithm remove the black center pixel, otherwise the pixel remains black.

Morphological filtering simplifies a segmented image to facilitate the search for object of interest by smoothing out object outlines, filling small holes, eliminating small projections, and using other similar techniques. The two principal morphological operations are dilation and erosion. Dilation allows object to expand, thus potentially filling in small holes and connecting disjoint objects. Erosion shrinks objects by etching away (eroding) their boundaries. These operations can be customized for an application by the proper selection of the structuring element, which determines exactly how the objects will be dilated or eroded. Grayscale modification methods are a point operations and function by changing the pixel's (gray level) values by a mapping equation. The mapping equation is typically linear and maps the original gray level values to other specified values. The gray level histogram of an image is the distribution of the gray levels in an image. Histogram equalization is a popular technique for improving the appearance of a poor image where the histogram of the resultant image is as flat as possible. The theoretical basis for histogram equalization involves probability theory where the histogram is treated as the probability distribution of the gray levels. This is reasonable, since the histogram is the distribution of gray levels for particular image.

Image scaling is the process of changing the size of a digital image. These involve either increase or reduction of image size by a fixed ratio. Two properties of image scaling are the contraction ratio is the same everywhere, although pixel distances are not preserved and the pixel lattice of the target image is a subset or superset the original image for an integer scaling ratio. The first property allows the use of spatially invariant filter, and the second property avoids the need for resampling when the scaling ratio is an integer. Scaling down process increases the incidence of high frequencies and causes several pixels to collapse into one. In order to minimize aliasing problems in the target image, Box filter (the smoothing filter) is applied.

11. Results and Discussion

BIOI²D feasibility is tested by setting-up a test environment in the laboratory. The experimental setup consists of a *Face Reader* prototype and a PC as a server. The *Face Reader* prototype and the server are connected to the LAN switch through wired Ethernet TCP/IP network cable. The evaluation is carried out for both stand-alone and network operation modes. In stand-alone mode, face recognition process is executed on the board (SBC), and for network-mode the face recognition process is implemented using external program run on a server using TCP/IP network through a 5 port switch. The experiments are made by using 100 face images of 10 different persons for the evaluation of the accuracy of biometric identification. This includes setting-up face template and database images. The person's face image is captured and pre-processed before biometric identification process is performed. Output image file from image preprocessing process and user ID are transmitted through the LAN to the server by utilizing socket programming interface. At the server, the image file and user ID's are used for biometric identification process and the result is sending back to the *Face Reader* through a LAN (whether the face is match with the information in the database). The *Face Reader* displays the result (such as "Authentication successful") though LCD panel. The delay measurement for both operation modes is counted from the beginning of image acquisition process until the ends, when the identification result is displayed.

Specification	Desktop PC	SBC
Processor Type	Intel(R) Core (TM) 2 CPU	AMD Elan 520
Processor Speed	1.8 GHz	133 MHz
RAM Size	1 GB	64 MB
Operating System	Mandriva 2006	TS-Linux

Table 7. Comparison desktop PC and SBC Specifications

BIOI²D hardware performance evaluation is performed by measuring the processing time for the overall BIOI²D operation, image pre-processing process and biometric identification process. For BIOI²D operation, the comparison is made to measure the performance for stand-alone and network mode. In image pre-processing and biometric identification process the performance of the 133 MHz SBC is compared to a desktop PC with Intel(R) Core (TM) 2 CPU running at 1.83 GHz (desktop). Table 7 shows the details of a desktop PC and SBC specifications. Overall BIOI²D processing time is measured starting from camera initializing until biometric identification results display on LCD Panel for both stand-alone and network modes. The processes include image capturing, user identification number input, image preprocessing, biometric identification and result display. Network mode requires additional process which involves the use of socket interfaces for network connectivity between *Face Reader* and a server for the face image, user identification number and result transfers. Table 8 shows the comparison for overall BIOI2D operations for both modes. Results show that the network mode is faster than stand-alone mode. The overall stand-alone mode processing speed is only 62.4% of a network mode.

BIOI²D Operation	Overall Processing (s)
Stand-alone	190.53
Network	118.95

Table 8. Comparison of overall BIOI²D operations execution time

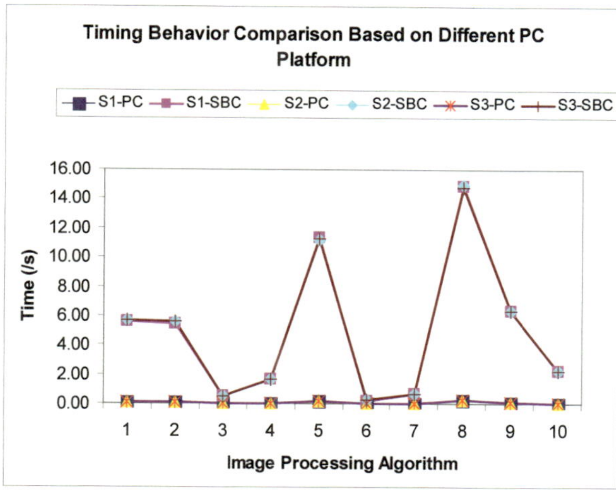

Fig. 3. Timing Behavior Comparison Based on Different PC Platform

The processing time for the image preprocessing process is evaluated by executing the algorithm by using 3 different image samples. The three (3) image samples differ in their background and local contrast. The speed for the *Face Reader* (SBC) is only 1.52 % of a desktop platform for image pre-processing process as shown in Figure 3 which illustrates timing behaviour comparison based on different PC platform. The pattern demonstrates that the processing time for image preprocessing algorithm is almost the same even though the complexity of the background image and the image contrast differs. Biometric identification performance evaluation is to measure the executing time for biometric identification process by executing the algorithm on both SBC and desktop platforms. Table 9 shows the result of the execution time which shows that processing is faster on desktop compare to SBC. For SBC platform the processing time are 0.01 operations per seconds while for desktop the execution time are 1.11 operations per second. The speed of SBC for biometric identification algorithm is slower than desktop that is only 0.9 % of a desktop speed.

As shown in Table 7, the SBC and server differ in processor type, processing speed, RAM size and OS. The hardware specification for the server is much faster than SBC. In stand-alone mode, all processes are execute on the prototype model itself, thus the processing time is dependence solely on the SBC hardware. For network mode, biometric identification process is performed on the server. This mean the processing time for biometric identification process on the server is much faster than in the *Face Reader*. The CPU processing speed and short term memory (RAM) are the key factors of determining the performance of the overall processing time for the system. The performance for network mode also depends on TCP/IP network performance such as speed, bandwidth, throughput and latency. Regardless of slower performance of SBC on the hardware performance, this functionality can still be a part of a successful embedded biometric identification system based on iris detection and the results also shows that the software is compatible for both platforms i.e. SBC and desktop.

Platform	Biometric Identification process (seconds)	Operations per second (ops)	% differences (SBC)
SBC	71.78 s	0.01 ops	0.9 %
Desktop	0.9 s	1.11 ops	

Table 9. Comparison of biometric identification process

The *Face Reader* is designed to operate in real-time mode, which requires the face identification and recognition software to identify the person face from the captured image. Image preprocessing processes are used to perform initial processing for the captured image. Face image is captured in YUV420P color format with complex background. Color space conversion technique is used for the conversion image colour format from, YUV420P to Greyscale format. Motion analysis technique is to locate the face and remove the background of the image. Histogram equalization technique improved image appearance by increase image local contrast and sharpness. The image is scaled down by using image scaling technique. Figure 4 shows the input, background and preprocessed output face image.

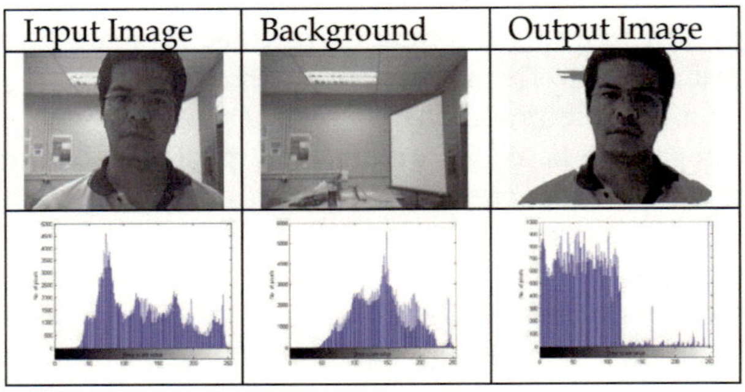

Fig. 4. Input, background and preprocessed output face image.

Figure 5 shows examples iris identification result of the face images which the biometric identification algorithm gave successful results and also biometric identification algorithm failed to detect the positions of the irises. All errors occurred in biometric identification were due to the biometric identification algorithm failures of iris detection. Figure 6, shows the matching percentages for difference image samples. The matching rate is the comparison between the same person in the database and image captured from the *Face Reader*. If the test successfully identifies the correct person, the result is success, vice versa it is fail. Table 10 shows the identification result for biometric identification software. The results show that the successful rate for the biometric identification system is 73% and percentage of matching that is reliable and should be used as a threshold for system implementation is 98%.

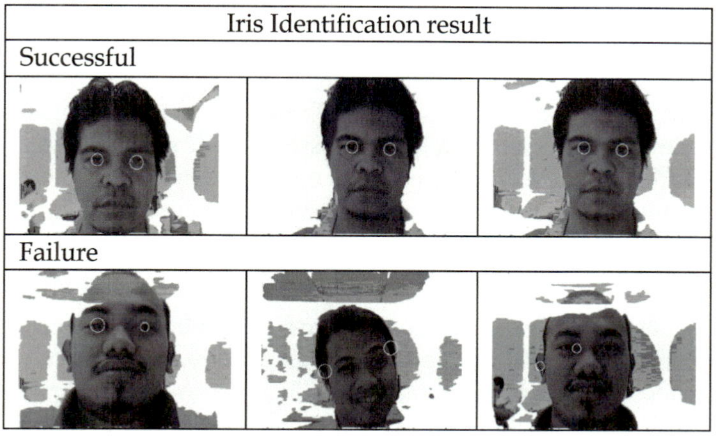

Fig. 5. Sample of the face images which the biometric identification algorithm gave successful and failure iris identification result.

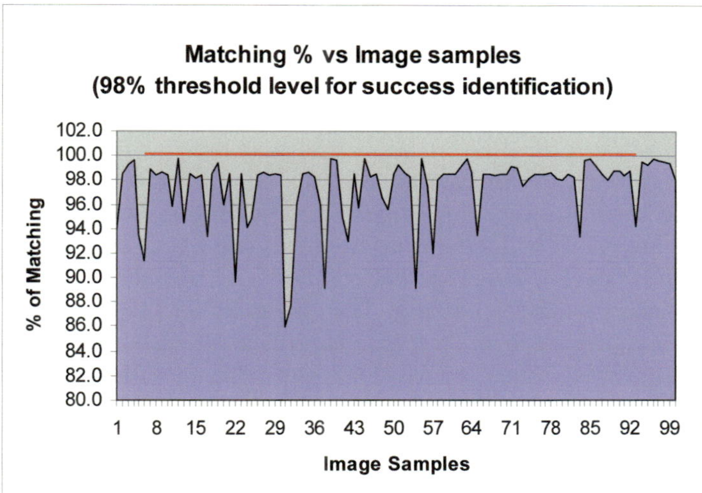

Fig. 6. Results for face recognition algorithm, graph show matching percentage vs. image samples, if percentage is 98% and above, identification is successful.

Total number of images	Number of successful images	Number of failed images	Success rate (%)
100	73	27	73

Table 10. Identification Results for Different Image Samples

12. Conclusion and Future Work

This chapter describes the design and implementation of an Embedded System for Biometric Identification from hardware and software perspectives. The first part of the chapter describes the idea of biometric identification. This includes the definition of biometric and general biometric system design. It also emphasize on the number biometric characteristics exist and are in use in various applications. A brief comparison of various biometric techniques based on seven factors and the applicability of a specific biometric technique depends on the requirements of the application domain. This part also highlights on face recognition as one of the most successful applications of image analysis and understanding with numerous practical applications. This chapter also discusses on the emerged of embedded systems and various projects with embedded hardware platforms. It also highlights several projects which focus on the integration of image acquisition and processing in single embedded device.

Hardware implementations focus on design, hardware integration and configuration in developing an embedded system for biometric identifications. It is based on single board computer (SBC) and utilizing GNU/Linux operating system (OS) which allows the use of open source resources such as libraries, kernels drivers and GNU C compiler in developing and implementing this system. This involves explaining the effort on finding compatible external devices I/O that can be integrate with the SBC, which include devices such as LCD Display, Matrix Keypad, Compact Flash Card, PCMCIA Wireless Network Card and USB Web camera. This embedded system is designed to operate in real-time mode to execute the following tasks: face (image) capture, pre-processing and matching with database using predetermine user identification number to reduce the processing tasks. Software design is structured in five modules namely as User Interface, Image Acquisition, Image Pre-processing, Network and Biometric Identification.

This chapter also present hardware and software design for BIOI^{2}D based on SBC and GNU/Linux. The hardware includes single board computer, USB webcam, LCD display panel and matrix keypad. The software components are based on GNU C programming language and Linux OS. The experimental results show that the algorithm is capable of performing the image pre-processing task. The system able to capture face image, execute image pre-processing and perform biometric identification based on iris detection. Future work includes reducing the face reader size, improving face recognition algorithm and increasing processing speed. This chapter demonstrate that embedded processing technology, in particular the x86 processor TS-5500 SBC, has been developed well enough to make it useable for implementing a computer vision system adequate for embedded biometric identification system.

13. Acknowledgement

The author acknowledges Universiti Malaysia Perlis (UniMAP) for providing the fundamental research grant (9003-00033) that enabled the production of this research project. The author would like to thank Associate Professor Dr. R. Badlishah Ahmad, Professor Dr. Ali Yeon Md Shakaff and Associate Professor Dr. Mohd Rizon Mohamed Juhari for their extraordinary support and understanding in guiding me through this project successfully.

14. References

Aaraj, N., Ravi, S., Raghunathan, A., and Jha, N. K., (2006) Architectures for efficient face authentication in embedded systems, *Proceedings of the conference on Design, automation and test in Europe: Designers' forum*, Munich, Germany, EDAA, p. 1-6,

Abreu, B., Botelho, L., Cavallaro, A., Douxchamps, D., Ebrahimi, T., Figueiredo, P., Macq, B., Mory, B., unes, L., Orri, J., Trigueiros, M.J. and Violante, A.,"Video-based multi-agent traffic surveillance system," in Intelligent Vehicles Symposium, 2000. IV 2000. Proceedings of the IEEE, 2000, pp. 457 - 462.

Al-Ali, A., Al-Rousan, M., and Al-Shaikh, M. (2003) Embedded system-based mobile patient monitoring device. In *Computer-Based Medical Systems, 2003. Proceedings. 16th IEEE Symposium*, pages 355- 360, 2.3.7

Baber, C. and Baumann, K., (2002) Embedded human computer interaction. *Applied Ergonomics*, 33(3):273- 287, 2.3.7

Badlishah, R. Ahmad, Wan Muhamad Azmi Mamat, Ahmad Nasir Che Rosli, (2006a) System Application Development : Single Board Computer (SBC) & Gnu/Linux for Robotic Application, *Proceedings of the International Conference on Underwater System Technology : Theory and Applications 2006 (USYS'06)*, USM, Penang.

Badlishah, R. Ahmad, Wan Muhamad Azmi Mamat, Ahmad Nasir Che Rosli, Suhizaz Sudin, (2006b) Embedded Linux in KUKUM: Towards High End Embedded System Product Design, *Malaysian Technical Universities Conference on Engineering and Technology 2006 (MUCET 2006)*, KUiTHHO

Bramberger, M., Doblander, A., Maier, A., Rinner, B. and Schwabach, H. (2006)"Distributed embedded smart camera for surveillance applications", Computer, vol. 39, no. 2, pp. 68-75.

Blackburn, D., Bone, M., and Phillips, P. J., (2001) Face Recognition vendor test 2000. Tech. rep. 2001. http://www.frvt.org.

Cao Z.Y., Ji, Z.Z. and Hu, M.Z. "An image sensor node for wireless sensor networks," in Proc. International Conference on Information Technology: Coding and Computing (ITCC 2005), Apr. 2005, vol. 2, pp. 740-745.

Chellappa, R., Wilson, C.L. and Sirohey, C., (1995) "Humain and machine recognition of faces: A survey," *Proc. IEEE*, vol. 83, no. 5, pp. 705-740.

Comerford, R., (1998) Pocket computers ignite OS battle. *IEEE Spectrum*, May. 2.2

Dan, H., (2003) An autonomous mobile robot development platform for teaching a graduate level mechatronics course. *33rd ASEE/IEEE Frontiers in Education Conference.*

Deb, S., Ghoshal, S., Malepati, V. and Kleinman, D., (2000) Tele-diagnosis: remote monitoring of large-scale systems. In *Aerospace Conference Proceedings, 2000 IEEE*, volume 6, pages 31-42, 2.3.7

Downes, I., Baghaei R.L. and Aghajan H., "Development of a mote for wireless image sensor networks," in Proc. COGnitive Systems with Interactive Sensors (COGIS 2006), Mar. 2006.

Dufey, J, Jost, B., Neufeld, N. and Zuin, M. (2000) Event building in an intelligent network interface card for the lhcb readout network. In *Nuclear Science Symposium Conference Record, 2000 IEEE*, volume 3, pages 26/50 -26/53, 2.3.7

Fleck S. and Straßer, W., "Adaptive Probabilistic Tracking Embedded in a Smart Camera," in IEEE Embedded Computer Vision Workshop (ECVW) in conjunction with IEEE CVPR 2005, 2005, pp. 134 - 134.

Fleck S., Busch, F., Biber, P. and Straßer, W. "3D Surveillance - A Distributed Network of Smart Cameras for Real-Time Tracking and its Visualization in 3D," in Computer Vision and Pattern Recognition Workshop, 2006 Conference on, Jun. 2006, pp. 118 - 118.

Fleck S., Busch, F., Biber, P. and Straßer, W. "Adaptive Probalistic Tracking Embedded in Smart Cameras for Distributed Surveillance in a 3D model", EURASIP Journal on Embedded Systems, 2007.

Fryer, R., (1998) Low and non-intrusive software instrumentation: a survey of requirements and methods. *In Digital Avionics Systems Conference, 1998. Proceedings., 17th DASC. The AIAA/IEEE/SAE*, volume 1, pages C22/1 -C22/8, 2.3.7

Garcia, R.L., Carlos Alberola-L'opez, Otman Aghzout and Juan Ruiz-Alzola, (2003) Biometric identification systems, Signal Processing, Vol. 83, Issue 12, pp. 2539 - 2557.

Galton, F., (1888) "Personal identification and description," *In Nature*, pp. 173-177, June 21.

Gori, L., Tommasini, R., Cautero, G., Giuressi, D., Barnaba, M., Accardo, A., Carrato, S. and Paolucci, G. (1999) An embedded control and acquisition system for multichannel detectors. *Nuclear Instruments and Methods in Physics Research Section A: Accelerators, Spectrometers, Detectors and Associated Equipment*, 431(1-2):338–346, 2.3.7

Hengstler, S. and Aghajan, H.,"A smart camera mote architecture for distributed intelligent surveillance" in International Workshop on Distributed Smart Cameras (DSC-06) in conjunction with The 4th ACM Conference on Embedded Networked Sensor Systems (SenSys 2006), 2006.

Jain, A.K. Bolle, R. and Pankanti, S. (eds.), (1998) *Biometrics, Personal Identification in Networked Society*, Kluwer Academic Publishers, Norwell, MA.

Jain, A.K., Hong, L. and Pankanti, S. (eds.), (2000) *Biometric Identification*, Communications of the ACM, February, ACM Press, New York USA, Vol. 43, Issue 2, pp 90-98.

Jain, A.K, Arun Ross and Salil Prabhakar, (2004) An Introduction to Biometric Identification, in IEEE Transaction on Circuits and Systems for Video Technology, Special Issue on Image and Video-Based Biometrics, Vol. 14, No. 1.

Kleihorst, P., Schueler, B., Danilin, A. and Heijligers, M., "Smart camera mote with high performance vision system" in International Workshop on Distributed Smart Cameras (DSC-06) in conjunction with The 4th ACM Conference on Embedded Networked Sensor Systems (SenSys 2006), 2006.

Kroll, M., Schütze, B., Geisbe, T., Lipinski, H.G., Grönemeyer, D.H.W. and Filler, T.J. (2003) Embedded systems for signing medical images using the dicom standard,. In *International Congress Series*, volume 1256, pages 849–854, 2.3.7

Lamberti, F and Demartini, C. (2003) Low-cost home monitoring using a java-based embedded computer. In *Information Technology Applications in Biomedicine, 2003. 4th International IEEE EMBS Special Topic Conference*, pages 342–345, 2.3.7.

LinuxDevices.com., (n.d.) A Linux-oriented Intro to Embeddable Single Board Computers. Citing Internet Sources. Retrieved on 2007-08-21 from URL http://www.linuxdevices.com/articles/AT6449817972.html.

Messer, K., Matas, J., Kittler, J., Luettin, J., and Maitre, G., (1999) XM2VTSDB: The Extended M2VTS Database. In *Proceedings, International Conference on Audio and Video-Based Person Authentication*. pp. 72-77.

Oliveira, F.D.R., Chalimbaund, P., Berry, F., Serot, J. and Marmoiton, F. "Embedded early vision systems: implementation proposal and hardware architecture," in Proc. COGnitive Systems with Interactive Sensors (COGIS 2006), Mar. 2006.

Perera, A., Papamichail, N. , Bârsan, N., Weimar, U., Marco, S., (2003) On-line Event Detection by Recursive Dynamic Principal Component Analysis and Gas Sensor Arrays under drift conditions, *In Proceedings of the 2nd IEEE international conference on sensors*, Toronto, Canada.

Phillips, P. J., Wechsler, H., Rizvi, S., and Rauss, P., (1998) The FERET database and evaluation procedure for face-recognition algorithms. Image Vis. Comput. 16, pp. 295-306.

Phillips, P. J., Moon, H., Rizvi, S., and Rauss, P., (2000) The FERET evaluation methodology for face recognition algorithms, IEEE Trans. Patt. Anal. Mach. Intell. 22.

Phillips, P. J., Grother, P. J. , Micheals, R. J., Blackburn, D. M., Tabassi, E., and Bone, J. M., (2003) Face Recognition vendor test 2002: Evaluation report. NISTIR 6965, http://www.frvt.org.

Quaritsch, M., Kreuzthaler, M., Rinner, B., Strobl, B.,"Decentralized Object Tracking in a Network of Embedded Smart Cameras" in International Workshop on Distributed Smart Cameras (DSC-06) in conjunction with The 4th ACM Conference on Embedded Networked Sensor Systems (SenSys 2006), 2006, pp. 99 - 104

Rahimi M, Baer, R., Iroezi, O.I., Garcia, J.C., Warrior, J., Estrin, D. and Srivastava, M. "Cyclops: In situ image sensing and interpretation in wireless sensor networks," in Proc. 3rn International Conference on Embedded Networked Sensor Systems (SenSys '2005), Nov 2005, pp. 192-204.

Ramamritham, K. and Arya, K. (2003) System support for embedded applications. In *Proceedings. 16th International Conference on VLSI Design, 2003*, pages 22–26, 2.3.7

Ratha, N.K., Senior, A., Bolle, R.M., (2001) Tutorial on automated biometrics, in *Proceedings of International Conference on Advances in Pattern Recognition*, Rio de Janeiro, Brazil.

Remagnino, P., Orwell, J., Greenhill, D., Jones, G.A. and Marchesotti, L., Multimedia Video Based Surveillance Systems: Requirements, Issues and Solutions. Kluwer Academic Publishers, 2001, ch. An Agent Society for Scene Interpretation, pp. 108 - 117.

Richard A. Sevenich, (2004), *An Introduction to Embedded Linux Development: Part 1*, Citing Internet Source, Retrieved March 20, 2006, URL: http://www.linuxdevices.com/.

Rizvi, S. A., Phillips, P. J., and Moon, H., (1998) A verification protocol and statistical performance analysis for face recognition algorithms. In *Proceedings, IEEE Conference on Computer Vision and Pattern Recognition*. Pp. 833-838.

Robert A. Burckle, (n.d.) The evolution of Single Board Computers. Citing Internet Sources. Retrieved on 2007-08-21 from URL http://www.winsystems.com

Rowe, A., Rosenberg, C. and Nourbakhsh, I. "A second generation low cost embedded color vision system," in IEEE Embedded Computer Vision Workshop (ECVW) in conjunction with IEEE CVPR 2005, vol. 3, 2005, pp. 136 - 136.

Stepner, D., Nagarajan Rajan, David Hui , (1999) Embedded Application Design Using a Real-Time OS, *Proceedings of the 36th ACM/IEEE conference on Design automation DAC '99*.

Tan, T., Raghunathan, A. and Jha, N. (2003) A simulation framework for energy-consumption analysis of os-driven embedded applications. *Computer-Aided Design of Integrated Circuits and Systems, IEEE Transactions on*, pages 1284- 1294, 2.3.7

Tolba, A. S., El-Baz, A. H. and El-Harby, A. A, (2005) Face Recognition: A Literature Review, International Journal of Signal Processing, Vol. 2, No. 2, pp 88-103.

Velipasalar, S., Schlessman, J., Chen, C.-Y., Wolf, W. and Singh J. P., "SCCS: A Scalable Clustered Camera System for Multiple Object Tracking Communicating via Message Passing Interface," in Multimedia and Expo, 2006. ICME 2006. IEEE International Conference on, 2006.

Wiencke, L., (2006) TS5500 Single Board Computer, Citing Internet sources URL http://www.physics.utah.edu/~wiencke/pc104html/5500.html

Williams, A., Xie, D., Ou, S., Grupen, R., Hanson, A. and Riseman, E. "Distributed smart cameras for aging in place" in International Workshop on Distributed Smart Cameras (DSC-06) in conjunction with The 4th ACM Conference on Embedded Networked Sensor Systems (SenSys 2006), 2006.

Wolf, W., Ozer, B. and Lv, T. "Smart cameras as embedded systems," Computer, vol.35. no 9, pp. 48-53, 2002.

Wood, S., (2006) Using many PC/104 serial ports. Citing Internet sources URL http://www.jlab.org/~Esaw/pc104/

Zaho, W., (1999) "*Robust image based 3D face recognition,*" Ph.D. Thesis, Maryland University.

Zhao, W., Rama Chellappa, P.J. Jonathon Phillips, and Azriel Rosenfeld, (2003) Face Recognition: A Literature Survey, ACM Computing Survey, December Issue, pp. 399-458.

Multi-Task Active-Vision in Robotics[1]

J. Cabrera, D. Hernandez, A. Dominguez and E. Fernandez
SIANI, ULPGC
Spain

1. Introduction

Vision constitutes the most important sense in the vast majority of animals. Researchers in robotic systems, where biological inspiration has been always a reference, frequently try to make use of vision as a primary sensor. The technological advances have notably favoured this, permitting the incorporation of cameras to a wide variety of robots, including even low cost models. Initially configured as passive devices, soon the same biological emulation led to the introduction of active stereo heads with several mechanical and optical degrees of freedom. However, the use of active vision is far from trivial and has and still is proposing challenging problems.

On the other hand, robots in general, and more specifically mobile robots, are extremely complex systems on their own. The "scientific pull" aiming at obtaining higher and higher levels of autonomy has contributed to create a great number of research lines, many of them remaining still open: obstacle avoidance, localization, navigation, SLAM.

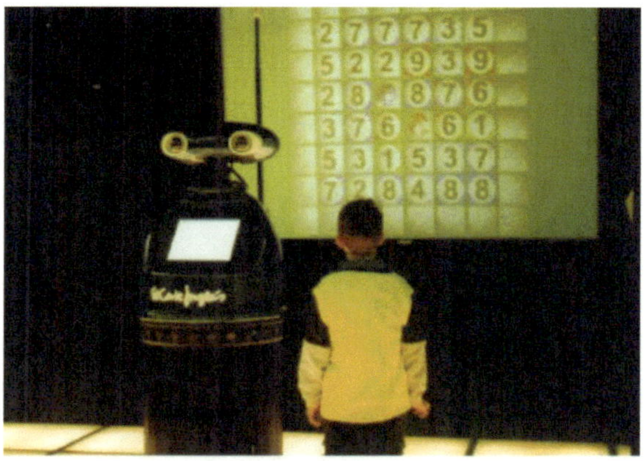

Fig. 1. Museum robot with active binocular head

[1] This work has been partially supported by project PI2007/039 from Canary Islands Government and FEDER funds, and by project TIN2008-060608 from Spanish MICINN.

¿What issues arise when we consider a system that integrates both elements, that is, when a mobile robot is equipped with an active head (see Fig. 1)? Obviously, the answer is too broad and depends on the perspective under which that system is analysed.

Here we will centre the discussion on attention mechanisms in multitasking environments, complemented with some software engineering considerations. Attention is relevant in the proposed scenario as it constitutes a common strategy used to optimize limited computational resources when high sensor data volumes are available. On the other hand, multitasking (see Fig. 2) is also present as it is frequently used in robotics to reduce the inherent complexity of the programming of these systems. Finally, this programming complexity makes highly desirable the use of good software engineering practices to promote reusability and facilitate upgrading and maintenance.

This chapter is organized in two main sections. The first one analyzes the general problems that can be defined for active vision robotics and reviews some works that have been developed in the area. The second one illustrates the most relevant problems stated in this context through the analysis of the solutions adopted in a case study, the MTVS system. The aspects considered include the control of the attention, task coordination and software engineering. Some experimental results obtained with MTVS in a real robot application will also be showed. The chapter ends with the analysis of the main conclusions obtained and the references.

2. Multi-Task Active-Vision

As commented previously, when configured as an active device (Clark & Ferrier, 1992; Bradshaw et al., 1994) cameras constitute a versatile and powerful source of information. However, in a dynamic context with real-time constraints, active vision has important limitations that must be taken into account: mechanical latencies and processing times.

An active binocular head is normally equipped with 6 motors for mechanical degrees of freedom (neck pan/tilt, and pan/tilt for each eye) and 6 more for optical degrees of freedom (zoom, iris and focus for each eye). Taken an image from a lateral position, for example, may result in a relatively high waiting time until the motors reach and stabilize at the final commanded angle, and the frame is captured. After that, the usually high processing time characteristic of visual sensors must be added. As a consequence, in order to preserve system performance, head movements should be economized and the processing should be applied to reduced regions of interest inside the image.

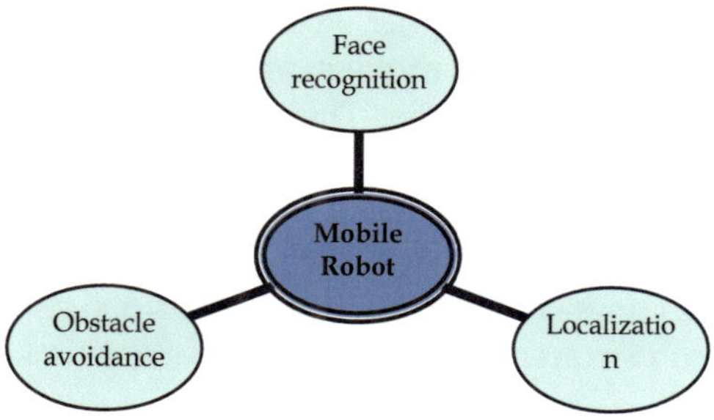

Fig. 2. Mobile robot multitask diagram

Autonomous robots have evolved in the last decade to systems able to develop more and more complex missions. As an example, humanoid robots demos are constantly improving, adding each time higher competence levels to their shows (always below expectations, inevitably).

As anticipated in the introduction, multitasking has been present in robotic systems from the beginning as a "divide and conquer" strategy, in terms of behaviours, actions, goals, etc (Arkin, 1998). In the proposed scenario, this fact automatically transforms an active vision head into a multipurpose shared sensor. Regarding again system performance, the question of which task gets the control of the head arises naturally and must be paid special attention by system developers.

2.1 Problem definitions

Several problems can be defined in this context. On one hand, the control of the gaze in an active vision system is usually formulated as a problem of detection of significant points in the image. The objective is to locate regions of interest on the image where processing can be focused. Under this perspective several aspects such as saliency, bottom-up vs. top-down control, computational modelling, etc, must be analyzed. No motors or, at most, only fast eye motors participate in this process, so the effects of mechanical delays are not so critical and can be neglected, if not ignored.

On the other hand, considering the shared resource nature of the sensor, the problem of management/coordination of the gaze in a multi-task environment should also be taken into account. The visual attention must be distributed among the tasks executing concurrently inside the robotic system. In this case, several motors, including the slower neck pan/tilt, can be operated, so the blind intervals induced by mechanical latencies play an important role and must be carefully handled.

Additionally, and from a more engineering point of view, is the fact that researchers and engineers involved in the development of vision systems are primarily concerned with the visual capabilities of the system in terms of performance, reliability, knowledge integration, etc. However, as important as that, is the problem of modular composition of vision capabilities in perception-action systems. Posing a simple analogy to clarify these issues, when we execute programs that read from or write to files that are kept in the hard disk, we aren't normally aware of any contention problem and need not to care if any other process is accessing the same disk at the same time. This is managed by the underlying services, simplifying the writing of programs that can be more easily codified as if they have exclusive access to the device.

According to the previous comments, the main objectives that must be pursued by a vision system, especially in the robotic area, can be summarized as follows:

- The system should offer a reduced set of services or visual primitives in pre-categorical terms to the clients.
- The control of the gaze must be assigned on the basis of a simple model of scheduler, allowing the results to be easily interpreted externally.
- The client's tasks should be integrated in the system individually with no coordination involved.
- It must be possible to change dynamically the set of tasks (activity) that the system manages.
- Some level of response time guarantee should be desirable or, at least, the system should offer high priority attention modes.
- Avoid monolithic developments with arbitration code embedded.
- Facilitate the integration of new vision capabilities and promote reusability.

2.2 Related work

As a selection of related work, several studies, systems and applications can be commented. Here we will centre on integrated systems, although many of them rely on basic attention mechanisms (Kundur & Raviv 2000; Itti, 2005).

In a first group, the problem of active vision applied to autonomous or assisted car driving has been analyzed by several authors. At a primary level, there is a long tradition of works that focus on human reactions while performing driving activities (Shinar, 1978; Land & Horwood, 1995; Underwood et al., 2003; Rogers et al., 2005).

Ernst Dickmanns and colleagues (Pellkoer et al., 2001; Dickmanns, 2003) have studied the problem of gaze control in the context of their MarVEye Project, where an active multi-camera head (see Fig. 3) is used to drive a car in a highway. In that project, several areas of interest are promoted and ranked by different modules of the control architecture using a measure of information gain.

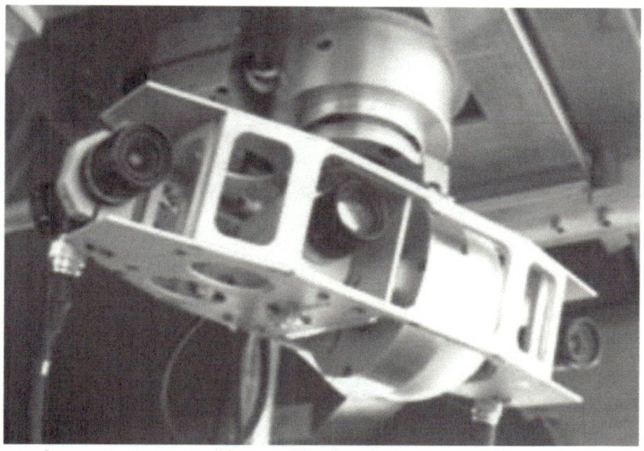

Fig. 3. MarVEye trinocular prototype (from Dickmanns et al.)

Other groups have explored the problem of gaze arbitration in the humanoid robots scenario, both in simulation and with real robots. Javier Seara and colleagues (Seara et al. 2001; Seara et al. 2003) have experimented with a biped robot that used a combination of two tasks to visually avoid obstacles and localize itself (see Fig. 4). The decision of where to look next was solved in two stages. Firstly, each task selects its next preferred focus of attention as that providing the largest reduction of incertitude in the robot localization, or in the location of obstacles. In a second stage, a multiagent decision schema, along with a winner-selection society model, was used to finally decide which task was granted the control of gaze.

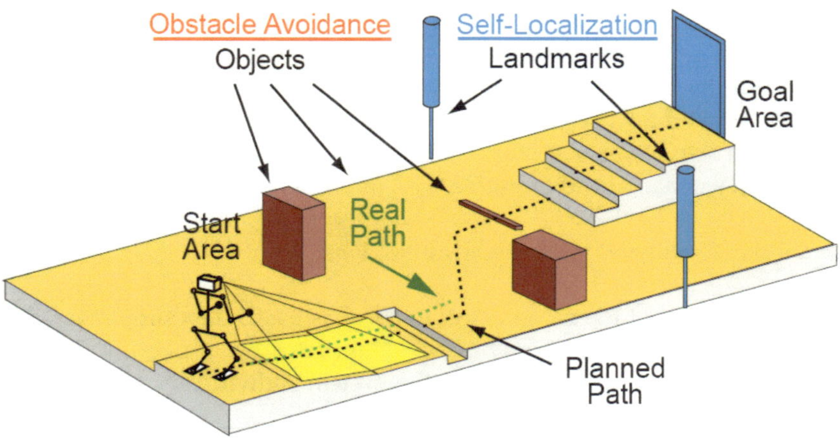

Fig. 4. Biped robot in scenario (from Seara et al.)

Nathan Sprague and colleagues (Sprague et al., 2005; Sprague et al. 2007) have designed a simulation environment where a biped robot must walk a lane while it picks up litter and avoids obstacles (see Fig. 5), using vision as the only sensor. These capabilities are implemented as visual behaviours using a reinforcement learning method for discovering the optimal gaze control policy for each task.

Fig. 5. Walter simulation (from Sprague et al.)

3. MTVS – A case study

Motivated by the previously stated description of the problem we have designed and implemented MTVS (Multi-Tasking Vision System), a proposal of architecture for active-vision systems in multi-tasking environments. MTVS has been designed to deal with the scheduling of concurrent visual tasks in such a way that resource arbitration is hidden to the user.

Similar in spirit to the systems described in the previous section, the aim of MTVS is two-fold: contribute to build a vision system more consistent from an engineering point of view, and to take a first step towards systems where the vision becomes integrated in an action context with higher semantic and cognitive level (an "intelligent" way of looking).

More in detail, MTVS pursues the following objectives:

- The assignment of the gaze control to a task is based on a simple scheduler model, so that the behaviour can be easily interpreted by an external observer.
- The client tasks are integrated in the system individually with no coordination requirements.
- The set of tasks managed (the activity) can change dynamically.
- The clients should not assume any a priori response time guarantee, though the system can offer high-priority attention modes.
- The system offers services based on a reduced set of visual primitives, in pre-categorical terms.

3.1 System architecture

The figure 6 shows an example with two clients and the basic elements making up the vision system architecture: a system server, a task scheduler and the data acquisition subsystem. Basically, the clients connect to the system server to ask for visual services with a given configuration (client A active). In response, the system server launches both a task-thread, to deal with internal scheduling issues, and a devoted server-thread that will be in charge of the interaction with the external client. The scheduler analyzes the tasks demands under a given scheduling policy and selects one to receive the gaze control. In combination, a second covert scheduler checks for compatibility between tasks to share images among them (FOA's overlapping). The data acquisition subsystem processes the different sensor data streams (images, head pose and robot pose) to generate as accurately as possible time stamps and pose labels for the served images.

3.2 Visual services

Clients can connect to the vision system and use it through a number of pre-categorical low-level services. The MTVS services are built around basic visual capabilities or primitives that have also been explored by other authors (Christensen & Granum, 1995):

- WATCH: Capture N images of a 3D point with a given camera configuration.
- SCAN: Take N images while the head is moving along a trajectory.
- SEARCH: Detect a model pre-categorically in a given image area.
- TRACK: Track a model pre-categorically.
- NOTIFY: Inform the client about movement, colour or other changes.

Except for WATCH, the rest of primitives can be executed discontinuously, allowing for the implementation of interruptible visual tasks.

The clients also regulate their activity in the system by means of the messages they interchange with their devoted server. Currently, the following messages have been defined for a task: creation, suspension, reconfiguration (modify parameters, change priority, commute primitive on success) and annihilation.

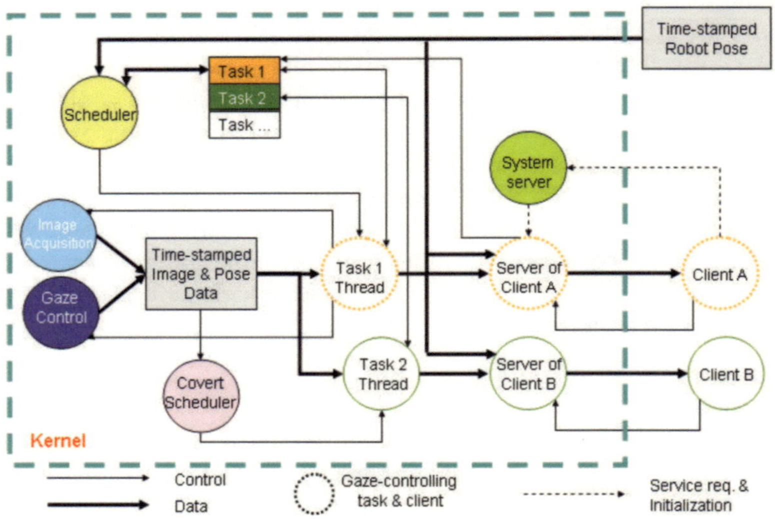

Fig. 6. Control Architecture: example with two clients

3.3 Scheduling policies

Several scheduling policies have been implemented and studied inside MTVS. This analysis has considered two main groups of schedulers: time-based and urgency based schedulers.

Time-based schedulers

Three types of time-based schedulers have been studied: Round-Robin (RR), Earliest Deadline First (EDF) and EDF with priorities (EDFP). The prioritized RR algorithm revealed rapidly as useless in a dynamic and contextual action schema. First, it makes no sense to assign similar time slices to different tasks, and second, the time assigned used for saccadic movements, especially when a slow neck is involved, becomes wasted.

The EDF algorithm yielded a slightly better performance than RR, but was difficult to generalize as visual tasks are not suitable for being modelled as periodic tasks.

The best results of this group were obtained by the EDFP algorithm combining critical tasks (strict deadline) with non-critical tasks. Each time a task is considered for execution and not selected its priority is incremented by a certain quantity (Kushleyeva et al., 2005).

Urgency-based schedulers

The concept of urgency is well correlated with a criterion of loss minimization, as a consequence of the task not receiving the control of the gaze within a time window. This measure can also be put into relation with uncertainty in many visual tasks.

Two schedulers have been studied in this group: lottery (Sprague & Ballard, 2003) and max-urgency. The lottery scheduler is based in a randomized scheme where the probability of a task being selected to obtain the gaze control is directly proportional to its urgency. Every task has the possibility of gaining the control of the gaze, but the random unpredictability can sometimes produce undesirable effects.

The max-urgency scheduler substitutes the weighted voting by a direct selection of the task with higher urgency value. This scheme has produced acceptable results provided that the urgency of a task is reduced significantly after gaining the control of the gaze (similar to an inhibition of return mechanism).

3.4 Experiments

A set of experiments were carried out to analyze the behaviour of MTVS on a real robotic application. The basic experimental setup consists of two ActivMedia Pioneer robots, one with the basic configuration and the other mounting an active monocular vision system (see Fig. 7). The active head is formed by a Directed Perception PTU (as a neck with two degrees of freedom) and a motorized Sony EVI-G21 camera (eye with two mechanical and two optical degrees of freedom).

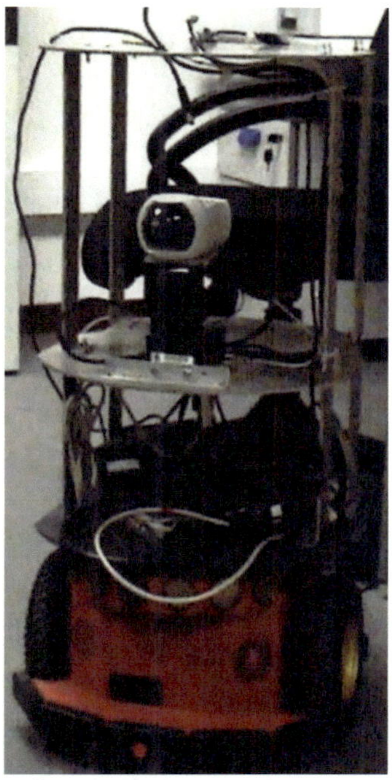

Fig. 7. Robot and active-vision system

Two main tasks were combined along the different experiments: target following and obstacle avoidance. The target following task commands the active vision robot (pursuer) to detect and follow a special square target mounted on other robot (leader), trying to keep a predefined constant distance between them. The obstacle avoidance task looks for coloured cylinders on the floor, estimating, as exactly as possible their 2D position. Kalman filtering is used to model both target and obstacles positions.

One-task experiments

As a reference for the maximum expected performance for each task some experiments where designed involving only one task.

Experiment 1: Follow Robot only

In this experiment, the leader robot is commanded to move forward at a constant speed of 200 mm/sec, while the pursuer must try to keep a constant separation of 2 meters. Several tests have been conducted along the main corridor of our lab following a 15 meters straight line path. The pursuer was able to stabilize the reference distance with a maximum error around 150 mm as shown in figure 8.

This experiment determines the base performance level for the follow task.

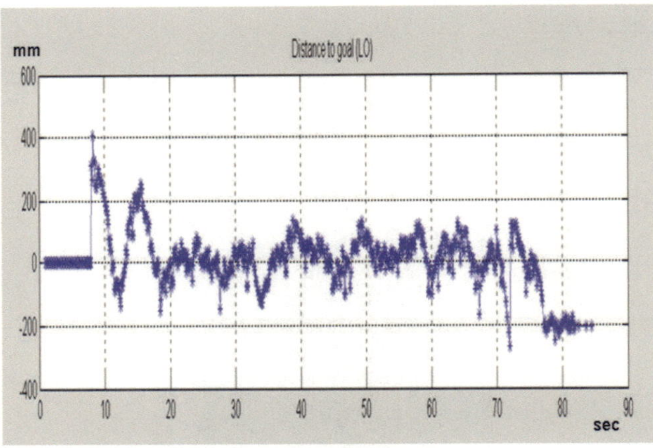

Fig. 8. Robot and active-vision system

Experiment 2: Obstacle avoidance only

The active vision robot is commanded to explore the environment looking for objects (yellow cylinders), trying to reduce their position uncertainty below a predefined threshold. The robot moves straight-line inside a corridor formed by 8 cylinders equally distributed in a zigzag pattern along the path.

The figure 9 illustrates the robot path and the different detections for each localized object, including their first (larger) and minimum uncertainty ellipses. The results show how the robot was able to localize all the objects with minimum uncertainty ellipses ranging from 100 to 200 mm in diameter.

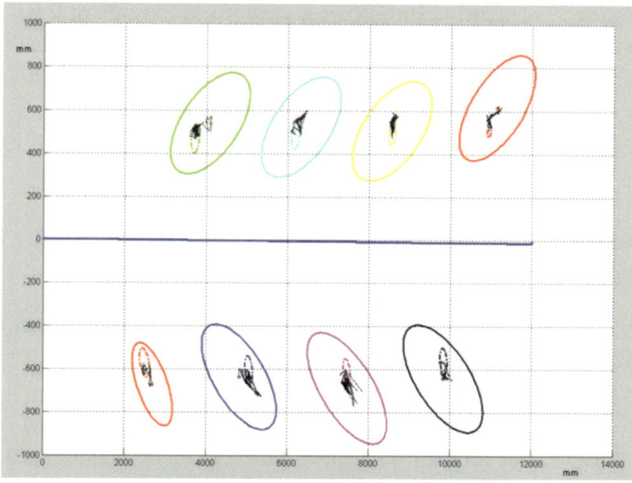

Fig. 9. Obstacle avoidance-Only experiment

This experiment determines the base performance level for the obstacle avoidance task.

Multiple-task experiments

The multiple-task experiments consider a scenario in which each task computes its desired camera configuration and urgency and asks the MTVS scheduler to obtain the gaze control. The scheduler uses this information to select where to look next and how to distribute images. The obstacle avoidance task is extended to classify special configurations of objects as "doors" (two objects aligned perpendicularly to robot initial orientation with a predefined separation).

The urgency of the following task is computed as a function of the distance error, the robot velocity and the time. This urgency increases as the distance between the robots differs from the reference, the velocity is high and the elapsed time since the last image was received becomes larger.

The urgency of the obstacle avoidance task is computed separately for three possible focus of attention: front (the urgency increases when the robot moves towards visually unexplored areas), worst estimated object (the urgency increases as the position of a previously detected object is not confirmed with new images), and closest door (the urgency increases with narrow doors).

The first simple multiple-task experiments try to illustrate the sharing images capability of MTVS. In experiment 5 a more complex scenario including doors is analyzed.

Experiment 3: Obstacle avoidance and robot following competing for the gaze (following priority)

In this experiment, the control of the gaze is only granted to the avoidance task when both the leader speed and the distance error are low. Typically, the following task performance is not affected significantly, but the avoidance task degrades yielding few objects localization with poor precision. As an example, the upper plot of the figure 10 presents the results of a non sharing run where only half the potential objects (all right sided due to the position of the closest obstacle) have been detected with large uncertainty ellipses. As the lower plot of the figure shows, the sharing of images permits a much better behaviour of the obstacle avoidance task.

Experiment 4: Obstacle avoidance and robot following competing for the gaze (obstacle avoidance priority)

In this experiment, the localization task has the priority, and the control of the gaze is only released in the best possible scenario, that is, all the objects have been precisely detected or left behind the robot position.

In the no-sharing context, the target robot goes away with no reaction from the pursuer, as the camera sensor is captured exclusively by the localization task. In the image-sharing mode, some initial frames can also be used by the following task, and the pursuer moves to reduce the gap. As the robot approaches to the first objects' position, the pan angle becomes larger and the images are not valid for the following task. Finally, the target robot also escapes from the pursuer.

Experiment 5: Localize doors and robot following competing for the gaze (narrow and wide doors)

The configuration of objects used for this experiment consists of a set of four "doors": two narrow type (600 mm width) and two wide type (1500 mm width).

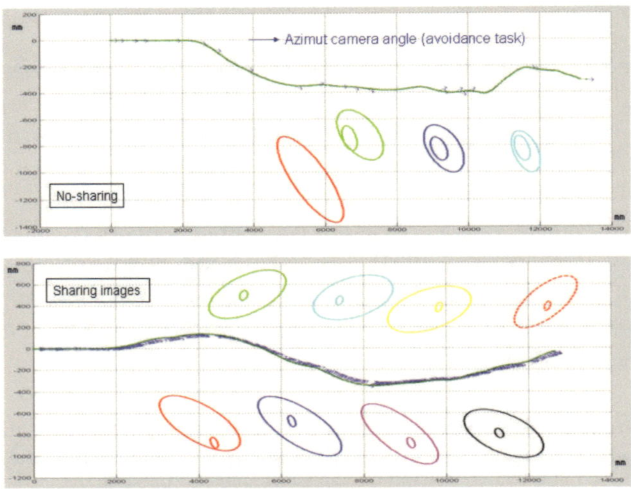

Fig. 10. Follow (priority) and avoidance experiment

All doors are located straight line in front of the robot, the first one (wide) three meters ahead and the rest every 1.5 meters, alternating narrow and wide types. The leader robot is commanded to move at constant speed crossing the doors centred.

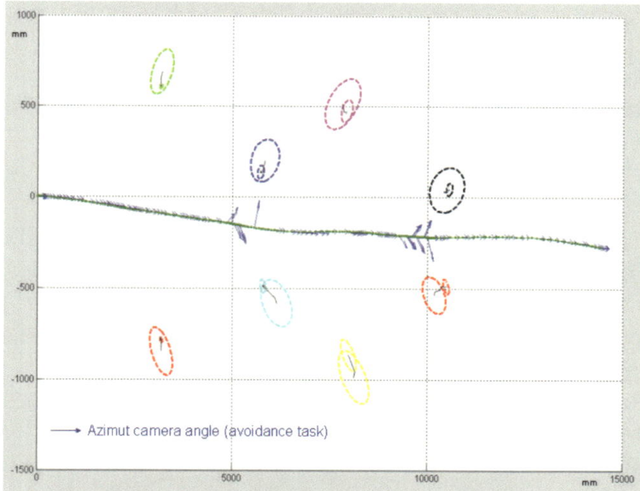

Fig. 11. Narrow and wide doors experiment

The figure 11 illustrates how the camera is pointed to both sides when crossing narrow doors. As a consequence of this behaviour, the pursuer robot slows down when approaching a narrow door until the doorframe position has been estimated with the required precision (compare final error ellipses for narrow and wide doors). After traversing the door, the robot accelerates to recover the desired following distance from the leader.

4. Conclusions

In this chapter we describe the main problems associated with the integration of active vision and multitasking. This configuration, though attractive, must be properly handled by means of simplification strategies that cope with its inherent complexity. Besides, the programming of this kind of complex system is prone to conclude often in monolithic ad-hoc solutions. These problems are illustrated through the analysis of MTVS, a prototype system that proposes an open architecture for the integration of concurrent visual tasks.

In MTVS the client's requests are articulated on the basis of a reduced set of services or visual primitives. All the low level control/coordination aspects are hidden to the clients simplifying the programming and allowing for an open and dynamic composition of visual activity from much simpler visual capabilities.

Regarding the gaze control assignation problem, several schedulers have been implemented. The best results are obtained by a contextual scheme governed by urgencies, taking the interaction of the agent with its environment as organization principle instead of temporal frequencies. Usually, a correspondence between urgency and uncertainty about a relevant task element can be established.

The internal structure of MTVS, its organization in terms of visual primitives and its separated scheduling mechanisms contribute to obtain modular software applications that facilitate maintenance and promote software reuse.

5. References

Arkin, R. (1998). *Behavior-Based Robotics*, MIT Press

Bradshaw, K.; McLauchlan, P.; Reid, I. & Murray, D. (1994). Saccade and Pursuit on an Active Head/Eye Platform in *Image and Vision Computing*

Christensen, H. & Granum, E. (1995). Control of perception in *Vision as process*, Springer-Verlag

Clark, J. & Ferrier, N. (1992). Attentive visual servoing in *Active Vision* MIT Press

Dickmanns, E. (2003). An Advanced Vision System for Ground Vehicles, *Proceedings of 1st Workshop on In-Vehicle Cognitive Computer Vision Systems (IVC2VS)*, Graz, Austria

Itti, L. (2005). Models of bottom-up attention and saliency in *Neurobiology of Attention*, Elsevier Academic Press

Kundur, S. & Raviv D. (2000). Active vision-based control schemes for autonomous navigation task in *Pattern Recognition*, Elsevier Academic Press

Kushleyeva, Y.; Salvucci, D.D. & Lee, F.J. (2005). Deciding when to switch tasks in time-critical multitasking in *Cognitive Systems Research*

Land, M. & Horwood, J. (1995). Which parts of the road guide steering? in *Nature*

Pellkoer, M.; Ltzeler, M. & Dickmanns, E. (2001). Interaction of perception and gaze control in autonomous vehicles, *Proceedings of SPIE: Intelligent Robots and Computer Vision XX: Algorithms, Techniques and Active Vision*, Newton, USA

Rogers, S.; Kadar, E. & Costall, A. (2005). Drivers' Gaze Patterns in Braking From Three Different Approaches to a Crash Barrier in *Ecological Psychology*, Lawrence Erlbaum Associates

Seara, J.; Lorch, O. & Schmidt, G. (2001). Gaze Control for Goal-Oriented Humanoid Walking, *Proceedings of the IEEE/RAS International Conference on Humanoid Robots (Humanoids)*, pp. 187-195, Tokio, Japan

Seara, J.; Strobl, & Schmidt, G. (2002). Information Management for Gaze Control in Vision Guided Biped Walking, *Proceedings of the IEEE/RAS International Conference on Humanoid Robots (Humanoids)*, pp. 187-195, Tokio, Japan

Seara, J., Strobl, K.H., Martin, E. & Schmidt, G. (2003). Task-oriented and Situation-dependent Gaze Control for Vision Guided Autonomous Walking, *Proceedings of the IEEE/RAS International Conference on Humanoid Robots (Humanoids)*, Munich and Karlsruhe, Germany

Shinar, D. (1978). *Psychology on the road*, New York: Wiley

Sprague, N. & Ballard, D. (2003). Eye movements for reward maximization in *Advances in Neural Information Processing Systems*, Vol. 16, MIT-Press

Sprague, N.; Ballard, D. & Robinson, A. (2005). Modeling attention with embodied visual Behaviours in *ACM Transactions on Applied Perception*

Sprague, N.; Ballard, D. & Robinson, A. (2007). Modeling Embodied Visual Behaviors in *ACM Transactions on Applied Perception*

Underwood, G.; Chapman, P.; Brocklehurst,N.; Underwood, J. & Crundall,D. (2003). Visual attention while driving: Sequences of eye fixations made by experienced and novice drivers in *Ergonomics*

An Approach to Perception Enhancement in Robotized Surgery using Computer Vision

Agustín A. Navarro[1], Albert Hernansanz[1], Joan Aranda[2] and Alícia Casals[2]
[1]*Centre of Bioengineering of Catalonia, Automatic Control Department, Technical University of Catalonia*
Barcelona, Spain
[2]*Institute for Bioengineering of Catalonia - Technical University of Catalonia*
Barcelona, Spain

1. Introduction

The knowledge of 3D scene information obtained from a video camera allows performing a diversity of action-perception tasks in which 2D data are the only inputs. Exterior orientation techniques are aimed to calculate the position and orientation of the camera with respect to other objects in the scene and perceptually contribute to control action in this kind of applications. In Minimally Invasive Surgery (MIS), the use of a 2D view on a 3D world is the most common procedure. The surgeon is limited to work without direct physical contact and must rely heavily on indirect perception (Healey, 2008). To effectively link action to perception it is necessary to assure the coherence between the surgeon body movements with the perceived information. Therefore, locating the instruments with respect to the surgeon body movements through computer vision techniques serves to enhance the cognitive mediation between action and perception and can be considered as an important assistance in MIS.

The 2D-3D pose estimation technique serves to map this relation by estimating the transformation between reference frames of surgical instruments and the endoscopic camera. There are several methods proposed to estimate the pose of a rigid object. The first step of those algorithms consists in the identification and location of some kind of features that represent an object in the image plane (Olensis, 2000); (Huang & Netravali, 1994). Most of them rely on singular points and apply closed-form or numerical solutions depending on the number of objects and image feature correspondences (Wrobel, 2001); (Harris, 1992). In this approach lines are the features selected as the most appropriate. As higher-order geometric primitives, lines can describe objects where part of its geometry is previously known. These kinds of features have been incorporated to take advantage of its inherent stability and robustness to solve pose estimation problems (Dornaika & Garcia, 1999); (Christy & Horaud, 1997). A diversity of methods has been proposed using line correspondences, parting from representing them as Plücker lines (Selig, 2000), to their combination with points (Horaud et al., 1995), or sets of lines (Park, 2005).

In the case of image sequences, motion and structure parameters of a scene can be determined. Motion parameters are calculated by establishing correspondences between selected features in successive images. The specific field of computer vision which studies features tracking and their correspondence is called dynamic vision (Dickmanns, 2004). The use of line correspondences, increases robustness. Nevertheless, the benefit from the gained stability introduces some disadvantages: more computationally intensive tracking algorithms, low sampling frequency and mathematic complexity (Rehbinder & Ghosh, 2003). Therefore, some early works have chosen solutions based on sets of nonlinear equations (Yen & Huang, 1983), or iterated Kalman filters through three perspective views (Faugeras et al., 1987). Recently, pose estimation algorithms have combined sets of lines and points for a linear estimation (Park, 2005), or used dynamic vision and inertial sensors (Rehbinder & Ghosh, 2003). The uniqueness of the structure and motion was discussed for combinations of lines and points correspondences, and their result was that three views with a set of homologue features, two lines and one point, or two points and one line give a unique solution (Holt & Netravali, 1996).

This approach focuses on the analysis of changes in the image plane determined by line correspondences. These changes are expressed as angular variations, which are represented differently depending on their orientation with respect to the camera. They are induced applying transformations to an object line. Some properties of these motions are useful to estimate the pose of an object addressing questions as the number of movements or motion patterns required which give a unique solution. Using a monocular view of a perspective camera, some of these questions are answered in this chapter by the development of a specific methodology. It is inspired in those monocular cues used by the human visual system for spatial perception, which is based on the proper content of the image. This algorithm focuses on the distortion of geometric configurations caused by perspective projection. Thus, the necessary information is completely contained within the captured camera view (Navarro, 2009).

The content of this chapter relies on the concept of biologically inspired vision methods as an appropriate tool to overcome limitations of artificial intelligence approaches. The main goal is highlighting the capacity of analysis of spatial cues to enhance visual perception, as a significant aid to improve the mediation between action and perception in MIS. The remainder of this chapter introduces the benefits of using computer vision for assistance in robotized surgery. It is followed by an analysis of the angular variation as a monocular cue for spatial perception, with a mathematical description of the proposed algorithm and experimental results the article finalizes with some concluding remarks.

2. Mediating action and perception in MIS

The introduction of minimally invasive surgery (MIS) as a common procedure in daily surgery practice is due to a number of advantages over some open surgery interventions. In MIS the patient body is accessed by inserting special instruments through small incisions. As a result tissue trauma is reduced and patients are able to recover faster. However, the nature of this technique forces the surgeon to work physically separated from the operation area. This fact implies a significant reduction of manipulation capabilities and a loss of direct perception. For this reason, robotic and computer-assisted systems have been developed as a solution to these restrictions to help the surgeon.

Some solutions have been proposed to overcome those limitations concerning the constrained workspace and the reduced manipulability restrictions. Approaches dedicated to assist the surgeon are basically aimed to provide an environment similar to conventional procedures. In this sense, robotic surgery developments are especially focused on the enhancement of dexterity, designing special hand-like tools or adding force-feedback through direct telerobotic systems (Grimberger & Jaspers, 2004); (Mayer, 2004). Other systems aid the surgeon through auxiliary robotic assistants, as is the case of a laparoscopic camera handler (Muñoz et al., 2004); (Hurteau et al., 1994). Nevertheless, though the limitation of the visual sense has been tackled by robotic vision systems capable of guiding the laparoscopic camera to a desired view (Doignon et al., 2007); (Casals et al., 1995), 3D perception and hand-eye coordination reduction in terms of cognitive mediation have not been extensively developed.

2.1 Computer assistance in MIS

The visual sense in MIS environments is limited because it imposes a 2D view of the operative site. Therefore, approaches focused to assist the surgeon are fundamentally based on image content recognition and presentation. As an example of this computer assistance, there are some approaches focused on surgical tool tracking (Dutkiewicz, 2005), the study of the distribution of markers to accurately track the instruments (Sun et al., 2005), the establishment of models of lens distortion (Payandeh, 2001). These examples constitute emergent techniques to assist the surgeon by the enhancement of the image content. The work in which this approach is addressed, however, is based on the integration of visual and motion information to perceptually locate the instruments with respect to the surgeon.

Healey in (Healey, 2008) describes the mediation between action and perception in MIS environments and states the necessity of effectively linking action to perception in egocentric coordinates. In this approach, it is suggested that the integration of egocentric information, as visual and limb movements, can be provided with the capacity of locating surgical instruments at a desired position in the operation scene and the knowledge of their orientation with respect to the laparoscopic camera. As a result, the surgeon perception is enhanced by a sense of presence. Thus, computer vision issues such as the 2D-3D pose estimation and exterior orientation, deal with this problem and can be applied to aid the surgeon in this kind of procedures.

The schematic of an application where exterior orientation is used and presented through enhanced visual information to assist the surgeon is shown in Fig. 1. This presentation is commonly performed using augmented reality. There have been early approaches in which this type of resource is used in different kinds of applications (Milgram et al. 1993), others, more specialized in surgery, recognize objects seen by the endoscope in cardiac MIS (Devernay et al., 2001), or design a system for surgical guidance (Pandya & Auner, 2005), being a visual enhancement which serves as a human-machine interface. In this approach, the position and orientation of surgical instruments is the information to be imposed over the image of the surgical scene. It serves to integrate egocentric information, as vision and limb movements, to provide a sense of presence and relate it with the external environment to help in becoming immersed in the working scenario. Nevertheless, the camera-tool calibration must be calculated. This problem can be tackled by computer vision techniques, as the perspective distortion model presented in this chapter. Thus, this computer assisted system can be expressed as a closed loop process, as shown in Fig. 2.

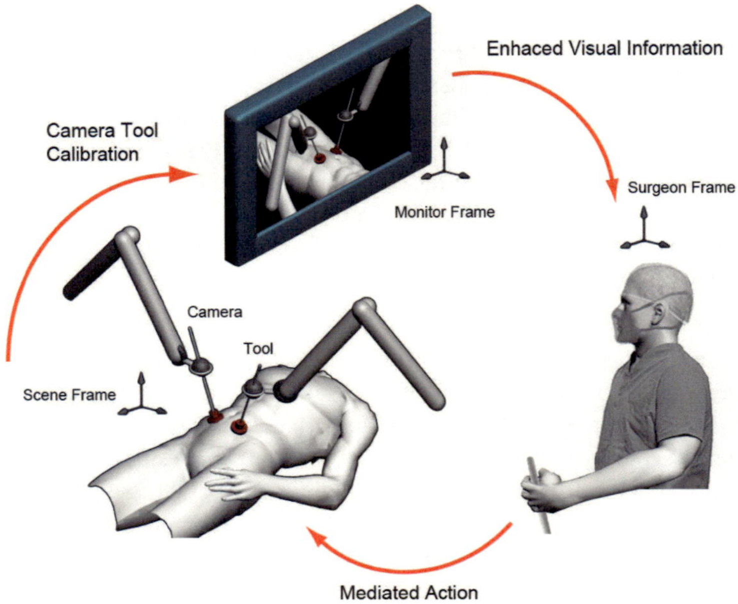

Fig. 1. Schematics of an application assisted surgery in MIS using computer vision.

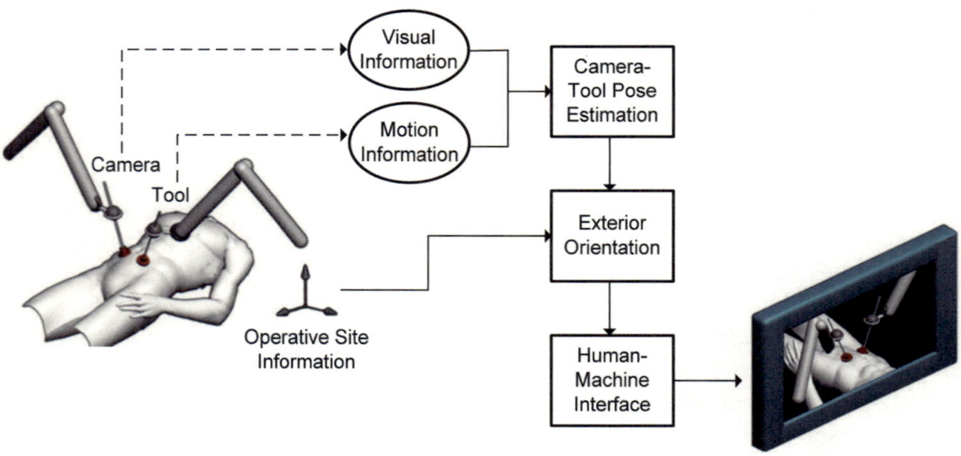

Fig. 2. Visual enhancement process to assist the surgeon. Motion and visual information is related to calibration of a surgical instrument with respect to the camera.

2.2 Robotic assistance in MIS

Assistant robots, as specialized handlers of surgical instruments, have been developed to facilitate surgeons' performance in MIS. Since a patient body is accessed by inserting surgical instruments through small incisions, passive wrists have been incorporated for free compliance through the entry port. With such wrist configuration, it is only possible to locate accurately an instrument tip, if its entry port or fulcrum point is known. The fulcrum is a 3D point external to the robotic system and though it has a significant influence on the passive wrist robot kinematics, its absolute position is uncertain.

A number of approaches focus on the control and manipulability of surgical instruments in MIS through robotic assistants. As can be seen in Fig. 3, 3D transformations are applied to produce pivoting motions through the fulcrum point. The more accurately estimate this entry port is, the more accurately the instrument tip is positioned at a desired location. Some approaches evade this difficulty by the incorporation of special mechanisms with actuated wrists (Taylor et al., 1995). Others, based on passive wrists tackle the problem through inverse kinematics approaches. Thus, error minimization methods are applied to determine the outside penetration (Ortmaier & Hirzinger, 2000) (Funda et al., 1995), and compensate the fulcrum location imprecision (Muñoz, 2004).

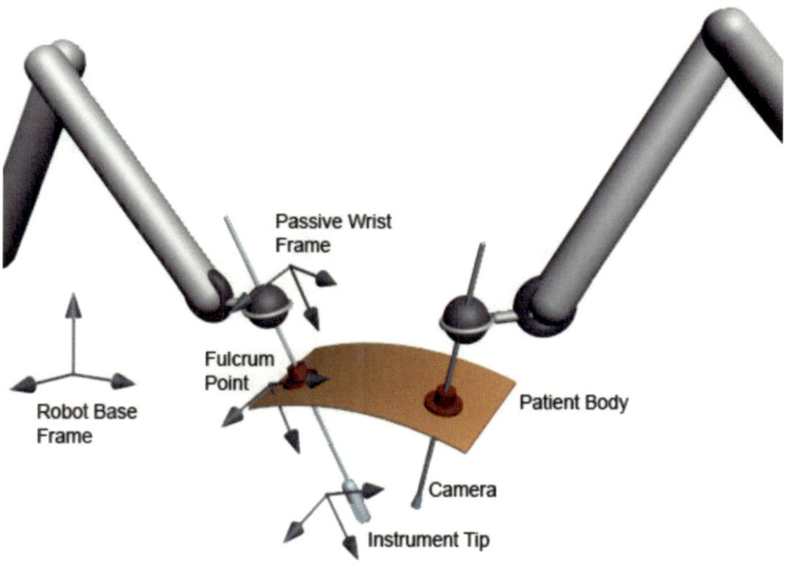

Fig. 3. Minimally invasive robotic surgery systems with passive wrist robotic assistants. The location of the instrument tip depends on the knowledge of the fulcrum point.

A reasonable alternative approach to tackle the passive robot wrist problem is the use of computer vision. Since the laparoscopic camera captures the workspace sight, specialized vision algorithms are capable of estimating 3D geometrical features of the scene. The 2D-3D pose estimation problem serves to map these geometric relations estimating the transformation between reference frames of the instruments and the camera. Several methods have been proposed to estimate the pose of a rigid object. The first step of their algorithms consists in the identification and location of some kind of features that represent an object in the image plane.

In case of image sequences, motion and structure parameters of a 3D scene can be determined. Correspondences between selected features in successive images must be established, which provide motion information and can be used, as is in this case, to estimate the pose of a moving object. Fig. 4 shows the pivoting motion of a surgical instrument on the fulcrum point. As can be seen, instruments are represented by feature lines and are visualized by the laparoscopic camera. In this example, three views after two different rotations generate three lines in the image plane. Each of them defines a 3D plane called the projection plane of the line. These planes pass through the projection center and their respective lines. Their intersection is a 3D line from the origin of the perspective camera frame to the fulcrum point.

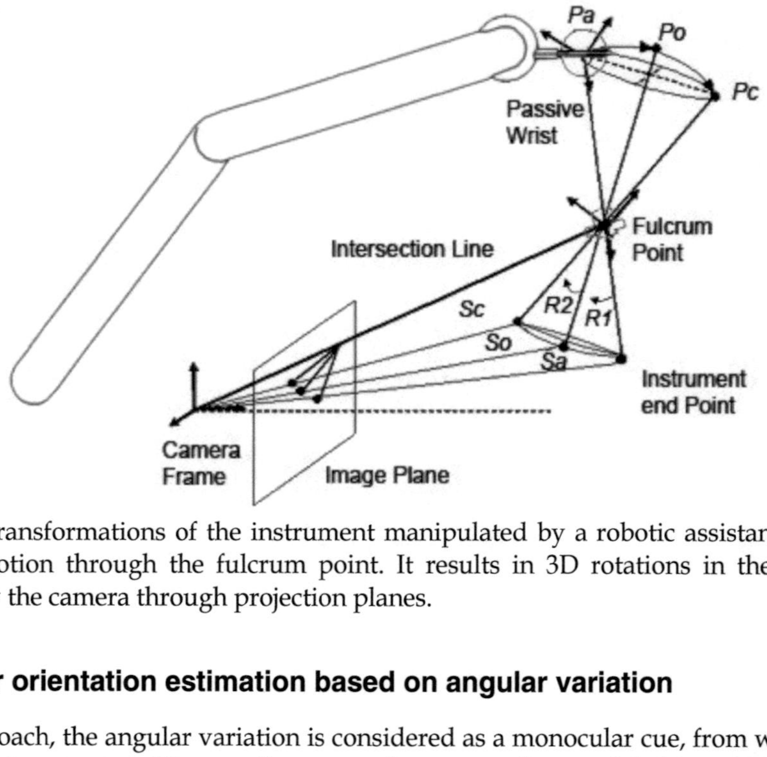

Fig. 4. 3D transformations of the instrument manipulated by a robotic assistant produce a pivoting motion through the fulcrum point. It results in 3D rotations in the workspace captured by the camera through projection planes.

3. Exterior orientation estimation based on angular variation

In this approach, the angular variation is considered as a monocular cue, from which spatial information is extracted. The specific monocular cue used to model this spatial perception property is linear perspective. It is related to the appearance of objects under perspective transformations on a flat surface. This bidimensional view generated by the representation of a 3D object is the result of a planar projection , obtained by mapping each point of the object onto a plane through passing lines emanated from a center of projection. Depending on the desired visual effect derived from this representation, this mapping may be different. It could show the general appearance of an object or depict its metric properties. When the center of projection is finite, a perspective projection is obtained , which presents an object as it is seen by the eye, as generally used in computer vision applications.

Perspective projection provides a realistic representation of an object. An impression of depth is created on a 2D surface and its 3D shape can be visualized. However, to provide this impression the geometry of the object is strongly distorted. Different parts are represented at different scales and parallel lines converge at a single point, implying that such a projection is not considered by the principles of Euclidean geometry (Mumford, 2002). Under perspective transformations, distances and angles, which are Euclidean invariants, are not preserved. Nevertheless, different properties of geometric configurations remain unchanged. For instance, a straight line is mapped into a straight line.

3.1 Linear perspective and angles

The change of geometric configurations under perspective transformations, particularly the angle between lines, plays an important role in modeling perspective distortion. However, certain configurations invariant to these transformations present essential properties necessary to describe the nature of the projection as well. The invariance of the cross-ratio defines the angular distribution of the projected pencil of uniformly separated coplanar lines. Fig. 5 shows first the 3D rotation of the circle in which the pencil is contained and afterward its resulting projection. There, a tendency of the projected lines to concentrate closer to the axis of rotation with progressive increments of the angular difference between them can be observed. This tendency grows with the applied angle of rotation, having the property of maintaining a constant cross-ratio.

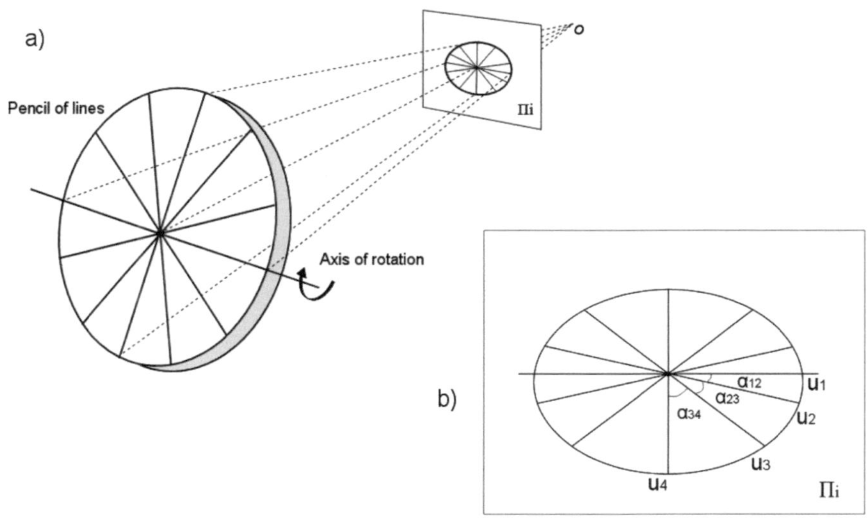

Fig. 5. Perspective projection of a pencil of lines: a) The rotated circle in which the pencil is contained is projected to an ellipse in the image plane; b) An angular variation pattern is produced bringing the lines closer as they approach the major axis of the ellipse.

The result of a projected circle is an ellipse if it is not parallel to the projection plane (Π_i). It is the locus of points that forms the pencil of lines, confirming the geometric property of the construction of conics from the cross-ratio (Mundy & Zisserman, 1992). The invariance of this property is strongly related to the angular distribution of the projected pencil of lines, and consequently, with the eccentricity of the ellipse. It provides information about the orientation of the object, knowing that the eccentricity (e) of the ellipse can be expressed as a function of the angle of rotation (γ) in the form $e = sin(\gamma)$.

3.2 Perspective distortion model

The angular variation pattern of a projected pencil of lines provides sufficient information to model the perspective distortion. It describes the resulting projection of a determined angle depending on the position of the point of incidence of the pencil and the orientation of the circle it forms. It could be seen as a circle rotated about an axis. In the case the center of projection is aligned with the point of incidence of the pencil, this axis is coplanar to the circle and parallel to the major axis of the resulting ellipse. Therefore, the pose of the pencil with respect to the center of projection is defined by the angle of rotation of the circle (γ), which is given by the eccentricity of its own projection.

3.2.1 Aligned center model

Aligning the centers is the simplest case to model. This model serves as starting point to analyze the projective properties of a rotated circle. If a sphere, with radius Z_0, is centered at the center of projection (o), the axis of rotation coplanar to a circle Γ_r is tangent to the sphere at the point of incidence $P_o=(0,0,z_0)$,as shown in Fig. 6. This implies the possibility of estimating the pose of the pencil of lines by an axis and an angle of rotation defined by the angular variation model. The axis is given by the tangent line, which is where the projected lines concentrate. The angle of rotation (γ), however, as the eccentricity of the ellipse (e), must be calculated from the angular variation model.

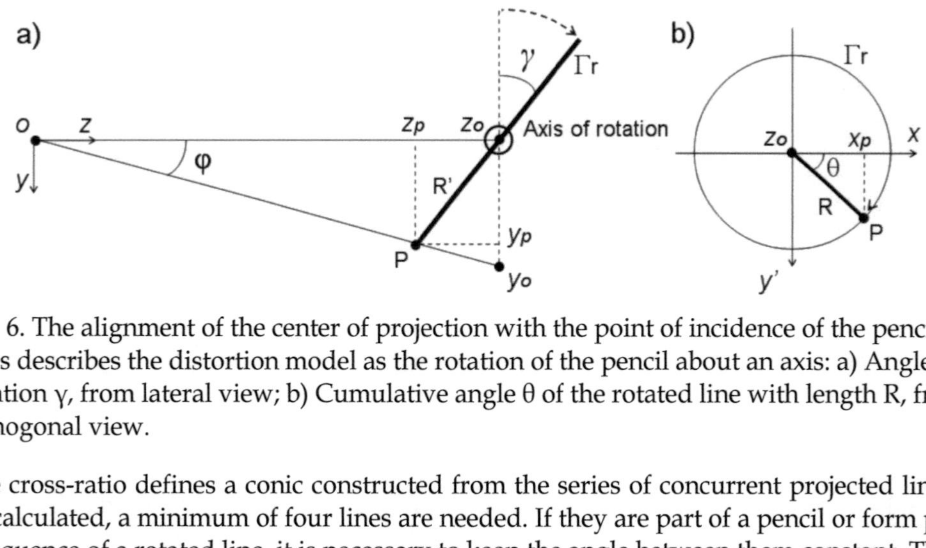

Fig. 6. The alignment of the center of projection with the point of incidence of the pencil of lines describes the distortion model as the rotation of the pencil about an axis: a) Angle of rotation γ, from lateral view; b) Cumulative angle θ of the rotated line with length R, from orthogonal view.

The cross-ratio defines a conic constructed from the series of concurrent projected lines. To be calculated, a minimum of four lines are needed. If they are part of a pencil or form part of a sequence of a rotated line, it is necessary to keep the angle between them constant. The rest of projected angles are calculated knowing the cross-ratio. Thus, parting from the axis of rotation, the angular variation pattern of a projected pencil of lines can be determined. It can be expressed by the relation between the 3D applied angular changes and their projected angular data.

In the case of aligned centers, the axis of rotation is perpendicular to the z axis, as shown in Fig. 6. Having the rotated circle with radius R, centered at P_o; an angle α is the projection of the 3D angle θ at plane Z_o, which is the position of the image plane Π_i. This 3D angle θ is the rotation angle of a line with length R, centered in P_o. Therefore, if the angle θ leads to a point $P=(x_p,y_p,z_p)$ along the circle, the projected angle α is formed by the angle between the projection of P at Z_o, and the axis of rotation of the circle. This can be expressed as:

$$\tan(\alpha) = y_p / x_p = y_0 / x_0 \tag{1}$$

Where, being x the axis of rotation, the slope of the projected line in Π_i describes the projected angle through x_p and y_p, the respective components of P in the xy plane. Thus, by the geometry of the configuration, under a rotation γ, in the yz plane:

$$\tan(\varphi) = R'\cos(\gamma)/(Z_0 - R'\sin(\gamma)) \tag{2}$$

Having R' as the component of R in the y axis, as:

$$R' = R\sin(\theta) \tag{3}$$

This leads to the expression of y_0 as:

$$y_0 = \frac{Z_0 R\sin(\theta)\cos(\gamma)}{Z_0 - R\sin(\theta)\sin(\gamma)} \tag{4}$$

Similarly, in the plane xz at Z_o, the component of P in the x axis is:

$$x_0 = \frac{Z_0 R\cos(\theta)}{Z_0 - R\sin(\theta)\sin(\gamma)} \tag{5}$$

It implies the function that describes the angular variation in an aligned center configuration, knowing the relation $e = \sin(\gamma)$, is defined as:

$$\tan(\alpha) = \tan(\theta)\sqrt{1-e^2} \tag{6}$$

This model satisfies the fact that length and scale do not influence in the angular variation pattern of a projected pencil of lines. It is function of the applied 3D angle and the eccentricity of the ellipse. Knowing this, the angular pattern extracted from the projected lines makes possible the calculation of the eccentricity of the ellipse. It is carried out by fitting the angular data to the model. Thus, the orientation of the circle, wich corresponds to the plane containing the pencil of lines, is calculated.

3.2.2 General case model

Generally the point of incidence of the pencil of lines is not aligned with the center of projection along the z axis. Its projection can be located at any position in the image plane Πi and represented, in this case, by a unit director vector v_d from the center of projection (o). Using the concept of the sphere centered at o, a tangent circle Γ_p is not parallel to the image plane, as would be in the aligned center case and consequently, the axis of rotation of the circle Γ_r is not parallel to the major axis of the projected ellipse. It implies an enhancement on the complexity of the configuration. However, the projective properties are equally satisfied by the angular variation pattern.

The methodology used in this general case approach is based on the aligned center model, on the calculation of the axis and angle of rotation of the circle Γ_r formed by the pencil of lines. Having the angular relation in (6) of two circles representing the rotation of a tangent circle about an angle, the general case configuration can be divided into two simpler aligned center models as shown in Fig. 7. This is due to the fact that in (6) it is assumed that the image plane Π_i is tangent to the sphere, and therefore, perpendicular to the axis of projection defined by v_d. Thus, the first part is conformed by the rotated circle Γ_r and a tangent circle Γ_p; and the second part by Γ_p and a circle Γ_i coplanar with Π_i. Both parts are individual aligned center models. It can be seen as the result of the projection of the rotated circle in a tangent plane, and its consecutive projection in the image plane.

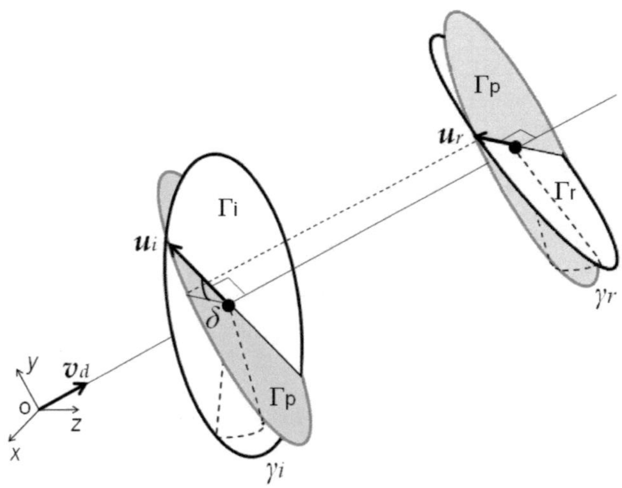

Fig. 7. Division of the general case configuration into two simpler aligned center models. The rotated circle Γr is projected over a tangent plane of the sphere, and its consecutive projection in the image plane.

The projection of the tangent circle Γ_p in the image plane could be considered as the first step to define the model, since the initial data is contained in the image. The extraction of the feature lines of the pencil defines the angular pattern of the projection; and the orientation of Γ_p with respect to Π_i through v_d provides the axis of rotation u_i. This permits to describe the relation between the angle of rotation θ_p, around Γ_p, and the angle θ_i, around Γ_i, which is the result of the rotation of Γ_p about a given angle γ_i. Applying the center aligned model, this relation can be expressed as:

$$\tan(\theta_p) = \tan(\theta_i)\cos(\gamma_i) \tag{7}$$

In the same way, the angular relation between the angle of rotation 3D θ_r, around Γ_r, and its projection in the tangent plane θ_p can be expressed by the aligned center model having γ_r as the angle of rotation of Γ_r and $\boldsymbol{u}_r$ as the axis determined from (7).

The two parts of the divided configuration are related to each other by the tangent circle Γ_p. However, the alignment of the two axes of rotation $\boldsymbol{u}_i$ and $\boldsymbol{u}_r$ is only a particular case of the model. Therefore, to relate the 3D angle θ_r with the angle projected in the image θ_i, the difference between these two axes must be taken into account. If this difference is defined by the angle δ, the angular variation pattern of Γ_r in the tangent plane is given by:

$$\tan(\theta_p + \delta) = \tan(\theta_r)\cos(\gamma_r) \tag{8}$$

which in conjunction with (7) express the angular variation of the 3D angle in the image plane as:

$$\tan(\theta_i) = \frac{\tan(\theta_r)\cos(\gamma_r) - \tan(\delta)}{\cos(\gamma_i)(1 + \tan(\theta_r)\cos(\gamma_r)\tan(\delta))} \tag{9}$$

This equation serves to model the perspective distortion through angular variations in a general case. This variation depends on the angles of rotation with the respective tangent and image plane, and the difference between their axes of rotation δ. If there is no difference between these axes and the image plane is tangent to the sphere, the equation is reduced to the aligned center model. In any other case, γ_i and δ are determined from the image data. Thus, through the fitting of the angular data to the model, γ_r can be estimated and consequently, the orientation of the circle with respect to the center of projection can be calculated.

4. Experimental results

The perspective distortion model developed in this approach was validated by using real world data. The experimental setup consisted on a fixed standard analog B/W camera equipped with known focal length optics and a mobile frontal frame able to reach a desired orientation. The tests carried out were aimed to analyze the response of the model to different 3D angle inputs under a range of rotations of the frontal frame. Two sets of tests were employed to analyze the angular variation and its response to the model. The first set was focused on a single rotated 3D angle, while the second on a pencil of lines.

A 3D angle is formed by the intersection of two lines. It can be seen as the difference of the slope of each line lying on a plane, which is how the projected angle in the image plane was calculated. This angle served as input to the model and had to be known, constituting the main drawback of the method. This problem can be solved with the use of a sequence of concurrent lines, as shown further on. In Fig. 8 the angular variation of three different single angles under rotation is shown.

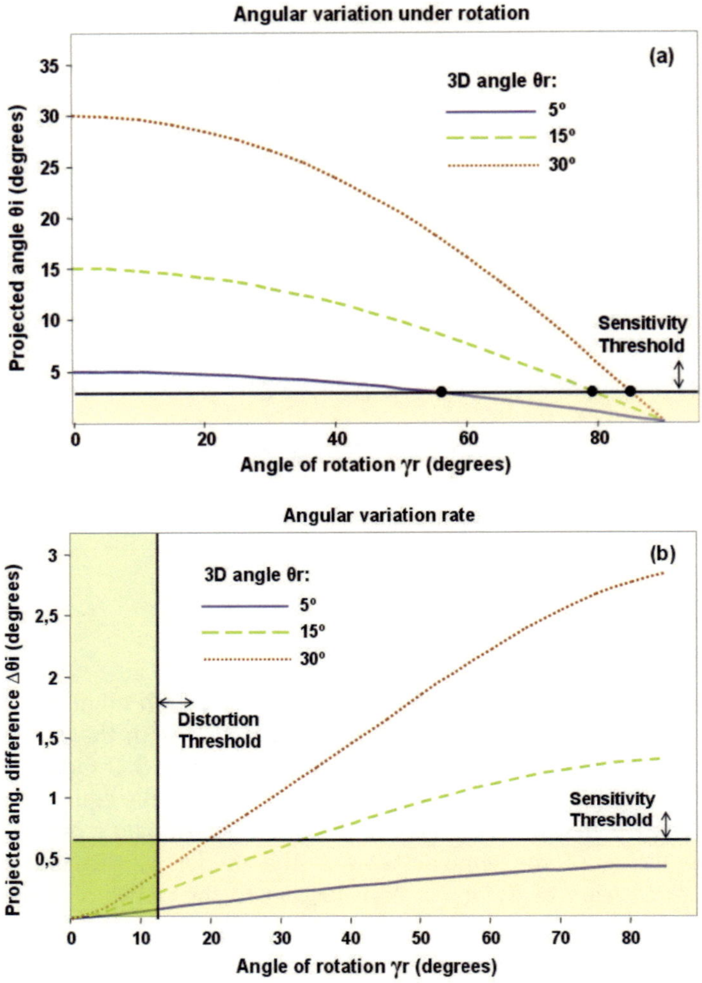

Fig. 8. Angular variation of a single projected angle under rotation. The response of the perspective distortion model is highly affected by line feature errors and the resolution of its acquisition method: a) reduced projected angles caused by long rotations produce unstable performance under a sensitivity threshold; b) the response resolution, dependent on the angular variation rate, misreads data under a distortion threshold.

Parting from the parallelism between the image and the frontal frame, the reduction of the projected angle under rotations can be seen. Likewise, as the resolution of the response depends on the detected angular variation, it does not only increase with higher 3D angles, but it also augments as the angle of rotation increases. As the area of extreme perspective provides enough angular variation with the more accurate response, the area of minor rotations provides negligible variations and consequently a misread response.

The sensitivity of the model is highly affected by the line feature error and the resolution of its acquisition method. Since the model response depends on the projected angle, its extraction using real world data is prone to inaccurate detections, particularly with small angles. The resulting effect of this line feature error is an unstable and poor performance of the model below a sensitivity threshold. However, a good resolution can be obtained from standard methods, which are enough for an accurate performance requirement. Equally, the negligible variation at minor rotations produces a misread response below a threshold caused by the low perspective distortion. Fig. 9 shows the performance error of the model in the single angle test having real world data as input.

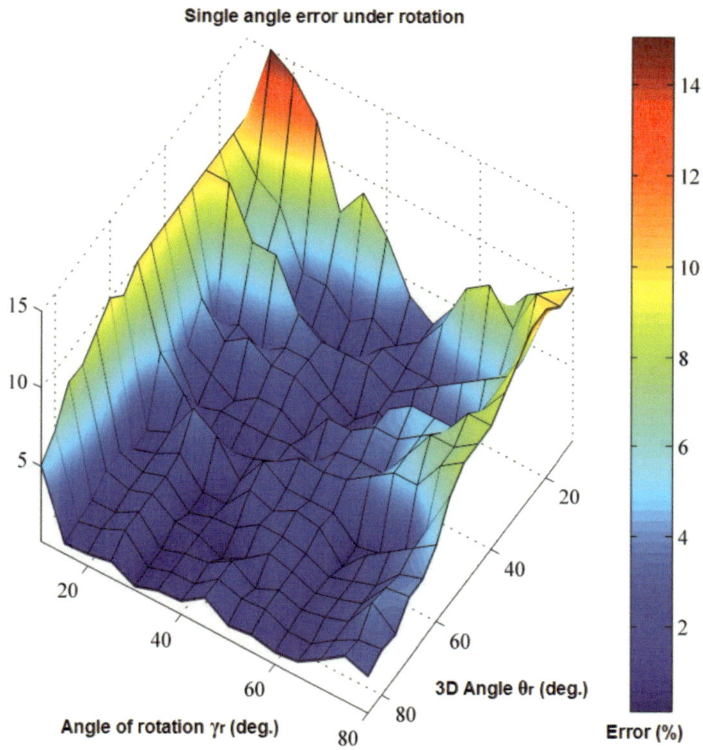

Fig. 9. Performance error of the single angle test. The response of the model is prone to errors with negligible variations at minor rotations and small projected angles. This improves as the 3D angles increases.

In general, the error decreases with increments of the 3D angle applied. Two areas of high error are differentiated along the applied rotations. The first is located below the distortion threshold, where minor rotations were applied. This is an area where the error is uniformly high independently of the 3D angle used. It is caused by the resolution of the line feature extraction method and the low perspective distortion. The second area, on the contrary, is located at long rotations. It decreases as the 3D angle applied increases, caused by the sensitivity of the model with reduced angles at long rotations.

The second set of tests employs pencils of lines of different constant angle separations. The method used to estimate the model parameters is based on fitting the projected measured angles. At least four line samples are required to calculate the cross-ratio or only three when the model is known. This permits to calculate the next angles of the sequence of concurrent lines and, consequently, more samples to obtain an improved fit. According to the invariant property of the pencil of lines, the distribution of the angles is unequal, while the cross-ratio is constant. Fig. 10 presents the performance sensitivity to lines orientation detection. The angular error increases with the amount of angle rotation. As in the previous set of tests, the model response is highly affected by the resolution and the error of the line extraction method, mainly at minor rotations.

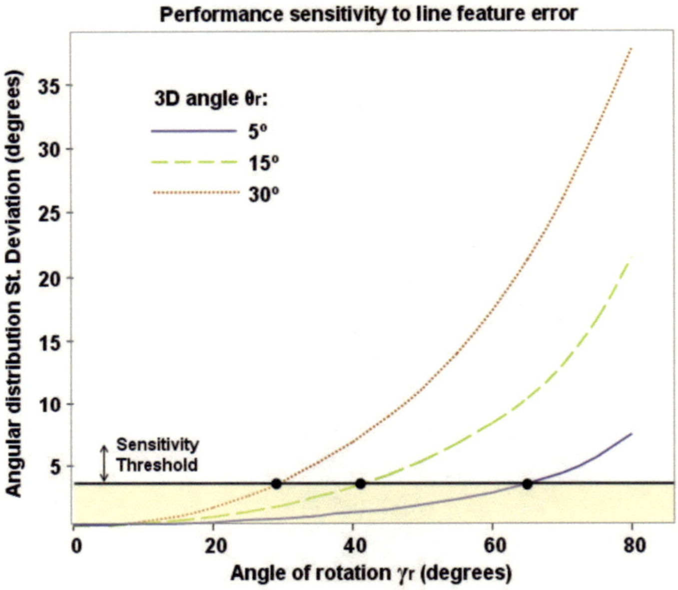

Fig. 10. Angular distribution variation in a rotated pencil of lines. The model response is highly affected under a sensitivity threshold caused by line feature errors at minor rotations.

The standard deviation of the angular distribution of the pencil indicates a superior performance of the model with pencils of higher 3D angle separation. It implies that the model response is prone to errors below a sensitivity threshold. This is depicted in Fig. 11, where real world data was used. Only one area presents a notable high error. It is located where minor rotations were applied. In contrast to the previous set of tests, this error is caused by the low angular distribution variation.

The change in this area is not only negligible, which depends on the resolution of the line feature extraction method, it is also highly sensitive to line feature errors since the pencil angles are similarly distributed.

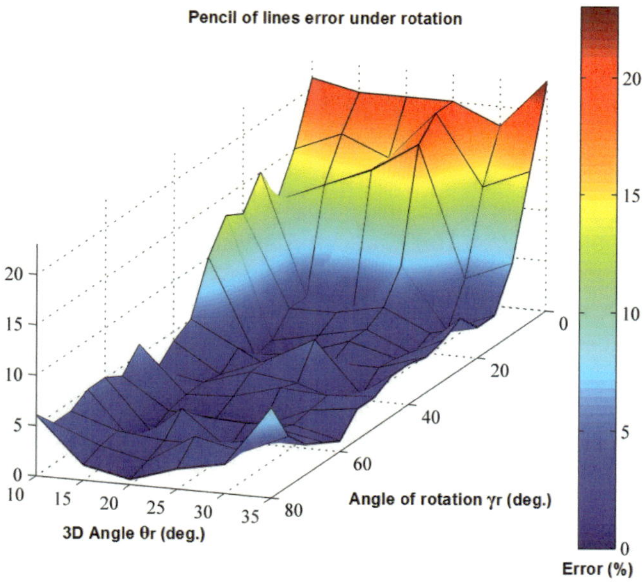

Fig. 11. Performance error of the pencil of lines test. The poor performance of the model at long rotations is improved, while the 3D separation angle of the pencil is limited.

In general the use of pencil of lines improves the performance of the model. It does not require the angular shift from the axis of rotation and provides a robust response at high 3D angle separations. Nevertheless, as the estimation is based on the fitting of sampled data, this 3D angle separation is limited due to the low number of measured samples. It is also suitable for real time applications, where a moving line feature forms the pencil of lines and its angular variation is modeled by its perspective distortion.

5. Conclusion

The capacity of the human visual system to perceive 3D space from a monocular view is characterized by a set of stimulus and processes. As human's perception of depth on a flat surface is enhanced by the use of linear perspective, a set of geometric properties from the projective transformation provide enough 3D information to effectively calculate the pose of an object from 2D images. In this work, a model of the variance of a geometric configuration under perspective transformation has been developed. Particularly, this geometric configuration is the angular variation caused by perspective distortion. Since the resulting projected variation depends on the position of the observer, the exterior orientation of the camera can be determined by the model.

In the presented approach the image plane contains the whole required information to solve the exterior orientation problem. Thus, there is no necessity to measure angular samples from determined 3D structures.

Experimental results show the efficiency and robustness of the method, in this case using a set of concurrent lines. Its accuracy can be affected by the reliability of the line feature extraction technique applied. The potential of this novel approach is prominent in various applications, parting from simple calibration tasks to presence enhancement in immersive teleoperation.

6. References

Casals, A., Amat, J., Prats, D. & Laporte, E. (1995). Vision guided robotic system for laparoscopic surgery, *IFAC Int. Cong. on Advanced Robotics.*

Christy, S. & Horaud, R. (1997). Fast and reliable object pose estimation from line correspondences, *Proc. Int. Conf. Computer Analysis Images Patterns,* pp. 432-439.

Devernay, F., Mourgues, F. & Coste-Maniere, E. (2001). Towards endoscopy augmented reality for robotically assisted minimally invasive cardiac surgery, *IEEE Proc. Int. Workshop on Medical Imaging and Augmented Reality,* pp. 16-20.

Dickmanns, E.D. (2004). Dynamic vision-based intelligence, *AI Magazine,* Vol. 25, No. 2, pp. 10-30.

Doignon, C., Nageotte, F., Maurin, B. & Krupa, A. (2007). Pose estimation and feature tracking for robot assisted surgery with medical imaging, in: *Unifying Perspectives in Computational and Robot Vision,* D. Kragic and V. Kyrki (Eds.), Springer-Verlag, Berlin, pp. 1-23.

Dornaika, F. & Garcia. C. (1999). Pose estimation using point and line correspondences, *Real-Time Imag.,* Vol. 5, pp. 215-230.

Dutkiewicz, P., Kielczewski, M., Kowalski, M., & Wroblewski, W. (2005). Experimental verification of visual tracking of surgical tools," *Fifth Int. Workshop on Robot Motion and Control.*

Faugeras, O., Lustran, F. & Toscani, G. (1987). Motion and structure from point and line matches, *Proc. Int. Conf. Computer Vision.*

Funda, J., Gruben, K., Eldridge, B., Gomory, S. & Taylor, R. (1995). Control and evaluation of a 7-axis surgical robot for laparoscopy, *IEEE Proc. Int. Conf. on Robotics and Automation,* pp. 1477-1484.

Grimberger, C.A. & Jaspers, J.E. (2004). Robotics in minimally invasive surgery, *Proc. IEEE Int. Conf. on Systems, Man and Cybernetics.*

Harris, C. (1992). Geometry from visual motion, In: *Active Vision,* A. Blake and A. Yuille (Eds.), Chapter 16, MIT Press, Cambridge, Mass.

Healey, A. (2008). Speculation on the neuropsychology of teleoperation: implications for presence research and minimally invasive surgery, *Presence: Teleoperators and Virtual Environments*, MIT Press, Vol. 17, No. 2, pp. 199-211.

Holt, J.R. & Netravali, A.N. (1996). Uniqueness of solution to structure and motion from combinations of point and line correspondences, *Journal of Visual Communication and Image Representation,* Vol. 7, No. 2, pp. 126-136.

Horaud, R., Phong, T.Q. and Tao, P.D. (1995). Object pose from 2-d to 3-d point and line correspondences, *Int. J. Computer Vision*, Vol. 15, pp. 225-243.

Huang, T.S. & Netravali, A.B. (1994). Motion and structure from feature correspondences: A review, *Proc. IEEE*, vol. 82, pp. 252-268.

Hurteau, R., DeSantis, S., Begin, E. & Gagner, M. (1994). Laparoscopic surgery assisted by a robotic cameraman: concept and experimental results, *Proc. IEEE Int. Conf. on Robotics and Automation.*

Mayer, H., Nagy, I., Knoll, A., Schirmbeck, E.U. & Bauernschmitt, R. (2004). The Endo[PA]R system for minimally invasive robotic surgery, *Proc. IEEE/RSJ Int. Conf. on Intelligent Robots and Systems.*

Milgram, P., Zhai, S., Drascic, D. & Grodski, J. (1993). Applications of augmented reality for human-robot communication, *IEEE/RSJ Proc. on Intelligent Robots and Systems,* pp. 1467-1472.

Mumford, D., Fogarty, J. & Kirwan, F. (2002) *Geometric Invariant Theory,* 3rd ed. Springer.

Mundy, J.L. & Zisserman, A. (1992). *Geometric Invariance in Computer Vision,* The MIT Press, Cambridge, Mass.

Muñoz, V.F., Garcia-Morales, I., Gomez-DeGabriel, J.M., Fernandez Lozano, J. & Garcia-Cerezo, A. (2004). Adaptive Cartesian motion control approach for a surgical robotic cameraman, *Proc. IEEE Int. Conf. on Robotics and Automation.*

Navarro, A.A. (2009), *Angular Variation as a Monocular Cue for Spatial Perception,* PhD Dissertation, UPC, Barcelona, Spain.

Olensis, J. (2000). A critique of structure-from-motion algorithms, *Computer Vision and Image Understanding,* Vol. 80, pp. 172-214.

Ortmaier, T., & Hirzinger, G. (2000). Cartesian control issues for minimally invasive robotic surgery, *IEEE/RSJ Int. Conf. on Intelligent Robots and Systems,* pp. 465-571.

Pandya, A. & Auner, G. (2005). Simultaneous augmented and virtual reality for surgical navigation, *IEEE Annual Meeting of the North American Fuzzy Information Processing Society.*

Park, J.S. (2005). Interactive 3D reconstruction from multiple images: a primitive-based approach, *Pattern Recognition Letters,* Vol. 26, No. 16, pp. 2558-2571.

Payandeh, S., Xiaoli, Z. & Li, A. (2001). Application of imaging to the laparoscopic surgery, *IEEE Int. Symp. Computer Intelligence in Robotics Automation,* pp. 432-437.

Rehbinder, H. & Ghosh, B.K. (2003). Pose estimation using line-based dynamic vision and inertial sensors, *IEEE Trans. Automatic Control,* Vol. 48, No. 2, pp. 186-199.

Selig, J.M. (2000). Some remarks on the statistics of pose estimation, *Technical report SBU-CISM-00-25,* South Bank University London.

Sun, J., Smith, M., Smith, L. & Nolte, L.P. (2005). Simulation of an optical-sensing technique for tracking surgical tools employed in computer assisted interventions, *IEEE Sensors Journal,* Vol. 5, No. 5.

Taylor, R., Funda, J., Eldridge, B., Gomory, S., Gruben, K., LaRose, D., Talamini, M., Kavoussi, J. & Anderson, J. (1995). A telerobotic assistant for laparoscopic surgery, *IEEE Engineering in Medicine and Biology Magazine,* Vol. 14, No. 3, pp. 279-288.

Wrobel, B. (2001). Minimum solutions for orientation, In: *Calibration and Orientation of Cameras in Computer Vision,* A. Gruen and T. Huang (Eds.), Chapter 2, Springer-Verlag.

Yen, B.L. & Huang, T.S. (1983). Determining 3-D motion and structure of a rigid body using straight line correspondences, *Image Sequence Processing and Dynamic Scene Analysis,* Springer-Verlag.